Preface

SPSS® is a comprehensive, integrated system for statistical data analysis. It is available on a wide variety of computers and operating systems, including IBM PC, PS/2, and compatible computers running OS/2 or Microsoft Windows; Apple Macintosh computers; workstations, minicomputers, and larger systems under UNIX and VAX/VMS; and many other mainframes. All of these versions contain an SPSS Processor that reads and carries out commands in the well-known SPSS language. No matter which version you use, you can issue the same commands and expect the same results.

This manual is a reference to the command syntax for the SPSS Base system. It opens with an introduction that provides a brief overview to help you determine which commands are best for the job at hand. Following the introduction is "Universals," which describes the rules of command syntax and documents those components of the command language that appear in many commands, such as the arithmetic, string, date, and other functions available in many data transformation commands. Following "Universals," SPSS commands are presented in alphabetical order, and the command syntax is illustrated with many examples. Appendixes provide additional information on command states, complex file definition, the macro facility, and import/export character sets.

This reference guide does *not* provide an overview of SPSS, teach you how to create jobs and interpret results, or show you how to run SPSS on your computer and operating system. This information is supplied in a separate *SPSS Base 9.0 User's Guide*.

Manuals for the Base System. Documentation for SPSS Release 9.0 consists of:

- The *SPSS Base User's Guide* provides detailed information on how to run SPSS on your computer's operating system, including complete documentation of the user interface provided for your system. It also explains many of the statistical concepts involved, how to use the statistical procedures correctly, and how to interpret the results.

- A companion book, the *SPSS Base Applications Guide*, provides examples of statistical procedures and related data transformations, with advice on screening data, using appropriate procedures, and interpreting the output.

- *SPSS Interactive Graphics* documents interactive charts, an important feature in the SPSS Base. Once you have created a chart, you can make many modifications dynamically, such as insert or delete graphical elements, change colors and textures, rotate 3-D graphs smoothly, and adjust fit lines and surfaces.

- The *SPSS Base Syntax Reference Guide* documents and provides examples of all the command syntax in the Base system. On some computer operating systems, the user interface makes it possible to obtain most of the features of SPSS without ever looking at command syntax. There are, however, some features that can be obtained only by entering and running SPSS commands.

SPSS Options. The following options are available as add-on enhancements to the SPSS Base system:

- **SPSS Regression Models**™ provides techniques for analyzing data that do not fit traditional linear statistical models. It includes procedures for probit analysis, logistic regression, weight estimation, two-stage least-squares regression, and general nonlinear regression.

- **SPSS Advanced Models**™ focuses on techniques often used in sophisticated experimental and biomedical research. It includes procedures for general linear models (GLM), variance components analysis, loglinear analysis, actuarial life tables, Kaplan-Meier survival analysis, and basic and extended Cox regression.

- **SPSS Tables**™ creates a variety of presentation-quality tabular reports, including complex stub-and-banner tables and displays of multiple response data.

- **SPSS Trends**™ performs comprehensive forecasting and time series analyses with multiple curve-fitting models, smoothing models, and methods for estimating autoregressive functions.

- **SPSS Categories**® performs optimal scaling procedures, including correspondence analysis.

- **SPSS Conjoint**™ performs conjoint analysis.

- **SPSS Exact Tests**™ calculates exact p values for statistical tests when small or very unevenly distributed samples could make the usual tests inaccurate.

- **SPSS Missing Value Analysis**™ describes patterns of missing data, estimates means and other statistics, and imputes values for missing observations.

Contacting SPSS

If you would like to be on our mailing list, contact one of our offices, listed on page v, or visit our WWW site at *http://www.spss.com*. We will send you a copy of our newsletter and let you know about SPSS Inc. activities in your area.

SPSS Inc.
Chicago, Illinois, U.S.A.
Tel: 1.312.651.3000
www.spss.com/corpinfo
Customer Service:
1.800.521.1337
Sales:
1.800.543.2185
sales@spss.com
Training:
1.800.543.6607
Technical Support:
1.312.651.3410
support@spss.com

SPSS Federal Systems
Tel: 1.703.527.6777
www.spss.com

SPSS Argentina srl
Tel: +541.814.5030
www.spss.com

SPSS Asia Pacific Pte. Ltd.
Tel: +65.245.9110
www.spss.com

SPSS Australasia Pty. Ltd.
Tel: +61.2.9954.5660
www.spss.com

SPSS Belgium
Tel: +32.162.389.82
www.spss.com

SPSS Benelux BV
Tel: +31.183.636711
www.spss.nl

**SPSS Central and
Eastern Europe**
Tel: +44.(0)1483.719200
www.spss.com

SPSS Czech Republic
Tel: +420.2.24813839
www.spss.cz

SPSS East Mediterranea and Africa
Tel: +972.9.9526701
www.spss.com

SPSS Finland Oy
Tel: +358.9.524.801
www.spss.com

SPSS France SARL
Tel: +33.1.5535.2700
www.spss.com

SPSS Germany
Tel: +49.89.4890740
www.spss.com

SPSS Hellas SA
Tel: +30.1.7251925/7251950
www.spss.com

SPSS Hispanoportuguesa S.L.
Tel: +34.91.447.37.00
www.spss.com

SPSS Ireland
Tel: +353.1.496.9007
www.spss.com

SPSS Israel Ltd.
Tel: +972.9.8655747
www.spss.com

SPSS Italia srl
Tel: +39.51.252573
www.spss.it

SPSS Japan Inc.
Tel: +81.3.5466.5511
www.spss.co.jp

SPSS Kenya Limited
Tel: +254.2.577.262
www.spss.com

SPSS Korea
Tel: +82.2.3446.7651
www.spss.com

SPSS Latin America
Tel: 1.312.494.3226
www.spss.com

SPSS Malaysia Sdn Bhd
Tel: +60.3.704.5877
www.spss.com

SPSS Mexico SA de CV
Tel: +52.5.682.87.68
www.spss.com

**SPSS Middle East and
South Asia**
Tel: +91.80.227.7436/221.8962
www.spss.com

SPSS Polska
Tel: +48.12.6369680
www.companion.krakow.pl

SPSS Russia
Tel: +7.095.125.0069
www.spss.com

SPSS Scandinavia AB
Tel: +46.8.506.105.50
www.spss.com

SPSS Schweiz AG
Tel: +41.1.266.90.30
www.spss.com

SPSS Singapore Pte. Ltd.
Tel: +65.533.3190
www.spss.com

SPSS South Africa
Tel: +27.11.706.7015
www.spss.com

SPSS Taiwan Corp.
Taipei, Republic of China
Tel: +886.2.25771100
www.spss.com

SPSS UK Ltd.
Tel: +44.1483.719200
www.spss.com

Contents

Introduction: A Guide to SPSS Command Syntax

Overview

The *SPSS Base Syntax Reference Guide* is arranged alphabetically by command name to provide quick access to detailed information on each command in the SPSS command language. This introduction is intended to help you determine which commands are best for the job at hand.

Most SPSS commands can be classified according to what they do to the **working data file**, which is simply the rectangular array of cases and variables with which SPSS is currently working. Operations with the working data file include:

- **Defining a working data file**. Data-definition commands define a new data file or read a previously defined data file and make it available for analysis.

- **Describing the working data file**. These commands add labels or other optional information to the data in the file.

- **Modifying data values**. The SPSS transformation language allows you to specify calculations, simple or elaborate, to be carried out with your data.

- **Defining complex data files**. More powerful "programming" commands let you take control of the process by which SPSS builds the working data file.

- **Selecting cases for processing**. Capabilities for logical case selection and random sampling are essential in data analysis.

- **Modifying the structure of the working data file**. You can easily rearrange, combine, or split up your data files.

- **Saving the working data file**. Save in SPSS format for efficiency or another format for portability.

- **Displaying data values**. Take a look at the data in your working data file.

- **Statistical analysis, tabulation, and graphics**. The analytical commands in SPSS calculate and display statistics, graphics, or tabulations. They are probably the reason you are using SPSS.

- **Other utilities**. This group includes utility commands that do not affect the working data file but that enhance or simplify the operation of SPSS itself.

The remainder of this introduction provides overviews of the commands that perform these functions. For details on the operation of any command, consult the appropriate section of this guide.

Defining a Working Data File

SPSS can read data files created in a wide variety of spreadsheet and database formats. Commands are also available for defining and reading data from simple, unformatted text files.

1

Data Files in SPSS, Spreadsheet, or Database Format

The easiest way to define a working data file is to open a data file that has already been defined, either in SPSS or in some other software. If you have data in such a file, use one of the following commands:

GET. Reads data files in SPSS format as created by the SAVE command in SPSS running under the same operating system or a compatible one. GET is the fastest way to define a working data file. Labels and missing-value definitions that were in effect when the file was saved are preserved.

IMPORT. Reads data files as created by the EXPORT command in SPSS on any machine under any operating system. IMPORT is noticeably slower than GET but preserves labels and missing-value definitions.

GET TRANSLATE. Reads data files created by popular spreadsheet and database software. Field names may be preserved as SPSS variable names. (Other GET commands for other software formats are available under some operating systems. Consult the appropriate sections of this guide for details.)

Unformatted Text Files

If your data are in an unformatted "text" file such as the ASCII files that can be saved by text editors or word processors, you must tell SPSS exactly where and how to read the variables in the file. Do this with:

DATA LIST. Specifies names, formats, and locations of variables to be read from a text file.

MATRIX DATA. Defines an SPSS matrix file to be read from a text or ASCII file. An SPSS matrix-format file can contain correlation, covariance, or other kinds of matrices. Statistical procedures are sometimes able to analyze a matrix-format file more efficiently than a case-oriented data file. The MCONVERT command converts between correlation and covariance matrix files.

Other Data Definition Commands

A utility command that can be useful in defining a data file is:

APPLY DICTIONARY. Applies labels, formats, and missing-value definitions to the working data file from a data file saved in SPSS format, when some or all of the variables in the two files have the same names.

If you are running SPSS under a suitable operating system, you can use:

KEYED DATA LIST and POINT. These commands read keyed (indexed sequential) or direct-access (VSAM) data files under certain operating systems.

Describing the Working Data File

Once you have defined a working data file, you can add other information to its dictionary. With the exception of the MISSING VALUES command, these commands are basically cosmetic and affect the appearance rather than the content of SPSS output.

MISSING VALUES. Specifies that certain values should be excluded from the analysis. These are typically codes used to represent absent or irrelevant data.

FORMATS. Specifies the format (numeric, date, dollar, etc.) by which data values should be displayed. You can also use PRINT FORMATS to specify one format for displayed values and WRITE FORMATS to specify another format (possibly nonprintable) for use with the WRITE command.

VARIABLE LABELS. Provides extended descriptive labels for variables. SPSS automatically uses variable labels to annotate its output.

VALUE LABELS. Provides extended descriptive labels for individual values of variables. These labels are particularly useful if you use numeric codes to represent categorical information, such as gender or race. SPSS automatically uses value labels to annotate its output.

ADD VALUE LABELS. Adds value labels without replacing those previously defined for a variable.

RENAME VARIABLES. Changes the names of variables in the working data file.

Related utilities include:

DISPLAY. Displays information on variables, documents, or macros defined in the working data file.

DOCUMENT. Adds documentary information to the working data file. Documents are preserved by the SAVE command.

Modifying Data Values

The SPSS transformation language makes it easy to change the values of your variables in almost any systematic way. (*Ad hoc* changes in individual values can be made in the Data Editor, available in some operating environments.)

Transformation commands are not executed immediately. Instead, they are stored in the computer's memory until a command that needs the data is processed. At that time, SPSS executes all transformation commands that are pending since the last time it read the data file. (See EXECUTE to override this behavior.)

COMPUTE. Evaluates an expression and assigns the result to the values of a new or existing variable. The expression can involve constants, variables in the working data file, arithmetic or logical operators, and any of several dozen functions.

IF. Evaluates an expression conditionally (depending on whether a logical expression is true for a particular case) and assigns the result of the expression to a new or existing variable.

DO IF and related commands (ELSE IF, ELSE, END IF). Delimit a block of transformation commands that are to be executed conditionally, depending on whether a logical expression is true for each particular case.

RECODE. Reassigns the values of individual variables or collapses ranges of values into single values, according to your specifications. This command can also create a new variable to contain the recoded or collapsed values.

AUTORECODE. Recodes values automatically into consecutive integers. This command works for both numeric and string (alphanumeric) variables.

COUNT. Counts how many of a set of variables have any of a set of specified values and sets a variable equal to the count.

DO REPEAT. Replicates a block of transformation commands, substituting different variables or constants into each copy.

RANK. Assigns rank orders to cases, based on a variable in the working data file. Unlike other commands listed here, RANK requires SPSS to process the data file immediately.

TEMPORARY. Indicates that a group of transformation commands should modify the working data file only temporarily.

Two utility commands do nothing but add variable names to the dictionary:

NUMERIC. Adds a list of numeric variables to the dictionary. Since new variables are numeric by default, the main use of this command is to specify in advance the order of a group of new variables.

STRING. Adds a string (alphanumeric) variable or a list of string variables to the dictionary. Since new variables are numeric by default, this command is required before any transformation command that uses a new string variable.

Defining Complex Data Files

The above commands all read or modify rectangular data files in ways that handle typical situations. When your data are not arranged in one of these typical ways, you can use the more powerful programming facilities of SPSS to take control of building the working data file. With these facilities, you can read a data file of almost any shape, or you can generate deterministic or random data in a file of your own creation.

INPUT PROGRAM. Marks the beginning of a program to define or create a working data file. The program usually includes control structures (such as LOOP or DO IF), one or more DATA LIST commands, and transformation commands (such as COMPUTE).

The following special-purpose commands are available within an input program:

END CASE. Sends a case to the working data file.

END FILE. Closes the working data file explicitly rather than waiting for the end of a data file being read by SPSS.

REREAD. Causes the next DATA LIST command executed to read the same record as the previously executed DATA LIST command. This lets you use part of a data record to determine the way in which the rest of the record is read.

REPEATING DATA. Allows more than one case to be defined by a single input record. This command can also be used in a FILE TYPE structure, described below.

LOOP. Marks the beginning of a group of transformation commands to be executed repeatedly. Loop termination can be controlled by a logical criterion, an index variable, or explicitly with the BREAK command. The LOOP command can also be used as a part of the transformation language, outside of an input program.

Certain commonly encountered data structures, where a data value on each record determines how that record should be treated, are handled automatically by the FILE TYPE and RECORD TYPE commands. Each variety of FILE TYPE provides "canned" logic for rereading data records, with automatic checks for such problems as invalid record types, missing or out-of-order records, and duplicate records. Subsequent RECORD TYPE commands provide the details for each record type.

FILE TYPE MIXED. Builds a case from each record that is read. Unwanted record types can be skipped, and each record type can be treated differently, but one case is built from each record processed.

FILE TYPE GROUPED. Builds a single case from a group of records.

FILE TYPE NESTED. Builds cases from hierarchical data files, spreading data values from higher-level (aggregated) records to lower-level records.

Utility commands that are particularly helpful in defining complex files include:

LEAVE. Retains the values of specified variables from one case to another, rather than reinitializing them between cases.

VECTOR. Defines a group of consecutive variables as a pseudo-vector. Transformation commands can then refer to individual variables by means of an index variable that is evaluated at run time. This facility is particularly helpful within a loop structure, since the loop index can also be used within the vector.

Selecting Cases for Processing

The following commands specify that subsequent processing should be based on selected cases only:

SELECT IF. Lets you specify a logical criterion for case selection.

FILTER. Lets you specify a logical criterion for temporary case selection.

SAMPLE. Lets you select a sample of the cases in the working data file, based on a pseudo-random number generated by SPSS.

N OF CASES. Specifies that only a certain number of cases from the beginning of the data file should be used.

Modifying the Structure of the Working Data File

The following commands, used singly or in combination, let you reorganize the working data file in almost any way you could want:

SORT CASES. Sorts the cases in the working data file into ascending or descending order of the values of one or more variables.

FLIP. Transposes the data matrix so that each variable becomes a case and each case becomes a variable.

WEIGHT. Simulates the replication of individual cases in statistical calculations and tables.

AGGREGATE. Combines groups of cases into single aggregated cases. Variables in the aggregated file contain statistical functions (such as sums or means) of the original variables, computed across a group of cases in the original, unaggregated file.

UPDATE. Replaces data values in a master file with values from one or more transaction files.

ADD FILES. Combines the cases in two or more data files, normally files containing many of the same variables.

MATCH FILES. Combines the variables in two or more data files, normally files containing many of the same cases. Can also perform table lookups, in which the value of a key variable is used to extract data from a table file.

SPLIT FILE. Specifies that analysis should be performed separately for each group of cases, as defined by one or more grouping variables.

Saving the Working Data File

A working data file exists only during the course of an SPSS session. The following commands save a copy of the working data file on any available storage device:

SAVE. Saves the working data file in native SPSS format, which can be read by the GET command under the same operating system or a compatible one. This is the best format in which to save data files that you will analyze repeatedly with SPSS. All dictionary information is preserved. SPSS reads and writes files much faster in its own format. Files in this format can be used only within SPSS.

XSAVE. Saves the working data file in native SPSS format while carrying out the next SPSS procedure, thus saving the processing time required to read the data file (provided that there is another SPSS procedure within the session).

EXPORT. Saves the working data file in SPSS portable format, which can be read by the SPSS Import command, on any machine under any operating system. EXPORT is noticeably slower than SAVE or XSAVE.

SAVE TRANSLATE. Saves the working data file in one of several formats that can be read by popular spreadsheet and database software.

WRITE. Saves the data values in the working data file in text (typically ASCII) format, with no dictionary information.

Displaying Data Values

The simplest thing that SPSS can do to the working data file is display it. The Data Editor (where available) provides the quickest and easiest way to view the contents of the working data file. The following commands display data in increasingly elaborate ways:

LIST. Displays the data in the working data file. This command offers minimal control over the data displayed or its format.

PRINT. Displays data values, or calculated values or constants, while carrying out the next SPSS procedure. This is an efficient and flexible way of displaying data, provided that there will be another procedure. It requires you to specify the format and to calculate any summary statistics using the transformation language.

REPORT. Produces reports containing summary statistics, listings of individual cases, or both. This is usually the easiest way to obtain reports more complex than simple case listings.

Statistical Analysis, Tabulation, and Graphics

The procedures performing these tasks are probably why you are using SPSS. Consult the *SPSS Base User's Guide* for your version of SPSS for assistance in choosing the right procedure and interpreting the results.

Analytical procedures read the working data file. As they do so, SPSS carries out any transformation commands that have been specified since the data file was last read. If the working data file has been modified, a new copy is written for subsequent use.

Summary Measures, Frequency Tables, and Crosstabulation

CROSSTABS. Builds cross-classification tables and calculates tests of independence and measures of association for categorical variables.

DESCRIPTIVES. Efficiently calculates univariate statistics, such as means and variances, that do not require tabulation.

EXAMINE. Displays exploratory plots and statistics.

FREQUENCIES. Displays frequency tables, as well as univariate statistics and plots.

MULT RESPONSE. Displays frequency tables and crosstabulations for multiple-response and multiple-dichotomy variables.

Comparing Means and Analysis of Variance

ANOVA. Performs factorial analysis of variance for single dependent variables and multiple factors.

MEANS. Displays subgroup means based on one or more grouping variables.

ONEWAY. Performs analysis of variance with one factor, allowing user-specified contrasts and displaying any of several multiple-comparison tests. See also ANOVA.

T-TEST. Performs the *t* test for a difference between two means, for either independent or paired samples.

Correlation and Linear Regression

CORRELATIONS. Calculates Pearson correlation coefficients.

REGRESSION. Performs least-squares regression analysis, displaying coefficients, significance tests, and a variety of diagnostic plots, statistics, and listings.

PARTIAL CORR. Calculates matrices of partial correlation coefficients.

Nonparametric Measures

NONPAR CORR. Calculates Spearman and Kendall nonparametric correlation coefficients.

NPAR TESTS. Calculates a variety of significance tests and measures of association for ordinal and nominal variables.

Graphical Display

GRAPH. Produces high-resolution charts and plots. This facility varies greatly from one operating environment to another.

PLOT. Displays high- or low-resolution (character-based) scatterplots.

Other Utilities

The following commands perform miscellaneous useful tasks whose implementation often differs widely from one operating environment to another. Such differences are noted, where possible, in the reference section for each command.

SET. Controls any of numerous settings that can be used to tailor the behavior or output of SPSS.

SHOW. Displays the current settings of the specifications controlled by SET.

PRESERVE and RESTORE. Allow you to "remember" the current settings of the SET specifications and restore them later. They are chiefly used in macros.

DEFINE (macro). The DEFINE command lets you define a macro, which is a block of SPSS command syntax (a command, part of a command, or multiple commands) that can be invoked by name. You can pass parameters to a macro when invoking it. See Appendix D for examples of how to use the macro facility.

HELP. The basic HELP facility described in this guide is replaced by a more powerful Help system in some environments. Consult the *SPSS Base User's Guide* for your version of SPSS.

EXECUTE. Causes SPSS to read the working data file and execute any commands that are pending, such as transformation commands. This is sometimes useful after commands that act like transformations (such as PRINT and XSAVE), carrying out their function during the next data pass.

INCLUDE. Reads and executes SPSS command syntax from a file.

HOST. Gives you access to native operating-system commands during an SPSS session, in operating systems where this facility is implemented.

ERASE. Deletes files during an SPSS session, in operating systems where this facility is implemented.

SYSFILE INFO. Displays information such as variable names from data files saved in SPSS format without disturbing the working data file.

TITLE and SUBTITLE. Include titles of your choice on each page of SPSS output.

COMMENT. Lets you annotate the listing of SPSS commands executed in a session. To save comments with a data file, use DOCUMENT.

Example

The following commands could be used in SPSS either as part of an SPSS session or as a complete batch job:

```
GET FILE=WEATHER.SAV.
COMPUTE AVTEMP=MEAN.2(TEMP1,TEMP2,TEMP3).
VARIABLE LABELS AVTEMP 'Average Daily Temperature'.
REGRESSION
 /DEPENDENT=NEWTEMP
 /ENTER=AVTEMP HUMID PRESSURE WINDDIR WINDSPD
 /SAVE=PRED(PREDICT).
SAVE OUTFILE=FORECAST.SAV.
```

- The GET command reads the SPSS data file *WEATHER.SAV* and uses it as the working data file.

- The COMPUTE command uses a statistical function to create a new variable, *AVTEMP*.

- The statistical function MEAN.2 indicates that the value of *AVTEMP* should be the mean of the three variables (*TEMP1, TEMP2, TEMP3*) and that at least two of the variables must have nonmissing values.

- The VARIABLE LABELS command supplies a descriptive label for the new variable.

- The REGRESSION command initiates a statistical procedure.

- The SAVE subcommand saves the predicted values generated by the REGRESSION procedure and assigns the variable name *PREDICT* to these values.

- The SAVE command creates a new SPSS data file, *FORECAST.SAV*, which contains all of the variables from *WEATHER.SAV* plus the two new variables, *AVTEMP* and *PREDICT*.

Universals

This part of the *SPSS Base Syntax Reference Guide* discusses general topics pertinent to using command syntax. The topics are divided into five sections:

- *Commands* explains command syntax, including command specification, command order, and running commands in different modes. In this section, you will learn how to read syntax charts, which summarize command syntax in diagrams and provide an easy reference. Discussions of individual commands are found in an alphabetical reference in the next part of this manual.

- *Files* discusses different types of files used by the program. Terms frequently mentioned in this manual are defined. This section provides an overview of how files are handled.

- *Variables* contains important information on general rules and conventions concerning variables and variable definition. In this section, you will find detailed information on variable formats.

- *Transformation Expressions* describes expressions that can be used in data transformation. Functions and operators are defined and illustrated. In this section, you will find a complete list of available functions and how to use them.

- *Date and Time* deals with functions and formats used with date and time expressions. In this section, you will find ways to read and convert date and time, use them in analysis, and display them in output.

Commands

Commands are the instructions that you give the program to initiate an action. For the program to interpret your commands correctly, you must follow certain rules.

Syntax Diagrams

Each command described in this manual includes a syntax diagram that shows all the subcommands, keywords, and specifications allowed for that command. By recognizing symbols and different type fonts, you can use the syntax diagram as a quick reference for any command. Figure 1 is an example.

- Lines of text in italics indicate limitation or operation mode of the command.

- Elements shown in upper case are keywords defined by SPSS to identify commands, subcommands, functions, operators, and other specifications. In Figure 1, T-TEST is the command and GROUPS is a subcommand.

- Elements in lower case describe specifications you supply. For example, varlist indicates that you need to supply a list of variables.

- Elements in bold are defaults. SPSS supports two types of defaults. When the default is followed by **, as ANALYSIS** is in Figure 1, the default (ANALYSIS) is in effect if the subcommand (MISSING) is not specified. If a default is not followed by **, it is in effect when the subcommand (or keyword) is specified by itself.

Figure 1   Syntax diagram

```
                                                            ┌──────────────► Subgrouping (in italics)
Independent samples:
                                                            ┌──────────────► Keywords (in all upper case)
T-TEST GROUPS=varname ({1,2**      }) /VARIABLES=varlist
                       {value      }                        ┐
                       {value,value}                        └─► User specification (in lower case)
                                                            ┌──────────────► Default (in bold)
[/MISSING={ANALYSIS**}   [INCLUDE]]
          {LISTWISE  }
                                                            ┌──────────────► Alternatives (in aligned { })
[/FORMAT={LABELS**}]
         {NOLABELS}
                                                            ──► Optional specification (in [ ])
Paired samples:

T-TEST PAIRS=varlist [WITH varlist [(PAIRED)]] [/varlist ...]
                                                            └──►Repeatable elements (with ...)
[/MISSING={ANALYSIS**}   [INCLUDE]]
          {LISTWISE  }
                                                            ──►Parentheses (cannot be omitted)
[/FORMAT={LABELS**}]
         {NOLABELS}

**Default if the subcommand is omitted.  ────────► Note
```

- Parentheses, apostrophes, and quotation marks are required where indicated.
- Elements enclosed in square brackets ([ ]) are optional. Wherever brackets would confuse the format, they are omitted. The command description explains which specifications are required and which are optional.
- Braces ({}) indicate a choice between elements. You can specify any one of the elements enclosed within the aligned braces.
- Ellipses indicate that you can repeat an element in the specification. The specification

  T-TEST PAIRS=varlist [WITH varlist [(PAIRED)]] [/varlist ...]

  means that you can specify multiple variable lists with optional WITH variables and the keyword PAIRED in parentheses.
- Most abbreviations are obvious; for example, varname stands for variable name and varlist stands for a variable list.
- The command terminator is not shown in the syntax diagram.

Command Specification

The following rules apply to all commands:

- Commands begin with a keyword that is the name of the command and often have additional specifications, such as subcommands and user specifications. Refer to the discussion of each command to see which subcommands and additional specifications are required.
- Commands and any command specifications can be entered in upper and lower case. Commands, subcommands, keywords, and variable names are translated to upper case

before processing. All user specifications, including labels and data values, preserve upper and lower case.

- Spaces can be added between specifications at any point where a single blank is allowed. In addition, lines can be broken at any point where a single blank is allowed. There are two exceptions: the END DATA command can have only one space between words, and string specifications on commands such as TITLE, SUBTITLE, VARIABLE LABELS, and VALUE LABELS can be broken across two lines only by specifying a + between string segments (see "String Values in Command Specifications" on p. 15).

- The first word of a command can be abbreviated to a minimum of three letters provided no duplicates result. For example, AGGREGATE can be abbreviated to AGG, but COMPUTE can only be abbreviated to COMP to avoid confusion with COMMENT. A very small number of commands can duplicate an internal command when abbreviated to three characters (for example, LIST) and at least four characters should be used. For internal command structure, DATA LIST cannot be abbreviated.

- If the first word of a multiple-word command has a duplicate (for example, FILE LABEL and FILE TYPE), the first word cannot be abbreviated.

- All keywords after the first command word can be abbreviated to three characters. For example, ADD VAL LAB is a valid abbreviation for ADD VALUE LABELS, and EXA VAR=varlist is valid for EXAMINE VARIABLES=varlist. END DATA is an exception. You must spell both command keywords in full; END DAT is *not* a valid abbreviation for END DATA.

- Three-character truncation does not apply to INFO command specifications. Spell out all keywords in full. For procedure names specified on INFO, spell out the first word in full and subsequent words through at least the first three characters.

Running Commands

You can run commands in either batch (production) or interactive mode. In batch mode, commands are read and acted upon as a batch, so the system knows that a command is complete when it encounters a new command. In interactive mode, commands are executed immediately, and you must use a command terminator to tell SPSS when a command is complete.

Interactive Mode

The following rules apply to command specifications in interactive mode:

- Each command ends with a command terminator. The default command terminator is a period. It is best to omit the terminator on BEGIN DATA, however, so that inline data is treated as one continuous specification.

- The command terminator must be the last nonblank character in a command.

- Commands can begin in any column of a command line and continue for as many lines as needed. The exception is the END DATA command, which must begin in the first column of the first line after the end of data.

- The maximum length of any command line is 80 characters, including the prompt and the command terminator.

You should observe interactive rules when you:

- Submit commands from a syntax window or with an SPSS Manager, either one command at a time or as a group.
- Enter commands at a command prompt on those systems that run prompted sessions.

See the *SPSS Base User's Guide* for your version of SPSS for more information.

Batch (Production) Mode

The following rules apply to command specifications in batch or production mode:

- All commands in the command file must begin in column 1. You can use plus (+) or minus (−) signs in the first column if you want to indent the command specification to make the command file more readable.
- If multiple lines are used for a command, column 1 of each continuation line must be blank.
- Command terminators are optional.
- An asterisk (*) in the first column indicates a comment line (see the COMMENT command).

You should observe batch rules when you:

- Construct a command file for use with the Production Facility.
- Construct a command file that will be submitted to your operating system for execution.
- Construct a command file that will be included using the INCLUDE command. You can include a command file when you are working in interactive mode. The included command file, however, must follow batch rules.

The way you submit a command file for execution varies from operating system to operating system. Command files do not necessarily need to be submitted to a batch queue, although they can be on operating systems that have a batch queue. In batch mode, the commands in the file are executed one after the other, and output is displayed when all commands are executed.

The following is a sample command file:

```
GET FILE=BANK.SAV /KEEP ID TIME SEX JOBCAT SALBEG SALNOW
        /RENAME SALNOW = SAL90.

DO IF TIME LT 82.
+   COMPUTE RATE=0.05.
ELSE.
+   COMPUTE RATE=0.04.
END IF.

COMPUTE SALNOW=(1+RATE)*SAL90.

EXAMINE VARIABLES=SALNOW BY SEX /PLOT=NONE.
```

Subcommands

Many commands include additional specifications called *subcommands* for locating data, handling data, and formatting the output.

- Subcommands begin with a keyword that is the name of the subcommand. Some subcommands include additional specifications.

- A subcommand keyword is separated from its specifications, if any, by an equals sign. The equals sign is usually optional but is required where ambiguity is possible in the specification. To avoid ambiguity, it is best to use the equals signs as shown in the syntax diagrams in this manual.

- Most subcommands can be named in any order. However, some commands require a specific subcommand order. The description of each command includes a section on subcommand order.

- Subcommands are separated from each other by a slash. To avoid ambiguity, it is best to use the slashes as shown in the syntax diagrams in this manual.

Keywords

Keywords identify commands, subcommands, functions, operators, and other specifications in SPSS.

- Keywords, including commands and subcommands, can often be truncated to the first three characters of each word. An exception is the keyword WITH, which must be spelled in full. See "Command Specification" on p. 12 for additional rules for three-character truncation of commands.

- Keywords identifying logical operators (AND, OR, and NOT), relational operators (EQ, GE, GT, LE, LT, and NE), and ALL, BY, TO, and WITH are reserved words and cannot be used as variable names.

Values in Command Specifications

The following rules apply to values specified in commands:

- A single lowercase character in the syntax diagram, such as *n*, *w*, or *d*, indicates a user-specified value.

- The value can be an integer or a real number within a restricted range, as required by the specific command or subcommand. For exact restrictions, read the individual command description.

- A number specified as an argument to a subcommand can be entered with or without leading zeros.

String Values in Command Specifications

- Each string specified in a command should be enclosed in a set of apostrophes or quotation marks.

- To specify an apostrophe within a string, either use quotation marks to enclose the string or specify double apostrophes. Both of the following specifications are valid:

```
'Client''s Satisfaction'
"Client's Satisfaction"
```

- To specify quotation marks within a string, use apostrophes to enclose the string:

  `'Categories Labeled "UNSTANDARD" in the Report'`

- String specifications can be broken across command lines by specifying each string segment within apostrophes or quotation marks and using a + sign to join segments. For example,

  `'One, Two'`

  can be specified as

  `'One,'`
  `+ ' Two'`

  The plus sign can be specified on either the first or the second line of the broken string. Any blanks separating the two segments must be enclosed within one or the other string segment.

- Blanks within apostrophes or quotation marks are significant.

Delimiters

Delimiters are used to separate data values, keywords, arguments, and specifications.

- A blank is usually used to separate one specification from another, except when another delimiter serves the same purpose or when a comma is required.

- Commas are required to separate arguments to functions. Otherwise, blanks are generally valid substitutes for commas.

- Arithmetic operators (+, −, *, and /) serve as delimiters in expressions.

- Blanks can be used before and after operators or equals signs to improve readability, but commas cannot.

- Special delimiters include parentheses, apostrophes, quotation marks, the slash, and the equals sign. Blanks before and after special delimiters are optional.

- The slash is used primarily to separate subcommands and lists of variables. Although slashes are sometimes optional, it is best to enter them as shown in the syntax diagrams.

- The equals sign is used between a subcommand and its specifications, as in STATISTICS= MEAN, and to show equivalence, as in COMPUTE target variable=expression. Equals signs following subcommands are frequently optional, but it is best to enter them for clarity.

Command Order

Command order is more often than not a matter of common sense and follows this logical sequence: variable definition, data transformation, and statistical analysis. For example, you cannot label, transform, analyze, or use a variable in any way before it exists. The following general rules apply:

- Commands that define variables for a session (DATA LIST, GET, MATRIX DATA, etc.) must precede commands that assign labels or missing values to those variables; they must also precede transformation and procedure commands that use those variables.

- Transformation commands (IF, COUNT, COMPUTE, etc.) that are used to create and modify variables must precede commands that assign labels or missing values to those variables, and they must also precede the procedures that use those variables.

- Generally, the logical outcome of command processing determines command order. For example, a procedure that creates new variables in the working data file must precede a procedure that uses those new variables.

- Some commands, such as REREAD and END CASE, can appear only in an *input program* where the cases are created. Other commands, such as SELECT IF, can appear only in a *transformation program* after cases have been created. Still other commands, such as COMPUTE, can appear in an input or transformation program. For a discussion of these program states and command order, see Appendix A.

In addition to observing the rules above, it is important to distinguish between commands that cause the data to be read and those that do not. Table 1 shows the commands that cause the data to be read. Most of the remaining commands (those that do not cause the data to be read) do not take effect immediately; they are read but are not executed until a command that causes the data to be read is encountered in the command sequence. This avoids unnecessary passes through the data.

Table 1   Commands that cause the data to be read [*]

AGGREGATE	FREQUENCIES	PARTIAL CORR
ALSCAL	GRAPH	PLOT
ANOVA	HILOGLINEAR	PROBIT
AUTORECODE	IMPORT	PROXIMITIES
BEGIN DATA	LIST	QUICK CLUSTER
CLUSTER	LOGISTIC REGRESSION	RANK
CNLR	LOGLINEAR	REGRESSION
CORRELATIONS	MANOVA	RELIABILITY
CROSSTABS	MATRIX	REPORT
DESCRIPTIVES	MCONVERT	SAVE
DISCRIMINANT	MEANS	SAVE SCSS
EXAMINE	MULTIPLE RESPONSE	SAVE TRANSLATE
EXECUTE	NLR	SORT
EXPORT	NONPAR CORR	SURVIVAL
FACTOR	NPAR TESTS	T-TEST
FLIP	ONEWAY	

[*] This table shows the procedures in the SPSS Base system and the Regression Models and Advanced Models options; it does not show commands in other SPSS options, such as SPSS Tables or SPSS Trends.

Transformation commands that alter the dictionary of the working data file, such as MISSING VALUES, and commands that do not affect the working data, such as SET, SHOW, and DISPLAY, take effect as soon as they are encountered in the command sequence, regardless of conditional statements that precede them. Table 2 lists all transformation commands that take effect immediately.

Table 2   Transformation commands that take effect immediately

ADD VALUE LABELS	PRINT FORMATS
DOCUMENT	SPLIT FILE
DROP DOCUMENTS	STRING
FORMATS	VALUE LABELS
LEAVE	VARIABLE LABELS
MISSING VALUES	VECTOR
N OF CASES	WEIGHT
NUMERIC	WRITE FORMATS

Since these transformations take effect regardless of the conditional statements that precede them, they cannot be applied selectively to individual cases, as shown in the following example:

```
DO IF AGE>69.
MISSING VALUES INCOME EXPENSES (0).
ELSE.
COMPUTE PROFIT=INCOME-EXPENSES.
END IF.
LIST.
```

The MISSING VALUES command is in effect when COMPUTE is executed, even if the condition defined on DO IF is false. To treat 0 income and expenses as missing only for those older than 69, use RECODE in the DO IF—END IF structure to selectively recode 0 to a negative number and declare the negative number as missing:

```
MISSING VALUES INCOME EXPENSES (-1).
DO IF (AGE>69).
RECODE INCOME EXPENSES (0=-1).
END IF.
COMPUTE PROFILE=INCOME-EXPENSES.
LIST.
```

In addition, the order of transformations that take effect immediately in the command sequence can be misleading. Consider the following:

```
COMPUTE PROFIT=INCOME-EXPENSES.
MISSING VALUES INCOME EXPENSES (0).
LIST.
```

- COMPUTE precedes MISSING VALUES and is processed first; however, execution is delayed until the data are being read.

- MISSING VALUES takes effect as soon as it is encountered.

- LIST causes the data to be read; thus, SPSS executes both COMPUTE and LIST during the same data pass. Because MISSING VALUES is already in effect by this time, all cases with the value 0 for either *INCOME* or *EXPENSES* return a missing value for *PROFIT*.

To prevent the MISSING VALUES command from taking effect before COMPUTE is executed, you must position MISSING VALUES after the LIST command. Alternatively, place an EXECUTE command between COMPUTE and MISSING VALUES.

Files

SPSS reads, creates, and writes different types of files. This section provides an overview of the types of files used in SPSS and discusses concepts and rules that apply to all files. Conventions for naming, printing, deleting, or permanently saving files, and for submitting command files for processing, differ from one computer and operating system to another. For specific information, consult the *SPSS Base User's Guide* for your version of SPSS.

Command File

Command files contain commands, sometimes with inline data. They can be created by a text editor. Wherever SPSS allows you to paste commands, either in a syntax window or with an SPSS manager, the resulting file is a command file. You can also edit a journal file to produce a command file (see "Journal File" below). The following is an example of a simple command file that contains both commands and inline data:

```
DATA LIST /ID 1-3 SEX 4 (A) AGE 5-6 OPINION1 TO OPINION5 7-11.
BEGIN DATA
001F2621221
002M5611122
003F3422212
329M2121212
END DATA.
LIST.
```

- Case does not matter for commands but is significant for inline data. If you specified *f* for female and *m* for male in column 4 of the data line, the value of *SEX* would be *f* or *m*, instead of *F* or *M* as it is now.
- Commands can be in upper or lower case. Uppercase characters are used for all commands throughout this manual only to distinguish them from other text.

Journal File

SPSS keeps a journal file to record all commands either entered in the syntax window or generated from a dialog box during a session. You can retrieve this file with any text editor and review it to learn how the session went. You can also edit the file to build a new command file and use it in another run. An edited and tested journal file can be saved and used later for repeated tasks. The journal file also records any error or warning messages generated by commands. You can rerun these commands after making corrections and removing the messages.

The default name for the journal file is *SPSS.JNL* on most operating systems. You can turn off the journal or assign a different name to it (see SET). SPSS erases an existing journal file with the default name when it starts a new session. If you want to save a journal file for future use, rename it before you start another session. On some operating systems, SPSS allows you to overwrite or append to journals from a previous session. Consult the *SPSS Base User's Guide* for your version of SPSS for specific information. Figure 2 is a journal file for a short session with a warning message.

Figure 2   Records from a journal file

```
DATA LIST /ID 1-3 SEX 4 (A) AGE 5-6 OPINION1 TO OPINION5 7-11.
BEGIN DATA
001F2621221
002M5611122
003F3422212
004F45112L2
>Warning # 1102
>An invalid numeric field has been found.  The result has been set to the
>system-missing value.
END DATA.
LIST.
```

- The warning message, marked by the > symbol, tells you that an invalid numeric field has been found. Checking the last data line, you will notice that column 10 is *L*, which is probably a typographic error. You can correct the typo (for example, by changing the *L* to 1), delete the warning message, and submit the file again.

Data Files

SPSS is capable of reading and writing a wide variety of data file formats, including raw data files created by a data entry device or a text editor, formatted data files produced by a data management program, data files generated by other software packages, and SPSS-format data files.

Raw Data File

Raw data files contain only data, either generated by a programming language, such as COBOL, FORTRAN, and Assembler, or entered with a data entry device or a text editor. SPSS can read raw data arranged in almost any format, including raw matrix materials and nonprintable codes. User-entered data can be embedded within a command file as inline data or saved on tape or disk as an external file. Nonprintable machine codes are usually stored in an external file.

Raw data must be defined before they can be used by procedures. Data definition commands such as DATA LIST, KEYED DATA LIST, and MATRIX DATA can be used to read in raw data. Appropriate input formats must be specified on these commands (see "Variable Formats" on p. 31). If for some reason you need to write a raw data file, use the WRITE command or specify WRITE on a procedure with that subcommand. On most operating systems, the default extension of a raw data file produced by SPSS is *.DAT*.

Files from Other Software Applications

You can read files from a variety of other software applications, including dBASE, Lotus, SYLK, and Excel. You can also read simple tab-delimited spreadsheet files. Use GET TRANSLATE with different TYPE specifications to read files from common spreadsheet and database programs. To produce data files for these programs, use SAVE TRANSLATE.

Consult the *SPSS Base User's Guide* for your version of SPSS for the types of files (if any) that your system can read and write.

SPSS-Format Data File

An SPSS-format data file is a file specifically formatted for use by SPSS, containing both data and the dictionary that defines the data. The **dictionary** contains names for the variables, formats for reading and displaying values, and optional variable and value labels and missing-value specifications. SPSS-format data files are created by using a SAVE or XSAVE command during a session. On most operating systems, the default extension of a saved SPSS-format data file is *.SAV*. An SPSS-format data file can also be a matrix file created with the MATRIX=OUT subcommand on procedures that write matrices.

To retrieve an SPSS-format data file, use GET. SPSS-format data files speed processing and are required as input for combining files during a session. For a discussion of the structure of SPSS-format data files, see "SPSS Data File Structure" below.

SPSS Portable File

A portable file contains all of the data and dictionary information stored in the working data file but is specially formatted for transporting files between installations with different versions of SPSS (such as the PRIME, VAX, or HONEYWELL GCOS computers) or for transporting files between SPSS, SPSS/PC+, and other software using the same portable file format. Use IMPORT to read a portable file and EXPORT to save the working data file as a portable file. On most operating systems, the default extension of a saved portable file is *.POR*. Since a portable file needs conversion, it is always simpler to transport a file as an SPSS-format data file whenever possible.

Working Data File

The working data file is the data file you build to use in the current session. You can retrieve an SPSS-format data file using GET, which in effect makes a working copy of the specified file. You can also build a new file with DATA LIST or other data definition commands.

The working data file is not created until SPSS encounters a command (usually a procedure) that causes it to read the data (see Table 1 on p. 17). At that point, SPSS executes all of the preceding data definition and transformation commands and the command that causes the data to be read. The working data file is then available for further transformations and procedures, and it remains available until replaced by a new working data file or until the end of the session.

Some procedures can add variables to the working data file. Others, such as AGGREGATE and procedures that write matrix materials, can replace the working data file.

Any transformations and statistical analyses that you request during a session are performed on the working data file. Transformations performed during a session apply to the working data file only. Changes to the file are lost if the working data file is erased or replaced before you have saved it. See SAVE and XSAVE.

SPSS Data File Structure

An SPSS-format data file is a self-documented file containing data and descriptive information. The descriptive information is called the **dictionary**. It contains variable names and locations, variable and value labels, print and write formats, and missing-value indicators. To use an SPSS-format data file, you must retrieve it with GET, which creates a working data file from the SPSS-format data file. Only a few commands can use an SPSS-format data file directly without first specifying GET; they include MATCH FILES, ADD FILES, and procedures that can read SPSS matrix data files.

To view the contents of an SPSS-format data file, retrieve it with GET and then use LIST to display the variables in the working data file. Figure 3 shows a partial listing of a working file. The values are displayed using their print format, which is different from the way they are internally stored.

Figure 3   Part of a listed working data file

ID	SALBEG	SEX	TIME	AGE	SALNOW	EDLEVEL	WORK	JOBCAT	MINORITY	SEXRACE
628	8400	0	81	28.50	16080	16	.25	4	0	1.00
630	24000	0	73	40.33	41400	16	12.50	5	0	1.00
632	10200	0	83	31.08	21960	15	4.08	5	0	1.00
633	8700	0	93	31.17	19200	16	1.83	4	0	1.00
635	17400	0	83	41.92	28350	19	13.00	5	0	1.00
637	12996	0	80	29.50	27250	18	2.42	4	0	1.00
641	6900	0	79	28.00	16080	15	3.17	1	0	1.00
649	5400	0	67	28.75	14100	15	.50	1	0	1.00
650	5040	0	96	27.42	12420	15	1.17	1	0	1.00
652	6300	0	77	52.92	12300	12	26.42	3	0	1.00
653	6300	0	84	33.50	15720	15	6.00	1	0	1.00
656	6000	0	88	54.33	8880	12	27.00	1	0	1.00
657	10500	0	93	32.33	22000	17	2.67	4	0	1.00
658	10800	0	98	41.17	22800	15	12.00	5	0	1.00

The dictionary is created when an SPSS-format data file is built. You can display or modify the dictionary of a working file. Use DISPLAY DICTIONARY to view the dictionary, and use commands such as VARIABLE LABELS, VALUE LABELS, and MISSING VALUES to modify specific information contained in the dictionary. Figure 4 shows part of the displayed dictionary information of the working data file displayed in Figure 3.

Figure 4   Displayed dictionary information

```
           List of variables on the active file

Name                                                      Position

ID          Employee Code                                       1
            Print Format: F4
            Write Format: F4

SALBEG      Beginning Salary                                    2
            Print Format: F5
            Write Format: F5
            Missing Values: 0

SEX         Sex of Employee                                     3
            Print Format: F1
            Write Format: F1
            Missing Values: 9

            Value    Label

               0     Males
               1     Females
TIME        Job Seniority                                       4
            Print Format: F2
            Write Format: F2
            Missing Values: 0
```

SPSS Matrix Data Files

An SPSS matrix data file is similar to any SPSS-format data file. It is a self-documented file containing data and descriptive information. The descriptive information, stored in the file dictionary, includes variable names, variable print and write formats, and optional variable and value labels. You can assign or change the names, labels, and formats of the variables in a matrix data file, just as you can in any SPSS-format data file. Many procedures can read raw matrix data and write a representative matrix of the data values to an SPSS matrix data file, which can be used as input for subsequent analysis.

Table 3 shows the types of matrix materials written by SPSS procedures. The *ROWTYPE_* values (discussed below) of each matrix are also included so that you can see which procedure matrices are readable by other procedures. If a procedure produces more than one type of matrix, the subcommands required for each type of matrix are listed.

Table 3   Types of matrices and their contents

Command	Subcommands/Notes	ROWTYPE_ values
ALSCAL		PROX
CLUSTER		PROX
CORRELATIONS		MEAN STDDEV N CORR
DISCRIMINANT	/CLASSIFY=POOLED	N (1 per cell) COUNT (1 per cell) MEAN (1 per cell) STDDEV (pooled) CORR (pooled)
	/CLASSIFY=SEPARATE, /STATISTICS=BOXM, or /STATISTICS=GCOV	N (1 per cell) COUNT (1 per cell) MEAN (1 per cell) STDDEV (1 per cell) CORR (1 per cell)
FACTOR	/MATRIX=OUT(CORR=file) /MATRIX=IN(CORR=file)	CORR
	/MATRIX=OUT(FAC=file) /MATRIX=IN(FAC=file)	FACTOR
MANOVA		N (cell and pooled) MEAN (1 per cell) STDDEV (pooled) CORR (pooled)
NONPAR CORR	/PRINT=SPEARMAN	N RHO
	/PRINT=KENDALL	N TAUB

Table 3   Types of matrices and their contents (Continued)

Command	Subcommands/Notes	ROWTYPE_ values
ONEWAY	Separate variance Can be input and output	MEAN (1 per cell) STDDEV (1 per cell) N (1 per cell)
	Pooled variance Can be input only	MEAN (1 per cell) N (1 per cell) MSE (pooled) DFE (pooled)
PARTIAL CORR		N CORR
PROXIMITIES		PROX
REGRESSION		MEAN STDDEV N CORR
RELIABILITY		N MEAN STDDEV CORR

- All SPSS procedures that handle matrix materials use the MATRIX subcommand. The MATRIX subcommand specifies the file from which the input matrix is read and/or the file to which the output matrix is written.

- Matrix materials can be read from an external file as long as a working data file has been created. The working file does not have to be the matrix data file.

- The procedures that read matrix materials cannot read every type of SPSS matrix data file. For example, REGRESSION cannot read a matrix data file written by NONPAR CORR.

Figure 5 lists the structure of a matrix file and Figure 6 shows the dictionary information for the same file.

Variable Order. The following variable order is standard for all SPSS matrix data files:

1. Split variables, if any. In Figure 5, the split variable is *SEX*.

2. *ROWTYPE_* variable. The values of the *ROWTYPE_* variable describe the contents of the matrix data file, such as *MEAN, STDDEV, N,* and *CORR*.

3. Factor or grouping variables, if any.

4. *VARNAME_* variable (or *FACTOR_* variable for factor-loading matrices). The values of the *VARNAME_* variable are the names of the variable used to form the matrix.

5. Continuous variables used to form the matrix.

Figure 5   A matrix data file (LIST output)

```
FILE:       MATRIX FILE
SEX:   1    FEMALE

SEX ROWTYPE_ VARNAME_      FOOD      RENT   PUBTRANS   TEACHER      COOK   ENGINEER

  1 MEAN              73.3750000 134.500000 53.5000000 46.8000000 72.4375000 59.8125000
  1 STDDEV            15.4483009 115.534699 25.8173069 19.4209018 29.5746936 21.5196616
  1 N        FOOD     16.0000000 16.0000000 16.0000000 15.0000000 16.0000000 16.0000000
  1 N        RENT     16.0000000 16.0000000 16.0000000 15.0000000 16.0000000 16.0000000
  1 N        PUBTRANS 16.0000000 16.0000000 16.0000000 15.0000000 16.0000000 16.0000000
  1 N        TEACHER  15.0000000 15.0000000 15.0000000 15.0000000 15.0000000 15.0000000
  1 N        COOK     16.0000000 16.0000000 16.0000000 15.0000000 16.0000000 16.0000000
  1 N        ENGINEER 16.0000000 16.0000000 16.0000000 15.0000000 16.0000000 16.0000000
  1 CORR     FOOD      1.0000000   .3658643   .5372333   .1733358   .1378010   .3778351
  1 CORR     RENT       .3658643  1.0000000   .1045105  -.0735708   .2026299   .1237062
  1 CORR     PUBTRANS   .5372333   .1045105  1.0000000   .6097397   .3877995   .6413121
  1 CORR     TEACHER    .1733358  -.0735708   .6097397  1.0000000   .4314755   .7312415
  1 CORR     COOK       .1378010   .2026299   .3877995   .4314755  1.0000000   .7807327
  1 CORR     ENGINEER   .3778351   .1237062   .6413121   .7312415   .7807327  1.0000000


NUMBER OF CASES READ =     14     NUMBER OF CASES LISTED =     14


FILE:       MATRIX FILE
SEX:   2    MALE

SEX ROWTYPE_ VARNAME_      FOOD      RENT   PUBTRANS   TEACHER      COOK   ENGINEER

  2 MEAN              68.8620690 112.137931 45.1379310 33.9310345 60.2142857 60.1785714
  2 STDDEV            20.4148478 81.3430672 24.1819356 26.9588722 30.2952840 28.8752792
  2 N        FOOD     29.0000000 29.0000000 29.0000000 29.0000000 28.0000000 28.0000000
  2 N        RENT     29.0000000 29.0000000 29.0000000 29.0000000 28.0000000 28.0000000
  2 N        PUBTRANS 29.0000000 29.0000000 29.0000000 29.0000000 28.0000000 28.0000000
  2 N        TEACHER  29.0000000 29.0000000 29.0000000 29.0000000 28.0000000 28.0000000
  2 N        COOK     28.0000000 28.0000000 28.0000000 28.0000000 28.0000000 28.0000000
  2 N        ENGINEER 28.0000000 28.0000000 28.0000000 28.0000000 28.0000000 28.0000000
  2 CORR     FOOD      1.0000000   .2012077   .5977491   .6417034   .4898941   .5190702
  2 CORR     RENT       .2012077  1.0000000  -.1405952  -.0540657   .0727153   .3508598
  2 CORR     PUBTRANS   .5977491  -.1405952  1.0000000   .7172945   .7170419   .6580408
  2 CORR     TEACHER    .6417034  -.0540657   .7172945  1.0000000   .6711871   .6650047
  2 CORR     COOK       .4898941   .0727153   .7170419   .6711871  1.0000000   .7688210
  2 CORR     ENGINEER   .5190702   .3508598   .6580408   .6650047   .7688210  1.0000000


NUMBER OF CASES READ =     14     NUMBER OF CASES LISTED =     14
```

Split Files. When split-file processing is in effect, a full set of matrix materials is written for each split-file group defined by the split variables.

- A split variable cannot have the same variable name as any other variable written to the matrix data file. Not all procedures allow split-file variables in their matrices.

- If split-file processing is in effect when a matrix is written, the same split file must be in effect when that matrix is read by any procedure.

Additional Statistics. Some procedures include statistics with their matrix materials. For example, CORRELATION matrices always include the mean, standard deviation, and number of cases used to compute each coefficient, as shown in Figure 5. Other procedures, for example PROXIMITIES and FACTOR, include no statistics with their matrices. See Table 3 for a list of the statistics written by each procedure. Refer to the description of each command for its requirements for a matrix input file.

Missing Values. The treatment of missing values in a procedure affects the matrix materials written to the data file. With pairwise treatment of missing values, the matrix of N's used to compute each coefficient is included in the matrix. With any other missing-value treatment, the single N used to calculate all coefficients in the matrix is included in the form of a vector. Figure 5 includes the matrix of N's written by CORRELATIONS when missing values are excluded pairwise from the analysis. Figure 7 shows the single N written by CORRELATIONS when missing values are excluded listwise.

The missing-value treatment that was in effect when the matrix was written must be compatible with the missing-value treatment in effect when the matrix is read. For example, REGRESSION can read a matrix written by CORRELATIONS but only if the missing-value treatment of both procedures is consistent. Either both must refer to a matrix of N's or both must refer to a single N. For all procedures, pairwise treatment of missing values generates a matrix of N's; any other treatment of missing values generates a single vector of N's.

Matrix File Dictionaries. As shown in Figure 6, print and write formats of A8 are assigned to the matrix variables that SPSS creates (for example, *ROWTYPE_*, *VARNAME_*, and *FACTOR_*). No labels are assigned to these variables. Print and write formats of F10.7 are assigned to all of the continuous variables in the matrix analysis; the names and variable labels defined for these variables in the original data file are retained, but their original values and value labels are dropped because they do not apply to the matrix data file. When split-file processing is in effect, the variable names, variable and value labels, and print and write formats of the split-file variables are read from the dictionary of the original data file.

Procedures read and write matrices in which each row corresponds to a single case in the matrix data file. For example, the matrix shown in Figure 7 has nine cases. The first three cases with the *ROWTYPE_* values of *MEAN*, *STDDEV*, and *N* have no values for *VARNAME_* but do have values for all the variables from *FOOD* to *ENGINEER*. The fourth case, *CORR*, in the matrix generated for the first split-file group has a value of *FOOD* for *VARNAME_*, a value of 0.3652366 when correlated with variable *RENT*, a value of 0.5371597 when correlated with variable *PUBTRANS*, and so on.

Figure 6   Dictionary of a matrix system file (DISPLAY output)

```
FILE:       MATRIX FILE

       LIST OF VARIABLES ON THE ACTIVE FILE

NAME                                                                POSITION

SEX                                                                    1
                    PRINT FORMAT: F2
                    WRITE FORMAT: F2

          VALUE    LABEL

            1      FEMALE
            2      MALE

ROWTYPE_                                                               2
                    PRINT FORMAT: A8
                    WRITE FORMAT: A8

VARNAME_                                                               3
                    PRINT FORMAT: A8
                    WRITE FORMAT: A8

FOOD      AVG FOOD PRICES                                              4
                    PRINT FORMAT: F10.7
                    WRITE FORMAT: F10.7

RENT      NORMAL RENT                                                  5
                    PRINT FORMAT: F10.7
                    WRITE FORMAT: F10.7

PUBTRANS  PRICE FOR PUBLIC TRANSPORT                                   6
                    PRINT FORMAT: F10.7
                    WRITE FORMAT: F10.7

TEACHER   NET TEACHER'S SALARY                                         7
                    PRINT FORMAT: F10.7
                    WRITE FORMAT: F10.7

COOK      NET COOK'S SALARY                                            8
                    PRINT FORMAT: F10.7
                    WRITE FORMAT: F10.7

ENGINEER  NET ENGINEER'S SALARY                                        9
                    PRINT FORMAT: F10.7
                    WRITE FORMAT: F10.7
```

Figure 7   Single N in the matrix system file

```
FILE:      MATRIX FILE
SEX:   1   FEMALE

SEX ROWTYPE_ VARNAME_      FOOD        RENT    PUBTRANS    TEACHER       COOK    ENGINEER

  1 MEAN              73.4666667 136.800000 54.0000000 46.8000000 73.8666667 60.0000000
  1 STDDEV            15.9860058 119.210019 26.6431444 19.4209018 30.0353760 22.2614337
  1 N                 15.0000000 15.0000000 15.0000000 15.0000000 15.0000000 15.0000000
  1 CORR     FOOD      1.0000000    .3652366   .5371597   .1733358   .1358120   .3773434
  1 CORR     RENT       .3652366  1.0000000    .0989524  -.0735708   .1914448   .1213899
  1 CORR     PUBTRANS   .5371597   .0989524  1.0000000    .6097397   .3811372   .6409265
  1 CORR     TEACHER    .1733358  -.0735708   .6097397  1.0000000    .4314755   .7312415
  1 CORR     COOK       .1358120   .1914448   .3811372   .4314755  1.0000000    .7893533
  1 CORR     ENGINEER   .3773434   .1213899   .6409265   .7312415   .7893533  1.0000000


NUMBER OF CASES READ =       9    NUMBER OF CASES LISTED =        9

                                                                         2

FILE:      MATRIX FILE
SEX:   2   MALE

SEX ROWTYPE_ VARNAME_      FOOD        RENT    PUBTRANS    TEACHER       COOK    ENGINEER

  2 MEAN              69.6428571 114.464286 46.1428571 33.7500000 60.2142857 60.1785714
  2 STDDEV            20.3437392 81.8474109 24.0011023 27.4356149 30.2952840 28.8752792
  2 N                 28.0000000 28.0000000 28.0000000 28.0000000 28.0000000 28.0000000
  2 CORR     FOOD      1.0000000    .1752920   .5784136   .6638084   .4898941   .5190702
  2 CORR     RENT       .1752920  1.0000000   -.1817862  -.0491139   .0727153   .3508598
  2 CORR     PUBTRANS   .5784136  -.1817862  1.0000000    .7447511   .7170419   .6580408
  2 CORR     TEACHER    .6638084  -.0491139   .7447511  1.0000000    .6711871   .6650047
  2 CORR     COOK       .4898941   .0727153   .7170419   .6711871  1.0000000    .7688210
  2 CORR     ENGINEER   .5190702   .3508598   .6580408   .6650047   .7688210  1.0000000


NUMBER OF CASES READ =       9    NUMBER OF CASES LISTED =        9
```

Variables

To prepare data for processing, you must define variables by assigning variable names and formats. You can also specify variable labels, value labels, and missing values, but they are optional. This section discusses the two essential components of variable definition: variable names and formats.

Variable Names

Each variable must have a unique name. Variable names are stored in the dictionary of an SPSS-format data file or working data file. Observe the following rules when establishing variable names or referring to variables by their names on commands:

- Variable names can contain up to eight characters, the first of which must be a letter or one of the characters @, #, or $.
- A # character in the first position of a variable name defines a scratch variable (see "Scratch Variables" on p. 31).
- A $ sign in the first position indicates that the variable is a system variable (see "System Variables" on p. 30). The $ sign is not allowed as the initial character of a user-defined variable.
- The period, underscore, and the characters $, #, and @ can be used within variable names. For example, *A._$@#1* is a valid variable name.
- Variable names ending with a period should be avoided, since the period may be interpreted as a command terminator.
- Variable names ending in underscores should be avoided, since such names may conflict with names of variables automatically created by a number of commands—for example, *YEAR_* and *DATE_* created by the DATE command.
- Variable names can be established on the DATA LIST, KEYED DATA LIST, MATRIX DATA, NUMERIC, STRING, COMPUTE, RECODE, and COUNT commands. They can be changed with the RENAME VARIABLES command.
- Reserved keywords cannot be used as variable names. Reserved keywords are

  | ALL | AND | BY | EQ | GE | GT | LE |
  | LT | NE | NOT | OR | TO | WITH | |

Keyword TO

You can establish names for a set of variables or to refer to any number of consecutive variables by specifying the beginning and the ending variables joined by the keyword TO.

To establish names for a set of variables with the keyword TO, use a character prefix with a numeric suffix.

- The prefix can be any valid name. Both the beginning and ending variables must use the same prefix.

- The numeric suffix can be any integer, but the first number must be smaller than the second. For example, ITEM1 TO ITEM5 establishes five variables named *ITEM1*, *ITEM2*, *ITEM3*, *ITEM4*, and *ITEM5*.

- Each variable name, including the number, must not exceed eight characters.

- Leading zeros used in numeric suffixes are included in the variable name. For example, V001 TO V100 establishes 100 variables, *V001*, *V002*, *V003*, ..., *V100*. V1 TO V100 establishes 100 variables, *V1*, *V2*, *V3*, ..., *V100*.

The keyword TO can also be used on procedures and other commands to refer to consecutive variables on the working data file. For example, AVAR TO VARB refers to the variables *AVAR* and all subsequent variables up to and including *VARB*.

- In most cases, the TO specification uses the variable order on the working data file. Use the DISPLAY command to see the order of variables on the working data file.

- On some subcommands, the order in which variables are named on a previous subcommand, usually the VARIABLES subcommand, is used to determine which variables are consecutive and therefore are implied by the TO specification. This is noted in the description of individual commands.

System Variables

System variables are special variables created during a working session to keep system-required information, such as the number of cases read by the system, the system-missing value, and the current date. System variables can be used in data transformations.

- The names of system variables begin with a dollar sign ($).

- You cannot modify a system variable or alter its print or write format. Except for these restrictions, you can use system variables anywhere a normal variable is used in the transformation language.

- System variables are not available for procedures.

$CASENUM   *Permanent case sequence number.* For each case, *$CASENUM* is the number of permanent cases read up to and including that case. The format is F8.0.The value of *$CASENUM* is not necessarily the row number in a Data Editor window (available in windowed environments).

$SYSMIS   *System-missing value.* The system-missing value displays as a period (.) or whatever is used as the decimal point.

$JDATE   *Current date in number of days from October 14, 1582* (day 1 of the Gregorian calendar). The format is F6.0.

$DATE   *Current date in international date format with two-digit year.* The format is A9 in the form dd-mmm-yy.

$DATE11   *Current date in international date format with four-digit year.* The format is A11 in the form dd-mmm-yyyy.

$TIME   *Current date and time. $TIME* represents the number of seconds from midnight, October 14, 1582, to the date and time when the transformation command is executed. The format is F20.

$LENGTH   *The current page length.* The format is F11.0. For more information, see SET.

$WIDTH   *The current page width.* The format is F3.0. For more information, see SET.

Scratch Variables

Scratch variables are variables created for the sole purpose of facilitating operations during a session.

- To create a scratch variable, specify a variable name that begins with the # character—for example, *#ID*. Scratch variables can be either numeric or string.
- Scratch variables are initialized to 0 for numeric variables or blank for string variables.
- SPSS does not reinitialize scratch variables when reading a new case. Their values are always carried across cases. Therefore, a scratch variable is a good choice for a looping index.
- Do not use LEAVE with a scratch variable.
- Scratch variables cannot be used in procedures and cannot be saved in a data file.
- Scratch variables cannot be assigned missing values, variable labels, or value labels.
- Scratch variables can be created between procedures but are always discarded as the next procedure begins.
- Scratch variables are discarded once a TEMPORARY command is specified.
- The keyword TO cannot refer to scratch variables and permanent variables at the same time.
- Scratch variables cannot be named on a WEIGHT command.

Variable Formats

SPSS accepts two variable types: numeric and string (also referred to as alphanumeric). Numeric values are stored internally as double-precision floating-point numbers and string values as codes listed in the SPSS character set (see Appendix B). Variable formats determine how SPSS reads raw data into storage and how it displays and writes values out.

Input and Output Formats

Values are read according to their *input* format and displayed on your terminal or written to a file according to their *output* format. The input and output formats differ in several ways.

- The input format is either specified or implied on the DATA LIST, KEYED DATA LIST, or other data definition commands. It is in effect only when SPSS builds cases in a working data file. Figure 8 shows the command printback for DATA LIST, which includes input format specifications.

Figure 8   Output showing input formats

```
   1  0  DATA LIST   /ID 1-4 SCORE 6-9 (F,2).

This command will read 1 records from the command file

Variable   Rec    Start      End        Format

ID           1       1        4          F4.0
SCORE        1       6        9          F4.2
```

- DATA LIST or any other data definition command automatically generates an output format from the input format and expands the output format to include punctuation characters such as decimal points, commas, dollar signs, and percent signs. To see the current output formats of variables in the working data file, use DISPLAY VARIABLES. The variables defined by the above DATA LIST command are displayed in Figure 9. Note that the output format for *SCORE* has been expanded one space to allow the display of the decimal point (the F4.2 input format indicates a four-character variable with two implied decimal places; the F5.2 output format includes one space for the decimal point).

Figure 9   Output showing output formats

```
List of variables on the active file

Name       Pos   Print Fmt    Write Fmt    Missing Values

ID           1   F4           F4
SCORE        2   F5.2         F5.2
```

- The formats (specified or default) on NUMERIC, COMPUTE, or other commands that create new variables are output formats. You must specify adequate widths to accommodate all punctuation characters.

- The output format is in effect during the entire working session (unless explicitly changed) and is saved in the dictionary of an SPSS-format data file.

- Output formats for numeric variables can be changed with the FORMATS, PRINT FORMATS, or WRITE FORMATS command.

- Output formats (widths) for string variables cannot be changed with command syntax. However, you can use STRING to declare a new variable with the desired format and then use COMPUTE to copy values from the existing string variable into the new variable.

- The format type cannot be changed from string to numeric, or vice versa, with command syntax. However, you can use RECODE to recode values from one variable into another variable of a different type.

See DATA LIST for information on specifying input data formats. See FORMATS, PRINT FORMATS, and WRITE FORMATS for information on specifying output data formats. See STRING for information on declaring new string variables.

Numeric Variable Formats

- The formats used in this manual use FORTRAN-like syntax—for example, Fw.d, where F denotes the format type (numeric), w represents the variable width, and d represents the number of decimal places.

- By default, the DATA LIST and KEYED DATA LIST commands assume that variables are numeric with an F format type. The default width depends on whether the data are in fixed or freefield format. For discussion of fixed data and freefield data, see DATA LIST.

- Numeric variables created by COMPUTE, COUNT, or other commands that create numeric variables are assigned a format type F8.2 (or the default format defined on SET FORMAT).

- If a data value exceeds its width specification, SPSS makes an attempt to display some value nevertheless. It first rounds the decimals, then takes out punctuation characters, then tries scientific notation, and if there is still not enough space, produces asterisks (***), indicating that a value is present but cannot be displayed in the assigned width.

- The output format does not affect the value stored in the file. A numeric value is always stored in double precision.

F, N, and E Formats

Table 4 lists the formats most commonly used to read in and write out numeric data.

Table 4   Common numeric formats

Format type	Description	Sample format	Sample input	Output for fixed input Format	Value	Output for freefield input Format	Value
Fw.d	Standard numeric	F5.0	1234	F5.0	1234	F5.0	1234
			1.234		1		1*
		F5.2	1234	F6.2	12.34	F6.2	1234.0
			1.234		1.23		1.23
Nw.d	Restricted numeric	N5.0	00123	F5.0	123	F5.0	123
			1.234		. †		1
		N5.2	12345	F6.2	123.45	F6.2	12345
			12.34		.		12.34
Ew.d	Scientific notation	E8.0	1234E3	E10.3	1.234E+06	E10.3	1.234E+06**
			1234		1.234E+03		1.234E+03

* Only the display is truncated. The value is stored in full precision.
† System-missing value. In this case, the value entered contains an illegal decimal point.
** Scientific notation is accepted in input data with F, COMMA, DOLLAR, DOT, and PCT formats. The same rules apply as specified below.

For fixed data:

- If a value has no coded decimal point but the input format specifies decimal positions, the rightmost positions are interpreted as implied decimal digits. For example, if the input F format specifies two decimal digits, the value 1234 is interpreted as 12.34; however, the value 123.4 is still interpreted as 123.4.

- With the N format, decimal places are always implied. Only unsigned integers are allowed. Values not padded with leading zeros to the specified width or those containing decimal points are assigned the system-missing value. This format is useful for reading and checking values that should be integers containing leading zeros.

- The E format reads all forms of scientific notation. If the sign is omitted, + is assumed. If the sign (+ or −) is specified before the exponent, the *E* or *D* can be omitted. A single space is permitted after the *E* or *D* and/or after the sign. If both the sign and the letter *E* or *D* are omitted, implied decimal places are assumed. For example, 1.234E3, 1.234+3, 1.234E+3, 1.234D3, 1.234D+3, 1.234E 3, and 1234 are all legitimate values. Only the last value can imply decimal places.

- E format input values can be up to 40 characters wide and include up to 15 decimal positions.

- The default output width (*w*) for the E format is either the specified input width or the number of specified decimal positions plus 7 (*d*+7), whichever is greater. The minimum width is 10 and the minimum decimal places are 3.

For freefield data:

- F format *w* and *d* specifications do not affect how data are read. They only determine the output formats (expanded, if necessary). 1234 is always read as 1234 in freefield data, but a specified F5.2 format will be expanded to F6.2 and the value will be displayed as 1234.0 (the last decimal place is rounded because of lack of space).

- The N format, when used for freefield data, is treated as the F format.

- The E format for freefield data follows the same rules as for fixed data except that no blank space is permitted in the value. Thus, 1.234E3 and 1.234+3 are allowed, but the value 1.234 3 will cause mistakes when the data are read.

- The default output E format and the width and decimal place limitations are the same as with fixed data.

COMMA, DOT, DOLLAR, and PCT Formats

Table 5 lists the formats that read and write data with embedded punctuation characters and symbols, such as commas, dots, and dollar and percent signs. The input data may or may not contain such characters. The data values read in are stored as numbers but displayed using the appropriate formats. Other formats that use punctuation characters and symbols are date and time formats and currency formats. Date and time are discussed in "Date and Time" on p. 60. Currency formats are output formats only. (See SET and FORMATS.)

Table 5   Numeric formats with punctuation and symbols

Format type	Description	Sample format	Sample input	Default output format	Displayed value
COMMAw.d	Commas in numbers	COMMA6.0	12345	COMMA7.0	12,345
			12,345		12,345
			123,45		12,345
		COMMA6.3	12345	COMMA7.3	12.345
			123,45		12.345
			1.2345		1.234
			1234.5		1234.50[*]
DOTw.d	Dots in numbers	DOT6.0	12345	DOT7.0	12.345
			123.45		12.345
			123.45		12.345
		DOT6.3	12345	DOT7.3	12,345
			123.45		12,345
			1,2345		1,234
			1234,5		1234,50*
DOLLARw.d	Dollar sign and comma in numbers	DOLLAR7.0	1234	DOLLAR10.0	$1,234
			1,234		$1,234
			$1234		$1,234
			$1,234		$1,234
		DOLLAR7.3	1234	DOLLAR10.3	$1.234
			1,234		$1.234
			$1,23.4		$123.400
			12345.6		$12345.600*
PCTw.d	Percent sign after numbers	PCT7.0	1234	PCT8.0	1234%
			12.34		12%
		PCT7.2	1234	PCT9.3	1.234%
			12.3		12.340%
			1234		12.34%

* When the decimal point is coded in input, SPSS displays all specified decimal places whether recorded in the data or not. When the width is inadequate, thousands separators are dropped before decimal places.

- Formats listed in Table 5 cannot be used to read freefield data.
- Data values can appear anywhere within the column specification. Both leading and trailing blanks are allowed.
- The sign (for example, "$" for DOLLAR format) or punctuation mark (for example, "." for DOT format) is ignored in the input data. Its position does not affect the value read into storage.
- The default output format expands the width of the input format by the number of the required signs or punctuation marks plus the decimal point if d is not 0. For example, COMMA9.2 is expanded to COMMA12.2 to accommodate two possible commas and one decimal point.
- DOT format is similar to COMMA format but reverses the symbols used for the thousands separator and the decimal point. For example, in DOT format, 1.234 has the value of one thousand, two hundred and thirty-four.

Binary and Hexadecimal Formats

SPSS is capable of reading and writing data in formats used by a number of programming languages such as PL/I, COBOL, FORTRAN, and Assembler. The data can be binary, hexadecimal, or zoned decimal. Formats described in this section can be used both as input formats and output formats, but with fixed data only. The described formats are not available on all systems. Consult the *SPSS Base User's Guide* for your version of SPSS for details.

The default output format for all formats described in this section is an equivalent F format, allowing the maximum number of columns for values with symbols and punctuation. To change the default, use FORMATS or WRITE FORMATS.

IBw.d (integer binary):

The IB format reads fields that contain fixed-point binary (integer) data. The data might be generated by COBOL using COMPUTATIONAL data items, by FORTRAN using INTEGER*2 or INTEGER*4, or by Assembler using fullword and halfword items. The general format is a signed binary number that is 16 or 32 bits in length.

The general syntax for the IB format is IBw.d, where w is the field width in bytes (omitted for column-style specifications) and d is the number of digits to the right of the decimal point. Since the width is expressed in bytes and the number of decimal positions is expressed in digits, d can be greater than w. For example, both of the following commands are valid:

```
DATA LIST FIXED /VAR1 (IB4.8).
```

```
DATA LIST FIXED /VAR1 1-4 (IB,8).
```

Widths of 2 and 4 represent standard 16-bit and 32-bit integers, respectively. Fields read with the IB format are treated as signed. For example, the one-byte binary value 11111111 would be read as −1.

PIBw.d (positive integer binary):

The PIB format is essentially the same as IB except that negative numbers are not allowed. This restriction allows one additional bit of magnitude. The same one-byte value 11111111 would be read as 255.

PIBHEXw (hexadecimal of PIB):

The PIBHEX format reads hexadecimal numbers as unsigned integers and writes positive integers as hexadecimal numbers. The general syntax for the PIBHEX format is PIBHEXw, where w indicates the total number of hexadecimal characters. The w specification must be an even number, with a maximum of 16.

For input data, each hexadecimal number must consist of the exact number of characters. No signs, decimal points, or leading and trailing blanks are allowed. For some operating systems (such as IBM CMS), hexadecimal characters must be upper case. The following example illustrates the kind of data the PIBHEX format can read:

```
DATA LIST FIXED
 /VAR1 1-4 (PIBHEX) VAR2 6-9 (PIBHEX) VAR3 11-14 (PIBHEX).
BEGIN DATA
0001 0002 0003
0004 0005 0006
0007 0008 0009
000A 000B 000C
000D 000E 000F
00F0 0B2C FFFF
END DATA.
LIST.
```

The values for *VAR1*, *VAR2*, and *VAR3* are listed in Figure 10. The PIBHEX format can also be used to write decimal values as hexadecimal numbers, which may be useful for programmers.

Figure 10   Output displaying values read in PIBHEX format

```
VAR1    VAR2    VAR3

   1       2       3
   4       5       6
   7       8       9
  10      11      12
  13      14      15
 240    2860   65535
```

Zw.d (zoned decimal):

The Z format reads data values that contain zoned decimal data. Such numbers may be generated by COBOL systems using DISPLAY data items, by PL/I systems using PICTURE data items, or by Assembler using zoned decimal data items.

In zoned decimal format, one digit is represented by one byte, generally hexadecimal F1 representing 1, F2 representing 2, and so on. The last byte, however, combines the sign for the number with the last digit. In the last byte, hexadecimal A, F, or C assigns +, and B, D, or E assigns −. For example, hexadecimal D1 represents 1 for the last digit and assigns the minus sign (−) to the number.

The general syntax of the Z format is Zw.d, where w is the total number of bytes (which is the same as columns) and d is the number of decimals. For input data, values can appear anywhere within the column specifications. Both leading and trailing blanks are allowed. Decimals can be implied by the input format specification or explicitly coded in the data. Explicitly coded decimals override the input format specifications.

The following example illustrates how the Z format reads zoned decimals in their printed forms on IBM mainframe and PC systems. The printed form for the sign zone (A to I for +1 to +9, and so on) may vary from system to system.

```
DATA LIST FIXED /VAR1 1-5 (Z) VAR2 7-11 (Z,2) VAR3 13-17 (Z)
 VAR4 19-23 (Z,2) VAR5 25-29 (Z) VAR6 31-35 (Z,2).
BEGIN DATA
1234A 1234A 1234B 1234B 1234C 1234C
1234D 1234D 1234E 1234E 1234F 1234F
1234G 1234G 1234H 1234H 1234I 1234I
1234J 1234J 1234K 1234K 1234L 1234L
1234M 1234M 1234N 1234N 1234O 1234O
1234P 1234P 1234Q 1234Q 1234R 1234R
1234{ 1234{ 1234} 1234} 1.23M 1.23M
END DATA.
LIST.
```

The values for *VAR1* to *VAR6* are listed in Figure 11.

Figure 11   Output displaying values read in Z format

```
VAR1     VAR2     VAR3     VAR4     VAR5     VAR6

 12341   123.41   12342   123.42   12343   123.43
 12344   123.44   12345   123.45   12346   123.46
 12347   123.47   12348   123.48   12349   123.49
-12341  -123.41  -12342  -123.42  -12343  -123.43
-12344  -123.44  -12345  -123.45  -12346  -123.46
-12347  -123.47  -12348  -123.48  -12349  -123.49
 12340   123.40  -12340  -123.40       -1    -1.23
```

The default output format for the Z format is the equivalent F format, as shown in Figure 11. The default output width is based on the input width specification plus one column for the sign and one column for the implied decimal point (if specified). For example, an input format of Z4.0 generates an output format of F5.0 and an input format of Z4.2 generates an output format of F6.2.

Pw.d (packed decimal):

The P format is used to read fields with packed decimal numbers. Such numbers are generated by COBOL using COMPUTATIONAL–3 data items and by Assembler using packed decimal data items. The general format of a packed decimal field is two four-bit digits in each byte of the field except the last. The last byte contains a single digit in its four leftmost bits and a four-bit sign in its rightmost bits. If the last four bits are 1111 (hexadecimal F), the value is positive; if they are 1101 (hexadecimal D), the value is negative. One byte under the P format can represent numbers from –9 to 9.

The general syntax of the P format is Pw.d, where w is the number of bytes (not digits) and d is the number of digits to the right of the implied decimal point. The number of digits in a field is (2*w–1).

PKw.d (unsigned packed decimal):

The PK format is essentially the same as P except that there is no sign. That is, even the rightmost byte contains two digits, and negative data cannot be represented. One byte under the PK format can represent numbers from 0 to 99. The number of digits in a field is 2*w.

RBw (real binary):

The RB format is used to read data values that contain internal format floating-point numbers. Such numbers are generated by COBOL using COMPUTATIONAL–1 or COMPUTATIONAL–2 data items, by PL/I using FLOATING DECIMAL data items, by FORTRAN using REAL or REAL*8 data items, or by Assembler using floating-point data items.

The general syntax of the RB format is RBw, where w is the total number of bytes. The width specification must be an even number between 2 and 8. Normally, a width specification of 8 is used to read double-precision values, and a width of 4 is used to read single-precision values.

RBHEXw (hexadecimal of RB):

The RBHEX format interprets a series of hexadecimal characters as a number that represents a floating-point number. This representation is system-specific. If the field width is less than twice the width of a floating-point number, the value is right-padded with binary zeros. For some operating systems (for example, IBM CMS), letters in hexadecimal values must be upper case.

The general syntax of the RBHEX format is RBHEXw, where w indicates the total number of columns. The width must be an even number. The values are real (floating-point) numbers. Leading and trailing blanks are not allowed. Any data values shorter than the specified input width must be padded with leading zeros.

String Variable Formats

- The values of string variables can contain numbers, letters, and special characters and can be up to 255 characters long.

- SPSS differentiates between long strings and short strings. Long strings can be displayed by some procedures and by the PRINT command, and they can be used as break variables to define subgroups in REPORT. They cannot, however, be tabulated in procedures such as CROSSTABS, and they cannot have user-missing values. Short strings, on the other hand, can be tabulated and can have user-missing values. The maximum length of a short string depends on the computer and operating system; it is typically 8 characters.

- System-missing values cannot be generated for string variables, since any character is a legal string value.

- When a transformation command that creates or modifies a string variable yields a missing or undefined result, a null string is assigned. The variable displays as blanks and is not treated as missing.

- String formats are used to read and write string variables. The input values can be alphanumeric characters (A format) or the hexadecimal representation of alphanumeric characters (AHEX format).

- For fixed data, the width can be explicitly specified on DATA LIST or KEYED DATA LIST or implied if column-style specifications are used. For freefield data, the default width is 1; if the input string may be longer, w must be explicitly specified. Input strings shorter than the specified width are right-padded with blanks.

- The output format for a string variable is always A. The width is determined by the input format or the format assigned on the STRING command. String formats can be displayed with DISPLAY VARIABLES but cannot be changed.

Aw (Standard Characters)

The A format is used to read standard characters. Characters can include letters, numbers, punctuation marks, blanks, and most other characters on your keyboard. Numbers entered as values for string variables cannot be used in calculations unless you convert them to numeric format with the NUMBER function (see "String Functions" on p. 51).

Fixed data:

With fixed-format input data, any punctuation—including leading, trailing, and embedded blanks—within the column specifications is included in the string value. For example, a string value of "Mr. Ed" (with one embedded blank) is distinguished from a value of "Mr. Ed" (with two embedded blanks). It is also distinguished from a string value of "MR. ED" (all upper case), and all three are treated as separate values. These can be important considerations for any procedures, transformations, or data selection commands involving string variables. Consider the following example:

```
DATA LIST FIXED /ALPHAVAR 1-10 (A).
BEGIN DATA
Mr. Ed
Mr. Ed
MR. ED
Mr.  Ed
 Mr. Ed
END DATA.
AUTORECODE ALPHAVAR /INTO NUMVAR.
LIST.
```

AUTORECODE recodes the values into consecutive integers. Figure 12 shows the recoded values.

Figure 12   Different string values illustrated

```
ALPHAVAR   NUMVAR

Mr. Ed        4
Mr. Ed        4
MR. ED        2
Mr.  Ed       3
 Mr. Ed       1
```

Freefield data:

With freefield data, blanks and commas are treated as delimiters for A format variables unless the value is enclosed in apostrophes or quotation marks. For example,

```
Ed, Mr.
```

is read as two separate values (Ed and Mr.). To include blanks and/or commas in a string value, enclose the value in apostrophes or quotation marks. For example, the following command file will generate a list of values as shown in Figure 13:

```
DATA LIST FREE /ALPHAVAR (A10).
BEGIN DATA
Mr.   Ed
Ed,Mr.
'Mr.   Ed'
'Ed, Mr.'
END DATA.
LIST.
```

Figure 13   Blanks and commas in freefield string input

```
ALPHAVAR

Mr.
Ed
Ed
Mr.
Mr.   Ed
Ed, Mr.
```

AHEXw (Hexadecimal Characters)

The AHEX format is used to read the hexadecimal representation of standard characters. Each set of two hexadecimal characters represents one standard character. For codes used on different operating systems, see Appendix B.

- The w specification refers to columns of the hexadecimal representation and must be an even number. Leading, trailing, and embedded blanks are not allowed, and only valid hexadecimal characters can be used in input values.

- For some operating systems (for example, IBM CMS), letters in hexadecimal values must be upper case.

- The default output format for variables read with the AHEX input format is the A format. The default width is half the specified input width. For example, an input format of AHEX14 generates an output format of A7.

- Used as an output format, the AHEX format displays the printable characters in the hexadecimal characters specific to your system. The following commands run on a UNIX system (where A=41 (decimal 65), a=61 (decimal 97), and so on) produce the output shown in Figure 14:

```
DATA LIST FIXED
   /A,B,C,D,E,F,G,H,I,J,K,L,M,N,O,P,Q,R,S,T,U,V,W,X,Y,Z 1-26 (A).
FORMATS ALL (AHEX2).
BEGIN DATA
ABCDEFGHIJKLMNOPQRSTUVWXYZ
abcdefghijklmnopqrstuvwxyz
END DATA.
LIST.
```

Figure 14   Display of hexadecimal representation of the character set with AHEX format

```
A  B  C  D  E  F  G  H  I  J  K  L  M  N  O  P  Q  R  S  T  U  V  W  X  Y  Z

41 42 43 44 45 46 47 48 49 4A 4B 4C 4D 4E 4F 50 51 52 53 54 55 56 57 58 59 5A
61 62 63 64 65 66 67 68 69 6A 6B 6C 6D 6E 6F 70 71 72 73 74 75 76 77 78 79 7A
```

FORTRAN-like Format Specifications

You can use FORTRAN-like format specifications to define formats for a set of variables, as in the following example:

```
DATA LIST FILE=HUBDATA RECORDS=3
     /MOHIRED, YRHIRED, DEPT1 TO DEPT4 (T12, 2F2.0, 4(1X,F1.0)).
```

- The specification T12 in parentheses tabs to the 12th column. The first variable (*MOHIRED*) will be read beginning from column 12.

- The specification 2F2.0 assigns the format F2.0 to two adjacent variables (*MOHIRED* and *YRHIRED*).

- The next four variables (*DEPT1* to *DEPT4*) are each assigned the format F1.0. The 4 in 4(1X,F1.0) distributes the same format to four consecutive variables. 1X skips one column before each variable. (The column-skipping specification placed within the parentheses is distributed to each variable.)

Transformation Expressions

Transformation expressions are used in commands like COMPUTE, IF, DO IF, LOOP IF, and SELECT IF. This section describes the three types of expressions: numeric, string, and logical, as well as available operators. For date and time functions, see "Date and Time" on p. 60.

Numeric Expressions

Numeric expressions can be used with the COMPUTE and IF command and as part of a logical expression for commands such as IF, DO IF, LOOP IF, and SELECT IF. Arithmetic expressions can also appear in the index portion of a LOOP command, on the REPEATING DATA command, and on the PRINT SPACES command.

Arithmetic Operations

The following arithmetic operators are available:

+   *Addition.*

–   *Subtraction.*

*   *Multiplication.*

/   *Division.*

**   *Exponentiation.*

- No two operators can appear consecutively.
- Arithmetic operators cannot be implied. For example, (VAR1)(VAR2) is not a legal specification; you must specify VAR1*VAR2.
- Arithmetic operators and parentheses serve as delimiters. To improve readability, blanks (not commas) can be inserted before and after an operator.
- To form complex expressions, you can use variables, constants, and functions with arithmetic operators.
- The order of execution is functions first, then exponentiation, then multiplication, division, and unary –, and then addition and subtraction.
- Operators at the same level are executed from left to right.
- To override the order of operation, use parentheses. Execution begins with the innermost set of parentheses and progresses out.

Numeric Constants

- Constants used in numeric expressions or as arguments to functions can be integer or non-integer, depending on the application or function.

43

- You can specify as many digits in a constant as needed, as long as you understand the precision restrictions of your computer.
- Numeric constants can be signed (+ or −) but cannot contain any other special characters such as the comma or dollar sign.
- Numeric constants can be expressed with scientific notation. Thus, the exponent for a constant in scientific notation is limited to two digits. The range of values allowed for exponents in scientific notation is from −99 to +99.

Complex Numeric Arguments

- Except where explicitly restricted, complex expressions can be formed by nesting functions and arithmetic operators as arguments to functions.
- The order of execution for complex numeric arguments is functions first, then exponentiation, then multiplication, division, and unary −, and then addition and subtraction.
- To control the order of execution in complex numeric arguments, use parentheses.

Numeric Functions

Numeric functions can be used in any numeric expression on IF, SELECT IF, DO IF, ELSE IF, LOOP IF, END LOOP IF, and COMPUTE commands. Numeric functions always return numbers (or the system-missing value whenever the result is indeterminate). The expression to be transformed by a function is called the *argument*. Most functions have a variable or a list of variables as arguments.

- In numeric functions with two or more arguments, each argument must be separated by a comma. Blanks alone cannot be used to separate variable names, expressions, or constants in transformation expressions.
- Arguments should be enclosed in parentheses, as in TRUNC(INCOME), where the TRUNC function returns the integer portion of the variable *INCOME*.
- Multiple arguments should be separated by commas, as in MEAN(Q1,Q2,Q3), where the MEAN function returns the mean of variables *Q1*, *Q2*, and *Q3*.

Arithmetic Functions

- All arithmetic functions except MOD have single arguments; MOD has two. The arguments to MOD must be separated by a comma.
- Arguments can be numeric expressions, as in RND(A**2/B).

ABS(arg)   *Absolute value.* ABS(SCALE) is 4.7 when *SCALE* equals 4.7 or −4.7.

RND(arg)   *Round the absolute value to an integer and reaffix the sign.* RND(SCALE) is −5 when *SCALE* equals −4.7.

TRUNC(arg)   *Truncate to an integer.* TRUNC(SCALE) is −4 when *SCALE* equals −4.7.

MOD(arg,arg) *Remainder (modulo) of the first argument divided by the second.* When *YEAR* equals 1983, MOD(YEAR,100) is 83.

SQRT(arg)   *Square root.* SQRT(SIBS) is 1.41 when *SIBS* equals 2.

EXP(arg)   *Exponential. e* is raised to the power of the argument. EXP(VARA) is 7.39 when *VARA* equals 2.

LG10(arg)   *Base 10 logarithm.* LG10(VARB) is 0.48 when *VARB* equals 3.

LN(arg)   *Natural or Naperian logarithm (base* e*).* LN(VARC) is 2.30 when *VARC* equals 10.

ARSIN(arg)   *Arcsine.* (Alias ASIN.) The result is given in radians. ARSIN(ANG) is 1.57 when *ANG* equals 1.

ARTAN(arg)   *Arctangent.* (Alias ATAN.) The result is given in radians. ARTAN(ANG2) is 0.79 when *ANG2* equals 1.

SIN(arg)   *Sine.* The argument must be specified in radians. SIN(VARD) is 0.84 when *VARD* equals 1.

COS(arg)   *Cosine.* The argument must be specified in radians. COS(VARE) is 0.54 when *VARE* equals 1.

Statistical Functions

- Each argument to a statistical function (expression, variable name, or constant) must be separated by a comma.
- The *.n* suffix can be used with all statistical functions to specify the number of valid arguments. For example, MEAN.2(A,B,C,D) returns the mean of the valid values for variables *A, B, C,* and *D* only if at least two of the variables have valid values. The default for *n* is 2 for SD, VARIANCE, and CFVAR, and 1 for other statistical functions.
- The keyword TO can be used to refer to a set of variables in the argument list.

SUM(arg list)   *Sum of the nonmissing values across the argument list.*

MEAN(arg list)   *Mean of the nonmissing values across the argument list.*

SD(arg list)   *Standard deviation of the nonmissing values across the argument list.*

VARIANCE(arg list)   *Variance of the nonmissing values across the argument list.*

CFVAR(arg list)   *Coefficient of variation of the nonmissing values across the argument list.* The coefficient of variation is the standard deviation divided by the mean.

MIN(arg list)   *Minimum nonmissing value across the argument list.*

MAX(arg list)   *Maximum nonmissing value across the argument list.*

Random Variable and Distribution Functions

- Random variable and distribution functions take both constants and variables for arguments.

- A function argument, if required, must come first and is denoted by q (quantile) for cumulative distribution functions and p (probability) for inverse distribution functions.

- All random variable and distribution functions must specify distribution parameters, denoted by a, b, and/or c, according to the number required.

- All arguments are real numbers.

- Cumulative distribution functions take the prefix CDF. A cumulative distribution function CDF.d_spec(q,a,...) returns a probability (p) that a variate with the specified distribution (d_spec) falls below q for continuous functions and at or below q for discrete functions.

- Inverse distribution functions take the prefix IDF. Inverse distribution functions are not available for discrete distributions. An inverse distribution function IDF.d_spec(p,a,...) returns a value q such that CDF.d_spec(q,a,...)=p with the specified distribution (d_spec).

- Random number generation functions take the prefix RV. A random number generation function RV.d_spec(a,...) generates an independent observation with the specified distribution (d_spec).

- Noncentral cumulative distribution functions take the prefix NCDF. A noncentral distribution function NCDF.d_spec(q,a,b,...) returns a probability (p) that a variate with the specified noncentral distribution falls below q. It is available only for beta, chi-square, F, and Student's t.

- Restrictions to distribution parameters a, b, and c apply to all functions for that distribution. Restrictions for the function parameter p or q apply to that particular distribution function. The program issues a warning and returns system missing when it encounters an out-of-range value for an argument.

The following are continuous distributions:

BETA *Beta distribution.* The beta distribution takes two shape parameters a and b; both must be positive. The functions are CDF.BETA(q,a,b), IDF.BETA(p,a,b), and RV.BETA(a,b), where both q and p must be between 0 and 1 inclusive. The noncentral beta distribution takes an extra noncentrality parameter c, which must be greater than or equal to 0. The noncentral cumulative distribution function is NCDF.BETA(q,a,b,c). The beta distribution is used in Bayesian analyses as a conjugate to the binomial distribution.

CAUCHY *Cauchy distribution.* The Cauchy distribution takes one location parameter (a) and one scale parameter (b); b must be positive. The functions are CDF.CAUCHY(q,a,b), IDF.CAUCHY(p,a,b), and RV.CAUCHY(a,b), where $0<p<1$. The Cauchy distribution is symmetric about the location parameter a and has slowly decaying tails that the expectation does not exist. The harmonic mean of variates that have positive density at 0 is typically distributed as Cauchy.

CHI-SQUARE *Chi-square distribution.* The chi-square distribution takes one shape parameter (a), which is the degrees of freedom and must be positive. The functions are CDF.CHISQ(q,a), IDF.CHISQ(p,a), and RV.CHISQ(a), where $q \geq 0$ and $0 \leq p < 1$. The noncentral chi-square distribution takes an extra noncentrality parameter c, which must be greater than or equal to 0. The noncentral cumulative distribution function is NCDF.CHISQ(q,a,c). Chi-square is a special case of the gamma distribution and is commonly used to test quadratic forms under the Gaussian assumption.

EXPONENTIAL   *Exponential distribution.* The exponential distribution takes one scale parameter (a), which can represent the rate of decay and must be positive. The functions are CDF.EXP(q,a), IDF.EXP(p,a), and RV.EXP(a), where $q \geq 0$ and $0 \leq p < 1$. The exponential distribution is a special case of the gamma distribution. A major use of this distribution is life testing.

F   F *distribution.* The F distribution takes two shape parameters a and b, which are the degrees of freedom and must be positive. The F distribution functions are CDF.F(q,a,b), IDF.F(p,a,b), and RV.F(a,b), where $q \geq 0$ and $0 \leq p < 1$. The noncentral F distribution takes an extra noncentrality parameter c, which must be greater than or equal to 0. The noncentral cumulative distribution function is NCDF.F(q,a,b,c). The F distribution is commonly used to test hypotheses under the Gaussian assumption.

GAMMA   *Gamma distribution.* The gamma distribution takes one shape parameter (a) and one scale parameter (b). Both parameters must be positive. The functions are CDF.GAMMA(q,a,b), IDF.GAMMA(p,a,b), and RV.GAMMA(a,b), where $q \geq 0$ and $0 \leq p < 1$. The gamma distribution is commonly used in queuing theory, inventory control, and precipitation processes. If a is an integer and $b=1$, it is the Erlang distribution.

LAPLACE   *Laplace or double exponential distribution.* The Laplace distribution takes one location parameter (a) and one scale parameter (b). Parameter b must be positive. The Laplace functions are CDF.LAPLACE(q,a,b), IDF.LAPLACE(p,a,b), and RV.LAPLACE(a,b), where $0 < p < 1$. The Laplace distribution is symmetric about 0 and has exponentially decaying tails on both ends.

LOGISTIC   *Logistic distribution.* The logistic distribution takes one location parameter (a) and one scale parameter (b). Parameter b must be positive. The logistic functions are CDF.LOGISTIC(q,a,b), IDF.LOGISTIC(p,a,b), and RV.LOGISTIC(a,b), where $0 < p < 1$. The logistic distribution is a unimodal, symmetric distribution with tails that are longer than the Gaussian distribution. It is used to model growth curves.

LOGNORMAL   *Lognormal distribution.* This distribution takes two parameters a and b. Both parameters must be positive. The functions are CDF.LOGNORMAL(q,a,b), IDF.LOGNORMAL(p,a,b), and RV.LOGNORMAL(a,b), where $q \geq 0$ and $0 \leq p < 1$. Lognormal is used in the distribution of particle sizes in aggregates, flood flows, concentrations of air contaminants, and failure time.

NORMAL   *Normal distribution.* The normal distribution takes one location parameter (a) and one scale parameter (b). Parameter b must be positive. The normal functions are CDF.NORMAL(q,a,b), IDF.NORMAL(p,a,b), and RV.NORMAL(a,b), where $0 < p < 1$. Three functions in SPSS releases earlier than 6.0 are special cases of the normal distribution functions:
CDFNORM(arg)=CDF.NORMAL(q,0,1)
where arg is $q;$
PROBIT(srg)=IDF.NORMAL(p,0,1)
where arg is $p;$ and
NORMAL(arg)=RV.NORMAL(0,b)

where arg is *b*. The normal or Gaussian distribution is symmetric about the mean and is the most widely used in statistics.

PARETO   *Pareto distribution.* The Pareto distribution takes a threshold parameter (*a*) and a shape parameter (*b*). Both parameters must be positive. The functions are CDF.PARETO(q,a,b), IDF.PARETO(p,a,b), and RV.PARETO(a,b), where $q \geq a$ and $0 \leq p < 1$. Pareto is commonly used in economics as a model for a density function with a slowly decaying tail.

STUDENT T   *Student* t *distribution.* The Student *t* distribution takes one shape parameter (*a*), which is the degrees of freedom and must be positive. The functions are CDF.T(q,a), IDF.T(p,a), and RV.T(a), where $0 < p < 1$. The Student *t* distribution is symmetric about 0 and approaches the Gaussian distribution as *a* approaches infinity. The noncentral Student *t* distribution takes an extra non-centrality parameter *b*. The noncentral cumulative distribution function is NCDF.T(q,a,b). The major use of the Student *t* distribution is to test hypotheses and construct confidence intervals for means of Gaussian data.

UNIFORM   *Uniform distribution.* The uniform distribution takes two parameters *a* and *b*. The first parameter *a* must be less than or equal to the second parameter *b*. The functions are CDF.UNIFORM(q,a,b), IDF.UNIFORM(p,a,b), and RV.UNIFORM(a,b), where $a \leq q \leq b$ and $0 \leq p \leq 1$. The uniform random number function in SPSS releases earlier than 6.0 is a special case:
UNIFORM(arg)=RV.UNIFORM(0,b)
where arg is parameter *b*. Among other uses, the uniform distribution commonly models the round-off error.

WEIBULL   *Weibull distribution.* The Weibull distribution takes two parameters *a* and *b*, both of which must be positive. The functions are CDF.WEIBULL(q,a,b), IDF.WEIBULL(p,a,b), and RV.WEIBULL(a,b), where $q \geq 0$ and $0 \leq p < 1$. The Weibull distribution is commonly used in survival analysis.

The following are discrete distributions:

BERNOULLI   *Bernoulli distribution.* The Bernoulli distribution takes one probability parameter *a*, which must be between 0 and 1 inclusive. The functions are CDF.BERNOULLI(q,a) and RV.BERNOULLI(a), where *a* is the probability of obtaining a success. The Bernoulli distribution is a special case of the binomial distribution and is used in simple success-failure experiments.

BINOMIAL   *Binomial distribution.* The binomial distribution takes one trial parameter (*a*) and one probability parameter (*b*). Parameter *a* must be a positive integer and parameter *b* must be between 0 and 1 inclusive. The functions are CDF.BINOM(q,a,b) and RV.BINOM(a,b), where *a* is the number of trials, *b* is the probability of obtaining a success in any single trial, and *q* is the number of successes in *a* trials. When *a*=1, it is the Bernoulli distribution. The binomial distribution is used in independently replicated success-failure experiments.

GEOMETRIC   *Geometric distribution.* The geometric distribution takes one probability parameter (*a*), which must be greater than 0 and less than or equal to 1. The functions are CDF.GEOM(q,a) and RV.GEOM(a), where *q* is the number of trials needed (including the last trial) before a success is observed and *a* is the probability of obtaining a success in a single trial.

HYPERGEOMETRIC   *Hypergeometric distribution.* The hypergeometric distribution takes three parameters *a*, *b*, and *c*. All three parameters are positive integers, and both *b* and *c* must be less than or equal to *a*. The functions are CDF.HYPER(q,a,b,c) and RV.HYPER(a,b,c), where *a* is the total number of objects in an urn model, *b* is the number of objects randomly drawn without replacement from the urn, *c* is the number of objects with distinct characteristics, and *q* is the number of objects with these distinct characteristics observed out of the withdrawn objects.

NEGATIVE BINOMIAL   *Negative binomial distribution.* The negative binomial distribution takes one threshold parameter (*a*) and one probability parameter (*b*). Parameter *a* must be an integer and parameter *b* must be greater than 0 and less than or equal to 1. The functions are CDF.NEGBIN(q,a,b) and RV.NEGBIN(a,b), where *q* is the number of trials needed (including the last trial) before *a* successes are observed and *b* is the probability of obtaining a success in a single trial. If *a*=1, it is a geometric distribution.

POISSON   *Poisson distribution.* The Poisson distribution takes one rate or mean parameter (*a*). Parameter *a* must be positive. The functions are CDF.POISSON(q,a) and RV.POISSON(a). The Poisson distribution is used in modeling the distribution of counts, such as traffic counts and insect counts.

Missing Values in Numeric Expressions

- Most numeric expressions receive the system-missing value when any one of the values in the expression is missing.
- Some arithmetic operations involving 0 can be evaluated even when the variables have missing values. These operations are:

Expression	Result
0 * missing	0
0 / missing	0
MOD(0,missing)	0

- The .*n* suffix can be used with the statistical functions SUM, MEAN, MIN, MAX, SD, VARIANCE, and CFVAR to specify the number of valid arguments you consider acceptable. The default of *n* is 2 for SD, VARIANCE, and CFVAR, and 1 for other statistical functions. For example,

```
COMPUTE FACTOR = SUM.2(SCORE1 TO SCORE3).
```

computes the variable *FACTOR* only if a case has valid information for at least two scores. *FACTOR* is assigned the system-missing value if a case has valid values for fewer than two scores.

Domain Errors

Domain errors occur when numeric expressions are mathematically undefined or cannot be represented numerically on the computer for reasons other than missing data. Two common examples are division by zero and the square root of a negative number. When SPSS detects a domain error, it issues a warning and assigns the system-missing value to the expression. For example, the command COMPUTE TESTVAR = TRUNC(SQRT(X/Y) * .5) returns system-missing if *X/Y* is negative or if *Y* is 0.

The following are domain errors in numeric expressions:

**   *A negative number to a non-integer power.*

/   *A divisor of 0.*

MOD   *A divisor of 0.*

SQRT   *A negative argument.*

EXP   *An argument that produces a result too large to be represented on the computer.*

LG10   *A negative or 0 argument.*

LN   *A negative or 0 argument.*

ARSIN   *An argument whose absolute value exceeds 1.*

NORMAL *A negative or 0 argument.*

PROBIT   *A negative or 0 argument, or an argument 1 or greater.*

String Expressions

Expressions involving string variables can be used on COMPUTE and IF commands and in logical expressions on commands such as IF, DO IF, LOOP IF, and SELECT IF.

- A string expression can be a constant enclosed in apostrophes (for example, 'IL'), a string function (see "String Functions" below), or a string variable.

- An expression must return a string if the target variable is a string.

- The string returned by a string expression does not have to be the same length as the target variable; no warning messages are issued if the lengths are not the same. If the target variable produced by a COMPUTE command is shorter, the result is right-trimmed. If the target variable is longer, the result is right-padded.

String Functions

- The target variable for each string function must be a string and *must have already been declared* (see STRING).
- Multiple arguments in a list must be separated by commas.
- When two strings are compared, the case in which they are entered is significant. The LOWER and UPCASE functions are useful for making comparisons of strings regardless of case.
- For certain functions (for example, MIN, MAX, ANY, and RANGE), the outcome will be affected by case and by whether the string includes numbers or special characters. The character set in use varies by system. With the ASCII character set, lower case follows upper case in the sort order. Therefore, if *NAME1* is in upper case and *NAME2* is in lower case, MIN(NAME1,NAME2) will return *NAME1* as the minimum. The reverse is true with the EBCDIC character set, which sorts lower case before upper case.

CONCAT(arg list) *Concatenate the arguments into a string.* String variables and strings can be intermixed as arguments. For example, CONCAT(A,'**') creates the string ABCD** for a case with the value *ABCD* for the string variable *A*.

LOWER(arg) *Convert upper case to lower case.* All other characters remain unchanged. The argument can be a string variable or value. For example, LOWER(NAME1) returns charles if the value of *NAME1* is *CHARLES*.

LPAD(a1, a2, a3) *Left-pad.* The variable a1 is left-padded up to the length specified by a2 using the optional single character a3 as the pad character. a2 must be a positive integer from 1 to 255. The default pad character is a blank. For example, LPAD(ALPHA1,10) adds four leading blanks to the target variable if *ALPHA1* has an A6 format. a3 can be any character enclosed in apostrophes or any expression that yields a single character.

LTRIM(a1, a2) *Left-trim.* The character a2 is trimmed from the beginning of a1. For example, LTRIM(ALPHA2,'0') trims leading zeros from the variable *ALPHA2*. a2 can be any character enclosed in apostrophes or any expression that yields a single character. The default for a2 is a blank.

RPAD(a1, a2, a3) *Right-pad.* The variable a1 is right-padded up to the length of a2 using the optional single character a3 as the pad character. a2 must be a positive integer from 1 to 255. The default pad character is a blank. For example, RPAD(ALPHA3,8,'*') adds two trailing asterisks to the target variable if *ALPHA3* has an A6 format. a3 can be any character enclosed in apostrophes or any expression that yields a single character.

RTRIM(a1, a2) *Right-trim.* The character a2 is trimmed from the end of a1. For example, RTRIM(ALPHA4,'*') trims trailing asterisks from variable *ALPHA4*. a2 can be any character enclosed in apostrophes or any expression that yields a single character. The default for a2 is a blank.

SUBSTR(a1, a2, a3) *Substring.* This function returns the substring within a1 beginning with the position specified by a2 and optionally for a length of a3. a2 can be a positive integer from 1 to the length of a1. a3, when added to a2, should not exceed the length of a1. If a3 is not specified, the substring is returned up to the end of a1. For example, if the variable *ALPHA5* has an A6 format, SUBSTR(ALPHA5,3) returns the last four characters of *ALPHA5*. SUBSTR (ALPHA5,3,1) returns the third character of *ALPHA5*.

When used on the left side of an equals sign, the substring is replaced by the string specified on the right side of the equals sign. The rest of the original string remains intact. For example, SUBSTR(ALPHA6,3,1)='*' changes the third character of all values for *ALPHA6* to *. If the replacement string is longer or shorter than the substring, the replacement is truncated or padded with blanks on the right to an equal length.

UPCASE(arg) — *Convert lower case to upper case.* The argument can be a string variable or a string. For example, UPCASE(NAME1) returns CHARLES if the value of *NAME1* is *Charles*.

MBLEN.BYTE(arg,a1) — *Return the number of bytes in the character at the specified position.* The argument is a string expression and a1 indicates the beginning byte of the character in the specified string.

Search Functions

- The values returned by INDEX and/or RINDEX can be used as arguments to SUBSTR to pull out substrings with the same beginning or ending character but with varying position and length.

INDEX(a1, a2, a3) — *Return a number that indicates the position of the first occurrence of a2 in a1.* a1 is the string that is searched. a2 is the string variable or string that is used in the search. If a3 is not specified, all of a2 is used. For example, INDEX(ALPHA8,'**X*') returns 2 for a case with the value *X**X**X** for the variable *ALPHA8*. The optional a3 is the number of characters used to divide a2 into separate strings. Each substring is used for searching and the function returns the first occurrence of any of the substrings. With the same value *X**X**X** for *ALPHA8*, both INDEX(ALPHA8, '**X*', 2) and INDEX(ALPHA8, '**X*', 1) return 1. a3 must be a positive integer and must divide evenly into the length of a2. The target variable must be numeric. If a2 is not found within a1, the value 0 is returned.

LENGTH(arg) — *Return the length of the specified string.* The argument can be a string variable or a string. For example, LENGTH(LNAME) always returns 6 if *LNAME* has an A6 format. The target variable must be numeric.

MAX(arg list) — *Return the maximum value across the argument list.* For example, MAX(LNAME,FNAME) selects the name that comes last in the sort order, the first or the last name. MAX is also available as a numeric function.

MIN(arg list) — *Return the minimum value across the argument list.* For example, MIN(LNAME,FNAME) selects the name that comes first in the sort order, the first or the last name. MIN is also available as a numeric function.

RINDEX(a1,a2,a3)   *Return a number indicating the position of the last occurrence of a2 in a1.* a1 is the string that is searched. a2 is the string variable or string that is used in the search. If a3 is not specified, all of a2 is used. For example, RINDEX(ALPHA8,'**X*') returns 5 for a case with the value $X{**}X{**}X{*}$ for the variable *ALPHA8.* The optional a3 is the number of characters used to divide a2 into separate strings. Each substring is used for searching, and the function returns the last occurrence of any of the substrings. With the same value $X{**}X{**}X{*}$ for *ALPHA8,* RINDEX (ALPHA8, '**X*', 2) returns 7, and RINDEX (ALPHA8, '**X*', 1) returns 8. a3 must be a positive integer and must divide evenly into the length of a2. The target variable must be numeric. If a2 is not found within a1, the value 0 is returned.

Conversion Functions

NUMBER(arg,format)   *Convert the argument into a number using the specified format.* The argument is string, the format is a numeric format, and the result is numeric. The string is essentially reread using the format and returned as a number. For example, NUMBER (XALPHA,F3.1) converts all values for *XALPHA* to numbers using the F3.1 format. The function returns the system-missing value if the conversion is invalid.

STRING(arg,format)   *Converts the argument into a string using the specified format.* The argument is numeric, the format is a numeric format, and the result is a string. The number is converted from internal representation according to the format and then stored as a string. For example, STRING (INCOME, DOLLAR8) converts the numeric values for *INCOME* to the dollar format and returns it as a string value. If the result is shorter than the string variable that receives the values, it is right-justified. If the result is longer, it is right-trimmed.

Missing Values in String Expressions

- If the numeric argument (which can be an expression) for functions LPAD and RPAD is illegal or missing, the result is a null string. If the padding or trimming is the only operation, the string is then padded to its entire length with blanks. If the operation is nested, the null string is passed to the next nested level.
- If a numeric argument to SUBSTR is illegal or missing, the result is a null string. If SUBSTR is the only operation, the string is blank. If the operation is nested, the null string is passed to the next nested level.
- If a numeric argument to INDEX or RINDEX is illegal or missing, the result is system-missing.

Logical Expressions

Logical expressions can appear on the IF, SELECT IF, DO IF, ELSE IF, LOOP IF, and END LOOP IF commands. SPSS evaluates a logical expression as true or false, or as missing if it is indeterminate. A logical expression returns 1 if the expression is true, 0 if it is false, or system-missing if it is missing. Thus, logical expressions can be any expressions that yield this three-value logic.

- The simplest logical expression is a logical variable. A logical variable is any numeric variable that has values 1, 0, or system-missing. Logical variables cannot be strings.

- Logical expressions can be simple logical variables or relations, or they can be complex logical tests involving variables, constants, functions, relational operators, logical operators, and parentheses to control the order of evaluation.

- On an IF command, a logical expression that is true causes the assignment expression to be executed. A logical expression that returns missing has the same effect as one that is false: the assignment expression is not executed and the value of the target variable is not altered.

- On a DO IF command, a logical expression that is true causes SPSS to execute the commands immediately following the DO IF, up to the next ELSE IF, ELSE, or END IF. If it is false, SPSS looks for the next ELSE IF or ELSE command. If the logical expression returns missing for each of these, the entire structure is skipped.

- On a SELECT IF command, a logical expression that is true causes the case to be selected. A logical expression that returns missing has the same effect as one that is false: the case is not selected.

- On a LOOP IF command, a logical expression that is true causes looping to begin (or continue). A logical expression that returns missing has the same effect as one that is false: the structure is skipped.

- On an END LOOP IF command, a logical expression that is false returns control to the LOOP command for that structure and looping continues. If it is true, looping stops and the structure is terminated. A logical expression that returns a missing value has the same effect as one that is true: the structure is terminated.

String Variables in Logical Expressions

String variables, like numeric variables, can be tested in logical expressions.

- String variables must be declared before they can be used in a string expression.

- String variables cannot be compared to numeric variables.

- If strings of different lengths are compared, the shorter string is right-padded with blanks to equal the length of the longer.

- The magnitude of strings can be compared using LT, GT, and so on, but the outcome depends on the sorting sequence of the computer. Use with caution.

Logical Functions

- Each argument to a logical function (expression, variable name, or constant) must be separated by a comma.

- The target variable for a logical function must be numeric.

- The functions RANGE and ANY can be useful shortcuts to more complicated specifications on the IF, DO IF, and other conditional commands. For example, the command

```
SELECT IF ANY(REGION, 'NW', 'NE', 'SE').
```

is equivalent to

```
SELECT IF (REGION EQ 'NW' OR REGION EQ 'NE' OR REGION EQ
'SE').
```

RANGE(arg,arg list)   *Return 1 or true if the value of the first argument is in the inclusive ranges; return 0 or false if not.* The first argument is usually a variable, and the second argument is a list of one or more pairs of values. The variable can be either numeric or string. For example, RANGE (AGE,1,17,62,99) returns 1 for ages 1 through 17 and 62 through 99, inclusive, and 0 for any other ages. RANGE (LNAME,'A','MZZZZZZ') returns 1 for last names that begin with a letter between A and M, inclusive, and 0 for last names beginning with other letters.

ANY(arg,arg list)   *Return 1 or true if the value of the first argument matches one of the arguments in the list; return 0 or false if not.* The first argument is usually a variable, either numeric or string. For example, ANY(PROJECT,3,4,7,9) returns 1 if the value for variable *PROJECT* is 3, 4, 7, or 9, and 0 for other values of *PROJECT*. Similarly, ANY (LNAME,'MARTIN','JONES','EVANS') returns 1 for people whose last names are *MARTIN*, *JONES*, or *EVANS*, and 0 for all other last names.

Relational Operators

A relation is a logical expression that compares two values using a *relational operator*. In the command

```
IF (X EQ 0) Y=1
```

the variable *X* and 0 are expressions that yield the values to be compared by the EQ relational operator. Relational operators are

EQ or =   *Equal to.*

NE or ~= ¬ = or <>   *Not equal to.*

LT or <   *Less than.*

LE or <=   *Less than or equal to.*

GT or >   *Greater than.*

GE or >=   *Greater than or equal to.*

- The symbols representing NE (~= or ¬=) are system dependent (see "NOT Logical Operator" below).

- The expressions in a relation can be variables, constants, or more complicated arithmetic expressions.

- Blanks (not commas) must be used to separate the relational operator from the expressions. To make the command more readable, use extra blanks or parentheses.

NOT Logical Operator

The NOT logical operator reverses the true/false outcome of the expression that immediately follows.

- The NOT operator affects only the expression that immediately follows, unless a more complex logical expression is enclosed in parentheses.
- The valid substitute for NOT varies from operating system to operating system. In general, the tilde (~) is valid for ASCII systems, while ¬ (or the symbol over number 6 on the keyboard) is valid for IBM EBCDIC systems. See the *SPSS Base User's Guide* for your version of SPSS.
- NOT can be used to check whether a numeric variable has the value 0, 1, or any other value. For example, all scratch variables are initialized to 0. Therefore, NOT (#ID) returns false or missing when #ID has been assigned a value other than 0.

AND and OR Logical Operators

Two or more relations can be logically joined using the logical operators AND and OR. Logical operators combine relations according to the following rules:

- The ampersand (&) symbol is a valid substitute for the logical operator AND. The vertical bar (|) is a valid substitute for the logical operator OR.
- Only one logical operator can be used to combine two relations. However, multiple relations can be combined into a complex logical expression.
- Regardless of the number of relations and logical operators used to build a logical expression, the result is either true, false, or indeterminate because of missing values.
- Operators or expressions cannot be implied. For example, X EQ 1 OR 2 is illegal; you must specify X EQ 1 OR X EQ 2.
- The ANY and RANGE functions can be used to simplify complex expressions.

AND   *Both relations must be true for the complex expression to be true.*

OR   *If either relation is true, the complex expression is true.*

Table 6 lists the outcome for AND and OR combinations.

Table 6   Outcome for AND and OR combinations

Expression	Outcome	Expression	Outcome
true AND true	= true	true OR true	= true
true AND false	= false	true OR false	= true
false AND false	= false	false OR false	= false
true AND missing	= missing	true OR missing	= true[*]
missing AND missing	= missing	missing OR missing	= missing

[*] Expressions where SPSS can evaluate the outcome with incomplete information. See "Missing Values in Logical Expressions" below.

Order of Evaluation

- When arithmetic operators and functions are used in a logical expression, the order of operations is functions and arithmetic operations first, then relational operators, and then logical operators.
- When more than one logical operator is used, NOT is evaluated first, then AND, and then OR.
- To change the order of evaluation, use parentheses.

Missing Values in Logical Expressions

In a simple relation, the logic is indeterminate if the expression on either side of the relational operator is missing. When two or more relations are joined by logical operators AND and OR, SPSS always returns a missing value if all of the relations in the expression are missing. However, if any one of the relations can be determined, SPSS tries to return true or false according to the logical outcomes shown in Table 6.

- When two relations are joined with the AND operator, the logical expression can never be true if one of the relations is indeterminate. The expression can, however, be false.
- When two relations are joined with the OR operator, the logical expression can never be false if one relation returns missing. The expression, however, can be true.

Other Functions

SPSS also includes a lag function and several missing-value functions.

LAG Function

LAG(arg,n)   *The value of the variable* n *cases before.* The first argument is a variable. The second argument, if specified, is a constant and must be a positive integer; the default is 1. For example, PREV4=LAG(GNP,4) returns the value of *GNP* for the fourth case before the current one. The first four cases have system-missing values for *PREV4*.

- The result is of the same type (numeric or string) as the variable specified as the first argument.
- The first *n* cases for string variables are set to blanks. For example, if PREV2=LAG (LNAME,2) is specified, blanks will be assigned to the first two cases for *PREV2*.
- When LAG is used with commands that select cases (for example, SELECT IF and SAMPLE), LAG counts cases *after* case selection, even if specified before these commands (see "Command Order" on p. 16).

Missing-Value Functions

- Each argument to a missing-value function (expression, variable name, or constant) must be separated by a comma.
- Only numeric values can be used as arguments in missing-value functions.
- The keyword TO can be used to refer to a set of variables in the argument list for functions NMISS and NVALID.
- The functions MISSING and SYSMIS are logical functions and can be useful shortcuts to more complicated specifications on the IF, DO IF, and other conditional commands.

VALUE(arg) *Ignore user-defined missing values.* The value is treated as is. The argument must be a variable name.

MISSING(arg) *True or 1 if the value is user-missing or system-missing; false or 0 otherwise.*

SYSMIS(arg) *True or 1 if the value is system-missing; false or 0 otherwise.*

NMISS(arg list) *Number of system-missing values in the argument list.*

NVALID(arg list) *Number of valid values in the argument list.*

Treatment of Missing Values in Arguments

If the logic of an expression is indeterminate because of missing values, the expression returns a missing value, and the command is not executed. Table 7 summarizes how missing values are handled in arguments to various functions.

Table 7   Missing values in arguments

Function	Returns system-missing if
MOD (x1,x2)	x1 is missing, or x2 is missing and x1 is not 0
MAX.n (x1,x2,...xk) MEAN.n (x1,x2,...xk) MIN.n (x1,x2,...x1) SUM.n (x1,x2,...xk)	fewer than *n* arguments are valid; the default *n* is 1

Table 7   Missing values in arguments (Continued)

Function	Returns system-missing if
CFVAR.n (x1,x2,...xk) SD.n (x1,x2,...xk) VARIANCE.n (x1,x2,...xk)	fewer than *n* arguments are valid; the default *n* is 2
LPAD(x1,x2,x3) LTRIM(x1,x2) RTRIM(x1,x2) RPAD(x1,x2,x3)	x1 or x2 is illegal or missing
SUBSTR(x1,x2,x3)	x2 or x3 is illegal or missing
NUMBER(x,format) STRING(x,format)	the conversion is invalid
INDEX(x1,x2,x3) RINDEX(x1,x2,x3)	x3 is invalid or missing
LAG (x,n)	x is missing *n* cases previously (and always for the first *n* cases); the default *n* is 1
ANY (x,x1,x2,...xk) RANGE (x,x1,x2,...xk)	x or all of x1, x2, ..., xk are missing
VALUE (x)	x is system-missing
MISSING (x) NMISS (x1,x2,...xk) NVALID (x1,x2,...xk) SYSMIS (x)	never

- Any function that is not listed in Table 7 returns the system-missing value when the argument is missing.
- The system-missing value is a displayed as a period (.) for numeric variables.
- String variables do not have system-missing values. An invalid string expression nested within a complex transformation yields a null string, which is passed to the next level of operation and treated as missing. However, an invalid string expression that is not nested is displayed as a blank string and is *not* treated as missing.

Date and Time

SPSS reads and writes date and time in many different formats but stores them as floating-point numbers. You can perform arithmetic operations on them, use them in statistical procedures, and display or print them in a format of your choice. This section discusses the input and output formats for date and time, arithmetic operations using date and time variables, and date and time functions.

Date and Time Formats

Date and time formats are both input and output formats. They can be used on DATA LIST and other variable definition commands to read in values representing dates or times or date-time combinations. Like numeric formats, each input format generates a default output format, automatically expanded (if necessary) to accommodate display width. In addition, you can assign or modify output formats using FORMATS, WRITE FORMATS, and PRINT FORMATS commands. The output formats are effective only with LIST, REPORT, and TABLES procedures and the PRINT and WRITE transformation commands. Other procedures use the F format and display the values as numbers.

- All date and time formats have a minimum input width, and some have a different minimum output. Wherever the input minimum width is less than the output minimum, SPSS expands the width automatically when displaying or printing values. However, when you specify output formats, you must allow enough space for displaying the date and time in the format you choose.

- Input data shorter than the specified width are correctly evaluated as long as all the necessary elements are present. For example, with the TIME format, 1:2, 01 2, and 01:02 are all correctly evaluated even though the minimum width is 5. However, if only one element (hours or minutes) is present, you must use a time function to aggregate or convert the data (see "Date and Time Functions" on p. 67).

- If a date or time value cannot be completely displayed in the specified width, values are truncated in the output. For example, an input time value of 1:20:59 (1 hour, 20 minutes, 59 seconds) displayed with a width of 5 will generate an output value of 01:20, not 01:21. The truncation of output does not affect the numeric value stored in the working file.

Table 8 shows all available date and time formats, where *w* indicates the total number of columns and *d* (if present), the number of decimal places for fractional seconds. The example shows the output format with the minimum width and default decimal positions (if applicable). The format allowed in the input data is much less restrictive (see "Input Data Specification" on p. 62).

Table 8   Date and time formats

Format type	Description	Min w In	Min w Out	Max w	Max d	General form	Example
DATEw	International date	8	9	40		dd-mmm-yy	28-OCT-90
		10	11			dd-mmm-yyyy	28-OCT-1990
ADATEw	American date	8	8	40		mm/dd/yy	10/28/90
		10	10			mm/dd/yyyy	10/28/1990
EDATEw	European date	8	8	40		dd.mm.yy	28.10.90
		10	10			dd.mm.yyyy	28.10.1990
JDATEw	Julian date	5	5	40		yyddd	90301
		7	7			yyyyddd	1990301
SDATEw	Sortable date*	8	8	40		yy/mm/dd	90/10/28
		10	10			yyyy/mm/dd	1990/10/28
QYRw	Quarter and year	4	6	40		q Q yy	4 Q 90
		6	8			q Q yyyy	4 Q 1990
MOYRw	Month and year	6	6	40		mmm yy	OCT 90
		8	8			mmm yyyy	OCT 1990
WKYRw	Week and year	6	8	40		ww WK yy	43 WK 90
		8	10			ww WK yyyy	43 WK 1990
WKDAYw	Day of the week	2	2	40		(name of the day)	SU
MONTHw	Month	3	3	40		(name of the month)	JAN
TIMEw	Time	5	5	40		hh:mm	01:02
TIMEw.d		10	10	40	16	hh:mm:ss.s	01:02:34.75
DTIMEw	Days and time	8	8	40		dd hh:mm	20 08:03
DTIMEw.d		13	13	40	16	dd hh:mm:ss.s	20 08:03:00
DATETIMEw	Date and time	17	17	40		dd-mmm-yyyy hh:mm	20-JUN-1990 08:03
DATETIMEw.d		22	22	40	16	dd-mmm-yyyy hh:mm:ss.s	20-JUN-1990 08:03:00

* All date and time formats produce sortable data. SDATE, a date format used in a number of Asian countries, can be sorted in its character form and is used as a sortable format by many programmers.

Input Data Specification

The following general rules apply to date and time input formats:

- Input data must be fixed. Data can appear anywhere within the specified columns. Leading and trailing blanks are allowed. If column-style specifications are used, the width specification can be omitted (see DATA LIST). For example,

```
DATA LIST /BIRTHDAY 1-8 (DATE).
```

is equivalent to

```
DATA LIST /BIRTHDAY (DATE8).
```

- You cannot use date and time formats to read freefield data.
- The century value for two-digit years is defined by the *SET EPOCH* value. By default, the century range begins 69 years prior to the current year and end 30 years after the current year. Whether all four digits or only two digits are displayed in output depends on the width specification on the format.
- Dashes, periods, commas, slashes, or blanks can be used as delimiters in the date-month-year input. For example, with the DATE format, the following input forms are all acceptable:

```
28-10-90     28/10/1990     28.OCT.90        October 28, 1990
```

The displayed values, however, will be the same: *28-OCT-90* or *28-OCT-1990*, depending on whether the specified width allows 11 characters in output.

- The JDATE format does not allow internal delimiters and requires leading zeros for day values less than 100 and two-digit year values less than 10. For example, for January 1, 1990, the following two specifications are acceptable:

```
90001            1990001
```

However, neither of the following is acceptable:

```
90 1                  90/1
```

- Months can be represented in digits, Roman numerals, or three-character abbreviations, and they can be fully spelled out. For example, all of the following specifications are acceptable for October:

```
10        X       OCT      October
```

- The quarter in QYR format is expressed as 1, 2, 3, or 4. It must be separated from the year by the letter *Q*. Blanks can be used as additional delimiters. For example, for the fourth quarter of 1990, all of the following specifications are acceptable:

```
4Q90       4Q1990      4 Q 90      4 Q 1990
```

On some operating systems, such as IBM CMS, *Q* must be upper case. The displayed output is *4 Q 90* or *4 Q 1990*, depending on whether the width specified allows all four digits of the year.

- The week in the WKYR format is expressed as a number from 1 to 53. Week 1 begins on January 1, week 2 on January 8, and so on. The value may be different from the number of the calendar week. The week and year must be separated by the string WK. Blanks can be used as additional delimiters. For example, for the 43rd week of 1990, all of the following specifications are acceptable:

```
43WK90      43WK1990      43 WK 90      43 WK 1990
```

On some operating systems, such as IBM CMS, WK must be upper case. The displayed output is *43 WK 90* or *43 WK 1990*, depending on whether the specified width allows enough space for all four digits of the year.

- In time specifications, colons can be used as delimiters between hours, minutes, and seconds. Hours and minutes are required but seconds are optional. A period is required to separate seconds from fractional seconds. Hours can be of unlimited magnitude, but the maximum value for minutes is 59 and for seconds 59.999. . . .

- Data values can contain a sign (+ or −) in TIME and DTIME formats to represent time intervals before or after a point in time.

Example

```
DATA LIST FIXED
 /VAR1 1-17 (DATE) VAR2 21-37 (ADATE) VAR3 41-47 (JDATE).
BEGIN DATA
28-10-90            10/28/90           90301
28.OCT.1990         X 28 1990          1990301
28 October, 2001    Oct. 28, 2001      2001301
END DATA.
LIST.
```

- Internally, all date format variables are stored as the number of seconds from 0 hours, 0 minutes, and 0 seconds of Oct. 14, 1582.

The LIST output from these commands is shown in Figure 15.

Figure 15   Output illustrating DATE, ADATE, and JDATE formats

```
     VAR1            VAR2            VAR3

28-OCT-1990      10/28/1990      1990301
28-OCT-1990      10/28/1990      1990301
28-OCT-2001      10/28/2001      2001301
```

Example

```
DATA LIST FIXED /VAR1 1-10 (QYR) VAR2 12-25 (MOYR) VAR3 28-37 (WKYR).
BEGIN DATA
4Q90        10/90           43WK90
4 Q 90      Oct-1990        43 WK 1990
4 Q 2001    October, 2001   43 WK 2001
END DATA.
LIST.
```

- Internally, the value of a QYR variable is stored as midnight of the first day of the first month of the specified quarter, the value of a MOYR variable is stored as midnight of the first day of the specified month, and the value of a WKYR format variable is stored as midnight of the first day of the specified week. Thus, *4Q90* and *10/90* are both equivalent to October 1, 1990, and *43WK90* is equivalent to October 22, 1990.

The LIST output from these commands is shown in Figure 16.

Figure 16   Output illustrating QYR, MOYR, and WKYR formats

```
      VAR1          VAR2              VAR3

 4 Q 1990      OCT 1990        43 WK 1990
 4 Q 1990      OCT 1990        43 WK 1990
 4 Q 2001      OCT 2001        43 WK 2001
```

Example

```
DATA LIST FIXED
 /VAR1 1-11 (TIME,2) VAR2 13-21 (TIME) VAR3 23-28 (TIME).
BEGIN DATA
1:2:34.75    1:2:34.75 1:2:34
END DATA.
LIST.
```

- TIME reads and writes time of the day or a time interval.
- Internally, the TIME values are stored as the number of seconds from midnight of the day or of the time interval.

The LIST output from these commands is shown in Figure 17.

Figure 17   Output illustrating TIME format

```
      VAR1         VAR2      VAR3

 1:02:34.75    1:02:34    1:02
```

Example

```
DATA LIST FIXED
 /VAR1 1-9 (WKDAY) VAR2 10-18 (WKDAY)
  VAR3 20-29 (MONTH) VAR4 30-32 (MONTH) VAR5 35-37 (MONTH).
BEGIN DATA
Sunday     Sunday     January     1     Jan
Monday     Monday     February    2     Feb
Tues       Tues       March       3     Mar
Wed        Wed        April       4     Apr
Th         Th         Oct        10     Oct
Fr         Fr         Nov        11     Nov
Sa         Sa         Dec        12     Dec
END DATA.
FORMATS VAR2 VAR5 (F2).
LIST.
```

- WKDAY reads and writes the day of the week; MONTH reads and writes the month of the year.
- Values for WKDAY are entered as strings but stored as numbers. They can be used in arithmetic operations but not in string functions.
- Values for MONTH can be entered either as strings or as numbers, but are stored as numbers. They can be used in arithmetic operations but not in string functions.
- To display the values as numbers, assign an F format to the variable, as was done for *VAR2* and *VAR5* in the above example.

The LIST output from these commands is shown in Figure 18.

Figure 18   Output illustrating WKDAY and MONTH formats

```
    VAR1 VAR2        VAR3 VAR4 VAR5

SUNDAY       1  JANUARY    JAN   1
MONDAY       2  FEBRUARY   FEB   2
TUESDAY      3  MARCH      MAR   3
WEDNESDAY    4  APRIL      APR   4
THURSDAY     5  OCTOBER    OCT  10
FRIDAY       6  NOVEMBER   NOV  11
SATURDAY     7  DECEMBER   DEC  12
```

Example

```
DATA LIST FIXED /VAR1 1-14 (DTIME) VAR2 18-42 (DATETIME).
BEGIN DATA
20 8:3            20-6-90 8:3
20:8:03:46        20/JUN/1990 8:03:46
20 08 03 46.75    20 June, 2001 08 03 46.75
END DATA.
LIST.
```

- DTIME and DATETIME read and write time intervals.

- The decimal point explicitly coded in the input data for fractional seconds.

- The DTIME format allows a − or + sign in the data value to indicate a time interval before or after a point in time.

- Internally, values for a DTIME variable are stored as the number of seconds of the time interval while those for a DATETIME variable are stored as the number of seconds from 0 hours, 0 minutes, and 0 seconds of Oct. 14, 1582.

The LIST output from these commands is shown in Figure 19.

Figure 19   Output illustrating DTIME and DATETIME formats

```
         VAR1                  VAR2

  20 08:03:00    20-JUN-1990 08:03:00
  20 08:03:46    20-JUN-1990 08:03:46
  20 08:03:46    20-JUN-2001 08:03:46
```

Arithmetic Operations with Date and Time Variables

Most date and time variables are stored internally as the number of seconds from a particular date or as a time interval and therefore can be used in arithmetic operations:

- A *date* is a floating-point number representing the number of seconds from midnight, October 14, 1582. Dates, which represent a particular point in time, are stored as the number of seconds to that date. For example, November 8, 1957, is stored as 1.2E+10.

- A date includes the time of day, which is the time interval past midnight. When time of day is not given, it is taken as 00:00 and the date is an even multiple of 86,400 (the number of seconds in a day).

- A *time interval* is a floating-point number representing the number of seconds in a time period, for example, an hour, minute, or day. For example, the value representing 5.5 days is 475,200; the value representing the time interval 14:08:17 is 50,897.

- QYR, MOYR, and WKYR variables are stored as midnight of the first day of the respective quarter, month, and week of the year. Therefore, *1 Q 90*, *1/90*, and *1 WK 90* are all equivalents of January 1, 1990 0:0:00. See "Date and Time Functions" on p. 67 for information on how to determine the quarter, month, or week of a year for a certain date.

- WKDAY variables are stored as 1 to 7, and MONTH variables as 1 to 12. For information on how to determine the day of the week or the month of the year for a certain date, see "Date and Time Functions" on p. 67.

- Both dates and time intervals can be used in arithmetic expressions. The results are stored as the number of seconds or days (see Table 9).

- Do not mix time variables (TIME and DTIME) with date variables (DATE, ADATE, EDATE, and so on) in computations. Since date variables have an implicit time value of 00:00:00, calculations involving time values that are not multiples of a whole day (for example, 24 hours, 0 minutes, 0 seconds) will yield unreliable results.

- Mixing a DATETIME variable with a date variable may yield an unreliable result. Operations involving date variables are accurate only to the days. To avoid possible misinterpretation, use the DTIME format and ignore the hours and minutes portion of the resulting value.

You can perform virtually any arithmetic operation with them. Of course, not all of these operations are particularly useful. You can calculate the number of days between two dates by subtracting one date from the other—but adding two dates does not produce a very meaningful result.

By default, any new numeric variables you compute are displayed in F format. In the case of calculations involving time and date variables, this means that the default output is expressed as a number of seconds or days. Use the FORMATS (or PRINT FORMATS) command to specify an appropriate format for the computed variable. Table 9 shows the recommended output formats for some of the calculations possible with date and time variables.

Table 9   Recommended output formats for date and time calculations

Arithmetic operation	Result	Recommended output format
time ± time[*]	time	TIME, DTIME
date – date [†]	time	DTIME
DATETIME – DATETIME	time	TIME, DTIME
DATETIME ± time	date	DATETIME

[*] Including TIME and DTIME formats.
[†] Including DATE, ADATE, EDATE, JDATE, and SDATE formats.

Example

```
DATA LIST RECORDS=2
 /TIME 1-8 (TIME) DTIME 10-19 (DTIME) DATE 21-29 (DATE)
  ADATE 31-38 (ADATE)
 /DATTIME1 1-18 (DATETIME) DATTIME2 20-37 (DATETIME).
BEGIN DATA
1:10:15  1 0:25:10   13-8-90  10/21/90
28-OCT-90 9:15:17  29/OCT/90 10:30:22
END DATA.
COMPUTE ADDTIME=TIME+DTIME.
COMPUTE DATEDIF1=ADATE-DATE..
COMPUTE DATEDIF2=DATTIME2-DATTIME1.
COMPUTE DATETIME=DATTIME2+DTIME.
LIST VARIABLES=ADDTIME DATEDIF1 DATEDIF2 DATETIME.
FORMATS ADDTIME DATEDIF2 (TIME15) DATEDIF1 (DTIME15)
 DATETIME (DATETIME25).
LIST VARIABLES=ADDTIME DATEDIF1 DATEDIF2 DATETIME.
```

The results of these commands are shown in Figure 20.

Figure 20   Results of arithmetic operations with date and time variables

```
    ADDTIME          DATEDIF1        DATEDIF2                    DATETIME

    25:35:25      69 00:00:00        25:15:05      30-OCT-1990 10:55:32
```

Date and Time Functions

Date and time functions provide aggregation, conversion, and extraction routines for dates and time intervals. Each function transforms an expression consisting of one or more arguments. Arguments can be complex expressions, variable names, or constants. Date and time expressions and variables are legitimate arguments.

All date functions that accept the argument of day—for example, DATE.DMY(d,m,y), DATE.MDY(m,d,y), and DATE.YRDAY(y,d)—check the validity of the argument. The value for day must be an integer between 1 and 31. If an invalid value is encountered, a warning is displayed and the value is set to system-missing. However, if the day value is invalid for a particular month—for example, 31 in September, April, June, and November or 29 through 31 for February in non-leap years—the resulting date is placed in the next month (for example, if you enter 2 for *MONTH*, 31 for *DAY*, and 91 for *YEAR*, the result becomes 03/02/91).

Aggregation Functions

Aggregation functions generate dates and time intervals from values that were not read by date and time input formats.

- All aggregation functions begin with DATE or TIME, depending on whether a date or a time interval is requested. This is followed by a subfunction that corresponds to the type of values found in the data.

- The subfunctions are separated from the function by a period (.) and are followed by an argument list specified in parentheses.

- The arguments to the DATE and TIME functions must be separated by commas and must contain integer values.

DATE.DMY(d,m,y)   *Combine day, month, and year.* The value of the argument for day must be expressed as an integer between 1 and 31. The value of the argument for month must be expressed as an integer between 1 and 13 (13 returns January of the following year). Years should be expressed in four digits. For example, the command

```
COMPUTE BIRTHDAY=DATE.DMY(DAY,MONTH,YEAR).
```

stores the value of approximately *1.184E+10* in *BIRTHDAY* when *DAY* is 8, *MONTH* is 11, and *YEAR* is 57. This value can be displayed with a DATE9 format as *08-NOV-57*.

DATE.MDY(m,d,y)   *Combine month, day, and year.* This function follows the same rules as DATE.DMY, except for the order of the arguments. For example, the command

```
COMPUTE BIRTHDAY=DATE.MDY(MONTH,DAY,YEAR).
```

stores the same value as the previous example in *BIRTHDAY* for the same values of *MONTH*, *DAY*, and *YEAR*. The value can be displayed as *11/08/57* with an ADATE8 format.

DATE.YRDAY(y,d)   *Combine year and day of the year.* The year can be expressed as either two or four digits. Years should be expressed in four digits. The day can be expressed as any integer between and including 1 and 366. For example, the command

```
COMPUTE BIRTHDAY=DATE.YRDAY(1688,301).
```

when combined with a DATE11 print format produces the date *27-OCT-1688* for *BIRTHDAY*.

DATE.QYR(q,y)   *Combine quarter and year.* The quarter must be expressed as a single digit between and including 1 and 4. The year can contain two or four digits. Years should be expressed in four digits. For example, the command

```
COMPUTE QUART=DATE.QYR(QTR,YEAR).
```

with a QDATE6 print format produces a value of *4 Q 57* for *QUART* when *QTR* is 4 and *YEAR* is 57. Since each quarter is assumed to begin on the first day of the first month of the quarter, a DATE9 print format for the same value is displayed as *01-OCT-57*.

DATE.MOYR(m,y)   *Combine month and year.* The value of the month must be expressed as an integer between and including 1 and 12. The year can be expressed as two or four digits. For example, the command

```
COMPUTE START=DATE.MOYR(MONTH,YEAR).
```

displays *NOV 57* for *START* when *MONTH* is 11 and *YEAR* is 57 and the print format is MOYR.

DATE.WKYR(w,y)   *Combine week and year.* The week must be an integer between and including 1 and 53. The year can be represented by two or four digits. For example, the command

```
COMPUTE WEEK=DATE.WKYR(WK,YEAR).
```

displays *26-NOV-57* for *WEEK* when *WK* is 48 and *YEAR* is 57 and the print format is DATE9. The number of the week in the WKYR format is calculated beginning with the first day of the year. It may be different from the number of the calendar week.

TIME.HMS(h,m,s)   *Combine hour, minute, and second into a time interval.* For example, the command

```
COMPUTE PERIOD1= TIME.HMS (HR,MIN,SEC).
```

produces an interval of 45,030 seconds for *PERIOD1* when *HR* equals 12, *MIN* equals 30, and *SEC* equals 30. The value can be displayed as *12:30:30* with a TIME8 print format.

You can supply one, two, or three arguments. Trailing arguments can be omitted and default to 0. The value of the first nonzero argument can spill over into the next higher argument. For example, the command

```
COMPUTE PERIOD2=TIME.HMS(HR,MIN).
```

produces an interval of 5400 seconds for *PERIOD2* when *HR* is 0 and *MIN* is 90. The value can be displayed as 01:30 with a TIME5 print format.

You can have a non-integer value for the last argument. For example, the command

```
COMPUTE PERIOD3=TIME.HMS(HR).
```

produces an interval of 5400 seconds for *PERIOD3* when *HR* equals 1.5 and is displayed as *01:30* with a TIME5 format. When you supply a nonzero argument to a function, each of the lower-level units must be within the range of −60 to +60.

TIME.DAYS(d)   *Aggregate days into a time interval.* The argument can be expressed as any numeric value. For example, the command

```
COMPUTE NDAYS=TIME.DAYS(SPELL).
```

with a value of 2.5 for *SPELL* generates a value for *NDAYS* that is displayed as *2 12:00* with a DTIME7 format.

Conversion Functions

The conversion functions convert time intervals from one unit of time to another. Time intervals are stored as the number of seconds in the interval; the conversion functions provide a means for calculating more appropriate units, for example, converting seconds to days.

Each conversion function consists of the CTIME function followed by a period (.), the target time unit, and an argument. The argument can consist of expressions, variable names, or constants. The argument must already be a time interval (see "Aggregation Functions" on p. 68). Time conversions produce non-integer results with a default format of F8.2.

Since time and dates are stored internally as seconds, a function that converts to seconds is not necessary.

CTIME.DAYS(arg)   *Convert a time interval to the number of days.* For example, the command

```
COMPUTE NDAYS=CTIME.DAYS(TIME.HMS(HR,MIN,SEC)).
```

with 12 for *HR*, 30 for *MIN*, and 30 for *SEC* yields a value of 0.52 for *NDAYS*. CTIME.DAYS(45030) yields the same result.

CTIME.HOURS(arg)   *Convert a time interval to the number of hours.* For example, the command

```
COMPUTE NHOURS=CTIME.HOURS(TIME.HMS(HR,MIN,SEC)).
```

using the same values as the previous example produces a value of 12.51 for *NHOURS*.

CTIME.MINUTES(arg)   *Convert a time interval to the number of minutes.* Using the same values as the previous example for *HR*, *MIN*, and, *SEC*, the command

```
COMPUTE NMINS=CTIME.MINUTES(TIME.HMS(HR,MIN,SEC)).
```

converts the interval to minutes and produces a value of 750.50 for *NMINS*.

YRMODA Function

YRMODA(arg list)   *Convert year, month, and day to a day number.* The number returned is the number of days since October 14, 1582 (day 0 of the Gregorian calendar).

- Arguments for YRMODA can be variables, constants, or any other type of numeric expression but must yield integers.
- Year, month, and day must be specified in that order.
- The first argument can be any year between 0 and 99, or between 1582 to 47516.
- If the first argument yields a number between 00 and 99, 1900 through 1999 is assumed.
- The month can range from 1 through 13. Month 13 with day 0 yields the last day of the year. For example, YRMODA(1990,13,0) produces the day number for December 31, 1990. Month 13 with any other day yields the day of the first month of the coming year, for example, YRMODA(1990,13,1) produces the day number for January 1, 1991.

- The day can range from 0 through 31. Day 0 is the last day of the previous month regardless of whether it is 28, 29, 30, or 31. For example, YRMODA(1990,3,0) yields 148791.00, the day number for February 28, 1990.
- The function returns the system-missing value if any of the three arguments is missing or if the arguments do not form a valid date *after* October 14, 1582.
- Since YRMODA yields the number of days instead of seconds, you can not display it in date format unless you convert it to the number of seconds.

Extraction Functions

The extraction functions extract subfields from dates or time intervals, targeting the day or a time from a date value. This permits you to classify events by day of the week, season, shift, and so forth.

- Each extraction function begins with XDATE, followed by a period, the subfunction name (what you want to extract), and an argument.
- The argument can be an expression, a variable name, or a constant, provided the argument is already in date form.
- In the following examples, the value for the variable *BIRTHDAY* is *05-DEC-1954 5:30:15*, read with a DATE20 input format.

XDATE.MDAY(arg)   *Return day number in a month from a date.* The result is an integer between 1 and 31. The date must have occurred after October 14, 1582. For example, you can extract the day number from *BIRTHDAY*, as in

```
COMPUTE DAYNUM=XDATE.MDAY(BIRTHDAY).
```

When the value for *BIRTHDAY* is *05-DEC-1954 5:30:15*, *DAYNUM* is 5.

XDATE.MONTH(arg)   *Return month number from a date.* The result is an integer between 1 and 12. The date must have occurred after October 14, 1582. For example, you can extract the month number from *BIRTHDAY*, as in

```
COMPUTE MONTHNUM=XDATE.MONTH(BIRTHDAY).
```

When the value for *BIRTHDAY* is *05-DEC-1954 5:30:15*, this command yields 12 for *MONTHNUM*. If you provide a print format of MONTH12, as in

```
PRINT FORMAT MONTHNUM(MONTH12).
```

the value would be displayed as *DECEMBER*.

XDATE.YEAR(arg)   *Return a four-digit year from a date.* The date must have occurred after October 14, 1582. For example, you can extract the year from *BIRTHDAY*, as in

```
COMPUTE YEAR=XDATE.YEAR(BIRTHDAY).
```

When the value for *BIRTHDAY* is *05-DEC-1954 5:30:15*, this command returns 1954 for *YEAR*.

XDATE.HOUR(arg)   *Return the hour from a date or time of day.* The result is an integer between 0 and 23. For example, you can extract the hour from *BIRTHDAY*, as in

```
COMPUTE HOUR=XDATE.HOUR(BIRTHDAY).
```

When the value for *BIRTHDAY* is *05-DEC-1954 5:30:15*, this command returns 5 for *HOUR*.

XDATE.MINUTE(arg)   *Return the minute of the hour from a date or time of day.* The result is an integer from 0 through 59. For example, you can extract the minute of the hour from *BIRTHDAY*, as in

```
COMPUTE MIN=XDATE.MINUTE(BIRTHDAY).
```

When the value for *BIRTHDAY* is *05-DEC-1954 5:30:15*, this command returns 30 for *MIN*.

XDATE.SECOND(arg)   *Return the second of the minute from a date or time of day.* The result is an integer or, if there are fractional seconds, a value with decimals. For example, you can extract the second of the minute from *BIRTHDAY*, as in

```
COMPUTE SEC=XDATE.SECOND(BIRTHDAY).
```

When the value for *BIRTHDAY* is *05-DEC-1954 5:30:15*, this command returns a value of 15.00 for *SEC*.

XDATE.WKDAY(arg)   *Return the day within a week from a date.* The result is an integer between and including 1 and 7, with Sunday being 1 and Saturday being 7. The date must have occurred after October 14, 1582. For example, you can extract the day of the week from *BIRTHDAY*, as in

```
COMPUTE DAYNAME=XDATE.WKDAY(BIRTHDAY).
```

When the value for *BIRTHDAY* is *05-DEC-1954 5:30:15*, this command returns the value 1 for *DAYNAME*. If you provide an output format of WKDAY, as in

```
PRINT FORMAT DAYNAME (WKDAY9).
```

the value for *DAYNAME* would display as *SUNDAY*.

XDATE.JDAY(arg)   *Return the day of the year from the date.* The result is an integer between 1 and 366 inclusive. The date must have occurred after October 14, 1582. For example, you can extract the day of the year from *BIRTHDAY*, as in

```
COMPUTE DAYNUM=XDATE.JDAY(BIRTHDAY).
```

When the value for *BIRTHDAY* is *05-DEC-1954 5:30:15*, this command returns the value 339 for *DAYNUM*.

XDATE.QUARTER(arg)   *Return quarter number within a year for a date.* The result is 1, 2, 3, or 4. The date must have occurred after October 14, 1582. To extract the quarter in which *BIRTHDAY* occurred, use the command

```
COMPUTE Q=XDATE.QUARTER(BIRTHDAY).
```

When *BIRTHDAY* equals *5-DEC-1954 05:30:15*, the value of *Q* is 4.

XDATE.WEEK(arg)   *Return the week number of a date.* The result is an integer between 1 and 53. The date must have occurred after October 14, 1582. For example, you can extract the week number from *BIRTHDAY*, as in

```
COMPUTE WEEKNUM=XDATE.WEEK(BIRTHDAY).
```

When the value for *BIRTHDAY* is *5-DEC-1954 05:30:15*, this command returns the value 49 for *WEEKNUM.*

XDATE.TDAY(arg)   *Return number of days in a time interval or from October 14, 1582.* The value returned is an integer (the fractional portion of a day is ignored). For example, the command

```
COMPUTE NDAYS=XDATE.TDAY(BIRTHDAY).
```

returns the value 135922 when the value for *BIRTHDAY* is *05-DEC-1954 5:30:15*, indicating the number of days between October 14, 1582 and December 5, 1954. The hours, minutes, and seconds are ignored.

XDATE.TIME(arg)   *Return time of day from a date.* The result is expressed as the number of elapsed seconds since midnight of that date. For example, when the value for *BIRTHDAY* is *05-DEC-1954 5:30:15*, the command

```
COMPUTE ELSEC=XDATE.TIME(BIRTHDAY).
```

returns the value 19815 for *ELSEC.* If you provide a TIME print format, as in

```
PRINT FORMAT ELSEC(TIME8).
```

the value is displayed as *5:30:15.*

XDATE.DATE(arg)   *Return the date portion of a date.* The result is the integral date portion of a date, which is the number of elapsed seconds between midnight October 14, 1582 and midnight of the date in question. The date must have occurred after October 14, 1582. To extract the date from variable *BIRTHDAY*, use

```
COMPUTE BRTHDATE=XDATE.DATE(BIRTHDAY).
```

The value for *BIRTHDATE* can then be displayed as *12/05/54* using ADATE8 format.

Precautions with Date and Time Variables

Dates and times are represented internally as seconds. The numbers for dates are very large, and arithmetic overflows can result. For example, dates in the 20th century are on the order of 10 to the 10th power (11 digits). For that reason, a few precautions are in order:

- Some machine environments cannot accommodate the computation of higher powers of date and time variables. For example, computations higher than the sixth power may cause overflows on some machines.
- The magnitude of the values may cause inaccuracies in some statistical procedures. It is advisable to subtract a fixed date if you want to keep seconds as the unit, or to convert

days using the XDATE.TDAYS function. REGRESSION, CORRELATIONS, ANOVA, and ONEWAY use an adaptive centering method, so their accuracy will not be affected.

- LIST, REPORT, and TABLES are the only procedures that display values in date and time formats. The PRINT and WRITE transformation commands can also display and write date and time formats. However, some summary variables in REPORT and calculated variables in TABLES display in F format, regardless of the print formats of variables used as arguments.

- All other procedures use F format in all cases. The default width and number of decimal places is taken from the print format, but the format type is ignored. For example, in a frequency table, the date 1/09/57 with a print format of DATE9 will be displayed as *11830147200*, not *01-SEP-57*.

- Changing the print format in no way alters the values that are stored. For example, if you assign a print format of DATE9 for a variable read with DATETIME format, the time of day will not display but continues to be part of the value. This means that seemingly identical values can be displayed as separate entries within procedures.

Commands

ACF

```
ACF [VARIABLES=] series names

 [/DIFF={1}]
       {n}

 [/SDIFF={1}]
        {n}

 [/PERIOD=n]

 [/{NOLOG**}]
   {LN     }

 [/SEASONAL]

 [/MXAUTO={16**}]
          {n   }

 [/SERROR={IND**}]
          {MA   }

 [/PACF]

 [/APPLY [='model name']]
```

**Default if the subcommand is omitted and there is no corresponding specification on the TSET command.

Example:

```
ACF TICKETS
  /LN
  /DIFF=1
  /SDIFF=1
  /PER=12
  /MXAUTO=50.
```

Overview

ACF displays and plots the sample autocorrelation function of one or more time series. You can also display and plot the autocorrelations of transformed series by requesting natural log and differencing transformations within the procedure.

Options

Modifying the Series. You can request a natural log transformation of the series using the LN subcommand and seasonal and nonseasonal differencing to any degree using the SDIFF and DIFF subcommands. With seasonal differencing, you can specify the periodicity on the PERIOD subcommand.

Statistical Output. With the MXAUTO subcommand, you can specify the number of lags for which you want autocorrelations displayed and plotted, overriding the maximum specified on TSET. You can also display and plot values only at periodic lags using the SEASONAL subcommand. In addition to autocorrelations, you can display and plot partial autocorrelations using the PACF subcommand.

Method of Calculating Standard Errors. You can specify one of two methods of calculating the standard errors for the autocorrelations on the SERROR subcommand.

Basic Specification

The basic specification is one or more series names.

- For each series specified, ACF automatically displays the autocorrelation value, standard error, Box-Ljung statistic, and probability for each lag.
- ACF plots the autocorrelations and marks the bounds of two standard errors on the plot. By default, ACF displays and plots autocorrelations for up to 16 lags or the number of lags specified on TSET.
- If a method has not been specified on TSET, the default method of calculating the standard error (IND) assumes the process is white noise.

Subcommand Order

- Subcommands can be specified in any order.

Syntax Rules

- VARIABLES can be specified only once.
- Other subcommands can be specified more than once, but only the last specification of each one is executed.

Operations

- Subcommand specifications apply to all series named on the ACF command.
- If the LN subcommand is specified, any differencing requested on that ACF command is done on the log-transformed series.
- Confidence limits are displayed in the plot, marking the bounds of two standard errors at each lag.

Limitations

- Maximum 1 VARIABLES subcommand. There is no limit on the number of series named on the list.

Example

```
ACF TICKETS
  /LN
  /DIFF=1
  /SDIFF=1
  /PER=12
  /MXAUTO=50.
```

- This example produces a plot of the autocorrelation function for the series *TICKETS* after a natural log transformation, differencing, and seasonal differencing have been applied. Along with the plot, the autocorrelation value, standard error, Box-Ljung statistic, and probability are displayed for each lag.
- LN transforms the data using the natural logarithm (base *e*) of the series.
- DIFF differences the series once.
- SDIFF and PERIOD apply one degree of seasonal differencing with a period of 12.
- MXAUTO specifies that the maximum number of lags for which output is to be produced is 50.

VARIABLES Subcommand

VARIABLES specifies the series names and is the only required subcommand. The actual keyword VARIABLES can be omitted.

DIFF Subcommand

DIFF specifies the degree of differencing used to convert a nonstationary series to a stationary one with a constant mean and variance before the autocorrelations are computed.

- You can specify any positive integer on DIFF.
- If DIFF is specified without a value, the default is 1.
- The number of values used in the calculations decreases by 1 for each degree-1 of differencing.

Example

```
ACF SALES
  /DIFF=1.
```

- In this example, the series *SALES* will be differenced once before the autocorrelations are computed and plotted.

SDIFF Subcommand

If the series exhibits a seasonal or periodic pattern, you can use the SDIFF subcommand to seasonally difference the series before obtaining autocorrelations.

- The specification on SDIFF indicates the degree of seasonal differencing and can be any positive integer.
- If SDIFF is specified without a value, the degree of seasonal differencing defaults to 1.
- The number of seasons used in the calculations decreases by 1 for each degree of seasonal differencing.
- The length of the period used by SDIFF is specified on the PERIOD subcommand. If the PERIOD subcommand is not specified, the periodicity established on the TSET or DATE command is used (see the PERIOD subcommand below).

PERIOD Subcommand

PERIOD indicates the length of the period to be used by the SDIFF or SEASONAL subcommands.

- The specification on PERIOD indicates how many observations are in one period or season and can be any positive integer.
- The PERIOD subcommand is ignored if it is used without the SDIFF or SEASONAL subcommands.
- If PERIOD is not specified, the periodicity established on TSET PERIOD is in effect. If TSET PERIOD is not specified, the periodicity established on the DATE command is used. If periodicity was not established anywhere, the SDIFF and SEASONAL subcommands will not be executed.

Example

```
ACF SALES
  /SDIFF=1M
  /PERIOD=12.
```

- This command applies one degree of seasonal differencing with a periodicity (season) of 12 to the series *SALES* before autocorrelations are computed.

LN and NOLOG Subcommands

LN transforms the data using the natural logarithm (base *e*) of the series and is used to remove varying amplitude over time. NOLOG indicates that the data should not be log transformed. NOLOG is the default.

- If you specify LN on an ACF command, any differencing requested on that command will be done on the log-transformed series.
- There are no additional specifications on LN or NOLOG.
- Only the last LN or NOLOG subcommand on an ACF command is executed.

- If a natural log transformation is requested when there are values in the series that are less than or equal to zero, the ACF will not be produced for that series because nonpositive values cannot be log transformed.

- NOLOG is generally used with an APPLY subcommand to turn off a previous LN specification.

Example

```
ACF SALES
  /LN.
```

- This command transforms the series *SALES* using the natural log transformation and then computes and plots autocorrelations.

SEASONAL Subcommand

Use the SEASONAL subcommand to focus attention on the seasonal component by displaying and plotting autocorrelations only at periodic lags.

- There are no additional specifications on SEASONAL.

- If SEASONAL is specified, values are displayed and plotted at the periodic lags indicated on the PERIOD subcommand. If PERIOD is not specified, the periodicity established on the TSET or DATE command is used (see the PERIOD subcommand on p. 78).

- If SEASONAL is not specified, autocorrelations for all lags up to the maximum are displayed and plotted.

Example

```
ACF SALES
  /SEASONAL
  /PERIOD=12.
```

- In this example, autocorrelations are displayed only at every 12th lag.

MXAUTO Subcommand

MXAUTO specifies the maximum number of lags for a series.

- The specification on MXAUTO must be a positive integer.

- If MXAUTO is not specified, the default number of lags is the value set on TSET MXAUTO. If TSET MXAUTO is not specified, the default is 16.

- The value on MXAUTO overrides the value set on TSET MXAUTO.

Example

```
ACF SALES
  /MXAUTO=14.
```

- This command sets the maximum number of autocorrelations to be displayed for series *SALES* to 14.

SERROR Subcommand

SERROR specifies the method of calculating the standard errors for the autocorrelations.

- You must specify either keyword IND or MA on SERROR.
- The method on SERROR overrides the method specified on the TSET ACFSE command.
- If SERROR is not specified, the method indicated on TSET ACFSE is used. If TSET ACFSE is not specified, the default is IND.

IND   *Independence model.* The method of calculating the standard errors assumes the underlying process is white noise.

MA   *MA model.* The method of calculating the standard errors is based on Bartlett's approximation. With this method, appropriate where the true MA order of the process is $k-1$, standard errors grow at increased lags (Pankratz, 1983).

Example

```
ACF SALES
 /SERROR=MA.
```

- In this example, the standard errors of the autocorrelations are computed using the MA method.

PACF Subcommand

Use the PACF subcommand to display and plot sample partial autocorrelations as well as autocorrelations for each series named on the ACF command.

- There are no additional specifications on PACF.
- PACF also displays the standard errors of the partial autocorrelations and indicates the bounds of two standard errors on the plot.
- With the exception of SERROR, all other subcommands specified on that ACF command apply to both the partial autocorrelations and the autocorrelations.

Example

```
ACF SALES
 /DIFFERENCE=1
 /PACF.
```

- This command requests both autocorrelations and partial autocorrelations for the series *SALES* after it has been differenced once.

APPLY Subcommand

APPLY allows you to use a previously defined ACF model without having to repeat the specifications.

- The only specification on APPLY is the name of a previous model in quotes. If a model name is not specified, the model specified on the previous ACF command is used.

- To change one or more model specifications, specify the subcommands of only those portions you want to change after the APPLY subcommand.
- If no series are specified on the ACF command, the series that were originally specified with the model being reapplied are used.
- To change the series used with the model, enter new series names before or after the APPLY subcommand.

Example

```
ACF TICKETS
  /LN
  /DIFF=1
  /SDIFF=1
  /PERIOD=12
  /MXAUTO=50.
ACF ROUNDTRP
  /APPLY.
ACF APPLY
  /NOLOG.
ACF APPLY 'MOD_2'
  /PERIOD=6.
```

- The first command requests a maximum of 50 autocorrelations for the series *TICKETS* after it has been natural log transformed, differenced once, and had one degree of seasonal differencing with a periodicity of 12 applied to it. This model is assigned the default name *MOD_1*.
- The second command displays and plots the autocorrelation function for the series *ROUNDTRP* using the same model that was used for the series *TICKETS*. This model is assigned the name *MOD_2*.
- The third command requests another autocorrelation function of the series *ROUNDTRP* using the same model but without the natural log transformation. Note that when APPLY is the first specification after the ACF command, the slash (/) before it is not necessary. This model is assigned the name *MOD_3*.
- The fourth command reapplies *MOD_2*, autocorrelations for the series *ROUNDTRP* with the natural log and differencing specifications, but this time with a periodicity of 6. This model is assigned the name *MOD_4*. It differs from *MOD_2* only in the periodicity.

References

Box, G. E. P., and G. M. Jenkins. 1976. *Time series analysis: Forecasting and control.* San Francisco: Holden-Day.

Pankratz, A. 1983. *Forecasting with univariate Box-Jenkins models: Concepts and cases.* New York: John Wiley and Sons.

ADD FILES

```
ADD FILES FILE={file}
              {*    }

[/RENAME=(old varnames=new varnames)...]

[/IN=varname]

/FILE=... [/RENAME=...] [/IN=...]

[/BY varlist]

[/MAP]

[/KEEP={ALL**  }] [/DROP=varlist]
       {varlist}

[/FIRST=varname]  [/LAST=varname]
```

**Default if the subcommand is omitted.

Example:

```
ADD FILES FILE=SCHOOL1 /FILE=SCHOOL2.
```

Overview

ADD FILES combines cases from 2 up to 50 SPSS-format data files by concatenating or interleaving cases. When cases are **concatenated,** all cases from one file are added to the end of all cases from another file. When cases are **interleaved,** cases in the resulting file are ordered according to the values of one or more key variables.

The files specified on ADD FILES can be SPSS-format data files created by the SAVE or XSAVE commands or the working data file. The combined file becomes the new working file. Statistical procedures following ADD FILES use this combined file unless you replace it by building another working file. You must use the SAVE or XSAVE commands if you want to save the combined file as an SPSS-format data file.

In general, ADD FILES is used to combine files containing the same variables but different cases. To combine files containing the same cases but different variables, use MATCH FILES. To update existing SPSS-format data files, use UPDATE. ADD FILES cannot concatenate raw data files. To concatenate raw data files, use DATA LIST within an INPUT PROGRAM structure (see p. 237 for an example). Alternatively, convert the raw data files to SPSS-format data files with the SAVE or XSAVE commands and then use ADD FILES to combine them.

Options

Variable Selection. You can specify which variables from each input file are included in the new working file using the DROP and KEEP subcommands.

Variable Names. You can rename variables in each input file before combining the files using the RENAME subcommand. This permits you to combine variables that are the same but whose names differ in different input files, or to separate variables that are different but have the same name.

Variable Flag. You can create a variable that indicates whether a case came from a particular input file using IN. When interleaving cases, you can use the FIRST or LAST subcommands to create a variable that flags the first or last case of a group of cases with the same value for the key variable.

Variable Map. You can request a map showing all variables in the new working file, their order, and the input files from which they came using the MAP subcommand.

Basic Specification

- The basic specification is two or more FILE subcommands, each of which specifies a file to be combined. If cases are to be interleaved, the BY subcommand specifying the key variables is also required.
- All variables from all input files are included in the new working file unless DROP or KEEP is specified.

Subcommand Order

- RENAME and IN must immediately follow the FILE subcommand to which they apply.
- BY, FIRST, and LAST must follow all FILE subcommands and their associated RENAME and IN subcommands.

Syntax Rules

- RENAME can be repeated after each FILE subcommand. RENAME applies only to variables in the file named on the FILE subcommand immediately preceding it.
- BY can be specified only once. However, multiple key variables can be specified on BY. When BY is used, all files must be sorted in ascending order by the key variables (see SORT CASES).
- FIRST and LAST can be used only when files are interleaved (when BY is used).
- MAP can be repeated as often as desired.

Operations

- ADD FILES reads all input files named on FILE and builds a new working data file that replaces any working file created earlier in the session. ADD FILES is executed when the data are read by one of the procedure commands or the EXECUTE, SAVE, or SORT CASES commands.

- The resulting file contains complete dictionary information from the input files, including variable names, labels, print and write formats, and missing-value indicators. It also contains the documents from each input file. See DROP DOCUMENTS for information on deleting documents.

- Variables are copied in order from the first file specified, then from the second file specified, and so on. Variables that are not contained in all files receive the system-missing value for cases that do not have values for those variables.

- If the same variable name exists in more than one file but the format type (numeric or string) does not match, the command is not executed.

- If a numeric variable has the same name but different formats (for example, F8.0 and F8.2) in different input files, the format of the variable in the first-named file is used.

- If a string variable has the same name but different formats (for example, A24 and A16) in different input files, the command is not executed.

- If the working file is named as an input file, any N and SAMPLE commands that have been specified are applied to the working file before files are combined.

- If only one of the files is weighted, the program turns weighting off when combining cases from the two files. To weight the cases, use the WEIGHT command again.

Limitations

- Maximum 50 files can be combined on one ADD FILES command.
- The TEMPORARY command cannot be in effect if the working data file is used as an input file.

Examples

```
ADD FILES FILE=SCHOOL1 /FILE=SCHOOL2.
```

- ADD FILES concatenates cases from the SPSS-format data files *SCHOOL*1 and SCHOOL2. All cases from *SCHOOL1* precede all cases from *SCHOOL2* in the resulting file.

```
SORT CASES BY LOCATN DEPT.
ADD FILES  FILE=SOURCE /FILE=* /BY LOCATN DEPT
 /KEEP AVGHOUR AVGRAISE LOCATN DEPT SEX HOURLY RAISE /MAP.
SAVE OUTFILE=PRSNNL.
```

- SORT CASES sorts cases in the working file in ascending order of their values for *LOCATN* and *DEPT*.

- ADD FILES combines two files: the SPSS-format data file *SOURCE* and the sorted working file. The file *SOURCE* must also be sorted by *LOCATN* and *DEPT*.

- BY indicates that the keys for interleaving cases are *LOCATN* and *DEPT*, the same variables used on SORT CASES.

- KEEP specifies the variables to be retained in the resulting file.

- MAP produces a list of variables in the resulting file and the two input files.

- SAVE saves the resulting file as a new SPSS-format data file named *PRSNNL*.

FILE Subcommand

FILE identifies the files to be combined. A separate FILE subcommand must be used for each input file.

- An asterisk may be specified on FILE to indicate the working data file.
- The order in which files are named determines the order of cases in the resulting file.

Raw Data Files

To add cases from a raw data file, you must first define the file as the working data file using the DATA LIST command. ADD FILES can then combine the working file with an SPSS-format data file.

Example

```
DATA LIST FILE=GASDATA/1 OZONE 10-12 CO 20-22 SULFUR 30-32.
ADD FILES  FILE=PARTICLE /FILE=*.
SAVE  OUTFILE=POLLUTE.
```

- The *GASDATA* file is a raw data file and is defined on the DATA LIST command.
- The *PARTICLE* file is a previously saved SPSS-format data file.
- FILE=* on ADD FILES specifies the working data file, which contains the gas data. FILE=PARTICLE specifies the SPSS-format data file *PARTICLE*.
- SAVE saves the resulting file as an SPSS-format data file with the filename *POLLUTE*. Cases from the *GASDATA* file follow cases from the *PARTICLE* file.

RENAME Subcommand

RENAME renames variables in input files *before* they are processed by ADD FILES. RENAME follows the FILE subcommand that specifies the file containing the variables to be renamed.

- RENAME applies only to the FILE subcommand immediately preceding it. To rename variables from more than one input file, enter a RENAME subcommand after each FILE subcommand that specifies a file with variables to be renamed.
- Specifications for RENAME consist of a left parenthesis, a list of old variable names, an equals sign, a list of new variable names, and a right parenthesis. The two variable lists must name or imply the same number of variables. If only one variable is renamed, the parentheses are optional.
- More than one such specification can be entered on a single RENAME subcommand, each enclosed in parentheses.
- The TO keyword can be used to refer to consecutive variables in the file and to generate new variable names (see "Keyword TO" on p. 29).
- RENAME takes effect immediately. KEEP and DROP subcommands entered prior to RENAME must use the old names, while those entered after RENAME must use the new names.
- All specifications within a single set of parentheses take effect simultaneously. For example, the specification RENAME (A,B = B,A) swaps the names of the two variables.
- Variables cannot be renamed to scratch variables.

- Input data files are not changed on disk; only the copy of the file being combined is affected.

Example

```
ADD FILES FILE=CLIENTS /RENAME=(TEL_NO, ID_NO = PHONE, ID)
/FILE=MASTER /BY ID.
```

- ADD FILES adds new client cases from the file *CLIENTS* to existing client cases in the file *MASTER*.
- Two variables on *CLIENTS* are renamed prior to the match. *TEL_NO* is renamed *PHONE* to match the name used for phone numbers in the master file. *ID_NO* is renamed *ID* so that it will have the same name as the identification variable in the master file and can be used on the BY subcommand.
- The BY subcommand orders the resulting file according to client ID number.

BY Subcommand

BY specifies one or more key variables that determine the order of cases in the resulting file. When BY is specified, cases from the input files are interleaved according to their values for the key variables.

- BY must follow the FILE subcommands and any associated RENAME and IN subcommands.
- The key variables specified on BY must be present and have the same names in all input files.
- Key variables can be long or short string variables or numerics.
- All input files must be sorted in ascending order of the key variables. If necessary, use SORT CASES before ADD FILES.
- Cases in the resulting file are ordered by the values of the key variables. All cases from the first file with the first value for the key variable are first, followed by all cases from the second file with the same value, followed by all cases from the third file with the same value, and so forth. These cases are followed by all cases from the first file with the next value for the key variable, and so on.
- Cases with system-missing values are first in the resulting file. User-missing values are interleaved with other values.

DROP and KEEP Subcommands

DROP and KEEP are used to include only a subset of variables in the resulting file. DROP specifies a set of variables to exclude and KEEP specifies a set of variables to retain.

- DROP and KEEP do not affect the input files on disk.
- DROP and KEEP must follow all FILE and RENAME subcommands.
- DROP and KEEP must specify one or more variables. If RENAME is used to rename variables, specify the new names on DROP and KEEP.
- DROP and KEEP take effect immediately. If a variable specified on DROP or KEEP does not exist in the input files, was dropped by a previous DROP subcommand, or was not retained by a previous KEEP subcommand, the program displays an error message and does not execute the ADD FILES command.

- DROP cannot be used with variables created by the IN, FIRST, or LAST subcommands.
- KEEP can be used to change the order of variables in the resulting file. With KEEP, variables are kept in the order they are listed on the subcommand. If a variable is named more than once on KEEP, only the first mention of the variable is in effect; all subsequent references to that variable name are ignored.
- The keyword ALL can be specified on KEEP. ALL must be the last specification on KEEP, and it refers to all variables not previously named on that subcommand. It is useful when you want to arrange the first few variables in a specific order.

Example

```
ADD FILES FILE=PARTICLE /RENAME=(PARTIC=POLLUTE1)
 /FILE=GAS /RENAME=(OZONE TO SULFUR=POLLUTE2 TO POLLUTE4)
 /KEEP=POLLUTE1 POLLUTE2 POLLUTE3 POLLUTE4.
```

- The renamed variables are retained in the resulting file. KEEP is specified after all the FILE and RENAME subcommands, and it refers to the variables by their new names.

IN Subcommand

IN creates a new variable in the resulting file that indicates whether a case came from the input file named on the preceding FILE subcommand. IN applies only to the file specified on the immediately preceding FILE subcommand.

- IN has only one specification, the name of the flag variable.
- The variable created by IN has value 1 for every case that came from the associated input file and value 0 for every case that came from a different input file.
- Variables created by IN are automatically attached to the end of the resulting file and cannot be dropped. If FIRST or LAST are used, the variable created by IN precedes the variables created by FIRST or LAST.

Example

```
ADD FILES  FILE=WEEK10 /FILE=WEEK11 /IN=INWEEK11 /BY=EMPID.
```

- IN creates the variable *INWEEK11*, which has value 1 for all cases in the resulting file that came from the input file *WEEK11* and value 0 for those cases that were not in the file *WEEK11*.

Example

```
ADD FILES  FILE=WEEK10 /FILE=WEEK11 /IN=INWEEK11 /BY=EMPID.
IF  (NOT INWEEK11) SALARY1=0.
```

- The variable created by IN is used to screen partially missing cases for subsequent analyses.
- Since IN variables have either value 1 or 0, they can be used as logical expressions, where 1=true and 0=false. The IF command sets variable *SALARY1* equal to 0 for all cases that came from the file *INWEEK11*.

FIRST and LAST Subcommands

FIRST and LAST create logical variables that flag the first or last case of a group of cases with the same value on the BY variables. FIRST and LAST must follow all FILE subcommands and their associated RENAME and IN subcommands.

- FIRST and LAST have only one specification, the name of the flag variable.
- FIRST creates a variable with value 1 for the first case of each group and value 0 for all other cases.
- LAST creates a variable with value 1 for the last case of each group and value 0 for all other cases.
- Variables created by FIRST and LAST are automatically attached to the end of the resulting file and cannot be dropped.

Example

```
ADD FILES  FILE=SCHOOL1 /FILE=SCHOOL2
 /BY=GRADE /FIRST=HISCORE.
```

- The variable *HISCORE* contains value 1 for the first case in each grade in the resulting file and value 0 for all other cases.

MAP Subcommand

MAP produces a list of the variables included in the new working file and the file or files from which they came. Variables are listed in the order in which they exist in the resulting file. MAP has no specifications and must follow after all FILE and RENAME subcommands.

- Multiple MAP subcommands can be used. Each MAP subcommand shows the current status of the working file and reflects only the subcommands that precede the MAP subcommand.
- To obtain a map of the working data file in its final state, specify MAP last.
- If a variable is renamed, its original and new names are listed. Variables created by IN, FIRST, and LAST are not included in the map, since they are automatically attached to the end of the file and cannot be dropped.
- MAP can be used with the EDIT command to obtain a listing of the variables in the resulting file without actually reading the data and combining the files.

ADD VALUE LABELS

```
ADD VALUE LABELS varlist value 'label' value 'label'...[/varlist...]
```

Example:
```
ADD VALUE LABELS JOBGRADE 'P' 'Parttime Employee'
                          'C' 'Customer Support'.
```

Overview

ADD VALUE LABELS adds or alters value labels without affecting other value labels already defined for that variable. In contrast, VALUE LABELS adds or alters value labels but deletes all existing value labels for that variable when it does so.

Basic Specification

The basic specification is a variable name and individual values with associated labels.

Syntax Rules

- Labels can be assigned to values of any previously defined variable. It is not necessary to enter value labels for all of a variable's values.
- Each value label must be enclosed in apostrophes or quotation marks.
- When an apostrophe occurs as part of a label, enclose the label in quotation marks or enter the internal apostrophe twice with no intervening space.
- Value labels can contain any characters, including blanks.
- The same labels can be assigned to the same values of different variables by specifying a list of variable names. For string variables, the variables on the list must have the same defined width (for example, A8).
- Multiple sets of variable names and value labels can be specified on one ADD VALUE LABELS command as long as each set is separated from the previous one by a slash.
- To continue a label from one command line to the next, specify a plus sign (+) before the continuation of the label and enclose each segment of the label, including the blank between them, in apostrophes or quotes.

Operations

- Unlike most transformations, ADD VALUE LABELS takes effect as soon as it is encountered in the command sequence. Thus, special attention should be paid to its position among commands. See "Command Order" on p. 16 for more information.

- The added value labels are stored in the working file dictionary.
- ADD VALUE LABELS can be used for variables that have no previously assigned value labels.
- Adding labels to some values does not affect labels previously assigned to other values.

Limitations

- Value labels cannot exceed 60 characters. Most procedures display only 20 characters.
- Value labels cannot be assigned to long string variables.

Example

```
ADD VALUE LABELS V1 TO V3 1 'Officials & Managers'
                          6 'Service Workers'
               /V4 'N' 'New Employee'.
```

- Labels are assigned to the values 1 and 6 of the variables between and including *V1* and *V3* in the working data file.
- Following the required slash, a label for value N for variable *V4* is specified. N is a string value and must be enclosed in apostrophes or quotation marks.
- If labels already exist for these values, they are changed in the dictionary. If labels do not exist for these values, new labels are added to the dictionary.
- Existing labels for other values for these variables are not affected.

Example

```
ADD VALUE LABELS OFFICE88 1 "EMPLOYEE'S OFFICE ASSIGNMENT PRIOR"
   + " TO 1988".
```

- The label for value 1 for *OFFICE88* is specified on two command lines. The plus sign concatenates the two string segments and a blank is included at the beginning of the second string in order to maintain correct spacing in the label.

Value Labels for String Variables

- For short string variables, the values and the labels must be enclosed in apostrophes or quotation marks.
- If a specified value is longer than the defined width of the variable, the program displays a warning and truncates the value. The added label will be associated with the truncated value.
- If a specified value is shorter than the defined width of the variable, the program adds blanks to right-pad the value without warning. The added label will be associated with the padded value.
- If a single set of labels is to be assigned to a list of string variables, the variables must have the same defined width (for example, A8).

Example

```
ADD VALUE LABELS  STATE 'TEX' 'TEXAS' 'TEN' 'TENNESSEE'
                        'MIN' 'MINNESOTA'.
```

- ADD VALUE LABELS assigns labels to three values of the variable *STATE*. Each value and each label is specified in apostrophes.
- Assuming that the variable *STATE* is defined as three characters wide, the labels *TEXAS*, *TENNESSEE*, and *MINNESOTA* will be appropriately associated with values TEX, TEN, and MIN. However, if *STATE* were defined as two characters wide, the program would truncate the specified values to two characters and would not be able to associate the labels correctly. Both TEX and TEN would be truncated to TE and would first be assigned the label *TEXAS*, which would then be changed to *TENNESSEE* by the second specification.

Example

```
ADD VALUE LABELS=STATE REGION "U" "UNKNOWN".
```

- The label *UNKNOWN* is assigned to value U for both *STATE* and *REGION*.
- *STATE* and *REGION* must have the same defined width. If they do not, a separate specification must be made for each, as in the following:

```
ADD VALUE LABELS STATE "U" "UNKNOWN" / REGION "U" "UNKNOWN".
```

AGGREGATE

```
AGGREGATE OUTFILE={file} [/MISSING=COLUMNWISE] [/DOCUMENT]
                {*    }

 [/PRESORTED]  /BREAK=varlist[({A})][varlist...]
                            {D}

 /aggvar['label']aggvar['label']...=function(arguments)

 [/aggvar ...]
```

Available functions:

SUM	Sum	MEAN	Mean
SD	Standard deviation	MAX	Maximum
MIN	Minimum	PGT	% of cases greater than value
PLT	% of cases less than value	PIN	% of cases between values
POUT	% of cases not in range	FGT	Fraction greater than value
FLT	Fraction less than value	FIN	Fraction between values
FOUT	Fraction not in range	N	Weighted number of cases
NU	Unweighted number of cases	NMISS	Weighted number of missing cases
NUMISS	Unweighted number of missing cases	FIRST	First nonmissing value
LAST	Last nonmissing value		

Example:

```
AGGREGATE OUTFILE=AGGEMP /BREAK=LOCATN DEPT /COUNT=N
  /AVGSAL AVGRAISE = MEAN(SALARY RAISE)
  /SUMSAL SUMRAISE = SUM(SALARY RAISE)
  /BLACKPCT 'Percentage Black' = PIN(RACE,1,1)
  /WHITEPCT 'Percentage White' = PIN(RACE,5,5).
```

Overview

AGGREGATE aggregates groups of cases in the working data file into single cases and creates a new, aggregated file. The values of one or more variables in the working file define the case groups. These variables are called **break variables.** A set of cases with identical values for each break variable is called a **break group.** A series of aggregate functions are applied to **source variables** in the working file to create new, aggregated variables that have one value for each break group.

AGGREGATE is often used with MATCH FILES to add variables with summary measures (sum, mean, etc.) to a file. Transformations performed on the combined file can create composite summary measures. With the REPORT procedure, the composite variables can be used to write reports with nested composite information.

Options

Aggregated File. You can produce either an SPSS-format data file or a new working file.

Documentary Text. You can copy documentary text from the original file into the aggregated file using the DOCUMENT subcommand. By default, documentary text is dropped.

Sorting. By default, cases in the aggregated file are sorted in ascending order of the values of each break variable. Alternatively, you can specify descending order. If the working file is already sorted by the break variables, you can skip this final sorting pass through the file using the PRESORTED subcommand.

Aggregated Variables. You can create aggregated variables using any of 19 aggregate functions. The functions SUM, MEAN, and SD can aggregate only numeric variables. All other functions can use both numeric and string variables.

Labels and Formats. You can specify variable labels for the aggregated variables. Variables created with the functions MAX, MIN, FIRST, and LAST assume the formats and value labels of their source variables. All other variables assume the default formats described under "Aggregate Functions" on p. 96.

Basic Specification

The basic specification is OUTFILE, BREAK, and at least one aggregate function and source variable. OUTFILE specifies a name for the aggregated file. BREAK names the case grouping (break) variables. The aggregate function creates a new aggregated variable.

Subcommand Order

- OUTFILE must be specified first.
- If specified, DOCUMENT and PRESORTED must precede BREAK. No other subcommand can be specified between these two subcommands.
- MISSING, if specified, must immediately follow OUTFILE.
- The aggregate functions must be specified last.

Operations

- When AGGREGATE produces an SPSS-format data file, the working file remains unchanged and is still available for analysis. When AGGREGATE creates a new working file, it replaces the old working file. Only the new working file is available for analysis.
- The aggregated file contains the break variables plus the variables created by the aggregate functions.
- AGGREGATE excludes cases with missing values from all aggregate calculations except those involving functions N, NU, NMISS, and NUMISS.
- Unless otherwise specified, AGGREGATE sorts cases in the aggregated file in ascending order of the values of the grouping variables.

- If PRESORTED is specified, a new aggregate case is created each time a different value or combination of values is encountered on variables named on the BREAK subcommand.
- AGGREGATE ignores split-file processing. To achieve the same effect, name the variable or variables used to split the file as break variables before any other break variables. AGGREGATE produces one file, but the aggregated cases are in the same order as the split files.

Example

```
AGGREGATE OUTFILE=AGGEMP /BREAK=LOCATN DEPT
 /COUNT=N
 /AVGSAL AVGRAISE = MEAN(SALARY RAISE)
 /SUMSAL SUMRAISE = SUM(SALARY RAISE)
 /BLACKPCT 'Percentage Black' = PIN(RACE,1,1)
 /WHITEPCT 'Percentage White' = PIN(RACE,5,5).
```

- AGGREGATE creates a new SPSS-format data file *AGGEMP*. *AGGEMP* contains two break variables (*LOCATN* and *DEPT*) and all the new aggregate variables (*COUNT, AVGSAL, AVGRAISE, SUMSAL, SUMRAISE, BLACKPCT,* and *WHITEPCT*).
- BREAK specifies *LOCATN* and *DEPT* as the break variables. In the aggregated file, cases are sorted in ascending order of *LOCATN* and in ascending order of *DEPT* within *LOCATN*. The working data file remains unsorted.
- Variable *COUNT* is created as the weighted number of cases in each break group. *AVGSAL* is the mean of *SALARY* and *AVGRAISE* is the mean of *RAISE*. *SUMSAL* is the sum of *SALARY* and *SUMRAISE* is the sum of *RAISE*. *BLACKPCT* is the percentage of cases with value 1 for *RACE*. *WHITEPCT* is the percentage of cases with value 5 for *RACE*.

Example

```
GET FILE=HUBEMPL /KEEP=LOCATN DEPT HOURLY RAISE SEX.
AGGREGATE OUTFILE=AGGFILE /BREAK=LOCATN DEPT
 /AVGHOUR AVGRAISE=MEAN(HOURLY RAISE).
SORT CASES BY LOCATN DEPT.
MATCH FILES  TABLE=AGGFILE /FILE=* /BY LOCATN DEPT
 /KEEP AVGHOUR AVGRAISE LOCATN DEPT SEX HOURLY RAISE /MAP.

COMPUTE HOURDIF=HOURLY/AVGHOUR.
COMPUTE RAISEDIF=RAISE/AVGRAISE.
LIST.
```

- GET reads the SPSS-format data file *HUBEMPL* and keeps a subset of variables.
- AGGREGATE creates a file aggregated by *LOCATN* and *DEPT* with the two new variables *AVGHOUR* and *AVGRAISE*, containing the means by location and department for *HOURLY* and *RAISE*. The aggregated file is saved as an SPSS-format data file named *AGGFILE*. Only the aggregated data file *AGGFILE* is sorted by *LOCATN* and *DEPT*; the working data file remains unchanged.
- SORT CASES sorts the working data file in ascending order of *LOCATN* and *DEPT*, the same variables used as AGGREGATE break variables.

- MATCH FILES specifies a table lookup match with *AGGFILE* as the table file and the sorted working data file as the case file.
- BY indicates that the keys for the match are *LOCATN* and *DEPT*.
- KEEP specifies the subset and order of variables to be retained in the resulting file.
- MAP provides a listing of the variables in the resulting file and the two input files.
- The COMPUTE commands calculate the ratios of each employee's hourly wage and raise to the department averages for wage and raise. The results are stored in the variables *HOURDIF* and *RAISEDIF*.
- LIST displays the resulting file.

OUTFILE Subcommand

OUTFILE specifies a name for the file created by AGGREGATE. If an asterisk is specified on OUTFILE, the aggregated file replaces the working file. OUTFILE must be the first subcommand specified on AGGREGATE.

- If the aggregated file replaces the working file, the file is not automatically saved on disk. To save the file, use the SAVE command.

Example

```
AGGREGATE OUTFILE=AGGEMP
 /BREAK=LOCATN
 /AVGSAL = MEAN(SALARY).
```

- OUTFILE creates an SPSS-format data file named *AGGEMP*. The working file remains unchanged and is available for further analysis.
- The file *AGGEMP* contains two variables, *LOCATN* and *AVGSAL*.

BREAK Subcommand

BREAK lists the grouping variables, also called break variables. Each unique combination of values of the break variables defines one break group.

- The variables named on BREAK can be any combination of variables in the working data file.
- Unless PRESORTED is specified, AGGREGATE sorts cases after aggregating. By default, cases are sorted in ascending order of the values of the break variables. AGGREGATE sorts first on the first break variable, then on the second break variable within the groups created by the first, and so on.
- Sort order can be controlled by specifying an A (for ascending) or D (for descending) in parentheses after any break variables.
- The designations A and D apply to all preceding undesignated variables.
- The subcommand PRESORTED overrides all sorting specifications.

Example

```
AGGREGATE OUTFILE=AGGEMP
 /BREAK=LOCATN DEPT (A) TENURE (D)
 /AVGSAL = MEAN(SALARY).
```

- BREAK names the variables *LOCATN*, *DEPT*, and *TENURE* as the break variables.
- Cases in the aggregated file are sorted in ascending order of *LOCATN*, in ascending order of *DEPT* within *LOCATN*, and in descending order of *TENURE* within *LOCATN* and *DEPT*. For each group defined by these variables, *AVGSAL* is computed as the mean of salary.

DOCUMENT Subcommand

DOCUMENT copies documentation from the original file into the aggregated file. By default, documents are dropped from the aggregated file, whether the file is the working file or an SPSS-format data file. DOCUMENT must appear after OUTFILE but before BREAK.

PRESORTED Subcommand

PRESORTED indicates that cases in the working data file are sorted according to the values of the break variables. This prevents AGGREGATE from sorting cases that have already been sorted and can save a considerable amount of processing time.

- If specified, PRESORTED must precede BREAK. The only specification is the keyword PRESORTED. PRESORTED has no additional specifications.
- When PRESORTED is specified, the program forms an aggregate case out of each group of *adjacent* cases with the same values for the break variables.
- If the working file is not sorted by the break variables in ascending order and PRESORTED is specified, a warning message is generated but the procedure is executed. Each group of adjacent cases with the same values for break variables forms a case in the aggregated file, which may produce multiple cases with the same values for the break variables.

Example

```
AGGREGATE OUTFILE=AGGEMP
 /PRESORTED
 /BREAK=LOCATN DEPT
 /AVGSAL = MEAN(SALARY).
```

- PRESORTED indicates that cases are already sorted by the variables *LOCATN* and *DEPT*.
- AGGREGATE does not make an extra data pass to sort the cases.

Aggregate Functions

An aggregated variable is created by applying an aggregate function to a variable in the working file. The variable in the working file is called the **source** variable, and the new aggregated variable is the **target** variable.

- The aggregate functions must be specified last on AGGREGATE.

- The simplest specification is a target variable list, followed by an equals sign, a function name, and a list of source variables.
- The number of target variables named must match the number of source variables.
- When several aggregate variables are defined at once, the first-named target variable is based on the first-named source variable, the second-named target is based on the second-named source, and so on.
- Only the functions MAX, MIN, FIRST, and LAST copy complete dictionary information from the source variable. For all other functions, new variables do not have labels and are assigned default dictionary print and write formats. The default format for a variable depends on the function used to create it (see the list of available functions below).
- You can provide a variable label for a new variable by specifying the label in apostrophes immediately following the new variable name. Value labels cannot be assigned in AGGREGATE.
- To change formats or add value labels to a working data file created by AGGREGATE, use the PRINT FORMATS, WRITE FORMATS, FORMATS, or VALUE LABELS commands. If the aggregate file is written to disk, first retrieve the file using GET, specify the new labels and formats, and resave the file.

The following is a list of available functions:

SUM(varlist)   *Sum across cases.* Default formats are F8.2.

MEAN(varlist)   *Mean across cases.* Default formats are F8.2.

SD(varlist)   *Standard deviation across cases.* Default formats are F8.2.

MAX(varlist)   *Maximum value across cases.* Complete dictionary information is copied from the source variables to the target variables.

MIN(varlist)   *Minimum value across cases.* Complete dictionary information is copied from the source variables to the target variables.

PGT(varlist,value)   *Percentage of cases greater than the specified value.* Default formats are F5.1.

PLT(varlist,value)   *Percentage of cases less than the specified value.* Default formats are F5.1.

PIN(varlist,value1,value2)   *Percentage of cases between value1 and value2, inclusive.* Default formats are F5.1.

POUT(varlist,value1,value2)   *Percentage of cases not between value1 and value2.* Cases where the source variable equals value1 or value2 are not counted. Default formats are F5.1.

FGT(varlist,value)   *Fraction of cases greater than the specified value.* Default formats are F5.3.

FLT(varlist,value)   *Fraction of cases less than the specified value.* Default formats are F5.3.

FIN(varlist,value1,value2)   *Fraction of cases between value1 and value2, inclusive.* Default formats are F5.3.

FOUT(varlist,value1,value2)   *Fraction of cases not between value1 and value2.* Cases where the source variable equals value1 or value2 are not counted. Default formats are F5.3.

N(varlist)   *Weighted number of cases in break group.* Default formats are F7.0 for unweighted files and F8.2 for weighted files.

NU(varlist)   *Unweighted number of cases in break group.* Default formats are F7.0.

NMISS(varlist)   *Weighted number of missing cases.* Default formats are F7.0 for unweighted files and F8.2 for weighted files.

NUMISS(varlist)   *Unweighted number of missing cases.* Default formats are F7.0.

FIRST(varlist)   *First nonmissing observed value in break group.* Complete dictionary information is copied from the source variables to the target variables.

LAST(varlist)   *Last nonmissing observed value in break group.* Complete dictionary information is copied from the source variables to the target variables.

- The functions SUM, MEAN, and SD can be applied only to numeric source variables. All other functions can use short and long string variables as well as numeric ones.
- The N and NU functions do not require arguments. Without arguments, they return the number of weighted and unweighted valid cases in a break group. If you supply a variable list, they return the number of weighted and unweighted valid cases for the variables specified.
- For several functions, the argument includes values as well as a source variable designation. Either blanks or commas can be used to separate the components of an argument list.
- For PIN, POUT, FIN, and FOUT, the first value should be less than or equal to the second. If the first is greater, AGGREGATE automatically reverses them and prints a warning message. If the two values are equal, PIN and FIN calculate the percentages and fractions of values equal to the argument. POUT and FOUT calculate the percentages and fractions of values not equal to the argument.
- String values specified in an argument should be enclosed in apostrophes. They are evaluated in alphabetical order.

Example

```
AGGREGATE OUTFILE=AGGEMP /BREAK=LOCATN
 /AVGSAL 'Average Salary' AVGRAISE = MEAN(SALARY RAISE).
```

- AGGREGATE defines two aggregate variables, *AVGSAL* and *AVGRAISE*.
- *AVGSAL* is the mean of *SALARY* for each break group, and *AVGRAISE* is the mean of *RAISE*.
- The label *Average Salary* is assigned to *AVGSAL*.

Example

```
AGGREGATE OUTFILE=* /BREAK=DEPT
/LOWVAC,LOWSICK = PLT (VACDAY SICKDAY,10).
```

- AGGREGATE creates two aggregated variables: *LOWVAC* and *LOWSICK. LOWVAC* is the percentage of cases with values less than 10 for *VACDAY* and *LOWSICK* is the percentage of cases with values less than 10 for *SICKDAY*.

Example

```
AGGREGATE OUTFILE=GROUPS /BREAK=OCCGROUP
/COLLEGE = FIN(EDUC,13,16).
```

- AGGREGATE creates the variable *COLLEGE*, which is the fraction of cases with 13 to 16 years of education (variable *EDUC*).

Example

```
AGGREGATE OUTFILE=* /BREAK=CLASS
/LOCAL = PIN(STATE,'IL','IO').
```

- AGGREGATE creates the variable *LOCAL*, which is the percentage of cases in each break group whose two-letter state code represents Illinois, Indiana, or Iowa. (The abbreviation for Indiana, IN, is between IL and IO in an alphabetical sort sequence.)

MISSING Subcommand

By default, AGGREGATE uses all nonmissing values of the source variable to calculate aggregated variables. An aggregated variable will have a missing value only if the source variable is missing for every case in the break group. You can alter the default missing-value treatment by using the MISSING subcommand. You can also specify the inclusion of user-missing values on any function.

- MISSING must immediately follow OUTFILE.
- COLUMNWISE is the only specification available for MISSING.
- If COLUMNWISE is specified, the value of an aggregated variable is missing for a break group if the source variable is missing for any case in the group.
- COLUMNWISE does not affect the calculation of the N, NU, NMISS, or NUMISS functions.
- COLUMNWISE does not apply to break variables. If a break variable has a missing value, cases in that group are processed and the break variable is saved in the file with the missing value. Use SELECT IF if you want to eliminate cases with missing values for the break variables.

Including Missing Values

You can force a function to include user-missing values in its calculations by specifying a period after the function name.

- AGGREGATE ignores periods used with functions N, NU, NMISS, and NUMISS if these functions have no argument.

- User-missing values are treated as valid when these four functions are followed by a period and have a variable as an argument. NMISS.(AGE) treats user-missing values as valid and thus gives the number of cases for which *AGE* has the system-missing value only.

The effect of specifying a period with N, NU, NMISS, and NUMISS is illustrated by the following:

N = N. = N(AGE) + NMISS(AGE) = N.(AGE) + NMISS.(AGE)

NU = NU. = NU(AGE) + NUMISS(AGE) = NU.(AGE) + NUMISS.(AGE)

- The function N (the same as N. with no argument) yields a value for each break group that equals the number of cases with valid values (N(AGE)) plus the number of cases with user- or system-missing values (NMISS(AGE)).
- This in turn equals the number of cases with either valid or user-missing values (N.(AGE)) plus the number with system-missing values (NMISS.(AGE)).
- The same identities hold for the NU, NMISS, and NUMISS functions.

Example

```
AGGREGATE OUTFILE=AGGEMP /MISSING=COLUMNWISE /BREAK=LOCATN
 /AVGSAL = MEAN(SALARY).
```

- *AVGSAL* is missing for an aggregated case if *SALARY* is missing for any case in the break group.

Example

```
AGGREGATE OUTFILE=* /BREAK=DEPT
 /LOVAC = PLT.(VACDAY,10).
```

- *LOVAC* is the percentage of cases within each break group with values less than 10 for *VACDAY*, even if some of those values are defined as user-missing.

Example

```
AGGREGATE OUTFILE=CLASS /BREAK=GRADE
 /FIRSTAGE = FIRST.(AGE).
```

- The first value of *AGE* in each break group is assigned to the variable *FIRSTAGE*.
- If the first value of *AGE* in a break group is user missing, that value will be assigned to *FIRSTAGE*. However, the value will retain its missing-value status, since variables created with FIRST take dictionary information from their source variables.

Comparing Missing-Value Treatments

Table 1 demonstrates the effects of specifying the MISSING subcommand and a period after the function name. Each entry in the table is the number of cases used to compute the specified function for the variable *EDUC*, which has 10 nonmissing cases, 5 user-missing cases, and 2 system-missing cases for the group. Note that columnwise treatment produces the same results as the default for every function except the MEAN function.

Table 1   Default versus columnwise missing-value treatments

Function	Default	Columnwise
N	17	17
N.	17	17
N(EDUC)	10	10
N.(EDUC)	15	15
MEAN(EDUC)	10	0
MEAN.(EDUC)	15	0
NMISS(EDUC)	7	7
NMISS.(EDUC)	2	2

ALSCAL

```
ALSCAL  VARIABLES=varlist

[/FILE=file]  [CONFIG  [({INITIAL})]]  [ROWCONF [({INITIAL})]]
                       {FIXED  }                 {FIXED  }

             [COLCONF [({INITIAL})]]  [SUBJWGHT[({INITIAL})]]
                      {FIXED  }                {FIXED  }


             [STIMWGHT[({INITIAL})]]
                      {FIXED  }

[/INPUT=ROWS ({ALL**})]
             { n  }

[/SHAPE={SYMMETRIC**}]
        {ASYMMETRIC }
        {RECTANGULAR}

[/LEVEL={ORDINAL**   [([UNTIE] [SIMILAR])]}]
        {INTERVAL[({1})]}                 }
        {        {n}    }                 }
        {RATIO[({1})]}                    }
        {      {n}   }                    }
        {NOMINAL                          }

[/CONDITION={MATRIX**    }]
            {ROW         }
            {UNCONDITIONAL}

[/{MODEL }={EUCLID**}]
  {METHOD} {INDSCAL }
           {ASCAL   }
           {AINDS   }
           {GEMSCAL }

[/CRITERIA=[NEGATIVE]  [CUTOFF({0**})]  [CONVERGE({.001})]
                              { n }               { n }

        [ITER({30})]  [STRESSMIN({.005})]  [NOULB]
              {n }               { n }

        [DIMENS({2**      })]  [DIRECTIONS(n)]
                {min[,max]}

        [CONSTRAIN]  [TIESTORE(n)]]

[/PRINT=[DATA] [HEADER]]    [/PLOT=[DEFAULT] [ALL]]

[/OUTFILE=file]

[/MATRIX=IN({file})]
            {*   }
```

**Default if the subcommand or keyword is omitted.

Example:

```
ALSCAL VARIABLES=ATLANTA TO TAMPA.
```

ALSCAL was originally designed and programmed by Forrest W. Young, Yoshio Takane, and Rostyslaw J. Lewyckyj of the Psychometric Laboratory, University of North Carolina.

Overview

ALSCAL uses an alternating least-squares algorithm to perform multidimensional scaling (MDS) and multidimensional unfolding (MDU). You can select one of the five models to obtain stimulus coordinates and/or weights in multidimensional space.

Options

Data Input. You can read inline data matrices, including all types of two- or three-way data, such as a single matrix or a matrix for each of several subjects, using the INPUT subcommand. You can read square (symmetrical or asymmetrical) or rectangular matrices of proximities with the SHAPE subcommand and proximity matrices created by PROXIMITIES and CLUSTER with the MATRIX subcommand. You can also read a file of coordinates and/or weights to provide initial or fixed values for the scaling process with the FILE subcommand.

Methodological Assumptions. You can specify data as matrix-conditional, row-conditional, or unconditional on the CONDITION subcommand. You can treat data as nonmetric (nominal or ordinal) or as metric (interval or ratio) using the LEVEL subcommand. You can also use LEVEL to identify ordinal-level proximity data as measures of similarity or dissimilarity and can specify tied observations as untied (continuous) or leave them tied (discrete).

Model Selection. You can specify most commonly used multidimensional scaling models by selecting the correct combination of ALSCAL subcommands, keywords, and criteria. In addition to the default Euclidean distance model, the MODEL subcommand offers the individual differences (weighted) Euclidean distance model (INDSCAL), the asymmetric Euclidean distance model (ASCAL), the asymmetric individual differences Euclidean distance model (AINDS), and the generalized Euclidean metric individual differences model (GEMSCAL).

Output. You can produce output that includes raw and scaled input data, missing-value patterns, normalized data with means, squared data with additive constants, each subject's scalar product and individual weight space, plots of linear or nonlinear fit, and plots of the data transformations using the PRINT and PLOT subcommands.

Basic Specification

The basic specification is VARIABLES followed by a variable list. By default, ALSCAL produces a two-dimensional nonmetric Euclidean multidimensional scaling solution. Input is assumed to be one or more square symmetric matrices with data elements that are dissimilarities at the ordinal level of measurement. Ties are not untied, and conditionality is by subject. Values less than 0 are treated as missing. The default output includes the improvement in Young's S-stress for successive iterations, two measures of fit for each input matrix (Kruskal's stress and the squared correlation, RSQ), and the derived configurations for each of the dimensions.

Subcommand Order

Subcommands can be named in any order.

Operations

- ALSCAL calculates the number of input matrices by dividing the total number of observations in the data set by the number of rows in each matrix. All matrices must contain the same number of rows. This number is determined by the settings on SHAPE and INPUT (if used). For square matrix data, the number of rows in the matrix equals the number of variables. For rectangular matrix data, it equals the number of rows specified or implied. For additional information, see the INPUT and SHAPE subcommands below.

- ALSCAL ignores user-missing specifications in all variables in the configuration/weights file (see the FILE subcommand on p. 107). The system-missing value is converted to 0.

- With split-file data, ALSCAL reads initial or fixed configurations from the configuration/weights file for each split-file group (see the FILE subcommand on p. 107). If there is only one initial configuration in the file, ALSCAL rereads these initial or fixed values for successive split-file groups.

- By default, ALSCAL estimates upper and lower bounds on missing values in the working data file in order to compute the initial configuration. To prevent this, specify CRITERIA=NOULB. Missing values are always ignored during the iterative process.

Limitations

- Maximum 100 variables on the VARIABLES subcommand.
- Maximum six dimensions can be scaled.
- ALSCAL does not recognize data weights created by the WEIGHT command.
- ALSCAL analyses can include no more than 32,767 values in each of the input matrices. Large analyses may require significant computing time.

Example

```
* Air distances among U.S. cities.
* Data are from Johnson and Wichern (1982), page 563.
DATA LIST
 /ATLANTA BOSTON CINCNATI COLUMBUS DALLAS INDNPLIS
   LITTROCK LOSANGEL MEMPHIS STLOUIS SPOKANE TAMPA 1-60.
BEGIN DATA
    0
1068    0
 461   867    0
 549   769   107    0
 805  1819   943  1050    0
 508   941   108   172   882    0
 505  1494   618   725   325   562    0
2197  3052  2186  2245  1403  2080  1701    0
 366  1355   502   586   464   436   137  1831    0
 558  1178   338   409   645   234   353  1848   294    0
2467  2747  2067  2131  1891  1959  1988  1227  2042  1820    0
 467  1379   928   985  1077   975   912  2480   779  1016  2821    0
END DATA.

ALSCAL VARIABLES=ATLANTA TO TAMPA
 /PLOT.
```

- By default, ALSCAL assumes a symmetric matrix of dissimilarities for ordinal-level variables. Only values below the diagonal are used. The upper triangle can be left blank. The 12 cities form the rows and columns of the matrix.
- The result is a classical MDS analysis that reproduces a map of the United States when the output is rotated to a north-south by east-west orientation.

VARIABLES Subcommand

VARIABLES identifies the columns in the proximity matrix or matrices that ALSCAL reads.
- VARIABLES is required and can name only numeric variables.
- Each matrix must have at least four rows and four columns.

INPUT Subcommand

ALSCAL reads data row by row, with each case in the working data file representing a single row in the data matrix. (VARIABLES specifies the columns.) Use INPUT when reading rectangular data matrices to specify how many rows are in each matrix.
- The specification on INPUT is ROWS. If INPUT is not specified or is specified without ROWS, the default is ROWS(ALL). ALSCAL assumes that each case in the working data file represents one row of a single input matrix, and the result is a square matrix.
- You can specify the number of rows (n) in each matrix in parentheses after the keyword ROWS. The number of matrices equals the number of observations divided by the number specified.
- The number specified on ROWS must be at least 4 and must divide evenly into the total number of rows in the data.
- With split-file data, n refers to the number of cases in each split-file group. All split-file groups must have the same number of rows.

Example

```
ALSCAL VARIABLES=V1 to V7 /INPUT=ROWS(8).
```

- INPUT indicates that there are eight rows per matrix, with each case in the working data file representing one row.
- The total number of cases must be divisible by 8.

SHAPE Subcommand

Use SHAPE to specify the structure of the input data matrix or matrices.
- You can specify one of the three keywords listed below.
- Both SYMMETRIC and ASYMMETRIC refer to square matrix data.

SYMMETRIC   *Symmetric data matrix or matrices.* For a symmetric matrix, ALSCAL looks only at the values below the diagonal. Values on and above the diagonal can be omitted. This is the default.

ASYMMETRIC	*Asymmetric data matrix or matrices.* The corresponding values in the upper and lower triangles are not all equal. The diagonal is ignored.
RECTANGULAR	*Rectangular data matrix or matrices.* The rows and columns represent different sets of items.

Example

```
ALSCAL VAR=V1 TO V8 /SHAPE=RECTANGULAR.
```

• ALSCAL performs a classical MDU analysis, treating the rows and columns as separate sets of items.

LEVEL Subcommand

LEVEL identifies the level of measurement for the values in the data matrix or matrices. You can specify one of the keywords defined below.

ORDINAL	*Ordinal-level data.* This specification is the default. It treats the data as ordinal, using Kruskal's (1964) least-squares monotonic transformation. The analysis is nonmetric. By default, the data are treated as discrete dissimilarities. Ties in the data remain tied throughout the analysis. To change the default, specify UNTIE and/or SIMILAR in parentheses. UNTIE treats the data as continuous and resolves ties in an optimal fashion; SIMILAR treats the data as similarities. UNTIE and SIMILAR cannot be used with the other levels of measurement.
INTERVAL(n)	*Interval-level data.* This specification produces a metric analysis of the data using classical regression techniques. You can specify any integer from 1 to 4 in parentheses for the degree of polynomial transformation to be fit to the data. The default is 1.
RATIO(n)	*Ratio-level data.* This specification produces a metric analysis. You can specify an integer from 1 to 4 in parentheses for the degree of polynomial transformation. The default is 1.
NOMINAL	*Nominal-level data.* This specification treats the data as nominal by using a least-squares categorical transformation (Takane et al., 1977). This option produces a nonmetric analysis of nominal data. It is useful when there are few observed categories, when there are many observations in each category, and when the order of the categories is not known.

Example

```
ALSCAL VAR=ATLANTA TO TAMPA /LEVEL=INTERVAL(2).
```

• This example identifies the distances between U.S. cities as interval-level data. The 2 in parentheses indicates a polynomial transformation with linear and quadratic terms.

CONDITION Subcommand

CONDITION specifies which numbers in a data set are comparable.

MATRIX   *Only numbers within each matrix are comparable.* If each matrix represents a different subject, this specification makes comparisons conditional by subject. This is the default.

ROW   *Only numbers within the same row are comparable.* This specification is appropriate only for asymmetric or rectangular data. They cannot be used when ASCAL or AINDS is specified on MODEL.

UNCONDITIONAL   *All numbers are comparable.* Comparisons can be made among any values in the input matrix or matrices.

Example

```
ALSCAL VAR=V1 TO V8 /SHAPE=RECTANGULAR /CONDITION=ROW.
```

- ALSCAL performs a Euclidean MDU analysis conditional on comparisons within rows.

FILE Subcommand

ALSCAL can read proximity data from the working data file or, with the MATRIX subcommand, from a matrix data file created by PROXIMITIES or CLUSTER. The FILE subcommand reads a file containing additional data: an initial or fixed configuration for the coordinates of the stimuli and/or weights for the matrices being scaled. This file can be created with the OUTFILE subcommand on ALSCAL or with an SPSS input program.

- The minimum specification is the file that contains the configurations and/or weights.

- FILE can include additional specifications that define the structure of the configuration/weights file.

- The variables in the configuration/weights file that correspond to successive ALSCAL dimensions must have the names *DIM1, DIM2,...DIMr,* where *r* is the maximum number of ALSCAL dimensions. The file must also contain the short string variable *TYPE_* to identify the types of values in all rows.

- Values for the variable *TYPE_* can be CONFIG, ROWCONF, COLCONF, SUBJWGHT, and STIMWGHT, in that order. Each value can be truncated to the first three letters. Stimulus coordinate values are specified as CONFIG; row stimulus coordinates as ROWCONF; column stimulus coordinates as COLCONF; and subject and stimulus weights as SUBJWGHT and STIMWGHT, respectively. ALSCAL accepts CONFIG and ROWCONF interchangeably.

- ALSCAL skips unneeded types as long as they appear in the file in their proper order. Generalized weights (GEM) and flattened subject weights (FLA) cannot be initialized or fixed and will always be skipped. (These weights can be generated by ALSCAL but cannot be used as input.)

The following list summarizes the optional specifications that can be used on FILE to define the structure of the configuration/weights file:

- Each specification can be further identified with option INITIAL or FIXED in parentheses.

- INITIAL is the default. INITIAL indicates that the external configuration or weights are to be used as initial coordinates and are to be modified during each iteration.
- FIXED forces ALSCAL to use the externally defined structure without modification to calculate the best values for all unfixed portions of the structure.

CONFIG *Read stimulus configuration.* The configuration/weights file contains initial stimulus coordinates. Input of this type is appropriate when SHAPE=SYMMETRIC or SHAPE=ASYMMETRIC, or when the number of variables in a matrix equals the number of variables on the ALSCAL command. The value of the *TYPE_* variable must be either CON or ROW for all stimulus coordinates for the configuration.

ROWCONF *Read row stimulus configuration.* The configuration/weights file contains initial row stimulus coordinates. This specification is appropriate if SHAPE=RECTANGULAR and if the number of ROWCONF rows in the matrix equals the number of rows specified on the INPUT subcommand (or, if INPUT is omitted, the number of cases in the working data file). The value of *TYPE_* must be either ROW or CON for the set of coordinates for each row.

COLCONF *Read column stimulus configuration.* The configuration/weights file contains initial column stimulus coordinates. This kind of file can be used only if SHAPE=RECTANGULAR and if the number of COLCONF rows in the matrix equals the number of variables on the ALSCAL command. The value of *TYPE_* must be COL for the set of coordinates for each column.

SUBJWGHT *Read subject (matrix) weights.* The configuration/weights file contains subject weights. The number of observations in a subject-weights matrix must equal the number of matrices in the proximity file. Subject weights can be used only if the model is INDSCAL, AINDS, or GEMSCAL. The value of *TYPE_* for each set of weights must be SUB.

STIMWGHT *Read stimulus weights.* The configuration/weights file contains stimulus weights. The number of observations in the configuration/weights file must equal the number of matrices in the proximity file. Stimulus weights can be used only if the model is AINDS or ASCAL. The value of *TYPE_* for each set of weights must be STI.

If the optional specifications for the configuration/weights file are not specified on FILE, ALSCAL sequentially reads the *TYPE_* values appropriate to the model and shape according to the defaults in Table 1.

Example

```
ALSCAL VAR=V1 TO V8 /FILE=ONE CON(FIXED) STI(INITIAL).
```

- ALSCAL reads the configuration/weights file *ONE*.
- The stimulus coordinates are read as fixed values, and the stimulus weights are read as initial values.

Table 1   Default specifications for the FILE subcommand

Shape	Model	Default specifications
SYMMETRIC	EUCLID	CONFIG (or ROWCONF)
	INDSCAL	CONFIG (or ROWCONF) SUBJWGHT
	GEMSCAL	CONFIG (or ROWCONF) SUBJWGHT
ASYMMETRIC	EUCLID	CONFIG (or ROWCONF)
	INDSCAL	CONFIG (or ROWCONF) SUBJWGHT
	GEMSCAL	CONFIG (or ROWCONF) SUBJWGHT
	ASCAL	CONFIG (or ROWCONF) STIMWGHT
	AINDS	CONFIG (or ROWCONF) SUBJWGHT STIMWGHT
RECTANGULAR	EUCLID	ROWCONF (or CONFIG) COLCONF
	INDSCAL	ROWCONF (or CONFIG) COLCONF SUBJWGHT
	GEMSCAL	ROWCONF (or CONFIG) COLCONF SUBJWGHT

MODEL Subcommand

MODEL (alias METHOD) defines the scaling model for the analysis. The only specification is MODEL (or METHOD) and any one of the five scaling and unfolding model types. EUCLID is the default.

EUCLID *Euclidean distance model.* This model can be used with any type of proximity matrix and is the default.

INDSCAL *Individual differences (weighted) Euclidean distance model.* ALSCAL scales the data using the weighted individual differences Euclidean distance model proposed by Carroll and Chang (1970). This type of analysis can be specified only if the analysis involves more than one data matrix and more than one dimension is specified on CRITERIA.

ASCAL *Asymmetric Euclidean distance model.* This model (Young, 1975) can be used only if SHAPE=ASYMMETRIC and more than one dimension is requested on CRITERIA.

AINDS *Asymmetric individual differences Euclidean distance model.* This option combines Young's (1975) asymmetric Euclidean model with the individual differences model proposed by Carroll and Chang (1970). This model can be used only when SHAPE=ASYMMETRIC, the analysis involves more than one data matrix, and more than one dimension is specified on CRITERIA.

GEMSCAL *Generalized Euclidean metric individual differences model.* The number of directions for this model is set with the DIRECTIONS option on CRITERIA. The number of directions specified can be equal to but cannot exceed the group space dimensionality. By default, the number of directions equals the number of dimensions in the solution.

Example

```
ALSCAL VARIABLES = V1 TO V6
 /SHAPE = ASYMMETRIC
 /CONDITION = ROW
 /MODEL = GEMSCAL
 /CRITERIA = DIM(4) DIRECTIONS(4).
```

- In this example, the number of directions in the GEMSCAL model is set to 4.

CRITERIA Subcommand

Use CRITERIA to control features of the scaling model and to set convergence criteria for the solution. You can specify one or more of the following:

CONVERGE(n) *Stop iterations if the change in S-stress is less than* n. S-stress is a goodness-of-fit index. By default, $n=0.001$. To increase the precision of a solution, specify a smaller value, for example, 0.0001. To obtain a less precise solution (perhaps to reduce computing time), specify a larger value, for example, 0.05. Negative values are not allowed. If $n=0$, the algorithm will iterate 30 times unless a value is specified with the ITER option.

ITER(n) *Set the maximum number of iterations to* n. The default value is 30. A higher value will give a more precise solution but will take longer to compute.

STRESSMIN(n) *Set the minimum stress value to* n. By default, ALSCAL stops iterating when the value of S-stress is 0.005 or less. STRESSMIN can be assigned any value from 0 to 1.

NEGATIVE *Allow negative weights in individual differences models.* By default, ALSCAL does not permit the weights to be negative. Weighted models include INDSCAL, ASCAL, AINDS, and GEMSCAL. The NEGATIVE option is ignored if the model is EUCLID.

CUTOFF(n) *Set the cutoff value for treating distances as missing to* n. By default, ALSCAL treats all negative similarities (or dissimilarities) as missing, and 0 and positive similarities as nonmissing ($n=0$). Changing the CUTOFF value causes ALSCAL to treat similarities greater than or equal to that value as nonmissing. User- and system-missing values are considered missing regardless of the CUTOFF specification.

NOULB   *Do not estimate upper and lower bounds on missing values.* By default, ALSCAL estimates the upper and lower bounds on missing values in order to compute the initial configuration. This specification has no effect during the iterative process, when missing values are ignored.

DIMENS(min[,max])   *Set the minimum and maximum number of dimensions in the scaling solution.* By default, ALSCAL calculates a solution with two dimensions. To obtain solutions for more than two dimensions, specify the minimum and the maximum number of dimensions in parentheses after DIMENS. The minimum and maximum can be integers between 2 and 6. A single value represents both the minimum and the maximum. For example, DIMENS(3) is equivalent to DIMENS(3,3). The minimum number of dimensions can be set to 1 only if MODEL=EUCLID.

DIRECTIONS(n)   *Set the number of principal directions in the generalized Euclidean model to* n. This option has no effect for models other than GEMSCAL. The number of principal directions can be any positive integer between 1 and the number of dimensions specified on the DIMENS option. By default, the number of directions equals the number of dimensions.

TIESTORE(n)   *Set the amount of storage needed for ties to* n. This option estimates the amount of storage needed to deal with ties in ordinal data. By default, the amount of storage is set to 1000 or the number of cells in a matrix, whichever is smaller. Should this be insufficient, ALSCAL terminates and displays a message that more space is needed.

CONSTRAIN   *Constrain multidimensional unfolding solution.* This option can be used to keep the initial constraints throughout the analysis.

PRINT Subcommand

PRINT requests output not available by default. You can specify the following:

DATA   *Display input data.* The display includes both the initial data and the scaled data for each subject according to the structure specified on SHAPE.

HEADER   *Display a header page.* The header includes the model, output, algorithmic, and data options in effect for the analysis.

- Data options listed by PRINT=HEADER include the number of rows and columns, number of matrices, measurement level, shape of the data matrix, type of data (similarity or dissimilarity), whether ties are tied or untied, conditionality, and data cutoff value.

- Model options listed by PRINT=HEADER are the type of model specified (EUCLID, INDSCAL, ASCAL, AINDS, or GEMSCAL), minimum and maximum dimensionality, and whether or not negative weights are permitted.

- Output options listed by PRINT=HEADER indicate whether the output includes the header page and input data, whether ALSCAL plotted configurations and transformations, whether an output data set was created, and whether initial stimulus coordinates, initial column stimulus coordinates, initial subject weights, and initial stimulus weights were computed.

- Algorithmic options listed by PRINT=HEADER include the maximum number of iterations permitted, the convergence criterion, the maximum S-stress value, whether or not missing data are estimated by upper and lower bounds, and the amount of storage allotted for ties in ordinal data.

Example

```
ALSCAL VAR=ATLANTA TO TAMPA /PRINT=DATA.
```

- In addition to scaled data, ALSCAL will display initial data.

PLOT Subcommand

PLOT controls the display of plots. The minimum specification is simply PLOT to produce the defaults.

DEFAULT   *Default plots.* Default plots include plots of stimulus coordinates, matrix weights (if the model is INDSCAL, AINDS, or GEMSCAL), and stimulus weights (if the model is AINDS or ASCAL). The default also includes a scatterplot of the linear fit between the data and the model and, for certain types of data, scatterplots of the nonlinear fit and the data transformation. If the SET command specifies HIGHRES=ON, ALSCAL sends all stimulus dimensions to the graphic editor and shows a 3-D plot with the first three dimensions if the solution has three or more dimensions. If HIGHRES=OFF, ALSCAL generates $d*(d-1)/2$ pages of plots for the stimulus space, where d is the number of dimensions in the solution. When appropriate, the same is true for the weight space.

ALL   *Transformation plots in addition to the default plots.* SPSS produces a separate plot for each subject if CONDITION=MATRIX and a separate plot for each row if CONDITION=ROW. For interval and ratio data, PLOT=ALL has the same effect as PLOT=DEFAULT. This option can generate voluminous output, particularly when CONDITION=ROW.

Example

```
ALSCAL VAR=V1 TO V8 /INPUT=ROWS(8) /PLOT=ALL.
```

- This command produces all the default plots (the number may be different depending on the setting of HIGHRES). It also produces a separate plot for each subject's data transformation and a plot of *V1* through *V8* in a two-dimensional space for each subject.

OUTFILE Subcommand

OUTFILE saves coordinate and weight matrices to an SPSS data file. The only specification is a name for the output file.

- The output data file has an alphanumeric (short string) variable named *TYPE_* that identifies the kind of values in each row, a numeric variable *DIMENS* that specifies the number of dimensions, a numeric variable *MATNUM* that indicates the subject (matrix) to which each set of coordinates corresponds, and variables *DIM1*, *DIM2*,...*DIMn* that correspond to the *n* dimensions in the model.
- The values of any split-file variables are also included in the output file.
- The file created by OUTFILE can be used by subsequent ALSCAL commands as initial data.

The following are the types of configurations and weights that can be included in the output file:

CONFIG   *Stimulus configuration coordinates.*

ROWCONF   *Row stimulus configuration coordinates.*

COLCONF   *Column stimulus configuration coordinates.*

SUBJWGHT   *Subject (matrix) weights.*

FLATWGHT   *Flattened subject (matrix) weights.*

GEMWGHT   *Generalized weights.*

STIMWGHT   *Stimulus weights.*

Only the first three characters of each identifier are written to variable *TYPE_* in the file. For example, CONFIG becomes CON. The structure of the file is determined by the SHAPE and MODEL subcommands, as shown in Table 2.

Table 2   Types of configurations and/or weights in output files

Shape	Model	TYPE_
SYMMETRIC	EUCLID	CON
	INDSCAL	CON SUB FLA
	GEMSCAL	CON SUB FLA GEM
ASYMMETRIC	EUCLID	CON
	INDSCAL	CON SUB FLA
	GEMSCAL	CON SUB FLA GEM
	ASCAL	CON STI
	AINDS	CON SUB FLA STI
RECTANGULAR	EUCLID	ROW COL
	INDSCAL	ROW COL SUB FLA
	GEMSCAL	ROW COL SUB FLA GEM

Example

```
ALSCAL VAR=ATLANTA TO TAMPA /OUTFILE=ONE.
```

• OUTFILE creates the SPSS configuration/weights file *ONE* from the example of air distances between cities.

MATRIX Subcommand

MATRIX reads SPSS matrix data files. It can read a matrix written by either PROXIMITIES or CLUSTER.

- Generally, data read by ALSCAL are already in matrix form. If the matrix materials are in the working data file, you do not need to use MATRIX to read them. Simply use the VARIABLES subcommand to indicate the variables (or columns) to be used. However, if the matrix materials are not in the working data file, MATRIX must be used to specify the matrix data file that contains the matrix.

- The proximity matrices ALSCAL reads have *ROWTYPE_* values of PROX. No additional statistics should be included with these matrix materials.

- ALSCAL ignores unrecognized *ROWTYPE_* values in the matrix file. In addition, it ignores variables present in the matrix file that are not specified on the VARIABLES subcommand in ALSCAL. The order of rows and columns in the matrix is unimportant.

- Since ALSCAL does not support case labeling, it ignores values for the *ID* variable (if present) in a CLUSTER or PROXIMITIES matrix.

- If split-file processing was in effect when the matrix was written, the same split file must be in effect when ALSCAL reads that matrix.

- The specification on MATRIX is the keyword IN and the matrix file in parentheses.

- MATRIX=IN cannot be used unless a working data file has already been defined. To read an existing matrix data file at the beginning of a session, first use GET to retrieve the matrix file and then specify IN(*) on MATRIX.

IN (filename)   *Read a matrix data file.* If the matrix data file is the working data file, specify an asterisk in parentheses (*). If the matrix data file is another file, specify the filename in parentheses. A matrix file read from an external file does not replace the working data file.

Example

```
PROXIMITIES V1 TO V8 /ID=NAMEVAR /MATRIX=OUT(*).
ALSCAL VAR=CASE1 TO CASE10 /MATRIX=IN(*).
```

- PROXIMITIES uses *V1* through *V8* in the working data file to generate a matrix file of Euclidean distances between each pair of cases based on the eight variables. The number of rows and columns in the resulting matrix equals the number of cases. MATRIX=OUT then replaces the working data file with this new matrix data file.

- MATRIX=IN on ALSCAL reads the matrix data file, which is the new working data file. In this instance, MATRIX is optional because the matrix materials are in the working data file.

- If there were 10 cases in the original working data file, ALSCAL performs a multidimensional scaling analysis in two dimensions on *CASE1* through *CASE10*.

Example

```
GET FILE PROXMTX.
ALSCAL VAR=CASE1 TO CASE10 /MATRIX=IN(*).
```

- GET retrieves the matrix data file *PROXMTX*.

- MATRIX=IN specifies an asterisk because the working data file is the matrix. MATRIX is optional, however, since the matrix materials are in the working data file.

Example

```
GET FILE PRSNNL.
FREQUENCIES VARIABLE=AGE.
ALSCAL VAR=CASE1 TO CASE10 /MATRIX=IN(PROXMTX).
```

- This example performs a frequencies analysis on file *PRSNNL* and then uses a different file containing matrix data for ALSCAL. The file is an existing matrix data file.
- MATRIX=IN is required because the matrix data file, *PROXMTX*, is not the working data file. *PROXMTX* does not replace *PRSNNL* as the working data file.

Specification of Analyses

Table 3 summarizes the analyses that can be performed for the major types of proximity matrices you can use with ALSCAL, Table 4 lists the specifications needed to produce these analyses for nonmetric models, and Table 5 lists the specifications for metric models. You can include additional specifications to control the precision of your analysis with CRITERIA.

Table 3   Models for types of matrix input

Matrix mode	Matrix form	Model class	Single matrix	Replications of single matrix	Two or more individual matrices
Object by object	Symmetric	Multi-dimensional scaling	CMDS Classical multi-dimensional scaling	RMDS Replicated multi-dimensional scaling	WMDS(INDSCAL) Weighted multi-dimensional scaling
	Asymmetric single process	Multi-dimensional scaling	CMDS(row conditional) Classical row conditional multi-dimensional scaling	RMDS(row conditional) Replicated row conditional multi-dimensional scaling	WMDS(row conditional) Weighted row conditional multi-dimensional scaling
	Asymmetric multiple process	Internal asymmetric multi-dimensional scaling	CAMDS Classical asymmetric multidimensional scaling	RAMDS Replicated asymmetric multidimensional scaling	WAMDS Weighted asymmetric multidimensional scaling
		External asymmetric multi-dimensional scaling	CAMDS(external) Classical external asymmetric multidimensional scaling	RAMDS(external) Replicated external asymmetric multi-dimensional scaling	WAMDS(external) Weighted external asymmetric multi-dimensional scaling
Object by attribute	Rectangular	Internal unfolding	CMDU Classical internal multidimensional unfolding	RMDU Replicated internal multidimensional unfolding	WMDU Weighted internal multi-dimensional unfolding
		External unfolding	CMDU(external) Classical external multidimensional unfolding	RMDU(external) Replicated external multidimensional unfolding	WMDU(external) Weighted external multi-dimensional unfolding

Table 4   ALSCAL specifications for nonmetric models

Matrix mode	Matrix form	Model class	Single matrix	Replications of single matrix	Two or more individual matrices
Object by object	Symmetric	Multi-dimensional scaling	ALSCAL VAR= varlist.	ALSCAL VAR= varlist.	ALSCAL VAR= varlist /MODEL=INDSCAL.
	Asymmetric single process	Multi-dimensional scaling	ALSCAL VAR= varlist /SHAPE=ASYMMETRIC /CONDITION=ROW.	ALSCAL VAR= varlist /SHAPE=ASYMMETRIC /CONDITION=ROW.	ALSCAL VAR= varlist /SHAPE=ASYMMETRIC /CONDITION=ROW /MODEL=INDSCAL.
	Asymmetric multiple process	Internal asymmetric multi-dimensional scaling	ALSCAL VAR= varlist /SHAPE=ASYMMETRIC /MODEL=ASCAL.	ALSCAL VAR= varlist /SHAPE=ASYMMETRIC /MODEL=ASCAL.	ALSCAL VAR= varlist /SHAPE=ASYMMETRIC /MODEL=AINDS.
		External asymmetric multi-dimensional scaling	ALSCAL VAR= varlist /SHAPE=ASYMMETRIC /MODEL=ASCAL /FILE=file COLCONF(FIX).	ALSCAL VAR= varlist /SHAPE=ASYMMETRIC /MODEL=ASCAL /FILE=file COLCONF(FIX).	ALSCAL VAR= varlist /SHAPE=ASYMMETRIC /MODEL=AINDS /FILE=file COLCONF(FIX).
Object by attribute	Rectangular	Internal unfolding	ALSCAL VAR= varlist /SHAPE=REC /INP=ROWS /CONDITION=ROW.	ALSCAL VAR= varlist /SHAPE=REC /INP=ROWS /CONDITION(ROW).	ALSCAL VAR= varlist /SHAPE=REC /INP=ROWS /CONDITION=ROW /MODEL=INDSCAL.
		External unfolding	ALSCAL VAR= varlist /SHAPE=REC /INP=ROWS /CONDITION=ROW /FILE=file ROWCONF(FIX).	ALSCAL VAR= varlist /SHAPE=REC /INP=ROWS /CONDITION=ROW /FILE=file ROWCONF(FIX).	ALSCAL VAR= varlist /SHAPE=REC /INP=ROWS /CONDITION=ROW /FILE=file ROWCONF(FIX) /MODEL=INDSCAL.

Table 5   ALSCAL specifications for metric models

Matrix mode	Matrix form	Model class	Single matrix	Replications of single matrix	Two or more individual matrices
Object by object	Symmetric	Multi-dimensional scaling	ALSCAL VAR= varlist /LEVEL=INT.	ALSCAL VAR= varlist /LEVEL=INT.	ALSCAL VAR= varlist /LEVEL=INT /MODEL=INDSCAL.
	Asymmetric single process	Multi-dimensional scaling	ALSCAL VAR= varlist /SHAPE=ASYMMETRIC /CONDITION=ROW /LEVEL=INT.	ALSCAL VAR= varlist /SHAPE=ASYMMETRIC /CONDITION=ROW /LEVEL=INT.	ALSCAL VAR= varlist /SHAPE=ASYMMETRIC /CONDITION=ROW /LEVEL=INT /MODEL=INDSCAL.
	Asymmetric multiple process	Internal asymmetric multi-dimensional scaling	ALSCAL VAR= varlist /SHAPE=ASYMMETRIC /LEVEL=INT /MODEL=ASCAL.	ALSCAL VAR= varlist /SHAPE=ASYMMETRIC /LEVEL=INT /MODEL=ASCAL.	ALSCAL VAR= varlist /SHAPE=ASYMMETRIC /LEVEL=INT /MODEL=AINDS.
		External asymmetric multi-dimensional scaling	ALSCAL VAR= varlist /SHAPE=ASYMMETRIC /LEVEL=INT /MODEL=ASCAL /FILE=file COLCONF(FIX).	ALSCAL VAR= varlist /SHAPE=ASYMMETRIC /LEVEL=INT /MODEL=ASCAL /FILE=file COLCONF(FIX).	ALSCAL VAR= varlist /SHAPE=ASYMMETRIC /LEVEL=INT /MODEL=AINDS /FILE=file COLCONF(FIX).
Object by attribute	Rectangular	Internal unfolding	ALSCAL VAR= varlist /SHAPE=REC /INP=ROWS /CONDITION=ROW /LEVEL=INT.	ALSCAL VAR= varlist /SHAPE=REC /INP=ROWS /CONDITION=ROW /LEVEL=INT.	ALSCAL VAR= varlist /SHAPE=REC /INP=ROWS /CONDITION=ROW /LEVEL=INT /MODEL=INDSCAL.
		External unfolding	ALSCAL VAR= varlist /SHAPE=REC /INP=ROWS /CONDITION=ROW /LEVEL=INT /FILE=file ROWCONF(FIX).	ALSCAL VAR= varlist /SHAPE=REC /INP=ROWS /CONDITION=ROW /LEVEL=INT /FILE=file ROWCONF(FIX).	ALSCAL VAR= varlist /SHAPE=REC /INP=ROWS /CONDITION=ROW /LEVEL=INT /FILE=file ROWCONF(FIX) /MODEL=INDSCAL.

ANOVA

```
ANOVA [VARIABLES=] varlist BY varlist(min,max)...varlist(min,max)
[WITH varlist] [/VARIABLES=...]

[/COVARIATES={FIRST** }]
             {WITH    }
             {AFTER   }

[/MAXORDERS={ALL**  }]
            {n      }
            {NONE   }

[/METHOD={UNIQUE**      }]
         {EXPERIMENTAL}
         {HIERARCHICAL}

[/STATISTICS=[MCA] [REG†] [MEAN] [ALL] [NONE]]

[/MISSING={EXCLUDE**}]
          {INCLUDE  }
```

**Default if the subcommand is omitted.
†REG (table of regression coefficients) is displayed only if the design is relevant.

Example:

```
ANOVA VARIABLES=PRESTIGE BY REGION(1,9) SEX,RACE(1,2)
/MAXORDERS=2
/STATISTICS=MEAN.
```

Overview

ANOVA performs analysis of variance for factorial designs. The default is the full factorial model if there are five or fewer factors. Analysis of variance tests the hypothesis that the group means of the dependent variable are equal. The dependent variable is interval level, and one or more categorical variables define the groups. These categorical variables are termed **factors**. ANOVA also allows you to include continuous explanatory variables, termed **covariates**. Other procedures that perform analysis of variance are ONEWAY, SUMMARIZE, and GLM. To perform a comparison of two means, use TTEST.

Options

Specifying Covariates. You can introduce covariates into the model using the WITH keyword on the VARIABLES subcommand.

Order of Entry of Covariates. By default, covariates are processed before main effects for factors. You can process covariates with or after main effects for factors using the COVARIATES subcommand.

Suppressing Interaction Effects. You can suppress the effects of various orders of interaction using the MAXORDERS subcommand.

Methods for Decomposing Sums of Squares. By default, the regression approach (keyword UNIQUE) is used. You can request the classic experimental or hierarchical approach using the METHOD subcommand.

Statistical Display. Using the STATISTICS subcommand, you can request means and counts for each dependent variable for groups defined by each factor and each combination of factors up to the fifth level. You also can request unstandardized regression coefficients for covariates and multiple classification analysis (MCA) results, which include the MCA table, the Factor Summary table, and the Model Goodness of Fit table. The MCA table shows **treatment effects** as deviations from the grand mean and includes a listing of unadjusted category effects for each factor, category effects adjusted for other factors, and category effects adjusted for all factors and covariates. The Factor Summary table displays eta and beta values. The Goodness of Fit table shows R and R^2 for each model.

Basic Specification

- The basic specification is a single VARIABLES subcommand with an analysis list. The minimum analysis list specifies a list of dependent variables, the keyword BY, a list of factor variables, and the minimum and maximum integer values of the factors in parentheses.
- By default, the model includes all interaction terms up to five-way interactions. The sums of squares are decomposed using the regression approach, in which all effects are assessed simultaneously, with each effect adjusted for all other effects in the model. A case that has a missing value for any variable in an analysis list is omitted from the analysis.

Subcommand Order

- The analysis list must be first if the keyword VARIABLES is omitted from the specification.
- The remaining subcommands can be named in any order.

Operations

A separate analysis of variance is performed for each dependent variable in an analysis list, using the same factors and covariates.

Limitations

- Maximum 5 analysis lists.
- Maximum 5 dependent variables per analysis list.
- Maximum 10 factor variables per analysis list.
- Maximum 10 covariates per analysis list.
- Maximum 5 interaction levels.
- Maximum 25 value labels per variable displayed in the MCA table.
- The combined number of categories for all factors in an analysis list plus the number of covariates must be less than the sample size.

Example

```
ANOVA VARIABLES=PRESTIGE BY REGION(1,9) SEX, RACE(1,2)
 /MAXORDERS=2
 /STATISTICS=MEAN.
```

- VARIABLES specifies a three-way analysis of variance—*PRESTIGE* by *REGION*, *SEX*, and *RACE*.
- The variables *SEX* and *RACE* each have two categories, with values 1 and 2 included in the analysis. *REGION* has nine categories, valued 1 through 9.
- MAXORDERS examines interaction effects up to and including the second order. All three-way interaction terms are pooled into the error sum of squares.
- STATISTICS requests a table of means of *PRESTIGE* within the combined categories of *REGION*, *SEX*, and *RACE*.

Example

```
ANOVA VARIABLES=PRESTIGE BY REGION(1,9) SEX,RACE(1,2)
 /RINCOME BY SEX,RACE(1,2).
```

- ANOVA specifies a three-way analysis of variance of *PRESTIGE* by *REGION*, *SEX*, and *RACE*, and a two-way analysis of variance of *RINCOME* by *SEX* and *RACE*.

VARIABLES Subcommand

VARIABLES specifies the analysis list. The actual keyword VARIABLES can be omitted.

- More than one design can be specified on the same ANOVA command by separating the analysis lists with a slash.
- Variables named before keyword BY are dependent variables. Value ranges are not specified for dependent variables.
- Variables named after BY are factor (independent) variables.
- Every factor variable must have a value range indicating its minimum and maximum values. The values must be separated by a space or a comma and enclosed in parentheses.
- Factor variables must have integer values. Noninteger values for factors are truncated.
- Cases with values outside the range specified for a factor are excluded from the analysis.
- If two or more factors have the same value range, you can specify the value range once following the last factor to which it applies. You can specify a single range that encompasses the ranges of all factors on the list. For example, if you have two factors, one with values 1 and 2 and the other with values 1 through 4, you can specify the range for both as 1,4. However, this may reduce performance and cause memory problems if the specified range is larger than some of the actual ranges.
- Variables named after the keyword WITH are covariates.
- Each analysis list can include only one BY and one WITH keyword.

COVARIATES Subcommand

COVARIATES specifies the order for assessing blocks of covariates and factor main effects.

- The order of entry is irrelevant when METHOD=UNIQUE.

FIRST   *Process covariates before factor main effects.* This is the default.

WITH   *Process covariates concurrently with factor main effects.*

AFTER   *Process covariates after factor main effects.*

MAXORDERS Subcommand

MAXORDERS suppresses the effects of various orders of interaction.

ALL   *Examine all interaction effects up to and including the fifth order.* This is the default.

n   *Examine all interaction effects up to and including the nth order.* For example, MAXORDERS=3 examines all interaction effects up to and including the third order. All higher-order interaction sums of squares are pooled into the error term.

NONE   *Delete all interaction terms from the model.* All interaction sums of squares are pooled into the error sum of squares. Only main and covariate effects appear in the ANOVA table.

METHOD Subcommand

METHOD controls the method for decomposing sums of squares.

UNIQUE   *Regression approach.* UNIQUE overrides any keywords on the COVARIATES subcommand. All effects are assessed simultaneously for their partial contribution. The MCA and MEAN specifications on the STATISTICS subcommand are not available with the regression approach. This is the default if METHOD is omitted.

EXPERIMENTAL   *Classic experimental approach.* Covariates, main effects, and ascending orders of interaction are assessed separately in that order.

HIERARCHICAL   *Hierarchical approach.*

Regression Approach

All effects are assessed simultaneously, with each effect adjusted for all other effects in the model. This is the default when the METHOD subcommand is omitted. Since MCA tables cannot be produced when the regression approach is used, specifying MCA or ALL on STATISTICS with the default method triggers a warning.

Some restrictions apply to the use of the regression approach:

- The lowest specified categories of all the independent variables must have a marginal frequency of at least 1, since the lowest specified category is used as the reference category. If this rule is violated, no ANOVA table is produced and a message identifying the first offending variable is displayed.

- Given an n-way crosstabulation of the independent variables, there must be no empty cells defined by the lowest specified category of any of the independent variables. If this restriction is violated, one or more levels of interaction effects are suppressed and a warning message is issued. However, this constraint does not apply to categories defined for an independent variable but not occurring in the data. For example, given two independent variables, each with categories of 1, 2, and 4, the (1,1), (1,2), (1,4), (2,1), and (4,1) cells must not be empty. The (1,3) and (3,1) cells will be empty but the restriction on empty cells will not be violated. The (2,2), (2,4), (4,2), and (4,4) cells may be empty, although the degrees of freedom will be reduced accordingly.

To comply with these restrictions, specify precisely the lowest nonempty category of each independent variable. Specifying a value range of (0,9) for a variable that actually has values of 1 through 9 results in an error, and no ANOVA table is produced.

Classic Experimental Approach

Each type of effect is assessed separately in the following order (unless WITH or AFTER is specified on the COVARIATES subcommand):

- Effects of covariates
- Main effects of factors
- Two-way interaction effects
- Three-way interaction effects
- Four-way interaction effects
- Five-way interaction effects

The effects within each type are adjusted for all other effects of that type and also for the effects of all prior types (see Table 1).

Hierarchical Approach

The hierarchical approach differs from the classic experimental approach only in the way it handles covariate and factor main effects. In the hierarchical approach, factor main effects and covariate effects are assessed hierarchically—factor main effects are adjusted only for the factor main effects already assessed, and covariate effects are adjusted only for the covariates already assessed (see Table 1). The order in which factors are listed on the ANOVA command determines the order in which they are assessed.

Example

The following analysis list specifies three factor variables named *A*, *B*, and *C*:

```
ANOVA VARIABLES=Y BY A,B,C(0,3).
```

Table 1 summarizes the three methods for decomposing sums of squares for this example.

- With the default *regression* approach, each factor or interaction is assessed with all other factors and interactions held constant.
- With the *classic experimental* approach, each main effect is assessed with the two other main effects held constant, and two-way interactions are assessed with all main effects and other two-way interactions held constant. The three-way interaction is assessed with all main effects and two-way interactions held constant.
- With the *hierarchical* approach, the factor main effects A, B, and C are assessed with all prior main effects held constant. The order in which the factors and covariates are listed on the ANOVA command determines the order in which they are assessed in the hierarchical analysis. The interaction effects are assessed the same way as in the experimental approach.

Table 1   Terms adjusted for under each option

Effect	Regression (UNIQUE)	Experimental	Hierarchical
A	All others	B,C	None
B	All others	A,C	A
C	All others	A,B	A,B
AB	All others	A,B,C,AC,BC	A,B,C,AC,BC
AC	All others	A,B,C,AB,BC	A,B,C,AB,BC
BC	All others	A,B,C,AB,AC	A,B,C,AB,AC
ABC	All others	A,B,C,AB,AC,BC	A,B,C,AB,AC,BC

Summary of Analysis Methods

Table 2 describes the results obtained with various combinations of methods for controlling entry of covariates and decomposing the sums of squares.

Table 2   Combinations of COVARIATES and METHOD subcommands

	Assessments between types of effects	Assessments within the same type of effect
METHOD=UNIQUE	**Covariates**, **Factors**, and **Interactions** simultaneously	**Covariates**: adjust for factors, interactions, and all other covariates **Factors**: adjust for covariates, interactions, and all other factors **Interactions**: adjust for covariates, factors, and all other interactions
METHOD=EXPERIMENTAL	**Covariates** then **Factors** then **Interactions**	**Covariates**: adjust for all other covariates **Factors**: adjust for covariates and all other factors **Interactions**: adjust for covariates, factors, and all other interactions of the same and lower orders
METHOD=HIERARCHICAL	**Covariates** then **Factors** then **Interactions**	**Covariates**: adjust for covariates that are preceding in the list **Factors**: adjust for covariates and factors preceding in the list **Interactions**: adjust for covariates, factors, and all other interactions of the same and lower orders
COVARIATES=WITH and METHOD=EXPERIMENTAL	**Factors** and **Covariates** concurrently then **Interactions**	**Covariates**: adjust for factors and all other covariates **Factors**: adjust for covariates and all other factors **Interactions**: adjust for covariates, factors, and all other interactions of the same and lower orders
COVARIATES=WITH and METHOD=HIERARCHICAL	**Factors** and **Covariates** concurrently then **Interactions**	**Factors**: adjust only for preceding factors **Covariates**: adjust for factors and preceding covariates **Interactions**: adjust for covariates, factors, and all other interactions of the same and lower orders
COVARIATES=AFTER and METHOD=EXPERIMENTAL	**Factors** then **Covariates** then **Interactions**	**Factors**: adjust for all other factors **Covariates**: adjust for factors and all other covariates **Interactions**: adjust for covariates, factors, and all other interactions of the same and lower orders
COVARIATES=AFTER and METHOD=HIERARCHICAL	**Factors** then **Covariates** then **Interactions**	**Factors**: adjust only for preceding factors **Covariates**: adjust factors and preceding covariates **Interactions**: adjust for covariates, factors, and all other interactions of the same and lower orders

STATISTICS Subcommand

STATISTICS requests additional statistics. STATISTICS can be specified by itself or with one or more keywords.

- If you specify STATISTICS without keywords, ANOVA calculates MEAN and REG (each defined below).
- If you specify a keyword or keywords on the STATISTICS subcommand, ANOVA calculates only the additional statistics you request.

MEAN *Means and counts table*. This statistic is not available when METHOD is omitted or when METHOD=UNIQUE. See "Cell Means" below.

REG *Unstandardized regression coefficients*. Displays unstandardized regression coefficients for the covariates. See "Regression Coefficients for the Covariates" below.

MCA *Multiple classification analysis*. The MCA, the Factor Summary, and the Goodness of Fit tables are not produced when METHOD is omitted or when METHOD=UNIQUE. See "Multiple Classification Analysis" on p. 127.

ALL *Means and counts table, unstandardized regression coefficients, and multiple classification analysis*.

NONE *No additional statistics*. ANOVA calculates only the statistics needed for analysis of variance. This is the default if the STATISTICS subcommand is omitted.

Cell Means

STATISTICS=MEAN displays the Cell Means table.

- This statistic is not available with METHOD=UNIQUE.
- The Cell Means table shows means and counts of each dependent variable for each cell defined by the factors and combinations of factors. Dependent variables and factors appear in their order on the VARIABLES subcommand.
- If MAXORDERS is used to suppress higher-order interactions, cell means corresponding to suppressed interaction terms are not displayed.
- The means displayed are the observed means in each cell, and they are produced only for dependent variables, not for covariates.

Regression Coefficients for the Covariates

STATISTICS=REG requests the unstandardized regression coefficients for the covariates.

- The regression coefficients are computed at the point where the covariates are entered into the equation. Thus, their values depend on the type of design specified by the COVARIATES or METHOD subcommands.
- The coefficients are displayed in the ANOVA table.

Multiple Classification Analysis

STATISTICS=MCA displays the MCA, the Factor Summary, and the Model Goodness of Fit tables.

- The MCA table presents counts, predicted means, and deviations of predicted means from the grand mean for each level of each factor. The predicted and deviation means each appear in up to three forms: unadjusted, adjusted for other factors, and adjusted for other factors and covariates.
- The Factor Summary table displays the correlation ratio (eta) with the unadjusted deviations (the square of eta indicates the proportion of variance explained by all categories of the factor), a partial beta equivalent to the standardized partial regression coefficient that would be obtained by assigning the unadjusted deviations to each factor category and regressing the dependent variable on the resulting variables, and the parallel partial betas from a regression that includes covariates in addition to the factors.
- The Model Goodness of Fit table shows R and R^2 for each model.
- The tables cannot be produced if METHOD is omitted or if METHOD=UNIQUE. When produced, the MCA table does not display values adjusted for factors if COVARIATES is omitted, if COVARIATES=FIRST, or if COVARIATES=WITH and METHOD=EXPERIMENTAL. A full MCA table is produced only if METHOD=HIERARCHICAL or if METHOD=EXPERIMENTAL and COVARIATES=AFTER.

MISSING Subcommand

By default, a case that has a missing value for any variable named in the analysis list is deleted for all analyses specified by that list. Use MISSING to include cases with user-missing data.

EXCLUDE   *Exclude cases with missing data.* This is the default.

INCLUDE   *Include cases with user-defined missing data.*

References

Andrews, F., J. Morgan, J. Sonquist, and L. Klein. 1973. *Multiple classification analysis.* 2nd ed. Ann Arbor: University of Michigan.

APPLY DICTIONARY

```
APPLY DICTIONARY FROM=file
```

Example:
```
APPLY DICTIONARY FROM = 'MASTER.SAV'.
```

Overview

APPLY DICTIONARY applies dictionary information from an external SPSS-format data file to the working data file. The applied dictionary information includes variable and value labels, missing-value flags, print and write formats, and weight. APPLY DICTIONARY does not add or remove variables, and it cannot apply dictionary information selectively to individual variables.

Basic Specification

The basic specification is the FROM subcommand and the name of an SPSS-format data file. The file specification may vary from operating system to operating system, but enclosing the filename in apostrophes generally works.

Syntax Rules

- The equals sign after FROM is optional.
- The file containing the dictionary information to be applied (the **source file**) must be an SPSS-format data file.
- The file to which the dictionary information is applied (the **target file**) must be the working data file. You cannot specify another file.

Operation

- APPLY DICTIONARY adds or replaces dictionary information variable by variable by matching variables that have the same name and the same type (string or numeric) in both files. Variables in the working data file that do not have a match in the source file are not changed.
- APPLY DICTIONARY does not add or remove variables from the working data file.
- If no matched variables are found, the program displays a warning message.
- Variables that have the same name but different types are not considered matching. The program displays a warning message and lists the variables with nonmatching types.

Variable Labels

APPLY DICTIONARY adds labels or replaces old labels with new ones. It cannot be used to remove a defined variable label in the working data file.

- If the variable label in the source file is blank, it will not replace an existing variable label, even if the blanks are in quotes.

Table 1 shows how variable labels are replaced between matched variables.

Table 1   Variable label replacement

Variable	Label in working file (target file)	Label in external file (source file)	Label in resulting file
VAR1	"AGE 86"	"AGE 91"	"AGE 91"
VAR2		"JOBCAT91"	"JOBCAT91"
VAR3	"WORK ID"		"WORK ID"
VAR4	"RACE"	" "	"RACE"

Value Labels

APPLY DICTIONARY treats the value labels of a variable as a set. It adds or replaces the entire set of value labels for a matched variable in the working data file. You cannot remove the defined value label set from a variable or selectively add or replace individual value labels.

- APPLY DICTIONARY does not merge the set of value labels for a variable in the SPSS-format data file with the labels for a matched variable in the working data file. The variable in the resulting file uses the labels from the SPSS-format data file only.

- If the variable in the SPSS-format data file does not have any defined value labels, the matching variable in the working data file keeps its original value labels.

- If the matched variable in the working data file is a long string, value labels are not applied even if the source variable is a short string and has value labels defined. The program displays a message when this occurs.

- If the matched variables are both short strings but the target variable is longer than the source variable, the values for the source variable are right-padded before their labels are applied to the target variable.

- If the matched variables are both short strings but the source variable is longer, the values for the source variable are right-trimmed if there are enough blank spaces on the right. If any one of the values that has labels defined does not have enough blank spaces to be trimmed, the entire set of value labels is not applied and the variable in the working data file maintains its original value label specifications.

Missing Values

APPLY DICTIONARY treats the missing-value specifications of a variable as a set. It adds or replaces the entire set of missing values for a matched variable in the working data file. You can remove the entire set of missing-value specifications from a variable but cannot selectively add or replace individual missing-value specifications.

- APPLY DICTIONARY does not merge the set of missing values for a variable in the SPSS-format data file with the missing-value specifications for a matched variable in the working data file. The variable in the resulting file uses the missing values defined in the SPSS-format data file only.
- If the variable in the SPSS-format data file does not define any missing values, the variable in the working data file keeps its missing-value specifications.
- If the matched variable in the working data file is a long string, missing-value specifications are not applied even if the source variable is a short string and has missing values defined. The program displays a message specifying the missing value and information about the length of the matched variables.
- If the matched variables are both short strings but the target variable is longer than the source variable, the missing values from the source variable are right-padded.
- If the matched variables are both short strings but the source variable is longer, the missing values from the source variable are right-trimmed if there are enough blank spaces on the right. If any one of the defined missing values does not have enough blank spaces to be trimmed, the entire set will not be applied. The variable in the working data file maintains its original missing-value specifications.

Print and Write Formats

APPLY DICTIONARY always replaces the print and write formats of matched numeric variables in the working data file.

- The print and write formats of string variables are not changed. They keep the original length defined on the DATA LIST or STRING command. To change the length of a string variable, define a new variable using STRING and then use the COMPUTE command.

Weight

APPLY DICTIONARY adds or replaces the weighting information in the working data file. Table 2 summarizes how weighting information is applied. In the table, *WTWORK* refers to the weight variable in the working file and *WTSPSS* to the weight variable in the SPSS-format data file.

- A message is displayed when either the weight status or the weight variable is changed.

Table 2   Weight information

Working file		External file		Resulting file	
Status	Weight	Status	Weight	Status	Weight
Weighted	*WTWORK*	Unweighted	N/A	Weighted	*WTWORK*
		Weighted	*WTSPSS*	Weighted	*WTSPSS** *WTWORK†*
Unweighted	N/A	Weighted	*WTSPSS*	Weighted Unweighted†	*WTSPSS** N/A

*If *WTSPSS* exists in the working file.
†If *WTSPSS* does not exist in the working file.

FROM Subcommand

FROM specifies an SPSS-format data file as the source file whose dictionary information is to be applied to the working file.

- FROM is required.
- Only one SPSS-format data file can be specified on FROM.
- The SPSS-format data file from which the current working file was built can be specified on FROM. This will restore dictionary information from the most recently saved version of the file.

AUTORECODE

```
AUTORECODE VARIABLES=varlist

 /INTO new varlist

 [/DESCENDING]

 [/PRINT]
```

Example:
```
AUTORECODE VARIABLES=COMPANY /INTO RCOMPANY.
```

Overview

AUTORECODE recodes the values of string and numeric variables to consecutive integers and puts the recoded values into a new variable called a **target variable**. The value labels or values of the original variable are used as value labels for the target variable. AUTORECODE is useful for creating numeric independent (grouping) variables from string variables for procedures like ONEWAY, ANOVA, MANOVA, and DISCRIMINANT. AUTORECODE can also recode the values of factor variables to consecutive integers, which is required by MANOVA and which reduces the amount of workspace needed by other statistical procedures like ANOVA. AUTORECODE is also useful with the TABLES procedure, where string values are truncated to eight characters but value labels can be displayed in full. (See the *SPSS Tables* manual for more information.)

AUTORECODE is similar to the RECODE command. The main difference is that AUTORECODE automatically generates the values. In RECODE, you must specify the new values.

Options

Displaying Recoded Variables. You can display the values of the original and recoded variables using the PRINT subcommand.

Ordering of Values. By default, values are recoded in ascending order (lowest to highest). You can recode values in descending order (highest to lowest) using the DESCENDING subcommand.

Basic Specification

The basic specification is VARIABLES, and INTO. VARIABLES specifies the variables to be recoded. INTO provides names for the target variables that store the new values. VARIABLES and INTO must name or imply the same number of variables.

Subcommand Order

- VARIABLES must be specified first.
- INTO must immediately follow VARIABLES.

Syntax Rules

A variable cannot be recoded into itself. More generally, target variable names cannot duplicate any variable names already in the working file.

Operations

- The values of each variable to be recoded are sorted and then assigned numeric values. By default, the values are assigned in ascending order: 1 is assigned to the lowest nonmissing value of the original variable, 2 to the second-lowest nonmissing value, and so on for each value of the original variable.
- Values of the original variables are unchanged.
- Missing values are recoded into values higher than any nonmissing values, with their order preserved. For example, if the original variable has 10 nonmissing values, the first missing value is recoded as 11 and retains its user-missing status. System-missing values remain system-missing.
- AUTORECODE does not sort the cases in the working file. As a result, the consecutive numbers assigned to the target variables may not be in order in the file.
- Target variables are assigned the same variable labels as the original source variables. To change the variable labels, use the VARIABLE LABELS command after AUTORECODE.
- Value labels are automatically generated for each value of the target variables. If the original value had a label, that label is used for the corresponding new value. If the original value did not have a label, the old value itself is used as the value label for the new value. The defined print format of the old value is used to create the new value label.
- AUTORECODE ignores SPLIT FILE specifications. However, any SELECT IF specifications are in effect for AUTORECODE.

Example

```
DATA LIST / COMPANY 1-21 (A) SALES 24-28.
BEGIN DATA
CATFOOD JOY            10000
OLD FASHIONED CATFOOD  11200
 . . .
PRIME CATFOOD          10900
CHOICE CATFOOD         14600
END DATA.

AUTORECODE VARIABLES=COMPANY /INTO=RCOMPANY /PRINT.

TABLES TABLE = SALES BY RCOMPANY
  /TTITLE='CATFOOD SALES BY COMPANY'.
```

- Because TABLES truncates string variables to eight characters, AUTORECODE is used to recode the string variable *COMPANY*, which contains the names of various hypothetical cat food companies.

- AUTORECODE recodes *COMPANY* into a numeric variable *RCOMPANY*. Values of *RCOMPANY* are consecutive integers beginning with 1 and ending with the number of different values entered for *COMPANY*. The values of *COMPANY* are used as value labels for *RCOMPANY*'s numeric values. The *PRINT* subcommand displays a table of the original and recoded values.

- The variable *RCOMPANY* is used as the banner variable in the TABLES procedure to produce a table of sales figures for each cat food company. The value labels for *RCOMPANY* are used as column headings. Since TABLES does not truncate value labels, the full company names appear.

Example

```
AUTORECODE VARIABLES=REGION /INTO=RREGION /PRINT.
ANOVA Y BY RREGION (1,5).
```

- In statistical procedures, empty cells can reduce performance and increase memory requirements. In this example, assume that the factor *REGION* has only five nonempty categories, represented by the numeric codes 1, 4, 6, 14, and 20. AUTORECODE recodes those values into 1, 2, 3, 4, and 5 for target variable *RREGION*.

- The variable *RREGION* is used in ANOVA. If the original variable *REGION* were used, the amount of memory required by ANOVA would be 4429 bytes. Using variable *RREGION*, ANOVA requires only 449 bytes of memory.

Example

```
DATA LIST / RELIGION 1-8 (A) Y 10-13.
MISSING VALUES RELIGION (' ').
BEGIN DATA
CATHOLIC 2013
PROTEST  3234
JEWISH   5169
NONE      714
OTHER    2321
  . . .
END DATA.
AUTORECODE VARIABLES=RELIGION /INTO=NRELIG /PRINT /DESCENDING.
MANOVA Y BY NRELIG(1,5).
```

- Because MANOVA requires consecutive integer values for factor levels, the string variable *RELIGION* is recoded into a numeric variable. The five values for *RELIGION* are first sorted in descending order (Z to A) and are then assigned values 1, 2, 3, 4, and 5 in target variable *NRELIG*.

- Since a blank space is specified as a user-missing value, it is assigned the value 6. In the table produced by PRINT, the value 6 is displayed as 6M for the variable *NRELIG* to flag it as a user-missing value.

- The values of *RELIGION* are used as value labels for the corresponding new values in *NRELIG*.

- Target variable *NRELIG* is used as a factor variable in MANOVA.

VARIABLES Subcommand

VARIABLES specifies the variables to be recoded. VARIABLES is required and must be specified first. The actual keyword VARIABLES is optional.

- Values from the specified variables are recoded and stored in the target variables listed on INTO. Values of the original variables are unchanged.

INTO Subcommand

INTO provides names for the target variables that store the new values. INTO is required and must immediately follow VARIABLES.

- The number of target variables named or implied on INTO must equal the number of source variables listed on VARIABLES.

Example

```
AUTORECODE VARIABLES=V1 V2 V3 /INTO=NEWV1 TO NEWV3 /PRINT.
```

- AUTORECODE stores the recoded values of *V1*, *V2*, and *V3* into target variables named *NEWV1*, *NEWV2*, and *NEWV3*.

PRINT Subcommand

PRINT displays a correspondence table of the original values of the source variables and the new values of the target variables. The new value labels are also displayed.

- The only specification is keyword PRINT. There are no additional specifications.

DESCENDING Subcommand

By default, values for the source variable are recoded in ascending order (from lowest to highest). DESCENDING assigns the values to new variables in descending order (from highest to lowest). The largest value is assigned 1, the second-largest, 2, and so on.

- The only specification is keyword DESCENDING. There are no additional specifications.

BEGIN DATA—END DATA

```
BEGIN DATA
data records
END DATA
```

Example:

```
BEGIN DATA
1   3424   274 ABU DHABI 2
2 39932    86 AMSTERDAM 4
3  8889   232 ATHENS
4   3424   294 BOGOTA     3
END DATA.
```

Overview

BEGIN DATA and END DATA are used when data are entered within the command sequence (inline data). BEGIN DATA and END DATA are also used for inline matrix data. BEGIN DATA signals the beginning of data lines and END DATA signals the end of data lines.

Basic Specification

The basic specification is BEGIN DATA, the data lines, and END DATA. BEGIN DATA must be specified by itself on the line that immediately precedes the first data line. END DATA is specified by itself on the line that immediately follows the last data line.

Syntax Rules

- BEGIN DATA, the data, and END DATA must precede the first procedure.
- The command terminator after BEGIN DATA is optional. It is best to leave it out so that the program will treat inline data as one continuous specification.
- END DATA must always begin in column 1. It must be spelled out in full and can have only one space between the words END and DATA. Procedures and additional transformations can follow the END DATA command.
- Data lines must *not* have a command terminator. For inline data formats, see DATA LIST.
- Inline data records are limited to a maximum of 80 columns. (On some systems, the maximum may be fewer than 80 columns.) If data records exceed 80 columns, they must be stored in an external file that is specified on the FILE subcommand of the DATA LIST (or similar) command.

Operations

- When the program encounters BEGIN DATA, it begins to read and process data on the next input line. All preceding transformation commands are processed as the working file is built.

- The program continues to evaluate input lines as data until it encounters END DATA, at which point it begins evaluating input lines as commands.

- No other commands are recognized between BEGIN DATA and END DATA.

- The INCLUDE command can specify a file that contains BEGIN DATA, data lines, and END DATA. The data in such a file are treated as inline data. Thus, the FILE subcommand should be omitted from the DATA LIST (or similar) command.

- When running the program from prompts, the prompt DATA> appears immediately after BEGIN DATA is specified. After END DATA is specified, the command line prompt returns.

Example

```
DATA LIST /XVAR 1 YVAR ZVAR 3-12 CVAR 14-22(A) JVAR 24.
BEGIN DATA
1   3424   274 ABU DHABI  2
2 39932    86 AMSTERDAM  4
3  8889   232 ATHENS
4  3424   294 BOGOTA      3
5 11323   332 HONG KONG  3
6   323   232 MANILA      1
7  3234   899 CHICAGO     4
8 78998 2344 VIENNA       3
9  8870   983 ZURICH      5
END DATA.
MEANS XVAR BY JVAR.
```

- DATA LIST defines the names and column locations of the variables. The FILE subcommand is omitted because the data are inline.

- There are nine cases in the inline data. Each line of data completes a case.

- END DATA signals the end of data lines. It begins in column 1 and has only a single space between END and DATA.

BREAK

Overview

BREAK controls looping that cannot be fully controlled with IF clauses. Generally, BREAK is used within a DO IF—END IF structure. The expression on the DO IF command specifies the condition in which BREAK is executed.

Basic Specification

- The only specification is keyword BREAK. There are no additional specifications.
- BREAK must be specified within a loop structure. Otherwise, an error results.

Operations

- A BREAK command inside a loop structure but not inside a DO IF—END IF structure terminates the first iteration of the loop for all cases, since no conditions for BREAK are specified.
- A BREAK command within an inner loop terminates only iterations in that structure, not in any outer loop structures.

Example

```
VECTOR          #X(10).
LOOP            #I = 1 TO #NREC.
+   DATA LIST       NOTABLE/ #X1 TO #X10 1-20.
+   LOOP        #J = 1 TO 10.
+     DO IF         SYSMIS(#X(#J)).
+       BREAK.
+     END IF.
+     COMPUTE       X = #X(#J).
+     END CASE.
+   END LOOP.
END LOOP.
```

- The inner loop terminates when there is a system-missing value for any of the variables *#X1* to *#X10*.
- The outer loop continues until all records are read.

CASEPLOT

```
CASEPLOT [VARIABLES=]varlist

[/DIFF={1}]
       {n}

[/SDIFF={1}]
        {n}

[/PERIOD=n]

[/{NOLOG**}]
  {LN    }

[/ID=varname]

[/MARK={varname          }]
       {date specification}

[/SPLIT {UNIFORM**}]
        {SCALE   }

[/APPLY [='model name']]
```

For plots with one variable:

```
[/FORMAT=[{NOFILL**}]  [{NOREFERENCE**}]
          {LEFT   }     {REFERENCE    }
          {RIGHT  }
```

For plots with multiple variables:

```
[/FORMAT={NOJOIN**}]
         {JOIN   }
         {HILO   }
```

**Default if the subcommand is omitted.

Example:

```
CASEPLOT TICKETS
  /LN
  /DIFF
  /SDIFF
  /PERIOD=12
  /FORMAT=REFERENCE
  /MARK=Y 55 M 6.
```

Overview

CASEPLOT produces a plot of one or more time series or sequence variables. You can request natural log and differencing transformations to produce plots of transformed variables. There are several plot formats available.

Options

Modifying the Variables. You can request a natural log transformation of the variable using the LN subcommand and seasonal and nonseasonal differencing to any degree using the SDIFF and DIFF subcommands. With seasonal differencing, you can also specify the periodicity on the PERIOD subcommand.

Plot Format. With the FORMAT subcommand, you can fill in the area on one side of the plotted values on plots with one variable. You can also plot a reference line indicating the variable mean. For plots with two or more variables, you can specify whether you want to join the values for each case with a horizontal line. With the ID subcommand, you can label the vertical axis with the values of a specified variable. You can mark the onset of an intervention variable on the plot with the MARK subcommand.

Split-File Processing. You can control how to plot data that have been divided into subgroups by a SPLIT FILE command using the SPLIT subcommand.

Basic Specification

The basic specification is one or more variable names.

- If the DATE command has been specified, the vertical axis is labeled with the *DATE_* variable at periodic intervals. Otherwise, sequence numbers are used. The horizontal axis is labeled with the value scale determined by the plotted variables.

Figure 1 shows a default high-resolution plot with DATE=YEAR 1900. Figure 2 shows the same default plot in low resolution.

Figure 1   CASEPLOT=PRICE (in high resolution)

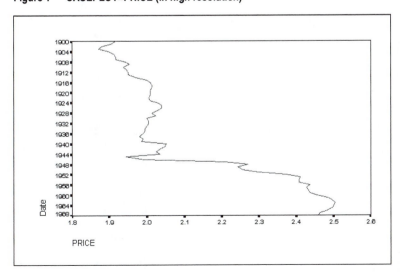

Figure 2   CASEPLOT=PRICE (low resolution)

The following plot symbols are used:
    P - Variable PRICE
    M - Missing Data (placed left of the vertical axis)

```
        1.7        1.9        2.1        2.3        2.5        2.7
YYYY  œ¡ffffffff¡ffffffff¡ffffffff¡ffffffff¡ffffffff¡ffffffff¡ø      PRICE
1900    £         P                                           £     1.9176
1901    £       P                                             £     1.9059
1902    £      P                                              £     1.8798
1903    £      P                                              £     1.8727
1904    £       P                                             £     1.8984
1905    £        P                                            £     1.9137
1906    £        P                                            £     1.9176
1907    £        P                                            £     1.9176
1908    £         P                                           £     1.9420
1909  ff£          P                                          £f    1.9547
1910    £         P                                           £     1.9379
1911    £         P                                           £     1.9462
1912    £          P                                          £     1.9504
1913    £          P                                          £     1.9504
1914    £           P                                         £     1.9723
1915    £            P                                        £     2.0000
1916    £            P                                        £     2.0097
1917    £             P                                       £     2.0146
1918    £             P                                       £     2.0146
1919  ff£            P                                        £f    2.0097
1920    £            P                                        £     2.0097
1921    £            P                                        £     2.0097
1922    £            P                                        £     2.0048
1923    £            P                                        £     2.0097
1924    £             P                                       £     2.0296
1925    £              P                                      £     2.0399
1926    £              P                                      £     2.0399
1927    £             P                                       £     2.0296
1928    £             P                                       £     2.0146
1929  ff£             P                                       £f    2.0245
1930    £            P                                        £     2.0000
1931    £            P                                        £     2.0048
1932    £            P                                        £     2.0048
1933    £            P                                        £     2.0000
1934    £            P                                        £     1.9952
1935    £            P                                        £     1.9952
1936    £            P                                        £     1.9905
1937    £           P                                         £     1.9813
1938    £            P                                        £     1.9905
1939  ff£           P                                         £f    1.9859
1940    £              P                                      £     2.0518
1941    £               P                                     £     2.0474
1942    £               P                                     £     2.0341
1943    £              P                                      £     2.0255
1944    £               P                                     £     2.0341
1945    £         P                                           £     1.9445
1946    £           P                                         £     1.9939
1947    £                  P                                  £     2.2082
1948    £                   P                                 £     2.2700
1949  ff£                  P                                  £f    2.2430
1950    £                   P                                 £     2.2567
1951    £                    P                                £     2.2988
1952    £                       P                             £     2.3723
1953    £                         P                           £     2.4105
1954    £                         P                           £     2.4081
1955    £                         P                           £     2.4081
1956    £                          P                          £     2.4367
1957    £                          P                          £     2.4284
1958    £                          P                          £     2.4310
1959  ff£                          P                          £f    2.4363
1960    £                           P                         £     2.4552
1961    £                            P                        £     2.4838
1962    £                             P                       £     2.4958
1963    £                             P                       £     2.5048
1964    £                             P                       £     2.5017
1965    £                             P                       £     2.4958
1966    £                            P                        £     2.4838
1967    £                           P                         £     2.4636
1968    £                           P                         £     2.4580
YYYY  ¿¶ffffffffff¶ffffffffff¶ffffffffff¶ffffffffff¶ffffffffff¶¶Ý  PRICE
        1.7        1.9        2.1        2.3        2.5        2.7
```

Subcommand Order

- Subcommands can be specified in any order.

Syntax Rules

- VARIABLES can be specified only once.
- Other subcommands can be specified more than once, but only the last specification of each one is executed.

Operations

- Subcommand specifications apply to all variables named on the CASEPLOT command.
- If the LN subcommand is specified, any differencing requested on that CASEPLOT command is done on the log-transformed variables.
- In high-resolution plots, split-file information is displayed as part of the subtitle and transformation information is displayed as part of the footnote.
- In low-resolution plots, values of plotted variables are displayed along the right axis. A wider page specification on SET allows you to display the values of more variables but does not change the plot frame size.

Limitations

- Maximum 1 VARIABLES subcommand. There is no limit on the number of variables named on the list.

Example

```
CASEPLOT TICKETS
  /LN
  /DIFF
  /SDIFF
  /PERIOD=12
  /FORMAT=REFERENCE
  /MARK=Y 55 M 6.
```

- This example produces a plot of *TICKETS* after a natural log transformation, differencing, and seasonal differencing have been applied.
- LN transforms the data using the natural logarithm (base e) of the variable.
- DIFF differences the variable once.
- SDIFF and PERIOD apply one degree of seasonal differencing with a period of 12.
- FORMAT=REFERENCE adds a reference line at the variable mean. In a low-resolution plot, the area between the plotted values and the mean is filled with the plotting symbol (T).

- MARK provides a marker on the plot at June 1955. The marker is displayed as a horizontal reference line in a high-resolution plot.

VARIABLES Subcommand

VARIABLES specifies the names of the variables to be plotted and is the only required subcommand. The actual keyword VARIABLES can be omitted.

DIFF Subcommand

DIFF specifies the degree of differencing used to convert a nonstationary variable to a stationary one with a constant mean and variance before plotting.
- You can specify any positive integer on DIFF.
- If DIFF is specified without a value, the default is 1.
- The number of values displayed decreases by 1 for each degree of differencing.

Example
```
CASEPLOT TICKETS
  /DIFF=2.
```
- In this example, TICKETS is differenced twice before plotting.

SDIFF Subcommand

If the variable exhibits a seasonal or periodic pattern, you can use the SDIFF subcommand to seasonally difference a variable before plotting.
- The specification on SDIFF indicates the degree of seasonal differencing and can be any positive integer.
- If SDIFF is specified without a value, the degree of seasonal differencing defaults to 1.
- The number of seasons displayed decreases by 1 for each degree of seasonal differencing.
- The length of the period used by SDIFF is specified on the PERIOD subcommand. If the PERIOD subcommand is not specified, the periodicity established on the TSET or DATE command is used (see the PERIOD subcommand below).

PERIOD Subcommand

PERIOD indicates the length of the period to be used by the SDIFF subcommand.
- The specification on PERIOD indicates how many observations are in one period or season and can be any positive integer.
- PERIOD is ignored if it is used without the SDIFF subcommand.
- If PERIOD is not specified, the periodicity established on TSET PERIOD is in effect. If TSET PERIOD is not specified either, the periodicity established on the DATE command

is used. If periodicity is not established anywhere, the SDIFF subcommand will not be executed.

Example

```
CASEPLOT TICKETS
  /SDIFF=1
  /PERIOD=12.
```

- This command applies one degree of seasonal differencing with 12 observations per season to *TICKETS* before plotting.

LN and NOLOG Subcommands

LN transforms the data using the natural logarithm (base *e*) of the variable and is used to remove varying amplitude over time. NOLOG indicates that the data should not be log transformed. NOLOG is the default.

- If you specify LN on CASEPLOT, any differencing requested on that command will be done on the log-transformed variable.
- There are no additional specifications on LN or NOLOG.
- Only the last LN or NOLOG subcommand on a CASEPLOT command is executed.
- If a natural log transformation is requested, any value less than or equal to zero is set to system-missing.
- NOLOG is generally used with an APPLY subcommand to turn off a previous LN specification.

Example

```
CASEPLOT TICKETS
  /LN.
```

- In this example, *TICKETS* is transformed using the natural logarithm before plotting.

ID Subcommand

ID names a variable whose values will be used as the left-axis labels.

- The only specification on ID is a variable name. If you have a variable named *ID* in your working data file, the equals sign after the subcommand is required.
- ID overrides the specification on TSET ID.
- If ID or TSET ID is not specified, the left vertical axis is labeled with the *DATE_* variable created by the DATE command. If the *DATE_* variable has not been created, the observation or sequence number is used as the label.

Example

```
CASEPLOT VARA
  /ID=VARB.
```

- In this example, the values of variable *VARB* will be used to label the left axis of the plot of *VARA*.

FORMAT Subcommand

FORMAT controls the plot format.

- The specification on FORMAT is one of the keywords listed below.
- Keywords NOFILL, LEFT, RIGHT, NOREFERENCE, and REFERENCE apply to plots with one variable. NOFILL, LEFT, and RIGHT are alternatives and indicate how the plot is filled. NOREFERENCE and REFERENCE are alternatives and specify whether a reference line is displayed. For low-resolution plots, only one keyword can be specified. One keyword *from each set* can be specified for high-resolution plots. NOFILL and NOREFERENCE are the defaults.
- Keywords JOIN, NOJOIN, and HILO apply to plots with multiple variables and are alternatives. NOJOIN is the default. Only one keyword can be specified on a FORMAT subcommand for plots with two variables.

The following formats are available for plots of one variable:

NOFILL   *Plot only the values for the variable with no fill.* NOFILL produces a plot with no fill to the left or right of the plotted values. This is the default format when one variable is specified.

LEFT   *Plot the values for the variable and fill in the area to the left.* For high-resolution plots, if the plotted variable has missing or negative values, keyword LEFT is ignored and the default NOFILL is used instead. Figure 3 contains a left-filled high-resolution plot. In low-resolution plots, the area to the left of the plotted curve is filled in with the first character of the variable name.

RIGHT   *Plot the values for the variable and fill in the area to the right.* In low-resolution plots, the area to the right of the plotted curve is filled in with the first character of the variable name. For high-resolution plots, RIGHT is ignored; if specified, the default NOFILL is used instead.

Figure 3   FORMAT=LEFT

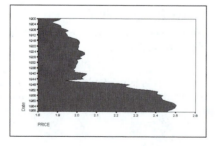

NOREFERENCE *Do not plot a reference line.* This is the default when one variable is specified.

REFERENCE   *Plot a reference line indicating the variable mean.* In low resolution, the area between the plotted curve and the reference line is filled in with the plotting character (the first character of the variable name). For low-resolution plots, you cannot specify REFERENCE together with either LEFT or RIGHT. In high resolution, a fill chart is displayed as an area chart with a reference line and a nofill chart is a line chart with a reference line. Figure 4 shows a high-resolution plot with a reference line indicating the mean of the variable.

Figure 4   FORMAT=REFERENCE

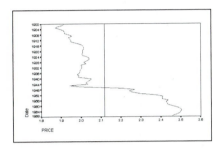

The following formats are available for plots of multiple variables:

NOJOIN   *Plot the values of each variable named.* In high-resolution plots, different colors or line patterns are used for multiple variables. In low-resolution plots, the plotting character for each variable is the first character of the variable name. Multiple occurrences of the same value for a single observation are plotted using a dollar sign ($). This is the default format for plots of multiple variables.

JOIN   *Plot the values of each variable and join the values for each case.* Values are plotted as described for NOJOIN and the values for each case are joined together by a line. Figure 5 contains a plot in this format with three variables (*PRICE, INCOME,* and *CONSUMP*).

HILO   *Plot the highest and lowest values across variables for each case and join the two values together.* The high and low values are plotted as a pair of vertical bars and are joined with a dashed line. For high-resolution plots, HILO is ignored if more than three variables are specified and the default NOJOIN is used instead. Figure 6 contains a plot in this format with three variables (*PRICE, INCOME,* and *CONSUMP*).

Figure 5   FORMAT=JOIN

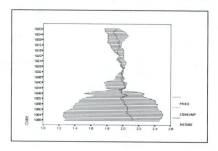

Figure 6   FORMAT=HILO

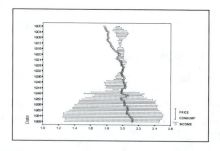

MARK Subcommand

Use MARK to indicate the onset of an intervention variable. Figure 7 shows a high-resolution plot with a reference line indicating the year 1945.

- In high resolution, the onset date is indicated by a horizontal reference line. In low resolution it is indicated by a tick mark on the left axis.

- The specification on MARK can be either a variable name or an onset date if the *DATE_* variable exists.

- If a variable is named, the reference line indicates where the values of that variable change.

- A date specification follows the same format as the DATE command, that is, a keyword followed by a value. For example, the specification for June 1955 is Y 1955 M 6 (or Y 55 M 6 if only the last two digits of the year are used on DATE).

Figure 7   MARK=Y 1945

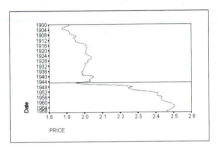

SPLIT Subcommand

SPLIT specifies how to plot data that have been divided into subgroups by a SPLIT FILE command. The specification on SPLIT is either SCALE or UNIFORM.

- If FORMAT=REFERENCE is specified when SPLIT=SCALE, the reference line is placed at the mean of the subgroup. If FORMAT=REFERENCE is specified when SPLIT=UNIFORM, the reference line is placed at the overall mean.

UNIFORM   *Uniform scale.* The horizontal axis is scaled according to the values of the entire data set. This is the default if SPLIT is not specified.

SCALE   *Individual scale.* The horizontal axis is scaled according to the values of each individual subgroup.

Example

```
SPLIT FILE BY REGION.
CASEPLOT TICKETS / SPLIT=SCALE.
```

- This example produces one plot for each *REGION* subgroup.
- The horizontal axis for each plot is scaled according to the values of *TICKETS* for each particular region.

APPLY Subcommand

APPLY allows you to produce a caseplot using previously defined specifications without having to repeat the CASEPLOT subcommands.

- The only specification on APPLY is the name of a previous model in quotes. If a model name is not specified, the specifications from the previous CASEPLOT command are used.

- If no variables are specified, the variables that were specified for the original plot are used.
- To change one or more plot specifications, specify the subcommands of only those portions you want to change after the APPLY subcommand.
- To plot different variables, enter new variable names before or after the APPLY subcommand.

Example

```
CASEPLOT TICKETS
  /LN
  /DIFF=1
  /SDIFF=1
  /PER=12.
CASEPLOT ROUNDTRP
  /APPLY.
CASEPLOT APPLY
  /NOLOG.
```

- The first command produces a plot of *TICKETS* after a natural log transformation, differencing, and seasonal differencing.
- The second command plots *ROUNDTRP* using the same transformations specified for *TICKETS*.
- The third command produces a plot of *ROUNDTRP*, but this time without any natural log transformation. The variable is still differenced once and seasonally differenced with a periodicity of 12.

CCF

```
CCF [VARIABLES=] series names [WITH series names]

[/DIFF={1}]
       {n}

[/SDIFF={1}]
        {n}

[/PERIOD=n]

[/{NOLOG**}]
  {LN    }

[/SEASONAL]

[/MXCROSS={7**}]
          {n  }

[/APPLY[='model name']]
```

**Default if the subcommand is omitted and there is no corresponding specification on the TSET command.

Example:

```
CCF VARX VARY
  /LN
  /DIFF=1
  /SDIFF=1
  /PERIOD=12
  /MXCROSS=25.
```

Overview

CCF displays and plots the cross-correlation functions of two or more time series. You can also display and plot the cross-correlations of transformed series by requesting natural log and differencing transformations within the procedure.

Options

Modifying the Series. You can request a natural log transformation of the series using the LN subcommand and seasonal and nonseasonal differencing to any degree using the SDIFF and DIFF subcommands. With seasonal differencing, you can also specify the periodicity on the PERIOD subcommand.

Statistical Display. You can control which series are paired by using the keyword WITH. You can specify the range of lags for which you want values displayed and plotted with the MXCROSS subcommand, overriding the maximum specified on TSET. You can also display and plot values only at periodic lags using the SEASONAL subcommand.

Basic Specification

The basic specification is two or more series names. By default, CCF automatically displays the cross-correlation coefficient and standard error for the negative lags (second series leading), the positive lags (first series leading), and the 0 lag for all possible pair combinations in the series list. It also plots the cross-correlations and marks the bounds of two standard errors on the plot. By default, CCF displays and plots values up to 7 lags (lags −7 to +7), or the range specified on TSET.

Subcommand Order

- Subcommands can be specified in any order.

Syntax Rules

- The VARIABLES subcommand can be specified only once.
- Other subcommands can be specified more than once, but only the last specification of each one is executed.

Operations

- Subcommand specifications apply to all series named on the CCF command.
- If the LN subcommand is specified, any differencing requested on that CCF command is done on the log transformed series.
- Confidence limits are displayed in the plot, marking the bounds of two standard errors at each lag.

Limitations

- Maximum 1 VARIABLES subcommand. There is no limit on the number of series named on the list.

Example

```
CCF VARX VARY
  /LN
  /DIFF=1
  /SDIFF=1
  /PERIOD=12
  /MXCROSS=25.
```

- This example produces a plot of the cross-correlation function for *VARX* and *VARY* after a natural log transformation, differencing, and seasonal differencing have been applied to both series. Along with the plot, the cross-correlation coefficients and standard errors are displayed for each lag.

- LN transforms the data using the natural logarithm (base e) of each series.
- DIFF differences each series once.
- SDIFF and PERIOD apply one degree of seasonal differencing with a period of 12.
- MXCROSS specifies 25 for the maximum range of positive and negative lags for which output is to be produced (lags −25 to +25).

VARIABLES Subcommand

VARIABLES specifies the series to be plotted and is the only required subcommand. The actual keyword VARIABLES can be omitted.

- The minimum VARIABLES specification is a pair of series names.
- If you do not use keyword WITH, each series is paired with every other series in the list.
- If you specify keyword WITH, every series named before WITH is paired with every series named after WITH.

Example

```
CCF VARIABLES=VARA VARB WITH VARC VARD.
```

- This example displays and plots the cross-correlation functions for the following pairs of series: *VARA* with *VARC*, *VARA* with *VARD*, *VARB* with *VARC*, and *VARB* with *VARD*.
- *VARA* is not paired with *VARB*, and *VARC* is not paired with *VARD*.

DIFF Subcommand

DIFF specifies the degree of differencing used to convert a nonstationary series to a stationary one with a constant mean and variance before obtaining cross-correlations.

- You can specify any positive integer on DIFF.
- If DIFF is specified without a value, the default is 1.
- The number of values used in the calculations decreases by 1 for each degree of differencing.

Example

```
CCF VARX VARY
   /DIFF=1.
```

- This command differences series *VARX* and *VARY* before calculating and plotting the cross-correlation function.

SDIFF Subcommand

If the series exhibits seasonal or periodic patterns, you can use SDIFF to seasonally difference the series before obtaining cross-correlations.

- The specification on SDIFF indicates the degree of seasonal differencing and can be any positive integer.
- If SDIFF is specified without a value, the degree of seasonal differencing defaults to 1.
- The number of seasons used in the calculations decreases by 1 for each degree of seasonal differencing.
- The length of the period used by SDIFF is specified on the PERIOD subcommand. If the PERIOD subcommand is not specified, the periodicity established on the TSET or DATE command is used (see the PERIOD subcommand below).

Example

```
CCF VAR01 WITH VAR02 VAR03
 /SDIFF=1.
```

- In this example, one degree of seasonal differencing using the periodicity established on the TSET or DATE command is applied to the three series.
- Two cross-correlation functions are then plotted, one for the pair *VAR01* and *VAR02*, and one for the pair *VAR01* and *VAR03*.

PERIOD Subcommand

PERIOD indicates the length of the period to be used by the SDIFF or SEASONAL subcommands.

- The specification on PERIOD indicates how many observations are in one period or season and can be any positive integer.
- PERIOD is ignored if it is used without the SDIFF or SEASONAL subcommands.
- If PERIOD is not specified, the periodicity established on TSET PERIOD is in effect. If TSET PERIOD is not specified, the periodicity established on the DATE command is used. If periodicity was not established anywhere, the SDIFF and SEASONAL subcommands will not be executed.

Example

```
CCF VARX WITH VARY
 /SDIFF=1
 /PERIOD=6.
```

- This command applies one degree of seasonal differencing with a periodicity of 6 to both series and computes and plots the cross-correlation function.

LN and NOLOG Subcommands

LN transforms the data using the natural logarithm (base *e*) of each series and is used to remove varying amplitude over time. NOLOG indicates that the data should not be log transformed. NOLOG is the default.

- There are no additional specifications on LN or NOLOG.
- Only the last LN or NOLOG subcommand on a CCF command is executed.
- LN and NOLOG apply to all series named on the CCF command.

- If a natural log transformation is requested and any values in either series in a pair are less than or equal to 0, the CCF for that pair will not be produced because nonpositive values cannot be log transformed.
- NOLOG is generally used with an APPLY subcommand to turn off a previous LN specification.

Example

```
CCF VAR01 VAR02
  /LN.
```

- This command transforms the series *VAR01* and *VAR02* using the natural log before computing cross-correlations.

SEASONAL Subcommand

Use SEASONAL to focus attention on the seasonal component by displaying and plotting cross-correlations only at periodic lags.

- There are no additional specifications on SEASONAL.
- If SEASONAL is specified, values are displayed and plotted at the periodic lags indicated on the PERIOD subcommand. If no PERIOD subcommand is specified, the periodicity first defaults to the TSET PERIOD specification and then to the DATE command periodicity. If periodicity is not established anywhere, SEASONAL is ignored (see the PERIOD subcommand on p. 154).
- If SEASONAL is not used, cross-correlations for all lags up to the maximum are displayed and plotted.

Example

```
CCF VAR01 VAR02 VAR03
  /SEASONAL.
```

- This command plots and displays cross-correlations at periodic lags.
- By default, the periodicity established on TSET PERIOD (or the DATE command) is used. If no periodicity is established, cross-correlations for all lags are displayed and plotted.

MXCROSS Subcommand

MXCROSS specifies the maximum range of lags for a series.

- The specification on MXCROSS must be a positive integer.
- If MXCROSS is not specified, the default range is the value set on TSET MXCROSS. If TSET MXCROSS is not specified, the default is 7 (lags −7 to +7).
- The value specified on the MXCROSS subcommand overrides the value set on TSET MXCROSS.

Example

```
CCF VARX VARY
  /MXCROSS=5.
```

- The maximum number of cross-correlations can range from lag −5 to lag +5.

APPLY Subcommand

APPLY allows you to use a previously defined CCF model without having to repeat the specifications.

- The only specification on APPLY is the name of a previous model enclosed in apostrophes. If a model name is not specified, the model specified on the previous CCF command is used.

- To change one or more model specifications, specify the subcommands of only those portions you want to change after the APPLY subcommand.

- If no series are specified on the command, the series that were originally specified with the model being applied are used.

- To change the series used with the model, enter new series names before or after the APPLY subcommand.

Example

```
CCF VARX VARY
   /LN
   /DIFF=1
   /MXCROSS=25.
CCF VARX VARY
   /LN
   /DIFF=1
   /SDIFF=1
   /PERIOD=12
   /MXCROSS=25.
CCF VARX VAR01
   /APPLY.
CCF VARX VAR01
   /APPLY='MOD_1'.
```

- The first command displays and plots the cross-correlation function for *VARX* and *VARY* after each series is log transformed and differenced. The maximum range is set to 25 lags. This model is assigned the name *MOD_1* as soon as the command is executed.

- The second command displays and plots the cross-correlation function for *VARX* and *VARY* after each series is log transformed, differenced, and seasonally differenced with a periodicity of 12. The maximum range is again set to 25 lags. This model is assigned the name *MOD_2*.

- The third command requests the cross-correlation function for the series *VARX* and *VAR01* using the same model and the same range of lags as used for *MOD_2*.

- The fourth command applies *MOD_1* (from the first command) to the series *VARX* and *VAR01*.

References

Box, G. E. P., and G. M. Jenkins. 1976. *Time series analysis: Forecasting and control.* San Francisco: Holden-Day.

CLEAR TRANSFORMATIONS

```
CLEAR TRANSFORMATIONS
```

Overview

CLEAR TRANSFORMATIONS discards previous data transformation commands.

Basic Specification

The only specification is the command itself. CLEAR TRANSFORMATIONS has no additional specifications.

Operations

- CLEAR TRANSFORMATIONS discards all data transformation commands that have accumulated since the last procedure.
- CLEAR TRANSFORMATIONS has no effect if a command file is submitted to your operating system for execution. It generates a warning when a command file is present.
- Be sure to delete CLEAR TRANSFORMATIONS and any unwanted transformation commands from the journal file if you plan to submit the file to the operating system for batch-mode execution. Otherwise, the unwanted transformations will cause problems.

Example

```
GET FILE=QUERY.
FREQUENCIES=ITEM1 ITEM2 ITEM3.
RECODE ITEM1, ITEM2, ITEM3 (0=1) (1=0) (2=-1).
COMPUTE INDEXQ=(ITEM1 + ITEM2 + ITEM3)/3.
VARIABLE LABELS INDEXQ 'SUMMARY INDEX OF QUESTIONS'.
CLEAR TRANSFORMATIONS.
DISPLAY DICTIONARY.
```

- The GET and FREQUENCIES commands are executed.
- The RECODE, COMPUTE, and VARIABLE LABELS commands are transformations. They do not affect the data until the next procedure is executed.
- The CLEAR TRANSFORMATIONS command discards the RECODE, COMPUTE, and VARIABLE LABELS commands.
- The DISPLAY command displays the working file dictionary. Data values and labels are exactly as they were when the FREQUENCIES command was executed. Variable *INDEXQ* does not exist because CLEAR TRANSFORMATIONS discarded the COMPUTE command.

CLUSTER

```
CLUSTER varlist [/MISSING=LISTWISE**] [INCLUDE]

[/MEASURE=[{SEUCLID**            }]
           {EUCLID               }
           {COSINE               }
           {CORRELATION          }
           {BLOCK                }
           {CHEBYCHEV            }
           {POWER(p,r)           }
           {MINKOWSKI(p)         }
           {CHISQ                }
           {PH2                  }
           {RR[(p[,np])]         }
           {SM[(p[,np])]         }
           {JACCARD[(p[,np])]    }
           {DICE[(p[,np])]       }
           {SS1[(p[,np])]        }
           {RT[(p[,np])]         }
           {SS2[(p[,np])]        }
           {K1[(p[,np])]         }
           {SS3[(p[,np])]        }
           {K2[(p[,np])]         }
           {SS4[(p[,np])]        }
           {HAMANN[(p[,np])]     }
           {OCHIAI[(p[,np])]     }
           {SS5[(p[,np])]        }
           {PHI[(p[,np])]        }
           {LAMBDA[(p[,np])]     }
           {D[(p[,np])]          }
           {Y[(p[,np])]          }
           {Q[(p[,np])]          }
           {BEUCLID[(p[,np])]    }
           {SIZE[(p[,np])]       }
           {PATTERN[(p[,np])]    }
           {BSEUCLID[(p[,np])]  ]}
           {BSHAPE[(p[,np])]     }
           {DISPER[(p[,np])]     }
           {VARIANCE[(p[,np])]  ]}
           {BLWMN[(p[,np])]      }


[/METHOD={BAVERAGE**}[(rootname)] [...]]
         {WAVERAGE   }
         {SINGLE     }
         {COMPLETE   }
         {CENTROID   }
         {MEDIAN     }
         {WARD       }
         {DEFAULT**  }

 [/SAVE=CLUSTER({level   })]  [/ID=varname]
               {min,max}

 [/PRINT=[CLUSTER({level   })] [DISTANCE] [SCHEDULE**] [NONE]]
                 {min,max}

 [/PLOT=[VICICLE**[(min[,max[,inc]])]]] [DENDROGRAM] [NONE]]
        [HICICLE[(min[,max[,inc]])]]]

 [/MATRIX=[IN({file})]] [OUT({file})]]
             {*    }          {*    }
```

** Default if subcommand or keyword is omitted.

Example:
```
CLUSTER V1 TO V4
 /PLOT=DENDROGRAM
 /PRINT=CLUSTER (2,4).
```

Overview

CLUSTER produces hierarchical clusters of items based on distance measures of dissimilarity or similarity. The items being clustered are usually cases from the working data file, and the distance measures are computed from their values for one or more variables. You can also cluster variables if you read in a matrix measuring distances between variables. Cluster analysis is discussed in Anderberg (1973).

Options

Cluster Measures and Methods. You can specify one of 37 similarity or distance measures on the MEASURE subcommand and any of the seven methods on the METHOD subcommand.

New Variables. You can save cluster membership for specified solutions as new variables in the working data file using the SAVE subcommand.

Display and Plots. You can display cluster membership, the distance or similarity matrix used to cluster variables or cases, and the agglomeration schedule for the cluster solution with the PRINT subcommand. You can request either a horizontal or vertical icicle plot or a dendrogram of the cluster solution and control the cluster levels displayed in the icicle plot with the PLOT subcommand. You can also specify a variable to be used as a case identifier in the display on the ID subcommand.

Matrix Input and Output. You can write out the distance matrix and use it in subsequent CLUSTER, PROXIMITIES, or ALSCAL analyses or read in matrices produced by other CLUSTER or PROXIMITIES procedures using the MATRIX subcommand.

Basic Specification

The basic specification is a variable list. CLUSTER assumes that the items being clustered are cases and uses the squared Euclidean distances between cases on the variables in the analysis as the measure of distance.

Subcommand Order

- The variable list must be specified first.
- The remaining subcommands can be specified in any order.

Syntax Rules

- The variable list and subcommands can each be specified once.

- More than one clustering method can be specified on the METHOD subcommand.

Operations

The CLUSTER procedure involves four steps:

- First, CLUSTER obtains distance measures of similarities between or distances separating initial clusters (individual cases or individual variables if the input is a matrix measuring distances between variables).
- Second, it combines the two nearest clusters to form a new cluster.
- Third, it recomputes similarities or distances of existing clusters to the new cluster.
- It then returns to the second step until all items are combined in one cluster.

This process yields a hierarchy of cluster solutions, ranging from one overall cluster to as many clusters as there are items being clustered. Clusters at a higher level can contain several lower-level clusters. Within each level, the clusters are disjoint (each item belongs to only one cluster).

- CLUSTER identifies clusters in solutions by sequential integers (1, 2, 3, and so on).

Limitations

- CLUSTER stores cases and a lower-triangular matrix of proximities in memory. Storage requirements increase rapidly with the number of cases. You should be able to cluster 100 cases using a small number of variables in an 80K workspace.
- CLUSTER does not honor weights.

Example

```
CLUSTER V1 TO V4
  /PLOT=DENDROGRAM
  /PRINT=CLUSTER (2 4).
```

- This example clusters cases based on their values for all variables between and including *V1* and *V4* in the working data file.
- The analysis uses the default measure of distance (squared Euclidean) and the default clustering method (average linkage between groups).
- PLOT requests a dendrogram.
- PRINT displays a table of the cluster membership of each case for the two-, three-, and four-cluster solutions.

Variable List

The variable list identifies the variables used to compute similarities or distances between cases.

- The variable list is required except when matrix input is used. It must be specified before the optional subcommands.
- If matrix input is used, the variable list can be omitted. The names for the items in the matrix are used to compute similarities or distances.
- You can specify a variable list to override the names for the items in the matrix. This allows you to read in a subset of cases for analysis. Specifying a variable that does not exist in the matrix results in an error.

MEASURE Subcommand

MEASURE specifies the distance or similarity measure used to cluster cases.

- If the MEASURE subcommand is omitted or included without specifications, squared Euclidean distances are used.
- Only one measure can be specified.

Measures for Interval Data

For interval data, use any one of the following keywords on MEASURE:

SEUCLID   *Squared Euclidean distance.* The distance between two items, x and y, is the sum of the squared differences between the values for the items. SEUCLID is the measure commonly used with centroid, median, and Ward's methods of clustering. SEUCLID is the default and can also be requested with keyword DEFAULT.

$$\text{SEUCLID}(x, y) = \Sigma_i(x_i - y_i)^2$$

EUCLID   *Euclidean distance.* This is the default specification for MEASURE. The distance between two items, x and y, is the square root of the sum of the squared differences between the values for the items.

$$\text{EUCLID}(x, y) = \sqrt{\Sigma_i(x_i - y_i)^2}$$

CORRELATION   *Correlation between vectors of values.* This is a pattern similarity measure.

$$\text{CORRELATION}(x, y) = \frac{\Sigma_i(Z_{xi}Z_{yi})}{N - 1}$$

where Z_{xi} is the Z-score (standardized) value of x for the ith case or variable, and N is the number of cases or variables.

COSINE   *Cosine of vectors of values.* This is a pattern similarity measure.

$$\text{COSINE}(x, y) = \frac{\Sigma_i(x_i y_i)}{\sqrt{(\Sigma_i x_i^2)(\Sigma_i y_i^2)}}$$

CHEBYCHEV   *Chebychev distance metric.* The distance between two items is the maximum absolute difference between the values for the items.

$$\text{CHEBYCHEV}(x, y) = \max_i |x_i - y_i|$$

BLOCK   *City-block or Manhattan distance.* The distance between two items is the sum of the absolute differences between the values for the items.

$$\text{BLOCK}(x, y) = \Sigma_i |x_i - y_i|$$

MINKOWSKI(p)   *Distance in an absolute Minkowski power metric.* The distance between two items is the *p*th root of the sum of the absolute differences to the *p*th power between the values for the items. Appropriate selection of the integer parameter *p* yields Euclidean and many other distance metrics.

$$\text{MINKOWSKI}(x, y) = (\Sigma_i |x_i - y_i|^p)^{1/p}$$

POWER(p,r)   *Distance in an absolute power metric.* The distance between two items is the *r*th root of the sum of the absolute differences to the *p*th power between the values for the items. Appropriate selection of the integer parameters *p* and *r* yields Euclidean, squared Euclidean, Minkowski, city-block, and many other distance metrics.

$$\text{POWER}(x, y) = (\Sigma_i |x_i - y_i|^p)^{1/r}$$

Measures for Frequency Count Data

For frequency count data, use any one of the following keywords on MEASURE:

CHISQ   *Based on the chi-square test of equality for two sets of frequencies.* The magnitude of this dissimilarity measure depends on the total frequencies of the two cases or variables whose dissimilarity is computed. Expected values are from the model of independence of cases or variables x and y.

$$\text{CHISQ}(x, y) = \sqrt{\frac{\Sigma_i (x_i - E(x_i))^2}{E(x_i)} + \frac{\Sigma_i (y_i - E(y_i))^2}{E(y_i)}}$$

PH2   *Phi-square between sets of frequencies.* This is the CHISQ measure normalized by the square root of the combined frequency. Therefore, its value does not depend on the total frequencies of the two cases or variables whose dissimilarity is computed.

$$\text{PH2}(x, y) = \sqrt{\frac{\dfrac{\Sigma_i (x_i - E(x_i))^2}{E(x_i)} + \dfrac{\Sigma_i (y_i - E(y_i))^2}{E(y_i)}}{N}}$$

Measures for Binary Data

Different binary measures emphasize different aspects of the relationship between sets of binary values. However, all the measures are specified in the same way. Each measure has two optional integer-valued parameters, p (present) and np (not present).

- If both parameters are specified, CLUSTER uses the value of the first as an indicator that a characteristic is present and the value of the second as an indicator that a characteristic is absent. CLUSTER skips all other values.

- If only the first parameter is specified, CLUSTER uses that value to indicate presence and all other values to indicate absence.

- If no parameters are specified, CLUSTER assumes that 1 indicates presence and 0 indicates absence.

Using the indicators for presence and absence within each item (case or variable), CLUSTER constructs a 2×2 contingency table for each pair of items in turn. It uses this table to compute a proximity measure for the pair.

	Item 2 characteristics	
	Present	**Absent**
Item 1 characteristics		
Present	a	b
Absent	c	d

CLUSTER computes all binary measures from the values of a, b, c, and d. These values are tallied across variables (when the items are cases) or across cases (when the items are variables). For example, if variables V, W, X, Y, Z have values 0, 1, 1, 0, 1 for case 1 and values 0, 1, 1, 0, 0 for case 2 (where 1 indicates presence and 0 indicates absence), the contingency table is as follows:

	Case 2 characteristics	
	Present	**Absent**
Case 1 characteristics		
Present	2	1
Absent	0	2

The contingency table indicates that both cases are present for two variables (W and X), both cases are absent for two variables (V and Y), and case 1 is present and case 2 is absent for one variable (Z). There are no variables for which case 1 is absent and case 2 is present.

The available binary measures include matching coefficients, conditional probabilities, predictability measures, and others.

Matching Coefficients. Table 1 shows a classification scheme for matching coefficients. In this scheme, *matches* are joint presences (value a in the contingency table) or joint absences (value d). *Nonmatches* are equal in number to value b plus value c. Matches and nonmatches may be weighted equally or not. The three coefficients JACCARD, DICE, and SS2 are related monotonically, as are SM, SS1, and RT. All coefficients in Table 1 are similarity measures, and all except two (K1 and SS3) range from 0 to 1. K1 and SS3 have a minimum value of 0 and no upper limit.

Table 1   Binary matching coefficients in CLUSTER

	Joint absences excluded from numerator	Joint absences included in numerator
All matches included in denominator		
Equal weight for matches and nonmatches	RR	SM
Double weight for matches		SS1
Double weight for nonmatches		RT
Joint absences excluded from denominator		
Equal weight for matches and nonmatches	JACCARD	
Double weight for matches	DICE	
Double weight for nonmatches	SS2	
All matches excluded from denominator		
Equal weight for matches and nonmatches	K1	SS3

RR[(p[,np])]   *Russell and Rao similarity measure.* This is the binary dot product.

$$RR(x, y) = \frac{a}{a + b + c + d}$$

SM[(p[,np])]   *Simple matching similarity measure.* This is the ratio of the number of matches to the total number of characteristics.

$$SM(x, y) = \frac{a + d}{a + b + c + d}$$

JACCARD[(p[,np])]   *Jaccard similarity measure.* This is also known as the *similarity ratio*.

$$JACCARD(x, y) = \frac{a}{a + b + c}$$

DICE[(p[,np])]

Dice (or Czekanowski or Sorenson) similarity measure.

$$\text{DICE}(x, y) = \frac{2a}{2a + b + c}$$

SS1[(p[,np])]

Sokal and Sneath similarity measure 1.

$$\text{SS1}(x, y) = \frac{2(a + d)}{2(a + d) + b + c}$$

RT[(p[,np])]

Rogers and Tanimoto similarity measure.

$$\text{RT}(x, y) = \frac{a + d}{a + d + 2(b + c)}$$

SS2[(p[,np])]

Sokal and Sneath similarity measure 2.

$$\text{SS2}(x, y) = \frac{a}{a + 2(b + c)}$$

K1[(p[,np])]

Kulczynski similarity measure 1. This measure has a minimum value of 0 and no upper limit. It is undefined when there are no nonmatches (b=0 and c=0). PROXIMITIES assigns an artificial upper limit of 10,000 to K1 when it is undefined or exceeds this value.

$$\text{K1}(x, y) = \frac{a}{b + c}$$

SS3[(p[,np])]

Sokal and Sneath similarity measure 3. This measure has a minimum value of 0 and no upper limit. It is undefined when there are no non-matches (b=0 and c=0). PROXIMITIES assigns an artificial upper limit of 10,000 to SS3 when it is undefined or exceeds this value.

$$\text{SS3}(x, y) = \frac{a + d}{b + c}$$

Conditional Probabilities. The following binary measures yield values that can be interpreted in terms of conditional probability. All three are similarity measures.

K2[(p[,np])]

Kulczynski similarity measure 2. This yields the average conditional probability that a characteristic is present in one item given that the characteristic is present in the other item. The measure is an average over both items acting as predictors. It has a range of 0 to 1.

$$\text{K2}(x, y) = \frac{a/(a + b) + a/(a + c)}{2}$$

SS4[(p[,np])]

Sokal and Sneath similarity measure 4. This yields the conditional probability that a characteristic of one item is in the same state (presence or absence) as the characteristic of the other item. The measure is an average over both items acting as predictors. It has a range of 0 to 1.

$$SS4(x, y) = \frac{a/(a+b) + a/(a+c) + d/(b+d) + d/(c+d)}{4}$$

HAMANN[(p[,np])]   *Hamann similarity measure.* This measure gives the probability that a characteristic has the same state in both items (present in both or absent from both) minus the probability that a characteristic has different states in the two items (present in one and absent from the other). HAMANN has a range of -1 to $+1$ and is monotonically related to SM, SS1, and RT.

$$HAMANN(x, y) = \frac{(a+d) - (b+c)}{a+b+c+d}$$

Predictability Measures. The following four binary measures assess the association between items as the predictability of one given the other. All four measures yield similarities.

LAMBDA[(p[,np])]   *Goodman and Kruskal's lambda (similarity).* This coefficient assesses the predictability of the state of a characteristic on one item (present or absent) given the state on the other item. Specifically, LAMBDA measures the proportional reduction in error using one item to predict the other when the directions of prediction are of equal importance. LAMBDA has a range of 0 to 1.

$$LAMBDA(x, y) = \frac{t_1 - t_2}{2(a+b+c+d) - t_2}$$

where
$t_1 = \max(a,b) + \max(c,d) + \max(a,c) + \max(b,d)$
$t_2 = \max(a+c, b+d) + \max(a+d, c+d).$

D[(p[,np])]   *Anderberg's D (similarity).* This coefficient assesses the predictability of the state of a characteristic on one item (present or absent) given the state on the other. D measures the actual reduction in the error probability when one item is used to predict the other. The range of D is 0 to 1.

$$D(x, y) = \frac{t_1 - t_2}{2(a+b+c+d)}$$

where
$t_1 = \max(a,b) + \max(c,d) + \max(a,c) + \max(b,d)$
$t_2 = \max(a+c, b+d) + \max(a+d, c+d)$

Y[(p[,np])]   *Yule's Y coefficient of colligation (similarity).* This is a function of the cross ratio for a 2×2 table. It has a range of -1 to $+1$.

$$Y(x, y) = \frac{\sqrt{ad} - \sqrt{bc}}{\sqrt{ad} + \sqrt{bc}}$$

Q[(p[,np])]   *Yule's* Q *(similarity).* This is the 2×2 version of Goodman and Kruskal's ordinal measure *gamma*. Like Yule's *Y*, *Q* is a function of the cross ratio for a 2×2 table and has a range of -1 to $+1$.

$$Q(x, y) = \frac{ad - bc}{ad + bc}$$

Other Binary Measures. The remaining binary measures available in CLUSTER are either binary equivalents of association measures for continuous variables or measures of special properties of the relationship between items.

OCHIAI[(p[,np])]   *Ochiai similarity measure.* This is the binary form of the cosine. It has a range of 0 to 1.

$$OCHIAI(x, y) = \sqrt{\frac{a}{a + b} \cdot \frac{a}{a + c}}$$

SS5[(p[,np])]   *Sokal and Sneath similarity measure 5.* The range is 0 to 1.

$$SS5(x, y) = \frac{ad}{\sqrt{(a + b)(a + c)(b + d)(c + d)}}$$

PHI[(p[,np])]   *Fourfold point correlation (similarity).* This is the binary form of the Pearson product-moment correlation coefficient.

$$PHI(x, y) = \frac{ad - bc}{\sqrt{(a + b)(a + c)(b + d)(c + d)}}$$

BEUCLID[(p[,np])]   *Binary Euclidean distance.* This is a distance measure. Its minimum value is 0, and it has no upper limit.

$$BEUCLID(x, y) = \sqrt{b + c}$$

BSEUCLID[(p[,np])]   *Binary squared Euclidean distance.* This is a distance measure. Its minimum value is 0, and it has no upper limit.

$$BSEUCLID(x, y) = b + c$$

SIZE[(p[,np])]   *Size difference.* This is a dissimilarity measure with a minimum value of 0 and no upper limit.

$$SIZE(x, y) = \frac{(b - c)^2}{(a + b + c + d)^2}$$

PATTERN[(p[,np])]   *Pattern difference.* This is a dissimilarity measure. The range is 0 to 1.

$$\text{PATTERN}(x, y) = \frac{bc}{(a + b + c + d)^2}$$

BSHAPE[(p[,np])]   *Binary shape difference.* This dissimilarity measure has no upper or lower limit.

$$\text{BSHAPE}(x, y) = \frac{(a + b + c + d)(b + c) - (b - c)^2}{(a + b + c + d)^2}$$

DISPER[(p[,np])]   *Dispersion similarity measure.* The range is −1 to +1.

$$\text{DISPER}(x, y) = \frac{ad - bc}{(a + b + c + d)^2}$$

VARIANCE[(p[,np])]   *Variance dissimilarity measure.* This measure has a minimum value of 0 and no upper limit.

$$\text{VARIANCE}(x, y) = \frac{b + c}{4(a + b + c + d)}$$

BLWMN[(p[,np])]   *Binary Lance-and-Williams nonmetric dissimilarity measure.* This measure is also known as the Bray-Curtis nonmetric coefficient. The range is 0 to 1.

$$\text{BLWMN}(x, y) = \frac{b + c}{2a + b + c}$$

METHOD Subcommand

METHOD specifies one or more clustering methods.

- If the METHOD subcommand is omitted or included without specifications, the method of average linkage between groups is used.
- Only one METHOD subcommand can be used, but more than one method can be specified on it.
- When the number of items is large, CENTROID and MEDIAN require significantly more CPU time than other methods.

BAVERAGE   *Average linkage between groups (UPGMA).* BAVERAGE is the default and can also be requested with keyword DEFAULT.

WAVERAGE   *Average linkage within groups.*

SINGLE   *Single linkage or nearest neighbor.*

COMPLETE   *Complete linkage or furthest neighbor.*

CENTROID   *Centroid clustering (UPGMC).* Squared Euclidean distances are commonly used with this method.

MEDIAN   *Median clustering (WPGMC).* Squared Euclidean distances are commonly used with this method.

WARD   *Ward's method.* Squared Euclidean distances are commonly used with this method.

Example

```
CLUSTER V1 V2 V3
 /METHOD=SINGLE COMPLETE WARDS.
```

• This example clusters cases based on their values for variables *V1*, *V2*, and *V3*, and uses three clustering methods: single linkage, complete linkage, and Ward's method.

SAVE Subcommand

SAVE allows you to save cluster membership at specified solution levels as new variables in the working data file.

• The specification on SAVE is the CLUSTER keyword, followed by either a single number indicating the level (number of clusters) of the cluster solution or a range separated by a comma indicating the minimum and maximum numbers of clusters when membership of more than one solution is to be saved. The number or range must be enclosed in parentheses and applies to all methods specified on METHOD.

• You can specify a rootname in parentheses after each method specification on the METHOD subcommand. CLUSTER forms new variable names by appending the number of the cluster solution to the rootname.

• If no rootname is specified, CLUSTER forms variable names using the formula *CLUn_m*, where *m* increments to create a unique rootname for the set of variables saved for one method and *n* is the number of the cluster solution.

• As *n* and *m* increase, the prefix *CLU* is truncated to keep names within eight characters.

• The names and descriptive labels of the new variables are displayed in the procedure information notes.

• You cannot use the SAVE subcommand if you are replacing the working data file with matrix materials (see "Matrix Output" on p. 172).

Example

```
CLUSTER A B C
 /METHOD=BAVERAGE SINGLE (SINMEM) WARD
 /SAVE=CLUSTERS(3,5).
```

• This command creates nine new variables: *CLU5_1*, *CLU4_1*, and *CLU3_1* for BAVERAGE, *SINMEM5*, *SINMEM4*, and *SINMEM3* for SINGLE, and *CLU5_2*, *CLU4_2*, and *CLU3_2* for WARD. The variables contain the cluster membership for each case at the five-, four-, and three-cluster solutions using the three clustering methods. Ward's method is the third specification on METHOD but uses the second set of default names since it is the second method specified without a rootname.

• The order of the new variables in the working data file is the same as listed above, since the solutions are obtained in the order from 5 to 3.

- New variables are listed in the procedure information notes.

ID Subcommand

ID names a string variable to be used as the case identifier in cluster membership tables, icicle plots, and dendrograms. If the ID subcommand is omitted, cases are identified by case numbers alone.

PRINT Subcommand

PRINT controls the display of cluster output (except plots, which are controlled by the PLOT subcommand).

- If the PRINT subcommand is omitted or included without specifications, an agglomeration schedule is displayed. If any keywords are specified on PRINT, the agglomeration schedule is displayed only if explicitly requested.
- CLUSTER automatically displays summary information (the method and measure used, the number of cases) for each method named on the METHOD subcommand. This summary is displayed regardless of specifications on PRINT.

You can specify any or all of the following on the PRINT subcommand:

SCHEDULE   *Agglomeration schedule.* The agglomeration schedule shows the order and distances at which items and clusters combine to form new clusters. It also shows the cluster level at which an item joins a cluster. SCHEDULE is the default and can also be requested with keyword DEFAULT.

CLUSTER(min,max)   *Cluster membership.* For each item, the display includes the value of the case identifier (or the variable name if matrix input is used), the case sequence number, and a value (1, 2, 3, and so on) identifying the cluster to which that case belongs in a given cluster solution. Specify either a single integer value in parentheses indicating the level of a single solution or a minimum value and a maximum value indicating a range of solutions for which display is desired. If the number of clusters specified exceeds the number produced, the largest number of clusters is used (the number of items minus 1). If CLUSTER is specified more than once, the last specification is used.

DISTANCE   *Proximities matrix.* The proximities matrix table displays the distances or similarities between items computed by CLUSTER or obtained from an input matrix. DISTANCE produces a large volume of output and uses significant CPU time when the number of cases is large.

NONE   *None of the above.* NONE overrides any other keywords specified on PRINT.

Example

```
CLUSTER V1 V2 V3 /PRINT=CLUSTER(3,5).
```

- This example displays cluster membership for each case for the three-, four-, and five-cluster solutions.

PLOT Subcommand

PLOT controls the plots produced for each method specified on the METHOD subcommand. For icicle plots, PLOT allows you to control the cluster solution at which the plot begins and ends and the increment for displaying intermediate cluster solutions.

- If the PLOT subcommand is omitted or included without specifications, a vertical icicle plot is produced.
- If any keywords are specified on PLOT, only those plots requested are produced.
- The icicle plots are generated as pivot tables and the dendrogram is generated as text output.
- If there is not enough memory for a dendrogram or an icicle plot, the plot is skipped and a warning is issued.
- The size of an icicle plot can be controlled by specifying range values or an increment for VICICLE or HICICLE. Smaller plots require significantly less workspace and time.

VICICLE(min,max,inc)   *Vertical icicle plot.* This is the default. The range specifications are optional. If used, they must be integer and must be enclosed in parentheses. The specification *min* is the cluster solution at which to start the display (the default is 1), and the specification *max* is the cluster solution at which to end the display (the default is the number of cases minus 1). If *max* is greater than the number of cases minus 1, the default is used. The increment to use between cluster solutions is *inc* (the default is 1). If *max* is specified, *min* must be specified, and if *inc* is specified, both *min* and *max* must be specified. If VICICLE is specified more than once, only the last range specification is used.

HICICLE(min,max,inc)   *Horizontal icicle plot.* The range specifications are the same as for VICICLE. If both VICICLE and HICICLE are specified, the last range specified is used for both. If a range is not specified on the last instance of VICICLE or HICICLE, the defaults are used even if a range is specified earlier.

DENDROGRAM   *Tree diagram.* The dendrogram is scaled by the joining distances of the clusters.

NONE   *No plots.*

Example

```
CLUSTER V1 V2 V3 /PLOT=VICICLE(1,20).
```

- This example produces a vertical icicle plot for the one-cluster through the twenty-cluster solution.

Example

```
CLUSTER V1 V2 V3 /PLOT=VICICLE(1,151,5).
```

- This example produces a vertical icicle plot for every fifth cluster solution starting with 1 and ending with 151 (1 cluster, 6 clusters, 11 clusters, and so on).

MISSING Subcommand

MISSING controls the treatment of cases with missing values. By default, a case that has a missing value for any variable on the variable list is omitted from the analysis.

LISTWISE   *Delete cases with missing values listwise.* Only cases with nonmissing values for all variables on the variable list are used. LISTWISE is the default and can also be requested with keyword DEFAULT.

INCLUDE   *Include cases with user-missing values.* Only cases with system-missing values are excluded.

MATRIX Subcommand

MATRIX reads and writes SPSS-format matrix data files.

- Either IN or OUT and a matrix file in parentheses are required. When both IN and OUT are used on the same CLUSTER procedure, they can be specified on separate MATRIX subcommands or on the same subcommand.
- The input or output matrix information is displayed in the procedure information notes.

OUT (filename)   *Write a matrix data file.* Specify either a filename or an asterisk in parentheses (*). If you specify a filename, the file is stored on disk and can be retrieved at any time. If you specify an asterisk (*), the matrix data file replaces the working data file but is not stored on disk unless you use SAVE or XSAVE.

IN (filename)   *Read a matrix data file.* If the matrix data file is the current working data file, specify an asterisk (*) in parentheses. If the matrix data file is another file, specify the filename in parentheses. A matrix file read from an external file does not replace the working data file.

Matrix Output

- CLUSTER writes proximity-type matrices with *ROWTYPE_* values of PROX. CLUSTER neither reads nor writes additional statistics with its matrix materials. See "Format of the Matrix Data File" on p. 173 for a description of the file.
- The matrices produced by CLUSTER can be used by subsequent CLUSTER procedures or by procedures PROXIMITIES and ALSCAL.

- Any documents contained in the working data file are not transferred to the matrix file.

Matrix Input

- CLUSTER can read matrices written by a previous CLUSTER command or by PROXIMITIES, or created by MATRIX DATA. When the input matrix contains distances between variables, CLUSTER clusters all or a subset of the variables.

- The order among rows and cases in the input matrix file is unimportant, as long as values for split-file variables precede values for ROWTYPE_.

- CLUSTER ignores unrecognized ROWTYPE_ values.

- When you are reading a matrix created with MATRIX DATA, you should supply a value label for PROX of either SIMILARITY or DISSIMILARITY so the matrix is correctly identified. If you do not supply a label, CLUSTER assumes DISSIMILARITY. (See "Format of the Matrix Data File" below.)

- The program reads variable names, variable and value labels, and print and write formats from the dictionary of the matrix data file.

- MATRIX=IN cannot be specified unless a working data file has already been defined. To read an existing matrix data file at the beginning of a session, use GET to retrieve the matrix file and then specify IN(*) on MATRIX.

- The variable list on CLUSTER can be omitted when a matrix data file is used as input. By default, all cases or variables in the matrix data file are used in the analysis. Specify a variable list when you want to read in a subset of items for analysis.

Format of the Matrix Data File

- The matrix data file can include three special variables created by the program: ROWTYPE_, ID, and VARNAME_.

- Variable ROWTYPE_ is a string variable with value PROX (for proximity measure). PROX is assigned value labels containing the distance measure used to create the matrix and either SIMILARITY or DISSIMILARITY as an identifier.

- ID is included only when an identifying variable is not specified on the ID subcommand. ID is a short string and takes the value CASE m, where m is the actual number of each case. Note that m may not be consecutive if cases have been selected.

- If an identifying variable is specified on the ID subcommand, it takes the place of ID between ROWTYPE_ and VARNAME_. Up to 20 characters can be displayed for the identifying variable.

- VARNAME_ is a string variable that takes the values VAR1, VAR2 ...VARn, to correspond to the names of the distance variables in the matrix (VAR1, VAR2 ... VARn, where n is the number of cases in the largest split file). The numeric suffix for the variable names is consecutive and may not be the same as the actual case number.

- The remaining variables in the matrix file are the distance variables used to form the matrix. The distance variables are assigned variable labels in the form of CASE m to identify the actual number of each case.

Split Files

- When split-file processing is in effect, the first variables in the matrix data file are the split variables, followed by *ROWTYPE_*, the case-identifier variable or *ID*, *VARNAME_*, and the distance variables.
- A full set of matrix materials is written for each split-file group defined by the split variables.
- A split variable cannot have the same name as any other variable written to the matrix data file.
- If split-file processing is in effect when a matrix is written, the same split file must be in effect when that matrix is read by any procedure.

Missing Values

Missing-value treatment affects the values written to a matrix data file. When reading a matrix data file, be sure to specify a missing-value treatment on CLUSTER that is compatible with the treatment that was in effect when the matrix materials were generated.

Example

```
DATA LIST FILE=ALMANAC1 RECORDS=3
  /1 CITY 6-18(A) POP80 53-60
  /2 CHURCHES 10-13 PARKS 14-17 PHONES 18-25 TVS 26-32
     RADIOST 33-35 TVST 36-38 TAXRATE 52-57(2).
N OF CASES 8.

CLUSTER CHURCHES TO TAXRATE
  /ID=CITY
  /MEASURE=EUCLID
  /MATRIX=OUT(CLUSMTX).
```

- CLUSTER reads raw data from file *ALMANAC1* and writes one set of matrix materials to file *CLUSMTX*.
- The working data file is still the *ALMANAC1* file defined on DATA LIST. Subsequent commands are executed on *ALMANAC1*.

Example

```
DATA LIST FILE=ALMANAC1 RECORDS=3
  /1 CITY 6-18(A) POP80 53-60
  /2 CHURCHES 10-13 PARKS 14-17 PHONES 18-25 TVS 26-32
     RADIOST 33-35 TVST 36-38 TAXRATE 52-57(2).
N OF CASES 8.

CLUSTER CHURCHES TO TAXRATE
  /ID=CITY
  /MEASURE=EUCLID
  /MATRIX=OUT(*).
LIST.
```

- CLUSTER writes the same matrix as in the previous example. However, the matrix data file replaces the working data file. The LIST command is executed on the matrix file, not on *ALMANAC1*.

Example

```
GET FILE=CLUSMTX.
CLUSTER
  /ID=CITY
  /MATRIX=IN(*).
```

- This example starts a new session and reads an existing matrix data file. GET retrieves the matrix data file *CLUSMTX*.
- MATRIX=IN specifies an asterisk because the matrix data file is the working data file. If MATRIX=IN(CLUSMTX) is specified, the program issues an error message.
- If the GET command is omitted, the program issues an error message.

Example

```
GET FILE=PRSNNL.
FREQUENCIES VARIABLE=AGE.

CLUSTER
  /ID=CITY
  /MATRIX=IN(CLUSMTX).
```

- This example performs a frequencies analysis on file *PRSNNL* and then uses a different file for CLUSTER. The file is an existing matrix data file.
- The variable list is omitted on the CLUSTER command. By default, all cases in the matrix file are used in the analysis.
- MATRIX=IN specifies the matrix data file *CLUSMTX*.
- *CLUSMTX* does not replace *PRSNNL* as the working data file.

Example

```
GET FILE=CRIME.
PROXIMITIES MURDER TO MOTOR
  /VIEW=VARIABLE
  /MEASURE=PH2
  /MATRIX=OUT(*).
CLUSTER
  /MATRIX=IN(*).
```

- GET retrieves an SPSS-format data file.
- PROXIMITIES uses the data from the *CRIME* file, which is now the working data file. The VIEW subcommand specifies computation of proximity values between variables. The MATRIX subcommand writes the matrix to the working data file.
- MATRIX=IN(*) on the CLUSTER command reads the matrix materials from the working data file. Since the matrix contains distances between variables, CLUSTER clusters vari-

ables based on distance measures in the input. The variable list is omitted on the CLUS-TER command, so all variables are used in the analysis. The slash preceding the MATRIX subcommand is required because there is an implied variable list. Without the slash, CLUSTER would attempt to interpret MATRIX as a variable name rather than a subcommand name.

COMMENT

```
{COMMENT} text
{   *   }
```

Overview

COMMENT inserts explanatory text within the command sequence. Comments are included among the commands printed back in the output; they do not become part of the information saved in an SPSS-format data file. To include commentary in the dictionary of a data file, use the DOCUMENT command.

Syntax Rules

- The first line of a comment can begin with the keyword COMMENT or with an asterisk (*). Comment text can extend for multiple lines and can contain any characters. A period is required at the end of the last line to terminate the comment.

- Use /* and */ to set off a comment within a command. The comment can be placed wherever a blank is valid (except within strings) and should be preceded by a blank. Comments within a command cannot be continued onto the next line.

- The closing */ is optional when the comment is at the end of the line. The command can continue onto the next line just as if the inserted comment was a blank.

- Comments cannot be inserted within data lines.

Example

```
* Create a new variable as a combination of two old variables;
  the new variable is a scratch variable used later in the
  session;  it will not be saved with the data file.

COMPUTE #XYVAR=0.
IF (XVAR EQ 1 AND YVAR EQ 1) #XYVAR=1.
```

- The three-line comment will be included in the display file but will not be part of the data file if the working data file is saved.

Example

```
IF (RACE EQ 1 AND SEX EQ 1) SEXRACE = 1   /*White males.
```

- The comment is entered on a command line. The closing */ is not needed because the comment is at the end of the line.

COMPUTE

```
COMPUTE target variable=expression
```

Arithmetic operators:

+	Addition	–	Subtraction
*	Multiplication	/	Division
**	Exponentiation		

Arithmetic functions:

ABS(arg)	Absolute value
RND(arg)	Round
TRUNC(arg)	Truncate
MOD(arg)	Modulus
SQRT(arg)	Square root
EXP(arg)	Exponential
LG10(arg)	Base 10 logarithm
LN(arg)	Natural logarithm
ARSIN(arg)	Arcsine
ARTAN(arg)	Arctangent
SIN(arg)	Sine
COS(arg)	Cosine

Statistical functions:

SUM[.n](arg list)	Sum of values across argument list
MEAN[.n](arg list)	Mean value across argument list
SD[.n](arg list)	Standard deviation of values across list
VAR[.n](arg list)	Variance of values across list
CFVAR[.n](arg list)	Coefficient of variation of values across list
MIN[.n](arg list)	Minimum value across list
MAX[.n](arg list)	Maximum value across list

Cumulative distribution functions (continuous):

CDF.BETA(q,a,b)	Return probability that the beta random variate falls below q ($0 \leq q \leq 1$; a>0; b>0).
CDF.CAUCHY(q,a,b)	Return probability that the Cauchy random variate falls below q ($q \geq 0$; b>0).
CDF.CHISQ (q,a)	Return probability that the chi-square random variate falls below q ($q \geq 0$; a>0).
CDF.EXP(q,a)	Return probability that the exponential random variate falls below q ($q \geq 0$; a>0).
CDF.F(q,a,b)	Return probability that the F random variate falls below q ($q \geq 0$; a>0; b>0).
CDF.GAMMA(q,a,b)	Return probability that the gamma random variate falls below q ($q \geq 0$; a>0; b>0).
CDF.LAPLACE(q,a,b)	Return probability that the Laplace random variate falls below q (b>0).
CDF.LOGISTIC(q,a,b)	Return probability that the logistic random variate falls below q (b>0).
CDF.LNORMAL(q,a,b)	Return probability that the lognormal random variate falls below q ($q \geq 0$; b>0).
CDF.NORMAL(q,a,b)	Return probability that the normal random variate falls below q (b>0). When $a=0$, $b=1$, alias CDFNORM(q).
CDF.PARETO(q,a,b)	Return probability that the Pareto random variate falls below q (q≥a>0; b>0).
CDF.T(q,a)	Return probability that the Student t random variate falls below q (a>0).
CDF.UNIFORM(q,a,b)	Return probability that the uniform random variate falls below q ($a \leq q \leq b$).
CDF.WEIBULL(q,a,b)	Return probability that the Weibull random variate falls below q ($q \geq 0$; a>0; b>0).

Inverse distribution functions (continuous):

IDF.BETA(p,a,b)	Return value q such that CDF.BETA(q,a,b)=p ($0 \leq p \leq 1$; a>0; b>0).
IDF.CAUCHY(p,a,b)	Return value q such that CDF.CAUCHY(q,a,b)=p ($0<p<1$; b>0).
IDF.CHISQ(p,a)	Return value q such that CDF.CHISQ(q,a)=p ($0 \leq p<1$; a>0).
IDF.EXP(p,a)	Return value q such that CDF.EXP(q,a)=p ($0 \leq p<1$; a>0).
IDF.F(p,a,b)	Return value q such that CDF.F(q,a,b)=p ($0 \leq p<1$; a>0; b>0).
IDF.GAMMA(p,a,b)	Return value q such that CDF.GAMMA(q,a,b)=p ($0 \leq p<1$; a>0; b>0).
IDF.LAPLACE(p,a,b)	Return value q such that CDF.LAPLACE(q,a,b)=p ($0<p<1$; b>0).
IDF.LOGISTIC(p,a,b)	Return value q such that CDF.LOGISTIC(q,a,b)=p ($0<p<1$; b>0).
IDF.LNORMAL(p,a,b)	Return value q such that CDF.LNORMAL(q,a,b)=p ($0 \leq p \leq 1$; b>0).
IDF.NORMAL(p,a,b)	Return value q such that CDF.NORMAL(q,a,b)=p ($0<p<1$; b>0). When $a=0$, $b=1$, alias PROBIT(p).
IDF.PARETO(p,a,b)	Return value q such that CDF.PARETO(q,a,b)=p ($0 \leq p<1$; a>0; b>0).
IDF.T(p,a)	Return value q such that CDF.T(q,a)=p ($0<p<1$; a>0).
IDF.UNIFORM(p,a,b)	Return value q such that CDF.UNIFORM(q,a,b)=p ($0 \leq p \leq 1$; a≤b).
IDF.WEIBULL(p,a,b)	Return value q such that CDF.WEIBULL(q,a,b)=p ($0 \leq p<1$; a>0; b>0).

Random variable functions (continuous distributions):

RV.BETA(a,b)	Generate a random variable of the beta distribution (a>0; b>0).
RV.CAUCHY(a,b)	Generate a random variable of the Cauchy distribution (b>0).
RV.CHISQ(a)	Generate a random variable of the chi-square distribution (a>0).
RV.EXP(a)	Generate a random variable of the exponential distribution (a>0).
RV.F(a,b)	Generate a random variable of the F distribution (a>0; b>0).
RV.GAMMA(a,b)	Generate a random variable of the gamma distribution (a>0; b>0).
RV.LAPLACE(a,b)	Generate a random variable of the Laplace distribution (b>0).

RV.LOGISTIC(a,b)	Generate a random variable of the logistic distribution (b>0).
RV.LNORMAL(a,b)	Generate a random variable of the lognormal distribution (b>0).
RV.NORMAL(a,b)	Generate a random variable of the normal distribution (b>0). When $a=0$, alias NORMAL(b).
RV.PARETO(x,a,b)	Generate a random variable of the Pareto distribution (b>0).
RV.T(a)	Generate a random variable of the Student t distribution (b>0).
RV.UNIFORM(a,b)	Generate a random variable of the uniform distribution. When $a=0$, alias UNIFORM(b).
RV.WEIBULL(a,b)	Generate a random variable of the Weibull distribution (a>0; b>0).

Cumulative distribution functions (discrete):

CDF.BERNOULLI(q,a)	Return probability that the Bernoulli distributed variate is less than or equal to q ($q=0$ or 1 only, $0 \le a \le 1$).
CDF.BINOM(q,a,b)	Return probability that the binomially distributed variate is less than or equal to q ($0 \le q \le a$ integer, $0 \le b \le 1$).
CDF.GEOM(q,a)	Return probability that the geometrically distributed variate is less than or equal to q ($q>0$ integer; $0<a \le 1$).
CDF.HYPER(q,a,b,c)	Return probability that the hypergeometrically distributed variate is less than or equal to q ($a>0$ integer, $0 \le c \le a$, $0 \le b \le a$; $\max(0,b-a+c) \le q \le \min(c,b)$).
CDF.NEGBIN(q,a,b)	Return probability that the negative binomially distributed variate is less than or equal to q ($a>0$ integer, $0 \le b \le 1$; $q \ge a$ integer).
CDF.POISSON(q,a)	Return probability that the Poisson distributed variate is less than or equal to q ($a>0$; $q \ge 0$ integer).

Random variable functions (discrete distributions):

RV.BERNOULLI(a)	Generate a random variable from the Bernoulli distribution.
RV.BINOM(a,b)	Generate a random variable from the binomial distribution.
RV.GEOM(a)	Generate a random variable from the geometric distribution.
RV.HYPER(a,b,c)	Generate a random variable from the hypergeometric distribution ($a>0$ integer, $0 \le c \le a$, $0 \le b \le a$).
RV.NEGBIN(a,b)	Generate a random variable from the negative binomial distribution ($a>0$ integer, $0 \le b \le 1$).
RV.POISSON(a)	Generate a random variable from the Poisson distribution ($a>0$).

Noncentral distribution functions:

NCDF.BETA(x,a,b,c)	Return probability that the noncentral beta distributed variate falls below x ($a>0, b>0, c \ge 0$; $0 \le x \le 1$).
NCDF.CHISQ(x,a,c)	Return probability that the noncentral chi-square distributed variate falls below x ($a>0$, $c \ge 0$; $x \ge 0$).
NCDF.F(x,a,b,c)	Return probability that the noncentral F distributed variate falls below x ($a>0$, $b>0$, $c \ge 0$; $x \ge 0$).
NCDF.T(x,a,c)	Return probability that the noncentral Student t distributed variate falls below x ($a>0$, $c \ge 0$).

Missing-value functions:

VALUE(varname)	Ignore user-missing.
MISSING(varname)	True if missing.
SYSMIS(varname)	True if system-missing.
NMISS(arg list)	Number of missing values across list.
NVALID(arg list)	Number of valid values across list.

Cross-case function:

LAG(varname,n)	Value of variable *n* cases before.

Logical functions:

RANGE(varname,range)	True if value of variable is in range.
ANY(arg,arg list)	True if value of first argument is included on argument list.

Other functions:

UNIFORM(arg)	Uniform pseudo-random number between 0 and *n*.
NORMAL(arg)	Normal pseudo-random number with mean of 0 and standard deviation of *n*.
CDFNORM(arg)	Probability that random variable falls below *n*.
PROBIT(arg)	Inverse of CDFNORM.

Date and time aggregation functions:

DATE.DMY(d,m,y)	Read day, month, year, and return date.
DATE.MDY(m,d,y)	Read month, day, year, and return date.
DATE.YRDAY(y,d)	Read year, day, and return date.
DATE.QYR(q,y)	Read quarter, year, and return quarter start date.
DATE.MOYR(m,y)	Read month, year, and return month start date.
DATE.WKYR(w,y)	Read week, year, and return week start date.
TIME.HMS(h,m,s)	Read hour, minutes, seconds, and return time interval.
TIME.DAYS(d)	Read days and return time interval.

Date and time conversion functions:

YRMODA(yr,mo,da)	Convert year, month, day to day number.
CTIME.DAYS(arg)	Convert time interval to days.
CTIME.HOURS(arg)	Convert time interval to hours.
CTIME.MINUTES(arg)	Convert time interval to minutes.

Date and time extraction functions:

XDATE.MDAY(arg)	Return day of the month.
XDATE.MONTH(arg)	Return month of the year.
XDATE.YEAR(arg)	Return four-digit year.
XDATE.HOUR(arg)	Return hour of a day.
XDATE.MINUTE(arg)	Return minute of an hour.
XDATE.SECOND(arg)	Return second of a minute.
XDATE.WKDAY(arg)	Return weekday number.
XDATE.JDAY(arg)	Return day number of day in given year.
XDATE.QUARTER(arg)	Return quarter of date in given year.
XDATE.WEEK(arg)	Return week number of date in given year.
XDATE.TDAY(arg)	Return number of days in time interval.
XDATE.TIME(arg)	Return time portion of given date and time.
XDATE.DATE(arg)	Return integral portion of date.

String functions:

ANY(arg,arg list)	Return 1 if value of argument is included on argument list.
CONCAT(arg list)	Join the arguments into a string.
INDEX(a1,a2,a3)	Return number indicating position of first occurrence of $a2$ in $a1$; optionally, $a2$ in $a3$ evenly divided substrings of $a1$.
LAG(arg,n)	Return value of argument n cases before.
LENGTH(arg)	Return length of argument.
LOWER(arg list)	Convert upper case to lower case.
LPAD(a1,a2,a3)	Left-pad beginning of $a1$ to length $a2$ with character $a3$.
LTRIM(a1,a2)	Trim character $a2$ from beginning of $a1$.
MAX(arg list)	Return maximum value of argument list.
MIN(arg list)	Return minimum value of argument list.
NUMBER(arg,format)	Convert argument into number using format.
RANGE(arg,arg list)	Return 1 if value of argument is in inclusive range of argument list.
RINDEX(a1,a2,a3)	Return number indicating rightmost occurrence of $a2$ in $a1$; optionally, $a2$ in $a3$ evenly divided substrings of $a1$.
RPAD(a1,a2,a3)	Right-pad end of $a1$ to length $a2$ with character $a3$.
RTRIM(a1,a2)	Trim character $a2$ from end of $a1$.
STRING(arg,format)	Convert argument into string using format.
SUBSTR(a1,a2,a3)	Return substring of $a1$ beginning with position $a2$ for length $a3$.
UPCASE(arg list)	Convert lower case to upper case.
MBLEN.BYTE(arg,a1)	Return the number of bytes for the character beginning at position $a1$ in the string argument. If $a1$ is not specified, it defaults to 1.

Example:

```
COMPUTE NEWVAR=RND((V1/V2)*100).
STRING DEPT(A20).
COMPUTE DEPT='PERSONNEL DEPARTMENT'.
```

Overview

COMPUTE creates new numeric variables or modifies the values of existing string or numeric variables. The variable named on the left of the equals sign is the **target variable**. The variables, constants, and functions on the right side of the equals sign form an **assignment expression**. For a complete discussion of functions, see "Transformation Expressions" on p. 43.

Numeric Transformations

Numeric variables can be created or modified with COMPUTE. The assignment expression for numeric transformations can include combinations of constants, variables, numeric operators, and functions.

String Transformations

String variables can be modified but cannot be created with COMPUTE. However, a new string variable can be declared and assigned a width with the STRING command and then assigned values by COMPUTE. The assignment expression can include string constants, string variables, and any of the string functions. All other functions are available for numeric transformations only.

Basic Specification

The basic specification is a target variable, an equals sign (required), and an assignment expression.

Syntax Rules

- The target variable must be named first, and the equals sign is required. Only one target variable is allowed per COMPUTE command.
- Numeric and string variables cannot be mixed in an expression. In addition, if the target variable is numeric, the expression must yield a numeric value; if the target variable is a string, the expression must yield a string value.
- Each function must specify at least one argument enclosed in parentheses. If a function has two or more arguments, the arguments must be separated by commas. For a complete discussion of the functions and their arguments, see "Transformation Expressions" on p. 43.
- You can use the TO keyword to refer to a set of variables where the argument is a list of variables.

Numeric Variables

- Parentheses are used to indicate the order of execution and to set off the arguments to a function.
- Numeric functions use simple or complex expressions as arguments. Expressions must be enclosed in parentheses.

String Variables

- String values and constants must be enclosed in apostrophes or quotation marks.
- When strings of different lengths are compared using the ANY or RANGE functions, the shorter string is right-padded with blanks so that its length equals that of the longer string.

Operations

- If the target variable already exists, its values are replaced.
- If the target variable does not exist and the assignment expression is numeric, the program creates a new variable.
- If the target variable does not exist and the assignment expression is a string, the program displays an error message and does not execute the command.
- COMPUTE is not executed if it contains invalid syntax. New variables are not created and existing target variables remain unchanged.

Numeric Variables

- New numeric variables created with COMPUTE are assigned a dictionary format of F8.2 and are initialized to the system-missing value for each case (unless the LEAVE command is used). Existing numeric variables transformed with COMPUTE retain their original dictionary formats. The format of a numeric variable can be changed with the FORMATS command.
- All expressions are evaluated in the following order: first functions, then exponentiation, and then arithmetic operations. The order of operations can be changed with parentheses.
- COMPUTE returns the system-missing value when it doesn't have enough information to evaluate a function properly. Arithmetic functions that take only one argument cannot be evaluated if that argument is missing. The date and time functions cannot be evaluated if any argument is missing. Statistical functions are evaluated if a sufficient number of arguments is valid. For example, in the command

```
COMPUTE FACTOR = SCORE1 + SCORE2 + SCORE3
```

FACTOR is assigned the system-missing value for a case if any of the three score values is missing. It is assigned a valid value only when all score values are valid. In the command

```
COMPUTE FACTOR = SUM(SCORE1 TO SCORE3).
```

FACTOR is assigned a valid value if at least one score value is valid. It is system-missing only when all three score values are missing.

String Variables

- String variables can be modified but not created on COMPUTE. However, a new string variable can be created and assigned a width with the STRING command and then assigned new values with COMPUTE.

- Existing string variables transformed with COMPUTE retain their original dictionary formats. String variables declared on STRING and transformed with COMPUTE retain the formats assigned to them on STRING.

- The format of string variables cannot be changed with FORMATS. Instead, use STRING to create a new variable with the desired width and then use COMPUTE to set the values of the new string equal to the values of the original.

- The string returned by a string expression does not have to be the same width as the target variable. If the target variable is shorter, the result is right-trimmed. If the target variable is longer, the result is right-padded. The program displays no warning messages when trimming or padding.

- To control the width of strings, use the functions that are available for padding (LPAD, RPAD), trimming (LTRIM, RTRIM), and selecting a portion of strings (SUBSTR).

- To determine whether a character in a string is single-byte or double-byte, use the MBLEN.BYTE function. Specify the string and, optionally, its beginning byte position. If the position is not specified, it defaults to 1.

Examples

The following examples illustrate the use of COMPUTE. For a complete discussion of each function, see "Transformation Expressions" on p. 43.

Arithmetic Operations

```
COMPUTE V1=25-V2.
COMPUTE V3=(V2/V4)*100.

DO IF TENURE GT 5.
COMPUTE RAISE=SALARY*.12.
ELSE IF TENURE GT 1.
COMPUTE RAISE=SALARY*.1.
ELSE.
COMPUTE RAISE=0.
END IF.
```

- *V1* is 25 minus *V2* for all cases. *V3* is *V2* expressed as a percentage of *V4*.

- *RAISE* is 12% of *SALARY* if *TENURE* is greater than 5. For remaining cases, *RAISE* is 10% of *SALARY* if *TENURE* is greater than 1. For all other cases, *RAISE* is 0.

Arithmetic Functions

```
COMPUTE WTCHANGE=ABS(WEIGHT1-WEIGHT2).
COMPUTE NEWVAR=RND((V1/V2)*100).
COMPUTE INCOME=TRUNC(INCOME).
COMPUTE MINSQRT=SQRT(MIN(V1,V2,V3,V4)).

COMPUTE TEST = TRUNC(SQRT(X/Y)) * .5.
COMPUTE PARENS = TRUNC(SQRT(X/Y) * .5).
```

- *WTCHANGE* is the absolute value of *WEIGHT1* minus *WEIGHT2*.

- *NEWVAR* is the percentage *V1* is of *V2*, rounded to an integer.

- *INCOME* is truncated to an integer.

- *MINSQRT* is the square root of the minimum value of the four variables *V1* to *V4*. MIN determines the minimum value of the four variables, and SQRT computes the square root.

- The last two examples above illustrate the use of parentheses to control the order of execution. For a case with value 2 for *X* and *Y*, *TEST* equals 0.5, since 2 divided by 2 (*X/Y*) is 1, the square root of 1 is 1, truncating 1 returns 1, and 1 times 0.5 is 0.5. However, *PARENS* equals 0 for the same case, since SQRT(*X/Y*) is 1, 1 times 0.5 is 0.5, and truncating 0.5 returns 0.

Statistical Functions

```
COMPUTE NEWSAL = SUM(SALARY,RAISE).
COMPUTE MINVAL = MIN(V1,V2,V3,V4).
COMPUTE MEANVAL = MEAN(V1,V2,V3,V4).
COMPUTE NEWMEAN = MEAN.3(V1,V2,V3,V4).
```

- *NEWSAL* is the sum of *SALARY* plus *RAISE*.

- *MINVAL* is the minimum of the values for *V1* to *V4*.

- *MEANVAL* is the mean of the values for *V1* to *V4*. Since the mean can be computed for one, two, three, or four values, *MEANVAL* is assigned a valid value as long as any one of the four variables has a valid value for that case.

- In the last example above, the .3 suffix specifies the minimum number of valid arguments required. *NEWMEAN* is the mean of variables *V1* to *V4* *only* if at least three of these variables have valid values. Otherwise, *NEWMEAN* is system-missing for that case.

Missing-Value Functions

```
MISSING VALUE V1 V2 V3 (0).
COMPUTE ALLVALID=V1 + V2 + V3.
COMPUTE UM=VALUE(V1) + VALUE(V2) + VALUE(V3).
COMPUTE SM=SYSMIS(V1) + SYSMIS(V2) + SYSMIS(V3).
COMPUTE M=MISSING(V1) + MISSING(V2) + MISSING(V3).
```

- The MISSING VALUE command declares value 0 as missing for *V1*, *V2*, and *V3*.

- *ALLVALID* is the sum of three variables only for cases with valid values for all three variables. *ALLVALID* is assigned the system-missing value for a case if any variable in the assignment expression has a system- or user-missing value.

- The VALUE function overrides user-missing value status. Thus, *UM* is the sum of *V1*, *V2*, and *V3* for each case, including cases with value 0 (the user-missing value) for any of the three variables. Cases with the system-missing value for *V1*, *V2*, and *V3* are system-missing.

- The SYSMIS function on the third COMPUTE returns the value 1 if the variable is system-missing. Thus, *SM* ranges from 0 to 3 for each case, depending on whether variables *V1*, *V2*, and *V3* are system-missing for that case.

- The MISSING function on the fourth COMPUTE returns the value 1 if the variable named is system- or user-missing. Thus, *M* ranges from 0 to 3 for each case, depending on whether variables *V1*, *V2*, and *V3* are user- or system-missing for that case.

- Alternatively, you could use the COUNT command to create variables *SM* and *M*.

```
* Test for listwise deletion of missing values.

DATA LIST /V1 TO V6 1-6.
BEGIN DATA
213 56
123457
123457
9234 6
END DATA.
MISSING VALUES V1 TO V6(6,9).

COMPUTE NOTVALID=NMISS(V1 TO V6).
FREQUENCIES VAR=NOTVALID.
```

- COMPUTE determines the number of missing values for each case. For each case without missing values, the value of *NOTVALID* is 0. For each case with one missing value, the value of *NOTVALID* is 1, and so on. Both system- and user-missing values are counted.

- FREQUENCIES generates a frequency table for *NOTVALID*. The table gives a count of how many cases have all valid values, how many cases have one missing value, how many cases have two missing values, and so on, for variables *V1* to *V6*. This table can be used to determine how many cases would be dropped in an analysis that uses listwise deletion of missing values. See p. 308 and p. 468 for other ways to check listwise deletion.

Cross-Case Operations

```
COMPUTE LV1=LAG(V1).
COMPUTE LV2=LAG(V2,3).
```

- *LV1* is the value of *V1* for the previous case.

- *LV2* is the value of *V2* for three cases previous. The first three cases of *LV2* receive the system-missing value.

Logical Functions

```
COMPUTE WORKERS=RANGE(AGE,18,65).
COMPUTE QSAME=ANY(Q1,Q2).
```

- *WORKERS* is 1 for cases where *AGE* is from 18 through 65, 0 for all other valid values of *AGE*, and system-missing for cases with a missing value for *AGE*.

- *QSAME* is 1 whenever *Q1* equals *Q2* and 0 whenever they are different.

Other Functions

```
COMPUTE V1=UNIFORM(10).
COMPUTE V2=NORMAL(1.5).
```

- *V1* is a pseudo-random number from a distribution with values ranging between 0 and the specified value of 10.
- *V2* is a pseudo-random number from a distribution with a mean of 0 and a standard deviation of the specified value of 1.5.
- You can change the seed value of the pseudo-random-number generator with the SEED specification on SET.

Date and Time Aggregation Functions

```
COMPUTE OCTDAY=DATE.YRDAY(1688,301).
COMPUTE QUART=DATE.QYR(QTR,YEAR).
COMPUTE WEEK=DATE.WKYR(WK,YEAR).
```

- *OCTDAY* is the 301st day of the year 1688. With a DATE format, *OCTDAY* displays as 27-OCT-1688.
- *QUART* reads values for the quarter from the variable *QTR* and values for the year from the variable *YEAR*. If *QTR* is 3 and *YEAR* is 88, *QUART* with a QDATE format displays as 3 Q 88.
- *WEEK* takes the value for the week from the variable *WK* and the value for the year from the variable *YEAR*. If *WK* is 48 and *YEAR* is 57, *WEEK* with a DATE format displays as 26-NOV-57.

Date and Time Conversion Functions

```
COMPUTE NMINS=CTIME.MINUTES(TIME.HMS(HR,MIN,SEC)).
COMPUTE AGER=(YRMODA(1992,10,01)-
              YRMODA(YRBIRTH,MOBIRTH,DABIRTH))/365.25.
```

- The CTIME.MINUTES function converts a time interval to number of minutes. If *HR* equals 12, *MIN* equals 30, and *SEC* equals 30, the TIME.HMS function returns an interval of 45,030, which CTIME.MINUTES converts to minutes. *NMINS* equals 750.50.
- The YRMODA function converts the current date (in this example, October 1, 1992) and birthdate to a number of days. The birthdate is subtracted from the current date and the remainder is divided by the number of days in a year to yield the age in years.

Date and Time Extraction Functions

```
COMPUTE MONTHNUM=XDATE.MONTH(BIRTHDAY).
COMPUTE DAYNUM=XDATE.JDAY(BIRTHDAY).
```

- The XDATE.MONTH function reads a date and returns the month number expressed as an integer from 1 to 12. If *BIRTHDAY* is formatted as DATETIME20 and contains the value 05-DEC-1954 5:30:15, *MONTHNUM* equals 12.

- The XDATE.JDAY function returns the day of the year, expressed as an integer between 1 and 366. For the value *BIRTHDAY* used by the first COMPUTE, *DAYNUM* equals 339.

Equivalence

```
STRING DEPT(A20).
COMPUTE DEPT='Personnel Department'.
COMPUTE OLDVAR=NEWVAL.
```

- *DEPT* is a new string variable and must be specified on STRING before it can be specified on COMPUTE. STRING assigns *DEPT* a width of 20 characters, and COMPUTE assigns the value *Personnel Department* to *DEPT* for each case.
- *OLDVAR* must already exist; otherwise, it would have to be declared on STRING. The values of *OLDVAR* are modified to equal the values of *NEWVAL*. *NEWVAL* must be an existing string variable. If the dictionary width of *NEWVAL* is longer than the dictionary width of *OLDVAR*, the modified values of *OLDVAR* are truncated.

String Functions

```
STRING NEWSTR(A7) / DATE(A8) / #MO #DA #YR (A2).
COMPUTE NEWSTR=LAG(OLDSTR,2).

COMPUTE #MO=STRING(MONTH,F2.0).
COMPUTE #DA=STRING(DAY,F2.0).
COMPUTE #YR=STRING(YEAR,F2.0).
COMPUTE DATE=CONCAT(#MO,'/',#DA,'/',#YR).

COMPUTE LNAME=UPCASE(LNAME).
```

- STRING declares *NEWSTR* as a new string variable with a width of seven characters, *DATE* with a width of eight characters, and scratch variables *#MO*, *#DA, and #YR* with a width of two characters each.
- The first COMPUTE sets *NEWSTR* equal to the value of *OLDSTR* for two cases previous. The first two cases receive the system-missing value for *NEWSTR*.
- The next three COMPUTE commands convert the existing numeric variables *MONTH*, *DAY*, and *YEAR* to the temporary string variables *#MO*, *#DA*, and *#YR* so that they can be used with the CONCAT function. The next COMPUTE assigns the concatenated value of *#MO*, *#DA*, and *#YR*, separated by slashes, to *DATE*. If *#MO* is 10, *#DA* is 16, and *#YR* is 49, *DATE* is 10/16/49.
- The final COMPUTE converts lowercase letters for the existing string variable *LNAME* to uppercase letters.

CORRELATIONS

```
CORRELATIONS [VARIABLES=] varlist [WITH varlist] [/varlist...]

 [/MISSING={PAIRWISE**}  [{INCLUDE}]]
           {LISTWISE }   {EXCLUDE}

 [/PRINT={TWOTAIL**}  {SIG**}]
         {ONETAIL }   {NOSIG}

 [/MATRIX=OUT({*    })]
              {file}

 [/STATISTICS=[DESCRIPTIVES] [XPROD] [ALL]]
```

**Default if the subcommand is omitted.

Example:

```
CORRELATIONS VARIABLES=FOOD RENT PUBTRANS TEACHER COOK ENGINEER
  /MISSING=INCLUDE.
```

Overview

CORRELATIONS (alias PEARSON CORR) produces Pearson product-moment correlations with significance levels and, optionally, univariate statistics, covariances, and cross-product deviations. Other procedures that produce correlation matrices are PARTIAL CORR, REGRESSION, DISCRIMINANT, and FACTOR.

Options

Types of Matrices. A simple variable list on the VARIABLES subcommand produces a square matrix. You can also request a rectangular matrix of correlations between specific pairs of variables or between variable lists using the keyword WITH on VARIABLES.

Significance Levels. By default, CORRELATIONS displays the number of cases and significance levels for each coefficient. Significance levels are based on a two-tailed test. You can request a one-tailed test, and you can display the significance level for each coefficient as an annotation using the PRINT subcommand.

Additional Statistics. You can obtain the mean, standard deviation, and number of nonmissing cases for each variable, and the cross-product deviations and covariance for each pair of variables using the STATISTICS subcommand.

Matrix Output. You can write matrix materials to a data file using the MATRIX subcommand. The matrix materials include the mean, standard deviation, number of cases used to compute each coefficient, and Pearson correlation coefficient for each variable. The matrix data file can be read by several other procedures.

Basic Specification

- The basic specification is the VARIABLES subcommand, which specifies the variables to be analyzed. The actual keyword VARIABLES can be omitted.
- By default, CORRELATIONS produces a matrix of correlation coefficients. The number of cases and the significance level are displayed for each coefficient. The significance level is based on a two-tailed test.

Subcommand Order

- The VARIABLES subcommand must be first.
- The remaining subcommands can be specified in any order.

Operations

- The correlation of a variable with itself is displayed as 1.0000.
- A correlation that cannot be computed is displayed as a period (.).
- CORRELATIONS does not execute if long or short string variables are specified on the variable list.

Limitations

- Maximum 40 variable lists.
- Maximum 500 variables total per command.
- Maximum 250 syntax elements. Each individual occurrence of a variable name, keyword, or special delimiter counts as 1 toward this total. Variables implied by the TO keyword do not count toward this total.

Example

```
CORRELATIONS VARIABLES=FOOD RENT PUBTRANS TEACHER COOK ENGINEER
  /VARIABLES=FOOD RENT WITH COOK TEACHER MANAGER ENGINEER
  /MISSING=INCLUDE.
```

- The first VARIABLES subcommand requests a square matrix of correlation coefficients among variables *FOOD*, *RENT*, *PUBTRANS*, *TEACHER*, *COOK*, and *ENGINEER*.
- The second VARIABLES subcommand requests a rectangular correlation matrix in which *FOOD* and *RENT* are the row variables and *COOK*, *TEACHER*, *MANAGER*, and *ENGINEER* are the column variables.
- MISSING requests that user-missing values be included in the computation of each coefficient.

VARIABLES Subcommand

VARIABLES specifies the variable list. The actual keyword VARIABLES is optional.

- A simple variable list produces a square matrix of correlations of each variable with every other variable.
- Variable lists joined by the keyword WITH produce a rectangular correlation matrix. Variables before WITH define the rows of the matrix and variables after WITH define the columns.
- The keyword ALL can be used on the variable list to refer to all user-defined variables.
- You can specify multiple VARIABLES subcommands on a single CORRELATIONS command. The slash between the subcommands is required; the keyword VARIABLES is not.

PRINT Subcommand

PRINT controls whether the significance level is based on a one- or two-tailed test and whether the number of cases and the significance level for each correlation coefficient are displayed.

TWOTAIL   *Two-tailed test of significance.* This test is appropriate when the direction of the relationship cannot be determined in advance, as is often the case in exploratory data analysis. This is the default.

ONETAIL   *One-tailed test of significance.* This test is appropriate when the direction of the relationship between a pair of variables can be specified in advance of the analysis.

SIG   *Display the significance level.* SIG is the default.

NOSIG   *Display the significance level in an annotation.*

STATISTICS Subcommand

The correlation coefficients are automatically displayed in the Correlations table for an analysis specified by a VARIABLES list. STATISTICS requests additional statistics.

DESCRIPTIVES   *Display mean, standard deviation, and number of nonmissing cases for each variable on the Variables list in the Descriptive Statistics table.* This table precedes all Correlations tables. Variables specified on more than one VARIABLES lists are displayed only once. Missing values are handled on a variable-by-variable basis regardless of the missing-value option in effect for the correlations.

XPROD   *Display cross-product deviations and covariance for each pair of variables in the Correlations table(s).*

ALL   *All additional statistics.* This produces the same statistics as DESCRIPTIVES and XPROD together.

MISSING Subcommand

MISSING controls the treatment of missing values.

- The PAIRWISE and LISTWISE keywords are alternatives; however, each can be specified with INCLUDE or EXCLUDE.
- The default is LISTWISE and EXCLUDE.

PAIRWISE *Exclude missing values pairwise.* Cases that have missing values for one or both of a pair of variables for a specific correlation coefficient are excluded from the computation of that coefficient. Since each coefficient is based on all cases that have valid values for that particular pair of variables, this can result in a set of coefficients based on a varying number of cases. The valid number of cases is displayed in the Correlations table. This is the default.

LISTWISE *Exclude missing values listwise.* Cases that have missing values for any variable named on any VARIABLES list are excluded from the computation of all coefficients across lists. The valid number of cases is the same for all analyses and is displayed in a single annotation.

INCLUDE *Include user-missing values.* User-missing values are included in the analysis.

EXCLUDE *Exclude all missing values.* Both user- and system-missing values are excluded from the analysis.

MATRIX Subcommand

MATRIX writes matrix materials to a data file. The matrix materials include the mean and standard deviation for each variable, the number of cases used to compute each coefficient, and the Pearson correlation coefficients. Several procedures can read matrix materials produced by CORRELATIONS, including PARTIAL CORR, REGRESSION, FACTOR, and CLUSTER (see "SPSS Matrix Data Files" on p. 23).

- CORRELATIONS cannot write rectangular matrices (those specified with the keyword WITH) to a file.
- If you specify more than one variable list on CORRELATIONS, only the last list that does not use the keyword WITH is written to the matrix data file.
- The keyword OUT specifies the file to which the matrix is written. The filename must be specified in parentheses.
- Documents from the original file will not be included in the matrix file and will not be present if the matrix file becomes the working data file.

OUT (filename) *Write a matrix data file.* Specify either a file or an asterisk (*), enclosed in parentheses. If you specify a file, the file is stored on disk and can be retrieved at any time. If you specify an asterisk, the matrix data file replaces the working file but is not stored on disk unless you use SAVE or XSAVE.

Format of the Matrix Data File

- The matrix data file has two special variables created by the program: *ROWTYPE_* and *VARNAME_*. The variable *ROWTYPE_* is a short string variable with values *MEAN*, *STDDEV*, *N*, and *CORR* (for Pearson correlation coefficient). The next variable, *VARNAME_*, is a short string variable whose values are the names of the variables used to form the correlation matrix. When *ROWTYPE_* is *CORR*, *VARNAME_* gives the variable associated with that row of the correlation matrix.
- The remaining variables in the file are the variables used to form the correlation matrix.

Split Files

- When split-file processing is in effect, the first variables in the matrix file will be split variables, followed by *ROWTYPE_*, *VARNAME_*, and the variables used to form the correlation matrix.
- A full set of matrix materials is written for each subgroup defined by the split variables.
- A split variable cannot have the same name as any other variable written to the matrix data file.
- If split-file processing is in effect when a matrix is written, the same split-file specifications must be in effect when that matrix is read by another procedure.

Missing Values

- With pairwise treatment of missing values (the default), a matrix of the number of cases used to compute each coefficient is included with the matrix materials.
- With listwise treatment, a single number indicating the number of cases used to calculate all coefficients is included.

Example

```
GET FILE=CITY /KEEP FOOD RENT PUBTRANS TEACHER COOK ENGINEER.
CORRELATIONS VARIABLES=FOOD TO ENGINEER
 /MATRIX OUT(CORRMAT).
```

- CORRELATIONS reads data from the file *CITY* and writes one set of matrix materials to the file *CORRMAT*. The working file is still *CITY*. Subsequent commands are executed on *CITY*.

Example

```
GET FILE=CITY /KEEP FOOD RENT PUBTRANS TEACHER COOK ENGINEER.
CORRELATIONS VARIABLES=FOOD TO ENGINEER
 /MATRIX OUT(*).
LIST.
DISPLAY DICTIONARY.
```

- CORRELATIONS writes the same matrix as in the example above. However, the matrix data file replaces the working file. The LIST and DISPLAY commands are executed on the matrix file, not on the *CITY* file.

Example

```
CORRELATIONS VARIABLES=FOOD RENT COOK TEACHER MANAGER ENGINEER
 /FOOD TO TEACHER /PUBTRANS WITH MECHANIC
 /MATRIX OUT(*).
```

- Only the matrix for *FOOD* TO *TEACHER* is written to the matrix data file because it is the last variable list that does not use the keyword WITH.

COUNT

```
COUNT varname=varlist(value list) [/varname=...]
```

Keywords for numeric value lists:

LOWEST, LO, HIGHEST, HI, THRU, MISSING, SYSMIS

Example:
```
COUNT TARGET=V1 V2 V3 (2).
```

Overview

COUNT creates a numeric variable that, for each case, counts the occurrences of the same value (or list of values) across a list of variables. The new variable is called the *target* variable. The variables and values that are counted are the *criterion* variables and values. Criterion variables can be either numeric or string.

Basic Specification

The basic specification is the target variable, an equals sign, the criterion variable(s), and the criterion value(s) enclosed in parentheses.

Syntax Rules

- Use a slash to separate the specifications for each target variable.
- The criterion variables specified for a single target variable must be either all numeric or all string.
- Each value on a list of criterion values must be separated by a comma or space. String values must be enclosed in apostrophes.
- The keywords THRU, LOWEST (LO), HIGHEST (HI), SYSMIS, and MISSING can be used only with numeric criterion variables.
- A variable can be specified on more than one criterion variable list.
- You can use the keyword TO to specify consecutive criterion variables that have the same criterion value or values.
- You can specify multiple variable lists for a single target variable to count different values for different variables.

Operations

- Target variables are always numeric and are initialized to 0 for each case. They are assigned a dictionary format of F8.2.
- If the target variable already exists, its previous values are replaced.
- COUNT ignores the missing-value status of user-missing values. It counts a value even if that value has been previously declared as missing.
- The target variable is never system-missing. To define user-missing values for target variables, use the RECODE or MISSING VALUES command.
- SYSMIS counts system-missing values for numeric variables.
- MISSING counts both user- and system-missing values for numeric variables.

Example

```
COUNT TARGET=V1 V2 V3 (2).
```

- The value of *TARGET* for each case will be either 0, 1, 2, or 3, depending on the number of times the value 2 occurs across the three variables for each case.
- *TARGET* is a numeric variable with an F8.2 format.

Example

```
COUNT QLOW=Q1 TO Q10 (LO THRU 0)
     /QSYSMIS=Q1 TO Q10 (SYSMIS).
```

- Assuming that there are 10 variables between and including *Q1* and *Q10* in the working data file, *QLOW* ranges from 0 to 10, depending on the number of times a case has a negative or 0 value across the variables *Q1* to *Q10*.
- *QSYSMIS* ranges from 0 to 10, depending on how many system-missing values are encountered for *Q1* to *Q10* for each case. User-missing values are not counted.
- Both *QLOW* and *QSYSMIS* are numeric variables and have F8.2 formats.

Example

```
COUNT SVAR=V1 V2 ('male  ') V3 V4 V5 ('female').
```

- *SVAR* ranges from 0 to 5, depending on the number of times a case has a value of male for *V1* and *V2* and a value of female for *V3*, *V4*, and *V5*.
- *SVAR* is a numeric variable with an F8.2 format.

CREATE

```
CREATE new series={CSUM (series)                              }
                   {DIFF (series, order)                       }
                   {FFT (series)                               }
                   {IFFT (series)                              }
                   {LAG (series, order [,order ])              }
                   {LEAD (series, order [,order ])             }
                   {MA (series, span [,minimum span])          }
                   {PMA (series, span)                         }
                   {RMED (series, span [,minimum span])        }
                   {SDIFF (series, order [,periodicity])}      }
                   {T4253H (series)                            }

[/new series=function (series {,span   {,minimum span}})]
                              {,order  {,order        }}
                                       {,periodicity  }
```

Function keywords:

CSUM	Cumulative sum
DIFF	Difference
FFT	Fast Fourier transform
IFFT	Inverse fast Fourier transform
LAG	Lag
LEAD	Lead
MA	Centered moving averages
PMA	Prior moving averages
RMED	Running medians
SDIFF	Seasonal difference
T4253H	Smoothing

Example:

```
CREATE NEWVAR1 NEWVAR2 = CSUM(TICKETS RNDTRP).
```

Overview

CREATE produces new series as a function of existing series. You can also use CREATE to replace the values of existing series. The new or revised series can be used in any procedure and can be saved in an SPSS-format data file.

CREATE displays a list of the new series, the case numbers of the first and last nonmissing cases, the number of valid cases, and the functions used to create the variables.

Basic Specification

The basic specification is a new series name, an equals sign, a function, and the existing series, along with any additional specifications needed.

Syntax Rules

- The existing series together with any additional specifications (order, span, or periodicity) must be enclosed in parentheses.
- The equals sign is required.
- Series names and additional specifications must be separated by commas or spaces.
- You can specify only one function per equation.
- You can create more than one new series per equation by specifying more than one new series name on the left side of the equation and either multiple existing series names or multiple orders on the right.
- The number of new series named on the left side of the equation must equal the number of series created on the right. Note that the FFT function creates two new series for each existing series, and IFFT creates one series from two existing series.
- You can specify more than one equation on a CREATE command. Equations are separated by slashes.
- A newly created series can be specified in subsequent equations on the same CREATE command.

Operations

- Each new series created is added to the working data file.
- If the new series named already exist, their values are replaced.
- If the new series named do not already exist, they are created.
- Series are created in the order in which they are specified on the CREATE command.
- If multiple series are created by a single equation, the first new series named is assigned the values of the first series created, the second series named is assigned the values of the second series created, and so on.
- CREATE automatically generates a variable label for each new series describing the function and series used to create it.
- The format of the new series is based on the function specified and the format of the existing series.
- CREATE honors the TSET MISSING setting that is currently in effect.
- CREATE does not honor the USE command.
- When an even-length span is specified for functions MA and RMED, the centering algorithm uses an average of two spans of the specified length. The first span ranges from span/2 cases before the current observation to the span length. The second span ranges from (span/2)−1 cases before the current observation to the span length.

Limitations

- Maximum 1 function per equation.
- There is no limit on the number of series created by an equation.
- There is no limit on the number of equations.

Example

```
CREATE NEWVAR1 = DIFF(OLDVAR,1).
```

- In this example, the series *NEWVAR1* is created by taking the first-order difference of *OLDVAR*.

CSUM Function

CSUM produces new series based on the cumulative sums of the existing series. Cumulative sums are the inverse of first-order differencing.

- The only specification on CSUM is the name or names of the existing series in parentheses.
- Cases with missing values in the existing series are not used to compute values for the new series. The values of these cases are system-missing in the new series.

Example

```
CREATE NEWVAR1 NEWVAR2 = CSUM(TICKETS RNDTRP).
```

- This example produces a new series called *NEWVAR1*, which is the cumulative sum of the series *TICKETS*, and a new series called *NEWVAR2*, which is the cumulative sum of the series *RNDTRP*.

DIFF Function

DIFF produces new series based on nonseasonal differences of existing series.

- The specification on DIFF is the name or names of the existing series and the degree of differencing, in parentheses.
- The degree of differencing must be specified; there is no default.
- Since one observation is lost for each order of differencing, system-missing values will appear at the beginning of the new series.
- You can specify only one degree of differencing per DIFF function.
- If either of the pair of values involved in a difference computation is missing, the result is set to system-missing in the new series.

Example

```
CREATE ADIF2 = DIFF(VARA,2) /
       YDIF1 ZDIF1 = DIFF(VARY VARZ,1).
```

- The series *ADIF2* is created by differencing *VARA* twice.
- The series *YDIF1* is created by differencing *VARY* once.
- The series *ZDIF1* is created by differencing *VARZ* once.

FFT Function

FFT produces new series based on fast Fourier transformations of existing series (Brigham, 1974).

- The only specification on FFT is the name or names of the existing series in parentheses.

- FFT creates two series, the cosine and sine parts (also called real and imaginary parts), for each existing series named. Thus, you must specify two new series names on the left side of the equation for each existing series specified on the right side.

- The first new series named becomes the real series, and the second new series named becomes the imaginary series.

- The existing series cannot have imbedded missing values.

- The existing series must be of even length. If an odd-length series is specified, FFT pads it with a 0 to make it even. Alternatively, you can make the series even by adding or dropping an observation.

- The new series will be only half as long as the existing series. The remaining cases are assigned the system-missing value.

Example

```
CREATE A B = FFT(C).
```

- Two series, *A* (real) and *B* (imaginary), are created by applying a fast Fourier transformation to series *C*.

IFFT Function

IFFT produces new series based on the inverse Fourier transformation of existing series.

- The only specification on IFFT is the name or names of the existing series in parentheses.

- IFFT needs two existing series to compute each new series. Thus, you must specify two existing series names on the right side of the equation for each new series specified on the left.

- The first existing series specified is the real series and the second series is the imaginary.

- The existing series cannot have imbedded missing values.

- The new series will be twice as long as the existing series. Thus, the last half of each existing series must be system-missing to allow enough room to create the new series.

Example

```
CREATE C = IFFT(A B).
```

- This command creates one new series, *C*, from the series *A* (real) and *B* (imaginary).

LAG Function

LAG creates new series by copying the values of the existing series and moving them forward the specified number of observations. This number is called the **lag order**. Table 1 shows a first-order lag for a hypothetical data set.

- The specification on LAG is the name or names of the existing series and one or two lag orders, in parentheses.

- At least one lag order must be specified; there is no default.

- Two lag orders indicate a range. For example, 2,6 indicates lag orders two through six. A new series is created for each lag order in the range.

- The number of new series specified must equal the number of existing series specified times the number of lag orders in the range.

- The first *n* cases at the beginning of the new series, where *n* is the lag order, are assigned the system-missing value.

- Missing values in the existing series are lagged and are assigned the system-missing value in the new series.

- A first-order lagged series can also be created using COMPUTE. COMPUTE does not cause a data pass (see COMPUTE).

Table 1   First-order lag and lead of series X

X	Lag	Lead
198	.	220
220	198	305
305	220	470
470	305	.

Example

```
CREATE LAGVAR2 TO LAGVAR5 = LAG(VARA,2,5).
```

- Four new variables are created based on lags on *VARA*. *LAGVAR2* is *VARA* lagged two steps, *LAGVAR3* is *VARA* lagged three steps, *LAGVAR4* is *VARA* lagged four steps, and *LAGVAR5* is *VARA* lagged five steps.

LEAD Function

LEAD creates new series by copying the values of the existing series and moving them back the specified number of observations. This number is called the lead order. Table 1 shows a first-order lead for a hypothetical data set.

- The specification on LEAD is the name or names of the existing series and one or two lead orders, in parentheses.

- At least one lead order must be specified; there is no default.

- Two lead orders indicate a range. For example, 1,5 indicates lead orders one through five. A new series is created for each lead order in the range.
- The number of new series must equal the number of existing series specified times the number of lead orders in the range.
- The last *n* cases at the end of the new series, where *n* equals the lead order, are assigned the system-missing value.
- Missing values in the existing series are moved back and are assigned the system-missing value in the new series.

Example

```
CREATE LEAD1 TO LEAD4 = LEAD(VARA,1,4).
```

- Four new series are created based on leads of *VARA*. *LEAD1* is *VARA* led one step, *LEAD2* is *VARA* led two steps, *LEAD3* is *VARA* led three steps, and *LEAD4* is *VARA* led four steps.

MA Function

MA produces new series based on the centered moving averages of existing series.

- The specification on MA is the name or names of the existing series and the span to be used in averaging, in parentheses.
- A span must be specified; there is no default.
- If the specified span is odd, the MA is naturally associated with the middle term. If the specified span is even, the MA is centered by averaging each pair of uncentered means (Velleman and Hoaglin, 1981).
- After the initial span, a second span can be specified to indicate the minimum number of values to use in averaging when the number specified for the initial span is unavailable. This makes it possible to produce nonmissing values at or near the ends of the new series.
- The second span must be greater than or equal to 1 and less than or equal to the first span.
- The second span should be even (or 1) if the first span is even; it should be odd if the first span is odd. Otherwise, the next higher span value will be used.
- If no second span is specified, the minimum span is simply the value of the first span.
- If the number of values specified for the span or the minimum span is not available, the case in the new series is set to system-missing. Thus, unless a minimum span of 1 is specified, the endpoints of the new series will contain system-missing values.
- When MA encounters an imbedded missing value in the existing series, it creates two subsets, one containing cases before the missing value and one containing cases after the missing value. Each subset is treated as a separate series for computational purposes.
- The endpoints of these subset series will have missing values according to the rules described above for the endpoints of the entire series. Thus, if the minimum span is 1, the endpoints of the subsets will be nonmissing; the only cases that will be missing in the new series are cases that were missing in the original series.

Example

```
CREATE TICKMA = MA(TICKETS,4,2).
```

- This example creates the series *TICKMA* based on centered moving average values of the series *TICKETS*.
- A span of 4 is used for computing averages. At the endpoints, where four values are not available, the average is based on the specified minimum of two values.

PMA Function

PMA creates new series based on the prior moving averages of existing series. The prior moving average for each case in the original series is computed by averaging the values of a span of cases preceding it.

- The specification on PMA is the name or names of the existing series and the span to be used, in parentheses.
- Only one span can be specified and it is required. There is no default span.
- If the number of values specified for the span is not available, the case is set to system-missing. Thus, the number of cases with system-missing values at the beginning of the new series equals the number specified for the span.
- When PMA encounters an imbedded missing value in the existing series, it creates two subsets, one containing cases before the missing value and one containing cases after the missing value. Each subset is treated as a separate series for computational purposes. The first n cases in the second subset will be system-missing, where n is the span.

Example

```
CREATE PRIORA = PMA(VARA,3).
```

- This command creates series *PRIORA* by computing prior moving averages for series *VARA*. Since the span is 3, the first three cases in series *PRIORA* are system-missing. The fourth case equals the average of cases 1, 2, and 3 of *VARA*, the fifth case equals the average of cases 2, 3, and 4 of *VARA*, and so on.

RMED Function

RMED produces new series based on the centered running medians of existing series.

- The specification on RMED is the name or names of the existing series and the span to be used in finding the median, in parentheses.
- A span must be specified; there is no default.
- If the specified span is odd, RMED is naturally the middle term. If the specified span is even, the RMED is centered by averaging each pair of uncentered medians (Velleman and Hoaglin, 1981).
- After the initial span, a second span can be specified to indicate the minimum number of values to use in finding the median when the number specified for the initial span is unavailable. This makes it possible to produce nonmissing values at or near the ends of the new series.

- The second span must be greater than or equal to 1 and less than or equal to the first span.
- The second span should be even (or 1) if the first span is even; it should be odd if the first span is odd. Otherwise, the next higher span value will be used.
- If no second span is specified, the minimum span is simply the value of the first span.
- If the number of values specified for the span or the minimum span is not available, the case in the new series is set to system-missing. Thus, unless a minimum span of 1 is specified, the endpoints of the new series will contain system-missing values.
- When RMED encounters an imbedded missing value in the existing series, it creates two subsets, one containing cases before the missing value and one containing cases after the missing value. Each subset is treated as a separate series for computational purposes.
- The endpoints of these subset series will have missing values according to the rules described above for the endpoints of the entire series. Thus, if the minimum span is 1, the endpoints of the subsets will be nonmissing; the only cases that will be missing in the new series are cases that were missing in the original series.

Example

```
CREATE TICKRMED = RMED(TICKETS,4,2).
```

- This example creates the series *TICKRMED* using centered running median values of the series *TICKETS*.
- A span of 4 is used for computing medians. At the endpoints, where four values are not available, the median is based on the specified minimum of two values.

SDIFF Function

SDIFF produces new series based on seasonal differences of existing series.
- The specification on SDIFF is the name or names of the existing series, the degree of differencing, and, optionally, the periodicity, all in parentheses.
- The degree of differencing must be specified; there is no default.
- Since the number of seasons used in the calculations decreases by 1 for each order of differencing, system-missing values will appear at the beginning of the new series.
- You can specify only one degree of differencing per SDIFF function.
- If no periodicity is specified, the periodicity established on TSET PERIOD is in effect. If TSET PERIOD has not been specified, the periodicity established on the DATE command is used. If periodicity was not established anywhere, the SDIFF function cannot be executed.
- If either of the pair of values involved in a seasonal difference computation is missing, the result is set to system-missing in the new series.

Example

```
CREATE SDVAR = SDIFF(VARA,1,12).
```

- The series *SDVAR* is created by applying one seasonal difference with a periodicity of 12 to the series *VARA*.

T4253H Function

T4253H produces new series by applying a compound data smoother to the original series. The smoother starts with a running median of 4, which is centered by a running median of 2. It then resmooths these values by applying a running median of 5, a running median of 3, and hanning (running weighted averages). Residuals are computed by subtracting the smoothed series from the original series. This whole process is then repeated on the computed residuals. Finally, the smoothed residuals are added to the smoothed values obtained the first time through the process (Velleman and Hoaglin, 1981).

- The only specification on T4253H is the name or names of the existing series in parentheses.
- The existing series cannot contain imbedded missing values.
- Endpoints are smoothed through extrapolation and are not system-missing.

Example

```
CREATE SMOOTHA = T4253H(VARA).
```

- The series *SMOOTHA* is a smoothed version of the series *VARA*.

References

Box, G. E. P., and G. M. Jenkins. 1976. *Time series analysis: Forecasting and control.* San Francisco: Holden-Day.

Brigham, E. O. 1974. *The fast Fourier transform.* Englewood Cliffs, N.J.: Prentice-Hall.

Cryer, J. D. 1986. *Time series analysis.* Boston: Duxbury Press.

Makridakis, S., S. C. Wheelwright, and V. E. McGee. 1983. *Forecasting: Methods and applications.* New York: John Wiley and Sons.

Monro, D. M. 1975. Algorithm AS 83: Complex discrete fast Fourier transform. *Applied Statistics,* 24: 153–160.

Monro, D. M., and J. L. Branch. 1977. Algorithm AS 117: The Chirp discrete Fourier transform of general length. *Applied Statistics,* 26: 351–361.

Velleman, P. F., and D. C. Hoaglin. 1981. *Applications, basics, and computing of exploratory data analysis.* Boston: Duxbury Press.

CROSSTABS

General mode:

```
CROSSTABS [TABLES=]varlist BY varlist [BY...] [/varlist...]

  [/MISSING={TABLE**}]
           {INCLUDE}

  [/WRITE[={NONE**}]]
          {CELLS }
```

Integer mode:

```
CROSSTABS VARIABLES=varlist(min,max) [varlist...]

  /TABLES=varlist BY varlist [BY...] [/varlist...]

  [/MISSING={TABLE**}]
           {INCLUDE}
           {REPORT }

  [/WRITE[={NONE**}]]
          {CELLS }
          {ALL   }
```

Both modes:

```
  [/FORMAT= {AVALUE**}   {TABLES**}]
            {DVALUE  }   {NOTABLES}

  [/CELLS=[{COUNT**}]  [ROW     ]  [EXPECTED]  [SRESID ]]
          {NONE    }   [COLUMN]    [RESID   ]  [ASRESID]
                       [TOTAL  ]               [ALL    ]

  [/STATISTICS=[CHISQ]  [LAMBDA]  [BTAU ]  [GAMMA   ]  [ETA    ]]
               [PHI  ]  [UC    ]  [CTAU ]  [D       ]  [CORR   ]
               [CC   ]  [RISK  ]  [KAPPA]  [MCNEMAR]   [CMH(1*)]
               [ALL  ]  [NONE  ]

  [/METHOD={MC [CIN({99.0 })] [SAMPLES({10000})]]}]††
               {value}               {value}
           {EXACT [TIMER({5     })]                 }
                        {value}

  [/BARCHART]
```

**Default if the subcommand is omitted.

†† The **METHOD** subcommand is available only if the Exact Tests option is installed.

Example:

```
CROSSTABS TABLES=FEAR BY SEX
 /CELLS=ROW COLUMN EXPECTED RESIDUALS
 /STATISTICS=CHISQ.
```

Overview

CROSSTABS produces contingency tables showing the joint distribution of two or more variables that have a limited number of distinct values. The frequency distribution of one variable is subdivided according to the values of one or more variables. The unique combination of values for two or more variables defines a cell.

CROSSTABS can operate in two different modes: *general* and *integer*. Integer mode builds some tables more efficiently but requires more specifications than general mode. Some subcommand specifications and statistics are available only in integer mode.

Options

Methods for building tables. To build tables in general mode, use the TABLES subcommand. Integer mode requires the TABLES and VARIABLES subcommands and minimum and maximum values for the variables.

Cell contents. By default, CROSSTABS displays only the number of cases in each cell. You can request row, column, and total percentages, and also expected values and residuals by using the CELLS subcommand.

Statistics. In addition to the tables, you can obtain measures of association and tests of hypotheses for each subtable using the STATISTICS subcommand.

Formatting options. With the FORMAT subcommand, you can control the display order for categories in rows and columns of subtables and suppress crosstabulation.

Writing and reproducing tables. You can write cell frequencies to a file and reproduce the original tables with the WRITE subcommand.

Basic Specification

In general mode, the basic specification is TABLES with a table list. The actual keyword TABLES can be omitted. In integer mode, the minimum specification is the VARIABLES subcommand, specifying the variables to be used and their value ranges, and the TABLES subcommand with a table list.

- The minimum table list specifies a list of row variables, the keyword BY, and a list of column variables.
- In integer mode, all variables must be numeric with integer values. In general mode, variables can be numeric (integer or non-integer) or string.
- The default table shows cell counts.

Subcommand Order

- In general mode, the table list must be first if the keyword TABLES is omitted. If the keyword TABLES is explicitly used, subcommands can be specified in any order.
- In integer mode, VARIABLES must precede TABLES. The keyword TABLES must be explicitly specified.

Operations

- Integer mode builds tables more quickly but requires more workspace if a table has many empty cells.
- If a long string variable is used in general mode, only the short string portion (first eight characters) is tabulated.
- Statistics are calculated separately for each two-way table or two-way subtable. Missing values are reported for the table as a whole.
- In general mode, the keyword TO on the TABLES subcommand refers to the order of variables in the working file. ALL refers to all variables in the working file. In integer mode, TO and ALL refer to the position and subset of variables specified on the VARIABLES subcommand.

Limitations

The following limitations apply to CROSSTABS in *general mode*:
- Maximum 200 variables named or implied on the TABLES subcommand
- Maximum 1000 non-empty rows or columns for each table
- Maximum 20 table lists per CROSSTABS command
- Maximum 10 dimensions (9 BY keywords) per table
- Maximum 400 value labels displayed on any single table

The following limitations apply to CROSSTABS in *integer mode*:
- Maximum 100 variables named or implied on the VARIABLES subcommand
- Maximum 100 variables named or implied on the TABLES subcommand
- Maximum 1000 non-empty rows or columns for each table
- Maximum 20 table lists per CROSSTABS command
- Maximum 8 dimensions (7 BY keywords) per table
- Maximum 20 rows or columns of missing values when REPORT is specified on MISSING
- Minimum value that can be specified is –99,999
- Maximum value that can be specified is 999,999

Example

```
CROSSTABS TABLES=FEAR BY SEX
 /CELLS=ROW COLUMN EXPECTED RESIDUALS
 /STATISTICS=CHISQ.
```

- CROSSTABS generates a Case Processing Summary table, a Crosstabulation table, and a Chi-Square Tests table.
- The variable *FEAR* defines the rows and the variable *SEX* defines the columns of the Crosstabulation table. CELLS requests row and column percentages, expected cell frequencies, and residuals.

- STATISTICS requests the chi-square statistics displayed in the Chi-Square Tests table.

Example

```
CROSSTABS TABLES=JOBCAT BY EDCAT BY SEX BY INCOME3.
```

- This table list produces a subtable of *JOBCAT* by *EDCAT* for each combination of values of *SEX* and *INCOME3*.

VARIABLES Subcommand

The VARIABLES subcommand is required for integer mode. VARIABLES specifies a list of variables to be used in the crosstabulations and the lowest and highest values for each variable. Values are specified in parentheses and must be integers. Non-integer values are truncated.

- Variables can be specified in any order. However, the order in which they are named on VARIABLES determines their implied order on TABLES (see the TABLES subcommand below).
- A range must be specified for each variable. If several variables can have the same range, it can be specified once after the last variable to which it applies.
- CROSSTABS uses the specified ranges to allocate tables. One cell is allocated for each possible combination of values of the row and column variables before the data are read. Thus, if the specified ranges are larger than the actual ranges, workspace will be wasted.
- Cases with values outside the specified range are considered missing and are not used in the computation of the table. This allows you to select a subset of values within CROSSTABS.
- If the table is sparse because the variables do not have values throughout the specified range, consider using general mode or recoding the variables.

Example

```
CROSSTABS VARIABLES=FEAR SEX RACE (1,2) MOBILE16 (1,3)
  /TABLES=FEAR BY SEX MOBILE16 BY RACE.
```

- VARIABLES defines values 1 and 2 for *FEAR*, *SEX*, and *RACE*, and values 1, 2, and 3 for *MOBILE16*.

TABLES Subcommand

TABLES specifies the table lists and is required in both integer mode and general mode. The following rules apply to both modes:

- You can specify multiple TABLES subcommands on a single CROSSTABS command. The slash between the subcommands is required; the keyword TABLES is required only in integer mode.
- Variables named before the first BY on a table list are row variables, and variables named after the first BY on a table list are column variables.

- When the table list specifies two dimensions (one BY keyword), the first variable before BY is crosstabulated with each variable after BY, then the second variable before BY with each variable after BY, and so on.
- Each subsequent use of the keyword BY on a table list adds a new dimension to the tables requested. Variables named after the second (or subsequent) BY are control variables.
- When the table list specifies more than two dimensions, a two-way subtable is produced for each combination of values of control variables. The value of the last specified control variable changes the most slowly in determining the order in which tables are displayed.
- You can name more than one variable in each dimension.

General Mode

- The actual keyword TABLES can be omitted in general mode.
- In general mode, both numeric and string variables can be specified. Long strings are truncated to short strings for defining categories.
- The keywords ALL and TO can be specified in any dimension. In general mode, TO refers to the order of variables in the working data file and ALL refers to all variables defined in the working data file.

Example

```
CROSSTABS  TABLES=FEAR BY SEX BY RACE.
```

- This example crosstabulates *FEAR* by *SEX* controlling for *RACE*. In each subtable, *FEAR* is the row variable and *SEX* is the column variable.
- A subtable is produced for each value of the control variable *RACE*.

Example

```
CROSSTABS  TABLES=CONFINAN TO CONARMY BY SEX TO REGION.
```

- This command produces crosstabulations of all variables in the working data file between and including *CONFINAN* and *CONARMY* by all variables between and including *SEX* and *REGION*.

Integer Mode

- In integer mode, variables specified on TABLES must first be named on VARIABLES.
- The keywords TO and ALL can be specified in any dimension. In integer mode, TO and ALL refer to the position and subset of variables specified on the VARIABLES subcommand, not to the variables in the working data file.

Example

```
CROSSTABS  VARIABLES=FEAR (1,2) MOBILE16 (1,3)
    /TABLES=FEAR BY MOBILE16.
```

- VARIABLES names two variables, *FEAR* and *MOBILE16*. Values 1 and 2 for *FEAR* are used in the tables, and values 1, 2, and 3 are used for the variable *MOBILE16*.

- TABLES specifies a Crosstabulation table with two rows (values 1 and 2 for *FEAR*) and three columns (values 1, 2, and 3 for *MOBILE16*). *FEAR* and *MOBILE16* can be named on TABLES because they were named on the previous VARIABLES subcommand.

Example

```
CROSSTABS  VARIABLES=FEAR SEX RACE DEGREE (1,2)
  /TABLES=FEAR BY SEX BY RACE BY DEGREE.
```

- This command produces four subtables. The first subtable crosstabulates *FEAR* by *SEX*, controlling for the first value of *RACE* and the first value of *DEGREE*; the second subtable controls for the second value of *RACE* and the first value of *DEGREE*; the third subtable controls for the first value of *RACE* and the second value of *DEGREE*; and the fourth subtable controls for the second value of *RACE* and the second value of *DEGREE*.

CELLS Subcommand

By default, CROSSTABS displays only the number of cases in each cell of the Crosstabulation table. Use CELLS to display row, column, or total percentages, expected counts, or residuals. These are calculated separately for each Crosstabulation table or subtable.

- CELLS specified without keywords displays cell counts plus row, column, and total percentages for each cell.
- If CELLS is specified with keywords, CROSSTABS displays only the requested cell information.
- Scientific notation is used for cell contents when necessary.

COUNT	*Observed cell counts.* This is the default if CELLS is omitted.
ROW	*Row percentages.* The number of cases in each cell in a row is expressed as a percentage of all cases in that row.
COLUMN	*Column percentages.* The number of cases in each cell in a column is expressed as a percentage of all cases in that column.
TOTAL	*Two-way table total percentages.* The number of cases in each cell of a subtable is expressed as a percentage of all cases in that subtable.
EXPECTED	*Expected counts.* Expected counts are the number of cases expected in each cell if the two variables in the subtable are statistically independent.
RESID	*Residuals.* Residuals are the difference between the observed and expected cell counts.
SRESID	*Standardized residuals* (Haberman, 1978).
ASRESID	*Adjusted standardized residuals* (Haberman, 1978).
ALL	*All cell information.* This includes cell counts; row, column, and total percentages; expected counts; residuals; standardized residuals; and adjusted standardized residuals.

NONE   *No cell information.* Use NONE when you want to write tables to a procedure output file without displaying them (see the WRITE subcommand on p. 216). This is the same as specifying NOTABLES on FORMAT.

STATISTICS Subcommand

STATISTICS requests measures of association and related statistics. By default, CROSSTABS does not display any additional statistics.

- STATISTICS without keywords displays the chi-square test.
- If STATISTICS is specified with keywords, CROSSTABS calculates only the requested statistics.
- In integer mode, values that are not included in the specified range are *not* used in the calculation of the statistics, even if these values exist in the data.
- If user-missing values are included with MISSING, cases with user-missing values are included in the calculation of statistics as well as in the tables.

CHISQ   *Display the Chi-Square Test table.* Chi-square statistics include Pearson chi-square, likelihood-ratio chi-square, and Mantel-Haenszel chi-square (linear-by-linear association). Mantel-Haenszel is valid only if both variables are numeric. Fisher's exact test and Yates' corrected chi-square are computed for all 2×2 tables. This is the default if STATISTICS is specified with no keywords.

PHI   *Display phi and Cramér's V in the Symmetric Measures table.*

CC   *Display contingency coefficient in the Symmetric Measures table.*

LAMBDA   *Display lambda (symmetric and asymmetric) and Goodman and Kruskal's tau in the Directional Measures table.*

UC   *Display uncertainty coefficient (symmetric and asymmetric) in the Directional Measures table.*

BTAU   *Display Kendall's tau-b in the Symmetric Measures table.*

CTAU   *Display Kendall's tau-c in the Symmetric Measures table.*

GAMMA   *Display gamma in the Symmetric Measures table or Zero-Order and Partial Gammas table.* The Zero-Order and Partial Gammas table is produced only for tables with more than two variable dimensions in integer mode.

D   *Display Somers' d (symmetric and asymmetric) in the Directional Measures table.*

ETA   *Display eta in the Directional Measures table.* Available for numeric data only.

CORR   *Display Pearson's r and Spearman's correlation coefficient in the Symmetric Measures table.* This is available for numeric data only.

KAPPA   *Display kappa coefficient* (Kraemer, 1982) *in the Symmetric Measures table.* Kappa can be computed only for square tables in which the row and column values are identical.

RISK   *Display relative risk* (Bishop et al., 1975) *in the Risk Estimate table.* Relative risk can be calculated only for 2×2 tables.

MCNEMAR   *Display a Crosstabulation table for each pair of related dichotomous variables and a Test Statistics table for all pairs showing the number of valid cases, chi-square, and probability for each pair.* Useful for detecting changes in responses due to experimental intervention in "before-and-after" designs.

CMH(1*)   *Conditional independence and homogeneity tests.* Cochran's and the Mantel-Haenszel statistics are computed for the test for conditional independence. The Breslow-Day and Taron's statistics are computed for the test for homogeneity. For each test, the chi-squared statistic with its degrees of freedom and asymptotic *p* value are computed. *Mantel-Haenszel relative risk (common odds ratio) estimate.* The Mantel-Haenszel relative risk (common odds ratio) estimate, the natural log of the estimate, the standard error of the natural log of the estimate, the asymptotic *p* value, and the asymptotic confidence intervals for common odds ratio and for the natural log of the common odds ratio are computed. The user can specify the null hypothesis for the common odds ratio in parentheses after the keyword. The passive default is 1. (The parameter value must be positive.)

ALL   *All statistics available.*

NONE   *No summary statistics.* This is the default if STATISTICS is omitted.

METHOD Subcommand

METHOD displays additional results for each statistic requested. If no METHOD subcommand is specified, the standard asymptotic results are displayed. If fractional weights have been specified, results for all methods will be calculated on the weight rounded to the nearest integer.

MC   Displays an unbiased point estimate and confidence interval based on the Monte Carlo sampling method, for all statistics. Asymptotic results are also displayed. When exact results can be calculated, they will be provided instead of the Monte Carlo results.

CIN(n)   Controls the confidence level for the Monte Carlo estimate. CIN is available only when /METHOD=MC is specified. CIN has a default value of 99.0. You can specify a confidence interval between 0.01 and 99.9, inclusive.

SAMPLES   Specifies the number of tables sampled from the reference set when calculating the Monte Carlo estimate of the exact *p* value. Larger sample sizes lead to narrower confidence limits but also take longer to calculate. You can specify any integer between 1 and 1,000,000,000 as the sample size. SAMPLES has a default value of 10,000.

EXACT   Computes the exact significance level for all statistics in addition to the asymptotic results. If both the EXACT and MC keywords are specified, only exact results are provided. Calculating the exact *p* value can be memory-intensive. If you have specified /METHOD=EXACT and find that you have insufficient memory to calculate results, you should first close any other applications that are currently running in order to make more memory available. You can also enlarge the size of your swap file (see your Windows manual for more information). If you still cannot obtain exact results, specify /METHOD=MC to obtain the Monte Carlo estimate of the exact *p* value. An optional TIMER keyword is available if you choose /METHOD=EXACT.

TIMER(n) Specifies the maximum number of minutes allowed to run the exact analysis for each statistic. If the time limit is reached, the test is terminated, no exact results are provided, and the program begins to calculate the next test in the analysis. TIMER is available only when /METHOD=EXACT is specified. You can specify any integer value for TIMER. Specifying a value of 0 for TIMER turns the timer off completely. TIMER has a default value of 5 minutes. If a test exceeds a time limit of 30 minutes, it is recommended that you use the Monte Carlo, rather than the exact, method.

Example

```
CROSSTABS TABLES=FEAR BY SEX
 /CELLS=ROW COLUMN EXPECTED RESIDUALS
 /STATISTICS=CHISQ
 /METHOD=MC SAMPLES(10000) CIN(95).
```

- This example requests chi-square statistics.
- An unbiased point estimate and confidence interval based on the Monte Carlo sampling method are displayed with the asymptotic results.

MISSING Subcommand

By default, CROSSTABS deletes cases with missing values on a table-by-table basis. Cases with missing values for any variable specified for a table are not used in the table or in the calculation of statistics. Use MISSING to specify alternative missing-value treatments.

- The only specification is a single keyword.
- The number of missing cases is always displayed in the Case Processing Summary table.
- If the missing values are not included in the range specified on VARIABLES, they are excluded from the table regardless of the keyword you specify on MISSING.

TABLE   *Delete cases with missing values on a table-by-table basis.* When multiple table lists are specified, missing values are handled separately for each list. This is the default.

INCLUDE   *Include user-missing values.* Available in integer mode only.

REPORT   *Report missing values in the tables.* This option includes missing values in tables but not in the calculation of percentages or statistics. The missing status is indicated on the categorical label. REPORT is available only in integer mode.

FORMAT Subcommand

By default, CROSSTABS displays tables and subtables. The values for the row and column variables are displayed in order from lowest to highest. Use FORMAT to modify the default table display.

AVALUE   *Display row and column variables from lowest to highest value.* This is the default.

DVALUE   *Display row and column variables from highest to lowest.*

TABLES   *Display tables.* This is the default.

NOTABLES   *Suppress Crosstabulation tables.* NOTABLES is useful when you want to write tables to a file without displaying them or when you want only the Statistics table. This is the same as specifying NONE on CELLS.

BARCHART Subcommand

BARCHART produces a clustered bar chart where bars represent categories defined by the first variable in a crosstabulation while clusters represent categories defined by the second variable in a crosstabulation. Any controlling variables in a crosstabulation are collapsed over before the clustered bar chart is created.

- BARCHART takes no further specification.
- If integer mode is in effect and MISSING=REPORT, BARCHART displays valid and user-missing values. Otherwise only valid values are used.

WRITE Subcommand

Use the WRITE subcommand to write cell frequencies to a file for subsequent use by the current program or another program. CROSSTABS can also use these cell frequencies as input to reproduce tables and compute statistics. When WRITE is specified, an Output File Summary table is displayed before all other tables.

- The only specification is a single keyword.
- The name of the file must be specified on the PROCEDURE OUTPUT command preceding CROSSTABS.
- If both CELLS and ALL are specified, CELLS is in effect and only the contents of non-empty cells are written to the file.
- If you include missing values with INCLUDE or REPORT on MISSING, no values are considered missing and all non-empty cells, including those with missing values, are written, even if CELLS is specified.
- If you exclude missing values on a table-by-table basis (the default), no records are written for combinations of values that include a missing value.
- If multiple tables are specified, the tables are written in the same order as they are displayed.

NONE   *Do not write cell counts to a file.* This is the default.

CELLS	*Write cell counts for non-empty and nonmissing cells to a file.* Combinations of values that include a missing value are not written to the file.
ALL	*Write cell counts for all cells to a file.* A record for each combination of values defined by VARIABLES and TABLES is written to the file. ALL is available only in integer mode.

The file contains one record for each cell. Each record contains the following:

Columns	Contents
1–4	*Split-file group number, numbered consecutively from 1.* Note that this is not the value of the variable or variables used to define the splits.
5–8	*Table number.* Tables are defined by the TABLES subcommand.
9–16	*Cell frequency.* The number of times this combination of variable values occurred in the data, or, if case weights are used, the sum of case weights for cases having this combination of values.
17–24	*The value of the row variable* (the one named before the first BY).
25–32	*The value of the column variable* (the one named after the first BY).
33–40	*The value of the first control variable* (the one named after the second BY).
41–48	*The value of the second control variable* (the one named after the third BY).
49–56	*The value of the third control variable* (the one named after the fourth BY).
57–64	*The value of the fourth control variable* (the one named after the fifth BY).
65–72	*The value of the fifth control variable* (the one named after the sixth BY).
73–80	*The value of the sixth control variable* (the one named after the seventh BY).

- The split-file group number, table number, and frequency are written as integers.
- In integer mode, the values of variables are also written as integers. In general mode, the values are written according to the print format specified for each variable. Alphanumeric values are written at the left end of any field in which they occur.
- Within each table, records are written from one column of the table at a time, and the value of the last control variable changes the most slowly.

Example

```
PROCEDURE OUTPUT  OUTFILE=CELLDATA.
CROSSTABS VARIABLES=FEAR SEX (1,2)
 /TABLES=FEAR BY SEX
 /WRITE=ALL.
```

- CROSSTABS writes a record for each cell in the table *FEAR* by *SEX* to the file *CELLDATA*. Figure 1 shows the contents of the *CELLDATA* file.

Figure 1   Cell records

```
1   1      55      1       1
1   1     172      2       1
1   1     180      1       2
1   1      89      2       2
```

Example

```
PROCEDURE OUTPUT  OUTFILE=XTABDATA.
CROSSTABS  TABLES=V1 TO V3 BY V4 BY V10 TO V15
  /WRITE=CELLS.
```

- CROSSTABS writes a set of records for each table to file *XTABDATA*.

- Records for the table *V1* by *V4* by *V10* are written first, followed by records for *V1* by *V4* by *V11*, and so on. The records for *V3* by *V4* by *V15* are written last.

Reading a CROSSTABS Procedure Output File

You can use the file created by WRITE in a subsequent session to reproduce a table and compute statistics for it. Each record in the file contains all the information used to build the original table. The cell frequency information can be used as a weight variable on the WEIGHT command to replicate the original cases.

Example

```
DATA LIST FILE=CELLDATA
  /WGHT 9-16 FEAR 17-24 SEX 25-32.
VARIABLE LABELS FEAR 'AFRAID TO WALK AT NIGHT IN NEIGHBORHOODS'.
VALUE LABELS  FEAR 1 'YES' 2 'NO'/ SEX 1 'MALE' 2 'FEMALE'.
WEIGHT BY WGHT.
CROSSTABS TABLES=FEAR BY SEX
  /STATISTICS=ALL.
```

- DATA LIST reads the cell frequencies and row and column values from the *CELLDATA* file shown in Figure 1. The cell frequency is read as a weighting factor (variable *WGHT*). The values for the rows are read as *FEAR*, and the values for the columns are read as *SEX*, the two original variables.

- The WEIGHT command recreates the sample size by weighting each of the four cases (cells) by the cell frequency.

If you do not have the original data or the CROSSTABS procedure output file, you can reproduce a crosstabulation and compute statistics simply by entering the values from the table:

```
DATA LIST   /FEAR 1 SEX 3 WGHT 5-7.
VARIABLE LABELS  FEAR 'AFRAID TO WALK AT NIGHT IN NEIGHBORHOOD'.
VALUE LABELS  FEAR 1 'YES' 2 'NO'/ SEX 1 'MALE' 2 'FEMALE'.
 WEIGHT  BY WGHT.
BEGIN DATA
1 1   55
2 1 172
1 2 180
2 2  89
END DATA.
CROSSTABS  TABLES=FEAR BY SEX
/STATISTICS=ALL.
```

References

Bishop, Y. M. M., S. E. Feinberg, and P. W. Holland. 1975. *Discrete multivariate analysis: Theory and practice.* Cambridge, Mass.: MIT Press.

Haberman, S. J. 1978. *Analysis of qualitative data.* Vol. 1. London: Academic Press.

Kraemer, H. C. 1982. Kappa coefficient. In: *Encyclopedia of Statistical Sciences*, S. Katz and N. L. Johnson, eds. New York: John Wiley and Sons.

CURVEFIT

```
CURVEFIT [VARIABLES=] varname [WITH varname]

  [/MODEL= [LINEAR**] [LOGARITHMIC] [INVERSE]

           [QUADRATIC] [CUBIC] [COMPOUND]

           [POWER] [S] [GROWTH] [EXPONENTIAL]

           [LGSTIC] [ALL]]

  [/CIN={95** }]
        {value}

  [/UPPERBOUND={NO**}]
              {n   }

  [/{CONSTANT† }
    {NOCONSTANT}

  [/PLOT={FIT**}]
         {NONE }

  [/ID = varname]

  [/PRINT=ANOVA]

  [/SAVE=[PRED] [RESID] [CIN]]

  [/APPLY [='model name'] [{SPECIFICATIONS}]]
                          {FIT           }
```

**Default if the subcommand is omitted.
†Default if the subcommand is omitted and there is no corresponding specification on the TSET command.

Example:

```
CURVEFIT VARY
  /MODEL=CUBIC.
```

Overview

CURVEFIT fits selected curves to a line plot, allowing you to examine the relationship between one or more dependent variables and one independent variable. CURVEFIT also fits curves to time series and produces forecasts, forecast errors, lower confidence limits, and upper confidence limits. You can choose curves from a variety of regression models.

Options

Model Specification. There are 11 regression models available on the MODEL subcommand. You can fit any or all of these to the data. The keyword ALL is available to fit all 11 models. You can control whether the regression equation includes a constant term using the CONSTANT or NOCONSTANT subcommand.

Upperbound Value. You can specify the upperbound value for the logistic model using the UPPERBOUND subcommand.

Output. You can produce an analysis-of-variance summary table using the PRINT subcommand. You can suppress the display of the curve-fitting plot using the PLOT subcommand.

New Variables. To evaluate the regression statistics without saving predicted and residual variables, specify TSET NEWVAR=NONE prior to CURVEFIT. To save the new variables and replace the variables saved earlier, use TSET NEWVAR=CURRENT (the default). To save the new variables without erasing variables saved earlier, use TSET NEWVAR=ALL or the SAVE subcommand on CURVEFIT.

Forecasting. When used with the PREDICT command, CURVEFIT can produce forecasts and confidence limits beyond the end of the series (see PREDICT).

Basic Specification

The basic specification is one or more dependent variables. If the variables are not time series, you must also specify the keyword WITH and an independent variable.

- By default, the LINEAR model is fit.
- A 95% confidence interval is used unless it is changed by a TSET CIN command prior to the procedure.
- CURVEFIT produces a plot of the curve, a regression summary table displaying the type of curve used, the R^2 coefficient, degrees of freedom, overall F test and significance level, and the regression coefficients.
- For each variable and model combination, CURVEFIT creates four variables: fit/forecast values, residuals, lower confidence limits, and upper confidence limits. These variables are automatically labeled and added to the working data file unless TSET NEWVAR=NONE is specified prior to CURVEFIT. For the new variable names, see the SAVE subcommand on p. 225.

Subcommand Order

- Subcommands can be specified in any order.

Syntax Rules

- VARIABLES can be specified only once.
- Other subcommands can be specified more than once, but only the last specification of each one is executed.

Operations

- When CURVEFIT is used with the PREDICT command to forecast values beyond the end of a time series, the original and residual series are assigned the system-missing value after the last case in the original series.

- If a model requiring a log transformation (COMPOUND, POWER, S, GROWTH, EXPONENTIAL, or LGSTIC) is requested and there are values in the dependent variable(s) less than or equal to 0, the model cannot be fit because nonpositive values cannot be log-transformed.

- CURVEFIT uses listwise deletion of missing values. Whenever one dependent variable is missing a value for a particular case or observation, that case or observation will not be included in any computations.

- For models QUADRATIC and CUBIC, a message is issued if the tolerance criterion is not met. (See TSET for information on changing the tolerance criterion.)

- Since CURVEFIT automatically generates four variables for each dependent variable and model combination, the ALL specification after MODEL should be used cautiously to avoid creating and adding to the working data file many more variables than are necessary.

- The residual variable is always reported in the original metric. To compute the logged residual (which should be used for diagnostic checks) for the models COMPOUND, POWER, S, GROWTH, and EXPONENTIAL, specify

```
COMPUTE NEWVAR = LN(VAR) - LN(FIT#n).
```

where *NEWVAR* is the logged residual, *VAR* is the name of the dependent variable or observed series, and *FIT#n* is the name of the fitted variable generated by CURVEFIT.

For the LGSTIC (logistic) model, the logged residual can be obtained by

```
COMPUTE NEWERR = LN(VAR) - LN(1/FIT#n).
```

or, if upperbound value *u* is specified on the UPPERBOUND subcommand, by

```
COMPUTE NEWVAR = LN(1/VAR - 1/u) - LN(1/FIT#n).
```

- CURVEFIT obeys the WEIGHT command when there is an independent variable. The WEIGHT specification is ignored if no independent variable is specified.

Limitations

- Maximum 1 VARIABLES subcommand. There is no limit on the number of dependent variables or series named on the subcommand.

- Maximum 1 independent variable can be specified after the keyword WITH.

Example

```
CURVEFIT VARY
  /MODEL=CUBIC.
```

- This example fits a cubic curve to the series *VARY*.

VARIABLES Subcommand

VARIABLES specifies the variables and is the only required subcommand. The actual keyword VARIABLES can be omitted.

- If the dependent variables specified are not time series, you must also specify the keyword WITH and an independent variable.

MODEL Subcommand

MODEL specifies the model or models to be fit to the data. The default model is LINEAR.

- You can fit any or all of the 11 available models.
- Model name keywords can be abbreviated to the first three characters.
- You can use the keyword ALL to fit all models.
- When the LGSTIC model is specified, the upperbound value is included in the output.

The following table lists the available models and their regression equations. The linear transformations for the last six models are also shown.

Keyword	Equation	Linear equation
LINEAR	$Y = b_0 + b_1 t$	
LOGARITHMIC	$Y = b_0 + b_1 \ln(t)$	
INVERSE	$Y = b_0 + b_1/t$	
QUADRATIC	$Y = b_0 + b_1 t + b_2 t^2$	
CUBIC	$Y = b_0 + b_1 t + b_2 t^2 + b_3 t^3$	
COMPOUND	$Y = b_0 b_1^{\,t}$	$\ln(Y) = \ln(b_0) + t \ln(b_1)$
POWER	$Y = b_0(t^{b_1})$	$\ln(Y) = \ln(b_0) + b_1 \ln(t)$
S	$Y = e^{b_0 + b_1/t}$	$\ln(Y) = b_0 + b_1/t$
GROWTH	$Y = e^{b_0 + b_1 t}$	$\ln(Y) = b_0 + b_1 t$
EXPONENTIAL	$Y = b_0(e^{b_1 t})$	$\ln(Y) = \ln(b_0) + b_1 t$
LGSTIC (logistic)	$Y = (1/u + b_0 b_1^{\,t})_{-1}$	$\ln(1/Y - 1/u) = \ln(b_0) + t \ln(b_1)$

where

b_0 = a constant
b_n = regression coefficient
t = independent variable or time value
$\ln$ = the natural log base
e = base e logs
u = upperbound value for LGSTIC

Example

```
CURVEFIT VARX.
```

- This command fits a curve to *VARX* using the linear regression model (the default).

Example

```
CURVEFIT VARY
  /MODEL=GROWTH EXPONENTIAL.
```

- This command fits two curves to *VARY*, one using the growth model and the other using the exponential model.

UPPERBOUND Subcommand

UPPERBOUND is used with the logistic model (keyword LGSTIC) to specify an upper boundary value to be used in the regression equation.

- The specification on UPPERBOUND must be a positive number and must be greater than the largest data value in any of the specified dependent variables.
- The default UPPERBOUND value is infinity, so that $1/u = 0$ and is dropped from the equation.
- You can specify UPPERBOUND NO to reset the value to infinity when applying a previous model.
- If you specify UPPERBOUND without LGSTIC, it is ignored.
- Note that UPPERBOUND is a subcommand and cannot be used within a MODEL subcommand. For example, the following specification is *not* valid:

```
/MODEL=CUBIC LGSTIC    /UPPER=99 LINEAR
```

The correct specification is:

```
/MODEL=CUBIC LGSTIC LINEAR
/UPPER=99
```

CONSTANT and NOCONSTANT Subcommands

CONSTANT and NOCONSTANT indicate whether a constant term should be estimated in the regression equation. The specification overrides the corresponding setting on the TSET command.

- CONSTANT indicates that a constant should be estimated. It is the default unless changed by TSET NOCONSTANT prior to the current procedure.
- NOCONSTANT eliminates the constant term from the model.

Example

```
CURVEFIT Y1
  /MODEL=COMPOUND
  /NOCONSTANT.
```

- In this example, a compound curve is fit to *Y1* with no constant term in the model.

CIN Subcommand

CIN controls the size of the confidence interval.
- The specification on CIN must be greater than 0 and less than 100.
- The default confidence interval is 95.
- The CIN subcommand overrides the TSET CIN setting.

PLOT Subcommand

PLOT specifies whether the curve-fitting plot is displayed. If PLOT is not specified, the default is FIT. The curve-fitting plot is displayed. PLOT=FIT is generally used with an APPLY subcommand to turn off a PLOT=NONE specification in the applied model.

FIT   *Display the curve-fitting plot.*

NONE   *Do not display the plot.*

ID Subcommand

ID specifies an identification variable. When in point selection mode, you can click on an individual chart point to display the value of the ID variable for the selected case.

SAVE Subcommand

SAVE saves the values of predicted, residual, and/or confidence interval variables generated during the current session in the working data file.
- SAVE saves the specified variables with default names: *PRED_n* for predicted values *RESID_n* for residuals, *LCL_n* for the lower confidence limit, and *UCL_n* for the upper confidence limit, where *n* increments each time any variable is saved for a model.
- SAVE overrides the CURRENT or NONE setting on TSET NEWVARS (see TSET).

PRED   *Predicted variable.*

RESID   *Residual variable.*

CIN   *Confidence interval.*

PRINT Subcommand

PRINT is used to produce an additional analysis-of-variance table for each model and variable.
- The only specification on PRINT is the keyword ANOVA.

APPLY Subcommand

APPLY allows you to use a previously defined CURVEFIT model without having to repeat the specifications.

- The specifications on APPLY can include the name of a previous model in quotes and one of two keywords. All of these specifications are optional.

- If a model name is not specified, the model specified on the previous CURVEFIT command is used.

- To change one or more of the specifications of the model, specify the subcommands of only those portions you want to change after the subcommand APPLY.

- If no variables or series are specified on the CURVEFIT command, the dependent variables that were originally specified with the model being reapplied are used.

- To change the dependent variables used with the model, enter new variable names before or after the APPLY subcommand.

The keywords available for APPLY on CURVEFIT are:

SPECIFICATIONS   *Use only the specifications from the original model.* This is the default.

FIT   *Use the coefficients estimated for the original model in the equation.*

Example

```
CURVEFIT X1
  /MODEL=QUADRATIC.
CURVEFIT Z1
  /APPLY.
```

- The first command fits a quadratic curve to *X1*.

- The second command fits the same type of curve to *Z1*.

Example

```
CURVEFIT X1 Y1 Z1
  /MODEL=QUADRATIC.
CURVEFIT APPLY
  /MODEL=CUBIC.
```

- The first command fits quadratic curves to *X1*, *Y1*, and *Z1*.

- The second command fits curves to the same three series using the cubic model.

References

Abraham, B., and J. Ledolter. 1983. *Statistical methods of forecasting.* New York: John Wiley and Sons.

Draper, N. R., and H. Smith. 1981. *Applied regression analysis.* New York: John Wiley and Sons.

Montgomery, D. C., and E. A. Peck. 1982. *Introduction to linear regression analysis.* New York: John Wiley and Sons.

DATA LIST

```
DATA LIST [FILE=file] [{FIXED}] [RECORDS={1}] [SKIP={n}] [{TABLE  }]
                                         {n}                {NOTABLE}

                      {FREE} [{("delimiter", "delimiter,..., TAB)}]
                      {LIST}

 /{1     } varname {col location [(format)]} [varname ...]
  {rec #}          {(FORTRAN-like format)  }

 [/{2     } ...] [/ ...]
   {rec #}
```

Numeric and string input formats:

Type	Column-style format	FORTRAN-like format
Numeric (default)	d or F,d	Fw.d
Restricted numeric	N,d	Nw.d
Scientific notation	E,d	Ew.d
Numeric with commas	COMMA,d	COMMAw.d
Numeric with dots	DOT,d	DOTw.d
Numeric with commas and dollar sign	DOLLAR,d	DOLLARw.d
Numeric with percent sign	PCT,d	PCTw.d
Zoned decimal	Z,d	Zw.d
String	A	Aw

Format elements to skip columns:
Some formats are not available on all implementations of the program.

Type	Column-style format	FORTRAN-like format
Tab to column *n*		Tn
Skip *n* columns		nX

Date and time input formats:

Type	Data input	Format	FORTRAN-like format
International date	dd-mmm-yyyy	DATE	DATEw
American date	mm/dd/yyyy	ADATE	ADATEw
European date	dd/mm/yy	EDATE	EDATEw
Julian date	yyddd	JDATE	JDATEw
Sorted date	yy/mm/dd	SDATE	SDATEw
Quarter and year	qQyyyy	QYR	QYRw

Month and year	mm/yyyy	MOYR	MOYRw
Week and year	wkWKyyyy	WKYR	WKYRw
Date and time	dd-mmm-yyyy hh:mm:ss.ss	DATETIME	DATETIMEw.d
Time	hh:mm:ss.ss	TIME	TIMEw.d
Days and time	ddd hh:mm:ss.ss	DTIME	DTIMEw.d
Day of the week	string	WKDAY	WKDAYw
Month	string	MONTH	MONTHw

Example:

```
DATA LIST /ID 1-3 SEX 5 (A) AGE 7-8 OPINION1 TO OPINION5 10-14.
```

Overview

DATA LIST defines a raw data file (a raw data file contains numbers and other alphanumeric characters) by assigning names and formats to each variable in the file. Raw data can be inline (entered with your commands between BEGIN DATA and END DATA) or stored in an external file. They can be in fixed format (values for the same variable are always entered in the same location on the same record for each case) or in freefield format (values for consecutive variables are not in particular columns but are entered one after the other, separated by blanks or commas).

For information on defining matrix materials, see MATRIX DATA. For information on defining complex data files that cannot be defined with DATA LIST, see FILE TYPE and REPEATING DATA. For information on reading SPSS-format data files and SPSS-format portable files, see GET and IMPORT.

The program can also read data files created by other software applications. Commands that read these files include GET CAPTURE and GET TRANSLATE.

Options

Data Source. You can use inline data or data from an external file.

Data Formats. You can define numeric (with or without decimal places) and string variables using an array of input formats (percent, dollar, date and time, and so forth). You can also specify column binary and unaligned positive integer binary formats (available only if used with the MODE=MULTIPUNCH setting on the FILE HANDLE command). For a complete list of available formats, see "Variable Formats" on p. 31.

Data Organization. You can define data that are in fixed format (values in the same location on the same record for each case), in freefield format with multiple cases per record, or in freefield format with one case on each record using the FIXED, FREE, and LIST keywords.

Multiple Records. For fixed-format data, you can indicate the number of records per case on the RECORDS subcommand. You can specify which records to read in the variable definition portion of DATA LIST.

Summary Table. For fixed-format data, you can display a table that summarizes the variable definitions using the TABLE subcommand. You can suppress this table using NOTABLE.

Value Delimiter. For freefield-format data (keywords FREE and LIST), you can specify the character(s) that separate data values, or you can use the keyword TAB to specify the tab character as the delimiter. Any delimiter other than the TAB keyword must be enclosed in quotation marks, and the specification must be enclosed in parentheses, as in DATA LIST FREE(",").

End-of-File Processing. You can specify a logical variable that indicates the end of the data using the END subcommand. This logical variable can be used to invoke special processing after all the cases from the data file have been read.

Basic Specification

- The basic specification is the FIXED, LIST, or FREE keyword, followed by a slash that signals the beginning of variable definition.
- FIXED is the default.
- If the data are in an external file, the FILE subcommand must be used.
- If the data are inline, the FILE subcommand is omitted and the data are specified between the BEGIN DATA and END DATA commands.
- Variable definition for fixed-format data includes a variable name, a column location, and a format (unless the default numeric format is used). The column location is not specified if FORTRAN-like formats are used, since these formats include the variable width.
- Variable definition for freefield data includes a variable name and, optionally, a delimiter specification and a FORTRAN-like format specification. If format specifications include a width and number of decimal positions (for example, F8.2), the width and decimal specifications are not used to read the data but are assigned as print and write formats for the variables.

Subcommand Order

Subcommands can be named in any order. However, all subcommands must precede the first slash, which signals the beginning of variable definition.

Syntax Rules

Subcommands on DATA LIST are separated by spaces or commas, not by slashes.

Operations

- DATA LIST clears the working data file and defines a new working file.
- Variable names are stored in the working file dictionary.
- Formats are stored in the working file dictionary and are used to display and write the values. To change output formats of numeric variables defined on DATA LIST, use the FORMATS command.

Fixed-Format Data

- The order of the variables in the working file dictionary is the order in which they are defined on DATA LIST, not their sequence in the input data file. This order is important if you later use the TO keyword to refer to variables on subsequent commands.

- In numeric format, blanks to the left or right of a number are ignored; imbedded blanks are invalid. When the program encounters a field that contains one or more blanks interspersed among the numbers, it issues a warning message and assigns the system-missing value to that case.

- Alphabetical and special characters, except the decimal point and leading plus and minus signs, are not valid in numeric variables and are set to system-missing if encountered in the data.

- The system-missing value is assigned to a completely blank field for numeric variables. The value assigned to blanks can be changed using the BLANKS specification on the SET command.

- The program ignores data contained in columns and records that are not specified in the variable definition.

Freefield Data

FREE can read freefield data with multiple cases recorded on one record or with one case recorded on more than one record. LIST can read freefield data with one case on each record.

- Line endings are read as delimiters between values.

- If you use FORTRAN-like format specifications (for example, DOLLAR12.2), width and decimal specifications are not used to read the data but are assigned as print and write formats for the variable.

For freefield data *without* explicitly specified value delimiters:

- Commas and blanks are interpreted as delimiters between values.

- Extra blanks are ignored.

- Multiple commas with or without blank space between them can be used to specify missing data.

- If a valid value contains commas or blank spaces, enclose the values in quotation marks or apostrophes.

For data with explicitly specified value delimiters (for example, DATA LIST FREE (",")):

- Multiple delimiters without any intervening space can be used to specify missing data.

- The specified delimiters cannot occur within a data value, even if you enclose the value in quotation marks or apostrophes.

Note: Freefield format with specified value delimiters is typically used to read data in text format written by a computer program, not for data manually entered in a text editor.

Example

```
* Column-style format specifications.

DATA LIST /ID 1-3 SEX 5 (A) AGE 7-8 OPINION1 TO OPINION5 10-14.
BEGIN DATA
001 m 28 12212
002 f 29 21212
003 f 45 32145
 ...
128 m 17 11194
END DATA.
```

- The data are inline between the BEGIN DATA and END DATA commands, so the FILE sub-command is not specified. The data are in fixed format. The keyword FIXED is not specified because it is the default.

- Variable definition begins after the slash. Variable *ID* is in columns 1 through 3. Because no format is specified, numeric format is assumed. Variable *ID* is therefore a numeric variable that is three characters wide.

- Variable *SEX* is a short string variable in column 5. Variable *SEX* is one character wide.

- *AGE* is a two-column numeric variable in columns 7 and 8.

- Variables *OPINION1*, *OPINION2*, *OPINION3*, *OPINION4*, and *OPINION5* are named using the TO keyword (see "Keyword TO" on p. 29). Each is a one-column numeric variable, with *OPINION1* located in column 10 and *OPINION5* located in column 14.

- The BEGIN DATA and END DATA commands enclose the inline data. Note that the values of *SEX* are lowercase letters and must be specified as such on subsequent commands.

FILE Subcommand

FILE specifies the raw data file. FILE is required when data are stored in an external data file. FILE must not be used when the data are stored in a file that is included with the INCLUDE command or when the data are inline (see INCLUDE and BEGIN DATA—END DATA).

- FILE must be separated from other DATA LIST subcommands by at least one blank or comma.

- FILE must precede the first slash, which signals the beginning of variable definition.

FIXED, FREE, and LIST Keywords

FIXED, FREE, or LIST indicates the format of the data. Only one of these keywords can be used on each DATA LIST. The default is FIXED.

FIXED *Fixed-format data.* Each variable is recorded in the same column location on the same record for each case in the data. FIXED is the default.

FREE *Freefield data.* The variables are recorded in the same order for each case but not necessarily in the same column locations. More than one case can be entered on the same record. By default, values are separated by blanks or commas. You can also specify different value delimiters.

LIST   *Freefield data with one case on each record.* The variables are recorded in freefield format as described for the keyword FREE except that the variables for each case must be recorded on one record.

- FIXED, FREE, or LIST must be separated from other DATA LIST subcommands by at least one blank or comma.

- FIXED, FREE, or LIST must precede the first slash, which signals the beginning of data definition.

- For fixed-format data, you can use column-style or FORTRAN-like formats, or a combination of both. For freefield data, you can use only FORTRAN-like formats.

- For fixed-format data, the program reads values according to the column locations specified or implied by the FORTRAN-like format. Values in the data do *not* have to be in the same order as the variables named on DATA LIST and do *not* have to be separated by a space or column.

- For freefield data, the program reads values sequentially in the order in which the variables are named on DATA LIST. Values in the data *must* be in the order in which the variables are named on DATA LIST and *must* be separated by at least one valid delimiter.

- For freefield data, multiple blank spaces can be used to indicate missing information only if a blank space is explicitly specified as the delimiter. In general, it is better to use multiple non-blank delimiters (for example, two commas with no intervening space) to specify missing data.

- In freefield format, a value cannot be split across records.

Example

```
* Data in fixed format.

DATA LIST FILE=HUBDATA FIXED RECORDS=3
  /1 YRHIRED 14-15 DEPT 19 SEX 20.
```

- FIXED indicates explicitly that the *HUBDATA* file is in fixed format. Because FIXED is the default, the keyword FIXED could have been omitted.

- Variable definition begins after the slash. Column locations are specified after each variable. Since formats are not specified, the default numeric format is used. Variable widths are determined by the column specifications: *YRHIRED* is two characters wide, and *DEPT* and *SEX* are each one character wide.

Example

```
* Data in freefield format.
DATA LIST FREE / POSTPOS NWINS.
BEGIN DATA
2, 19, 7, 5, 10, 25, 5, 17, 8, 11, 3,, 6, 8, 1, 29
END DATA.
```

- Data are inline, so FILE is omitted. The keyword FREE is used because data are in freefield format with multiple cases on a single record. Two variables, *POSTPOS* and *NWINS*, are defined. Since formats are not specified, both variables receive the default F8.2 format.

- All of the data are recorded on one record. The first two values build the first case in the working data file. For the first case, *POSTPOS* has value 2 and *NWINS* has value 19. For the second case, *POSTPOS* has value 7 and *NWINS* has value 5, and so on. The working data file will contain eight cases.

- The two commas without intervening space after the data value 3 indicate a missing data value.

Example

```
* Data in list format.

DATA LIST LIST (",")/ POSTPOS NWINS.
BEGIN DATA
2,19
7,5
10,25
5,17
8,11
3,
6,8
1,29
END DATA.
```

- This example defines the same data as the previous example, but LIST is used because each case is recorded on a separate record. FREE could also be used. However, LIST is less prone to errors in data entry. If you leave out a value in the data with FREE format, all values after the missing value are assigned to the wrong variable. Since LIST format reads a case from each record, a missing value will affect only one case.
- A comma is specified as the delimiter between values.
- Since line endings are interpreted as delimiters between values, the second comma after the value 3 (in the sixth line of data) is not necessary to indicate that the value of *NWINS* is missing for that case.

Example

```
* Freefield format with formats specified and embedded commas.

DATA LIST LIST / datevar(DATE12) numvar(COMMA8.2).
BEGIN DATA
28 Oct 1986, 12345
"28,10,86", "1,2345"
END DATA.

DATA LIST LIST (",") / datevar(DATE12) numvar(COMMA8.2).
BEGIN DATA
28 Oct 1986, 12345
"28,10,86", "1,2345"
END DATA.
```

- This example specifies a date format variable and a comma format variable. The width and decimal specifications are not used to read the data but are assigned as print and write formats for the variables.
- In the first DATA LIST command, the two data records are read exactly the same. The values on the second line are enclosed in quotation marks because they contain commas, which is the default delimiter.

- In the second DATA LIST command, neither value on the second line is read correctly because both values contain commas, and a comma is explicitly specified as the delimiter. With an explicitly specified delimiter, you cannot include the delimiter in a data value, even if you enclose the value in apostrophes or quotation marks.

TABLE and NOTABLE Subcommands

TABLE displays a table summarizing the variable definitions supplied on DATA LIST. NOTABLE suppresses the summary table. TABLE is the default.

- TABLE and NOTABLE can be used only for fixed-format data.
- TABLE and NOTABLE must be separated from other DATA LIST subcommands by at least one blank or comma.
- TABLE and NOTABLE must precede the first slash, which signals the beginning of variable definition.

RECORDS Subcommand

RECORDS indicates the number of records per case for fixed-format data. In the variable definition portion of DATA LIST, each record is preceded by a slash. By default, DATA LIST reads one record per case.

- The only specification on RECORDS is a single integer indicating the *total* number of records for each case (even if the DATA LIST command does not define all the records).
- RECORDS can be used only for fixed-format data and must be separated from other DATA LIST subcommands by at least one blank or comma. RECORDS must precede the first slash, which signals the beginning of variable definition.
- Each slash in the variable definition portion of DATA LIST indicates the beginning of a new record. The first slash indicates the first (or only) record. The second and any subsequent slashes tell the program to go to a new record.
- To skip a record, specify a slash without any variables for that record.
- The number of slashes in the variable definition cannot exceed the value of the integer specified on RECORDS.
- The sequence number of the record being defined can be specified after each slash. DATA LIST reads the number to determine which record to read. If the sequence number is used, you *do not* have to use a slash for any skipped records. However, the records to be read must be in their sequential order.
- The slashes for the second and subsequent records can be specified within the variable list, or they can be specified on a format list following the variable list (see the example below).
- All variables to be read from one record should be defined before you proceed to the next record.
- Since RECORDS can be used only with fixed format, it is not necessary to define all the variables on a given record or to follow their order in the input data file.

Example

```
DATA LIST FILE=HUBDATA RECORDS=3
 /2 YRHIRED 14-15 DEPT 19 SEX 20.
```

- DATA LIST defines fixed-format data. RECORDS can be used only for fixed-format data.

- RECORDS indicates that there are three records per case in the data. Only one record per case is defined in the data definition.

- The sequence number (2) before the first variable definition indicates that the variables being defined are on the second record. Because the sequence number is provided, a slash is not required for the first record, which is skipped.

- The variables *YRHIRED*, *DEPT*, and *SEX* are defined and will be included in the working data file. Any other variables on the second record or on the other records are not defined and are not included in the working file.

Example

```
DATA LIST FILE=HUBDATA RECORDS=3
 / /YRHIRED 14-15 DEPT 19 SEX 20.
```

- This command is equivalent to the one in the previous example. Because the record sequence number is omitted, a slash is required to skip the first record.

Example

```
DATA LIST FILE=HUBDATA RECORDS=3
 /YRHIRED (T14,F2.0) /  /NAME (T25,A24).
```

- RECORDS indicates there are three records for each case in the data.

- *YRHIRED* is the only variable defined on the first record. The FORTRAN-like format specification T14 means tab over 14 columns. Thus, *YRHIRED* begins in column 14 and has format F2.0.

- The second record is skipped. Because the record sequence numbers are not specified, a slash must be used to skip the second record.

- *NAME* is the only variable defined for the third record. *NAME* begins in column 25 and is a string variable with a width of 24 characters (format A24).

Example

```
DATA LIST FILE=HUBDATA RECORDS=3
 /YRHIRED NAME (T14,F2.0 /  / T25,A24).
```

- This command is equivalent to the one in the previous example. *YRHIRED* is located on the first record, and *NAME* is located on the third record.

- The slashes that indicate the second and third records are specified within the format specifications. The format specifications follow the complete variable list.

END Subcommand

END provides control of end-of-file processing by specifying a variable that is set to a value of 0 until the end of the data file is encountered, at which point the variable is set to 1. The values of all variables named on DATA LIST are left unchanged. The logical variable created with END can then be used on DO IF and LOOP commands to invoke special processing after all the cases from a particular input file have been built.

- DATA LIST and the entire set of commands used to define the cases must be enclosed within an INPUT PROGRAM—END INPUT PROGRAM structure. The END FILE command must also be used to signal the end of case generation.
- END can be used only with fixed-format data. An error is generated if the END subcommand is used with FREE or LIST.

Example

```
INPUT PROGRAM.
NUMERIC         TINCOME (DOLLAR8.0).                    /* Total income
LEAVE           TINCOME.
DO IF           $CASENUM EQ 1.
+   PRINT       EJECT.
+   PRINT       / 'Name          Income'.
END IF
DATA LIST       FILE=INCOME END=#EOF NOTABLE / NAME 1-10(A)
                                               INCOME 16-20(F).
DO IF           #EOF.
+   PRINT       / 'TOTAL       ', TINCOME.
+   END FILE.
ELSE.
+   PRINT       / NAME, INCOME (A10,COMMA8).
+   COMPUTE     TINCOME = TINCOME+INCOME.  /* Accumulate total income
END IF.
END INPUT PROGRAM.

EXECUTE.
```

- The data definition commands are enclosed within an INPUT PROGRAM—END INPUT PROGRAM structure.
- NUMERIC indicates that a new numeric variable, *TINCOME*, will be created.
- LEAVE tells the program to leave variable *TINCOME* at its value for the previous case as each new case is read, so that it can be used to accumulate totals across cases.
- The first DO IF structure, enclosing the PRINT EJECT and PRINT commands, tells the program to display the headings *Name* and *Income* at the top of the display (when *$CASENUM* equals 1).
- DATA LIST defines variables *NAME* and *INCOME*, and it specifies the scratch variable *#EOF* on the END subcommand.
- The second DO IF prints the values for *NAME* and *INCOME* and accumulates the variable *INCOME* into *TINCOME* by passing control to ELSE as long as *#EOF* is not equal to 1. At the end of the file, *#EOF* equals 1, and the expression on DO IF is true. The label *TOTAL* and the value for *TINCOME* are displayed, and control is passed to END FILE.

Example

```
* Concatenate three raw data files.

INPUT PROGRAM.
NUMERIC #EOF1 TO #EOF3.   /*These will be used as the END variables.

DO IF #EOF1 & #EOF2 & #EOF3.
+    END FILE.
ELSE IF #EOF1 & #EOF2.
+    DATA LIST  FILE=THREE END=#EOF3 NOTABLE / NAME 1-20(A)
            AGE 25-26 SEX 29(A).
+    DO IF NOT #EOF3.
+       END CASE.
+    END IF.
ELSE IF #EOF1.
+    DATA LIST  FILE=TWO END=#EOF2 NOTABLE / NAME 1-20(A)
            AGE 21-22 SEX 24(A).
+    DO IF NOT #EOF2.
+       END CASE.
+    END IF.
ELSE.
+    DATA LIST  FILE=ONE END=#EOF1 NOTABLE /1 NAME 1-20(A)
            AGE 21-22 SEX 24 (A).
+    DO IF NOT #EOF1.
+       END CASE.
+    END IF.
END IF.
END INPUT PROGRAM.

REPORT FORMAT AUTOMATIC LIST /VARS=NAME AGE SEX.
```

- The input program contains a DO IF—ELSE IF—END IF structure.
- Scratch variables are used on each END subcommand so the value will not be reinitialized to the system-missing value after each case is built.
- Three data files are read, two of which contain data in the same format. The third requires a slightly different format for the data items. All three DATA LIST commands are placed within the DO IF structure.
- END CASE builds cases from each record of the three files. END FILE is used to trigger end-of-file processing once all data records have been read.
- This application can also be handled by creating three separate SPSS-format data files and using ADD FILES to put them together. The advantage of using the input program is that additional files are not required to store the separate data files prior to performing ADD FILES.

Variable Definition

The variable definition portion of DATA LIST assigns names and formats to the variables in the data. Depending on the format of the file, you may also need to specify record and column location. The following sections describe variable names, location, and formats.

Variable Names

- Variable names can contain up to eight characters. All variable names must begin with a letter or the @ or # character. A # symbol as the first character of the variable name defines the variable as a scratch variable. System variables (beginning with a $) cannot be defined on DATA LIST. An underscore can be used within a variable name, provided the underscore is not the first character.

- The keyword TO can be used to generate names for consecutive variables in the data. Leading zeros in the number are preserved in the name. *X1* TO *X100* and *X001* TO *X100* both generate 100 variable names, but the first 99 names are not the same in the two lists. *X01* TO *X9* is not a valid specification. For more information on the TO keyword and other variable-naming rules, see "Variable Names" on p. 29.

- The order in which variables are named on DATA LIST determines their order in the working data file. If the working file is saved as an SPSS-format data file, the variables are saved in this order unless they are explicitly reordered on the SAVE or XSAVE command.

Example

```
DATA LIST FREE / ID SALARY #V1 TO #V4.
```

- The FREE keyword indicates that the data are in freefield format. Six variables are defined: *ID*, *SALARY*, *#V1*, *#V2*, *#V3*, and *#V4*. *#V1* to *#V4* are scratch variables that are not stored in the working data file. Their values can be used in transformations but not in procedure commands.

Variable Location

For fixed-format data, variable locations are specified either explicitly using column locations or implicitly using FORTRAN-like formats. For freefield data, variable locations are not specified. Values are read sequentially in the order in which variables are named on the variable list.

Fixed-Format Data

- If column-style formats are used, you must specify the column location of each variable after the variable name. If the variable is one column wide, specify the column number. Otherwise, specify the first column number followed by a dash (–) and the last column number.

- If several adjacent variables on the same record have the same width and format type, you can use one column specification after the last variable name. Specify the beginning column location of the first variable, a dash, and the ending column location of the last variable. the program divides the total number of columns specified equally among the variables. If the number of columns does not divide equally, an error message is issued.

- The same column locations can be used to define multiple variables.

- For FORTRAN-like formats, column locations are implied by the width specified on the formats (see "Variable Formats" on p. 240). To skip columns, use the Tn or nX format specifications.

- With fixed format, column-style and FORTRAN-like specifications can be mixed on the same DATA LIST command.
- Record location is indicated by a slash or a slash and record number before the names of the variables on that record. See the RECORDS subcommand on p. 234 for information on specifying record location.
- The program ignores data in columns and on records that are not specified on DATA LIST.
- In the data, values do not have to be separated by a space or comma.

Example

```
DATA LIST  FILE=HUBDATA RECORDS=3
 /1 YRHIRED 14-15 DEPT 19 SEX 20
 /2 SALARY 21-25.
```

- The data are in fixed format (the default) and are read from the file *HUBDATA*.
- Three variables, *YRHIRED*, *DEPT*, and *SEX*, are defined on the first record of the *HUBDATA* file. One variable, *SALARY*, is read from columns 21 through 25 on the second record. The total number of records per case is specified as 3 even though no variables are defined on the third record. The third record is simply skipped in data definition.

Example

```
DATA LIST  FILE=HUBDATA RECORDS=3
 /1 DEPT 19 SEX 20 YRHIRED 14-15 MOHIRED 12-13 HIRED 12-15
 /2 SALARY 21-25.
```

- The first two defined variables are *DEPT* and *SEX*, located in columns 19 and 20 on record 1. The next three variables, *YRHIRED*, *MOHIRED*, and *HIRED*, are also located on the first record.
- *YRHIRED* is read from columns 14 and 15, *MOHIRED* from columns 12 and 13, and *HIRED* from columns 12 through 15. The variable *HIRED* is a four-column variable with the first two columns representing the month when an employee was hired (the same as *MOHIRED*) and the last two columns representing the year of employment (the same as *YRHIRED*).
- The order of the variables in the dictionary is the order in which they are defined on DATA LIST, not their sequence in the *HUBDATA* file.

Example

```
DATA LIST  FILE=HUBDATA RECORDS=3
 /1 DEPT 19 SEX 20 MOHIRED YRHIRED 12-15
 /2 SALARY 21-25.
```

- A single column specification follows *MOHIRED* and *YRHIRED*. DATA LIST divides the total number of columns specified equally between the two variables. Thus, each variable has a width of two columns.

Example

```
* Mixing column-style and FORTRAN-like format specifications.

DATA LIST FILE=PRSNL / LNAME M_INIT STREET (A20,A1,1X,A10)
    AGE 35-36.
```

- FORTRAN-like format specifications are used for string variables *LNAME, M_INIT*, and *STREET*. These variables must be adjacent in the data file. *LNAME* is 20 characters wide and is located in columns 1–20. *M_INIT* is one character wide and is located in column 21. The 1X specification defines a blank column between *M_INIT* and *STREET. STREET* is 10 characters wide and is located in columns 23–32.
- A column-style format is used for the variable *AGE. AGE* begins in column 35, ends in column 36, and by default has numeric format.

Freefield Data

- In freefield data, column location is irrelevant, since values are not in fixed column positions. Instead, values are simply separated from each other by blanks or by commas or a specified delimiter. Any number of consecutive blanks are interpreted as one delimiter unless a blank space is explicitly specified as the value delimiter. A value cannot be split across records.
- If there are not enough values to complete the last case, a warning is issued and the incomplete case is dropped.
- The specified delimiter can only be used within data values if the value is enclosed in quotations marks or apostrophes.
- To include an apostrophe in a string value, enclose the value in quotation marks. To include quotation marks in a value, enclose the value in apostrophes (see "String Values in Command Specifications" on p. 15).

Variable Formats

Two types of format specifications are available: column-style and FORTRAN-like. With each type, you can specify both numeric and string formats. The difference between the two types is that FORTRAN-like formats include the width of the variable and column-style formats do not.

- Column-style formats are available only for fixed-format data.
- Column-style and FORTRAN-like formats can be mixed on the same DATA LIST to define fixed-format data.
- A value that cannot be read according to the format type specified is assigned the system-missing value and a warning message is issued.

The following sections discuss the rules for specifying column-style and FORTRAN-like formats, followed by additional considerations for numeric and string formats. See p. 227 for a partial list of available formats. For a complete discussion of formats, see "Variable Formats" on p. 31.

Column-Style Format Specifications

The following rules apply to column-style formats:

- Data must be in a fixed format.

- Column locations must be specified after variable names. The width of a variable is determined by the number of specified columns. See "Fixed-Format Data" on p. 238 for information on specifying column location.

- Following the column location, specify the format type in parentheses. The format type applies only to the variable or the list of variables associated with the column location specification immediately before it. If no format type is specified, numeric (F) format is used.

- To include decimal positions in the format, specify the format type followed by a comma and the number of decimal positions. For example, (DOLLAR) specifies only whole dollar amounts; (DOLLAR,2) specifies DOLLAR format with two decimal positions.

- Since column positions are explicitly specified, the variables can be named in any order.

FORTRAN-like Format Specifications

The following rules apply to FORTRAN-like formats:

- Data can be in either fixed or freefield format.

- Column locations cannot be specified. The width of a variable is determined by the width portion (w) of the format specification. The width must specify the number of characters in the widest value.

- One format specification applies to only one variable. The format is specified in parentheses after the variable to which it applies. Alternatively, a variable list can be followed by an equal number of format specifications contained in one set of parentheses. When a number of consecutive variables have the same format, the number can be used as a multiplying factor preceding the format. For example, (3F5.2) assigns the format F5.2 to three consecutive variables.

- For fixed data, the number of formats specified (either explicitly or implied by the multiplication factor) must be the same as the number of variables. Otherwise, the program issues an error message. If no formats are specified, all variables have the default format F8.2.

- For freefield data, variables with no specified formats take the default F8.2 format. However, an asterisk (*) must be used to indicate where the default format stops. Otherwise, the program tries to apply the next specified format to every variable before it and issues an error message if the number of formats specified is less than the number of variables.

- For freefield data, width and decimal specifications are not used to read the data but are assigned as print and write formats for the variable.

- For fixed data, Tn can be used before a format to indicate that the variable begins at the nth column, and nX can be used to skip n columns before reading the variable. When Tn is specified, variables named do not have to follow the order of the variables in the data.

- For freefield data, variables are located according to the sequence in which they are named on DATA LIST. The order of variables on DATA LIST must correspond to the order of variables in the data.

- To include decimal positions in the format for fixed-format data, specify the total width followed by a decimal point and the number of decimal positions. For example, (DOLLAR5) specifies a five-column DOLLAR format without decimal positions; (DOLLAR5.2) specifies a five-column DOLLAR format, two columns of which are decimal positions.

Numeric Formats

- Format specifications on DATA LIST are input formats. Based on the width specification and format type, the program generates output (print and write) formats for each variable. The program automatically expands the output format to accommodate punctuation characters such as decimal points, commas, dollar signs, or date and time delimiters. (The program does not automatically expand the output formats you assign on the FORMATS, PRINT FORMATS, and WRITE FORMATS commands. For information on assigning output formats, refer to these commands.)
- Scientific notation is accepted in input data with F, COMMA, DOLLAR, DOT, and PCT formats. The same rules apply to these formats as to E format. The values 1.234E3, 1.234+3, and 1.234E 3 are all legitimate. The last value (with a blank space) will cause freefield data to be misread and therefore should be avoided when LIST or FREE is specified.

Implied Decimal Positions

- For fixed-format data, decimal positions can be coded in the data or implied by the format. If decimal positions are implied but are not entered in the data, the program interprets the rightmost digits in each value as the decimal digits. A coded decimal point in a value overrides the number of implied decimal places. For example, (DOLLAR,2) specifies two decimal positions. The value 123 is interpreted as 1.23; however, the value 12.3 is interpreted as 12.3 because the coded decimal position overrides the number of implied decimal positions.
- For freefield data, decimal positions cannot be implied but must be coded in the data. If decimal positions are specified in the format but a data value does not include a decimal point, the program fills the decimal places with zeros. For example, with F3.1 format (three columns with one decimal place), the value 22 is displayed as 22.0. If a value in the data has more decimal digits than are specified in the format, the additional decimals are truncated in displayed output (but not in calculations). For example, with F3.1 format, the value 2.22 is displayed as 2.2 even though in calculations it remains 2.22.

Table 1 compares how values are interpreted for fixed and freefield formats. Values in the table are for a four-column numeric variable.

Table 1   Interpretation of values in fixed and freefield format

Values	Fixed		Freefield	
	Default	Two defined decimal places	Default	Two defined decimal places
2001	2001	20.01	2001.00	2001.00
201	201	2.01	201.00	201.00
−201	−201	−2.01	−201.00	−201.00

Table 1   Interpretation of values in fixed and freefield format (Continued)

2	2	.02	2.00	2.00
20	20	.20	20.00	20.00
2.2	2.2	2.2	2.20	2.20
.201	.201	.201	.201	.201
2 01	Undefined	Undefined	Two values	Two values

Example

```
DATA LIST
  /MODEL 1 RATE 2-6(PCT,2) COST 7-11(DOLLAR) READY 12-21(ADATE).
BEGIN DATA
1935   7878811-07-1988
2 16754654606-08-1989
3 17684783612-09-1989
END DATA.
```

- Data are inline and in fixed format (the default).

- Each variable is followed by its column location. After the column location, a column-style format is specified in parentheses.

- *MODEL* begins in column 1, is one column wide, and receives the default numeric F format.

- *RATE* begins in column 2 and ends in column 6. The PCT format is specified with two decimal places. A comma is used to separate the format type from the number of decimal places. Decimal points are not coded in the data. Thus, the program reads the rightmost digits of each value as decimal digits. The value 935 for the first case in the data is interpreted as 9.35. Note that it does not matter where numbers are entered within the column width.

- *COST* begins in column 7 and ends in column 11. DOLLAR format is specified.

- *READY* begins in column 12 and ends in column 21. ADATE format is specified.

Example

```
DATA LIST FILE=DATA1
  /MODEL (F1) RATE (PCT5.2) COST (DOLLAR5) READY (ADATE10).
```

- In this example, the FILE subcommand is used because the data are in an external file.

- The variable definition is the same as in the preceding example except that FORTRAN-like format specifications are used rather than column-style. Column locations are not specified. Instead, the format specifications include a width for each format type.

- The width (w) portion of each format must specify the total number of characters in the widest value. DOLLAR5 format for *COST* accepts the five-digit value 78788, which displays as $78,788. Thus, the specified input format DOLLAR5 generates an output format DOLLAR7. The program automatically expands the width of the output format to accommodate the dollar sign and comma in displayed output.

String Formats

String (alphanumeric) variables can contain any numbers, letters, or characters, including special characters and imbedded blanks. Numbers entered as values for string variables cannot be used in calculations unless you convert them to numeric format (see RECODE). On DATA LIST, a string variable is defined with an A format if data are in standard character form or an AHEX format if data are in hexadecimal form. For further discussion of string formats, see "String Variable Formats" on p. 39.

- For fixed-format data, the width of a string variable is either implied by the column location specification or specified by the *w* on the FORTRAN-like format. For freefield data, the width must be specified on the FORTRAN-like format.

- The string formats defined on DATA LIST are both input and output formats. You cannot change the format of a defined string variable in this program. However, you can use the STRING command to define a new string variable and COMPUTE to copy the values from the old variable (see COMPUTE).

- AHEX format is available only for fixed-format data. Since each set of two hexadecimal characters represents one standard character, the width specification must be an even number. The output format for a variable in AHEX format is A format with half the specified width.

- If a string in the data is longer than its specified width, the string is truncated and a warning message is displayed. If the string in the data is shorter, it is right-padded with blanks and no warning message is displayed.

- For fixed-format data, all characters within the specified or implied columns, including leading, trailing, and imbedded blanks and punctuation marks, are read as the value of the string.

- For freefield data without a specified delimiter, string values in the data must be enclosed in apostrophes or quotation marks if the string contains a blank or a comma. Otherwise, the blank or comma is treated as a delimiter between values. Apostrophes can be included in a string by enclosing the string in quotation marks. Quotation marks can be included in a string by enclosing the string in apostrophes.

Example

```
DATA LIST FILE=WINS FREE /POSTPOS NWINS * POSNAME (A24).
```

- *POSNAME* is specified as a 24-character string. The asterisk preceding *POSNAME* indicates that *POSTPOS* and *NWINS* are read with the default format. If the asterisk was not specified, the program would apply the A24 format to *POSNAME* and then issue an error message indicating that there are more variables than specified formats.

Example

```
DATA LIST FILE=WINS FREE /POSTPOS * NWINS (A5) POSWINS.
```

- Both *POSTPOS* and *POSWINS* receive the default numeric format F8.2.
- *NWINS* receives the specified format of A5.

DATE

```
DATE  keyword [starting value [periodicity]]

    [keyword [starting value [periodicity]]]

    [BY increment]
```

Keywords for long time periods:

Keyword	Abbreviation	Default starting value	Default periodicity
YEAR	Y	1	none
QUARTER	Q	1	4
MONTH	M	1	12

Keywords for short time periods:

Keyword	Abbreviation	Default starting value	Default periodicity
WEEK	W	1	none
DAY	D	1	7
HOUR	H	0	24
MINUTE	MI	0	60
SECOND	S	0	60

Keywords for any time periods:

Keyword	Abbreviation	Default starting value	Default periodicity
CYCLE	C	1	none
OBS	O	none	none

Example:

```
DATE Y 1960 M.
```

Overview

DATE generates date identification variables. You can use these variables to label plots and other output, establish periodicity, and distinguish between historical, validation, and forecasting periods.

Options

You can specify the starting value and periodicity. You can also specify an increment for the lowest-order keyword specified.

Basic Specification

The basic specification on DATE is a single keyword.

- For each keyword specified, DATE creates a numeric variable whose name is the keyword with an underscore as a suffix. Values for this variable are assigned to observations sequentially, beginning with the specified starting value. DATE also creates a string variable named *DATE_*, which combines the information from the numeric date variables and is used for labeling.

- If no starting value is specified, either the default is used or the value is inferred from the starting value of another DATE keyword.

- All variables created by DATE are automatically assigned variable labels that describe periodicity and associated formats. DATE produces a list of the names of the variables it creates and their variable labels.

Subcommand Order

- Keywords can be specified in any order.

Syntax Rules

- You can specify more than one keyword per command.
- If a keyword is specified more than once, only the last one is executed.
- Keywords that describe long time periods (YEAR, QUARTER, MONTH) cannot be used on the same command with keywords that describe short time periods (WEEK, DAY, HOUR, MINUTE, SECOND).
- Keywords CYCLE and OBS can be used with any other keyword.
- The lowest-order keyword specified should correspond to the level at which observations occur. For example, if observations are daily, the lowest-order keyword should be DAY.
- Keywords (except MINUTE) can be abbreviated down to the first character. MINUTE must have at least two characters (MI) to distinguish it from keyword MONTH.
- Keywords and additional specifications are separated by commas or spaces.

Starting Value and Periodicity

- A starting value and periodicity can be entered for any keyword except CYCLE. CYCLE can have only a starting value.
- Starting value and periodicity *must* be specified for keyword OBS.

- The starting value is specified first, followed by the periodicity, if any.
- You cannot specify a periodicity without first specifying a starting value.
- Starting values for HOUR, MINUTE, and SECOND can range from 0 to the periodicity minus 1 (for example, 0 to 59). For all other keywords, the range is 1 to the periodicity.
- If both MONTH and QUARTER are specified, DATE can infer the starting value of one from the other (see "Example 5" on p. 251).
- Specifying conflicting starting values for MONTH and QUARTER, such as Q 1 M 4, results in an error.
- For keyword YEAR, the starting value can be specified as the last two digits (93) instead of the whole year (1993) when the series and any forecasting are all within the same century. The same format (2 digits or 4 digits) must be used in all other commands that use year values.
- If you specify keywords that describe short time periods and skip over a level of measurement (for example, if you specify HOUR and SECOND but not MINUTE), you must specify the starting value and periodicity of the keyword after the skipped keywords. Otherwise, inappropriate periodicities will be generated (see "Example 7" on p. 252).

BY Keyword

- Keyword BY and a positive integer can be specified after the lowest-order keyword on the command to indicate an increment value. This value indicates how much to increment values of the lowest-order date variable as they are assigned to observations (see "Example 4" on p. 250).
- The increment value must divide evenly into the periodicity of the lowest-order DATE variable specified.

Operations

- DATE creates a numeric variable for every keyword specified, plus a string variable *DATE_*, which combines information from all the specified keywords.
- DATE automatically creates variable labels for each keyword specified indicating the variable name and its periodicity. For the *DATE_* variable, the label indicates the variable name and format.
- If the highest-order DATE variable specified has a periodicity, the *CYCLE_* variable will automatically be created. *CYCLE_* cannot have a periodicity (see "Example 3" on p. 249).
- Default periodicities are not used for the highest-order keyword specified. The exception is QUARTER, which will always have a default periodicity.
- The periodicity of the lowest-order variable is the default periodicity used by the procedures when periodicity is not defined either within the procedure or by the TSET command.
- The keyword name with an underscore is always used as the new variable name, even if keyword abbreviations are used in the specifications.
- Each time the DATE command is used, any DATE variables already in the working data file are deleted.

- The DATE command invalidates any previous USE and PREDICT commands specified. The USE and PREDICT periods must be respecified after DATE.

Limitations

- There is no limit on the number of keywords on the DATE command. However, keywords that describe long time periods (YEAR, QUARTER, MONTH) cannot be used on the same command with keywords that describe short time periods (WEEK, DAY, HOUR, MINUTE, SECOND).
- User-defined variable names must not conflict with DATE variable names.

Example 1

```
DATE Y 1960 M.
```

- This command generates variables *DATE_*, *YEAR_*, and *MONTH_*.
- *YEAR_* has a starting value of 1960. *MONTH_* starts at the default value of 1.
- By default, *YEAR_* has no periodicity, and *MONTH_* has a periodicity of 12.

DATE reports the following:

```
Name        Label

YEAR_       YEAR, not periodic
MONTH_      MONTH, period 12
DATE_       DATE.  FORMAT:  "MMM YYYY"
```

The following is a partial listing of the new variables:

```
YEAR_ MONTH_ DATE_

 1960     1   JAN 1960
 1960     2   FEB 1960
 1960     3   MAR 1960
 1960     4   APR 1960
 ...
 1960    10   OCT 1960
 1960    11   NOV 1960
 1960    12   DEC 1960
 1961     1   JAN 1961
 1961     2   FEB 1961
 ...
 1999     4   APR 1999
 1999     5   MAY 1999
 1999     6   JUN 1999
```

Example 2

```
DATE WEEK DAY 1 5 HOUR 1 8.
```

- This command creates four variables (*DATE_*, *WEEK_*, *DAY_*, and *HOUR_*) in a file where observations occur hourly in a 5-day, 40-hour week.
- For *WEEK_*, the default starting value is 1 and the default periodicity is none.

- For *DAY_*, the starting value has to be specified, even though it is the same as the default, because a periodicity is specified. The periodicity of 5 means that observations are measured in a 5-day week.
- For *HOUR_*, a starting value of 1 is specified. The periodicity of 8 means that observations occur in an 8-hour day.

DATE reports the following:

```
Name         Label

WEEK_        WEEK, not periodic
DAY_         DAY, period 5
HOUR_        HOUR, period 24
DATE_        DATE.  FORMAT:  "WWW D HH"
```

The following is a partial listing of the new variables:

```
WEEK_ DAY_ HOUR_ DATE_

   1    1     1    1 1  1
   1    1     2    1 1  2
   1    1     3    1 1  3
   1    1     4    1 1  4
   1    1     5    1 1  5
  ...
   1    1    22    1 1 22
   1    1    23    1 1 23
   1    2     0    1 2  0
   1    2     1    1 2  1
   1    2     2    1 2  2
  ...
   4    5    16    4 5 16
   4    5    17    4 5 17
   4    5    18    4 5 18
```

Example 3

```
DATE DAY 1 5 HOUR 3 8.
```

- This command creates four variables (*DATE_*, *CYCLE_*, *DAY_*, and *HOUR_*) in a file where observations occur hourly.
- For *HOUR_*, the starting value is 3 and the periodicity is 8.
- For *DAY_*, the starting value is 1 and the periodicity is 5. Since *DAY_* is the highest-order variable and it has a periodicity assigned, variable *CYCLE_* is automatically created.

DATE reports the following:

```
Name         Label

CYCLE_       CYCLE, not periodic
DAY_         DAY, period 5
HOUR_        HOUR, period 8
DATE_        DATE.  FORMAT:  "CCCC D H"
```

The following is a partial listing of the new variables:

```
CYCLE_ DAY_ HOUR_ DATE_

    1    1    3        1 1 3
    1    1    4        1 1 4
    1    1    5        1 1 5
    1    1    6        1 1 6
    1    1    7        1 1 7
    1    2    0        1 2 0
    1    2    1        1 2 1
   ...
   12    4    6       12 4 6
   12    4    7       12 4 7
   12    5    0       12 5 0
   12    5    1       12 5 1
   12    5    2       12 5 2
   12    5    3       12 5 3
   12    5    4       12 5 4
```

Example 4

```
DATE DAY HOUR 1 24 BY 2.
```

- This command creates three variables (*DATE_*, *DAY_*, and *HOUR_*) in a file where observations occur every two hours in a 24-hour day.
- *DAY_* uses the default starting value of 1. It has no periodicity, since none is specified, and it is the highest-order keyword on the command.
- *HOUR_* starts with a value of 1 and has a periodicity of 24.
- Keyword BY specifies an increment of 2 to use in assigning hour values.

DATE reports the following:

```
Name         Label

DAY_         DAY, not periodic
HOUR_        HOUR, period 24 by 2
DATE_        DATE.  FORMAT:  "DDDD HH"
```

The following is a partial listing of the new variables:

```
DAY_ HOUR_ DATE_

    1    1        1  1
    1    3        1  3
    1    5        1  5
   ...
   39   17       39 17
   39   19       39 19
   39   21       39 21
   39   23       39 23
   40    1       40  1
   40    3       40  3
   40    5       40  5
   40    7       40  7
   40    9       40  9
   40   11       40 11
```

Example 5

```
DATE Y 1950 Q 2 M.
```

- This example creates four variables (*DATE_*, *YEAR_*, *QUARTER_*, and *MONTH_*) in a file where observations are quarterly, starting with April 1950.
- The starting value for *MONTH_* is inferred from *QUARTER_*.
- This specification is equivalent to DATE Y 1950 Q M 4. Here, the starting value for *QUARTER_* (2) would be inferred from MONTH.

DATE reports the following:

```
Name        Label

YEAR_       YEAR, not periodic
QUARTER_    QUARTER, period 4
MONTH_      MONTH, period 12
DATE_       DATE.  FORMAT:  "MMM YYYY"
```

The following is a partial listing of the new variables:

```
YEAR_  QUARTER_  MONTH_  DATE_

1950      2         4     APR 1950
1950      2         5     MAY 1950
1950      2         6     JUN 1950
1950      3         7     JUL 1950
1950      3         8     AUG 1950
...
1988      4        11     NOV 1988
1988      4        12     DEC 1988
1989      1         1     JAN 1989
1989      1         2     FEB 1989
1989      1         3     MAR 1989
1989      2         4     APR 1989
1989      2         5     MAY 1989
1989      2         6     JUN 1989
1989      3         7     JUL 1989
1989      3         8     AUG 1989
1989      3         9     SEP 1989
```

Example 6

```
DATE OBS 9 17.
```

- This command creates variables *DATE_*, *CYCLE_*, and *OBS_* and assigns values to observations sequentially, starting with value 9. The periodicity is 17.

DATE reports the following:

```
Name        Label

CYCLE_      CYCLE, not periodic
OBS_        OBS, period 17
DATE_       DATE.  FORMAT:  "CCCC OO"
```

The following is a partial listing of the new variables:

```
CYCLE_ OBS_ DATE_

     1    9     1   9
     1   10     1  10
     1   11     1  11
     1   12     1  12
     1   13     1  13
     1   14     1  14
     1   15     1  15
     1   16     1  16
     1   17     1  17
     2    1     2   1
     2    2     2   2
   ...
    28   15    28  15
    28   16    28  16
    28   17    28  17
    29    1    29   1
    29    2    29   2
    29    3    29   3
    29    4    29   4
    29    5    29   5
    29    6    29   6
```

Example 7

```
DATE W H 1 168
```

- This example creates three variables (*DATE_*, *WEEK_*, and *HOUR_*) in a file where observations occur hourly.
- Since the DAY keyword is not specified, a periodicity must be specified for HOUR. The value 168 indicates that there are 168 hours in a week.
- The starting value of HOUR is specified as 1.

DATE reports the following:

```
Name        Label

WEEK_       WEEK, not periodic
HOUR_       HOUR, period 168
DATE_       DATE.  FORMAT:  "WWWW HHH"
```

The following is a partial listing of the new variables:

```
WEEK_  HOUR_  DATE_

  1      1    1    1
  1      2    1    2
  1      3    1    3
  1      4    1    4
  1      5    1    5
  1      6    1    6
. . .
  1    161    1  161
  1    162    1  162
  1    163    1  163
  1    164    1  164
  1    165    1  165
  1    166    1  166
  1    167    1  167
  2      0    2    0
  2      1    2    1
  2      2    2    2
  2      3    2    3
  2      4    2    4
  2      5    2    5
. . .
  3    131    3  131
  3    132    3  132
  3    133    3  133
  3    134    3  134
  3    135    3  135
  3    136    3  136
  3    137    3  137
  3    138    3  138
```

DEFINE—!ENDDEFINE

```
DEFINE macro name

 ([{argument name=} [!DEFAULT (string)] [!NOEXPAND] {!TOKENS  (n)               }]
    {!POSITIONAL=  }                                {!CHAREND ('char')          }
                                                    {!ENCLOSE ('char', 'char')}
                                                    {!CMDEND                    }


 [/{argument name=} ...])
    {!POSITIONAL=  }

macro body

!ENDDEFINE
```

SET command controls:

```
PRESERVE
RESTORE
```

Assignment:

```
!LET var=expression
```

Conditional processing:

```
!IF (expression) !THEN statements
    [!ELSE statements]
!IFEND
```

Looping constructs:

```
!DO !varname=start !TO finish [BY step]
    statements  [!BREAK]
!DOEND

!DO !varname !IN (list)
    statements  [!BREAK]
!DOEND
```

Macro directives:

```
!OFFEXPAND
!ONEXPAND
```

String manipulation functions:

```
!LENGTH (string)
!CONCAT (string1,string2)
!SUBSTR (string,from,[length])
!INDEX (string1,string2)
!HEAD (string)
!TAIL (string)
!QUOTE (string)
!UNQUOTE (string)
!UPCASE (string)
!BLANKS (n)
!NULL
!EVAL (string)
```

Example:

```
DEFINE sesvars ()
  age sex educ religion.
!ENDDEFINE.
```

Overview

DEFINE—!ENDDEFINE defines a program macro, which can then be used within a command sequence. A macro can be useful in several different contexts. For example, it can be used to:

- Issue a series of the same or similar commands repeatedly, using looping constructs rather than redundant specifications.
- Specify a set of variables.
- Produce output from several program procedures with a single command.
- Create complex input programs, procedure specifications, or whole sessions that can then be executed.

A macro is defined by specifying any part of a valid command and giving it a macro name. This name is then specified in a macro call within a command sequence. When the program encounters the macro name, it expands the macro.

In the examples of macro definition throughout this reference, the macro name, body, and arguments are shown in lower case for readability. Macro keywords, which are always preceded by an exclamation point (!), are shown in upper case. For additional examples of the macro facility, see Appendix D.

Options

Macro Arguments. You can declare and use arguments in the macro definition and then assign specific values to these arguments in the macro call. You can define defaults for the arguments and indicate whether an argument should be expanded when the macro is called. (See pp. 258–265.)

Macro Directives. You can turn macro expansion on and off (see p. 265).

String Manipulation Functions. You can process one or more character strings and produce either a new character string or a character representation of a numeric result (see pp. 265–267).

Conditional Processing. You can build conditional and looping constructs (see p. 269).

Macro Variables. You can directly assign values to macro variables (see p. 271).

Basic Specification

All macros must start with the DEFINE command and end with the macro command !ENDDEFINE. These commands identify the beginning and end of a macro definition and are used to separate the macro definition from the rest of the command sequence.

- Immediately after DEFINE, specify the **macro name**. All macros must have a name. The name is used in the macro call to refer to the macro. Macro names can begin with an exclamation point (!), but other than this, follow the usual naming conventions. Starting a name with an ! ensures that it will not conflict with the other text or variables in the session.

- Immediately after the macro name, specify an optional **argument** definition in parentheses. This specification indicates the arguments that will be read when the macro is called. If you do not want to include arguments, specify just the parentheses; *the parentheses are required, whether or not they enclose an argument.*

- Next specify the body of the macro. The **macro body** can include commands, parts of commands, or macro statements (macro directives, string manipulation statements, and looping and conditional processing statements).

- At the end of the macro body, specify the !ENDDEFINE command.

To invoke the macro, issue a **macro call** in the command sequence. To call a macro, specify the macro name and any necessary arguments. If there are no arguments, only the macro name is required.

Operations

- When macros are used in a prompted session, the command line prompt changes to DEFINE> between the DEFINE and !ENDDEFINE commands.

- When the program reads the macro definition, it translates into upper case all text (except arguments) not enclosed in quotation marks. Arguments are read in upper and lower case.

- The macro facility does not build and execute commands; rather, it expands strings in a process called **macro expansion**. A macro call initiates macro expansion. After the strings are expanded, the commands (or parts of commands) that contain the expanded strings are executed as part of the command sequence.

- Any elements on the macro call that are not used in the macro expansion are read and combined with the expanded strings.

- The expanded strings and the remaining elements from the macro call, if any, must conform to the syntax rules for the program. If not, the program generates either a warning or an error message, depending on the nature of the syntax problem.

Limitations

- The BEGIN DATA—END DATA commands are not allowed within a macro.

- The DEFINE command is not allowed within a macro.

Example

```
* Macro without arguments: Specify a group of variables.

DEFINE sesvars ()
   age sex educ religion.
!ENDDEFINE.

FREQUENCIES VARIABLES=sesvars.
```

- The macro name is sesvars. Because the parentheses are empty, sesvars has no arguments. The macro body defines four variables: *AGE*, *SEX*, *EDUC*, and *RELIGION*.
- The macro call is specified on FREQUENCIES. When the call is executed, sesvars is expanded into the variables *AGE*, *SEX*, *EDUC*, and *RELIGION*.
- After the macro expansion, FREQUENCIES is executed.

Example

```
* Macro without arguments: Repeat a sequence of commands.

DATA LIST FILE = MAC4D /GROUP 1   REACTIME 3-5 ACCURACY 7-9.
VALUE LABELS GROUP     1'normal'
                       2'learning disabled'.
* Macro definition.
DEFINE check ().
split file by group.
frequencies variables = reactime accuracy
  /histogram.
descriptives reactime accuracy.
list.
split file off.
regression variables = group reactime accuracy
  /dependent = accuracy
  /enter
  /scatterplot (reactime, accuracy).
!ENDDEFINE.

check.                    /* First call of defined macro check

COMPUTE REACTIME = SQRT (REACTIME).
COMPUTE ACCURACY = SQRT (ACCURACY).

check.                    /* Second call of defined macro check

COMPUTE REACTIME = lg10 (REACTIME * REACTIME).
COMPUTE ACCURACY = lg10 (ACCURACY * ACCURACY).

check.                    /* Third call of defined macro check
```

- The name of the macro is *CHECK*. The empty parentheses indicate that there are no arguments to the macro.
- The macro definition (between DEFINE and !ENDDEFINE) contains the command sequence to be repeated: SPLIT FILE, FREQUENCIES, DESCRIPTIVES, LIST, SPLIT FILE, and REGRESSION.

- The macro is called three times. Every time check is encountered, it is replaced with the command sequence SPLIT FILE, FREQUENCIES, DESCRIPTIVES, LIST, SPLIT FILE OFF, and REGRESSION. The command sequence using the macro facility is identical to the command sequence in which the specified commands are explicitly stated three separate times.

Example

```
* Macro with an argument.

DEFINE myfreq (vars = !CHAREND('/')).
frequencies variables = !vars
  /format = notable
  /hbar = normal
  /statistics = default skewness kurtosis.
!ENDDEFINE.

myfreq vars = AGE SEX EDUC RELIGION /.
```

- The macro definition defines vars as the macro argument. In the macro call, four variables are specified as the argument to the macro myfreq. When the program expands the myfreq macro, it substitutes the argument, AGE, SEX, EDUC, and RELIGION, for !vars and executes the resulting commands.

Macro Arguments

The macro definition can include macro arguments, which can be assigned specific values in the macro call. There are two types of arguments: keyword and positional. Keyword arguments are assigned names in the macro definition; in the macro call, they are identified by name. Positional arguments are defined after the keyword !POSITIONAL in the macro definition; in the macro call, they are identified by their relative position within the macro definition.

- There is no limit to the number of arguments that can be specified in a macro.

- All arguments are specified in parentheses and must be separated by slashes.

- If both keyword and positional arguments are defined in the same definition, the positional arguments must be defined, used in the macro body, and invoked in the macro call before the keyword arguments.

Example
```
* A keyword argument.

DEFINE macname (arg1 = !TOKENS(1)).
frequencies variables = !arg1.
!ENDDEFINE.

macname arg1 = V1.
```

- The macro definition defines macname as the macro name and arg1 as the argument. The argument arg1 has one token and can be assigned any value in the macro call.

- The macro call expands the macname macro. The argument is identified by its name, arg1, and is assigned the value V1. V1 is substituted wherever !arg1 appears in the macro body. The macro body in this example is the FREQUENCIES command.

Example

```
* A positional argument.

DEFINE macname (!POSITIONAL !TOKENS(1)
               /!POSITIONAL !TOKENS(2)).
frequencies variables = !1 !2.
!ENDDEFINE.

macname V1 V2 V3.
```

- The macro definition defines macname as the macro name with two positional arguments. The first argument has one token and the second argument has two tokens. The tokens can be assigned any values in the macro call.
- The macro call expands the macname macro. The arguments are identified by their positions. V1 is substituted for !1 wherever !1 appears in the macro body. V2 and V3 are substituted for !2 wherever !2 appears in the macro body. The macro body in this example is the FREQUENCIES command.

Keyword Arguments

Keyword arguments are called with user-defined keywords that can be specified in any order. In the macro body, the argument name is preceded by an exclamation point. On the macro call, the argument is specified without the exclamation point.

- Keyword argument definitions contain the argument name, an equals sign, and the !TOKENS, !ENCLOSE, !CHAREND, or !CMDEND keyword (see "Assigning Tokens to Arguments" on p. 261).
- Argument names are limited to seven characters and cannot match the character portion of a macro keyword, such as DEFINE, TOKENS, CHAREND, and so forth. See the syntax chart on p. 254 for a list of macro keywords for the program.
- The keyword !POSITIONAL cannot be used in keyword argument definitions.
- Keyword arguments do not have to be called in the order they were defined.

Example

```
DATA LIST FILE=MAC / V1 1-2 V2 4-5 V3 7-8.

* Macro definition.
DEFINE macdef2 (arg1 = !TOKENS(1)
               /arg2 = !TOKENS(1)
               /arg3 = !TOKENS(1)).
frequencies  variables = !arg1 !arg2 !arg3.
!ENDDEFINE.

* Macro call.
macdef2 arg1=V1  arg2=V2  arg3=V3.
macdef2 arg3=V3  arg1=V1  arg2=V2.
```

- Three arguments are defined: arg1, arg2, and arg3, each with one token. In the first macro call, arg1 is assigned the value V1, arg2 is assigned the value V2, and arg3 is assigned the value V3. V1, V2, and V3 are then used as the variables in the FREQUENCIES command.
- The second macro call yields the same results as the first one. With keyword arguments, you do not need to call the arguments in the order in which they were defined.

Positional Arguments

Positional arguments must be defined in the order in which they will be specified on the macro call. In the macro body, the first positional argument is referred to by !1, the second positional argument defined is referred to by !2, and so on. Similarly, the value of the first argument in the macro call is assigned to !1, the value of the second argument is assigned to !2, and so on.

- Positional arguments can be collectively referred to in the macro body by specifying !*. The !* specification concatenates arguments, separating individual arguments with a blank.

Example

```
DATA LIST FILE=MAC / V1 1-2 V2 4-5 V3 7-8.

* Macro definition.
DEFINE macdef (!POS !TOKENS(1).
               /!POS !TOKENS(1).
               /!POS !TOKENS(1)).
frequencies variables = !1 !2 !3.
!ENDDEFINE.

* Macro call.
macdef  V1    V2    V3.
macdef  V3    V1    V2.
```

- Three positional arguments with one token each are defined. The first positional argument is referred to by !1 on the FREQUENCIES command, the second by !2, and the third by !3.
- When the first call expands the macro, the first positional argument (!1) is assigned the value V1, the second positional argument (!2) is assigned the value V2, and the third positional argument (!3) is assigned the value V3.
- In the second call, the first positional argument is assigned the value V3, the second positional argument is assigned the value V1, and the third positional argument is assigned the value V2.

Example

```
DEFINE macdef (!POS !TOKENS(3)).
frequencies variables = !1.
!ENDDEFINE.

macdef  V1    V2    V3.
```

- This example is the same as the previous one, except that it assigns three tokens to one argument instead of assigning one token to each of three arguments. The result is the same.

Example

```
DEFINE macdef (!POS !TOKENS(1)
               /!POS !TOKENS(1)
               /!POS !TOKENS(1)).
frequencies variables = !*.
!ENDDEFINE.

macdef  V1    V2    V3.
```

- This is a third alternative for achieving the macro expansion shown in the previous two examples. It specifies three arguments but then joins them all together on one FREQUENCIES command using the symbol !*.

Assigning Tokens to Arguments

A **token** is a character or group of characters that has a predefined function in a specified context. The argument definition must include a keyword that indicates which tokens following the macro name are associated with each argument.

- Any program keyword, variable name, or delimiter (a slash, comma, etc.) is a valid token.
- The arguments for a given macro can use a combination of the token keywords.

!TOKENS (n)   *Assign the next n tokens to the argument.* The value *n* can be any positive integer and must be enclosed in parentheses. !TOKENS allows you to specify exactly how many tokens are desired.

!CHAREND ('char')   *Assign all tokens up to the specified character to the argument.* The character must be a one-character string specified in apostrophes and enclosed in parentheses. !CHAREND specifies the character that ends the argument assignment. This is useful when the number of assigned tokens is arbitrary or not known in advance.

!ENCLOSE ('char','char') *Assign all tokens between the indicated characters to the argument.* The starting and ending characters can be any one-character strings, and they do not need to be the same. The characters are each enclosed in apostrophes and separated by a comma. The entire specification is enclosed in parentheses. !ENCLOSE allows you to group multiple tokens within a specified pair of symbols. This is useful when the number of tokens to be assigned to an argument is indeterminate, or when the use of an ending character is not sufficient.

!CMDEND   *Assign to the argument all of the remaining text on the macro call, up to the start of the next command.* !CMDEND is useful for changing the defaults on an existing command. Since !CMDEND reads up to the next command, only the last argument on the argument list can be specified with !CMDEND. If !CMDEND is not the final argument, the arguments following !CMDEND are read as text.

Example

```
* Keyword !TOKENS.

DEFINE macname (!POSITIONAL !TOKENS (3)).
frequencies variables = !1.
!ENDDEFINE.

macname ABC DEFG HI.
```

- The three tokens following macname (ABC, DEFG, and HI) are assigned to the positional argument !1, and FREQUENCIES is then executed.

Example

```
* Keyword !TOKENS.

* Macro definition.
DEFINE earnrep (varrep = !TOKENS (1)).
sort cases by !varrep.
report variables = earnings
  /break = !varrep
  /summary = mean.
!ENDDEFINE.

* Call the macro three times.
earnrep varrep= SALESMAN.    /*First macro call
earnrep varrep = REGION.     /*Second macro call
earnrep varrep = MONTH.      /*Third macro call
```

- This macro runs a REPORT command three times, each time with a different break variable.
- The macro name is earnrep, and there is one keyword argument, varrep, which has one token.
- In the first macro call, the token SALESMAN is substituted for !varrep when the macro is expanded. REGION and MONTH are substituted for !varrep when the macro is expanded in the second and third calls.

Example

```
* Keyword !CHAREND'.

DEFINE macname (!POSITIONAL !CHAREND ('/')
               /!POSITIONAL !TOKENS(2)).
frequencies variables = !1.
correlations variables= !2.
!ENDDEFINE.

macname A B C D / E F.
```

- When the macro is called, all tokens up to the slash (A, B, C, and D) are assigned to the positional argument !1. E and F are assigned to the positional argument !2.

Example

```
* Keyword !CHAREND.

DEFINE macname (!POSITIONAL !CHAREND ('/')).
frequencies variables = !1.
!ENDDEFINE.

macname A B C D / E F.
```

- Although E and F are not part of the positional argument and are not used in the macro expansion, the program still reads them as text and interprets them in relation to where the macro definition ends. In this example, macro definition ends after the expanded variable list (D). E and F are names of variables. Thus, E and F are added to the variable list and FREQUENCIES is executed with six variables: *A*, *B*, *C*, *D*, *E*, and *F*.

Example

```
* Keyword !ENCLOSE.

DEFINE macname (!POSITIONAL !ENCLOSE('(',')')).
frequencies variables = !1
  /statistics = default skewness.
!ENDDEFINE.

macname (A B C) D E.
```

- When the macro is called, the three tokens enclosed in parentheses, A, B, and C, are assigned to the positional argument !1 in the macro body.
- After macro expansion is complete, the program reads the remaining characters on the macro call as text. In this instance, the macro definition ends with keyword SKEWNESS on the STATISTICS subcommand. Adding variable names to the STATISTICS subcommand is not valid syntax. The program generates a warning message but is still able to execute the frequencies command. Frequency tables and the specified statistics are generated for the variables *A*, *B*, and *C*.

Example

```
* Keyword !CMDEND'.

DEFINE macname (!POSITIONAL !TOKENS(2)
                /!POSITIONAL !CMDEND).
frequencies variables = !1.
correlations variables= !2.
!ENDDEFINE.

macname A B C D E.
```

- When the macro is called, the first two tokens following macname (A and B) are assigned to the positional argument !1. C, D, and E are assigned to the positional argument !2. Thus, the variables used for FREQUENCIES are *A* and *B*, and the variables used for CORRELATION are *C*, *D*, and *E*.

Example

```
* Incorrect order for !CMDEND.

DEFINE macname  (!POSITIONAL !CMDEND
                 /!POSITIONAL !tokens(2)).
frequencies variables = !1.
correlations variables= !2.
!ENDDEFINE.

macname  A B C D E.
```

- When the macro is called, all five tokens, A, B, C, D, and E, are assigned to the first positional argument. No variables are included on the variable list for CORRELATIONS, causing the program to generate an error message. The previous example declares the arguments in the correct order.

Example

```
* Using !CMDEND.
SUBTITLE 'CHANGING DEFAULTS ON A COMMAND'.

DEFINE myfreq (!POSITIONAL !CMDEND ).
frequencies !1
  /statistics=default skewness  /* Modify default statistics.
!ENDDEFINE.

myfreq VARIABLES = A B /HIST.
```

- The macro myfreq contains options for the FREQUENCIES command. When the macro is called, myfreq is expanded to perform a FREQUENCIES analysis on the variables *A* and *B*. The analysis produces default statistics and the skewness statistic, plus a histogram, as requested on the macro call.

Example

```
* Keyword arguments: Using a combination of token keywords.

DATA LIST FREE / A B C D E.
DEFINE macdef3 (arg1 = !TOKENS(1)
                /arg2 = !ENCLOSE ('(',')')
                /arg3 = !CHAREND('%')).
frequencies variables = !arg1  !arg2 !arg3.
!ENDDEFINE.
macdef arg1 = A  arg2=(B C)  arg3=DE %.
```

- Because arg1 is defined with the !TOKENS keyword, the value for arg1 is simply specified as A. The value for arg2 is specified in parentheses, as indicated by !ENCLOSE. The value for arg3 is followed by a percent sign, as indicated by !CHAREND.

Defining Defaults

The optional !DEFAULT keyword in the macro definition establishes default settings for arguments.

!DEFAULT   *Default argument.* After !DEFAULT, specify the value you want to use as a default for that argument. A default can be specified for each argument.

Example

```
DEFINE macdef (arg1 = !DEFAULT (V1) !TOKENS(1)
               /arg2 = !TOKENS(1)
               /arg3 = !TOKENS(1)).
frequencies variables = !arg1 !arg2 !arg3.
!ENDDEFINE.

macdef arg2=V2  arg3=V3.
```

- V1 is defined as the default value for argument **arg1**. Since **arg1** is not specified on the macro call, it is set to V1.
- If !DEFAULT (V1) were not specified, the value of **arg1** would be set to a null string.

Controlling Expansion

!NOEXPAND indicates that an argument should not be expanded when the macro is called.

!NOEXPAND   *Do not expand the specified argument.* !NOEXPAND applies to a single argument and is useful only when a macro calls another macro (imbedded macros).

Macro Directives

!ONEXPAND and !OFFEXPAND determine whether macro expansion is on or off. !ONEXPAND activates macro expansion and !OFFEXPAND stops macro expansion. All symbols between !OFFEXPAND and !ONEXPAND in the macro definition will not be expanded when the macro is called.

!ONEXPAND   *Turn macro expansion on.*

!OFFEXPAND   *Turn macro expansion off.* !OFFEXPAND is effective only when SET MEXPAND is ON (the default).

Macro Expansion in Comments

When macro expansion is on, a macro is expanded when its name is specified in a comment line beginning with *. To use a macro name in a comment, specify the comment within slashes and asterisks (/*...*/) to avoid unwanted macro expansion. (See COMMENT.)

String Manipulation Functions

String manipulation functions process one or more character strings and produce either a new character string or a character representation of a numeric result.

- The result of any string manipulation function is treated as a character string.

- The arguments to string manipulation functions can be strings, variables, or even other macros. A macro argument or another function can be used in place of a string.
- The strings within string manipulation functions must be either single tokens, such as ABC, or delimited by apostrophes or quotation marks, as in 'A B C'. See Table 1 for a set of expressions and their results.

Table 1   Expressions and results

Expression	Result
!UPCASE(abc)	ABC
!UPCASE('abc')	ABC
!UPCASE(a b c)	error
!UPCASE('a b c')	A B C
!UPCASE(a/b/c)	error
!UPCASE('a/b/c')	A/B/C
!UPCASE(!CONCAT(a,b,c))	ABC
!UPCASE(!CONCAT('a','b','c'))	ABC
!UPCASE(!CONCAT(a, b, c))	ABC
!UPCASE(!CONCAT('a ','b ','c '))	A B C
!UPCASE(!CONCAT('a,b,c'))	A,B,C
!QUOTE(abc)	'ABC'
!QUOTE('abc')	abc
!QUOTE('Bill''s')	'Bill''s'
!QUOTE("Bill's")	"Bill's"
!QUOTE(Bill's)	error
!QUOTE(!UNQUOTE('Bill''s'))	'Bill''s'

!LENGTH (str) — *Return the length of the specified string.* The result is a character representation of the string length. !LENGTH(abcdef) returns 6. If the string is specified with apostrophes around it, each apostrophe adds 1 to the length. !LENGTH ('abcdef') returns 8. If an argument is used in place of a string and it is set to null, this function will return 0.

!CONCAT(str1,str2 . . .) — *Return a string that is the concatenation of the strings.* For example, !CONCAT (abc,def) returns abcdef.

!SUBSTR (str,from,[length]) — *Return a substring of the specified string.* The substring starts at the *from* position and continues for the specified *length*. If the length is not specified, the substring ends at the end of the input string. For example, !SUBSTR (abcdef, 3, 2) returns cd.

!INDEX (haystack,needle) — *Return the position of the first occurrence of the needle in the haystack.* If the needle is not found in the haystack, the function returns 0. !INDEX (abcdef,def) returns 4.

!HEAD (str)	*Return the first token within a string.* The input string is not changed. !HEAD ('a b c') returns a.
!TAIL (str)	*Return all tokens except the head token.* The input string is not changed. !TAIL('a b c') returns b c.
!QUOTE (str)	*Put apostrophes around the argument.* !QUOTE replicates any imbedded apostrophe. !QUOTE(abc) returns 'abc'. If !1 equals Bill's, !QUOTE(!1) returns 'Bill''s'.
!UNQUOTE (str)	*Remove quotation marks and apostrophes from the enclosed string.* If !1 equals 'abc', !UNQUOTE(!1) is abc. Internal paired quotation marks are unpaired; if !1 equals 'Bill''s', !UNQUOTE(!1) is Bill's. The specification !UNQUOTE(!QUOTE(Bill)) returns Bill.
!UPCASE (str)	*Convert all lowercase characters in the argument to upper case.* !UPCASE('abc def') returns ABC DEF.
!BLANKS (n)	*Generate a string containing the specified number of blanks.* The *n* specification must be a positive integer. !BLANKS(5) returns a string of five blank spaces. Unless the blanks are quoted, they cannot be processed, since the macro facility compresses blanks.
!NULL	*Generate a string of length 0.* This can help determine whether an argument was ever assigned a value, as in !IF (!1 !EQ !NULL) !THEN. . . .
!EVAL (str)	*Scan the argument for macro calls.* During macro definition, an argument to a function or an operand in an expression is not scanned for possible macro calls unless the !EVAL function is used. It returns a string that is the expansion of its argument. For example, if mac1 is a macro, then !EVAL(mac1) returns the expansion of mac1. If mac1 is not a macro, !EVAL(mac1) returns mac1.

SET Subcommands for Use with Macro

Four subcommands on the SET command were designed for use with the macro facility.

MPRINT	*Display a list of commands after macro expansion.* The specification on MPRINT is YES or NO (alias ON or OFF). By default, the output does not include a list of commands after macro expansion (MPRINT NO). The MPRINT subcommand on SET is independent of the PRINTBACK command.
MEXPAND	*Macro expansion.* The specification on MEXPAND is YES or NO (alias ON or OFF). By default, MEXPAND is on. SET MEXPAND OFF prevents macro expansion. Specifying SET MEXPAND ON reestablishes macro expansion.
MNEST	*Maximum nesting level for macros.* The default number of levels that can be nested is 50. The maximum number of levels depends on storage capacity.

MITERATE   *Maximum loop iterations permitted in macro expansions.* The default number of iterations is 1000.

Restoring SET Specifications

The PRESERVE and RESTORE commands bring more flexibility and control over SET. PRESERVE and RESTORE are available generally within the program but are especially useful with macros.

- The settings of all SET subcommands—those set explicitly and those set by default (except MEXPAND)—are saved with PRESERVE. PRESERVE has no further specifications.
- With RESTORE, all SET subcommands are changed to what they were when the PRESERVE command was executed. RESTORE has no further specifications.
- PRESERVE...RESTORE sequences can be nested up to five levels.

PRESERVE   *Store the SET specifications that are in effect at this point in the session.*

RESTORE   *Restore the SET specifications to what they were when PRESERVE was specified.*

Example

```
* Two nested levels of preserve and restore'.

DEFINE macdef ().
preserve.
set format F5.3.
descriptives v1 v2.
+ preserve.
set format F3.0 blanks=999.
descriptives v3 v4.
+ restore.
descriptives v5 v6.
restore.
!ENDDEFINE.
```

- The first PRESERVE command saves all of the current SET conditions. If none have been specified, the default settings are saved.
- Next, the format is set to F5.3 and descriptive statistics for *V1* and *V2* are obtained.
- The second PRESERVE command saves the F5.3 format setting and all other settings in effect.
- The second SET command changes the format to F3.0 and sets BLANKS to 999 (the default is SYSMIS). Descriptive statistics are then obtained for *V3* and *V4*.
- The first RESTORE command restores the format to F5.3 and BLANKS to the default, the setting in effect at the second PRESERVE. Descriptive statistics are then obtained for *V5* and *V6*.
- The last RESTORE restores the settings in effect when the first PRESERVE was specified.

Conditional Processing

The !IF construct specifies conditions for processing. The syntax is as follows:

```
!IF (expression) !THEN statements
                 [!ELSE statements]
!IFEND
```

- !IF, !THEN, and !IFEND are all required. !ELSE is optional.
- If the result of the expression is true, the statements following !THEN are executed. If the result of the expression is false and !ELSE is specified, the statements following !ELSE are executed. Otherwise, the program continues.
- Valid operators for the expressions include !EQ, !NE, !GT, !LT, !GE, !LE, !OR, !NOT, and !AND, or =, ~= (¬=), >, <, >=, <=, |, ~ (¬), and & (see "Relational Operators" on p. 55).
- When a macro is expanded, conditional processing constructs are interpreted after arguments are substituted and functions are executed.
- !IF statements can be nested whenever necessary. Parentheses can be used to specify the order of evaluation. The default order is the same as for transformations: !NOT has precedence over !AND, which has precedence over !OR.

Looping Constructs

Looping constructs accomplish repetitive tasks. Loops can be nested to whatever depth is required, but loops cannot be crossed. The macro facility has two looping constructs: the index loop (DO loop) and the list-processing loop (DO IN loop).

- When a macro is expanded, looping constructs are interpreted after arguments are substituted and functions are executed.

Index Loop

The syntax of an index loop is as follows:

```
!DO !var = start !TO finish [ !BY step ]
    statements
!BREAK
!DOEND
```

- The indexing variable is *!var* and must begin with an exclamation point.
- The start, finish, and step values must be numbers or expressions that evaluate to numbers.
- The loop begins at the start value and continues until it reaches the finish value (unless a !BREAK statement is encountered). The step value is optional and can be used to specify a subset of iterations. If start is set to 1, finish to 10, and step to 3, the loop will be executed four times with the index variable assigned values 1, 4, 7, and 10.
- The statements can be any valid commands or macro keywords. !DOEND specifies the end of the loop.
- !BREAK is an optional specification. It can be used in conjunction with conditional processing to exit the loop.

Example

```
DEFINE macdef (arg1 = !TOKENS(1)
                /arg2 = !TOKENS(1)).
!DO !i = !arg1 !TO !arg2.
frequencies variables = !CONCAT(var,!i).
!DOEND.
!ENDDEFINE.
macdef arg1 = 1 arg2 = 3.
```

- The variable *!i* is initially assigned the value 1 (arg1) and is incremented until it equals 3 (arg2), at which point the loop ends.
- The first loop concatenates var and the value for *!i*, which is 1 in the first loop. The second loop concatenates var and 2, and the third concatenates var and 3. The result is that FREQUEN-CIES is executed three times, with variables *VAR1*, *VAR2*, and *VAR3*, respectively.

List-processing Loop

The syntax of a list-processing loop is as follows:

```
!DO !var !IN (list)
    statements
!BREAK
!DOEND
```

- The !DO and !DOEND statements begin and end the loop. !BREAK is used to exit the loop.
- The !IN function requires one argument, which must be a list of items. The number of items on the list determines the number of iterations. At each iteration, the index variable *!var* is set to each item on the list.
- The list can be any expression, although it is usually a string. Only one list can be speci-fied in each list-processing loop.

Example

```
DEFINE macdef (!POS !CHAREND('/') ).
!DO !i !IN ( !1).
frequencies variables = !i.
!DOEND.
!ENDDEFINE.
macdef VAR1 VAR2 VAR3  /.
```

- The macro call assigns three variables, *VAR1*, *VAR2*, and *VAR3*, to the positional argument !1. Thus, the loop completes three iterations.
- In the first iteration, *!i* is set to value *VAR1*. In the second and third iterations, *!i* is set to *VAR2* and *VAR3*, respectively. Thus, FREQUENCIES is executed three times, respectively with *VAR1*, *VAR2*, and *VAR3*.

Example

```
DEFINE macdef (!POS !CHAREND('/') ).
!DO !i !IN ( !1).
sort cases by !i.
report var = earnings
  /break = !i
  /summary = mean.
!DOEND.
!ENDDEFINE.

macdef SALESMAN REGION MONTH /.
```

- The positional argument !1 is assigned the three variables *SALESMAN*, *REGION*, and *MONTH*. The loop is executed three times and the index variable *!i* is set to each of the variables in succession. The macro creates three reports.

Direct Assignment of Macro Variables

The macro command !LET assigns values to macro variables. The syntax is as follows:

```
!LET !var = expression
```

- The expression must be either a single token or enclosed in parentheses.
- The macro variable *!var* cannot be a macro keyword (see the syntax chart on p. 254 for a list of macro keywords), and it cannot be the name of one of the arguments within the macro definition. Thus, !LET cannot be used to change the value of an argument.
- The macro variable *!var* can be a new variable or one previously assigned by a !DO command or another !LET command.

Example

```
!LET !a = 1.
!LET !b = !CONCAT(ABC,!SUBSTR(!1,3,1),DEF).
!LET !c = (!2 ~= !NULL).
```

- The first !LET sets *!a* equal to 1.
- The second !LET sets *!b* equal to ABC followed by 1 character taken from the third position of !1 followed by DEF.
- The last !LET sets *!c* equal to 0 (false) if !2 is a null string or to 1 (true) if !2 is not a null string.

DESCRIPTIVES

```
DESCRIPTIVES [VARIABLES=] varname[(zname)] [varname...]

 [/MISSING={VARIABLE**}  [INCLUDE]]
          {LISTWISE  }

 [/SAVE]

 [/STATISTICS=[DEFAULT**]  [MEAN**]  [MIN**]  [SKEWNESS]]
              [STDDEV** ]  [SEMEAN]  [MAX**]  [KURTOSIS]
              [VARIANCE ]  [SUM   ]  [RANGE]  [ALL]

 [/SORT=[{MEAN    }] [{(A)}]]
         {SMEAN   }   {(D)}
         {STDDEV  }
         {VARIANCE}
         {KURTOSIS}
         {SKEWNESS}
         {RANGE   }
         {MIN     }
         {MAX     }
         {SUM     }
         {NAME    }
```

**Default if the subcommand is omitted.

Example:

```
DESCRIPTIVES VARIABLES=FOOD RENT, APPL TO COOK, TELLER, TEACHER
  /STATISTICS=VARIANCE DEFAULT
  /MISSING=LISTWISE.
```

Overview

DESCRIPTIVES computes univariate statistics, including the mean, standard deviation, minimum, and maximum, for numeric variables. Because it does not sort values into a frequency table, DESCRIPTIVES is an efficient means of computing descriptive statistics for continuous variables. Other procedures that display descriptive statistics include FREQUENCIES, MEANS, and EXAMINE.

Options

Z Scores. You can create new variables that contain z scores (standardized deviation scores from the mean) and add them to the working data file by specifying z-score names on the VARIABLES subcommand or by using the SAVE subcommand.

Statistical Display. Optional statistics available with the STATISTICS subcommand include the standard error of the mean, variance, kurtosis, skewness, range, and sum. DESCRIPTIVES does not compute the median or mode (see FREQUENCIES or EXAMINE).

Display Order. You can list variables in ascending or descending alphabetical order or by the numerical value of any of the available statistics using the SORT subcommand.

Basic Specification

The basic specification is the VARIABLES subcommand with a list of variables. The actual keyword VARIABLES can be omitted. All cases with valid values for a variable are included in the calculation of statistics for that variable. Statistics include the mean, standard deviation, minimum, maximum, and number of cases with valid values.

Subcommand Order

- Subcommands can be used in any order.

Operations

- If a string variable is specified on the variable list, no statistics are displayed for that variable.
- If there is insufficient memory available to calculate statistics for all variables requested, DESCRIPTIVES truncates the variable list.

Example

```
DESCRIPTIVES VARIABLES=FOOD RENT, APPL TO COOK, TELLER, TEACHER
/STATISTICS=VARIANCE DEFAULT
/MISSING=LISTWISE.
```

- DESCRIPTIVES requests statistics for the variables *FOOD*, *RENT*, *TELLER*, *TEACHER*, and all of the variables between and including *APPL* and *COOK* in the working data file.
- STATISTICS requests the variance and the default statistics: mean, standard deviation, minimum, and maximum.
- MISSING specifies that cases with missing values for any variable on the variable list will be omitted from the calculation of statistics for all variables.

Example

```
DESCRIPTIVES VARS=ALL.
```

- DESCRIPTIVES requests statistics for all variables in the working file.
- Because no STATISTICS subcommand is included, only the mean, standard deviation, minimum, and maximum are displayed.

VARIABLES Subcommand

VARIABLES names the variables for which you want to compute statistics. The actual keyword VARIABLES can be omitted.

- The keyword ALL can be used to refer to all user-defined variables in the working data file.
- Only one variable list can be specified.

Z Scores

The z-score transformation standardizes variables to the same scale, producing new variables with a mean of 0 and a standard deviation of 1. These variables are added to the working data file.

- To obtain z scores for all specified variables, use the SAVE subcommand.
- To obtain z scores for a subset of variables, name the new variable in parentheses following the source variable on the VARIABLES subcommand and do not use the SAVE subcommand.
- Specify new names individually; a list in parentheses is not recognized.
- The new variable name can be any acceptable eight-character name that is not already part of the working data file.

Example

```
DESCRIPTIVES VARIABLES=NTCSAL NTCPUR (PURCHZ) NTCPRI (PRICEZ).
```

- DESCRIPTIVES creates z-score variables named *PURCHZ* and *PRICEZ* for *NTCPUR* and *NTCPRI*, respectively. No z-score variable is created for *NTCSAL*.

SAVE Subcommand

SAVE creates a z-score variable for each variable specified on the VARIABLES subcommand. The new variables are added to the working data file.

- When DESCRIPTIVES creates new z-score variables, it displays the source variable names, the new variable names, and their labels in the Notes table.
- DESCRIPTIVES automatically supplies variable names for the new variables. The new variable name is created by prefixing the letter Z to the first seven characters of the source variable name. For example, *ZNTCPRI* is the z-score variable for *NTCPRI*.
- If the default naming convention duplicates variable names in the working data file, DESCRIPTIVES uses an alternative naming convention: first *ZSC001* through *ZSC099*, then *STDZ01* through *STDZ09*, then *ZZZZ01* through *ZZZZ09*, and then *ZQZQ01* through *ZQZQ09*.
- Variable labels are created by prefixing *ZSCORE* to the first 31 characters of the source variable label. If the alternative naming convention is used, DESCRIPTIVES prefixes *ZSCORE(varname)* to the first 31 characters of the label. If the source variable does not have a label, DESCRIPTIVES uses *ZSCORE(varname)* for the label.
- If you specify new names on the VARIABLES subcommand *and* use the SAVE subcommand, DESCRIPTIVES creates one new variable for each variable on the VARIABLES subcommand, using default names for variables not assigned names on VARIABLES.
- If at any time you want to change any of the variable names, whether those DESCRIPTIVES created or those you previously assigned, you can do so with the RENAME VARIABLES command.

Example

```
DESCRIPTIVES VARIABLES=ALL
  /SAVE.
```

- SAVE creates a *z*-score variable for all variables in the working file. All *z*-score variables receive the default name.

Example

```
DESCRIPTIVES VARIABLES=NTCSAL NTCPUR (PURCHZ) NTCPRI (PRICEZ)
  /SAVE.
```

- DESCRIPTIVES creates three *z*-score variables named *ZNTCSAL* (the default name), *PURCHZ*, and *PRICEZ*.

Example

```
DESCRIPTIVES VARIABLES=SALARY86 SALARY87 SALARY88
  /SAVE.
```

- In this example, the default naming convention would produce duplicate names. Thus, the names of the three *z*-score variables are *ZSALARY8*, *ZSC001*, and *ZSC002*.

STATISTICS Subcommand

By default, DESCRIPTIVES displays the mean, standard deviation, minimum, and maximum. Use the STATISTICS subcommand to request other statistics.

- When you use STATISTICS, DESCRIPTIVES displays *only* those statistics you request.
- The keyword ALL obtains all statistics.
- You can specify the keyword DEFAULT to obtain the default statistics without having to name MEAN, STDDEV, MIN, and MAX.
- The median and mode, which are available in FREQUENCIES and EXAMINE, are not available in DESCRIPTIVES. These statistics require that values be sorted, and DESCRIPTIVES does not sort values (the SORT subcommand does not sort values, it simply lists variables in the order you request).
- If you request a statistic that is not available, DESCRIPTIVES issues an error message and the command is not executed.

MEAN	*Mean.*
SEMEAN	*Standard error of the mean.*
STDDEV	*Standard deviation.*
VARIANCE	*Variance.*
KURTOSIS	*Kurtosis and standard error of kurtosis.*
SKEWNESS	*Skewness and standard error of skewness.*
RANGE	*Range.*
MIN	*Minimum observed value.*

MAX   *Maximum observed value.*

SUM   *Sum.*

DEFAULT   *Mean, standard deviation, minimum, and maximum.* These are the default statistics.

ALL   *All statistics available in DESCRIPTIVES.*

SORT Subcommand

By default, DESCRIPTIVES lists variables in the order in which they are specified on VARIABLES. Use SORT to list variables in ascending or descending alphabetical order of variable name or in ascending or descending order of numeric value of any of the statistics.

- If you specify SORT without any keywords, variables are sorted in ascending order of the mean.
- SORT can sort variables by the value of any of the statistics available with DESCRIPTIVES, but only those statistics specified on STATISTICS (or the default statistics) are displayed.

Only one of the following keywords can be specified on SORT:

MEAN   *Sort by mean.* This is the default when SORT is specified without a keyword.

SEMEAN   *Sort by standard error of the mean.*

STDDEV   *Sort by standard deviation.*

VARIANCE   *Sort by variance.*

KURTOSIS   *Sort by kurtosis.*

SKEWNESS   *Sort by skewness.*

RANGE   *Sort by range.*

MIN   *Sort by minimum observed value.*

MAX   *Sort by maximum observed value.*

SUM   *Sort by sum.*

NAME   *Sort by variable name.*

Sort order can be specified in parentheses following the specified keyword:

A   *Sort in ascending order.* This is the default when SORT is specified without keywords.

D   *Sort in descending order.*

Example

```
DESCRIPTIVES VARIABLES=A B C
 /STATISTICS=DEFAULT RANGE
 /SORT=RANGE (D).
```

- DESCRIPTIVES sorts variables *A*, *B*, and *C* in descending order of range and displays the mean, standard deviation, minimum and maximum values, range, and the number of valid cases.

MISSING Subcommand

MISSING controls missing values.

- By default, DESCRIPTIVES deletes cases with missing values on a variable-by-variable basis. A case with a missing value for a variable will not be included in the summary statistics for that variable, but the case *will* be included for variables where it is not missing.

- The VARIABLE and LISTWISE keywords are alternatives; however, each can be specified with INCLUDE.

- When either the keyword VARIABLE or the default missing-value treatment is used, DESCRIPTIVES reports the number of valid cases for each variable. It always displays the number of cases that would be available if listwise deletion of missing values had been selected.

VARIABLE   *Exclude cases with missing values on a variable-by-variable basis.* This is the default.

LISTWISE   *Exclude cases with missing values listwise.* Cases with missing values for any variable named are excluded from the computation of statistics for all variables.

INCLUDE   *Include user-missing values.*

DISCRIMINANT

```
DISCRIMINANT GROUPS=varname(min,max) /VARIABLES=varlist

 [/SELECT=varname(value)]

 [/ANALYSIS=varlist[(level)] [varlist...]]

 [/METHOD={DIRECT**}] [/TOLERANCE={0.001}]
          {WILKS    }                { n   }
          {MAHAL    }
          {MAXMINF  }
          {MINRESID}
          {RAO      }

 [/MAXSTEPS={n}]

 [/FIN={3.84**}] [/FOUT={2.71**}] [/PIN={n}]
       { n    }         { n    }

 [/POUT={n}] [/VIN={0**}]
                  { n }

 [/FUNCTIONS={g-1,100.0,1.0**}] [/PRIORS={EQUAL**    }]
             {n₁ , n₂  ,n₃  }            {SIZE       }
                                         {value list}
 [/SAVE=[CLASS[=varname]] [PROBS[=rootname]]

        [SCORES[=rootname]]]

 [/ANALYSIS=...]

 [/MISSING={EXCLUDE**}]
           {INCLUDE  }

 [/MATRIX=[OUT({*   })] [IN({*   })]]
              {file}      {file}

 [/HISTORY={STEP**} ]
           {NONE   }

 [/ROTATE={NONE**   }]
          {COEFF    }
          {STRUCTURE}

 [/CLASSIFY={NONMISSING  }  {POOLED  }  [MEANSUB]]
            {UNSELECTED  }  {SEPARATE}
            {UNCLASSIFIED}

 [/STATISTICS=[MEAN]  [COV  ]  [FPAIR]  [RAW ]  [STDDEV]
              [GCOV]  [UNIVF]  [COEFF]  [CORR]  [TCOV ]
              [BOXM]  [TABLE]  [CROSSVALID]
              [ALL]]

 [/PLOT=[MAP]  [SEPARATE]  [COMBINED]  [CASES[(n)]]  [ALL]]
```

**Default if subcommand or keyword is omitted.

Example:

```
DISCRIMINANT GROUPS=OUTCOME (1,4)
  /VARIABLES=V1 TO V7
  /SAVE CLASS=PREDOUT.
```

Overview

DISCRIMINANT performs linear discriminant analysis for two or more groups. The goal of discriminant analysis is to classify cases into one of several mutually exclusive groups based on their values for a set of predictor variables. In the analysis phase, a classification rule is developed using cases for which group membership is known. In the classification phase, the rule is used to classify cases for which group membership is not known. The grouping variable must be categorical, and the independent (predictor) variables must be interval or dichotomous, since they will be used in a regression-type equation.

Options

Variable Selection Method. In addition to the direct-entry method, you can specify any of several stepwise methods for entering variables into the discriminant analysis using the METHOD subcommand. You can set the values for the statistical criteria used to enter variables into the equation using the TOLERANCE, FIN, PIN, FOUT, POUT, and VIN subcommands, and you can specify inclusion levels on the ANALYSIS subcommand. You can also specify the maximum number of steps in a stepwise analysis using the MAXSTEPS subcommand.

Case Selection. You can select a subset of cases for the analysis phase using the SELECT subcommand.

Prior Probabilities. You can specify prior probabilities for membership in a group using the PRIORS subcommand. Prior probabilities are used in classifying cases.

New Variables. You can add new variables to the working data file containing the predicted group membership, the probability of membership in each group, and discriminant function scores using the SAVE subcommand.

Classification Options. With the CLASSIFY subcommand, you can classify only those cases that were not selected for inclusion in the discriminant analysis, or only those cases whose value for the grouping variable was missing or fell outside the range analyzed. In addition, you can classify cases based on the separate-group covariance matrices of the functions instead of the pooled within-groups covariance matrix.

Statistical Display. You can request any of a variety of statistics on the STATISTICS subcommand. You can rotate the pattern or structure matrices using the ROTATE subcommand. You can compare actual with predicted group membership using a classification results table requested with the STATISTICS subcommand or compare any of several types of plots or histograms using the PLOT subcommand.

Basic Specification

The basic specification requires two subcommands:

- GROUPS specifies the variable used to group cases.
- VARIABLES specifies the predictor variables.

By default, DISCRIMINANT enters all variables simultaneously into the discriminant equation (the DIRECT method), provided that they are not so highly correlated that multicollinearity problems arise. Default output includes analysis case processing summary, valid numbers of cases in group statistics, variables failing tolerance test, a summary of canonical discriminant functions, standardized canonical discriminant function coefficients, a structure matrix showing pooled within-groups correlations between the discriminant functions and the predictor variables, and functions at group centroids.

Subcommand Order

- The GROUPS, VARIABLES, and SELECT subcommands must precede all other subcommands and may be entered in any order.
- The analysis block follows, which may include ANALYSIS, METHOD, TOLERANCE, MAXSTEPS, FIN, FOUT, PIN, POUT, VIN, FUNCTIONS, PRIORS, and SAVE. Each analysis block performs a single analysis. To do multiple analyses, specify multiple analysis blocks.
- The keyword ANALYSIS is optional for the first analysis block. Each new analysis block must begin with an ANALYSIS subcommand. Remaining subcommands in the block may be used in any order and apply only to the analysis defined within the same block.
- No analysis block subcommands can be specified after any of the global subcommands, which apply to all analysis blocks. The global subcommands are MISSING, MATRIX, HISTORY, ROTATE, CLASSIFY, STATISTICS, and PLOT. If an analysis block subcommand appears after a global subcommand, the program displays a warning and ignores it.

Syntax Rules

- Only one GROUPS, one SELECT, and one VARIABLES subcommand can be specified per DISCRIMINANT command.

Operations

- DISCRIMINANT first estimates one or more discriminant functions that best distinguish among the groups.
- Using these functions, DISCRIMINANT then classifies cases into groups (if classification output is requested).
- If more than one analysis block is specified, the above steps are repeated for each block.

Limitations

- Pairwise deletion of missing data is not available.

Example

```
DISCRIMINANT GROUPS=OUTCOME (1,4)
  /VARIABLES=V1 TO V7
  /SAVE CLASS=PREDOUT
  /STATISTICS=COV GCOV TCOV.
```

- Only cases with values 1, 2, 3, or 4 for the grouping variable *GROUPS* will be used in computing the discriminant functions.
- The variables in the working data file between and including *V1* and *V7* will be used to compute the discriminant functions and to classify cases.
- Predicted group membership will be saved in the variable *PREDOUT*.
- In addition to the default output, the STATISTICS subcommand requests the pooled within-groups covariance matrix and the group and total covariance matrices.
- Since SAVE is specified, DISCRIMINANT also displays a classification processing summary table and a priori probabilities for groups table.

GROUPS Subcommand

GROUPS specifies the name of the grouping variable, which defines the categories or groups, and a range of categories.

- GROUPS is required and can be specified only once.
- The specification consists of a variable name followed by a range of values in parentheses.
- Only one grouping variable may be specified; its values must be integers. To use a string variable as the grouping variable, first use AUTORECODE to convert the string values to integers and then specify the recoded variable as the grouping variable.
- Empty groups are ignored and do not affect calculations. For example, if there are no cases in group 2, the value range (1, 5) will define only four groups.
- Cases with values outside the value range or missing are ignored during the analysis phase but are classified during the classification phase.

VARIABLES Subcommand

VARIABLES identifies the predictor variables, which are used to classify cases into the groups defined on the GROUPS subcommand. The list of variables follows the usual conventions for variable lists.

- VARIABLES is required and can be specified only once. Use the ANALYSIS subcommand to obtain multiple analyses.
- Only numeric variables can be used.
- Variables should be suitable for use in a regression-type equation, either measured at the interval level or dichotomous.

SELECT Subcommand

SELECT limits cases used in the analysis phase to those with a specified value for any one variable.

- Only one SELECT subcommand is allowed. It can follow the GROUPS and VARIABLES subcommands but must precede all other subcommands.

- The specification is a variable name and a single integer value in parentheses. Multiple variables or values are not permitted.
- The selection variable does not have to be specified on the VARIABLES subcommand.
- Only cases with the specified value for the selection variable are used in the analysis phase.
- All cases, whether selected or not, are classified by default. Use CLASSIFY=UNSELECTED to classify only the unselected cases.
- When SELECT is used, classification statistics are reported separately for selected and unselected cases, unless CLASSIFY=UNSELECTED is used to restrict classification.

Example

```
DISCRIMINANT GROUPS=APPROVAL(1,5)
    /VARS=Q1 TO Q10
    /SELECT=COMPLETE(1)
    /CLASSIFY=UNSELECTED.
```

- Using only cases with the value 1 for the variable *COMPLETE*, DISCRIMINANT estimates a function of *Q1* to *Q10* that discriminates between the categories 1 to 5 of the grouping variable *APPROVAL*.
- Because CLASSIFY=UNSELECTED is specified, the discriminant function will be used to classify only the unselected cases (cases for which *COMPLETE* does not equal 1).

ANALYSIS Subcommand

ANALYSIS is used to request several different discriminant analyses using the same grouping variable, or to control the order in which variables are entered into a stepwise analysis.

- ANALYSIS is optional for the first analysis block. By default, all variables specified on the VARIABLES subcommand are included in the analysis.
- The variables named on ANALYSIS must first be specified on the VARIABLES subcommand.
- The keyword ALL includes all variables on the VARIABLES subcommand.
- If the keyword TO is used to specify a list of variables on an ANALYSIS subcommand, it refers to the order of variables on the VARIABLES subcommand, which is not necessarily the order of variables in the working data file.

Example

```
DISCRIMINANT GROUPS=SUCCESS(0,1)
    /VARIABLES=V10 TO V15, AGE, V5
    /ANALYSIS=V15 TO V5
    /ANALYSIS=ALL.
```

- The first analysis will use the variables *V15*, *AGE*, and *V5* to discriminate between cases where *SUCCESS* equals 0 and *SUCCESS* equals 1.
- The second analysis will use all variables named on the VARIABLES subcommand.

Inclusion Levels

When you specify a stepwise method on the METHOD subcommand (any method other than the default direct-entry method), you can control the order in which variables are considered for entry or removal by specifying inclusion levels on the ANALYSIS subcommand. By default, all variables in the analysis are entered according to the criterion requested on the METHOD subcommand.

- An **inclusion level** is an integer between 0 and 99, specified in parentheses after a variable or list of variables on the ANALYSIS subcommand.
- The default inclusion level is 1.
- Variables with higher inclusion levels are considered for entry before variables with lower inclusion levels.
- Variables with even inclusion levels are entered as a group.
- Variables with odd inclusion levels are entered individually, according to the stepwise method specified on the METHOD subcommand.
- Only variables with an inclusion level of 1 are considered for removal. To make a variable with a higher inclusion level eligible for removal, name it twice on the ANALYSIS subcommand, first specifying the desired inclusion level and then an inclusion level of 1.
- Variables with an inclusion level of 0 are never entered. However, the statistical criterion for entry is computed and displayed.
- Variables that fail the tolerance criterion are not entered regardless of their inclusion level.

The following are some common methods of entering variables and the inclusion levels that could be used to achieve them. These examples assume that one of the stepwise methods is specified on the METHOD subcommand (otherwise, inclusion levels have no effect).

Direct. ANALYSIS=ALL(2) forces all variables into the equation. (This is the default and can be requested with METHOD=DIRECT or simply by omitting the METHOD subcommand.)

Stepwise. ANALYSIS=ALL(1) yields a stepwise solution in which variables are entered and removed in stepwise fashion. (This is the default when anything other than DIRECT is specified on the METHOD subcommand.)

Forward. ANALYSIS=ALL(3) enters variables into the equation stepwise but does not remove variables.

Backward. ANALYSIS=ALL(2) ALL(1) forces all variables into the equation and then allows them to be removed stepwise if they satisfy the criterion for removal.

Example
```
DISCRIMINANT GROUPS=SUCCESS(0,1)
  /VARIABLES=A, B, C, D, E
  /ANALYSIS=A TO C (2) D, E (1)
  /METHOD=WILKS.
```

- A, B, and C are entered into the analysis first, assuming that they pass the tolerance criterion. Since their inclusion level is even, they are entered together.
- D and E are then entered stepwise. The one that minimizes the overall value of Wilks' lambda is entered first.

- After entering *D* and *E*, the program checks whether the partial *F* for either one justifies removal from the equation (see the FOUT and POUT subcommands on p. 285).

Example

```
DISCRIMINANT GROUPS=SUCCESS(0,1)
  /VARIABLES=A, B, C, D, E
  /ANALYSIS=A TO C (2) D, E (1).
```

- Since no stepwise method is specified, inclusion levels have no effect and all variables are entered into the model at once.

METHOD Subcommand

METHOD is used to select a method for entering variables into an analysis.

- A variable will never be entered into the analysis if it does not pass the tolerance criterion specified on the TOLERANCE subcommand (or the default).
- A METHOD subcommand applies only to the *preceding* ANALYSIS subcommand, or to an analysis using all predictor variables if no ANALYSIS subcommand has been specified before it.
- If more than one METHOD subcommand is specified within one analysis block, the last is used.

Any one of the following methods can be specified on the METHOD subcommand:

DIRECT   *All variables passing the tolerance criteria are entered simultaneously.* This is the default method.

WILKS   *At each step, the variable that minimizes the overall Wilks' lambda is entered.*

MAHAL   *At each step, the variable that maximizes the Mahalanobis distance between the two closest groups is entered.*

MAXMINF   *At each step, the variable that maximizes the smallest* F *ratio between pairs of groups is entered.*

MINRESID   *At each step, the variable that minimizes the sum of the unexplained variation for all pairs of groups is entered.*

RAO   *At each step, the variable that produces the largest increase in Rao's* V *is entered.*

TOLERANCE Subcommand

TOLERANCE specifies the minimum tolerance a variable can have and still be entered into the analysis. The tolerance of a variable that is a candidate for inclusion in the analysis is the proportion of its within-groups variance not accounted for by other variables in the analysis. A variable with very low tolerance is nearly a linear function of the other variables; its inclusion in the analysis would make the calculations unstable.

- The default tolerance is 0.001.

- You can specify any decimal value between 0 and 1 as the minimum tolerance.

PIN and POUT Subcommands

PIN specifies the minimum probability of F that a variable can have to enter the analysis and POUT specifies the maximum probability of F that a variable can have and not be removed from the model.

- PIN and POUT take precedence over FIN and FOUT. That is, if all are specified, PIN and POUT values are used.

- If PIN and POUT are omitted, FIN and FOUT are used by default.

- You can set PIN and POUT to any decimal value between 0 and 1. However, POUT should be greater than PIN if PIN is also specified.

- PIN and POUT apply only to the stepwise methods and are ignored if the METHOD subcommand is omitted or if DIRECT is specified on METHOD.

FIN and FOUT Subcommands

FIN specifies the minimum partial F value that a variable must have to enter the analysis. As additional variables are entered into the analysis, the partial F for variables already in the equation changes. FOUT specifies the smallest partial F that a variable can have and not be removed from the model.

- PIN and POUT take precedence over FIN and FOUT. That is, if all are specified, PIN and POUT values are used.

- If PIN and POUT are omitted, FIN and FOUT are used by default. If FOUT is specified but FIN is omitted, the default value for FIN is 3.84. If FIN is specified, the default value for FOUT is 2.71.

- You can set FIN and FOUT to any non-negative number. However, FOUT should be less than FIN if FIN is also specified.

- FIN and FOUT apply only to the stepwise methods and are ignored if the METHOD subcommand is omitted or if DIRECT is specified on METHOD.

VIN Subcommand

VIN specifies the minimum Rao's *V* that a variable must have to enter the analysis. When you use METHOD=RAO, variables satisfying one of the other criteria for entering the equation may actually cause a decrease in Rao's *V* for the equation. The default VIN prevents this but does not prevent the addition of variables that provide no additional separation between groups.

- You can specify any value for VIN. The default is 0.

- VIN should be used only when you have specified METHOD=RAO. Otherwise, it is ignored.

MAXSTEPS Subcommand

MAXSTEPS is used to decrease the maximum number of steps allowed. By default, the maximum number of steps allowed in a stepwise analysis is the number of variables with inclusion levels greater than 1 plus twice the number of variables with inclusion levels equal to 1. This is the maximum number of steps possible without producing a loop in which a variable is repeatedly cycled in and out.

- MAXSTEPS applies only to the stepwise methods (all except DIRECT).

- MAXSTEPS applies only to the preceding METHOD subcommand.

- The format is MAX=*n*, where *n* is the maximum number of steps desired.

- If multiple MAXSTEPS subcommands are specified, the last is used.

FUNCTIONS Subcommand

By default, DISCRIMINANT computes all possible functions. This is either the number of groups minus 1 or the number of predictor variables, whichever is less. Use FUNCTIONS to set more restrictive criteria for the extraction of functions.

FUNCTIONS has three parameters:

n_1 *Maximum number of functions.* The default is the number of groups minus 1 or the number of predictor variables, whichever is less.

n_2 *Cumulative percentage of the sum of the eigenvalues.* The default is 100.

n_3 *Significance level of function.* The default is 1.0.

- The parameters must always be specified in sequential order (n_1, n_2, n_3). To specify n_2, you must explicitly specify the default for n_1. Similarly, to specify n_3, you must specify the defaults for n_1 and n_2.

- If more than one restriction is specified, the program stops extracting functions when any one of the restrictions is met.

- When multiple FUNCTIONS subcommands are specified, the program uses the last; however, if n_2 or n_3 are omitted on the last FUNCTIONS subcommand, the corresponding specifications on the previous FUNCTIONS subcommands will remain in effect.

Example

```
DISCRIMINANT  GROUPS=CLASS(1,5)
  /VARIABLES = SCORE1 TO SCORE20
  /FUNCTIONS=4,100,.80.
```

- The first two parameters on the FUNCTIONS subcommand are defaults: the default for n_1 is 4 (the number of groups minus 1), and the default for n_2 is 100.
- The third parameter tells DISCRIMINANT to use fewer than four discriminant functions if the significance level of a function is greater than 0.80.

PRIORS Subcommand

By default, DISCRIMINANT assumes equal prior probabilities for groups when classifying cases. You can provide different prior probabilities with the PRIORS subcommand.

- Prior probabilities are used only during classification.
- If you provide unequal prior probabilities, DISCRIMINANT adjusts the classification coefficients to reflect this.
- If adjacent groups have the same prior probability, you can use the notation $n*c$ on the value list to indicate that n adjacent groups have the same prior probability c.
- You can specify a prior probability of 0. No cases are classified into such a group.
- If the sum of the prior probabilities is not 1, the program rescales the probabilities to sum to 1 and issues a warning.

EQUAL   *Equal prior probabilities.* This is the default.

SIZE   *Proportion of the cases analyzed that fall into each group.* If 50% of the cases included in the analysis fall into the first group, 25% in the second, and 25% in the third, the prior probabilities are 0.5, 0.25, and 0.25, respectively. Group size is determined after cases with missing values for the predictor variables are deleted.

Value list   *User-specified prior probabilities.* The list of probabilities must sum to 1.0. The number of prior probabilities named or implied must equal the number of groups.

Example

```
DISCRIMINANT  GROUPS=TYPE(1,5)
  /VARIABLES=A TO H
  /PRIORS = 4*.15,.4.
```

- The PRIORS subcommand establishes prior probabilities of 0.15 for the first four groups and 0.4 for the fifth group.

SAVE Subcommand

SAVE allows you to save casewise information as new variables in the working data file.

- SAVE applies only to the current analysis block. To save casewise results from more than one analysis, specify a SAVE subcommand in each analysis block.

- You can specify a variable name for CLASS and rootnames for SCORES and PROBS to obtain descriptive names for the new variables.

- If you do not specify a variable name for CLASS, the program forms variable names using the formula *DSC_m*, where *m* increments to distinguish group membership variables saved on different SAVE subcommands for different analysis blocks.

- If you do not specify a rootname for SCORES or PROBS, the program forms new variable names using the formula *DSCn_m*, where *m* increments to create unique rootnames and *n* increments to create unique variable names. For example, the first set of default names assigned to discriminant scores or probabilities are *DSC1_1*, *DSC2_1*, *DSC3_1*, and so on. The next set of default names assigned will be *DSC1_2*, *DSC2_2*, *DSC3_2*, and so on, regardless of whether discriminant scores or probabilities are being saved or whether they are saved by the same SAVE subcommand.

- As *m* and/or *n* increase, the prefix *DSC* is truncated to keep variable names within eight characters. For example, *DS999_12* increases to *D1000_12*. The initial character *D* is required.

- The keywords CLASS, SCORES, and PROBS can be used in any order, but the new variables are always added to the end of the working data file in the following order: first the predicted group, then the discriminant scores, and finally probabilities of group membership.

- Appropriate variable labels are automatically generated. The labels describe whether the variables contain predictor group membership, discriminant scores, or probabilities, and for which analysis they are generated.

- The CLASS variable will use the value labels (if any) from the grouping variable specified for the analysis.

- When SAVE is specified with any keyword, DISCRIMINANT displays a classification processing summary table and a prior probabilities for groups table.

- You cannot use the SAVE subcommand if you are replacing the working data file with matrix materials (see "Matrix Output" on p. 293).

CLASS [(varname)]   *Predicted group membership.*

SCORES [(rootname)]   *Discriminant scores.* One score is saved for each discriminant function derived. If a rootname is specified, DISCRIMINANT will append a sequential number to the name to form new variable names for the discriminant scores.

PROBS [(rootname)]   *For each case, the probabilities of membership in each group.* As many variables are added to each case as there are groups. If a rootname is specified, DISCRIMINANT will append a sequential number to the name to form new variable names.

Example

```
DISCRIMINANT GROUPS=WORLD(1,3)
 /VARIABLES=FOOD TO FSALES
 /SAVE CLASS=PRDCLASS SCORES=SCORE PROBS=PRB
 /ANALYSIS=FOOD SERVICE COOK MANAGER FSALES
 /SAVE CLASS SCORES PROBS.
```

- Two analyses are specified. The first uses all variables named on the VARIABLES subcommand and the second narrows down to five variables. For each analysis, a SAVE subcommand is specified.

- For each analysis, DISCRIMINANT displays a classification processing summary table and a prior probabilities for groups table.

- On the first SAVE subcommand, a variable name and two rootnames are provided. With three groups, the following variables are added to each case:

Name	Variable label	Description
PRDCLASS	Predicted group for analysis 1	Predicted group membership
SCORE1	Function 1 for analysis 1	Discriminant score for function 1
SCORE2	Function 2 for analysis 1	Discriminant score for function 2
PRB1	Probability 1 for analysis 1	Probability of being in group 1
PRB2	Probability 2 for analysis 1	Probability of being in group 2
PRB3	Probability 3 for analysis 1	Probability of being in group 3

- Since no variable name or rootnames are provided on the second SAVE subcommand, DISCRIMINANT uses default names. Note that m serves only to distinguish variables saved as a set and does not correspond to the sequential number of an analysis. To find out what information a new variable holds, read the variable label, as shown in the following table:

Name	Variable label	Description
DSC_1	Predicted group for analysis 2	Predicted group membership
DSC1_1	Function 1 for analysis 2	Discriminant score for function 1
DSC2_1	Function 2 for analysis 2	Discriminant score for function 2
DSC1_2	Probability 1 for analysis 2	Probability of being in group 1
DSC2_2	Probability 2 for analysis 2	Probability of being in group 2
DSC3_2	Probability 3 for analysis 2	Probability of being in group 3

STATISTICS Subcommand

By default, DISCRIMINANT produces the following statistics for each analysis: analysis case processing summary, valid numbers of cases in group statistics, variables failing tolerance test, a summary of canonical discriminant functions, standardized canonical discriminant function coefficients, a structure matrix showing pooled within-groups correlations between the discriminant functions and the predictor variables, and functions at group centroids.

- *Group statistics.* Only valid number of cases is reported.

- *Summary of canonical discriminant functions.* Displayed in two tables: an eigenvalues table with percentage of variance, cumulative percentage of variance, and canonical correlations and a Wilks' lambda table with Wilks' lambda, chi-square, degrees of freedom, and significance.

- *Stepwise statistics.* Wilks' lambda, equivalent F, degrees of freedom, significance of F and number of variables are reported for each step. Tolerance, F-to-remove, and the value of the statistic used for variable selection are reported for each variable in the equation. Tolerance, minimum tolerance, F-to-enter, and the value of the statistic used for variable selection are reported for each variable not in the equation. (These statistics can be suppressed with HISTORY=NONE.)

- *Final statistics.* Standardized canonical discriminant function coefficients, the structure matrix of discriminant functions and all variables named in the analysis (whether they were entered into the equation or not), and functions evaluated at group means are reported following the last step.

In addition, you can request optional statistics on the STATISTICS subcommand. STATISTICS can be specified by itself or with one or more keywords.

- STATISTICS without keywords displays MEAN, STDDEV, and UNIVF. If you include a keyword or keywords on STATISTICS, only the statistics you request are displayed.

MEAN *Means.* Total and group means for all variables named on the ANALYSIS subcommand are displayed.

STDDEV *Standard deviations.* Total and group standard deviations for all variables named on the ANALYSIS subcommand are displayed.

UNIVF *Univariate* F *ratios.* The analysis-of-variance F statistic for equality of group means for each predictor variable is displayed. This is a one-way analysis-of-variance test for equality of group means on a single discriminating variable.

COV *Pooled within-groups covariance matrix.*

CORR *Pooled within-groups correlation matrix.*

FPAIR *Matrix of pairwise* F *ratios.* The F ratio for each pair of groups is displayed. This F is the significance test for the Mahalanobis distance between groups. This statistic is available only with stepwise methods.

BOXM *Box's* M *test.* This is a test for equality of group covariance matrices.

GCOV *Group covariance matrices.*

TCOV *Total covariance matrix.*

RAW   *Unstandardized canonical discriminant functions.*

COEFF   *Classification function coefficients.* Although DISCRIMINANT does not directly use these coefficients to classify cases, you can use them to classify other samples (see the CLASSIFY subcommand below).

TABLE   *Classification results.* If both selected and unselected cases are classified, the results are reported separately. To obtain cross-validated results for selected cases, specify CROSSVALID.

CROSSVALID   *Cross-validated classification results.* The cross-validation is done by treating $n-1$ out of n observations as the training data set to determine the discrimination rule and using the rule to classify the one observation left out. The results are displayed only for selected cases.

ALL   *All optional statistics.*

ROTATE Subcommand

The coefficient and correlation matrices can be rotated to facilitate interpretation of results. To control varimax rotation, use the ROTATE subcommand.

- Neither COEFF nor STRUCTURE affects the classification of cases.

COEFF   *Rotate pattern matrix.* DISCRIMINANT displays a varimax transformation matrix, a rotated standardized canonical discriminant function coefficients table, and a correlations between variables and rotated functions table.

STRUCTURE   *Rotate structure matrix.* DISCRIMINANT displays a varimax transformation matrix, a rotated structure matrix, and a rotated standardized canonical discriminant function coefficients table.

NONE   *Do not rotate.* This is the default.

HISTORY Subcommand

HISTORY controls the display of stepwise and summary output.

- By default, HISTORY displays both the step-by-step output and the summary table (keyword STEP, alias END).

STEP   *Display step-by-step and summary output.* Alias END. This is the default. See *Stepwise statistics* in "STATISTICS Subcommand" on p. 290.

NONE   *Suppress the step-by-step and summary table.* Alias NOSTEP, NOEND.

CLASSIFY Subcommand

CLASSIFY determines how cases are handled during classification.

- By default, all cases with nonmissing values for all predictors are classified, and the pooled within-groups covariance matrix is used to classify cases.

- The default keywords for CLASSIFY are NONMISSING and POOLED.

NONMISSING *Classify all cases that do not have missing values on any predictor variables.* Two sets of classification results are produced, one for selected cases (those specified on the SELECT subcommand) and one for unselected cases. This is the default.

UNSELECTED *Classify only unselected cases.* The classification phase is suppressed for cases selected via the SELECT subcommand. If all cases are selected (when the SELECT subcommand is omitted), the classification phase is suppressed for all cases and no classification results are produced.

UNCLASSIFIED *Classify only unclassified cases.* The classification phase is suppressed for cases that fall within the range specified on the GROUPS subcommand.

POOLED *Use the pooled within-groups covariance matrix to classify cases.* This is the default.

SEPARATE *Use separate-groups covariance matrices of the discriminant functions for classification.* DISCRIMINANT displays the group covariances of canonical discriminant functions and Box's test of equality of covariance matrices of canonical discriminant functions. Since classification is based on the discriminant functions and not the original variables, this option is not necessarily equivalent to quadratic discrimination.

MEANSUB *Substitute means for missing predictor values during classification.* During classification, means are substituted for missing values and cases with missing values are classified. Cases with missing values are not used during analysis.

PLOT Subcommand

PLOT requests additional output to help you examine the effectiveness of the discriminant analysis.

- If PLOT is specified without keywords, the default is COMBINED and CASES.
- If any keywords are requested on PLOT, only the requested plots are displayed.
- If PLOT is specified with any keyword except MAP, DISCRIMINANT displays a classification processing summary table and a prior probabilities for groups table.

COMBINED *All-groups plot.* For each case, the first two function values are plotted.

CASES(n) *Casewise statistics.* For each case, classification information, squared Mahalanobis distance to centroid for the highest and second highest groups, and discriminant scores of all functions are plotted. Validated statistics are displayed for selected cases if CROSSVALID is specified on STATISTICS. If n is specified, DISCRIMINANT displays the first n cases only.

MAP *Territorial map.* A plot of group centroids and boundaries used for classifying groups.

SEPARATE   *Separate-groups plots.* These are the same types of plots produced by the keyword COMBINED, except that a separate plot is produced for each group. If only one function is used, a histogram is displayed.

ALL   *All available plots.*

MISSING Subcommand

MISSING controls the treatment of cases with missing values in the analysis phase. By default, cases with missing values for any variable named on the VARIABLES subcommand are not used in the analysis phase but are used in classification.

• The keyword INCLUDE includes cases with user-missing values in the analysis phase.

• Cases with missing or out-of-range values for the grouping variable are always excluded.

EXCLUDE   *Exclude all cases with missing values.* Cases with user- or system-missing values are excluded from the analysis. This is the default.

INCLUDE   *Include cases with user-missing values.* User-missing values are treated as valid values. Only the system-missing value is treated as missing.

MATRIX Subcommand

MATRIX reads and writes SPSS-format matrix data files.

• Either IN or OUT and the matrix file in parentheses are required. When both IN and OUT are used in the same DISCRIMINANT procedure, they can be specified on separate MATRIX subcommands or on the same subcommand.

OUT (filename)   *Write a matrix data file.* Specify either a filename or an asterisk in parentheses (*). If you specify a filename, the file is stored on disk and can be retrieved at any time. If you specify an asterisk (*), the matrix data file replaces the working data file but is not stored on disk unless you use SAVE or XSAVE.

IN (filename)   *Read a matrix data file.* If the matrix data file is the working data file, specify an asterisk (*) in parentheses. If the matrix file is another file, specify the filename in parentheses. A matrix file read from an external file does not replace the working data file.

Matrix Output

• In addition to Pearson correlation coefficients, the matrix materials written by DISCRIMINANT include weighted and unweighted numbers of cases, means, and standard deviations. (See "Format of the Matrix Data File" on p. 294 for a description of the file.) These materials can be used in subsequent DISCRIMINANT procedures.

• Any documents contained in the working data file are not transferred to the matrix file.

• If BOXM or GCOV is specified on the STATISTICS subcommand or SEPARATE is specified on the CLASSIFY subcommand when a matrix file is written, the *STDDEV* and *CORR* records in the matrix materials represent within-cell data, and separate covariance matrices are written to the file. When the matrix file is used as input for a subsequent DISCRIMINANT procedure, at least one of these specifications must be used on that DISCRIMINANT command.

Matrix Input

- DISCRIMINANT can read correlation matrices written by a previous DISCRIMINANT command or by other procedures. Matrix materials read by DISCRIMINANT must contain records with *ROWTYPE_* values *MEAN*, *N* or *COUNT* (or both), *STDDEV*, and *CORR*.

- If the data do not include records with *ROWTYPE_* value *COUNT* (unweighted number of cases), DISCRIMINANT uses information from records with *ROWTYPE_* value *N* (weighted number of cases). Conversely, if the data do not have *N* values, DISCRIMINANT uses the *COUNT* values. These records can appear in any order in the matrix input file with the following exceptions: the order of split-file groups cannot be violated and all *CORR* vectors must appear consecutively within each split-file group.

- If you want to use a covariance-type matrix as input to DISCRIMINANT, you must first use the MCONVERT command to change the covariance matrix to a correlation matrix.

- DISCRIMINANT can use a matrix from a previous data set to classify data in the working data file. The program checks to make sure that the grouping variable (specified on GROUPS) and the predictor variables (specified on VARIABLES) are the same in the working data file as in the matrix file. If they are not, the program displays an error message and the classification will not be executed.

- MATRIX=IN cannot be used unless a working data file has already been defined. To read an existing matrix data file at the beginning of a session, first use GET to retrieve the matrix file and then specify IN(*) on MATRIX.

Format of the Matrix Data File

- The matrix data file has two special variables created by the program: *ROWTYPE_* and *VARNAME_*. Variable *ROWTYPE_* is a short string variable having values *N*, *COUNT*, *MEAN*, *STDDEV*, and *CORR* (for Pearson correlation coefficient). The variable *VARNAME_* is a short string variable whose values are the names of the variables used to form the correlation matrix.

- When *ROWTYPE_* is *CORR*, *VARNAME_* gives the variable associated with that row of the correlation matrix.

- Between *ROWTYPE_* and *VARNAME_* is the grouping variable, which is specified on the GROUPS subcommand of DISCRIMINANT.

- The remaining variables are the variables used to form the correlation matrix.

Split Files

- When split-file processing is in effect, the first variables in the matrix data file will be split variables, followed by *ROWTYPE_*, the grouping variable, *VARNAME_*, and then the variables used to form the correlation matrix.

- A full set of matrix materials is written for each subgroup defined by the split variables.
- A split variable cannot have the same variable name as any other variable written to the matrix data file.
- If split-file processing is in effect when a matrix is written, the same split file must be in effect when that matrix is read by another procedure.

STDDEV and CORR Records

Records written with *ROWTYPE_* values *STDDEV* and *CORR* are influenced by specifications on the STATISTICS and CLASSIFY subcommands.

- If BOXM or GCOV is specified on STATISTICS or SEPARATE is specified on CLASSIFY, the *STDDEV* and *CORR* records represent within-cell data and receive values for the grouping variable.
- If none of the above specifications is in effect, the *STDDEV* and *CORR* records represent pooled values. The *STDDEV* vector contains the square root of the mean square error for each variable, and *STDDEV* and *CORR* records receive the system-missing value for the grouping variable.

Missing Values

Missing-value treatment affects the values written to a matrix data file. When reading a matrix data file, be sure to specify a missing-value treatment on DISCRIMINANT that is compatible with the treatment that was in effect when the matrix materials were generated.

Example

```
GET FILE=UNIONBK /KEEP WORLD FOOD SERVICE BUS MECHANIC
                      CONSTRUC COOK MANAGER FSALES APPL RENT.
DISCRIMINANT   GROUPS=WORLD(1,3)
 /VARIABLES=FOOD SERVICE BUS MECHANIC CONSTRUC COOK MANAGER FSALES
 /METHOD=WILKS
 /PRIORS=SIZE
 /MATRIX=OUT(DISCMTX).
```

- DISCRIMINANT reads data from the SPSS-format data file *UNIONBK* and writes one set of matrix materials to the file *DISCMTX*.
- The working data file is still *UNIONBK*. Subsequent commands are executed on this file.

Example

```
* Use matrix output to classify data in a different file.

GET FILE=UB2 /KEEP WORLD FOOD SERVICE BUS MECHANIC
                CONSTRUC COOK MANAGER FSALES APPL RENT.
DISCRIMINANT  GROUPS=WORLD(1,3)
 /VARIABLES=FOOD SERVICE BUS MECHANIC CONSTRUC COOK MANAGER FSALES
 /METHOD=WILKS
 /PRIORS=SIZE
 /MATRIX=IN(DISCMTX).
```

- The matrix data file created in the previous example is used to classify data from the file *UB2*.

Example

```
GET FILE=UNIONBK /KEEP WORLD FOOD SERVICE BUS MECHANIC
                    CONSTRUC COOK MANAGER FSALES APPL RENT.
DISCRIMINANT  GROUPS=WORLD(1,3)
 /VARIABLES=FOOD SERVICE BUS MECHANIC CONSTRUC COOK MANAGER FSALES
 /METHOD=WILKS
 /PRIORS=SIZE
 /MATRIX=OUT(*).
LIST.
```

- DISCRIMINANT writes the same matrix as in the first example. However, the matrix data file replaces the working data file.
- The LIST command is executed on the matrix file, not on the *UNIONBK* file.

Example

```
GET FILE=DISCMTX.
DISCRIMINANT  GROUPS=WORLD(1,3)
 /VARIABLES=FOOD SERVICE BUS MECHANIC CONSTRUC COOK MANAGER FSALES
 /METHOD=RAO
 /MATRIX=IN(*).
```

- This example assumes that you are starting a new session and want to read an existing matrix data file. GET retrieves the matrix data file *DISCMTX*.
- MATRIX=IN specifies an asterisk because the matrix data file is the working data file. If MATRIX=IN(DISCMTX) is specified, the program issues an error message.
- If the GET command is omitted, the program issues an error message.

Example

```
GET FILE=UNIONBK /KEEP WORLD FOOD SERVICE BUS MECHANIC
                    CONSTRUC COOK MANAGER FSALES APPL RENT.
DISCRIMINANT  GROUPS=WORLD(1,3)
 /VARIABLES=FOOD SERVICE BUS MECHANIC CONSTRUC COOK MANAGER FSALES
 /CLASSIFY=SEPARATE
 /MATRIX=OUT(*).
DISCRIMINANT  GROUPS=WORLD(1,3)
 /VARIABLES=FOOD SERVICE BUS MECHANIC CONSTRUC COOK MANAGER FSALES
 /STATISTICS=BOXM
 /MATRIX=IN(*).
```

- The first DISCRIMINANT command creates a matrix with CLASSIFY=SEPARATE in effect. To read this matrix, the second DISCRIMINANT command must specify either BOXM or GCOV on STATISTICS or SEPARATE on CLASSIFY. STATISTICS=BOXM is used.

DISPLAY

```
DISPLAY [SORTED] [{NAMES**   }] [/VARIABLES=varlist]
                 {INDEX      }
                 {VARIABLES  }
                 {LABELS     }
                 {DICTIONARY}

         {[SCRATCH]   }
         {[VECTOR]    }
         {[MACROS]    }
         {[DOCUMENTS]}
```

**Default if the subcommand is omitted.

Example:
```
DISPLAY SORTED DICTIONARY /VARIABLES=DEPT SALARY SEX TO JOBCAT.
```

Overview

DISPLAY exhibits information from the dictionary of the working data file. The information can be sorted, and it can be limited to selected variables.

Basic Specification

The basic specification is simply the command keyword, which displays an unsorted list of the variables in the working data file.

Syntax Rules

DISPLAY can be specified by itself or with one of the keywords defined below. NAMES is the default. To specify two or more keywords, use multiple DISPLAY commands.

NAMES
Variable names. A list of the variables in the working data file is displayed. The names are not sorted and display in a compressed format, about eight names across the page. This is the default.

DOCUMENTS
Documentary text. Documentary text is provided on the DOCUMENT command. No error message is issued if there is no documentary information in the working data file.

DICTIONARY
Complete dictionary information for variables. Information includes variable names, labels, sequential position of each variable in the file, print and write formats, missing values, and value labels. Up to 60 characters can be displayed for variable and value labels.

INDEX
Variable names and positions.

VARIABLES	*Variable names, positions, print and write formats, and missing values.*
LABELS	*Variable names, positions, and variable labels.*
SCRATCH	*Scratch variable names.*
VECTOR	*Vector names.*
MACROS	*Currently defined macros.* The macro names are always sorted.

Operations

- DISPLAY directs information to the output.
- If SORTED is not specified, information is displayed according to the order of variables in the working data file.
- DISPLAY is executed as soon as it is encountered in the command sequence, as long as a dictionary has been defined.

Example

```
GET FILE=HUB.
DISPLAY DOCUMENTS.
DISPLAY DICTIONARY.
```

- Each DISPLAY command specifies only one keyword. The first requests documentary text and the second requests complete dictionary information for the *HUB* file.

SORTED Keyword

SORTED alphabetizes the display by variable name. SORTED can precede the keywords NAMES, DICTIONARY, INDEX, VARIABLES, LABELS, SCRATCH, or VECTOR.

Example

```
DISPLAY SORTED DICTIONARY.
```

- This command displays complete dictionary information for variables in the working data file, sorted alphabetically by variable name.

VARIABLES Subcommand

VARIABLES (alias NAMES) limits the displayed information to a set of specified variables. VARIABLES must be the last specification on DISPLAY and can follow any specification that requests information about variables (all except VECTOR, SCRATCH, DOCUMENTS, and MACROS).

- The only specification is a slash followed by a list of variables. The slash is optional.

- If the keyword SORTED is not specified, information is displayed in the order in which variables are stored in the working data file, regardless of the order in which variables are named on VARIABLES.

Example

```
DISPLAY SORTED DICTIONARY
 /VARIABLES=DEPT, SALARY, SEX TO JOBCAT.
```

- DISPLAY exhibits dictionary information only for the variables named and implied by the keyword TO on the VARIABLES subcommand, sorted alphabetically by variable name.

DOCUMENT

```
DOCUMENT text
```

Example:
```
DOCUMENT    This file contains a subset of variables from the
            General Social Survey data.  For each case it records
            only the age, sex, education level, marital status,
            number of children, and type of medical insurance
            coverage.
```

Overview

DOCUMENT saves a block of text of any length in an SPSS-format data file. The documentation can be displayed with the DISPLAY command.

When GET retrieves a data file, or when ADD FILES, MATCH FILES, or UPDATE is used to combine data files, all documents from each specified file are copied into the working file. DROP DOCUMENTS can be used to drop those documents from the working file. Whether or not DROP DOCUMENTS is used, new documents can be added to the working file with the DOCUMENT command.

Basic Specification

The basic specification is DOCUMENT followed by any length of text. The text is stored in the file dictionary when the data are saved in an SPSS-format data file.

Syntax Rules

- The text can be entered on as many lines as needed.
- Blank lines can be used to separate paragraphs.
- A period at the end of a line terminates the command, so you should not place a period at the end of any line but the last.
- Multiple DOCUMENT commands can be used within the command sequence. However, the DISPLAY command cannot be used to exhibit the text from a particular DOCUMENT command. DISPLAY shows all existing documentation.

Operations

- The documentation and the date it was entered are saved in the data file's dictionary. New documentation is saved along with any documentation already in the working data file.

- If a DROP DOCUMENTS command *follows* a DOCUMENT command anywhere in the command sequence, the documentation added by that DOCUMENT command is dropped from the working file along with all other documentation.

Example

```
GET FILE=GENSOC /KEEP=AGE SEX EDUC MARITAL CHILDRN MED_INS.
FILE LABEL   General Social Survey subset.

DOCUMENT     This file contains a subset of variables from the
             General Social Survey data.  For each case it records
             only the age, sex, education level, marital status,
             number of children, and type of medical insurance
             coverage.

SAVE OUTFILE=SUBSOC.
```

- GET keeps only a subset of variables from the file *GENSOC*. All documentation from the file *GENSOC* is copied into the working file.
- FILE LABEL creates a label for the new working file.
- DOCUMENT specifies the new document text. Both existing documents from the file *GENSOC* and the new document text are saved in the file *SUBSOC*.

Example

```
GET FILE=GENSOC /KEEP=AGE SEX EDUC MARITAL CHILDRN MED_INS.

DROP DOCUMENTS.

FILE LABEL   General Social Survey subset.

DOCUMENT     This file contains a subset of variables from the
             General Social Survey data.  For each case it records
             only the age, sex, education level, marital status,
             number of children, and type of medical insurance
             coverage.

SAVE OUTFILE=SUBSOC.
```

- DROP DOCUMENTS drops the documentation from the file *GENSOC* as data are copied into the working file. Only the new documentation specified on DOCUMENT is saved in the file *SUBSOC*.

DO IF

```
DO IF [(]logical expression[)]

transformation commands

[ELSE IF [(]logical expression[)]]

transformation commands

[ELSE IF [(]logical expression[)]]
   .
   .
   .
[ELSE]

transformation commands

END IF
```

The following relational operators can be used in logical expressions:

Symbol	Definition	Symbol	Definition
EQ or =	Equal to	NE or <>*	Not equal to
LT or <	Less than	LE or <=	Less than or equal to
GT or >	Greater than	GE or >=	Greater than or equal to

* On ASCII systems (for example, UNIX, VAX, and all PC's), you can also use ~=; on IBM EBCDIC systems (for example, IBM 360 and IBM 370), you can also use ¬=.

The following logical operators can be used in logical expressions:

Symbol	Definition
AND or &	Both relations must be true
OR or |	Either relation can be true
NOT*	Reverses the outcome of an expression

* On ASCII systems, you can also use ~; on IBM EBCDIC systems, you can also use ¬ (or the symbol above number 6).

Example:

```
DO IF (YRHIRED GT 87).
COMPUTE           BONUS = 0.
ELSE IF (DEPT87 EQ 3).
COMPUTE           BONUS = .1*SALARY87.
ELSE IF (DEPT87 EQ 1).
COMPUTE           BONUS = .12*SALARY87.
ELSE IF (DEPT87 EQ 4).
COMPUTE           BONUS = .08*SALARY87.
ELSE IF (DEPT87 EQ 2).
COMPUTE           BONUS = .14*SALARY87.
END IF.
```

Overview

The DO IF—END IF structure conditionally executes one or more transformations on subsets of cases based on one or more logical expressions. The ELSE command can be used within the structure to execute one or more transformations when the logical expression on DO IF is not true. The ELSE IF command within the structure provides further control.

The DO IF—END IF structure is best used for conditionally executing multiple transformation commands, such as COMPUTE, RECODE, and COUNT. IF is more efficient for executing a single conditional COMPUTE-like transformation. DO IF—END IF transforms data for subsets of cases defined by logical expressions. To perform repeated transformations on the same case, use LOOP—END LOOP.

A DO IF—END IF structure can be used within an input program to define complex files that cannot be handled by standard file definition facilities. See "Complex File Structures" on p. 310 for an example.

See END FILE for information on using DO IF—END IF to instruct the program to stop reading data before it encounters the end of the file or to signal the end of the file when creating data. See p. 237 for an example of using DO IF—END IF with END FILE to concatenate raw data files.

Basic Specification

The basic specification is DO IF followed by a logical expression, a transformation command, and the END IF command, which has no specifications.

Syntax Rules

- The ELSE IF command is optional and can be repeated as many times as needed.
- The ELSE command is optional. It can be used only once and must follow any ELSE IF commands.
- The END IF command must follow any ELSE IF and ELSE commands.
- A logical expression must be specified on the DO IF and ELSE IF commands. Logical expressions are not used on the ELSE and END IF commands.
- String values used in expressions must be specified in quotation marks and must include any leading or trailing blanks. Lowercase letters are distinguished from uppercase letters.
- To create a new string variable within a DO IF—END IF structure, you must first declare the variable on the STRING command.
- DO IF—END IF structures can be nested to any level permitted by available memory. They can be nested within LOOP—END LOOP structures, and loop structures can be nested within DO IF structures.

Logical Expressions

- Logical expressions can be simple logical variables or relations, or they can be complex logical tests involving variables, constants, functions, relational operators, and logical operators. Logical expressions can use any of the numeric or string functions allowed in COMPUTE transformations (see COMPUTE).

- Parentheses can be used to enclose the logical expression itself and to specify the order of operations within a logical expression. Extra blanks or parentheses can be used to make the expression easier to read.

- Blanks (*not* commas) are used to separate relational operators from expressions.

- A relation can include variables, constants, or more complicated arithmetic expressions. Relations cannot be abbreviated. For example, the first relation below is valid; the second is not:

Valid: (A EQ 2 OR A EQ 5)
Not valid: (A EQ 2 OR 5)

- A relation cannot compare a string variable to a numeric value or variable, or vice versa. A relation cannot compare the result of a logical function (SYSMIS, MISSING, ANY, or RANGE) to a number.

Operations

- DO IF marks the beginning of the control structure and END IF marks the end. Control for a case is passed out of the structure as soon as a logical condition is met on a DO IF, ELSE IF, or ELSE command.

- A logical expression is evaluated as true, false, or missing. A transformation specified for a logical expression is executed only if the expression is true.

- Logical expressions are evaluated in the following order: functions, exponentiation, arithmetic operations, relations, and finally, logical operators. (For strings, the order is functions, relations, and then logical operators.) When more than one logical operator is used, NOT is evaluated first, followed by AND and then OR. You can change the order of operations using parentheses.

- Numeric variables created within a DO IF structure are initially set to the system-missing value. By default, they are assigned an F8.2 format.

- New string variables created within a DO IF structure are initially set to a blank value and are assigned the format specified on the STRING command that creates them.

- If the transformed value of a string variable exceeds the variable's defined format, the value is truncated. If the value is shorter than the format, the value is right-padded with blanks.

- If WEIGHT is specified within a DO IF structure, it takes effect unconditionally.

- Commands like SET, DISPLAY, SHOW, and so forth specified within a DO IF structure are executed when they are encountered in the command file.

- The DO IF—END IF structure (like LOOP—END LOOP) can include commands such as DATA LIST, END CASE, END FILE, and REREAD, which define complex file structures.

Flow of Control

- If the logical expression on DO IF is true, the commands immediately following DO IF are executed up to the next ELSE IF, ELSE, or END IF command. Control then passes to the first statement following END IF.

- If the expression on DO IF is false, control passes to the following ELSE IF command. Multiple ELSE IF commands are evaluated in the order in which they are specified until the logical expression on one of them is true. Commands following that ELSE IF command are executed up to the ELSE or END IF command, and control passes to the first statement following END IF.

- If none of the expressions are true on the DO IF or any of the ELSE IF commands, the commands following ELSE are executed and control passes out of the structure. If there is no ELSE command, a case goes through the entire structure with no change.

- Missing values returned by the logical expression on DO IF or on any ELSE IF cause control to pass to the END IF command at that point.

Missing Values and Logical Operators

When two or more relations are joined by logical operators AND and OR, the program always returns missing if all of the relations in the expression are missing. However, if any one of the relations can be determined, the program tries to return true or false according to the logical outcomes shown in Table 1. The asterisk indicates situations where the program can evaluate the outcome with incomplete information.

Table 1 Logical outcome

Expression	Outcome	Expression	Outcome
true AND true	= true	true OR true	= true
true AND false	= false	true OR false	= true
false AND false	= false	false OR false	= false
true AND missing	= missing	true OR missing	= true*
missing AND missing	= missing	missing OR missing	= missing
false AND missing	= false*	false OR missing	= missing

Example

```
DO IF (YRHIRED LT 87).
RECODE RACE(1=5)(2=4)(4=2)(5=1).
END IF.
```

- The RECODE command recodes *RACE* for those individuals hired before 1987 (*YRHIRED* is less than 87). The *RACE* variable is not recoded for individuals hired in 1987 or later.

- The RECODE command is skipped for any case with a missing value for *YRHIRED*.

Example

```
DATA LIST        FREE / X(F1).
NUMERIC          #QINIT.
DO IF            NOT #QINIT.
+   PRINT EJECT.
+   COMPUTE      #QINIT = 1.
END IF.
PRINT            / X.

BEGIN DATA
1 2  3  4  5
END DATA.
EXECUTE.
```

• This example shows how to execute a command only once.

• The NUMERIC command creates scratch variable *#QINIT*, which is initialized to 0.

• The NOT logical operator on DO IF reverses the outcome of a logical expression. In this example, the logical expression is a numeric variable that takes only 0 (false) or 1 (true) as its values. The PRINT EJECT command is executed only once, when the value of scratch variable *#QINIT* equals 0. After the COMPUTE command sets *#QINIT* to 1, the DO IF structure is skipped for all subsequent cases. A scratch variable is used because it is initialized to 0 and is not reinitialized after each case.

ELSE Command

ELSE executes one or more transformations when none of the logical expressions on DO IF or any ELSE IF commands is true.

• Only one ELSE command is allowed within a DO IF—END IF structure.

• ELSE must follow all ELSE IF commands (if any) in the structure.

• If the logical expression on DO IF or any ELSE IF command is true, the program ignores the commands following ELSE.

Example

```
DO IF (X EQ 0).
COMPUTE Y=1.
ELSE.
COMPUTE Y=2.
END IF.
```

• *Y* is set to 1 for all cases with value 0 for *X*, and *Y* is 2 for all cases with any other valid value for *X*.

• The value of *Y* is not changed by this structure if *X* is missing.

Example

```
DO IF    (YRHIRED GT 87).
COMPUTE            BONUS = 0.
ELSE.
IF (DEPT87 EQ 1) BONUS = .12*SALARY87.
IF (DEPT87 EQ 2) BONUS = .14*SALARY87.
IF (DEPT87 EQ 3) BONUS = .1*SALARY87.
IF (DEPT87 EQ 4) BONUS = .08*SALARY87.
END IF.
```

- If an individual was hired after 1987 (*YRHIRED* is greater than 87), *BONUS* is set to 0 and control passes out of the structure. Otherwise, control passes to the IF commands following ELSE.

- Each IF command evaluates every case. The value of *BONUS* is transformed only when the case meets the criteria specified on IF. Compare this structure with ELSE IF in the second example on p. 309, which performs the same task more efficiently.

Example

```
* Test for listwise deletion of missing values.

DATA LIST / V1 TO V6 1-6.
BEGIN DATA
123456
     56
1 3456
123456
123456
END DATA.

DO IF NMISS(V1 TO V6)=0.
+   COMPUTE SELECT='V'.
ELSE
+   COMPUTE SELECT='M'.
END IF.

FREQUENCIES VAR=SELECT.
```

- If there are no missing values for any of the variables *V1* to *V6*, COMPUTE sets the value of *SELECT* equal to V (for valid). Otherwise, COMPUTE sets the value of *SELECT* equal to M (for missing).

- FREQUENCIES generates a frequency table for *SELECT*. The table gives a count of how many cases have missing values for one or more variables, and how many cases have valid values for all variables. Commands in this example can be used to determine how many cases are dropped from an analysis that uses listwise deletion of missing values. See pp. 187 and 468 for alternative ways to check listwise deletion of missing values.

ELSE IF Command

ELSE IF executes one or more transformations when the logical expression on DO IF is not true.

- Multiple ELSE IF commands are allowed within the DO IF—END IF structure.

- If the logical expression on DO IF is true, the program executes the commands immediately following DO IF up to the first ELSE IF. Then control passes to the command following the END IF command.

- If the result of the logical expression on DO IF is false, control passes to ELSE IF.

Example

```
STRING STOCK(A9).
DO IF (ITEM EQ 0).
COMPUTE STOCK='New'.
ELSE IF (ITEM LE 9).
COMPUTE STOCK='Old'.
ELSE.
COMPUTE STOCK='Cancelled'.
END IF.
```

- STRING declares string variable *STOCK* and assigns it a width of nine characters.

- The first COMPUTE is executed for cases with value 0 for *ITEM*, and then control passes out of the structure. Such cases are not reevaluated by ELSE IF, even though 0 is less than 9.

- When the logical expression on DO IF is false, control passes to the ELSE IF command, where the second COMPUTE is executed only for cases with *ITEM* less than or equal to 9. Then control passes out of the structure.

- If the logical expressions on both the DO IF and ELSE IF commands are false, control passes to ELSE, where the third COMPUTE is executed.

- The DO IF—END IF structure sets *STOCK* equal to New when *ITEM* equals 0, to Old when *ITEM* is less than or equal to 9 but not equal to 0 (including negative numbers if they are valid), and to Cancelled for all valid values of *ITEM* greater than 9. The value of *STOCK* remains blank if *ITEM* is missing.

Example

```
DO IF (YRHIRED GT 87).
COMPUTE           BONUS = 0.
ELSE IF (DEPT87 EQ 3).
COMPUTE           BONUS = .1*SALARY87.
ELSE IF (DEPT87 EQ 1).
COMPUTE           BONUS = .12*SALARY87.
ELSE IF (DEPT87 EQ 4).
COMPUTE           BONUS = .08*SALARY87.
ELSE IF (DEPT87 EQ 2).
COMPUTE           BONUS = .14*SALARY87.
END IF.
```

- For cases hired after 1987, *BONUS* is set to 0 and control passes out of the structure. For a case that was hired before 1987 with value 3 for *DEPT87*, *BONUS* equals 10% of salary. Control then passes out of the structure. The other three ELSE IF commands are not evaluated for that case. This differs from the example on p. 308, where the IF command is evaluated for every case. The DO IF—ELSE IF structure shown here is more efficient.

- If Department 3 is the largest, Department 1 the next largest, and so forth, control passes out of the structure quickly for many cases. For a large number of cases or a command file that will be executed frequently, these efficiency considerations can be important.

Nested DO IF Structures

To perform transformations involving logical tests on two variables, you can use nested DO IF—END IF structures.

- There must be an END IF command for every DO IF command in the structure.

Example

```
DO IF (RACE EQ 5).          /*Do whites
+   DO IF (SEX EQ 2).       /*White female
+   COMPUTE SEXRACE=3.
+   ELSE.                   /*White male
+   COMPUTE SEXRACE=1.
+   END IF.                 /*Whites done
ELSE IF (SEX EQ 2).         /*Nonwhite female
COMPUTE SEXRACE=4.
ELSE.                       /*Nonwhite male
COMPUTE SEXRACE=2.
END IF.                     /*Nonwhites done
```

- This structure creates variable *SEXRACE*, which indicates both the sex and minority status of an individual.
- An optional plus sign, minus sign, or period in the first column allows you to indent commands so you can easily see the nested structures.

Complex File Structures

Some complex file structures may require you to imbed more than one DATA LIST command inside a DO IF—END IF structure. For example, consider a data file that has been collected from various sources. The information from each source is basically the same, but it is in different places on the records:

```
111295100FORD       CHAPMAN AUTO SALES
121199005VW     MIDWEST VOLKSWAGEN SALES
11 395025FORD       BETTER USED CARS
11        CHEVY 195005      HUFFMAN SALES & SERVICE
11        VW    595020      MIDWEST VOLKSWAGEN SALES
11        CHEVY 295015      SAM'S AUTO REPAIR
12        CHEVY 210 20      LONGFELLOW CHEVROLET
 9555032 VW               HYDE PARK IMPORTS
```

In the above file, an automobile part number always appears in columns 1 and 2, and the automobile manufacturer always appears in columns 10 through 14. The location of other information, such as price and quantity, depends on both the part number and the type of automobile. The DO IF—END IF structure in the following example reads records for part type 11.

Example

```
INPUT PROGRAM.
DATA LIST FILE=CARPARTS /PARTNO 1-2 KIND 10-14 (A).

DO IF (PARTNO EQ 11 AND KIND EQ 'FORD').
+ REREAD.
+ DATA LIST /PRICE 3-6 (2) QUANTITY 7-9 BUYER 20-43 (A).
+ END CASE.

ELSE IF (PARTNO EQ 11 AND (KIND EQ 'CHEVY' OR KIND EQ 'VW')).
+ REREAD.
+ DATA LIST /PRICE 15-18 (2) QUANTITY 19-21 BUYER 30-53 (A).
+ END CASE.
END IF.
END INPUT PROGRAM.

PRINT FORMATS PRICE (DOLLAR6.2).
PRINT /PARTNO TO BUYER.
WEIGHT BY QUANTITY.
DESCRIPTIVES PRICE.
```

- The first DATA LIST extracts the part number and the type of automobile.

- Depending on the information from the first DATA LIST, the records are reread, pulling the price, quantity, and buyer from different places.

- The two END CASE commands limit the working file to only those cases with Part 11 and automobile type Ford, Chevrolet, or Volkswagen. Without the END CASE commands, cases would be created in the working file for other part numbers and automobile types with missing values for price, quantity, and buyer.

- The results of the PRINT command are shown in Figure 1.

Figure 1   Printed information for part 11

```
11 FORD   $12.95 100 CHAPMAN AUTO SALES
11 FORD    $3.95  25 BETTER USED CARS
11 CHEVY   $1.95   5 HUFFMAN SALES & SERVICE
11 VW      $5.95  20 MIDWEST VOLKSWAGEN SALES
11 CHEVY   $2.95  15 SAM'S AUTO REPAIR
```

DO REPEAT—END REPEAT

```
DO REPEAT stand-in var={varlist   } [/stand-in var=...]
                      {value list}

transformation commands

END REPEAT [PRINT]
```

Example:
```
DO REPEAT R=REGION1 TO REGION5.
COMPUTE R=0.
END REPEAT.
```

Overview

The DO REPEAT—END REPEAT structure repeats the same transformations on a specified set of variables, reducing the number of commands you must enter to accomplish a task. This utility does not reduce the number of commands the program executes, just the number of commands you enter. To display the expanded set of commands the program generates, specify PRINT on END REPEAT.

DO REPEAT uses a *stand-in variable* to represent a *replacement list* of variables or values. The stand-in variable is specified as a place holder on one or more transformation commands within the structure. When the program repeats the transformation commands, the stand-in variable is replaced, in turn, by each variable or value specified on the replacement list.

The following commands can be used within a DO REPEAT—END REPEAT structure:

- Data transformations: COMPUTE, RECODE, IF, COUNT, and SELECT IF
- Data declarations: VECTOR, STRING, NUMERIC, and LEAVE
- Data definition: DATA LIST, MISSING VALUES (but not VARIABLE LABELS or VALUE LABELS)
- Loop structure commands: LOOP, END LOOP, and BREAK
- Do-if structure commands: DO IF, ELSE IF, ELSE, and END IF
- Print and write commands: PRINT, PRINT EJECT, PRINT SPACE, and WRITE
- Format commands: PRINT FORMATS, WRITE FORMATS, and FORMATS

Basic Specification

The basic specification is DO REPEAT, a stand-in variable followed by a required equals sign and a replacement list of variables or values, and at least one transformation command. The structure must end with the END REPEAT command. On the transformation commands, a single stand-in variable represents every variable or value specified on the replacement list.

Syntax Rules

- Multiple stand-in variables can be specified on a DO REPEAT command. Each stand-in variable must have its own equals sign and associated variable or value list and must be separated from other stand-in variables by a slash. All lists must name or generate the same number of items.

- Stand-in variables can be assigned any valid variable names: permanent, temporary, scratch, system, and so forth. A stand-in variable does not exist outside the DO REPEAT— END REPEAT structure and has no effect on variables with the same name that exist outside the structure. However, two stand-in variables cannot have the same name within the same DO REPEAT structure.

- A replacement variable list can include new or existing variables, and they can be string or numeric. Keyword TO can be used to name consecutive existing variables and to create a set of new variables. New string variables must be declared on the STRING command either before DO REPEAT or within the DO REPEAT structure. All replacement variable and value lists must have the same number of items.

- A replacement value list can be a list of strings or numeric values, or it can be of the form n_1 TO n_2, where n_1 is less than n_2 and both are integers. (Note that the keyword is TO, not THRU.)

Operations

- DO REPEAT marks the beginning of the control structure and END REPEAT marks the end. Once control passes out of the structure, all stand-in variables defined within the structure cease to exist.

- The program repeats the commands between DO REPEAT and END REPEAT once for each variable or value on the replacement list.

- Numeric variables created within the structure are initially set to the system-missing value. By default, they are assigned an F8.2 format.

- New string variables declared within the structure are initially set to a blank value and are assigned the format specified on the STRING command that creates them.

- If DO REPEAT is used to create new variables, the order in which they are created depends on how the transformation commands are specified. Variables created by specifying the TO keyword (for example, *V1* TO *V5*) are not necessarily consecutive in the working data file. See the PRINT subcommand on p. 315 for examples.

Example

```
DO REPEAT R=REGION1 TO REGION5.
COMPUTE R=0.
END REPEAT.
```

- DO REPEAT defines the stand-in variable *R*, which represents five new numeric variables: *REGION1*, *REGION2*, *REGION3*, *REGION4*, and *REGION5*.

- The five variables are initialized to 0 by a single COMPUTE specification that is repeated for each variable on the replacement list. Thus, the program generates five COMPUTE commands from the one specified.
- Stand-in variable *R* ceases to exist once control passes out of the DO REPEAT structure.

Example

```
* This example shows a typical application of INPUT PROGRAM, LOOP,
    and DO REPEAT. A data file containing random numbers is generated.

INPUT PROGRAM.
+   LOOP #I = 1 TO 1000.
+      DO REPEAT RESPONSE = R1 TO R400.
+         COMPUTE RESPONSE = UNIFORM(1) > 0.5.
+      END REPEAT.
+      COMPUTE AVG = MEAN(R1 TO R400).
+      END CASE.
+   END LOOP.
+   END FILE.
END INPUT PROGRAM.

FREQUENCIES VARIABLE=AVG
 /FORMAT=CONDENSE
 /HISTOGRAM
 /STATISTICS=MEAN MEDIAN MODE STDDEV MIN MAX.
```

- The INPUT PROGRAM—END INPUT PROGRAM structure encloses an input program that builds cases from transformation commands.
- The indexing variable (*#I*) on LOOP—END LOOP indicates that the loop should be executed 1000 times.
- The DO REPEAT—END REPEAT structure generates 400 variables, each with a 50% chance of being 0 and a 50% chance of being 1. This is accomplished by specifying a logical expression on COMPUTE that compares the values returned by UNIFORM(1) to the value 0.5. (UNIFORM(1) generates random numbers between 0 and 1.) Logical expressions are evaluated as false (0), true (1), or missing. Thus, each random number returned by UNIFORM that is 0.5 or less is evaluated as false and assigned the value 0, and each random number returned by UNIFORM that is greater than 0.5 is evaluated as true and assigned the value 1.
- The second COMPUTE creates variable *AVG*, which is the mean of *R1* to *R400* for each case.
- END CASE builds a case with the variables created within each loop. Thus, the loop structure creates 1000 cases, each with 401 variables (*R1* to *R400*, and *AVG*).
- END FILE signals the end of the data file generated by the input program. If END FILE were not specified in this example, the input program would go into an infinite loop. No working file would be built, and the program would display an error message for every procedure that follows the input program.
- FREQUENCIES produces a condensed frequency table, histogram, and statistics for *AVG*. The histogram for *AVG* shows a normal distribution.

PRINT Subcommand

The PRINT subcommand on END REPEAT displays the commands generated by the DO REPEAT—END REPEAT structure. PRINT can be used to verify the order in which commands are executed.

Example

```
DO REPEAT Q=Q1 TO Q5/ R=R1 TO R5.
COMPUTE Q=0.
COMPUTE R=1.
END REPEAT PRINT.
```

- The DO REPEAT—END REPEAT structure initializes one set of variables to 0 and another set to 1.

- The output from the PRINT subcommand is shown in Figure 1. The generated commands are preceded by plus signs.

- The COMPUTE commands are generated in such a way that variables are created in alternating order: *Q1*, *R1*, *Q2*, *R2*, and so forth. If you plan to use the TO keyword to refer to *Q1* to *Q5* later, you should use two separate DO REPEAT utilities; otherwise, *Q1* to *Q5* will include four of the five *R* variables. Alternatively, use the NUMERIC command to predetermine the order in which variables are added to the working file, or specify the replacement value lists as shown in the next example.

Figure 1   Output from the PRINT subcommand

```
 2   0        DO REPEAT Q=Q1 TO Q5/ R=R1 TO R5
 3   0        COMPUTE Q=0
 4   0        COMPUTE R=1
 5   0        END REPEAT PRINT

 6   0        +COMPUTE Q1=0
 7   0        +COMPUTE R1=1
 8   0        +COMPUTE Q2=0
 9   0        +COMPUTE R2=1
10   0        +COMPUTE Q3=0
11   0        +COMPUTE R3=1
12   0        +COMPUTE Q4=0
13   0        +COMPUTE R4=1
14   0        +COMPUTE Q5=0
15   0        +COMPUTE R5=1
```

Example

```
DO REPEAT Q=Q1 TO Q5,R1 TO R5/ N=0,0,0,0,0,1,1,1,1,1.
COMPUTE Q=N.
END REPEAT PRINT.
```

- In this example, a series of constants is specified as a stand-in value list for *N*. All the *Q* variables are initialized first, and then all the *R* variables, as shown in Figure 2.

Figure 2   Output from the PRINT subcommand

```
 2  0            DO REPEAT Q=Q1 TO Q5,R1 TO R5/ N=0,0,0,0,0,1,1,1,1,1
 3  0            COMPUTE Q=N
 4  0            END REPEAT PRINT

 5  0            +COMPUTE  Q1=0
 6  0            +COMPUTE  Q2=0
 7  0            +COMPUTE  Q3=0
 8  0            +COMPUTE  Q4=0
 9  0            +COMPUTE  Q5=0
10  0            +COMPUTE  R1=1
11  0            +COMPUTE  R2=1
12  0            +COMPUTE  R3=1
13  0            +COMPUTE  R4=1
14  0            +COMPUTE  R5=1
```

Example

```
DO REPEAT R=REGION1 TO REGION5/ X=1 TO 5.
COMPUTE R=REGION EQ X.
END REPEAT PRINT.
```

- In this example, stand-in variable *R* represents the variable list *REGION1* to *REGION5*. Stand-in variable *X* represents the value list 1 to 5.

- The DO REPEAT—END REPEAT structure creates dummy variables *REGION1* to *REGION5* that equal 0 or 1 for each of 5 regions, depending on whether variable *REGION* equals the current value of stand-in variable *X*.

- PRINT on END REPEAT causes the program to display the commands generated by the structure, as shown in Figure 3.

Figure 3   Commands generated by DO REPEAT

```
 2  0  DO REPEAT R=REGION1 TO REGION5/ X=1 TO 5
 3  0  COMPUTE R=REGION EQ X
 4  0  END REPEAT PRINT

 5  0  +COMPUTE REGION1=REGION EQ 1
 6  0  +COMPUTE REGION2=REGION EQ 2
 7  0  +COMPUTE REGION3=REGION EQ 3
 8  0  +COMPUTE REGION4=REGION EQ 4
 9  0  +COMPUTE REGION5=REGION EQ 5
```

DROP DOCUMENTS

```
DROP DOCUMENTS
```

Overview

When GET retrieves an SPSS-format data file, or when ADD FILES, MATCH FILES, or UPDATE are used to combine SPSS-format data files, all documents from each specified file are copied into the working file. DROP DOCUMENTS is used to drop these or any documents added with the DOCUMENT command from the working file. Whether or not DROP DOCUMENTS is used, new documents can be added to the working file with the DOCUMENT command.

Basic Specification

The only specification is DROP DOCUMENTS. There are no additional specifications.

Operations

- Documents are dropped from the working data file only. The original data file is unchanged, unless it is resaved.
- DROP DOCUMENTS drops all documentation, including documentation added by any DOCUMENT commands specified prior to the DROP DOCUMENTS command.

Example

```
GET FILE=GENSOC /KEEP=AGE SEX EDUC MARITAL CHILDRN MED_INS.

DROP DOCUMENTS.

FILE LABEL   General Social Survey Subset.
DOCUMENT     This file contains a subset of variables from the
             General Social Survey data.  For each case it records
             only the age, sex, education level, marital status,
             number of children, and type of medical insurance
             coverage.

SAVE OUTFILE=SUBSOC.
```

- DROP DOCUMENTS drops the documentation text from file *GENSOC*. Only the new documentation added with the DOCUMENT command is saved in file *SUBSOC*.
- The original file *GENSOC* is unchanged.

END CASE

```
END CASE
```

Example:
```
* Restructure a data file to make each data item into a single case.

INPUT PROGRAM.
DATA LIST /#X1 TO #X3 (3(F1,1X)).

VECTOR V=#X1 TO #X3.

LOOP #I=1 TO 3.
- COMPUTE X=V(#I).
- END CASE.
END LOOP.
END INPUT PROGRAM.
```

Overview

END CASE is used in an INPUT PROGRAM—END INPUT PROGRAM structure to signal that a case is complete. Control then passes to the commands immediately following the input program. After these commands are executed for the newly created case, the program returns to the input program and continues building cases by processing the commands immediately after the last END CASE command that was executed. For more information about the flow control in an input program, see INPUT PROGRAM—END INPUT PROGRAM.

END CASE is especially useful for restructuring files, either building a single case from several cases or building several cases from a single case. It can also be used to generate data without any data input (see p. 314 for an example).

Basic Specification

The basic specification is simply END CASE. There are no additional specifications.

Syntax Rules

- END CASE is available only within an input program and is generally specified within a loop.
- Multiple END CASE commands can be used within an input program. Each builds a case from the transformation and data definition commands executed since the last END CASE command.
- If no END CASE is explicitly specified, an END CASE command is implied immediately before END INPUT PROGRAM and the input program loops until an end-of-file is encountered or specified (see END FILE).

Operations

- When an END CASE command is encountered, the program suspends execution of the rest of the commands before the END INPUT PROGRAM command and passes control to the commands after the input program. After these commands are executed for the new case, control returns to the input program. The program continues building cases by processing the commands immediately after the most recent END CASE command. Use a loop to build cases from the same set of transformation and data definition commands.

- When multiple END CASE commands are specified, the program follows the flow of the input program and builds a case whenever it encounters an END CASE command, using the set of commands executed since the last END CASE.

- Unless LEAVE is specified, all variables are reinitialized each time the input program is resumed.

- When transformations such as COMPUTE, definitions such as VARIABLE LABELS, and utilities such as PRINT are specified between the last END CASE command and END INPUT PROGRAM, they are executed while a case is being initialized, not when it is complete. This may produce undesirable results (see the example beginning on p. 324).

Example

```
* Restructuring a data file to make each data item a single case.

INPUT PROGRAM.
DATA LIST /#X1 TO #X3 (3(F1,1X)).

VECTOR V=#X1 TO #X3.

LOOP #I=1 TO 3.
- COMPUTE X=V(#I).
- END CASE.
END LOOP.
END INPUT PROGRAM.

BEGIN DATA
2 1 1
3 5 1
END DATA.
FORMAT X(F1.0).
PRINT / X.
EXECUTE.
```

- The input program encloses the commands that build cases from the input file. An input program is required because END CASE is used to create multiple cases from single input records.

- DATA LIST defines three variables. In the format specification, the number 3 is a repetition factor that repeats the format in parentheses three times, once for each variable. The specified format is F1 and the 1X specification skips 1 column.

- VECTOR creates the vector *V* with the original scratch variables as its three elements. The indexing expression on the LOOP command increments the variable *#I* three times to control the number of iterations per input case and to provide the index for the vector *V*.

- COMPUTE sets *X* equal to each of the scratch variables. END CASE tells the program to build a case. Thus, the first loop (for the first case) sets *X* equal to the first element of vector *V*. Since *V(1)* references *#X1*, and *#X1* is 2, the value of *X* is 2. Variable *X* is then formatted and printed before control returns to the command END LOOP. The loop continues, since indexing is not complete. Thus, the program then sets *X* to *#X2*, which is 1, builds the second case, and passes it to the FORMAT and PRINT commands. After the third iteration, which sets *X* equal to 1, the program formats and prints the case and terminates the loop. Since the end of the file has not been encountered, END INPUT PROGRAM passes control to the first command in the input program, DATA LIST, to read the next input case. After the second loop, however, the program encounters END DATA and completes building the working data file.
- The six new cases are shown in Figure 1.

Figure 1   Outcome for multiple cases read from a single case

```
2
1
1
3
5
1
```

Example

```
*Restructuring a data file to create a separate case for
 each book order.

INPUT PROGRAM.
DATA LIST   /ORDER 1-4 #X1 TO #X22 (1X,11(F3.0,F2.0,1X)).

LEAVE ORDER.
VECTOR BOOKS=#X1 TO #X22.

LOOP #I=1 TO 21 BY 2 IF NOT SYSMIS(BOOKS(#I)).
- COMPUTE ISBN=BOOKS(#I).
- COMPUTE QUANTITY=BOOKS(#I+1).
- END CASE.
END LOOP.
END INPUT PROGRAM.
BEGIN DATA
1045 182 2 155 1 134 1 153 5
1046 155 3 153 5 163 1
1047 161 5 182 2 163 4 186 6
1048 186 2
1049 155 2 163 2 153 2 074 1 161 1
END DATA.

SORT CASES ISBN.
DO IF $CASENUM EQ 1.
- PRINT EJECT /'Order ISBN Quantity'.
- PRINT SPACE.
END IF.

FORMATS ISBN (F3)/ QUANTITY (F2).
PRINT /' ' ORDER ' ' ISBN '  ' QUANTITY.

EXECUTE.
```

- Data are extracted from a file whose records store values for an invoice number and a series of book codes and quantities ordered. For example, invoice 1045 is for four different titles and a total of nine books: two copies of book 182, one copy each of 155 and 134, and five copies of book 153. The task is to break each individual book order into a record, preserving the order number on each new case.

- The input program encloses the commands that build cases from the input file. They are required because the END CASE command is used to create multiple cases from single input records.

- DATA LIST specifies *ORDER* as a permanent variable and defines 22 scratch variables to hold the book numbers and quantities (this is the maximum number of numbers and quantities that will fit in 72 columns). In the format specification, the first element skips one space after the value for the variable *ORDER*. The number 11 repeats the formats that follow it 11 times: once for each book number and quantity pair. The specified format is F3.0 for book numbers and F2.0 for quantities. The 1X specification skips 1 column after each quantity value.

- LEAVE preserves the value of the variable *ORDER* across the new cases to be generated.

- VECTOR sets up the vector *BOOKS* with the 22 scratch variables as its elements. The first element is *#X1*, the second is *#X2*, and so on.

- If the element for the vector *BOOKS* is not system-missing, LOOP initiates the loop structure that moves through the vector *BOOKS*, picking off the book numbers and quantities. The indexing clause initiates the indexing variable *#I* at 1, to be increased by 2 to a maximum of 21.

- The first COMPUTE command sets the variable *ISBN* equal to the element in the vector *BOOKS* indexed by *#I*, which is the current book number. The second COMPUTE sets the variable *QUANTITY* equal to the next element in the vector *BOOKS*, *#I* +1, which is the quantity associated with the book number in *BOOKS(#I)*.

- END CASE tells the program to write out a case with the current values of the three variables: *ORDER*, *ISBN*, and *QUANTITY*.

- END LOOP terminates the loop structure and control is returned to the LOOP command, where *#I* is increased by 2 and looping continues until the entire input case is read or until *#I* exceeds the maximum value of 21.

- SORT CASES sorts the new cases by book number.

- The DO IF structure encloses a PRINT EJECT command and a PRINT SPACE command to set up titles for the output.

- FORMATS establishes dictionary formats for the new variables *ISBN* and *QUANTITY*. PRINT displays the new cases.

- EXECUTE runs the commands. The output is shown in Figure 2.

Figure 2   PRINT output showing new cases

```
Order ISBN Quantity

1049   74    1
1045  134    1
1045  153    5
1046  153    5
1049  153    2
1045  155    1
1046  155    3
1049  155    2
1047  161    5
1049  161    1
1046  163    1
1047  163    4
1049  163    2
1045  182    2
1047  182    2
1047  186    6
1048  186    2
```

Example

```
* Create variable that approximates a log-normal distribution.

SET FORMAT=F8.0.

INPUT PROGRAM.
LOOP I=1 TO 1000.
+ COMPUTE SCORE=EXP(NORMAL(1)).
+ END CASE.
END LOOP.
END FILE.
END INPUT PROGRAM.

FREQUENCIES VARIABLES=SCORE /FORMAT=NOTABLE /HISTOGRAM
  /PERCENTILES=1 10 20 30 40 50 60 70 80 90 99
  /STATISTICS=ALL.
```

- The input program creates 1000 cases with a single variable *SCORE*. Values for *SCORE* approximate a log-normal distribution.

Example

```
* Restructure a data file to create a separate case for each
  individual.
INPUT PROGRAM.
DATA LIST  /#RECS 1 HEAD1 HEAD2 3-4(A).     /*Read header info
LEAVE   HEAD1 HEAD2.

LOOP  #I=1 TO #RECS.
DATA LIST  /INDIV 1-2(1).                    /*Read individual info
PRINT  /#RECS HEAD1 HEAD2 INDIV.
END CASE.                                    /*Create combined case
END LOOP.
END INPUT PROGRAM.
```

```
BEGIN DATA
1 AC
91
2 CC
35
43
0 XX
1 BA
34
3 BB
42
96
37
END DATA.
LIST.
```

- Data are in a file with header records that indicate the type of record and the number of individual records that follow. The number of records following each header record varies. For example, the 1 in the first column of the first header record (AC) says that only one individual record (91) follows. The 2 in the first column of the second header record (CC) says that two individual records (35 and 43) follow. The next header record has no individual records, indicated by the 0 in column 1, and so on.

- The first DATA LIST reads the expected number of individual records for each header record into temporary variable *#RECS*. *#RECS* is then used as the terminal value in the indexing variable to read the correct number of individual records using the second DATA LIST.

- The variables *HEAD1* and *HEAD2* contain the information in columns 3 and 4, respectively, in the header records. The LEAVE command retains *HEAD1* and *HEAD2* so that this information can be spread to the individual records.

- The variable *INDIV* is the information from the individual record. *INDIV* is combined with *#RECS*, *HEAD1*, and *HEAD2* to create the new case. Notice in the output from the PRINT command in Figure 3 that no case is created for the header record with 0 for *#RECS*.

- END CASE passes each case out of the input program to the LIST command. Without END CASE, the PRINT command would still display the cases as shown in Figure 3 because it is inside the loop. However, only one (the last) case per header record would pass out of the input program. The outcome for LIST will be quite different (compare Figure 4 with Figure 5).

Figure 3 PRINT output

```
1 A C 9.1
2 C C 3.5
2 C C 4.3
1 B A 3.4
3 B B 4.2
3 B B 9.6
3 B B 3.7
```

Figure 4   LIST output when END CASE is specified

```
HEAD1 HEAD2 INDIV

A       C       9.1
C       C       3.5
C       C       4.3
B       A       3.4
B       B       4.2
B       B       9.6
B       B       3.7
```

Figure 5   LIST output when END CASE is not specified

```
HEAD1 HEAD2 INDIV

A       C       9.1
C       C       4.3
X       X       .
B       A       3.4
B       B       3.7
```

Example

```
* Note: the following is an erroneous program! The COMPUTE and
  PRINT commands that follow END CASE are misplaced. They should
  be specified after the END INPUT PROGRAM command.

INPUT PROGRAM.
DATA LIST   /#X1 TO #X3 (3(F1,1X)).

VECTOR V=#X1 TO #X3.

LOOP #I=1 TO 3.
COMPUTE X=V(#I).
END CASE.
END LOOP.

COMPUTE Y=X**2.     /* This should be specified after the input program
VARIABLE LABELS X 'TEST VARIABLE' Y 'SQUARE OF X'.
PRINT FORMATS X Y (F2).
END INPUT PROGRAM.

BEGIN DATA
2 1 1
3 5 1
END DATA.

FREQUENCIES VARIABLES=X Y.
```

- No error or warning is issued for these commands, but the result is not what was intended. The computed value for X is passed out of the input program when the END CASE command is encountered. Thus, Y is computed from the initialized value of X, which is the system-missing value. As Figure 6 shows, all six cases computed for Y within the input program have the system-missing value, represented by a period (.).

- The frequencies table for *X* is as expected, because *X* is computed from inline data and no computation is done between END CASE and END INPUT PROGRM.
- The VARIABLE LABELS and PRINT FORMATS commands have their desired effects even though they are executed with the COMPUTE command, because they do not act on any data read in.
- Moving COMPUTE before END CASE will solve the problem, but the preferred solution is to specify END INPUT PROGRAM before all commands in the transformation program, since they operate on the cases created by the input program.

Figure 6   FREQUENCIES output

```
X         TEST VARIABLE

                                              VALID      CUM
     VALUE LABEL          VALUE  FREQUENCY  PERCENT  PERCENT  PERCENT

                            1         3      50.0    50.0     50.0
                            2         1      16.7    16.7     66.7
                            3         1      16.7    16.7     83.3
                            5         1      16.7    16.7    100.0
                                   -------  -------  -------
                         TOTAL       6     100.0    100.0

VALID CASES      6    MISSING CASES      0
- - - - - - - - - - - - - - - - - - - - - - - - - - - - - - - - - - -


Y         SQUARE OF X

                                              VALID      CUM
     VALUE LABEL          VALUE  FREQUENCY  PERCENT  PERCENT  PERCENT

                            .         6     100.0   MISSING
                                   -------  -------  -------
                         TOTAL       6     100.0    100.0
```

END FILE

```
END FILE
```

Example:
```
INPUT PROGRAM.
DATA LIST FILE=PRICES /YEAR 1-4 QUARTER 6 PRICE 8-12(2).
DO IF (YEAR GE 1881).  /*Stop reading before 1881
END FILE.
END IF.
END INPUT PROGRAM.
```

Overview

END FILE is used in an INPUT PROGRAM—END INPUT PROGRAM structure to tell the program to stop reading data before it actually encounters the end of the file. END FILE can be used with END CASE to concatenate raw data files by causing the program to delay end-of-file processing until it has read multiple data files (see p. 237 for an example). END FILE can also be used with LOOP and END CASE to generate data without any data input (see p. 314 for an example).

Basic Specification

The basic specification is simply END FILE. There are no additional specifications. The end of file is defined according to the conditions specified for END FILE in the input program.

Syntax Rules

- END FILE is available only within an INPUT PROGRAM structure.
- Only one END FILE command can be executed per input program. However, multiple END FILE commands can be specified within a conditional structure in the input program.

Operations

- When END FILE is encountered, the program stops reading data and puts an end of file in the working data file it was building. The case that causes the execution of END FILE is not read. To include this case, use the END CASE command before END FILE (see the examples below).
- END FILE has the same effect as the end of the input data file. It terminates the input program (see INPUT PROGRAM—END INPUT PROGRAM).

Example

```
*Select cases.

INPUT PROGRAM.
DATA LIST FILE=PRICES /YEAR 1-4 QUARTER 6 PRICE 8-12(2).

DO IF (YEAR GE 1881).  /*Stop reading before 1881
END FILE.
END IF.

END INPUT PROGRAM.

LIST.
```

- This example assumes that data records are entered chronologically by year. The DO IF—END IF structure specifies an end of file when the first case with a value of 1881 or later for *YEAR* is reached.
- LIST executes the input program and lists cases in the working data file. The case that causes the end of the file is not included in the working data file.
- As an alternative to an input program with END FILE, you can use N OF CASES to select cases if you know the exact number of cases. Another alternative is to use SELECT IF to select cases before 1881, but then the program would unnecessarily read the entire input file.

Example

```
Select cases but retain the case that causes end-of-file processing.

INPUT PROGRAM.
DATA LIST FILE=PRICES /YEAR 1-4 QUARTER 6 PRICE 8-12(2).

DO IF (YEAR GE 1881).   /*Stop reading before 1881 (or at end of file)
END CASE.               /*Create case 1881
END FILE.

ELSE.
END CASE.               /*Create all other cases
END IF.
END INPUT PROGRAM.

LIST.
```

- The first END CASE command forces the program to retain the case that causes end-of-file processing.
- The second END CASE indicates the end of case for all other cases and passes them out of the input program one at a time. It is required because the first END CASE command causes the program to abandon default end-of-case processing (see END CASE).

ERASE

```
ERASE FILE='file'
```

Example:
```
ERASE FILE='PRSNL.DAT'.
```

Overview

ERASE removes a file from a disk.

Basic Specification

The basic specification is the keyword FILE followed by a file specification. The specified file is erased from the disk. The file specification may vary from operating system to operating system, but enclosing the filename in apostrophes generally works.

Syntax Rules

- The keyword FILE is required but the equals sign is optional.
- ERASE allows one file specification only and does not accept wildcard characters. To erase more than one file, specify multiple ERASE commands.
- The file to be erased must be specified in full. ERASE does not recognize any default file extension.

Operations

ERASE deletes the specified file regardless of its type. No message is displayed unless the command cannot be executed. Use ERASE with caution.

Example

```
ERASE FILE 'PRSNL.DAT'.
```

- The file *PRSNL.SAV* is deleted from the current directory. Whether it is an SPSS-format data file or a file of any other type makes no difference.

EXAMINE

```
EXAMINE VARIABLES=varlist [[BY varlist] [varname BY varname]]

[/COMPARE={GROUPS** }]
         {VARIABLES}

[/{TOTAL**}]
  {NOTOTAL}

[/ID={case number**}]
     {varname    }

[/PERCENTILES [[({5,10,25,50,75,90,95})=[{HAVERAGE  }] [NONE]]
                {value list           }  {WAVERAGE  }
                                         {ROUND     }
                                         {AEMPIRICAL}
                                         {EMPIRICAL }

[/PLOT=[STEMLEAF**] [BOXPLOT**] [NPPLOT] [SPREADLEVEL(n)] [HISTOGRAM]]

        [{ALL  }]
         {NONE}

[/STATISTICS=[DESCRIPTIVES**] [EXTREME({5})]]
                                       {n}
             [{ALL }]
              {NONE}

[/CINTERVAL {95**}]
            {n   }

[/MESTIMATOR=[{NONE**}]]
             {ALL   }

             [HUBER({1.339})] [ANDREW({1.34}]
                   {c    }           {c    }

             [HAMPEL({1.7,3.4,8.5})]
                    {a  ,b  ,c  }

             [TUKEY({4.685})]
                   {c    }

[/MISSING=[{LISTWISE**}] [{EXCLUDE**}] [{NOREPORT**}]]
           {PAIRWISE }   {INCLUDE  }   {REPORT    }
```

**Default if the subcommand is omitted.

Examples:

```
EXAMINE VARIABLES=ENGSIZE,COST.

EXAMINE VARIABLES=MIPERGAL BY MODEL,MODEL BY CYLINDERS.
```

Overview

EXAMINE provides stem-and-leaf plots, histograms, boxplots, normal plots, robust estimates of location, tests of normality, and other descriptive statistics. Separate analyses can be obtained for subgroups of cases.

Options

Cells. You can subdivide cases into cells based on their values for grouping (factor) variables using the BY keyword on the VARIABLES subcommand.

Output. You can control the display of output using the COMPARE subcommand. You can specify the computational method and break points for percentiles with the PERCENTILES subcommand, and you can assign a variable to be used for labeling outliers on the ID subcommand.

Plots. You can request stem-and-leaf plots, histograms, vertical boxplots, spread-versus-level plots with Levene tests for homogeneity of variance, and normal and detrended probability plots with tests for normality. These plots are available through the PLOT subcommand.

Statistics. You can request univariate statistical output with the STATISTICS subcommand and maximum-likelihood estimators with the MESTIMATORS subcommand.

Basic Specification

- The basic specification is VARIABLES and at least one dependent variable.
- The default output includes a Descriptives table displaying univariate statistics (mean, median, standard deviation, standard error, variance, kurtosis, kurtosis standard error, skewness, skewness standard error, sum, interquartile range (IQR), range, minimum, maximum, and 5% trimmed mean), a vertical boxplot and a stem-and-leaf plot. Outliers are labeled on the boxplot with the system variable *$CASENUM*.

Subcommand Order

Subcommands can be named in any order.

Limitations

- When string variables are used as factors, only the first eight characters are used to form cells. String variables cannot be specified as dependent variables.
- When more than eight crossed factors (for example, A, B, ... in the specification Y by A by B by ...) are specified, the command is not executed.

Example

```
EXAMINE VARIABLES=ENGSIZE,COST.
```

- *ENGSIZE* and *COST* are the dependent variables.
- EXAMINE produces univariate statistics for *ENGSIZE* and *COST* in the Descriptives table and a vertical boxplot and a stem-and-leaf plot for each variable.

Example

```
EXAMINE VARIABLES=MIPERGAL BY MODEL,MODEL BY CYLINDERS.
```

- *MIPERGAL* is the dependent variable. The cell specification follows the first BY keyword. Cases are subdivided based on values of *MODEL* and also based on the combination of values of *MODEL* and *CYLINDERS*.
- Assuming that there are three values for *MODEL* and two values for *CYLINDERS*, this example produces a Descriptives table, a stem-and-leaf plot, and a boxplot for the total sample, a Descriptives table and a boxplot for each factor defined by the first BY (*MIPERGAL* by *MODEL* and *MIPERGAL* by *MODEL* by *CYLINDERS*), and a stem-and-leaf plot for each of the nine cells (three defined by *MODEL* and six defined by *MODEL* and *CYLINDERS* together).

VARIABLES Subcommand

VARIABLES specifies the dependent variables and the cells. The dependent variables are specified first, followed by the keyword BY and the variables that define the cells. Repeated models on the same EXAMINE are discarded.

- To create cells defined by the combination of values of two or more factors, specify the factor names separated by the keyword BY.

Caution. Large amounts of output can be produced if many cells are specified. If there are many factors or if the factors have many values, EXAMINE will produce a large number of separate analyses.

Example

```
EXAMINE VARIABLES=SALARY,YRSEDUC BY RACE,SEX,DEPT,RACE BY SEX.
```

- *SALARY* and *YRSEDUC* are dependent variables.
- Cells are formed first for the values of *SALARY* and *YRSEDUC* individually, and then each by values for *RACE, SEX, DEPT,* and the combination of *RACE* and *SEX*.
- By default, EXAMINE produces Descriptives tables, stem-and-leaf plots, and boxplots.

COMPARE Subcommand

COMPARE controls how boxplots are displayed. This subcommand is most useful if there is more than one dependent variable and at least one factor in the design.

GROUPS *For each dependent variable, boxplots for all cells are displayed together.* With this display, comparisons across cells for a single dependent variable are easily made. This is the default.

VARIABLES *For each cell, boxplots for all dependent variables are displayed together.* With this display, comparisons of several dependent variables are easily made. This is useful in situations where the dependent variables are repeated measures of the same variable (see the following example) or have similar scales, or when the dependent variable has very different values for different cells, and plotting all cells on the same scale would cause information to be lost.

Example

```
EXAMINE VARIABLES=GPA1 GPA2 GPA3 GPA4 BY MAJOR   /COMPARE=VARIABLES.
```

- The four GPA variables are summarized for each value of *MAJOR*.
- COMPARE=VARIABLES groups the boxplots for the four GPA variables together for each value of *MAJOR*.

Example

```
EXAMINE VARIABLES=GPA1 GPA2 GPA3 GPA4 BY MAJOR /COMPARE=GROUPS.
```

- COMPARE=GROUPS groups the boxplots for *GPA1* for all majors together, followed by boxplots for *GPA2* for all majors, and so on.

TOTAL and NOTOTAL Subcommands

TOTAL and NOTOTAL control the amount of output produced by EXAMINE when factor variables are specified.

- TOTAL is the default. By default, or when TOTAL is specified, EXAMINE produces statistics and plots for each dependent variable overall and for each cell specified by the factor variables.
- NOTOTAL suppresses overall statistics and plots.
- TOTAL and NOTOTAL are alternatives.
- NOTOTAL is ignored when the VARIABLES subcommand does not specify factor variables.

ID Subcommand

ID assigns a variable from the working data file to identify the cases in the output. By default the case number is used for labeling outliers and extreme cases in boxplots.

- The identification variable can be either string or numeric. If it is numeric, value labels are used to label cases. If no value labels exist, the values are used.
- Only one identification variable can be specified.

Example

```
EXAMINE VARIABLES=SALARY BY RACE BY SEX /ID=LASTNAME.
```

- ID displays the value of *LASTNAME* for outliers and extreme cases in the boxplots.

PERCENTILES Subcommand

PERCENTILES displays the Percentiles table. If PERCENTILES is omitted, no percentiles are produced. If PERCENTILES is specified without keywords, HAVERAGE is used with default break points of 5, 10, 25, 50, 75, 90, and 95.

- Values for break points are specified in parentheses following the subcommand. EXAMINE displays up to six decimal places for user-specified percentile values.

- The method keywords follow the specifications for break points.

In the following formulas, cases are assumed to be ranked in ascending order. The following notation is used: w is the sum of the weights for all nonmissing cases, p is the specified percentile divided by 100, i is the rank of each case, and X_i is the value of the ith case.

HAVERAGE   *Weighted average at* $X_{(w+1)p}$. The percentile value is the weighted average of X_i and X_{i+1} using the formula $(1-f)X_i + fX_{i+1}$, where $(w+1)p$ is decomposed into an integer part i and a fractional part f. This is the default if PERCENTILES is specified without a keyword.

WAVERAGE   *Weighted average at* X_{wp}. The percentile value is the weighted average of X_i and $X_{(i+1)}$ using the formula $(1-f)X_i + fX_{i+1}$, where i is the integer part of wp and f is the fractional part of wp.

ROUND   *Observation closest to* wp. The percentile value is X_i, where i is the integer part of $(wp + 0.5)$.

EMPIRICAL   *Empirical distribution function.* The percentile value is X_i when the fractional part of wp is equal to 0. The percentile value is X_{i+1} when the fractional part of wp is greater than 0.

AEMPIRICAL   *Empirical distribution with averaging.* The percentile value is $(X_i + X_{i+1})/2$ when the fractional part of wp equals 0. The percentile value is X_{i+1} when the fractional part of wp is greater than 0.

NONE   *Suppress percentile output.* This is the default if PERCENTILES is omitted.

Example

```
EXAMINE VARIABLE=SALARY /PERCENTILES(10,50,90)=EMPIRICAL.
```

- PERCENTILES produces the 10th, 50th, and 90th percentiles for the dependent variable *SALARY* using the EMPIRICAL distribution function.

PLOT Subcommand

PLOT controls plot output. The default is a vertical boxplot and a stem-and-leaf plot for each dependent variable for each cell in the model.

- Spread-versus-level plots can be produced only if there is at least one factor variable on the VARIABLES subcommand. If you request a spread-versus-level plot and there are no factor variables, the program issues a warning and no spread-versus-level plot is produced.
- If you specify the PLOT subcommand, only those plots explicitly requested are produced.

BOXPLOT   *Vertical boxplot.* The boundaries of the box are Tukey's hinges. The median is identified by an asterisk. The length of the box is the interquartile range (IQR) computed from Tukey's hinges. Values more than three IQR's from the end of a box are labeled as extreme (E). Values more than 1.5 IQR's but less than 3 IQR's from the end of the box are labeled as outliers (O).

STEMLEAF *Stem-and-leaf plot.* In a stem-and-leaf plot, each observed value is divided into two components—leading digits (stem) and trailing digits (leaf).

HISTOGRAM *Histogram.*

SPREADLEVEL(n) *Spread-versus-level plot with the Test of Homogeneity of Variance table.* If the keyword appears alone, the natural logs of the interquartile ranges are plotted against the natural logs of the medians for all cells. If a power for transforming the data (n) is given, the IQR and median of the transformed data are plotted. If 0 is specified for n, a natural log transformation of the data is done. The slope of the regression line and Levene tests for homogeneity of variance are also displayed. The Levene tests are based on the original data if no transformation is specified and on the transformed data if a transformation is requested.

NPPLOT *Normal and detrended Q-Q plots with the Tests of Normality table presenting Shapiro-Wilk's statistic and a Kolmogorov-Smirnov statistic with a Lilliefors significance level for testing normality.* Shapiro-Wilk's statistic is not calculated when the sample size exceeds 50.

ALL *All available plots.*

NONE *No plots.*

Example

```
EXAMINE VARIABLES=CYCLE BY TREATMNT /PLOT=NPPLOT.
```

- PLOT produces normal and detrended Q-Q plots for each value of *TREATMNT* and a Tests of Normality table.

Example

```
EXAMINE VARIABLES=CYCLE BY TREATMNT /PLOT=SPREADLEVEL(.5).
```

- PLOT produces a spread-versus-level plot of the medians and interquartile ranges of the square root of *CYCLE*. Each point on the plot represents one of the *TREATMNT* groups.
- A Test of Homogeneity of Variance table displays Levene statistics.

Example

```
EXAMINE VARIABLES=CYCLE BY TREATMNT /PLOT=SPREADLEVEL(0).
```

- PLOT generates a spread-versus-level plot of the medians and interquartile ranges of the natural logs of *CYCLE* for each *TREATMENT* group.
- A Test of Homogeneity of Variance table displays Levene statistics.

Example

```
EXAMINE VARIABLES=CYCLE BY TREATMNT /PLOT=SPREADLEVEL.
```

- PLOT generates a spread-versus-level plot of the natural logs of the medians and interquartile ranges of *CYCLE* for each *TREATMNT* group.
- A Test of Homogeneity of Variance table displays Levene statistics.

STATISTICS Subcommand

STATISTICS requests univariate statistics and determines how many extreme values are displayed. DESCRIPTIVES is the default. If you specify keywords on STATISTICS, only the requested statistics are displayed.

DESCRIPTIVES *Display the Descriptives table showing univariate statistics (the mean, median, 5% trimmed mean, standard error, variance, standard deviation, minimum, maximum, range, interquartile range, skewness, skewness standard error, kurtosis, and kurtosis standard error).* This is the default.

EXTREME(n) *Display the Extreme Values table presenting cases with the* n *largest and* n *smallest values.* If *n* is omitted, the five largest and five smallest values are displayed. Extreme cases are labeled with their values for the identification variable if the ID subcommand is used or with their values for the system variable *$CASENUM* if ID is not specified.

ALL *Display the Descriptives and Extreme Values tables.*

NONE *Display neither the Descriptives nor the Extreme Values tables.*

Example

```
EXAMINE VARIABLE=FAILTIME /ID=BRAND
  /STATISTICS=EXTREME(10) /PLOT=NONE.
```

- STATISTICS identifies the cases with the 10 lowest and 10 highest values for *FAILTIME*. These cases are labeled with the first characters of their values for the variable *BRAND*. The Descriptives table is not displayed.

CINTERVAL Subcommand

CINTERVAL controls the confidence level when the default DESCRIPTIVES statistics is displayed. CINTERVAL has a default value of 95.

- You can specify a CINTERVAL value (*n*) between 50 and 99.99 inclusive. If the value you specify is out of range, the program issues a warning and uses the default 95% intervals.

- If you specify a keyword on STATISTICS subcommand that turns off the default DESCRIPTIVES, the CINTERVAL subcommand is ignored.

- The confidence interval appears in the output with the label *n% CI for Mean*, followed by the confidence interval in parentheses. For example,

```
95% CI for Mean (.0001,.00013)
```

The *n* in the label shows up to six decimal places. That is, input `/CINTERVAL 95` displays as *95% CI* while input `/CINTERVAL 95.975` displays as *95.975% CI*.

MESTIMATORS Subcommand

M-estimators are robust maximum-likelihood estimators of location. Four M-estimators are available for display in the M-Estimators table. They differ in the weights they apply to the cases. MESTIMATORS with no keywords produces Huber's M-estimator with c=1.339; Andrews' wave with c=1.34π; Hampel's M-estimator with a=1.7, b=3.4, and c=8.5; and Tukey's biweight with c=4.685.

HUBER(c)   *Huber's M-estimator.* The value of weighting constant c can be specified in parentheses following the keyword. The default is c=1.339.

ANDREW(c)   *Andrews' wave estimator.* The value of weighting constant c can be specified in parentheses following the keyword. Constants are multiplied by π. The default is 1.34π.

HAMPEL(a,b,c)   *Hampel's M-estimator.* The values of weighting constants a, b, and c can be specified in order in parentheses following the keyword. The default values are a=1.7, b=3.4, and c=8.5.

TUKEY(c)   *Tukey's biweight estimator.* The value of weighting constant c can be specified in parentheses following the keyword. The default is c=4.685.

ALL   *All four above M-estimators.* This is the default when MESTIMATORS is specified with no keyword. The default values for weighting constants are used.

NONE   *No M-estimators.* This is the default if MESTIMATORS is omitted.

Example

```
EXAMINE VARIABLE=CASTTEST /MESTIMATORS.
```

- MESTIMATORS generates all four M-estimators computed with the default constants.

Example

```
EXAMINE VARIABLE=CASTTEST /MESTIMATORS=HAMPELS(2,4,8).
```

- MESTIMATOR produces Hampel's M-estimator with weighting constants a=2, b=4, and c=8.

MISSING Subcommand

MISSING controls the processing of missing values in the analysis. The default is LISTWISE, EXCLUDE, and NOREPORT.

- LISTWISE and PAIRWISE are alternatives and apply to all variables. They are modified for dependent variables by INCLUDE/EXCLUDE and for factor variables by REPORT/NOREPORT.
- INCLUDE and EXCLUDE are alternatives; they apply only to dependent variables.
- REPORT and NOREPORT are alternatives; they determine if missing values for factor variables are treated as valid categories.

LISTWISE   *Delete cases with missing values listwise.* A case with missing values for any dependent variable or any factor in the model specification is excluded from statistics and plots unless modified by INCLUDE or REPORT. This is the default.

PAIRWISE   *Delete cases with missing values pairwise.* A case is deleted from the analysis only if it has a missing value for the dependent variable or factor being analyzed.

EXCLUDE   *Exclude user-missing values.* User-missing values and system-missing values for dependent variables are excluded. This is the default.

INCLUDE   *Include user-missing values.* Only system-missing values for dependent variables are excluded from the analysis.

NOREPORT   *Exclude user- and system-missing values for factor variables.* This is the default.

REPORT   *Include user- and system-missing values for factor variables.* User- and system-missing values for factors are treated as valid categories and are labeled as missing.

Example

```
EXAMINE VARIABLES=RAINFALL MEANTEMP BY REGION.
```

- MISSING is not specified and the default is used. Any case with a user- or system-missing value for *RAINFALL*, *MEANTEMP*, or *REGION* is excluded from the analysis and display.

Example

```
EXAMINE VARIABLES=RAINFALL MEANTEMP BY REGION
  /MISSING=PAIRWISE.
```

- Only cases with missing values for *RAINFALL* are excluded from the analysis of *RAINFALL*, and only cases with missing values for *MEANTEMP* are excluded from the analysis of *MEANTEMP*. Missing values for *REGION* are not used.

Example

```
EXAMINE VARIABLES=RAINFALL MEANTEMP BY REGION
  /MISSING=REPORT.
```

- Missing values for *REGION* are considered valid categories and are labeled as missing.

References

Frigge, M., D. C. Hoaglin, and B. Iglewicz. 1987. Some implementations of the boxplot. In: *Computer Science and Statistics Proceedings of the 19th Symposium on the Interface,* R. M. Heiberger and M. Martin, eds. Alexandria, Virginia: American Statistical Association.

Hoaglin, D. C., F. Mosteller, and J. W. Tukey. 1983. *Understanding robust and exploratory data analysis.* New York: John Wiley and Sons.

_____. 1985. *Exploring data tables, trends, and shapes.* New York: John Wiley and Sons.

Tukey, J. W. 1977. *Exploratory data analysis.* Reading, Mass.: Addison-Wesley.

Velleman, P. F., and D. C. Hoaglin. 1981. *Applications, basics, and computing of exploratory data analysis.* Boston: Duxbury Press.

EXECUTE

Overview

EXECUTE forces the data to be read and executes the transformations that precede it in the command sequence.

Basic Specification

The basic specification is simply the command keyword. EXECUTE has no additional specifications.

Operations

- EXECUTE causes the data to be read but has no other influence on the session.
- EXECUTE is designed for use with transformation commands and facilities such as ADD FILES, MATCH FILES, UPDATE, PRINT, and WRITE, which do not read data and are not executed unless followed by a data-reading procedure.

Example

```
DATA LIST  FILE=RAWDATA / 1 LNAME 1-13 (A)  FNAME 15-24 (A)
  MMAIDENL 40-55.
VAR LABELS  MMAIDENL 'MOTHER''S MAIDEN NAME'.
DO IF (MMAIDENL EQ 'Smith').
WRITE OUTFILE=SMITHS/LNAME FNAME.
END IF.
EXECUTE.
```

- This example writes the last and first names of all people whose mother's maiden name was Smith to the data file *SMITHS*.
- DO IF—END IF and WRITE do not read data and are executed only when data are read for a procedure. Because there is no procedure in this session, EXECUTE is used to read the data and execute all of the preceding transformation commands. Otherwise, the commands would not be executed.

EXPORT

```
EXPORT OUTFILE=file

[/TYPE={COMM**}]
       {TAPE  }

[/UNSELECTED=[{RETAIN}]
             {DELETE}

[/KEEP={ALL**  }] [/DROP=varlist]
       {varlist}

[/RENAME=(old varnames=new varnames)...]

[/MAP]

[/DIGITS=n]
```

**Default if the subcommand is omitted.

Example:

```
EXPORT OUTFILE=NEWDATA /RENAME=(V1 TO V3=ID, SEX, AGE) /MAP.
```

Overview

EXPORT produces a portable data file. A portable data file is a data file created used to transport data between different types of computers and operating systems (such as between IBM CMS and Digital VAX/VMS) or between SPSS, SPSS/PC+, or other software using the same portable file format. Like an SPSS-format data file, a portable file contains all of the data and dictionary information stored in the working data file from which it was created. (To send data to a computer and operating system the same as your own, send an SPSS-format data file, which is easier and faster to process than a portable file.)

EXPORT is similar to the SAVE command. It can occur in the same position in the command sequence as the SAVE command and saves the working data file. The file includes the results of all permanent transformations and any temporary transformations made just prior to the EXPORT command. The working data file is unchanged after the EXPORT command.

Options

Format. You can control the format of the portable file using the TYPE subcommand.

Variables. You can save a subset of variables from the working file and rename the variables using the DROP, KEEP, and RENAME subcommands. You can also produce a record of all variables and their names on the exported file with the MAP subcommand.

Precision. You can specify the number of decimal digits of precision for the values of all numeric variables on the DIGITS subcommand.

Basic Specification

The basic specification is the OUTFILE subcommand with a file specification. All variables from the working data file are written to the portable file, with variable names, variable and value labels, missing-value flags, and print and write formats.

Subcommand Order

Subcommands can be named in any order.

Operations

- Portable files are written with 80-character record lengths.
- Portable files may contain some unprintable characters.
- The working data file is still available for transformations and procedures after the portable file is created.
- The system variables *$CASENUM* and *$DATE* are assigned when the file is read by IMPORT.
- If the WEIGHT command is used before EXPORT, the weighting variable is included in the portable file.

Example

```
EXPORT OUTFILE=NEWDATA /RENAME=(V1 TO V3=ID,SEX,AGE) /MAP.
```

- The portable file is written to *NEWDATA*.
- The variables *V1*, *V2*, and *V3* are renamed *ID*, *SEX*, and *AGE* in the portable file. Their names remain *V1*, *V2*, and *V3* in the working file. None of the other variables written to the portable file are renamed.
- MAP requests a display of the variables in the portable file.

Methods of Transporting Portable Files

Portable files can be transported on magnetic tape or by a communications program.

Magnetic Tape

Before transporting files on a magnetic tape, make sure the receiving computer can read the tape being sent. The following tape specifications must be known before you write the portable file on the tape:

- Number of tracks—either 7 or 9.
- Tape density—200, 556, 800, 1600, or 6250 bits per inch (BPI).
- Parity—even or odd. This must be known only when writing a 7-track tape.

- Tape labeling—labeled or unlabeled. Check whether the site can use tape labels. Also make sure that the site has the ability to read multivolume tape files if the file being written uses more than one tape.
- Blocksize—the maximum blocksize the receiving computer can accept.

A tape written with the following characteristics can be read by most computers: 9 track, 1600 BPI, unlabeled, and a blocksize of 3200 characters. However, there is no guarantee that a tape written with these characteristics can be read successfully. The best policy is to know the requirements of the receiving computer ahead of time.

The following advice may help ensure successful file transfers by magnetic tape:

- Unless you are certain that the receiving computer can read labels, prepare an unlabeled tape.
- Make sure the record length of 80 is not changed.
- Do not use a separate character translation program, especially ASCII/EBCDIC translations. EXPORT/IMPORT takes care of this for you.
- Make sure the same blocking factor is used when writing and reading the tape. A blocksize of 3200 is frequently a good choice.
- If possible, write the portable file directly to tape to avoid possible interference from copy programs. Read the file directly from the tape for the same reason.
- Use the INFO LOCAL command to find out about using the program on your particular computer and operating system. INFO LOCAL generally includes additional information about reading and writing portable files.

Communications Programs

Transmission of a portable file by a communications program may not be possible if the program misinterprets any characters in the file as control characters (for example, as a line feed, carriage return, or end of transmission). This can be prevented by specifying TYPE=COMM on EXPORT. This specification replaces each control character with the character 0. The affected control characters are in positions 0–60 of the IMPORT/EXPORT character set (see Appendix B).

The line length that the communications program uses must be set to 80 to match the 80-character record length of portable files. A transmitted file must be checked for blank lines or special characters inserted by the communications program. These must be edited out prior to reading the file with the IMPORT command.

Character Translation

Portable files are character files, not binary files, and they have 80-character records so they can be transmitted over data links. A receiving computer may not use the same character set as the computer where the portable file was written. When it imports a portable file, the program translates characters in the file to the character set used by the receiving computer. Depending on the character set in use, some characters in labels and in string data may be lost in the translation. For example, if a file is transported from a computer using a seven-bit ASCII character set to a computer using a six-bit ASCII character set, some characters in the file may have no matching characters in six-bit ASCII. For a character that has no match, the program generates an appropriate nonprintable character (the null character in most cases).

For a table of the character-set translations available with IMPORT and EXPORT, refer to Appendix B. A blank in a column of the table means that there is no matching character for that character set and an appropriate nonprintable character will be generated when you import a file.

OUTFILE Subcommand

OUTFILE specifies the portable file. OUTFILE is the only required subcommand on EXPORT.

TYPE Subcommand

TYPE indicates whether the portable file should be formatted for magnetic tape or for a communications program. You can specify either COMM or TAPE. See "Methods of Transporting Portable Files" on p. 340 for more information on magnetic tapes and communications programs.

COMM   *Transport portable files by a communications program.* When COMM is specified on TYPE, the program removes all control characters and replaces them with the character 0. This is the default.

TAPE   *Transport portable files on magnetic tape.*

Example

```
EXPORT TYPE=TAPE /OUTFILE=HUBOUT.
```

- File *HUBOUT* is saved as a tape-formatted portable file.

UNSELECTED Subcommand

UNSELECTED determines whether cases excluded on a previous FILTER or USE command are to be retained or deleted in the SPSS-format data file. The default is RETAIN. The UNSELECTED subcommand has no effect when the working data file does not contain unselected cases.

RETAIN   *Retain the unselected cases.* All cases in the working data file are saved. This is the default when UNSELECTED is specified by itself.

DELETE   *Delete the unselected cases.* Only cases that meet the FILTER or USE criteria are saved in the SPSS-format data file.

DROP and KEEP Subcommands

DROP and KEEP save a subset of variables in the portable file.

- DROP excludes a variable or list of variables from the portable file. All variables not named are included in the portable file.
- KEEP includes a variable or list of variables in the portable file. All variables not named are excluded.
- Variables can be specified on DROP and KEEP in any order. With the DROP subcommand, the order of variables in the portable file is the same as their order in the working file. With the KEEP subcommand, the order of variables in the portable file is the order in which they are named on KEEP. Thus, KEEP can be used to reorder variables in the portable file.
- Both DROP and KEEP can be used on the same EXPORT command; the effect is cumulative. If you specify a variable already named on a previous DROP or one not named on a previous KEEP, the variable is considered nonexistent and the program displays an error message. The command is aborted and no portable file is saved.

Example

```
EXPORT OUTFILE=NEWSUM /DROP=DEPT TO DIVISION.
```

- The portable file is written to file *NEWSUM*. Variables between and including *DEPT* and *DIVISION* in the working file are excluded from the portable file.
- All other variables are saved in the portable file.

RENAME Subcommand

RENAME renames variables being written to the portable file. The renamed variables retain their original variable and value labels, missing-value flags, and print formats. The names of the variables are not changed in the working data file.

- To rename a variable, specify the name of the variable in the working data file, an equals sign, and the new name.
- A variable list can be specified on both sides of the equals sign. The number of variables on both sides must be the same, and the entire specification must be enclosed in parentheses.
- The keyword TO can be used for both variable lists (see "Keyword TO" on p. 29).
- If you specify a renamed variable on a subsequent DROP or KEEP subcommand, the new variable name must be used.

Example

```
EXPORT OUTFILE=NEWSUM /DROP=DEPT TO DIVISION
    /RENAME=(NAME,WAGE=LNAME,SALARY).
```

- RENAME renames *NAME* and *WAGE* to *LNAME* and *SALARY*.
- *LNAME* and *SALARY* retain the variable and value labels, missing-value flags, and print formats assigned to *NAME* and *WAGE*.

MAP Subcommand

MAP displays any changes that have been specified by the RENAME, DROP, or KEEP subcommands.

- MAP can be specified as often as desired.
- Each MAP subcommand maps the results of subcommands that precede it; results of subcommands that follow it are not mapped. When MAP is specified last, it also produces a description of the portable file.

Example

```
EXPORT OUTFILE=NEWSUM /DROP=DEPT TO DIVISION /MAP
/RENAME NAME=LNAME WAGE=SALARY /MAP.
```

- The first MAP subcommand produces a listing of the variables in the file after DROP has dropped the specified variables.
- RENAME renames *NAME* and *WAGE*.
- The second MAP subcommand shows the variables in the file after renaming. Since this is the last subcommand, the listing will show the variables as they are written in the portable file.

DIGITS Subcommand

DIGITS specifies the degree of precision for all noninteger numeric values written to the portable file.

- DIGITS has the general form DIGITS=n, where n is the number of digits of precision.
- DIGITS applies to all numbers for which rounding is required.
- Different degrees of precision *cannot* be specified for different variables. Thus, DIGITS should be set according to the requirements of the variable that needs the most precision.
- Default precision methods used by EXPORT work perfectly for integers that are not too large and for fractions whose denominators are products of 2, 3, and 5 (all decimals, quarters, eighths, sixteenths, thirds, thirtieths, sixtieths, and so forth.) For other fractions and for integers too large to be represented exactly in the working data file (usually more than 9 digits, often 15 or more), the representation used in the working file contains some error already, so no exact way of sending these numbers is possible. The program sends enough digits to get very close. The number of digits sent in these cases depends on the originating computer: on mainframe IBM versions of the program, it is the equivalent of 13 decimal digits (integer and fractional parts combined). If many numbers on a file require this level of precision, the file can grow quite large. If you do not need the full default precision, you can save some space in the portable file by using the DIGITS subcommand.

Example

```
EXPORT OUTFILE=NEWSUM /DROP=DEPT TO DIVISION /MAP /DIGITS=4.
```

- DIGITS guarantees the accuracy of values to four significant digits. For example, 12.34567890876 will be rounded to 12.35.

FACTOR

```
FACTOR VARIABLES=varlist† [/MISSING=[{LISTWISE**}] [INCLUDE]]
                                      {PAIRWISE }
                                      {MEANSUB  }
                                      {DEFAULT** }

[/MATRIX=[IN({COR=file})]  [OUT({COR=file})]]
             {COR=*    }         {COR=*    }
             {COV=file}          {COV=file}
             {COV=*   }          {COV=*    }
             {FAC=file}          {FAC=file}
             {FAC=*   }          {FAC=*    }

[/METHOD = {CORRELATION**}]
           {COVARIANCE   }

[/SELECT=varname(value)]

[/ANALYSIS=varlist...]

[/PRINT=[DEFAULT**] [INITIAL**] [EXTRACTION**] [ROTATION**]
        [UNIVARIATE] [CORRELATION] [COVARIANCE] [DET] [INV]
        [REPR] [AIC] [KMO] [FSCORE] [SIG] [ALL]]

[/PLOT=[EIGEN] [ROTATION [(n1,n2)]]]

[/DIAGONAL={value list}]
           {DEFAULT** }

[/FORMAT=[SORT] [BLANK(n)] [DEFAULT**]]

[/CRITERIA=[FACTORS(n)] [MINEIGEN({1.0**})] [ITERATE({25**})]
                                  {n    }             {n  }

           [RCONVERGE({0.0001**})]  [{KAISER**}]
                      {n        }    {NOKAISER}

           [ECONVERGE({0.001**})] [DEFAULT**]]
                      {n       }

[/EXTRACTION={PC**    }] [/ROTATION={VARIMAX**   }]
             {PA1**   }             {EQUAMAX     }
             {PAF     }             {QUARTIMAX   }
             {ALPHA   }             {OBLIMIN({0})}
             {IMAGE   }                     {n}
             {ULS     }             {PROMAX({4} }
             {GLS     }                    {n}
             {ML      }             {NOROTATE    }
             {DEFAULT**}            {DEFAULT**   }

[/SAVE=[{REG    } ({ALL}[rootname])]]
        {BART   } {n }
        {AR     }
        {DEFAULT}
```

† Omit VARIABLES with matrix input.
**Default if subcommand or keyword is omitted.

Example:

```
FACTOR VARIABLES=V1 TO V12.
```

Overview

FACTOR performs factor analysis based either on correlations or covariances and using one of the seven extraction methods. FACTOR also accepts matrix input in the form of correlation matrices, covariance matrices, or factor loading matrices and can write the matrix materials to a matrix data file.

Options

Analysis Phase Options. You can choose to analyze a correlation or covariance matrix using the METHOD subcommand. You can select a subset of cases for the analysis phase using the SELECT subcommand. You can tailor the statistical display for an analysis using the PRINT subcommand. You can sort the output in the factor pattern and structure matrices with the FORMAT subcommand. You can also request scree plots and plots of the variables in factor space on the PLOT subcommand.

Extraction Phase Options. With the EXTRACTION subcommand you can specify one of six extraction methods in addition to the default principal components extraction: principal axis factoring, alpha factoring, image factoring, unweighted least squares, generalized least squares, and maximum likelihood. You can supply initial diagonal values for principal axis factoring on the DIAGONAL subcommand. On the CRITERIA subcommand, you can alter the default statistical criteria used in the extraction.

Rotation Phase Options. You can control the criteria for factor rotation with the CRITERIA subcommand. On the ROTATION subcommand you can choose among four rotation methods (equamax, quartimax, promax, and oblimin) in addition to the default varimax rotation, or you can specify no rotation.

Factor Scores. You can save factor scores as new variables in the working data file using any of the three methods available on the SAVE subcommand.

Matrix Input and Output. With the MATRIX subcommand, you can write a correlation matrix, a covariance matrix, or a factor loading matrix. You can also read matrix materials written either by a previous FACTOR procedure or by a procedure that writes correlation or covariance matrices.

Basic Specification

The basic specification is the VARIABLES subcommand with a variable list. FACTOR performs principal components analysis with a varimax rotation on all variables in the analysis using default criteria.

- When matrix materials are used as input, do not specify VARIABLES. Use the ANALYSIS subcommand to specify a subset of the variables in the matrix.

Subcommand Order

- METHOD and SELECT can be specified anywhere. VARIABLES must be specified before any other subcommands, unless an input matrix is specified. MISSING must be specified before ANALYSIS.

- The ANALYSIS, EXTRACTION, ROTATION, and SAVE subcommands must be specified in the order they are listed here. If you specify these subcommands out of order, you may get unpracticed results. For example, if you specify EXTRACTION before ANALYSIS and SAVE before ROTATION, EXTRACTION and SAVE are ignored. If no EXTRACTION and SAVE subcommands are specified in proper order, the default will be used, that is, PC for EXTRACTION and no SAVE.

- The FORMAT subcommand can be specified anywhere after the VARIABLES subcommand.

- If an ANALYSIS subcommand is present, the statistical display options on PRINT, PLOT, or DIAGONAL must be specified after it. PRINT, PLOT, and DIAGONAL subcommands specified before the ANALYSIS subcommand are ignored. If no such commands are specified after the ANALYSIS subcommand, the default is used.

- The CRITERIA subcommand can be specified anywhere, but applies only to the subcommands that follow. If no CRITERIA subcommand is specified before EXTRACTION or ROTATION, the default criteria for the respective subcommand are used.

Example

```
FACTOR VAR=V1 TO V12
  /ANALYSIS=V1 TO V8
  /CRITERIA=FACTORS(3)
  /EXTRACTION=PAF
  /ROTATION=QUARTIMAX.
```

- The default CORRELATION method is used. FACTOR performs a factor analysis of the correlation matrix based on the first eight variables in the working data file (*V1* to *V8*).

- The procedure extracts three factors using the principal axis method and quartimax rotation.

- LISTWISE (the default for MISSING) is in effect. Cases with missing values for any one of the variables from *V1* to *V12* are omitted from the analysis. As a result, if you ask for the factor analysis using VAR=V1 TO V8 and ANALYSIS=ALL, the results may be different even though the variables used in the analysis are the same.

Syntax Rules

- Each FACTOR procedure performs only one analysis with one extraction and one rotation. Use multiple FACTOR commands to perform multiple analyses.

- VARIABLES or MATRIX=IN can be specified only once. Any other subcommands can be specified multiple times but only the last in proper order takes effect.

Operations

- VARIABLES calculates a correlation and a covariance matrix. If SELECT is specified, only the selected cases are used.
- The correlation or covariance matrix (either calculated from the data or read in) is the basis for the factor analysis.
- Factor scores are calculated for all cases (selected and unselected).

Example

```
FACTOR VARIABLES=V1 TO V12.
```

- This example uses the default CORRELATION method.
- It produces the default principal components analysis of 12 variables. Those with eigenvalues greater than 1 (the default criterion for extraction) are rotated using varimax rotation (the default).

VARIABLES Subcommand

VARIABLES names all the variables to be used in the FACTOR procedure.

- VARIABLES is required except when matrix input is used. When FACTOR reads a matrix data file, the VARIABLES subcommand cannot be used.
- The specification on VARIABLES is a list of numeric variables.
- Keyword ALL on VARIABLES refers to all variables in the working data file.
- Only one VARIABLES subcommand can be specified, and it must be specified first.

MISSING Subcommand

MISSING controls the treatment of cases with missing values.

- If MISSING is omitted or included without specifications, listwise deletion is in effect.
- MISSING must precede the ANALYSIS subcommand.
- The LISTWISE, PAIRWISE, and MEANSUB keywords are alternatives, but any one of them can be used with INCLUDE.

LISTWISE   *Delete cases with missing values listwise.* Only cases with nonmissing values for all variables named on the VARIABLES subcommand are used. Cases are deleted even if they have missing values only for variables listed on VARIABLES and have valid values for all variables listed on ANALYSIS. Alias DEFAULT.

PAIRWISE   *Delete cases with missing values pairwise.* All cases with nonmissing values for each pair of variables correlated are used to compute that correlation, regardless of whether the cases have missing values for any other variable.

MEANSUB   *Replace missing values with the variable mean.* All cases are used after the substitution is made. If INCLUDE is also specified, user-missing values are included in the computation of the means, and means are substituted only for the system-missing value. If SELECT is in effect, only the values of selected cases are used in calculating the means used to replace missing values for selected cases in analysis and for all cases in computing factor scores.

INCLUDE   *Include user-missing values.* Cases with user-missing values are treated as valid.

METHOD Subcommand

METHOD specifies whether the factor analysis is performed on a correlation matrix or a covariance matrix.

- Only one METHOD subcommand is allowed. If more than one is specified, the last is in effect.

CORRELATION   *Perform a correlation matrix analysis.* This is the default.

COVARIANCE   *Perform a covariance matrix analysis.* Valid only with principal components, principal axis factoring, or image factoring methods of extraction. The program issues an error if this keyword is specified when the input is a factor loading matrix or a correlation matrix that does not contain standard deviations (STDDEV or SD).

SELECT Subcommand

SELECT limits cases used in the analysis phase to those with a specified value for any one variable.

- Only one SELECT subcommand is allowed. If more than one is specified, the last is in effect.
- The specification is a variable name and a valid value in parentheses. A string value must be specified within quotes. Multiple variables or values are not permitted.
- The selection variable does not have to be specified on the VARIABLES subcommand.
- Only cases with the specified value for the selection variable are used in computing the correlation or covariance matrix. You can compute and save factor scores for the unselected cases as well as the selected cases.
- SELECT is not valid if MATRIX = IN is specified.

Example

```
FACTOR VARIABLES = V1 TO V10
  /SELECT=COMPLETE(1)
  /SAVE (4).
```

- FACTOR analyzes all ten variables named on VARIABLES, using only cases with a value of 1 for the variable *COMPLETE*.

- By default, FACTOR uses the CORRELATION method and performs the principal components analysis of the selected cases. Those with eigenvalues greater than 1 are rotated using varimax rotation.
- Four factor scores, for both selected and unselected cases, are computed using the default regression method and four new variables are saved in the working data file.

ANALYSIS Subcommand

The ANALYSIS subcommand specifies a subset of the variables named on VARIABLES for use in an analysis.

- The specification on ANALYSIS is a list of variables, all of which must have been named on the VARIABLES subcommand. For matrix input, ANALYSIS can specify a subset of the variables in a correlation or covariance matrix.
- Only one ANALYSIS subcommand is allowed. When multiple ANALYSIS subcommands are specified, the last is in effect.
- If no ANALYSIS is specified, all variables named on the VARIABLES subcommand (or included in the matrix input file) are used.
- Keyword TO in a variable list on ANALYSIS refers to the order in which variables are named on the VARIABLES subcommand, not to their order in the working data file.
- Keyword ALL refers to all variables named on the VARIABLES subcommand.

Example

```
FACTOR VARIABLES=V1 V2 V3 V4 V5 V6
  /ANALYSIS=V4 TO V6.
```

- This example requests a factor analysis of *V4*, *V5*, and *V6*. Keyword TO on ANALYSIS refers to the order of variables on VARIABLES, not the order in the working data file.
- Cases with missing values for all variables specified on VARIABLES are omitted from the analysis. (The default setting for MISSING.)
- By default, the CORRELATION method is used and a principal components analysis with a varimax rotation is performed.

FORMAT Subcommand

FORMAT modifies the format of factor pattern and structure matrices.

- FORMAT can be specified anywhere after VARIABLES and MISSING. If more than one FORMAT is specified, the last is in effect.
- If FORMAT is omitted or included without specifications, variables appear in the order in which they are named on ANALYSIS and all matrix entries are displayed.

SORT	*Order the factor loadings in descending order.*
BLANK(n)	*Suppress coefficients lower than* n *in absolute value.*
DEFAULT	*Turn off keywords SORT and BLANK.*

Example

```
FACTOR VARIABLES=V1 TO V12
  /MISSING=MEANSUB
  /FORMAT=SORT BLANK(.3)
  /EXTRACTION=ULS
  /ROTATION=NOROTATE.
```

- This example specifies an analysis of all variables between and including *V1* and *V12* in the working data file.
- The default CORRELATION method is used.
- The MISSING subcommand substitutes variable means for missing values.
- The FORMAT subcommand orders variables in factor pattern matrices by descending value of loadings. Factor loadings with an absolute value less than 0.3 are omitted.
- Factors are extracted using unweighted least squares and are not rotated.

PRINT Subcommand

PRINT controls the statistical display in the output.

- Keywords INITIAL, EXTRACTION, and ROTATION are the defaults if PRINT is omitted or specified without keywords.
- If any keywords are specified, only the output specifically requested is produced.
- The requested statistics are displayed only for variables specified on the last ANALYSIS subcommand.
- If more than one PRINT subcommand is specified, the last is in effect.
- If any ANALYSIS subcommand is explicitly specified, all PRINT subcommands specified before the last ANALYSIS subcommand are ignored. If no PRINT subcommand is specified after the last ANALYSIS subcommand, the default takes effect.

INITIAL	*Initial communalities for each variable, eigenvalues of the unreduced correlation matrix, and percentage of variance for each factor.*
EXTRACTION	*Factor pattern matrix, revised communalities, the eigenvalue of each factor retained, and the percentage of variance each eigenvalue represents.*
ROTATION	*Rotated factor pattern matrix, factor transformation matrix, factor correlation matrix, and the post-rotation sums of squared loadings.*
UNIVARIATE	*Valid number of cases, means, and standard deviations.* (Not available with matrix input.) If MISSING=MEANSUB or PAIRWISE, the output also includes the number of missing cases.
CORRELATION	*Correlation matrix.* Ignored if the input is a factor loading matrix.
COVARIANCE	*Covariance matrix.* Ignored if the input is a factor loading matrix or a correlation matrix that does not contain standard deviations (STDDEV or SD).
SIG	*Matrix of significance levels of correlations.*

DET	*Determinant of the correlation or covariance matrix, depending on the specification on* METHOD.
INV	*Inverse of the correlation or covariance matrix, depending on the specification on* METHOD.
AIC	*Anti-image covariance and correlation matrices* (Kaiser, 1970). The measure of sampling adequacy for the individual variable is displayed on the diagonal of the anti-image correlation matrix.
KMO	*Kaiser-Meyer-Olkin measure of sampling adequacy and Bartlett's test of sphericity.* Always based on the correlation matrix. Not computed for an input matrix when it does not contain *N* values.
REPR	*Reproduced correlations and residuals or reproduced covariance and residuals, depending on the specification on* METHOD.
FSCORE	*Factor score coefficient matrix.* Factor score coefficients are calculated using the method requested on the SAVE subcommand. The default is the regression method.
ALL	*All available statistics.*
DEFAULT	INITIAL, EXTRACTION, *and* ROTATION.

Example

```
FACTOR VARS=V1 TO V12
  /SELECT=COMPLETE ('yes')
  /MISS=MEANSUB
  /PRINT=DEF AIC KMO REPR
  /EXTRACT=ULS
  /ROTATE=VARIMAX.
```

- This example specifies a factor analysis that includes all variables between and including *V1* and *V12* in the working data file.
- Only cases with the value "yes" on *COMPLETE* are used.
- Variable means are substituted for missing values. Only values for the selected cases are used in computing the mean. This mean is used to substitute missing values in analyzing the selected cases and in computing factor scores for all cases.
- The output includes the anti-image correlation and covariance matrices, the Kaiser-Meyer-Olkin measure of sampling adequacy, the reproduced correlation and residual matrix, as well as the default statistics.
- Factors are extracted using unweighted least squares.
- The factor pattern matrix is rotated using the varimax rotation.

PLOT Subcommand

Use PLOT to request scree plots or plots of variables in rotated factor space.

- If PLOT is omitted, no plots are produced. If PLOT is used without specifications, it is ignored.

- If more than one PLOT subcommand is specified, only the last one is in effect.
- If any ANALYSIS subcommand is explicitly specified, all PLOT subcommands specified before the last ANALYSIS subcommand are ignored. If no PLOT subcommand is specified after the last ANALYSIS subcommand, no plot is produced.

EIGEN   *Scree plot* (Cattell, 1966). The eigenvalues from each extraction are plotted in descending order.

ROTATION   *Plots of variables in factor space.* When used without any additional specifications, ROTATION can produce only high-resolution graphics. If three or more factors are extracted, a 3-D plot is produced with the factor space defined by the first three factors. You can request two-dimensional plots by specifying pairs of factor numbers in parentheses; for example, PLOT ROTATION(1,2)(1,3)(2,3) requests three plots, each defined by two factors. When SET HIGHRES is OFF, ROTATION can produce only two-dimensional plots, and they must be explicitly requested; otherwise, the program issues an error message. The ROTATION subcommand must be explicitly specified when you enter the keyword ROTATION on the PLOT subcommand.

DIAGONAL Subcommand

DIAGONAL specifies values for the diagonal in conjunction with principal axis factoring.

- If DIAGONAL is omitted or included without specifications, FACTOR uses the default method for specifying the diagonal.
- DIAGONAL is ignored with extraction methods other than PAF. The values are automatically adjusted by corresponding variances if METHOD=COVARIANCE.
- If more than one DIAGONAL subcommand is specified, only the last one is in effect.
- If any ANALYSIS subcommand is explicitly specified, DIAGONAL subcommands specified before the last ANALYSIS subcommand are ignored. If no DIAGONAL is specified after the last ANALYSIS subcommand, the default is used.
- Default communality estimates for PAF are squared multiple correlations. If these cannot be computed, the maximum absolute correlation between the variable and any other variable in the analysis is used.

valuelist   *Diagonal values.* The number of values supplied must equal the number of variables in the analysis block. Use the notation n* before a value to indicate that the value is repeated *n* times.

DEFAULT   *Initial communality estimates.*

Example

```
FACTOR VARIABLES=V1 TO V12
  /DIAGONAL=.56 .55 .74 2*.56 .70 3*.65 .76 .64 .63
  /EXTRACTION=PAF
  /ROTATION=VARIMAX.
```

- The factor analysis includes all variables between and including *V1* and *V12* in the working data file.

- DIAGONAL specifies 12 values to use as initial estimates of communalities in principal axis factoring.
- The factor pattern matrix is rotated using varimax rotation.

CRITERIA Subcommand

CRITERIA controls extraction and rotation criteria.

- CRITERIA can be specified anywhere after VARIABLES and MISSING.
- Only explicitly specified criteria are changed. Unspecified criteria keep their defaults.
- Multiple CRITERIA subcommands are allowed. Changes made by a previous CRITERIA subcommand are overwritten by a later CRITERIA subcommand.
- Any CRITERIA subcommands specified after the last EXTRACTION subcommand have no effect on extraction.
- Any CRITERIA subcommands specified after the last ROTATION subcommand have no effect on rotation.

The following keywords on CRITERIA apply to extractions:

FACTORS(n)   *Number of factors extracted.* The default is the number of eigenvalues greater than MINEIGEN. When specified, FACTORS overrides MINEIGEN.

MINEIGEN(n)   *Minimum eigenvalue used to control the number of factors extracted.* If METHOD=CORRELATION, the default is 1. If METHOD=COVARIANCE, the default is computed as *(Total Variance/Number of Variables)*n*, where *Total Variance* is the total weighted variance principal components or principal axis factoring extraction and the total image variance for image factoring extraction.

ECONVERGE(n)   *Convergence criterion for extraction.* The default is 0.001.

The following keywords on CRITERIA apply to rotations:

RCONVERGE(n)   *Convergence criterion for rotation.* The default is 0.0001.

KAISER   *Kaiser normalization in the rotation phase.* This is the default. The alternative is NOKAISER.

NOKAISER   *No Kaiser normalization.*

The following keywords on CRITERIA apply to both extractions and rotations:

ITERATE(n)   *Maximum number of iterations for solutions in the extraction or rotation phases.* The default is 25.

DEFAULT   *Reestablish default values for all criteria.*

Example

```
FACTOR VARIABLES=V1 TO V12
  /CRITERIA=FACTORS(6)
  /EXTRACTION=PC
  /ROTATION=NOROTATE
  /PLOT=ROTATION.
```

- This example analyzes all variables between and including *V1* and *V12* in the working data file.
- Six factors are extracted using the default principal components method, and the factor pattern matrix is not rotated.
- PLOT sends all extracted factors to the graphics editor and shows a 3-D plot of the first three factors. If HIGHRES is set to OFF, the program displays an error message.

EXTRACTION Subcommand

EXTRACTION specifies the factor extraction technique.

- Only one EXTRACTION subcommand is allowed. If multiple EXTRACTION subcommands are specified, only the last is performed.
- If any ANALYSIS subcommand is explicitly specified, all EXTRACTION subcommands before the last ANALYSIS subcommand are ignored. If no EXTRACTION subcommand is specified after the last ANALYSIS subcommand, the default extraction is performed.
- If EXTRACTION is not specified or is included without specifications, principal components extraction is used.
- If you specify criteria for EXTRACTION, the CRITERIA subcommand must precede the EXTRACTION subcommand.
- When you specify EXTRACTION, you should always explicitly specify the ROTATION subcommand. If ROTATION is not specified, the factors are not rotated.

PC   *Principal components analysis* (Harman, 1967). This is the default. PC can also be requested with keyword PA1 or DEFAULT.

PAF   *Principal axis factoring*. PAF can also be requested with keyword PA2.

ALPHA   *Alpha factoring* (Kaiser & Caffry, 1965). Invalid if METHOD=COVARIANCE.

IMAGE   *Image factoring* (Kaiser, 1963).

ULS   *Unweighted least squares* (Harman & Jones, 1966). Invalid if METHOD=COVARIANCE.

GLS   *Generalized least squares*. Invalid if METHOD=COVARIANCE.

ML   *Maximum likelihood* (Jöreskog & Lawley, 1968). Invalid if METHOD=VARIANCE.

Example

```
FACTOR VARIABLES=V1 TO V12
  /ANALYSIS=V1 TO V6
  /EXTRACTION=ULS
  /ROTATE=NOROTATE.
```

- This example analyzes variables *V1* through *V6* with an unweighted least-squares extraction. No rotation is performed.

ROTATION Subcommand

ROTATION specifies the factor rotation method. It can also be used to suppress the rotation phase entirely.

- Only one ROTATION subcommand is allowed. If multiple ROTATION subcommands are specified, only the last is performed.
- If any ANALYSIS subcommand is explicitly specified, all ROTATION subcommands before the last ANALYSIS subcommand are ignored. If any EXTRACTION subcommand is explicitly specified, all ROTATION subcommands before the last EXTRACTION subcommand are ignored.
- If ROTATION is omitted together with EXTRACTION, varimax rotation is used.
- If ROTATION is omitted but EXTRACTION is not, factors are not rotated.
- Keyword NOROTATE on the ROTATION subcommand produces a plot of variables in unrotated factor space if the PLOT subcommand is also included for the analysis.

VARIMAX	*Varimax rotation.* This is the default if ROTATION is entered without specifications or if EXTRACTION and ROTATION are both omitted. Varimax rotation can also be requested with keyword DEFAULT.
EQUAMAX	*Equamax rotation.*
QUARTIMAX	*Quartimax rotation.*
OBLIMIN(n)	*Direct oblimin rotation.* This is a nonorthogonal rotation; thus, a factor correlation matrix will also be displayed. You can specify a delta ($n \leq 0.8$) in parentheses. The value must be less than or equal to 0.8. The default is 0.
PROMAX(n)	*Promax rotation.* This is a nonorthogonal rotation; thus, a factor correlation matrix will also be displayed. For this method, you can specify a real-number value greater than 1. The default is 4.
NOROTATE	*No rotation.*

Example

```
FACTOR VARIABLES=V1 TO V12
  /EXTRACTION=ULS
  /ROTATION
  /ROTATION=OBLIMIN.
```

- The first ROTATION subcommand specifies the default varimax rotation.
- The second ROTATION subcommand specifies an oblimin rotation based on the same extraction of factors.

SAVE Subcommand

SAVE allows you to save factor scores from any rotated or unrotated extraction as new variables in the working data file. You can use any of the three methods for computing the factor scores.

- Only one SAVE subcommand is executed. If you specify multiple SAVE subcommands, only the last is executed.
- SAVE must follow the last ROTATION subcommand.
- If no ROTATION subcommand is specified after the last EXTRACTION subcommand, SAVE must follow the last EXTRACTION subcommand and no rotation is used.
- If neither ROTATION nor EXTRACTION is specified, SAVE must follow the last ANALYSIS subcommand and the default extraction and rotation are used to compute the factor scores.
- SAVE subcommands before any explicitly specified ANALYSIS, EXTRACTION, or ROTATION subcommands are ignored.
- You cannot use the SAVE subcommand if you are replacing the working data file with matrix materials (see "Matrix Output" on p. 358).
- The new variables are added to the end of the working data file.

Keywords to specify the method of computing factor scores are:

REG   *Regression method.* This is the default.

BART   *Bartlett method.*

AR   *Anderson-Rubin method.*

DEFAULT *The same as REG.*

- After one of the above keywords, specify in parentheses the number of scores to save and a rootname to use in naming the variables.
- You can specify either an integer or the keyword ALL. The maximum number of scores you can specify is the number of factors in the solution.
- FACTOR forms variable names by appending sequential numbers to the rootname you specify. The rootname must begin with a letter and conform to the rules for variable names. It must be short enough that the variable names formed will not exceed eight characters.
- If you do not specify a rootname, FACTOR forms unique variable names using the formula *FACn_m,* where *m* increments to create a new rootname and *n* increments to create a unique variable name. For example, *FAC1_1, FAC2_1, FAC3_1,* and so on will be generated for the first set of saved scores and *FAC1_2, FAC2_2, FAC3_2,* and so on for the second set. As *m* and *n* increase, the prefix *FAC* is truncated to keep the variable names within eight characters. For example, *FAC999_12* is increased to *F1000_12.* The initial *F* is required.
- FACTOR automatically generates variable labels for the new variables. Each label contains information about the method of computing the factor score, its sequential number, and the sequential number of the analysis.

Example

```
FACTOR VARIABLES=V1 TO V12
  /CRITERIA FACTORS(4)
  /ROTATION
  /SAVE REG (4,PCOMP).
```

- Since there is no EXTRACTION subcommand before the ROTATION subcommand, the default principal components extraction is performed.
- The CRITERIA subcommand specifies that four principal components should be extracted.
- The ROTATION subcommand requests the default varimax rotation for the principal components.
- The SAVE subcommand calculates scores using the regression method. Four scores will be added to the file: *PCOMP1*, *PCOMP2*, *PCOMP3*, and *PCOMP4*.

MATRIX Subcommand

MATRIX reads and writes SPSS-format matrix data files.

- MATRIX must always be specified first.
- Only one IN and one OUT keyword can be specified on the MATRIX subcommand. If either IN or OUT is specified more than once, the FACTOR procedure is not executed.
- The matrix type must be indicated on IN or OUT. The types are COR for a correlation matrix, COV for a covariance matrix, and FAC for a factor loading matrix. Indicate the matrix type within parentheses immediately before you identify the matrix file.
- If you use both IN and OUT on MATRIX, you can specify them in either order. You cannot write a covariance matrix if the input matrix is a factor loading matrix or a correlation matrix that does not contain standard deviations (STDDEV or SD).
- If you read in a covariance matrix and write out a factor loading matrix, the output factor loadings are rescaled.

OUT (filename)   *Write a matrix data file.* Specify the matrix type (COR, COV, or FAC) and the matrix file in parentheses. For the matrix data file, specify a filename to store the matrix materials on disk or an asterisk to replace the working data file. If you specify an asterisk, the matrix data file is not stored on disk unless you use SAVE or XSAVE.

IN (filename)   *Read a matrix data file.* Specify the matrix type (COR, COV, or FAC) and the matrix file in parentheses. For the matrix data file, specify an asterisk if the matrix data file is the working data file. If the matrix file is another file, specify the filename in parentheses. A matrix file read from an external file does not replace the working data file.

Matrix Output

- FACTOR can write matrix materials in the form of a correlation matrix, a covariance matrix, or a factor loading matrix. The correlation and covariance matrix materials include counts, means, and standard deviations in addition to correlations or covariances. The factor loading matrix materials contain only factor values and no additional statistics. See "Format of the Matrix Data File" below for a description of the file.

- FACTOR generates one matrix per split file.
- Any documents contained in the working data file are not transferred to the matrix file.

Matrix Input

- FACTOR can read matrix materials written either by a previous FACTOR procedure or by a procedure that writes correlation or covariance matrices. For more information, see Universals on p. 11.
- MATRIX=IN cannot be used unless a working data file has already been defined. To read an existing matrix data file at the beginning of a session, first use GET to retrieve the matrix file and then specify IN(COR=*), IN(COV=*) or IN(FAC=*) on MATRIX.
- The VARIABLES subcommand cannot be used with matrix input.
- For correlation and covariance matrix input, the ANALYSIS subcommand can specify a subset of the variables in the matrix. You cannot specify a subset of variables for factor loading matrix input. By default, the ANALYSIS subcommand uses all variables in the matrix.

Format of the Matrix Data File

- For correlation or covariance matrices, the matrix data file has two special variables created by the program: ROWTYPE_ and VARNAME_. Variable ROWTYPE_ is a short string variable with the value CORR (for Pearson correlation coefficient) or COV (for covariance) for each matrix row. Variable VARNAME_ is a short string variable whose values are the names of the variables used to form the correlation matrix.
- For factor loading matrices, the program generates two special variables named ROWTYPE_ and FACTOR_. The value for ROWTYPE_ is always FACTOR. The values for FACTOR_ are the ordinal numbers of the factors.
- The remaining variables are the variables used to form the matrix.

Split Files

- FACTOR can read or write split-file matrices.
- When split-file processing is in effect, the first variables in the matrix data file are the split variables, followed by ROWTYPE_, VARNAME_ (or FACTOR_), and then the variables used to form the matrix.
- A full set of matrix materials is written for each split-file group defined by the split variables.
- A split variable cannot have the same variable name as any other variable written to the matrix data file.
- If split-file processing is in effect when a matrix is written, the same split file must be in effect when that matrix is read by any other procedure.

Example

```
GET FILE=GSS80 /KEEP ABDEFECT TO ABSINGLE.
FACTOR VARIABLES=ABDEFECT TO ABSINGLE
  /MATRIX OUT(COR=CORMTX).
```

- FACTOR retrieves the *GSS80* file and writes a factor correlation matrix to the file *CORMTX*.
- The working data file is still *GSS80*. Subsequent commands will be executed on this file.

Example

```
GET FILE=GSS80 /KEEP ABDEFECT TO ABSINGLE.
FACTOR VARIABLES=ABDEFECT TO ABSINGLE
  /MATRIX OUT(COR=*).
LIST.
```

- FACTOR writes the same matrix as in the previous example.
- The working data file is replaced with the correlation matrix. The LIST command is executed on the matrix file, not on *GSS80*.

Example

```
GET FILE=GSS80 /KEEP ABDEFECT TO ABSINGLE.
FACTOR VARIABLES=ABDEFECT TO ABSINGLE
  /MATRIX OUT(FAC=*).
```

- FACTOR generates a factor loading matrix that replaces the working data file.

Example

```
GET FILE=COUNTRY /KEEP SAVINGS POP15 POP75 INCOME GROWTH.
REGRESSION MATRIX OUT(*)
  /VARS=SAVINGS TO GROWTH
  /MISS=PAIRWISE
  /DEP=SAVINGS /ENTER.
FACTOR MATRIX IN(COR=*) /MISSING=PAIRWISE.
```

- The GET command retrieves the *COUNTRY* file and selects the variables needed for the analysis.
- The REGRESSION command computes correlations among five variables with pairwise deletion. MATRIX=OUT writes a matrix data file, which replaces the working data file.
- MATRIX IN(COR=*) on FACTOR reads the matrix materials REGRESSION has written to the working data file. An asterisk is specified because the matrix materials are in the working data file. FACTOR uses pairwise deletion, since this is what was in effect when the matrix was built.

Example

```
GET FILE=COUNTRY /KEEP SAVINGS POP15 POP75 INCOME GROWTH.
REGRESSION
  /VARS=SAVINGS TO GROWTH
  /MISS=PAIRWISE
  /DEP=SAVINGS /ENTER.
FACTOR MATRIX IN(COR=CORMTX).
```

- This example performs a regression analysis on file *COUNTRY* and then uses a different file for FACTOR. The file is an existing matrix data file.
- MATRIX=IN specifies the matrix data file *CORMTX*.
- *CORMTX* does not replace *COUNTRY* as the working data file.

Example

```
GET FILE=CORMTX.
FACTOR MATRIX IN(COR=*).
```

- This example starts a new session and reads an existing matrix data file. GET retrieves the matrix data file *CORMTX*.
- MATRIX=IN specifies an asterisk because the matrix data file is the working data file. If MATRIX=IN(CORMTX) is specified, the program issues an error message.
- If the GET command is omitted, the program issues an error message.

FILE HANDLE

```
FILE HANDLE handle /NAME=file specifications
                [/MODE={CHARACTER }] [/RECFORM \={FIXED    } [/LRECL=n]
                      {BINARY    }              {VARIABLE}
                      {MULTIPUNCH}              {SPANNED }
                      {IMAGE     }
                      {360       }
```

Overview

FILE HANDLE assigns a unique *file handle* to a file and supplies operating system specifications for the file. A defined file handle can be specified on any subsequent FILE, OUTFILE, MATRIX, or WRITE subcommands of various procedures.

Syntax Rules

- A file handle cannot exceed eight characters and must begin with an alphabetical character (A–Z) or a $, #, or @. It can contain numeric digits (0–9) but not imbedded blanks.
- FILE HANDLE is required for reading IBM VSAM data sets, EBCDIC data files, binary data files, and character data files that are not delimited by ASCII line feeds.
- If you specify 360 on the MODE subcommand, you must specify RECFORM.
- If you specify IMAGE on the MODE subcommand, you must specify LRECL.

Operations

A file handle is used only during the current work session. The handle is never saved as part of an SPSS-format data file.

NAME Subcommand

NAME specifies the file you want to refer to by the file handle. The file specifications must conform to the file naming convention for the type of computer and operating system on which the program is run. See the documentation for your system for specific information about the file naming convention.

MODE Subcommand

MODE specifies the type of file you want to refer to by the file handle.

CHARACTER   *Character file whose logical records are delimited by ASCII line feeds.*

BINARY	*Unformatted binary file generated by Microsoft FORTRAN.*
MULTIPUNCH	*Column binary file.*
IMAGE	*Binary file consisting of fixed-length records.*
360	*EBCDIC data file.*

Example

```
FILE HANDLE ELE48 /NAME='OSPS:[SPSSUSER]ELE48.DAT' /MODE=MULTIPUNCH.
DATA LIST FILE=ELE48.
```

- FILE HANDLE defines *ELE48* as the handle for the file.
- The MODE subcommand indicates that the file contains multipunch data.
- The file specification on NAME conforms to VMS convention: the file *ELE48.DAT* is located in the directory *OSPS:[SPSSUSER]*.
- The FILE subcommand on DATA LIST refers to the handle defined on the FILE HANDLE command.

RECFORM Subcommand

RECFORM specifies the record format and is necessary when you specify 360 on MODE. RECFORM has no effect with other specifications on MODE.

FIXED	*Fixed-length record.* All records have the same length. Alias F. When FIXED is specified, the record length must be specified on the LRECL subcommand.
VARIABLE	*Variable-length record.* No logical record is larger than one physical block. Alias V.
SPANNED	*Spanned record.* Records may be larger than fixed-length physical blocks. Alias VS.

LRECL Subcommand

LRECL specifies the length of each record in the file. When you specify IMAGE under UNIX, OS/2, or Microsoft Windows, or 360 for IBM360 EBCDIC data files, you must specify LRECL. You can specify a record length greater than the default (8192) for an image file, a character file, or a binary file. Do not use LRECL with MULTIPUNCH.

Example

```
FILE HANDLE TRGT1 /NAME='OSPS:RGT.DAT'
                  /MODE=IMAGE LRECL=16.
DATA LIST FILE=TRGT1.
```

- IMAGE is specified on the MODE subcommand. Subcommand LRECL must be specified.
- The file handle is used on the DATA LIST command.

FILE LABEL

```
FILE LABEL label
```

Overview

FILE LABEL provides a descriptive label for a data file.

Syntax Rules

The only specification is a label up to 60 characters long.

Operations

- The file label is printed on the first line of each page of output displayed by the program.
- If the specified label is longer than 60 characters, the program truncates the label to 60 characters without warning.
- If the file is saved, the label is included in the dictionary of the SPSS-format data file.

Example

```
FILE LABEL  Hubbard Industrial Consultants Inc. employee data.
SAVE OUTFILE=HUBEMPL
   /RENAME=(AGE JOBCAT=AGE80 JOBCAT82) /MAP.
```

- FILE LABEL assigns a file label to the Hubbard Consultants Inc. employee data.
- The SAVE command saves the file as an SPSS-format data file, renaming two variables and mapping the results to check the renamed variables.

FILE TYPE—END FILE TYPE

For mixed file types:

```
FILE TYPE MIXED [FILE=file] RECORD=[varname] column location [(format)]

                 [WILD={NOWARN}]
                       {WARN  }
```

For grouped file types:

```
FILE TYPE GROUPED [FILE=file] RECORD=[varname] column location [(format)]

  CASE=[varname] column location [(format)]

  [WILD={WARN  }] [DUPLICATE={WARN  }]
        {NOWARN}             {NOWARN}

  [MISSING={WARN  }] [ORDERED={YES}]
           {NOWARN}           {NO }
```

For nested file types:

```
FILE TYPE NESTED [FILE=file] RECORD=[varname] column location [(format)]

  [CASE=[varname] column location [(format)]]

  [WILD={NOWARN}] [DUPLICATE={NOWARN}]
        {WARN  }             {WARN  }
                             {CASE  }

  [MISSING={NOWARN}]
           {WARN  }

END FILE TYPE
```

Example:

```
FILE TYPE  MIXED RECORD=RECID 1-2.
RECORD TYPE 23.
DATA LIST   /SEX 5 AGE 6-7 DOSAGE 8-10 RESULT 12.
END FILE TYPE.

BEGIN DATA
21  145010 1
22  257200 2
25  235   250  2
35  167           300     3
24  125150 1
23  272075 1
21  149050 2
25  134   035  3
30  138           300     3
32  229           500     3
END DATA.
```

Overview

The FILE TYPE—END FILE TYPE structure defines data for any one of the three types of complex raw data files: *mixed files,* which contain several types of records that define different types of cases; *hierarchical* or *nested files,* which contain several types of records with a defined relationship among the record types; or *grouped files,* which contain several records for each case with some records missing or duplicated. A fourth type of complex file, files with *repeating groups* of information, can be defined with the REPEATING DATA command.

FILE TYPE must be followed by at least one RECORD TYPE command and one DATA LIST command. Each pair of RECORD TYPE and DATA LIST commands defines one type of record in the data. END FILE TYPE signals the end of file definition.

Within the FILE TYPE structure, the lowest-level record in a nested file can be read with a REPEATING DATA command rather than a DATA LIST command. In addition, any record in a mixed file can be read with REPEATING DATA.

Basic Specification

The basic specification on FILE TYPE is one of the three file type keywords (MIXED, GROUPED, or NESTED) and the RECORD subcommand. RECORD names the record identification variable and specifies its column location. If keyword GROUPED is specified, the CASE subcommand is also required. CASE names the case identification variable and specifies its column location.

The FILE TYPE—END FILE TYPE structure must enclose at least one RECORD TYPE and one DATA LIST command. END FILE TYPE is required to signal the end of file definition.

- RECORD TYPE specifies the values of the record type identifier (see RECORD TYPE).
- DATA LIST defines variables for the record type specified on the preceding RECORD TYPE command (see DATA LIST).
- Separate pairs of RECORD TYPE and DATA LIST commands must be used to define each different record type.

The resulting working data file is always a rectangular file, regardless of the structure of the original data file.

Specification Order

- FILE TYPE must be the first command in the FILE TYPE—END FILE TYPE structure. FILE TYPE subcommands can be named in any order.
- Each RECORD TYPE command must precede its corresponding DATA LIST command.
- END FILE TYPE must be the last command in the structure.

Syntax Rules

- For mixed files, if the record types have different variables or if they have the same variables recorded in different locations, separate RECORD TYPE and DATA LIST commands are required for each record type.

- For mixed files, the same variable name can be used on different DATA LIST commands, since each record type defines a separate case.

- For mixed files, if the same variable is defined for more than one record type, the format type and length of the variable should be the same on all DATA LIST commands. The program refers to the *first* DATA LIST command that defines a variable for the print and write formats to include in the dictionary of the working data file.

- For grouped and nested files, the variable names on each DATA LIST must be unique, since a case is built by combining all record types together into a single record.

- For nested files, the order of the RECORD TYPE commands defines the hierarchical structure of the file. The first RECORD TYPE defines the highest-level record type, the next RECORD TYPE defines the next highest-level record, and so forth. The last RECORD TYPE command defines a case in the working data file. By default, variables from higher-level records are spread to the lowest-level record.

- For nested files, the SPREAD subcommand on RECORD TYPE can be used to spread the values in a record type only to the *first* case built from each record of that type. All other cases associated with that record are assigned the system-missing value for the variables defined on that type. See RECORD TYPE for more information.

- String values specified on the RECORD TYPE command must be enclosed in apostrophes or quotation marks.

Operations

- For mixed file types, the program skips all records that are not specified on one of the RECORD TYPE commands.

- If different variables are defined for different record types in mixed files, the variables are assigned the system-missing value for those record types on which they are not defined.

- For nested files, the first record in the file should be the type specified on the first RECORD TYPE command—the highest level of the hierarchy. If the first record in the file is not the highest-level type, the program skips all records until it encounters a record of the highest-level type. If MISSING or DUPLICATE has been specified, these records may produce warning messages but will not be used to build a case in the working file.

- When defining complex files, you are effectively building an input program and can use only commands that are allowed in the input state. See Appendix A for information on program states.

Example

```
* Reading multiple record types from a mixed file.

FILE TYPE  MIXED FILE=TREATMNT RECORD=RECID 1-2.
+ RECORD TYPE 21,22,23,24.
+ DATA LIST    /SEX 5 AGE 6-7 DOSAGE 8-10 RESULT 12.
+ RECORD TYPE 25.
+ DATA LIST    /SEX 5 AGE 6-7 DOSAGE 10-12 RESULT 15.
END FILE TYPE.
```

- Variable *DOSAGE* is read from columns 8–10 for record types 21, 22, 23, and 24 and from columns 10–12 for record type 25. *RESULT* is read from column 12 for record types 21, 22, 23, and 24, and from column 15 for record type 25.

- The working data file contains values for all variables defined on the DATA LIST commands for record types 21 through 25. All other record types are skipped.

Example

```
* Reading only one record type from a mixed file.

FILE TYPE  MIXED RECORD=RECID 1-2.
RECORD TYPE 23.
DATA LIST    /SEX 5 AGE 6-7 DOSAGE 8-10 RESULT 12.
END FILE TYPE.

BEGIN DATA
21   145010 1
22   257200 2
25   235   250   2
35   167            300      3
24   125150 1
23   272075 1
21   149050 2
25   134   035   3
30   138            300      3
32   229            500      3
END DATA.
```

- FILE TYPE begins the file definition and END FILE TYPE indicates the end of file definition. FILE TYPE specifies a mixed file type. Since the data are included between BEGIN DATA—END DATA, the FILE subcommand is omitted. The record identification variable *RECID* is located in columns 1 and 2.

- RECORD TYPE indicates that records with value 23 for variable *RECID* will be copied into the working data file. All other records are skipped. the program does not issue a warning when it skips records in mixed files.

- DATA LIST defines variables on records with the value 23 for variable *RECID*.

Example

```
* A grouped file of student test scores.

FILE TYPE GROUPED RECORD=#TEST 6 CASE=STUDENT 1-4.
RECORD TYPE 1.
DATA LIST  /ENGLISH 8-9 (A).
RECORD TYPE 2.
DATA LIST /READING 8-10.
RECORD TYPE 3.
DATA LIST /MATH 8-10.
END FILE TYPE.

BEGIN DATA
0001 1 B+
0001 2  74
0001 3  83
0002 1 A
0002 2 100
0002 3  71
0003 1 B-
0003 2  88
0003 3  81
0004 1 C
0004 2  94
0004 3  91
END DATA.
```

- FILE TYPE identifies the file as a grouped file. As required for grouped files, all records for a single case are together in the data. The record identification variable *#TEST* is located in column 6. A scratch variable is specified so it won't be saved in the working data file. The case identification variable *STUDENT* is located in columns 1–4.

- Because there are three record types, there are three RECORD TYPE commands. For each RECORD TYPE, there is a DATA LIST to define variables on that record type.

- END FILE TYPE signals the end of file definition.

- The program builds four cases—one for each student. Each case includes the case identification variable plus the variables defined for each record type (the test scores). The values for *#TEST* are not saved in the working data file. Thus, each case in the working file has four variables: *STUDENT*, *ENGLISH*, *READING*, and *MATH*.

Example

```
* A nested file of accident records.

FILE TYPE NESTED RECORD=6 CASE=ACCID 1-4.
RECORD TYPE 1.
DATA LIST /ACC_ID 9-11 WEATHER 12-13 STATE 15-16 (A) DATE 18-24 (A).
RECORD TYPE 2.
DATA LIST /STYLE 11 MAKE 13 OLD 14 LICENSE 15-16(A) INSURNCE 18-21 (A).
RECORD TYPE 3.
DATA LIST /PSNGR_NO 11 AGE 13-14 SEX 16 (A) INJURY 18 SEAT 20-21 (A)
          COST 23-24.
END FILE TYPE.

BEGIN DATA
0001 1   322 1 IL 3/13/88    /* Type 1:   accident record
0001 2     1 44MI 134M       /* Type 2:    vehicle record
0001 3     1 34 M 1 FR   3   /* Type 3:     person record
0001 2     2 16IL 322F       /*             vehicle record
0001 3     1 22 F 1 FR  11   /*              person record
0001 3     2 35 M 1 FR   5   /*              person record
0001 3     3 59 M 1 BK   7   /*              person record
0001 2     3 21IN 146M       /*             vehicle record
0001 3     1 46 M 0 FR   0   /*              person record
END DATA.
```

- FILE TYPE specifies a nested file type. The record identifier, located in column 6, is not assigned a variable name, so the default scratch variable name *####RECD* is used. The case identification variable *ACCID* is located in columns 1–4.

- Because there are three record types, there are three RECORD TYPE commands. For each RECORD TYPE, there is a DATA LIST command to define variables on that record type. The order of the RECORD TYPE commands defines the hierarchical structure of the file.

- END FILE TYPE signals the end of file definition.

- The program builds a case for each lowest-level (type 3) record, representing each person in the file. There can be only one type 1 record for each type 2 record, and one type 2 record for each type 3 record. Each vehicle can be in only one accident, and each person can be in only one vehicle. The variables from the type 1 and type 2 records are spread to their corresponding type 3 records.

Types of Files

The first specification on FILE TYPE is a file type keyword, which defines the structure of the data file. There are three file type keywords: MIXED, GROUPED, and NESTED. Only one of the three types can be specified on FILE TYPE.

MIXED   *Mixed file type.* MIXED specifies a file in which each record type named on a RECORD TYPE command defines a case. You do not need to define all types of records in the file. In fact, FILE TYPE MIXED is useful for reading only one type of record because the program can decide whether to execute the DATA LIST for a record by simply reading the variable that identifies the record type.

GROUPED   *Grouped file type.* GROUPED defines a file in which cases are defined by grouping together record types with the same identification number. Each case usually has one record of each type. All records for a single case must be together in the file. By default, the program assumes that the records are in the same sequence within each case.

NESTED   *Nested file type.* NESTED defines a file in which the record types are related to each other hierarchically. The record types are grouped together by a case identification number that identifies the highest level—the first record type—of the hierarchy. Usually, the last record type specified—the lowest level of the hierarchy—defines a case. For example, in a file containing household records and records for each person living in the household, each person record defines a case. Information from higher record types may be *spread* to each case. For example, the value for a variable on the household record, such as *CITY*, can be spread to the records for each person in the household.

Subcommands and Their Defaults for Each File Type

The specifications on the FILE TYPE differ for each type of file. Table 1 shows whether each subcommand is required or optional and, where applicable, what the default specification is for each file type. N/A indicates that the subcommand is not applicable to that type of file.

Table 1   Summary of FILE TYPE subcommands for different file types

Subcommand	Mixed	Grouped	Nested
FILE	Conditional	Conditional	Conditional
RECORD	Required	Required	Required
CASE	Not Applicable	Required	Optional
WILD	NOWARN	WARN	NOWARN
DUPLICATE	N/A	WARN	NOWARN
MISSING	N/A	WARN	NOWARN
ORDERED	N/A	YES	N/A

- FILE is required unless data are inline (included between BEGIN DATA—END DATA).
- RECORD is always required.
- CASE is required for grouped files.
- The subcommands CASE, DUPLICATE, and MISSING can also be specified on the associated RECORD TYPE commands for grouped files. However, `DUPLICATE=CASE` is invalid.
- For nested files, CASE and MISSING can be specified on the associated RECORD TYPE commands.
- If the subcommands CASE, DUPLICATE, or MISSING are specified on a RECORD TYPE command, the specification on the FILE TYPE command (or the default) is overridden only for the record types listed on that RECORD TYPE command. The FILE TYPE specification or default applies to all other record types.

FILE Subcommand

FILE specifies a text file containing the data. FILE is not used when the data are inline.

Example

```
FILE TYPE  MIXED FILE=TREATMNT RECORD=RECID 1-2.
```

- Data are in file *TREATMNT*. The file type is mixed. The record identification variable *RECID* is located in columns 1 and 2 of each record.

RECORD Subcommand

RECORD specifies the name and column location of the record identification variable.
- The column location of the record identifier is required. The variable name is optional.
- If you do not want to save the record type variable, you can assign a scratch variable name by using the # character as the first character of the name. If a variable name is not specified on RECORD, the record identifier is defined as the scratch variable *####RECD*.
- The value of the identifier for each record type must be unique and must be in the same location on all records. However, records do not have to be sorted according to type.
- A column-style format can be specified for the record identifier. For example, the following two specifications are valid:

```
RECORD=V1  1-2(N)
RECORD=V1  1-2(F,1)
```

FORTRAN-like formats cannot be used because the column location must be specified explicitly.

- Specify A in parentheses after the column location to define the record type variable as a string variable.

Example

```
FILE TYPE  MIXED FILE=TREATMNT RECORD=RECID 1-2.
```

- The record identifier is variable *RECID*, located in columns 1 and 2 of the hospital treatment data file.

CASE Subcommand

CASE specifies a name and column location for the case identification variable. CASE is required for grouped files and optional for nested files. It cannot be used with mixed files.
- For grouped files, each unique value for the case identification variable defines a case in the working data file.
- For nested files, the case identification variable identifies the highest-level record of the hierarchy. The program issues a warning message for each record with a case identification number not equal to the case identification number on the last highest-level record. However, the record with the invalid case number is used to build the case.

- The column location of the case identifier is required. The variable name is optional.
- If you do not want to save the case identification variable, you can assign a scratch variable name by using the # character as the first character of the name. If a variable name is not specified on CASE, the case identifier is defined as the scratch variable *####CASE*.
- A column-style format can be specified for the case identifier. For example, the following two specifications are valid:

```
CASE=V1 1-2(N)
CASE=V1 1-2(F,1)
```

FORTRAN-like formats cannot be used because the column location must be specified explicitly.

- Specify A in parentheses after the column location to define the case identification variable as a string variable.
- If the case identification number is not in the same columns on all record types, use the CASE subcommand on the RECORD TYPE commands as well as on the FILE TYPE command (see RECORD TYPE).

Example

```
* A grouped file of student test scores.

FILE TYPE GROUPED RECORD=#TEST 6 CASE=STUDENT 1-4.
RECORD TYPE 1.
DATA LIST  /ENGLISH 8-9 (A).
RECORD TYPE 2.
DATA LIST /READING 8-10.
RECORD TYPE 3.
DATA LIST /MATH 8-10.
END FILE TYPE.

BEGIN DATA
0001 1 B+
0001 2  74
0001 3  83
0002 1 A
0002 2 100
0002 3  71
0003 1 B-
0003 2  88
0003 3  81
0004 1 C
0004 2  94
0004 3  91
END DATA.
```

- CASE is required for grouped files. CASE specifies variable *STUDENT*, located in columns 1–4, as the case identification variable.
- The data contain four different values for *STUDENT*. The working data file therefore has four cases, one for each value of *STUDENT*. In a grouped file, each unique value for the case identification variable defines a case in the working file.
- Each case includes the case identification variable plus the variables defined for each record type. The values for *#TEST* are not saved in the working data file. Thus, each case in the working file has four variables: *STUDENT, ENGLISH, READING*, and *MATH*.

Example

```
* A nested file of accident records.

FILE TYPE NESTED RECORD=6 CASE=ACCID 1-4.
RECORD TYPE 1.
DATA LIST    /ACC_ID 9-11 WEATHER 12-13 STATE 15-16 (A) DATE 18-24 (A).
RECORD TYPE 2.
DATA LIST /STYLE 11 MAKE 13 OLD 14 LICENSE 15-16 (A) INSURNCE 18-21 (A).
RECORD TYPE 3.
DATA LIST /PSNGR_NO 11 AGE 13-14 SEX 16 (A) INJURY 18 SEAT 20-21 (A)
          COST 23-24.
END FILE TYPE.

BEGIN DATA
0001 1  322 1 IL 3/13/88    /* Type 1:   accident record
0001 2    1 44MI 134M        /* Type 2:     vehicle record
0001 3    1 34 M 1 FR  3     /* Type 3:        person record
0001 2    2 16IL 322F        /*             vehicle record
0001 3    1 22 F 1 FR 11     /*                person record
0001 3    2 35 M 1 FR  5     /*                person record
0001 3    3 59 M 1 BK  7     /*                person record
0001 2    3 21IN 146M        /*             vehicle record
0001 3    1 46 M 0 FR  0     /*                person record
END DATA.
```

- CASE specifies variable *ACCID*, located in columns 1–4, as the case identification variable. *ACCID* identifies the highest level of the hierarchy: the level for the accident records.

- As each case is built, the value of the variable *ACCID* is checked against the value of *ACCID* on the last highest-level record (record type 1). If the values do not match, a warning message is issued. However, the record is used to build the case.

- The data in this example contain only one value for *ACCID*, which is spread across all cases. In a nested file, the lowest-level record type determines the number of cases in the working data file. In this example, the working file has five cases because there are five person records.

Example

```
* Specifying case on the RECORD TYPE command.

FILE TYPE GROUPED FILE=HUBDATA RECORD=#RECID 80 CASE=ID 1-5.
RECORD TYPE 1.
DATA LIST    /MOHIRED YRHIRED 12-15 DEPT79 TO DEPT82 SEX 16-20.
RECORD TYPE 2.
DATA LIST    /SALARY79 TO SALARY82 6-25 HOURLY81 HOURLY82 40-53 (2)
             PROMO81 72   AGE 54-55 RAISE82 66-70.
RECORD TYPE 3   CASE=75-79.
DATA LIST    /JOBCAT 6 NAME 25-48 (A).
END FILE TYPE.
```

- The CASE subcommand on FILE TYPE indicates that the case identification number is located in columns 1–5. However, for type 3 records, the case identification number is located in columns 75–79. The CASE subcommand is therefore specified on the third RECORD TYPE command to override the case setting for type 3 records.

- The format of the case identification variable must be the same on all records. If the case identification variable is defined as a string on the FILE TYPE command, it cannot be defined as a numeric variable on the RECORD TYPE command, and vice versa.

WILD Subcommand

WILD determines whether the program issues a warning when it encounters undefined record types in the data file. Regardless of whether the warning is issued, undefined records are not included in the working data file.

- The only specification on WILD is keyword WARN or NOWARN.
- WARN cannot be specified if keyword OTHER is specified on the last RECORD TYPE command to indicate all other record types (see RECORD TYPE).

WARN   *Issue warning messages.* The program displays a warning message and the first 80 characters of the record for each record type that is not mentioned on a RECORD TYPE command. This is the default for grouped file types.

NOWARN   *Suppress warning messages.* The program simply skips all record types not mentioned on a RECORD TYPE command and does not display warning messages. This is the default for mixed and nested file types.

Example

```
FILE TYPE  MIXED FILE=TREATMNT RECORD=RECID 1-2 WILD=WARN.
```

- WARN is specified on the WILD subcommand. The program displays a warning message and the first 80 characters of the record for each record type that is not mentioned on a RECORD TYPE command.

DUPLICATE Subcommand

DUPLICATE determines how the program responds when it encounters more than one record of each type for a single case. DUPLICATE is optional for grouped and nested files. DUPLICATE cannot be used with mixed files.

- The only specification on DUPLICATE is keyword WARN, NOWARN, or CASE.

WARN   *Issue warning messages.* The program displays a warning message and the first 80 characters of the last record of the duplicate set of record types. Only the *last* record from a set of duplicates is included in the working data file. This is the default for grouped files.

NOWARN   *Suppress warning messages.* The program does not display warning messages when it encounters duplicate record types. Only the *last* record from a set of duplicates is included in the working data file. This is the default for nested files.

CASE   *Build a case in the working data file for each duplicate record.* The program builds one case in the working file for each duplicate record, spreading information from any higher-level records and assigning system-missing values to the variables defined on lower-level records. This option is available only for nested files.

Example

```
* A nested file of accident records.
* Issue a warning for duplicate record types.

FILE TYPE NESTED RECORD=6 CASE=ACCID 1-4 DUPLICATE=WARN.
RECORD TYPE 1.
DATA LIST  /ACC_ID 9-11 WEATHER 12-13 STATE 15-16 (A) DATE 18-24 (A).
RECORD TYPE 2.
DATA LIST /STYLE 11 MAKE 13 OLD 14 LICENSE 15-16 (A) INSURNCE 18-21 (A).
RECORD TYPE 3.
DATA LIST /PSNGR_NO 11 AGE 13-14 SEX 16 (A) INJURY 18 SEAT 20-21 (A)
          COST 23-24.
END FILE TYPE.

BEGIN DATA
0001 1  322 1 IL 3/13/88  /*              accident record
0001 2    1 44MI 134M     /*               vehicle record
0001 3    1 34 M 1 FR  3  /*                person record
0001 2    1 31IL 134M     /* duplicate vehicle record
0001 2    2 16IL 322F     /*               vehicle record
0001 3    1 22 F 1 FR 11  /*                person record
0001 3    2 35 M 1 FR  5  /*                person record
0001 3    3 59 M 1 BK  7  /*                person record
0001 2    3 21IN 146M     /*               vehicle record
0001 3    1 46 M 0 FR  0  /*                person record
END DATA.
```

- In the data, there are two vehicle (type 2) records above the second set of person (type 3) records. This implies that an empty (for example, parked) vehicle was involved, or that each of the three persons was in two vehicles, which is impossible.

- DUPLICATE specifies keyword WARN. The program displays a warning message and the first 80 characters of the second of the duplicate set of type 2 records. The first duplicate record is skipped, and only the second is included in the working data file. This assumes that no empty vehicles were involved in the accident.

- If the duplicate record represents an empty vehicle, it can be included in the working data file by specifying keyword CASE on DUPLICATE. The program builds one case in the working data file for the first duplicate record, spreading information to that case from the previous type 1 record and assigning system-missing values to the variables defined for type 3 records. The second record from the duplicate set is used to build the three cases for the associated type 3 records.

MISSING Subcommand

MISSING determines whether the program issues a warning when it encounters a missing record type for a case. Regardless of whether the program issues the warning, it builds the case in the working file with system-missing values for the variables defined on the missing record. MISSING is optional for grouped and nested files.

- MISSING cannot be used with mixed files and is optional for grouped and nested files.

- For grouped and nested files, the program verifies that each defined case includes one record of each type.

- The only specification is keyword WARN or NOWARN.

WARN   *Issue a warning message when a record type is missing for a case.* This is the default for grouped files.

NOWARN   *Suppress the warning message when a record type is missing for a case.* This is the default for nested files.

Example

```
* A grouped file with missing records.

FILE TYPE GROUPED RECORD=#TEST 6 CASE=STUDENT 1-4 MISSING=NOWARN.
RECORD TYPE 1.
DATA LIST  /ENGLISH 8-9 (A).
RECORD TYPE 2.
DATA LIST /READING 8-10.
RECORD TYPE 3.
DATA LIST /MATH 8-10.
END FILE TYPE.

BEGIN DATA
0001 1 B+
0001 2  74
0002 1 A
0002 2 100
0002 3  71
0003 3  81
0004 1 C
0004 2  94
0004 3  91
END DATA.
```

- The data contain records for three tests administered to four students. However, not all students took all tests. The first student took only the English and reading tests. The third student took only the math test.

- One case in the working data file is built for each of the four students. If a student did not take a test, the system-missing value is assigned in the working file to the variable for the missing test. Thus, the first student has the system-missing value for the math test, and the third student has missing values for the English and reading tests.

- Keyword NOWARN is specified on MISSING. Therefore, no warning messages are issued for the missing records.

Example

```
* A nested file with missing records.

FILE TYPE NESTED RECORD=6 CASE=ACCID 1-4 MISSING=WARN.
RECORD TYPE 1.
DATA LIST  /ACC_ID 9-11 WEATHER 12-13 STATE 15-16 (A) DATE 18-24 (A).
RECORD TYPE 2.
DATA LIST /STYLE 11 MAKE 13 OLD 14 LICENSE 15-16 (A) INSURNCE 18-21 (A).
RECORD TYPE 3.
DATA LIST /PSNGR_NO 11 AGE 13-14 SEX 16 (A) INJURY 18 SEAT 20-21 (A)
          COST 23-24.
END FILE TYPE.
```

```
BEGIN DATA
0001 1   322 1 IL 3/13/88    /*              accident record
0001 3     1 34 M 1 FR   3   /*               person record
0001 2     2 16IL 322F       /*              vehicle record
0001 3     1 22 F 1 FR 11    /*               person record
0001 3     2 35 M 1 FR   5   /*               person record
0001 3     3 59 M 1 BK   7   /*               person record
0001 2     3 21IN 146M       /*              vehicle record
0001 3     1 46 M 0 FR   0   /*               person record
END DATA.
```

- The data contain records for one accident. The first record is a type 1 (accident) record, and the second record is a type 3 (person) record. However, there is no type 2 record, and therefore no vehicle associated with the first person. The person may have been a pedestrian, but it is also possible that the vehicle record is missing.

- One case is built for each person record. The first case has missing values for the variables specified on the vehicle record.

- Keyword WARN is specified on MISSING. A warning message is issued for the missing record.

ORDERED Subcommand

ORDERED indicates whether the records are in the same order as they are defined on the RECORD TYPE commands. Regardless of the order of the records in the data file and the specification on ORDERED, the program builds cases in the working data file with records in the order defined on the RECORD TYPE commands.

- ORDERED can be used only for grouped files.

- The only specification is keyword YES or NO.

- If YES is in effect but the records are not in the order defined on the RECORD TYPE commands, the program issues a warning for each record that is out of order. The program still uses these records to build cases.

YES *Records for each case are in the same order as they are defined on the RECORD TYPE commands.* This is the default.

NO *Records are not in the same order within each case.*

Example

```
* A grouped file with records out of order.

FILE TYPE GROUPED RECORD=#TEST 6 CASE=STUDENT 1-4  MISSING=NOWARN
   ORDERED=NO.
RECORD TYPE 1.
DATA LIST  /ENGLISH 8-9 (A).
RECORD TYPE 2.
DATA LIST  /READING 8-10.
RECORD TYPE 3.
DATA LIST  /MATH 8-10.
END FILE TYPE.
```

```
BEGIN DATA
0001 2   74
0001 1  B+
0002 3   71
0002 2  100
0002 1  A
0003 2   81
0004 2   94
0004 1  C
0004 3   91
END DATA.
```

- The first RECORD TYPE command specifies record type 1, the second specifies record type 2, and the third specifies record type 3. However, records for each case are not always ordered type 1, type 2, and type 3.

- NO is specified on ORDERED. The program builds cases without issuing a warning that they are out of order in the data.

- Regardless of whether YES or NO is in effect for ORDERED, the program builds cases in the working data file in the same order specified on the RECORD TYPE commands.

FILTER

```
FILTER  {BY var}
        {OFF   }
```

Example:

```
FILTER BY SEX.
FREQUENCIES BONUS.
```

Overview

FILTER is used to exclude cases from program procedures without deleting them from the working data file. When FILTER is in effect, cases with a zero or missing value for the specified variable are not used in program procedures. Those cases are not actually deleted and are available again if the filter is turned off. To see the current filter status, use the SHOW command.

Basic Specification

The basic specification is keyword BY followed by a variable name. Cases that have a zero or missing value for the filter variable are excluded from subsequent procedures.

Syntax Rules

- Only one numeric variable can be specified. The variable can be one of the original variables in the data file or a variable computed with transformation commands.
- Keyword OFF turns off the filter. All cases in the working data file become available to subsequent procedures.
- If FILTER is specified without a keyword, FILTER OFF is assumed but the program displays a warning message.
- FILTER can be specified anywhere in the command sequence. Unlike SELECT IF, FILTER has the same effect within an input program as it does outside an input program. Attention must be paid to the placement of any transformation command used to compute values for the filter variable (see INPUT PROGRAM).

Operations

- FILTER performs case selection without changing the working data file. Cases that have a zero or missing value are excluded from subsequent procedures but are not deleted from the file.

380

- Both system-missing and user-missing values are treated as missing. The FILTER command does not offer options for changing selection criteria. To set up different criteria for exclusion, create a numeric variable and conditionally compute its values before specifying it on FILTER.

- If FILTER is specified after TEMPORARY, FILTER affects the next procedure only. After that procedure, the filter status reverts to whatever it was before the TEMPORARY command.

- The filter status does not change until another FILTER command is specified or the working data file is replaced.

- If the specified filter variable is renamed, it is still in effect. The SHOW command will display the new name of the filter variable. However, the filter is turned off if the filter variable is recoded into a string variable or is deleted from the file.

- If the working data file is replaced after a MATCH FILES, ADD FILES, or UPDATE command and the working file is one of the input files, the filter remains in effect if the new working file has a numeric variable with the name of the filter variable. If the working data file does not have a numeric variable with that name (for example, if the filter variable was dropped or renamed), the filter is turned off.

- If the working data file is replaced by an entirely new data file (for example, by a DATA LIST, GET, and IMPORT command), the filter is turned off.

- The FILTER command changes the filter status and takes effect when a procedure is executed or an EXECUTE command is encountered.

Example

```
FILTER BY SEX.
FREQUENCIES BONUS.
```

- This example assumes that *SEX* is a numeric variable, with male and female coded as 0 and 1, respectively. The FILTER command excludes males and cases with missing values for *SEX* from the subsequent procedures. The FREQUENCIES command generates a frequency table of *BONUS* for females only.

Example

```
RECODE SEX (1=0)(0=1).
FILTER BY SEX.
FREQUENCIES BONUS.
```

- This example assumes the same coding scheme for *SEX* as the previous example. Before FILTER is specified, variable *SEX* is recoded. The FILTER command then excludes females and cases with missing values for *SEX*. The FREQUENCIES command generates a frequency table of *BONUS* for males only.

FINISH

```
FINISH
```

Overview

FINISH causes the program to stop reading commands.

Basic Specification

The basic specification is keyword FINISH. There are no additional specifications.

Command Files

- FINISH is optional in a command file and is used to mark the end of a session.
- FINISH causes the program to stop reading commands. Anything following FINISH in the command file is ignored. Any commands following FINISH in an INCLUDE file are ignored.
- FINISH cannot be used within a DO IF structure to end a session conditionally. FINISH within a DO IF structure will end the session unconditionally.

Prompted Sessions

- FINISH is required in a prompted session to terminate the session.
- Because FINISH is a program command, it can be used only after the command line prompt for the program, which expects a procedure name. FINISH cannot be used to end a prompted session from a DATA>, CONTINUE>, HELP>, or DEFINE> prompt.

Operations

- FINISH immediately causes the program to stop reading commands.
- The appearance of FINISH on the printback of commands in the display file indicates that the session has been completed.
- When issued within the SPSS Manager (not available on all systems), FINISH terminates command processing and causes the program to query whether you want to continue working. If you answer *yes*, you can continue creating and editing files in both the input window and the output window; however, you can no longer run commands.

Example

```
* A command file.

DATA LIST FILE=RAWDATA /NAME 1-15(A) V1 TO V15 16-30.
LIST.
FINISH.
REPORT FORMAT=AUTO LIST /VARS=NAME V1 TO V10.
```

- FINISH causes the program to stop reading commands after LIST is executed. The REPORT command is not executed.

Example

```
SPSS> * A prompted session.

SPSS> DATA LIST FILE=RAWDATA /NAME 1-15(A) V1 TO V15 16-30.
SPSS> LIST.
SPSS> FINISH.
```

- FINISH terminates the prompted session.

FIT

```
FIT [[ERRORS=] residual series names]

    [/OBS=observed series names]

    [/{DFE=error degrees of freedom      }]
       {DFH=hypothesis degrees of freedom}
```

Example:

```
FIT ERR_4  ERR_8.
```

Overview

FIT displays a variety of descriptive statistics computed from the residual series as an aid in evaluating the goodness of fit of one or more models.

Options

Statistical Output. You can produce statistics for a particular residual series by specifying the names of the series after FIT. You can also obtain percent error statistics for specified residual series by specifying observed series on the OBS subcommand.

Degrees of Freedom. You can specify the degrees of freedom for the residual series using the DFE or DFH subcommands.

Basic Specification

The basic specification is simply the command keyword FIT. All other specifications are optional.

- By default, FIT calculates the mean error, mean percent error, mean absolute error, mean absolute percent error, sum of squared errors, mean square error, root mean square error, and the Durbin-Watson statistic for the last ERR_n (residual) series generated and the corresponding observed series in the working data file.

- If neither residual nor observed series are specified, percent error statistics for the default residual and observed series are included.

Syntax Rules

- If OBS is specified, the ERRORS subcommand naming the residual series is required.

Operations

- Observed series and degrees of freedom are matched with residual series according to the order in which they are specified.
- If residual series are explicitly specified but observed series are not, percent error statistics are not included in the output. If neither residual nor observed series are specified, percent error statistics for the default residual and observed series are included.
- If subcommand DFH is specified, FIT calculates the DFE (error degrees of freedom) by subtracting the DFH (hypothesis degrees of freedom) from the number of valid cases in the series.
- If a PREDICT period (validation period) starts before the end of the observed series, statistics are reported separately for the USE period (historical period) and the PREDICT period.

Limitations

- There is no limit on the number of residual series specified. However, the number of observed series must equal the number of residual series.

Example

```
FIT ERR_4 ERR_5 ERR_6.
```

- This command requests goodness-of-fit statistics for the residual series *ERR_4*, *ERR_5*, and *ERR_6*, which were generated by previous procedures. Percent error statistics are not included in the output, since only residual series are named.

ERRORS Subcommand

ERRORS specifies the residual (error) series.
- The actual keyword ERRORS can be omitted. VARIABLES is an alias for ERRORS.
- The minimum specification on ERRORS is a residual series name.
- The ERRORS subcommand is required if the OBS subcommand is specified.

OBS Subcommand

OBS specifies the observed series to use for calculating the mean percentage error and mean absolute percentage error.
- OBS can be used only when the residual series are explicitly specified.
- The number and order of observed series must be the same as that of the residual series.

- If more than one residual series was calculated from a single observed series, the observed series is specified once for each residual series that is based on it.

Example

```
FIT ERRORS=ERR#1 ERR#2
 /OBS=VAR1 VAR1.
```

- This command requests FIT statistics for two residual series, *ERR#1* and *ERR#2*, which were computed from the same observed series, *VAR1*.

DFE and DFH Subcommands

DFE and DFH specify the degrees of freedom for each residual series. With DFE, error degrees of freedom are entered directly. DFH specifies hypothesis degrees of freedom so FIT can compute the DFE.

- Only one DFE or DFH subcommand should be specified. If both are specified, only the last one is in effect.
- The specification on DFE or DFH is a list of numeric values. The order of these values should correspond to the order of the residual series list.
- The error degrees of freedom specified on DFE are used to compute the mean square error (MSE) and root mean square (RMS).
- The value specified for DFH should equal the number of parameters in the model (including the constant if it is present). Differencing is not considered in calculating DFH, since any observations lost due to differencing are system-missing.
- If neither DFE or DFH are specified, FIT sets DFE equal to the number of observations.

Example

```
FIT ERR#1 ERR#2
 /OBS=VAR1 VAR2
 /DFE=47 46.
```

- In this example, the error degrees of freedom for the first residual series, *ERR#1*, is 47. The error degrees of freedom for the second residual series, *ERR#2*, is 46.

Output Considerations for SSE

The sum of squared errors (SSE) reported by FIT may not be the same as the SSE reported by the estimation procedure. The SSE from the procedure is an estimate of sigma squared for that model. The SSE from FIT is simply the sum of the squared residuals.

References

Makridakis, S., S. C. Wheelwright, and V. E. McGee. 1983. *Forecasting: Methods and applications*. New York: John Wiley and Sons.

McLaughlin, R. L. 1984. *Forecasting techniques for decision making*. Rockville, Md.: Control Data Management Institute.

FLIP

```
FLIP [[VARIABLES=] {ALL      }]
                  {varlist}

     [/NEWNAMES=variable]
```

Example:

```
FLIP VARIABLES=WEEK1 TO WEEK52 /NEWNAMES=DEPT.
```

Overview

The program requires a file structure in which the variables are the columns and observations (cases) are the rows. If a file is organized such that variables are in rows and observations are in columns, you need to use FLIP to reorganize it. FLIP transposes the rows and columns of the data in the working data file so that, for example, row 1, column 2 becomes row 2, column 1, and so forth.

Options

Variable Subsets. You can transpose specific variables (columns) from the original file using the VARIABLES subcommand.

Variable Names. You can use the values of one of the variables from the original file as the variable names in the new file, using the NEWNAMES subcommand.

Basic Specification

The basic specification is the command keyword FLIP, which transposes all rows and columns.

- By default, FLIP assigns variable names *VAR001* to *VARn* to the variables in the new file. It also creates the new variable *CASE_LBL*, whose values are the variable names that existed before transposition.

Subcommand Order

VARIABLES must precede NEWNAMES.

Operations

- FLIP replaces the working data file with the transposed file and displays a list of variable names in the transposed file.

- FLIP discards any previous VARIABLE LABELS, VALUE LABELS, and WEIGHT settings. Values defined as user-missing in the original file are translated to system-missing in the transposed file.
- FLIP obeys any SELECT IF, N, and SAMPLE commands in effect.
- FLIP does not obey the TEMPORARY command. Any transformations become permanent when followed by FLIP.
- String variables in the original file are assigned system-missing values after transposition.
- Numeric variables are assigned a default format of F8.2 after transposition (with the exceptions of *CASE_LBL* and the variable specified on NEWNAMES).
- The variable *CASE_LBL* is created and added to the working data file each time FLIP is executed.
- If *CASE_LBL* already exists as the result of a previous FLIP, its current values are used as the names of variables in the new file (if NEWNAMES is not specified).

Example

The following is the LIST output for a data file arranged in a typical spreadsheet format, with variables in rows and observations in columns:

```
A            B           C           D

Income    22.00      31.00       43.00
Price     34.00      29.00       50.00
Year     1970.00   1971.00     1972.00
```

The command

```
FLIP.
```

transposes all variables in the file. The LIST output for the transposed file is as follows:

```
CASE_LBL    VAR001    VAR002     VAR003

A              .         .          .
B            22.00     34.00     1970.00
C            31.00     29.00     1971.00
D            43.00     50.00     1972.00
```

- The values for the new variable *CASE_LBL* are the variable names from the original file.
- Case A has system-missing values, since variable *A* had the string values Income, Price, and Year.
- The names of the variables in the new file are *CASE_LBL, VAR001, VAR002,* and *VAR003*.

VARIABLES Subcommand

VARIABLES names one or more variables (columns) to be transposed. The specified variables become observations (rows) in the new working file.

- The VARIABLES subcommand is optional. If it is not used, all variables are transposed.
- The actual keyword VARIABLES can be omitted.
- If the VARIABLES subcommand is specified, variables that are not named are discarded.

Example

Using the untransposed file from the previous example, the command

```
FLIP VARIABLES=A TO C.
```

transposes only variables *A* through *C*. Variable *D* is not transposed and is discarded from the working data file. The LIST output for the transposed file is as follows:

```
CASE_LBL    VAR001    VAR002    VAR003

A              .         .         .
B            22.00     34.00    1970.00
C            31.00     29.00    1971.00
```

NEWNAMES Subcommand

NEWNAMES specifies a variable whose values are used as the new variable names.

- The NEWNAMES subcommand is optional. If it is not used, the new variable names are either *VAR001* to *VARn*, or the values of *CASE_LBL* if it exists.
- Only one variable can be specified on NEWNAMES.
- The variable specified on NEWNAMES does not become an observation (case) in the new working data file, regardless of whether it is specified on the VARIABLES subcommand.
- If the variable specified is numeric, its values become a character string beginning with the letter *V*.
- If the variable specified is a long string, only the first eight characters are used.
- Lowercase character values of a string variable are converted to upper case, and any bad character values, such as blank spaces, are replaced with underscore (_) characters.
- If the variable's values are not unique, a numeric extension *n* is added to the end of a value after its first occurrence, with *n* increasing by 1 at each subsequent occurrence.

Example

Using the untransposed file from the first example, the command

```
FLIP NEWNAMES=A.
```

uses the values for variable *A* as variable names in the new file. The LIST output for the transposed file is as follows:

```
CASE_LBL    INCOME    PRICE     YEAR

B            22.00     34.00    1970.00
C            31.00     29.00    1971.00
D            43.00     50.00    1972.00
```

- Variable *A* does not become an observation in the new file. The string values for *A* are converted to upper case.

The following command transposes this file back to a form resembling its original structure:

```
FLIP.
```

The LIST output for the transposed file is as follows:

```
CASE_LBL        B          C          D

INCOME      22.00      31.00      43.00
PRICE       34.00      29.00      50.00
YEAR      1970.00    1971.00    1972.00
```

- Since the NEWNAMES subcommand is not used, the values of *CASE_LBL* from the previous FLIP (*B, C,* and *D*) are used as variable names in the new file.
- The values of *CASE_LBL* are now INCOME, PRICE, and YEAR.

FORMATS

```
FORMATS varlist(format) [varlist...]
```

Example:
```
FORMATS SALARY (DOLLAR8) / HOURLY (DOLLAR7.2) / RAISE BONUS (PCT2).
```

Overview

FORMATS changes variable print and write formats. In this program, print and write formats are *output* formats. Print formats, also called display formats, control the form in which values are displayed by a procedure or by the PRINT command; write formats control the form in which values are written by the WRITE command.

FORMATS changes both print and write formats. To change only print formats, use PRINT FORMATS. To change only write formats, use WRITE FORMATS. For information on assigning input formats during data definition, see DATA LIST.

Table 1 shows the output formats that can be assigned with the FORMATS, PRINT FORMATS, and WRITE FORMATS commands. For additional information on formats, see "Variable Formats" on p. 31.

Basic Specification

The basic specification is a variable list followed by a format specification in parentheses. All variables on the list receive the new format.

Syntax Rules

- You can specify more than one variable or variable list, followed by a format in parentheses. Only one format can be specified after each variable list. For clarity, each set of specifications can be separated by a slash.
- You can use keyword TO to refer to consecutive variables in the working data file.
- The specified width of a format must include enough positions to accommodate any punctuation characters such as decimal points, commas, dollar signs, or date and time delimiters. (This differs from assigning an *input* format on DATA LIST, where the program automatically expands the input format to accommodate punctuation characters in output.)
- Custom currency formats (CCw, CCw.d) must first be defined on the SET command before they can be used on FORMATS.
- FORMATS cannot be used with string variables. To change the length of a string variable, declare a new variable of the desired length with the STRING command and then use COMPUTE to copy values from the existing string into the new variable.
- To save the new print and write formats, you must save the working data file as an SPSS-format data file with the SAVE or XSAVE command.

Table 1 shows the formats that can be assigned by FORMATS, PRINT FORMATS, or WRITE FORMATS. The first column of the table lists the FORTRAN-like specification. The column labeled *PRINT* indicates whether the format can be used to display values. The columns labeled *Min w* and *Max w* refer to the minimum and maximum widths allowed for the format type. The column labeled *Max d* refers to the maximum decimal places.

Table 1   Output data formats

Type	PRINT	Min w	Max w	Max d
Numeric				
Fw, Fw.d	yes	1*	40	16
COMMAw, COMMAw.d	yes	1*	40	16
DOTw, DOTw.d	yes	1*	40	16
DOLLARw, DOLLARw.d	yes	2*	40	16
CCw, CCw.d	yes	2*	40	16
PCTw, PCTw.d	yes	1*	40	16
PIBHEXw	yes	2†	16†	
RBHEXw	yes	4†	16†	
Zw, Zw.d	yes	1	40	16
IBw, IBw.d	no	1	8	16
PIBw, PIBw.d	no	1	8	16
Nw.d	yes	1	40	16
Pw, Pw.d	no	1	16	16
Ew, Ew.d	yes	6	40	
PKw, PKw.d	no	1	16	16
RBw	no	2	8	
String				
Aw	yes	1	254	
AHEXw	yes	2†	510	

Type	PRINT	Min w	Max w	Resulting form
Date and time				
DATEw	yes	9	40	dd-mmm-yy
		11		dd-mmm-yyyy
ADATEw	yes	8	40	mm/dd/yy
		10		mm/dd/yyyy
EDATEw	yes	8	40	dd/mm/yy
		10		dd/mm/yyyy
JDATEw	yes	5	40	yyddd
		7		yyyyddd
SDATEw	yes	8	40	yy/mm/dd
		10		yyyy/mm/dd
QYRw	yes	6	40	q Q yy

Table 1   Output data formats (Continued)

Type	PRINT	Min w	Max w	Max d	
		8			q Q yyyy
MOYRw	yes	6	40		mmm yy
		8			mmm yyyy
WKYRw	yes	8	40		ww WK yy
		10			ww WK yyyy
WKDAYw	yes	2**	40		
MONTHw	yes	3**	40		
TIMEw	yes	5††	40		hh:mm
TIMEw.d	yes	10	40	16	hh:mm:ss.s
DTIMEw	yes	8††	40		dd hh:mm
DTIMEw.d	yes	13	40	16	dd hh:mm:ss.s
DATETIMEw	yes	17††	40		dd-mmm-yyyy hh:mm
DATETIMEw.d	yes	22	40	16	dd-mmm-yyyy hh:mm:ss.s

*Add number of decimals plus 1 if number of decimals is more than 0. Total width cannot exceed 40 characters.
†Must be a multiple of 2.
**As the field width is expanded, the output string is expanded until the entire name of the day or month is produced.
††Add 3 to display seconds.

Operations

- Unlike most transformations, FORMATS takes effect as soon as it is encountered in the command sequence. Special attention should be paid to its position among commands. For more information, see "Command Order" on p. 16.

- Variables not specified on FORMATS retain their current print and write formats in the working file. To see the current formats, use the DISPLAY command.

- The new formats are changed only in the working file and are in effect for the duration of the current session or until changed again with a FORMATS, PRINT FORMATS, or WRITE FORMATS command. Formats in the original data file (if one exists) are not changed unless the file is resaved with the SAVE or XSAVE command.

- New numeric variables created with transformation commands are assigned default print and write formats of F8.2 (or the format specified on the FORMAT subcommand of SET). The FORMATS command can be used to change the new variable's print and write formats.

- New string variables created with transformation commands are assigned the format specified on the STRING command that declares the variable. FORMATS cannot be used to change the format of a new string variable.

- If a numeric data value exceeds its width specification, the program attempts to display some value nevertheless. The program first rounds decimal values, then removes punctuation characters, then tries scientific notation, and finally, if there is still not enough space, produces asterisks indicating that a value is present but cannot be displayed in the assigned width.

Example

```
FORMATS SALARY (DOLLAR8) /HOURLY (DOLLAR7.2)
       /RAISE BONUS (PCT2).
```

- The print and write formats for *SALARY* are changed to DOLLAR format with eight positions, including the dollar sign and comma when appropriate. The value 11550 is displayed as $11,550. An eight-digit number would require a DOLLAR11 format: eight characters for the digits, two characters for commas, and one character for the dollar sign.

- The print and write formats for *HOURLY* are changed to DOLLAR format with seven positions, including the dollar sign, decimal point, and two decimal places. The value 115 is displayed as $115.00. If DOLLAR6.2 had been specified, the value 115 would be displayed as $115.0. The program would truncate the last 0 because a width of 6 is not enough to display the full value.

- The print and write formats for both *RAISE* and *BONUS* are changed to PCT with two positions: one position for the percentage and one position for the percent sign. The value 9 is displayed as 9%. Since the width allows for only two positions, the value 10 is displayed as 10, since the percent sign is truncated.

Example

```
COMPUTE V3=V1 + V2.
FORMATS V3 (F3.1).
```

- COMPUTE creates the new numeric variable *V3*. By default, *V3* is assigned an F8.2 format (or the default format specified on SET).

- FORMATS changes both the print and write formats for *V3* to F3.1.

Example

```
SET CCA='-/-.Dfl ..-'.
FORMATS COST (CCA14.2).
```

- SET defines a European currency format for the custom currency format type CCA.

- FORMATS assigns format CCA to variable *COST*. With the format defined for CCA on SET, the value 37419 is displayed as Dfl 37.419,00. See the SET command for more information on custom currency formats.

FREQUENCIES

```
FREQUENCIES [VARIABLES=]varlist [varlist...]

[/FORMAT= [{NOTABLE }] [{AVALUE}]
          {LIMIT(n)}   {DVALUE}
                       {AFREQ }
                       {DFREQ }

[/MISSING=INCLUDE]

[/BARCHART=[MINIMUM(n)] [MAXIMUM(n)] [{FREQ(n)    }]]
                                     {PERCENT(n)}

[/PIECHART=[MINIMUM(n)] [MAXIMUM(n)] [{FREQ    }] [{MISSING  }]]
                                     {PERCENT}   {NOMISSING}

[/HISTOGRAM=[MINIMUM(n)] [MAXIMUM(n)] [{FREQ(n)   }] [{NONORMAL}] ]
                                                     {NORMAL  }

[/GROUPED=varlist [{(width)        }]]
                  {(boundary list)}

[/NTILES=n]

[/PERCENTILES=value list]

[/STATISTICS=[DEFAULT] [MEAN] [STDDEV] [MINIMUM] [MAXIMUM]
             [SEMEAN] [VARIANCE] [SKEWNESS] [SESKEW] [RANGE]
             [MODE] [KURTOSIS] [SEKURT] [MEDIAN] [SUM] [ALL]
                [NONE]]

[/ORDER=[{ANALYSIS}] [{VARIABLE}]
```

Example:

```
FREQUENCIES VAR=RACE /STATISTICS=ALL.
```

Overview

FREQUENCIES produces Frequency tables showing frequency counts and percentages of the values of individual variables. You can also use FREQUENCIES to obtain Statistics tables for categorical variables and to obtain Statistics tables and graphical displays for continuous variables.

Options

Display Format. You can suppress tables and alter the order of values within tables using the FORMAT subcommand.

Statistical Display. Percentiles and ntiles are available for numeric variables with the PERCENTILES and NTILES subcommands. The following statistics are available with the STATISTICS subcommand: mean, median, mode, standard deviation, variance, skewness, kurtosis, and sum.

Plots. Histograms can be specified for numeric variables on the HISTOGRAM subcommand. Bar charts can be specified for numeric or string variables on the BARCHART subcommand.

Input Data. On the GROUPED subcommand, you can indicate whether the input data are grouped (or collapsed) so that a better estimate can be made of percentiles.

Basic Specification

The basic specification is the VARIABLES subcommand and the name of at least one variable. By default, FREQUENCIES produces a Frequency table.

Subcommand Order

Subcommands can be named in any order.

Syntax Rules

- You can specify multiple NTILES subcommands.
- BARCHART and HISTOGRAM are mutually exclusive.
- You can specify numeric variables (with or without decimal values) or string variables. Only the short-string portion of long string variables are tabulated.
- Keyword ALL can be used on VARIABLES to refer to all user-defined variables in the working data file.

Operations

- Variables are tabulated in the order they are mentioned on the VARIABLES subcommand.
- If a requested ntile or percentile cannot be calculated, a period (.) is displayed.
- FREQUENCIES dynamically builds the table, setting up one cell for each unique value encountered in the data.

Limitations

- Maximum 500 variables total per FREQUENCIES command.
- Maximum of 32,767 observed values over all variables.

Example

```
FREQUENCIES VAR=RACE /STATISTICS=ALL.
```

- FREQUENCIES requests a Frequency table and a Statistics table showing all statistics for the categorical variable *RACE*.

Example

```
FREQUENCIES STATISTICS=ALL /HISTOGRAM
/VARIABLES=SEX TVHOURS SCALE1 TO SCALE5
/FORMAT=NOTABLE.
```

- FREQUENCIES requests statistics and histograms for *SEX, TVHOURS,* and all variables between and including *SCALE1* and *SCALE5* in the working data file.
- FORMAT suppresses the Frequency tables, which are not useful for continuous variables.

VARIABLES Subcommand

VARIABLES names the variables to be tabulated and is the only required subcommand. The actual keyword VARIABLES can be omitted.

FORMAT Subcommand

FORMAT controls various features of the output, including order of categories and suppression of tables.
- The minimum specification is a single keyword.
- By default, FREQUENCIES displays the Frequency table and sort categories in ascending order of values for numeric variables and in alphabetical order for string variables.

Table Order

AVALUE   *Sort categories in ascending order of values (numeric variables) or in alphabetical order (string variables).* This is the default.

DVALUE   *Sort categories in descending order of values (numeric variables) or in reverse alphabetical order (string variables).* This is ignored when HISTOGRAM, NTILES, or PERCENTILES is requested.

AFREQ   *Sort categories in ascending order of frequency.* This is ignored when HISTOGRAM, NTILES, or PERCENTILES is requested.

DFREQ   *Sort categories in descending order of frequency.* This is ignored when HISTOGRAM, NTILES, or PERCENTILES is requested.

Table Suppression

LIMIT(n)   *Suppress frequency tables with more than* n *categories.* The number of missing and valid cases and requested statistics are displayed for suppressed tables.

NOTABLE   *Suppress all frequency tables.* The number of missing and valid cases are displayed for suppressed tables. NOTABLE overrides LIMIT.

BARCHART Subcommand

BARCHART produces a bar chart for each variable named on the VARIABLES subcommand. By default, the horizontal axis for each bar chart is scaled in frequencies, and the interval width is determined by the largest frequency count for the variable being plotted. Bar charts are labeled with value labels or with the value if no label is defined.

- The minimum specification is the BARCHART keyword, which generates default bar charts.
- BARCHART cannot be used with HISTOGRAM.

MIN(n) *Lower bound below which values are not plotted.*

MAX(n) *Upper bound above which values are not plotted.*

FREQ(n) *Vertical axis scaled in frequencies, where optional* n *is the maximum.* If *n* is not specified or if it is too small, FREQUENCIES chooses 5, 10, 20, 50, 100, 200, 500, 1000, 2000, and so forth, depending on the largest category. This is the default.

PERCENT(n) *Vertical axis scaled in percentages, where optional* n *is the maximum.* If *n* is not specified or if it is too small, FREQUENCIES chooses 5, 10, 25, 50, or 100, depending on the frequency count for the largest category.

Example

```
FREQUENCIES VAR=RACE /BARCHART.
```

- FREQUENCIES produces a frequency table and the default bar chart for variable *RACE*.

Example

```
FREQUENCIES VAR=V1 V2 /BAR=MAX(10).
```

- FREQUENCIES produces a frequency table and bar chart with values through 10 for each of variables *V1* and *V2*.

PIECHART Subcommand

PIECHART produces a pie chart for each variable named on the VARIABLES subcommand. By default, one slice corresponds to each category defined by the variable with one slice representing all missing values. Pie charts are labeled with value labels or with the value if no label is defined.

- The minimum specification is the PIECHART keyword, which generates default pie charts.
- PIECHART can be requested together with either BARCHART or HISTOGRAM.
- FREQ and PERCENT are mutually exclusive. If both are specified, only the first specification is in effect.
- MISSING and NOMISSING are mutually exclusive. If both are specified, only the first specification is in effect.

MIN(n) *Lower bound below which values are not plotted.*

MAX(n) *Upper bound above which values are not plotted.*

FREQ   *The pie charts are based on frequencies.* Frequencies are displayed when you request values in the Chart Editor. This is the default.

PERCENT   *The pie charts are based on percentage.* Percentage is displayed when you request values in the Chart Editor.

MISSING   *User-missing and system-missing values are treated as one category.* This is the default. Specify INCLUDE on the MISSING subcommand to display system-missing and user-missing values as separate slices.

NOMISSING   *Missing values are excluded from the chart.* If you specify INCLUDE on the MISSING subcommand, each user-missing value is represented by one slice.

Example

```
FREQUENCIES VAR=RACE /PIECHART.
```

- FREQUENCIES produces a frequency table and the default pie chart for variable *RACE*.

Example

```
FREQUENCIES VAR=V1 V2 /PIE=MAX(10).
```

- For each variable *V1* and *V2*, FREQUENCIES produces a frequency table and a pie chart with values through 10.

HISTOGRAM Subcommand

HISTOGRAM displays a plot for each numeric variable named on the VARIABLES subcommand. By default, the horizontal axis of each histogram is scaled in frequencies and the interval width is determined by the largest frequency count of the variable being plotted.

- The minimum specification is the HISTOGRAM keyword, which generates default histograms.
- HISTOGRAM cannot be used with BARCHART.

MIN(n)   *Lower bound below which values are not plotted.*

MAX(n)   *Upper bound above which values are not plotted.*

FREQ(n)   *Vertical axis scaled in frequencies, where optional* n *is the scale.* If *n* is not specified or if it is too small, FREQUENCIES chooses 5, 10, 20, 50, 100, 200, 500, 1000, 2000, and so forth, depending on the largest category. This is the default.

NORMAL   *Superimpose a normal curve.* The curve is based on all valid values for the variable, including values excluded by MIN and MAX.

NONORMAL   *Suppress the normal curve.* This is the default.

Example

```
FREQUENCIES VAR=V1 /HIST=NORMAL.
```

- FREQUENCIES requests a histogram with a superimposed normal curve.

GROUPED Subcommand

When the values of a variable represent grouped or collapsed data, it is possible to estimate percentiles for the original, ungrouped data from the grouped data. The GROUPED subcommand specifies which variables have been grouped. It affects only the output from the PERCENTILES and NTILES subcommands and the MEDIAN statistic from the STATISTICS subcommand.

- Multiple GROUPED subcommands can be used on a single FREQUENCIES command. Multiple variable lists, separated by slashes, can appear on a single GROUPED subcommand.

- The variables named on GROUPED must have been named on the VARIABLES subcommand.

- The value or value list in the parentheses is optional. When it is omitted, the program treats the values of the variables listed on GROUPED as midpoints. If the values are not midpoints, they must first be recoded with the RECODE command.

- A single value in parentheses specifies the width of each grouped interval. The data values must be group midpoints, but there can be empty categories. For example, if you have data values of 10, 20, and 30 and specify an interval width of 5, the categories are 10 ± 2.5, 20 ± 2.5, and 30 ± 2.5. The categories 15 ± 2.5 and 25 ± 2.5 are empty.

- A value list in the parentheses specifies interval boundaries. The data values do not have to represent midpoints, but the lowest boundary must be lower than any value in the data. If any data values exceed the highest boundary specified (the last value within the parentheses), they will be assigned to an open-ended interval. In this case, some percentiles cannot be calculated.

Example

```
RECODE AGE (1=15) (2=25) (3=35) (4=45) (5=55)
           (6=65) (7=75) (8=85) (9=95)
    /INCOME (1=5)  (2=15) (3=25) (4=35) (5=45)
           (6=55) (7=65) (8=75) (9=100).

FREQUENCIES VARIABLES=AGE, SEX, RACE, INCOME
    /GROUPED=AGE, INCOME
    /PERCENTILES=5,25,50,75,95.
```

- The *AGE* and *INCOME* categories of 1, 2, 3, and so forth are recoded to category midpoints. Note that data can be recoded to category midpoints on any scale; here *AGE* is recoded in years, but *INCOME* is recoded in thousands of dollars.

- The GROUPED subcommand on FREQUENCIES allows more accurate estimates of the requested percentiles.

Example

```
FREQUENCIES VARIABLES=TEMP
    /GROUPED=TEMP (0.5)
    /NTILES=10.
```

- The values of *TEMP* (temperature) in this example were recorded using an inexpensive thermometer whose readings are precise only to the nearest half degree.

- The observed values of 97.5, 98, 98.5, 99, and so on, are treated as group midpoints, smoothing out the discrete distribution. This yields more accurate estimates of the deciles.

Example

```
FREQUENCIES VARIABLES=AGE
  /GROUPED=AGE (17.5, 22.5, 27.5, 32.5, 37.5, 42.5, 47.5
               52.5, 57.5, 62.5, 67.5, 72.5, 77.5, 82.5)
  /PERCENTILES=5, 10, 25, 50, 75, 90, 95.
```

- The values of *AGE* in this example have been estimated to the nearest five years. The first category is 17.5 to 22.5, the second is 22.5 to 27.5, and so forth. The artificial clustering of age estimates at multiples of five years is smoothed out by treating *AGE* as grouped data.

- It is not necessary to recode the ages to category midpoints, since the interval boundaries are explicitly given.

PERCENTILES Subcommand

PERCENTILES displays the value below which the specified percentage of cases falls. The desired percentiles must be explicitly requested. There are no defaults.

Example

```
FREQUENCIES VAR=V1 /PERCENTILES=10 25 33.3 66.7 75.
```

- FREQUENCIES requests the values for percentiles 10, 25, 33.3, 66.7, and 75 for *V1*.

NTILES Subcommand

NTILES calculates the percentages that divide the distribution into the specified number of categories and displays the values below which the requested percentages of cases fall. There are no default ntiles.

- Multiple NTILES subcommands are allowed. Each NTILES subcommand generates separate percentiles. Any duplicate percentiles generated by different NTILES subcommands are consolidated in the output.

Example

```
FREQUENCIES VARIABLE=V1 /NTILES=4.
```

- FREQUENCIES requests quartiles (percentiles 25, 50, and 75) for *V1*.

Example

```
FREQUENCIES VARIABLE=V1 /NTILES=4 /NTILES=10.
```

- The first NTILES subcommand requests percentiles 25, 50, and 75.

- The second NTILES subcommand requests percentiles 10 through 90 in increments of 10.

- The 50th percentile is produced by both specifications but is displayed only once in the output.

STATISTICS Subcommand

STATISTICS controls the display of statistics. By default, cases with missing values are excluded from the calculation of statistics.

- The minimum specification is the keyword STATISTICS, which generates the mean, standard deviation, minimum, and maximum (these statistics are also produced by keyword DEFAULT).

MEAN	*Mean.*
SEMEAN	*Standard error of the mean.*
MEDIAN	*Median.* Ignored when AFREQ or DFREQ are specified on the FORMAT subcommand.
MODE	*Mode.* If there is more than one mode, only the first mode is displayed.
STDDEV	*Standard deviation.*
VARIANCE	*Variance.*
SKEWNESS	*Skewness.*
SESKEW	*Standard error of the skewness statistic.*
KURTOSIS	*Kurtosis.*
SEKURT	*Standard error of the kurtosis statistic.*
RANGE	*Range.*
MINIMUM	*Minimum.*
MAXIMUM	*Maximum.*
SUM	*Sum.*
DEFAULT	*Mean, standard deviation, minimum, and maximum.*
ALL	*All available statistics.*
NONE	*No statistics.*

Example

```
FREQUENCIES VAR=AGE /STATS=MODE.
```

- STATISTICS requests the mode of *AGE*.

Example

```
FREQUENCIES VAR=AGE /STATS=DEF MODE.
```

- STATISTICS requests the default statistics (mean, standard deviation, minimum, and maximum) plus the mode of *AGE*.

MISSING Subcommand

By default, both user-missing and system-missing values are labeled as missing in the table but are not included in the valid and cumulative percentages, in the calculation of descriptive statistics, or in charts and histograms.

INCLUDE   *Include cases with user-missing values.* Cases with user-missing values are included in statistics and plots.

ORDER Subcommand

You can organize your output by variable or by analysis. Frequencies output that is organized by analysis has a single statistics table for all variables. Output organized by variable has a statistics table and a frequency table for each variable.

ANALYSIS   *Organize output by analysis.* Displays a single statistics table for all variables. This is the default.

VARIABLE   *Organize output by variable.* Displays a statistics table and a frequency table for each variable.

GET

```
GET FILE=file

 [/KEEP={ALL**  }] [/DROP=varlist]
        {varlist}

 [/RENAME=(old varnames=new varnames)...]

 [/MAP]
```

**Default if the subcommand is omitted.

Example:

```
GET FILE=EMPL.
```

Overview

GET reads an SPSS-format data file that was created by the SAVE or XSAVE command. An SPSS-format data file contains data plus a dictionary. The dictionary contains a name for each variable in the data file, plus any assigned variable and value labels, missing-value flags, and variable print and write formats. The dictionary also contains document text created with the DOCUMENTS command.

GET is used only for reading SPSS-format data files. See DATA LIST for information on reading and defining data in a text data file. See MATRIX DATA for information on defining matrix materials in a text data file. For information on defining complex data files that cannot be defined with DATA LIST alone, see FILE TYPE and REPEATING DATA.

The program can also read data files created for other software applications. See IMPORT for information on reading *portable files* created with EXPORT. See commands such as GET TRANSLATE, GET SAS, and GET BMDP for information on reading files created by other software programs.

Options

Variable Subsets and Order. You can read a subset of variables and reorder the variables that are copied into the working data file using the DROP and KEEP subcommands.

Variable Names. You can rename variables as they are copied into the working data file with the RENAME subcommand.

Variable Map. To confirm the names and order of variables in the working data file, use the MAP subcommand. MAP displays the variables in the working file next to their corresponding names in the SPSS-format data file.

Basic Specification

- The basic specification is the FILE subcommand, which specifies the SPSS-format data file to be read.
- By default, GET copies all variables from the SPSS-format data file into the working data file. Variables in the working file are in the same order and have the same names as variables in the SPSS-format data file. Documentary text from the SPSS-format data file is copied into the dictionary of the working file.

Subcommand Order

- FILE must be specified first.
- The remaining subcommands can be specified in any order.

Syntax Rules

- FILE is required and can be specified only once.
- KEEP, DROP, RENAME, and MAP can be used as many times as needed.
- Documentary text copied from the SPSS-format data file can be dropped from the working data file with the DROP DOCUMENTS command.
- GET cannot be used inside a DO IF—END IF or LOOP—END LOOP structure.

Operations

- GET reads the dictionary of the SPSS-format data file.
- If KEEP is not specified, variables in the working data file are in the same order as variables in the SPSS-format data file.
- A file saved with weighting in effect maintains the values of the variable *$WEIGHT*. For a discussion of turning off weights, see WEIGHT.
- The order of cases in the working data file is the same as their order in the SPSS-format data file. The values of *$CASENUM* are those from the original text data file before any selecting (see SELECT IF) or sorting (see SORT). The value of *$CASENUM* may differ from the actual number of a case after selecting or sorting.

FILE Subcommand

FILE specifies the SPSS-format data file to be read. FILE is required and can be specified only once. It must be the first specification on GET.

DROP and KEEP Subcommands

DROP and KEEP are used to copy a subset of variables into the working data file. DROP specifies variables that should not be copied into the working file. KEEP specifies variables that should be copied. Variables not specified on KEEP are dropped.

- Variables can be specified in any order. The order of variables on KEEP determines the order of variables in the working file. The order of variables on DROP does not affect the order of variables in the working file.

- The keyword ALL on KEEP refers to all remaining variables not previously specified on KEEP. ALL must be the last specification on KEEP.

- If a variable is specified twice on the same subcommand, only the first mention is recognized.

- Multiple DROP and KEEP subcommands are allowed. However, specifying a variable named on a previous DROP or not named on a previous KEEP results in an error, and the GET command is not executed.

- The keyword TO can be used to specify a group of consecutive variables in the SPSS-format data file.

Example

```
GET FILE=HUBTEMP /DROP=DEPT79 TO DEPT84 SALARY79.
```

- The working data file is copied from SPSS-format data file *HUBTEMP*. All variables between and including *DEPT79* and *DEPT84*, as well as *SALARY79*, are excluded from the working file. All other variables are copied into the working file.

- Variables in the working data file are in the same order as the variables in the *HUBTEMP* file.

Example

```
GET FILE=PRSNL /DROP=GRADE STORE
               /KEEP=LNAME NAME TENURE JTENURE ALL.
```

- The variables *GRADE* and *STORE* are dropped when the file *PRSNL* is copied into the working data file.

- KEEP specifies that *LNAME*, *NAME*, *TENURE*, and *JTENURE* are the first four variables in the working file, followed by all remaining variables (except those dropped by the previous DROP). These remaining variables are copied into the working file in the same sequence in which they appear in the *PRSNL* file.

RENAME Subcommand

RENAME changes the names of variables as they are copied into the working data file.

- The specification on RENAME is a list of old variable names followed by an equals sign and a list of new variable names. The same number of variables must be specified on both lists. The keyword TO can be used on the first list to refer to consecutive variables in the SPSS-format data file and on the second list to generate new variable names (see "Keyword TO" on p. 29). The entire specification must be enclosed in parentheses.

- Alternatively, you can specify each old variable name individually, followed by an equals sign and the new variable name. Multiple sets of variable specifications are allowed. The parentheses around each set of specifications are optional.
- Old variable names do not need to be specified according to their order in the SPSS-format data file.
- Name changes take place in one operation. Therefore, variable names can be exchanged between two variables.
- Variables cannot be renamed to scratch variables.
- Multiple RENAME subcommands are allowed.
- On a subsequent DROP or KEEP subcommand, variables are referred to by their new names.

Example

```
GET FILE=EMPL88 /RENAME  AGE=AGE88 JOBCAT=JOBCAT88.
```

- RENAME specifies two name changes for the working data file. *AGE* is renamed to *AGE88* and *JOBCAT* is renamed to *JOBCAT88*.

Example

```
GET FILE=EMPL88 /RENAME (AGE JOBCAT=AGE88 JOBCAT88).
```

- The name changes are identical to those in the previous example. *AGE* is renamed to *AGE88* and *JOBCAT* is renamed to *JOBCAT88*. The parentheses are required with this method.

MAP Subcommand

MAP displays a list of the variables in the working data file and their corresponding names in the SPSS-format data file.

- The only specification is the keyword MAP. There are no additional specifications.
- Multiple MAP subcommands are allowed. Each MAP subcommand maps the results of subcommands that precede it; results of subcommands that follow it are not mapped.

Example

```
GET FILE=EMPL88 /RENAME=(AGE=AGE88) (JOBCAT=JOBCAT88)
 /KEEP=LNAME NAME JOBCAT88 ALL /MAP.
```

- MAP is specified to confirm the new names for the variables *AGE* and *JOBCAT* and the order of variables in the working data file (*LNAME*, *NAME*, and *JOBCAT88*, followed by all remaining variables in the SPSS-format data file).

GET BMDP

This command is not available on all operating systems.

```
GET BMDP FILE=file

 [/SCAN={YES }] [/CODE=name]
        {ONLY}

 [/CONTENT=name] [/LABEL=quoted string]

 [/KEEP={ALL** }] [/DROP=varlist]
        {varlist}

 [/RENAME=(old varnames=new varnames)...]

 [/MAP]
```

**Default if the subcommand is omitted.

Example:

```
GET BMDP FILE=BMDPFIL3.
```

Overview

GET BMDP reads a save file from a BMDP data set. The specified save file from the data set becomes the working data file. If necessary, BMDP variable names and missing values are automatically converted to comply with SPSS conventions.

Options

Save Files. You can read a particular save file within the data set to read using the CONTENT, CODE, and LABEL subcommands.

Variable Subsets and Order. You can read a subset of variables and reorder the variables that are copied into the working data file using the DROP and KEEP subcommands.

Variable Names. You can rename variables as they are copied into the working data file with the RENAME subcommand.

Variable Map. To confirm the names and order of variables copied into the working data file, use the MAP subcommand. MAP displays the variables in the working file next to their corresponding names in the BMDP save file.

Basic Specification

- The basic specification is the FILE subcommand, which specifies the BMDP data set.

- By default, the program reads the first save file within the data set with the content field *DATA*. All variables from the BMDP save file are copied into the working data file. However, the program may have to rename BMDP variables so that they conform to specific naming conventions (see "BMDP to SPSS Data Conversion" below).

Subcommand Order

- FILE is required and must be specified first.
- If specified, SCAN must immediately follow FILE.
- CONTENT, CODE, and LABEL can appear in any order but must follow FILE and SCAN.
- KEEP, DROP, RENAME, and MAP can be specified more than once and in any order but must follow all other subcommands.

Operations

- If KEEP is not specified, variables in the working data file are in the same order as variables in the BMDP save file.
- The program makes assumptions about the record format and other characteristics of the BMDP data set based on your computer and operating system. See the *SPSS Base User's Guide* for your version of SPSS for information.
- Although it is possible for the program to read files with content other than *DATA*, such files are likely to be interpreted incorrectly. A certain amount of trial and error may be necessary to read and redefine such files.
- Information generated by the BMDP GROUPS paragraph is ignored.

Case Selection

In a BMDP save file, each case includes an automatic variable *USE*, whose value determines whether the case is included in an analysis. Only cases in which *USE* has a positive, nonmissing value are included in BMDP analyses. GET BMDP retains all cases, and it retains the variable *USE* unless the KEEP or DROP subcommands indicate otherwise. The program can use the same case selection if the SELECT IF command is used before an analysis, as in SELECT IF USE > 0.

BMDP to SPSS Data Conversion

The program makes the following conversions to force BMDP data to comply with SPSS conventions:

Variable Names

- Initial blanks and special characters are changed to @. For example, *$VAR*, *.VAR*, */VAR*, and *VAR* preceded by a blank all become *@VAR* (see below about duplicate names).

- Internal blanks and special characters are changed to underscores. *VAR ONE* and *VAR/ONE* both become *VAR_ONE*.
- Parentheses are removed. *X(1)* becomes *X1*.
- If a reserved keyword is used as a BMDP variable name, the program appends the # symbol to the name and issues a warning message. The reserved keywords are ALL, AND, BY, GE, GT, LE, LT, NE, NOT, OR, TO, and WITH. A BMDP variable named *AND*, for example, would be converted to *AND#*.
- If conversion produces duplicate variable names, the program creates names of the form *Vn*, in which *n* is an integer.

Missing Values

All three BMDP missing values (missing, lower than the minimum, and higher than the maximum) are converted to the system-missing value.

Print and Write Formats

- GET BMDP supplies print and write formats of F8.2 for all numeric variables and A4 for all string variables. FORMATS, PRINT FORMATS, and WRITE FORMATS can be used to change these numeric formats if they are inappropriate.
- The program recognizes as string variables only those identified by the LABEL clause of BMDP's VARIABLE paragraph. Other string variables might not be detected and may be read as numeric. You can change these variables back to string using the REFORMAT command (see REFORMAT).

FILE Subcommand

FILE specifies the BMDP data set, which can include more than one BMDP save file. Unless the CODE, CONTENT, or LABEL subcommands are specified, the program reads the first save file within the specified data set with the content field *DATA*.

- FILE is required and must be the first specification on GET BMDP.

SCAN Subcommand

SCAN displays information about the save files within the BMDP data set. The information includes the content, code, and label fields for the save files. Code and label are specified by the user within BMDP; content is supplied by BMDP to identify the type of file (data, correlation matrix, and so on).

- When used, SCAN must immediately follow FILE.

YES   *Read the save file and display the code, content, and label fields and other information from the file.*

ONLY   *Do not read the save file but display the code, content, and label fields and other information from the file.*

Example

```
GET BMDP FILE=BMDPFIL3  /SCAN ONLY.
```

- FILE specifies the *BMDPFIL3* data set.
- SCAN displays information about the save files within the data set. However, no files are read. Information about the save file can be used on the CONTENT, CODE, or LABEL subcommands of another GET BMDP command.

CONTENT, CODE, and LABEL Subcommands

CONTENT, CODE, and LABEL are used to specify a particular save file within a single data set. The specification is a name or a string enclosed in apostrophes, according to BMDP conventions.

- If CONTENT is not specified, the program assumes DATA.
- If CODE or LABEL are not specified, the program reads the first save file with the specified content (DATA by default).
- If CODE or LABEL are specified, the program reads the first file that matches all of the information provided.

Example

```
GET BMDP FILE=BMDPFIL /LABEL= 'OLD DATA'.
```

- The program reads the first save file in data set *BMDPFIL* with content DATA and label OLD DATA.

DROP and KEEP Subcommands

DROP and KEEP are used to copy a subset of variables into the working data file. DROP specifies variables that should not be copied into the working file. KEEP specifies variables that should be copied. Variables not specified on KEEP are dropped.

- DROP and KEEP cannot precede the FILE, CONTENT, CODE, or LABEL subcommands.
- DROP and KEEP must use SPSS variable names, not BMDP variable names (see "BMDP to SPSS Data Conversion" on p. 409).
- Variables can be specified in any order. The order of variables on KEEP determines the order of variables in the working file. The order of variables on DROP does not affect the order of variables in the working file.
- The keyword ALL on KEEP refers to all remaining variables not previously specified. ALL must be the last specification on KEEP.
- If a variable is specified twice on the same subcommand, only the first mention is recognized.
- Multiple DROP and KEEP subcommands are allowed. However, specifying a variable named on a previous DROP or not named on a previous KEEP results in an error and the command is not executed.
- The keyword TO can be used to specify a group of consecutive variables in the BMDP save file.

Example

```
GET BMDP FILE=BMDPFIL /DROP=X1 TO X4, X9 /KEEP=X7 X6 ALL.
```

- GET BMDP reads the BMDP data set *BMDPFIL*; the first save file with content *DATA* is copied into the working data file. The save file contains variables *X(1)* to *X(20)*. Note that DROP and KEEP use the SPSS variable names, not the BMDP variable names: the parentheses are dropped from the variable names.

- DROP excludes from the working data file all variables between and including *X1* and *X4*, as well as *X9*. All other variables are copied into the working file.

- KEEP specifies that *X7* and *X6* are the first two variables in the working data file, followed by all remaining variables (except those specified on DROP). The remaining variables are copied into the working file in the same sequence they appear in the original BMDP save file.

RENAME Subcommand

RENAME changes the names of variables as they are copied into the working data file.

- RENAME cannot precede the FILE, CONTENT, CODE, or LABEL subcommands.

- The specification on RENAME is a list of old variable names followed by an equals sign and a list of new variable names. The same number of variables must be specified on both lists, and you can use the keyword TO. The entire specification must be enclosed in parentheses.

- Alternatively, you can specify each old variable name individually, followed by an equals sign and the new variable name. Multiple sets of variable specifications are allowed. The parentheses around each set of specifications are optional.

- The list of old variable names must use SPSS variable names, not BMDP variable names (see "BMDP to SPSS Data Conversion" on p. 409).

- Old variable names do not need to be specified according to their order in the BMDP save file.

- Name changes take place in one operation. Therefore, variable names can be exchanged between two variables.

- Variables cannot be renamed to scratch variables.

- Multiple RENAME subcommands are allowed.

- On a subsequent DROP or KEEP subcommand, variables are referred to by their new names.

Example

```
GET BMDP FILE= BMDPFIL4  /SCAN YES
  /KEEP = X1 X2 V1 V2
  /RENAME = (X1 X2 V1 V2 = X1_A X2_A X1_B X2_B).
```

- Assume that the save file within the data set *BMDPFIL4* contains variables named *X(1)*, *X(2)*, *X1*, and *X2* (and some others), in that order. The program converts the variable names *X(1)* and *X(2)* to *X1* and *X2*. Then, because of duplication, it converts *X1* and *X2* to *V1* and

V2 (see "BMDP to SPSS Data Conversion" on p. 409). Note that the KEEP and RENAME specifications use the SPSS names.

- RENAME changes variable names *X1* to *X1_A*, *X2* to *X2_A*, *V1* to *X1_B*, and *V2* to *X2_B*.

MAP Subcommand

MAP displays a list of the variables in the working data file and their corresponding names in the BMDP save file.

- MAP cannot precede the FILE, CONTENT, CODE, or LABEL subcommands.
- The only specification is the keyword MAP. There are no additional specifications.
- Multiple MAP subcommands are allowed. Each MAP subcommand maps the results of subcommands that precede it; results of subcommands that follow it are not mapped.

Example

```
GET BMDP FILE=BMDPFIL4   /SCAN YES
  /KEEP=X1 X2 V1 V2 ALL
  /RENAME=(X1 X2 V1 V2 = X1_A X2_A X1_B X2_B)
  /MAP.
```

- MAP is specified to confirm the new names and the order of variables in the working data file (*X1_A*, *X2_A*, *X1_B*, and *X2_B*, followed by all remaining variables in the BMDP save file).

GET CAPTURE

```
GET CAPTURE {ODBC    }*

[/CONNECT='connection string']
[/LOGIN=login] [/PASSWORD=password]
[/SERVER=host] [/DATABASE=database name]†

/SELECT any select statement
```

* You can import data from any database for which you have an ODBC driver installed.

† Optional subcommands are database-specific. See "Syntax Rules" below for the subcommand(s) required by a database type.

Example:

```
GET CAPTURE ODBC
 /CONNECT='DSN=Sample DBASE files;CollatingSequence=ASCII;'
         'DBQ=C:\CRW; DefaultDir=C:\CRW; Deleted=1;'
         'Driverid=21;Fil=dBaseIII;PageTimeout=600;'
         'Statistics=0;UID=admin;'
 /SELECT EMPLOYEE.LASTNAME,EMPLOYEE.FIRSTNAME,EMPLOYEE.ADDRESS,
         EMPDATA.DATA FROM {oj employee LEFT OUTER JOIN EMPDATA ON
         'EMPLOYEE','LASTNAME'='EMPDATA','LASTNAME'}.
```

Overview

GET CAPTURE retrieves data from a database and converts them to a format that can be used by program procedures. GET CAPTURE retrieves data and data information and builds a working data file for the current session.

Basic Specification

The basic specification is one of the subcommands specifying the database type followed by the SELECT subcommand and any SQL select statement.

Subcommand Order

The subcommand specifying the type of database must be the first specification. The SELECT subcommand must be the last.

Syntax Rules

- Only one subcommand specifying the database type can be used.
- The CONNECT subcommand must be specified if you use the Microsoft ODBC (Open Database Connectivity) driver.

Operations

- GET CAPTURE retrieves the data specified on SELECT.
- The variables are in the same order in which they are specified on the SELECT subcommand.
- The data definition information captured from the database is stored in the working data file dictionary.

Limitations

- Maximum 3800 characters (approximately) can be specified on the SELECT subcommand. This translates to 76 lines of 50 characters. Characters beyond the limit are ignored.

CONNECT Subcommand

CONNECT is required to access any database that has an installed Microsoft ODBC driver.

- You cannot specify the connection string directly in the syntax window, but you can paste it with the rest of the command from the Results dialog box, which is the last of the series of dialog boxes opened with the Database Capture command from the File menu.

SELECT Subcommand

SELECT specifies any SQL select statement accepted by the database you access. With ODBC, you can now select columns from more than one related table in an ODBC data source using either the inner join or the outer join.

Example

```
GET CAPTURE ODBC
 /CONNECT='DSN=Sample DBASE files;CollatingSequence=ASCII;'
          'DBQ=C:\CRW; DefaultDir=C:\CRW; Deleted=1;'
          'Driverid=21;Fil=dBaseIII;PageTimeout=600;'
          'Statistics=0;UID=admin;'
 /SELECT EMPLOYEE.LASTNAME,EMPLOYEE.FIRSTNAME,EMPLOYEE.ADDRESS,
          EMPDATA.DATA FROM {oj EMPLOYEE LEFT OUTER JOIN EMPDATA ON
          'EMPLOYEE'.'LASTNAME'='EMPDATA'.'LASTNAME'}.
```

- This example retrieves data from two related tables in a dBASE III database.
- The SQL select statement retrieves the employee's first name, last name, and address from the EMPLOYEE table and, if the last name is also in the EMPDATA table, the DATA column of the employee's data table will be retrieved.
- GET CAPTURE converts the data to a format used by program procedures and builds a working data file.

Data Conversion

GET CAPTURE converts variable names, labels, missing values, and data types, wherever necessary, to a format that conforms to SPSS-format conventions.

Variable Names and Labels

Database columns are read as variables.

* A column name is converted to a variable name if it conforms to SPSS-format naming conventions and is different from all other names created for the working data file. If not, GET CAPTURE gives the column a name formed from the first few letters of the column and its column number. If this is not possible, the letters COL followed by the column number are used. For example, the seventh column specified in the select statement could be *COL7*.

* GET CAPTURE labels each variable with its full column name specified in the original database.

* You can display a table of variable names with their original database column names using the DISPLAY LABELS command.

Missing Values

Null values in the database are transformed into the system-missing value in numeric variables or into blanks in string variables.

Example

```
GET CAPTURE ORACLE
    /LOGIN=SCOTT /PASSWORD=TIGER
    /SELECT EMP.ENAME, EMP.JOB,
            EMP.HIREDATE, EMP.SAL,
            DEPT.DNAME
            FROM EMP, DEPT, DEPT_SAL
            WHERE EMP.DEPTNO = DEPT.DEPTNO
            AND EMP.DEPTNO = DEPT_SAL.DEPTNO
            AND EMP.SAL = DEPT_SAL.HISAL.
LIST.
```

* The indentation of the select statement illustrates how GET CAPTURE considers everything after the word SELECT to be part of the database statement. These lines are passed directly to the database, including all spaces and punctuation, except for the command terminator (.). The LIST output from these commands may look like the following:

```
FILE:    File built with ORACLE Capture

ENAME      JOB        HIREDATE     SAL     DNAME

KING       PRESIDENT  17-NOV-1981 5500.00 ACCOUNTING
MASON      ANALYST    24-APR-1982 3910.00 RESEARCH
BLAKE      MANAGER    01-MAY-1981 2992.50 SALES
```

GET SAS

```
GET SAS DATA=file [DSET(data set)]

  [/FORMATS=file [FSET(data set)]]
```

Example:

```
GET SAS DATA='ELECT' DSET(Y1948).
```

Overview

GET SAS builds an SPSS-format working data file from a data set contained in a SAS transport file. A SAS transport file is a sequential file written in SAS transport format and can be created by the SAS export engine available in SAS Release 6.06 or higher or by the EXPORT option on the COPY or XCOPY procedure in earlier versions. (See "Tips for Creating and Moving a SAS Transport File" on p. 423.) In most instances, GET SAS retrieves data and data definition items stored in the SAS transport file, including variable labels, print and write formats, missing values, and, optionally, value labels. GET SAS automatically modifies these data definition items where necessary to conform with SPSS conventions.

Note that the terms "file" and "data set" used to describe GET SAS follow the SAS convention. A SAS data set is approximately equivalent to an SPSS data file that contains both the data values and the descriptor information.

Options

Retrieving User-defined Formats in SAS. You can specify a SAS transport file on the FORMATS subcommand to retrieve user-defined formats associated with the data being read. GET SAS retrieves user-defined formats from a data set contained in the file, either applying them as output formats or using them as value labels.

Specifying the Data Set. You can name a data set contained in a specified SAS transport file, using DSET on the DATA subcommand or FSET on the FORMATS subcommand. GET SAS reads the specified data set from the SAS transport file.

Basic Specification

The basic specification is the DATA subcommand followed by the name of the SAS transport file to read. By default, the first SAS data set is copied into the working data file and any necessary data conversions are made (see "SAS to SPSS Data Conversion" on p. 419).

Syntax Rules

- The subcommand DATA and the SAS transport file are required and must be specified first.

- The subcommand FORMATS is optional. When specified, it requires a file specification whether it is the same as or different from the file specification on the DATA subcommand.

- GET SAS does not allow KEEP, DROP, RENAME, and MAP subcommands. To use a subset of the variables, rename them, or display the file content, you can specify the appropriate commands after the SPSS working data file is created.

Operations

- GET SAS reads data from the specified or default data set contained in the SAS transport file named on the DATA subcommand.

- When GET SAS encounters an unknown format name, it inspects the data set specified on FSET. If the format exists, it is applied after any necessary modifications are made (see "SAS to SPSS Data Conversion" on p. 419); otherwise, GET SAS applies the default format for the SPSS session (see SET).

- Value labels retrieved from a SAS user-defined format are used for variables associated with that format, becoming part of the SPSS dictionary.

- All variables from the SAS data set are included in the working data file, and they are in the same order as in the SAS data set.

DATA Subcommand

DATA specifies the transport file that contains the SAS data set to be read.

- DATA is required and must be the first specification on GET SAS.

- The file specification varies from operating system to operating system. Enclosing the filename within apostrophes always works.

- The optional DSET keyword on DATA determines which data set within the specified SAS transport file is to be read. The default is the first data set.

DSET (data set)   *Data set to be read.* Specify the name of the data set in parentheses. If the specified data set does not exist in the SAS transport file, GET SAS displays a message informing you that the data set was not found. Names of the data sets in the file are then listed.

Example

```
GET SAS DATA='ELECT' DSET(Y1948).
```

- The SAS transport file *ELECT* is opened and the data set named *Y1948* is used to build the working file for the SPSS session.

FORMATS Subcommand

FORMATS specifies the SAS transport file with the data set containing user-defined formats to be applied to the retrieved data. User-defined formats in SAS may contain value labels and/or user-defined output formats. In most cases, SPSS reads in value labels, if specified, and sets user-defined output formats to SPSS defaults.

• The file specification varies from operating system to operating system. Enclosing the filename within apostrophes always works.

• FORMATS is optional. If the user-defined formats reside in the same transport file as the data, you can specify FSET directly on the DATA subcommand. The data set named on FSET must be different from that named on DSET.

• If FORMATS is omitted and FSET is not specified on DATA either, no value labels are available and all user-defined formats used in the data are set to the default for the session.

The optional keyword FSET specifies the data set containing the formats. The default is the first data set in the specified transport file.

FSET (data set)   *Data set containing formats.* Specify the data set from which user-defined formats and value labels are to be obtained. The data set name must be enclosed in parentheses. If the specified data set does not exist in the SAS transport file, GET SAS displays a message informing you that the data set was not found. Names of the data sets in the file are then listed.

Example

```
GET SAS /DATA='ELECT' DSET(Y1948)
 /FORMATS='ELECTFM' FSET(F1948).
```

• The user-defined formats reside in a different transport file. The FORMATS subcommand is required.

• FSET specifies *F1948* as the data set to read for user-specified formats.

• Value labels and formats read from the SAS transport file *ELECTFM* are converted to conform to SPSS conventions.

Example

```
GET SAS /DATA='ELECT' DSET(Y1948) FSET(F1948).
```

• The SAS transport file *ELECT* contains both the data and the user-defined formats.

• DSET specifies *Y1948* as the data set to read for input data.

• FSET specifies *F1948* as the data set to read for user-specified formats.

SAS to SPSS Data Conversion

Although SAS and SPSS data files have similar attributes, they are not identical. SPSS makes the following conversions to force SAS data sets to comply with SPSS conventions.

File Label

The file label for the SPSS file is obtained from the name specified on the LABEL option of the SAS DATA statement.

Variable Names

• Like SPSS, SAS allows variable names up to eight characters long, but the SAS naming conventions are different from those in SPSS. A SAS variable name must begin with a letter or an underscore. The underscore can be used within SPSS variable names but not at the beginning of a name. All leading underscores in SAS files are changed to the @ symbol.

• If an SPSS reserved keyword is used as a SAS variable name, SPSS appends the # symbol to the name and issues a warning message. The SPSS reserved keywords are ALL, AND, BY, GE, GT, LE, LT, NE, NOT, OR, TO, and WITH. A SAS variable named *AND*, for example, would be converted to *AND#*.

Variable Labels

SAS variable labels specified on the LABEL statement in the DATA step are used as variable labels in SPSS.

Value Labels

SAS value formats that assign value labels are read from the data set specified on the FORMATS subcommand. The SAS value labels are then converted to SPSS value labels in the following manner:

• Labels assigned to single values are retained.

• Labels assigned to a range of values are assigned to the beginning and end points of the range. For example, if SAS assigns the label *LOW* to values 1–3, in the resulting SPSS working data file the label *LOW* is assigned only to values 1 and 3.

• Labels assigned to SAS keywords LOW, HIGH, and OTHER are ignored.

• Labels assigned to long string variables are ignored.

• Labels over 60 characters long are truncated.

Missing Values

Since SAS has no user-defined missing values, all SAS missing codes are converted to SPSS system-missing values.

Variable Types

- Both SAS and SPSS allow two types of variables: numeric and character string. During conversion, SAS numeric variables become SPSS numeric variables, and SAS string variables become SPSS string variables of the same length.

- Values for SAS variables that can be identified in date format are converted to the number of seconds from October 15, 1582, to the given date. Similarly, values for any SAS variables that are clearly in date-time format are converted to the number of seconds from October 15, 1582, to the given date and time.

Print and Write Formats

SAS formats are converted to their closest representation within SPSS. Esoteric formats are converted to the default print format and the closest write format. If a numeric variable does not have a SAS format, the default SPSS format is used for both print and write formats. (The default numeric format for an SPSS session can be specified on SET FORMAT. If SET FORMAT is not specified for the session, the default numeric format is F8.2.)

Table 1 shows the correspondence between SPSS and SAS formats.

Table 1   Output format correspondence

SAS	SPSS print format	SPSS write format	Notes
BEST	default	default	
BINARYw.d	PIBHEXk	IBw.d	k=ceil(w/4)
Fw.d	Fw.d	Fw.d	
NEGPARENw.d	Fw.d	Fw.d	Prints negative numbers in parentheses in SAS
COMMAw.d	COMMAw.d	COMMAw.d	
COMMAXw.d	DOTw.d	DOTw.d	
DOLLARw.d	DOLLARw.d	DOLLARw.d	
DOLLARXw.d	DOTw.d	DOTw.d	Prints dollar format with comma as decimal delimiter in SAS
Ew.d	Ew.d	Ew.d	
FRACT	default	default	Prints n/m format in SAS
HEXw	PIBHEXw	PIBHEXw	
IBw	Fk.0	IBw	k=2w+1
OCTALw	PIBHEXk.d	PIBHEXk.d	k=3/4w
PDw	Fk.d	PW	k=2w+1
PERCENTw.d	PCTw.d	PCTw.d	
PIBw.d	default	PIBw.d	
PKw.d	Fk.d	PKw.d	k=2w+1
RBw	default	RBw	
ROMAN	F8.0	F8.0	

Table 1   Output format correspondence (Continued)

SAS	SPSS print format	SPSS write format	Notes
SSNw	Fw.0	Fw.0	
WORDFw.d	Fw.d	Fw.d	Prints numeric values as words in SAS
WORDSw.d	Fw.d	Fw.d	Prints numeric values as words and decimals as fractions in SAS
Zw	Nw	Nw	
ZDw	Zw	Zw	
$w	Aw	Aw	
$CHARw	Aw	Aw	
$ASCIIw	Aw	Aw	
$EBCDIC	Aw	Aw	
$HEXw	AHEXw	AHEXw	
$OCTALw	AHEXk	AHEXk	k=2/3w
$BINARYw	AHEXk	AHEXk	k=w/4
$VARYINGw	Aw	Aw	
DATEw	DATEw	DATEw	Minimum width for SPSS is 9
DATETIMEw	DATETIMEw	DATETIMEw	Minimum width for SPSS is 17
DAYw	DATE9	DATE9	Prints day of month in SAS
DDMMYYw	EDATEw	EDATEw	Minimum width for SPSS is 9
DOWNAMEw	WKDAYw	WKDAYw	
HHMMw.d	TIMEw+d	TIMEw+d	Minimum width for SPSS is 5
HOURw.d	TIME5.0	TIME5.0	No equivalent format for fractions of an hour in SPSS
JULIANw	JDATEw	JDATEw	
JULDAYw	JDATEw	JDATEW	
MMDDYYw	ADATEw	ADATEw	Minimum width for SPSS is 8
MMSSw.d	TIMEw.d	TIMEw.d	
MMYYw	MOYRw+1	MOYRw+1	
MONNAMEw	MONTHw	MONTHw	Prints name of the month in SAS
MONTH	MONTHw	MONTHw	
MONYYw	MOYRw+1	MOYRw+1	
NENGOw	JDATEw	JDATEw	Prints Japanese date format in SAS
QTRw	QYR8	QYR8	SPSS assumes the current year
QTRRw	QYR8	QYR8	Prints quarter in Roman numerals in SAS
TIMEw.d	TIMEw.d	TIMEw.d	Minimum width for SPSS is 5
TODw	DATETIMEw	DATETIMEw	Minimum width for SPSS is 21
WEEKDATEw	DATE12	DATE12	Prints day of week and date in SAS (day-of-week, month-name dd yy)
WEEKDATEXw	EDATE12	EDATE12	Prints day of week and date in SAS (day-of-week, dd month-name yy)

Table 1   Output format correspondence (Continued)

SAS	SPSS print format	SPSS write format	Notes
WEEKDAYw	WKDAYw	WKDAYw	
WORDDATEw	ADATE12	ADATE12	
WORDDATXw	DATE12	DATE12	
YEARw	SDATE10	SDATE10	
YYMMXw	MOYR8	MOYR8	
YYMONw	MOYR8	MOYR8	
YYMMDDw	MOYR6	MOYR6	SDATE10 if width is 6 or more
YYQXw	QYRw+2	QYRw+2	
YYQRw	QYRw+2	QYRw+2	Prints quarter in Roman numerals in SAS

Tips for Creating and Moving a SAS Transport File

Most versions of SAS are capable of creating a transport file using a machine-independent portable format. Here are some tips for creating and moving a SAS transport file with a data set containing either data or user-defined formats, or both:

- Use the SAS export engine available in SAS Release 6.06 and higher to create a transport file containing two data sets, one of data and the other of formats:

```
LIBNAME OUTLIB XPORT 'dir/filename';
PROC FORMAT CNTLOUT=format_set_name;
VALUE format_name 1='value label' 2='value label' ... ;

DATA data_set_name; INPUT var1 ...;
ATTRIB var1 FORMAT=format_name.;
CARDS;
1 ...
2 ...
...
;
PROC COPY IN=WORK OUT=OUTLIB;
SELECT data_set_name format_set_name;
RUN;
```

where `filename` is the name of the transport file, `dir` is the directory to save the transport file to, `format_set_name` is the name of the data set that will contain your formats, `format_name` is the name of a format defined on **PROC FORMAT** and later to be associated with *var1* in the data set, `value label` stands for the labels specified for numeric values 1 and so on, and `data_set_name` is the name of the data set created from the input. Note that the SAS export engine on PCs is **SASV5XPT**. Use `SASV5XPT` in place of `XPORT` if you are on a PC.

- Use the SAS export engine to write a SAS data set (either with data or with user-defined formats) into a transport format:

```
LIBNAME TRANFILE XPORT 'dir/filename';
LIBNAME OLDLIB 'dir';

PROC COPY IN=OLDLIB OUT=TRANFILE;
SELECT data_set_name;
RUN;
```

where `filename` is the name of the transport file, `dir` is the directory containing the data set file, and `data_set_name` is the name of the data set to be written into the transport file. Note that the SAS export engine on PCs is **SASV5XPT**. Use `SASV5XPT` in place of `XPORT` if you are on a PC.

- If the user-defined formats have been stored in a format library, you must create a SAS data set first:

```
LIBNAME=libref;
PROC FORMAT LIBRARY=LIBRARY CNTLOUT=libname.data_set_name;
RUN;
```

where `libref` is the name of the format library you want to convert to a data set and `libname.data_set_name` is the name of the data set containing the formats. You can now write it to a transport file.

- The SAS transport file is a binary file. When you move it through your network or to a different platform, transport it in binary mode. For example, you can FTP it with the binary switch on.

GET TRANSLATE

```
GET TRANSLATE FILE=file

[/TYPE={WK }]
       {WK1}
       {WKS}
       {WR1}
       {WRK}
       {SLK}
       {XLS}
       {DBF}
       {TAB}

  [/FIELDNAMES]*

  [/RANGE={range name }]*
         {start..stop}
         {start:stop }

  [/KEEP={ALL** }] [/DROP=varlist]
        {varlist}

[/MAP]
```

*Available only for spreadsheet and tab-delimited ASCII files.
**Default if the subcommand is omitted.

Keyword	Type of file
WK	Any Lotus 1-2-3 or Symphony file
WK1	1-2-3 Release 2.0
WKS	1-2-3 Release 1A
WR1	Symphony Release 2.0
WRK	Symphony Release 1.0
SLK	Microsoft Excel and Multiplan in SYLK (symbolic link) format
XLS	Microsoft Excel
DBF	All dBASE files
TAB	Tab-delimited ASCII file

Example:

```
GET TRANSLATE FILE='PROJECT.WKS'
 /FIELDNAMES
 /RANGE=D3..J279.
```

Overview

GET TRANSLATE creates a working data file from files produced by other software applications. Supported formats are 1-2-3, Symphony, Multiplan, Excel, dBASE II, dBASE III, dBASE IV, and tab-delimited ASCII files.

425

Options

Variable Subsets. You can use the DROP and KEEP subcommands to specify variables to omit or retain in the resulting working data file.

Variable Names. You can rename variables as they are translated using the RENAME subcommand.

Variable Map. To confirm the names and order of the variables in the working data file, use the MAP subcommand. MAP displays the variables in the working data file and their corresponding names in the other application.

Spreadsheet Files. You can use the RANGE subcommand to translate a subset of cells from a spreadsheet file. You can use the FIELDNAMES subcommand to translate field names in the spreadsheet file to variable names.

Basic Specification

- The basic specification is FILE with a file specification enclosed in apostrophes.
- If the file's extension is not the default for the type of file you are reading, TYPE must also be specified.

Subcommand Order

Subcommands can be named in any order.

Operations

GET TRANSLATE replaces an existing working data file.

Spreadsheets

A spreadsheet file suitable for this program should be arranged so that each row represents a case and each column a variable.

- By default, the new working data file contains all rows and up to 256 columns from Lotus 1-2-3, Symphony, or Excel, or up to 255 columns from Multiplan.
- By default, GET TRANSLATE uses the column letters as variable names in the working data file.
- The first row of a spreadsheet or specified range may contain field labels immediately followed by rows of data. These names can be transferred as SPSS variable names (see the FIELDNAMES subcommand on p. 430).
- The current value of a formula is translated to the working data file.
- Blank, ERR, and NA values in 1-2-3 and Symphony and error values such as #N/A in Excel are translated as system-missing values in the working data file.

- Hidden columns and cells in 1-2-3 Release 2 and Symphony files are translated and copied into the working data file.
- Column width and format type are transferred to the dictionary of the working data file.
- The format type is assigned from values in the first data row. By default, the first data row is row 1. If RANGE is specified, the first data row is the first row in the range. If FIELDNAMES is specified, the first data row follows immediately after the single row containing field names.
- If a cell in the first data row is empty, the variable is assigned the global default format from the spreadsheet.

The formats from 1-2-3, Symphony, Excel, and Multiplan are translated as follows:

1-2-3/Symphony	Excel	SYLK	SPSS
Fixed	0.00; #,##0.00	Fixed	F
	0; #,##0	Integer	F
Scientific	0.00E+00	Exponent	E
Currency	$#,##0_);...	$ (dollar)	DOLLAR
, (comma)			COMMA
General	General	General	F
+/ -		* (bargraph)	F
Percent	0%; 0.00%	Percent	PCT
Date	m/d/yy;d-mmm-yy...		DATE
Time	h:mm; h:mm:ss...		TIME
Text/Literal			F
Label		Alpha	String

- If a string is encountered in a column with numeric format, it is converted to the system-missing value in the working data file.
- If a numeric value is encountered in a column with string format, it is converted to a blank in the working data file.
- Blank lines are translated as cases containing the system-missing value for numeric variables and blanks for string variables.
- 1-2-3 and Symphony date and time indicators (shown at the bottom of the screen) are not transferred from *WKS*, *WK1*, *WRK*, or *WR1* files.

Databases

Database files are logically very similar to SPSS-format data files.

- By default, all fields and records from dBASE II, dBASE III, or dBASE IV files are included in the working data file.
- Field names are automatically translated into variable names. If the FIELDNAMES subcommand is used with database files, it is ignored.

- Field names to be translated should comply with SPSS-format variable naming conventions. Names longer than eight characters are truncated. If a field name is not unique in the first eight characters, the field will be dropped.
- Colons used in dBASE II field names are translated to underscores.
- Records in dBASE II, dBASE III, or dBASE IV that have been marked for deletion but that have not actually been purged are included in the working data file. To differentiate these cases, GET TRANSLATE creates a new string variable *D_R*, which contains an asterisk for cases marked for deletion. Other cases contain a blank for *D_R*.
- Character, floating, and numeric fields are transferred directly to variables. Logical fields are converted into string variables. Memo fields are ignored.

dBASE formats are translated as follows:

dBASE	SPSS
Character	String
Logical	String
Date	Date
Numeric	Number
Floating	Number
Memo	Ignored

Tab-delimited ASCII Files

Tab-delimited ASCII files are simple spreadsheets produced by a text editor, with the columns delimited by tabs and rows by carriage returns. The first row is usually occupied by column headings.

- By default all columns of all rows are treated as data. Default variable names *VAR1*, *VAR2*, and so on are assigned to each column. The data type (numeric or string) for each variable is determined by the first data value in the column.
- If FIELDNAMES is specified, the program reads in the first row as variable names and determines data type by the values in from the second row.
- Any value that contains non-numeric characters is considered a string value. Dollar and date formats are not recognized and are treated as strings. When string values are encountered for a numeric variable, they are converted to the system-missing value.
- For numeric variables, the assigned format is F8.2 or the format of the first data value in the column, whichever is wider. Values that exceed the defined width are rounded for display, but the entire value is stored internally.
- For string variables, the assigned format is A8 or the format of the first data value in the column, whichever is wider. Values that exceed the defined width are truncated.
- ASCII data files delimited by space (instead of tabs) or in fixed format should be read by DATA LIST.

Limitations

The maximum number of variables that can be translated into the working data file depends on the maximum number of variables the other software application can handle:

Application	Maximum variables
1-2-3	256
Symphony	256
Multiplan	255
Excel	256
dBASE IV	255
dBASE III	128
dBASE II	32

FILE Subcommand

FILE names the file to read. The only specification is the name of the file.

- On some systems, file specifications should be enclosed in quotation marks or apostrophes.

Example

```
GET TRANSLATE FILE='PROJECT.WKS'.
```

- GET TRANSLATE creates a working data file from the 1-2-3 Release 1.0 spreadsheet with the name *PROJECT.WKS*.
- The working file contains all rows and columns and uses the column letters as variable names.
- The format for each variable is determined by the format of the value in the first row of each column.

TYPE Subcommand

TYPE indicates the format of the file.

- TYPE can be omitted if the file extension named on FILE is the default for the type of file you are reading.
- The TYPE subcommand takes precedence over the file extension.
- You can create a Lotus format file in Multiplan and translate it to an working data file by specifying WKS on TYPE.

WK   *Any Lotus 1-2-3 or Symphony file.*

WK1   *1-2-3 Release 2.0.*

WKS   *1-2-3 Release 1A.*

WR1   *Symphony Release 2.0.*

WRK	*Symphony Release 1.0.*
SLK	*Microsoft Excel and Multiplan saved in SYLK (symbolic link) format.*
XLS	*Microsoft Excel, Release 4.0 or earlier. (For Excel 5 or later, use* GET CAPTURE.*)*
DBF	*All dBASE files.*
TAB	*Tab-delimited ASCII data file.*

Example

```
GET TRANSLATE FILE='PROJECT.OCT' /TYPE=SLK.
```

• GET TRANSLATE creates a working data file from the Multiplan file *PROJECT.OCT*.

FIELDNAMES Subcommand

FIELDNAMES translates spreadsheet field names into variable names.

• FIELDNAMES can be used with spreadsheet and tab-delimited ASCII files only. FIELDNAMES is ignored when used with database files.

• Each cell in the first row of the spreadsheet file (or the specified range) must contain a field name. If a column does not contain a name, the column is dropped.

• Field names to be translated should conform to SPSS-format naming conventions. They must be unique in the first eight characters and cannot have leading blanks.

• Field names that exceed eight characters are truncated.

• If two or more columns in the spreadsheet have the same field name, digits are appended to all field names after the first, making them unique.

• Illegal characters in field names are changed to underscores in this program.

• If the spreadsheet file uses reserved words (ALL, AND, BY, EQ, GE, GT, LE, LT, NE, NOT, OR, TO, or WITH) as field names, GET TRANSLATE appends a dollar sign ($) to the variable name. For example, columns named *GE*, *GT*, *EQ*, and *BY* will be renamed *GE$*, *GT$*, *EQ$*, and *BY$* in the working data file.

Example

```
GET TRANSLATE FILE='MONTHLY.WRK' /FIELDNAMES.
```

• GET TRANSLATE creates a working data file from a Symphony 1.0 spreadsheet. The first row in the spreadsheet contains field names that are used as variable names in the working file.

RANGE Subcommand

RANGE translates a specified set of cells from a spreadsheet file.

• RANGE cannot be used for translating database files.

- For 1-2-3 or Symphony, specify the beginning of the range with a column letter and row number followed by two periods and the end of the range with a column letter and row number, as in A1..K14.
- For Multiplan spreadsheets, specify the beginning and ending cells of the range separated by a colon, as in R1C1:R14C11.
- For Excel files, specify the beginning column letter and row number, a colon, and the ending column letter and row number, as in A1:K14.
- You can also specify the range using range names supplied in Symphony, 1-2-3, or Multiplan.
- If you specify FIELDNAMES with RANGE, the first row of the range must contain field names.

Example

```
GET TRANSLATE FILE='PROJECT.WKS' /FIELDNAMES /RANGE=D3..J279.
```

- GET TRANSLATE creates an SPSS working data file from the 1-2-3 Release 1A file *PROJECT.WKS*.
- The field names in the first row of the range (row 3) are used as variable names.
- Data from cells D4 through J279 are transferred to the working data file.

DROP and KEEP Subcommands

DROP and KEEP are used to copy a subset of variables into the working data file. DROP specifies the variables not to copy into the working file. KEEP specifies variables to copy. Variables not specified on KEEP are dropped.

- DROP and KEEP cannot precede the FILE or TYPE subcommands.
- DROP and KEEP specifications use variable names. By default, this program uses the column letters from spreadsheets and the field names from databases as variable names.
- If FIELDNAMES is specified when translating from a spreadsheet, the DROP and KEEP subcommands must refer to the field names, not the default column letters.
- Variables can be specified in any order. Neither DROP nor KEEP affects the order of variables in the resulting file. Variables are kept in their original order.
- If a variable is referred to twice on the same subcommand, only the first mention of the variable is recognized.
- Multiple DROP and KEEP subcommands are allowed; the effect is cumulative. Specifying a variable named on a previous DROP or not named on a previous KEEP results in an error and the command is not executed.
- If you specify both RANGE and KEEP, the resulting file contains only variables that are both within the range and specified on KEEP.
- If you specify both RANGE and DROP, the resulting file contains only variables within the range and excludes those mentioned on DROP, even if they are within the range.

Example

```
GET TRANSLATE FILE='ADDRESS.DBF' /DROP=PHONENO, ENTRY.
```

- GET TRANSLATE creates an SPSS working data file from the dBASE file *ADDRESS.DBF*, omitting the fields named *PHONENO* and *ENTRY*.

Example

```
GET TRANSLATE FILE='PROJECT.OCT' /TYPE=WK1 /FIELDNAMES
/KEEP=NETINC, REP, QUANTITY, REGION, MONTH, DAY, YEAR.
```

- GET TRANSLATE creates a working data file from the 1-2-3 Release 2.0 file called *PROJECT.OCT*.
- The subcommand FIELDNAMES indicates that the first row of the spreadsheet contains field names, which will be translated into variable names in the working file.
- The subcommand KEEP translates columns with the field names *NETINC*, *REP*, *QUANTITY*, *REGION*, *MONTH*, *DAY*, and *YEAR* to the working file.

MAP Subcommand

MAP displays a list of the variables in the working data file and their corresponding names in the other application.

- The only specification is the keyword MAP. There are no additional specifications.
- Multiple MAP subcommands are allowed. Each MAP subcommand maps the results of subcommands that precede it; results of subcommands that follow it are not mapped.

Example

```
GET TRANSLATE FILE='ADDRESS.DBF' /DROP=PHONENO, ENTRY /MAP.
```

- MAP is specified to confirm that variables *PHONENO* and *ENTRY* have been dropped.

GRAPH

This command is available only on systems with high-resolution graphics capabilities.

```
GRAPH

  [/TITLE='line 1' ['line 2']]
  [/SUBTITLE='line 1']
  [/FOOTNOTE='line 1' ['line 2']]

  {/BAR  [{(SIMPLE)     }]=function/variable specification†      }
         {(GROUPED)     }
         {(STACKED)     }
         {(RANGE)       }

  {/LINE [{(SIMPLE)    }]=function/variable specification†       }
         {(MULTIPLE)   }
         {(DROP)       }
         {(AREA)       }
         {(DIFFERENCE) }

  {/PIE                                                          }

  {/PARETO[{(CUM)  }][{(SIMPLE) }]=function/variable specification†}
          {(NOCUM)}   {(STACKED)}

  {/HILO[{(SIMPLE) }]=function/variable specification††           }
        {(GROUPED)}

  {/HISTOGRAM [(NORMAL)]=var                                     }

  {/SCATTERPLOT[{(BIVARIATE)}]=variable specification†††         }
               {(OVERLAY)  }
               {(MATRIX)   }
               {(XYZ)      }

  {/ERRORBAR[{(CI[{95}])     }]={var [var var ...][BY var]}      }
            {n }                {var BY var BY var        }
            {(STERRIR[{12}])}
                      {n }
            {(STDDEV[{2}])  }
                      {n}

  [/TEMPLATE=file]

  [/MISSING=[{LISTWISE**}][{NOREPORT**}][{EXCLUDE**}]]
            {VARIABLE  }] {REPORT   } {INCLUDE  }
```

** Default if the subcommand is omitted.

The following table shows all possible function/variable specifications for BAR, LINE, PIE, BLOCK, and PARETO subcommands. For special restrictions, see individual subcommands. In the table, valuef refers to the value function, countf refers to the count functions, and sumf refers to the summary functions.

	Simple Bar, Simple or Area Line, Pie, Simple High-Low, and Simple Pareto Charts	Grouped or Stacked Bar, Multiple, Drop or Difference Line, and Stacked Pareto Charts
Categorical Charts	[countf BY] var	[countf BY] var BY var
	sumf(var) BY var	sumf(var) BY var BY var
	sumf(varlist)	sumf(varlist) BY var
	sumf(var) sumf(var)...	sumf(var) sumf(var)... BY var
Noncategorical Charts	valuef(var) [BY var]	valuef(varlist) [BY var]

The following table shows all possible function/variable specifications for the HILO subcommand. Categorical variables for simple high-low-close charts must be dichotomous or trichotomous.

Simple Range Bar and Simple High-Low-Close Charts	Clustered Range Bar and Clustered High-Low-Close Charts
[countf BY] var	(sumf(var) sumf(var) [sumf(var)]) (...) ...BY var
sumf(var) sumf(var) sumf(var) BY var	sumf(var) sumf(var) [sumf(var)] BY var BY var
sumf(var) BY var BY var	
valuef(varlist) [BY var]	valuef(varlist) (...) ... [BY var]

Variable specification is required on all types of scatterplots. The following table shows all possible specifications:

BIVARIATE	var WITH var [BY var] [BY var ({NAME })] {IDENTIFY}
OVERLAY	varlist WITH varlist [(PAIR)] [BY var ({NAME })] {IDENTIFY}
MATRIX	varlist [BY var] [BY var ({NAME })] {IDENTIFY}
XYZ	var WITH var WITH var [BY var] [BY var ({NAME })] {IDENTIFY}

Value function:

The VALUE function yields the value of the specified variable for each case. It always produces one bar, point, or slice for each case. The VALUE(X) specification implies the value of X by n, where n is the number of each case. You can specify multiple variables, as in:

```
GRAPH /BAR = VALUE(SALARY BONUS BENEFIT).
```

This command draws a bar chart with the values of *SALARY, BONUS,* and *BENEFIT* for each employee (case). A BY variable can be used to supply case labels, but it does not affect the layout of the chart, even if values of the BY variable are the same for multiple cases.

GRAPH   435

Aggregation functions:

Two groups of aggregation functions are available: count functions and summary functions.

Count functions:

COUNT   *Frequency of cases in each category.*

PCT   *Frequency of cases in each category expressed as a percentage of the whole.*

CUPCT   *Cumulative percentage sorted by category value.*

CUFREQ   *Cumulative frequency sorted by category value.*

- Count functions yield the count or percentage of valid cases within categories determined by one or more BY variables, as in

  ```
  GRAPH /BAR (SIMPLE) = PCT BY REGION.
  ```

- Count functions do not have any arguments.

- You can omit the keyword COUNT and subsequent keyword BY and specify just a variable, as in

  ```
  GRAPH /BAR = DEPT.
  ```

  This command is interpreted as

  ```
  GRAPH /BAR = COUNT BY DEPT.
  ```

Summary functions:

MINIMUM   *Minimum value of the variable.*

MAXIMUM   *Maximum value of the variable.*

N   *Number of cases for which the variable has a nonmissing value.*

SUM   *Sum of the values of the variable.*

CUSUM   *Sum of the summary variable accumulated across values of the category variable.*

MEAN   *Mean.*

STDDEV   *Standard deviation.*

VARIANCE   *Variance.*

MEDIAN   *Median.*

GMEDIAN   *Group median.*

MODE   *Mode.*

PTILE(x)   *Xth percentile value of the variable. X must be greater than 0 and less than 100.*

PLT(x)   *Percentage of cases for which the value of the variable is less than x.*

PGT(x)   *Percentage of cases for which the value of the variable is greater than x.*

NLT(x)   *Number of cases for which the value of the variable is less than x.*

NGT(x)   *Number of cases for which the value of the variable is greater than* x.

PIN(x1,x2)   *Percentage of cases for which the value of the variable is greater than or equal to* x1 *and less than or equal to* x2. x1 *cannot exceed* x2.

NIN(x1,x2)   *Number of cases for which the value of the variable is greater than or equal to* x1 *and less than or equal to* x2. x1 *cannot exceed* x2.

- Summary functions are usually used with summary variables (variables that record continuous values, like age or expenses). To use a summary function, specify the name of one or more variables in parentheses after the name of the function, as in

```
GRAPH /BAR = SUM(SALARY) BY DEPT.
```

- You can specify multiple summary functions for more chart types. For example, the same function can be applied to a list of variables, as in

```
GRAPH /BAR = SUM(SALARY BONUS BENEFIT) BY DEPT.
```

This syntax is equivalent to

```
GRAPH /BAR = SUM(SALARY) SUM(BONUS) SUM(BENEFIT) BY DEPT.
```

Different functions can be applied to the same variable, as in

```
GRAPH /BAR = MEAN(SALARY) MEDIAN(SALARY) BY DEPT.
```

Different functions and variables can be combined, as in

```
GRAPH /BAR = MIN(SALARY81) MAX(SALARY81)
             MIN(SALARY82) MAX(SALARY82) BY JOBCAT.
```

The effect of multiple summary functions on the structure of the charts is illustrated under the discussion of specific chart types.

Overview

GRAPH generates a high-resolution chart by computing statistics from variables in the working data file and constructing the chart according to your specification. The chart can be a bar chart, pie chart, line chart, error bar chart, high-low-close histogram, scatterplot, or Pareto chart. The chart is displayed where high-resolution display is available and can be edited with a chart editor and saved as a chart file.

Options

Titles and Footnotes. You can specify a title, subtitle, and footnote for the chart using the TITLE, SUBTITLE, and FOOTNOTE subcommands.

Chart Type. You can request a specific type of chart using the BAR, LINE, PIE, ERRORBAR, HILO, HISTOGRAM, SCATTERPLOT, or PARETO subcommand.

Chart Content. You can specify an aggregated categorical chart using various aggregation functions or a nonaggregated categorical chart using the VALUE function (see pp. 434–436 for a list of available functions).

Templates. You can specify a template, using the TEMPLATE subcommand, to override the default chart attribute settings on your system.

GRAPH   437

Basic Specification

The basic specification is a chart type subcommand. By default, the generated chart will have no title, subtitle, or footnote.

Subcommand Order

Subcommands can be specified in any order.

Syntax Rules

- Only one chart type subcommand can be specified.
- The function/variable specification is required for all subtypes of bar, line, error bar, hilo, and Pareto charts; the variable specification is required for histograms and all subtypes of scatterplots.
- The function/variable or variable specifications should match the subtype keywords. If there is a discrepancy, GRAPH produces the default chart for the function/variable or variable specification regardless of the specified keyword.

Operations

- GRAPH computes aggregated functions to obtain the values needed for the requested chart and calculates an optimal scale for charting.
- The chart title, subtitle, and footnote are assigned as they are specified on TITLE, SUBTITLE, and FOOTNOTE subcommands. If you do not use these subcommands, the chart title, subtitle, and footnote are null. The split-file information is displayed as a subtitle if split-file is in effect.
- GRAPH creates labels that provide information on the source of the values being plotted. Labeling conventions vary for different subtypes. Where variable or value labels are defined in the working data file, GRAPH uses the labels; otherwise, variable names or values are used.

Limitations

Categorical charts cannot display fewer than 2 or more than 3000 categories.

Example

```
GRAPH /BAR=SUM (MURDER) BY CITY.
```

- This command generates a simple (default) bar chart showing the number of murders in each city.
- The category axis (*x* axis) labels are defined by the value labels (or values if no value labels exit) of the variable *CITY*.

- The default span (2) and sigma value (3) are used.
- Since no BY variable is specified, the *x* axis is labeled by sequence numbers.

TITLE, SUBTITLE, and FOOTNOTE Subcommands

TITLE, SUBTITLE, and FOOTNOTE specify lines of text placed at the top or bottom of the chart.

- One or two lines of text can be specified for TITLE or FOOTNOTE, and one line of text can be specified for SUBTITLE.
- Each line of text must be enclosed in apostrophes or quotation marks. The maximum length of any line is 72 characters.
- The default font sizes and types are used for the title, subtitle, and footnote.
- By default, the title, subtitle, and footnote are left-aligned with the *y* axis.
- If you do not specify TITLE, the default title, subtitle, and footnote are null, which leaves more space for the chart. If split-file processing is in effect, the split-file information is provided as a default subtitle.

Example

```
GRAPH TITLE = 'Murder in Major U.S. Cities'
 /SUBTITLE='per 100,000 people'
 /FOOTNOTE='The above data was reported on August 26, 1987'
 /BAR=SUM(MURDER) BY CITY.
```

BAR Subcommand

BAR creates one of five types of bar charts using keywords SIMPLE, COMPOSITIONAL, GROUPED, STACKED, or RANGE.

- Only one keyword can be specified, and it must be specified in the parentheses.
- When no keyword is specified, the default is either SIMPLE or GROUPED, depending on the type of function/variable specification.

SIMPLE *Simple bar chart.* This is the default if no keyword is specified on the BAR subcommand and the variables define a simple bar chart. A simple bar chart can be defined by a single summary or count function and a single BY variable, or by multiple summary functions and no BY variable (see Figure 1 to Figure 4).

GROUPED *Clustered bar chart.* A clustered bar chart is defined by a single function and two BY variables, or by multiple functions and a single BY variable. This is the default if no keyword is specified on the BAR subcommand and the variables define a clustered bar chart (see Figure 5 to Figure 8).

STACKED *Stacked bar chart.* A stacked bar chart displays a series of bars, each divided into segments stacked one on top of the other. The height of each segment represents the value of the category. Like a clustered bar

GRAPH   439

chart, it is defined by a single function and two BY variables or by multiple functions and a single BY variable (see Figure 9 to Figure 11).

RANGE   *Range bar chart.* A range bar chart displays a series of floating bars. The height of each bar represents the range of the category and its position in the chart indicates the minimum and maximum values. A range bar chart can be defined by a single function and two BY variables or by multiple functions and a single BY variable. If a variable list is used as the argument for a function, the list must be of an even number. If a second BY variable is used to define the range, the variable must be dichotomous (see Figure 12 to Figure 14).

Figure 1   /BAR=COUNT BY JOBCAT

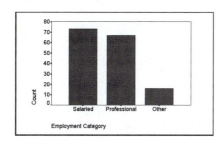

Specification: count_function BY var
                or: sum_function(var) BY var

y-axis title:	fn name [+fn var label]
y-axis labels:	fn value scale
x-axis title:	BY var label
x-axis labels:	BY var value labels

Each bar shows the number of cases in the indicated job categories.

Figure 2   /BAR=MEAN(SALBEG, SALNOW)

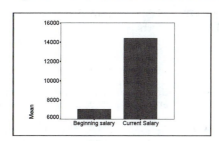

Specification: sum_function (varlist)

y-axis title:	fn name
y-axis labels:	fn value scale
x-axis title:	none
x-axis labels:	fn var labels

One bar is produced for each variable, representing the summary function of that variable across all cases.

Figure 3   **/BAR=MEAN(SALBEG) MEDIAN(SALBEG) MEAN(SALNOW) MEDIAN(SALNOW)**

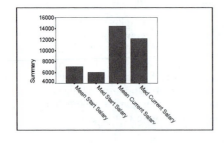

Specification: sum_function list

y-axis title:	Summary
y-axis labels:	fn value scale
x-axis title:	none
x-axis labels:	fn names +var names

One bar is produced for each summary function. The arguments can be the same or different.

Figure 4   **/BAR=VALUE(SALNOW) BY ID**

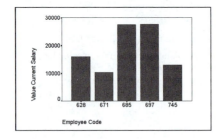

Specification: value_function(var) [BY var]

y-axis title:	value + var label
y-axis labels:	fn value scale
x-axis title:	BY var value labels
x-axis labels:	BY var label

Each bar shows the value of a single case. If no BY variable is specified, the *x*-axis title will be Case Number and the *x*-axis labels will be case numbers.

Figure 5   **/BAR=COUNT BY JOBCAT BY SEX**

Specification: count_function BY var1 BY var2
or: sum_function(var) BY var1 BY var2

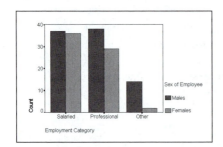

Legend title:	2nd BY var label
Legend labels:	2nd BY var value labels
y-axis title:	fn name [+var label]
y-axis labels:	fn value scale
x-axis title:	1st BY var label
x-axis labels:	1st BY value labels

Cases are broken down into categories by *VAR1* and then by *VAR2*. Each bar shows the valid number of cases or the summary function value within each subcategory.

GRAPH   441

Figure 6   /BAR=MEAN(SALBEG SALNOW) BY JOBCAT

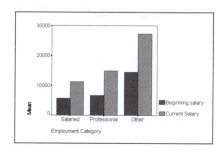

Specification: sum_function (varlist) BY var

Legend title:	none
Legend labels:	fn var labels
y-axis title:	fn name
y-axis labels:	fn value scale
x-axis title:	var label
x-axis labels:	BY value labels

The variables are broken down into categories. Within a category, each bar shows the value of the function for each variable.

Figure 7   /BAR=MEDIAN(SALNOW) MEAN(SALNOW) BY SEX

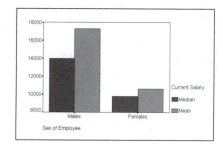

Specification: sum_function list BY var

Legend title:	fn var label (if only one fn var)
Legend labels:	fn name
y-axis title:	none
y-axis labels:	fn value scale
x-axis title:	BY var label
x-axis labels:	BY var value label

The variable is broken down into categories. Within a category, each bar shows a different function of the same variable.

Figure 8   /BAR=VALUE(SALBEG SALNOW) BY ID

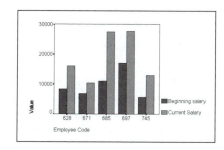

Specification: value_function(varlist) [BY var]

Legend title:	none
Legend labels:	fn var name
y-axis title:	value
y-axis labels:	values
x-axis title:	BY var label
x-axis labels:	BY var value label

Each group shows one case identified by the category variable following BY. Each bar within the case shows the value of one variable for that case.

Figure 9   /BAR(STACKED)=COUNT BY JOBCAT BY SEX

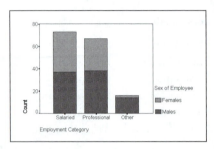

Specification: count_function BY var1 BY var2
              or: sum_function(var) BY var1 BY var2

Legend title:	2nd BY var label
Legend labels:	2nd BY var value labels
y-axis title:	fn name [+fn var label]
y-axis labels:	fn value scale
x-axis title:	1st BY var label
x-axis labels:	1st BY var value labels

Each bar represents one subcategory defined by the two category variables. The bars are stacked within each category defined by the first category variable.

Figure 10   /BAR(STACKED)=SUM(THEFT AUTO BURGLARY) BY YEAR

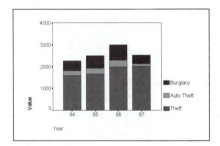

Specification: sum_function (varlist) BY var

Legend title:	none
Legend labels:	fn var labels
y-axis title:	fn name
y-axis labels:	fn value scale
x-axis title:	BY var label
x-axis labels:	BY var value labels

Each bar represents the function value of one variable broken down into categories. Bars within each category are stacked.

Figure 11   /BAR(STACKED)=VALUE(SALNOW FRINGE) BY ID

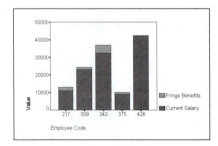

Specification: value_function(varlist)[BY var]

Legend title:	none
Legend labels:	var labels
y-axis title:	fn name
y-axis labels:	fn value scale
x-axis title:	BY var label
x-axis labels:	BY var value labels

Each bar shows the value of each variable for the indicated case. If no BY variable is specified, the *x* axis is labeled by case numbers and its title is Case Number.

GRAPH   443

Figure 12   /BAR(RANGE)=COUNT BY JOBCAT BY RACE

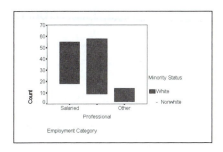

Specification: count_function BY var1 BY var2

Legend title:	var2 label
Legend labels:	var2 value labels
y-axis title:	fn name
y-axis labels:	fn value scale
x-axis title:	var1 label
x-axis labels:	var1 value labels

The height of each bar represents the difference between the two categories defined by *var2*, which must be dichotomous. The direction of difference, that is, whether nonwhite employees in each category defined by *var1* are more or less, is not shown.

Figure 13   /BAR(RANGE)=VALUE(SWI_HI SWI_LO) BY DAY

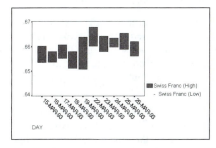

Specification: value_function(var1 var2)[BY var]

Legend title:	none
Legend labels:	var1 label–var2 label
y-axis title:	none
y-axis labels:	fn value scale
x-axis title:	BY var label
x-axis labels:	BY var value labels

The height of each bar represents the difference between the high and the low values of the day. The position of each bar shows the fluctuation over the two-week period.

Figure 14   /BAR(RANGE)=MEAN(SWI_HI SWI_LO GER_HI GER_LO CAN_HI CAN_LO) BY WEEK

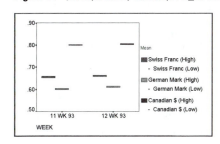

Specification: sum_function (varlist) BY var

Legend title:	fn name
Legend labels:	pairs of var labels
y-axis title:	none
y-axis labels:	fn value scale
x-axis title:	BY var label
x-axis labels:	BY var value labels

The variable list must contain an even number of variables. Each pair of variables is plotted as a separate series.

LINE Subcommand

LINE creates one of five types of line charts using keywords SIMPLE, MULTIPLE, DROP, AREA, or DIFFERENCE.

- Only one keyword can be specified, and it must be specified in the parentheses.
- When no keyword is specified, the default is either SIMPLE or MULTIPLE, depending on the type of function/variable specification.

SIMPLE   *Simple line chart.* A simple line chart is defined by a single function and a single BY variable or by multiple functions and no BY keyword. This is the default if no keyword is specified on LINE and the data define a simple line (see Figure 15 to Figure 17).

MULTIPLE   *Multiple line chart.* A multiple line chart is defined by a single function and two BY variables or by multiple functions and a single BY variable. This is the default if no keyword is specified on LINE and the data define a multiple line (see Figure 18 to Figure 20).

DROP   *Drop-line chart.* A drop-line chart shows the difference between two or more fluctuating variables. It is defined by a single function and two BY variables or by multiple functions and a single BY variable (see Figure 21 to Figure 24).

AREA   *Area line chart.* An area line chart fills the area beneath each line with a color or pattern. When multiple lines are specified, the second line is the sum of the first and second variables, the third line is the sum of the first, second, and third variables, and so on. The specification is the same as that for a simple or multiple line chart. Figure 25 to Figure 27 show area line charts with multiple lines.

DIFFERENCE   *Difference line chart.* A difference line chart fills the area between a pair of lines. It highlights the difference between two variables or two groups. A difference line chart is defined by a single function and two BY variables or by two summary functions and a single BY variable. If a second BY variable is used to define the two groups, the variable must be dichotomous (see Figure 28 to Figure 31).

Figure 15   /LINE=COUNT BY TIME

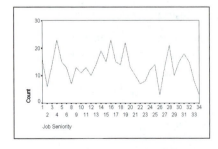

Specification: count_function BY var
          or: sum_function(var) BY var

y-axis title: fn name [+fn var label]

y-axis labels: fn value scale

x-axis title: BY var label

x-axis labels: BY var value labels

Each point on the line represents the number of valid cases for one category.

GRAPH   445

Figure 16   /LINE=MEAN(SPRING SUMMER FALL WINTER)

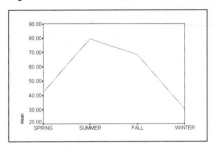

Specification: sum_function (varlist)

y-axis title:	fn name
y-axis labels:	fn value scale
x-axis title:	none
x-axis labels:	fn var labels

Each point on the line shows the function value for one variable across all valid cases.

Figure 17   /LINE=VALUE(POUND) BY DAY

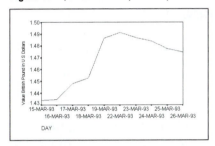

Specification: value_function (var) [BY var]

y-axis title:	value + var name
y-axis labels:	value labels
x-axis title:	BY var label
x-axis label:	BY var value labels

Each point on the line shows the value of a single case. If a BY variable is not specified, the *x*-axis title will be Case Number and the *x*-axis labels will be the number of each case.

Figure 18   /LINE=COUNT BY TIME BY SEX

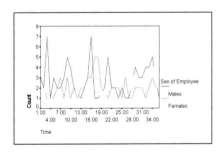

Specification: count_function BY var1 BY var2
            or: sum_function(var) BY var1 BY var2

Legend title:	2nd BY var label
Legend labels:	2nd BY var value labels
y-axis title:	fn name [+fn var label]
y-axis labels:	fn value scale
x-axis title:	1st BY var label
x-axis labels:	1st BY var value labels

Each line represents one category defined by the second BY variable. Each point on the line shows the number of valid cases for one category defined by the first BY variable. Missing values are indicated by unconnected lines.

Figure 19   /LINE=MEAN(THEFT AUTO BURGLARY) BY YEAR

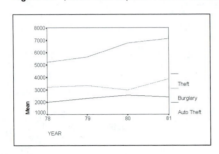

Specification: sum_function (varlist) BY var

Legend title:	none
Legend labels:	fn var labels
y-axis title:	fn name
y-axis labels:	fn value scale
x-axis title:	BY var label
x-axis labels:	BY var value labels

Each line represents one variable. Each point on the line shows the value for one category.

Figure 20   /LINE=VALUE(SALBEG SALNOW) BY ID

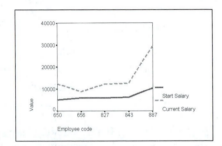

Specification: value_function (varlist) [BY var]

Legend title:	none
Legend labels:	var labels
y-axis title:	value
y-axis labels:	values
x-axis title:	BY var label
x-axis labels:	BY var value labels

Each line represents one variable. Each point shows the value of each case for the variable. If no BY variable is specified, the *x*-axis title will be Case Number and the *x*-axis labels will be the number of each individual case.

Figure 21   LINE(DROP)=NEAN (SALBEG SALNOW) BY SEXRACE

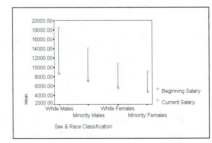

Specification: sum_function (varlist) BY var

Legend title:	none
Legend labels:	var labels
y-axis title:	fn name
y-axis labels:	fn value scale
x-axis title:	BY var label
x-axis labels:	BY var value labels

Each line represents the difference in each sex and race category between summary function values computed from the two variables. If more variables are specified, each will be represented by a symbol on the lines.

GRAPH   447

Figure 22   LINE(DROP)=MEAN(SALNOW) BY SEXRACE BY JOBCAT

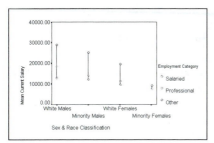

Specification: sum_function BY var BY var

Legend title:	2nd BY var label
Legend labels:	2nd BY var value labels
y-axis title:	fn name[+var label]
y-axis labels:	fn value scale
x-axis title:	1st BY var label
x-axis labels:	1st BY var value labels

Each line represents the difference in each sex and race category between job categories.

Figure 23   LINE(DROP)=COUNT BY JOBCAT BY SEX

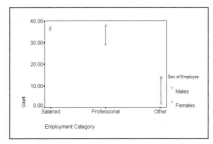

Specification: count_function BY var1 BY var2

Legend title:	2nd BY var label
Legend labels:	2nd BY var value labels
y-axis title:	fn name
y-axis labels:	fn value scale
x-axis title:	1st BY var label
x-axis labels:	1st BY var value labels

Each line represents the difference in number of valid cases in each job category between male and female.

Figure 24   LINE(DROP)=VALUE(SALBEG SALNOW) BY ID

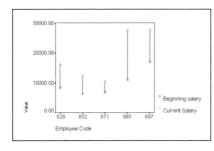

Specification: value_function (varlist) [BY var]

Legend title:	none
Legend labels:	var labels
y-axis title:	fn name
y-axis labels:	value scale
x-axis title:	BY var label
x-axis labels:	BY var value labels

If no BY variable is specified, the *x*-axis title is Case Number and the *x*-axis labels are the numbers of cases.

Figure 25   /LINE(AREA)=COUNT BY TIME

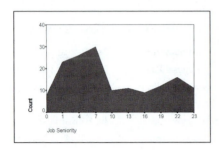

Specification: count_function BY var
or: sum_function(var) BY var

y-axis title:	fn name [+fn var label]
y-axis labels:	fn value scale
x-axis title:	BY var label
x-axis labels:	BY var value labels

The area shows the number of valid cases for categories defined by the BY variable.

Figure 26   /LINE(AREA)=COUNT BY TIME BY SEX

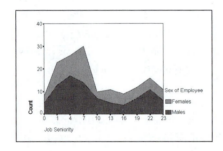

Specification: count_function BY var1 BY var2
or: sum_function(var) BY var1 BY var2

Legend title:	2nd BY var label
Legend labels:	2nd BY var value labels
y-axis title:	fn name [+fn var label]
y-axis labels:	fn value scale
x-axis title:	1st BY var label
x-axis labels:	1st BY var value labels

The two areas respectively represent the categories defined by the second BY variable.

Figure 27   /LINE(AREA)=SUM(VIOLENT PROPERTY) BY YEAR

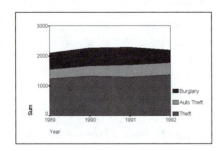

Specification: sum_function (varlist) BY var

Legend title:	none
Legend labels:	fn var labels
y-axis title:	fn name
y-axis labels:	fn value scale
x-axis title:	BY var label
x-axis labels:	BY var value labels

Each area represents one function variable.

GRAPH   449

Figure 28   LINE(DIFFERENCE)=MEAN(SALBEG SALNOW) BY TIME

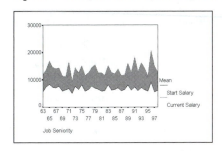

Specification: sum_function (varlist) BY var

Legend title:	fn name
Legend labels:	fn var labels
y-axis title:	none
y-axis labels:	fn value scale
x-axis title:	BY var label
x-axis labels:	BY var value labels

Figure 29   LINE(DIFFERENCE)=MEAN(SALNOW) BY TIME BY SEX

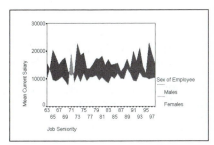

Specification: sum_function(var) BY var BY var

Legend title:	2nd BY var label
Legend labels:	2nd BY var value labels
y-axis title:	fn name [+var label]
y-axis labels:	fn value scale
x-axis title:	1st BY var label
x-axis labels:	1st BY var value labels

The second BY variable must be dichotomous.

Figure 30   LINE(DIFFERENCE)=COUNT BY TIME BY SEX

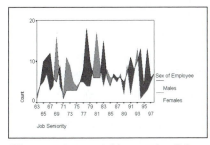

Specification: count_function BY var BY var

Legend title:	2nd BY var label
Legend labels:	2nd BY var value labels
y-axis title:	fn name
y-axis labels:	fn value scale
x-axis title:	1st BY var label
x-axis labels:	1st BY var value labels

The second BY variable must be dichotomous.

Figure 31   LINE(DIFFERENCE)=VALUE(SALBEG SALNOW) BY TIME

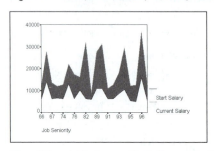

Specification: value_function(var1 var2 [BY var]

Legend title:	2nd BY var label
Legend labels:	2nd BY var value labels
y-axis title:	fn name
y-axis labels:	fn value scale
x-axis title:	1st BY var label
x-axis labels:	1st BY var value labels

If no BY variable is specified, the x-axis title is Case Number and x-axis labels are the case numbers.

PIE Subcommand

PIE creates pie charts. A pie chart can be defined by a single function and a single BY variable or by multiple summary functions and no BY variable. A pie chart divides a circle into slices. The size of each slice indicates the value of the category relative to the whole (see Figure 32 to Figure 34). Cumulative functions (CUPCT, CUFREQ, and CUSUM) are inappropriate for pie charts but are not prohibited. When specified, all cases except those in the last category are counted more than once in the resulting pie.

Figure 32   /PIE=COUNT BY JOBCAT

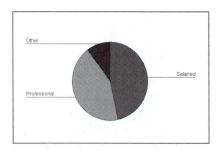

Specification: count_function BY var

Labels:	BY var value labels

Each pie slice shows proportionally the number of cases in each category defined by the BY variable.

GRAPH   451

Figure 33   /PIE=SUM(THEFT AUTO BURGLARY)

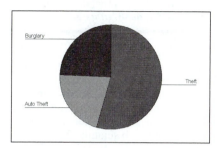

Specification: summary_function(varlist)

Labels: fn var labels

Each pie slice proportionally shows the function value for one variable.

Figure 34   /PIE=VALUE(SALNOW) BY ID

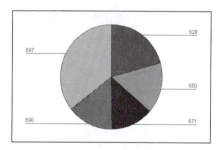

Specification: value_function (var) [BY var]

Labels: BY variable value labels

Each pie slice shows the value of one case. If no BY variable is specified, the number of each case is used as the label.

HILO Subcommand

HILO creates one of two types of high-low-close charts using keywords SIMPLE or GROUPED. High-low-close charts show the range and the closing (or average) value of a series.

- Only one keyword can be specified.
- When a keyword is specified, it must be specified in the parentheses.
- When no keyword is specified, the default is either SIMPLE or GROUPED, depending on the type of function/variable specification.

SIMPLE   *Simple high-low-close chart.* A simple high-low-close chart can be defined by a single summary or count function and two BY variables, by three summary functions and one BY variable, or by three values with one or no BY variable. When a second BY variable is used to define a high-low-close chart, the variable must be dichotomous or trichotomous. If dichotomous, the first value defines low and the second value defines high; if trichotomous, the first value defines high, the second defines low and the third defines close (see Figure 35 to Figure 37).

GROUPED   *Grouped high-low-close chart.* A grouped high-low-close chart is defined by a single function and two BY variables or by multiple functions and a single BY variable. When a variable list is used for a single function, the list must contain two or three variables. If it contains two variables, the first defines the high value, and the second defines the low value. If it contains three variables, the first defines the high value, the second defines the low value, and the third defines the close value. Likewise, if multiple functions are specified, they must be either in groups of two or in groups of three. The first function defines the high value, the second defines the low value, and the third, if specified, defines the close value (see Figure 38 and Figure 39).

Figure 35   HILO=MEAN(HIGH LOW CLOSE) BY DATE

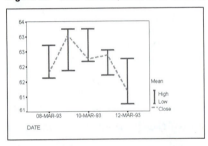

Specification: sum_function(varlist) BY var

Legend title:	fn name
Legend labels:	fn var labels
y-axis title:	none
y-axis labels:	fn value scale
x-axis title:	BY var label
x-axis labels:	BY var value labels

You can specify three variables with one summary function or three summary functions each with one variable. The line represents the close or average series defined by the function. If you specify only two, they are used as high and low values.

Figure 36   HILO=MEAN(VALUE) BY DATE BY HILO

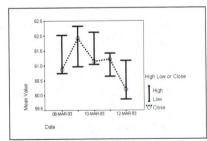

Specification: sum_function(var) BY var BY var

Legend title:	2nd BY var label
Legend labels:	2nd BY var value labels
y-axis title:	fn name+fn var label
y-axis labels:	fn value scale
x-axis title:	1st BY var label
x-axis labels:	1st BY var value labels

The second BY variable must be dichotomous or trichotomous. If dichotomous, the first value defines the high and the second value defines the low value. If trichotomous, the first value defines the high value, the second value defines the low, and the last value defines the close.

GRAPH   453

Figure 37   HILO=VALUE(HIGH LOW CLOSE) BY TIME

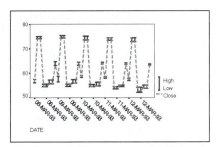

Specification: value_function(varlist) BY var

Legend title:	none
Legend labels:	var labels
y-axis title:	none
y-axis labels:	value scale
x-axis title:	BY var label
x-axis labels:	BY var value labels

The first variable represents the high value, the second, the low value, and the third, the close value.

Figure 38   HILO=MEAN(HIGH) MEAN(LOW) MEAN(CLOSE) BY DATE BY COMPANY

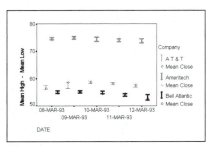

Specification: sum_function list BY var BY var

Legend title:	2nd BY var label
Legend labels:	2nd BY var value labels 3rd fn name + var label
y-axis title:	1st 2 fn names+var labels
y-axis labels:	fn value scale
x-axis title:	1st BY var label
x-axis labels:	1st BY var value labels

The function-variable specification automatically produces a clustered high-low-close chart. The function list must consist of two or three functions. If two functions are specified, they represent the high and the low; if three functions are specified, they represent the high, the low, and the close.

Figure 39   HILO=VALUE(RH RL RA) VALUE(FH HL HA)   VALUE(GH GL HA) BY WEEK

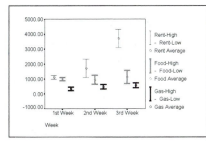

Specification: value_function list BY var

Legend title:	none
Legend labels:	var labels
y-axis title:	none
y-axis labels:	value scale
x-axis title:	BY var label
x-axis labels:	BY var value labels

Each function must have two or three variables to represent high and low values or high, low, and close values. If no BY variable is specified, case numbers are used as *x*-axis labels.

ERRORBAR Subcommand

ERRORBAR creates either a simple or a clustered error bar chart, depending on the variable specification on the subcommand. A simple error bar chart is defined by one numeric variable with or without a BY variable or a variable list. A clustered error bar chart is defined by one numeric variable with two BY variables or a variable list with a BY variable (see Figure 40 to Figure 43).

Error bar charts can display confidence intervals, standard deviations, or standard errors of the mean. To specify the statistics to be displayed, one of the following keywords is required:

CI value   *Display confidence intervals for mean.* You can specify a confidence level between 50 and 99.9. The default is 95.

STERROR n   *Display standard errors of mean.* You can specify any positive number for n. The default is 2.

STDDEV n   *Display standard deviations.* You can specify any positive number for n. The default is 2.

Figure 40   ERRORBAR=SALNOW BY SEXRACE

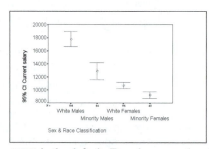

Specification: var by var

Legend title:	none
Legend labels:	none
y-axis title:	display + var label
y-axis labels:	value scale
x-axis title:	BY var label
x-axis labels:	BY var value labels

CI(95) is the default. Error bars can also display standard errors of the mean or standard deviations if you specify the appropriate keyword in the parentheses.

Figure 41   ERRORBAR=FRINGE SALBEG SALNOW

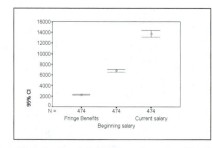

Specification: varlist

Legend title:	none
Legend labels:	none
y-axis title:	displayed statistics
y-axis labels:	value scale
x-axis title:	none
x-axis labels:	var labels

CI(95) is the default. Error bars can also display standard errors of the mean or standard deviations if you specify the appropriate keyword in the parentheses. Numbers of valid cases for each variable are displayed.

GRAPH   455

Figure 42   ERRORBAR=SALNOW BY JOBCAT BY SEXRACE

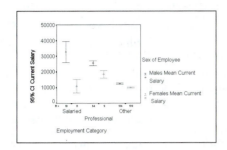

Specification: var1 BY var2 BY var3

Legend title:	var3 label
Legend labels:	var3 value labels+Mean +var1 label
y-axis title:	display+var1 label
y-axis labels:	value scale
x-axis title:	var2 label
x-axis labels:	var2 value labels

Figure 43   ERRORBAR=FRINGE SALBEG SALNOW BY SEX

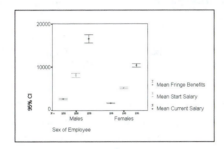

Specification: varlist BY var

Legend title:	none
Legend labels:	Mean+var labels
y-axis title:	displayed statistics
y-axis labels:	values
x-axis title:	BY var label
x-axis labels:	BY var value labels

SCATTERPLOT Subcommand

SCATTERPLOT produces two- or three-dimensional scatterplots. Multiple two-dimensional plots can be plotted within the same frame or as a scatterplot matrix. Only variables can be specified; aggregated functions cannot be plotted. When SCATTERPLOT is specified without keywords, the default is BIVARIATE.

BIVARIATE   *One two-dimensional scatterplot.* A basic scatterplot is defined by two variables separated by the keyword WITH (see Figure 44 to Figure 46). This is the default when SCATTERPLOT is specified without keywords.

OVERLAY   *Multiple plots drawn within the same frame.* Specify a variable list on both sides of WITH. By default, one scatterplot is drawn for each combination of variables on the left of WITH with variables on the right (see Figure 47). You can specify PAIR in parentheses to indicate that the first variable on the left is paired with the first variable on the right, the second variable on the left with the second variable on the right, and so on. All plots are drawn within the same frame and are differentiated by color or pattern. The axes are scaled to accommodate the minimum and maximum values across all variables.

MATRIX   *Scatterplot matrix.* Specify at least two variables. One scatterplot is drawn for each combination of the specified variables above the diagonal and a second below the diagonal in a square matrix (see Figure 48).

XYZ   *One three-dimensional plot.* Specify three variables, each separated from the next with the keyword WITH (see Figure 49).

• If you specify a control variable using BY, GRAPH produces a control scatterplot where values of the BY variable are indicated by different colors or patterns. A control variable cannot be specified for overlay plots.

• You can display the value label of an identification variable at the plotting position for each case by adding BY *var* (NAME) or BY *var* (IDENTIFY) to the end of any valid scatterplot specification. When the chart is created, NAME turns the labels on while IDENTIFY turns the labels off. You can use the Point Selection tool to turn individual labels off or on in the scatterplot. Figure 46 shows a simple scatterplot with labels turned on.

Figure 44   /SCATTERPLOT=PROFITS WITH COMPS

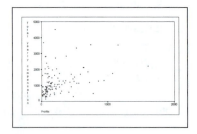

Specification: var1 WITH var2
                                    [BY var] [BY var (NAME)]

y-axis title: var2 var label

y-axis labels: scaled values

x-axis title: var1 var label

x-axis labels: scaled values

Figure 45   /SCATTERPLOT=SALBEG WITH SALNOW BY SEX

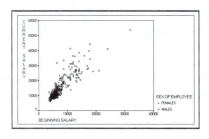

Specification: var1 WITH var2 BY var3*

Legend title   marker var (var3) label

Legend labels: marker var value [label]

y-axis title: var2 var label

y-axis labels: scaled values

x-axis title: var1 var label

x-axis labels: scaled values

*VAR3 is a marker variable. For specification of a label variable, see Figure 46.

GRAPH 457

Figure 46   /SCATTERPLOT=JOBCAT WITH SALNOW BY ID (NAME)

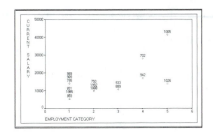

Specification: var1 WITH var2 BY var3(NAME)*

Point labels:	Label var (*VAR3)* value labels
y-axis title:	var2 var label
y-axis labels:	scaled values
x-axis title:	var1 var label
x-axis labels:	scaled values

*When keyword NAME is specified, *VAR3* serves as a label variable. For the specification of a marker variable, see Figure 45. You can specify both a marker variable and a label variable for a simple scatterplot.

Figure 47   /SCATTERPLOT(OVERLAY)=VERBAL MATH WITH AARATIO)

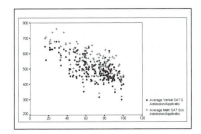

Specification: varlist WITH varlist [BY var(NAME)]*

Legend title:	none
Legend labels:	pairs of var names
y-axis title:	none
y-axis labels:	scaled values**
x-axis title:	none
x-axis labels:	scaled values**

*You can specify only a label variable after BY for an overlay scatterplot. The keyword NAME is required if a BY variable is specified.
**Values are scaled to accommodate the maximum and minimum values of each pair.

Figure 48   /SCATTERPLOT(MATRIX)=SCORE COST SFRATIO

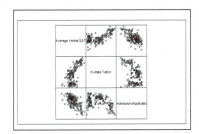

Specification: varlist [BY var] [BY var(NAME)]*

Legend title:	marker var name
Legend labels:	marker var value labels
Point labels:	label value labels
Diagonal titles:	var labels

*Matrix scatterplots can have both marker variable and label variable specifications.

Figure 49   /SCATTERPLOT(XYZ)=JOBCAT WITH SALARY WITH EDLEVEL BY SEX BY ID (NAME)

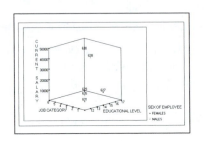

Specification:
xvar WITH yvar WITH zvar [BY var] [BY var(NAME)]

Legend title:	1st BY var label
Legend labels:	1st BY var value labels
Point labels:	2nd BY var value labels
x-axis title:	xvar label
y-axis title:	yvar label
z-axis title:	zvar label

*3-D scatterplots allow both marker variable and label variable specifications.

HISTOGRAM Subcommand

HISTOGRAM creates a histogram (see Figure 50 and Figure 51).

- Only one variable can be specified on this subcommand.
- GRAPH divides the values of the variable into several evenly spaced intervals and produces a bar chart showing the number of times the values for the variable fall within each interval.
- You can request a normal distribution line by specifying the keyword NORMAL in parentheses (see Figure 51).

Figure 50   /HISTOGRAM=RATIO

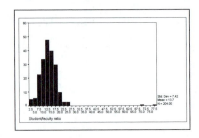

Specification: var

y-axis title:	none
y-axis label:	number of valid cases
x-axis title:	var label
x-axis label:	scaled values

The standard deviation, mean, and number of valid cases are displayed.

GRAPH 459

Figure 51 /HISTOGRAM(NORMAL)=VERBAL

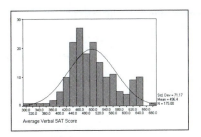

Specification: var

y-axis title:	none
y-axis labels:	number of valid cases
x-axis title:	var label
x-axis labels:	scaled values

The normal distribution line as well as the standard deviation, mean, and number of valid cases are displayed.

PARETO Subcommand

PARETO creates one of two types of Pareto charts. A Pareto chart is used in quality control to identify the few problems that create the majority of nonconformities. Only SUM, VALUE, and COUNT can be used with the PARETO subcommand.

Before plotting, PARETO sorts the plotted values in descending order by category. The right axis is always labeled by the cumulative percentage from 0 to 100. By default, a cumulative line is displayed. You can eliminate the cumulative line or explicitly request it by specifying one of the following keywords:

CUM *Display the cumulative line.* This is the default.

NOCUM *Do not display the cumulative line.*

You can request a simple or a stacked Pareto chart by specifying one of the following keywords and define it with appropriate function/variable specifications:

SIMPLE *Simple Pareto chart.* Each bar represents one type of nonconformity. A simple Pareto chart can be defined by a single variable, a single VALUE function, a single SUM function with a BY variable, or a SUM function with a variable list as an argument with no BY variable (see Figure 52 and Figure 53).

STACKED *Stacked Pareto chart.* Each bar represents one or more types of nonconformity within the category. A stacked Pareto chart can be defined by a single SUM function with two BY variables, a single variable with a BY variable, a VALUE function with a variable list as an argument, or a SUM function with a variable list as an argument and a BY variable (see Figure 54 and Figure 55).

Figure 52   PARETO(CUM SIMPLE)=SUM(DEF1 TO DEF7)

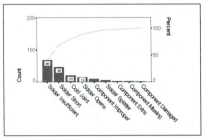

Specification: sum_fun (varlist)

Right axis title:	Percent
Right axis labels:	Cumulative percentage
y-axis title:	Count
y-axis labels:	defect count
x-axis title:	none
x-axis labels:	var labels

The data are sorted in descending order. The cumulative line is displayed. The first two defects account for over 75% of the returned products.

Figure 53   PARETO(CUM SIMPLE)=SUM(DEFECTS) BY SHIFT

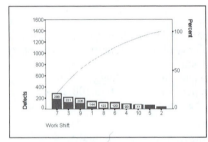

Specification: sum_fun (var) BY var

Right axis title:	Percent
Right axis labels:	Cumulative percentage
y-axis title:	fn var label
y-axis labels:	defect count
x-axis title:	BY var label
x-axis labels:	var labels

The data are sorted in descending order. The cumulative line is displayed. The work shifts 7, 3, and 9 account for 60% of the defective products.

Figure 54   PARETO(CUM STACKED)=SUM(DEF1 TO DEF5) BY SHIFT

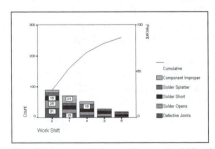

Specification: sum_fn(varlist) BY var

Legend title:	none
Legend labels:	fn variable labels
y-axis title:	Count
y-axis labels:	defect count
x-axis title:	BY var label
x-axis labels:	BY var value labels

The Pareto chart shows the work shifts that are responsible for most of the defects. It also shows the type of defects each work shift produces.

GRAPH   461

Figure 55   PARETO(CUM STACKED)=SUM(DEFECTS) BY SHIFT BY TYPE

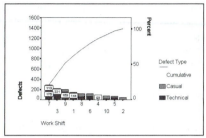

Specification: sum_fn(var1) BY var2 BY var3

Legend title:	var3 label
Legend labels:	var3 value labels
y-axis title:	var1 label
y-axis labels:	defect count
x-axis title:	var2 label
x-axis labels:	var2 value labels

The stacks are defined by the second BY variable (*TYPE*); the categories are defined by the first BY variable (*SHIFT*).

TEMPLATE Subcommand

TEMPLATE uses an existing chart as a template and applies it to the chart requested by the current GRAPH command.

- The specification on TEMPLATE is a chart file saved during a previous session.

- The general rule of application is that the template overrides the default setting, but the specifications on the current GRAPH command override the template. Nonapplicable elements and attributes are ignored.

- Three types of elements and attributes can be applied from a chart template: those dependent on data, those dependent on the chart type, and those dependent on neither.

Elements and Attributes Independent of Chart Types or Data

Elements and attributes common to all chart types are always applied unless overridden by the specifications on the current GRAPH command.

- The title, subtitle, and footnote, including text, color, font type and size, and line alignment are always applied. To give your chart a new title, subtitle, or footnote, specify the text on the TITLE, SUBTITLE, or FOOTNOTE subcommand. You cannot change other attributes.

- The outer frame of the chart, including line style, color, and fill pattern, is always applied. The inner frame is applied except for those charts that do not have an inner frame. The template overrides the system default.

- Label formats are applied wherever applicable. The template overrides the system default. Label text, however, is not applied. GRAPH automatically provides axis labels according to the function/variable specification.

- Legends and the legend title attributes, including color, font type and size, and alignment, are applied provided the current chart requires legends. The legend title text, however, is not applied. GRAPH provides the legend title according to the function/variable specification.

Elements and Attributes Dependent on Chart Type

Elements and attributes dependent on the chart type are those that exist only in a specific chart type. They include bars (in bar charts), lines and areas (in line charts), markers (in scatterplots), boxes (in boxplots), and pie sectors (in pie charts). These elements and their attributes are usually applied only when the template chart and the requested chart are of the same type. Some elements or their attributes may override the default settings across chart type.

- Color and pattern are always applied except for pie charts. The template overrides the system default.
- Scale axis lines are applied across chart types. Scale axis range is never applied.
- Interval axis lines are applied from interval axis to interval axis. Interval axis bins are never applied.
- If the template is a 3-D bar chart and you request a chart with one category axis, attributes of the first axis are applied from the template. If you request a 3-D bar chart and the template is not a 3-D chart, no category axis attributes are applied.

Elements and Attributes Dependent on Data

Data-dependent elements and attributes are applied only when the template and the requested chart are of the same type and the template has at least as many series assigned to the same types of chart elements as the requested chart.

- Category attributes and elements, including fill, border, color, pattern, line style, weight of pie sectors, pie sector explosion, reference lines, projection lines, and annotations, are applied only when category values in the requested chart match those in the template.
- The attributes of data-related elements with on/off states are always applied. For example, the line style, weight, and color of a quadratic fit in a simple bivariate scatterplot are applied if the requested chart is also a simple bivariate scatterplot. The specification on the GRAPH command, for example, HISTOGRAM(NORMAL), overrides the applied on/off status; in this case, a normal curve is displayed regardless of whether the template displays a normal curve.
- In bar, line, and area charts, the assignment of series to bars, lines, and areas is not applied.
- Case weighting status for histograms and scatterplots is not applied. You must turn weighting on or off before specifying the GRAPH command.

MISSING Subcommand

MISSING controls the treatment of missing values in the chart drawn by GRAPH.

- The default is LISTWISE.
- The MISSING subcommand has no effect on variables used with the VALUE function to create nonaggregated charts. User-missing and system-missing values create empty cells.
- LISTWISE and VARIABLE are alternatives and apply to variables used in summary functions for a chart or to variables being plotted in a scatterplot.

GRAPH   463

- REPORT and NOREPORT are alternatives and apply only to category variables. They control whether categories and series with missing values are created. NOREPORT is the default.

- INCLUDE and EXCLUDE are alternatives and apply to both summary and category variables. EXCLUDE is the default.

- When a case has a missing value for the name variable but contains valid values for the dependent variable in a scatterplot, the case is always included. User-missing values are displayed as point labels; system-missing values are not displayed.

- For an aggregated categorical chart, if every aggregated series is empty in a category, the empty category is excluded.

- A nonaggregated categorical chart created with the VALUE function can contain completely empty categories. There are always as many categories as rows of data. However, at least one nonempty cell must be present; otherwise the chart is not created.

LISTWISE   *Listwise deletion of cases with missing values.* A case with a missing value for any dependent variable is excluded from computations and graphs.

VARIABLE   *Variable-wise deletion.* A case is deleted from the analysis only if it has a missing value for the dependent variable being analyzed.

NOREPORT   *Suppress missing-value categories.* This is the default.

REPORT   *Report and graph missing-value categories.*

EXCLUDE   *Exclude user-missing values.* Both user- and system-missing values for dependent variables are excluded from computations and graphs. This is the default.

INCLUDE   *Include user-missing values.* Only system-missing values for dependent variables are excluded from computations and graphs.

IF

```
IF [(]logical expression[)] target variable=expression
```

The following relational operators can be used in logical expressions:

Symbol	Definition	Symbol	Definition
EQ or =	Equal to	NE or <>[*]	Not equal to
LT or <	Less than	LE or <=	Less than or equal to
GT or >	Greater than	GE or >=	Greater than or equal to

* On ASCII systems (for example, UNIX, VAX, and all PC's) you can also use ~=;
on IBM EBCDIC systems (for example, IBM 360 and IBM 370) you can also use ¬=.

The following logical operators can be used in logical expressions:

Symbol	Definition
AND or &	Both relations must be true
Or or |	Either relation can be true
Not*	Reverses the outcome of an expression[*]

* On ASCII systems you can also use ~; on IBM EBCDIC systems
you can also use ¬ (or the symbol above number 6).

Example:

```
IF (AGE > 20 AND SEX = 1) GROUP=2.
```

Overview

IF conditionally executes a single transformation command based upon logical conditions found in the data. The transformation can create a new variable or modify the values of an existing variable for each case in the working data file. You can create or modify the values of both numeric and string variables. If you create a new string variable, you must first declare it on the STRING command.

IF has three components: a *logical expression* (see "Logical Expressions" on p. 53) that sets up the logical criteria, a *target variable* (the one to be modified or created), and an *assignment expression*. The target variable's values are modified according to the assignment expression.

IF is most efficient when used to execute a single, conditional, COMPUTE-like transformation. If you need multiple IF statements to define the condition, it is usually more efficient to use the RECODE command or a DO IF—END IF structure.

Basic Specification

The basic specification is a logical expression followed by a target variable, a required equals sign, and the assignment expression. The assignment is executed only if the logical expression is true.

Syntax Rules

- Logical expressions can be simple logical variables or relations, or complex logical tests involving variables, constants, functions, relational operators, and logical operators. Both the logical expression and the assignment expression can use any of the numeric or string functions allowed in COMPUTE transformations (see COMPUTE and "Transformation Expressions" on p. 43).
- Parentheses can be used to enclose the logical expression. Parentheses can also be used within the logical expression to specify the order of operations. Extra blanks or parentheses can be used to make the expression easier to read.
- A relation can compare variables, constants, or more complicated arithmetic expressions. Relations cannot be abbreviated. For example, (A EQ 2 OR A EQ 5) is valid, while (A EQ 2 OR 5) is not. Blanks (not commas) must be used to separate relational operators from the expressions being compared.
- A relation cannot compare a string variable to a numeric value or variable, or vice versa. A relation cannot compare the result of the logical functions SYSMIS, MISSING, ANY, or RANGE to a number.
- String values used in expressions must be specified in quotes and must include any leading or trailing blanks. Lowercase letters are considered distinct from uppercase letters.
- String variables that are used as target variables must already exist. To declare a new string variable, first create the variable with the STRING command and then specify the new variable as the target variable on IF.

Operations

- Each IF command evaluates every case in the data. Compare IF with DO IF, which passes control for a case out of the DO IF—END IF structure as soon as a logical condition is met.
- The logical expression is evaluated as true, false, or missing. The assignment is executed only if the logical expression is true. If the logical expression is false or missing, the assignment is not made. Existing target variables remain unchanged; new numeric variables retain their initial (system-missing) values.
- In general, a logical expression is evaluated as missing if any one of the variables used in the logical expression is system- or user-missing. However, when relations are joined by the logical operators AND or OR, the expression can sometimes be evaluated as true or false even when variables have missing values (see "Missing Values and Logical Operators" on p. 466).

Numeric Variables

- Numeric variables created with IF are initially set to the system-missing value. By default, they are assigned an F8.2 format.
- Logical expressions are evaluated in the following order: functions, followed by exponentiation, arithmetic operations, relations, and logical operators. When more than one logical operator is used, NOT is evaluated first, followed by AND and then OR. You can change the order of operations using parentheses.
- Assignment expressions are evaluated in the following order: functions, then exponentiation, and then arithmetic operators.

String Variables

- New string variables declared on IF are initially set to a blank value and are assigned the format specified on the STRING command that creates them.
- Logical expressions are evaluated in the following order: string functions, then relations, and then logical operators. When more than one logical operator is used, NOT is evaluated first, followed by AND and then OR. You can change the order of operations using parentheses.
- If the transformed value of a string variable exceeds the variable's defined width, the transformed value is truncated. If the transformed value is shorter than the defined width, the string is right-padded with blanks.

Missing Values and Logical Operators

When two or more relations are joined by logical operators AND or OR, the program always returns a missing value if all of the relations in the expression are missing. However, if any one of the relations can be determined, the program interprets the expression as true or false according to the logical outcomes shown in Table 1. The asterisk flags expressions where the program can evaluate the outcome with incomplete information.

Table 1   Logical outcome

Expression	Outcome	Expression	Outcome
true AND true	= true	true OR true	= true
true AND false	= false	true OR false	= true
false AND false	= false	false OR false	= false
true AND missing	= missing	true OR missing	= true*
missing AND missing	= missing	missing OR missing	= missing
false AND missing	= false*	false OR missing	= missing

Example

```
IF (AGE > 20 AND SEX = 1) GROUP=2.
```

- The numeric variable *GROUP* is set to 2 for cases where *AGE* is greater than 20 *and SEX* is equal to 1.
- When the expression is false or missing, the value of *GROUP* remains unchanged. If *GROUP* has not been previously defined, it contains the system-missing value.

Example

```
IF (SEX EQ 'F') EEO=QUOTA+GAIN.
```

- The logical expression tests the string variable *SEX* for the value *F*.
- When the expression is true (when *SEX* equals *F*), the value of the numeric variable *EEO* is assigned the value of *QUOTA* plus *GAIN*. Both *QUOTA* and *GAIN* must be previously defined numeric variables.
- When the expression is false or missing (for example, if *SEX* equals *F*), the value of *EEO* remains unchanged. If *EEO* has not been previously defined, it contains the system-missing value.

Example

```
COMPUTE V3=0.
IF ((V1-V2) LE 7) V3=V1**2.
```

- COMPUTE assigns *V3* the value 0.
- The logical expression tests whether *V1* minus *V2* is less than or equal to 7. If it is, the value of *V3* is assigned the value of *V1* squared. Otherwise, the value of *V3* remains at 0.

Example

```
IF (ABS(A-C) LT 100) INT=100.
```

- IF tests whether the absolute value of the variable *A* minus the variable *C* is less than 100. If it is, *INT* is assigned the value 100. Otherwise, the value is unchanged. If *INT* has not been previously defined, it is system-missing.

Example

```
IF (MEAN(V1 TO V5) LE 7) INDEX=1.
```

- If the mean of variables *V1* through *V5* is less than or equal to 7, *INDEX* equals 1.

Example

```
* Test for listwise deletion of missing values.

DATA LIST   /V1 TO V6 1-6.
STRING SELECT(A1).
COMPUTE SELECT='V'.
VECTOR V=V1 TO V6.

LOOP #I=1 TO 6.
IF MISSING(V(#I)) SELECT='M'.
END LOOP.

BEGIN DATA
123456
    56
1 3456
123456
123456
END DATA.

FREQUENCIES VAR=SELECT.
```

- STRING creates the string variable *SELECT* with an A1 format and COMPUTE sets the value of *SELECT* to *V*.

- VECTOR defines the vector *V* as the original variables *V1* to *V6*. Variables on a single vector must be all numeric or all string variables. In this example, because the vector *V* is used as an argument on the MISSING function of IF, the variables must be numeric (MISSING is not available for string variables).

- The loop structure executes six times: once for each VECTOR element. If a value is missing for any element, SELECT is set equal to *M*. In effect, if any case has a missing value for any of the variables *V1* to *V6*, SELECT is set to *M*.

- FREQUENCIES generates a frequency table for SELECT. The table gives a count of how many cases have missing values for at least one variable and how many cases have valid values for all variables. This table can be used to determine how many cases would be dropped from an analysis that uses listwise deletion of missing values. See pp. 187 and 308 for alternative ways to test for listwise deletion of missing values.

Example

```
IF YRHIRED LT 1980 RATE=0.02.
IF DEPT='SALES' DIVISION='TRANSFERRED'.
```

- The logical expression on the first IF command tests whether *YRHIRED* is less than 1980 (hired before 1980). If so, the variable *RATE* is set to 0.02.

- The logical expression on the second IF command tests whether *DEPT* equals *SALES*. When the condition is true, the value for the string variable *DIVISION* is changed to *TRANSFERRED* but is truncated if the format for *DIVISION* is not at least 11 characters wide. For any other value of *DEPT*, the value of *DIVISION* remains unchanged.

- Although there are two IF statements, each defines a separate and independent condition. The IF command is used rather than the DO IF—END IF structure in order to test both conditions on every case. If DO IF—END IF is used, control passes out of the structure as soon as the first logical condition is met.

Example

```
IF (STATE EQ 'IL' AND CITY EQ 13) COST=1.07 * COST.
```

- The logical expression tests whether *STATE* equals *IL* and *CITY* equals 13.
- If the logical expression is true, the numeric variable *COST* is increased by 7%.
- For any other value of *STATE* or *CITY*, the value of *COST* remains unchanged.

Example

```
STRING GROUP (A18).
IF (HIRED GE 1988) GROUP='Hired after merger'.
```

- STRING declares the string variable *GROUP* and assigns it a width of 18 characters.
- When *HIRED* is greater than or equal to 1988, *GROUP* is assigned the value *Hired after merger*. When *HIRED* is less than 1988, *GROUP* remains blank.

Example

```
IF (RECV GT DUE OR (REVNUES GE EXPNS AND BALNCE GT 0))STATUS='SOLVENT.
```

- First, the program tests whether *REVNUES* is greater than or equal to *EXPNS* and whether *BALNCE* is greater than 0.
- Second, the program evaluates if *RECV* is greater than *DUE*.
- If either of these expressions is true, *STATUS* is assigned the value *SOLVENT*.
- If both expressions are false, *STATUS* remains unchanged.
- *STATUS* is an existing string variable in the working data file. Otherwise, it would have to be declared on a preceding STRING command.

IGRAPH

```
IGRAPH

  [/Y=[VAR(varname1)]
      [TYPE={SCALE ([MIN=value] [MAX=value])})]
            {CATEGORICAL                       }
      [TITLE='string']]

  [/X1=[VAR(varname2)]]
      [TYPE={SCALE([MIN=value] [MAX=value])})]
            {CATEGORICAL                      }
      [TITLE='string']]

  [/X2=[VAR(varname3)]]
      [TYPE={SCALE([MIN=value] [MAX=value])})]
            {CATEGORICAL                      }
      [TITLE='string']]

  [/YLENGTH=value]

  [/X1LENGTH=value]

  [/X2LENGTH=value]

  [/CATORDER VAR(varname)
    ({COUNT      }   [{ASCENDING }] [{SHOWEMPTY]})]
    {OCCURRENCE}     {DESCENDING}   {OMITEMPTY}
    {LABEL}
    {VALUE}

  [/COLOR=varname
      [TYPE={SCALE([MIN=value] [MAX=value])})]
            {CATEGORICAL                     }
      [LEGEND={ON|OFF}]
      [TITLE='string']]
      [{CLUSTER}]]
       {STACK  }

  [/REFLINE varname value [LABEL={ON|OFF}]
                          [SPIKE = {ON|OFF}]]
                          [COLOR={ON|OFF}]
                          [STYLE={ON|OFF}]

  [/STYLE=varname
      [LEGEND={ON|OFF}]
      [TITLE='string']]
      [{CLUSTER}]
       {STACK  }

  [/NORMALIZE]

  [/SIZE=varname
      [TYPE={SCALE([MIN=value] [MAX=value])})]
            {CATEGORICAL                     }
      [LEGEND={ON|OFF}]
      [TITLE='string']]

  [/CLUSTER=varname]

  [/SUMMARYVAR=varname]

  [/PANEL varlist]

  [/POINTLABEL=varname]

  [/COORDINATE={HORIZONTAL}]
```

```
                     {VERTICAL  }
                     {THREE     }

[/EFFECT={NONE }]
         {THREE}

[/TITLE='string']

[/SUBTITLE='string']

[/CAPTION='string']

[/VIEWNAME='line 1']

[/CHARTLOOK='filename']

[/SCATTER
     [COINCIDENT={NONE             }]
                 {JITTER[(amount)]}]

[/BAR [(summary function)]
     [LABEL {INSIDE }[VAL][N]]
            {OUTSIDE}
     [SHAPE={RECTANGLE}]
            {PYRAMID  }
            {OBELISK  }
     [BARBASE={SQUARE}]
             {ROUND }
     [BASELINE (value)]]

[/PIE [(summary function)]
      [START value]
      [{CW|CCW}]
      [SLICE={INSIDE } [LABEL] [PCT] [VAL] [N]]
             {OUTSIDE}
             {TEXTIN }
             {NUMIN  }
      [CLUSTER={URIGHT} [LABEL] [PCT] [VAL] [N]]]
               {LRIGHT}
               {ULEFT }
               {LLEFT }

[/BOX [OUTLIERS={ON|OFF}] [EXTREME={ON|OFF}]
      [MEDIAN={ON|OFF}]
      [LABEL=[N]]
      [BOXBASE={SQUARE}]
               {ROUND }
      [WHISKER={T    }]
               {FANCY}
               {LINE }
      [CAPWIDTH (pct)]]

[/LINE [(summary function)]
     STYLE={DOTLINE}
           {LINE   }
           {DOT    }
           {NONE   }
     [DROPLINE={ON|OFF}]
     [LABEL=[VAL] [N] [PCT]]
     [LINELABEL=[CAT] [N] [PCT]]
     [INTERPOLATE={STRAIGHT}]
                  {LSTEP    }
                  {CSTEP    }
                  {RSTEP    }
                  {LJUMP    }
                  {RJUMP    }
                  {CJUMP    }
                  {SPLINE   }
                  {LAGRANGE3}
                  {LAGRANGE5}
```

```
            [BREAK={MISSING}]]
                   {NONE    }

    [/ERRORBAR [{CI(pctvalue)}]
                {SD(sdval)   }
                {SE(seval)   }
               [LABEL [VAL][N]]
               [DIRECTION={BOTH|UP|DOWN|SIGN}
               [CAPWIDTH (pct)]
               [CAPSTYLE {NONE }]
                         {T    }
                         {FANCY}
               [SYMBOL={ON|OFF}]
               [BASELINE value]]

    [/HISTOGRAM [CUM]
                [SHAPE={HISTOGRAM}]
                [X1INTERVAL={AUTO    }]
                            {NUM=n   }
                            {WIDTH=n}
                [X2INTERVAL={AUTO    }]
                            {NUM=n   }
                            {WIDTH=n}
                [X1START=n]
                [X2START=n]
                [CURVE={OFF|ON}]
                [SURFACE={OFF|ON}]]

    [/FITLINE [METHOD={NONE              }]
                      {REGRESSION LINEAR}
                      {ORIGIN LINEAR    }
                      {MEAN             }
                      {LLR [(NORMAL|EPANECHNIKOV|UNIFORM)]
                           [BANDWIDTH={FAST|CONSTRAINED}]
                           [X1MULTIPLIER=multiplier]
                           [X2MULTIPLIER=multiplier]}
               [INTERVAL[(cval)]=[MEAN] [INDIVIDUAL]]
               [LINE=[TOTAL] [MEFFECT]]]

    [/SPIKE  {X1                         }]
             {X2                         }
             {Y                          }
             {CORNER                     }
             {ORIGIN                     }
             {FLOOR                      }
             {CENTROID [TOTAL] [MEFFECT]}

     [/FORMAT [ SPIKE [COLOR={ON|OFF}] [STYLE={ON|OFF}]]]
```

Summary function names are found beginning on p. 492.

Example:

```
IGRAPH
/VIEWNAME='Scatterplot'
/X1=VAR(trial1) TYPE=SCALE
/Y=VAR(trial3) TYPE=SCALE
/X2=VAR(trial2) TYPE=SCALE
/COORDINATE=THREE
/X1LENGTH=3.0
/YLENGTH=3.0
/X2LENGTH=3.0
/SCATTER COINCIDENT=NONE
/FITLINE METHOD=REGRESSION LINEAR INTERVAL(90.0)=MEAN  LINE=TOTAL.
```

Overview

The interactive Chart Editor is designed to emulate the experience of drawing a statistical chart with a pencil and paper. The Chart Editor is a highly interactive, direct manipulation environment that automates the data manipulation and drawing tasks required to draw a chart by hand, such as determining data ranges for axes; drawing ticks and labels; aggregating and summarizing data; drawing data representations such as bars, boxes, or clouds; and incorporating data dimensions as legends when the supply of dependent axes is exhausted.

The IGRAPH command creates a chart in an interactive environment. The interactive Chart Editor allows you to make extensive and fundamental changes to this chart instead of creating a new chart. The Chart Editor allows you to replace data, add new data, change dimensionality, create separate chart panels for different groups, or change the way data are represented in a chart (that is, change a bar chart into a boxplot). The Chart Editor is not a "typed" chart system. You can use chart elements in any combination, and you are not limited by "types" that the application recognizes.

To create a chart, you assign data dimensions to the domain (independent) and range (dependent) axes to create a "data region." You also add data representations such as bars or clouds to the data region. Data representations automatically position themselves according to the data dimensions assigned to the data region.

There is no required order for assigning data dimensions or adding data representations; you can add the data dimensions first or add the data representations first. When defining the data region, you can define the range axis first or the domain axis first.

Options

Titles and Captions. You can specify a title, subtitle, and caption for the chart.

Chart Type. You can request a specific type of chart using the BAR, PIE, BOX, LINE, ERRORBAR, HISTOGRAM, and SCATTERPLOT subcommands.

Chart Content. You can combine elements in a single chart. For example, you can add error bars to a bar chart.

Chart Legends. You can specify either scale legends or categorical legends. Moreover, you can define which properties of the chart reflect the legend variables.

Chart Appearance. You can specify a template, using the CHARTLOOK subcommand, to override the default chart attribute settings.

Basic Specification

The minimum syntax to create a graph is simply the IGRAPH command, without any variable assignment. This will create an empty graph. To create an element in a chart, a dependent variable must be assigned and a chart element specified.

Subcommand Order

- Subcommands can be used in any order.

Syntax Rules

- EFFECT=THREE and COORDINATE=THREE cannot be specified together. If they are, the EFFECT keyword will be ignored.

Operations

- The chart title, subtitle, and caption are assigned as they are specified on the TITLE, SUBTITLE, and CAPTION subcommands. In the absence of any of these subcommands, the missing title, subtitle, or caption are null.

General Syntax

Following are the most general-purpose subcommands. Even so, not all plots will use all subcommands. For example, if the only element in a chart is a bar, the SIZE subcommand will not be shown in the graph.

Each general subcommand may be specified only once. If one of these subcommands appears more than once, the last one is used.

X1, Y, and X2 Subcommands

X1, Y, and X2 assign variables to the *X1*, *Y*, and *X2* dimensions of the chart.

- The variable must be enclosed in parentheses after the VAR keyword.
- Each of these subcommands can include the TITLE keyword, specifying a string with which to title the corresponding axis.
- Each variable must be either a scale variable, a categorical variable, or a built-in data dimension. If a type is not specified, a default type is used from the variable's definition.

SCALE   A scale dimension is interpreted as a measurement on some continuous scale for each case. Optionally, the minimum (MIN) and maximum (MAX) scale values can be specified. In the absence of MIN and MAX, the entire data range is used.

CATEGORICAL   A categorical dimension partitions cases into exclusive groups (each case is a member of exactly one group). The categories are represented by evenly spaced ticks.

A built-in dimension is a user interface object used to create a chart of counts or percentages and to make a casewise chart of elements that usually aggregate data like bars or lines. The built-in dimensions are **count** ($COUNT), **percentage** ($PCT), and **case** ($CASE).

- To create a chart that displays counts or percentages, one of the built-in data dimensions is assigned to the range (*Y*) axis. The VAR keyword is not used for built-in dimensions.
- Built in count and percentage data dimensions cannot be assigned to a domain axis (*X1* or *X2*) or to a legend subcommand.
- The count and percentage data dimensions are all scales and cannot be changed into categorizations.

CATORDER Subcommand

The CATORDER subcommand defines the order in which categories are displayed in a chart and controls the display of empty categories, based on the characteristics of a variable specified in parenthesis after the subcommand name.

- You can display categories in ascending or descending order based on category values, category value labels, counts, or values of a summary variable.
- You can either show or hide empty categories (categories with no cases).

Keywords for the CATORDER subcommand include:

ASCENDING   *Display categories in ascending order of the specified order keyword.*

DESCENDING   *Display categories in descending order of the specified order keyword.*

SHOWEMPTY   *Include empty categories in the chart.*

OMITEMPTY   *Do not include empty categories in the chart.*

ASCENDING and DESCENDING are mutually exclusive. SHOWEMPTY and OMITEMPTY are mutually exclusive.

Order keywords include:

COUNT   *Sort categories based on the number of observations in each category.*

OCCURRENCE   *Sort categories based on the first occurrence of each unique value in the data file.*

LABEL   *Sort categories based on defined value labels for each category.* For categories without defined value labels, the category value is used.

VALUE   *Sort categories based on the values of the categories or the values of a specified summary function for the specified variable.* Summary functions are defined on p. 492.

Order keywords are mutually exclusive. You can specify only one order keyword on each CATORDER subcommand.

X1LENGTH, YLENGTH, and X2LENGTH Subcommands

X1LENGTH, YLENGTH, and X2LENGTH define the length in inches of the corresponding axis.

Example:

```
IGRAPH
 /VIEWNAME='Scatterplot'
 /Y=VAR(sales96) TYPE=SCALE
 /X1=VAR(sales95) TYPE=SCALE
 /X2=VAR(region) TYPE=CATEGORICAL
 /X1LENGTH=2.39
 /YLENGTH=2.42
 /X2LENGTH=2.47
 /SCATTER.
```

- Y assigns *sales96* to the dependent axis, defining it to be continuous.
- X1 assigns *sales95* to the *X1* axis, defining it to be a scale variable (continuous).
- X2 assigns *region* to the *X2* axis, defining it to be categorical.
- X1LENGTH, YLENGTH, and X2LENGTH define the length of each axis in inches.

COLOR, STYLE, and SIZE Subcommands

COLOR, STYLE, and SIZE specify variables used to create a legend. Each value of these variables corresponds to a unique property of the chart. The effect of these variables depends on the type of chart.

- Most charts use color in a similar fashion; casewise elements draw each case representation using the color value for the case, and summary elements draw each group representation in the color that represents a summarized value in the color data dimension.
- For dot-line charts, dot charts, and scatterplots, symbol shape is used for style variables and symbol size is used for size variables.
- For line charts and lines in a scatterplot, dash patterns encode style variables and line thickness encodes size variables.
- For bar charts, pie charts, boxplots, histograms, and error bars, fill pattern encodes style variables. Typically, these charts are not sensitive to size variables.

CATEGORICAL legend variables split the elements in the chart into categories. A categorical legend shows the reader which color, style, or size is associated with which category of the variable. The colors, styles, or sizes are assigned according to the discrete categories of the variable.

SCALE legend variables apply color or size to the elements by the value or a summary value of the legend variable, creating a continuum across the values. COLOR and SIZE can create either scale legends or categorical legends. STYLE can create categorical legends only.

Scale variables have the following keywords:

MIN   *Defines the minimum value of the scale.*

MAX   *Defines the maximum value of the scale.*

- The keywords MIN and MAX and their assigned values must be enclosed in parentheses.

In addition, the following keywords are available for COLOR, STYLE, and SIZE:

LEGEND   *Determines if the legend is displayed or not.* The legend explains how to decode color, size, or style in a chart.

TITLE   *Specifies a string used to title the legend.*

The following keywords are available for COLOR and STYLE:

CLUSTER   *Creates clustered charts based on color or size variables.*

STACK   *Creates stacked charts based on color or size variables.*

CLUSTER and STACK are mutually exclusive. Only one can be specified.

Example:

```
IGRAPH
 /VIEWNAME='Scatterplot'
 /Y=VAR(sales96) TYPE=SCALE
 /X1=VAR(sales95) TYPE=SCALE
 /X2=VAR(region) TYPE=CATEGORICAL
 /COLOR=VAR(tenure) TYPE=SCALE
 /STYLE=VAR(vol94)
 /SCATTER.
```

- The chart contains a three-dimensional scatterplot.
- COLOR defines a scale legend corresponding to the variable *TENURE*. Points appear in a continuum of colors, with the point color reflecting the value of *TENURE*.
- STYLE defines a categorical legend. Points appear with different shapes, with the point shape reflecting the value of *VOL94*.

CLUSTER Subcommand

CLUSTER defines the variable used to create clustered pie charts. The variable specified must be categorical. The cluster will contain as many pies as there are categories in the cluster variable.

SUMMARYVAR Subcommand

SUMMARYVAR specifies the variable or function for summarizing a pie element. It can only have the built-in variables $COUNT or $PCT or a user-defined variable name.

Specifying a user-defined variable on SUMMARYVAR requires specifying a summary function on the PIE subcommand. Valid summary functions include SUM, SUMAV, SUMSQ, NLT(x), NLE(x), NEQ(x), NGT(x), and NGE(x). The slices of the pie represent categories defined by the values of the summary function applied to SUMMARYVAR.

PANEL Subcommand

PANEL specifies a categorical variable or variables for which separate charts will be created.

- Specifying a single panel variable results in a separate chart for each level of the panel variable.
- Specifying multiple panel variables results in a separate chart for each combination of levels of the panel variables.

POINTLABEL Subcommand

POINTLABEL specifies a variable used to label points in a boxplot or scatterplot.

- If a label variable is specified without ALL or NONE, no labels are turned on (NONE).
- The keyword NONE turns all labels off.

COORDINATE Subcommand

COORDINATE specifies the orientation of the chart. Three-dimensional charts (THREE) have a default orientation that cannot be altered. Keywords available for two-dimensional charts include:

HORIZONTAL   *The* Y *variable appears along the horizontal axis and the* X1 *variable appears along the vertical axis.*

VERTICAL   *The* Y *variable appears along the vertical axis and the* X1 *variable appears along the horizontal axis.*

Example:

```
IGRAPH
 /VIEWNAME='Scatterplot'
 /Y=VAR(sales96) TYPE=SCALE
 /X1=VAR(region) TYPE=CATEGORICAL
 /COORDINATE=HORIZONTAL
 /BAR (mean).
```

- The COORDINATE subcommand defines the bar chart as horizontal with *region* on the vertical dimension and means of *sales96* on the horizontal dimension.

EFFECT Subcommand

EFFECT displays a two-dimensional chart with additional depth along a third dimension. Two-dimensional objects are displayed as three-dimensional solids.
- EFFECT is unavailable for three-dimensional charts.

TITLE, SUBTITLE, and CAPTION Subcommands

TITLE, SUBTITLE, and CAPTION specify lines of text placed at the top or bottom of a chart.
- Multiple lines of text can be entered using the carriage control character (\n).
- Each title, subtitle, or caption must be enclosed in apostrophes or quotation marks.
- The maximum length of a title, subtitle, or caption is 255 characters.
- The font, point size, color, alignment, and orientation of the title, subtitle, and caption text is determined by the ChartLook.

VIEWNAME Subcommand

VIEWNAME assigns a name to the chart, which will appear in the outline pane of the Viewer. The name can have a maximum of 255 characters.

CHARTLOOK Subcommand

CHARTLOOK identifies a file containing specifications concerning the initial visual properties of a chart, such as fill, color, font, style, and symbol. By specifying a ChartLook, you can control cosmetic properties that are not explicitly available as syntax keywords.

Valid ChartLook files have a *.clo* extension. Files designated on CHARTLOOK must either be included with the software or created using the Chart Properties and ChartLooks options on the Format menu.

A ChartLook contains values for the following properties:

- Color sequence for categorical color legends
- Color range for scale color legends
- Line style sequence for categorical style legends
- Symbol style sequence for categorical style legends
- Categorical legend fill styles
- Categorical symbol size sequence for categorical size legends
- Symbol size sequence for scale size sequences
- Categorical line weight sequence for categorical size legends
- Font, size, alignment, bold, and italic properties for text objects
- Fill and border for filled objects
- Style, weight, and color for line objects
- Font, shape, size, and color for symbol objects
- Style, weight, and color for visual connectors
- Axis properties: axis line style, color, weight; major tick shape, location, color, size.

Example:

```
IGRAPH
/VIEWNAME='Slide 1'
/X1=VAR(sales95) TYPE=SCALE
/Y=VAR(sales96) TYPE=SCALE
/X2=VAR(region) TYPE=CATEGORICAL
/COORDINATE=THREE
/POINTLABEL=VAR(division) NONE
/TITLE='Scatterplot Comparing Regions'
/SUBTITLE='Predicting 1996 Sales\nfrom 1995 Sales'
/CHARTLOOK='Classic.clo'
/SCATTER.
```

- VIEWNAME assigns the name *Slide 1* to the chart. The outline pane of the Viewer uses this name for the chart.
- Points in the chart are labeled with the values of *division*. Initially, all labels are off. Labels for individual points can be turned on interactively after creating the chart.
- TITLE and SUBTITLE define text to appear of the plot. The subtitle contains a carriage return between *Sales* and *from*.
- The appearance of the chart is defined in the Classic ChartLook.

REFLINE Subcommand

The REFLINE subcommand inserts a reference line for the specified variable at the specified value. Optional keywords are:

LABEL={ON|OFF}   *Display a label for the reference line.* For variables with defined value labels, the value label for the specified value is displayed. If there is no defined value label for the specified value, the specified value is displayed.

SPIKE={ON|OFF}   *Display spikes from the reference line to individual data points.*

Example:

```
IGRAPH
  /X1 = VAR(gender) TYPE = CATEGORICAL
  /Y = VAR(salary) TYPE = SCALE
  /BAR(MEAN)
  /REFLINE salary 30000 LABEL=ON.
```

SPIKE Subcommand

The SPIKE subcommand inserts spikes from individual data points to the specified location. Keywords for location include:

X1   *Display spikes to the* X1 *axis.*

X2   *Display spikes to the* X2 *axis.*

Y   *Display spikes to the* Y *axis.*

CORNER   *Display spikes to the corner defined by the lowest displayed values of the* X1, X2, *and* Y *axes.*

ORIGIN   *Display spikes to the origin. The origin is the point defined by the 0 values for the* X1, X2, *and* Y *axes.*

FLOOR   *Display spikes to the "floor" defined by the* X1 *and* X2 *axes.*

CENTROID   *Display spikes to the point defined by the mean values of the* X1, X2, *and* Y *variables.* CENTROID=TOTAL displays spikes to the overall mean. CENTROID=MEFFECT displays spikes to subgroup means defined by color and/or style variables.

Example:

```
IGRAPH
  /X1 = VAR(salbegin) TYPE = SCALE
  /Y = VAR(salary) TYPE = SCALE
  /COLOR = VAR(gender) TYPE = CATEGORICAL
  /SPIKE CENTROID=MEFFECT.
```

FORMAT Subcommand

For charts with color or style variables, the FORMAT subcommand controls the color and style attributes of spikes. The keywords are:

SPIKE   *Applies color and style specifications to spikes.* This keyword is required.

COLOR{ON|OFF}   *Controls use of color in spikes as defined by color variable.* The default is ON.

STYLE {ON|OFF}   *Controls use of line style in spikes as defined by style variable.* The default is ON.

Example:

```
IGRAPH
  /X1 = VAR(salbegin) TYPE = SCALE
  /Y = VAR(salary) TYPE = SCALE
  /COLOR = VAR(gender) TYPE = CATEGORICAL
  /SPIKE CENTROID=MEFFECT
  /FORMAT COLOR=OFF.
```

KEY Keyword

All interactive chart types except histograms include a key element that identifies the summary measures displayed in the chart (for example, counts, means, medians). The KEY keyword controls the display of the key in the chart. The default is ON, which displays the key. The OFF specification hides the key. The KEY specification is part of the subcommand that defines the chart type.

Example:

```
IGRAPH
  /X1 = VAR(jobcat) TYPE = CATEGORICAL
  /Y = $count
  /BAR KEY=OFF.
```

Element Syntax

The following subcommands add elements to a chart. The same subcommand can be specified more than once. Each subcommand adds another element to the chart.

SCATTER Subcommand

SCATTER produces two- or three-dimensional scatterplots. Scatterplots can use either categorical or scale dimensions to create color or size legends. Categorical dimensions are required to create style legends.

The keyword COINCIDENT controls the placement of markers that have identical values on all axes. COINCIDENT can have one of the following two values:

NONE   *Places coincident markers on top of one another.* This is the default value.

JITTER(amount) *Adds a small amount of random noise to all scale axis dimensions.* Amount indicates the percentage of noise added and ranges from 0 to 10.

Example:

```
IGRAPH
 /Y=VAR(sales96) TYPE=SCALE
 /X1=VAR(sales95) TYPE=SCALE
 /COORDINATE=VERTICAL
 /SCATTER COINCIDENT=JITTER(5).
```

- COORDINATE defines the chart as two-dimensional with *sales96* on the vertical dimension.
- SCATTER creates a scatterplot of *sales96* and *sales95*.
- The scale axes have 5% random noise added by the JITTER keyword allowing separation of coincident points.

AREA Subcommand

AREA creates area charts. These charts summarize categories of one or more variables. The following keywords are available:

summary function *Defines a function used to summarize the variable defined on the Y subcommand. If the Y axis assignment is* $COUNT *or* $PCT*, the AREA subcommand cannot have a summary function. If the Y subcommand specifies* TYPE=CATEGORICAL*, then AREA can only specify* MODE *as the summary function. Otherwise, all summary functions described on* p. 492 *are available.*

POINTLABEL   *Labels points with the actual values corresponding to the dependent axis (*VAL*), the percentage of cases (*PCT*), and the number of cases included in each data point (*N*).* The default is no labels.

AREALABEL   *Labels area with category labels (*CAT*), the percentage of cases (*PCT*), and the number of cases included in each line (*N*).* The default is no labels.

BREAK   *Indicates whether the lines break at missing values (*MISSING*) or not (*NONE*).*

BASELINE   *The baseline value determines the location from which the areas will hang (vertical) or extend (horizontal).* The default value is 0.

The INTERPOLATE keyword determines how the lines connecting the points are drawn. Options include:

STRAIGHT   *Straight lines.*

LSTEP   *A horizontal line extends from each data point.* A vertical riser connects the line to the next data point.

| CSTEP | *Each data point is centered on a horizontal line that extends half of the distance between consecutive points.* Vertical risers connect the line to the next horizontal line. |
| RSTEP | *A horizontal line terminates at each data point.* A vertical riser extends from each data point, connecting to the next horizontal line. |

BAR Subcommand

BAR creates a bar element in a chart, corresponding to the *X1*, *X2*, and *Y* axis assignments. Bars can by clustered by assigning variables to COLOR or STYLE. Horizontal or vertical orientation is specified by the COORDINATE subcommand.

summary function	*Defines a function used to summarize the variable defined on the Y subcommand.* If the *Y* axis assignment is $COUNT or $PCT, the BAR subcommand cannot have a summary function. If the Y subcommand specifies TYPE=CATEGORICAL, then BAR can specify only MODE as the summary function. Otherwise, all summary functions described on p. 492 are available.
LABEL	*Bars can be labeled with the actual values corresponding to the dependent axis* (VAL) *or with the number of cases included in each bar* (N). The default is no labels. The placement of the labels is inside the bars (INSIDE) or outside the bars (OUTSIDE).
SHAPE	*Determines whether the bars are drawn as rectangles* (RECTANGLE), *pyramids* (PYRAMID), *or obelisks* (OBELISK). The default is rectangular bars.
BARBASE	*For three-dimensional bars, the base can be round* (ROUND) *or square* (SQUARE). The default is square.
BASELINE	*The baseline value determines the location from which the bars will hang (vertical) or extend (horizontal).* The default value is 0.

Example:

```
IGRAPH
 /X1=VAR(volume96) TYPE=CATEGORICAL
 /Y=$count
 /COORDINATE=VERTICAL
 /EFFECT=THREE
 /BAR LABEL INSIDE N SHAPE=RECTANGLE.
```

- X1 assigns the categorical variable *volume96* to the *X1* axis.
- Y assigns the built-in dimension *$count* to the range axis.
- VERTICAL defines the counts to appear along the vertical dimension.
- BAR adds a bar element to the chart.
- LABEL labels the bars in the chart with the number of cases included in the bars. These labels appear inside the bars.

- SHAPE indicates that the bars are rectangles. However, EFFECT adds a third dimension to the chart, yielding three-dimensional solids.

Example:

```
IGRAPH
/X1=VAR(volume94) TYPE=CATEGORICAL
/Y=VAR(sales96) TYPE=SCALE
/COORDINATE=HORIZONTAL
/EFFECT=NONE
/BAR (MEAN) LABEL OUTSIDE VAL SHAPE=PYRAMID BASELINE=370.00.
```

- X1 assigns the categorical variable *volume94* to the *X1* axis.
- Y assigns the scale variable *sales96* to the range axis.
- HORIZONTAL defines *sales96* to appear along the horizontal dimension.
- EFFECT defines the chart as two-dimensional.
- BAR adds a bar element to the chart.
- MEAN defines the summary function to apply to *sales96*. Each bar represents the mean *sales96* value for the corresponding category of *volume94*.
- LABEL labels the bars in the chart with the mean *sales96* value. These labels appear outside the bars.
- SHAPE indicates that the bars are pyramids.
- BASELINE indicates that bars should extend from 370. Any bar with a mean value above 370 extends to the right. Any bar with a mean value below 370 extends to the left.

PIE Subcommand

A simple pie chart summarizes categories defined by a single variable or by a group of related variables. A clustered pie chart contains a cluster of simple pies, all of which are stacked into categories by the same variable. The pies are of different sizes and appear to be stacked on top of one another. The cluster contains as many pies as there are categories in the cluster variable. For both simple and clustered pie charts, the size of each slice represents the count, the percentage, or a summary function of a variable.

The following keywords are available:

summary function	*Defines a function used to summarize the variable defined on the* SUMMARYVAR *subcommand.* If the SUMMARYVAR assignment is $COUNT or $PCT, the PIE subcommand cannot have a summary function. Otherwise, of the summary functions described on p. 492, SUM, SUMAV, SUMSQ, NGT(x), NLE(x), NEQ(x), NGE(x), NGT(x), and NIN(x1,x2) are available.
START num	*Indicates the starting position of the smallest slice of the pie chart.* Any integer can be specified for num. The value is converted to a number between 0 and 360, which represents the degree of rotation of the smallest slice.

CW I CCW	*Sets the positive rotation of the pie to either clockwise (CW) or counterclockwise (CCW).* The default rotation is clockwise.
SLICE	*Sets the labeling characteristics for the slices of the pie.* The pie slices can be labeled with the category labels (LABEL), the category percentages (PCT), the number of cases (N), and the category values (VAL). Label position is either all labels inside the pie (INSIDE), all labels outside the pie (OUTSIDE), text labels inside the pie with numeric labels outside (TEXTIN), or numeric labels inside the pie with text labels outside (NUMIN).
CLUSTER	*Sets the labeling characteristics for the pies from clusters.* The pies can be labeled with the category labels (LABEL), the category percentages (PCT), the number of cases (N), and the category values (VAL). Label position is either upper left (ULEFT), upper right (URIGHT), lower left (LLEFT), or lower right (LRIGHT) of the figure.

Example:

```
IGRAPH
 /SUMMARYVAR=$count
 /COLOR=VAR(volume96) TYPE=CATEGORICAL
 /EFFECT=THREE
 /PIE START 180 CW SLICE=TEXTIN LABEL PCT N.
```

- The pie slices represent the number of cases (SUMMARYVAR=$count) in each category of *volume96* (specified on the COLOR subcommand).
- EFFECT yields a pie chart with an additional third dimension.
- PIE creates a pie chart.
- The first slice begins at 180 degrees and the rotation of the pie is clockwise.
- SLICE labels the slices with category labels, the percentage in each category, and the number of cases in each category. TEXTIN places the text labels (category labels) inside the pie slices and the numeric labels outside.

Example:

```
IGRAPH
 /SUMMARYVAR=VAR(sales96)
 /COLOR=VAR(volume95) TYPE=CATEGORICAL
 /X1=VAR(region) TYPE=CATEGORICAL
 /Y=VAR(division) TYPE=CATEGORICAL
 /COORDINATE=VERTICAL
 /PIE (SUM) START 0 CW SLICE=INSIDE VAL.
```

- The pie slices represent the sums of *sales96* values for each category of *volume95* (specified on the COLOR subcommand).
- X1 and Y define two axes representing *region* and *division*. A pie chart is created for each combination of these variables.
- The first slice in each pie begins at 0 degrees and the rotation of the pie is clockwise.
- SUM indicates the summary function applied to the summary variable, *sales96*. The pie slices represent the sum of the *sales96* values.

- SLICE labels the slices with the value of the summary function. INSIDE places the labels inside the pie slices.

BOX Subcommand

BOX creates a boxplot, sometimes called a box-and-whiskers plot, showing the median, quartiles, and outlier and extreme values for a scale variable. The interquartile range (IQR) is the difference between the 75th and 25th percentiles and corresponds to the length of the box.

The following keywords are available:

OUTLIERS	*Indicates whether outliers should be displayed.* Outliers are values between 1.5 IQR's and 3 IQR's from the end of a box. By default, the boxplot displays outliers (ON).
EXTREME	*Indicates whether extreme values should be displayed.* Values more than 3 IQR's from the end of a box are defined as extreme. By default, the boxplot displays extreme values (ON).
MEDIAN	*Indicates whether a line representing the median should be included in the box.* By default, the boxplot displays the median line (ON).
LABEL	*Displays the number of cases (N) represented by each box.*
BOXBASE	*Controls the shape of the box for three dimensional plots.* SQUARE results in rectangular solids. ROUND yields cylinders.
WHISKER	*Controls the appearance of the whiskers.* Whiskers can be straight lines (LINE), end in a *T*-shape (T), or end in a fancy *T*-shape (FANCY). Fancy whiskers are unavailable for three-dimensional boxplots.
CAPWIDTH(pct)	*Controls the width of the whisker cap relative to the corresponding box.* Pct equals the percentage of the box width. The default value for pct is 45.

Example:

```
IGRAPH
/X1=VAR(region) TYPE=CATEGORICAL
/Y=VAR(sales96) TYPE=SCALE
/COORDINATE=HORIZONTAL
/BOX OUTLIERS=ON EXTREME=ON MEDIAN=ON WHISKER=FANCY.
```

- X1 assigns the variable *region* to the *X1* axis.
- Y assigns the variable *sales96* to the range axis.
- COORDINATE positions the range axis along the horizontal dimension.
- BOX creates a boxplot. The outliers and extreme vales are shown. In addition, a line representing the median is added to the box.
- WHISKER yields whiskers ending in a fancy *T*.

Example:

```
IGRAPH
 /X1=VAR(region) TYPE=CATEGORICAL
 /Y=VAR(sales96) TYPE=SCALE
 /X2=VAR(division) TYPE=CATEGORICAL
 /COORDINATE=THREE
 /BOX OUTLIERS=OFF EXTREME=ON MEDIAN=OFF LABEL=N BOXBASE=ROUND WHISKER=T.
```

- X2 adds a third dimension, corresponding to *division*, to the boxplot in the previous example.
- COORDINATE indicates that the chart displays the third dimension.
- BOX creates a boxplot without outliers or a median line. Extreme values are shown.
- LABEL labels each box with the number of cases represented by each box.
- BOXBASE defines the three-dimensional representation of the boxes to be cylindrical.

LINE Subcommand

LINE creates line charts, dot charts, and ribbon charts. These charts summarize categories of one or more variables. Line charts tend to emphasize flow or movement instead of individual values. They are commonly used to display data over time and therefore can be used to give a good sense of trends. A ribbon chart is similar to a line chart, with the lines displayed as ribbons in a third dimension. Ribbon charts can either have two dimensions displayed with a 3-D effect, or they can have three dimensions.

The following keywords are available:

summary function	*Defines a function used to summarize the variable defined on the* Y *subcommand. If the Y axis assignment is* $COUNT *or* $PCT*, the* LINE *subcommand cannot have a summary function. If the Y subcommand specifies* TYPE=CATEGORICAL*, then* LINE *can specify only* MODE *as the summary function. Otherwise, all summary functions described on p. 492 are available.*
STYLE	*Chart can include dots and lines (*DOTLINE*), lines only (*LINE*), or dots only (*DOT*). The keyword* NONE *creates an empty chart.*
DROPLINE	*Indicates whether drop lines between points having the same value of a variable are included in the chart (*ON*) or not (*OFF*). To include drop lines, specify a categorical variable on the* STYLE*,* COLOR*, or* SIZE *subcommands.*
LABEL	*Labels points with the actual values corresponding to the dependent axis (*VAL*), the percentage of cases (*PCT*), and the number of cases included in each data point (*N*). The default is no labels.*
LINELABEL	*Labels lines with category labels (*CAT*), the percentage of cases (*PCT*), and the number of cases included in each line (*N*). The default is no labels.*
BREAK	*Indicates whether the lines break at missing values (*MISSING*) or not (*NONE*).*

The INTERPOLATE keyword determines how the lines connecting the points are drawn. Options include:

STRAIGHT   *Straight lines.*

LSTEP   *A horizontal line extends from each data point.* A vertical riser connects the line to the next data point.

CSTEP   *Each data point is centered on a horizontal line that extends half of the distance between consecutive points.* Vertical risers connect the line to the next horizontal line.

RSTEP   *A horizontal line terminates at each data point.* A vertical riser extends from each data point, connecting to the next horizontal line.

LJUMP   *A horizontal line extends from each data point.* No vertical risers connect the lines to the points.

RJUMP   *A horizontal line terminates at each data point.* No vertical risers connect the points to the next horizontal line.

CJUMP   *A horizontal line is centered at each data point, extending half of the distance between consecutive points.* No vertical risers connect the lines.

SPLINE   *Connects data points with a cubic spline.*

LAGRANGE3   *Connects data points with third-order Lagrange interpolations, in which a third-order polynomial is fit to the nearest four points.*

LAGRANGE5   *Connects data points with fifth-order Lagrange interpolations, in which a fifth-order polynomial is fit to the nearest six points.*

Example:

```
IGRAPH
/X1=VAR(volume95) TYPE=CATEGORICAL
/Y=VAR(sales96) TYPE=SCALE
/COLOR=VAR(volume94) TYPE=CATEGORICAL
/COORDINATE=VERTICAL
/LINE (MEAN) STYLE=LINE DROPLINE=ON LABEL VAL
        INTERPOLATE=STRAIGHT BREAK=MISSING.
```

- LINE creates a line chart. The lines represent the mean value of *sales96* for each category of *volume95*.

- The chart contains a line for each category of *volume94*, with droplines connecting the lines at each category of *volume95*.

- LABEL labels the lines with the mean *sales96* value for each category of *volume95*.

- INTERPOLATE specifies that straight lines connect the mean *sales96* values across the *volume95* categories.

- BREAK indicates that the lines will break at any missing values.

ERRORBAR Subcommand

Error bars help you to visualize distributions and dispersion by indicating the variability of the measure being displayed. The mean of a scale variable is plotted for a set of categories, and the length of an error bar on either side of the mean value indicates a confidence interval or a specified number of standard errors or standard deviations. Error bars can extend in one direction or in both directions from the mean. Error bars are sometimes displayed in the same chart with other chart elements, such as bars.

One of the following three keywords indicating the statistic and percentage/multiplier applied to the error bars must be specified:

CI(Pct)   *Error bars represent confidence intervals.* Pct indicates the level of confidence and varies from 0 to 100.

SD(sdval)   *Error bars represent standard deviations.* Sdval indicates how many standard deviations above and below the mean the error bars extend. Sdval must between 0 and 6.

SE(seval)   *Error bars represent standard errors.* Seval indicates how many standard errors above and below the mean the error bars extend. Seval must between 0 and 6.

In addition, the following keywords can be specified:

LABEL   *Labels error bars with means (VAL) and the number of cases (N).*

DIRECTION   *Error bars can extend both above and below the mean values (BOTH), only above the mean values (UP), only below the mean values (DOWN), or above for error bars above the baseline and below for error bars below the baseline (SIGN).*

CAPSTYLE   *For error bars, the style can be T-shaped (T), no cap (NONE), or a cap with end pieces (FANCY). The default style is T-shaped.*

SYMBOL   *Displays the mean marker (ON). For no symbol, specify OFF.*

BASELINE val   *Defines the value (val) above which the error bars extend above the bars and below which the error bars extend below the bars.*

CAPWIDTH(pct) *Controls the width of the cap relative to the distance between categories. Pct equals the percent of the distance. The default value for pct is 45.*

Example:

```
IGRAPH
/X1=VAR(volume94) TYPE=CATEGORICAL
/Y=VAR(sales96) TYPE=SCALE
/BAR (MEAN) LABEL INSIDE VAL SHAPE=RECTANGLE BASELINE=0.00
/ERRORBAR SE(2.0) DIRECTION=BOTH CAPWIDTH (45) CAPSTYLE=FANCY.
```

- BAR creates a bar chart with rectangular bars. The bars represent the mean *sales96* values for the *volume94* categories.

- ERRORBAR adds error bars to the bar chart. The error bars extend two standard errors above and below the mean.

HISTOGRAM Subcommand

HISTOGRAM creates a histogram element in a chart, corresponding to the *X1*, *X2*, and *Y* axis assignments. Horizontal or vertical orientation is specified by the COORDINATE subcommand. A histogram groups the values of a variable into evenly spaced groups (intervals or bins) and plots a count of the number of cases in each group. The count can be expressed as a percentage. Percentages are useful for comparing data sets of different sizes. The count or percentage can also be accumulated across the groups.

- $COUNT or $PCT must be specified on the Y subcommand.

The following keywords are available:

SHAPE	*Defines the shape of the histogram.* Currently, the only value for SHAPE is HISTOGRAM.
CUM	*Specifies a cumulative histogram.* Counts or percentages are aggregated across the values of the domain variables.
X1INTERVAL	*Intervals on the* X1 *axis can be set automatically, or you can specify the number of intervals (1 to 250) along the axis* (NUM) *or the width of an interval* (WIDTH).
X2INTERVAL	*Intervals on the* X2 *axis can be set automatically, or you can specify the number of intervals (1 to 250) along the axis* (NUM) *or the width of an interval* (WIDTH).
CURVE	*Superimposes a normal curve on a 2-D histogram.* The normal curve has the same mean and variance as the data.
X1START	*The starting point along the* X1 *axis.* Indicates the percentage of an interval width above the minimum value along the *X1* axis at which to begin the histogram. The value can range from 0 to 99.
X2START	*The starting point along the* X2 *axis.* Indicates the percentage of an interval width above the minimum value along the *X2* axis at which to begin the histogram. The value can range from 0 to 99.

Example:

```
IGRAPH
/X1=VAR(sales96) TYPE=SCALE
/Y=$count
/Histogram SHAPE=HISTOGRAM CURVE=ON X1INTERVAL WIDTH=100.
```

- Histogram creates a histogram of *sales96*. The *sales96* intervals are 100 units wide.
- CURVE superimposes a normal curve on the histogram.

FITLINE Subcommand

FITLINE adds a line or surface to a scatterplot to help you discern the relationship shown in the plot. The following general methods are available:

NONE	*No line is fit.*

REGRESSION   *Fits a straight line (or surface) using ordinary least squares.* Must be followed by the keyword LINEAR.

ORIGIN   *Fits a straight line (or surface) through the origin.* Must be followed by the keyword LINEAR.

MEAN   *For a 2-D chart, fits a line at the mean of the dependent (Y) variable.* For a 3-D chart, the *Y* mean is shown as a plane.

LLR   *Fits a local linear regression curve or surface.* A normal (NORMAL) kernel is the default. With EPANECHNIKOV, the curve is not as smooth as with a normal kernel and is smoother than with a uniform (UNIFORM) kernel. (For more information, see Simonoff, J. S. 1966. *Smoothing methods in statistics.* New York: Springer-Verlag.)

The keyword LINE indicates the number of fit lines. TOTAL fits the line to all of the cases. MEFFECT fits a separate line to the data for each value of a legend variable.

The REGRESSION, ORIGIN, and MEAN methods offer the option of including prediction intervals with the following keyword:

INTERVAL[(cval)]   *The intervals are based on the mean* (MEAN) *or on the individual cases* (INDIVIDUAL). Cval indicates the size of the interval and ranges from 50 to 100.

The local linear regression (LLR) smoother offers the following controls for the smoothing process:

BANDWIDTH   *Constrains the bandwidth to be constant across subgroups or panels* (CONSTRAINED). The default is unconstrained (FAST).

X1MULTIPLIER   *Specifies the bandwidth multiplier for the X1 axis.* The bandwidth multiplier changes the amount of data that is included in each calculation of a small part of the smoother. The multiplier can be adjusted to emphasize specific features of the plot that are of interest. Any positive multiplier (including fractions) is allowed. The larger the multiplier, the smoother the curve. The range between 0 and 10 should suffice in most applications.

X2MULTIPLIER   *Specifies the bandwidth multiplier for the X2 axis.* The bandwidth multiplier changes the amount of data that is included in each calculation of a small part of the smoother. The multiplier can be adjusted to emphasize specific features of the plot that are of interest. Any positive multiplier (including fractions) is allowed. The larger the multiplier, the smoother the curve. The range between 0 and 10 should suffice in most applications.

Example:

```
IGRAPH
/X1=VAR(sales95) TYPE=SCALE
/Y=VAR(sales96) TYPE=SCALE
/COLOR=VAR(region) TYPE=CATEGORICAL
/SCATTER
/FITLINE METHOD=LLR EPANECHNIKOV BANDWIDTH=CONSTRAINED
        X1MULTIPLIER=2.00 LINE=MEFFECT.
```

- SCATTER creates a scatterplot of *sales95* and *sales96*.
- FITLINE adds a local linear regression smoother to the scatterplot. The Epanechnikov smoother is used with an *X1* multiplier of 2. A separate line is fit for each category of region and the bandwidth is constrained to be equal across region categories.

Summary Functions

Summary functions apply to scale variables selected for a dependent axis or a slice summary. Percentages are based on the specified percent base. For a slice summary, only summary functions appropriate for the type of chart are available.

The following summary functions are available:

First Values (FIRST). The value found in the first case for each category in the data file at the time the summary was defined.

Kurtosis (KURTOSIS). A measure of the extent to which observations cluster around a central point. For a normal distribution, the value of the kurtosis statistic is 0. Positive kurtosis indicates that the observations cluster more and have longer tails than those in the normal distribution, and negative kurtosis indicates the observations cluster less and have shorter tails.

Last Values (LAST). The value found in the last case for each category in the data file at the time the summary was defined.

Maximum Values (MAXIMUM). The largest value for each category.

Minimum Values (MINIMUM). The smallest value within the category.

Means (MEAN). The arithmetic average for each category.

Medians (MEDIAN). The values below which half of the cases fall in each category.

Modes (MODE). The most frequently occurring value within each category.

Number of Cases Above (NGT(x)). The number of cases having values above the specified value.

Number of Cases Between (NIN(x1,x2)). The number of cases between two specified values.

Number of Cases Equal to (NEQ(x)). The number of cases equal to the specified value.

Number of Cases Greater Than or Equal to (NGE(x)). The number of cases having values above or equal to the specified value.

Number of Cases Less Than (NLT(x)). The number of cases below the specified value.

Number of Cases Less Than or Equal to (NLE(x)). The number of cases below or equal to the specified value.

Percentage of Cases Above (PGT(x)). The percentage of cases having values above the specified value.

Percentage of Cases Between (PIN(x1,x2)). The percentage of cases between two specified values.

Percentage of Cases Equal to (PEQ(x)). The percentage of cases equal to the specified value.

Percentage of Cases Greater Than or Equal to (PGE(x)). The percentage of cases having values above or equal to the specified value.

Percentage of Cases Less Than (PLT(x)). The percentage of cases having values below the specified value.

Percentage of Cases Less Than or Equal to (PLE(x)). The percentage of cases having values below or equal to the specified value.

Percentiles (PTILE(x)). The data value below which the specified percentage of values fall within each category.

Skewness (SKEW). A measure of the asymmetry of a distribution. The normal distribution is symmetric and has a skewness value of 0. A distribution with a significant positive skewness has a long right tail. A distribution with a significant negative skewness has a long left tail.

Standard Deviations (STDDEV). A measure of dispersion around the mean, expressed in the same units of measurement as the observations, equal to the square root of the variance. In a normal distribution, 68% of cases fall within one SD of the mean and 95% of cases fall within two SD's.

Standard Errors of Kurtosis (SEKURT). The ratio of kurtosis to its standard error can be used as a test of normality (that is, you can reject normality if the ratio is less than –2 or greater than +2). A large positive value for kurtosis indicates that the tails of the distribution are longer than those of a normal distribution; a negative value for kurtosis indicates shorter tails (becoming like those of a box-shaped uniform distribution).

Standard Errors of the Mean (SEMEAN). A measure of how much the value of the mean may vary from sample to sample taken from the same distribution. It can be used to roughly compare the observed mean to a hypothesized value (that is, you can conclude the two values are different if the ratio of the difference to the standard error is less than –2 or greater than +2).

Standard Errors of Skewness (SESKEW). The ratio of skewness to its standard error can be used as a test of normality (that is, you can reject normality if the ratio is less than –2 or greater than +2). A large positive value for skewness indicates a long right tail; an extreme negative value, a long left tail.

Sums (SUM). The sums of the values within each category.

Sums of Absolute Values (SUMAV). The sums of the absolute values within each category.

Sums of Squares (SUMSQ). The sums of the squares of the values within each category.

Variances (VARIANCE). A measure of how much observations vary from the mean, expressed in squared units.

IMPORT

```
IMPORT FILE=file

[/TYPE={COMM}]
       {TAPE}

[/KEEP={ALL**  }] [/DROP=varlist]
       {varlist}

[/RENAME=(old varnames=new varnames)...]

[/MAP]
```

**Default if the subcommand is omitted.

Example:

```
IMPORT FILE=NEWDATA /RENAME=(V1 TO V3=ID, SEX, AGE) /MAP.
```

Overview

IMPORT reads SPSS-format portable data files created with the EXPORT command. A portable data file is a data file created by the program and used to transport data between different types of computers and operating systems (such as between IBM CMS and Digital VAX/VMS) or between SPSS, SPSS/PC+, or other software using the same portable file format. Like an SPSS-format data file, a portable file contains all of the data and dictionary information stored in the working data file from which it was created.

The program can also read data files created by other software programs. See GET TRANSLATE for information on reading files created by spreadsheet and database programs such as dBASE, Lotus, and Excel.

Options

Format. You can specify the format of the portable file (magnetic tape or communications program) on the TYPE subcommand. For more information on magnetic tapes and communications programs, see "Methods of Transporting Portable Files" on p. 340.

Variables. You can read a subset of variables from the working data file with the DROP and KEEP subcommands. You can rename variables using RENAME. You can also produce a record of all variables and their names in the working file with the MAP subcommand.

Basic Specification

The basic specification is the FILE subcommand with a file specification. All variables from the portable file are copied into the working data file with their original names, variable and value labels, missing-value flags, and print and write formats.

Subcommand Order

- FILE and TYPE must precede all other subcommands.
- No specific order is required between FILE and TYPE or among other subcommands.

Operations

- The portable data file and dictionary become the working data file and dictionary.
- A file saved with weighting in effect (using the WEIGHT command) automatically uses the case weights when the file is read.

Example

```
IMPORT FILE=NEWDATA /RENAME=(V1 TO V3=ID,SEX,AGE) /MAP.
```

- The working data file is generated from the portable file *NEWDATA*.
- Variables *V1*, *V2*, and *V3* are renamed *ID*, *SEX*, and *AGE* in the working file. Their names remain *V1*, *V2*, and *V3* in the portable file. None of the other variables copied into the working file are renamed.
- MAP requests a display of the variables in the working data file.

FILE Subcommand

FILE specifies the portable file. FILE is the only required subcommand on IMPORT.

TYPE Subcommand

TYPE indicates whether the portable file is formatted for magnetic tape or for a communications program. TYPE can specify either COMM or TAPE. For more information on magnetic tapes and communications programs, see EXPORT.

COMM   *Communications-formatted file*. This is the default.

TAPE   *Tape-formatted file.*

Example

```
IMPORT TYPE=TAPE /FILE=HUBOUT.
```

- The file *HUBOUT* is read as a tape-formatted portable file.

DROP and KEEP Subcommands

DROP and KEEP are used to read a subset of variables from the portable file.

- DROP excludes a variable or list of variables from the working data file. All variables not named are included in the file.
- KEEP includes a variable or list of variables in the working file. All variables not specified on KEEP are excluded.
- DROP and KEEP cannot precede the FILE or TYPE subcommands.
- Variables can be specified in any order. The order of variables on KEEP determines the order of variables in the working file. The order on DROP does not affect the order of variables in the working file.
- If a variable is referred to twice on the same subcommand, only the first mention is recognized.
- Multiple DROP and KEEP subcommands are allowed; the effect is cumulative. Specifying a variable named on a previous DROP or not named on a previous KEEP results in an error and the command is not executed.
- The keyword TO can be used to specify a group of consecutive variables in the portable file.
- The portable file is not affected by DROP or KEEP.

Example

```
IMPORT FILE=NEWSUM /DROP=DEPT TO DIVISION.
```

- The working data file is generated from the portable file *NEWSUM*. Variables between and including *DEPT* and *DIVISION* in the portable file are excluded from the working file.
- All other variables are copied into the working file.

RENAME Subcommand

RENAME renames variables being read from the portable file. The renamed variables retain the variable and value labels, missing-value flags, and print formats contained in the portable file.

- To rename a variable, specify the name of the variable in the portable file, a required equals sign, and the new name.
- A variable list can be specified on both sides of the equals sign. The number of variables on both sides must be the same, and the entire specification must be enclosed in parentheses.
- The keyword TO can be used for both variable lists (see "Keyword TO" on p. 29).
- Any DROP or KEEP subcommand after RENAME must use the new variable names.

Example

```
IMPORT FILE=NEWSUM /DROP=DEPT TO DIVISION
 /RENAME=(NAME,WAGE=LNAME,SALARY).
```

- RENAME renames *NAME* and *WAGE* to *LNAME* and *SALARY*.
- *LNAME* and *SALARY* retain the variable and value labels, missing-value flags, and print formats assigned to *NAME* and *WAGE*.

MAP Subcommand

MAP displays a list of variables in the working data file, showing all changes that have been specified on the RENAME, DROP, or KEEP subcommands.

- MAP can be specified as often as desired.
- MAP confirms only the changes specified on the subcommands that precede the MAP request.
- Results of subcommands that follow MAP are not mapped. When MAP is specified last, it also produces a description of the file.

Example

```
IMPORT FILE=NEWSUM /DROP=DEPT TO DIVISION /MAP
  /RENAME NAME=LNAME WAGE=SALARY /MAP.
```

- The first MAP subcommand produces a listing of the variables in the file after DROP has dropped the specified variables.
- RENAME renames *NAME* and *WAGE*.
- The second MAP subcommand shows the variables in the file after renaming.

INCLUDE

```
INCLUDE FILE=file
```

Example:

```
INCLUDE FILE=GSSLABS.
```

Overview

INCLUDE includes a file of commands in a session. INCLUDE is especially useful for including a long series of data definition statements or transformations. Another use for INCLUDE is to set up a library of commonly used commands and include them in the command sequence as they are needed.

INCLUDE allows you to run multiple commands together during a session and can save time. Complex or repetitive commands can be stored in a command file and included in the session, while simpler commands or commands unique to the current analysis can be entered during the session, before and after the included file.

Basic Specification

The only specification is the FILE subcommand, which specifies the file to include. When INCLUDE is executed, the commands in the specified file are processed.

Syntax Rules

- Commands in an included file must begin in column 1, and continuation lines for each command must be indented at least one column.

- A raw data file can be used as an include file if the first line of the included file contains the BEGIN DATA command and the last line contains the END DATA command. However, because the data are specified between BEGIN DATA and END DATA, they are limited to a maximum of 80 columns (the maximum may be fewer than 80 columns on some systems).

- As many INCLUDE commands as needed can be used in a session.

- INCLUDE commands can be nested so that one set of included commands includes another set of commands. This nesting can go to five levels. However, a file cannot be included that is still open from a previous step.

Operations

- If an included file contains a FINISH command, the session ends and no further commands are processed.

498

- If a journal file is created for the session, INCLUDE is copied to the journal file. Commands from the included file are also copied to the journal file but are treated like printed messages. Thus, INCLUDE can be executed from the journal file if the journal file is later used as a command file. Commands from the included file are executed only once.

FILE Subcommand

FILE identifies the file containing commands. FILE is the only specification on INCLUDE and is required.

Example

```
INCLUDE FILE=GSSLABS.
```

- INCLUDE includes the file *GSSLABS* in the prompted session. When INCLUDE is executed, the commands in *GSSLABS* are processed.
- Assume that the include file *GSSLABS* contains the following:

```
DATA LIST FILE=DATA52
  /RELIGION 5 OCCUPAT 7 SES 12 ETHNIC 15
   PARTY 19 VOTE48 33 VOTE52 41.
```

The working data file will be defined and ready for analysis after INCLUDE is executed.

INFO

This command is not available on all operating systems.

```
INFO [OUTFILE = file]
     [OVERVIEW]
     [LOCAL]
     [ERRORS]
     [FACILITIES]
     [PROCEDURES]
     [ALL]
     [procedure name] [/procedure name...]
     [SINCE release number]
```

Example:

```
INFO LOCAL.
```

Overview

INFO makes available two kinds of online documentation: local and update.

Local Documentation

Local documentation concerns the environment in which the program is run. It includes some or all of the following, depending on the operating system:

- Commands or job control language for running the program.
- Conventions for referring to files. These include instructions on how your computer's operating system accesses or creates a particular file.
- Conventions for handling tapes and other input/output devices.
- Data formats. The formats the program reads and writes may differ from one computer and operating system to another.
- Default values for parameters controlled by the SET command. Many defaults for these parameters are set at the individual installation. The SHOW command displays the values that are currently in effect. Local documentation may contain information on why one setting is preferred over another.
- Information about your computer and operating system or your individual installation.

Update Documentation

Update documentation includes changes to existing procedures and facilities made after publication of this manual, new procedures and facilities, and corrections to this manual. Update documentation can be requested for all available releases, or for releases after a particular release.

Basic Specification

- The minimum specification is the command name. When specified by itself, the program displays an overview of available documents.

Syntax Rules

- Multiple keywords and/or procedure names can be specified on a single INFO command.
- Multiple procedure names must be separated by slashes.
- The order of specifications is unimportant and does not affect the order in which the documentation is printed.
- Three- or four-character truncation does *not* apply to INFO command specifications. Spell all keywords in full. For procedure names, spell the first word in full and subsequent words through at least the first three characters.

Operations

- By default, the INFO command produces update information only for the current release. Documentation for earlier releases may also be available; read the INFO overview to find out whether it is available on your system.
- If overlapping sets of information are requested, only one copy is printed.
- If there is no available documentation for the requested information, only a copyright page is printed.
- If information is requested for an unrecognized topic, the program prints an error message.
- The characteristics of the output produced by the INFO command may vary by computer type. As implemented at SPSS Inc., the output includes carriage control, with the maximum length of a page determined by the LENGTH subcommand on SET. A printer width of 132 characters is assumed for some examples, although the text is generally much narrower.
- The program requires more computer resources than most printing utilities. Your installation may therefore provide an alternative method for printing INFO documentation. In this case, the INFO command may simply provide instructions for using the alternative method.

Example

```
INFO  OVERVIEW FACILITIES FREQUENCIES / CROSSTABS.
```

- INFO produces an overview and documentation for any changes made to system facilities and to the FREQUENCIES and CROSSTABS procedures.
- Because the keyword SINCE is not specified, INFO prints only documentation for the current release.

Types of Information

The following types of information can be requested on INFO:

OVERVIEW   *Overview of available documentation.* This includes a table of contents for the documentation available with INFO, along with information about SPSS manuals.

LOCAL   *Local documentation.* See "Local Documentation" on p. 500.

ERRORS   *List of known unfixed errors.* This lists the known unfixed errors in the current release of the program. Since ERRORS applies only to the current release, the SINCE keyword (described below) has no effect with ERRORS.

FACILITIES   *Update information for system facilities.* This covers all differences, except in procedures, between the system as documented in this manual and the system as installed on your computer—whether those differences result from updates to the system, revisions required for conversions to particular operating systems, or errors in this manual. Only updates for the most current release are printed unless keyword SINCE is specified.

PROCEDURES   *Update information for procedures.* This includes full documentation for procedures new in the current release and update information for procedures that existed prior to the current release.

PROCEDURE   *Documentation for the procedure named.* This is the same information as that printed by the PROCEDURES keyword, but limited to the procedure named. You can specify multiple procedures, separating each from the other with a slash.

ALL   *All available documentation.* ALL includes OVERVIEW, LOCAL, ERRORS, FACILITIES, and PROCEDURES.

SINCE Keyword

Releases of SPSS are numbered by integers, with decimal digits indicating maintenance releases between major releases. The release number appears in the default heading for SPSS output. Each SPSS manual is identified in the preface by the number of the release it documents.

The keyword SINCE obtains information for earlier releases or limits the information to maintenance releases since the last major release.

- The minimum specification is the keyword SINCE followed by a release number.

- SINCE is not inclusive. Specifying 3.0 does not include changes made to the system in release 3.0.

- To identify a maintenance release, enter the exact number, with decimal, as in 3.1.

- Information for some earlier releases may not be available. For example, information for release 2.2 and earlier is not available if INFO is run with SPSS release 5.0 or later.

Example

```
INFO   OVERVIEW FACILITIES FREQUENCIES / CROSSTABS SINCE 3.
```

- INFO prints documentation for all changes to system facilities and to procedures FREQUENCIES and CROSSTABS since release 3.0.

OUTFILE Subcommand

By default, the information generated by INFO is part of the output. OUTFILE sends INFO output to a separate file.

Example

```
INFO OUTFILE=SPSSDOC ALL SINCE 3.
```

- INFO creates a text file that includes an overview, local documentation, error, and update information for facilities and procedures since release 3.0.
- The OUTFILE subcommand sends the documentation to the file *SPSSDOC*.

INPUT PROGRAM—END INPUT PROGRAM

```
INPUT PROGRAM

commands to create or define cases

END INPUT PROGRAM
```

Example:
```
INPUT PROGRAM.
DATA LIST FILE=PRICES /YEAR 1-4 QUARTER 6 PRICE 8-12(2).

DO IF (YEAR GE 1881).   /*Stop reading before 1881
END FILE.
END IF.
END INPUT PROGRAM.
```

Overview

The INPUT PROGRAM and END INPUT PROGRAM commands enclose data definition and transformation commands that build cases from input records. The input program often encloses one or more DO IF—END IF or LOOP—END LOOP structures, and it must include at least one file definition command, such as DATA LIST. One of the following utility commands is also usually used:

END CASE   *Build cases from the commands within the input program and pass the cases to the commands immediately following the input program.*

END FILE   *Terminate processing of a data file before the actual end of the file or define the end of the file when the input program is used to read raw data.*

REREAD   *Reread the current record using a different DATA LIST.*

REPEATING DATA *Read repeating groups of data from the same input record.*

For more information on the commands used in an input program, see the discussion of each command.

Input programs create a dictionary and data for a working file from raw data files; they cannot be used to read SPSS-format data files. They can be used to process direct-access and keyed data files. For details, see KEYED DATA LIST.

Input Programs

The program builds the working data file dictionary when it encounters commands that create and define variables. At the same time, the program builds an *input program* that constructs cases and an optional *transformation program* that modifies cases prior to analysis or display. By the time the program encounters a procedure command that tells it to read the data, the working file dictionary is ready, and the programs that construct and modify the cases in the working file are built.

The internal input program is usually built from either a single DATA LIST command or from any of the commands that read or combine SPSS-format data files (for example, GET, ADD FILES, MATCH FILES, UPDATE, and so on). The input program can also be built from the FILE TYPE—END FILE TYPE structure used to define nested, mixed, or grouped files. The third type of input program is specified with the INPUT PROGRAM—END INPUT PROGRAM commands.

With INPUT PROGRAM—END INPUT PROGRAM, you can create your own input program to perform many different operations on raw data. You can use transformation commands to build cases. You can read nonrectangular files, concatenate raw data files, and build cases selectively. You can also create a working data file without reading any data at all.

Input State

There are four program states in the program: the *initial state,* in which there is no working file dictionary; the *input state,* in which cases are created from the input file; the *transformation state,* in which cases are transformed; and the *procedure state,* in which procedures are executed. When you specify INPUT PROGRAM—END INPUT PROGRAM, you must pay attention to which commands are allowed within the input state, which commands can appear only within the input state, and which are not allowed within the input state. See Appendix A for a discussion of program states, command order, and a table that describes what happens to each command when it is encountered in each of the four states.

Basic Specification

The basic specification is INPUT PROGRAM, the commands used to create cases and define the working data file, and END INPUT PROGRAM.

- INPUT PROGRAM and END INPUT PROGRAM each must be specified on a separate line and have no additional specifications.

- To define a working data file, the input program must include at least one DATA LIST or END FILE command.

Operations

- The INPUT PROGRAM—END INPUT PROGRAM structure defines a working data file and is not executed until the program encounters a procedure or the EXECUTE command.

- INPUT PROGRAM clears the current working data file.

Example

```
* Select cases with an input program.

INPUT PROGRAM.
DATA LIST FILE=PRICES /YEAR 1-4 QUARTER 6 PRICE 8-12(2).

DO IF (YEAR GE 1881).   /*Stop reading when reaching 1881
END FILE.
END IF.
END INPUT PROGRAM.

LIST.
```

- The input program is defined between the INPUT PROGRAM and END INPUT PROGRAM commands.
- This example assumes that data records are entered chronologically by year. The DO IF— END IF structure specifies an end of file when the first case with a value of 1881 or later for *YEAR* is reached.
- LIST executes the input program and lists cases in the working data file. The case that causes the end of the file is not included in the working file generated by the input program.
- As an alternative to this input program, you can use N OF CASES to select cases if you know the exact number of cases. Another alternative is to use SELECT IF to select cases before 1881, but then the program would unnecessarily read the entire input file.

Example

```
* Skip the first n records in a file.

INPUT PROGRAM.
NUMERIC         #INIT.
DO IF           NOT (#INIT).
+  LOOP         #I = 1 TO 5.
+     DATA LIST    NOTABLE/.   /* No data - just skip record
+  END LOOP.
+  COMPUTE      #INIT = 1.
END IF.
DATA LIST       NOTABLE/ X 1.
END INPUT PROGRAM.

BEGIN DATA
A                           /* The first 5 records are skipped
B
C
D
E
1
2
3
4
5
END DATA.
LIST.
```

- NUMERIC declares the scratch variable *#INIT*, which is initialized to system-missing.

- The DO IF structure is executed as long as *#INIT* does not equal 1.

- LOOP is executed five times. Within the loop, DATA LIST is specified without variable names, causing the program to read records in the data file without copying them into the working file. LOOP is executed five times, so the program reads five records in this manner. END LOOP terminates this loop.

- COMPUTE creates the scratch variable *#INIT* and sets it equal to 1. The DO IF structure is therefore not executed again.

- END IF terminates the DO IF structure.

- The second DATA LIST specifies numeric variable *X*, which is located in column 1 of each record. Because the program has already read five records, the first value for *X* that is copied into the working file is read from record 6.

More Examples

For additional examples of input programs, refer to DATA LIST (p. 237), DO IF (p. 311), DO REPEAT (p. 314), END CASE, END FILE, LOOP, NUMERIC (p. 653), POINT (p. 689), REPEATING DATA, REREAD, and VECTOR (p. 1004).

KEYED DATA LIST

```
KEYED DATA LIST KEY=varname IN=varname

 FILE=file [{TABLE  }]
           {NOTABLE}

 /varname {col location [(format)]} [varname ..]
          {(FORTRAN-like format)  }
```

Example:
```
FILE HANDLE EMPL/ file specifications.
KEYED DATA LIST FILE=EMPL KEY=#NXTCASE IN=#FOUND
        /YRHIRED 1-2 SEX 3 JOBCLASS 4.
```

Overview

KEYED DATA LIST reads raw data from two types of nonsequential files: direct-access files, which provide direct access by a record number, and keyed files, which provide access by a record key. An example of a direct-access file is a file of 50 records, each corresponding to one of the United States. If you know the relationship between the states and the record numbers, you can retrieve the data for any specific state. An example of a keyed file is a file containing social security numbers and other information about a firm's employees. The social security number can be used to identify the records in the file.

Direct-Access Files

There are various types of direct-access files. This program's concept of a direct-access file, however, is very specific. The file must be one from which individual records can be selected according to their number. The records in a 100-record direct-access file, for example, are numbered from 1 to 100.

Although the concept of record number applies to almost any file, not all files can be treated by this program as direct-access files. In fact, some operating systems provide no direct-access capabilities at all, and others permit only a narrowly defined subset of all files to be treated as direct access.

Very few files turn out to be good candidates for direct-access organization. In the case of an inventory file, for example, the usual large gaps in the part numbering sequence would result in large amounts of wasted file space. Gaps are not a problem, however, if they are predictable. For example, if you recognize that telephone area codes have first digits of 2 through 9, second digits of 0 or 1, and third digits of 0 through 9, you can transform an area code into a record number by using the following COMPUTE statement:

```
COMPUTE RECNUM = 20*(DIGIT1-2) + 10*DIGIT2 + DIGIT3 + 1.
```

where *DIGIT1*, *DIGIT2*, and *DIGIT3* are variables corresponding to the respective digits in the area code, and *RECNUM* is the resulting record number. The record numbers would range from 1, for the non-existent area code 200, through 160, for area code 919. The file would then have a manageable number of unused records.

Keyed Files

Of the many kinds of keyed files, the ones to which the program can provide access are generally known as *indexed sequential files*. A file of this kind is basically a sequential file in which an index is maintained so that the file can be processed either sequentially or selectively. In effect, there is an underlying data file that is accessed through a file of index entries. The file of index entries may, for example, contain the fact that data record 797 is associated with social security number 476-77-1359. Depending on the implementation, the underlying data may or may not be maintained in sequential order.

The key for each record in the file generally comprises one or more pieces of information found within the record. An example of a complex key is a customer's last name and house number, plus the consonants in the street name, plus the zip code, plus a unique digit in case there are duplicates. Regardless of the information contained in the key, the program treats it as a character string.

On some systems, more than one key is associated with each record. That is, the records in a file can be identified according to different types of information. Although the primary key for a file normally must be unique, sometimes the secondary keys need not be. For example, the records in an employee file might be identified by social security number and job classification.

Options

Data Source. You can specify the name of the keyed file on the FILE subcommand. By default, the last file that was specified on an input command, such as DATA LIST or REPEATING DATA, is read.

Summary Table. You can display a table that summarizes the variable definitions.

Basic Specification

- The basic specification requires FILE, KEY, and IN, each of which specifies one variable, followed by a slash and variable definitions.
- FILE specifies the direct-access or keyed file. The file must have a file handle already defined.
- KEY specifies the variable whose value will be used to read a record. For direct-access files, the variable must be numeric; for keyed files, it must be string.
- IN creates a logical variable that flags whether a record was successfully read.
- Variable definitions follow all subcommands; the slash preceding them is required. Variable definitions are similar to those specified on DATA LIST.

Subcommand Order

- Subcommands can be named in any order.
- Variable definitions must follow all specified subcommands.

Syntax Rules

- Specifications for the variable definitions are the same as those described for DATA LIST. The only difference is that only one record can be defined per case.
- The FILE HANDLE command must be used if the FILE subcommand is specified on KEYED DATA LIST.
- KEYED DATA LIST can be specified in an input program, or it can be used as a transformation language to change an existing working data file. This differs from all other input commands, such as GET and DATA LIST, which create new working files.

Operations

- Variable names are stored in the working file dictionary.
- Formats are stored in the working file dictionary and are used to display and write the values. To change output formats of numeric variables, use the FORMATS command.

Example

```
FILE HANDLE EMPL/ file specifications.
KEYED DATA LIST FILE=EMPL KEY=#NXTCASE IN=#FOUND
         /YRHIRED 1-2 SEX 3 JOBCLASS 4.
```

- FILE HANDLE defines the handle for the data file to be read by KEYED DATA LIST. The handle is specified on the FILE subcommand of KEYED DATA LIST.
- KEY on KEYED DATA LIST specifies the variable to be used as the access key. For a direct-access file, the value of the variable must be between 1 and the number of records in the file. For a keyed file, the value must be a string.
- IN creates the logical scratch variable *#FOUND*, whose value will be 1 if the record is successfully read, or 0 if the record is not found.
- The variable definitions are the same as those used for DATA LIST.

Example

```
* Reading a direct-access file: sampling 1 out of every 25 records.

FILE HANDLE     EMPL/ file specifications.
INPUT PROGRAM.
COMPUTE #INTRVL = TRUNC(UNIF(48))+1. /* Mean interval = 25
COMPUTE #NXTCASE = #NXTCASE+#INTRVL. /* Next record number
COMPUTE #EOF = #NXTCASE > 1000.      /* End of file check
DO IF    #EOF.
+   END FILE.
ELSE.
+   KEYED DATA LIST  FILE=EMPL, KEY=#NXTCASE, IN=#FOUND, NOTABLE
                    /YRHIRED 1-2 SEX 3 JOBCLASS 4.
+   DO IF      #FOUND.
+      END CASE.                     /* Return a case
+   ELSE.
+      PRINT / 'Oops. #NXTCASE=' #NXTCASE.
+   END IF.
END IF.
END INPUT PROGRAM.
EXECUTE.
```

- FILE HANDLE defines the handle for the data file to be read by the KEYED DATA LIST command. The record numbers for this example are generated by the transformation language; they are not based on data taken from another file.

- The INPUT PROGRAM and END INPUT PROGRAM commands begin and end the block of commands that build cases from the input file. Since the session generates cases, an input program is required.

- The first two COMPUTE statements determine the number of the next record to be selected. This is done in two steps. First, the integer portion is taken from the sum of 1 and a uniform pseudo-random number between 1 and 49. The result is a mean interval of 25. Second, the variable *#NXTCASE* is added to this number to generate the next record number. This record number, *#NXTCASE*, will be used for the key variable on the KEYED DATA LIST command. The third COMPUTE creates a logical scratch variable, *#EOF*, that has a value of 0 if the record number is less than or equal to 1000, or 1 if the value of the record number is greater than 1000.

- The DO IF—END IF structure controls the building of cases. If the record number is greater than 1000, *#EOF* equals 1, and the END FILE command tells the program to stop reading data and end the file.

- If the record number is less than or equal to 1000, the record is read via KEYED DATA LIST using the value of *#NXTCASE*. A case is generated if the record exists (*#FOUND* equals 1). If not, the program displays the record number and continues to the next case. The sample will have about 40 records.

- EXECUTE causes the transformations to be executed.

- This example illustrates the difference between DATA LIST, which always reads the next record in a file, and KEYED DATA LIST, which reads only specified records. The record numbers must be generated by another command or be contained in the working data file.

Example

```
* Reading a keyed file: reading selected records.

GET FILE=STUDENTS/KEEP=AGE,SEX,COURSE.
FILE HANDLE COURSES/ file specifications.
STRING #KEY(A4).
COMPUTE #KEY = STRING(COURSE,N4). /* Create a string key
KEYED DATA LIST FILE=COURSES KEY=#KEY IN=#FOUND NOTABLE
      /PERIOD 13 CREDITS 16.
SELECT IF #FOUND.
LIST.
```

- GET reads the *STUDENTS* file, which contains information on students, including a course identification for each student. The course identification will be used as the key for selecting one record from a file of courses.

- The FILE HANDLE command defines a file handle for the file of courses.

- The STRING and COMPUTE commands transform the course identification from numeric to string for use as a key. For keyed files, the key variable must be a string.

- KEYED DATA LIST uses the value of the newly created string variable *#KEY* as the key to search the course file. If a record that matches the value of *#KEY* is found, *#FOUND* is set to 1; otherwise, it is set to 0. Note that KEYED DATA LIST appears outside an input program in this example.

- If the course file contains the requested record, *#FOUND* equals 1. The variables *PERIOD* and *CREDITS* are added to the case and the case is selected via the SELECT IF command; otherwise, the case is dropped.

- LIST lists the values of the selected cases.

- This example shows how existing cases can be updated on the basis of information read from a keyed file.

- This task could also be accomplished by reading the entire course file with DATA LIST and combining it with the student file via the MATCH FILES command. The technique you should use depends on the percentage of the records in the course file that need to be accessed. If fewer than 10% of the course file records are read, KEYED DATA LIST is probably more efficient. As the percentage of the records that are read increases, reading the entire course file and using MATCH makes more sense.

FILE Subcommand

FILE specifies the handle for the direct-access or keyed data file. The file handle must have been defined on a previous FILE HANDLE command (or, in the case of the IBM OS environment, on a DD statement in the JCL).

KEY Subcommand

KEY specifies the variable whose value will be used as the key. This variable must already exist as the result of a prior DATA LIST, KEYED DATA LIST, GET, or transformation command.

- KEY is required. Its only specification is a single variable. The variable can be a permanent variable or a scratch variable.

- For direct-access files, the key variable must be numeric, and its value must be between 1 and the number of records in the file.

- For keyed files, the key variable must be string. If the keys are numbers, such as social security numbers, the STRING function can be used to convert the numbers to strings. For example, the following might be required to get the value of a numeric key into exactly the same format as used on the keyed file:

```
COMPUTE #KEY=STRING(123,IB4).
```

IN Subcommand

IN creates a numeric variable whose value indicates whether or not the specified record is found.

- IN is required. Its only specification is a single numeric variable. The variable can be a permanent variable or a scratch variable.

- The value of the variable is 1 if the record is successfully read or 0 if the record is not found. The IN variable can be used to select all cases that have been updated by KEYED DATA LIST.

Example

```
FILE HANDLE EMPL/ file specifications.
KEYED DATA LIST FILE=EMPL KEY=#NXTCASE IN=#FOUND
        /YRHIRED 1-2 SEX 3 JOBCLASS 4.
```

- IN creates the logical scratch variable *#FOUND*. The values of *#FOUND* will be 1 if the record indicated by the key value in *#NXTCASE* is found or 0 if the record does not exist.

TABLE and NOTABLE Subcommands

TABLE and NOTABLE determine whether the program displays a table that summarizes the variable definitions. TABLE, the default, displays the table. NOTABLE suppresses the table.

- TABLE and NOTABLE are optional and mutually exclusive.

- The only specification for TABLE or NOTABLE is the subcommand keyword. Neither subcommand has additional specifications.

LEAVE

```
LEAVE varlist
```

Example:
```
COMPUTE TSALARY=TSALARY+SALARY.
LEAVE TSALARY.
FORMAT TSALARY (DOLLAR8)/ SALARY (DOLLAR7).
EXECUTE.
```

Overview

Normally, the program reinitializes variables each time it prepares to read a new case. LEAVE suppresses reinitialization and retains the current value of the specified variable or variables when the program reads the next case. It also sets the initial value received by a numeric variable to 0 instead of system-missing. LEAVE is frequently used with COMPUTE to create a variable to store an accumulating sum. LEAVE is also used to spread a variable's values across multiple cases when VECTOR is used within an input program to restructure a data file (see p. 320 for an example).

LEAVE cannot be used with scratch variables. For information on using scratch variables, see "Scratch Variables" on p. 31.

Basic Specification

The basic specification is the variable(s) whose values are not to be reinitialized as each new case is read.

Syntax Rules

- Variables named on LEAVE must already exist and cannot be scratch variables.
- Multiple variables can be named. The keyword TO can be used to refer to a list of consecutive variables.
- String and numeric variables can be specified on the same LEAVE command.

Operations

- Unlike most transformations, which do not take effect until the data are read, LEAVE takes effect as soon as it is encountered in the command sequence. Thus, special attention should be paid to its position among commands. For more information, see "Command Order" on p. 16.

- Numeric variables named on LEAVE are initialized to 0 for the first case, and string variables are initialized to blanks. These variables are not reinitialized when new cases are read.

Example

```
COMPUTE TSALARY=TSALARY+SALARY.
LEAVE TSALARY.
FORMAT TSALARY (DOLLAR8)/ SALARY (DOLLAR7).
```

- These commands keep a running total of salaries across all cases. *SALARY* is the variable containing the employee's salary, and *TSALARY* is the new variable containing the cumulative salaries for all previous cases.
- For the first case, *TSALARY* is initialized to 0, and *TSALARY* equals *SALARY*. For the rest of the cases, *TSALARY* stores the cumulative totals for *SALARY*.
- LEAVE follows COMPUTE because *TSALARY* must first be defined before it can be specified on LEAVE.
- If LEAVE were not specified for this computation, *TSALARY* would be initialized to system-missing for all cases. *TSALARY* would remain system-missing because its value would be missing for every computation.

Example

```
SORT CASES DEPT.
IF DEPT NE LAG(DEPT,1) TSALARY=0.   /*Initialize for new dept
COMPUTE TSALARY=TSALARY+SALARY.     /*Sum salaries
LEAVE TSALARY.                      /*Prevent  initialization
each case
FORMAT TSALARY (DOLLAR8)/ SALARY (DOLLAR7).
```

- These commands accumulate a sum across cases for each department.
- SORT first sorts cases by the values of variable *DEPT*.
- IF specifies that if the value of *DEPT* for the current case is not equal to the value of *DEPT* for the previous case, *TSALARY* equals 0. Thus, *TSALARY* is reset to 0 each time the value of *DEPT* changes. (For the first case in the file, the logical expression on IF is missing. However, the desired effect is obtained because LEAVE initializes *TSALARY* to 0 for the first case, independent of the IF statement.)
- LEAVE prevents *TSALARY* from being initialized for cases within the same department.

LIST

```
LIST [[VARIABLES=]{ALL**  }] [/FORMAT=[{WRAP**}] [{UNNUMBERED**}]]
               {varlist}               {SINGLE}   {NUMBERED    }

[/CASES=[FROM {1**}] [TO {eof**}] [BY {1**}]]
              {n  }        {n   }      {n  }
```

**Default if the subcommand is omitted.

Example:

```
LIST VARIABLES=V1 V2 /CASES=FROM 10 TO 100 BY 2.
```

Overview

LIST displays case values for variables in the working data file. The output is similar to the output produced by the PRINT command. However, LIST is a procedure and reads data, whereas PRINT is a transformation and requires a procedure (or the EXECUTE command) to execute it.

Options

Selecting and Ordering Variables. You can specify a list of variables to be listed using the VARIABLES subcommand.

Format. You can limit each case listing to a single line, and you can display the case number for each listed case with the FORMAT subcommand.

Selecting Cases. You can limit the listing to a particular sequence of cases using the CASES subcommand.

Basic Specification

- The basic specification is simply LIST, which displays the values for all variables in the working data file.
- By default, cases wrap to multiple lines if all the values do not fit within the page width (the page width is determined by the SET WIDTH command). Case numbers are not displayed for the listed cases.

Subcommand Order

All subcommands are optional and can be named in any order.

Operations

- If VARIABLES is not specified, variables are listed in the order in which they appear in the working file.
- LIST does not display values for scratch or system variables.
- LIST uses print formats contained in the dictionary of the working data file. Alternative formats cannot be specified on LIST. See FORMATS or PRINT FORMATS for information on changing print formats.
- LIST output uses the width specified on SET.
- If a numeric value is longer than its defined width, the program first attempts to list the value by removing punctuation characters, then uses scientific notation, and finally prints asterisks.
- If a long string variable cannot be listed within the output width, it is truncated.
- Values of the variables listed for a case are always separated by at least one blank.
- System-missing values are displayed as a period for numeric variables and a blank for string variables.
- If cases fit on one line, the column width for each variable is determined by the length of the variable name or the format, whichever is greater. If the variable names do not fit on one line, they are printed vertically.
- If cases do not fit on one line within the output width specified on SET, they are wrapped. LIST displays a table illustrating the location of the variables in the output and prints the name of the first variable in each line at the beginning of the line.
- Each execution of LIST begins at the top of a new page. If SPLIT FILE is in effect, each split also begins at the top of a new page.

Example

```
LIST.
```

- LIST by itself requests a display of the values for all variables in the working file.

Example

```
LIST VARIABLES=V1 V2 /CASES=FROM 10 TO 100 BY 2.
```

- LIST produces a list of every second case for variables *V1* and *V2*, starting with case 10 and stopping at case 100.

VARIABLES Subcommand

VARIABLES specifies the variables to be listed. The actual keyword VARIABLES can be omitted.

- The variables must already exist, and they cannot be scratch or system variables.
- If VARIABLES is used, only the specified variables are listed.

- Variables are listed in the order in which they are named on VARIABLES.
- If a variable is named more than once, it is listed more than once.
- The keyword ALL (the default) can be used to request all variables. ALL can also be used with a variable list (see example below).

ALL   *List all user-defined variables.* Variables are listed in the order in which they appear in the working data file. This is the default if VARIABLES is omitted.

Example

```
LIST VARIABLES=V15 V31 ALL.
```

- VARIABLES is used to list values for *V15* and *V31* before all other variables. The keyword ALL then lists all variables, including *V15* and *V31*, in the order in which they appear in the working data file. Values for *V15* and *V31* are therefore listed twice.

FORMAT Subcommand

FORMAT controls whether cases wrap if they cannot fit on a single line and whether the case number is displayed for each listed case. The default display uses more than one line per case (if necessary) and does not number cases.

- The minimum specification is a single keyword.
- WRAP and SINGLE are alternatives, as are NUMBERED and UNNUMBERED. Only one of each pair can be specified.
- If SPLIT FILE is in effect for NUMBERED, case numbering restarts at each split. To get sequential numbering regardless of splits, create a variable and set it equal to the system variable *$CASENUM* and then name this variable as the first variable on the VARIABLES subcommand. An appropriate format should be specified for the new variable before it is used on LIST.

WRAP   *Wrap cases if they do not fit on a single line.* Page width is determined by the SET WIDTH command. This is the default.

SINGLE   *Limit each case to one line.* Only variables that fit on a single line are displayed.

UNNUMBERED   *Do not include the sequence number of each case.* This is the default.

NUMBERED   *Include the sequence number of each case.* The sequence number is displayed to the left of the listed values.

CASES Subcommand

CASES limits the number of cases listed. By default, all cases in the working data file are listed.

- Any or all of the keywords below can be used. Defaults that are not changed remain in effect.
- If LIST is preceded by a SAMPLE or SELECT IF command, case selections specified by CASES are taken from those cases that were selected by SAMPLE or SELECT IF.

- If SPLIT FILE is in effect, case selections specified by CASES are restarted for each split.

FROM n   *Number of the first case to be listed.* The default is 1.

TO n   *Number of the last case to be listed.* The default is the end of the working file. CASES 100 is interpreted as CASES TO 100.

BY n   *Increment used to choose cases for listing.* The default is 1.

Example

```
LIST CASES BY 3 /FORMAT=NUMBERED.
```

- Every third case is listed for all variables in the working data file. The listing begins with the first case and includes every third case up to the end of the file.
- FORMAT displays the case number of each listed case.

Example

```
LIST CASES FROM 10 TO 20.
```

- Cases from case 10 through case 20 are listed for all variables in the working file.

LOOP—END LOOP

```
LOOP [varname=n TO m [BY {1**}]]   [IF [(]logical expression[)]]
                         {n  }

transformation commands

END LOOP [IF [(]logical expression[)]]
```

**Default if the subcommand is omitted.

Examples:

```
SET MXLOOPS=10.      /*Maximum number of loops allowed
LOOP.                /*Loop with no limit other than MXLOOPS
COMPUTE X=X+1.
END LOOP.

LOOP #I=1 TO 5.      /*Loop five times
COMPUTE X=X+1.
END LOOP.
```

Overview

The LOOP—END LOOP structure performs repeated transformations specified by the commands within the loop until they reach a specified cutoff. The cutoff can be specified by an indexing clause on the LOOP command, an IF clause on the END LOOP command, or a BREAK command within the loop structure (see BREAK). In addition, the maximum number of iterations within a loop can be specified on the MXLOOPS subcommand on SET. The default MXLOOPS is 40.

The IF clause on the LOOP command can be used to perform repeated transformations on a subset of cases. The effect is similar to nesting the LOOP—END LOOP structure within a DO IF—END IF structure, but using IF on LOOP is simpler and more efficient. You have to use the DO IF—END IF structure, however, if you want to perform different transformations on different subsets of cases. You can also use IF on LOOP to specify the cutoff, especially when the cutoff may be reached before the first iteration.

LOOP and END LOOP are usually used within an input program or with the VECTOR command. Since the loop structure repeats transformations on a single case or on a single input record containing information on multiple cases, it allows you to read complex data files or to generate data for a working data file. For more information, see INPUT PROGRAM—END INPUT PROGRAM and VECTOR.

The loop structure repeats transformations on single cases across variables. It is different from the DO REPEAT—END REPEAT structure, which replicates transformations on a specified set of variables. When both can be used to accomplish a task, such as selectively transforming data for some cases on some variables, LOOP and END LOOP are generally more efficient and more flexible, but DO REPEAT allows selection of nonadjacent variables and use of replacement values with different intervals.

Options

Missing Values. You can prevent cases with missing values for any of the variables used in the loop structure from entering the loop (see "Missing Values" on p. 527).

Creating Data. A loop structure within an input program can be used to generate data (see "Creating Data" on p. 528).

Defining Complex File Structures. A loop structure within an input program can be used to define complex files that cannot be handled by standard file definition facilities (see pp. 319, 320, and 322 for examples).

Basic Specification

The basic specification is LOOP followed by at least one transformation command. The structure must end with the END LOOP command. Commands within the loop are executed until the cutoff is reached.

Syntax Rules

- If LOOP and END LOOP are specified before a working data file exists, they must be specified within an input program.
- If both an indexing and an IF clause are used on LOOP, the indexing clause must be first.
- Loop structures can be nested within other loop structures or within DO IF structures, and vice versa.

Operations

- The LOOP command defines the beginning of a loop structure and the END LOOP command defines its end. The END LOOP command returns control to LOOP unless the cutoff has been reached. When the cutoff has been reached, control passes to the command immediately following END LOOP.
- When specified within a loop structure, definition commands (such as MISSING VALUES and VARIABLE LABELS) and utility commands (such as SET and SHOW) are invoked only once, when they are encountered for the first time within the loop.

Example

```
SET MXLOOPS=10.
LOOP.    /*Loop with no limit other than MXLOOPS
COMPUTE X=X+1.
END LOOP.
```

- This and the following examples assume that a working data file and all of the variables mentioned in the loop exist.

- The SET MXLOOPS command limits the number of times the loop is executed to 10. The function of MXLOOPS is to prevent infinite loops when there is no iteration clause.
- Within the loop structure, each iteration increments X by 1. After 10 iterations, the value of X for all cases is increased by 10, and, as specified on the SET command, the loop is terminated.

IF Keyword

The keyword IF and a logical expression can be specified on LOOP or on END LOOP to control iterations through the loop.

- The specification on IF is a logical expression enclosed in parentheses. For more information, see "Logical Expressions" on p. 53.

Example

```
LOOP.
COMPUTE X=X+1.
END LOOP IF (X EQ 5).        /*Loop until X is 5
```

- Iterations continue until the logical expression on END LOOP is true, which for every case is when X equals 5. Each case does not go through the same number of iterations.
- This corresponds to the programming notion of DO UNTIL. The loop is always executed at least once.

Example

```
LOOP IF (X LT 5).            /*Loop while X is less than 5
COMPUTE X=X+1.
END LOOP.
```

- The IF clause is evaluated each trip through the structure, so looping stops once X equals 5.
- This corresponds to the programming notion of DO WHILE. The loop may not be executed at all.

Example

```
LOOP IF (Y GT 10).           /*Loop only for cases with Y GT 10
COMPUTE X=X+1.
END LOOP IF (X EQ 5).        /*Loop until X IS 5
```

- The IF clause on LOOP allows transformations to be performed on a subset of cases. X is increased by 5 only for cases with values greater than 10 for Y. X is not changed for all other cases.

Indexing Clause

The indexing clause limits the number of iterations for a loop by specifying the number of times the program should execute commands within the loop structure. The indexing clause is specified on the LOOP command and includes an indexing variable followed by initial and terminal values.

- The program sets the *indexing variable* to the *initial value* and increases it by the specified increment each time the loop is executed for a case. When the indexing variable reaches the specified *terminal value*, the loop is terminated for that case.

- By default, the program increases the indexing variable by 1 for each iteration. The keyword BY overrides this increment.

- The indexing variable can have any valid variable name. Unless you specify a scratch variable, the indexing variable is treated as a permanent variable and is saved on the working data file. If the indexing variable is assigned the same name as an existing variable, the values of the existing variable are altered by the LOOP structure as it is executed, and the original values are lost.

- The indexing clause overrides the maximum number of loops specified by SET MXLOOPS.

- The initial and terminal values of the indexing clause can be numeric expressions. Non-integer and negative expressions are allowed.

- If the expression for the initial value is greater than the terminal value, the loop is not executed. For example, #J=X TO Y is a zero-trip loop if X is 0 and Y is -1.

- If the expressions for the initial and terminal values are equal, the loop is executed once. #J=0 TO Y is a one-trip loop when Y is 0.

- If the loop is exited via BREAK or a conditional clause on the END LOOP statement, the iteration variable is not updated. If the LOOP statement contains both an indexing clause and a conditional clause, the indexing clause is executed first, and the iteration variable is updated regardless of which clause causes the loop to terminate.

Example

```
LOOP #I=1 TO 5.              /*LOOP FIVE TIMES
COMPUTE X=X+1.
END LOOP.
```

- The scratch variable #I (the indexing variable) is set to the initial value of 1 and increased by 1 each time the loop is executed for a case. When #I increases beyond the terminal value 5, no further loops are executed. Thus, the value of X will be increased by 5 for every case.

Example

```
LOOP #I=1 TO 5 IF (Y GT 10). /*Loop to X=5 only if Y GT 10
COMPUTE X=X+1.
END LOOP.
```

- Both an indexing clause and an IF clause are specified on LOOP. X is increased by 5 for all cases where Y is greater than 10.

Example

```
LOOP #I=1 TO Y.              /*Loop to the value of Y
COMPUTE X=X+1.
END LOOP.
```

- The number of iterations for a case depends on the value of the variable Y for that case. For a case with value 0 for the variable Y, the loop is not executed and X is unchanged. For a case with value 1 for the variable Y, the loop is executed once and X is increased by 1.

Example

```
* Factorial routine.

DATA LIST FREE / X.
BEGIN DATA
1 2 3 4 5 6 7
END DATA.

COMPUTE FACTOR=1.
LOOP #I=1 TO X.
COMPUTE FACTOR=FACTOR * #I.
END LOOP.
LIST.
```

- The loop structure computes *FACTOR* as the factorial value of *X*.

Example

```
* Example of nested loops: compute every possible combination of values
  for each variable.

INPUT PROGRAM.
-LOOP #I=1 TO 4.        /* LOOP TO NUMBER OF VALUES FOR I
+    LOOP #J=1 TO 3.      /* LOOP TO NUMBER OF VALUES FOR J
@        LOOP #K=1 TO 4.     /* LOOP TO NUMBER OF VALUES FOR K

@              COMPUTE I=#I.
@              COMPUTE J=#J.
@              COMPUTE K=#K.
@              END CASE.

@        END LOOP.
+    END LOOP.
-END LOOP.
END FILE.
END INPUT PROGRAM.
LIST.
```

- The first loop iterates four times. The first iteration sets the indexing variable *#I* equal to 1 and then passes control to the second loop. *#I* remains 1 until the second loop has completed all of its iterations.

- The second loop is executed 12 times, three times for each value of *#I*. The first iteration sets the indexing variable *#J* equal to 1 and then passes control to the third loop. *#J* remains 1 until the third loop has completed all of its iterations.

- The third loop results in 48 iterations ($4 \times 3 \times 4$). The first iteration sets *#K* equal to 1. The COMPUTE statements set the variables *I, J,* and *K* each to 1, and END CASE creates a case. The third loop iterates a second time, setting *#K* equal to 2. Variables *I, J,* and *K* are then computed with values 1, 1, 2, respectively, and a second case is created. The third and fourth iterations of the third loop produce cases with *I, J,* and *K*, equal to 1, 1, 3 and 1, 1, 4, respectively. After the fourth iteration within the third loop, control passes back to the second loop.

- The second loop is executed again. *#I* remains 1, while *#J* increases to 2, and control returns to the third loop. The third loop completes its iterations, resulting in four more cases with *I* equal to 1, *J* to 2, and *K* increasing from 1 to 4. The second loop is executed a third time, resulting in cases with $I=1$, $J=3$, and K increasing from 1 to 4. Once the second loop has completed three iterations, control passes back to the first loop, and the entire cycle is repeated for the next increment of $\#I$.

- Once the first loop completes four iterations, control passes out of the looping structures to END FILE. END FILE defines the resulting cases as a data file, the input program terminates, and the LIST command is executed.

- This example does not require a LEAVE command because the iteration variables are scratch variables. If the iteration variables were I, J, and K, LEAVE would be required because the variables would be reinitialized after each END CASE command.

Example

```
* Modifying the loop iteration variable.
INPUT PROGRAM.
PRINT SPACE    2.
LOOP           A = 1 TO 3.                    /*Simple iteration
+   PRINT          /'A WITHIN LOOP: ' A(F1).
+   COMPUTE        A = 0.
END LOOP
PRINT          /'A AFTER LOOP:  ' A(F1).

NUMERIC        #B.
LOOP           B = 1 TO 3.                    /*Iteration + UNTIL
+   PRINT          /'B WITHIN LOOP: ' B(F1).
+   COMPUTE        B = 0.
+   COMPUTE        #B = #B+1.
END LOOP       IF #B = 3.
PRINT          /'B AFTER LOOP:  ' B(F1).

NUMERIC        #C.
LOOP           C = 1 TO 3 IF #C NE 3.   /*Iteration + WHILE
+   PRINT          /'C WITHIN LOOP: ' C(F1).
+   COMPUTE        C = 0.
+   COMPUTE        #C = #C+1.
END LOOP.
PRINT          /'C AFTER LOOP:  ' C(F1).

NUMERIC        #D.
LOOP           D = 1 TO 3.                    /*Iteration + BREAK
+   PRINT          /'D WITHIN LOOP: ' D(F1).
+   COMPUTE        D = 0.
+   COMPUTE        #D = #D+1.
+   DO IF          #D = 3.
+       BREAK.
+   END IF.
END LOOP.
PRINT          /'D AFTER LOOP:  ' D(F1).

LOOP           E = 3 TO 1.                    /*Zero-trip iteration
+   PRINT          /'E WITHIN LOOP: ' E(F1).
+   COMPUTE        E = 0.
END LOOP.
PRINT          /'E AFTER LOOP:  ' E(F1).
END FILE.
END INPUT PROGRAM.
EXECUTE.
```

- If a loop is exited via BREAK or a conditional clause on the END LOOP statement, the iteration variable is not updated.
- If the LOOP statement contains both an iteration clause and a conditional clause, the iteration clause is executed first, and the actual iteration variable will be updated regardless of which clause causes termination of the loop.

Figure 1 shows the output from this example.

Figure 1   Modify the loop iteration variable

```
A WITHIN LOOP: 1
A WITHIN LOOP: 2
A WITHIN LOOP: 3
A AFTER LOOP:  4
B WITHIN LOOP: 1
B WITHIN LOOP: 2
B WITHIN LOOP: 3
B AFTER LOOP:  0
C WITHIN LOOP: 1
C WITHIN LOOP: 2
C WITHIN LOOP: 3
C AFTER LOOP:  4
D WITHIN LOOP: 1
D WITHIN LOOP: 2
D WITHIN LOOP: 3
D AFTER LOOP:  0
E AFTER LOOP:  3
```

BY Keyword

By default, the program increases the indexing variable by 1 for each iteration. The keyword BY overrides this increment.

- The *increment value* can be a numeric expression and can therefore be non-integer or negative. Zero causes a warning and results in a zero-trip loop.
- If the initial value is greater than the terminal value and the increment is positive, the loop is never entered. #I=1 TO 0 BY 2 results in a zero-trip loop.
- If the initial value is less than the terminal value and the increment is negative, the loop is never entered. #I=1 TO 2 BY −1 also results in a zero-trip loop.
- Order is unimportant: 2 BY 2 TO 10 is equivalent to 2 TO 10 BY 2.

Example

```
LOOP #I=2 TO 10 BY 2.          /*Loop five times by 2'S
COMPUTE X=X+1.
END LOOP.
```

- The scratch variable *#I* starts at 2 and increases by 2 for each of five iterations until it equals 10 for the last iteration.

Example

```
LOOP #I=1 TO Y BY Z.           /*Loop to Y incrementing by Z
COMPUTE X=X+1.
END LOOP.
```

- The loop is executed once for a case with Y equal to 2 and Z equal to 2 but twice for a case with Y equal to 3 and Z equal to 2.

Example

```
* Repeating data using LOOP.

INPUT PROGRAM.
DATA LIST        NOTABLE/ ORDER 1-4(N) #BKINFO 6-71(A).
LEAVE ORDER.
LOOP             #I = 1 TO 66 BY 6 IF SUBSTR(#BKINFO,#I,6) <> ' '.
+  REREAD           COLUMN = #I+5.
+  DATA LIST        NOTABLE/ ISBN 1-3(N) QUANTITY 4-5.
+  END CASE.
END LOOP.
END INPUT PROGRAM.
SORT CASES       BY ISBN ORDER.
BEGIN DATA
1045 182 2 155 1 134 1 153 5
1046 155 3 153 5 163 1
1047 161 5 182 2 163 4 186 6
1048 186 2
1049 155 2 163 2 153 2 074 1 161 1
END DATA.

DO IF            $CASENUM = 1.
+  PRINT EJECT      /'Order' 1  'ISBN' 7  'Quantity' 13.
END IF.
PRINT            /ORDER 2-5(N) ISBN 8-10(N) QUANTITY 13-17.
EXECUTE.
```

- This example uses LOOP to simulate a REPEATING DATA command.

- DATA LIST specifies the scratch variable *#BKINFO* as a string variable (format A) to allow blanks in the data.

- LOOP is executed if the SUBSTR function returns anything other than a blank or null value. SUBSTR returns a six-character substring of *#BKINFO*, beginning with the character in the position specified by the value of the indexing variable *#I*. As specified on the indexing clause, *#I* begins with a value of 1 and is increased by 6 for each iteration of LOOP, up to a maximum *#I* value of 61 ($1 + 10 \times 6 = 61$). The next iteration would exceed the maximum *#I* value ($1 + 11 \times 6 = 67$).

Missing Values

- If the program encounters a case with a missing value for the initial, terminal, or increment value or expression, or if the conditional expression on the LOOP command returns missing, a zero-trip loop results and control is passed to the first command after the END LOOP command.

- If a case has a missing value for the conditional expression on an END LOOP command, the loop is terminated after the first iteration.

- To prevent cases with missing values for any variable used in the loop structure from entering the loop, use the IF clause on the LOOP command (see third example below).

Example

```
LOOP #I=1 TO Z   IF (Y GT 10). /*Loop to X=Z for cases with Y GT 10
COMPUTE X=X+1.
END LOOP.
```

- The value of *X* remains unchanged for cases with a missing value for *Y* or a missing value for *Z* (or if *Z* is less than 1).

Example

```
MISSING VALUES X(5).
LOOP.
COMPUTE X=X+1.
END LOOP IF (X GE 10). /*Loop until X is at least 10 or missing
```

- Looping is terminated when the value of *X* is 5 because 5 is defined as missing for *X*.

Example

```
LOOP IF NOT MISSING(Y).      /*Loop only when Y isn't missing
COMPUTE X=X+Y.
END LOOP IF (X GE 10).       /*Loop until X is at least 10
```

- The variable *X* is unchanged for cases with a missing value for *Y*, since the loop is never entered.

Creating Data

A loop structure and an END CASE command within an input program can be used to create data without any data input. The END FILE command must be used outside the loop (but within the input program) to terminate processing.

Example

```
INPUT PROGRAM.
LOOP #I=1 TO 20.
COMPUTE AMOUNT=RND(UNIFORM(5000))/100.
END CASE.
END LOOP.
END FILE.
END INPUT PROGRAM.

PRINT FORMATS AMOUNT (DOLLAR6.2).
PRINT /AMOUNT.
EXECUTE.
```

- This example creates 20 cases with a single variable, *AMOUNT. AMOUNT* is a uniformly distributed number between 0 and 5000, rounded to an integer and divided by 100 to provide a variable in dollars and cents.
- The END FILE command is required to terminate processing once the loop structure is complete.

See pp. 314 and 322 for other examples of creating data without any data input.

MATCH FILES

```
MATCH FILES FILE={file}  [TABLE={file}]
                {*   }          {*   }

 [/RENAME=(old varnames=new varnames)...]

 [/IN=varname]

 /FILE==...  [TABLE= ...]

 [/BY varlist]

 [/MAP]

 [/KEEP={ALL** }] [/DROP=varlist]
        {varlist}

 [/FIRST=varname]  [/LAST=varname]
```

**Default if the subcommand is omitted.

Example:

```
MATCH FILES FILE=PART1 /FILE=PART2 /FILE=*.
```

Overview

MATCH FILES combines variables from 2 up to 50 SPSS-format data files. MATCH FILES can make parallel or nonparallel matches between different files or perform table lookups. **Parallel matches** combine files sequentially by case (they are sometimes referred to as **sequential matches**). **Nonparallel matches** combine files according to the values of one or more key variables. In a table lookup, MATCH FILES looks up variables in one file and transfers those variables to a case file.

The files specified on MATCH FILES can be SPSS-format data files created with SAVE or XSAVE or the working data file. The combined file becomes the new working data file. Statistical procedures following MATCH FILES use this combined file unless you replace it by building another working file. You must use the SAVE or XSAVE commands if you want to save the combined file as an SPSS-format data file.

In general, MATCH FILES is used to combine files containing the same cases but different variables. To combine files containing the same variables but different cases, use ADD FILES. To update existing SPSS-format data files, use UPDATE.

MATCH FILES is often used with the AGGREGATE command to add variables with summary measures (sum, mean, and so forth) to the data. For an example, see p. 94.

Options

Variable Selection. You can specify which variables from each input file are included in the new working file using the DROP and KEEP subcommands.

Variable Names. You can rename variables in each input file before combining the files using the RENAME subcommand. This permits you to combine variables that are the same but whose names differ in different input files, or to separate variables that are different but have the same name.

Variable Flag. You can create a variable that indicates whether a case came from a particular input file using IN. You can use the FIRST or LAST subcommands to create a variable that flags the first or last case of a group of cases with the same value for the key variable.

Variable Map. You can request a map showing all variables in the new working file, their order, and the input files from which they came using the MAP subcommand.

Basic Specification

The basic specification is two or more FILE subcommands, each of which specifies a file to be matched. In addition, BY is required to specify the key variables for nonparallel matches. Both BY and TABLE are required to match table-lookup files.

- All variables from all input files are included in the new working file unless DROP or KEEP is specified.

Subcommand Order

- RENAME and IN must immediately follow the FILE subcommand to which they apply.
- BY must follow the FILE and TABLE subcommands and any associated RENAME and IN subcommands.
- FIRST and LAST must follow all TABLE and FILE subcommands and any associated RENAME and IN subcommands.
- MAP, DROP, and KEEP must follow all FILE, TABLE, and RENAME subcommands.

Syntax Rules

- RENAME can be repeated after each FILE or TABLE subcommand and applies only to variables in the file named on the immediately preceding FILE or TABLE.
- IN can be used only for a nonparallel match or for a table lookup. (Thus, IN can be used only if BY is specified.)
- BY can be specified only once. However, multiple variables can be specified on BY. When BY is used, all files must be sorted in ascending order of the key variables named on BY.
- MAP can be repeated as often as desired.

Operations

- MATCH FILES reads all files named on FILE or TABLE and builds a new working data file that replaces any working file created earlier in the session.

- The new working data file contains complete dictionary information from the input files, including variable names, labels, print and write formats, and missing-value indicators. The new file also contains the documents from each of the input files. See DROP DOCUMENTS for information on deleting documents.

- Variables are copied in order from the first file specified, then from the second file specified, and so on.

- If the same variable name is used in more than one input file, data are taken from the file specified first. Dictionary information is taken from the first file containing value labels, missing values, or a variable label for the common variable. If the first file has no such information, MATCH FILES checks the second file, and so on, seeking dictionary information.

- All cases from all input files are included in the combined file. Cases that are absent from one of the input files will be assigned system-missing values for variables unique to that file.

- BY specifies that cases should be combined according to a common value on one or more key variables. All input files must be sorted in ascending order of the key variables.

- If BY is not used, the program performs a parallel (sequential) match, combining the first case from each file, then the second case from each file, and so on, without regard to any identifying values that may be present.

- If the working file is named as an input file, any N and SAMPLE commands that have been specified are applied to that file before files are matched.

Limitations

- Maximum 50 files can be combined on one MATCH FILES command.
- Maximum one BY subcommand. However, BY can specify multiple variables.
- The TEMPORARY command cannot be in effect if the working data file is used as an input file.

Example

```
MATCH FILES FILE=PART1 /FILE=PART2 /FILE=*.
```

- MATCH FILES combines three files (the working data file and two SPSS-format data files) in a parallel match. Cases are combined according to their order in each file.

- The new working data file contains as many cases as are contained in the largest of the three input files.

FILE Subcommand

FILE identifies the files to be combined (except table files). At least one FILE subcommand is required on MATCH FILES. A separate FILE subcommand must be used for each input file.

- An asterisk can be specified on FILE to refer to the working data file.

- The order in which files are specified determines the order of variables in the new working file. In addition, if the same variable name occurs in more than one input file, the variable is taken from the file specified first.

- If the files have unequal numbers of cases, cases are generated from the longest file. Cases that do not exist in the shorter files have system-missing values for variables that are unique to those files.

Raw Data Files

To add variables from a raw data file, you must first define the raw data as the working data file using the DATA LIST command. MATCH FILES can then combine the working data file with an SPSS-format data file.

Example

```
DATA LIST FILE=GASDATA/1 OZONE 10-12 CO 20-22 SULFUR 30-32.

VARIABLE LABELS OZONE 'LEVEL OF OZONE'
  CO 'LEVEL OF CARBON MONOXIDE'
  SULFUR 'LEVEL OF SULFUR DIOXIDE'.

MATCH FILES  FILE=PARTICLE /FILE=*.

SAVE  OUTFILE=POLLUTE.
```

- The *PARTICLE* file is a previously saved SPSS-format data file.
- The *GASDATA* file is a raw data file and is defined on the DATA LIST command. Variable labels are assigned on the VARIABLE LABELS command.
- MATCH FILES adds the working data file (*), which now contains the gas data, to SPSS-format data file *PARTICLE*.
- SAVE saves the new working file as an SPSS-format data file with the filename *POLLUTE*.

BY Subcommand

BY specifies one or more identification, or key, variables that determine which cases are to be combined. When BY is specified, cases from one file are matched only with cases from other files that have the same values for the key variables. BY is required unless all input files are to be matched sequentially according to the order of cases.

- BY must follow the FILE and TABLE subcommands and any associated RENAME and IN subcommands.
- BY specifies the names of one or more key variables. The key variables must exist in all input files. The key variables can be numeric or long or short strings.
- All input files must be sorted in ascending order of the key variables. If necessary, use SORT CASES before MATCH FILES.
- Missing values for key variables are handled like any other values.
- Unmatched cases are assigned system-missing values (for numeric variables) or blanks (for string variables) for variables from files that do not contain a match.

Duplicate Cases

Duplicate cases are those with the same values for the key variables named on the BY subcommand.

- Duplicate cases are permitted in any input files except table files.
- When there is no table file, the first duplicate case in each file is matched with the first matching case (if any) from the other files; the second duplicate case is matched with a second matching duplicate, if any; and so on. (In effect, a parallel match is performed within groups of duplicate cases.) Unmatched cases are assigned system-missing values (for numeric variables) or blanks (for string variables) for variables from files that do not contain a match.
- The program displays a warning if it encounters duplicate keys in one or more of the files being matched.

TABLE Subcommand

TABLE specifies a table lookup (or keyed table) file. A lookup file contributes variables but not cases to the new working file. Variables from the table file are added to all cases from other files that have matching values for the key variables. FILE specifies the files that supply the cases.

- A separate TABLE subcommand must be used to specify each lookup file, and a separate FILE subcommand must be used to specify each case file.
- The BY subcommand is required when TABLE is used.
- All specified files must be sorted in ascending order of the key variables. If necessary, use SORT CASES before MATCH FILES.
- A lookup file cannot contain duplicate cases (cases for which the key variable(s) named on BY have identical values).
- An asterisk on TABLE refers to the working data file.
- Cases in a case file that do not have matches in a table file are assigned system-missing values (for numeric variables) or blanks (for string variables) for variables from that table file.
- Cases in a table file that do not match any cases in a case file are ignored.

Example

```
MATCH FILES FILE=* /TABLE=MASTER /BY EMP_ID.
```

- MATCH FILES combines variables from the SPSS-format data file *MASTER* with the working data file, matching cases by the variable *EMP_ID*.
- No new cases are added to the working file as a result of the table lookup.
- Cases whose value for *EMP_ID* is not included in the *MASTER* file are assigned system-missing values for variables taken from the table.

RENAME Subcommand

RENAME renames variables on the input files *before* they are processed by MATCH FILES. RENAME must follow the FILE or TABLE subcommand that contains the variables to be renamed.

- RENAME applies only to the immediately preceding FILE or TABLE subcommand. To rename variables from more than one input file, specify a RENAME subcommand after each FILE or TABLE subcommand.

- Specifications for RENAME consist of a left parenthesis, a list of old variable names, an equals sign, a list of new variable names, and a right parenthesis. The two variable lists must name or imply the same number of variables. If only one variable is renamed, the parentheses are optional.

- More than one rename specification can be specified on a single RENAME subcommand, each enclosed in parentheses.

- The TO keyword can be used to refer to consecutive variables in the file and to generate new variable names. (See the TO keyword on p. 29.)

- RENAME takes effect immediately. Any KEEP and DROP subcommands entered prior to a RENAME must use the old names, while KEEP and DROP subcommands entered after a RENAME must use the new names.

- All specifications within a single set of parentheses take effect simultaneously. For example, the specification RENAME (A,B = B,A) swaps the names of the two variables.

- Variables cannot be renamed to scratch variables.

- Input SPSS-format data files are not changed on disk; only the copy of the file being combined is affected.

Example

```
MATCH FILES FILE=UPDATE /RENAME=(NEWID = ID)
 /FILE=MASTER /BY ID.
```

- MATCH FILES matches a master SPSS-format data file (*MASTER*) with an update data file (*UPDATE*).

- Variable *NEWID* in the *UPDATE* file is renamed *ID* so that it will have the same name as the identification variable in the master file and can be used on the BY subcommand.

DROP and KEEP Subcommands

DROP and KEEP are used to include a subset of variables in the new working data file. DROP specifies a set of variables to exclude and KEEP specifies a set of variables to retain.

- DROP and KEEP do not affect the input files on disk.

- DROP and KEEP must follow all FILE, TABLE, and RENAME subcommands.

- DROP and KEEP must specify one or more variables. If RENAME is used to rename variables, specify the new names on DROP and KEEP.

- The keyword ALL can be specified on KEEP. ALL must be the last specification on KEEP, and it refers to all variables not previously named on KEEP.

- DROP cannot be used with variables created by the IN, FIRST, or LAST subcommands.
- KEEP can be used to change the order of variables in the resulting file. By default, MATCH FILES first copies the variables in order from the first file, then copies the variables in order from the second file, and so on. With KEEP, variables are kept in the order in which they are listed on the subcommand. If a variable is named more than once on KEEP, only the first mention of the variable is in effect; all subsequent references to that variable name are ignored.

Example

```
MATCH FILES FILE=PARTICLE /RENAME=(PARTIC=POLLUTE1)
   /FILE=GAS /RENAME=(OZONE TO SULFUR=POLLUTE2 TO POLLUTE4)
   /DROP=POLLUTE4 .
```

- The renamed variable *POLLUTE4* is dropped from the resulting file. DROP is specified after all of the FILE and RENAME subcommands, and it refers to the dropped variable by its new name.

IN Subcommand

IN creates a new variable in the resulting file that indicates whether a case came from the input file named on the preceding FILE subcommand. IN applies only to the file specified on the immediately preceding FILE subcommand.

- IN can be used only for a nonparallel match or table lookup.
- IN has only one specification—the name of the flag variable.
- The variable created by IN has the value 1 for every case that came from the associated input file and the value 0 if the case came from a different input file.
- Variables created by IN are automatically attached to the end of the resulting file and cannot be dropped. If FIRST or LAST is used, the variable created by IN precedes the variables created by FIRST or LAST.

Example

```
MATCH FILES  FILE=WEEK10 /FILE=WEEK11 /IN=INWEEK11 /BY=EMPID.
```

- IN creates the variable *INWEEK11*, which has the value 1 for all cases in the resulting file that had values in the input file *WEEK11* and the value 0 for those cases that were not in file *WEEK11*.

FIRST and LAST Subcommands

FIRST and LAST create logical variables that flag the first or last case of a group of cases with the same value for the BY variables.

- FIRST and LAST must follow all TABLE and FILE subcommands and any associated RENAME and IN subcommands.
- FIRST and LAST have only one specification—the name of the flag variable.

- FIRST creates a variable with the value 1 for the first case of each group and the value 0 for all other cases.
- LAST creates a variable with the value 1 for the last case of each group and the value 0 for all other cases.
- Variables created by FIRST and LAST are automatically attached to the end of the resulting file and cannot be dropped.
- If one file has several cases with the same values for the key variables, FIRST or LAST can be used to create a variable that flags the first or last case of the group.

Example

```
MATCH FILES  TABLE=HOUSE /FILE=PERSONS
 /BY=HOUSEID /FIRST=HEAD.
```

- The variable *HEAD* contains the value 1 for the first person in each household and the value 0 for all other persons. Assuming that the *PERSONS* file is sorted with the head of household as the first case for each household, the variable *HEAD* identifies the case for the head of household.

Example

```
* Using match files with only one file.

* This example flags the first of several cases with
  the same value for a key variable.

MATCH FILES  FILE=PERSONS /BY HOUSEID /FIRST=HEAD.
SELECT IF  (HEAD EQ 1).
CROSSTABS  JOBCAT BY SEX.
```

- MATCH FILES is used instead of GET to read the SPSS-format data file *PERSONS*. The BY subcommand identifies the key variable (*HOUSEID*), and FIRST creates the variable *HEAD* with the value 1 for the first case in each household and the value 0 for all other cases.
- SELECT IF selects only the cases with the value 1 for *HEAD*, and the CROSSTABS procedure is run on these cases.

MAP Subcommand

MAP produces a list of the variables that are in the new working file and the file or files from which they came. Variables are listed in the order in which they appear in the resulting file. MAP has no specifications and must be placed after all FILE, TABLE, and RENAME subcommands.

- Multiple MAP subcommands can be used. Each MAP shows the current status of the working data file and reflects only the subcommands that precede the MAP subcommand.
- To obtain a map of the resulting file in its final state, specify MAP last.
- If a variable is renamed, its original and new names are listed. Variables created by IN, FIRST, and LAST are not included in the map, since they are automatically attached to the end of the file and cannot be dropped.
- MAP can be used with the EDIT command to obtain a list of the variables in the resulting file without actually reading the data and combining the files.

MATRIX—END MATRIX

This command is not available on all operating systems.

```
MATRIX
matrix statements
END MATRIX
```

The following matrix language statements can be used in a matrix program:

BREAK	DO IF	END LOOP	MSAVE	SAVE
CALL	ELSE	GET	PRINT	WRITE
COMPUTE	ELSE IF	LOOP	READ	
DISPLAY	END IF	MGET	RELEASE	

The following functions can be used in matrix language statements:

ABS	Absolute values of matrix elements
ALL	Test if all elements are positive
ANY	Test if any element is positive
ARSIN	Arcsines of matrix elements
ARTAN	Arctangents of matrix elements
BLOCK	Create block diagonal matrix
CDFNORM	Cumulative normal distribution function
CHICDF	Cumulative chi-squared distribution function
CHOL	Cholesky decomposition
CMAX	Column maxima
CMIN	Column minima
COS	Cosines of matrix elements
CSSQ	Column sums of squares
CSUM	Column sums
DESIGN	Create design matrix
DET	Determinant
DIAG	Diagonal of matrix
EOF	Check end of file
EVAL	Eigenvalues of symmetric matrix
EXP	Exponentials of matrix elements
FCDF	Cumulative F distribution function
GINV	Generalized inverse
GRADE	Rank elements in matrix, using sequential integers for ties
GSCH	Gram-Schmidt orthonormal basis
IDENT	Create identity matrix

INV	Inverse
KRONECKER	Kronecker product of two matrices
LG10	Logarithms to base 10 of matrix elements
LN	Logarithms to base e of matrix elements
MAGIC	Create magic square
MAKE	Create a matrix with all elements equal
MDIAG	Create a matrix with the given diagonal
MMAX	Maximum element in matrix
MMIN	Minimum element in matrix
MOD	Remainders after division
MSSQ	Matrix sum of squares
MSUM	Matrix sum
NCOL	Number of columns
NROW	Number of rows
RANK	Matrix rank
RESHAPE	Change shape of matrix
RMAX	Row maxima
RMIN	Row minima
RND	Round off matrix elements to nearest integer
RNKORDER	Rank elements in matrix, averaging ties
RSSQ	Row sums of squares
RSUM	Row sums
SIN	Sines of matrix elements
SOLVE	Solve systems of linear equations
SQRT	Square roots of matrix elements
SSCP	Sums of squares and cross-products
SVAL	Singular values
SWEEP	Perform sweep transformation
T	(Synonym for TRANSPOS)
TCDF	Cumulative normal t distribution function
TRACE	Calculate trace (sum of diagonal elements)
TRANSPOS	Transposition of matrix
TRUNC	Truncation of matrix elements to integer
UNIFORM	Create matrix of uniform random numbers

Example:

```
MATRIX.
READ A /FILE=MATRDATA /SIZE={6,6} /FIELD=1 TO 60.
CALL EIGEN(A,EIGENVEC,EIGENVAL).
LOOP J=1 TO NROW(EIGENVAL).
+ DO IF (EIGENVAL(J) > 1.0).
+    PRINT EIGENVAL(J) / TITLE="Eigenvalue:" /SPACE=3.
+    PRINT T(EIGENVEC(:,J)) / TITLE="Eigenvector:" /SPACE=1.
+ END IF.
END LOOP.
END MATRIX.
```

Overview

The MATRIX and END MATRIX commands enclose statements that are executed by the SPSS matrix processor. Using matrix programs, you can write your own statistical routines in the compact language of matrix algebra. Matrix programs can include mathematical calculations, control structures, display of results, and reading and writing matrices as character files or SPSS data files.

As discussed below, a matrix program is for the most part independent of the rest of the SPSS session, although it can read and write SPSS data files, including the working data file.

This section does not attempt to explain the rules of matrix algebra. Many textbooks, such as Hadley (1961) and O'Nan (1971), teach the application of matrix methods to statistics.

The SPSS MATRIX procedure was originally developed at the Madison Academic Computing Center, University of Wisconsin.

Terminology

A variable within a matrix program represents a **matrix**, which is simply a set of values arranged in a rectangular array of rows and columns.

- An $n \times m$ (read "n by m") matrix is one that has n rows and m columns. The integers n and m are the dimensions of the matrix. An $n \times m$ matrix contains $n \times m$ elements, or data values.

- An $n \times 1$ matrix is sometimes called a **column vector**, and a $1 \times n$ matrix is sometimes called a **row vector**. A vector is a special case of a matrix.

- A 1×1 matrix, containing a single data value, is often called a **scalar**. A scalar is also a special case of a matrix.

- An **index** to a matrix or vector is an integer that identifies a specific row or column. Indexes normally appear in printed works as subscripts, as in A_{31}, but are specified in the matrix language within parentheses, as in $A(3,1)$. The row index for a matrix precedes the column index.

- The **main diagonal** of a matrix consists of the elements whose row index equals their column index. It begins at the top left corner of the matrix; in a square matrix, it runs to the bottom right corner.

- The **transpose** of a matrix is the matrix with rows and columns interchanged. The transpose of an $n \times m$ matrix is an $m \times n$ matrix.

- A **symmetric matrix** is a square matrix that is unchanged if you flip it about the main diagonal. That is, the element in row i, column j equals the element in row j, column i. A symmetric matrix equals its transpose.

- Matrices are always rectangular, although it is possible to read or write symmetric matrices in triangular form. Vectors and scalars are considered degenerate rectangles.

- It is an error to try to create a matrix whose rows have different numbers of elements.

A matrix program does not process individual cases unless you so specify, using the control structures of the matrix language. Unlike ordinary SPSS variables, matrix variables do not have distinct values for different cases. A matrix is a single entity.

Vectors in matrix processing should not be confused with the vectors temporarily created by the VECTOR command in SPSS. The latter are shorthand for a list of SPSS variables and, like all ordinary SPSS variables, are unavailable during matrix processing.

Matrix Variables

A matrix variable is created by a matrix statement that assigns a value to a variable name.

- A matrix variable name follows the same rules as those applicable to an ordinary SPSS variable name.

- The names of matrix functions and procedures cannot be used as variable names within a matrix program. (In particular, the letter T cannot be used as a variable name because T is an alias for the TRANSPOS function.)

- The COMPUTE, READ, GET, MGET, and CALL statements create matrices. An index variable named on a LOOP statement creates a scalar with a value assigned to it.

- A variable name can be redefined within a matrix program without regard to the dimensions of the matrix it represents. The same name can represent scalars, vectors, and full matrices at different points in the matrix program.

- MATRIX—END MATRIX does not include any special processing for missing data. When reading a data matrix from an SPSS data file, you must therefore specify whether missing data are to be accepted as valid or excluded from the matrix.

String Variables in Matrix Programs

Matrix variables can contain short string data. Support for string variables is limited, however.

- MATRIX will attempt to carry out calculations with string variables if you so request. The results will not be meaningful.

- You must specify a format (such as A8) when you display a matrix that contains string data.

Syntax of Matrix Language

A matrix program consists of statements. Matrix statements must appear in a matrix program, between the MATRIX and END MATRIX commands. They are analogous to SPSS commands and follow the rules of the SPSS command language regarding the abbreviation of keywords; the equivalence of upper and lower case; the use of spaces, commas, and equals signs; and the splitting of statements across multiple lines. However, commas are required to separate arguments to matrix functions and procedures and to separate variable names on the RELEASE statement.

Matrix statements are composed of the following elements:

- Keywords, such as the names of matrix statements.
- Variable names.
- Explicitly written matrices, which are enclosed within braces ({ }).
- Arithmetic and logical operators.
- Matrix functions.
- The SPSS command terminator, which serves as a statement terminator within a matrix program.

Comments in Matrix Programs

Within a matrix program, you can enter comments in any of the forms recognized by SPSS: on lines beginning with the COMMENT command, on lines beginning with an asterisk, or between the characters /* and */ on a command line.

Matrix Notation in SPSS

To write a matrix explicitly:

- Enclose the matrix within braces ({ }).
- Separate the elements of each row by commas.
- Separate the rows by semicolons.
- String elements must be enclosed in either apostrophes or quotation marks, as is generally true in the SPSS command language.

Example

`{1,2,3;4,5,6}`

- The example represents the following matrix:

$$\begin{bmatrix} 1 & 2 & 3 \\ 4 & 5 & 6 \end{bmatrix}$$

Example

`{1,2,3}`

- This example represents a row vector:

$$\begin{bmatrix} 1 & 2 & 3 \end{bmatrix}$$

Example

```
{11;12;13}
```

- This example represents a column vector:

$$\begin{bmatrix} 11 \\ 12 \\ 13 \end{bmatrix}$$

Example

```
{3}
```

- This example represents a scalar. The braces are optional. You can specify the same scalar as 3.

Matrix Notation Shorthand

You can simplify the construction of matrices using notation shorthand.

Consecutive Integers. Use a colon to indicate a range of consecutive integers. For example, the vector `{1,2,3,4,5,6}` can be written as `{1:6}`.

Incremented Ranges of Integers. Use a second colon followed by an integer to indicate the increment. The matrix `{1,3,5,7;2,5,8,11}` can be written as `{1:7:2;2:11:3}`, where `1:7:2` indicates the integers from 1 to 7 incrementing by 2, and `2:11:3` indicates the integers from 2 to 11 incrementing by 3.

- You must use integers when specifying a range in either of these ways. Numbers with fractional parts are truncated to integers.
- If an arithmetic expression is used, it should be enclosed in parentheses.

Extraction of an Element, a Vector, or a Submatrix

You can use indexes in parentheses to extract an element from a vector or matrix, a vector from a matrix, or a submatrix from a matrix. In the following discussion, an **integer index** refers to an integer expression used as an index, which can be a scalar matrix with an integer value or an integer element extracted from a vector or matrix. Similarly, a **vector index** refers to a vector expression used as an index, which can be a vector matrix or a vector extracted from a matrix.

For example, if S is a scalar matrix, $S = \begin{bmatrix} 2 \end{bmatrix}$, R is a row vector, $R = \begin{bmatrix} 1 & 3 & 5 \end{bmatrix}$, C is a

column vector, $C = \begin{bmatrix} 2 \\ 3 \\ 4 \end{bmatrix}$, and A is a 5×5 matrix, $A = \begin{bmatrix} 11 & 12 & 13 & 14 & 15 \\ 21 & 22 & 23 & 24 & 25 \\ 31 & 32 & 33 & 34 & 35 \\ 41 & 42 & 43 & 44 & 45 \\ 51 & 52 & 53 & 54 & 55 \end{bmatrix}$, then:

$R(S) = R(2) = \{3\}$
$C(S) = C(2) = \{3\}$
- An integer index extracts an element from a vector matrix.
- The distinction between a row and a column vector does not matter when an integer index is used to extract an element from it.

$A(2,3) = A(S,3) = \{23\}$
- Two integer indexes separated by a comma extract an element from a rectangular matrix.

$A(R,2)=A(1:5:2,2)=\{12; 32; 52\}$
$A(2,R)=A(2,1:5:2)=\{21, 23, 25\}$
$A(C,2)=A(2:4,2)= \{22;32;42\}$
$A(2,C)=A(2,2:4)= \{22,23,24\}$
- An integer and a vector index separated by a comma extract a vector from a matrix.
- The distinction between a row and a column vector does not matter when used as indexes in this way.

$A(2,:)=A(S,:) = \{21, 22, 23, 24, 25\}$
$A(:,2) =A(:,S)= \{12; 22; 32; 42; 52\}$
- A colon by itself used as an index extracts an entire row or column vector from a matrix.

$A(R,C)=A(R,2:4)=A(1:5:2,C)=A(1:5:2,2:4)=\{12,13,14;32,33,34;52,53,54\}$
$A(C,R)=A(C,1:5:2)=A(2:4,R)=A(2:4,1:5:2)=\{21,23,25;31,33,35;41,43,45\}$
- Two vector indexes separated by a comma extract a submatrix from a matrix.
- The distinction between a row and a column vector does not matter when used as indexes in this way.

Construction of a Matrix from Other Matrices

You can use vector or rectangular matrices to construct a new matrix, separating row expressions by semicolons and components of row expressions by commas. If a column vector V_c has n elements and matrix M has the dimensions $n \times m$, then $\{M, V_c\}$ is an $n \times (m + 1)$ matrix. Similarly, if the row vector V_r has m elements and M is the same, then $\{M;V_r\}$ is an $(n + 1) \times m$ matrix. In fact, you can paste together any number of matrices and vectors this way.

- All of the components of each column expression must have the same number of actual rows, and all of the row expressions must have the same number of actual columns.
- The distinction between row vectors and column vectors must be observed carefully when constructing matrices in this way, so that the components will fit together properly.
- Several of the matrix functions are also useful in constructing matrices; see in particular the MAKE, UNIFORM, and IDENT functions in "Matrix Functions" on p. 551.

Example

```
COMPUTE M={CORNER, COL3; ROW3}.
```

- This example constructs the matrix *M* from the matrix *CORNER*, the column vector *COL3*, and the row vector *ROW3*.
- *COL3* supplies new row components and is separated from *CORNER* by a comma.
- *ROW3* supplies column elements and is separated from previous expressions by a semicolon.
- *COL3* must have the same number of rows as *CORNER*.
- *ROW3* must have the same number of columns as the matrix resulting from the previous expressions.

- For example, if $CORNER = \begin{bmatrix} 11 & 12 \\ 21 & 22 \end{bmatrix}$, $COL3 = \begin{bmatrix} 13 \\ 23 \end{bmatrix}$, and $ROW3 = \begin{bmatrix} 31 & 32 & 33 \end{bmatrix}$,

then: $M = \begin{bmatrix} 11 & 12 & 13 \\ 21 & 22 & 23 \\ 31 & 32 & 33 \end{bmatrix}$

Matrix Operations

You can perform matrix calculations according to the rules of matrix algebra and compare matrices using relational or logical operators.

Conformable Matrices

Many operations with matrices make sense only if the matrices involved have "suitable" dimensions. Most often, this means that they should be the same size, with the same number of rows and the same number of columns. Matrices that are the right size for an operation are said to be **conformable matrices**. If you attempt to do something in a matrix program with a matrix that is not conformable for that operation—a matrix that has the wrong dimensions—you will receive an error message, and the operation will not be performed. An important exception, where one of the matrices is a scalar, is discussed below.

Requirements for carrying out matrix operations include:

- Matrix addition and subtraction require that the two matrices be the same size.

- The relational and logical operations described below require that the two matrices be the same size.
- Matrix multiplication requires that the number of columns of the first matrix equal the number of rows of the second matrix.
- Raising a matrix to a power can be done only if the matrix is square. This includes the important operation of *inverting* a matrix, where the power is −1.
- Conformability requirements for matrix functions are noted in "Matrix Functions" on p. 551 and in "COMPUTE Statement" on p. 550.

Scalar Expansion

When one of the matrices involved in an operation is a scalar, the scalar is treated as a matrix of the correct size in order to carry out the operation. This internal scalar expansion is performed for the following operations:

- Addition and subtraction.
- Elementwise multiplication, division, and exponentiation. Note that multiplying a matrix elementwise by an expanded scalar is equivalent to ordinary scalar multiplication—each element of the matrix is multiplied by the scalar.
- All relational and logical operators.

Arithmetic Operators

You can add, subtract, multiply, or exponentiate matrices according to the rules of matrix algebra, or you can perform elementwise arithmetic, in which you multiply, divide, or exponentiate each element of a matrix separately. The arithmetic operators are listed below.

Unary −   *Sign reversal.* A minus sign placed in front of a matrix reverses the sign of each element. (The unary + is also accepted but has no effect.)

+   *Matrix addition.* Corresponding elements of the two matrices are added. The matrices must have the same dimensions, or one must be a scalar.

−   *Matrix subtraction.* Corresponding elements of the two matrices are subtracted. The matrices must have the same dimensions, or one must be a scalar.

*   *Multiplication.* There are two cases. First, *scalar multiplication*: if either of the matrices is a scalar, each element of the other matrix is multiplied by that scalar. Second, *matrix multiplication*: if A is an $m \times n$ matrix and B is an $n \times p$ matrix, $A*B$ is an $m \times p$ matrix in which the element in row i, column k, is equal to $\Sigma_{j=1}^{n} A(i,j) \times B(j,k)$.

/   *Division.* The division operator performs elementwise division (described below). True matrix division, the inverse operation of matrix multiplication, is accomplished by taking the INV function (square matrices) or the GINV function (rectangular matrices) of the denominator and multiplying.

**   *Matrix exponentiation.* A matrix can be raised only to an integer power. The matrix, which must be square, is multiplied by itself as many times as the absolute value of the exponent. If the exponent is negative, the result is then inverted.

&*   *Elementwise multiplication.* Each element of the matrix is multiplied by the corresponding element of the second matrix. The matrices must have the same dimensions, or one must be a scalar.

&/   *Elementwise division.* Each element of the matrix is divided by the corresponding element of the second matrix. The matrices must have the same dimensions, or one must be a scalar.

&**   *Elementwise exponentiation.* Each element of the first matrix is raised to the power of the corresponding element of the second matrix. The matrices must have the same dimensions, or one must be a scalar.

:   *Sequential integers.* This operator creates a vector of consecutive integers from the value preceding the operator to the value following it. You can specify an optional increment following a second colon. See "Matrix Notation Shorthand" on p. 542 for the principal use of this operator.

- Use these operators only with numeric matrices. The results are undefined when they are used with string matrices.

Relational Operators

The relational operators are used to compare two matrices, element by element. The result is a matrix of the same size as the (expanded) operands and containing either 1 or 0. The value of each element, 1 or 0, is determined by whether the comparison between the corresponding element of the first matrix with the corresponding element of the second matrix is true or false, 1 for true and 0 for false. The matrices being compared must be of the same dimensions unless one of them is a scalar. The relational operators are listed in Table 1.

Table 1   Relational operators in matrix programs

>	GT	Greater than
<	LT	Less than
<> or ~= (¬=)	NE	Not equal to
<=	LE	Less than or equal to
>=	GE	Greater than or equal to
=	EQ	Equal to

- The symbolic and alphabetic forms of these operators are equivalent.
- The symbols representing NE ($\sim=$ or $\neg=$) are system dependent. In general, the tilde ($\sim$) is valid for ASCII systems, while the logical-not sign ($\neg$), or whatever symbol is over the number 6 on the keyboard, is valid for IBM EBCDIC systems.
- Use these operators only with numeric matrices. The results are undefined when they are used with string matrices.

Logical Operators

Logical operators combine two matrices, normally containing values of 1 (true) or 0 (false). When used with other numerical matrices, they treat all positive values as true and all negative and 0 values as false. The logical operators are:

NOT   *Reverses the truth of the matrix that follows it.* Positive elements yield 0, and negative or 0 elements yield 1.

AND   *Both must be true.* The matrix A AND B is 1 where the corresponding elements of A and B are both positive, and 0 elsewhere.

OR   *Either must be true.* The matrix A OR B is 1 where the corresponding element of either A or B is positive, and 0 where both elements are negative or 0.

XOR   *Either must be true, but not both.* The matrix A XOR B is 1 where one, but not both, of the corresponding elements of A and B is positive, and 0 where both are positive or neither is positive.

Precedence of Operators

Parentheses can be used to control the order in which complex expressions are evaluated. When the order of evaluation is not specified by parentheses, operations are carried out in the order listed below. The operations higher on the list take precedence over the operations lower on the list.

```
+ - (Unary)
:
** &**
* &* &/
+ - (Addition and Subtraction)
> >= < <= <>=
NOT
AND
OR XOR
```

Operations of equal precedence are performed left to right of the expressions.

Examples

```
COMPUTE A = {1,2,3;4,5,6}.
COMPUTE B = A + 4.
COMPUTE C = A &** 2.
COMPUTE D = 2 &** A.
COMPUTE E = A < 5.
COMPUTE F = (C &/ 2) < B.
```

- The results of these COMPUTE statements are:

$$A = \begin{bmatrix} 1 & 2 & 3 \\ 4 & 5 & 6 \end{bmatrix} \qquad B = \begin{bmatrix} 5 & 6 & 7 \\ 8 & 9 & 10 \end{bmatrix} \qquad C = \begin{bmatrix} 1 & 4 & 9 \\ 16 & 25 & 36 \end{bmatrix}$$

$$D = \begin{bmatrix} 2 & 4 & 8 \\ 16 & 32 & 64 \end{bmatrix} \qquad E = \begin{bmatrix} 1 & 1 & 1 \\ 1 & 0 & 0 \end{bmatrix} \qquad F = \begin{bmatrix} 1 & 1 & 1 \\ 0 & 0 & 0 \end{bmatrix}$$

MATRIX and Other SPSS Commands

A matrix program is a single procedure within an SPSS session.

- No working data file is needed to run a matrix program. If one exists, it is ignored during matrix processing unless you specifically reference it (with an asterisk) on the GET, SAVE, MGET, or MSAVE statements.

- Variables defined in the SPSS working data file are unavailable during matrix processing, except with the GET or MGET statements.

- Matrix variables are unavailable after the END MATRIX command, unless you use SAVE or MSAVE to write them to the working data file.

- You cannot run a matrix program from a syntax window if split-file processing is in effect. If you save the matrix program into a syntax file, however, you can use the INCLUDE command to run the program even if split-file processing is in effect.

Matrix Statements

Table 2 lists all of the statements that are accepted within a matrix program. Most of them have the same name as an analogous SPSS command and perform an exactly analogous function. Use only these statements between the MATRIX and END MATRIX commands. Any command not recognized as a valid matrix statement will be rejected by the matrix processor.

Table 2   Valid matrix statements

BREAK	ELSE IF	MSAVE
CALL	END IF	PRINT
COMPUTE	END LOOP	READ
DISPLAY	GET	RELEASE
DO IF	LOOP	SAVE
ELSE	MGET	WRITE

Exchanging Data with SPSS Data Files

Matrix programs can read and write SPSS data files.

- The GET and SAVE statements read and write ordinary (case-oriented) SPSS data files, treating each case as a row of a matrix and each ordinary variable as a column.

- The MGET and MSAVE statements read and write matrix-format SPSS data files, respecting the structure defined by SPSS when it creates the file. These statements are discussed below.
- Case weighting in an SPSS data file is ignored when the file is read into a matrix program.

Using a Working Data File

You can use the GET statement to read a case-oriented working data file into a matrix variable. The result is a rectangular data matrix in which cases have become rows and variables have become columns. Special circumstances can affect the processing of this data matrix.

Split-File Processing. After a SPLIT FILE command in SPSS, a matrix program executed with the INCLUDE command will read one split-file group with each execution of a GET statement. This enables you to process the subgroups separately within the matrix program.

Case Selection. When a subset of cases is selected for processing, as the result of a SELECT IF, SAMPLE, or N OF CASES command, only the selected cases will be read by the GET statement in a matrix program.

Temporary Transformations. The entire matrix program is treated as a single procedure by the SPSS system. Temporary transformations—those preceded by the TEMPORARY command—entered immediately before a matrix program are in effect throughout that program (even if you GET the working data file repeatedly) and are no longer in effect at the end of the matrix program.

Case Weighting. Case weighting in a working data file is ignored when the file is read into a matrix program.

MATRIX and END MATRIX Commands

The MATRIX command, when encountered in an SPSS session, invokes the matrix processor, which reads matrix statements until the END MATRIX or FINISH command is encountered.

- MATRIX is a procedure and cannot be entered inside a transformation structure such as DO IF or LOOP.
- The MATRIX procedure does not require a working data file.
- Comments are removed before subsequent lines are passed to the matrix processor.
- Macros are expanded before subsequent lines are passed to the matrix processor.

The END MATRIX command terminates matrix processing and returns control to the SPSS command processor.

- The contents of matrix variables are lost after an END MATRIX command.
- The working data file, if present, becomes available again after an END MATRIX command.

COMPUTE Statement

The COMPUTE statement carries out most of the calculations in the matrix program. It closely resembles the COMPUTE command in the SPSS transformation language.

- The basic specification is the target variable, an equals sign, and the assignment expression. Values of the target variable are calculated according to the specification on the assignment expression.
- The target variable must be named first, and the equals sign is required. Only one target variable is allowed per COMPUTE statement.
- Expressions that extract portions of a matrix, such as $M(1,:)$ or $M(1:3,4)$, are allowed to assign values. (See "Matrix Notation Shorthand" on p. 542.) The target variable must be specified as a variable.
- Matrix functions must specify at least one argument enclosed in parentheses. If an expression has two or more arguments, each argument must be separated by a comma. For a complete discussion of the functions and their arguments, see "Matrix Functions" on p. 551.

String Values on COMPUTE Statements

Matrix variables, unlike those in the SPSS transformation language, are not checked for data type (numeric or string) when you use them in a COMPUTE statement.

- Numerical calculations with matrices containing string values will produce meaningless results.
- One or more elements of a matrix can be set equal to string constants by enclosing the string constants in apostrophes or quotation marks on a COMPUTE statement.
- String values can be copied from one matrix to another with the COMPUTE statement.
- There is no way to display a matrix that contains both numeric and string values, if you compute one for some reason.

Example

```
COMPUTE LABELS={"Observe", "Predict", "Error"}.
PRINT LABELS /FORMAT=A7.
```

- *LABELS* is a row vector containing three string values.

Arithmetic Operations and Comparisons

The expression on a COMPUTE statement can be formed from matrix constants and variables, combined with the arithmetic, relational, and logical operators discussed above. Matrix constructions and matrix functions are also allowed.

Examples

```
COMPUTE PI = 3.14159265.
COMPUTE RSQ = R * R.
COMPUTE FLAGS = EIGENVAL >= 1.
COMPUTE ESTIM = {OBS, PRED, ERR}.
```

- The first statement computes a scalar. Note that the braces are optional on a scalar constant.
- The second statement computes the square of the matrix *R*. *R* can be any square matrix, including a scalar.
- The third statement computes a vector named *FLAGS*, which has the same dimension as the existing vector *EIGENVAL*. Each element of *FLAGS* equals 1 if the corresponding element of *EIGENVAL* is greater than or equal to 1, and 0 if the corresponding element is less than 1.
- The fourth statement constructs a matrix *ESTIM* by concatenating the three vectors or matrices *OBS*, *PRED*, and *ERR*. The component matrices must have the same number of rows.

Matrix Functions

The following functions are available in the matrix program. Except where noted, each takes one or more numeric matrices as arguments and returns a matrix value as its result. The arguments must be enclosed in parentheses, and multiple arguments must be separated by commas.

On the following list, matrix arguments are represented by names beginning with *M*. Unless otherwise noted, these arguments can be vectors or scalars. Arguments that must be vectors are represented by names beginning with *V*, and arguments that must be scalars are represented by names beginning with *S*.

ABS(M)
Absolute value. Takes a single argument. Returns a matrix having the same dimensions as the argument, containing the absolute values of its elements.

ALL(M)
Test for all elements nonzero. Takes a single argument. Returns a scalar: 1 if all elements of the argument are nonzero and 0 if any element is zero.

ANY(M)
Test for any element nonzero. Takes a single argument. Returns a scalar: 1 if any element of the argument is nonzero and 0 if all elements are zero.

ARSIN(M)
Inverse sine. Takes a single argument, whose elements must be between -1 and 1. Returns a matrix having the same dimensions as the argument, containing the inverse sines (arcsines) of its elements. The results are in radians and are in the range from $-\pi/2$ to $\pi/2$.

ARTAN(M)
Inverse tangent. Takes a single argument. Returns a matrix having the same dimensions as the argument, containing the inverse tangents (arctangents) of its elements, in radians. To convert radians to degrees, multiply by $180/\pi$, which you can compute as `45/ARTAN(1)`. For example, the statement `COMPUTE DEGREES=ARTAN(M)*45/ARTAN(1)` returns a matrix containing inverse tangents in degrees.

BLOCK(M1,M2,...)
Create a block diagonal matrix. Takes any number of arguments. Returns a matrix with as many rows as the sum of the rows in all the arguments, and as many columns as the sum of the columns in all the arguments, with the argument matrices down the diagonal and zeros elsewhere. For example, if:

$$A = \begin{bmatrix} 1 & 1 & 1 \\ 1 & 1 & 1 \end{bmatrix}, \quad B = \begin{bmatrix} 2 & 2 \\ 2 & 2 \end{bmatrix}, \quad C = \begin{bmatrix} 3 & 3 & 3 \\ 3 & 3 & 3 \\ 3 & 3 & 3 \\ 3 & 3 & 3 \end{bmatrix}, \quad \text{and} \quad D = \begin{bmatrix} 4 & 4 & 4 \end{bmatrix},$$

then: $\text{BLOCK}(A, B, C, D) = \begin{bmatrix} 1 & 1 & 1 & 0 & 0 & 0 & 0 & 0 & 0 & 0 \\ 1 & 1 & 1 & 0 & 0 & 0 & 0 & 0 & 0 & 0 \\ 0 & 0 & 0 & 2 & 2 & 0 & 0 & 0 & 0 & 0 \\ 0 & 0 & 0 & 2 & 2 & 0 & 0 & 0 & 0 & 0 \\ 0 & 0 & 0 & 0 & 0 & 3 & 3 & 3 & 0 & 0 & 0 \\ 0 & 0 & 0 & 0 & 0 & 3 & 3 & 3 & 0 & 0 & 0 \\ 0 & 0 & 0 & 0 & 0 & 3 & 3 & 3 & 0 & 0 & 0 \\ 0 & 0 & 0 & 0 & 0 & 3 & 3 & 3 & 0 & 0 & 0 \\ 0 & 0 & 0 & 0 & 0 & 0 & 0 & 0 & 4 & 4 & 4 \end{bmatrix}$

CDFNORM(M)

Standard normal cumulative distribution function of elements. Takes a single argument. Returns a matrix having the same dimensions as the argument, containing the values of the cumulative normal distribution function for each of its elements. If an element of the argument is x, the corresponding element of the result is a number between 0 and 1, giving the proportion of a normal distribution that is less than x. For example, CDFNORM({-1.96,0,1.96}) results in, approximately, {.025,.5,.975}.

CHICDF(M,S)

Chi-square cumulative distribution function of elements. Takes two arguments, a matrix of chi-square values and a scalar giving the degrees of freedom (which must be positive). Returns a matrix having the same dimensions as the first argument, containing the values of the cumulative chi-square distribution function for each of its elements. If an element of the first argument is x and the second argument is S, the corresponding element of the result is a number between 0 and 1, giving the proportion of a chi-square distribution with S degrees of freedom that is less than x. If x is not positive, the result is 0.

CHOL(M)

Cholesky decomposition. Takes a single argument, which must be a symmetric positive-definite matrix (a square matrix, symmetric about the main diagonal, with positive eigenvalues). Returns a matrix having the same dimensions as the argument. If M is a symmetric positive-definite matrix and B=CHOL(M), then T(B)*B=M, where T is the transpose function defined below.

CMAX(M) *Column maxima.* Takes a single argument. Returns a row vector with the same number of columns as the argument. Each column of the result contains the maximum value of the corresponding column of the argument.

CMIN(M) *Column minima.* Takes a single argument. Returns a row vector with the same number of columns as the argument. Each column of the result contains the minimum value of the corresponding column of the argument.

COS(M) *Cosines.* Takes a single argument. Returns a matrix having the same dimensions as the argument, containing the cosines of the elements of the argument. Elements of the argument matrix are assumed to be measured in radians. To convert degrees to radians, multiply by $\pi/180$, which you can compute as $ARTAN(1)/45$. For example, the statement `COMPUTE COSINES=COS(DEGREES*ARTAN(1)/45)` returns cosines from a matrix containing elements measured in degrees.

CSSQ(M) *Column sums of squares.* Takes a single argument. Returns a row vector with the same number of columns as the argument. Each column of the result contains the sum of the squared values of the elements in the corresponding column of the argument.

CSUM(M) *Column sums.* Takes a single argument. Returns a row vector with the same number of columns as the argument. Each column of the result contains the sum of the elements in the corresponding column of the argument.

DESIGN(M) *Main-effects design matrix from the columns of a matrix.* Takes a single argument. Returns a matrix having the same number of rows as the argument, and as many columns as the sum of the numbers of unique values in each column of the argument. Constant columns in the argument are skipped with a warning message. The result contains 1 in the row(s) where the value in question occurs in the argument and 0 otherwise. For example, if:

$$A = \begin{bmatrix} 1 & 2 & 8 \\ 1 & 3 & 8 \\ 2 & 6 & 5 \\ 3 & 3 & 8 \\ 3 & 6 & 5 \end{bmatrix}, \text{ then: } DESIGN(A) = \begin{bmatrix} 1 & 0 & 0 & 1 & 0 & 0 & 1 & 0 \\ 1 & 0 & 0 & 0 & 1 & 0 & 1 & 0 \\ 0 & 1 & 0 & 0 & 0 & 1 & 0 & 1 \\ 0 & 0 & 1 & 0 & 1 & 0 & 1 & 0 \\ 0 & 0 & 1 & 0 & 0 & 1 & 0 & 1 \end{bmatrix}$$

The first three columns of the result correspond to the three distinct values 1, 2, and 3 in the first column of A; the fourth through sixth columns of the result correspond to the three distinct values 2, 3, and 6 in the second column of A; and the last two columns of the result correspond to the two distinct values 8 and 5 in the third column of A.

DET(M)	*Determinant.* Takes a single argument, which must be a square matrix. Returns a scalar, which is the determinant of the argument.
DIAG(M)	*Diagonal of a matrix.* Takes a single argument. Returns a column vector with as many rows as the minimum of the number of rows and the number of columns in the argument. The *i*th element of the result is the value in row *i*, column *i*, of the argument.
EOF(file)	*End of file indicator.* Normally used after a READ statement. Takes a single argument, which must be either a filename in apostrophes or quotation marks, or a file handle defined on a FILE HANDLE command that precedes the matrix program. Returns a scalar equal to 1 if the last attempt to read that file encountered the last record in the file, and equal to 0 if the last attempt did not encounter the last record in the file. Calling the EOF function causes a REREAD specification on the READ statement to be ignored on the next attempt to read the file.
EVAL(M)	*Eigenvalues of a symmetric matrix.* Takes a single argument, which must be a symmetric matrix. Returns a column vector with the same number of rows as the argument, containing the eigenvalues of the argument in decreasing numerical order.
EXP(M)	*Exponentials of matrix elements.* Takes a single argument. Returns a matrix having the same dimensions as the argument, in which each element equals *e* raised to the power of the corresponding element in the argument matrix.
FCDF(M,S1,S2)	*Cumulative* F *distribution function of elements.* Takes three arguments, a matrix of *F* values and two scalars giving the degrees of freedom (which must be positive). Returns a matrix having the same dimensions as the first argument *M*, containing the values of the cumulative *F* distribution function for each of its elements. If an element of the first argument is *x* and the second and third arguments are *S1* and *S2*, the corresponding element of the result is a number between 0 and 1, giving the proportion of an *F* distribution with *S1* and *S2* degrees of freedom that is less than *x*. If *x* is not positive, the result is 0.
GINV(M)	*Moore-Penrose generalized inverse of a matrix.* Takes a single argument. Returns a matrix with the same dimensions as the transpose of the argument. If *A* is the generalized inverse of a matrix *M*, then $M*A*M=M$ and $A*M*A=A$. Both $A*M$ and $M*A$ are symmetric.
GRADE(M)	*Ranks elements in a matrix.* Takes a single argument. Uses sequential integers for ties.
GSCH(M)	*Gram-Schmidt orthonormal basis for the space spanned by the column vectors of a matrix.* Takes a single argument, in which there must be as many linearly independent columns as there are rows. (That is, the rank of the argument must equal the number of rows.) Returns a square matrix with as many rows as the argument. The columns of the result form a basis for the space spanned by the columns of the argument.

IDENT(S1 [,S2])   *Create an identity matrix.* Takes either one or two arguments, which must be scalars. Returns a matrix with as many rows as the first argument and as many columns as the second argument, if any. If the second argument is omitted, the result is a square matrix. Elements on the main diagonal of the result equal 1, and all other elements equal 0.

INV(M)   *Inverse of a matrix.* Takes a single argument, which must be square and nonsingular (that is, its determinant must not be 0). Returns a square matrix having the same dimensions as the argument. If A is the inverse of M, then $M*A=A*M=I$, where I is the identity matrix.

KRONEKER(M1,M2)   *Kronecker product of two matrices.* Takes two arguments. Returns a matrix whose row dimension is the product of the row dimensions of the arguments and whose column dimension is the product of the column dimensions of the arguments. The Kronecker product of two matrices A and B takes the form of an array of scalar products:

$$A(1,1)*B \quad A(1,2)*B \quad ...A(1,N)*B$$
$$A(2,1)*B \quad A(2,2)*B \quad ...A(2,N)*B$$
$$...$$
$$A(M,1)*B \quad A(M,2)*B \quad ...A(M,N)*B$$

LG10(M)   *Base 10 logarithms of the elements.* Takes a single argument, all of whose elements must be positive. Returns a matrix having the same dimensions as the argument, in which each element is the logarithm to base 10 of the corresponding element of the argument.

LN(M)   *Natural logarithms of the elements.* Takes a single argument, all of whose elements must be positive. Returns a matrix having the same dimensions as the argument, in which each element is the logarithm to base e of the corresponding element of the argument.

MAGIC(S)   *Magic square.* Takes a single scalar, which must be 3 or larger, as an argument. Returns a square matrix with S rows and S columns containing the integers from 1 through S^2. All the row sums and all the column sums are equal in the result matrix. (The result matrix is only one of several possible magic squares.)

MAKE(S1,S2,S3)   *Create a matrix, all of whose elements equal a specified value.* Takes three scalars as arguments. Returns an $S1 \times S2$ matrix, all of whose elements equal $S3$.

MDIAG(V)   *Create a square matrix with a specified main diagonal.* Takes a single vector as an argument. Returns a square matrix with as many rows and columns as the dimension of the vector. The elements of the vector appear on the main diagonal of the matrix, and the other matrix elements are all 0.

MMAX(M)   *Maximum element in a matrix.* Takes a single argument. Returns a scalar equal to the numerically largest element in the argument M.

MMIN(M)   *Minimum element in a matrix.* Takes a single argument. Returns a scalar equal to the numerically smallest element in the argument M.

MOD(M,S)   *Remainders after division by a scalar.* Takes two arguments, a matrix and a scalar (which must not be 0). Returns a matrix having the same dimensions as *M*, each of whose elements is the remainder after the corresponding element of *M* is divided by *S*. The sign of each element of the result is the same as the sign of the corresponding element of the matrix argument *M*.

MSSQ(M)   *Matrix sum of squares.* Takes a single argument. Returns a scalar that equals the sum of the squared values of all the elements in the argument.

MSUM(M)   *Matrix sum.* Takes a single argument. Returns a scalar that equals the sum of all of the elements in the argument.

NCOL(M)   *Number of columns in a matrix.* Takes a single argument. Returns a scalar that equals the number of columns in the argument.

NROW(M)   *Number of rows in a matrix.* Takes a single argument. Returns a scalar that equals the number of rows in the argument.

RANK(M)   *Rank of a matrix.* Takes a single argument. Returns a scalar that equals the number of linearly independent rows or columns in the argument.

RESHAPE(M,S1,S2)   *Matrix of different dimensions.* Takes three arguments, a matrix and two scalars, whose product must equal the number of elements in the matrix. Returns a matrix whose dimensions are given by the scalar arguments. For example, if *M* is any matrix with exactly 50 elements, then `RESHAPE(M, 5, 10)` is a matrix with 5 rows and 10 columns. Elements are assigned to the reshaped matrix in order by row.

RMAX(M)   *Row maxima.* Takes a single argument. Returns a column vector with the same number of rows as the argument. Each row of the result contains the maximum value of the corresponding row of the argument.

RMIN(M)   *Row minima.* Takes a single argument. Returns a column vector with the same number of rows as the argument. Each row of the result contains the minimum value of the corresponding row of the argument.

RND(M)   *Elements rounded to the nearest integers.* Takes a single argument. Returns a matrix having the same dimensions as the argument. Each element of the result equals the corresponding element of the argument rounded to an integer.

RNKORDER(M)   *Ranking of matrix elements in ascending order.* Takes a single argument. Returns a matrix having the same dimensions as the argument *M*. The smallest element of the argument corresponds to a result element of 1, and the largest element of the argument to a result element equal to the number of elements, except that ties (equal elements in *M*) are resolved by assigning a rank equal to the arithmetic mean of the applicable ranks. For example, if:

$$M = \begin{bmatrix} -1 & -21.7 & 8 \\ 0 & 3.91 & -21.7 \\ 8 & 9 & 10 \end{bmatrix}, \text{ then: } \text{RNKORDER}(M) = \begin{bmatrix} 3 & 1.5 & 6.5 \\ 4 & 5 & 1.5 \\ 6.5 & 8 & 9 \end{bmatrix}$$

RSSQ(M)   *Row sums of squares.* Takes a single argument. Returns a column vector having the same number of rows as the argument. Each row of the result contains the sum of the squared values of the elements in the corresponding row of the argument.

RSUM(M)   *Row sums.* Takes a single argument. Returns a column vector having the same number of rows as the argument. Each row of the result contains the sum of the elements in the corresponding row of the argument.

SIN(M)   *Sines.* Takes a single argument. Returns a matrix having the same dimensions as the argument, containing the sines of the elements of the argument. Elements of the argument matrix are assumed to be measured in radians. To convert degrees to radians, multiply by $\pi/180$, which you can compute as $\text{ARTAN}(1)/45$. For example, the statement `COMPUTE SINES=SIN(DEGREES*ARTAN(1)/45)` computes sines from a matrix containing elements measured in degrees.

SOLVE(M1,M2)   *Solution of systems of linear equations.* Takes two arguments, the first of which must be square and nonsingular (its determinant must be non-zero), and the second of which must have the same number of rows as the first. Returns a matrix with the same dimensions as the second argument. If $M1*X=M2$, then $X=\text{SOLVE}(M1, M2)$. In effect, this function sets its result X equal to $\text{INV}(M1)*M2$.

SQRT(M)   *Square roots of elements.* Takes a single argument, whose elements must not be negative. Returns a matrix having the same dimensions as the arguments, whose elements are the positive square roots of the corresponding elements of the argument.

SSCP(M)   *Sums of squares and cross-products.* Takes a single argument. Returns a square matrix having as many rows (and columns) as the argument has columns. $\text{SSCP}(M)$ equals $\text{T}(M)*M$, where T is the transpose function defined below.

SVAL(M)   *Singular values of a matrix.* Takes a single argument. Returns a column vector containing as many rows as the minimum of the numbers of rows and columns in the argument, containing the singular values of the argument in decreasing numerical order. The singular values of a matrix M are the square roots of the eigenvalues of $\text{T}(M)*M$, where T is the transpose function discussed below.

SWEEP(M,S)   *Sweep transformation of a matrix.* Takes two arguments, a matrix and a scalar, which must be less than or equal to both the number of rows and the number of columns of the matrix. In other words, the pivot element of the matrix, which is $M(S,S)$, must exist. Returns a matrix of the same dimensions as M. Suppose that $S=\{k\}$ and $A=\text{SWEEP}(M,S)$. If $M(k,k)$ is not 0, then

$$A(k, k) = 1/M(k, k)$$
$$A(i, k) = -M(i, k)/M(k, k) \quad \text{for } i \text{ not equal to } k$$
$$A(k, j) = M(k, j)/(M(k, k)) \quad \text{for } j \text{ not equal to } k$$
$$A(i, j) = (M(k, k)*M(i, j) - M(i, k)*M(k, j))/M(k, k)$$
$$\text{for } i,j \text{ not equal to } k$$

and if $M(k,k)$ equals 0, then

$$A(i, k) = A(k, i) = 0 \quad \text{for all } i$$
$$A(i, j) = M(i, j) \quad \text{for } i,j \text{ not equal to } k$$

TCDF(M,S)   *Cumulative* t *distribution function of elements.* Takes two arguments, a matrix of *t* values and a scalar giving the degrees of freedom (which must be positive). Returns a matrix having the same dimensions as M, containing the values of the cumulative *t* distribution function for each of its elements. If an element of the first argument is x and the second argument is S, then the corresponding element of the result is a number between 0 and 1, giving the proportion of a *t* distribution with S degrees of freedom that is less than x.

TRACE(M)   *Sum of the main diagonal elements.* Takes a single argument. Returns a scalar, which equals the sum of the elements on the main diagonal of the argument.

TRANSPOS(M)   *Transpose of the matrix.* Takes a single argument. Returns the transpose of the argument. TRANSPOS can be shortened to T.

TRUNC(M)   *Truncation of elements to integers.* Takes a single argument. Returns a matrix having the same dimensions as the argument, whose elements equal the corresponding elements of the argument truncated to integers.

UNIFORM(S1,S2)   *Uniformly distributed pseudo-random numbers between 0 and 1.* Takes two scalars as arguments. Returns a matrix with the number of rows specified by the first argument and the number of columns specified by the second argument, containing pseudo-random numbers uniformly distributed between 0 and 1.

CALL Statement

Closely related to the matrix functions are the matrix procedures, which are invoked with the CALL statement. Procedures, similarly to functions, accept arguments enclosed in parentheses and separated by commas. They return their result in one or more of the arguments as noted in the individual descriptions below. They are implemented as procedures rather than as functions so that they can return more than one value or (in the case of SETDIAG) modify a matrix without making a copy of it.

EIGEN(M,var1,var2)   *Eigenvectors and eigenvalues of a symmetric matrix.* Takes three arguments: a symmetric matrix and two valid variable names to which the results are assigned. If M is a symmetric matrix, the statement

CALL EIGEN(M, A, B) will assign to A a matrix having the same dimensions as M, containing the eigenvectors of M as its columns, and will assign to B a column vector having as many rows as M, containing the eigenvalues of M in descending numerical order. The eigenvectors in A are ordered to correspond with the eigenvalues in B; thus, the first column corresponds to the largest eigenvalue, the second to the second largest, and so on.

SETDIAG(M,V)   *Set the main diagonal of a matrix.* Takes two arguments, a matrix and a vector. Elements on the main diagonal of M are set equal to the corresponding elements of V. If V is a scalar, all the diagonal elements are set equal to that scalar. Otherwise, if V has fewer elements than the main diagonal of M, remaining elements on the main diagonal are unchanged. If V has more elements than are needed, the extra elements are not used. See also MDIAG on p. 555.

SVD(M,var1,var2,var3)   *Singular value decomposition of a matrix.* Takes four arguments: a matrix and three valid variable names to which the results are assigned. If M is a matrix, the statement CALL SVD(M,U,Q,V) will assign to Q a diagonal matrix of the same dimensions as M, and to U and V unitary matrices (matrices whose inverses equal their transposes) of appropriate dimensions, such that $M=U*Q*T(V)$, where T is the transpose function defined above. The singular values of M are in the main diagonal of Q.

PRINT Statement

The PRINT statement displays matrices or matrix expressions. Its syntax is as follows:

```
PRINT [matrix expression]
      [/FORMAT="format descriptor"]
      [/TITLE="title"]
      [/SPACE={NEWPAGE}]
             {n      }
      [{/RLABELS=list of quoted names}]
       {/RNAMES=vector of names      }

      [{/CLABELS=list of quoted names}]
       {/CNAMES=vector of names      }
```

Matrix Expression

Matrix expression is a single matrix variable name or an expression that evaluates to a matrix. PRINT displays the specified matrix.

- The matrix specification must precede any other specifications on the PRINT statement. If no matrix is specified, no data will be displayed, but the TITLE and SPACE specifications will be honored.

- You can specify a matrix name, a matrix raised to a power, or a matrix function (with its arguments in parentheses) by itself, but you must enclose other matrix expressions in parentheses. For example, PRINT A, PRINT INV(A), and PRINT B**DET(T(C)*D) are all legal, but PRINT A+B is not. You must specify PRINT (A+B).

- Constant expressions are allowed.
- A matrix program can consist entirely of PRINT statements, without defining any matrix variables.

FORMAT Keyword

FORMAT specifies a single format descriptor for display of the matrix data.

- All matrix elements are displayed with the same format.
- You can use any printable numeric format (for numeric matrices) or string format (for string matrices) as defined in FORMATS.
- The matrix processor will choose a suitable numeric format if you omit the FORMAT specification, but a string format such as A8 is essential when displaying a matrix containing string data.
- String values exceeding the width of a string format are truncated.
- See "Scaling Factor in Displays" on p. 561 for default formatting of matrices containing large or small values.

TITLE Keyword

TITLE specifies a title for the matrix displayed. The title must be enclosed in quotation marks or apostrophes. If it exceeds the maximum display width, it is truncated. The slash preceding TITLE is required, even if it is the only specification on the PRINT statement. If you omit the TITLE specification, the matrix name or expression from the PRINT statement is used as a default title.

SPACE Keyword

SPACE controls output spacing before printing the title and the matrix. You can specify either a positive number or the keyword NEWPAGE. The slash preceding SPACE is required, even if it is the only specification on the PRINT statement.

NEWPAGE   *Start a new page before printing the title.*

n   *Skip n lines before displaying the title.*

RLABELS Keyword

RLABELS allows you to supply row labels for the matrix.

- The labels must be separated by commas.
- Enclose individual labels in quotation marks or apostrophes if they contain imbedded commas or if you want to preserve lowercase letters. Otherwise, quotation marks or apostrophes are optional.
- If too many names are supplied, the extras are ignored. If not enough names are supplied, the last rows remain unlabeled.

RNAMES Keyword

RNAMES allows you to supply the name of a vector or a vector expression containing row labels for the matrix.

- Either a row vector or a column vector can be used, but the vector must contain string data.
- If too many names are supplied, the extras are ignored. If not enough names are supplied, the last rows remain unlabeled.

CLABELS Keyword

CLABELS allows you to supply column labels for the matrix.

- The labels must be separated by commas.
- Enclose individual labels in quotation marks or apostrophes if they contain imbedded commas or if you want to preserve lowercase letters. Otherwise, quotation marks or apostrophes are optional.
- If too many names are supplied, the extras are ignored. If not enough names are supplied, the last columns remain unlabeled.

CNAMES Keyword

CNAMES allows you to supply the name of a vector or a vector expression containing column labels for the matrix.

- Either a row vector or a column vector can be used, but the vector must contain string data.
- If too many names are supplied, the extras are ignored. If not enough names are supplied, the last columns remain unlabeled.

Scaling Factor in Displays

When a matrix contains very large or very small numbers, it may be necessary to use scientific notation to display the data. If you do not specify a display format, the matrix processor chooses a power-of-10 multiplier that will allow the largest value to be displayed, and it displays this multiplier on a heading line before the data. The multiplier is not displayed for each element in the matrix. The displayed values, multiplied by the power of 10 that is indicated in the heading, equal the actual values (possibly rounded).

- Values that are very small, relative to the multiplier, are displayed as 0.
- If you explicitly specify a scientific-notation format ($Ew.d$), each matrix element is displayed using that format. This permits you to display very large and very small numbers in the same matrix without losing precision.

Example

```
COMPUTE M = {.0000000001357, 2.468, 3690000000}.
PRINT M /TITLE "Default format".
PRINT M /FORMAT "E13" /TITLE "Explicit exponential format".
```

- The first PRINT subcommand uses the default format with 10^9 as the multiplier for each element of the matrix. This results in the following output:

```
Default format
  10 ** 9   X
  .000000000    .000000002   3.690000000
```

Note that the first element is displayed as 0 and the second is rounded to one significant digit.

- An explicitly specified exponential format on the second PRINT subcommand allows each element to be displayed with full precision, as the following output shows:

```
Explicit exponential format
 1.3570000E-10 2.4680000E+00 3.6900000E+09
```

Matrix Control Structures

The matrix language includes two structures that allow you to alter the flow of control within a matrix program.

- The DO IF statement tests a logical expression to determine whether one or more subsequent matrix statements should be executed.

- The LOOP statement defines the beginning of a block of matrix statements that should be executed repeatedly until a termination criterion is satisfied or a BREAK statement is executed.

These statements closely resemble the DO IF and LOOP commands in the SPSS transformation language. In particular, these structures can be nested within one another as deeply as the available memory allows.

DO IF Structures

A DO IF structure in a matrix program affects the flow of control exactly as the analogous commands affect an SPSS transformation program, except that missing-value considerations do not arise in a matrix program. The syntax of the DO IF structure is as follows:

```
DO IF [(]logical expression[)]

  matrix statements

[ELSE IF [(]logical expression[)]]

  matrix statements

[ELSE IF...]

  .
  .
  .

[ELSE]

 matrix statements

END IF.
```

- The DO IF statement marks the beginning of the structure, and the END IF statement marks its end.

- The ELSE IF statement is optional and can be repeated as many times as desired within the structure.
- The ELSE statement is optional. It can be used only once and must follow any ELSE IF statements.
- The END IF statement must follow any ELSE IF and ELSE statements.
- The DO IF and ELSE IF statements must contain a logical expression, normally one involving the relational operators EQ, GT, and so on. However, the matrix language allows any expression that evaluates to a scalar to be used as the logical expression. Scalars greater than 0 are considered true, and scalars less than or equal to 0 are considered false.

A DO IF structure affects the flow of control within a matrix program as follows:

- If the logical expression on the DO IF statement is true, the statements immediately following the DO IF are executed up to the next ELSE IF or ELSE in the structure. Control then passes to the first statement following the END IF for that structure.
- If the expression on the DO IF statement is false, control passes to the first ELSE IF, where the logical expression is evaluated. If this expression is true, statements following the ELSE IF are executed up to the next ELSE IF or ELSE statement, and control passes to the first statement following the END IF for that structure.
- If the expressions on the DO IF and the first ELSE IF statements are both false, control passes to the next ELSE IF, where that logical expression is evaluated. If none of the expressions is true on any of the ELSE IF statements, statements following the ELSE statement are executed up to the END IF statement, and control falls out of the structure.
- If none of the expressions on the DO IF statement or the ELSE IF statements is true and there is no ELSE statement, control passes to the first statement following the END IF for that structure.

LOOP Structures

A LOOP structure in a matrix program affects the flow of control exactly as the analogous commands affect an SPSS transformation program, except that missing-value considerations do not arise in a matrix program. Its syntax is as follows:

```
LOOP [varname=n TO m [BY k]] [IF [(]logical expression[)]]

matrix statements

[BREAK]

matrix statements

END LOOP [IF [(]logical expression[)]]
```

The matrix statements specified between LOOP and END LOOP are executed repeatedly until one of the following four conditions is met:

- A logical expression on the IF clause of the LOOP statement is evaluated as false.
- An index variable used on the LOOP statement passes beyond its terminal value.
- A logical expression on the IF clause of the END LOOP statement is evaluated as true.
- A BREAK statement is executed within the loop structure (but outside of any nested loop structures).

Index Clause on the LOOP Statement

An index clause on a LOOP statement creates an index variable whose name is specified immediately after the keyword LOOP. The variable is assigned an initial value of n. Each time through the loop, the variable is tested against the terminal value m and incremented by the increment value k if k is specified, or by 1 if k is not specified. When the index variable is greater than m for positive increments or less than m for negative increments, control passes to the statement after the END LOOP statement.

- Both the index clause and the IF clause are optional. If both are present, the index clause must appear first.
- The index variable must be scalar with a valid matrix variable name.
- The initial value, n, the terminal value, m, and the increment, k (if present), must be scalars or matrix expressions evaluating to scalars. Non-integer values are truncated to integers before use.
- If the keyword BY and the increment k are absent, an increment of 1 is used.

IF Clause on the LOOP Statement

The logical expression is evaluated before each iteration of the loop structure. If it is false, the loop terminates and control passes to the statement after END LOOP.

- The IF clause is optional. If both the index clause and the IF clause are present, the index clause must appear first.
- As in the DO IF structure, the logical expression of the IF clause is evaluated as scalar, with positive values being treated as true and 0 or negative values, as false.

IF Clause on the END LOOP Statement

When an IF clause is present on an END LOOP statement, the logical expression is evaluated after each iteration of the loop structure. If it is true, the loop terminates and control passes to the statement following the END LOOP statement.

- The IF clause is optional.
- As in the LOOP statement, the logical expression of the IF clause is evaluated as scalar, with positive values being treated as true and 0 or negative values, as false.

BREAK Statement

The BREAK statement within a loop structure transfers control immediately to the statement following the (next) END LOOP statement. It is normally placed within a DO IF structure inside the LOOP structure to exit the loop when specified conditions are met.

Example

```
LOOP LOCATION = 1, NROW(VEC).
+   DO IF (VEC(LOCATION) = TARGET).
+       BREAK.

+   END IF.
END LOOP.
```

- This loop searches for the (first) location of a specific value, *TARGET*, in a vector, *VEC*.
- The DO IF statement checks whether the vector element indexed by *LOCATION* equals the target.
- If so, the BREAK statement transfers control out of the loop, leaving *LOCATION* as the index of *TARGET* in *VEC*.

READ Statement: Reading Character Data

The READ statement reads data into a matrix or submatrix from a character-format file—that is, a file containing ordinary numbers or words in readable form. The syntax for the READ statement is:

```
READ  variable reference
   [/FILE = file reference]
    /FIELD = c1 TO c2 [BY w]
   [/SIZE = size expression]
   [/MODE = {RECTANGULAR}]
            {SYMMETRIC  }
   [/REREAD]
   [/FORMAT = format descriptor]
```

- The file can contain values in freefield or fixed-column format. The data can appear in any of the field formats supported by DATA LIST.
- More than one matrix can be read from a single input record by rereading the record.
- If the end of the file is encountered during a READ operation (that is, fewer values are available than the number of elements required by the specified matrix size), a warning message is displayed and the contents of the unread elements of the matrix are unpredictable.

Variable Specification

The variable reference on the READ statement is a matrix variable name, with or without indexes.

For a name without indexes:

- READ creates the specified matrix variable.
- The matrix need not exist when READ is executed.
- If the matrix already exists, it is replaced by the matrix read from the file.
- You must specify the size of the matrix using the SIZE specification.

For an indexed name:

- READ creates a submatrix from an existing matrix.

- The matrix variable named must already exist.
- You can define any submatrix with indexes; for example, M(:,I). To define an entire existing matrix, specify M(:,:).
- The SIZE specification can be omitted. If specified, its value must match the size of the specified submatrix.

FILE Specification

FILE designates the character file containing the data. It can be an actual filename in apostrophes or quotation marks, or a file handle defined on a FILE HANDLE command that precedes the matrix program.

- The filename or handle must specify an existing file containing character data, not an SPSS data file or a specially formatted file of another kind, such as a spreadsheet file.
- The FILE specification is required on the first READ statement in a matrix program (first in order of appearance, not necessarily in order of execution). If you omit the FILE specification from a later READ statement, the statement uses the most recently named file (in order of appearance) on a READ statement in the same matrix program.

FIELD Specification

FIELD specifies the column positions of a fixed-format record where the data for matrix elements are located.

- The FIELD specification is required.
- Startcol is the number of the leftmost column of the input area.
- Endcol is the number of the rightmost column of the input area.
- Both startcol and endcol are required and both must be constants. For example, FIELD = 9 TO 72 specifies that values to be read appear between columns 9 and 72 (inclusive) of each input record.
- The BY clause, if present, indicates that each value appears within a fixed set of columns on the input record; that is, one value is separated from the next by its column position rather than by a space or comma. Width is the width of the area designated for each value. For example, FIELD = 1 TO 80 BY 10 indicates that there are eight possible values per record and that one will appear between columns 1 and 10 (inclusive), another between columns 11 and 20, and so on, up to columns 71 and 80. The BY value must evenly divide the length of the field. That is, endcol – startcol + 1 must be a multiple of the width.
- You can use the FORMAT specification (see p. 568) to supply the same information as the BY clause of the FIELD specification. If you omit the BY clause and do not specify a format on the FORMAT specification, READ assumes that values are separated by blanks or commas within the designated field.

SIZE Specification

The SIZE specification is a matrix expression that, when evaluated, specifies the size of the matrix to be read.

- The expression should evaluate to a two-element row or column vector. The first element designates the number of rows in the matrix to be read; the second element gives the number of columns.
- Values of the SIZE specification are truncated to integers if necessary.
- The size expression may be a constant, such as {5;5}, or a matrix variable name, such as MSIZE, or any valid expression, such as INFO(1,:).
- If you use a scalar as the size expression, a column vector containing that number of rows is read. Thus, SIZE=1 reads a scalar, and SIZE=3 reads a 3 × 1 column vector.

You must include a SIZE specification whenever you name an entire matrix (rather than a submatrix) on the READ statement. If you specify a submatrix, the SIZE specification is optional but, if included, must agree with the size of the specified submatrix.

MODE Specification

MODE specifies the format of the matrix to be read in. It can be either rectangular or symmetric. If the MODE specification is omitted, the default is RECTANGULAR.

RECTANGULAR   *Matrix is completely represented in file.* Each row begins on a new record, and all entries in that row are present on that and (possibly) succeeding records. This is the default if the MODE specification is omitted.

SYMMETRIC   *Elements of the matrix below the main diagonal are the same as those above it.* Only matrix elements on and below the main diagonal are read; elements above the diagonal are set equal to the corresponding symmetric elements below the diagonal. Each row is read beginning on a new record, although it may span more than one record. Only a single value is read from the first record, two values are read from the second, and so on.

- If SYMMETRIC is specified, the matrix processor first checks that the number of rows and the number of columns are the same. If the numbers, specified either on SIZE or on the variable reference, are not the same, an error message is displayed and the command is not executed.

REREAD Specification

The REREAD specification indicates that the current READ statement should begin with the last record read by a previous READ statement.

- REREAD has no further specifications.
- REREAD cannot be used on the first READ statement to read from a file.
- If you omit REREAD, the READ statement begins with the first record following the last one read by the previous READ statement.
- The REREAD specification is ignored on the first READ statement following a call to the EOF function for the same file.

FORMAT Specification

FORMAT specifies how the matrix processor should interpret the input data. The format descriptor can be any valid SPSS data format, such as F6, E12.2, or A6, or it can be a type code; for example, F, E, or A.

- If you omit the FORMAT specification, the default is F.

- You can specify the width of fixed-size data fields with either a FORMAT specification or a BY clause on a FIELD specification. You can include it in both places only if you specify the same value.

- If you do not include either a FORMAT or a BY clause on FIELD, READ expects values separated by blanks or commas.

- An additional way of specifying the width is to supply a repetition factor without a width (for example, 10F, 5COMMA, or 3E). The field width is then calculated by dividing the width of the whole input area on the FIELD specification by the repetition factor. A format with a digit for the repetition factor must be enclosed in quotes.

- Only one format can be specified. A specification such as FORMAT='5F2.0 3F3.0 F2.0' is invalid.

WRITE Statement: Writing Character Data

WRITE writes the value of a matrix expression to an external file. The syntax of the WRITE statement is:

```
WRITE  matrix expression
    [/OUTFILE = file reference]
     /FIELD = startcol TO endcol [BY width]
    [/MODE = {RECTANGULAR}]
            {TRIANGULAR }
    [/HOLD]
    [/FORMAT = format descriptor]
```

Matrix Expression Specification

Specify any matrix expression that evaluates to the value(s) to be written.

- The matrix specification must precede any other specifications on the WRITE statement.

- You can specify a matrix name, a matrix raised to a power, or a matrix function (with its arguments in parentheses) by itself, but you must enclose other matrix expressions in parentheses. For example, WRITE A, WRITE INV(A), or WRITE B**DET(T(C)*D) is legal, but WRITE A+B is not. You must specify WRITE (A+B).

- Constant expressions are allowed.

OUTFILE Specification

OUTFILE designates the character file to which the matrix expression is to be written. The file reference can be an actual filename in apostrophes or quotation marks, or a file handle defined on a FILE HANDLE command that precedes the matrix program. The filename or file handle must be a valid file specification.

- The OUTFILE specification is required on the first WRITE statement in a matrix program (first in order of appearance, not necessarily in order of execution).

- If you omit the OUTFILE specification from a later WRITE statement, the statement uses the most recently named file (in order of appearance) on a WRITE statement in the same matrix program.

FIELD Specification

FIELD specifies the column positions of a fixed-format record to which the data should be written.

- The FIELD specification is required.

- The start column, $c1$, is the number of the leftmost column of the output area.

- The end column, $c2$, is the number of the rightmost column of the output area.

- Both $c1$ and $c2$ are required, and both must be constants. For example, FIELD = 9 TO 72 specifies that values should be written between columns 9 and 72 (inclusive) of each output record.

- The BY clause, if present, indicates how many characters should be allocated to the output value of a single matrix element. The value w is the width of the area designated for each value. For example, FIELD = 1 TO 80 BY 10 indicates that up to eight values should be written per record, and that one should go between columns 1 and 10 (inclusive), another between columns 11 and 20, and so on up to columns 71 and 80. The value on the BY clause must evenly divide the length of the field. That is, $c2 - c1 + 1$ must be a multiple of w.

- You can use the FORMAT specification (see below) to supply the same information as the BY clause. If you omit the BY clause from the FIELD specification and do not specify a format on the FORMAT specification, WRITE uses freefield format, separating matrix elements by single blank spaces.

MODE Specification

MODE specifies the format of the matrix to be written. If MODE is not specified, the default is RECTANGULAR.

RECTANGULAR   *Write the entire matrix.* Each row starts a new record, and all of the values in that row are present in that and (possibly) subsequent records. This is the default if the MODE specification is omitted.

TRIANGULAR   *Write only the lower triangular entries and the main diagonal.* Each row begins a new record and may span more than one record. This mode may save file space.

- A matrix written with MODE = TRIANGULAR must be square, but it need not be symmetric. If it is not, values in the upper triangle are not written.

- A matrix written with MODE = TRIANGULAR may be read with MODE = SYMMETRIC.

HOLD Specification

HOLD causes the last line written by the current WRITE statement to be held so that the next WRITE to that file will write on the same line. Use HOLD to write more than one matrix on a line.

FORMAT Specification

FORMAT indicates how the internal (binary) values of matrix elements should be converted to character format for output.

- The format descriptor is any valid SPSS data format, such as F6, E12.2, or A6, or it can be a format type code, such as F, E, or A. It specifies how the written data are encoded and, if a width is specified, how wide the fields containing the data are. (See FORMATS for valid formats.)

- If you omit the FORMAT specification, the default is F.

- The data field widths may be specified either here or after BY on the FIELD specification. You may specify the width in both places only if you give the same value.

- An additional way of specifying the width is to supply a repetition factor without a width (for example, 10F or 5COMMA). The field width is then calculated by dividing the width of the whole output area on the FIELD specification by the repetition factor. A format with a digit for the repetition factor must be enclosed in quotes.

- If the field width is not specified in any of these ways, then the freefield format is used—matrix values are written separated by one blank, and each value occupies as many positions as necessary to avoid the loss of precision. Each row of the matrix is written starting with a new output record.

- Only one format descriptor can be specified. Do *not* try to specify more than one format; for example, '5F2.0 3F3.0 F2.0' is invalid as a FORMAT specification on WRITE.

GET Statement: Reading SPSS Data Files

GET reads matrices from an external SPSS data file or from the working data file. The syntax of GET is as follows:

```
GET variable reference
   [/FILE={file reference}]
         {*              }
   [/VARIABLES = variable list]
   [/NAMES = names vector]
   [/MISSING = {ACCEPT}]
               {OMIT  }
               {value }
   [/SYSMIS = {OMIT }]
             {value}
```

Variable Specification

The variable reference on the GET statement is a matrix variable name with or without indexes.

For a name without indexes:

- GET creates the specified matrix variable.
- The size of the matrix is determined by the amount of data read from the SPSS data file or the working file.
- If the matrix already exists, it is replaced by the matrix read from the file.

For an indexed name:

- GET creates a submatrix from an existing matrix.
- The matrix variable named must already exist.
- You can define any submatrix with indexes; for example, $M(:,I)$. To define an entire existing matrix, specify $M(:,:)$.
- The indexes, along with the size of the existing matrix, specify completely the size of the submatrix, which must agree with the dimensions of the data read from the SPSS data file.
- The specified submatrix is replaced by the matrix elements read from the SPSS data file.

FILE Specification

FILE designates the SPSS data file to be read. Use an asterisk, or simply omit the FILE specification, to designate the current working data file.

- The file reference can be either a filename enclosed in apostrophes or quotation marks, or a file handle defined on a FILE HANDLE command that precedes the matrix program.
- If you omit the FILE specification, the working data file is used.
- In a matrix program executed with the INCLUDE command, if a SPLIT FILE command is in effect, a GET statement that references the working data file will read a single split-file group of cases. (A matrix program cannot be executed from a syntax window if a SPLIT FILE command is in effect.)

VARIABLES Specification

VARIABLES specifies a list of variables to be read from the SPSS data file.

- The variable list is entered much the same as in other SPSS procedures except that the variable names *must* be separated by commas.
- The keyword TO can be used to reference consecutive variables on the SPSS data file.
- The variable list can consist of the keyword ALL to get all the variables in the SPSS data file. ALL is the default if the VARIABLES specification is omitted.
- All variables read from the SPSS data file should be numeric. If a string variable is specified, a warning message is issued and the string variable is skipped.

Example

```
GET M /VARIABLES = AGE, RESIDE, INCOME TO HEALTH.
```

- The variables *AGE*, *RESIDE*, and *INCOME* to *HEALTH* from the working data file will form the columns of the matrix *M*.

NAMES Specification

NAMES specifies a vector to store the variable names from the SPSS data file.

- If you omit the NAMES specification, the variable names are not available to the MATRIX procedure.

- In place of a vector name, you can use a matrix expression that evaluates to a vector, such as A(N+1,:).

MISSING Specification

MISSING specifies how missing values declared for the SPSS data file should be handled.

- The MISSING specification is required if the SPSS data file contains missing values for any variable being read.

- If you omit the MISSING specification and a missing value is encountered for a variable being read, an error message is displayed and the GET statement is not executed.

The following keywords are available on the MISSING specification. There is no default.

ACCEPT   *Accept user-missing values for entry.* If the system-missing value exists for a variable to be read, you must specify SYSMIS to indicate how the system-missing value should be handled (see "SYSMIS Specification" below).

OMIT   *Skip an entire observation when a variable with a missing value is encountered.*

value   *Recode all missing values encountered (including the system-missing value) to the specified value for entry.* The replacement value can be any numeric constant.

SYSMIS Specification

SYSMIS specifies how system-missing values should be handled when you have specified ACCEPT on MISSING.

- The SYSMIS specification is ignored unless ACCEPT is specified on MISSING.

- If you specify ACCEPT on MISSING but omit the SYSMIS specification, and a system-missing value is encountered for a variable being read, an error message is displayed and the GET statement is not executed.

The following keywords are available on the SYSMIS specification. There is no default.

OMIT   *Skip an entire observation when a variable with a system-missing value is encountered.*

value   *Recode all system-missing values encountered to the specified value for entry.* The replacement value can be any numeric constant.

Example

```
GET SCORES
  /VARIABLES = TEST1,TEST2,TEST3
  /NAMES = VARNAMES
  /MISSING = ACCEPT
  /SYSMIS = -1.0.
```

- A matrix named *SCORES* is read from the working data file.
- The variables *TEST1*, *TEST2*, and *TEST3* form the columns of the matrix, while the cases in the working file form the rows.
- A vector named *VARNAMES*, whose three elements contain the variable names *TEST1*, *TEST2*, and *TEST3*, is created.
- User-missing values defined in the working data file are accepted into the matrix *SCORES*.
- System-missing values in the working data file are converted to the value −1 in the matrix *SCORES*.

SAVE Statement: Writing SPSS Data Files

SAVE writes matrices to an SPSS data file or to the current working data file. The rows of the matrix expression become cases, and the columns become variables. The syntax of the SAVE statement is as follows:

```
SAVE matrix expression
  [/OUTFILE = {file reference}]
             {*             }
  [/VARIABLES = variable list]
  [/NAMES = names vector]
  [/STRINGS = variable list]
```

Matrix Expression Specification

The matrix expression following the keyword SAVE is any matrix language expression that evaluates to the value(s) to be written to an SPSS data file.

- The matrix specification must precede any other specifications on the SAVE statement.
- You can specify a matrix name, a matrix raised to a power, or a matrix function (with its arguments in parentheses) by itself, but you must enclose other matrix expressions in parentheses. For example, SAVE A, SAVE INV(A), or SAVE B**DET(T(C)*D) is legal, but SAVE A+B is not. You must specify SAVE (A+B).
- Constant expressions are allowed.

OUTFILE Specification

OUTFILE designates the file to which the matrix expression is to be written. It can be an actual filename in apostrophes or quotation marks, or a file handle defined on a FILE HANDLE command that precedes the matrix program. The filename or handle must be a valid file specification.

- To save a matrix expression as the working data file, specify an asterisk (*). If there is no working data file, one will be created; if there is one, it is replaced by the saved matrices.
- The OUTFILE specification is required on the first SAVE statement in a matrix program (first in order of appearance, not necessarily in order of execution). If you omit the OUTFILE specification from a later SAVE statement, the statement uses the most recently named file (in order of appearance) on a SAVE statement in the same matrix program.

- If more than one SAVE statement writes to the working data file in a single matrix program, the dictionary of the new working data file is written on the basis of the information given by the first such SAVE. All the subsequently saved matrices are appended to the new working data file as additional cases. If the number of columns differs, an error occurs.

- When you execute a matrix program with the INCLUDE command, the SAVE statement creates a new SPSS data file at the end of the matrix program's execution, so any attempt to GET the data file obtains the original data file, if any.

- When you execute a matrix program from a syntax window, SAVE creates a new SPSS data file immediately, but the file remains open, so you cannot GET it until after the END MATRIX statement.

VARIABLES Specification

You can provide variable names for the SPSS data file with the VARIABLES specification. The variable list is a list of valid SPSS variable names separated by commas.

- You can use the TO convention, as shown in the example below.

- You can also use the NAMES specification, discussed below, to provide variable names.

Example

```
SAVE {A,B,X,Y} /OUTFILE=*
  /VARIABLES = A,B,X1 TO X50,Y1,Y2.
```

- The matrix expression on the SAVE statement constructs a matrix from two column vectors A and B and two matrices X and Y. All four matrix variables must have the same number of rows so that this matrix construction will be valid.

- The VARIABLES specification provides descriptive names so that the SPSS variable names in the new working data file will resemble the names used in the matrix program.

NAMES Specification

As an alternative to the explicit list on the VARIABLES specification, you can specify a name list with a matrix expression that evaluates to a vector containing string values. The elements of this vector are used as names for the variables.

- The NAMES specification on SAVE is designed to complement the NAMES specification on the GET statement. Names extracted from an SPSS data file can be used in a new data file by specifying the same vector name on both NAMES specifications.

- If you specify both VARIABLES and NAMES, a warning message is displayed and the VARIABLES specification is used.

- If you omit both the VARIABLES and NAMES specifications, or if you do not specify names for all columns of the matrix, the MATRIX procedure creates default names. The names have the form *COLn*, where n is the column number.

STRINGS Specification

The STRINGS specification provides the names of variables that contain short string data rather than numeric data.

- By default, all variables are assumed to be numeric.
- The variable list specification following STRINGS consists of a list of SPSS variable names separated by commas. The names must be among those used by SAVE.

MGET Statement: Reading SPSS Matrix Data Files

MGET reads an SPSS matrix-format data file. MGET puts the data it reads into separate matrix variables. It also names these new variables automatically. The syntax of MGET is as follows:

```
MGET [ [/] FILE = file reference]
   [/TYPE = {COV    }]
            {CORR   }
            {MEAN   }
            {STDDEV}
            {N      }
            {COUNT  }
```

- Since MGET assigns names to the matrices it reads, do not specify matrix names on the MGET statement.

FILE Specification

FILE designates an SPSS matrix-format data file. (See MATRIX DATA for a discussion of matrix-format data files.) To designate the working data file (if it is a matrix-format data file), use an asterisk, or simply omit the FILE specification.

- The file reference can be either a filename enclosed in apostrophes or quotation marks, or a file handle defined on a FILE HANDLE command that precedes the matrix program.
- The same matrix-format SPSS data file can be read more than once.
- If you omit the FILE specification, the current working data file is used.
- MGET ignores the SPLIT FILE command in SPSS when reading the working data file. It does honor the split-file groups that were in effect when the matrix-format data file was created.
- The maximum number of split-file groups that can be read is 99.
- The maximum number of cells that can be read is 99.

TYPE Specification

TYPE specifies the rowtype(s) to read from the matrix-format data file.

- By default, records of all rowtypes are read.
- If the matrix-format data file does not contain rows of the requested type, an error occurs.

Valid keywords on the TYPE specification are:

COV   *A matrix of covariances.*

CORR   *A matrix of correlation coefficients.*

MEAN   *A vector of means.*

STDDEV *A vector of standard deviations.*

N   *A vector of numbers of cases.*

COUNT   *A vector of counts.*

Names of Matrix Variables from MGET

- The MGET statement automatically creates matrix variable names for the matrices it reads.
- All new variables created by MGET are reported to the user.
- If a matrix variable already exists with the same name that MGET chose for a new variable, the new variable is not created and a warning is issued. The RELEASE statement can be used to get rid of a variable. A COMPUTE statement followed by RELEASE can be used to change the name of an existing matrix variable.

MGET constructs variable names in the following manner:

- The first two characters of the name identify the row type. If there are no cells and no split file groups, these two characters constitute the name:

    CV   A covariance matrix (rowtype COV)
    CR   A correlation matrix (rowtype CORR)
    MN   A vector of means (rowtype MEAN)
    SD   A vector of standard deviations (rowtype STDDEV)
    NC   A vector of numbers of cases (rowtype N)
    CN   A vector of counts (rowtype COUNT)

- Characters 3–5 of the variable name identify the cell number or the split-group number. Cell identifiers consist of the letter *F* and a two-digit cell number. Split-group identifiers consist of the letter *S* and a two-digit split-group number; for example, *MNF12* or *SDS22*.
- If there are both cells and split groups, characters 3–5 identify the cell and characters 6–8 identify the split group. The same convention for cell or split-file numbers is used—for example, *CRF12S21*.
- After the name is constructed as described above, any leading zeros are removed from the cell number and the split-group number—for example, *CNF2S99* or *CVF2S1*.

MSAVE Statement: Writing SPSS Matrix Data Files

The MSAVE statement writes matrix expressions to an SPSS matrix-format data file that can be used as matrix input to other SPSS procedures. (See MATRIX DATA for a discussion of matrix-format data files.) The syntax of MSAVE is as follows:

```
MSAVE matrix expression
   /TYPE = {COV   }
           {CORR  }
           {MEAN  }
           {STDDEV}
           {N     }
           {COUNT }
  [/OUTFILE = {file reference}]
             {*             }
  [/VARIABLES = variable list]
  [/SNAMES = variable list]
  [/SPLIT = split vector]
  [/FNAMES = variable list]
  [/FACTOR = factor vector]
```

- Only one matrix-format data file can be saved in a single matrix program.

- Each MSAVE statement writes records of a single rowtype. Therefore, several MSAVE statements will normally be required to write a complete matrix-format data file.

- Most specifications are retained from one MSAVE statement to the next so that it is not necessary to repeat the same specifications on a series of MSAVE statements. The exception is the FACTOR specification, as noted below.

Example

```
MSAVE M /TYPE=MEAN /OUTFILE=CORRMAT /VARIABLES=V1 TO V8.
MSAVE S /TYPE STDDEV.
MSAVE MAKE(1,8,24) /TYPE N.
MSAVE C /TYPE CORR.
```

- The series of MSAVE statements save the matrix variables *M*, *S*, and *C*, which contain, respectively, vectors of means and standard deviations and a matrix of correlation coefficients. The SPSS matrix-format data file thus created is suitable for use in a procedure such as FACTOR.

- The first MSAVE statement saves *M* as a vector of means. This statement specifies OUTFILE, a previously defined file handle, and VARIABLES, a list of variable names to be used in the SPSS data file.

- The second MSAVE statement saves *S* as a vector of standard deviations. Note that the OUTFILE and VARIABLES specifications do not have to be repeated.

- The third MSAVE statement saves a vector of case counts. The matrix function MAKE constructs an eight-element vector with values equal to the case count (24 in this example).

- The last MSAVE statement saves *C*, an 8×8 matrix, as the correlation matrix.

Matrix Expression Specification

- The matrix expression must be specified first on the MSAVE statement.

- The matrix expression specification can be any matrix language expression that evaluates to the value(s) to be written to the matrix-format file.
- You can specify a matrix name, a matrix raised to a power, or a matrix function (with its arguments in parentheses) by itself, but you must enclose other matrix expressions in parentheses. For example, MSAVE A, SAVE INV(A), or MSAVE B**DET(T(C)*D) is legal, but MSAVE N * WT is not. You must specify MSAVE (N * WT).
- Constant expressions are allowed.

TYPE Specification

TYPE specifies the rowtype to write to the matrix-format data file. Only a single rowtype can be written by any one MSAVE statement. Valid keywords on the TYPE specification are:

COV   *A matrix of covariances.*

CORR   *A matrix of correlation coefficients.*

MEAN   *A vector of means.*

STDDEV   *A vector of standard deviations.*

N   *A vector of numbers of cases.*

COUNT   *A vector of counts.*

OUTFILE Specification

OUTFILE designates the SPSS matrix-format data file to which the matrices are to be written. It can be an asterisk, an actual filename in apostrophes or quotation marks, or a file handle defined on a FILE HANDLE command that precedes the matrix program. The filename or handle must be a valid file specification.

- The OUTFILE specification is required on the first MSAVE statement in a matrix program.
- To save a matrix expression as the working data file (replacing any working data file created before the matrix program), specify an asterisk (*).
- Since only one matrix-format data file can be written in a single matrix program, any OUTFILE specification on the second and later MSAVE statements in one matrix program must be the same as that on the first MSAVE statement.

VARIABLES Specification

You can provide variable names for the matrix-format data file with the VARIABLES specification. The variable list is a list of valid SPSS variable names separated by commas. You can use the TO convention.

- The VARIABLES specification names only the data variables in the matrix. Split-file variables and grouping or factor variables are named on the SNAMES and FNAMES specifications.
- The names in the VARIABLES specification become the values of the special variable *VARNAME_* in the matrix-format data file for rowtypes of CORR and COV.

- You cannot specify the reserved names *ROWTYPE_* and *VARNAME_* on the VARIABLES specification.
- If you omit the VARIABLES specification, the default names *COL1*, *COL2*,..., etc., are used.

FACTOR Specification

To write an SPSS matrix-format data file with factor or group codes, you must use the FACTOR specification to provide a row matrix containing the values of each of the factors or group variables for the matrix expression being written by the current MSAVE statement.

- The factor vector must have the same number of columns as there are factors in the matrix data file being written. You can use a scalar when the groups are defined by a single variable. For example, FACTOR=1 indicates that the matrix data being written are for the value 1 of the factor variable.
- The values of the factor vector are written to the matrix-format data file as values of the factors in the file.
- To create a complete matrix-format data file with factors, you must execute an MSAVE statement for every combination of values of the factors or grouping variables (in other words, for every group). If split-file variables are also present, you must execute an MSAVE statement for every combination of factor codes within every combination of values of the split-file variables.

Example

```
MSAVE M11 /TYPE=MEAN /OUTFILE=CORRMAT /VARIABLES=V1 TO V8
    /FNAMES=SEX, GROUP /FACTOR={1,1}.
MSAVE S11 /TYPE STDDEV.
MSAVE MAKE(1,8,N(1,1)) /TYPE N.
MSAVE C11 /TYPE CORR.

MSAVE M12 /TYPE=MEAN /FACTOR={1,2}.
MSAVE S12 /TYPE STDDEV.
MSAVE MAKE(1,8,N(1,2)) /TYPE N.
MSAVE C12 /TYPE CORR.

MSAVE M21 /TYPE=MEAN /FACTOR={2,1}.
MSAVE S21 /TYPE STDDEV.
MSAVE MAKE(1,8,N(2,1)) /TYPE N.
MSAVE C21 /TYPE CORR.

MSAVE M22 /TYPE=MEAN /FACTOR={2,2}.
MSAVE S22 /TYPE STDDEV.
MSAVE MAKE(1,8,N(2,2)) /TYPE N.
MSAVE C22 /TYPE CORR.
```

- The first four MSAVE statements provide data for a group defined by the variables *SEX* and *GROUP*, with both factors having the value 1.
- The second, third, and fourth groups of four MSAVE statements provide the corresponding data for the other groups, in which *SEX* and *GROUP*, respectively, equal 1 and 2, 2 and 1, and 2 and 2.
- Within each group of MSAVE statements, a suitable number-of-cases vector is created with the matrix function MAKE.

FNAMES Specification

To write an SPSS matrix-format data file with factor or group codes, you can use the FNAMES specification to provide variable names for the grouping or factor variables.

- The variable list following the keyword FNAMES is a list of valid SPSS variable names, separated by commas.
- If you omit the FNAMES specification, the default names *FAC1*, *FAC2*,..., etc., are used.

SPLIT Specification

To write an SPSS matrix-format data file with split-file groups, you must use the SPLIT specification to provide a row matrix containing the values of each of the split-file variables for the matrix expression being written by the current MSAVE statement.

- The split vector must have the same number of columns as there are split-file variables in the matrix data file being written. You can use a scalar when there is only one split-file variable. For example, SPLIT=3 indicates that the matrix data being written are for the value 3 of the split-file variable.
- The values of the split vector are written to the matrix-format data file as values of the split-file variable(s).
- To create a complete matrix-format data file with split-file variables, you must execute MSAVE statements for every combination of values of the split-file variables. (If factor variables are present, you must execute MSAVE statements for every combination of factor codes within every combination of values of the split-file variables.)

SNAMES Specification

To write an SPSS matrix-format data file with split-file groups, you can use the SNAMES specification to provide variable names for the split-file variables.

- The variable list following the keyword SNAMES is a list of valid SPSS variable names separated by commas.
- If you omit the SNAMES specification, the default names *SPL1*, *SPL2*,..., etc., are used.

DISPLAY Statement

DISPLAY provides information on the matrix variables currently defined in a matrix program and on usage of internal memory by the matrix processor. Two keywords are available on DISPLAY:

DICTIONARY   *Display variable name and row and column dimensions for each matrix variable currently defined.*

STATUS   *Display the status and size of internal tables.* This display is intended as a debugging aid when writing large matrix programs that approach the memory limitations of your system.

If you enter the DISPLAY statement with no specifications, both DICTIONARY and STATUS information is displayed.

RELEASE Statement

Use the RELEASE statement to release the work areas in memory assigned to matrix variables that are no longer needed.

- Specify a list of currently defined matrix variables. Variable names on the list must be separated by commas.
- RELEASE discards the contents of the named matrix variables. Releasing a large matrix when it is no longer needed makes memory available for additional matrix variables.
- All matrix variables are released when the END MATRIX statement is encountered.

Macros Using the Matrix Language

Macro expansion (see DEFINE—END DEFINE) occurs before command lines are passed to the matrix processor. Therefore, previously defined macro names can be used within a matrix program. If the macro name expands to one or more valid matrix statements, the matrix processor will execute those statements. Similarly, you can define an entire matrix program, including the MATRIX and END MATRIX commands, as a macro, but you cannot define a macro within a matrix program, since DEFINE and END DEFINE are not valid matrix statements.

MATRIX DATA

```
MATRIX DATA VARIABLES=varlist    [/FILE={INLINE**}]
                                       {file    }

[/FORMAT=[{LIST**}]  [{LOWER**}]  [{DIAGONAL**}]]
          {FREE  }    {UPPER  }    {NODIAGONAL}
                      {FULL   }

[/SPLIT=varlist]    [/FACTORS=varlist]

[/CELLS=number of cells]    [/N=sample size]

[/CONTENTS= [CORR**]  [COV]  [MAT]  [MSE]  [DFE]  [MEAN]  [PROX]

            [{STDDEV}]  [N_SCALAR]  [{N_VECTOR}]  [N_MATRIX]  [COUNT]]
             {SD    }               {N        }
```

**Default if the subcommand is omitted.

Example:
```
MATRIX DATA VARIABLES=ROWTYPE_ SAVINGS POP15 POP75 INCOME GROWTH.
BEGIN DATA
MEAN 9.6710 35.0896 2.2930 1106.7784 3.7576
STDDEV 4.4804 9.1517 1.2907 990.8511 2.8699
N 50 50 50 50 50
CORR 1
CORR -.4555 1
CORR .3165 -.9085 1
CORR .2203 -.7562 .7870 1
CORR .3048 -.0478 .0253 -.1295  1
END DATA.
```

Overview

MATRIX DATA reads raw matrix materials and converts them to a matrix data file that can be read by procedures that handle matrix materials. The data can include vector statistics such as means and standard deviations as well as matrices.

MATRIX DATA is similar to a DATA LIST command: it defines variable names and their order in a raw data file. However, MATRIX DATA can read only data that conform to the general format of SPSS-format matrices.

Matrix Files

Like the matrix data files created by procedures, the file that MATRIX DATA creates contains the following variables in the indicated order. If the variables are in a different order in the raw data file, MATRIX DATA rearranges them in the working data file.

- *Split-file variables.* These optional variables define split files. There can be up to eight split variables, and they must have numeric values. Split-file variables will appear in the order in which they are specified on the SPLIT subcommand.

- *ROWTYPE_*. This is a string variable with A8 format. Its values define the data type for each record. For example, it might identify a row of values as means, standard deviations, or correlation coefficients. Every SPSS-format matrix data file has a *ROWTYPE_* variable.

- *Factor variables*. There can be any number of factors. They occur only if the data include within-cells information, such as the within-cells means. Factors have the system-missing value on records that define pooled information. Factor variables appear in the order in which they are specified on the FACTORS subcommand.

- *VARNAME_*. This is a string variable with A8 format. MATRIX DATA automatically generates *VARNAME_* and its values based on the variables named on VARIABLES. You never enter values for *VARNAME_*. Values for *VARNAME_* are blank for records that define vector information. Every matrix in the program has a *VARNAME_* variable.

- *Continuous variables*. These are the variables that were used to generate the correlation coefficients or other aggregated data. There can be any number of them. Continuous variables appear in the order in which they are specified on VARIABLES.

Options

Data Files. You can define both inline data and data in an external file.

Data Format. By default, data are assumed to be entered in freefield format with each vector or row beginning on a new record (the keyword LIST on the FORMAT subcommand). If each vector or row does not begin on a new record, use the keyword FREE. You can also use FORMAT to indicate whether matrices are entered in upper or lower triangular or full square or rectangular format, and whether or not they include diagonal values.

Variable Types. You can specify split-file and factor variables using the SPLIT and FACTORS subcommands. You can identify record types by specifying ROWTYPE_ on the VARIABLES subcommand if *ROWTYPE_* values are included in the data, or by implying *ROWTYPE_* values on CONTENTS.

Basic Specification

The basic specification is VARIABLES and a list of variables. Additional specifications are required as follows:

- FILE is required to specify the data file if the data are not inline.

- If data are in any format other than lower-triangular with diagonal values included, FORMAT is required.

- If the data contain values in addition to matrix coefficients, such as the mean and standard deviation, either variable *ROWTYPE_* must be specified on VARIABLES and *ROWTYPE_* values must be included in the data, or CONTENTS must be used to describe the data.

- If the data include split-file variables, SPLIT is required. If there are factors, FACTORS is required.

Specifications on most MATRIX DATA subcommands depend on whether *ROWTYPE_* is included in the data and specified on VARIABLES, or whether it is implied using CONTENTS.

Table 1 summarizes the status of each MATRIX DATA subcommand in relation to the *ROWTYPE_* specification.

Table 1   Subcommand requirements in relation to ROWTYPE_

Subcommand	Implicit ROWTYPE_ using CONTENTS	Explicit ROWTYPE_ on VARIABLES
FILE	Defaults to INLINE	Defaults to INLINE
VARIABLES	Required	Required
FORMAT	Defaults to LOWER DIAG	Defaults to LOWER DIAG
SPLIT	Required if split files[*]	Required if split files
FACTORS	Required if factors	Required if factors
CELLS	Required if factors	Inapplicable
CONTENTS	Defaults to CORR	Optional
N	Optional	Optional

[*] If the data do not contain values for the split-file variables, this subcommand can specify a single variable, which is not specified on the VARIABLES subcommand.

Subcommand Order

- SPLIT and FACTORS, when used, must follow VARIABLES.
- The remaining subcommands can be specified in any order.

Syntax Rules

- No commands can be specified between MATRIX DATA and BEGIN DATA, not even a VARIABLE LABELS or FORMAT command. Data transformations cannot be used until after MATRIX DATA is executed.

Operations

- MATRIX DATA defines and writes data in one step.
- MATRIX DATA clears the working data file and defines a new working file.
- If CONTENTS is not specified and *ROWTYPE_* is not specified on VARIABLES, MATRIX DATA assumes that the data contain only CORR values and issues warning messages to alert you to its assumptions.
- With the default format, data values, including diagonal values, must be in the lower triangle of the matrix. If MATRIX DATA encounters values in the upper triangle, it ignores those values and issues a series of warnings.
- With the default format, if any matrix rows span records in the data file, MATRIX DATA cannot form the matrix properly.
- MATRIX DATA does not allow format specifications for matrix materials. The procedure assigns the formats shown in Table 2. To change data formats, execute MATRIX DATA

and then assign new formats with the FORMATS, PRINT FORMATS, or WRITE FORMATS commands.

Table 2   Print and write formats for matrix variables

Variable type	Format
*ROWTYPE_, VARNAME_*	A8
Split-file variables	F4.0
Factors	F4.0
Continuous variables	F10.4

Format of the Raw Matrix Data File

- If LIST is in effect on the FORMAT subcommand, the data are entered in freefield format, with blanks and commas used as separators and each scalar, vector, or row of the matrix beginning on a new record. Unlike LIST format with DATA LIST, a vector or row of the matrix can be contained on multiple records. The continuation records do not have a value for *ROWTYPE_*.

- *ROWTYPE_* values can be enclosed in apostrophes or quotes.

- The order of variables in the raw data file must match the order in which they are specified on VARIABLES. However, this order does not have to correspond to the order of variables in the resulting SPSS-format matrix data file.

- The way records are entered for pooled vectors or matrices when factors are present depends upon whether *ROWTYPE_* is specified on the VARIABLES subcommand (see the FACTORS subcommand on p. 594).

- MATRIX DATA recognizes plus and minus signs as field separators when they are not preceded by the letter *D* or *E*. This allows MATRIX DATA to read scientific notation as well as correlation matrices written by FORTRAN in F10.8 format. A plus sign preceded by a *D* or *E* is read as part of the number in scientific notation.

Example

```
MATRIX DATA
    VARIABLES=ROWTYPE_ SAVINGS POP15 POP75 INCOME GROWTH.
BEGIN DATA
MEAN 9.6710 35.0896 2.2930 1106.7784 3.7576
STDDEV 4.4804 9.1517 1.2907 990.8511 2.8699
N 50 50 50 50 50
CORR 1
CORR -.4555 1
CORR .3165 -.9085 1
CORR .2203 -.7562 .7870 1
CORR .3048 -.0478 .0253 -.1295  1
END DATA.
```

- The variable *ROWTYPE_* is specified on VARIABLES. *ROWTYPE_* values are included in the data.

- No other specifications are required.

Example

```
* Matrix data with procedure DISCRIMINANT'.
MATRIX DATA VARIABLES=WORLD ROWTYPE_ FOOD APPL SERVICE RENT
   /FACTORS=WORLD.
BEGIN DATA
1 N       25 25 25 25
1 MEAN    76.64 77.32 81.52 101.40
2 N       7 7 7 7
2 MEAN    76.1428571 85.2857143 60.8571429 249.571429
3 N       13 13 13 13
3 MEAN    55.5384615 76 63.4615385 86.3076923
. SD      16.4634139 22.5509310 16.8086768 77.1085326
. CORR    1
. CORR    .1425366 1
. CORR    .5644693 .2762615 1
. CORR    .2133413 -.0499003 .0417468 1
END DATA.

DISCRIMINANT GROUPS=WORLD(1,3)
   /VARIABLES=FOOD APPL SERVICE RENT /METHOD=WILKS /MATRIX=IN(*).
```

- MATRIX DATA is used to generate a working data file that DISCRIMINANT can read. DISCRIMINANT reads the mean, count (unweighted *N*), and *N* (weighted *N*) for each cell in the data, as well as pooled values for the standard deviation and correlation coefficients. If count equals *N*, only *N* needs to be supplied.
- *ROWTYPE_* is specified on VARIABLES to identify record types in the data. Though CONTENTS and CELLS can be used to identify record types and distinguish between within-cells data and pooled values, it is usually easier to specify *ROWTYPE_* on VARIABLES and enter the *ROWTYPE_* values in the data.
- Because factors are present in the data, the continuous variables (*FOOD, APPL, SERVICE,* and *RENT*) must be specified last on VARIABLES and must be last in the data.
- The FACTORS subcommand identifies *WORLD* as the factor variable.
- BEGIN DATA immediately follows MATRIX DATA.
- *N* and *MEAN* values for each cell are entered in the data.
- *ROWTYPE_* values for the pooled records are *SD* and *COR*. MATRIX DATA assigns the values *STDDEV* and *CORR* to the corresponding vectors in the matrix. Records with pooled information have the system-missing value (.) for the factors.
- The DISCRIMINANT procedure reads the data matrix. An asterisk (*) is specified as the input file on the MATRIX subcommand because the data are in the working file.

Example

```
* Matrix data with procedure REGRESSION.

MATRIX DATA VARIABLES=SAVINGS POP15 POP75 INCOME GROWTH
  /CONTENTS=MEAN SD N CORR /FORMAT=UPPER NODIAGONAL.

BEGIN DATA
9.6710 35.0896 2.2930 1106.7784 3.7576
4.4804 9.1517 1.2908 990.8511 2.8699
50 50 50 50 50
-.4555 .3165 .2203 .3048
-.9085 -.7562 -.0478
 .7870 .0253
-.1295
END DATA.

REGRESSION MATRIX=IN(*)  /VARIABLES=SAVINGS TO GROWTH
  /DEP=SAVINGS /ENTER.
```

- MATRIX DATA is used to generate a matrix that REGRESSION can read. REGRESSION reads and writes matrices that always contain the mean, standard deviation, N, and Pearson correlation coefficients. Data in this example do not have *ROWTYPE_* values, and the correlation values are from the upper triangle of the matrix without the diagonal values.

- *ROWTYPE_* is not specified on VARIABLES because its values are not included in the data.

- Because there are no *ROWTYPE_* values, CONTENTS is required to define the record types and the order of the records in the file.

- By default, MATRIX DATA reads values from the lower triangle of the matrix, including the diagonal values. FORMAT is required in this example to indicate that the data are in the upper triangle and do not include diagonal values.

- BEGIN DATA immediately follows the MATRIX DATA command.

- The REGRESSION procedure reads the data matrix. An asterisk (*) is specified as the input file on the MATRIX subcommand because the data are in the working file. Since there is a single vector of N's in the data, missing values are handled listwise (the default for REGRESSION).

Example

```
* Matrix data with procedure ONEWAY.

MATRIX DATA VARIABLES=EDUC ROWTYPE_ WELL /FACTORS=EDUC.
BEGIN DATA
1 N 65
2 N 95
3 N 181
4 N 82
5 N 40
6 N 37
1 MEAN 2.6462
2 MEAN 2.7737
3 MEAN 4.1796
4 MEAN 4.5610
5 MEAN 4.6625
6 MEAN 5.2297
. MSE 6.2699
. DFE 494
END DATA.

ONEWAY WELL BY EDUC(1,6) /MATRIX=IN(*)
```

- One of the two types of matrices that the ONEWAY procedure reads includes a vector of frequencies for each factor level, a vector of means for each factor level, a record containing the pooled variance (within-group mean square error), and the degrees of freedom for the mean square error. MATRIX DATA is used to generate a working data file containing this type of matrix data for the ONEWAY procedure.

- *ROWTYPE_* is explicit on VARIABLES and identifies record types.

- Because factors are present in the data, the continuous variables (*WELL*) must be specified last on VARIABLES and must be last in the data.

- The FACTORS subcommand identifies *EDUC* as the factor variable.

- *MSE* is entered in the data as the *ROWTYPE_* value for the vector of square pooled standard deviations.

- *DFE* is entered in the data as the *ROWTYPE_* value for the vector of degrees of freedom.

- Records with pooled information have the system-missing value (.) for the factors.

VARIABLES Subcommand

VARIABLES specifies the names of the variables in the raw data and the order in which they occur.

- VARIABLES is required.

- There is no limit to the number of variables that can be specified.

- If *ROWTYPE_* is specified on VARIABLES, the continuous variables must be the last variables specified on the subcommand and must be last in the data.

- If split-file variables are present, they must also be specified on SPLIT.

- If factor variables are present, they must also be specified on FACTORS.

When either of the following is true, the only variables that must be specified on VARIABLES are the continuous variables:

1. The data contain only correlation coefficients. There can be no additional information, such as the mean and standard deviation, and no factor information or split-file variables. MATRIX DATA assigns the record type *CORR* to all records.

2. CONTENTS is used to define all record types. The data can then contain information such as the mean and standard deviation, but no factor, split-file, or *ROWTYPE_* variables. MATRIX DATA assigns the record types defined on the CONTENTS subcommand.

Variable VARNAME_

*VARNAME_* cannot be specified on the VARIABLES subcommand or anywhere on MATRIX DATA, and its values cannot be included in the data. The MATRIX DATA command generates the variable *VARNAME_* automatically.

Variable ROWTYPE_

*   *ROWTYPE_* is a string variable with A8 format. Its values define the data types. All SPSS-format matrix data files contain a *ROWTYPE_* variable.

*   If *ROWTYPE_* is specified on VARIABLES and its values are entered in the data, MATRIX DATA is primarily used to define the names and order of the variables in the raw data file.

*   *ROWTYPE_* must precede the continuous variables.

*   Valid values for *ROWTYPE_* are *CORR, COV, MAT, MSE, DFE, MEAN, STDDEV* (or *SD*), *N_VECTOR* (or *N*), *N_SCALAR, N_MATRIX, COUNT,* or *PROX*. For definitions of these values, see the CONTENTS subcommand on p. 596. Three-character abbreviations for these values are permitted. These values can also be enclosed in quotes or apostrophes.

*   If *ROWTYPE_* is not specified on VARIABLES, CONTENTS must be used to define the order in which the records occur within the file. MATRIX DATA follows these specifications strictly and generates a *ROWTYPE_* variable according to the CONTENTS specifications. A data-entry error, especially skipping a record, can cause the procedure to assign the wrong values to the wrong records.

Example

```
* ROWTYPE_ is specified on VARIABLES.

MATRIX DATA
     VARIABLES=ROWTYPE_ SAVINGS POP15 POP75 INCOME GROWTH.
BEGIN DATA
MEAN 9.6710 35.0896 2.2930 1106.7784 3.7576
STDDEV 4.4804 9.1517 1.2907 990.8511 2.8699
N 50 50 50 50 50
CORR 1
CORR -.4555 1
CORR .3165 -.9085 1
CORR .2203 -.7562 .7870 1
CORR .3048 -.0478 .0253 -.1295  1
END DATA.
```

- *ROWTYPE_* is specified on VARIABLES. *ROWTYPE_* values in the data identify each record type.
- Note that *VARNAME_* is not specified on VARIABLES, and its values are not entered in the data.

Example

```
* ROWTYPE_ is specified on VARIABLES.

MATRIX DATA
    VARIABLES=ROWTYPE_ SAVINGS POP15 POP75 INCOME GROWTH.
BEGIN DATA
'MEAN     ' 9.6710 35.0896 2.2930 1106.7784 3.7576
'SD       ' 4.4804 9.1517 1.2907 990.8511 2.8699
'N        ' 50 50 50 50 50
"CORR     " 1
"CORR     " -.4555 1
"CORR     " .3165 -.9085 1
"CORR     " .2203 -.7562 .7870 1
"CORR     " .3048 -.0478 .0253 -.1295  1
END DATA.
```

- *ROWTYPE_* values for the mean, standard deviation, *N*, and Pearson correlation coefficients are abbreviated and enclosed in apostrophes or quotations.

Example

```
* ROWTYPE_ is not specified on VARIABLES.

MATRIX DATA VARIABLES=SAVINGS POP15 POP75 INCOME GROWTH
    /CONTENTS=MEAN SD N CORR.
BEGIN DATA
9.6710 35.0896 2.2930 1106.7784 3.7576
4.4804 9.1517 1.2907 990.8511 2.8699
50 50 50 50 50
 1
-.4555 1
 .3165 -.9085 1
 .2203 -.7562 .7870 1
 .3048 -.0478 .0253 -.1295 1
END DATA.
```

- *ROWTYPE_* is not specified on VARIABLES, and its values are not included in the data.
- CONTENTS is required to define the record types and the order of the records in the file.

FILE Subcommand

FILE specifies the matrix file containing the data. The default specification is INLINE, which indicates that the data are included within the command sequence between the BEGIN DATA and END DATA commands.

- If the data are in an external file, FILE must specify the file.
- If the FILE subcommand is omitted, the data must be inline.

Example

```
MATRIX DATA FILE=RAWMTX /VARIABLES=varlist.
```

- FILE indicates that the data are in the file *RAWMTX*.

FORMAT Subcommand

FORMAT indicates how the matrix data are formatted. It applies only to matrix values in the data, not to vector values, such as the mean and standard deviation.

- FORMAT can specify up to three keywords: one to specify the data-entry format, one to specify matrix shape, and one to specify whether the data include diagonal values.
- The minimum specification is a single keyword.
- Default settings remain in effect unless explicitly overridden.

Data-Entry Format

FORMAT has two keywords that specify the data-entry format:

LIST   *Each scalar, vector, and matrix row must begin on a new record.* A vector or row of the matrix may be continued on multiple records. This is the default.

FREE   *Matrix rows do not need to begin on a new record.* Any item can begin in the middle of a record.

Matrix Shape

FORMAT has three keywords that specify the matrix shape. With either triangular shape, no values—not even missing indicators—are entered for the implied values in the matrix.

LOWER   *Read data values from the lower triangle.* This is the default.

UPPER   *Read data values from the upper triangle.*

FULL   *Read the full square matrix of data values.* FULL cannot be specified with NODIAGONAL.

Diagonal Values

FORMAT has two keywords that refer to the diagonal values:

DIAGONAL   *Data include the diagonal values.* This is the default.

NODIAGONAL   *Data do not include diagonal values.* The diagonal value is set to the system-missing value for all matrices except the correlation matrices. For correlation matrices, the diagonal value is set to 1. NODIAGONAL cannot be specified with FULL.

Table 3 shows how data might be entered for each combination of FORMAT settings that govern matrix shape and diagonal values. With UPPER NODIAGONAL and LOWER NODIAGONAL, you do not enter the matrix row that has blank values for the continuous variables. If you enter that row, MATRIX DATA cannot properly form the matrix.

Table 3   Various FORMAT settings

FULL	UPPER DIAGONAL	UPPER NODIAGONAL	LOWER DIAGONAL	LOWER NODIAGONAL
MEAN 5 4 3	MEAN 5 4 3	MEAN 5 4 3	MEAN 5 4 3	MEAN 5 4 3
SD 3 2 1	SD 3 2 1	SD 3 2 1	SD 3 2 1	SD 3 2 1
N 9 9 9	N 9 9 9	N 9 9 9	N 9 9 9	N 9 9 9
CORR 1 .6 .7	CORR 1 .6 .7	CORR .6 .7	CORR 1	CORR .6
CORR .6 1 .8	CORR 1 .8	CORR .8	CORR .6 1	CORR .7 .8
CORR .7 .8 1	CORR 1		CORR .7 .8 1	

Example

```
MATRIX DATA VARIABLES=ROWTYPE_ V1 TO V3
   /FORMAT=UPPER NODIAGONAL.
BEGIN DATA
MEAN     5    4    3
SD       3    2    1
N        9    9    9
CORR        .6   .7
CORR             .8
END DATA.
LIST.
```

• FORMAT specifies the upper-triangle format with no diagonal values. The default LIST is in effect for the data-entry format.

Example

```
MATRIX DATA VARIABLES=ROWTYPE_ V1 TO V3
   /FORMAT=UPPER NODIAGONAL.
BEGIN DATA
MEAN 5 4 3
SD 3 2 1
N 9 9 9
CORR .6 .7
CORR .8
END DATA.
LIST.
```

• This example is identical to the previous example. It shows that data do not have to be aligned in columns. Data throughout this section are aligned in columns to emphasize the matrix format.

SPLIT Subcommand

SPLIT specifies the variables whose values define the split files. SPLIT must follow the VARIABLES subcommand.

- SPLIT can specify a subset of up to eight of the variables named on VARIABLES. All split variables must be numeric. The keyword TO can be used to imply variables in the order in which they are named on VARIABLES.

- A separate matrix must be included in the data for each value of each split variable. MATRIX DATA generates a complete set of matrix materials for each.

- If the data contain neither *ROWTYPE_* nor split-file variables, a single split-file variable can be specified on SPLIT. This variable is *not* specified on the VARIABLES subcommand. MATRIX DATA generates a complete set of matrix materials for each set of matrix materials in the data and assigns values 1, 2, 3, etc., to the split variable until the end of the data is encountered.

Example

```
MATRIX DATA   VARIABLES=S1 ROWTYPE_ V1 TO V3 /SPLIT=S1.
BEGIN DATA
0 MEAN     5   4   3
0 SD       1   2   3
0 N        9   9   9
0 CORR     1
0 CORR    .6   1
0 CORR    .7  .8   1
1 MEAN     9   8   7
1 SD       5   6   7
1 N        9   9   9
1 CORR     1
1 CORR    .4   1
1 CORR    .3  .2   1
END DATA.
LIST.
```

- The split variable *S1* has two values: 0 and 1. Two separate matrices are entered in the data, one for each value *S1*.

- *S1* must be specified on both VARIABLES and SPLIT.

Example

```
MATRIX DATA VARIABLES=V1 TO V3 /CONTENTS=MEAN SD N CORR
   /SPLIT=SPL.
BEGIN DATA
   5   4   3
   1   2   3
   9   9   9
   1
  .6   1
  .7  .8   1
   9   8   7
   5   6   7
   9   9   9
   1
  .4   1
  .3  .2   1
END DATA.
LIST.
```

- The split variable *SPL* is not specified on VARIABLES, and values for *SPL* are not included in the data.

- Two sets of matrix materials are included in the data. MATRIX DATA therefore assigns values 1 and 2 to variable *SPL* and generates two matrices in the matrix data file.

FACTORS Subcommand

FACTORS specifies the variables whose values define the cells represented by the within-cells data. FACTORS must follow the VARIABLES subcommand.

- FACTORS specifies a subset of the variables named on the VARIABLES subcommand. The keyword TO can be used to imply variables in the order in which they are named on VARIABLES.

- If *ROWTYPE_* is explicit on VARIABLES and its values are included in the data, records that represent pooled information have the system-missing value (indicated by a period) for the factors, since the values of *ROWTYPE_* are ambiguous.

- If *ROWTYPE_* is not specified on VARIABLES and its values are not in the data, enter data values for the factors only for records that represent within-cells information. Enter nothing for the factors for records that represent pooled information. CELLS must be specified to indicate the number of within-cells records, and CONTENTS must be specified to indicate which record types have within-cells data.

Example

```
* Rowtype is explicit.

MATRIX DATA VARIABLES=ROWTYPE_ F1 F2  VAR1 TO VAR3
  /FACTORS=F1 F2.
BEGIN DATA
MEAN 1 1   1   2   3
SD   1 1   5   4   3
N    1 1   9   9   9
MEAN 1 2   4   5   6
SD   1 2   6   5   4
N    1 2   9   9   9
MEAN 2 1   7   8   9
SD   2 1   7   6   5
N    2 1   9   9   9
MEAN 2 2   9   8   7
SD   2 2   8   7   6
N    2 2   9   9   9
CORR . . .1
CORR . . .6  1
CORR . . .7 .8  1
END DATA.
```

- *ROWTYPE_* is specified on VARIABLES.
- Factor variables must be specified on both VARIABLES and FACTORS.
- Periods in the data represent missing values for the *CORR* factor values.

Example

```
* Rowtype is implicit.
MATRIX DATA VARIABLES=F1 F2  VAR1 TO VAR3
   /FACTORS=F1 F2 /CONTENTS=(MEAN SD N) CORR /CELLS=4.
BEGIN DATA
1 1  1   2   3
1 1  5   4   3
1 1  9   9   9
1 2  4   5   6
1 2  6   5   4
1 2  9   9   9
2 1  7   8   9
2 1  7   6   5
2 1  9   9   9
2 2  9   8   7
2 2  8   7   6
2 2  9   9   9
     1
    .6  1
    .7 .8 1
END DATA.
```

- *ROWTYPE_* is not specified on VARIABLES.
- Nothing is entered for the *CORR* factor values because the records contain pooled information.
- CELLS is required because there are factors in the data and *ROWTYPE_* is implicit.
- CONTENTS is required to define the record types and to differentiate between the within-cells and pooled types.

CELLS Subcommand

CELLS specifies the number of within-cells records in the data. The only valid specification for CELLS is a single integer, which indicates the number of sets of within-cells information that MATRIX DATA must read.

- CELLS is required when there are factors in the data and *ROWTYPE_* is implicit.
- If CELLS is used when *ROWTYPE_* is specified on VARIABLES, MATRIX DATA issues a warning and ignores the CELLS subcommand.

Example

```
MATRIX DATA VARIABLES=F1 VAR1 TO VAR3 /FACTORS=F1 /CELLS=2
   /CONTENTS=(MEAN SD N) CORR.
BEGIN DATA
1   5   4   3
1   3   2   1
1   9   9   9
2   8   7   6
2   6   7   8
2   9   9   9
    1
   .6  1
   .7 .8  1
END DATA.
```

- The specification for CELLS is 2 because the factor variable *F1* has two values (1 and 2) and there are therefore two sets of within-cells information.
- If there were two factor variables, *F1* and *F2*, and each had two values, 1 and 2, CELLS would equal 4 to account for all four possible factor combinations (assuming all 4 combinations are present in the data).

CONTENTS Subcommand

CONTENTS defines the record types when *ROWTYPE_* is not included in the data. The minimum specification is a single keyword indicating a type of record. The default is CORR.

- CONTENTS is required to define record types and record order whenever *ROWTYPE_* is not specified on VARIABLES and its values are not in the data. The only exception to this rule is the rare situation in which all data values represent pooled correlation records and there are no factors. In that case, MATRIX DATA reads the data values and assigns the default *ROWTYPE_* of *CORR* to all records.
- The order in which keywords are specified on CONTENTS must correspond to the order in which records appear in the data. If the keywords on CONTENTS are in the wrong order, MATRIX DATA will incorrectly assign values.

CORR   *Matrix of correlation coefficients.* This is the default. If *ROWTYPE_* is not specified on the VARIABLES subcommand and you omit the CONTENTS subcommand, MATRIX DATA assigns the *ROWTYPE_* value *CORR* to all matrix rows.

COV   *Matrix of covariance coefficients.*

MAT   *Generic square matrix.*

MSE   *Vector of mean squared errors.*

DFE   *Vector of degrees of freedom.*

MEAN   *Vector of means.*

STDDEV   *Vector of standard deviations.* SD is a synonym for STDDEV. MATRIX DATA assigns the *ROWTYPE_* value STDDEV to the record if either STDDEV or SD is specified.

N_VECTOR   *Vector of counts.* N is a synonym for N_VECTOR. MATRIX DATA assigns the *ROWTYPE_* value *N* to the record.

N_SCALAR   *Count.* Scalars are a shorthand mechanism for representing vectors in which all elements have the same value, such as when a vector of *N*'s is calculated using listwise deletion of missing values. Enter N_SCALAR as the *ROWTYPE_* value in the data and then the N_SCALAR value for the first continuous variable only. MATRIX DATA assigns the *ROWTYPE_* value *N* to the record and copies the specified N_SCALAR value across all the continuous variables.

N_MATRIX   *Square matrix of counts.* Enter N_MATRIX as the *ROWTYPE_* value for each row of counts in the data. MATRIX DATA assigns the *ROWTYPE_* value *N* to each of those rows.

COUNT   *Count vector accepted by procedure DISCRIMINANT.* This contains unweighted *N*'s.

Example

```
MATRIX DATA VARIABLES=V1 TO V3 /CONTENTS=MEAN SD N_SCALAR CORR.
BEGIN DATA
   5   4   3
   3   2   1
   9
   1
  .6   1
  .7  .8   1
END DATA.
LIST.
```

- *ROWTYPE_* is not specified on VARIABLES, and *ROWTYPE_* values are not in the data. CONTENTS is therefore required to identify record types.
- CONTENTS indicates that the matrix records are in the following order: mean, standard deviation, *N*, and correlation coefficients.
- The *N_SCALAR* value is entered for the first continuous variable only.

Within-Cells Record Definition

When the data include factors and *ROWTYPE_* is not specified, CONTENTS distinguishes between within-cells and pooled records by enclosing the keywords for within-cells records in parentheses.
- If the records associated with the within-cells keywords appear together for each set of factor values, enclose the keywords together within a single set of parentheses.
- If the records associated with each within-cells keyword are grouped together across factor values, enclose the keyword within its own parentheses

Example

```
MATRIX DATA VARIABLES=F1 VAR1 TO VAR3 /FACTORS=F1 /CELLS=2
   /CONTENTS=(MEAN SD N) CORR.
```

- MEAN, SD, and N contain within-cells information and are therefore specified within parentheses. CORR is outside the parentheses because it identifies pooled records.
- CELLS is required because there is a factor specified and *ROWTYPE_* is implicit.

Example

```
MATRIX DATA VARIABLES=F1 VAR1 TO VAR3 /FACTORS=F1 /CELLS=2
  /CONTENTS=(MEAN SD N) CORR.
BEGIN DATA
1   5   4   3
1   3   2   1
1   9   9   9
2   4   5   6
2   6   5   4
2   9   9   9
    1
   .6   1
   .7  .8   1
END DATA.
```

- The parentheses around the CONTENTS keywords indicate that the mean, standard deviation, and *N* for value 1 of factor *F1* are together, followed by the mean, standard deviation, and *N* for value 2 of factor *F1*.

Example

```
MATRIX DATA VARIABLES=F1 VAR1 TO VAR3 /FACTORS=F1 /CELLS=2
  /CONTENTS=(MEAN) (SD) (N) CORR.
BEGIN DATA
1   5   4   3
2   4   5   6
1   3   2   1
2   6   5   4
1   9   9   9
2   9   9   9
    1
   .6   1
   .7  .8   1
END DATA.
```

- The parentheses around each CONTENTS keyword indicate that the data include the means for all cells, followed by the standard deviations for all cells, followed by the *N* values for all the cells.

Example

```
MATRIX DATA VARIABLES=F1 VAR1 TO VAR3 /FACTORS=F1 /CELLS=2
  /CONTENTS=(MEAN SD) (N) CORR.
BEGIN DATA
1   5   4   3
1   3   2   1
2   4   5   6
2   6   5   4
1   9   9   9
2   9   9   9
    1
   .6   1
   .7  .8   1
END DATA.
```

- The parentheses around the CONTENTS keywords indicate that the data include the mean and standard deviation for value 1 of *F1*, followed by the mean and standard deviation for value 2 of *F1*, followed by the *N* values for all cells.

Optional Specification When ROWTYPE_ Is Explicit

When *ROWTYPE_* is explicitly named on VARIABLES, MATRIX DATA uses *ROWTYPE_* values to determine record types.

- When *ROWTYPE_* is explicitly named on VARIABLES, CONTENTS can be used for informational purposes. However, *ROWTYPE_* values in the data determine record types.
- If MATRIX DATA reads values for *ROWTYPE_* that are not specified on CONTENTS, it issues a warning.
- Missing values for factors are entered as periods, even though CONTENTS is specified (see the FACTORS subcommand on p. 594).

Example

```
MATRIX DATA VARIABLES=ROWTYPE_ F1 F2 VAR1 TO VAR3
     /FACTORS=F1 F2 /CONTENTS=(MEAN SD N) CORR.
BEGIN DATA
MEAN 1 1   1   2   3
SD   1 1   5   4   3
N    1 1   9   9   9
MEAN 1 2   4   5   6
SD   1 2   6   5   4
N    1 2   9   9   9
CORR . .   1
CORR . .  .6   1
CORR . .  .7  .8   1
END DATA.
```

- *ROWTYPE_* is specified on VARIABLES. MATRIX DATA therefore uses *ROWTYPE_* values in the data to identify record types.
- Because *ROWTYPE_* is specified on VARIABLES, CONTENTS is optional. However, CONTENTS is specified for informational purposes. This is most useful when data are in an external file and the *ROWTYPE_* values cannot be seen in the data.
- Missing values for factors are entered as periods, even though CONTENTS is specified.

N Subcommand

N specifies the population *N* when the data do not include it. The only valid specification is an integer, which indicates the population *N*.

- MATRIX DATA generates one record with a *ROWTYPE_* of N for each split file, and it uses the specified *N* value for each continuous variable.

Example

```
MATRIX DATA VARIABLES=V1 TO V3 /CONTENTS=MEAN SD CORR
   /N=99.
BEGIN DATA
   5   4   3
   3   4   5
   1
  .6   1
  .7  .8   1
END DATA.
```

- MATRIX DATA uses 99 as the N value for all continuous variables.

MCONVERT

```
MCONVERT [[/MATRIX=] [IN({*    })] [OUT({*    })]]
                          {file}        {file}
          [{/REPLACE}]
           {/APPEND }
```

Example:
```
MCONVERT MATRIX=OUT(CORMTX) /APPEND.
```

Overview

MCONVERT converts covariance matrix materials to correlation matrix materials, or vice versa. For MCONVERT to convert a correlation matrix, the matrix data must contain *CORR* values (Pearson correlation coefficients) and a vector of standard deviations (*STDDEV*). For MCONVERT to convert a covariance matrix, only *COV* values are required in the data.

Options

Matrix Files. MCONVERT can read matrix materials from an external matrix data file, and it can write converted matrix materials to an external file.

Matrix Materials. MCONVERT can write the converted matrix only or both the converted matrix and the original matrix to the resulting matrix data file.

Basic Specification

The minimum specification is the command itself. By default, MCONVERT reads the original matrix from the working data file and then replaces it with the converted matrix.

Syntax Rules

- The keywords IN and OUT cannot specify the same external file.
- The APPEND and REPLACE subcommands cannot be specified on the same MCONVERT command.

Operations

- If the data are covariance matrix materials, MCONVERT converts them to a correlation matrix plus a vector of standard deviations.
- If the data are a correlation matrix and vector of standard deviations, MCONVERT converts them to a covariance matrix.

- If there are multiple *CORR* or *COV* matrices (for example, one for each grouping (factor) or one for each split variable), each will be converted to a separate matrix, preserving the values of any factor or split variables.
- All cases with *ROWTYPE_* values other than *CORR* or *COV*, such as *MEAN*, *N*, and *STDDEV*, are always copied into the new matrix data file.
- MCONVERT cannot read raw matrix values. If your data are raw values, use the MATRIX DATA command.
- Split variables (if any) must occur first in the file that MCONVERT reads, followed by the variable *ROWTYPE_*, the grouping variables (if any), and the variable *VARNAME_*. All variables following *VARNAME_* are the variables for which a matrix will be read and created.

Limitations

- The total number of split variables plus grouping variables cannot exceed eight.

Example

```
MATRIX DATA VARIABLES=ROWTYPE_ SAVINGS POP15 POP75 INCOME GROWTH
   /FORMAT=FULL.
BEGIN DATA
COV    20.0740459  -18.678638    1.8304990  978.181242 3.9190106
COV   -18.678638    83.7541100 -10.731666 -6856.9888   -1.2561071
COV     1.8304990  -10.731666    1.6660908 1006.52742    .0937992
COV   978.181242  -6856.9888    1006.52742 981785.907 -368.18652
COV     3.9190106   -1.2561071    .0937992 -368.18652  8.2361574
END DATA.
MCONVERT.
```

- MATRIX DATA defines the variables in the file and creates a working data file of matrix materials. The values for the variable *ROWTYPE_* are *COV*, indicating that the matrix contains covariance coefficients. The FORMAT subcommand indicates that data are in full square format.
- MCONVERT converts the covariance matrix to a correlation matrix plus a vector of standard deviations. By default, the converted matrix is written to the working data file.

MATRIX Subcommand

The MATRIX subcommand specifies the file for the matrix materials. By default, MATRIX reads the original matrix from the working data file and replaces the working data file with the converted matrix.

- MATRIX has two keywords, IN and OUT. The specification on both IN and OUT is the name of an external file in parentheses or an asterisk (*) to refer to the working data file (the default).
- The actual keyword MATRIX is optional.
- IN and OUT cannot specify the same external file.

- MATRIX=IN cannot be specified unless a working data file has already been defined. To convert an existing matrix at the beginning of a session, use GET to retrieve the matrix file and then specify IN(*) on MATRIX.

IN   *The matrix file to read.*

OUT   *The matrix file to write.*

Example

```
GET FILE=COVMTX.
MCONVERT MATRIX=OUT(CORMTX).
```

- GET retrieves the SPSS-format matrix data file *COVMTX*. *COVMTX* becomes the working data file.
- By default, MCONVERT reads the original matrix from the working data file. IN(*) can be specified to make the default explicit.
- The keyword OUT on MATRIX writes the converted matrix to file *CORMTX*.

REPLACE and APPEND Subcommands

By default, MCONVERT writes only the converted matrix to the resulting matrix file. Use APPEND to copy both the original matrix and the converted matrix.

- The only specification is the keyword REPLACE or APPEND.
- REPLACE and APPEND are alternatives.
- REPLACE and APPEND affect the resulting matrix file only. The original matrix materials, whether in the working file or in an external file, remain intact.

APPEND   *Write the original matrix followed by the converted matrix to the matrix file. If there are multiple sets of matrix materials, APPEND appends each converted matrix to the end of a copy of its original matrix.*

REPLACE   *Write the original matrix followed by the covariance matrix to the matrix file.*

Example

```
MCONVERT MATRIX=OUT(COVMTX) /APPEND.
```

- MCONVERT reads matrix materials from the working file.
- The APPEND subcommand copies original matrix materials, appends each converted matrix to the end of the copy of its original matrix, and writes both sets to the file *COVMTX*.

MEANS

```
MEANS [TABLES=]{varlist} BY varlist [BY...] [/varlist...]
                {ALL     }

 [/MISSING={TABLE      }]
           {INCLUDE   }
           {DEPENDENT}

 [/CELLS= [MEAN**  ] [COUNT**  ] [STDDEV**]
          [MEDIAN] [GMEDIAN] [SEMEAN] [SUM ]
          [MIN] [MAX] [RANGE] [VARIANCE]
          [KURT] [SEKURT] [SKEW] [SESKEW]
          [FIRST] [LAST]
          [NPCT] [SPCT] [NPCT(var)] [SPCT(var)]
          [HARMONIC] [GEOMETRIC]
          [DEFAULT]
          [ALL] [NONE]   ]

 [/STATISTICS=[ANOVA] [{LINEARITY}]  [NONE**]]
                      {ALL      }
```

**Default if the subcommand is omitted.

Example:

```
MEANS TABLES=V1 TO V5 BY GROUP
  /STATISTICS=ANOVA.
```

Overview

By default, MEANS (alias BREAKDOWN) displays means, standard deviations, and group counts for a numeric dependent variable and group counts for a string variable within groups defined by one or more control (independent) variables. Other procedures that display univariate statistics are SUMMARIZE, FREQUENCIES, and DESCRIPTIVES.

Options

Cell Contents. By default, MEANS displays means, standard deviations, and cell counts for a dependent variable across groups defined by one or more control variables. You can also display sums and variances using the CELLS subcommand.

Statistics. In addition to the statistics displayed for each cell of the table, you can obtain a one-way analysis of variance and test of linearity using the STATISTICS subcommand.

Basic Specification

The basic specification is TABLES with a table list. The actual keyword TABLES can be omitted.

- The minimum table list specifies a dependent variable, the keyword BY, and a control variable.

- By default, MEANS displays means, standard deviations, and number of cases.

Subcommand Order

The table list must be first if the keyword TABLES is omitted. If the keyword TABLES is explicitly used, subcommands can be specified in any order.

Operations

- MEANS displays the number and percentage of the processed and missing cases in the Case Process Summary table.
- MEANS displays univariate statistics for the population as a whole and for each value of each successive control variable defined by the BY keyword on the TABLE subcommand in the Group Statistics table.
- ANOVA and linearity statistics, if requested, are displayed in the ANOVA and Measures of Association tables.
- If a control variable is a long string, only the short-string portion is used to identify groups in the analysis.
- If a string variable is specified as a dependent variable on any table lists, the MEANS procedure produces limited statistics (COUNT, FIRST, and LAST).

Limitations

- Maximum 200 variables total per MEANS command.
- Maximum 250 tables.

Example

```
MEANS TABLES=V1 TO V5 BY GROUP
   /STATISTICS=ANOVA.
```

- TABLES specifies that *V1* through *V5* are the dependent variables. *GROUP* is the control variable.
- Assuming that variables *V2, V3,* and *V4* lie between *V1* and *V5* in the working data file, five tables are produced: *V1* by *GROUP*, *V2* by *GROUP*, *V3* by *GROUP*, and so on.
- STATISTICS requests one-way analysis-of-variance tables of *V1* through *V5* by *GROUP*.

Example

```
MEANS VARA BY VARB BY VARC/V1 V2 BY V3 V4 BY V5.
```

- This command contains two TABLES subcommands that omit the optional TABLES keyword.

- The first table list produces a Group Statistics table for *VARA* within groups defined by each combination of values as well as the totals of *VARB* and *VARC*.
- The second table list produces a Group Statistics table displaying statistics for *V1* by *V3* by *V5*, *V1* by *V4* by *V5*, *V2* by *V3* by *V5*, and *V2* by *V4* by *V5*.

TABLES Subcommand

TABLES specifies the table list.

- You can specify multiple TABLES subcommands on a single MEANS command. The slash between the subcommands is required. You can also name multiple table lists separated by slashes on one TABLES subcommand.
- The dependent variable is specified first. If the dependent variable is a string variable, MEANS produces only limited statistics (COUNT, FIRST, and LAST). The control (independent) variables follow the BY keyword and can be numeric (integer or non-integer) or string.
- Each use of the keyword BY in a table list adds a dimension to the table requested. Statistics are displayed for each dependent variable by each combination of values and the totals of the control variables across dimensions.
- The order in which control variables are displayed is the same as the order in which they are specified on TABLES. The values of the first control variable defined for the table appear in the leftmost column of the table and change the most slowly in the definition of groups.
- More than one dependent variable can be specified in a table list, and more than one control variable can be specified in each dimension of a table list.

CELLS Subcommand

By default, SUMMARIZE displays the means, standard deviations, and cell counts in each cell. Use CELLS to modify cell information.

- If CELLS is specified without keywords, SUMMARIZE displays the default statistics.
- If any keywords are specified on CELLS, only the requested information is displayed.
- MEDIAN and GMEDIAN are expensive in terms of computer resources and time. Requesting these statistics (via these keywords or ALL) may slow down performance.

DEFAULT	*Means, standard deviations, and cell counts.* This is the default if CELLS is omitted.
MEAN	*Cell means.*
STDDEV	*Cell standard deviations.*
COUNT	*Cell counts.*
MEDIAN	*Cell median.*
GMEDIAN	*Grouped median.*

SEMEAN	*Standard error of cell mean.*
SUM	*Cell sums.*
MIN	*Cell minimum.*
MAX	*Cell maximum.*
RANGE	*Cell range.*
VARIANCE	*Variances.*
KURT	*Cell kurtosis.*
SEKURT	*Standard error of cell kurtosis.*
SKEW	*Cell skewness.*
SESKEW	*Standard error of cell skewness.*
FIRST	*First value.*
LAST	*Last value.*
NPCT	*Percentage of the total number of cases.*
SPCT	*Percentage of the total sum.*
NPCT(var)	*Percentage of the total number of cases within the specified variable.* The specified variable must be one of the control variables.
SPCT(var)	*Percentage of the total sum within the specified variable.* The specified variable must be one of the control variables.
HARMONIC	*Harmonic mean.*
GEOMETRIC	*Geometric mean.*
ALL	*All cell information.*

STATISTICS Subcommand

Use STATISTICS to request a one-way analysis of variance and a test of linearity for each TABLE list.

- Statistics requested on STATISTICS are computed in addition to the statistics displayed in the Group Statistics table.
- If STATISTICS is specified without keywords, MEANS computes ANOVA.
- If two or more dimensions are specified, the second and subsequent dimensions are ignored in the analysis-of-variance table. To obtain a two-way and higher analysis of variance, use the ANOVA or MANOVA procedure. The ONEWAY procedure calculates a one-way analysis of variance with multiple comparison tests.

ANOVA	*Analysis of variance.* ANOVA displays a standard analysis-of-variance table and calculates eta and eta squared (displayed in the Measures of Association table). This is the default if STATISTICS is specified without keywords.

LINEARITY   *Test of linearity.* LINEARITY (alias ALL) displays additional statistics to the tables created by the ANOVA keyword: the sums of squares, degrees of freedom, and mean square associated with linear and nonlinear components, the F ratio, and significance level for the ANOVA table and Pearson's r and r^2 for the Measures of Association table. LINEARITY is ignored if the control variable is a string.

NONE   *No additional statistics.* This is the default if STATISTICS is omitted.

Example

```
MEANS TABLES=INCOME BY SEX BY RACE
  /STATISTICS=ANOVA.
```

- MEANS produces a Group Statistics table of *INCOME* by *RACE* within *SEX* and computes an analysis of variance only for *INCOME* by *SEX*.

MISSING Subcommand

MISSING controls the treatment of missing values. If no MISSING subcommand is specified each combination of a dependent variable and control variables is handled separately.

TABLE   *Delete cases with missing values on a tablewise basis.* A case with a missing value for any variable specified for a table is not used. Thus, every case contained in a table has a complete set of nonmissing values for all variables in that table. When you separate table requests with a slash, missing values are handled separately for each list. Any MISSING specification will result in tablewise treatment of missing values.

INCLUDE   *Include user-missing values.* This option treats user-missing values as valid values.

DEPENDENT   *Exclude user-missing values for dependent variables only.* DEPENDENT treats user-missing values for all control variables as valid.

References

Hays, W. L. 1981. *Statistics for the social sciences*, 3rd ed. New York: Holt, Rinehart, and Wilson.

MISSING VALUES

```
MISSING VALUES {varlist}(value list) [[/]{varlist} ...]
               {ALL    }               {ALL       }
```

Keywords for numeric value lists:

LO, LOWEST, HI, HIGHEST, THRU

Example:
```
MISSING VALUES V1 (8,9) V2 V3 (0) V4 ('X') V5 TO V9 ('   ').
```

Overview

MISSING VALUES declares values for numeric and short string variables as user-missing. These values can then receive special treatment in data transformations, statistical calculations, and case selection. By default, user-missing values are treated the same as the system-missing values. System-missing values are automatically assigned by the program when no legal value can be produced, such as when an alphabetical character is encountered in the data for a numeric variable, or when an illegal calculation, such as division by 0, is requested in a data transformation.

Basic Specification

The basic specification is a single variable followed by the user-missing value or values in parentheses. Each specified value for the variable is treated as user-missing for any analysis.

Syntax Rules

- Each variable can have a maximum of three individual user-missing values. A space or comma must separate each value. For numeric variables, you can also specify a range of missing values. See "Specifying Ranges of Missing Values" on p. 611.
- The missing-value specification must correspond to the variable type (numeric or string).
- The same values can be declared missing for more than one variable by specifying a variable list followed by the values in parentheses. Variable lists must have either all numeric or all string variables.
- Different values can be declared missing for different variables by specifying separate values for each variable. An optional slash can be used to separate specifications.
- Missing values cannot be assigned to long string variables or to scratch variables.

- Missing values for short string variables must be enclosed in apostrophes or quotation marks. The value specifications must include any leading or trailing blanks. (See "String Values in Command Specifications" on p. 15.)

- A variable list followed by an empty set of parentheses ( ) deletes any user-missing specifications for those variables.

- The keyword ALL can be used to refer to all user-defined variables in the working file, provided the variables are either all numeric or all string. ALL can refer to both numeric and string variables if it is followed by an empty set of parentheses. This will delete all user-missing specifications in the working data file.

- More than one MISSING VALUES command can be specified per session.

Operations

- Unlike most transformations, MISSING VALUES takes effect as soon as it is encountered. Special attention should be paid to its position among commands. See "Command Order" on p. 16 for more information.

- Missing-value specifications can be changed between procedures. New specifications replace previous ones. If a variable is mentioned more than once on one or more MISSING VALUES commands before a procedure, only the last specification is used.

- Missing-value specifications are saved in SPSS-format data files (see SAVE) and portable files (see EXPORT).

Example

```
MISSING VALUES V1 (8,9) V2 V3 (0) V4 ('X') V5 TO V9 ('    ').
```

- The values 8 and 9 are declared missing for the numeric variable *V1*.
- The value 0 is declared missing for the numeric variables *V2* and *V3*.
- The value X is declared missing for the string variable *V4*.
- Blanks are declared missing for the string variables between and including *V5* and *V9*. All of these variables must have a width of four columns.

Example

```
MISSING VALUES V1 ().
```

- Any previously declared missing values for *V1* are deleted.

Example

```
MISSING VALUES ALL (9).
```

- The value 9 is declared missing for all variables in the working data file; the variables must all be numeric. All previous user-missing specifications are overridden.

Example

```
MISSING VALUES ALL ().
```

- All previously declared user-missing values for all variables in the working data file are deleted. The variables in the working data file can be both numeric and string.

Specifying Ranges of Missing Values

A range of values can be specified as missing for numeric variables but *not* for string variables.

- The keyword THRU indicates an inclusive list of values. Values must be separated from THRU by at least one blank space.
- The keywords HIGHEST and LOWEST with THRU indicate the highest and lowest values of a variable. HIGHEST and LOWEST can be abbreviated to HI and LO.
- Only one THRU specification can be used for each variable or variable list. Each THRU specification can be combined with one additional missing value.

Example

```
MISSING VALUES  V1 (LOWEST THRU 0).
```

- All negative values and 0 are declared missing for the variable *V1*.

Example

```
MISSING VALUES  V1 (0 THRU 1.5).
```

- Values from 0 through and including 1.5 are declared missing.

Example

```
MISSING VALUES V1 (LO THRU 0, 999).
```

- All negative values, 0, and 999 are declared missing for the variable *V1*.

MULT RESPONSE

```
MULT RESPONSE†

{/GROUPS=groupname['label'](varlist ({value1,value2})))}
                                     {value          }
     ...[groupname...]

{/VARIABLES=varlist(min,max)   [varlist...]              }

{/FREQUENCIES=varlist                                    }

{/TABLES=varlist BY varlist... [BY varlist] [(PAIRED)]}
      [/varlist BY...]


[/MISSING=[{TABLE**}]  [INCLUDE]]
          {MDGROUP}
          {MRGROUP}

[/FORMAT={LABELS**}  {TABLE**  }  [DOUBLE]]
         {NOLABELS}  {CONDENSE}
                     {ONEPAGE }

[/BASE={CASES**  }]
       {RESPONSES}

[/CELLS=[COUNT**]  [ROW]  [COLUMN]  [TOTAL]  [ALL]]
```

†A minimum of two subcommands must be used: at least one from the pair GROUPS or VARIABLES and one from the pair FREQUENCIES or TABLES.
**Default if the subcommand is omitted.

Example:

```
MULT RESPONSE  GROUPS=MAGS (TIME TO STONE (2))
   /FREQUENCIES=MAGS.
```

Overview

MULT RESPONSE displays frequencies and optional percentages for multiple-response items in univariate tables and multivariate crosstabulations. Another procedure that analyzes multiple-response items is TABLES, which has most, but not all, of the capabilities of MULT RESPONSE. TABLES has special formatting capabilities that make it useful for presentations.

Multiple-response items are questions that can have more than one value for each case. For example, the respondent may have been asked to circle all magazines read within the last month in a list of magazines. You can organize multiple-response data in one of two ways for use in the program. For each possible response, you can create a variable that can have one of two values, such as 1 for *no* and 2 for *yes*; this is the multiple-dichotomy method. Alternatively, you can estimate the maximum number of possible answers from a respondent and create that number of variables, each of which can have a value representing one of the possible answers, such as 1 for *Time*, 2 for *Newsweek*, and 3 for *PC Week*. If an individual did not give the maximum number of answers, the extra variables receive a missing-value code. This is the multiple-response or multiple-category method of coding answers.

To analyze the data entered by either method, you combine variables into groups. The technique depends on whether you have defined multiple-dichotomy or multiple-response variables. When you create a multiple-dichotomy group, each component variable with at least one *yes* value across cases becomes a category of the group variable. When you create a multiple-response group, each value becomes a category and the program calculates the frequency for a particular value by adding the frequencies of all component variables with that value. Both multiple-dichotomy and multiple-response groups can be crosstabulated with other variables in MULT RESPONSE.

Options

Cell Counts and Percentages. By default, crosstabulations include only counts and no percentages. You can request row, column, and total table percentages using the CELLS subcommand. You can also base percentages on responses instead of respondents using BASE.

Format. You can suppress the display of value labels and request condensed format for frequency tables using the FORMAT subcommand.

Basic Specification

The subcommands required for the basic specification fall into two groups: GROUPS and VARIABLES name the elements to be included in the analysis; FREQUENCIES and TABLES specify the type of table display to be used for tabulation. The basic specification requires at least one subcommand from each group:

- GROUPS defines groups of multiple-response items to be analyzed and specifies how the component variables will be combined.
- VARIABLES identifies all individual variables to be analyzed.
- FREQUENCIES requests frequency tables for the groups and/or individual variables specified on GROUPS and VARIABLES.
- TABLES requests crosstabulations of groups and/or individual variables specified on GROUPS and VARIABLES.

Subcommand Order

- The basic subcommands must be used in the following order: GROUPS, VARIABLES, FREQUENCIES, and TABLES. Only one set of basic subcommands can be specified.
- All basic subcommands must precede all optional subcommands. Optional subcommands can be used in any order.

Operations

- Empty categories are not displayed in either frequency tables or crosstabulations.
- If you define a multiple-response group with a very wide range, the tables require substantial amounts of workspace. If the component variables are sparsely distributed, you should recode them to minimize the workspace required.
- MULT RESPONSE stores category labels in the workspace. If there is insufficient space to store the labels after the tables are built, the labels are not displayed.

Limitations

- The component variables must have integer values. Non-integer values are truncated.
- Maximum 100 existing variables named or implied by GROUPS and VARIABLES together.
- Maximum 20 groups defined on GROUPS.
- Maximum 32,767 categories for a multiple-response group or an individual variable.
- Maximum 10 table lists on TABLES.
- Maximum 5 dimensions per table.
- Maximum 100 groups and variables named or implied on FREQUENCIES and TABLES together.
- Maximum 200 non-empty rows and 200 non-empty columns in a single table.

GROUPS Subcommand

GROUPS defines both multiple-dichotomy and multiple-response groups.
- Specify a name for the group and an optional label, followed by a list of the component variables and the value or values to be used in the tabulation.
- Enclose the variable list in parentheses and enclose the values in an inner set of parentheses following the last variable in the list.
- The label for the group is optional and can be up to 40 characters in length, including imbedded blanks. Apostrophes or quotes around the label are not required.
- To define a multiple-dichotomy group, specify only one tabulating value (the value that represents *yes*) following the variable list. Each component variable becomes a value of the group variable, and the number of cases that have the tabulating value becomes the frequency. If there are no cases with the tabulating value for a given component variable, that variable does not appear in the tabulation.
- To define a multiple-response group, specify two values following the variable list. These are the minimum and maximum values of the component variables. The group variable will have the same range of values. The frequency for each value is tabulated across all component variables in the list.
- You can use any valid variable name for the group except the name of an existing variable specified on the same MULT RESPONSE command. However, you can reuse a group name on another MULT RESPONSE command.

- The group names and labels exist only during MULT RESPONSE and disappear once MULT RESPONSE has been executed. If group names are referred to in other procedures, an error results.

- For a multiple-dichotomy group, the category labels come from the variable labels defined for the component variables.

- For a multiple-response group, the category labels come from the value labels for the first component variable in the group. If categories are missing for the first variable but are present for other variables in the group, you must define value labels for the missing categories. (You can use the ADD VALUE LABELS command to define extra value labels.)

Example

```
MULT RESPONSE   GROUPS=MAGS 'MAGAZINES READ' (TIME TO STONE (2))
   /FREQUENCIES=MAGS.
```

- The GROUPS subcommand creates a multiple-dichotomy group named *MAGS*. The variables between and including *TIME* and *STONE* become categories of *MAGS*, and the frequencies are cases with the value 2 (indicating *yes, read the magazine*) for the component variables.

- The group label is *MAGAZINES READ*.

Example

```
MULT RESPONSE   GROUPS=PROBS 'PERCEIVED NATIONAL PROBLEMS'
   (PROB1 TO PROB3 (1,9))
   /FREQUENCIES=PROBS.
```

- The GROUPS subcommand creates the multiple-response group *PROBS*. The component variables are the existing variables between and including *PROB1* and *PROB3*, and the frequencies are tabulated for the values 1 through 9.

- The frequency for a given value is the number of cases that have that value in any of the variables *PROB1* to *PROB3*.

VARIABLES Subcommand

VARIABLES specifies existing variables to be used in frequency tables and crosstabulations. Each variable is followed by parentheses enclosing a minimum and a maximum value, which are used to allocate cells for the tables for that variable.

- You can specify any numeric variable on VARIABLES, but non-integer values are truncated.

- If GROUPS is also specified, VARIABLES follows GROUPS.

- To provide the same minimum and maximum for each of a set of variables, specify a variable list followed by a range specification.

- The component variables specified on GROUPS can be used in frequency tables and crosstabulations, but you must specify them again on VARIABLES, along with a range for the values. You do not have to respecify the component variables if they will not be used as individual variables in any tables.

Example

```
MULT RESPONSE  GROUPS=MAGS 'MAGAZINES READ' (TIME TO STONE (2))
  /VARIABLES SEX(1,2) EDUC(1,3)
  /FREQUENCIES=MAGS SEX EDUC.
```

- The VARIABLES subcommand names the variables *SEX* and *EDUC* so that they can be used in a frequencies table.

Example

```
MULT RESPONSE  GROUPS=MAGS 'MAGAZINES READ' (TIME TO STONE (2))
  /VARIABLES=EDUC (1,3) TIME (1,2).
  /TABLES=MAGS BY EDUC TIME.
```

- The variable *TIME* is used in a group and also in a table.

FREQUENCIES Subcommand

FREQUENCIES requests frequency tables for groups and individual variables. By default, a frequency table contains the count for each value, the percentage of responses, and the percentage of cases. For another method of producing frequency tables for individual variables, see the FREQUENCIES procedure.

- All groups must be created by GROUPS, and all individual variables to be tabulated must be named on VARIABLES.
- You can use the keyword TO to imply a set of group or individual variables. TO refers to the order in which variables are specified on the GROUPS or VARIABLES subcommand.

Example

```
MULT RESPONSE  GROUPS=MAGS 'MAGAZINES READ' (TIME TO STONE (2))
  /FREQUENCIES=MAGS.
```

- The FREQUENCIES subcommand requests a frequency table for the multiple-dichotomy group *MAGS*, tabulating the frequency of the value 2 for each of the component variables *TIME* to *STONE*.

Example

```
MULT RESPONSE
 GROUPS=MAGS 'MAGAZINES READ' (TIME TO STONE (2))
      PROBS 'PERCEIVED NATIONAL PROBLEMS' (PROB1 TO PROB3 (1,9))
      MEMS 'SOCIAL ORGANIZATION MEMBERSHIPS' (VFW AMLEG ELKS (1))
 /VARIABLES SEX(1,2) EDUC(1,3)
 /FREQUENCIES=MAGS TO MEMS SEX EDUC.
```

- The FREQUENCIES subcommand requests frequency tables for *MAGS, PROBS, MEMS, SEX*, and *EDUC*.
- You cannot specify MAGS TO EDUC because *SEX* and *EDUC* are individual variables, and *MAGS, PROBS*, and *MEMS* are group variables.

TABLES Subcommand

TABLES specifies the crosstabulations to be produced by MULT RESPONSE. Both individual variables and group variables can be tabulated together.

- The first list defines the rows of the tables; the next list (following BY) defines the columns. Subsequent lists following BY keywords define control variables, which produce subtables. Use the keyword BY to separate the dimensions. You can specify up to five dimensions (four BY keywords) for a table.
- To produce more than one table, name one or more variables for each dimension of the tables. You can also specify multiple table lists separated by a slash. If you use the keyword TO to imply a set of group or individual variables, TO refers to the order in which groups or variables are specified on the GROUPS or VARIABLES subcommand.
- If FREQUENCIES is also specified, TABLES follows FREQUENCIES.
- The value labels for columns are displayed on three lines with eight characters per line. To avoid splitting words, reverse the row and column variables, or redefine the variable or value labels (depending on whether the variables are multiple-dichotomy or multiple-response variables).

Example

```
MULT RESPONSE  GROUPS=MAGS 'MAGAZINES READ' (TIME TO STONE (2))
   /VARIABLES=EDUC (1,3)/TABLES=EDUC BY MAGS.
```

- The TABLES subcommand requests a crosstabulation of variable *EDUC* by the multiple-dichotomy group *MAGS*.

Example

```
MULT RESPONSE  GROUPS=MAGS 'MAGAZINES READ' (TIME TO STONE (2))
   MEMS 'SOCIAL ORGANIZATION MEMBERSHIPS' (VFW AMLEG ELKS (1))
   /VARIABLES EDUC (1,3)/TABLES=MEMS MAGS BY EDUC.
```

- The TABLES subcommand specifies two crosstabulations—*MEMS* by *EDUC*, and *MAGS* by *EDUC*.

Example

```
MULT RESPONSE  GROUPS=MAGS 'MAGAZINES READ' (TIME TO STONE (2))
   /VARIABLES SEX (1,2) EDUC (1,3)
   /TABLES=MAGS BY EDUC SEX/EDUC BY SEX/MAGS BY EDUC BY SEX.
```

- The TABLES subcommand uses slashes to separate three table lists. It produces two tables from the first table list (*MAGS* by *EDUC* and *MAGS* by *SEX*) and one table from the second table list (*EDUC* by *SEX*). The third table list produces separate tables for each sex (*MAGS* by *EDUC* for male and for female).

Example

```
MULT RESPONSE  GROUPS=MAGS 'MAGAZINES READ' (TIME TO STONE (2))
   PROBS 'NATIONAL PROBLEMS MENTIONED' (PROB1 TO PROB3 (1,9))
   /TABLES=MAGS BY PROBS.
```

- The TABLES subcommand requests a crosstabulation of the multiple-dichotomy group *MAGS* with the multiple-response group *PROBS*.

PAIRED Keyword

When MULT RESPONSE crosstabulates two multiple-response groups, by default it tabulates each variable in the first group with each variable in the second group and sums the counts for each cell. Thus, some responses can appear more than once in the table. Use PAIRED to pair the first variable in the first group with the first variable in the second group, the second variable in the first group with the second variable in the second group, and so on.

- The keyword PAIRED is specified in parentheses on the TABLES subcommand following the last variable named for a specific table list.
- When you request paired crosstabulations, the order of the component variables on the GROUPS subcommand determines the construction of the table.
- Although the tables can contain individual variables and multiple-dichotomy groups in a paired table request, only variables within multiple-response groups are paired.
- PAIRED also applies to a multiple-response group used as a control variable in a three-way or higher-order table.
- Paired tables are identified in the output by the label *PAIRED GROUP*.
- Percentages in paired tables are always based on responses rather than cases.

Example

```
MULT RESPONSE GROUPS=PSEX 'SEX OF CHILD'(P1SEX P2SEX P3SEX (1,2))
  /PAGE 'AGE OF ONSET OF PREGNANCY' (P1AGE P2AGE P3AGE (1,4))
  /TABLES=PSEX BY PAGE (PAIRED).
```

- The PAIRED keyword produces a paired crosstabulation of *PSEX* by *PAGE*, which is a combination of the tables *P1SEX* by *P1AGE*, *P2SEX* by *P2AGE*, and *P3SEX* by *P3AGE*.

Example

```
MULT RESPONSE GROUPS=PSEX 'SEX OF CHILD'(P1SEX P2SEX P3SEX (1,2))
  PAGE 'AGE OF ONSET OF PREGNANCY' (P1AGE P2AGE P3AGE (1,4))
  /VARIABLES=EDUC (1,3)
  /TABLES=PSEX BY PAGE BY EDUC (PAIRED).
```

- The TABLES subcommand pairs only *PSEX* with *PAGE*. *EDUC* is not paired because it is an individual variable, not a multiple-response group.

CELLS Subcommand

By default, MULT RESPONSE displays cell counts but not percentages in crosstabulations. CELLS requests percentages for crosstabulations.

- If you specify one or more keywords on CELLS, MULT RESPONSE displays cell counts plus the percentages you request. The count cannot be eliminated from the table cells.

COUNT   *Cell counts.* This is the default if you omit the CELLS subcommand.

ROW   *Row percentages.*

COLUMN   *Column percentages.*

TOTAL   *Two-way table total percentages.*

ALL   *Cell counts, row percentages, column percentages, and two-way table total percentages.* This is the default if you specify the CELLS subcommand without keywords.

Example

```
MULT RESPONSE  GROUPS=MAGS 'MAGAZINES READ' (TIME TO STONE (2))
  /VARIABLES=SEX (1,2) (EDUC (1,3)
  /TABLES=MAGS BY EDUC SEX
  /CELLS=ROW COLUMN.
```

• The CELLS subcommand requests row and column percentages in addition to counts.

BASE Subcommand

BASE lets you obtain cell percentages and marginal frequencies based on responses rather than respondents. Specify one of two keywords:

CASES   *Base cell percentages on cases.* This is the default if you omit the BASE subcommand and do not request paired tables. You cannot use this specification if you specify PAIRED on TABLE.

RESPONSES   *Base cell percentages on responses.* This is the default if you request paired tables.

Example

```
MULT RESPONSE  GROUPS=PROBS 'NATIONAL PROBLEMS MENTIONED'
  (PROB1 TO PROB3 (1,9))/VARIABLES=EDUC (1,3)
  /TABLES=EDUC BY PROBS
  /CELLS=ROW COLUMN
  /BASE=RESPONSES.
```

• The BASE subcommand requests marginal frequencies and cell percentages based on responses.

MISSING Subcommand

MISSING controls missing values. Its minimum specification is a single keyword.

• By default, MULT RESPONSE deletes cases with missing values on a table-by-table basis for both individual variables and groups. In addition, values falling outside the specified range are not tabulated and are included in the missing category. Thus, specifying a range that excludes missing values is equivalent to the default missing-value treatment.

• For a multiple-dichotomy group, a case is considered missing by default if none of the component variables contains the tabulating value for that case. Keyword MDGROUP overrides the default and specifies listwise deletion for multiple-dichotomy groups.

• For a multiple-response group, a case is considered missing by default if none of the components has valid values falling within the tabulating range for that case. Thus, cases with missing or excluded values on some (but not all) of the components of a group are included in tabulations of the group variable. The keyword MRGROUP overrides the default and specifies listwise deletion for multiple-response groups.

* You can use INCLUDE with MDGROUP, MRGROUP, or TABLE. The user-missing value is tabulated if it is included in the range specification.

TABLE   *Exclude missing values on a table-by-table basis.* Missing values are excluded on a table-by-table basis for both component variables and groups. This is the default if you omit the MISSING subcommand.

MDGROUP   *Exclude missing values listwise for multiple-dichotomy groups.* Cases with missing values for any component dichotomy variable are excluded from the tabulation of the multiple-dichotomy group.

MRGROUP   *Exclude missing values listwise for multiple-response groups.* Cases with missing values for any component variable are excluded from the tabulation of the multiple-response group.

INCLUDE   *Include user-missing values.* User-missing values are treated as valid values if they are included in the range specification on the GROUPS or VARIABLES subcommands.

Example

```
MULT RESPONSE  GROUPS=FINANCL 'FINANCIAL PROBLEMS MENTIONED'
  (FINPROB1 TO FINPROB3 (1,3))
  SOCIAL 'SOCIAL PROBLEMS MENTIONED'(SOCPROB1 TO SOCPROB4 (4,9))
  /VARIABLES=EDUC (1,3)
  /TABLES=EDUC BY FINANCL SOCIAL
  /MISSING=MRGROUP.
```

* The MISSING subcommand indicates that a case will be excluded from counts in the first table if any of the variables in the group *FINPROB1* to *FINPROB3* has a missing value or a value outside the range 1 to 3. A case is excluded from the second table if any of the variables in the group *SOCPROB1* to *SOCPROB4* has a missing value or value outside the range 4 to 9.

FORMAT Subcommand

FORMAT controls table formats. The minimum specification on FORMAT is a single keyword.

Labels are controlled by two keywords:

LABELS   *Display value labels in frequency tables and crosstabulations.* This is the default.

NOLABELS   *Suppress value labels in frequency tables and crosstabulations for multiple-response variables and individual variables.* You cannot suppress the display of variable labels used as value labels for multiple-dichotomy groups.

The following keywords apply to the format of frequency tables:

DOUBLE   *Double spacing for frequency tables.* By default, MULT RESPONSE uses single spacing.

TABLE   *One-column format for frequency tables.* This is the default if you omit the FORMAT subcommand.

CONDENSE   *Condensed format for frequency tables.* This option uses a three-column condensed format for frequency tables for all multiple-response groups and individual variables. Labels are suppressed. This option does not apply to multiple-dichotomy groups.

ONEPAGE   *Conditional condensed format for frequency tables.* Three-column condensed format is used if the resulting table would not fit on a page. This option does not apply to multiple-dichotomy groups.

Example

```
MULT RESPONSE   GROUPS=PROBS 'NATIONAL PROBLEMS MENTIONED'
   (PROB1 TO PROB3 (1,9))/VARIABLES=EDUC (1,3)
   /FREQUENCIES=EDUC PROBS
   /FORMAT=CONDENSE.
```

- The FORMAT subcommand specifies condensed format, which eliminates category labels and displays the categories in three parallel sets of columns, each set containing one or more rows of categories (rather than displaying one set of columns aligned vertically down the page).

N OF CASES

```
N OF CASES n
```

Example:
```
N OF CASES 100.
```

Overview

N OF CASES (alias N) limits the number of cases in the working data file to the first n cases.

Basic Specification

The basic specification is N OF CASES followed by at least one space and a positive integer. Cases in the working data file are limited to the specified number.

Syntax Rules

- To limit the number of cases for the next procedure only, use the TEMPORARY command before N OF CASES (see TEMPORARY).
- In some versions of the program, N OF CASES can be specified only after a working data file is defined.

Operations

- Unlike most transformations, N OF CASES takes effect as soon as it is encountered in the command sequence. Thus, special attention should be paid to its position among commands. See "Command Order" on p. 16 for more information.
- N OF CASES limits the number of cases analyzed by all subsequent procedures in the session. The working data file will have no more than n cases after the first data pass following the N OF CASES command. Any subsequent N OF CASES command specifying a greater number of cases will be ignored.
- If N OF CASES specifies more cases than can actually be built, the program builds as many cases as possible.
- If N OF CASES is used with SAMPLE or SELECT IF, the program reads as many records as required to build the specified n cases. It makes no difference whether the N OF CASES precedes or follows the SAMPLE or SELECT IF command.

622

Example

```
GET FILE=CITY.
N 100.
```

- N OF CASES limits the number of cases on the working data file to the first 100 cases. Cases are limited for all subsequent analyses.

Example

```
DATA LIST FILE=PRSNNL / NAME 1-20 (A) AGE 22-23 SALARY 25-30.
N 25.
SELECT IF (SALARY GT 20000).
LIST.
```

- DATA LIST defines variables from file *PRSNNL*.
- N OF CASES limits the working data file to 25 cases after cases have been selected by SELECT IF.
- SELECT IF selects only cases in which *SALARY* is greater than $20,000.
- LIST produces a listing of the cases in the working data file. If the original working data file has fewer than 25 cases in which salary is greater than 20,000, fewer than 25 cases will be listed.

Example

```
DATA LIST FILE=PRSNNL / NAME 1-20(A) AGE 22-23
                        SALARY 25-30 DEPT 32.
LIST.
TEMPORARY.
N 25.
FREQUENCIES VAR=SALARY.
N 50.
FREQUENCIES VAR=AGE.
REPORT FORMAT=AUTO /VARS=NAME AGE SALARY /BREAK=DEPT
  / SUMMARY=MEAN.
```

- The first N OF CASES command is temporary. Only 25 cases are used in the first FREQUENCIES procedure.
- The second N OF CASES command is permanent. The second frequency table and the report are based on 50 cases from file *PRSNNL*. The working data file now contains 50 cases (assuming the original working file had at least that many).

NEW FILE

```
NEW FILE
```

Overview

The NEW FILE command clears the working data file. It is used when you want to build a new working data file by generating data within an input program (see INPUT PROGRAM— END INPUT PROGRAM).

Basic Specification

NEW FILE is always specified by itself. No other keyword is required or allowed.

Operations

- NEW FILE clears the working data file. The command takes effect as soon as it is encountered. You *must* build a new working data file after this command to continue your session. Transformations or procedures cannot be used before a working data file is created.

- When you build a working data file with GET, DATA LIST, or other file definition commands (such as ADD FILES or MATCH FILES), the working data file is automatically replaced. It is not necessary to specify NEW FILE.

NONPAR CORR

```
NONPAR CORR [VARIABLES=] varlist [WITH varlist] [/varlist...]

[/PRINT={TWOTAIL**}  {SIG**}  {SPEARMAN**}]
         {ONETAIL  }  {NOSIG}  {KENDALL   }
                              {BOTH      }

[/SAMPLE]

[/MISSING=[{PAIRWISE**} [INCLUDE]]
           {LISTWISE  }

[/MATRIX=OUT({*   })]
             {file}
```

**Default if the subcommand is omitted.

Example:

```
NONPAR CORR VARIABLES=PRESTIGE SPPRES PAPRES16 DEGREE PADEG MADEG.
```

Overview

NONPAR CORR computes two rank-order correlation coefficients, Spearman's rho and Kendall's tau-b, with their significance levels. You can obtain either or both coefficients. NONPAR CORR automatically computes the ranks and stores the cases in memory. Therefore, memory requirements are directly proportional to the number of cases being analyzed.

Options

Coefficients and Significance Levels. By default, NONPAR CORR computes Spearman coefficients and displays the two-tailed significance level. You can request a one-tailed test, and you can display the significance level for each coefficient as an annotation using the PRINT subcommand.

Random Sampling. You can request a random sample of cases using the SAMPLE subcommand when there is not enough space to store all the cases.

Matrix Output. You can write matrix materials to an SPSS-format data file using the MATRIX subcommand. The matrix materials include the number of cases used to compute each coefficient and the Spearman or Kendall coefficients for each variable. These materials can be read by other procedures.

Basic Specification

The basic specification is VARIABLES and a list of numeric variables. The actual keyword VARIABLES can be omitted. By default, Spearman correlation coefficients are calculated.

Subcommand Order

- VARIABLES must be specified first.
- The remaining subcommands can be used in any order.

Operations

- NONPAR CORR produces one or more matrices of correlation coefficients. For each coefficient, NONPAR CORR displays the number of cases used and the significance level.
- The number of valid cases is always displayed. Depending on the specification on the MISSING subcommand, it can be displayed for each pair or in a single annotation.
- If all cases have a missing value for a given pair of variables, or if they all have the same value for a variable, the coefficient cannot be computed. If a correlation cannot be computed, NONPAR CORR displays a decimal point.
- If both Spearman and Kendall coefficients are requested and MATRIX is used to write matrix materials to an SPSS-format matrix data file, only Spearman's coefficient will be written with the matrix materials.

Limitations

- Maximum 25 variable lists.
- Maximum 100 variables total per NONPAR CORR command.

Example

```
NONPAR CORR VARIABLES=PRESTIGE SPPRES PAPRES16 DEGREE PADEG MADEG.
```

- By default, Spearman correlation coefficients are calculated. The number of cases upon which the correlations are based and the two-tailed significance level are displayed for each correlation.

VARIABLES Subcommand

VARIABLES specifies the variable list. The keyword VARIABLES is optional.

- All variables must be numeric.
- If keyword WITH is not used, NONPAR CORR displays the correlations of each variable with every other variable in the list.
- To obtain a rectangular matrix, specify two variable lists separated by keyword WITH. NONPAR CORR writes a rectangular matrix of variables in the first list correlated with variables in the second list.
- Keyword WITH cannot be used when the MATRIX subcommand is used.
- You can request more than one analysis. Use a slash to separate the specifications for each analysis.

Example

```
NONPAR CORR VARS=PRESTIGE SPPRES PAPRES16 WITH DEGREE PADEG MADEG.
```

- The three variables listed before WITH define the rows; the three variables listed after WITH define the columns of the correlation matrix.
- Spearman's rho is displayed by default.

Example

```
NONPAR CORR VARIABLES=SPPRES PAPRES16 PRESTIGE
                 /SATCITY WITH SATHOBBY SATFAM.
```

- NONPAR CORR produces two Correlations tables.
- By default, Spearman's rho is displayed.

PRINT Subcommand

By default, NONPAR CORR displays Spearman correlation coefficients. The significance level(s) are displayed below the coefficients. The significance level is based on a two-tailed test. Use PRINT to change these defaults.

- The Spearman and Kendall coefficients are both based on ranks.

SPEARMAN   *Spearman's rho.* Only Spearman coefficients are displayed. This is the default.

KENDALL   *Kendall's tau*-b. Only Kendall coefficients are displayed.

BOTH   *Kendall and Spearman coefficients.* Both coefficients are displayed. If MATRIX is used to write the correlation matrix to a matrix data file, only Spearman coefficients are written with the matrix materials.

SIG   *Display the significance level.* This is the default.

NOSIG   *Display the significance level in an annotation.*

TWOTAIL   *Two-tailed test of significance.* This test is appropriate when the direction of the relationship cannot be determined in advance, as is often the case in exploratory data analysis. This is the default.

ONETAIL   *One-tailed test of significance.* This test is appropriate when the direction of the relationship between a pair of variables can be specified in advance of the analysis.

SAMPLE Subcommand

NONPAR CORR must store cases in memory to build matrices. SAMPLE selects a random sample of cases when computer resources are insufficient to store all the cases. To request a random sample, simply specify the subcommand. SAMPLE has no additional specifications.

MISSING Subcommand

MISSING controls missing-value treatments.

- PAIRWISE and LISTWISE are alternatives. You can specify INCLUDE with either PAIRWISE or LISTWISE.

PAIRWISE *Exclude missing values pairwise.* Cases with a missing value for one or both of a pair of variables for a specific correlation coefficient are excluded from the computation of that coefficient. This allows the maximum information available to be used in every calculation. This also results in a set of coefficients based on a varying number of cases. The number is displayed for each pair. This is the default.

LISTWISE *Exclude missing values listwise.* Cases with a missing value for any variable named in a list are excluded from the computation of all coefficients in the Correlations table. The number of cases used is displayed in a single annotation. Each variable list on a command is evaluated separately. Thus, a case missing for one matrix might be used in another matrix. This option decreases the amount of memory required and significantly decreases computational time.

INCLUDE *Include user-missing values.* User-missing values are treated as valid values.

MATRIX Subcommand

MATRIX writes matrix materials to a matrix data file. The matrix materials always include the number of cases used to compute each coefficient, and either the Spearman or the Kendall correlation coefficient for each variable, whichever is requested. See "Format of the Matrix Data File" on page 629 for a description of the file.

- You cannot write both Spearman's and Kendall's coefficients to the same matrix data file. To obtain both Spearman's and Kendall's coefficients in matrix format, specify separate NONPAR CORR commands for each coefficient and define different matrix data files for each command.

- If PRINT=BOTH is in effect, NONPAR CORR displays a matrix in the listing file for both coefficients but writes only the Spearman coefficients to the matrix data file.

- NONPAR CORR cannot write matrix materials for rectangular matrices (variable lists containing keyword WITH). If more than one variable list is specified, only the last variable list that does not use keyword WITH is written to the matrix data file.

- The specification on MATRIX is keyword OUT and the name of the matrix file in parentheses.

- If you want to use a correlation matrix written by NONPAR CORR in another procedure, change the *ROWTYPE_* value RHO or TAUB to CORR using the RECODE command.

- Any documents contained in the working data file are not transferred to the matrix file.

OUT (filename) *Write a matrix data file.* Specify either a file or an asterisk, enclosed in parentheses. If you specify a file, the file is stored on disk and can be retrieved at any time. If you specify an asterisk (*), the matrix data file replaces the working file but is not stored on disk unless you use SAVE or XSAVE.

Format of the Matrix Data File

- The matrix data file has two special variables created by the program: *ROWTYPE_* and *VARNAME_*.
- Variable *ROWTYPE_* is a short string variable with values N and RHO for Spearman's correlation coefficient. If you specify Kendall's coefficient, the values are N and TAUB.
- *VARNAME_* is a short string variable whose values are the names of the variables used to form the correlation matrix. When *ROWTYPE_* is RHO (or TAUB), VARNAME_ gives the variable associated with that row of the correlation matrix.
- The remaining variables in the file are the variables used to form the correlation matrix.

Split Files

- When split-file processing is in effect, the first variables in the matrix data file are the split variables, followed by *ROWTYPE_*, *VARNAME_*, and the variables used to form the correlation matrix.
- A full set of matrix materials is written for each split-file group defined by the split variables.
- A split variable cannot have the same name as any other variable written to the matrix data file.
- If split-file processing is in effect when a matrix is written, the same split file must be in effect when that matrix is read by a procedure.

Missing Values

- With PAIRWISE treatment of missing values (the default), the matrix of N's used to compute each coefficient is included with the matrix materials.
- With LISTWISE or INCLUDE treatments, a single N used to calculate all coefficients is included with the matrix materials.

Example

```
GET FILE GSS80 /KEEP PRESTIGE SPPRES PAPRES16 DEGREE PADEG MADEG.
NONPAR CORR VARIABLES=PRESTIGE TO MADEG
    /MATRIX OUT(NPMAT).
```

- NONPAR CORR reads data from file *GSS80* and writes one set of correlation matrix materials to the file *NPMAT*.
- The working data file is still *GSS80*. Subsequent commands are executed on file *GSS80*.

Example

```
GET FILE GSS80 /KEEP PRESTIGE SPPRES PAPRES16 DEGREE PADEG MADEG.
NONPAR CORR VARIABLES=PRESTIGE TO MADEG
   /MATRIX OUT(*).
LIST.
DISPLAY DICTIONARY.
```

- NONPAR CORR writes the same matrix as in the example above. However, the matrix data file replaces the working file. The LIST and DISPLAY commands are executed on the matrix file, not on the original working file *GSS80*.

Example

```
NONPAR CORR VARIABLES=PRESTIGE SPPRES PAPRES16 DEGREE PADEG MADEG
      /PRESTIGE TO DEGREE /PRESTIGE WITH DEGREE
/MATRIX OUT(NPMAT).
```

- Only the matrix for *PRESTIGE* to *DEGREE* is written to the matrix data file because it is the last variable list that does not use keyword WITH.

NPAR TESTS

```
NPAR TESTS [CHISQUARE=varlist[(lo,hi)]/] [/EXPECTED={EQUAL    }]
                                                     {f1,f2,...fn}

[/K-S({UNIFORM [min,max]    })=varlist]
      {NORMAL [mean,stddev]}
      {POISSON [mean]      }
      {EXPONENTIAL [mean]  }

[/RUNS({MEAN   })=varlist]
       {MEDIAN}
       {MODE  }
       {value }

[/BINOMIAL[({.5})]=varlist[({value1,value2})]]
           { p}              {value          }

[/MCNEMAR=varlist [WITH varlist [(PAIRED)]]]

[/SIGN=varlist [WITH varlist [(PAIRED)]]]

[/WILCOXON=varlist [WITH varlist [(PAIRED)]]]

|/MH=varlist [WITH varlist [(PAIRED)]]]††

[/COCHRAN=varlist]

[/FRIEDMAN=varlist]

[/KENDALL=varlist]

[/M-W=varlist BY var (value1,value2)]

[/K-S=varlist BY var (value1,value2)]

[/W-W=varlist BY var (value1,value2)]

[/MOSES[(n)]=varlist BY var (value1,value2)]

[/K-W=varlist BY var (value1,value2)]

[/J-T=varlist BY var (value1, value2)]††

[/MEDIAN[(value)]=varlist BY var (value1,value2)]

[/MISSING=[{ANALYSIS**}]  [INCLUDE]]
           {LISTWISE  }

[/SAMPLE]

[/STATISTICS=[DESCRIPTIVES]  [QUARTILES] [ALL]]

[/METHOD={MC [CIN({99.0 })] [SAMPLES({10000})] }]††
                  {value}            {value}
          {EXACT [TIMER({5    })]                }
                        {value}
```

**Default if the subcommand is omitted.

††Available only if the Exact Tests option is installed.

Example:
```
NPAR TESTS K-S(UNIFORM)=V1 /K-S(NORMAL,0,1)=V2.
```

Overview

NPAR TESTS is a collection of nonparametric tests. These tests make minimal assumptions about the underlying distribution of the data and are described in Siegel (1956). In addition to the nonparametric tests available in NPAR TESTS, the k-sample chi-square and Fisher's exact test are available in procedure CROSSTABS.

The tests available in NPAR TESTS can be grouped into three broad categories based on how the data are organized: one-sample tests, related-samples tests, and independent-samples tests. A one-sample test analyzes one variable. A test for related samples compares two or more variables for the same set of cases. An independent-samples test analyzes one variable grouped by categories of another variable.

The one-sample tests available in procedure NPAR TESTS are:

- BINOMIAL
- CHISQUARE
- K-S (Kolmogorov-Smirnov)
- RUNS

Tests for two related samples are:

- MCNEMAR
- SIGN
- WILCOXON

Tests for k related samples are:

- COCHRAN
- FRIEDMAN
- KENDALL

Tests for two independent samples are:

- M-W (Mann-Whitney)
- K-S (Kolmogorov-Smirnov)
- W-W (Wald-Wolfowitz)
- MOSES

Tests for k independent samples are:

- K-W (Kruskal-Wallis)
- MEDIAN

Tests are described below in alphabetical order.

Options

Statistical Display. In addition to the tests, you can request univariate statistics, quartiles, and counts for all variables specified on the command. You can also control the pairing of variables in tests for two related samples.

Random Sampling. NPAR TESTS must store cases in memory when computing tests that use ranks. You can use random sampling when there is not enough space to store all cases.

Basic Specification

The basic specification is a single test subcommand and a list of variables to be tested. Some tests require additional specifications. CHISQUARE has an optional subcommand.

Subcommand Order

Subcommands can be used in any order.

Syntax Rules

- The STATISTICS, SAMPLE, and MISSING subcommands are optional. Each can be specified only once per NPAR TESTS command.
- You can request any or all tests, and you can specify a test subcommand more than once on a single NPAR TESTS command.
- If you specify a variable more than once on a test subcommand, only the first is used.
- Keyword ALL in any variable list refers to all user-defined variables in the working data file.
- Keyword WITH controls pairing of variables in two-related-samples tests.
- Keyword BY introduces the grouping variable in two- and k-independent-samples tests.
- Keyword PAIRED can be used with keyword WITH on the MCNEMAR, SIGN, and WILCOXON subcommands to obtain sequential pairing of variables for two related samples.

Operations

- If a string variable is specified on any subcommand, NPAR TESTS will stop executing.
- When ALL is used, requests for tests of variables with themselves are ignored and a warning is displayed.

Limitations

- Maximum 100 subcommands.
- Maximum 500 variables total per NPAR TESTS command.
- Maximum 200 values for subcommand CHISQUARE.

BINOMIAL Subcommand

```
NPAR TESTS BINOMIAL [({.5})]=varlist[({value,value})]
                      {p }                {value      }
```

BINOMIAL tests whether the observed distribution of a dichotomous variable is the same as that expected from a specified binomial distribution. By default, each variable named is assumed to have only two values, and the distribution of each variable named is compared to a binomial distribution with p (the proportion of cases expected in the first category) equal to 0.5. The default output includes the number of valid cases in each group, the test proportion, and the two-tailed probability of the observed proportion.

Syntax

- The minimum specification is a list of variables to be tested.
- To change the default 0.5 test proportion, specify a value in parentheses immediately after keyword BINOMIAL.
- A single value in parentheses following the variable list is used as a cutting point. Cases with values equal to or less than the cutting point form the first category; the remaining cases form the second.
- If two values appear in parentheses after the variable list, cases with values equal to the first value form the first category, and cases with values equal to the second value form the second category.
- If no values are specified, the variables must be dichotomous.

Operations

- The proportion observed in the first category is compared to the test proportion. The probability of the observed proportion occurring given the test proportion and a binomial distribution is then computed. A test statistic is calculated for each variable specified.
- If the test proportion is the default (0.5), a two-tailed probability is displayed. For any other test proportion, a one-tailed probability is displayed. The direction of the one-tailed test depends on the observed proportion in the first category. If the observed proportion is more than the test proportion, the significance of observing that many or more in the first category is reported. If the observed proportion is less than or equal to the test proportion, the significance of observing that many or fewer in the first category is reported. In other words, the test is always done in the observed direction.

Example

```
NPAR TESTS BINOMIAL(.667)=V1(0,1).
```

- NPAR TESTS displays the Binomial Test table showing the number of cases, observed proportion, test proportion (0.667), and the one-tailed significance for each category.

- If more than 0.667 of the cases have value 0 for *V1*, BINOMIAL gives the probability of observing that many or more values of 0 in a binomial distribution with probability 0.667. If fewer than 0.667 of the cases are 0, the test will be of observing that many or fewer.

CHISQUARE Subcommand

```
NPAR TESTS CHISQUARE=varlist [(lo,hi)] [/EXPECTED={EQUAL**    }]
                                                  {f1,f2,... fn}
```

The CHISQUARE (alias CHI-SQUARE) one-sample test computes a chi-square statistic based on the differences between the observed and expected frequencies of categories of a variable. By default, equal frequencies are expected in each category. The output includes the frequency distribution, expected frequencies, residuals, chi-square, degrees of freedom, and probability.

Syntax

- The minimum specification is a list of variables to be tested. Optionally, you can specify a value range in parentheses following the variable list. You can also specify expected proportions with the EXPECTED subcommand.
- If you use the EXPECTED subcommand to specify unequal expected frequencies, you must specify a value greater than 0 for each observed category of the variable. The expected frequencies are specified in ascending order of category value. You can use the notation $n*f$ to indicate that frequency f is expected for n consecutive categories.
- Specifying keyword EQUAL on the EXPECTED subcommand has the same effect as omitting the EXPECTED subcommand.
- EXPECTED applies to all variables specified on the CHISQUARE subcommand. Use multiple CHISQUARE and EXPECTED subcommands to specify different expected proportions for variables.

Operations

- If no range is specified for the variables to be tested, a separate Chi-Square Frequency table is produced for each variable. Each distinct value defines a category.
- If a range is specified, integer-valued categories are established for each value within the range. Noninteger values are truncated before classification. Cases with values outside the specified range are excluded. One combined Chi-Square Frequency table is produced for all specified variables.
- Expected values are interpreted as proportions, not absolute values. Values are summed, and each value is divided by the total to calculate the proportion of cases expected in the corresponding category.
- A test statistic is calculated for each variable specified.

Example

```
NPAR TESTS CHISQUARE=V1 (1,5) /EXPECTED= 12, 3*16, 18.
```

- This example requests the chi-square test for values 1 through 5 of variable *V1*.
- The observed frequencies for variable *V1* are compared with the hypothetical distribution of 12/78 occurrences of value 1; 16/78 occurrences each of values 2, 3, and 4; and 18/78 occurrences of value 5.

COCHRAN Subcommand

```
NPAR TESTS COCHRAN=varlist
```

COCHRAN calculates Cochran's *Q*, which tests whether the distribution of values is the same for *k* related dichotomous variables. The output shows the frequency distribution for each variable in the Cochran Frequencies table and the number of cases, Cochran's *Q*, degrees of freedom, and probability in the Test Statistics table.

Syntax

- The minimum specification is a list of two variables.
- The variables must be dichotomous and must be coded with the same two values.

Operations

- A $k \times 2$ contingency table (variables by categories) is constructed for dichotomous variables and the proportions for each variable are computed. A single test comparing all variables is calculated.
- Cochran's *Q* statistic has approximately a chi-square distribution.

Example

```
NPAR TESTS COCHRAN=RV1 TO RV3.
```

- This example tests whether the distribution of values 0 and 1 for *RV1*, *RV2*, and *RV3* is the same.

FRIEDMAN Subcommand

```
NPAR TESTS FRIEDMAN=varlist
```

FRIEDMAN tests whether *k* related samples have been drawn from the same population. The output shows the mean rank for each variable in the Friedman Ranks table and the number of valid cases, chi-square, degrees of freedom, and probability in the Test Statistics table.

Syntax

- The minimum specification is a list of two variables.
- Variables should be at least at the ordinal level of measurement.

Operations

- The values of k variables are ranked from 1 to k for each case, and the mean rank is calculated for each variable over all cases.
- The test statistic has approximately a chi-square distribution. A single test statistic comparing all variables is calculated.

Example

```
NPAR TESTS FRIEDMAN=V1 V2 V3
  /STATISTICS=DESCRIPTIVES.
```

- This example tests variables *V1*, *V2*, and *V3*, and requests univariate statistics for all three.

J-T Subcommand

```
NPAR TESTS /J-T=varlist BY variable(value1,value2)
```

J-T (alias JONCKHEERE-TERPSTRA) performs the Jonckheere-Terpstra test, which tests whether k independent samples defined by a grouping variable are from the same population. This test is particularly powerful when the k populations have a natural ordering. The output shows the number of levels in the grouping variable, the total number of cases, observed, standardized, mean, and standard deviation of the test statistic, the two-tailed asymptotic significance, and, if a /METHOD subcommand is specified, one-tailed and two-tailed exact or Monte Carlo probabilities. This subcommand is available only if the SPSS Exact Tests option is installed.

Syntax

- The minimum specification is a test variable, the keyword BY, a grouping variable, and a pair of values in parentheses.
- Every value in the range defined by the pair of values for the grouping variable forms a group.
- If the /METHOD subcommand is specified, and the number of populations, k, is greater than 5, the p value is estimated using the Monte Carlo sampling method. The exact p value is not available when k exceeds 5.

Operations

- Cases from the k groups are ranked in a single series, and the rank sum for each group is computed. A test statistic is calculated for each variable specified before BY.
- The Jonckheere-Terpstra statistic has approximately a normal distribution.
- Cases with values other than those in the range specified for the grouping variable are excluded.
- The direction of a one-tailed inference is indicated by the sign of the standardized test statistic.

Example

```
NPAR TESTS /J-T=V1 BY V2(0,4)
  /METHOD=EXACT.
```

- This example performs the Jonckheere-Terpstra test for groups defined by values 0 through 4 of *V2*. The exact *p* values are calculated.

K-S Subcommand (One-Sample)

```
NPAR TESTS K-S({NORMAL [mean,stddev]})=varlist
              {POISSON [mean]      }
              {UNIFORM [min,max]   }
              {EXPONENTIAL [mean]  }
```

The K-S (alias KOLMOGOROV-SMIRNOV) one-sample test compares the cumulative distribution function for a variable with a uniform, normal, Poisson, or exponential distribution, and it tests whether the distributions are homogeneous. The parameters of the test distribution can be specified; the defaults are the observed parameters. The output shows the number of valid cases, parameters of the test distribution, most-extreme absolute, positive, and negative differences, Kolmogorov-Smirnov Z, and two-tailed probability for each variable.

Syntax

The minimum specification is a distribution keyword and a list of variables. The distribution keywords are NORMAL, POISSON, EXPONENTIAL, and UNIFORM.

- The distribution keyword and its optional parameters must be enclosed within parentheses.
- The distribution keyword must be separated from its parameters by blanks or commas.

NORMAL [mean, stdev]   *Normal distribution.* The default parameters are the observed mean and standard deviation.

POISSON [mean]   *Poisson distribution.* The default parameter is the observed mean.

UNIFORM [min,max]   *Uniform distribution.* The default parameters are the observed minimum and maximum values.

EXPONENTIAL [mean]   *Exponential distribution.* The default parameter is the observed mean.

Operations

- The Kolmogorov-Smirnov Z is computed from the largest difference in absolute value between the observed and test distribution functions.
- The K-S probability levels assume that the test distribution is specified entirely in advance. The distribution of the test statistic and resulting probabilities are different when the parameters of the test distribution are estimated from the sample. No correction is made.
- For a mean of 100,000 or larger, a normal approximation to the Poisson distribution is used.
- A test statistic is calculated for each variable specified.

Example

```
NPAR TESTS K-S(UNIFORM)=V1 /K-S(NORMAL,0,1)=V2.
```

- The first K-S subcommand compares the distribution of *V1* with a uniform distribution that has the same range as *V1*.
- The second K-S subcommand compares the distribution of *V2* with a normal distribution that has a mean of 0 and a standard deviation of 1.

K-S Subcommand (Two-Sample)

```
NPAR TESTS K-S=varlist BY variable(value1,value2)
```

K-S (alias KOLMOGOROV-SMIRNOV) tests whether the distribution of a variable is the same in two independent samples defined by a grouping variable. The test is sensitive to any difference in median, dispersion, skewness, and so forth, between the two distributions. The output shows the valid number of cases in each group in the Frequency table and the largest absolute, positive, and negative differences between the two groups, the Kolmogorov-Smirnov Z, and the two-tailed probability for each variable in the Test Statistics table.

Syntax

- The minimum specification is a test variable, the keyword BY, a grouping variable, and a pair of values in parentheses.
- The test variable should be at least at the ordinal level of measurement.
- Cases with the first value form one group and cases with the second value form the other. The order in which values are specified determines which difference is the largest positive and which is the largest negative.

Operations

- The observed cumulative distributions for both groups are computed, as are the maximum positive, negative, and absolute differences. A test statistic is calculated for each variable named before BY.
- Cases with values other than those specified for the grouping variable are excluded.

Example

```
NPAR TESTS K-S=V1 V2 BY V3(0,1).
```

- This example specifies two tests. The first compares the distribution of *V1* for cases with value 0 for *V3* with the distribution of *V1* for cases with value 1 for *V3*.
- A parallel test is calculated for *V2*.

K-W Subcommand

```
NPAR TESTS K-W=varlist BY variable(value1,value2)
```

K-W (alias **KRUSKAL-WALLIS**) tests whether k independent samples defined by a grouping variable are from the same population. The output shows the number of valid cases and the mean rank of the variable in each group in the Ranks table and the chi-square, degrees of freedom, and probability in the Test Statistics table.

Syntax

- The minimum specification is a test variable, the keyword BY, a grouping variable, and a pair of values in parentheses.
- Every value in the range defined by the pair of values for the grouping variable forms a group.

Operations

- Cases from the k groups are ranked in a single series, and the rank sum for each group is computed. A test statistic is calculated for each variable specified before BY.
- Kruskal-Wallis H has approximately a chi-square distribution.
- Cases with values other than those in the range specified for the grouping variable are excluded.

Example

```
NPAR TESTS K-W=V1 BY V2(0,4).
```

- This example tests *V1* for groups defined by values 0 through 4 of *V2*.

KENDALL Subcommand

```
NPAR TESTS KENDALL=varlist
```

KENDALL tests whether k related samples are from the same population. W is a measure of agreement among judges or raters where each case is one judge's rating of several items (variables). The output includes the mean rank for each variable in the Ranks table and the valid number of cases, Kendall's W, chi-square, degrees of freedom, and probability in the Test Statistics table.

Syntax

The minimum specification is a list of two variables.

Operations

- The values of the k variables are ranked from 1 to k for each case, and the mean rank is calculated for each variable over all cases. Kendall's W and a corresponding chi-square statistic are calculated, correcting for ties. In addition, a single test statistic is calculated for all variables.

- W ranges between 0 (no agreement) and 1 (complete agreement).

Example

```
DATA LIST /V1 TO V5 1-10.
BEGIN DATA
2 5 4 5 1
3 3 4 5 3
3 4 4 6 2
2 4 3 6 2
END DATA.
NPAR TESTS KENDALL=ALL.
```

- This example tests four judges (cases) on five items (variables *V1* through *V5*).

M-W Subcommand

```
NPAR TESTS M-W=varlist BY variable(value1,value2)
```

M-W (alias MANN-WHITNEY) tests whether two independent samples defined by a grouping variable are from the same population. The test statistic uses the rank of each case to test whether the groups are drawn from the same population. The output shows the number of valid cases of each group, the mean rank of the variable within each group and the sum of ranks in the Ranks table and the Mann-Whitney U, Wilcoxon W (the rank sum of the smaller group), Z statistic, and probability in the Test Statistics table.

Syntax

- The minimum specification is a test variable, the keyword BY, a grouping variable, and a pair of values in parentheses.

- Cases with the first value form one group and cases with the second value form the other. The order in which the values are specified is unimportant.

Operations

- Cases are ranked in order of increasing size, and test statistic U (the number of times a score from group 1 precedes a score from group 2) is computed.

- An exact significance level is computed if there are 40 or fewer cases. For more than 40 cases, U is transformed into a normally distributed Z statistic, and a normal approximation p value is computed.

- A test statistic is calculated for each variable named before BY.

- Cases with values other than those specified for the grouping variable are excluded.

Example

```
NPAR TESTS M-W=V1 BY V2(1,2).
```

- This example tests *V1* based on the two groups defined by values 1 and 2 of *V2*.

MCNEMAR Subcommand

```
NPAR TESTS MCNEMAR=varlist [WITH varlist [(PAIRED)]]
```

MCNEMAR tests whether combinations of values between two dichotomous variables are equally likely. The output includes a Crosstabulation table for each pair and a Test Statistics table for all pairs showing the number of valid cases, chi-square, and probability for each pair.

Syntax

- The minimum specification is a list of two variables. Variables must be dichotomous and must have the same two values.
- If keyword WITH is not specified, each variable is paired with every other variable in the list.
- If WITH is specified, each variable before WITH is paired with each variable after WITH. If PAIRED is also specified, the first variable before WITH is paired with the first variable after WITH, the second variable before WITH with the second variable after WITH, and so on. PAIRED cannot be specified without WITH.
- With PAIRED, the number of variables specified before and after WITH must be the same. PAIRED must be specified in parentheses after the second variable list.

Operations

- In computing the test statistics, only combinations for which the values for the two variables are different are considered.
- If fewer than 25 cases change values from the first variable to the second variable, the binomial distribution is used to compute the probability.

Example

```
NPAR TESTS MCNEMAR=V1 V2 V3.
```

- This example performs the MCNEMAR test on variable pairs *V1* and *V2*, *V1* and *V3*, and *V2* and *V3*.

MEDIAN Subcommand

```
NPAR TESTS MEDIAN [(value)]=varlist BY variable(value1,value2)
```

MEDIAN determines if k independent samples are drawn from populations with the same median. The independent samples are defined by a grouping variable. For each variable, the output shows a table of the number of cases greater than and less than or equal to the median in each category in the Frequency table and the number of valid cases, the median, chi-square, degrees of freedom, and probability in the Test Statistics table.

Syntax

- The minimum specification is a single test variable, the keyword BY, a grouping variable, and two values in parentheses.
- If the first grouping value is less than the second, every value in the range defined by the pair of values forms a group and a k-sample test is performed.
- If the first value is greater than the second, two groups are formed using the two values and a two-sample test is performed.
- By default, the median is calculated from all cases included in the test. To override the default, specify a median value in parentheses following the MEDIAN subcommand keyword.

Operations

- A $2 \times k$ contingency table is constructed with counts of the number of cases greater than the median and less than or equal to the median for the k groups.
- Test statistics are calculated for each variable specified before BY.
- For more than 30 cases, a chi-square statistic is computed. For 30 or fewer cases, Fisher's exact procedure (two-tailed) is used instead of chi-square.
- For a two-sample test, cases with values other than the two specified are excluded.

Example

```
NPAR TESTS MEDIAN(8.4)=V1 BY V2(1,2) /MEDIAN=V1 BY V2(1,2)
  /MEDIAN=V1 BY V3(1,4) /MEDIAN=V1 BY V3(4,1).
```

- The first two MEDIAN subcommands test variable *V1* grouped by values 1 and 2 of variable *V2*. The first test specifies a median of 8.4 and the second uses the observed median.
- The third MEDIAN subcommand requests a four-samples test, dividing the sample into four groups based on values 1, 2, 3, and 4 of variable *V3*.
- The last MEDIAN subcommand requests a two-samples test, grouping cases based on values 1 and 4 of *V3* and ignoring all other cases.

MH Subcommand

```
NPAR TESTS /MH=varlist [WITH varlist [(PAIRED)]]
```

MH performs the marginal homogeneity test, which tests whether combinations of values between two paired ordinal variables are equally likely. The marginal homogeneity test is typically used in repeated measures situations. This test is an extension of the McNemar test from binary response to multinomial response. The output shows the number of distinct values for all test variables, the number of valid off-diagonal cell counts, mean, standard deviation, observed and standardized values of the test statistics, the asymptotic two-tailed probability for each pair of variables, and, if a /METHOD subcommand is specified, one-tailed and two-tailed exact or Monte Carlo probabilities. This subcommand is available only if the SPSS Exact Tests option has been installed.

Syntax

- The minimum specification is a list of two variables. Variables must be polychotomous and must have more than two values. If the variables contain only two values, the McNemar test is performed.

- If keyword WITH is not specified, each variable is paired with every other variable in the list.

- If WITH is specified, each variable before WITH is paired with each variable after WITH. If PAIRED is also specified, the first variable before WITH is paired with the first variable after WITH, the second variable before WITH with the second variable after WITH, and so on. PAIRED cannot be specified without WITH.

- With PAIRED, the number of variables specified before and after WITH must be the same. PAIRED must be specified in parentheses after the second variable list.

Operations

- The data consist of paired, dependent responses from two populations. The marginal homogeneity test tests the equality of two multinomial $c \times 1$ tables, and the data can be arranged in the form of a square $c \times c$ contingency table. A $2 \times c$ table is constructed for each off-diagonal cell count. The marginal homogeneity test statistic is computed for cases with different values for the two variables. Only combinations for which the values for the two variables are different are considered. The first row of each $2 \times c$ table specifies the category chosen by population 1, and the second row specifies the category chosen by population 2. The test statistic is calculated by summing the first row scores across all $2 \times c$ tables.

Example

```
NPAR TESTS /MH=V1 V2 V3
  /METHOD=MC.
```

- This example performs the marginal homogeneity test on variable pairs *V1* and *V2*, *V1* and *V3*, and *V2* and *V3*. The exact *p* values are estimated using the Monte Carlo sampling method.

MOSES Subcommand

```
NPAR TESTS MOSES[(n)]=varlist BY variable(value1,value2)
```

The MOSES test of extreme reactions tests whether the range of an ordinal variable is the same in a control group and a comparison group. The control and comparison groups are defined by a grouping variable. The output includes a Frequency table showing for each variable before *BY* the total number of cases and the number of cases in each group and a Test Statistics table showing the number of outliers removed, span of the control group before and after outliers are removed, and one-tailed probability of the span with and without outliers.

Syntax

- The minimum specification is a test variable, the keyword BY, a grouping variable, and two values in parentheses.
- The test variable must be at least at the ordinal level of measurement.
- The first value of the grouping variable defines the control group and the second value defines the comparison group.
- By default, 5% of the cases are trimmed from each end of the range of the control group to remove outliers. You can override the default by specifying a value in parentheses following the MOSES subcommand keyword. This value represents an actual number of cases, not a percentage.

Operations

- Values from the groups are arranged in a single ascending sequence. The span of the control group is computed as the number of cases in the sequence containing the lowest and highest control values.
- No adjustments are made for tied cases.
- Cases with values other than those specified for the grouping variable are excluded.
- Test statistics are calculated for each variable named before BY.

Example

```
NPAR TESTS MOSES=V1 BY V3(0,1) /MOSES=V1 BY V3(1,0).
```

- The first MOSES subcommand tests *V1* using value 0 of *V3* to define the control group and value 1 for the comparison group. The second MOSES subcommand reverses the comparison and control groups.

RUNS Subcommand

```
NPAR TESTS RUNS({MEAN  })=varlist
               {MEDIAN}
               {MODE  }
               {value }
```

RUNS tests whether the sequence of values of a dichotomized variable is random. The output includes a Run Test table showing the test value (cut point used to dichotomize the variable tested), number of runs, number of cases below the cut point, number of cases greater than or equal to the cut point, and test statistic Z with its two-tailed probability for each variable.

Syntax

- The minimum specification is a cut point in parentheses followed by a test variable.
- The cut point can be specified by an exact value or one of the keywords MEAN, MEDIAN, or MODE.

Operations

- All variables tested are treated as dichotomous: cases with values less than the cut point form one category, and cases with values greater than or equal to the cut point form the other category.
- Test statistics are calculated for each variable specified.

Example

```
NPAR TESTS RUNS(MEDIAN)=V2 /RUNS(24.5)=V2 /RUNS(1)=V3.
```

- This example performs three runs tests. The first tests variable V2 using the median as the cut point. The second also tests V2, this time using 24.5 as the cut point. The third tests variable V3 with value 1 specified as the cut point.

SIGN Subcommand

```
NPAR TESTS SIGN=varlist [WITH varlist [(PAIRED)] ]
```

SIGN tests whether the distribution of two paired variables in a two-related-samples test is the same. The output includes a Frequency table showing for each pair the number of positive differences, number of negative differences, number of ties, and the total number and a Test Statistics table showing the Z statistic and two-tailed probability.

Syntax

- The minimum specification is a list of two variables.
- Variables should be at least at the ordinal level of measurement.

- If keyword WITH is not specified, each variable in the list is paired with every other variable in the list.
- If keyword WITH is specified, each variable before WITH is paired with each variable after WITH. If PAIRED is also specified, the first variable before WITH is paired with the first variable after WITH, the second variable before WITH with the second variable after WITH, and so on. PAIRED cannot be specified without WITH.
- With PAIRED, the number of variables specified before and after WITH must be the same. PAIRED must be specified in parentheses after the second variable list.

Operations

- The positive and negative differences between the pair of variables are counted. Ties are ignored.
- The probability is taken from the binomial distribution if 25 or fewer differences are observed. Otherwise, the probability comes from the Z distribution.
- Under the null hypothesis for large sample sizes, Z is approximately normally distributed with a mean of 0 and a variance of 1.

Example

```
NPAR TESTS SIGN=N1,M1 WITH N2,M2 (PAIRED).
```

- *N1* is tested with *N2*, and *M1* is tested with *M2*.

W-W Subcommand

```
NPAR TESTS W-W=varlist BY variable(value1,value2)
```

W-W (alias WALD-WOLFOWITZ) tests whether the distribution of a variable is the same in two independent samples. A runs test is performed with group membership as the criterion. The output includes a Frequency table showing the total number of valid cases for each variable specified before BY and the number of valid cases in each group, and a Test Statistics table showing the number of runs, Z, and one-tailed probability of Z. If ties are present, the minimum and maximum number of runs possible, their Z statistics, and one-tailed probabilities are displayed.

Syntax

- The minimum specification is a single test variable, the keyword BY, a grouping variable, and two values in parentheses.
- Cases with the first value form one group and cases with the second value form the other. The order in which values are specified is unimportant.

Operations

- Cases are combined from both groups and ranked from lowest to highest, and a runs test is performed using group membership as the criterion. For ties involving cases from both groups, both the minimum and maximum number of runs possible are calculated. Test statistics are calculated for each variable specified before BY.
- For a sample size of 30 or less, the exact one-tailed probability is calculated. For a sample size greater than 30, the normal approximation is used.
- Cases with values other than those specified for the grouping variable are excluded.

Example

```
NPAR TESTS W-W=V1 BY V3(0,1).
```

- This example ranks cases from lowest to highest based on their values for *V1* and a runs test is performed. Cases with value 0 for *V3* form one group and cases with value 1 form the other.

WILCOXON Subcommand

```
NPAR TESTS WILCOXON=varlist [WITH varlist [(PAIRED)] ]
```

WILCOXON tests whether the distribution of two paired variables in two related samples is the same. This test takes into account the magnitude of the differences between two paired variables. The output includes a Ranks table showing for each pair the number of valid cases, positive and negative differences, their respective mean and sum of ranks, and the number of ties and a Test Statistics table showing *Z* and probability of *Z*.

Syntax

- The minimum specification is a list of two variables.
- If keyword WITH is not specified, each variable is paired with every other variable in the list.
- If keyword WITH is specified, each variable before WITH is paired with each variable after WITH. If PAIRED is also specified, the first variable before WITH is paired with the first variable after WITH, the second variable before WITH with the second variable after WITH, and so on. PAIRED cannot be specified without WITH.
- With PAIRED, the number of variables specified before and after WITH must be the same. PAIRED must be specified in parentheses after the second variable list.

Operations

- The differences between the pair of variables are counted, the absolute differences ranked, the positive and negative ranks summed, and the test statistic *Z* computed from the positive and negative rank sums.

- Under the null hypothesis for large sample sizes, Z is approximately normally distributed with a mean of 0 and a variance of 1.

Example

```
NPAR TESTS WILCOXON=A B WITH C D (PAIRED).
```

- This example pairs *A* with *C* and *B* with *D*. If PAIRED were not specified, it would also pair *A* with *D* and *B* with *C*.

STATISTICS Subcommand

STATISTICS requests summary statistics for variables named on the NPAR TESTS command. Summary statistics are displayed in the Descriptive Statistics table before all test output.

- If STATISTICS is specified without keywords, univariate statistics (keyword DESCRIPTIVES) are displayed.

DESCRIPTIVES   *Univariate statistics.* The displayed statistics include the mean, maximum, minimum, standard deviation, and number of valid cases for each variable named on the command.

QUARTILES   *Quartiles and number of cases.* The 25th, 50th, and 75th percentiles are displayed for each variable named on the command.

ALL   *All statistics available on* NPAR TESTS.

MISSING Subcommand

MISSING controls the treatment of cases with missing values.

- ANALYSIS and LISTWISE are alternatives. However, each can be specified with INCLUDE.

ANALYSIS   *Exclude cases with missing values on a test-by-test basis.* Cases with missing values for a variable used for a specific test are omitted from that test. On subcommands that specify several tests, each test is evaluated separately. This is the default.

LISTWISE   *Exclude cases with missing values listwise.* Cases with missing values for any variable named on any subcommand are excluded from all analyses.

INCLUDE   *Include user-missing values.* User-missing values are treated as valid values.

SAMPLE Subcommand

NPAR TESTS must store cases in memory. SAMPLE allows you to select a random sample of cases when there is not enough space on your computer to store all the cases. SAMPLE has no additional specifications.

- Because sampling would invalidate a runs test, this option is ignored when the RUNS sub-command is used.

METHOD Subcommand

METHOD displays additional results for each statistic requested. If no METHOD subcommand is specified, the standard asymptotic results are displayed. If fractional weights have been specified, results for all methods will be calculated on the weight rounded to the nearest integer. This subcommand is available only if the SPSS Exact Tests option has been installed.

MC
Displays an unbiased point estimate and confidence interval based on the Monte Carlo sampling method, for all statistics. Asymptotic results are also displayed. When exact results can be calculated, they will be provided instead of the Monte Carlo results. See *SPSS Exact Tests* for details of the situations under which exact results are provided instead of Monte Carlo results.

CIN(n)
Controls the confidence level for the Monte Carlo estimate. CIN is available only when /METHOD=MC is specified. CIN has a default value of 99.0. You can specify a confidence interval between 0.01 and 99.9, inclusive.

SAMPLES
Specifies the number of tables sampled from the reference set when calculating the Monte Carlo estimate of the exact *p* value. Larger sample sizes lead to narrower confidence limits but also take longer to calculate. You can specify any integer between 1 and 1,000,000,000 as the sample size. SAMPLES has a default value of 10,000.

EXACT
Computes the exact significance level for all statistics, in addition to the asymptotic results. If both the EXACT and MC keywords are specified, only exact results are provided. Calculating the exact *p* value can be memory-intensive. If you have specified /METHOD=EXACT and find that you have insufficient memory to calculate results, you should first close any other applications that are currently running in order to make more memory available. You can also enlarge the size of your swap file (see your Windows manual for more information). If you still cannot obtain exact results, specify /METHOD=MC to obtain the Monte Carlo estimate of the exact *p* value. An optional TIMER keyword is available if you choose /METHOD=EXACT.

TIMER(n)
Specifies the maximum number of minutes allowed to run the exact analysis for each statistic. If the time limit is reached, the test is terminated, no exact results are provided, and the program begins to calculate the next test in the analysis. TIMER is available only when /METHOD=EXACT is specified. You can specify any integer value for TIMER. Specifying a value of 0 for TIMER turns the timer off completely. TIMER has a default value of 5 minutes. If a test exceeds a time limit of 30 minutes, it is recommended that you use the Monte Carlo, rather than the exact, method.

References

Siegel, S. 1956. *Nonparametric statistics for the behavioral sciences.* New York: McGraw-Hill.

NUMBERED and UNNUMBERED

This command is not available on all operating systems.

```
{NUMBERED   }
{UNNUMBERED}
```

Overview

NUMBERED and UNNUMBERED are IBM-specific commands. Usually IBM systems reserve columns 73–80 of each input line for line numbers. NUMBERED reserves columns 73–80 for those line numbers; UNNUMBERED indicates that the columns are not reserved for numbers. The default may vary by installation. Use the SHOW command to see the default for your installation.

Basic Specification

The only specification is either NUMBERED or UNNUMBERED. NUMBERED instructs the program to check only the first 72 columns for data. UNNUMBERED instructs the program to check all 80 columns for data.

Operations

- If NUMBERED is in effect and data extend beyond column 72, the program issues a warning message.
- NUMBERED and UNNUMBERED column settings apply only to inline data; they do not apply to data in an external file.

Example

```
UNNUMBERED.
```

- The program checks up to 80 columns of each input line for data.

NUMERIC

NUMERIC varlist[(format)] [/varlist...]

Example:

NUMERIC V1 V2 (F4.0) / V3 (F1.0).

Overview

NUMERIC declares new numeric variables that can be referred to in the transformation language before they are assigned values. Commands such as COMPUTE, IF, RECODE, and COUNT can be used to assign values to the new numeric variables.

Basic Specification

The basic specification is the name of the new variables. By default, variables are assigned a format of F8.2 (or the format specified on the SET command).

Syntax Rules

- A FORTRAN-like format can be specified in parentheses following a variable or variable list. Each format specified applies to all variables in the list. To specify different formats for different groups of variables, separate each format group with a slash.
- Keyword TO can be used to declare multiple numeric variables. The specified format applies to each variable named and implied by the TO construction.
- NUMERIC can be used within an input program to predetermine the order of numeric variables in the dictionary of the working data file. When used for this purpose, NUMERIC must precede DATA LIST in the input program.

Operations

- Unlike most transformations, NUMERIC takes effect as soon as it is encountered in the command sequence. Special attention should be paid to its position among commands. For more information, see "Command Order" on p. 16.
- The specified formats (or the defaults) are used as both print and write formats.
- Permanent or temporary variables are initialized to the system-missing value. Scratch variables are initialized to 0.
- Variables named on NUMERIC are added to the working file in the order in which they are specified. The order in which they are used in transformations does not affect their order in the working data file.

Example

```
NUMERIC V1 V2 (F4.0) / V3 (F1.0).
```

- NUMERIC declares variables *V1* and *V2* with format F4.0, and variable *V3* with format F1.0.

Example

```
NUMERIC V1 TO V6 (F3.1) / V7 V10 (F6.2).
```

- NUMERIC declares variables *V1*, *V2*, *V3*, *V4*, *V5*, and *V6* each with format F3.1, and variables *V7* and *V10*, each with format F6.2.

Example

```
NUMERIC SCALE85 IMPACT85 SCALE86 IMPACT86 SCALE87 IMPACT87
        SCALE88 IMPACT88.
```

- Variables *SCALE85* to *IMPACT88* are added to the working data file in the order specified on NUMERIC. The order in which they are used in transformations does not affect their order in the working data file.

Example

```
* Predetermine variable order.

INPUT PROGRAM.
STRING CITY (A24).
NUMERIC POP81 TO POP83 (F9)/ REV81 TO REV83(F10).
DATA LIST FILE=POPDATA RECORDS=3
  /1 POP81 22-30 REV81 31-40
  /2 POP82 22-30 REV82 31-40
  /3 POP83 22-30 REV83 31-40
  /4 CITY 1-24(A).
END INPUT PROGRAM.
```

- STRING and NUMERIC are specified within an input program to predetermine variable order in the working data file. Though data in the file are in a different order, the working file dictionary uses the order specified on STRING and NUMERIC. Thus, *CITY* is the first variable in the dictionary, followed by *POP81*, *POP82*, *POP83*, *REV81*, *REV82*, and *REV83*.

- Formats are specified for the variables on NUMERIC. Otherwise, the program uses the default numeric format (F8.2) from the NUMERIC command for the dictionary format, even though it uses the format on DATA LIST to read the data. In other words, the dictionary uses the first formats specified, even though DATA LIST may use different formats to read cases.

OLAP CUBE

```
OLAP CUBE {varlist} BY varlist [BY...]

[/CELLS= [MEAN**] [COUNT**] [STDDEV**]
         [NPCT**] [SPCT**] [SUM** ]
         [MEDIAN] [GMEDIAN] [SEMEAN]
         [MIN] [MAX] [RANGE]
         [VARIANCE] [KURT] [SEKURT]
         [SKEW] [SESKEW] [FIRST] [LAST]
         [NPCT(var)][SPCT(var)]
         [HARMONIC] [GEOMETRIC]
         [DEFAULT]
         [ALL] [NONE] ]

[/TITLE ='string'][FOOTNOTE= 'string']
```

**Default if the subcommand is omitted.

Example:

```
OLAP CUBE sales BY region by industry
  /CELLS=MEAN MEDIAN SUM SPCT(region).
```

Overview

OLAP CUBE produces summary statistics for continuous, quantitative variables within categories defined by one or more categorical grouping variables.

Options

Cell Contents. By default, OLAP CUBE displays means, standard deviations, cell counts, sums, percentage of total N, and percentage of total sum. Optionally, you can request any combination of available statistics.

Format. You can specify a title and a caption for the report using the TITLE and FOOTNOTE subcommands.

Basic Specification

The basic specification is the command name, OLAP CUBE, with a summary variable, the keyword BY, and one or more grouping variables.

- The minimum specification is a summary variable, the keyword BY, and a grouping variable.
- By default, OLAP CUBE displays a Case Processing Summary table showing the number and percentage of cases included, excluded, and their total, and a Layered Report showing means, standard deviations, sums, number of cases for each category, percentage of total N, and percentage of total sum.

654

Syntax Rules

- Both numeric and string variables can be specified. String variables can be short or long. Summary variables must be numeric.
- String specifications for TITLE and FOOTNOTE cannot exceed 255 characters. Quotation marks or apostrophes are required. When the specification breaks on multiple lines, enclose each line in apostrophes or quotes and separate the specifications for each line by at least one blank. To specify line breaks in titles and footnotes, use the /n specification.
- Each subcommand can be specified only once. Multiple use results in a warning, and the last specification is used.
- When a variable is specified more than once, only the first occurrence is honored. The same variables specified after different BY keywords will result in an error.

Limitations

- Only 5 BY keywords can be specified.

Operations

- The data are processed sequentially. It is not necessary to sort the cases before processing. If a BY keyword is used, the output is always sorted.
- A Case Processing Summary table is always generated, showing the number and percentage of the cases included, excluded, and the total.
- For each combination of grouping variables specified after different BY keywords, OLAP CUBE produces a group in the report.

Example

```
OLAP CUBE SALES BY REGION BY INDUSTRY
  /CELLS=MEAN MEDIAN SUM.
```

- A Case Processing Summary table lists the number and percentage of cases included, excluded, and the total.
- A Layered Report displays the requested statistics for sales for each group defined by each combination of *REGION* and *INDUSTRY*.

TITLE and FOOTNOTE Subcommands

TITLE and FOOTNOTE provide a title and a caption for the Layered Report.

- TITLE and FOOTNOTE are optional and can be placed anywhere.
- The specification on TITLE or FOOTNOTE is a string within apostrophes or quotation marks. To specify a multiple-line title or footnote, enclose each line in apostrophes or quotation marks and separate the specifications for each line by at least one blank.

- To insert line breaks in the displayed title or footnote, use the /n specification.
- The string you specify cannot exceed 255 characters.

CELLS Subcommand

By default, OLAP CUBE displays the means, standard deviations, number of cases, sum, percentage of total cases, and percentage of total sum.

- If CELLS is specified without keywords, OLAP CUBE displays the default statistics.
- If any keywords are specified on CELLS, only the requested information is displayed.

DEFAULT	*Means, standard deviations, cell counts, sum, percentage of total N, and percentage of total sum.* This is the default if CELLS is omitted.
MEAN	*Cell means.*
STDDEV	*Cell standard deviations.*
COUNT	*Cell counts.*
MEDIAN	*Cell median.*
GMEDIAN	*Grouped median.*
SEMEAN	*Standard error of cell mean.*
SUM	*Cell sums.*
MIN	*Cell minimum.*
MAX	*Cell maximum.*
RANGE	*Cell range.*
VARIANCE	*Variances.*
KURT	*Cell kurtosis.*
SEKURT	*Standard error of cell kurtosis.*
SKEW	*Cell skewness.*
SESKEW	*Standard error of cell skewness.*
FIRST	*First value.*
LAST	*Last value.*
SPCT	*Percentage of total sum.*
NPCT	*Percentage of total number of cases.*
SPCT(var)	*Percentage of total sum within specified variable.* The specified variable must be one of the grouping variables.
NPCT(var)	*Percentage of total number of cases within specified variable.* The specified variable must be one of the grouping variables.
HARMONIC	*Harmonic mean.*

GEOMETRIC   *Geometric mean.*

ALL   *All cell information.*

ONEWAY

```
ONEWAY   varlist BY varname

[/POLYNOMIAL=n]   [/CONTRAST=coefficient list]  [/CONTRAST=... ]

[/POSTHOC=([SNK] [TUKEY] [BTUKEY] [DUNCAN] [SCHEFFE] [DUNNETT[refcat]]
          [DUNNETTL(refcat)] [DUNNETTR(refcat)] [BONFERRONI] [;SD]
          [SIDAK] [GT2] [GABRIEL] [FREGW] [QREGW] [T2] [T3] [GH] [C]
          [WALLER({100** })]) [ALPHA({0.05**})]
                  {Kratio}            {α       }

[/RANGES={LSD     }([{0.05**}])]  [/RANGES=...]
         {DUNCAN  } {α      }
         {SNK     }
         {TUKEYB  }
         {TUKEY   }
         {MODLSD  }
         {SCHEFFE }

[/STATISTICS=[NONE**] [DESCRIPTIVES]  [EFFECTS]  [HOMOGENEITY]  [ALL]

[/PLOT MEANS

[/MISSING=[{ANALYSIS**}]  [{EXCLUDE**}]]
          {LISTWISE  }    {INCLUDE  }

[/MATRIX =[IN({*   })]  [OUT({*   })]   [NONE]]
             {file}          {file}
```

**Default if the subcommand is omitted.

Example:

```
ONEWAY V1 BY V2(1,4).
```

Overview

ONEWAY produces a one-way analysis of variance for an interval-level dependent variable by one numeric independent variable that defines the groups for the analysis. Other procedures that perform an analysis of variance are SUMMARIZE, UNIANOVA, and GLM (GLM is available in the SPSS Advanced Models option). Some tests not included in the other procedures are available as options in ONEWAY.

Options

Trend and Contrasts. You can partition the between-groups sums of squares into linear, quadratic, cubic, and higher-order trend components using the POLYNOMIAL subcommand. You can specify up to 10 contrasts to be tested with the t statistic on the CONTRAST subcommand.

Post Hoc Tests. You can specify 20 different post hoc tests for comparisons of all possible pairs of group means or multiple comparisons using the POSTHOC subcommand.

Statistical Display. In addition to the default display, you can obtain means, standard deviations, and other descriptive statistics for each group using the STATISTICS subcommand. Fixed- and random-effects statistics as well as Leven's test for homogeneity of variance are also available.

Matrix Input and Output. You can write means, standard deviations, and category frequencies to a matrix data file that can be used in subsequent ONEWAY procedures using the MATRIX subcommand. You can also read matrix materials consisting of means, category frequencies, pooled variance, and degrees of freedom for the pooled variance.

Basic Specification

The basic specification is a dependent variable, keyword BY, and an independent variable. ONEWAY produces an ANOVA table displaying the between- and within-groups sums of squares, mean squares, degrees of freedom, the F ratio, and the probability of F for each dependent variable by the independent variable.

Subcommand Order

- The variable list must be specified first.
- The remaining subcommands can be specified in any order.

Operations

- All values of the independent variable are used. Each different value creates one category.
- If a string variable is specified as an independent or dependent variable, ONEWAY is not executed.

Limitations

- Maximum 100 dependent variables and 1 independent variable.
- An unlimited number of categories for the independent variable. However, post hoc tests are not performed if the number of nonempty categories exceeds 50. Contrast tests are not performed if the total of empty and nonempty categories exceeds 50.
- Maximum 1 POLYNOMIAL subcommand.
- Maximum 1 POSTHOC subcommand.
- Maximum 10 CONTRAST subcommands.

Example

```
ONEWAY V1 BY V2.
```

- ONEWAY names *V1* as the dependent variable and *V2* as the independent variable.

Analysis List

The analysis list consists of a list of dependent variables, keyword BY, and an independent (grouping) variable.

- Only one analysis list is allowed, and it must be specified before any of the optional subcommands.
- All variables named must be numeric.

POLYNOMIAL Subcommand

POLYNOMIAL partitions the between-groups sums of squares into linear, quadratic, cubic, or higher-order trend components. The display is an expanded analysis-of-variance table that provides the degrees of freedom, sums of squares, mean square, F, and probability of F for each partition.

- The value specified on POLYNOMIAL indicates the highest-degree polynomial to be used.
- The polynomial value must be a positive integer less than or equal to 5 and less than the number of groups. If the polynomial specified is greater than the number of groups, the highest-degree polynomial possible is assumed.
- Only one POLYNOMIAL subcommand can be specified per ONEWAY command. If more than one is used, only the last one specified is in effect.
- ONEWAY computes the sums of squares for each order polynomial from weighted polynomial contrasts, using the category of the independent variable as the metric. These contrasts are orthogonal.
- With unbalanced designs and equal spacing between groups, ONEWAY also computes sums of squares using the unweighted polynomial contrasts. These contrasts are not orthogonal.
- The deviation sums of squares are always calculated from the weighted sums of squares (Speed, 1976).

Example

```
ONEWAY WELL BY EDUC6
  /POLYNOMIAL=2.
```

- ONEWAY requests an analysis of variance of WELL by EDUC6 with second-order (quadratic) polynomial contrasts.
- The ANOVA table is expanded to include both linear and quadratic terms.

CONTRAST Subcommand

CONTRAST specifies a priori contrasts to be tested by the t statistic. The specification on CONTRAST is a vector of coefficients, where each coefficient corresponds to a category of the independent variable. The Contrast Coefficients table displays the specified contrasts for each group and the Contrast Tests table displays the value of the contrast and its standard error, the *t* statistic, and the degrees of freedom and two-tailed probability of *t* for each variable. Both pooled- and separate-variance estimates are displayed.

- A contrast coefficient must be specified or implied for every group defined for the independent variable. If the number of contrast values is not equal to the number of groups, the contrast test is not performed.
- The contrast coefficients for a set should sum to 0. If they do not, a warning is issued. ONEWAY will still give an estimate of this contrast.
- Coefficients are assigned to groups defined by ascending values of the independent variable.
- The notation $n*c$ can be used to indicate that coefficient c is repeated n times.

Example

```
ONEWAY V1 BY V2
    /CONTRAST = -1 -1 1 1
    /CONTRAST = -1 0 0 1
    /CONTRAST = -1 0 .5 .5.
```

- *V2* has four levels.
- The first CONTRAST subcommand contrasts the combination of the first two groups with the combination of the last two groups.
- The second CONTRAST subcommand contrasts the first group with the last group.
- The third CONTRAST subcommand contrasts the first group with the combination of the third and fourth groups.

Example

```
ONEWAY V1 BY V2
    /CONTRAST = -1 1 2*0
    /CONTRAST = -1 1 0 0
    /CONTRAST = -1 1.
```

- The first two CONTRAST subcommands specify the same contrast coefficients for a four-group analysis. The first group is contrasted with the second group in both cases.
- The first CONTRAST uses the $n*c$ notation.
- The last CONTRAST does not work because only two coefficients are specified for four groups.

POSTHOC Subcommand

POSTHOC produces post hoc tests for comparisons of all possible pairs of group means or multiple comparisons. In contrast to a priori analyses specified on the CONTRAST subcommand, post hoc analyses are usually not planned at the beginning of the study but are suggested by the data in the course of the study.

- Twenty post hoc tests are available. Some detect homogeneity subsets among the groups of means, some produce pairwise comparisons, and others perform both. POSTHOC produces a Multiple Comparison table showing up to 10 test categories. Nonempty group means are sorted in ascending order, with asterisks indicating significantly different groups. In addition, homogeneous subsets are calculated and displayed in the Homogeneous Subsets table if the test is designed to detect homogeneity subsets.

- When the number of valid cases in the groups varies, the harmonic mean of the group sizes is used as the sample size in the calculation for homogeneity subsets except for QREGW and FREGW. For QREGW and FREGW and tests for pairwise comparison, the sample sizes of individual groups are always used.

- You can specify only one POSTHOC subcommand per ONEWAY command. If more than one is specified, the last specification takes effect.

- You can specify one alpha value used in all POSTHOC tests using keyword ALPHA. The default is 0.05.

SNK	*Student-Newman-Keuls procedure based on the Studentized range test.* Used for detecting homogeneity subsets.
TUKEY	*Tukey's honestly significant difference.* This test uses the Studentized range statistic to make all pairwise comparisons between groups. Used for pairwise comparison and for detecting homogeneity subsets.
BTUKEY	*Tukey's b.* Multiple comparison procedure based on the average of Studentized range tests. Used for detecting homogeneity subsets.
DUNCAN	*Duncan's multiple comparison procedure based on the Studentized range test.* Used for detecting homogeneity subsets.
SCHEFFE	*Scheffé's multiple comparison t test.* Used for pairwise comparison and for detecting homogeneity subsets.
DUNNETT(refcat)	*Dunnett's two-tailed t test.* Used for pairwise comparison. Each group is compared to a reference category. You can specify a reference category in parentheses. The default is the last category. This keyword must be spelled out in full.
DUNNETTL(refcat)	*Dunnett's one-tailed t test.* Used for pairwise comparison. This test indicates whether the mean of each group (except the reference category) is *smaller* than that of the reference category. You can specify a reference category in parentheses. The default is the last category. This keyword must be spelled out in full.
DUNNETTR(refcat)	*Dunnett's one-tailed t test.* Used for pairwise comparison. This test indicates whether the mean of each group (except the reference category) is *larger* than that of the reference category. You can specify a reference category in parentheses. The default is the last category. This keyword must be spelled out in full.
BONFERRONI	*Bonferroni t test.* This test is based on Student's t statistic and adjusts the observed significance level for the fact that multiple comparisons are made. Used for pairwise comparison.
LSD	*Least significant difference t test.* Equivalent to multiple t tests between all pairs of groups. Used for pairwise comparison. This test does not control the overall probability of rejecting the hypotheses that some pairs of means are different, while in fact they are equal.

SIDAK	*Sidak* t *test.* Used for pairwise comparison. This test provides tighter bounds than the Bonferroni test.
GT2	*Hochberg's GT2.* Used for pairwise comparison and for detecting homogeneity subsets. This test is based on the Studentized maximum modulus test. Unless the cell sizes are extremely unbalanced, this test is fairly robust even for unequal variances.
GABRIEL	*Gabriel's pairwise comparisons test based on the Studentized maximum modulus test.* Used for pairwise comparison and for detecting homogeneity subsets.
FREGW	*Ryan-Einot-Gabriel-Welsch's multiple stepdown procedure based on an* F *test.* Used for detecting homogeneity subsets.
QREGW	*Ryan-Einot-Gabriel-Welsch's multiple stepdown procedure based on the Studentized range test.* Used for detecting homogeneity subsets.
T2	*Tamhane's T2.* Used for pairwise comparison. This test is based on a *t* test and can be applied in situations where the variances are unequal.
T3	*Tamhane's T3.* Used for pairwise comparison. This test is based on the Studentized maximum modulus test and can be applied in situations where the variances are unequal.
GH	*Games and Howell's pairwise comparisons test based on the Studentized range test.* Used for pairwise comparison. This test can be applied in situations where the variances are unequal.
C	*Dunnett's* C. Used for pairwise comparison. This test is based on the weighted average of Studentized ranges and can be applied in situations where the variances are unequal.
WALLER(kratio)	*Waller-Duncan* t *test.* Used for detecting homogeneity subsets. This test uses a Bayesian approach. The k-ratio is the Type 1/Type 2 error seriousness ratio. The default value is 100. You can specify an integer greater than 1 within parentheses.

Example

```
ONEWAY WELL BY EDUC6
  /POSTHOC=SNK SCHEFFE ALPHA=.01.
```

- ONEWAY requests two different post hoc tests. The first uses the Student-Newman-Keuls test and the second uses Scheffé's test. Both tests use an alpha of 0.01.

RANGES Subcommand

RANGES produces results for some post hoc tests. It is available only through syntax. You can always produce the same results using the POSTHOC subcommand.

- Up to 10 RANGE subcommands are allowed. The effect is cumulative. If you specify more than one alpha value for different range tests, the last specified value takes effect for all tests. The default is 0.05.

- Keyword MODLSD on the RANGE subcommand is equivalent to keyword BONFERRONI on the POSTHOC subcommand. Keyword LSDMOD is an alias for MODLSD.

PLOT MEANS Subcommand

PLOT MEANS produces a chart that plots the subgroup means (the means for each group defined by values of the factor variable).

STATISTICS Subcommand

By default, ONEWAY displays the ANOVA table showing between- and within-groups sums of squares, mean squares, degrees of freedom, F ratio, and probability of F. Use STATISTICS to obtain additional statistics.

DESCRIPTIVES   *Group descriptive statistics.* The statistics include the number of cases, mean, standard deviation, standard error, minimum, maximum, and 95% confidence interval for each dependent variable for each group.

EFFECTS   *Fixed- and random-effects statistics.* The statistics include the standard deviation, standard error, and 95% confidence interval for the fixed-effects model, and the standard error, 95% confidence interval, and estimate of between-components variance for the random-effects model.

HOMOGENEITY   *Homogeneity-of-variance tests.* The statistics include Levene statistic, degrees of freedom, and the significance level displayed in the Test of Homogeneity of Variances table.

NONE   *No optional statistics.* This is the default.

ALL   *All statistics available for ONEWAY.*

MISSING Subcommand

MISSING controls the treatment of missing values.

- Keywords ANALYSIS and LISTWISE are alternatives. Each can be used with INCLUDE or EXCLUDE. The default is ANALYSIS and EXCLUDE.
- A case outside the range specified for the grouping variable is not used.

ANALYSIS   *Exclude cases with missing values on a pair-by-pair basis.* A case with a missing value for the dependent or grouping variable for a given analysis is not used for that analysis. This is the default.

LISTWISE   *Exclude cases with missing values listwise.* Cases with missing values for any variable named are excluded from all analyses.

EXCLUDE   *Exclude cases with user-missing values.* User-missing values are treated as missing. This is the default.

INCLUDE   *Include user-missing values.* User-missing values are treated as valid values.

MATRIX Subcommand

MATRIX reads and writes matrix data files.

- Either IN or OUT and a matrix file in parentheses are required.
- You cannot specify both IN and OUT on the same ONEWAY procedure.
- Use MATRIX=NONE to explicitly indicate that a matrix data file is not being written or read.

OUT (filename)   *Write a matrix data file.* Specify either a filename or an asterisk, enclosed in parentheses. If you specify a filename, the file is stored on disk and can be retrieved at any time. If you specify an asterisk (*), the matrix data file replaces the working file but is not stored on disk unless you use SAVE or XSAVE.

IN (filename)   *Read a matrix data file.* If the matrix data file is the working data file, specify an asterisk (*) in parentheses. If the matrix data file is another file, specify the filename in parentheses. A matrix file read from an external file does not replace the working data file.

NONE   *Do not read or write matrix data materials.* This is the default.

Matrix Output

- ONEWAY writes means, standard deviations, and frequencies to a matrix data file that can be used by subsequent ONEWAY procedures. See "Format of the Matrix Data File" below for a description of the file.

Matrix Input

- ONEWAY can read the matrices it writes, and it can also read matrix materials that include the means, category frequencies, pooled variance, and degrees of freedom for the pooled variance. The pooled variance has a *ROWTYPE_* value MSE, and the vector of degrees of freedom for the pooled variance has the *ROWTYPE_* value DFE.
- The dependent variables named on ONEWAY can be a subset of the dependent variables in the matrix data file.
- MATRIX=IN cannot be specified unless a working data file has already been defined. To read an existing matrix data file at the beginning of a session, use GET to retrieve the matrix file and then specify IN(*) on MATRIX.

Format of the Matrix Data File

- The matrix data file includes two special variables created by the program: *ROWTYPE_* and *VARNAME_*.
- *ROWTYPE_* is a short string variable with values MEAN, STDDEV, and N.

- *VARNAME_* is a short string variable that never has values for procedure ONEWAY. *VARNAME_* is included with the matrix materials so that matrices written by ONEWAY can be read by procedures that expect to read a *VARNAME_* variable.
- The independent variable is between variables *ROWTYPE_* and *VARNAME_*.
- The remaining variables in the matrix file are the dependent variables.

Split Files

- When split-file processing is in effect, the first variables in the matrix data file are the split variables, followed by *ROWTYPE_*, the independent variable, *VARNAME_*, and the dependent variables.
- A full set of matrix materials is written for each split-file group defined by the split variable(s).
- A split variable cannot have the same variable name as any other variable written to the matrix data file.
- If split-file processing is in effect when a matrix is written, the same split file must be in effect when that matrix is read by any procedure.
- Generally, matrix rows, independent variables, and dependent variables can be in any order in the matrix data file read by keyword IN. However, all split-file variables must precede variable *ROWTYPE_*, and all split-group rows must be consecutive. ONEWAY ignores unrecognized *ROWTYPE_* values.

Missing Values

Missing-value treatment affects the values written to an matrix data file. When reading a matrix data file, be sure to specify a missing-value treatment on ONEWAY that is compatible with the treatment that was in effect when the matrix materials were generated.

Example

```
GET FILE=GSS80.
ONEWAY  WELL BY EDUC6
  /MATRIX=OUT(ONEMTX).
```

- ONEWAY reads data from file *GSS80* and writes one set of matrix materials to the file *ONEMTX*.
- The working data file is still *GSS80*. Subsequent commands are executed on *GSS80*.

Example

```
GET FILE=GSS80.
ONEWAY  WELL BY EDUC6
  /MATRIX=OUT(*).
LIST.
```

- ONEWAY writes the same matrix as in the example above. However, the matrix data file replaces the working data file. The LIST command is executed on the matrix file, not on the *GSS80* file.

Example

```
GET FILE=PRSNNL.
FREQUENCIES VARIABLE=AGE.
ONEWAY  WELL BY EDUC6
 /MATRIX=IN(ONEMTX).
```

- This example performs a frequencies analysis on *PRSNNL* and then uses a different file for ONEWAY. The file is an existing matrix data file.
- MATRIX=IN specifies the matrix data file.
- *ONEMTX* does not replace *PRSNNL* as the working data file.

Example

```
GET FILE=ONEMTX.
ONEWAY  WELL BY EDUC6
 /MATRIX=IN(*).
```

- The GET command retrieves the matrix data file *ONEMTX*.
- MATRIX=IN specifies an asterisk because the working data file is the matrix data file *ONEMTX*. If MATRIX=IN(ONEMTX) is specified, the program issues an error message, since *ONEMTX* is already open.
- If the GET command is omitted, the program issues an error message.

References

Speed, M. F. 1976. Response curves in the one way classification with unequal numbers of observations per cell. *Proceedings of the Statistical Computing Section.* American Statistical Association.

PACF

```
PACF [VARIABLES=] series names

[/DIFF={1}]
       {n}

[/SDIFF={1}]
        {n}

[/PERIOD=n]

[/{NOLOG**}]
  {LN    }

[/SEASONAL]

[/MXAUTO={16**}]
         {n   }

[/APPLY [='model name']]
```

**Default if the subcommand is omitted and there is no corresponding specification on the TSET command.

Example:
```
PACF TICKETS
  /LN
  /DIFF=1
  /SDIFF=1
  /PERIOD=12
  /MXAUTO=25.
```

Overview

PACF displays and plots the sample partial autocorrelation function of one or more time series. You can also display and plot the partial autocorrelations of transformed series by requesting natural log and differencing transformations from within the procedure.

Options

Modifying the Series. You can request a natural log transformation of the series using the LN subcommand and seasonal and nonseasonal differencing to any degree using the SDIFF and DIFF subcommands. With seasonal differencing, you can specify the periodicity on the PERIOD subcommand.

Statistical Output. With the MXAUTO subcommand, you can specify the number of lags for which you want values displayed and plotted, overriding the maximum specified on TSET. You can also display and plot values only at periodic lags using the SEASONAL subcommand.

Basic Specification

The basic specification is one or more series names. For each series specified, PACF automatically displays the partial autocorrelation value and standard error value for each lag. It also plots the partial autocorrelations and marks the bounds of two standard errors on the plot. By default, PACF displays and plots partial autocorrelations for up to 16 lags or the number of lags specified on TSET.

Subcommand Order

- Subcommands can be specified in any order.

Syntax Rules

- VARIABLES can be specified only once.
- Other subcommands can be specified more than once, but only the last specification of each one is executed.

Operations

- Subcommand specifications apply to all series named on the PACF command.
- If the LN subcommand is specified, any differencing requested on that PACF command is done on log-transformed series.
- Confidence limits are displayed in the plot, marking the bounds of two standard errors at each lag.

Limitations

- Maximum 1 VARIABLES subcommand. There is no limit on the number of series named on the list.

Example

```
PACF TICKETS
 /LN
 /DIFF=1
 /SDIFF=1
 /PERIOD=12
 /MXAUTO=25.
```

- This example produces a plot of the partial autocorrelation function for the series *TICKETS* after a natural log transformation, differencing, and seasonal differencing have been applied to the series. Along with the plot, the partial autocorrelation value and standard error are displayed for each lag.

- LN transforms the data using the natural logarithm (base e) of the series.
- DIFF differences the series once.
- SDIFF and PERIOD apply one degree of seasonal differencing with a period of 12.
- MXAUTO specifies that the maximum number of lags for which output is to be produced is 25.

VARIABLES Subcommand

VARIABLES specifies the series names and is the only required subcommand. The actual keyword VARIABLES can be omitted.

DIFF Subcommand

DIFF specifies the degree of differencing used to convert a nonstationary series to a stationary one with a constant mean and variance before the partial autocorrelations are computed.

- You can specify any positive integer on DIFF.
- If DIFF is specified without a value, the default is 1.
- The number of values used in the calculations decreases by 1 for each degree of differencing.

Example

```
PACF SALES
  /DIFF=1.
```

- In this example, the series *SALES* will be differenced once before the partial autocorrelations are computed and plotted.

SDIFF Subcommand

If the series exhibits a seasonal or periodic pattern, you can use the SDIFF subcommand to seasonally difference the series before obtaining partial autocorrelations.

- The specification on SDIFF indicates the degree of seasonal differencing and can be any positive integer.
- If SDIFF is specified without a value, the degree of seasonal differencing defaults to 1.
- The number of seasons used in the calculations decreases by 1 for each degree of seasonal differencing.
- The length of the period used by SDIFF is specified on the PERIOD subcommand. If the PERIOD subcommand is not specified, the periodicity established on the TSET or DATE command is used (see the PERIOD subcommand below).

PERIOD Subcommand

PERIOD indicates the length of the period to be used by the SDIFF or SEASONAL subcommand.

- The specification on PERIOD indicates how many observations are in one period or season and can be any positive integer.
- PERIOD is ignored if it is used without the SDIFF or SEASONAL subcommand.
- If PERIOD is not specified, the periodicity established on TSET PERIOD is in effect. If TSET PERIOD is not specified, the periodicity established on the DATE command is used. If periodicity was not established anywhere, the SDIFF and SEASONAL subcommands will not be executed.

Example

```
PACF SALES
  /SDIFF=1
  /PERIOD=12.
```

- This PACF command applies one degree of seasonal differencing with a periodicity of 12 to the series *SALES* before partial autocorrelations are computed and plotted.

LN and NOLOG Subcommands

LN transforms the data using the natural logarithm (base *e*) of the series and is used to remove varying amplitude over time. NOLOG indicates that the data should not be log transformed. NOLOG is the default.

- If you specify LN on a PACF command, any differencing requested on that command will be done on the log-transformed series.
- There are no additional specifications on LN or NOLOG.
- Only the last LN or NOLOG subcommand on a PACF command is executed.
- If a natural log transformation is requested when there are values in the series that are less than or equal to 0, the PACF will not be produced for that series because nonpositive values cannot be log transformed.
- NOLOG is generally used with an APPLY subcommand to turn off a previous LN specification.

Example

```
PACF SALES
  /LN.
```

- This command transforms the series *SALES* using the natural log transformation and then computes and plots partial autocorrelations.

SEASONAL Subcommand

Use SEASONAL to focus attention on the seasonal component by displaying and plotting autocorrelations only at periodic lags.

- There are no additional specifications on SEASONAL.

- If SEASONAL is specified, values are displayed and plotted at the periodic lags indicated on the PERIOD subcommand. If PERIOD is not specified, the periodicity established on the TSET or DATE command is used (see the PERIOD subcommand on p. 671).
- If SEASONAL is not specified, partial autocorrelations for all lags up to the maximum are displayed and plotted.

Example

```
PACF SALES
 /SEASONAL
 /PERIOD=12.
```

- In this example, partial autocorrelations are displayed and plotted at every 12th lag.

MXAUTO Subcommand

MXAUTO specifies the maximum number of lags for a series.
- The specification on MXAUTO must be a positive integer.
- If MXAUTO is not specified, the default number of lags is the value set on TSET MXAUTO. If TSET MXAUTO is not specified, the default is 16.
- The value on MXAUTO overrides the value set on TSET MXAUTO.

Example

```
PACF SALES
 /MXAUTO=14.
```

- This command specifies 14 for the maximum number of partial autocorrelations that can be displayed and plotted for series *SALES*.

APPLY Subcommand

APPLY allows you to use a previously defined PACF model without having to repeat the specifications.
- The only specification on APPLY is the name of a previous model enclosed in apostrophes. If a model name is not specified, the model specified on the previous PACF command is used.
- To change one or more model specifications, specify the subcommands of only those portions you want to change after the APPLY subcommand.
- If no series are specified on the PACF command, the series that were originally specified with the model being reapplied are used.
- To change the series used with the model, enter new series names before or after the APPLY subcommand.

Example

```
PACF TICKETS
 /LN
 /DIFF=1
 /SDIFF=1
 /PER=12
 /MXAUTO=25.
PACF ROUNDTRP
 /APPLY.
```

- The first command specifies a maximum of 25 partial autocorrelations for the series *TICKETS* after it has been log transformed, differenced once, and had one degree of seasonal differencing with a periodicity of 12 applied to it. This model is assigned the default name *MOD_1*.

- The second command displays and plots partial autocorrelations for series *ROUNDTRP* using the same model that was specified for series *TICKETS*.

References

Box, G. E. P., and G. M. Jenkins. 1976. *Time series analysis: Forecasting and control.* San Francisco: Holden-Day.

PARTIAL CORR

```
PARTIAL CORR [VARIABLES=] varlist [WITH varlist]
    BY varlist [(levels)] [/varlist...]

[/SIGNIFICANCE={TWOTAIL**}]
               {ONETAIL }

[/STATISTICS=[NONE**] [CORR] [DESCRIPTIVES] [BADCORR] [ALL]]

[/FORMAT={MATRIX** }]
         {SERIAL   }
         {CONDENSED}

[/MISSING=[{LISTWISE**}] [{EXCLUDE**}]]
           {ANALYSIS  }   {INCLUDE  }

[/MATRIX= [IN({*    })] [OUT({*    })]]
              {file}        {file}
```

**Default if the subcommand is omitted.

Example:

```
PARTIAL CORR VARIABLES=PUBTRANS MECHANIC BUSDRVER BY NETPURSE(1).
```

Overview

PARTIAL CORR produces partial correlation coefficients that describe the relationship between two variables while adjusting for the effects of one or more additional variables. PARTIAL CORR calculates a matrix of Pearson product-moment correlations. It can also read the zero-order correlation matrix as input. Other procedures producing zero-order correlation matrices that can be read by PARTIAL CORR include CORRELATIONS, REGRESSION, DISCRIMINANT, and FACTOR.

Options

Significance Levels. By default, the significance level for each partial correlation coefficient is based on a two-tailed test. Optionally, you can request a one-tailed test using the SIGNIFICANCE subcommand.

Statistics. In addition to the partial correlation coefficient, degrees of freedom, and significance level, you can obtain the mean, standard deviation, and number of nonmissing cases for each variable, and zero-order correlation coefficients for each pair of variables using the STATISTICS subcommand.

Format. You can specify condensed format, which suppresses the degrees of freedom and significance level for each coefficient, and you can print only nonredundant coefficients in serial string format using the FORMAT subcommand.

Matrix Input and Output. You can read and write zero-order correlation matrices using the MATRIX subcommand.

674

Basic Specification

The basic specification is the VARIABLES subcommand, which specifies a list of variables to be correlated and one or more control variables following keyword BY. PARTIAL CORR calculates the partial correlation of each variable with every other variable specified on the correlation variable list.

Subcommand Order

Subcommands can be specified in any order.

- If VARIABLES is the first subcommand used on PARTIAL CORR, keyword VARIABLES can be omitted.
- If VARIABLES is not the first subcommand specified on PARTIAL CORR, both the subcommand keyword VARIABLES and the equals sign are required.

Operations

PARTIAL CORR produces one matrix of partial correlation coefficients for each of up to five order values. For each coefficient, PARTIAL CORR prints the degrees of freedom and the significance level.

Limitations

- Maximum 25 variable lists on a single PARTIAL CORR command. Each variable list contains a correlation list, a control list, and order values.
- Maximum 400 variables total can be named or implied per PARTIAL CORR command.
- Maximum 100 control variables.
- Maximum 5 different order values per single list. The largest order value that can be specified is 100.

Example

```
PARTIAL CORR VARIABLES=PUBTRANS MECHANIC BUSDRVER BY NETPURSE(1).
```

- PARTIAL CORR produces a square matrix containing three unique first-order partial correlations: *PUBTRANS* with *MECHANIC* controlling for *NETPURSE*; *PUBTRANS* with *BUSDRVER* controlling for *NETPURSE*; and *MECHANIC* with *BUSDRVER* controlling for *NETPURSE*.

VARIABLES Subcommand

VARIABLES requires a *correlation list* of one or more pairs of variables for which partial correlations are desired and a *control list* of one or more variables that will be used as controls for the variables in the correlation list, followed by optional order values in parentheses.

- The correlation list specifies pairs of variables to be correlated while controlling for the variables in the control list.

- To request a square or lower-triangular matrix, do not use keyword WITH in the correlation list. This obtains the partial correlation of every variable with every other variable in the list.

- To request a rectangular matrix, specify a list of correlation variables followed by keyword WITH and a second list of variables. This obtains the partial correlation of specific variable pairs. The first variable list defines the rows of the matrix and the second list defines the columns.

- The control list is specified after keyword BY.

- The correlation between a pair of variables is referred to as a zero-order correlation. Controlling for one variable produces a first-order partial correlation, controlling for two variables produces a second-order partial, and so on.

- You can specify order values in parentheses following the control list to indicate the exact partials to be computed. These values also determine the partial correlation matrix or matrices to be printed. Up to five order values can be specified. Separate each value with at least one space or comma. The default order value is the number of control variables.

- One partial is produced for every unique combination of control variables for each order value.

- To specify multiple analyses, use multiple VARIABLES subcommands or a slash to separate each set of specifications on one VARIABLES subcommand. PARTIAL CORR computes the zero-order correlation matrix for each analysis list separately.

Example

```
PARTIAL CORR RENT FOOD PUBTRANS WITH TEACHER MANAGER BY NETSALRY(1).
```

- PARTIAL CORR produces a rectangular matrix. Variables *RENT*, *FOOD*, and *PUBTRANS* form the matrix rows, and variables *TEACHER* and *MANAGER* form the columns.

- Keyword VARIABLES is omitted. This is allowed because the variable list is the first specification on PARTIAL CORR.

Example

```
PARTIAL CORR   RENT WITH TEACHER BY NETSALRY, NETPRICE (1).
PARTIAL CORR   RENT WITH TEACHER BY NETSALRY, NETPRICE (2).
PARTIAL CORR   RENT WITH TEACHER BY NETSALRY, NETPRICE (1,2).
PARTIAL CORR   RENT FOOD PUBTRANS BY NETSALRY NETPURSE NETPRICE
(1,3).
```

- The first PARTIAL CORR produces two first-order partials: *RENT* with *TEACHER* controlling for *NETSALRY*, and *RENT* with *TEACHER* controlling for *NETPRICE*.

- The second PARTIAL CORR produces one second-order partial of *RENT* with *TEACHER* controlling simultaneously for *NETSALRY* and *NETPRICE*.
- The third PARTIAL CORR specifies both sets of partials specified by the previous two commands.
- The fourth PARTIAL CORR produces three first-order partials (controlling for *NETSALRY*, *NETPURSE*, and *NETPRICE* individually) and one third-order partial (controlling for all three control variables simultaneously).

Example

```
PARTIAL CORR RENT FOOD WITH TEACHER BY NETSALRY NETPRICE (1,2)
    /WCLOTHES MCLOTHES BY NETPRICE (1).
```

- PARTIAL CORR produces three matrices for the first correlation list, control list, and order values.
- The second correlation list, control list, and order value produce one matrix.

SIGNIFICANCE Subcommand

SIGNIFICANCE determines whether the significance level is based on a one-tailed or two-tailed test.

- By default, the significance level is based on a two-tailed test. This is appropriate when the direction of the relationship between a pair of variables cannot be specified in advance of the analysis.
- When the direction of the relationship can be determined in advance, a one-tailed test is appropriate.

TWOTAIL *Two-tailed test of significance.* This is the default.

ONETAIL *One-tailed test of significance.*

STATISTICS Subcommand

By default, the partial correlation coefficient, degrees of freedom, and significance level are displayed. Use STATISTICS to obtain additional statistics.

- If both CORR and BADCORR are requested, CORR takes precedence over BADCORR and the zero-order correlations are displayed.

CORR *Zero-order correlations with degrees of freedom and significance level.*

DESCRIPTIVES *Mean, standard deviation, and number of nonmissing cases.* Descriptive statistics are not available with matrix input.

BADCORR *Zero-order correlation coefficients only if any of the zero-order correlations cannot be computed.* Noncomputable coefficients are displayed as a period.

NONE *No additional statistics.* This is the default.

ALL *All additional statistics available with* PARTIAL CORR.

FORMAT Subcommand

FORMAT determines page format.

- If both CONDENSED and SERIAL are specified, only SERIAL is in effect.

MATRIX   *Display degrees of freedom and significance level in matrix format.* This format requires four lines per matrix row and displays the degrees of freedom and the significance level. The output includes redundant coefficients. This is the default.

CONDENSED   *Suppress the degrees of freedom and significance level.* This format requires only one line per matrix row and suppresses the degrees of freedom and significance. A single asterisk (*) following a coefficient indicates a significance level of 0.05 or less. Two asterisks (**) following a coefficient indicate a significance level of 0.01 or less.

SERIAL   *Display only the nonredundant coefficients in serial string format.* The coefficients, degrees of freedom, and significance levels from the first row of the matrix are displayed first, followed by all the unique coefficients from the second row and so on for all the rows of the matrix.

MISSING Subcommand

MISSING controls the treatment of cases with missing values.

- When multiple analysis lists are specified, missing values are handled separately for each analysis list. Thus, different sets of cases can be used for different lists.
- When pairwise deletion is in effect (keyword ANALYSIS), the degrees of freedom for a particular partial coefficient are based on the smallest number of cases used in the calculation of any of the simple correlations.
- LISTWISE and ANALYSIS are alternatives. However, each can be used with either INCLUDE or EXCLUDE. The default is LISTWISE and EXCLUDE.

LISTWISE   *Exclude cases with missing values listwise.* Cases with missing values for any of the variables listed for an analysis, including control variables, are not used in the calculation of the zero-order correlation coefficient. This is the default.

ANALYSIS   *Exclude cases with missing values on a pair-by-pair basis.* Cases with missing for one or both of a pair of variables are not used in the calculation of zero-order correlation coefficients.

EXCLUDE   *Exclude user-missing values.* User-missing values are treated as missing. This is the default.

INCLUDE   *Include user-missing values.* User-missing values are treated as valid values.

MATRIX Subcommand

MATRIX reads and writes matrix data files.

- Either IN or OUT and a matrix file in parentheses is required. When both IN and OUT are used on the same PARTIAL CORR procedure, they can be specified on separate MATRIX subcommands or both on the same subcommand.

OUT (filename)   *Write the (zero-order) correlation matrix to a file.* Specify either a filename or an asterisk, enclosed in parentheses. If you specify a filename, the file is stored on disk and can be retrieved at any time. If you specify an asterisk (*), the matrix data file replaces the working data file but is not stored on disk unless you use SAVE or XSAVE.

IN (filename)   *Read a matrix data file.* If the matrix data file is the working data file, specify an asterisk (*) in parentheses. If the matrix data file is another file, specify a filename in parentheses. Both the working data file and the matrix data file must contain all the variables specified on the VARIABLES subcommands on PARTIAL CORR. A matrix file read from an external file does not replace the working data file.

Matrix Output

- The matrix materials that PARTIAL CORR writes can be used by subsequent PARTIAL CORR procedures or by other procedures that read correlation-type matrices.

- In addition to the Pearson correlation coefficients, the matrix materials PARTIAL CORR writes include the mean, standard deviation, and number of cases used to compute each coefficient (see "Format of the Matrix Data File" on p. 680 for a description of the file). If PARTIAL CORR reads matrix data and then writes matrix materials based on those data, the matrix data file that it writes will not include means and standard deviations.

- PARTIAL CORR writes a full square matrix for the analysis specified on the first VARIABLES subcommand (or the first analysis list if keyword VARIABLES is omitted). No matrix is written for subsequent variable lists.

- Any documents contained in the working data file are not transferred to the matrix file.

Matrix Input

- When matrix materials are read from a file other than the working data file, both the working data file and the matrix data file specified on IN must contain all the variables specified on the VARIABLES subcommands.

- MATRIX=IN cannot be specified unless a working data file has already been defined. To read an existing matrix data file at the beginning of a session, use GET to retrieve the matrix file and then specify IN(*) on MATRIX.

- PARTIAL CORR can read correlation-type matrices written by other procedures.

- The program reads variable names, variable and value labels, and print and write formats from the dictionary of the matrix data file.

Format of the Matrix Data File

- The matrix data file includes two special variables created by the program: *ROWTYPE_* and *VARNAME_*.
- *ROWTYPE_* is a short string variable with values N, MEAN, STDDEV, and CORR (for Pearson's correlation coefficient).
- *VARNAME_* is a short string variable whose values are the names of the variables used to form the correlation matrix. When *ROWTYPE_* is CORR, *VARNAME_* gives the variable associated with that row of the correlation matrix.
- The remaining variables in the file are the variables used to form the correlation matrix.

Split Files

- When split-file processing is in effect, the first variables in the matrix data file are the split variables, followed by *ROWTYPE_*, *VARNAME_*, and the variables used to form the correlation matrix.
- A full set of matrix materials is written for each split-file group defined by the split variables.
- A split variable cannot have the same variable name as any other variable written to the matrix data file.
- If split-file processing is in effect when a matrix is written, the same split file must be in effect when that matrix is read by any procedure.

Missing Values

- With pairwise treatment of missing values (MISSING=ANALYSIS is specified), the matrix of N's used to compute each coefficient is included with the matrix materials.
- With LISTWISE treatment, a single N used to calculate all coefficients is included with the matrix materials.
- When reading a matrix data file, be sure to specify a missing-value treatment on PARTIAL CORR that is compatible with the missing-value treatment that was in effect when the matrix materials were produced.

Example

```
GET FILE=CITY.
PARTIAL CORR VARIABLES=BUSDRVER MECHANIC ENGINEER TEACHER COOK
                       BY  NETSALRY(1)
   /MATRIX=OUT(PTMTX).
```

- PARTIAL CORR reads data from file *CITY* and writes one set of matrix materials to file *PTMTX*.
- The working data file is still *CITY*. Subsequent commands are executed on *CITY*.

Example

```
GET FILE=CITY.
PARTIAL CORR VARIABLES=BUSDRVER MECHANIC ENGINEER TEACHER COOK
  BY  NETSALRY(1)    /MATRIX=OUT(*).
LIST.
```

- PARTIAL CORR writes the same matrix as in the example above. However, the matrix data file replaces the working data file. The LIST command is executed on the matrix file, not on the *CITY* file.

Example

```
GET FILE=PRSNNL.
FREQUENCIES VARIABLE=AGE.
PARTIAL CORR VARIABLES=BUSDRVER MECHANIC ENGINEER TEACHER COOK
    BY  NETSALRY(1)    /MATRIX=IN(CORMTX).
```

- This example performs a frequencies analysis on file *PRSNNL* and then uses a different file for PARTIAL CORR. The file is an existing matrix data file.
- MATRIX=IN specifies the matrix data file. Both the working data file and the *CORMTX* file must contain all variables specified on the VARIABLES subcommand on PARTIAL CORR.
- *CORMTX* does not replace *PRSNNL* as the working data file.

Example

```
GET FILE=CORMTX.
PARTIAL CORR VARIABLES=BUSDRVER MECHANIC ENGINEER TEACHER COOK
                    BY NETSALRY(1)
  /MATRIX=IN(*).
```

- The GET command retrieves the matrix data file *CORMTX*.
- MATRIX=IN specifies an asterisk because the working data file is the matrix file *CORMTX*. If MATRIX=IN(CORMTX) is specified, the program issues an error message.
- If the GET command is omitted, the program issues an error message.

Example

```
GET FILE=CITY.
REGRESSION MATRIX=OUT(*)
  /VARIABLES=NETPURSE PUBTRANS MECHANIC BUSDRVER
  /DEPENDENT=NETPURSE /ENTER.
PARTIAL CORR  PUBTRANS MECHANIC BUSDRVER BY NETPURSE(1) /MATRIX=IN(*).
```

- GET retrieves the SPSS-format data file *CITY*.

- REGRESSION computes correlations among the specified variables. MATRIX=OUT(*) writes a matrix data file that replaces the working data file.
- The MATRIX=IN(*) specification on PARTIAL CORR reads the matrix materials in the working data file.

PLOT

```
PLOT
 [/MISSING=[{PLOTWISE**}] [INCLUDE] [DEFAULT**]]
            {LISTWISE  }

 [/FORMAT={DEFAULT**         }]
          {OVERLAY           }
          {CONTOUR††[({10})]}
          {            {n }  }
          {REGRESSION        }

 [/TITLE='title']

 [/HORIZONTAL=['label'] [STANDARDIZE] [REFERENCE(value list)]
              [MIN(n)] [MAX(n)] [UNIFORM]]

 [/VERTICAL=['label'] [STANDARDIZE] [REFERENCE(value list)]
            [MIN(n)] [MAX(n)] [UNIFORM]]

 /PLOT={varlist} WITH varlist [(PAIR)] [BY varname] [;varlist...]
       {ALL     }

 [/PLOT=...]
```

**Default if the subcommand is omitted.

Example:

```
PLOT FORMAT=OVERLAY
  /TITLE='Marriage and Divorce Rates'
  /VERTICAL='Rates per 1000 population'
  /HORIZONTAL='Year' REFERENCE (1918, 1945) MIN (1880) MAX (2000)
  /PLOT=MARRATE DIVRATE WITH YEAR.
```

Overview

PLOT produces two-dimensional plots, including simple bivariate scatterplots, scatterplots with a control variable, contour plots, and overlay plots. You can also request bivariate regression statistics. You can choose from a variety of options for plot symbols, and you can add reference lines. You have control over size, labeling, and scaling of each axis, and you can constrain the axes to be uniform for a series of plots. Many of these plots can also be produced with the GRAPH command.

Options

Types of Plots. You can introduce a control variable for bivariate scatterplots and request regression plots with or without a control variable, contour plots, and overlay plots using the FORMAT subcommand.

Basic Specification

The basic specification is a PLOT subcommand that names the variables for the vertical (y) axis, keyword WITH, and the variables for the horizontal (x) axis. By default, PLOT produces separate bivariate scatterplots for all combinations formed by each variable on the left side of WITH with each variable on the right.

Subcommand Order

- No subcommand can be specified after the last PLOT subcommand specified. Other than this, subcommands can be specified in any order.

Syntax Rules

- The PLOT subcommand can be specified more than once.
- Subcommands HORIZONTAL, VERTICAL, FORMAT, and TITLE can be specified more than once and apply only to the following PLOT subcommand.

Limitations

There are no limitations on the number of plots requested or on the number of variables specified on a PLOT command. The following limitations apply to the optional subcommands:

- Maximum 60 characters for a title specified on TITLE.
- Maximum 10 reference points on each HORIZONTAL or VERTICAL subcommand.
- Maximum 40 characters per label on each HORIZONTAL or VERTICAL subcommand.

Example

```
PLOT FORMAT=OVERLAY
 /TITLE='Marriage and Divorce Rates'
 /VERTICAL='Rates per 1000 population'
 /HORIZONTAL='Year' REFERENCE (1918, 1945) MIN (1900) MAX (1983)
 /PLOT=MARRATE DIVRATE WITH YEAR.
```

- This example produces an overlay plot of marriage and divorce rates by year.
- TITLE specifies a plot title.
- VERTICAL provides a title for the vertical axis.
- HORIZONTAL provides a title for the horizontal axis. The REFERENCE keyword provides reference lines at values 1918 and 1945. MIN and MAX specify minimum and maximum scale values for the horizontal axis.

PLOT Subcommand

The PLOT subcommand names the variables to be plotted on each axis. PLOT can also name a control or contour variable.

- PLOT is the only required subcommand.
- Multiple PLOT subcommands are allowed.
- No other subcommands can follow the last PLOT subcommand.
- The basic specification on PLOT is a list of variables to be plotted on the vertical axis, keyword WITH, and a list of variables to be plotted on the horizontal axis.
- By default, PLOT creates a separate plot for each variable specified before WITH with each variable specified after WITH.
- To request special pairing of variables, specify keyword PAIR in parentheses following the second variable list. The first variable before WITH is plotted against the first variable after WITH, the second against the second, and so on.
- Use semicolons to separate multiple plot lists on a single PLOT subcommand.
- Keyword ALL can be used to refer to all user-defined variables.
- An optional control variable can be specified following keyword BY. Only one control variable can be specified on any plot list.
- If a control variable is specified for a bivariate scatterplot (the default), PLOT uses the first character of the control variable's value label as the plot symbol. If value labels have not been specified, the first character of the value is used. The symbol $ indicates that more than one control value occurs at that position.

Example

```
PLOT PLOT=MARRATE WITH YEAR AGE;
          BIRTHS DEATHS WITH INCOME1 INCOME2 (PAIR);
          DIVRATE WITH AGE BY YEAR.
```

- The PLOT subcommand contains three plot lists. The first requests a plot of *MARRATE* with *YEAR* and of *MARRATE* with *AGE*.
- The second uses the keyword PAIR to request two plots: *BIRTHS* with *INCOME1* and *DEATHS* with *INCOME2*.
- The third requests a plot of *DIVRATE* with *AGE* using *YEAR* as a control variable. The first character of the value labels for *YEAR* is used as the plot symbol.

FORMAT Subcommand

FORMAT controls the type of plot produced.

- FORMAT can be specified once before each PLOT subcommand and applies only to plots requested on that PLOT subcommand.
- If FORMAT is not used or keyword DEFAULT is specified, bivariate scatterplots are displayed.
- Only one keyword can be specified on each FORMAT subcommand.

DEFAULT	*Bivariate scatterplot.* When there is no control variable, each symbol represents the case count at that position. When a control variable is specified, each symbol represents the first character of the control variable's value label, or the first character of the value if no labels have been defined.
OVERLAY	*Overlay plots.* All bivariate plots on the next PLOT subcommand appear in one plot frame. PLOT selects a unique symbol for each plot to be overlaid, plus a symbol to represent multiple plot points at one position.
REGRESSION	*Regression of the y axis variable on the x axis variable.* The regression-line intercepts are marked with the letter *R*. When there is no control variable, each symbol represents the frequency of cases at that position. If a control variable is specified, regression statistics are pooled over all categories and each symbol represents the first character of the control variable's value label, or the first character of the value if no labels have been defined.

VERTICAL and HORIZONTAL Subcommands

VERTICAL and HORIZONTAL control labeling and scaling for the vertical and horizontal axes.

- VERTICAL and HORIZONTAL can each be specified once before each PLOT subcommand and apply only to plots requested by that subcommand.
- If VERTICAL and HORIZONTAL are omitted, all defaults are in effect. If VERTICAL and HORIZONTAL are included, only those defaults explicitly altered are changed.

The following keywords are available for both VERTICAL and HORIZONTAL:

'label'	*Label for axis.* The label can contain up to 40 characters. A label that cannot fit in the frame is truncated. The default is the variable label for the variable plotted on that axis, or the variable name if no variable label has been specified.
MIN (n)	*Minimum axis value.* If you specify a minimum value greater than the observed minimum value, some points will not be included in the plot. The default is the minimum observed value.
MAX (n)	*Maximum axis value.* If you specify a maximum value less than the observed maximum value, some points will not be included in the plot. The default is the maximum observed value.
UNIFORM	*Uniform values on axis.* All plots specified on that PLOT subcommand will have the same scale on that axis. A uniform scale is implied when both MIN and MAX are specified. If UNIFORM is specified, PLOT determines the minimum and maximum observed values across all variables on the PLOT subcommand.
REFERENCE(values)	*Reference lines.* The values at which reference lines should be drawn are separated by blanks or commas. The default is no reference lines.
STANDARDIZE	*Plot standardized variables.* Standardized variables are useful for overlay plots of variables with different scales. The default is to plot observed values.

TITLE Subcommand

TITLE provides titles for plots.

- TITLE can be specified once before each PLOT subcommand and applies to all plots named on that PLOT subcommand.
- The default title for a bivariate scatterplot or regression plot is the names of the variables in the plot. For other plots, the default is the plot type requested on FORMAT.
- The title can be up to 60 characters long and follows the usual rules for specifying strings (see "String Values in Command Specifications" on p. 15).
- The title is truncated if it exceeds the width specified on the HSIZE subcommand.

MISSING Subcommand

MISSING controls the treatment of cases with missing values.

- MISSING can be specified only once per PLOT command and applies to all plots requested.
- Keywords LISTWISE and PLOTWISE are alternatives. Either one can be specified with INCLUDE. The default is PLOTWISE.

DEFAULT   *Exclude cases with system-missing or user-missing values for any variables in a plot from that plot.*

PLOTWISE   *Delete cases with missing values plotwise.* Cases with missing values for any variable in a plot are not included in that plot. In overlay plots, PLOTWISE applies separately to each overlaid plot in the frame, not to the full list specified on the PLOT subcommand.

LISTWISE   *Delete cases with missing values listwise.* Cases with missing values for any variable named on the PLOT subcommand are deleted from all plots specified on that PLOT subcommand.

INCLUDE   *Treat user-missing values as valid values.* Only cases with system-missing values are excluded according to the missing-value treatment specified.

POINT

```
POINT KEY=varname [FILE=file]
```

Example:

```
FILE HANDLE DRIVERS/ file specifications.
POINT FILE=DRIVERS /KEY=#FRSTAGE.
```

Overview

POINT establishes the location at which sequential access begins (or resumes) in a keyed file. A keyed file is a file that provides access to information by a record key. An example of a keyed file is a file containing a social security number and other information about a firm's employees. The social security number can be used to identify the records in the file. For additional information on keyed files, see KEYED DATA LIST.

POINT prepares for reading the key-sequenced data set sequentially from a point that the key value controls. Data selection commands can then be used to limit the file to the portion you want to analyze. A DATA LIST command is used to read the data. To read keyed files (and also direct access files), see the KEYED DATA LIST command.

Basic Specification

The basic specification is the KEY subcommand and a string variable. The value of the string variable is used as the file key for determining where sequential retrieval (via DATA LIST) begins or resumes.

Subcommand Order

- Subcommands can be named in any order.
- Each POINT command must precede its corresponding DATA LIST command.

Syntax Rules

- POINT can be used more than once to change the order of retrieval during processing.
- POINT must be specified in an input program and therefore cannot be used to add cases to an existing file.

Operations

- The next DATA LIST command executed after the POINT command (for the same file) will read a record whose key value is at least as large as that of the specified key. To prevent an infinite loop in which the same record is read again and again, either the value of the variable specified on KEY must change from case to case or the POINT command must be set up to execute only once.

- If the file contains a record whose key exactly matches the value of the KEY variable, the next execution of DATA LIST will read that record, the second execution of DATA LIST will read the next record, and so on.

- If an exact match is not found, the results depend on the operating system. On IBM implementations, reading will begin or resume at the record that has the next higher key. If the value of the key is shorter than the file key, the value of the key variable is logically extended with the lowest character in the collating sequence. For example, if the value of the key variable is the single letter M, retrieval would begin or resume at the first record that had a key (regardless of length) beginning with the letter M or a character higher in the collating sequence.

- POINT does not report on whether the file contains a record that exactly matches the specified key. The only way to check for missing records is to display the data read by the subsequent DATA LIST command using LIST.

Example

```
* Select a subset of records from a keyed file.

FILE HANDLE    DRIVERS/ file specifications.
INPUT PROGRAM.
STRING         #FRSTAGE(A2).
DO IF          #FRSTAGE = ' '.     /* First case check
+  COMPUTE     #FRSTAGE = '26'.    /* Initial key
+  POINT       FILE=DRIVERS /KEY=#FRSTAGE.
END IF.
DATA LIST      FILE=DRIVERS NOTABLE/
               AGE 19-20(A) SEX 21(A) TICKETS 12-13.
DO IF          AGE > '30'.
+  END FILE.
END IF.
END INPUT PROGRAM.
LIST.
```

- This example illustrates how to execute POINT for only the first case. The file contains information about traffic violations, and it uses the individual's age as the key. Ages between 26 and 30 are selected.

- FILE HANDLE specifies the file handle DRIVERS.

- The INPUT PROGRAM and END INPUT PROGRAM commands begin and end the block of commands that build cases. POINT must appear in an input program.

- STRING declares the string variable *#FRSTAGE*, whose value will be used as the key on the POINT command. Since *#FRSTAGE* is a string variable, it is initialized as blanks.

- The first DO IF—END IF structure is executed only if no records have been read; that is, when *#FRSTAGE* is blank. When *#FRSTAGE* is blank, COMPUTE resets *#FRSTAGE* to 26, which is the initial value. POINT is executed, and it causes the first execution of DATA LIST to read a record whose key is at least 26. Since the value of *#FRSTAGE* is now 26, the DO IF—END IF structure is not executed again.

- DATA LIST reads the variables *AGE*, *SEX*, and *TICKETS* from the file *DRIVERS*.
- The second DO IF—END IF structure executes an END FILE command as soon as a record is read that contains a driver's age greater than 30. The program does not add this last case to the working file when it ends the file (see END FILE).

Example

```
FILE HANDLE DRIVERS/ file specifications.
POINT FILE=DRIVERS /KEY=#FRSTAGE.
```

- FILE HANDLE defines the handle for the data file to be read by POINT. The handle is specified on the FILE subcommand on POINT.
- KEY on POINT specifies the key variable. The key variable must be a string, and it must already exist as the result of a prior DATA LIST, KEYED DATA LIST, or transformation command.

FILE Subcommand

FILE specifies a file handle for the keyed data file. The file handle must have been previously defined on a FILE HANDLE command.

- FILE is optional.
- If FILE is omitted, POINT reads from the last file specified on an input command, such as DATA LIST.

Example

```
FILE HANDLE DRIVERS/ file specifications.
POINT FILE=DRIVERS /KEY=#NXTCASE.
```

- FILE HANDLE specifies *DRIVERS* as the file handle for the data. The FILE subcommand on POINT specifies file handle *DRIVERS*.

KEY Subcommand

KEY specifies the variable whose value will be used as the file key for determining where sequential retrieval by DATA LIST will begin or resume. This variable must be a string variable, and it must already exist as the result of a prior DATA LIST, KEYED DATA LIST, or transformation command.

- KEY is required. Its only specification is a single variable. The variable can be a permanent variable or a scratch variable.
- Where the keys on a file are inherently numbers, such as social security numbers, the STRING function can be used to convert the numeric variable to a string (see "Conversion Functions" on p. 53).

Example

```
FILE HANDLE DRIVERS/ file specifications.
POINT FILE=DRIVERS /KEY=#NXTCASE.
```

- KEY indicates that the value of the existing scratch variable *#FRSTAGE* will be used as the key to reading each record.

- Variable *#FRSTAGE* must be an existing string variable.

PPLOT

```
PPLOT [VARIABLES=] varlist

[/DISTRIBUTION={NORMAL(a,b)** }   ]
              {EXPONENTIAL(a) }
              {WEIBUL(a,b)    }
              {PARETO(a,b)    }
              {LNORMAL(a,b)   }
              {BETA(a,b)      }
              {GAMMA(a,b)     }
              {LOGISTIC(a,b)  }
              {LAPLACE(a,b)   }
              {UNIFORM(a,b)   }
              {HNORMAL(a)     }
              {CHI(df)        }
              {STUDENT(df)    }

[/FRACTION={BLOM**}]
           {RANKIT}
           {TUKEY }
           {VW    }

[/TIES={MEAN**  }]
       {LOW     }
       {HIGH    }
       {CONDENSE}

[/{NOSTANDARDIZE**}]
  {STANDARDIZE    }

[/TYPE={Q-Q**}]
       {P-P  }

[/PLOT={BOTH**    }]
       {NORMAL    }
       {DETRENDED}

[/DIFF={1}]
       {n}

[/SDIFF={1}]
        {n}

[/PERIOD=n]

[/{NOLOG**}]
  {LN    }

[/APPLY [='model name']]
```

**Default if the subcommand is omitted.

Example:

```
PPLOT VARX
  /FRACTION=TUKEY
  /DIFF=2.
```

Overview

PPLOT (alias NPPLOT) produces probability plots of one or more sequence or time series variables. The variables can be standardized, differenced, and/or transformed before plotting. Expected normal values or deviations from expected normal values can be plotted.

Options

Modifying the Variables. You can request a natural log transformation of the sequence or time series variables using the LN subcommand and seasonal and nonseasonal differencing to any degree using the SDIFF and DIFF subcommands. With seasonal differencing, you can specify the periodicity on the PERIOD subcommand. You can also plot standardized series using the STANDARDIZE subcommand.

Plot Type. You can request p-p (proportion-proportion) or q-q (quantile-quantile) plots on the TYPE subcommand. With the PLOT subcommand you can display normal plots, detrended plots, or both.

Distribution Type. You can specify the distribution type on the DISTRIBUTION subcommand. The cumulative distribution function (CDF) and the inverse distribution function (IDF) for the specified distribution type are used to compute the expected values in the p-p and q-q plots, respectively.

Score Calculations. On the FRACTION subcommand, you can specify one of several fractional rank formulas to use for estimating the empirical distribution in p-p plots and computing expected quantiles in q-q plots. You can specify the treatment of tied values on the TIE subcommand.

Basic Specification

The basic specification is one or more variable names.

- For each variable specified, PPLOT produces two q-q plots of the observed values, one versus expected normal values and the other versus deviations from normal values. By default, expected normal values are calculated using Blom's transformation.
- Observed values define the horizontal axis, and expected normal values or deviations define the vertical axis.

Subcommand Order

- Subcommands can be specified in any order.

Syntax Rules

- VARIABLES can be specified only once.
- Other subcommands can be specified more than once, but only the last specification of each one is executed.

Operations

- Subcommand specifications apply to all plots produced by PPLOT.
- If the LN subcommand is specified, any differencing or standardization requested on that PPLOT is done on the log-transformed series.
- If differencing (DIFF or SDIFF) is specified, any standardization is done on the differenced series.

Limitations

- Maximum 1 VARIABLES subcommand. There is no limit on the number of variables named on the list.

Example

```
PPLOT VARX
 /FRACTION=TUKEY
 /DIFF=2.
```

- This command produces two normal q-q plots of *VARX*, one not detrended and the other detrended.
- The expected quantile values are calculated using Tukey's transformation.
- The variable is differenced twice before plotting.

VARIABLES Subcommand

VARIABLES specifies the sequence or time series variables to be plotted and is the only required subcommand. The actual keyword VARIABLES can be omitted.

DISTRIBUTION Subcommand

DISTRIBUTION specifies the distribution type of your data. The default is NORMAL if the subcommand is not specified or is specified without a keyword. If the parameters of the distribution type are not specified, DISTRIBUTION estimates them from the sample data and displays them with the plots.

NORMAL(a,b)   *Normal distribution.* The location parameter *a* can be any numeric value, while the scale parameter *b* must be positive. If they are not specified, DISTRIBUTION estimates them from the sample mean and sample standard deviation.

EXPONENTIAL(a)   *Exponential distribution.* The scale parameter *a* must be positive. If the parameter is not specified, DISTRIBUTION estimates it from the sample mean. Negative observations are not allowed.

WEIBULL(a,b)	*Weibull distribution.* The scale and shape parameters *a* and *b* must be positive. If they are not specified, DISTRIBUTION estimates them using the least square method. Negative observations are not allowed.
PARETO(a,b)	*Pareto distribution.* The threshold and shape parameters *a* and *b* must be positive. If they are not specified, DISTRIBUTION assumes *a* equals the minimum observation and estimates *b* by the maximum likelihood method. Negative observations are not allowed.
LNORMAL(a,b)	*Lognormal distribution.* The scale and shape parameters *a* and *b* must be positive. If they are not specified, DISTRIBUTION estimates them from the mean and standard deviation of the natural logarithm of the sample data. Negative observations are not allowed.
BETA(a,b)	*Beta distribution.* The shape1 and shape2 parameters *a* and *b* must be positive. If they are not specified, DISTRIBUTION estimates them from the sample mean and sample standard deviation. All observations must be between 0 and 1, inclusive.
GAMMA(a,b)	*Gamma distribution.* The shape and scale parameters *a* and *b* must be positive. If they are not specified, DISTRIBUTION estimates them from the sample mean and sample standard deviation if they are not specified. Negative observations are not allowed.
LOGISTIC(a,b)	*Logistic distribution.* LOGISTIC takes a location and a scale parameter (*a* and *b*). The scale parameter (*b*) must be positive. If the parameters are not specified, DISTRIBUTION estimates them from the sample mean and sample standard deviation.
LAPLACE(a,b)	*Laplace or double exponential distribution.* LAPLACE takes a location and a scale parameter (*a* and *b*). The scale parameter (*b*) must be positive. If the parameters are not specified, DISTRIBUTION estimates them from the sample mean and sample standard deviation.
UNIFORM(a,b)	*Uniform distribution.* UNIFORM takes a minimum and a maximum parameter (*a* and *b*). *a* must be equal to or greater than *b*. If the parameters are not specified, DISTRIBUTION assumes them from the sample data.
HNORMAL(a)	*Half-normal distribution.* Data are assumed to be location free or centralized. (Location parameter=0.) You can specify the scale parameter *a* or let DISTRIBUTION estimate it using the maximum likelihood method.
CHI (df)	*Chi-square distribution.* You must specify the degrees of freedom *df*. Negative observations are not allowed.
STUDENT(df)	*Student's* t *distribution.* You must specify the degrees of freedom *df*.

FRACTION Subcommand

FRACTION specifies the formula to be used in estimating the empirical distribution in p-p plots and calculating the expected quantile values in q-q plots.

- Only one formula can be specified. If more than one is specified, only the first is used.
- If the FRACTION subcommand is not specified, BLOM is used by default.
- These formulas will produce noticeable differences only for short series.

Four formulas are available:

BLOM   Blom's transformation, defined by the formula $(r - (3/8)) / (n + (1/4))$, where n is the number of observations and r is the rank, ranging from 1 to n (Blom, 1958).

RANKIT   Uses the formula $(r - (1/2)) / n$, where n is the number of observations and r is the rank, ranging from 1 to n (Chambers et al., 1983).

TUKEY   Tukey's transformation, defined by the formula $(r - (1/3)) / (n + (1/3))$, where n is the number of observations and r is the rank, ranging from 1 to n (Tukey, 1962).

VW   Van der Waerden's transformation, defined by the formula $r / (n + 1)$, where n is the number of observations and r is the rank, ranging from 1 to n (Lehmann, 1975).

Example

```
PPLOT VARX
  /FRACTION=VW.
```

- This PPLOT command uses van der Waerden's transformation to approximate the proportion estimate p, which is used in the inverse distribution function.
- By default, two q-q plots are produced.

TIES Subcommand

TIES determines the way tied values are handled. The default method is MEAN.

MEAN   *Mean rank of tied values is used for ties.* This is the default.

LOW   *Lowest rank of tied values is used for ties.*

HIGH   *Highest rank of tied values is used for ties.*

CONDENSE   *Consecutive ranks with ties sharing the same value.* Each distinct value of the ranked variable is assigned a consecutive rank. Ties share the same rank.

TYPE Subcommand

TYPE specifies the type of plot to produce. The default is Q-Q. Figure 1 shows a quantile-quantile plot and Figure 2 shows a proportion-proportion plot using the same data (with a normal distribution).

Q-Q   *Quantile-quantile plots.* The quantiles of the observed values are plotted against the quantiles of the specified distribution.

P-P   *Proportion-proportion plots*. The observed cumulative proportion is plotted against the expected cumulative proportion if the data were a sample from a specified distribution.

Figure 1   Normal q-q plot of current salary

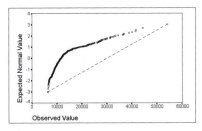

Figure 2   Normal p-p plot of current salary

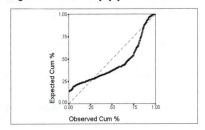

PLOT Subcommand

PLOT specifies whether to produce a plot of observed values versus expected values, a plot of observed values versus deviations from expected values, or both. Figure 1 and Figure 2 are nondetrended plots. Figure 3 shows a detrended q-q plot.

BOTH   *Display both detrended and nondetrended normal plots.* This is the default.

NORMAL   *Display nondetrended normal plots.* The observed values are plotted against the expected values.

DETRENDED   *Display detrended plots.* The observed values are plotted against the deviations from the expected values.

- If you specify PLOT more than once, only the last specification is executed.
- Deviations are calculated by subtracting the expected value from the observed value.

- In low resolution, a dash is used in a detrended plot to indicate where the deviation from the expected is 0.

Figure 3   Detrended normal q-q plot of current salary

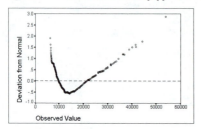

STANDARDIZE and NOSTANDARDIZE Subcommands

STANDARDIZE transforms the sequence or time series variables into a sample with a mean of 0 and a standard deviation of 1. NOSTANDARDIZE indicates that the series should not be standardized and is the default.

- There are no additional specifications on the STANDARDIZE or NOSTANDARDIZE subcommands.
- Only the last STANDARDIZE or NOSTANDARDIZE subcommand on the PPLOT command is executed.
- The STANDARDIZE and NOSTANDARDIZE subcommands have no effect on expected values, which are always standardized.
- NOSTANDARDIZE is generally used with an APPLY subcommand to turn off a previous STANDARDIZE specification.

Example

```
PPLOT VARX
  /STANDARDIZE.
```

- This example produces two q-q normal probability plots of *VARX* with standardized observed values.

DIFF Subcommand

DIFF specifies the degree of differencing used before plotting to convert a nonstationary variable to a stationary one with a constant mean and variance.

- You can specify any positive integer on DIFF.
- If DIFF is specified without a value, the default is 1.
- The number of values plotted decreases by 1 for each degree of differencing.

Example

```
PPLOT TICKETS
  /DIFF=2.
```

- In this example, *TICKETS* is differenced twice before the expected and observed values are plotted.

SDIFF Subcommand

If the variable exhibits a seasonal or periodic pattern, you can use the SDIFF subcommand to seasonally difference the variable before plotting.

- The specification on SDIFF indicates the degree of seasonal differencing and can be any positive integer.

- If SDIFF is specified without a value, the degree of seasonal differencing defaults to 1.

- The number of seasons plotted decreases by 1 for each degree of seasonal differencing.

- The length of the period used by SDIFF is specified on the PERIOD subcommand. If the PERIOD subcommand is not specified, the periodicity established on the TSET or DATE command is used (see the PERIOD subcommand below).

PERIOD Subcommand

PERIOD indicates the length of the period to be used by the SDIFF subcommand.

- The specification on PERIOD indicates how many observations are in one period or season. You can specify any positive integer on PERIOD.

- The PERIOD subcommand is ignored if it is used without the SDIFF subcommand.

- If PERIOD is not specified, the periodicity established on TSET PERIOD is in effect. If TSET PERIOD is not specified either, the periodicity established on the DATE command is used. If periodicity was not established anywhere, the SDIFF subcommand will not be executed.

Example

```
PPLOT TICKETS
  /SDIFF=1
  /PERIOD=12.
```

- This command applies 1 degree of seasonal differencing with 12 observations per season to the variable *TICKETS*.

LN and NOLOG Subcommands

LN transforms the data using the natural logarithm (base e) to remove varying amplitude. NOLOG indicates that the data should not be log transformed. NOLOG is the default.

- There are no additional specifications on LN or NOLOG.

- Only the last LN or NOLOG subcommand on a PPLOT command is executed.

- If a natural log transformation is requested, cases with values that are less than or equal to 0 will be set to system-missing, since nonpositive values cannot be log-transformed.
- NOLOG is generally used with an APPLY subcommand to turn off a previous LN specification.

Example

```
PPLOT TICKETS
  /FRACTION=TUKEY
  /DIFF=1
  /LN.
PPLOT EARNINGS
  /APPLY
  /NOLOG.
```

- The first command requests a natural log transformation of variable *TICKETS* before plotting.
- The second command applies the previous PPLOT specifications to variable *EARNINGS*. However, *EARNINGS* is not log-transformed before plotting.

APPLY Subcommand

APPLY allows you to produce a plot using previously defined specifications without having to repeat the PPLOT subcommands.

- The only specification on APPLY is the name of a previous model in quotes. If a model name is not specified, the model specified on the previous PPLOT command is used.
- To change any plot specifications, specify the subcommands of only those portions you want to change after the APPLY subcommand.
- If no variables are specified, the variables that were specified for the original plot are used.
- To change the variables used with the model, enter new variable names before or after the APPLY subcommand.
- The distribution type is applied but the parameters are not.

Example

```
PPLOT X1
  /FRACTION=TUKEY.
PPLOT Z1
  /APPLY.
```

- The first command produces two q-q normal probability plots of *X1* using Tukey's transformation to compute the expected values.
- The second command requests the same plots for variable *Z1*.

Example

```
PPLOT X1 Y1 Z1
  /FRACTION=VW.
PPLOT APPLY
  /FRACTION=BLOM.
```

- The first command uses van der Waerden's transformation to calculate expected normal values of *X1*, *Y1*, and *Z1*.
- The second command uses Blom's transformation for the same three series.

Example

```
PPLOT VARX
  /FRACTION=RANKIT
  /DIFF
  /STANDARDIZE.
PPLOT VARY
  /APPLY
  /NOSTANDARDIZE.
```

- The first command differences and standardizes series *VARX* and then produces a normal probability plot using the RANKIT transformation.
- The second command applies the previous plot specifications to *VARY* but does not standardize the series.

References

Blom, G. 1958. *Statistical estimates and transformed beta variables.* New York: John Wiley and Sons.

Chambers, J. M., W. S. Cleveland, B. Kleiner, and P. A. Tukey. 1983. *Graphical methods for data analysis.* Belmont, Calif.: Wadsworth International Group; Boston: Duxbury Press.

Lehmann, E. L. 1975. *Nonparametrics: Statistical methods based on ranks.* San Francisco: Holden-Day.

Tukey, J. W. 1962. The future of data analysis. *Annals of Mathematical Statistics,* 33:22.

PREDICT

```
PREDICT   [{start date        }] [THRU [{end date         }]]
          {start case number}         {end case number}
                                      {END              }
```

Example:
```
PREDICT Y 61 THRU Y 65.
```

Overview

PREDICT specifies the observations that mark the beginning and end of the forecast period. If the forecast period extends beyond the length of the series, PREDICT extends the series in the working data file to allow room for the forecast observations.

Basic Specification

The minimum specification on PREDICT is either the start or the end of the range, or keyword THRU. PREDICT sets up a forecast period beginning and ending with the dates or case numbers specified. The default starting point is the observation immediately after the end of the series or, if USE is specified, the observation immediately after the end of the use range (the historical period). The default end is the last observation in the series.

Syntax Rules

- You can specify a start, an end, or both.
- The start and end are specified as either date specifications or case (observation) numbers.
- Date specifications and case numbers cannot be mixed on one PREDICT command.
- Keyword THRU is required if the end of the range is specified.
- Keyword THRU by itself defines a PREDICT range starting with the first observation after the use range and ending with the end of the series. If USE has not been specified, PREDICT THRU is meaningless.

Date Specifications

- A date specification consists of DATE keyword(s) and value(s) (see DATE). These specifications must correspond to existing date variables.
- If more than one date variable exists, the highest-order one must be included in the date specification.

702

- Values on keyword YEAR must have the same format (2 or 4 digits) as the YEAR specifications on the DATE command.

Case Specifications

The case number specification is the sequence number of the case (observation) as it is read by the program.

Valid Range

- The start date must precede the end date.
- The start case number must be less than the end case number.
- The start can be any observation ranging from the second observation in the historical period specified on USE to the observation immediately following the end of the historical period. If USE is not specified, the start can be any observation ranging from the second observation in the series to the observation immediately following the end of the series.
- For most models, the start of the predict period should not be too close to the start of the use period.
- The predict and use periods should not be exactly the same.
- The start of the predict period should not precede the start of the use period.

Operations

- PREDICT is executed when the data are read for the next forecasting procedure (ARIMA in SPSS Trends, CURVEFIT in SPSS Base system, and 2SLS in SPSS Regression Models).
- PREDICT is ignored by non-forecasting procedures.
- Case number specifications refer to the sequential numbers assigned to cases as they are read.
- If the forecast period extends beyond the length of the series, PREDICT extends the series in the working data file to allow room for the forecast observations.
- New observations added to the end of existing series will contain non-missing date variables, forecast values (variable *FIT#n*), confidence interval limits (variables *LCL#n* and *UCL#n*), and, for ARIMA models, standard error of the predicted value (*SEP#n*). For all other variables, including the original series, the new cases will be system-missing.
- PREDICT cannot forecast beyond the end of the series for ARIMA with regressors and 2SLS. However, it *can* forecast values for the dependent variable if the independent variables have valid values in the predict period.
- If the use and predict periods overlap, the model is still estimated using all observations in the use period.
- USE and PREDICT can be used together to perform forecasting validation. To do this, specify a use period that ends before the existing end of the series, and specify a predict period starting with the next observation.

- If there is a gap between the end of the use period and the start of the specified predict period, the program will use the first observation after the end of the use period as the start of the predict period. (This is the default.)
- The DATE command turns off all existing USE and PREDICT specifications.
- PREDICT remains in effect in a session until it is changed by another PREDICT command or until a new DATE command is issued.
- If more than one forecasting procedure is specified after PREDICT, the USE command should be specified between procedures so that the original series without any new, system-missing cases will be used each time. Alternatively, you can specify

```
TSET NEWVAR = NONE
```

before the first forecasting procedure so that you can evaluate model statistics without creating new variables or adding new cases with missing values to the original series.

Limitations

Maximum 1 range (one start and/or one end) can be specified per PREDICT command.

Example

```
PREDICT Y 61 THRU Y 65.
```

- This command specifies a forecast period from 1961 to 1965.
- The working data file must include variable *YEAR_*, which in this example contains only the last 2 digits of each year.
- If variable *MONTH_* also exists, the above command is equivalent to

```
PREDICT Y 61 M 1 THRU Y 65 M 12.
```

Example

```
PREDICT 61 THRU 65.
```

- This command specifies a forecast period from the 61st case (observation) to the 65th case.

Example

```
PREDICT W 28 THRU W 56.
```

- This command specifies a forecast period from the 28th week to the 56th week.
- The working data file must include variable *WEEK_*.

- If variable *DAY_* also exists, the above command is equivalent to

  ```
  PREDICT W 28 D 1 THRU W 56 D 7.
  ```

Example

```
PREDICT THRU Y 65.
```

- This command uses the default start date, which is the observation immediately following the end of the use period. If USE is not specified, the default start is the observation immediately following the end of the series.
- The forecast period extends from the start date through year '65.
- The working data file must include variable *YEAR_*.
- Keyword THRU is required.

Example

```
PREDICT THRU CYCLE 4 OBS 17.
```

- This example uses the date variables *OBS_* and *CYCLE_*, which must exist in the working data file.
- *CYCLE*, the highest order, must be included on PREDICT.
- Keyword THRU is required.
- The forecast period extends from the default start up to the 17th observation of cycle 4.

PRESERVE

PRESERVE

Overview

PRESERVE stores current SET specifications that can later be restored by the RESTORE command. PRESERVE and RESTORE are especially useful with the macro facility. PRESERVE—RESTORE sequences can be nested up to five levels.

Basic Specification

The only specification is the command keyword. PRESERVE has no additional specifications.

Example

```
GET FILE=PRSNNL.
FREQUENCIES VAR=DIVISION /STATISTICS=ALL.
PRESERVE.
SET XSORT=NO WIDTH=90 UNDEFINED=NOWARN BLANKS=000 CASE=UPLOW.
SORT CASES BY DIVISION.
REPORT FORMAT=AUTO LIST /VARS=LNAME FNAME DEPT SOCSEC SALARY
  /BREAK=DIVISION /SUMMARY=MEAN.
RESTORE.
```

- GET reads SPSS-format data file *PRSNNL*.
- FREQUENCIES requests a Frequency table and all statistics for variable *DIVISION*.
- PRESERVE stores all current SET specifications.
- SET changes several subcommand settings.
- SORT sorts cases in preparation for a report. Because SET XSORT=NO, the sort program is not used to sort cases; another sort program must be available.
- REPORT requests a report organized by variable *DIVISION*.
- RESTORE reestablishes the SET specifications that were in effect when PRESERVE was specified.

PRINT

```
PRINT [OUTFILE=file] [RECORDS={1}] [{NOTABLE}]
                               {n}   {TABLE  }

 /{1     } varlist [{col location [(format)]}] [varlist...]
  {rec #}          {(format list)            }
                   {*                        }

 [/{2     }...]
   {rec #}
```

Example:

```
PRINT / MOHIRED YRHIRED DEPT SALARY NAME.
EXECUTE.
```

Overview

PRINT displays the values of variables for each case in the data. PRINT is designed to be simple enough for a quick check on data definitions and transformations and yet flexible enough for formatting simple reports.

Options

Formats. You can specify formats for the variables (see "Formats" on p. 709).

Strings. You can specify string values within the variable specifications. The strings can be used to label values or to create extra space between values. Strings can also be used as column headings. (See "Strings" on p. 710.)

Output File. You can direct the output to a specified file using the OUTFILE subcommand.

Summary Table. You can display a table that summarizes variable formats with the TABLE subcommand.

Basic Specification

The basic specification is a slash followed by a variable list. The values for all variables named on the list are displayed in the output.

Subcommand Order

Subcommands can be specified in any order. However, all subcommands must be specified before the slash that precedes the start of the variable specifications.

Syntax Rules

- A slash must precede the variable specifications. The first slash begins the definition of the first (and possibly only) line per case of the PRINT display.
- Specified variables must already exist, but they can be numeric, string, scratch, temporary, or system variables. Subscripted variable names, such as *X(1)* for the first element in vector *X,* cannot be used.
- Keyword ALL can be used to display the values of all user-defined variables in the working data file.

Operations

- PRINT is executed once for each case constructed from the data file.
- PRINT is a transformation and will not be executed unless it is followed by a procedure or the EXECUTE command.
- Because PRINT is a transformation command, the output might be mixed with casewise procedure output. Procedures that produce individual case listings (such as LIST) should not be used immediately after PRINT. An intervening EXECUTE or procedure command should be specified.
- Values are displayed with a blank space between them. However, if a format is specified for a variable, the blank space for that variable's values is suppressed.
- Values are displayed in the output as the data are read. The PRINT output appears before the output from the first procedure.
- If more variables are specified than can be displayed in 132 columns or within the width specified on SET WIDTH, the program displays an error message. You must reduce the number of variables or split the output into several records.
- User-missing values are displayed just like valid values. System-missing values are represented by a period.

Example

```
PRINT   / MOHIRED YRHIRED DEPT SALARY NAME.
FREQUENCIES VARIABLES=DEPT.
```

- PRINT displays values for each variable on the variable list. The FREQUENCIES procedure reads the data and causes PRINT to be executed.
- All variables are displayed using their dictionary formats. One blank space separates the values of each variable.

Example

```
PRINT /ALL.
EXECUTE.
```

- PRINT displays values for all user-defined variables in the working data file. The EXECUTE command executes PRINT.

Formats

By default, PRINT uses the dictionary print formats. You can specify formats for some or all variables specified on PRINT. For a string variable, the specified format must have a width at least as large as that of the dictionary format. String values are truncated if the specified width is smaller than that of the dictionary format.

- Format specifications can be either column-style or FORTRAN-like (see DATA LIST). The column location specified with column-style formats or implied with FORTRAN-like formats refers to the column in which the variable will be displayed.

- A format specification following a list of variables applies to all of the variables in the list. Use an asterisk to prevent the specified format from applying to variables preceding the asterisk. The specification of columns locations implies a default print format, and that format will apply to all previous variables if no asterisk is used.

- Printable numeric formats are F, COMMA, DOLLAR, CC, DOT, N, E, PCT, PIBHEX, RBHEX, Z, and the date and time formats. Printable string formats are A and AHEX. Note that hex and binary formats use different widths. For example, the AHEX format must have a width twice that of the corresponding A format. For more information on specifying formats and on the formats available, see DATA LIST and "Variable Formats" on p. 31.

- Format specifications are in effect only for the PRINT command. They do not change the dictionary print formats.

- When a format is specified for a variable, the automatic blank following the variable in the output is suppressed. To preserve the blank between variables, use a string (see "Strings" on p. 710), specify blank columns in the format, or use an X or T format element (see DATA LIST for information on X and T).

Example

```
PRINT / TENURE (F2.0) ' ' MOHIRED YRHIRED DEPT *
      SALARY85 TO SALARY88 (4(DOLLAR8,1X)) NAME.
EXECUTE.
```

- Format F2.0 is specified for *TENURE*. A blank string is specified after *TENURE* because the automatic blank following the variable is suppressed by the format specification.

- *MOHIRED*, *YRHIRED*, and *DEPT* are displayed with default formats because the asterisk prevents them from receiving the DOLLAR8 format specified for *SALARY85* to *SALARY88*. The automatic blank is preserved for *MOHIRED*, *YRHIRED*, and *DEPT*, but the blank is suppressed for *SALARY85* to *SALARY88* by the format specification. The 1X format element is therefore specified with DOLLAR8 to add one blank after each value of *SALARY85* to *SALARY88*.

- NAME uses the default dictionary format.

Strings

You can specify string values within the variable list. Strings must be enclosed in apostrophes or quotation marks.

- If a format is specified for a variable list, the application of the format is interrupted by a specified string. Thus, the string has the same effect within a variable list as an asterisk.

- Strings can be used to create column headings for the displayed variables. The PRINT command that specifies the column headings must be used within a DO IF—END IF structure. If you want the column headings to begin a new page in the output, use a PRINT EJECT command rather than PRINT to specify the headings (see PRINT EJECT).

Example

```
PRINT / NAME 'HIRED=' MOHIRED(F2) '/' YRHIRED
             ' SALARY=' SALARY (DOLLAR8).
EXECUTE.
```

- Three strings are specified. The strings HIRED= and SALARY= label the values being displayed. The slash specified between month hired (*MOHIRED*) and year hired (*YRHIRED*) creates a composite hiring date. The F2 format is supplied for variable *MOHIRED* in order to suppress the blank that would follow it if the dictionary format were used.

- *NAME* and *YRHIRED* are displayed with default formats. The 'HIRED=' specification prevents the F2 format from applying to *NAME*, and the 'SALARY=' specification prevents the DOLLAR8 format from applying to *YRHIRED*.

Example

```
DO IF $CASENUM EQ 1.
PRINT /'   NAME ' 1 'DEPT' 25 'HIRED' 30 '  SALARY' 35.
END IF.
PRINT / NAME DEPT *
        MOHIRED 30-31 '/' YRHIRED *
        SALARY 35-42(DOLLAR).
EXECUTE.
```

- The first PRINT command specifies strings only. The integer after each string specifies the beginning column number of the string. The strings will be used as column headings for the variables. DO IF $CASENUM EQ 1 causes the first PRINT command to be executed only once, as the first case is processed. END IF closes the structure.

- The second PRINT command specifies the variables to be displayed. It is executed once for each case in the data. Column locations are specified to align the values with the column headings. In this example, the T format element could also have been used to align the variables and the column headings. For example, MOHIRED (T30,F2) begins the display of values for variable *MOHIRED* in column 30.

- The asterisk after *DEPT* prevents the format specified for *MOHIRED* from applying to *NAME* and *DEPT*. The asterisk after *YRHIRED* prevents the format specified for *SALARY* from applying to *YRHIRED*.

RECORDS Subcommand

RECORDS indicates the total number of lines displayed per case. The number specified on RECORDS is informational only. The actual specification that causes variables to display on a new line is a slash within the variable specifications. Each new line is requested by another slash.

- RECORDS must be specified before the slash that precedes the start of the variable specifications.
- The only specification on RECORDS is an integer to indicate the number of records for the output. If the number does not agree with the actual number of records indicated by slashes, the program issues a warning and ignores the specification on RECORDS.
- Specifications for each line of output must begin with a slash. An integer can follow the slash, indicating the line on which values are to be displayed. The integer is informational only. It cannot be used to rearrange the order of records in the output. If the integer does not agree with the actual record number indicated by the number of slashes in the variable specifications, the integer is ignored.
- A slash that is not followed by a variable list generates a blank line in the output.

Example

```
PRINT RECORDS=3 /EMPLOYID NAME DEPT
                /EMPLOYID TENURE SALARY
                /.
EXECUTE.
```

- PRINT displays the values of an individual's name and department on one line, tenure and salary on the next line, and the employee identification number on both lines, followed by a blank third line. Two lines are displayed for each case, and cases in the output are separated by a blank line.

Example

```
PRINT RECORDS=3 /1 EMPLOYID NAME DEPT
                /2 EMPLOYID TENURE SALARY
                /3.
```

- This PRINT command is equivalent to that in the preceding example.

Example

```
PRINT / EMPLOYID NAME DEPT / EMPLOYID TENURE SALARY /.
```

- This PRINT command is equivalent to those in the two preceding examples.

OUTFILE Subcommand

OUTFILE specifies a file for the output from the PRINT command. By default, PRINT output is included with the rest of the output from the session.

- OUTFILE must be specified before the slash preceding the start of the variable specifications.
- The output from PRINT cannot exceed 132 characters, even if the external file is defined with a longer record length.

Example

```
PRINT OUTFILE=PRINTOUT
   /1 EMPLOYID DEPT SALARY /2 NAME.
EXECUTE.
```

- OUTFILE specifies *PRINTOUT* as the file that receives the PRINT output.

TABLE Subcommand

TABLE requests a table showing how the variable information is formatted. NOTABLE, which suppresses the format table, is the default.

- TABLE must be specified before the slash that precedes the start of the variable specifications.

Example

```
PRINT TABLE /1 EMPLOYID DEPT SALARY /2  NAME.
EXECUTE.
```

- TABLE requests a summary table describing the PRINT specifications. The table is included with the PRINT output.

PRINT EJECT

```
PRINT EJECT [OUTFILE=file] [RECORDS={1}] [{NOTABLE}]
                                     {n}   {TABLE  }

 /{1    } varlist [{col location [(format)]}] [varlist...]
  {rec #}          {(format list)           }
                   {*                       }

[/{2    }...]
  {rec #}
```

Example:

```
DO IF $CASENUM EQ 1.
PRINT EJECT /'   NAME ' 1 'DEPT' 25 'HIRED' 30 '   SALARY' 35.
END IF.
PRINT / NAME DEPT *
        MOHIRED(T30,F2) '/' YRHIRED *
        SALARY (T35,DOLLAR8).
EXECUTE.
```

Overview

PRINT EJECT displays specified information at the top of a new page of the output. PRINT EJECT causes a page ejection each time it is executed. If PRINT EJECT is not used in a DO IF—END IF structure, it is executed for each case in the data, and each case is displayed on a separate page.

PRINT EJECT is designed to be used with the PRINT command to insert titles and column headings above the values displayed by PRINT. PRINT can also generate titles and headings, but PRINT cannot be used to control page ejections.

PRINT EJECT and PRINT can be used for writing simple reports.

Options

The options available for PRINT EJECT are identical to those available for PRINT:

- You can specify formats for the variables.
- You can specify string values within the variable specifications. With PRINT EJECT, the strings are usually used as titles or column headings and often include a specification for column location.
- You can display each case on more than one line using the RECORDS subcommand.
- You can direct the output to a specified file using the OUTFILE subcommand.
- You can display a table that summarizes variable formats with the TABLE subcommand.

All of these features are documented in detail for the PRINT command and work identically for PRINT EJECT. Refer to PRINT for additional information.

Basic Specification

The basic specification is a slash followed by a variable list and/or a list of string values that will be used as column headings or titles. The values for each variable or string are displayed on the top line of a new page in the output. PRINT EJECT is usually used within a DO IF—END IF structure to control the page ejections.

Operations

- PRINT EJECT is a transformation and will not be executed unless it is followed by a procedure or the EXECUTE command.
- If PRINT EJECT is not used within a DO IF—END IF structure, it is executed for each case in the data and displays the values for each case on a separate page.
- Values are displayed with a blank space between them. However, if a format is specified for a variable, the blank space for that variable's values is suppressed.
- Values are displayed in the output as the data are read. The PRINT output appears before the output from the first procedure.
- If more variables are specified than can be displayed in 132 columns or within the width specified on SET WIDTH, the program displays an error message. You must reduce the number of variables or split the output into several records.
- User-missing values are displayed just like valid values. System-missing values are represented by a period.

Example

```
DO IF $CASENUM EQ 1.
PRINT EJECT /'   NAME ' 1 'DEPT' 25 'HIRED' 30 '   SALARY' 35.
END IF.
PRINT / NAME DEPT *
        MOHIRED(T30,F2) '/' YRHIRED *
        SALARY (T35,DOLLAR8).
EXECUTE.
```

- PRINT EJECT specifies strings to be used as column headings and causes a page ejection. DO IF—END IF causes the PRINT EJECT command to be executed only once, when the system variable $CASENUM$ equals 1 (the value assigned to the first case in the file). Thus, column headings are displayed on the first page of the output only. The next example shows how to display column headings at the top of every page of the output.
- If a PRINT command were used in place of PRINT EJECT, the column headings would begin immediately after the command printback.

Example

```
DO IF MOD($CASENUM,50) = 1.
PRINT   EJECT
FILE=OUT /'    NAME ' 1 'DEPT' 25 'HIRED' 30 '    SALARY' 35.
END IF.
PRINT FILE=OUT / NAME DEPT *
        MOHIRED 30-31 '/' YRHIRED *
        SALARY 35-42(DOLLAR).
EXECUTE.
```

- In this example, DO IF specifies that PRINT EJECT is executed if MOD (the remainder) of *$CASENUM* divided by 50 equals 1 (see p. 44 for a description of MOD). Thus, column headings are displayed on a new page after every 50th case.

- If PRINT were used instead of PRINT EJECT, column headings would display after every 50th case but would not appear at the top of a new page.

- Both PRINT EJECT and PRINT specify the same file for the output. If the FILE subcommands on PRINT EJECT and PRINT do not specify the same file, the column headings and the displayed values end up in different files.

PRINT FORMATS

```
PRINT FORMATS varlist(format) [varlist...]
```

Example:
```
PRINT FORMATS SALARY (DOLLAR8) / HOURLY (DOLLAR7.2)
             / RAISE BONUS (PCT2).
```

Overview

PRINT FORMATS changes variable print formats. Print formats are output formats and control the form in which values are displayed by a procedure or by the PRINT command.

PRINT FORMATS changes only print formats. To change write formats, use the WRITE FORMATS command. To change both the print and write formats with a single specification, use the FORMATS command. For information on assigning input formats during data definition, see DATA LIST. For a more detailed discussion of input and output formats, see "Variable Formats" on p. 31.

Basic Specification

The basic specification is a variable list followed by the new format specification in parentheses. All specified variables receive the new format.

Syntax Rules

- You can specify more than one variable or variable list, followed by a format in parentheses. Only one format can be specified after each variable list. For clarity, each set of specifications can be separated by a slash.
- You can use keyword TO to refer to consecutive variables in the working data file.
- The specified width of a format must include enough positions to accommodate any punctuation characters such as decimal points, commas, dollar signs, or date and time delimiters. (This differs from assigning an *input* format on DATA LIST, where the program automatically expands the input format to accommodate punctuation characters in output.)
- Custom currency formats (CCw, CCw.d) must first be defined on the SET command before they can be used on PRINT FORMATS.
- PRINT FORMATS cannot be used with string variables. To change the length of a string variable, declare a new variable of the desired length with the STRING command and then use COMPUTE to copy values from the existing string into the new string.

Operations

- Unlike most transformations, PRINT FORMATS takes effect as soon as it is encountered in the command sequence. Special attention should be paid to its position among commands.

- Variables not specified on PRINT FORMATS retain their current print formats in the working data file. To see the current formats, use the DISPLAY command.

- The new print formats are changed only in the working file and are in effect for the duration of the session or until changed again with a PRINT FORMATS or FORMATS command. Print formats in the original data file (if one exists) are not changed, unless the file is re-saved with the SAVE or XSAVE command.

- New numeric variables created with transformation commands are assigned default print formats of F8.2 (or the format specified on the FORMAT subcommand of SET). The FORMATS command can be used to change the new variable's print formats.

- New string variables created with transformation commands are assigned the format specified on the STRING command that declares the variable. PRINT FORMATS cannot be used to change the format of a new string variable.

- If a numeric data value exceeds its width specification, the program attempts to display some value nevertheless. First the program rounds decimal values, then removes punctuation characters, then tries scientific notation, and finally, if there is still not enough space, produces asterisks indicating that a value is present but cannot be displayed in the assigned width.

Example

```
PRINT FORMATS SALARY (DOLLAR8) / HOURLY (DOLLAR7.2)
          / RAISE BONUS (PCT2).
```

- The print format for *SALARY* is changed to DOLLAR with eight positions, including the dollar sign and comma when appropriate. The value 11550 is displayed as $11,550. An eight-digit number would require a DOLLAR11 format specification: eight characters for digits, two characters for commas, and one character for the dollar sign.

- The print format for *HOURLY* is changed to DOLLAR with seven positions, including the dollar sign, decimal point, and two decimal places. The number 115 is displayed as $115.00. If DOLLAR6.2 had been specified, the value 115 would be displayed as $115.0. the program would truncate the last 0 because a width of 6 is not enough to display the full value.

- The print format for both *RAISE* and *BONUS* is changed to PCT with two positions: one position for the percentage and one position for the percent sign. The value 9 displays as 9%. Because the width allows for only two positions, the value 10 displays as 10, since the percent sign is truncated.

Example

```
COMPUTE V3=V1 + V2.
PRINT FORMATS V3 (F3.1).
```

- COMPUTE creates the new numeric variable *V3*. By default, *V3* is assigned an F8.2 format (or the default format specified on SET).
- PRINT FORMATS changes the print format for *V3* to F3.1.

Example

```
SET CCA='-/-.Dfl ..-'.
PRINT FORMATS COST (CCA14.2).
```

- SET defines a European currency format for the custom currency format type CCA.
- PRINT FORMATS assigns the print format CCA to variable *COST*. With the format defined for CCA on SET, the value 37419 is displayed as Dfl'37.419,00. See the SET command for more information on custom currency formats.

PRINT SPACE

```
PRINT SPACE [OUTFILE=file] [numeric expression]
```

Example:

```
PRINT / NAME DEPT82 *
       MOHIRED(T30,F2) '/' YRHIRED *
       SALARY82 (T35,DOLLAR8).
PRINT SPACE.
EXECUTE.
```

Overview

PRINT SPACE displays blank lines in the output and is generally used with a PRINT or WRITE command. Because PRINT SPACE displays a blank line each time it is executed, it is often used in a DO IF—END IF structure.

Basic Specification

The basic specification is simply the command PRINT SPACE.

Syntax Rules

- To display more than one blank line, specify a numeric expression after PRINT SPACE. The expression can be an integer or a complex expression.
- OUTFILE directs the output to a specified file. OUTFILE should be specified if an OUTFILE subcommand is specified on the PRINT or WRITE command that is used with PRINT SPACE. The OUTFILE subcommand on PRINT SPACE and PRINT or WRITE should specify the same file.

Operations

- If PRINT SPACE is not used in a DO IF—END IF structure, it is executed for each case in the data and displays a blank line for every case.

Example

```
PRINT / NAME DEPT82 *
       MOHIRED(T30,F2) '/' YRHIRED *
       SALARY82 (T35,DOLLAR8).
PRINT SPACE.
EXECUTE.
```

- PRINT SPACE displays one blank line each time it is executed. Because PRINT SPACE is not used in a DO IF—END IF structure, it is executed once for each case. In effect, the output is double-spaced.

Example

```
NUMERIC #LINE.
DO IF MOD(#LINE,5) = 0.
PRINT SPACE 2.
END IF.
COMPUTE #LINE=#LINE + 1.
PRINT / NAME DEPT *
       MOHIRED 30-31 '/' YRHIRED *
       SALARY 35-42(DOLLAR).
EXECUTE.
```

- DO IF specifies that PRINT SPACE will be executed if MOD (the remainder) of *#LINE* divided by 5 equals 1. Since *#LINE* is incremented by 1 for each case, PRINT SPACE is executed once for every five cases. (See p. 44 for information on the MOD function.)
- PRINT SPACE specifies two blank lines. Cases are displayed in groups of five with two blank lines between each group.

Example

```
* Printing addresses on labels.

COMPUTE #LINES=0.                     /*Initiate #LINES to 0
DATA LIST FILE=ADDRESS/RECORD 1-40 (A).  /*Read a record
COMPUTE #LINES=#LINES+1.              /*Bump counter and print
WRITE OUTFILE=LABELS /RECORD.

DO IF RECORD EQ ' '.                  /*Blank between addresses
+   PRINT SPACE OUTFILE=LABELS 8 - #LINES.  /*Add extra blank #LINES
+   COMPUTE #LINES=0.
END IF.
EXECUTE.
```

- PRINT SPACE uses a complex expression for specifying the number of blank lines to display. The data contain a variable number of input records for each name and address, which must be printed in a fixed number of lines for mailing labels. The goal is to know when the last line for each address has been printed, how many lines have printed, and therefore how many blank records must be printed in order for the next address to fit on the next label. The example assumes that there is already one blank line between each address on input and that you want to print eight lines per label.
- The DATA LIST command defines the data. Each line of the address is contained in columns 1–40 of the data file and is assigned the variable name *RECORD*. For the blank line between each address, *RECORD* is blank.
- Variable *#LINES* is the key to this example. *#LINES* is initialized to 0 as a scratch variable. It is incremented for each record written. When the program encounters a blank line

(RECORD EQ ' '), PRINT SPACE prints a number of blank lines equal to 8 minus the number already printed, and *#LINES* is then reset to 0.

- OUTFILE on PRINT SPACE specifies the same file specified by OUTFILE on WRITE.

PROCEDURE OUTPUT

```
PROCEDURE OUTPUT OUTFILE=file
```

Example:

```
PROCEDURE OUTPUT OUTFILE=CELLDATA.
CROSSTABS VARIABLES=FEAR SEX (1,2)
  /TABLES=FEAR BY SEX
  /WRITE=ALL.
```

Overview

PROCEDURE OUTPUT specifies the files to which CROSSTABS, FREQUENCIES, and SURVIVAL (included in the SPSS Advanced Models option) can write procedure output. PROCEDURE OUTPUT has no other applications.

Basic Specification

The only specification is OUTFILE and the file specification. PROCEDURE OUTPUT must precede the command to which it applies.

Operations

Commands with the WRITE subcommand or keyword write to the output file specified on the most recent PROCEDURE OUTPUT command. If only one output file has been specified, the output from the last such procedure overwrites all previous ones.

Example

```
PROCEDURE OUTPUT OUTFILE=CELLDATA.
CROSSTABS VARIABLES=FEAR SEX (1,2)
  /TABLES=FEAR BY SEX
  /WRITE=ALL.
```

- PROCEDURE OUTPUT precedes CROSSTABS and specifies *CELLDATA* as the file to receive the cell frequencies.
- The WRITE subcommand on CROSSTABS is required for writing cell frequencies to a procedure output file.

Example

```
PROCEDURE OUTPUT OUTFILE=CODEBOOK.
FREQUENCIES VARIABLES=ALL
  /FORMAT=ONEPAGE WRITE.
PROCEDURE OUTPUT OUTFILE=CELLDATA.
CROSSTABS VARIABLES=FEAR SEX (1 2)
  /TABLES=FEAR BY SEX
  /WRITE=ALL.
```

- The first PROCEDURE OUTPUT command precedes FREQUENCIES and specifies *CODEBOOK* as the file to receive frequency tables.
- The WRITE keyword on the FORMAT subcommand on FREQUENCIES is required for writing the display to a procedure output file.
- The second PROCEDURE OUTPUT command is required to specify *CELLDATA* as the file to receive the cell frequencies of the crosstabulation. Without this command, the cell frequencies would overwrite the FREQUENCIES output.

Example

```
PROCEDURE OUTPUT OUTFILE=SURVTBL.
SURVIVAL  TABLES=ONSSURV,RECSURV BY TREATMNT(1,3)
  /STATUS = RECURSIT(1,9) FOR RECSURV
  /STATUS = STATUS(3,4) FOR ONSSURV
  /INTERVAL=THRU 50 BY 5 THRU 100 BY 10/PLOTS/COMPARE
  /CALCULATE=CONDITIONAL PAIRWISE
  /WRITE=TABLES.
```

- PROCEDURE OUTPUT precedes SURVIVAL and specifies *SURVTBL* as the file to receive the survival tables.
- The WRITE subcommand on SURVIVAL is required for writing survival tables to a procedure output file.

PROXIMITIES

```
PROXIMITIES  varlist  [/VIEW={CASE**  }]
                             {VARIABLE}

   [/STANDARDIZE=[{VARIABLE}] [{NONE**  }]]
                  {CASE    }  {Z      }
                              {SD     }
                              {RANGE  }
                              {MAX    }
                              {MEAN   }
                              {RESCALE}

      [/MEASURE=[{EUCLID**          }] [ABSOLUTE] [REVERSE] [RESCALE]
                 {SEUCLID           }
                 {COSINE            }
                 {CORRELATION       }
                 {BLOCK             }
                 {CHEBYCHEV         }
                 {POWER(p,r)        }
                 {MINKOWSKI(p)      }
                 {CHISQ             }
                 {PH2               }
                 {RR[(p[,np])]      }
                 {SM[(p[,np])]      }
                 {JACCARD[(p[,np])] }
                 {DICE[(p[,np])]    }
                 {SS1[(p[,np])]     }
                 {RT[(p[,np])]      }
                 {SS2[(p[,np])]     }
                 {K1[(p[,np])]      }
                 {SS3[(p[,np])]     }
                 {K2[(p[,np])]      }
                 {SS4[(p[,np])]     }
                 {HAMANN[(p[,np])]  }
                 {OCHIAI[(p[,np])]  }
                 {SS5[(p[,np])]     }
                 {PHI[(p[,np])]     }
                 {LAMBDA[(p[,np])]  }
                 {D[(p[,np])]       }
                 {Y[(p[,np])]       }
                 {Q[(p[,np])]       }
                 {BEUCLID[(p[,np])] }
                 {SIZE[(p[,np])]    }
                 {PATTERN[(p[,np])] }
                 {BSEUCLID[(p[,np])]}
                 {BSHAPE[(p[,np])]  }
                 {DISPER[(p[,np])]  }
                 {VARIANCE[(p[,np])]}
                 {BLWMN[(p[,np])]   }
                 {NONE              }

   [/PRINT=[{PROXIMITIES**}]]  [/ID=varname]
            {NONE         }

   [/MISSING=[LISTWISE**]  [INCLUDE]

   [/MATRIX=[IN({file})]  [OUT({file})]]
              {*    }        {*    }
```

**Default if subcommand or keyword is omitted.

Example:

```
PROXIMITIES A B C.
```

Overview

PROXIMITIES computes a variety of measures of similarity, dissimilarity, or distance between pairs of cases or pairs of variables for moderate-sized data sets (see "Limitations" below). PROXIMITIES matrix output can be used as input to procedures ALSCAL, CLUSTER, and FACTOR. To learn more about proximities matrices and their uses, consult Anderberg (1973) and Romesburg (1984).

Options

Standardizing Data. With the STANDARDIZE subcommand you can standardize the values for each variable or for each case by any of several different methods.

Proximity Measures. You can compute a variety of similarity, dissimilarity, and distance measures using the MEASURE subcommand. (Similarity measures increase with greater similarity; dissimilarity and distance measures decrease.) MEASURE can compute measures for interval data, frequency count data, and binary data. Only one measure can be requested in any one PROXIMITIES procedure. With the VIEW subcommand, you can control whether proximities are computed between variables or between cases.

Output. You can display a computed matrix using the PRINT subcommand.

Matrix Input and Output. You can write a computed proximities matrix to an SPSS-format data file using the MATRIX subcommand. This matrix can be used as input to procedures CLUSTER, ALSCAL, and FACTOR. You can also use MATRIX to read a similarity, dissimilarity, or distance matrix. This option lets you rescale or transform existing proximity matrices.

Basic Specification

The basic specification is a variable list, which obtains Euclidean distances between cases based on the values of each specified variable.

Subcommand Order

- The variable list must be first.
- Subcommands can be named in any order.

Operations

- PROXIMITIES ignores case weights when computing coefficients.

Limitations

- PROXIMITIES keeps the raw data for the current split-file group in memory. Storage requirements increase rapidly with the number of cases and the number of items (cases or variables) for which PROXIMITIES computes coefficients.

Example

```
PROXIMITIES A B C.
```

- PROXIMITIES computes Euclidean distances between cases based on the values of variables *A*, *B*, and *C*.

Variable Specification

- The variable list must be specified first.
- The variable list can be omitted when an input matrix data file is specified. A slash must then be specified before the first subcommand to indicate that the variable list is omitted.

STANDARDIZE Subcommand

Use STANDARDIZE to standardize data values for either cases or variables before computing proximities. One of two options can be specified to control the direction of standardization:

VARIABLE *Standardize the values for each variable.* This is the default.

CASE *Standardize the values within each case.*

Several standardization methods are available. These allow you to equalize selected properties of the values. All methods can be used with either VARIABLE or CASE. Only one standardization method can be specified.

- If STANDARDIZE is omitted, proximities are computed using the original values (keyword NONE).
- If STANDARDIZE is used without specifications, proximities are computed using Z scores (keyword Z).
- STANDARDIZE cannot be used with binary measures.

NONE *Do not standardize.* Proximities are computed using the original values. This is the default if STANDARDIZE is omitted.

Z *Standardize values to Z scores, with a mean of 0 and a standard deviation of 1.* PROXIMITIES subtracts the mean value for the variable or case from each value being standardized and then divides by the standard deviation. If the standard deviation is 0, PROXIMITIES sets all values for the case or variable to 0. This is the default if STANDARDIZE is used without specifications.

RANGE   *Standardize values to have a range of 1.* PROXIMITIES divides each value being standardized by the range of values for the variable or case. If the range is 0, PROXIMITIES leaves all values unchanged.

RESCALE   *Standardize values to have a range from 0 to 1.* From each value being standardized, PROXIMITIES subtracts the minimum value and then divides by the range for the variable or case. If a range is 0, PROXIMITIES sets all values for the case or variable to 0.50.

MAX   *Standardize values to a maximum magnitude of 1.* PROXIMITIES divides each value being standardized by the maximum value for the variable or case. If the maximum of the values is 0, PROXIMITIES divides each value by the absolute magnitude of the smallest value and adds 1.

MEAN   *Standardize values to a mean of 1.* PROXIMITIES divides each value being standardized by the mean of the values for the variable or case. If the mean is 0, PROXIMITIES adds 1 to all values for the case or variable to produce a mean of 1.

SD   *Standardize values to unit standard deviation.* PROXIMITIES divides each value being standardized by the standard deviation of the values for the variable or case. PROXIMITIES does not change the values if their standard deviation is 0.

Example

```
PROXIMITIES A B C
   /STANDARDIZE=CASE RANGE.
```

- Within each case, values are standardized to have ranges of 1.

VIEW Subcommand

VIEW indicates whether proximities are computed between cases or between variables.

CASE   *Compute proximity values between cases.* This is the default.

VARIABLE   *Compute proximity values between variables.*

MEASURE Subcommand

MEASURE specifies the similarity, dissimilarity, or distance measure that PROXIMITIES computes. Three transformations are available with any of these measures:

ABSOLUTE   *Take the absolute values of the proximities.* Use ABSOLUTE when the sign of the values indicates the direction of the relationship (as with correlation coefficients) but only the magnitude of the relationship is of interest.

REVERSE   *Transform similarity values into dissimilarities, or vice versa.* Use this specification to reverse the ordering of the proximities by negating the values.

RESCALE   *Rescale the proximity values to a range of 0 to 1.* RESCALE standardizes the proximities by first subtracting the value of the smallest and then dividing by the range. You would not usually use RESCALE with measures that are already standardized on meaningful scales, as are correlations, cosines, and many binary coefficients.

PROXIMITIES can compute any one of a number of measures between items. You can choose among measures for interval data, frequency count data, or binary data. Available keywords for each of these types of measures are defined in the following sections.

- Only one measure can be specified. However, each measure can be specified with any of the transformations ABSOLUTE, REVERSE, or RESCALE. To apply a transformation to an existing matrix of proximity values without computing any measures, use keyword NONE (see p. 736).

- If more than one transformation is specified, PROXIMITIES does them in the order listed above: first ABSOLUTE, then REVERSE, and then RESCALE regardless of the order they are specified.

- Each entry in the resulting proximity matrix represents a pair of items. The items can be either cases or variables, whichever is specified on the VIEW subcommand.

- When the items are cases, the computation for each pair of cases involves pairs of values for the specified variables.

- When the items are variables, the computation for each pair of variables involves pairs of values for the variables across all cases.

Example

```
PROXIMITIES A B C
  /MEASURE=EUCLID REVERSE.
```

- MEASURE specifies a EUCLID measure and a REVERSE transformation.

Measures for Interval Data

To obtain proximities for interval data, use any one of the following keywords on MEASURE:

EUCLID   *Euclidean distance.* The distance between two items, x and y, is the square root of the sum of the squared differences between the values for the items. This is the default.

$$EUCLID(x, y) = \sqrt{\Sigma_i(x_i - y_i)^2}$$

SEUCLID   *Squared Euclidean distance.* The distance between two items is the sum of the squared differences between the values for the items.

$$SEUCLID(x, y) = \Sigma_i(x_i - y_i)^2$$

CORRELATION   *Correlation between vectors of values.* This is a pattern similarity measure.

$$\text{CORRELATION}(x, y) = \frac{\Sigma_i(Z_{xi}Z_{yi})}{N-1}$$

where Z_{xi} is the Z-score (standardized) value of x for the ith case or variable, and N is the number of cases or variables.

COSINE
Cosine of vectors of values. This is a pattern similarity measure.

$$\text{COSINE}(x, y) = \frac{\Sigma_i(x_iy_i)}{\sqrt{(\Sigma_i x_i^2)(\Sigma_i y_i^2)}}$$

CHEBYCHEV
Chebychev distance metric. The distance between two items is the maximum absolute difference between the values for the items.

$$\text{CHEBYCHEV}(x, y) = \max_i|x_i - y_i|$$

BLOCK
City-block or Manhattan distance. The distance between two items is the sum of the absolute differences between the values for the items.

$$\text{BLOCK}(x, y) = \Sigma_i|x_i - y_i|$$

MINKOWSKI(p)
Distance in an absolute Minkowski power metric. The distance between two items is the pth root of the sum of the absolute differences to the pth power between the values for the items. Appropriate selection of the integer parameter p yields Euclidean and many other distance metrics.

$$\text{MINKOWSKI}(x, y) = (\Sigma_i|x_i - y_i|^p)^{1/p}$$

POWER(p,r)
Distance in an absolute power metric. The distance between two items is the rth root of the sum of the absolute differences to the pth power between the values for the items. Appropriate selection of the integer parameters p and r yields Euclidean, squared Euclidean, Minkowski, city-block, and many other distance metrics.

$$\text{POWER}(x, y) = (\Sigma_i|x_i - y_i|^p)^{1/r}$$

Measures for Frequency Count Data

To obtain proximities for frequency count data, use either of the following keywords on MEASURE:

CHISQ
Based on the chi-square test of equality for two sets of frequencies. The magnitude of this dissimilarity measure depends on the total frequencies of the two cases or variables whose dissimilarity is computed. Expected values are from the model of independence of cases or variables x and y.

$$\mathrm{CHISQ}(x, y) = \sqrt{\frac{\Sigma_i (x_i - E(x_i))^2}{E(x_i)} + \frac{\Sigma_i (y_i - E(y_i))^2}{E(y_i)}}$$

PH2　　　　　　*Phi-square between sets of frequencies.* This is the CHISQ measure normalized by the square root of the combined frequency. Therefore, its value does not depend on the total frequencies of the two cases or variables whose dissimilarity is computed.

$$\mathrm{PH2}(x, y) = \sqrt{\frac{\dfrac{\Sigma_i (x_i - E(x_i))^2}{E(x_i)} + \dfrac{\Sigma_i (y_i - E(y_i))^2}{E(y_i)}}{N}}$$

Measures for Binary Data

Different binary measures emphasize different aspects of the relationship between sets of binary values. However, all the measures are specified in the same way. Each measure has two optional integer-valued parameters, p (present) and np (not present).

- If both parameters are specified, PROXIMITIES uses the value of the first as an indicator that a characteristic is present and the value of the second as an indicator that a characteristic is absent. PROXIMITIES skips all other values.

- If only the first parameter is specified, PROXIMITIES uses that value to indicate presence and all other values to indicate absence.

- If no parameters are specified, PROXIMITIES assumes that 1 indicates presence and 0 indicates absence.

Using the indicators for presence and absence within each item (case or variable), PROXIMITIES constructs a 2×2 contingency table for each pair of items in turn. It uses this table to compute a proximity measure for the pair.

	Item 2 characteristics	
	Present	**Absent**
Item 1 characteristics		
Present	a	b
Absent	c	d

PROXIMITIES computes all binary measures from the values of a, b, c, and d. These values are tallied across variables (when the items are cases) or cases (when the items are variables). For example, if variables V, W, X, Y, Z have values 0, 1, 1, 0, 1 for case 1 and values 0, 1, 1,

0, 0 for case 2 (where 1 indicates presence and 0 indicates absence), the contingency table is as follows:

	Case 2 characteristics	
	Present	**Absent**
Case 1 characteristics		
Present	2	1
Absent	0	2

The contingency table indicates that both cases are present for two variables (W and X), both cases are absent for two variables (V and Y), and case 1 is present and case 2 is absent for one variable (Z). There are no variables for which case 1 is absent and case 2 is present.

The available binary measures include matching coefficients, conditional probabilities, predictability measures, and others.

Matching Coefficients. Table 1 shows a classification scheme for PROXIMITIES matching coefficients. In this scheme, *matches* are joint presences (value a in the contingency table) or joint absences (value d). *Nonmatches* are equal in number to value b plus value c. Matches and nonmatches may be weighted equally or not. The three coefficients JACCARD, DICE, and SS2 are related monotonically, as are SM, SS1, and RT. All coefficients in Table 1 are similarity measures, and all except two (K1 and SS3) range from 0 to 1. K1 and SS3 have a minimum value of 0 and no upper limit.

Table 1   Binary matching coefficients in PROXIMITIES

	Joint absences excluded from numerator	Joint absences included in numerator
All matches included in denominator		
Equal weight for matches and nonmatches	RR	SM
Double weight for matches		SS1
Double weight for nonmatches		RT
Joint absences excluded from denominator		
Equal weight for matches and nonmatches	JACCARD	
Double weight for matches	DICE	

Table 1   Binary matching coefficients in PROXIMITIES (Continued)

	Joint absences excluded from numerator	Joint absences included in numerator
Double weight for nonmatches	SS2	
All matches excluded from denominator		
Equal weight for matches and nonmatches	K1	SS3

RR[(p[,np])]

Russell and Rao similarity measure. This is the binary dot product.

$$RR(x, y) = \frac{a}{a + b + c + d}$$

SM[(p[,np])]

Simple matching similarity measure. This is the ratio of the number of matches to the total number of characteristics.

$$SM(x, y) = \frac{a + d}{a + b + c + d}$$

JACCARD[(p[,np])]

Jaccard similarity measure. This is also known as the *similarity ratio*.

$$JACCARD(x, y) = \frac{a}{a + b + c}$$

DICE[(p[,np])]

Dice (or Czekanowski or Sorenson) similarity measure.

$$DICE(x, y) = \frac{2a}{2a + b + c}$$

SS1[(p[,np])]

Sokal and Sneath similarity measure 1.

$$SS1(x, y) = \frac{2(a + d)}{2(a + d) + b + c}$$

RT[(p[,np])]

Rogers and Tanimoto similarity measure.

$$RT(x, y) = \frac{a + d}{a + d + 2(b + c)}$$

SS2[(p[,np])]

Sokal and Sneath similarity measure 2.

$$SS2(x, y) = \frac{a}{a + 2(b + c)}$$

K1[(p[,np])]

Kulczynski similarity measure 1. This measure has a minimum value of 0 and no upper limit. It is undefined when there are no nonmatches

($b=0$ and $c=0$). PROXIMITIES assigns an artificial upper limit of 10,000 to K1 when it is undefined or exceeds this value.

$$K1(x, y) = \frac{a}{b + c}$$

SS3[(p[,np])]   *Sokal and Sneath similarity measure 3.* This measure has a minimum value of 0 and no upper limit. It is undefined when there are no non-matches ($b=0$ and $c=0$). PROXIMITIES assigns an artificial upper limit of 10,000 to SS3 when it is undefined or exceeds this value.

$$SS3(x, y) = \frac{a + d}{b + c}$$

Conditional Probabilities. The following binary measures yield values that can be interpreted in terms of conditional probability. All three are similarity measures.

K2[(p[,np])]   *Kulczynski similarity measure 2.* This yields the average conditional probability that a characteristic is present in one item given that the characteristic is present in the other item. The measure is an average over both items acting as predictors. It has a range of 0 to 1.

$$K2(x, y) = \frac{a/(a + b) + a/(a + c)}{2}$$

SS4[(p[,np])]   *Sokal and Sneath similarity measure 4.* This yields the conditional probability that a characteristic of one item is in the same state (presence or absence) as the characteristic of the other item. The measure is an average over both items acting as predictors. It has a range of 0 to 1.

$$SS4(x, y) = \frac{a/(a + b) + a/(a + c) + d/(b + d) + d/(c + d)}{4}$$

HAMANN[(p[,np])]   *Hamann similarity measure.* This measure gives the probability that a characteristic has the same state in both items (present in both or absent from both) minus the probability that a characteristic has different states in the two items (present in one and absent from the other). HAMANN has a range of -1 to $+1$ and is monotonically related to SM, SS1, and RT.

$$HAMANN(x, y) = \frac{(a + d) - (b + c)}{a + b + c + d}$$

Predictability Measures. The following four binary measures assess the association between items as the predictability of one given the other. All four measures yield similarities.

LAMBDA[(p[,np])]   *Goodman and Kruskal's lambda (similarity).* This coefficient assesses the predictability of the state of a characteristic on one item (present or absent) given the state on the other item. Specifically, LAMBDA measures the proportional reduction in error using one item to predict the other when the directions of prediction are of equal importance. LAMBDA has a range of 0 to 1.

$$\text{LAMBDA}(x, y) = \frac{t_1 - t_2}{2(a + b + c + d) - t_2}$$

where

$t_1 = \max(a,b) + \max(c,d) + \max(a,c) + \max(b,d)$
$t_2 = \max(a + c, b + d) + \max(a + d, c + d).$

D[(p[,np])]   *Anderberg's D (similarity).* This coefficient assesses the predictability of the state of a characteristic on one item (present or absent) given the state on the other. D measures the actual reduction in the error probability when one item is used to predict the other. The range of D is 0 to 1.

$$D(x, y) = \frac{t_1 - t_2}{2(a + b + c + d)}$$

where

$t_1 = \max(a,b) + \max(c,d) + \max(a,c) + \max(b,d)$
$t_2 = \max(a + c, b + d) + \max(a + d, c + d)$

Y[(p[,np])]   *Yule's Y coefficient of colligation (similarity).* This is a function of the cross ratio for a 2×2 table. It has a range of -1 to $+1$.

$$Y(x, y) = \frac{\sqrt{ad} - \sqrt{bc}}{\sqrt{ad} + \sqrt{bc}}$$

Q[(p[,np])]   *Yule's Q (similarity).* This is the 2×2 version of Goodman and Kruskal's ordinal measure *gamma.* Like Yule's Y, Q is a function of the cross ratio for a 2×2 table and has a range of -1 to $+1$.

$$Q(x, y) = \frac{ad - bc}{ad + bc}$$

Other Binary Measures. The remaining binary measures available in PROXIMITIES are either binary equivalents of association measures for continuous variables or measures of special properties of the relationship between items.

OCHIAI[(p[,np])]   *Ochiai similarity measure.* This is the binary form of the cosine. It has a range of 0 to 1.

$$\text{OCHIAI}(x, y) = \sqrt{\frac{a}{a + b} \cdot \frac{a}{a + c}}$$

SS5[(p[,np])]   *Sokal and Sneath similarity measure 5.* The range is 0 to 1.

$$SS5(x, y) = \frac{ad}{\sqrt{(a + b)(a + c)(b + d)(c + d)}}$$

PHI[(p[,np])]

Fourfold point correlation (similarity). This is the binary form of the Pearson product-moment correlation coefficient.

$$PHI(x, y) = \frac{ad - bc}{\sqrt{(a + b)(a + c)(b + d)(c + d)}}$$

BEUCLID[(p[,np])]

Binary Euclidean distance. This is a distance measure. Its minimum value is 0, and it has no upper limit.

$$BEUCLID(x, y) = \sqrt{b + c}$$

BSEUCLID[(p[,np])]

Binary squared Euclidean distance. This is a distance measure. Its minimum value is 0, and it has no upper limit.

$$BSEUCLID(x, y) = b + c$$

SIZE[(p[,np])]

Size difference. This is a dissimilarity measure with a minimum value of 0 and no upper limit.

$$SIZE(x, y) = \frac{(b - c)^2}{(a + b + c + d)^2}$$

PATTERN[(p[,np])]

Pattern difference. This is a dissimilarity measure. The range is 0 to 1.

$$PATTERN(x, y) = \frac{bc}{(a + b + c + d)^2}$$

BSHAPE[(p[,np])]

Binary shape difference. This dissimilarity measure has no upper or lower limit.

$$BSHAPE(x, y) = \frac{(a + b + c + d)(b + c) - (b - c)^2}{(a + b + c + d)^2}$$

DISPER[(p[,np])]

Dispersion similarity measure. The range is −1 to +1.

$$DISPER(x, y) = \frac{ad - bc}{(a + b + c + d)^2}$$

VARIANCE[(p[,np])]

Variance dissimilarity measure. This measure has a minimum value of 0 and no upper limit.

$$VARIANCE(x, y) = \frac{b + c}{4(a + b + c + d)}$$

BLWMN[(p[,np])]   *Binary Lance-and-Williams nonmetric dissimilarity measure.* This measure is also known as the Bray-Curtis nonmetric coefficient. The range is 0 to 1.

$$\text{BLWMN}(x, y) = \frac{b + c}{2a + b + c}$$

Example

```
PROXIMITIES A B C
  /MEASURE=RR(1,2).
```

• MEASURE computes Russell and Rao coefficients from data in which 1 indicates the presence of a characteristic and 2 indicates the absence. Other values are ignored.

Example

```
PROXIMITIES A B C
  /MEASURE=SM(2).
```

• MEASURE computes simple matching coefficients from data in which 2 indicates presence and all other values indicate absence.

Transforming Measures in Proximity Matrix

Use keyword NONE to apply the ABSOLUTE, REVERSE, and/or RESCALE transformations to an existing matrix of proximity values without computing any proximity measures.

NONE   *Do not compute proximity measures.* Use NONE only if you have specified an existing proximity matrix on keyword IN on the MATRIX subcommand.

PRINT Subcommand

PROXIMITIES always prints the name of the measure it computes and the number of cases. Use PRINT to control printing of the proximity matrix.

PROXIMITIES   *Print the matrix of the proximities between items.* This is the default. The matrix may have been either read or computed. When the number of cases or variables is large, this specification produces a large volume of output and uses significant CPU time.

NONE   *Do not print the matrix of proximities.*

ID Subcommand

By default, PROXIMITIES identifies cases by case number alone. Use ID to specify an identifying string variable for cases.

• Any string variable in the working data file can be named as the identifier. PROXIMITIES uses the first eight characters of this variable to identify cases in the output.

MISSING Subcommand

MISSING controls the treatment of cases with missing values.

- By default, PROXIMITIES deletes cases with missing values listwise and excludes user-missing values from the analysis.

LISTWISE   *Delete cases with missing values listwise.* This is the default.

INCLUDE   *Include cases with user-missing values.* Only cases with system-missing values are deleted.

MATRIX Subcommand

MATRIX reads and writes matrix data files.

- Either IN or OUT and the matrix file in parentheses are required. When both IN and OUT are used on the same PROXIMITIES command, they can be specified on separate MATRIX subcommands or on the same subcommand.

OUT (filename)   *Write a matrix data file.* Specify either a filename or an asterisk (*), enclosed in parentheses. If you specify a filename, the file is stored on disk and can be retrieved at any time. If you specify an asterisk, the matrix data file replaces the working data file but is not stored on disk unless you use SAVE or XSAVE.

IN (filename)   *Read a matrix data file.* If the matrix data file is the working data file, specify an asterisk in parentheses. If the matrix data file is another file, specify the filename in parentheses. A matrix file read from an external file does not replace the working data file.

Matrix Output

- PROXIMITIES writes a variety of proximity matrices, each with *ROWTYPE_* values of PROX. PROXIMITIES neither reads nor writes additional statistics with its matrix materials. See "Format of the Matrix Data File" on p. 738 for a description of the file.
- The matrices PROXIMITIES writes can be used by PROXIMITIES or other procedures. Procedures CLUSTER and ALSCAL can read a proximity matrix directly. Procedure FACTOR can read a correlation matrix written by PROXIMITIES, but RECODE must first be used to change the *ROWTYPE_* value PROX to *ROWTYPE_* value CORR. Also, the ID subcommand cannot be used on PROXIMITIES if the matrix will be used in FACTOR. For more information, see "Universals" on p. 11.
- If VIEW=VARIABLE, the variables in the matrix file will have the names and labels of the original variables.
- If VIEW=CASE (the default), the variables in the matrix file will be named *VAR1, VAR2, ...VARn*, where *n* is the sequential number of the variable in the new file. The numeric suffix *n* is consecutive and does not necessarily match the number of the actual case. If there are no split files, the case number appears in the variable label in the form *CASE m*. The numeric suffix *m* is the actual case number and may not be consecutive (for example, if cases were selected before PROXIMITIES was executed).

- The new file preserves the names and values of any split-file variables in effect. When split-file processing is in effect, no labels are generated for variables in the new file. The actual case number is retained by the variable *ID*.
- Any documents contained in the working data file are not transferred to the matrix file.

Matrix Input

- PROXIMITIES can read a matrix file written by a previous PROXIMITIES procedure.
- The order among rows and variables in the input matrix file is unimportant as long as values for split-file variables precede values for *ROWTYPE_*.
- PROXIMITIES ignores unrecognized *ROWTYPE_* values. In addition, it ignores variables present in the matrix file that are not specified (or used by default) on the PROXIMITIES variable list.
- The program reads variable names, variable and value labels, and print and write formats from the dictionary of the matrix data file.
- MATRIX=IN cannot be used unless a working data file has already been defined. To read an existing matrix data file at the beginning of a session, first use GET to retrieve the matrix file and then specify IN(*) on MATRIX.
- When you read a matrix created with MATRIX DATA, you should supply a value label for PROX of either *SIMILARITY* or *DISSIMILARITY* so the matrix is correctly identified. If you do not supply a label, PROXIMITIES assumes *DISSIMILARITY*. (See "Format of the Matrix Data File" below.)
- The variable list on PROXIMITIES can be omitted when a matrix file is used as input. When the variable list is omitted, all variables in the matrix data file are used in the analysis. If a variable list is specified, the specified variables can be a subset of the variables in the matrix file.
- With a large number of variables, the matrix data file will wrap when it is displayed (as with LIST) and will be difficult to read. Nonetheless, the matrix values are accurate and can be used as matrix input.

Format of the Matrix Data File

- The matrix data file includes two special variables created by the program: *ROWTYPE_* and *VARNAME_*. Variable *ROWTYPE_* is a short string variable with value PROX (for proximity measure). PROX is assigned value labels containing the distance measure used to create the matrix and either *SIMILARITY* or *DISSIMILARITY* as an identifier. Variable *VARNAME_* is a short string variable whose values are the names of the new variables.
- The matrix file includes the string variable named on the ID subcommand. This variable is used to identify cases. Up to 20 characters can be displayed for the identifier variable; longer values are truncated. The identifier variable is present only when VIEW=CASE (the default) and when the ID subcommand is used.
- The remaining variables in the matrix file are the variables used to form the matrix.

Split Files

- When split-file processing is in effect, the first variables in the matrix system file are the split variables, followed by *ROWTYPE_*, the case-identifier variable (if VIEW=CASE and ID are used), *VARNAME_*, and the variables that make up the matrix.
- A full set of matrix materials is written for each split-file group defined by the split variables.
- A split variable cannot have the same name as any other variable written to the matrix data file.
- If split-file processing is in effect when a matrix is written, the same split file must be in effect when that matrix is read by any procedure.

Example

```
PROXIMITIES  V1 TO V20
  /MATRIX=OUT(DISTOUT).
```

- PROXIMITIES produces a default Euclidean distance matrix for cases using variables *V1* through *V20* and saves the matrix in the SPSS-format file *DISTOUT*.
- The names of the variables on the matrix file will be *VAR1, VAR2, ...VARn*.

Example

```
GET FILE=CRIME.
PROXIMITIES MURDER TO MOTOR
  /ID=CITY
  /MEASURE=EUCLID
  /MATRIX=OUT(PROXMTX).
```

- PROXIMITIES reads data from the SPSS-format data file *CRIME* and writes one set of matrix materials to file *PROXMTX*.
- The working data file is still *CRIME*. Subsequent commands are executed on this file.

Example

```
GET FILE=CRIME.
PROXIMITIES MURDER TO MOTOR
  /ID=CITY
  /MEASURE=EUCLID
  /MATRIX=OUT(*).
LIST.
```

- PROXIMITIES writes the same matrix as in the example above. However, the matrix data file replaces the working data file. The LIST command is executed on the matrix file, not on the *CRIME* file.

Example

```
GET FILE PRSNNL.
FREQUENCIES VARIABLE=AGE.

PROXIMITIES CASE1 TO CASE8
  /ID=CITY
  /MATRIX=IN(PROXMTX).
```

- This example performs a frequencies analysis on file *PRSNNL* and then uses a different file containing matrix data for PROXIMITIES.
- MATRIX=IN specifies the matrix data file *PROXMTX*. *PROXMTX* does not replace *PRSNNL* as the working data file.

Example

```
GET FILE PROXMTX.
PROXIMITIES CASE1 TO CASE8
  /ID=CITY
  /MATRIX=IN(*).
```

- This example assumes that you are starting a new session and want to read an existing matrix data file. GET retrieves the matrix file *PROXMTX*.
- MATRIX=IN specifies an asterisk because the matrix data file is the working data file. If MATRIX=IN(PROXMTX) is specified, the program issues an error message.
- If the GET command is omitted, the program issues an error message.

Example

```
GET FILE=CRIME.
PROXIMITIES MURDER TO MOTOR
  /ID=CITY
  /MATRIX=OUT(*).
PROXIMITIES
  /MATRIX=IN(*)
  /STANDARDIZE.
```

- GET retrieves the SPSS-format data file *CRIME*.
- The first PROXIMITIES command specifies variables for the analysis and reads data from file *CRIME*. ID specifies *CITY* as the case identifier. MATRIX writes the resulting matrix to the working data file.
- The second PROXIMITIES command uses the matrix file written by the first PROXIMITIES command as input. The asterisk indicates that the matrix file is the working data file. The variable list is omitted, indicating that all variables in the matrix are to be used.
- The slash preceding the MATRIX subcommand on the second PROXIMITIES is required. Without the slash, PROXIMITIES would attempt to interpret MATRIX as a variable name rather than as a subcommand.

Example

In this example, PROXIMITIES and FACTOR are used for a Q-factor analysis, in which factors account for variance shared among observations rather than among variables. Procedure

FACTOR does not perform *Q*-factor analysis without some preliminary transformation such as that provided by PROXIMITIES. Because the number of cases exceeds the number of variables, the model is not of full rank and FACTOR will print a warning. This is a common occurrence when case-by-case matrices from PROXIMITIES are used as input to FACTOR.

```
* Recoding a PROXIMITIES matrix for procedure FACTOR.

GET FILE=CRIME.
PROXIMITIES    MURDER TO MOTOR
  /MEASURE=CORR
  /MATRIX=OUT(TEMPFILE).
GET FILE=TEMPFILE/DROP=ID.
RECODE ROWTYPE_ ('PROX' = 'CORR').
FACTOR MATRIX IN(COR=*).
```

- The MATRIX subcommand on PROXIMITIES writes the correlation matrix to the working data file. Because the matrix materials will be used in procedure FACTOR, the ID subcommand is not specified.

- RECODE recodes *ROWTYPE_* values PROX to CORR so procedure FACTOR can read the matrix.

- When FACTOR reads matrix materials, it reads all the variables in the file. The MATRIX subcommand on FACTOR indicates that the matrix is a correlation matrix and data are in the working data file.

QUICK CLUSTER

```
QUICK CLUSTER {varlist}
             {ALL     }

[/MISSING=[{LISTWISE**}] [INCLUDE]]
          {PAIRWISE  }
          {DEFAULT   }

[/FILE=file]

[/INITIAL=(value list)]

.[/CRITERIA=[CLUSTER({2**})][NOINITIAL][MXITER({10**})] [CONVERGE({0**})]]
                    {n  }                       {n  }              {n  }

[/METHOD=[{KMEANS[(NOUPDATE)]**}]
          {KMEANS(UPDATE)}      }
          {CLASSIFY             }

[/PRINT=[INITIAL**] [CLUSTER] [ID(varname)] [DISTANCE] [ANOVA] [NONE]]

[/OUTFILE=file]

[/SAVE=[CLUSTER[(varname)]] [DISTANCE[(varname)]]]
```

**Default if subcommand or keyword is omitted.

Example:

```
QUICK CLUSTER V1 TO V4
  /CRITERIA=CLUSTER(4)
  /SAVE=CLUSTER(GROUP) .
```

Overview

When the desired number of clusters is known, QUICK CLUSTER groups cases efficiently into clusters. It is not as flexible as CLUSTER, but it uses considerably less processing time and memory, especially when the number of cases is large.

Options

Algorithm Specifications. You can specify the number of clusters to form with the CRITERIA subcommand. You can also use CRITERIA to control initial cluster selection and the criteria for iterating the clustering algorithm. With the METHOD subcommand, you can specify how to update cluster centers, and you can request classification only when working with very large data files (see "Operations" on p. 743).

Initial Cluster Centers. By default, QUICK CLUSTER chooses the initial cluster centers. Alternatively, you can provide initial centers on the INITIAL subcommand. You can also read initial cluster centers from an SPSS-format data file using the FILE subcommand.

Optional Output. With the PRINT subcommand you can display the cluster membership of each case and the distance of each case from its cluster center. You can also display the distances between the final cluster centers and a univariate analysis of variance between clusters for each clustering variable.

Saving Results. You can write the final cluster centers to an SPSS-format data file using the OUTFILE subcommand. In addition, you can save the cluster membership of each case and the distance from each case to its classification cluster center as new variables in the working data file using the SAVE subcommand.

Basic Specification

The basic specification is a list of variables. By default, QUICK CLUSTER produces two clusters. The two cases that are farthest apart based on the values of the clustering variables are selected as initial cluster centers and the rest of the cases are assigned to the nearer center. The new cluster centers are calculated as the means of all cases in each cluster, and if neither the minimum change nor the maximum iteration criterion is met, all cases are assigned to the new cluster centers again. When one of the criteria is met, iteration stops, the final cluster centers are updated, and the distance of each case is computed.

Subcommand Order

- The variable list must be specified first.
- Subcommands can be named in any order.

Operations

The procedure generally involves four steps:
- First, initial cluster centers are selected, either by choosing one case for each cluster requested or by using the specified values.
- Second, each case is assigned to the nearest cluster center, and the mean of each cluster is calculated to obtain the new cluster centers.
- Third, the maximum change between the new cluster centers and the initial cluster centers is computed. If the maximum change is not less than the minimum change value and the maximum iteration number is not reached, the second step is repeated and the cluster centers are updated. The process stops when either the minimum change or maximum iteration criterion is met. The resulting clustering centers are used as classification centers in the last step.
- In the last step, all cases are assigned to the nearest classification center. The final cluster centers are updated and the distance for each case is computed.

When the number of cases is large, directly clustering all cases may be impractical. As an alternative, you can cluster a sample of cases and then use the cluster solution for the sample to classify the entire group. This can be done in two phases:
- The first phase obtains a cluster solution for the sample. This involves all four steps of the QUICK CLUSTER algorithm. OUTFILE then saves the final cluster centers to an SPSS-format data file.

- The second phase requires only one pass through the data. First, the FILE subcommand specifies the file containing the final cluster centers from the first analysis. These final cluster centers are used as the initial cluster centers for the second analysis. CLASSIFY is specified on the METHOD subcommand to skip the second and third steps of the clustering algorithm, and cases are classified using the initial cluster centers. When all cases are assigned, the cluster centers are updated and the distance of each case is computed. This phase can be repeated until final cluster centers are stable.

Example

```
QUICK CLUSTER V1 TO V4
  /CRITERIA=CLUSTERS(4)
  /SAVE=CLUSTER(GROUP).
```

- This example clusters cases based on their values for all variables between and including *V1* and *V4* in the working data file.
- Four clusters, rather than the default two, will be formed.
- Initial cluster centers are chosen by finding four widely spaced cases. This is the default.
- The cluster membership of each case is saved in variable *GROUP* in the working data file. *GROUP* has integer values from 1 to 4, indicating the cluster to which each case belongs.

Variable List

The variable list identifies the clustering variables.

- The variable list is required and must be the first specification on QUICK CLUSTER.
- You can use keyword ALL to refer to all user-defined variables in the working data file.
- QUICK CLUSTER uses squared Euclidean distances, which equally weight all clustering variables. If the variables are measured in units that are not comparable, the procedure will give more weight to variables with large variances. Therefore, you should standardize variables measured on different scales using procedure DESCRIPTIVES before performing QUICK CLUSTER.

CRITERIA Subcommand

CRITERIA specifies the number of clusters to form and controls options for the clustering algorithm. You can use any or all of the keywords below.

- The NOINITIAL option followed by the remaining steps of the default QUICK CLUSTER algorithm makes QUICK CLUSTER equivalent to MacQueen's n-means clustering method.

CLUSTER(n)   *Number of clusters.* QUICK CLUSTER assigns cases to n clusters. The default is 2.

NOINITIAL   *No initial cluster center selection.* By default, initial cluster centers are formed by choosing one case (with valid data for the clustering variables) for each cluster requested. The initial selection requires a pass through the data to ensure that the centers are well separated from one another. If NOINITIAL is specified, QUICK CLUSTER selects the first *n* cases without missing values as initial cluster centers.

MXITER(n)   *Maximum number of iterations for updating cluster centers.* The default is 10. Iteration stops when the maximum number of iterations has been reached. MXITER is ignored when METHOD=CLASSIFY.

CONVERGE(n)   *Convergence criterion controlling minimum change in cluster centers.* The default value for *n* is 0. The minimum change value equals the convergence value (*n*) times the minimum distance between initial centers. Iteration stops when the largest change of any cluster center is less than or equal to the minimum change value. CONVERGE is ignored when METHOD=CLASSIFY.

METHOD Subcommand

By default, QUICK CLUSTER recalculates cluster centers after assigning all the cases and repeats the process until one of the criteria is met. You can use the METHOD subcommand to recalculate cluster centers after each case is assigned or to suppress recalculation until after classification is complete. When METHOD=KMEANS is specified, QUICK CLUSTER displays the iteration history table.

KMEANS(NOUPDATE)   *Recalculate cluster centers after all cases are assigned for each iteration.* This is the default.

KMEANS(UPDATE)   *Recalculate a cluster center each time a case is assigned.* QUICK CLUSTER calculates the mean of cases currently in the cluster and uses this new cluster center in subsequent case assignment.

CLASSIFY   *Do not recalculate cluster centers.* QUICK CLUSTER uses the initial cluster centers for classification and computes the final cluster centers as the means of all the cases assigned to the same cluster. When CLASSIFY is specified, the CONVERGE or MXITER specifications on CRITERIA are ignored.

INITIAL Subcommand

INITIAL specifies the initial cluster centers. Initial cluster centers can also be read from an SPSS-format data file (see the FILE subcommand on p. 746).

- One value for each clustering variable must be included for each cluster requested. Values are specified in parentheses cluster by cluster.

Example

```
QUICK CLUSTER  A B C D
  /CRITERIA = CLUSTER(3)
  /INITIAL = (13 24  1  8
               7 12  5  9
              10 18 17 16).
```

- This example specifies four clustering variables and requests three clusters. Thus, twelve values are supplied on INITIAL.
- The initial center of the first cluster has a value of 13 for variable *A*, 24 for variable *B*, 1 for *C*, and 8 for *D*.

FILE Subcommand

Use FILE to obtain initial cluster centers from an SPSS-format data file.

- The only specification is the name of the file.

Example
```
QUICK CLUSTER  A B C D
  /FILE=INIT
  /CRITERIA = CLUSTER(3) .
```

- In this example, the initial cluster centers are read from file *INIT*. The file must contain cluster centers for the same four clustering variables specified (*A*, *B*, *C*, and *D*).

PRINT Subcommand

QUICK CLUSTER always displays in a Final Cluster Centers table listing the centers used to classify cases and the mean values of the cases in each cluster and a Number of Cases in Each Cluster table listing the number of weighted (if weighting is on) and unweighted cases in each cluster. Use PRINT to request other types of output.

- If PRINT is not specified or is specified without keywords, the default is INITIAL.

INITIAL   *Initial cluster centers.* When SPLIT FILES is in effect, the initial cluster center for each split file is displayed. This is the default.

CLUSTER   *Cluster membership.* Each case displays an identifying number or value, the number of the cluster to which it was assigned, and its distance from the center of that cluster. This output is extensive when the number of cases is large.

ID(varname)   *Case identification.* The value of the specified variable is used in addition to the case numbers to identify cases in output. Case numbers may not be sequential if cases have been selected.

DISTANCE   *Pairwise distances between all final cluster centers.* This output can consume a great deal of processing time when the number of clusters requested is large.

ANOVA   *Descriptive univariate F tests for the clustering variables.* Since cases are systematically assigned to clusters to maximize differences on the clustering variables, these tests are descriptive only and should not be used to test the null hypothesis that there are no differences between clusters. Statistics after clustering are also available through procedure DISCRIMINANT or GLM (GLM is available in the SPSS Advanced Models option).

NONE   *No additional output.* Only the default output is displayed. NONE overrides any other specifications on PRINT.

Example

```
QUICK CLUSTER A B C D E
  /CRITERIA=CLUSTERS(6)
  /PRINT=CLUSTER ID(CASEID) DISTANCE.
```

- Six clusters are formed on the basis of the five variables *A*, *B*, *C*, *D*, and *E*.
- For each case in the file, cluster membership and distance from cluster center are displayed. Cases are identified by the values of the variable *CASEID*.
- Distances between all cluster centers are printed.

OUTFILE Subcommand

OUTFILE saves the final cluster centers in an SPSS-format data file. You can later use these final cluster centers as initial cluster centers for a different sample of cases that use the same variables. You can also cluster the final cluster centers themselves to obtain clusters of clusters.

- The only specification is a filename for the file.
- The program displays the name of the saved file in the procedure information notes.

Example

```
QUICK CLUSTER A B C D
  /CRITERIA = CLUSTER(3)
  /OUTFILE = QC1.
```

- QUICK CLUSTER writes the final cluster centers to the file *QC1*.

SAVE Subcommand

Use SAVE to save results of cluster analysis as new variables in the working data file.

- You can specify a variable name in parentheses following either keyword. If no variable name is specified, QUICK CLUSTER forms unique variable names by appending an underscore and a sequential number to the rootname *QCL*. The number increments with each new variable saved.
- The program displays the new variables and a short description of each in the procedure information notes.

CLUSTER[(varname)]   *The cluster number of each case.* The value of the new variable is set to an integer from 1 to the number of clusters.

DISTANCE[(varname)]   *The distance of each case from its classification cluster center.*

Example

```
QUICK CLUSTER A B C D
  /CRITERIA=CLUSTERS(6)
  /SAVE=CLUSTER DISTANCE.
```

- Six clusters of cases are formed on the basis of the variables *A*, *B*, *C*, and *D*.
- A new variable *QCL_1* is created and set to an integer between 1 and 6 to indicate cluster membership for each case.
- Another new variable *QCL_2* is created and set to the Euclidean distance between a case and the center of the cluster to which it is assigned.

MISSING Subcommand

MISSING controls the treatment of cases with missing values.

- LISTWISE, PAIRWISE, and DEFAULT are alternatives. However, each can be used with INCLUDE.

LISTWISE   *Delete cases with missing values listwise.* A case with a missing value for any of the clustering variables is deleted from the analysis and will not be assigned to a cluster. This is the default.

PAIRWISE   *Assign each case to the nearest cluster on the basis of the clustering variables for which the case has nonmissing values.* Only cases with missing values for *all* clustering variables are deleted.

INCLUDE   *Treat user-missing values as valid.*

DEFAULT   *Same as LISTWISE.*

RANK

```
RANK [VARIABLES=] varlist [({A**})] [BY varlist]
                           {D  }

[/TIES={MEAN**   }]
       {LOW      }
       {HIGH     }
       {CONDENSE}

[/FRACTION={BLOM**}]
           {TUKEY }
           {VW    }
           {RANKIT}

[/PRINT={YES**}]
        {NO   }

[/MISSING={EXCLUDE**}]
          {INCLUDE  }
```

The following function subcommands can each be specified once:

```
[/RANK**] [/NTILES(k)] [/NORMAL] [/PERCENT]

[/RFRACTION] [/PROPORTION] [/N] [/SAVAGE]
```

The following keyword can be used with any function subcommand:

```
[INTO varname]
```

**Default if the subcommand is omitted.

Example:

```
RANK VARIABLES=SALARY JOBTIME.
```

Overview

RANK produces new variables containing ranks, normal scores, and Savage and related scores for numeric variables.

Options

Methods. You can rank variables in ascending or descending order by specifying A or D on the VARIABLES subcommand. You can compute different rank functions and also name the new variables using the function subcommands. You can specify the method for handling ties on the TIES subcommand, and you can specify how the proportion estimate is computed for the NORMAL and PROPORTIONAL functions on the FRACTION subcommand.

Format. You can suppress the display of the summary table that lists the ranked variables and their associated new variables in the working data file using the PRINT subcommand.

Basic Specification

The basic specification is VARIABLES and at least one variable from the working data file. By default, the ranking function is RANK. Direction is ascending, and ties are handled by assigning the mean rank to tied values. A summary table that lists the ranked variables and the new variables into which computed ranks have been stored is displayed.

Subcommand Order

- VARIABLES must be specified first.
- The remaining subcommands can be specified in any order.

Operations

- RANK does not change the way the working data file is sorted.
- If new variable names are not specified with the INTO keyword on the function subcommand, RANK creates default names. (See the INTO keyword on p. 752.)
- RANK automatically assigns variable labels to the new variables. The labels identify the source variables. For example, the label for a new variable with the default name *RSALARY* is *RANK of SALARY*.

Example

```
RANK VARIABLES=SALARY JOBTIME.
```

- RANK ranks *SALARY* and *JOBTIME* and creates two new variables in the working file, *RSALARY* and *RJOBTIME*, which contain the ranks.

VARIABLES Subcommand

VARIABLES specifies the variables to be ranked. Keyword VARIABLES can be omitted.

- VARIABLES is required and must be the first specification on RANK. The minimum specification is a single numeric variable. To rank more than one variable, specify a variable list.
- After the variable list you can specify the direction for ranking in parentheses. Specify A for ascending (smallest value gets smallest rank) or D for descending (largest value gets smallest rank). A is the default.
- To rank some variables in ascending order and others in descending order, use both A and D in the same variable list. A or D applies to all preceding variables in the list up to the previous A or D specification.
- To organize ranks into subgroups, specify keyword BY followed by the variable whose values determine the subgroups. The working data file does not have to be sorted by this variable.

- String variables cannot be specified. Use AUTORECODE to recode string variables for ranking.

Example

```
RANK VARIABLES=MURDERS ROBBERY (D).
```

- RANK ranks *MURDERS* and *ROBBERY* and creates two new variables in the working data file: *RMURDERS* and *RROBBERY*.
- D specifies descending order of rank. D applies to both *MURDERS* and *ROBBERY*.

Example

```
RANK VARIABLES=MURDERS (D) ROBBERY (A) BY ETHNIC.
```

- Ranks are computed within each group defined by *ETHNIC*. *MURDERS* is ranked in descending order and *ROBBERY* in ascending order within each group of *ETHNIC*. The working data file does not have to be sorted by *ETHNIC*.

Function Subcommands

The optional function subcommands specify different rank functions. RANK is the default function.

- Any combination of function subcommands can be specified for a RANK procedure, but each function can be specified only once.
- Each function subcommand must be preceded by a slash.
- The functions assign default names to the new variables unless keyword INTO is specified (see the INTO keyword on p. 752).

RANK	*Simple ranks.* The values for the new variable are the ranks. Rank can either be ascending or descending, as indicated on the VARIABLES subcommand. Rank values can be affected by the specification on the TIES subcommand.
RFRACTION	*Fractional ranks.* The values for the new variable equal the ranks divided by the sum of the weights of the nonmissing cases. If HIGH is specified on TIES, fractional rank values are an empirical cumulative distribution.
NORMAL	*Normal scores* (Lehmann, 1975). The new variable contains the inverse of the standard normal cumulative distribution of the proportion estimate defined by the FRACTION subcommand. The default for FRACTION is BLOM.
PERCENT	*Fractional ranks as a percentage.* The new variable contains fractional ranks multiplied by 100.
PROPORTION	*Proportion estimates.* The estimation method is specified by the FRACTION subcommand. The default for FRACTION is BLOM.
N	*Sum of case weights.* The new variable is a constant.
SAVAGE	*Savage scores* (Lehmann, 1975). The new variable contains Savage (exponential) scores.

NTILES(k)   *Percentile groups.* The new variable contains values from 1 to k, where k is the number of groups to be generated. Each case is assigned a group value, which is the integer part of $1+rk/(w+1)$, where r is the rank of the case, k is the number of groups specified on NTILES, and w is the sum of the case weights. Group values can be affected by the specification on TIES. There is no default for k.

INTO Keyword

INTO specifies variable names for the new variable(s) added to the working data file. INTO can be used with any of the function subcommands.

- INTO must follow a function subcommand. You must specify the INTO subcommand to assign names to the new variables created by the function.

- You can specify multiple variable names on INTO. The names are assigned to the new variables in the order they are created (the order the variables are specified on the VARIABLES subcommand).

- If you specify fewer names than the new variables, default names are used for the remaining new variables. If you specify more names, the program issues a message and the command is not executed.

If INTO is not specified on a function, RANK creates default names for the new variables according to the following rules:

- The first letter of the ranking function is added to the first seven characters of the original variable name.

- New variable names cannot duplicate variable names in the working data file or names specified after INTO or generated by default.

- If a new default name is a duplicate, the scheme *XXXnnn* is used, where *XXX* represents the first three characters of the function and *nnn* is a three-digit number starting with 001 and increased by 1 for each variable. (If the ranking function is N, *XXX* is simply *N*.) If this naming scheme generates duplicate names, the duplicates are named *RNKXXnn*, where *XX* is the first two characters of the function and *nn* is a two-digit number starting with 01 and increased by 1 for each variable.

- If it is not possible to generate unique names, an error results.

Example

```
RANK VARIABLES=SALARY
 /NORMAL INTO SALNORM
 /SAVAGE INTO SALSAV
 /NTILES(4) INTO SALQUART.
```

- RANK generates three new variables from variable *SALARY*.

- NORMAL produces the new variable *SALNORM*. *SALNORM* contains normal scores for *SALARY* computed with the default formula BLOM.

- SAVAGE produces the new variable *SALSAV*. *SALSAV* contains Savage scores for *SALARY*.

- NTILES(4) produces the new variable *SALQUART*. *SALQUART* contains the value 1, 2, 3, or 4 to represent one of the four percentile groups of *SALARY*.

TIES Subcommand

TIES determines the way tied values are handled. The default method is MEAN.

MEAN   *Mean rank of tied values is used for ties.* This is the default.

LOW   *Lowest rank of tied values is used for ties.*

HIGH   *Highest rank of tied values is used for ties.*

CONDENSE   *Consecutive ranks with ties sharing the same value.* Each distinct value of the ranked variable is assigned a consecutive rank. Ties share the same rank.

Example

```
RANK VARIABLES=BURGLARY /RANK INTO RMEAN /TIES=MEAN.
RANK VARIABLES=BURGLARY /RANK INTO RCONDS /TIES=CONDENSE.
RANK VARIABLES=BURGLARY /RANK INTO RHIGH /TIES=HIGH.
RANK VARIABLES=BURGLARY /RANK INTO RLOW /TIES=LOW.
```

- The values of *BURGLARY* and the four new ranking variables are shown below:

BURGLARY	RMEAN	RCONDS	RHIGH	RLOW
0	3	1	5	1
0	3	1	5	1
0	3	1	5	1
0	3	1	5	1
0	3	1	5	1
1	6.5	2	7	6
1	6.5	2	7	6
3	8	3	8	8

FRACTION Subcommand

FRACTION specifies the way to compute a proportion estimate P for the NORMAL and PRO-PORTION rank functions.

- FRACTION can be used only with function subcommands NORMAL or PROPORTION. If it is used with other function subcommands, FRACTION is ignored and a warning message is displayed.

- Only one formula can be specified for each RANK procedure. If more than one is specified, an error results.

In the following formulas, r is the rank and w is the sum of case weights.

BLOM   *Blom's transformation, defined by the formula $(r - 3/8)/(w + 1/4)$.* (Blom, 1958.) This is the default.

RANKIT   *The formula is $(r - 1/2)/w$.* (Chambers et al., 1983.)

TUKEY   *Tukey's transformation, defined by the formula $(r - 1/3)/(w + 1/3)$.* (Tukey, 1962.)

VW   *Van der Waerden's transformation, defined by the formula $r/(w + 1)$.* (Lehmann, 1975.)

Example

```
RANK VARIABLES=MORTGAGE VALUE /FRACTION=BLOM
  /NORMAL INTO MORTNORM VALNORM.
```

- RANK generates new variables *MORTNORM* and *VALNORM*. *MORTNORM* contains normal scores for *MORTGAGE*, and *VALNORM* contains normal scores for *VALUE*.

PRINT Subcommand

PRINT determines whether the summary tables are displayed. The summary table lists the ranked variables and their associated new variables in the working data file.

YES   *Display the summary tables.* This is the default.

NO   *Suppress the summary tables.*

MISSING Subcommand

MISSING controls the treatment of user-missing values.

INCLUDE   *Include user-missing values.* User-missing values are treated as valid values.

EXCLUDE   *Exclude all missing values.* User-missing values are treated as missing. This is the default.

Example

```
MISSING VALUE SALARY (0).
RANK VARIABLES=SALARY /RANK INTO SALRANK /MISSING=INCLUDE.
```

- RANK generates the new variable *SALRANK*.
- INCLUDE causes the user-missing value 0 to be included in the ranking process.

References

Blom, G. 1958. *Statistical estimates and transformed beta variables.* New York: John Wiley and Sons.

Chambers, J. M., W. S. Cleveland, B. Kleiner, and P. A. Tukey. 1983. *Graphical methods for data analysis.* Belmont, California: Wadsworth International Group; Boston: Duxbury Press.

Fisher, R. A. 1973. *Statistical methods for research workers.* 14th ed. New York: Hafner Publishing Company.

Frigge, M., D. C. Hoaglin, and B. Iglewicz. 1987. Some implementations of the boxplot. In: *Computer Science and Statistics Proceedings of the 19th Symposium on the Interface*, R. M. Heiberger and M. Martin, eds. Alexandria, Virginia: American Statistical Association.

Lehmann, E. L. 1975. *Nonparametrics: Statistical methods based on ranks.* San Francisco: Holden-Day.

Tukey, J. W. 1962. The future of data analysis. *Annals of Mathematical Statistics*, 33:22.

RECODE

For numeric variables:

```
RECODE varlist (value list=value)...(value list=value) [INTO varlist]
       [/varlist...]
```

Input keywords:

LO, LOWEST, HI, HIGHEST, THRU, MISSING, SYSMIS, ELSE

Output keywords:

COPY, SYSMIS

For string variables:

```
RECODE varlist [('string',['string'...]='string')][INTO varlist]
       [/varlist...]
```

Input keywords:

CONVERT, ELSE

Output keyword:

COPY

Examples:

```
RECODE V1 TO V3 (0=1) (1=0) (2,3=-1) (9=9) (ELSE=SYSMIS).

RECODE STRNGVAR ('A','B','C'='A')('D','E','F'='B')(ELSE=' ').
```

Overview

RECODE changes, rearranges, or consolidates the values of an existing variable. RECODE can be executed on a value-by-value basis or for a range of values. Where it can be used, RECODE is much more efficient than the series of IF commands that produce the same transformation.

With RECODE, you must specify the new values. Use AUTORECODE to automatically recode the values of string or numeric variables to consecutive integers.

Options

You can generate a new variable as the recoded version of an existing variable using keyword INTO. You can also use INTO to recode a string variable into a new numeric variable for more efficient processing, or to recode a numeric variable into a new string variable to provide more descriptive values.

755

Basic Specification

The basic specification is a variable name and, within parentheses, the original values followed by a required equals sign and a new value. RECODE changes the values on the left of the equals sign into the single value on the right of the equals sign.

Syntax Rules

- The variables to be recoded must already exist and must be specified before the value specifications.
- Value specifications are enclosed in parentheses. The original value or values must be specified to the left of an equals sign. A single new value is specified to the right of the equals sign.
- Multiple values can be consolidated into a single recoded value by specifying, to the left of the equals sign, a list of values separated by blanks or commas. Only one recoded value per set is allowed to the right of the equals sign.
- Multiple sets of value specifications are permitted. Each set must be enclosed in parentheses and can result in only one new value.
- To recode multiple variables using the same set of value specifications, specify a variable list before the value specifications. Each variable in the list is recoded identically.
- To recode variables using different value specifications, separate each variable (or variable list) and its specifications from the others by a slash.
- Original values that are not mentioned remain unchanged unless keyword ELSE is used. ELSE refers to all original values not previously mentioned, including the system-missing value. ELSE should be the last specification for the variable.
- COPY replicates original values without recoding them.
- INTO is required to recode a string variable into a numeric variable or a numeric variable into a string variable (see the INTO keyword on p. 758).

Numeric Variables

- Keywords that can be used in the list of original values are LO (or LOWEST), HI (or HIGHEST), THRU, MISSING, SYSMIS, and ELSE. Keywords that can be used in place of a new value are COPY and SYSMIS.
- THRU specifies a value range and includes the specified end values.
- LOWEST and HIGHEST (LO and HI) specify the lowest and highest values encountered in the data. LOWEST and HIGHEST include user-missing values but not the system-missing value.
- MISSING specifies user-missing and system-missing values for recoding. MISSING can be used in the list of original values only.
- SYSMIS specifies the system-missing value and can be used as both an original value and a new value.
- See "Syntax Rules" above for a description of ELSE and COPY.

String Variables

- Keywords that can be used in the list of original values are CONVERT and ELSE. The only keyword that can be used in place of a new value is COPY. See p. 759 for a description of CONVERT, and "Syntax Rules" on p. 756 for a description of ELSE and COPY.
- Both short and long string variables can be recoded.
- Values must be enclosed in apostrophes or quotation marks.
- Blanks are significant characters.

Operations

- Value specifications are scanned left to right.
- A value is recoded only once per RECODE command.
- Invalid specifications on a RECODE command that result in errors stop all processing of that RECODE command. No variables are recoded.

Numeric Variables

- Blank fields for numeric variables are handled according to the SET BLANKS specification prior to recoding.
- When you recode a value that was previously defined as user-missing on the MISSING VALUE command, the new value is not missing.

String Variables

- If the original or new value specified is shorter than the format width defined for the variable, the string is right-padded with blanks.
- If the original or recoded value specified is longer than the format width defined for that variable, the program issues an error message and RECODE is not executed.

Limitations

- You can recode (and count using the COUNT command) approximately 400 values.

Example

```
RECODE V1 TO V3 (0=1) (1=0) (2,3=-1) (9=9) (ELSE=SYSMIS)
  /QVAR(1 THRU 5=1)(6 THRU 10=2)(11 THRU HI=3)(ELSE=0).
```

- The numeric variables between and including *V1* and *V3* are recoded: original values 0 and 1 are switched respectively to 1 and 0; 2 and 3 are changed to −1; 9 remains 9; and any other value is changed to the system-missing value.

- Variable *QVAR* is also recoded: original values 1 through 5 are changed to 1; 6 through 10 are changed to 2; 11 through the highest value in the data are changed to 3; and any other value, including system-missing, is changed to 0.

Example

```
RECODE STRNGVAR ('A','B','C'='A')('D','E','F'='B')(ELSE=' ').
RECODE PET ('IGUANA', 'SNAKE ' = 'WILD  ').
```

- Values A, B, and C are changed to value A. Values D, E, and F are changed to value B. All other values are changed to a blank.
- Values IGUANA and SNAKE are changed to value WILD. The defined width of variable *PET* is 6. Thus, values SNAKE and WILD include trailing blanks for a total of six characters. If blanks are not specified, the values are right-padded. In this example, the results will be the same.
- Each string value is enclosed within apostrophes.

INTO Keyword

INTO specifies a **target** variable to receive recoded values from the original, or **source**, variable. Source variables remain unchanged after the recode.

- INTO must follow the value specifications for the source variables that are being recoded into the target variables.
- The number of target variables must equal the number of source variables.

Numeric Variables

- Target variables can be existing or new variables. For existing variables, cases with values not mentioned in the value specifications are not changed. For new variables, cases with values not mentioned are assigned the system-missing value.
- New numeric variables have default print and write formats of F8.2 (or the format specified on SET FORMAT).

Example

```
RECODE AGE (MISSING=9) (18 THRU HI=1) (0 THRU 18=0) INTO VOTER.
```

- The recoded *AGE* values are stored in target variable *VOTER*, leaving *AGE* unchanged.
- Value 18 and higher values are changed to value 1. Values between 0 and 18, but not including 18, are recoded to 0. If the specification 0 THRU 18 preceded the specification 18 THRU HI, value 18 would be recoded to 0.

Example

```
RECODE V1 TO V3 (0=1) (1=0) (2=-1) INTO DEFENSE WELFARE HEALTH.
```

- Values for *V1* through *V3* are recoded and stored in *DEFENSE*, *WELFARE*, and *HEALTH*. *V1, V2,* and *V3* are not changed.

String Variables

- Target variables must already exist. To create a new string variable, declare the variable with the STRING command before specifying it on RECODE.
- The new string values cannot be longer than the defined width of the target variable.
- If the new values are shorter than the defined width of the target variable, the values are right-padded with blanks.
- Multiple target variables are allowed. The target variables must all be the same defined width; the source variables can have different widths.
- If the source and target variables have different widths, the criterion for the width of the original values is the width defined for the source variable; the criterion for the width of the recoded values is the width defined for the target variable.

Example

```
STRING STATE1 (A2).
RECODE STATE ('IO'='IA') (ELSE=COPY) INTO STATE1.
```

- STRING declares variable *STATE1* so that it can be used as a target variable on RECODE.
- RECODE specifies *STATE* as the source variable and *STATE1* as the target variable. The original value IO is recoded to IA. Keywords ELSE and COPY copy all other state codes over unchanged. Thus, *STATE* and *STATE1* are identical except for cases with the original value IO.

Example

```
RECODE SEX ('M'=1) ('F'=2) INTO NSEX.
```

- RECODE recodes string variable *SEX* into numeric variable *NSEX*. Any value other than M or F becomes system-missing.
- The program can process a large number of cases more efficiently with the numeric variable *NSEX* than it can with the string variable *SEX*.

CONVERT Keyword

CONVERT recodes the string representation of numbers to their numeric representation.

- If keyword CONVERT precedes the value specifications, cases with numbers are recoded immediately and blanks are recoded to the system-missing value, even if you specifically recode blanks into a value.
- To recode blanks to a value other than system-missing or to recode a string value to a non-corresponding numeric value (for example '0' to 10), you must specify a recode specification *before* the keyword CONVERT.
- RECODE converts numbers as if the variable were being reread using the F format.
- If RECODE encounters a value that cannot be converted, it scans the remaining value specifications. If there is no specific recode specification for that value, the target variable will be system-missing for that case.

Example

```
RECODE #JOB (CONVERT) ('-'=11) ('&'=12) INTO JOB.
```

- RECODE first recodes all numbers in string variable #JOB to numbers. The target variable is JOB.
- RECODE then specifically recodes the minus sign (the "eleven" punch) to 11 and the ampersand (or "twelve" punch in EBCDIC) to 12. Keyword CONVERT is specified first as an efficiency measure to recode cases with numbers immediately. Blanks are recoded to the system-missing value.

Example

```
RECODE #JOB (' '=-99) (CONVERT) ('-'=11) ('&'=12) INTO JOB.
```

- The result is the same as in the above example, except that blanks are changed to −99.

RECORD TYPE

For mixed file types:

```
RECORD TYPE {value list} [SKIP]
            {OTHER     }
```

For grouped file types:

```
RECORD TYPE {value list} [SKIP] [CASE=col loc]
            {OTHER     }

 [DUPLICATE={WARN  }] [MISSING={WARN  }]
           {NOWARN}           {NOWARN}
```

For nested file types:

```
RECORD TYPE {value list} [SKIP] [CASE=col loc]
            {OTHER     }

 [SPREAD={YES}] [MISSING={WARN  }]
         {NO }          {NOWARN}
```

Example:

```
FILE TYPE  MIXED RECORD=RECID 1-2.
RECORD TYPE 23.
DATA LIST   /SEX 5 AGE 6-7 DOSAGE 8-10 RESULT 12.
END FILE TYPE.

BEGIN DATA
21   145010 1
22   257200 2
25   235  250  2
35   167           300     3
24   125150 1
23   272075 1
21   149050 2
25   134  035  3
30   138           300     3
32   229           500     3
END DATA.
```

Overview

RECORD TYPE is used with DATA LIST within a FILE TYPE—END FILE TYPE structure to define any one of the three types of complex raw data files: **mixed files**, which contain several types of records that define different types of cases; **hierarchical** or **nested files**, which contain several types of records with a defined relationship among the record types; or **grouped files**, which contain several records for each case with some records missing or duplicated (see FILE TYPE for more complete information). A fourth type of complex file, files with **repeating groups** of information, can be read with the REPEATING DATA command. REPEATING DATA can also be used to read mixed files and the lowest level of nested files.

Each type of complex file has varying types of records. One set of RECORD TYPE and DATA LIST commands is used to define each type of record in the data. The specifications available for RECORD TYPE vary according to whether MIXED, GROUPED, or NESTED is specified on FILE TYPE.

Basic Specification

For each record type being defined, the basic specification is the value of the record type variable defined on the RECORD subcommand on FILE TYPE.

- RECORD TYPE must be followed by a DATA LIST command defining the variables for the specified records, unless SKIP is used.
- One pair of RECORD TYPE and DATA LIST commands must be used for each defined record type.

Syntax Rules

- A list of values can be specified if a set of different record types has the same variable definitions. Each value must be separated by a space or comma.
- String values must be enclosed in apostrophes or quotation marks.
- For mixed files, each DATA LIST can specify variables with the same variable name, since each record type defines a separate case. For grouped and nested files, the variable names on each DATA LIST must be unique, since a case is built by combining all record types together onto a single record.
- For mixed files, if the same variable is defined for more than one record type, the format type and width of the variable should be the same on all DATA LIST commands. The program refers to the first DATA LIST command that defines a variable for the print and write formats to include in the dictionary of the working data file.
- For nested files, the order of the RECORD TYPE commands defines the hierarchical structure of the file. The first RECORD TYPE defines the highest-level record type, the next RECORD TYPE defines the next highest-level record, and so forth. The last RECORD TYPE command defines a case in the working data file.

Operations

- If a record type is specified on more than one RECORD TYPE command, the program uses the DATA LIST command associated with the first specification and ignores all others.
- For NESTED files, the first record in the file should be the type specified on the first RECORD TYPE command—the highest-level record of the hierarchy. If the first record in the file is not the highest-level type, the program skips all records until it encounters a record of the highest-level type. If the MISSING or DUPLICATE subcommands have been specified on the FILE TYPE command, these records may produce warning messages but will not be used to build a case in the working data file.

Example

```
* Reading only one record type from a mixed file.

FILE TYPE  MIXED RECORD=RECID 1-2.
RECORD TYPE 23.
DATA LIST    /SEX 5 AGE 6-7 DOSAGE 8-10 RESULT 12.
END FILE TYPE.

BEGIN DATA
21  145010 1
22  257200 2
25  235  250  2
35  167         300   3
24  125150 1
23  272075 1
21  149050 2
25  134  035  3
30  138         300   3
32  229         500   3
END DATA.
```

- FILE TYPE begins the file definition, and END FILE TYPE indicates the end of file definition. FILE TYPE specifies a mixed file type. Since the data are included between BEGIN DATA—END DATA, the FILE subcommand is omitted. The record identification variable *RECID* is located in columns 1 and 2.

- RECORD TYPE indicates that records with value 23 for variable *RECID* will be copied into the working data file. All other records are skipped. The program does not issue a warning when it skips records in mixed files.

- DATA LIST defines variables on records with the value 23 for variable *RECID*.

Example

```
* Reading multiple record types from a mixed file.

FILE TYPE  MIXED FILE=TREATMNT RECORD=RECID 1-2.
+ RECORD TYPE 21,22,23,24.
+ DATA LIST    /SEX 5 AGE 6-7 DOSAGE 8-10 RESULT 12.
+ RECORD TYPE 25.
+ DATA LIST    /SEX 5 AGE 6-7 DOSAGE 10-12 RESULT 15.
END FILE TYPE.
```

- Variable *DOSAGE* is read from columns 8–10 for record types 21, 22, 23, and 24 and from columns 10–12 for record type 25. *RESULT* is read from column 12 for record types 21, 22, 23, and 24 and from column 15 for record type 25.

- The working data file contains values for all variables defined on the DATA LIST commands for record types 21 through 25. All other record types are skipped.

Example

```
* A nested file of accident records.

FILE TYPE NESTED RECORD=6 CASE=ACCID 1-4.
RECORD TYPE 1.
DATA LIST /ACC_ID 9-11 WEATHER 12-13 STATE 15-16 (A) DATE 18-24 (A).
RECORD TYPE 2.
DATA LIST /STYLE 11 MAKE 13 OLD 14 LICENSE 15-16(A) INSURNCE 18-21 (A).
RECORD TYPE 3.
DATA LIST /PSNGR_NO 11 AGE 13-14 SEX 16 (A) INJURY 18 SEAT 20-21 (A)
          COST 23-24.
END FILE TYPE.

BEGIN DATA
0001 1  322 1 IL 3/13/88   /* Type 1:  accident record
0001 2    1 44MI 134M      /* Type 2:    vehicle record
0001 3    1 34 M 1 FR   3  /* Type 3:      person record
0001 2    2 16IL 322F      /*             vehicle record
0001 3    1 22 F 1 FR 11   /*               person record
0001 3    2 35 M 1 FR   5  /*               person record
0001 3    3 59 M 1 BK   7  /*               person record
0001 2    3 21IN 146M      /*             vehicle record
0001 3    1 46 M 0 FR   0  /*               person record
END DATA.
```

- FILE TYPE specifies a nested file type. The record identifier, located in column 6, is not assigned a variable name, so the default scratch variable name *####RECD* is used. The case identification variable *ACCID* is located in columns 1–4.

- Because there are three record types, there are three RECORD TYPE commands. For each RECORD TYPE there is a DATA LIST command to define variables on that record type. The order of the RECORD TYPE commands defines the hierarchical structure of the file.

- END FILE TYPE signals the end of file definition.

- The program builds a case for each lowest-level (type 3) record, representing each person in the file. There can be only one type 1 record for each type 2 record, and one type 2 record for each type 3 record. Each vehicle can be in only one accident, and each person can be in only one vehicle. The variables from the type 1 and type 2 records are spread to their corresponding type 3 records.

OTHER Keyword

OTHER specifies all record types that have not been mentioned on previous RECORD TYPE commands.

- OTHER can be specified only on the last RECORD TYPE command in the file definition.

- OTHER can be used with SKIP to skip all undefined record types.

- For nested files, OTHER can be used only with SKIP. Neither can be used separately.

- If WILD=WARN is in effect for the FILE TYPE command, OTHER cannot be specified on the RECORD TYPE command.

Example

```
* A mixed file.

FILE TYPE  MIXED FILE=TREATMNT RECORD=RECID 1-2.
RECORD TYPE 21,22,23,24.
DATA LIST    /SEX 5 AGE 6-7 DOSAGE 8-10 RESULT 12.
RECORD TYPE 25.
DATA LIST    /SEX 5 AGE 6-7 DOSAGE 10-12 RESULT 15.
RECORD TYPE OTHER.
DATA LIST    /SEX 5 AGE 6-7 DOSAGE 18-20 RESULT 25.
END FILE TYPE.
```

- The first two RECORD TYPE commands specify record types 21–25. All other record types are specified by the third RECORD TYPE.

Example

```
* A nested file.

FILE TYPE NESTED FILE=ACCIDENT RECORD=#RECID 6 CASE=ACCID 1-4.
RECORD TYPE 1.       /* Accident record
DATA LIST    /WEATHER 12-13.
RECORD TYPE 2.       /* Vehicle record
DATA LIST /STYLE 16.
RECORD TYPE OTHER SKIP.
END FILE TYPE.
```

- The third RECORD TYPE specifies OTHER SKIP. Type 2 records are therefore the lowest-level records included in the working data file. These commands build one case for each vehicle record. The person records are skipped.
- Because the data are in a nested file, OTHER can be specified only with SKIP.

SKIP Subcommand

SKIP specifies record types to skip.

- To skip selected record types, specify the values for the types you want to skip and then specify SKIP. To skip all record types other than those specified on previous RECORD TYPE commands, specify OTHER and then SKIP.
- For nested files, SKIP can be used only with OTHER. Neither can be used separately.
- For grouped files, OTHER cannot be specified on SKIP if WILD=WARN (the default) is in effect for FILE TYPE.
- For mixed files, all record types that are not specified on a RECORD TYPE command are skipped by default. No warning is issued (WILD=NOWARN on FILE TYPE is the default for mixed files).
- For grouped files, a warning message is issued by default for all record types not specified on a RECORD TYPE command (WILD=WARN on FILE TYPE is the default for grouped files). If the record types are explicitly specified on SKIP, no warning is issued.

Example

```
FILE TYPE GROUPED FILE=HUBDATA RECORD=#RECID 80 CASE=ID 1-5
                              WILD=NOWARN.
RECORD TYPE 1.
DATA LIST    /MOHIRED YRHIRED 12-15 DEPT79 TO DEPT82 SEX 16-20.
RECORD TYPE OTHER SKIP.
END FILE TYPE.
```

- The program reads variables from type 1 records and skips all other types.
- WILD=NOWARN on the FILE TYPE command suppresses the warning messages that is issued by default for undefined record types for grouped files. Keyword OTHER cannot be used when the default WILD=WARN specification is in effect.

Example

```
FILE TYPE GROUPED FILE=HUBDATA RECORD=#RECID 80 CASE=ID 1-5.
RECORD TYPE 1.
DATA LIST    /MOHIRED YRHIRED 12-15 DEPT79 TO DEPT82 SEX 16-20.
RECORD TYPE 2,3 SKIP.
END FILE TYPE.
```

- Record type 1 is defined for each case, and record types 2 and 3 are skipped.
- WILD=WARN (the default) on FILE TYPE GROUPED is in effect. The program therefore issues a warning message for any record types it encounters other than types 1, 2, and 3. No warning is issued for record types 2 and 3 because they are explicitly specified on a RECORD TYPE command.

CASE Subcommand

CASE specifies the column locations of the case identification variable when that variable is not in the location defined by the CASE subcommand on FILE TYPE.

- CASE on RECORD TYPE applies only to those records specified by that RECORD TYPE command. The identifier for record types without CASE on RECORD TYPE must be in the location specified by CASE on FILE TYPE.
- CASE can be used for nested and grouped files only. CASE cannot be used for mixed files.
- CASE can be used on RECORD TYPE only if a CASE subcommand is specified on FILE TYPE.
- The format type of the case identification variable must be the same on all records, and the same format must be assigned on the RECORD TYPE and FILE TYPE commands. For example, if the case identification variable is defined as a string on FILE TYPE, it cannot be defined as a numeric variable on RECORD TYPE.

Example

```
* Specifying case on the record type command for a grouped file.

FILE TYPE GROUPED FILE=HUBDATA RECORD=#RECID 80 CASE=ID 1-5.
RECORD TYPE 1.
DATA LIST    /MOHIRED YRHIRED 12-15 DEPT79 TO DEPT82 SEX 16-20.
RECORD TYPE 2.
DATA LIST    /SALARY79 TO SALARY82 6-25
             HOURLY81 HOURLY82 40-53 (2)
             PROMO81 72   AGE 54-55 RAISE82 66-70.
RECORD TYPE 3  CASE=75-79.
DATA LIST    /JOBCAT 6 NAME 25-48 (A).
END FILE TYPE.
```

- CASE on FILE TYPE indicates that the case identification variable is located in columns 1–5. On the third RECORD TYPE command, the CASE subcommand overrides the identifier location for type 3 records. For type 3 records, the case identification variable is located in columns 75–79.

MISSING Subcommand

MISSING controls whether the program issues a warning when it encounters a missing record type for a case. Regardless of whether the program issues the warning, it builds the case in the working data file with system-missing values for the variables defined on the missing record.

- The only specification is a single keyword. NOWARN is the default for nested files. WARN is the default for grouped files. MISSING cannot be used with MIXED files.
- MISSING on RECORD TYPE applies only to those records specified by that RECORD TYPE command. The treatment of missing records for record types without the MISSING specification on RECORD TYPE is determined by the MISSING subcommand on FILE TYPE.
- For grouped files, the program checks whether there is a record for each case identification number. For nested files, the program verifies that each defined case includes one record of each type.

WARN *Issue a warning message when a record type is missing for a case.* This is the default for grouped files.

NOWARN *Suppress the warning message when a record type is missing for a case.* This is the default for nested files.

Example

```
FILE TYPE GROUPED FILE=HUBDATA RECORD=#RECID 80 CASE=ID 1-5.
RECORD TYPE 1.
DATA LIST    /MOHIRED YRHIRED 12-15 DEPT79 TO DEPT82 SEX 16-20.
RECORD TYPE 2  MISSING=NOWARN.
DATA LIST    /SALARY79 TO SALARY82 6-25
  HOURLY81 HOURLY82 40-53 (2) PROMO81 72 AGE 54-55 RAISE82 66-70.
RECORD TYPE 3.
DATA LIST    /JOBCAT 6 NAME 25-48 (A).
END FILE TYPE.
```

- MISSING is not specified on FILE TYPE. Therefore the default MISSING=WARN is in effect for all record types.
- MISSING=NOWARN is specified on the second RECORD TYPE, overriding the default setting for type 2 records. WARN is still in effect for type 1 and type 3 records.

DUPLICATE Subcommand

DUPLICATE controls whether the program issues a warning when it encounters more than one record of each type for a single case.

- DUPLICATE on RECORD TYPE can be used for grouped files only. DUPLICATE cannot be used for mixed or nested files.
- The only specification is a single keyword. WARN is the default.
- DUPLICATE on RECORD TYPE applies only to those records specified by that RECORD TYPE command. The treatment of duplicate records for record types without DUPLICATE specification is determined by the DUPLICATE subcommand on FILE TYPE.
- Regardless of the specification on DUPLICATE, only the last record from a set of duplicates is included in the working data file.

WARN   *Issue a warning message.* The program issues a message and the first 80 characters of the last record of the duplicate set of record types. This is the default.

NOWARN   *Suppress the warning message.*

Example

```
* Specifying DUPLICATE on RECORD TYPE for a grouped file.

FILE TYPE GROUPED FILE=HUBDATA RECORD=#RECID 80 CASE=ID 1-5.
RECORD TYPE 1.
DATA LIST   /MOHIRED YRHIRED 12-15 DEPT79 TO DEPT82 SEX 16-20.
RECORD TYPE 2  DUPLICATE=NOWARN.
DATA LIST   /SALARY79 TO SALARY82 6-25
  HOURLY81 HOURLY82 40-53 (2) PROMO81 72  AGE 54-55 RAISE82 66-70.
RECORD TYPE 3.
DATA LIST   /JOBCAT 6 NAME 25-48 (A).
END FILE TYPE.
```

- DUPLICATE is not specified on FILE TYPE. Therefore the default DUPLICATE=WARN is in effect for all record types.
- DUPLICATE=NOWARN is specified on the second RECORD TYPE, overriding the FILE TYPE setting for type 2 records. WARN is still in effect for type 1 and type 3 records.

SPREAD Subcommand

SPREAD controls whether the values for variables defined for a record type are spread to all related cases.

- SPREAD can be used for nested files only. SPREAD cannot be used for mixed or grouped files.

- The only specification is a single keyword. YES is the default.

- SPREAD=NO applies only to the record type specified on that RECORD TYPE command. The default YES is in effect for all other defined record types.

YES   *Spread the values from the specified record type to all related cases.* This is the default.

NO   *Spread the values from the specified type only to the first related case.* All other cases built from the same record are assigned the system-missing value for the variables defined on the record type.

Example

```
* A nested file.

FILE TYPE NESTED RECORD=#RECID 6 CASE=ACCID 1-4.
RECORD TYPE 1.
DATA LIST    /ACC_NO 9-11 WEATHER 12-13
                STATE 15-16 (A) DATE 18-24 (A).
RECORD TYPE 2   SPREAD=NO.
DATA LIST /STYLE 11 MAKE 13 OLD 14
             LICENSE 15-16 (A) INSURNCE 18-21 (A).
RECORD TYPE 3.
DATA LIST /PSNGR_NO 11 AGE 13-14 SEX 16 (A)
          INJURY 18 SEAT 20-21 (A) COST 23-24.
END FILE TYPE.

BEGIN DATA
0001 1   322 1 IL 3/13/88    /* Type 1:   accident record
0001 2     1 44MI 134M       /* Type 2:    vehicle record
0001 3     1 34 M 1 FR   3   /* Type 3:      person record
0001 2     2 16IL 322F       /*             vehicle record
0001 3     1 22 F 1 FR 11    /*               person record
0001 3     2 35 M 1 FR   5   /*               person record
0001 3     3 59 M 1 BK   7   /*               person record
0001 2     3 21IN 146M       /*             vehicle record
0001 3     1 46 M 0 FR   0   /*               person record
END DATA.
```

- The accident record (type 1) is spread to all related cases (in this example, all cases).

- The first vehicle record has one related person record. The values for *STYLE, MAKE, OLD, LICENSE,* and *INSURNCE* are spread to the case built for the person record.

- The second vehicle record has three related person records. The values for *STYLE, MAKE, OLD, LICENSE,* and *INSURNCE* are spread only to the case built from the first person record. The other two cases have the system-missing values for *STYLE, MAKE, OLD, LICENSE,* and *INSURNCE*.

- The third vehicle record has one related person record, and the values for type 2 records are spread to that case.

REFORMAT

```
REFORMAT  {ALPHA  } = varlist [/...]
          {NUMERIC}
```

Example:

```
REFORMAT ALPHA=STATE /NUMERIC=HOUR1 TO HOUR6.
```

Overview

REFORMAT converts variables from BMDP files to variables for SPSS-format data files. It also converts very old versions of SPSS-format data files to current SPSS-format data files. REFORMAT can change the print formats, write formats, and missing-value specifications for variables from alphanumeric to numeric, or from numeric to alphanumeric.

Basic Specification

The basic specification is ALPHA and a list of variables or NUMERIC and a list of variables.

- The ALPHA subcommand declares variables as string variables. The NUMERIC subcommand declares variables as numeric variables.
- If both ALPHA and NUMERIC are specified, they must be separated by a slash.

Operations

- REFORMAT always assigns the print and write format F8.2 (or the format specified on the SET command) to variables specified after NUMERIC and format A4 to variables specified after ALPHA.
- Formats cannot be specified on REFORMAT. To define different formats for numeric variables, use the PRINT FORMATS, WRITE FORMATS, or FORMATS commands. To declare new format widths for string variables, use the STRING and COMPUTE commands to perform data transformations.
- Missing-value specifications for variables named with both ALPHA and NUMERIC are also changed to conform to the new formats.
- The SAVE or XSAVE commands can be used to save the reformatted variables in an SPSS-format data file. This avoids having to reformat the variables each time the SPSS-format or BMDP data set is used.

Example

```
* Convert an old SPSS-format file to a new SPSS-format data file.

GET FILE R9FILE.
REFORMAT ALPHA=STATE /NUMERIC=HOUR1 TO HOUR6.
STRING XSTATE (A2) /NAME1 TO NAME6 (A15).
COMPUTE XSTATE=STATE.
FORMATS HOUR1 TO HOUR6 (F2.0).
SAVE OUTFILE=NEWFILE /DROP=STATE
    /RENAME=(XSTATE=STATE).
```

- GET accesses the old SPSS-format data file.

- REFORMAT converts variable STATE to a string variable with an A4 format and variables *HOUR1* to *HOUR6* to numeric variables with F8.2 formats.

- STRING declares *XSTATE* as a string variable with two positions.

- COMPUTE transfers the information from the variable *STATE* to the new string variable *XSTATE*.

- FORMATS changes the F8.2 formats for *HOUR1* to *HOUR6* to F2.0 formats.

- SAVE saves a new SPSS-format data file. The DROP subcommand drops the old variable *STATE*. RENAME renames the new string variable *XSTATE* to the original variable name *STATE*.

REGRESSION

```
REGRESSION [MATRIX=[IN({file})]   [OUT({file})]]
                      {*   }            {*   }

[/VARIABLES={varlist     }]
            {(COLLECT)**}
            {ALL         }

[/DESCRIPTIVES=[DEFAULTS] [MEAN] [STDDEV] [CORR] [COV]
               [VARIANCE] [XPROD] [SIG] [N] [BADCORR]
               [ALL] [NONE**]]

[/SELECT={varname relation value}

[/MISSING=[{LISTWISE**       }] [INCLUDE]]
           {PAIRWISE         }
           {MEANSUBSTITUTION }

[/REGWGT=varname]

[/STATISTICS=[DEFAULTS**] [R**] [COEFF**] [ANOVA**] [OUTS**]
             [ZPP] [LABEL] [CHA] [CI] [F] [BCOV] [SES]
             [XTX] [COLLIN] [TOL] [SELECTION] [ALL]]

[/CRITERIA=[DEFAULTS**] [TOLERANCE({0.0001**})] [MAXSTEPS(n)]
                                   {value   }

           [PIN[({0.05**})]] [POUT[({0.10**})]]
                {value }            {value }

           [FIN[({3.84 })]] [FOUT[({2.71 })]]
                {value }           {value}

           [CIN[({ 95**})]]]]
                {value}

[/{NOORIGIN**}]
  {ORIGIN   }

 /DEPENDENT=varlist

[/METHOD=]{STEPWISE [varlist]    } [...] [/...]
          {FORWARD [varlist]     }
          {BACKWARD [varlist]    }
          {ENTER [varlist]       }
          {REMOVE varlist        }
          {TEST(varlist)(varlist)...}

  [/OUTFILE={COVB (filename)}]
            {CORB (filename)}
```

**Default if the subcommand is omitted.

Example:

```
REGRESSION VARIABLES=POP15,POP75,INCOME,GROWTH,SAVINGS
 /DEPENDENT=SAVINGS
 /METHOD=ENTER POP15,POP75,INCOME
 /METHOD=ENTER GROWTH.
```

Overview

REGRESSION calculates multiple regression equations and associated statistics and plots. REGRESSION also calculates collinearity diagnostics, predicted values, residuals, measures of fit and influence, and several statistics based on these measures (see the section on residuals beginning on p. 788).

Options

Input and Output Control Subcommands. DESCRIPTIVES requests descriptive statistics on the variables in the analysis. SELECT estimates the model based on a subset of cases. REGWGT specifies a weight variable for estimating weighted least-squares models. MISSING specifies the treatment of cases with missing values. MATRIX reads and writes matrix data files.

Equation-Control Subcommands. These optional subcommands control the calculation and display of statistics for each equation. STATISTICS controls the statistics displayed for the equation(s) and the independent variable(s), CRITERIA specifies the criteria used by the variable selection method, and ORIGIN specifies whether regression is through the origin.

Analysis of Residuals, Fit, and Influence. The optional subcommands that analyze and plot residuals and add new variables to the working data file containing predicted values, residuals, measures of fit and influence, or related information, are described starting on p. 788. These subcommands apply to the final equation.

Basic Specification

The basic specification is DEPENDENT, which initiates the equation(s) and defines at least one dependent variable, followed by METHOD, which specifies the method for selecting independent variables.

- By default, all variables named on DEPENDENT and METHOD are used in the analysis.
- The default display for each equation includes a Model Summary table showing R^2, an ANOVA table, a Coefficients table displaying related statistics for variables in the equation, and an Excluded Variables table displaying related statistics for variables not yet in the equation.
- By default, all cases in the working data file with valid values for all selected variables are used to compute the correlation matrix on which the regression equations are based. The default equations include a constant (intercept).

Subcommand Order

The standard subcommand order for REGRESSION is

```
REGRESSION MATRIX=...
    /VARIABLES=...
    /DESCRIPTIVES=...
    /SELECT=...
    /MISSING=...
    /REGWGT=...
```

```
┌─────────────────────────────────────────────────────────────────────┐
│                          Equation Block                              │
│  /STATISTICS=...                                                     │
│  /CRITERIA=...                                                       │
│  /ORIGIN                                                             │
│  /DEPENDENT=...                                                      │
│  ┌─────────────────────────────────────────────────────────────┐   │
│  │                     Method Block(s)                          │   │
│  │  /METHOD=...                                                 │   │
│  │  [/METHOD...]...                                            │   │
│  └─────────────────────────────────────────────────────────────┘   │
│  /RESIDUALS=...                                                     │
│  /SAVE=...                                                          │
│  /CASEWISE=...                                                      │
│  /SCATTERPLOT=...                                                   │
│  /PARTIALPLOT=...                                                   │
│  /OUTFILE = ...                                                     │
└─────────────────────────────────────────────────────────────────────┘
```

- Only one equation block is allowed per REGRESSION command.

- Subcommands listed outside the equation block must be specified before any subcommands within the block.

- When used, MATRIX must be specified first.

- An equation block can contain multiple METHOD subcommands. These methods are applied, one after the other, to the estimation of the equation for that block.

- The STATISTICS, CRITERIA, and ORIGIN/NOORIGIN subcommands must precede the DEPENDENT subcommand.

- The RESIDUALS, CASEWISE, SCATTERPLOT, SAVE, PARTIALPLOT and OUTFILE subcommands must follow the last METHOD subcommand in an equation block and apply only to the final equation after all METHOD subcommands have been processed. These subcommands are discussed in the section on residuals beginning on p. 788.

Syntax Rules

- VARIABLES can be specified only once. If omitted, VARIABLES defaults to COLLECT.

- The DEPENDENT subcommand can be specified only once and must be followed immediately by one or more METHOD subcommands.
- CRITERIA, STATISTICS, and ORIGIN must be specified before DEPENDENT and METHOD. If any of these subcommands are specified more than once, only the last specified is in effect for all subsequent equations.
- More than one variable can be specified on the DEPENDENT subcommand. An equation is estimated for each.
- If no variables are specified on METHOD, all variables named on VARIABLES but not on DEPENDENT are considered for selection.

Operations

- REGRESSION calculates a correlation matrix that includes all variables named on VARIABLES. All equations requested on the REGRESSION command are calculated from the same correlation matrix.
- The MISSING, DESCRIPTIVES, and SELECT subcommands control the calculation of the correlation matrix and associated displays.
- If multiple METHOD subcommands are specified, they operate in sequence on the equations defined by the preceding DEPENDENT subcommand.
- Only independent variables that pass the tolerance criterion are candidates for entry into the equation (see the CRITERIA subcommand on p. 780).

Example

```
REGRESSION VARIABLES=POP15,POP75,INCOME,GROWTH,SAVINGS
 /DEPENDENT=SAVINGS
 /METHOD=ENTER POP15,POP75,INCOME
 /METHOD=ENTER GROWTH.
```

- VARIABLES calculates a correlation matrix of five variables for use by REGRESSION.
- DEPENDENT defines a single equation, with *SAVINGS* as the dependent variable.
- The first METHOD subcommand enters *POP15*, *POP75*, and *INCOME* into the equation.
- The second METHOD subcommand adds *GROWTH* to the equation containing *POP15* to *INCOME*.

VARIABLES Subcommand

VARIABLES names all the variables to be used in the analysis.

- The minimum specification is a list of two variables or the keyword ALL or COLLECT. COLLECT, which must be specified in parentheses, is the default.
- Only one VARIABLES subcommand is allowed and it must precede any DEPENDENT or METHOD subcommands.
- You can use keyword TO to refer to consecutive variables in the working data file.

- The order of variables in the correlation matrix constructed by REGRESSION is the same as their order on VARIABLES. If (COLLECT) is used, the order of variables in the correlation matrix is the order in which they are first listed on the DEPENDENT and METHOD subcommands.

ALL   *Include all user-defined variables in the working data file.*

(COLLECT)   *Include all variables named on the DEPENDENT and METHOD subcommands.* COLLECT is the default if the VARIABLES subcommand is omitted. COLLECT must be specified in parentheses. If COLLECT is used, the METHOD subcommands must specify variable lists.

Example

```
REGRESSION VARIABLES=(COLLECT)
 /DEPENDENT=SAVINGS
 /METHOD=STEP POP15 POP75 INCOME
 /METHOD=ENTER GROWTH.
```

- COLLECT requests that the correlation matrix include *SAVINGS, POP15, POP75, INCOME,* and *GROWTH.* Since COLLECT is the default, the VARIABLES subcommand could have been omitted.
- The DEPENDENT subcommand defines a single equation in which *SAVINGS* is the dependent variable.
- The first METHOD subcommand requests that the block of variables *POP15, POP75,* and *INCOME* be considered for inclusion using a stepwise procedure.
- The second METHOD subcommand adds variable *GROWTH* to the equation.

DEPENDENT Subcommand

DEPENDENT specifies a list of variables and requests that an equation be built for each. DEPENDENT is required.

- The minimum specification is a single variable. There is no default variable list.
- Only one DEPENDENT subcommand can be specified. It must be followed by at least one METHOD subcommand.
- Keyword TO on a DEPENDENT subcommand refers to the order in which variables are specified on the VARIABLES subcommand. If VARIABLES=(COLLECT), TO refers to the order of variables in the working data file.
- If DEPENDENT names more than one variable, an equation is built for each using the same independent variables and methods.

METHOD Subcommand

METHOD specifies a variable selection method and names a block of variables to be evaluated using that method. METHOD is required.

- The minimum specification is a method keyword and, for some methods, a list of variables. The actual keyword METHOD can be omitted.

- When more than one METHOD subcommand is specified, each METHOD subcommand is applied to the equation that resulted from the previous METHOD subcommands.
- The default variable list for methods FORWARD, BACKWARD, STEPWISE, and ENTER consists of all variables named on VARIABLES that are not named on the DEPENDENT subcommand. If VARIABLES=(COLLECT), the variables must be specified for these methods.
- There is no default variable list for the REMOVE and TEST methods.
- Keyword TO in a variable list on METHOD refers to the order in which variables are specified on the VARIABLES subcommand. If VARIABLES=(COLLECT), TO refers to the order of variables in the working data file.

The available stepwise methods are as follows:

BACKWARD [varlist]   *Backward elimination.* Variables in the block are considered for removal. At each step, the variable with the largest probability-of-*F* value is removed, provided that the value is larger than POUT (see the CRITERIA subcommand on p. 780). If no variables are in the equation when BACKWARD is specified, all independent variables in the block are first entered.

FORWARD [varlist]   *Forward entry.* Variables in the block are added to the equation one at a time. At each step, the variable not in the equation with the smallest probability of *F* is entered if the value is smaller than PIN (see the CRITERIA subcommand on p. 780).

STEPWISE [varlist]   *Stepwise selection.* If there are independent variables already in the equation, the variable with the largest probability of *F* is removed if the value is larger than POUT. The equation is recomputed without the variable and the process is repeated until no more independent variables can be removed. Then, the independent variable not in the equation with the smallest probability of *F* is entered if the value is smaller than PIN. All variables in the equation are again examined for removal. This process continues until no variables in the equation can be removed and no variables not in the equation are eligible for entry, or until the maximum number of steps has been reached (see the CRITERIA subcommand on p. 780).

The methods that enter or remove the entire variable block in a single step are as follows:

ENTER [varlist]   *Forced entry.* All variables specified are entered in a single step in order of decreasing tolerance. You can control the order in which variables are entered by specifying the variables on multiple METH-OD=ENTER subcommands.

REMOVE varlist   *Forced removal.* All variables specified are removed in a single step. REMOVE requires a variable list.

TEST (varlist) (varlist) R^2 *change and its significance for sets of independent variables.* This method first adds all variables specified on TEST to the current equation. It then removes in turn each subset from the equation and displays requested statistics. Specify test subsets in parentheses. A variable can be used in more than one subset, and each subset can include any number of variables. Variables named on TEST remain in the equation when the method is completed.

Example

```
REGRESSION VARIABLES=POP15 TO GROWTH, SAVINGS
 /DEPENDENT=SAVINGS
 /METHOD=STEPWISE
 /METHOD=ENTER.
```

- STEPWISE applies the stepwise procedure to variables *POP15* to *GROWTH*.

- All variables not in the equation when the STEPWISE method is completed will be forced into the equation with ENTER.

Example

```
REGRESSION VARIABLES=(COLLECT)
 /DEPENDENT=SAVINGS
 /METHOD=TEST(MEASURE3 TO MEASURE9)(MEASURE3,INCOME)
 /METHOD=ENTER GROWTH.
```

- The VARIABLES=(COLLECT) specification assembles a correlation matrix that includes all variables named on the DEPENDENT and METHOD subcommands.

- REGRESSION first builds the full equation of all the variables named on the first METHOD subcommand: *SAVINGS* regressed on *MEASURE3* to *MEASURE9* and *INCOME*. For each set of test variables (MEASURE3 to MEASURE9, and MEASURE3 and INCOME), the R^2 change, *F*, probability, sums of squares, and degrees of freedom are displayed.

- *GROWTH* is added to the equation by the second METHOD subcommand. Variables *MEASURE3* to *MEASURE9* and *INCOME* are still in the equation when this subcommand is executed.

STATISTICS Subcommand

STATISTICS controls the display of statistics for the equation and for the independent variables.

- If STATISTICS is omitted or if it is specified without keywords, R, ANOVA, COEFF, and OUTS are displayed (see below).

- If any statistics are specified on STATISTICS, only those statistics specifically requested are displayed.

- STATISTICS must be specified before DEPENDENT and METHOD subcommands. The last specified STATISTICS affects all equations.

Global Statistics

DEFAULTS   *R, ANOVA, COEFF, and OUTS*. These are displayed if STATISTICS is omitted or if it is specified without keywords.

ALL   *All statistics except F.*

Equation Statistics

R
Multiple R. R includes R^2, adjusted R^2, and standard error of the estimate displayed in the Model Summary table.

ANOVA
Analysis of variance table. This option includes regression and residual sums of squares, mean square, *F*, and probability of *F* displayed in the ANOVA table.

CHA
Change in R^2. This option includes the change in R^2 between steps, along with the corresponding *F* and its probability, in the Model Summary table. For each equation, *F* and its probability are also displayed.

BCOV
Variance-covariance matrix for unstandardized regression coefficients. The statistics are displayed in the Coefficient Correlations table.

XTX
Swept correlation matrix.

COLLIN
Collinearity diagnostics (Belsley et al., 1980). COLLIN includes the variance-inflation factors (VIF) displayed in the Coefficients table, and the eigenvalues of the scaled and uncentered cross-products matrix, condition indexes, and variance-decomposition proportions displayed in the Collinearity Diagnostics table.

SELECTION
Selection statistics. This option includes Akaike information criterion (AIK), Ameniya's prediction criterion (PC), Mallows conditional mean squared error of prediction criterion (C_p), and Schwarz Bayesian criterion (SBC) (Judge et al., 1980). The statistics are displayed in the Model Summary table.

Statistics for the Independent Variables

COEFF
Regression coefficients. This option includes regression coefficients (B), standard errors of the coefficients, standardized regression coefficients (beta), *t*, and two-tailed probability of *t*. The statistics are displayed in the Coefficients table.

OUTS
Statistics for variables not yet in the equation that have been named on METHOD subcommands for the equation. OUTS displays the Excluded Variables table showing beta, *t*, two-tailed probability of *t*, and minimum tolerance of the variable if it were the only variable entered next.

ZPP
Zero-order, part, and partial correlation. The statistics are displayed in the Coefficients table.

CI
95% confidence interval for the unstandardized regression coefficients. The statistics are displayed in the Coefficients table.

SES
Approximate standard error of the standardized regression coefficients. (Meyer & Younger, 1976.) The statistics are displayed in the Coefficients table.

TOL
Tolerance. This option displays tolerance for variables in the equation in the Coefficients table. For variables not yet entered into the equation, TOL displays in the

Excluded Variables table the tolerance each variable would have if it were the only variable entered next.

F   *F value for B and its probability.* This is displayed instead of the *t* value in the Coefficients or Excluded Variables table.

CRITERIA Subcommand

CRITERIA controls the statistical criteria used to build the regression equations. The way in which these criteria are used depends on the method specified on METHOD. The default criteria are noted in the description of each CRITERIA keyword below.

- The minimum specification is a criterion keyword and its arguments, if any.
- If CRITERIA is omitted or included without specifications, the default criteria are in effect.
- The CRITERIA subcommand must be specified before DEPENDENT and METHOD subcommands. The last specified CRITERIA affects all equations.

Tolerance and Minimum Tolerance Tests

Variables must pass both tolerance and minimum tolerance tests in order to enter and remain in a regression equation. Tolerance is the proportion of the variance of a variable in the equation that is not accounted for by other independent variables in the equation. The minimum tolerance of a variable not in the equation is the smallest tolerance any variable already in the equation would have if the variable being considered were included in the analysis.

If a variable passes the tolerance criteria, it is eligible for inclusion based on the method in effect.

Criteria for Variable Selection

- The ENTER, REMOVE, and TEST methods use only the TOLERANCE criterion.
- BACKWARD removes variables according to the probability of *F*-to-remove (keyword POUT). Specify FOUT to use *F*-to-remove instead.
- FORWARD enters variables according to the probability of *F*-to-enter (keyword PIN). Specify FIN to use *F*-to-enter instead.
- STEPWISE uses both PIN and POUT (or FIN and FOUT) as criteria. If the criterion for entry (PIN or FIN) is less stringent than the criterion for removal (POUT or FOUT), the same variable can cycle in and out until the maximum number of steps is reached. Therefore, if PIN is larger than POUT or FIN is smaller than FOUT, REGRESSION adjusts POUT or FOUT and issues a warning.
- The values for these criteria are specified in parentheses. If a value is not specified, the default values are used.

DEFAULTS   *PIN(0.05), POUT(0.10), and TOLERANCE(0.0001).* These are the defaults if CRITERIA is omitted. If criteria have been changed, DEFAULTS restores these defaults.

PIN[(value)]	*Probability of* F-*to-enter*. The default value is 0.05. Either PIN or FIN can be specified. If more than one is used, the last one specified is in effect.
FIN[(value)]	F-*to-enter*. The default value is 3.84. Either PIN or FIN can be specified. If more than one is used, the last one specified is in effect.
POUT[(value)]	*Probability of* F-*to-remove*. The default value is 0.10. Either POUT or FOUT can be specified. If more than one is used, the last one specified is in effect.
FOUT[(value)]	F-*to-remove*. The default value is 2.71. Either POUT or FOUT can be specified. If more than one is used, the last one specified is in effect.
TOLERANCE[(value)]	*Tolerance*. The default value is 0.0001. If the specified tolerance is very low, REGRESSION issues a warning.
MAXSTEPS[(n)]	*Maximum number of steps*. The value of MAXSTEPS is the sum of the maximum number of steps for each method for the equation. The default values are, for the BACKWARD or FORWARD methods, the number of variables meeting PIN/POUT or FIN/FOUT criteria, and for the STEPWISE method, twice the number of independent variables.

Confidence Intervals

CIN[(value)]	*Reset the value of the percent for confidence intervals*. The default is 95%. The specified value sets the percentage interval used in the computation of temporary variable types MCIN and ICIN. (See the list of temporary variable types on p. 789.)

Example

```
REGRESSION VARIABLES=POP15 TO GROWTH, SAVINGS
 /CRITERIA=PIN(.1) POUT(.15)
 /DEPENDENT=SAVINGS
 /METHOD=FORWARD.
```

- The CRITERIA subcommand relaxes the default criteria for entry and removal for the FORWARD method. Note that the specified PIN is less than POUT.

ORIGIN and NOORIGIN Subcommands

ORIGIN and NOORIGIN control whether or not the constant is suppressed. By default, the constant is included in the model (NOORIGIN).

- The specification is either the ORIGIN or NOORIGIN subcommand.
- ORIGIN and NOORIGIN must be specified before the DEPENDENT and METHOD subcommands. The last specified remains in effect for all equations.
- ORIGIN requests regression through the origin. The constant term is suppressed.

- If you specify ORIGIN, statistics requested on the DESCRIPTIVES subcommand are computed as if the mean were 0.
- ORIGIN and NOORIGIN affect the way the correlation matrix is built. If matrix materials are used as input to REGRESSION, the keyword that was in effect when the matrix was written should be in effect when that matrix is read.

Example

```
REGRESSION VAR=(COL)
 /ORIGIN
 /DEP=HOMICIDE
 /METHOD=ENTER POVPCT.
```

- The REGRESSION command requests an equation that regresses *HOMICIDE* on *POVPCT* and suppresses the constant (ORIGIN).

REGWGT Subcommand

The only specification on REGWGT is the name of the variable containing the weights to be used in estimating a weighted least-squares model. With REGWGT the default display is the usual REGRESSION display.

- REGWGT is a global subcommand.
- If more than one REGWGT subcommand is specified on a REGRESSION procedure, only the last one is in effect.
- REGWGT can be used with MATRIX OUT but not with MATRIX IN.
- Residuals saved from equations using the REGWGT command are not weighted. To obtain weighted residuals, multiply the residuals created with SAVE by the square root of the weighting variable in a COMPUTE statement.
- REGWGT is in effect for all equations and affects the way the correlation matrix is built. Thus, if REGWGT is specified on a REGRESSION procedure that writes matrix materials to a matrix data file, subsequent REGRESSION procedures using that file will be automatically weighted.

Example

```
REGRESSION VARIABLES=GRADE GPA STARTLEV TREATMNT
 /DEPENDENT=GRADE
 /METHOD=ENTER
 /SAVE PRED(P).
COMPUTE WEIGHT=1/(P*(1-P)).
REGRESSION VAR=GRADE GPA STARTLEV TREATMNT
 /REGWGT=WEIGHT
 /DEP=GRADE
 /METHOD=ENTER.
```

- VARIABLES builds a correlation matrix that includes *GRADE*, *GPA*, *STARTLEV*, and *TREATMNT*.
- DEPENDENT identifies *GRADE* as the dependent variable.
- METHOD regresses *GRADE* on *GPA*, *STARTLEV*, and *TREATMNT*.

- SAVE saves the predicted values from the regression equation as variable *P* in the working data file (see the SAVE subcommand on p. 795).
- COMPUTE creates the variable *WEIGHT* as a transformation of *P*.
- The second REGRESSION procedure performs a weighted regression analysis on the same set of variables using *WEIGHT* as the weighting variable.

Example

```
REGRESSION VAR=GRADE GPA STARTLEV TREATMNT
 /REGWGT=WEIGHT
 /DEP=GRADE
 /METHOD=ENTER
 /SAVE RESID(RGRADE).
COMPUTE WRGRADE=RGRADE * SQRT(WEIGHT).
```

- This example illustrates the use of COMPUTE with SAVE to weight residuals.
- REGRESSION performs a weighted regression analysis of *GRADE* on *GPA*, *STARTLEV*, and *TREATMNT*, using *WEIGHT* as the weighting variable.
- SAVE saves the residuals as *RGRADE* (see the SAVE subcommand on p. 795). These residuals are not weighted.
- COMPUTE creates variable *WRGRADE*, which contains the weighted residuals.

DESCRIPTIVES Subcommand

DESCRIPTIVES requests the display of correlations and descriptive statistics. By default, descriptive statistics are not displayed.

- The minimum specification is simply the subcommand keyword DESCRIPTIVES, which obtains MEAN, STDDEV, and CORR.
- If DESCRIPTIVES is specified with keywords, only those statistics specifically requested are displayed.
- Descriptive statistics are displayed only once for all variables named or implied on VARIABLES.
- Descriptive statistics are based on all valid cases for each variable if PAIRWISE or MEANSUBSTITUTION has been specified on MISSING. Otherwise, only cases with valid values for all variables named or implied on the VARIABLES subcommand are included in the calculation of descriptive statistics.
- If regression through the origin has been requested (subcommand ORIGIN), statistics are computed as if the mean were 0.

NONE   *No descriptive statistics.* This is the default if the subcommand is omitted.

DEFAULTS *MEAN, STDDEV, and CORR.* This is the same as specifying DESCRIPTIVES without specifications.

MEAN   *Display variable means in the Descriptive Statistics table.*

STDDEV   *Display variable standard deviations in the Descriptive Statistics table.*

VARIANCE *Display variable variances in the Descriptive Statistics table.*

CORR	*Display Pearson correlation coefficients in the Correlations table.*
SIG	*Display one-tailed probabilities of the correlation coefficients in the Correlations table.*
BADCORR	*Display the correlation coefficients only if some coefficients cannot be computed.*
COV	*Display covariance in the Correlations table.*
XPROD	*Display sum of squares and cross-product deviations from the mean in the Correlations table.*
N	*Display numbers of cases used to compute correlation coefficients in the Correlations table.*
ALL	*All descriptive statistics.*

Example

```
REGRESSION DESCRIPTIVES=DEFAULTS SIG COV
 /VARIABLES=AGE,FEMALE,YRS_JOB,STARTPAY,SALARY
 /DEPENDENT=SALARY
 /METHOD=ENTER STARTPAY
 /METHOD=ENTER YRS_JOB.
```

- The variable means, standard deviations, and number of cases are displayed in the Descriptive Statistics table and the correlation coefficients, one-tailed probabilities of the correlation coefficients, and covariance are displayed in the Correlations table.
- Statistics are displayed for all variables named on VARIABLES, even though only variables *SALARY, STARTPAY*, and *YRS_JOB* are used to build the equations.
- *STARTPAY* is entered into the equation by the first METHOD subcommand. *YRS_JOB* is entered by the second METHOD subcommand.

SELECT Subcommand

By default, all cases in the working data file are considered for inclusion on REGRESSION. Use SELECT to include a subset of cases in the correlation matrix and resulting regression statistics.

- The required specification on SELECT is a logical expression.
- The syntax for the SELECT subcommand is as follows:

```
/SELECT=varname relation value
```

- The variable named on SELECT should not be specified on the VARIABLES subcommand.
- The relation can be EQ, NE, LT, LE, GT, or GE.
- Only cases for which the logical expression on SELECT is true are included in the calculation of the correlation matrix and regression statistics.
- All other cases, including those with missing values for the variable named on SELECT, are not included in the computations.

- If SELECT is specified, residuals and predicted values are calculated and reported separately for both selected and unselected cases by default (see the RESIDUALS subcommand on p. 791).

- Cases deleted from the working data file with SELECT IF, a temporary SELECT IF, or SAMPLE are not passed to REGRESSION and are not included among either the selected or unselected cases.

- You should not use a variable from a temporary transformation as a selection variable, since REGRESSION reads the data file more than once if any residuals subcommands are specified. A variable created from a temporary transformation (with IF and COMPUTE statements) will disappear when the data are read a second time, and a variable that is the result of a temporary RECODE will change.

Example

```
REGRESSION SELECT SEX EQ 'M'
 /VARIABLES=AGE,STARTPAY,YRS_JOB,SALARY
 /DEPENDENT=SALARY
 /METHOD=STEP
 /RESIDUALS=NORMPROB.
```

- Only cases with the value M for *SEX* are included in the correlation matrix calculated by REGRESSION.

- Separate normal P_P plots are displayed for cases with *SEX* equal to M and for other cases (see the RESIDUALS subcommand on p. 791).

MATRIX Subcommand

MATRIX reads and writes matrix data files. It can read files written by previous REGRESSION procedures or files written by other procedures such as CORRELATIONS. The matrix materials REGRESSION writes also include the mean, standard deviation, and number of cases used to compute each coefficient. This information immediately precedes the correlation matrix in the matrix file (see "Format of the Matrix Data File" on p. 786).

- Either IN or OUT and a matrix file in parentheses are required on MATRIX.

- When used, MATRIX must be the first subcommand specified in a REGRESSION procedure.

- ORIGIN and NOORIGIN affect the way the correlation matrix is built. If matrix materials are used as input to REGRESSION, the keyword that was in effect when the matrix was written should be in effect when that matrix is read.

OUT (filename)   *Write a matrix data file.* Specify either a filename or an asterisk, enclosed in parentheses. If you specify a filename, the file is stored on disk and can be retrieved at any time. If you specify an asterisk (*), the matrix data file replaces the working file but is not stored on disk unless you use SAVE or XSAVE.

IN (filename)   *Read a matrix data file.* If the matrix data file is the working data file, specify an asterisk (*) in parentheses. If the matrix data file is another file, specify the filename in parentheses. A matrix file read from an external file does not replace the working data file.

Format of the Matrix Data File

- The file has two special variables created by the program: *ROWTYPE_* and *VARNAME_*.
- *ROWTYPE_* is a short string variable with values MEAN, STDDEV, N, and CORR (for Pearson correlation coefficient).
- *VARNAME_* is a short string variable whose values are the names of the variables used to form the correlation matrix. When *ROWTYPE_* is CORR, *VARNAME_* gives the variable associated with that row of the correlation matrix.
- The remaining variables in the file are the variables used to form the correlation matrix.
- To suppress the constant term when ORIGIN is used in the analysis, value OCORR (rather than value CORR) is written to the matrix system file. OCORR indicates that the regression passes through the origin.

Split Files

- When split-file processing is in effect, the first variables in the matrix data file are the split variables, followed by *ROWTYPE_*, the independent variable, *VARNAME_*, and the dependent variables.
- A full set of matrix materials is written for each subgroup defined by the split variable(s).
- A split variable cannot have the same variable name as any other variable written to the matrix data file.
- If a split file is in effect when a matrix is written, the same split file must be in effect when that matrix is read.

Missing Values

- With PAIRWISE treatment of missing values, the matrix of N's used to compute each coefficient is included with the matrix materials.
- With LISTWISE treatment (the default) or MEANSUBSTITUTION, a single N used to calculate all coefficients is included.

Example

```
REGRESSION MATRIX IN(PAY_DATA) OUT(*)
 /VARIABLES=AGE,STARTPAY,YRS_JOB,SALARY
 /DEPENDENT=SALARY
 /METHOD=STEP.
```

- MATRIX IN reads the matrix data file *PAY_DATA*.
- A stepwise regression analysis of *SALARY* is performed using *AGE*, *STARTPAY*, and *YRS_JOB*.
- MATRIX OUT replaces the working data file with the matrix data file that was previously stored in the *PAY_DATA* file.

MISSING Subcommand

MISSING controls the treatment of cases with missing values. By default, a case that has a user-missing or system-missing value for any variable named or implied on VARIABLES is omitted from the computation of the correlation matrix on which all analyses are based.

- The minimum specification is a keyword specifying a missing-value treatment.

LISTWISE   *Delete cases with missing values listwise.* Only cases with valid values for all variables named on the current VARIABLES subcommand are used. If INCLUDE is also specified, only cases with system-missing values are deleted listwise. LISTWISE is the default if the MISSING subcommand is omitted.

PAIRWISE   *Delete cases with missing values pairwise.* Each correlation coefficient is computed using cases with complete data for the pair of variables correlated. If INCLUDE is also specified, only cases with system-missing values are deleted pairwise.

MEANSUBSTITUTION   *Replace missing values with the variable mean.* All cases are included and the substitutions are treated as valid observations. If INCLUDE is also specified, user-missing values are treated as valid and are included in the computation of the means.

INCLUDE   *Includes cases with user-missing values.* All user-missing values are treated as valid values. This keyword can be specified along with the methods LISTWISE, PAIRWISE, or MEANSUBSTITUTION.

Example

```
REGRESSION   VARIABLES=POP15,POP75,INCOME,GROWTH,SAVINGS
 /DEPENDENT=SAVINGS
 /METHOD=STEP
 /MISSING=MEANSUBSTITUTION.
```

- System-missing and user-missing values are replaced with the means of the variables when the correlation matrix is calculated.

References

Belsley, D. A., E. Kuh, and R. E. Welsch. 1980. *Regression diagnostics: Identifying influential data and sources of collinearity.* New York: John Wiley and Sons.

Berk, K. N. 1977. Tolerance and condition in regression computation. *Journal of the American Statistical Association,* 72: 863–66.

Judge, G. G., W. E. Griffiths, R. C. Hill, H. Lutkepohl, and T. C. Lee. 1980. *The theory and practice of econometrics.* 2nd ed. New York: John Wiley and Sons.

Meyer, L. S., and M. S. Younger. 1976. Estimation of standardized coefficients. *Journal of the American Statistical Association,* 71: 154–57.

REGRESSION: Residuals

```
REGRESSION VARIABLES=varlist /DEPENDENT=varname /METHOD=method

 [/RESIDUALS=[DEFAULTS] [DURBIN] [OUTLIERS({ZRESID })] [ID (varname)]
                                          {tempvars}

       [NORMPROB({ZRESID })] [HISTOGRAM({ZRESID })]
                {tempvars}              {tempvars}

       [SIZE({SEPARATE})]
             {POOLED  }

 [/CASEWISE=[DEFAULTS]   [{OUTLIERS({3     })}]   [PLOT({ZRESID })]
                         {         {value} }            {tempvar}
                         {ALL             }

       [{DEPENDENT PRED RESID}]]
        {tempvars           }

 [/SCATTERPLOT [varname,varname]...[

 [/PARTIALPLOT=[{ALL    }]
               {varlist}

 [/OUTFILE={COVB (filename)}]
           {CORB (filename)}

 [/SAVE=tempvar[(newname)]  [tempvar[(newname)]...]  [FITS]]
```

Temporary residual variables are:

PRED, ADJPRED, SRESID, MAHAL, RESID, ZPRED, SDRESID, COOK, DRESID, ZRESID,
SEPRED, LEVER, DFBETA, SDBETA, DFFIT, SDFFIT, COVRATIO, MCIN, ICIN

SAVE FITS saves:

DFFIT, SDFIT, DFBETA, SDBETA, COVRATIO

Example:

```
REGRESSION VARIABLES=SAVINGS INCOME POP15 POP75
  /WIDTH=132
  /DEPENDENT=SAVINGS
  /METHOD=ENTER
  /RESIDUALS
  /CASEWISE
  /SCATTERPLOT (*ZRESID *ZPRED)
  /PARTIALPLOT
  /SAVE ZRESID(STDRES) ZPRED(STDPRED).
```

Overview

REGRESSION creates temporary variables containing predicted values, residuals, measures of fit and influence, and several statistics based on these measures. These temporary variables can be analyzed within REGRESSION in Casewise Diagnostics tables (CASEWISE subcommand), scatterplots (SCATTERPLOT subcommand), histograms and normal probability plots

(RESIDUALS subcommand), and partial regression plots (PARTIALPLOT subcommand). Any of the residuals subcommands can be specified to obtain descriptive statistics for the predicted values, residuals, and their standardized versions. Any of the temporary variables can be added to the working data file with the SAVE subcommand.

Basic Specification

All residuals analysis subcommands are optional. Most have defaults that can be requested by including the subcommand without any further specifications. These defaults are described in the discussion of each subcommand below.

Subcommand Order

- The residuals subcommands RESIDUALS, CASEWISE, SCATTERPLOT, and PARTIALPLOT follow the last METHOD subcommand of any equation for which residuals analysis is requested. Statistics are based on this final equation.
- Residuals subcommands can be specified in any order. All residuals subcommands must follow the DEPENDENT and METHOD subcommands.

Operations

- Residuals subcommands affect all equations.
- The temporary variables *PRED* (unstandardized predicted value), *ZPRED* (standardized predicted value), *RESID* (unstandardized residual), and *ZRESID* (standardized residual) are calculated and descriptive statistics are displayed whenever any residuals subcommand is specified. If any of the other temporary variables are referred to on the command, they are also calculated.
- Predicted values and statistics based on predicted values are calculated for every observation that has valid values for all variables in the equation. Residuals and statistics based on residuals are calculated for all observations that have a valid predicted value and a valid value for the dependent variable. The missing-values option therefore affects the calculation of residuals and predicted values.
- No residuals or predictors are generated for cases deleted from the working data file with SELECT IF, a temporary SELECT IF, or SAMPLE.
- All variables are standardized before plotting. If the unstandardized version of a variable is requested, the standardized version is plotted.
- Residuals processing is not available when the working data file is a matrix file or is replaced by a matrix file with MATRIX OUT(*) on REGRESSION. If RESIDUALS, CASEWISE, SCATTERPLOT, PARTIALPLOT, or SAVE are used when MATRIX IN(*) or MATRIX OUT(*) is specified, the REGRESSION command is not executed.

For each analysis, REGRESSION can calculate the following types of temporary variables:

PRED   *Unstandardized predicted values.*

RESID   *Unstandardized residuals.*

DRESID   *Deleted residuals.*

ADJPRED   *Adjusted predicted values.*

ZPRED   *Standardized predicted values.*

ZRESID   *Standardized residuals.*

SRESID   *Studentized residuals.*

SDRESID   *Studentized deleted residuals.* (See Hoaglin & Welsch, 1978.)

SEPRED   *Standard errors of the predicted values.*

MAHAL   *Mahalanobis distances.*

COOK   *Cook's distances.* (See Cook, 1977.)

LEVER   *Centered leverage values.* (See Velleman & Welsch, 1981.)

DFBETA   *Change in the regression coefficient that results from the deletion of the ith case.* A DFBETA value is computed for each case for each regression coefficient generated by a model. (See Belsley et al., 1980.)

SDBETA   *Standardized DFBETA.* An SDBETA value is computed for each case for each regression coefficient generated by a model. (See Belsley et al., 1980.)

DFFIT   *Change in the predicted value when the ith case is deleted.* (See Belsley et al., 1980.)

SDFIT   *Standardized DFFIT.* (See Belsley et al., 1980.)

COVRATIO   *Ratio of the determinant of the covariance matrix with the ith case deleted to the determinant of the covariance matrix with all cases included.* (See Belsley et al., 1980.)

MCIN   *Lower and upper bounds for the prediction interval of the mean predicted response.* A lowerbound *LMCIN* and an upperbound *UMCIN* are generated. The default confidence interval is 95%. The confidence interval can be reset with the CIN subcommand. (See Dillon & Goldstein, 1984.)

ICIN   *Lower and upper bounds for the prediction interval for a single observation.* A lowerbound *LICIN* and an upperbound *UICIN* are generated. The default confidence interval is 95%. The confidence interval can be reset with the CIN subcommand. (See Dillon & Goldstein, 1984.)

Example

```
REGRESSION VARIABLES=SAVINGS INCOME POP15 POP75
  /DEPENDENT=SAVINGS
  /METHOD=ENTER
  /RESIDUALS
  /CASEWISE
  /SCATTERPLOT (*ZRESID *ZPRED)
  /PARTIALPLOT
  /SAVE ZRESID(STDRES) ZPRED(STDPRED).
```

- REGRESSION requests a single equation in which *SAVINGS* is the dependent variable and *INCOME*, *POP15*, and *POP75* are independent variables.
- RESIDUALS requests the default residuals output.
- Because residuals processing has been requested, statistics for predicted values, residuals, and standardized versions of predicted values and residuals are displayed in a Residuals Statistics table.
- CASEWISE requests a Casewise Diagnostics table for cases whose absolute value of *ZRESID* is greater than 3. Values of the dependent variable, predicted value, and residual are listed for each case.
- SCATTERPLOT requests a plot of the standardized predicted value and the standardized residual.
- PARTIALPLOT requests partial regression plots for all independent variables.
- SAVE adds the standardized residual and the standardized predicted value to the working data file as new variables named *STDRES* and *STDPRED*.

RESIDUALS Subcommand

RESIDUALS controls the display and labeling of summary information on outliers as well as the display of the Durbin-Watson statistic and histograms and normal probability plots for the temporary variables.

- If RESIDUALS is specified without keywords, it displays a histogram of residuals, a normal probability plot of residuals, the values of *$CASENUM* and *ZRESID* for the 10 cases with the largest absolute value of *ZRESID*, and the Durbin-Watson test statistic. The histogram and the normal plot are standardized.
- If any keywords are specified on RESIDUALS, only the requested information and plots are displayed.

DEFAULTS   *DURBIN, NORMPROB(ZRESID), HISTOGRAM(ZRESID), OUTLI-ERS(ZRESID).* These are the defaults if RESIDUALS is used without specifications.

HISTOGRAM(tempvars) *Histogram of the temporary variable or variables.* The default is *ZRESID*. You can request histograms for *PRED, RESID, ZPRED, DRESID, ADJPRED, SRESID, SDRESID, SEPRED, MAHAL, COOK,* and *LEVER*. The specification of any other temporary variable will result in an error.

NORMPROB(tempvars) *Normal probability (P-P) plot.* The default is *ZRESID.* The other temporary variables for which normal probability plots are available are *PRED, RESID, ZPRED, DRESID, SRESID,* and *SDRESID.* The specification of any other temporary variable will result in an error. Normal probability plots are always displayed in standardized form; therefore, when *PRED, RESID,* or *DRESID* is requested, the standardized equivalent *ZPRED, ZRESID* or *SDRESID* is displayed.

OUTLIERS(tempvars) *The 10 cases with the largest absolute values of the specified temporary variables.* The default is *ZRESID.* The output includes the values of *$CASENUM* and of the temporary variables for the 10 cases. The other temporary variables available for OUTLIERS are *RESID, SRESID, SDRESID, DRESID, MAHAL,* and *COOK.* The specification of any temporary variable other than these will result in an error.

DURBIN *Display Durbin-Watson test statistic in the Model Summary table.*

ID(varname) *ID variable providing case labels for use with point selection mode in the Chart Editor.* Applicable to scatterplots produced by SCATTERPLOT, PARTIALPLOT, and RESIDUALS. Any variable in the working data file can be named.

SEPARATE *Separate reporting of residuals statistics and plots for selected and unselected cases.* This is the default.

POOLED *Pooled plots and statistics using all cases in the working file when the SELECT subcommand is in effect.* (See the SELECT subcommand on p. 784.) This is an alternative to SEPARATE.

Example

```
/RESID=DEFAULT ID(SVAR)
```

- DEFAULT produces the default residuals statistics: Durbin-Watson statistic, a normal probability plot and histogram of *ZRESID,* and an outlier listing for *ZRESID.*
- Descriptive statistics for *ZRESID, RESID, PRED,* and *ZPRED* are automatically displayed.
- *SVAR* is specified as the case identifier on the outlier output.

CASEWISE Subcommand

CASEWISE requests a Casewise Diagnostics table of residuals. You can specify a temporary residual variable for casewise listing (via the PLOT keyword). You can also specify variables to be listed in the table for each case.

- If CASEWISE is used without any additional specifications, it displays a Casewise Diagnostics table of *ZRESID* for cases whose absolute value of *ZRESID* is at least 3. By default, the values of the case sequence number, *DEPENDENT, PRED,* and *RESID* are listed for each case.
- Defaults remain in effect unless specifically altered.

DEFAULTS   *OUTLIERS(3), PLOT(ZRESID), DEPENDENT, PRED, and RESID*. These are the defaults if the subcommand is used without specifications.

OUTLIERS(value) *List only cases for which the absolute standardized value of the listed variable is at least as large as the specified value.* The default value is 3. Keyword OUTLIERS is ignored if keyword ALL is also present.

ALL   *Include all cases in the Casewise Diagnostic table.* ALL is the alternative to keyword OUTLIERS.

PLOT(tempvar)   *List the values of the temporary variable in the Casewise Diagnostics table.* The default temporary variable is *ZRESID*. Other variables that can be listed are *RESID, DRESID, SRESID,* and *SDRESID*. The specification of any temporary variable other than these will result in an error. When requested, *RESID* is standardized and *DRESID* is Studentized in the output.

tempvars   *Display the values of these variables next to the casewise list entry for each case.* The default variables are *DEPENDENT* (the dependent variable), *PRED,* and *RESID*. Any of the other temporary variables can be specified. If an ID variable is specified on RESIDUALS, the ID variable is also listed.

Example

```
/CASEWISE=DEFAULT ALL SRE MAH COOK SDR
```

- This example requests a Casewise Diagnostics table of the standardized residuals for all cases.
- *ZRESID*, the dependent variable, and the temporary variables *PRED, RESID, SRESID, MAHAL, COOK,* and *SDRESID* are for all cases.

SCATTERPLOT Subcommand

SCATTERPLOT names pairs of variables for scatterplots.

- The minimum specification for SCATTERPLOT is a pair of variables in parentheses. There are no default specifications.
- You can specify as many pairs of variables in parentheses as you want.
- The first variable named in each set of parentheses is plotted along the vertical axis, and the second variable is plotted along the horizontal axis.
- Plotting symbols are used to represent multiple points occurring at the same position.
- You can specify any variable named on the VARIABLES subcommand.
- You can specify *PRED, RESID, ZPRED, ZRESID, DRESID, ADJPRED, SRESID, SDRESID, SEPRED, MAHAL, COOK,* and *LEVER*. The specification of any other temporary variables will result in an error.
- Specify an asterisk before temporary variable names to distinguish them from user-defined variables. For example, use *PRED* to specify *PRED*.

Example

```
/SCATTERPLOT (*RES,*PRE)(*RES,SAVINGS)
```

- This example specifies two scatterplots: residuals against predicted values and residuals against the values of the variable *SAVINGS*.

PARTIALPLOT Subcommand

PARTIALPLOT requests partial regression plots. Partial regression plots are scatterplots of the residuals of the dependent variable and an independent variable when both of these variables are regressed on the rest of the independent variables.

- If PARTIALPLOT is included without any additional specifications, it produces a partial regression plot for every independent variable in the equation. The plots appear in the order the variables are specified or implied on the VARIABLES subcommand.
- If variables are specified on PARTIALPLOT, only the requested plots are displayed. The plots appear in the order the variables are listed on the PARTIALPLOT subcommand.
- At least two independent variables must be in the equation for partial regression plots to be produced.

ALL   *Plot all independent variables in the equation.* This is the default.

varlist   *Plot the specified variables.* Any variable entered into the equation can be specified.

Example

```
REGRESSION VARS=PLOT15 TO SAVINGS
  /DEP=SAVINGS
  /METH=ENTER
  /RESID=DEFAULTS
  /PARTIAL.
```

- A partial regression plot is produced for every independent variable in the equation.

OUTFILE Subcommand

OUTFILE saves in an SPSS-format data file the parameter covariance or correlation matrix with parameter estimates, standard errors, significance values, and residual degrees of freedom for each term in the final equation.

- The OUTFILE subcommand must follow the last METHOD subcommand.
- Only one OUTFILE subcommand is allowed. If you specify more than one, only the last one is executed.
- You must specify one keyword and a valid filename in parentheses. There is no default.
- You cannot save the parameter statistics as the working data file.

COVB (filename) *Write the parameter covariance matrix with other statistics.* Specify the filename in full. REGRESSION does not supply an extension.

CORB (filename) *Write the parameter correlation matrix with other statistics.* Specify the filename in full. REGRESSION does not supply an extension.

Example

```
REGRESSION DEPENDENT=Y
 /METHOD=ENTER X1 X2
 /OUTFILE CORB (covx1x2y.sav).
```

- The OUTFILE subcommand saves the parameter correlation matrix, and the parameter estimates, standard errors, significance values and residual degrees of freedom for the constant term, *X1* and *X2*.

SAVE Subcommand

Use SAVE to add one or more residual or fit variables to the working data file.

- The specification on SAVE is one or more of the temporary variable types listed on pp. 789–790, each followed by an optional name in parentheses for the new variable.
- New variable names must be unique.
- If new names are not specified, REGRESSION generates a rootname using a shortened form of the temporary variable name with a suffix to identify its creation sequence.
- If you specify DFBETA or SDBETA on the SAVE subcommand, the number of new variables saved is the total number of variables in the equation.

FITS   *Save all influence statistics.* FITS saves *DFFIT, SDFIT, DFBETA, SDBETA*, and *COVRATIO.* You cannot specify new variable names when using this keyword. Default names are generated.

Example

```
/SAVE=PRED(PREDVAL) RESID(RESIDUAL) COOK(CDISTANC)
```

- This subcommand adds three variables to the end of the working data file: *PREDVAL*, containing the unstandardized predicted value for each case; *RESIDUAL*, containing the unstandardized residual; and *CDISTANC*, containing Cook's distance.

Example

```
/SAVE=PRED RESID
```

- This subcommand adds two variables named *PRE_1* and *RES_1* to the end of the working data file.

Example

```
REGRESSION DEPENDENT=Y
 /METHOD=ENTER X1 X2
 /SAVE DFBETA(DFBVAR).
```

- The SAVE subcommand creates and saves three new variables with the names *DFBVAR0*, *DFBVAR1*, and *DFBVAR2*.

Example

```
REGRESSION VARIABLES=SAVINGS INCOME POP15 POP75 GROWTH
 /DEPENDENT=SAVINGS
 /METHOD=ENTER INCOME POP15 POP75
 /SAVE=PRED(PREDV) SDBETA(BETA) ICIN.
```

- The SAVE subcommand adds seven variables to the end of the file: *PREDV*, containing the unstandardized predicted value for the case; *BETA0*, the standardized *DFBETA* for the intercept; *BETA1*, *BETA2*, and *BETA3*, the standardized *DFBETA*'s for the three independent variables in the model; *LICI_1*, the lower bound for the prediction interval for an individual case; and *UICI_1*, the upper bound for the prediction interval for an individual case.

References

Belsley, D. A., E. Kuh, and R. E. Welsch. 1980. *Regression diagnostics: Identifying influential data and sources of collinearity.* New York: John Wiley and Sons.

Cook, R. D. 1977. Detection of influential observations in linear regression. *Technometrics*, 19: 15–18.

Dillon, W. R., and M. Goldstein. 1984. *Multivariate analysis: Methods and applications.* New York: John Wiley and Sons.

Hoaglin, D. C., and R. E. Welsch. 1978. The hat matrix in regression and ANOVA. *American Statistician*, 32: 17–22.

Velleman, P. F., and R. E. Welsch. 1981. Efficient computing of regression diagnostics. *American Statistician*, 35: 234–42.

RELIABILITY

```
RELIABILITY VARIABLES={varlist}
                      {ALL     }

[/SCALE(scalename)=varlist [/SCALE... ]]

[/MODEL={ALPHA         }] [/VARIABLES...]
        {SPLIT[(n)]    }
        {GUTTMAN       }
        {PARALLEL      }
        {STRICTPARALLEL}

[/STATISTICS=[DESCRIPTIVE]  [SCALE]      [{ANOVA         }]  [ALL]]
             [COVARIANCES]  [TUKEY]       {ANOVA FRIEDMAN}
             [CORRELATIONS] [HOTELLING]   {ANOVA COCHRAN }

[/SUMMARY=[MEANS] [VARIANCE] [COV] [CORR] [TOTAL] [ALL]]

[/ICC=[MODEL({MIXED**})][TYPE({CONSISTENCY**})][CIN={95**}]]
             {RANDOM}         {ABSOLUTE    }        {n  }
      [TESTVAL={0**}]
              {p  }


[/METHOD=COVARIANCE]

[/FORMAT={NOLABELS**}]
         {LABELS    }

[/MISSING={EXCLUDE**}]
          {INCLUDE  }

[/MATRIX =[IN({*   })] [OUT({*   })] [NOPRINT]]
             {file}         {file}
```

**Default if the subcommand or keyword is omitted.

Example:

```
RELIABILITY  VARIABLES=SCORE1 TO SCORE10
  /SCALE (OVERALL) = ALL
  /MODEL = ALPHA
  /SUMMARY = MEANS TOTAL.
```

Overview

RELIABILITY estimates reliability statistics for the components of multiple-item additive scales. It uses any one of five models for reliability analysis and offers a variety of statistical displays. RELIABILITY can also be used to perform a repeated measures analysis of variance, a two-way factorial analysis of variance with one observation per cell, Tukey's test for additivity, Hotelling's *T*-square test for equality of means in repeated measures designs, and Friedman's two-way analysis of variance on ranks. For more complex repeated measures designs, use the GLM procedure (available in the SPSS Advanced Models option).

Options

Model Type. You can specify any one of five models on the MODEL subcommand.

Statistical Display. Statistics available on the STATISTICS subcommand include descriptive statistics, correlation and covariance matrices, a repeated measures analysis of variance table, Hotelling's T-square, Tukey's test for additivity, Friedman's chi-square for the analysis of ranked data, and Cochran's Q.

Computational Method. You can force RELIABILITY to use the covariance method, even when you are not requesting any output that requires it, by using the METHOD subcommand.

Matrix Input and Output. You can read data in the form of correlation matrices and you can write correlation-type matrix materials to a data file using the MATRIX subcommand.

Basic Specification

The basic specification is VARIABLES and a variable list. By default, RELIABILITY displays the number of cases, number of items, and Cronbach's alpha. Whenever possible, it uses an algorithm that does not require the calculation of the covariance matrix.

Subcommand Order

- VARIABLES must be specified first.
- The remaining subcommands can be named in any order.

Operations

- STATISTICS and SUMMARY are cumulative. If you enter them more than once, all requested statistics are produced for each scale.
- If you request output that is not available for your model or for your data, RELIABILITY ignores the request.
- RELIABILITY uses an economical algorithm whenever possible but calculates a covariance matrix when necessary (see the METHOD subcommand on p. 802).

Limitations

- Maximum 10 VARIABLES subcommands.
- Maximum 50 SCALE subcommands.
- Maximum 500 variables on the combined VARIABLES subcommands. Each occurrence of a variable counts as 1 toward this limit.
- Maximum 500 variables on one SCALE subcommand.
- Maximum 1000 variables on all SCALE subcommands combined. Each mention of a variable counts one toward this limit.
- If the available workspace is insufficient to handle multiple VARIABLES subcommands, RELIABILITY deletes them in the reverse order of specification until the workspace is sufficient.

Example

```
RELIABILITY  VARIABLES=SCORE1 TO SCORE10
  /SCALE (OVERALL) = ALL
  /SCALE (ODD) = SCORE1 SCORE3 SCORE5 SCORE7 SCORE9
  /SUMMARY = MEANS TOTAL.
```

- This example analyzes two additive scales.
- One scale (labeled *OVERALL* in the output) includes all 10 items. Another (labeled *ODD*) includes every other item.
- Summary statistics are displayed for each scale, showing item means and the relationship of each item to the total scale.

Example

```
RELIABILITY  VARIABLES=SCORE1 TO SCORE10.
```

- This example analyzes one scale (labeled *ALL* in the display output) that includes all 10 items.
- Because there is no SUMMARY subcommand, no summary statistics are displayed.

VARIABLES Subcommand

VARIABLES specifies the variables to be used in the analysis. Only numeric variables can be used.

- VARIABLES is required and must be specified first.
- You can use keyword ALL to refer to all user-defined variables in the working data file.
- You can specify VARIABLES more than once on a single RELIABILITY command. A reliability analysis is performed on each set of variables.

SCALE Subcommand

SCALE defines a scale for analysis, providing a label for the scale and specifying its component variables. If SCALE is omitted, all variables named on VARIABLES are used, and the label for the scale is *ALL*.

- The label is specified in parentheses after SCALE. It can have a maximum of eight characters and can use only the letters A to Z and the numerals 0 to 9.
- RELIABILITY does not add any new variables to the working data file. The label is used only to identify the output. If the analysis is satisfactory, use COMPUTE to create a new variable containing the sum of the component items.
- Variables named on SCALE must have been named on the previous VARIABLES subcommand. Use the keyword ALL to refer to all variables named on the preceding VARIABLES subcommand.
- To analyze different groups of component variables, specify SCALE more than once following a VARIABLES subcommand.

Example

```
RELIABILITY VARIABLES = ITEM1 TO ITEM20
  /SCALE (A) = ITEM1 TO ITEM10
  /SCALE (B) = ITEM1 ITEM3 ITEM5 ITEM16 TO ITEM20
  /SCALE (C) = ALL.
```

- This command analyzes three different scales: scale A has 10 items, scale B has 8 items, and scale C has 20 items.

MODEL Subcommand

MODEL specifies the type of reliability analysis for the scale named on the preceding SCALE subcommand.

ALPHA   *Cronbach's* α. Standardized item α is displayed. This is the default.

SPLIT [(n)]   *Split-half coefficients.* You can specify a number in parentheses to indicate how many items should be in the second half. For example, MODEL SPLIT (6) uses the last six variables for the second half and all others for the first. By default, each half has an equal number of items, with the odd item, if any, going to the first half.

GUTTMAN   *Guttman's lower bounds for true reliability.*

PARALLEL   *Maximum-likelihood reliability estimate under parallel assumptions.* This model assumes that items have the same variance but not necessarily the same mean.

STRICTPARALLEL   *Maximum-likelihood reliability estimate under strictly parallel assumptions.* This model assumes that items have the same means, the same true score variances over a set of objects being measured, and the same error variance over replications.

STATISTICS Subcommand

STATISTICS displays optional statistics. There are no default statistics.

- STATISTICS is cumulative. If you enter it more than once, all requested statistics are produced for each scale.

DESCRIPTIVES   *Item means and standard deviations.*

COVARIANCES   *Inter-item variance-covariance matrix.*

CORRELATIONS   *Inter-item correlation matrix.*

SCALE   *Scale means and scale variances.*

TUKEY   *Tukey's test for additivity.* This helps determine whether a transformation of the items is needed to reduce nonadditivity. The test displays an estimate of the power to which the items should be raised in order to be additive.

HOTELLING	*Hotelling's* T-*square.* This is a test for equality of means among the items.
ANOVA	*Repeated measures analysis of variance table.*
FRIEDMAN	*Friedman's chi-square and Kendall's coefficient of concordance.* These apply to ranked data. You must request ANOVA in addition to FRIEDMAN; Friedman's chi-square appears in place of the usual *F* test.
COCHRAN	*Cochran's Q.* This applies when all items are dichotomies. You must request ANOVA in addition to COCHRAN; the *Q* statistic appears in place of the usual *F* test.
ALL	*All applicable statistics.*

ICC Subcommand

ICC displays intraclass correlation coefficients for single measure and average measure. Single measure applies to single measurements, for example, the rating of judges, individual item scores, or the body weights of individuals. Average measure, however, applies to average measurements, for example, the average rating of *k* judges, or the average score for a *k*-item test.

MODEL	*Model.* You can specify the model for the computation of ICC. There are three keywords for this option. ONEWAY is the one-way random effects model (people effects are random). RANDOM is the two-way random effect model (people effects and the item effects are random). MIXED is the two-way mixed (people effects are random and the item effects are fixed). MIXED is the default. Only one model can be specified.
TYPE	*Type of definition.* There are two keywords for this option. CONSISTENCY is the consistency definition and ABSOLUTE is the absolute agreement definition. For the consistency coefficient, the between measures variance is excluded from the denominator variance, and for absolute agreement, it is not.
CIN	*The value of the percent for confidence interval and significance level of the hypothesis testing.*
TESTVAL	*The value with which an estimate of ICC is compared.* The value should be between 0 and 1.

SUMMARY Subcommand

SUMMARY displays summary statistics for each individual item in the scale.

- SUMMARY is cumulative. If you enter it more than once, all requested statistics are produced for each scale.
- You can specify one or more of the following:

MEANS	*Statistics on item means.* The average, minimum, maximum, range, ratio of maximum to minimum, and variance of the item means.
VARIANCE	*Statistics on item variances.* This displays the same statistics as for MEANS.
COVARIANCES	*Statistics on item covariances.* This displays the same statistics as for MEANS.
CORRELATIONS	*Statistics on item correlations.* This displays the same statistics as for MEANS.
TOTAL	*Statistics comparing each individual item to the scale composed of the other items.* The output includes the scale mean, variance, and Cronbach's α without the item, and the correlation between the item and the scale without it.
ALL	*All applicable summary statistics.*

METHOD Subcommand

By default, RELIABILITY uses a computational method that does not require the calculation of a covariance matrix wherever possible. METHOD forces RELIABILITY to calculate the covariance matrix. Only a single specification applies to METHOD:

COVARIANCE   *Calculate and use the covariance matrix, even if it is not needed.*

If METHOD is not specified, RELIABILITY computes the covariance matrix for all variables on each VARIABLES subcommand only if any of the following is true:

• You specify a model other than ALPHA or SPLIT.
• You request COV, CORR, FRIEDMAN, or HOTELLING on the STATISTICS subcommand.
• You request anything other than TOTAL on the SUMMARY subcommand.
• You write the matrix to a matrix data file, using the MATRIX subcommand.

FORMAT Subcommand

FORMAT controls the initial display of variable names and labels before the analysis.

NOLABELS   *Do not display names and labels before the analysis.* This is the default.

LABELS   *Display names and labels for all items before the analysis.*

MISSING Subcommand

MISSING controls the deletion of cases with user-missing data.

• RELIABILITY deletes cases from analysis if they have a missing value for any variable named on the current VARIABLES subcommand. By default, both system-missing and user-missing values are excluded.

EXCLUDE *Exclude user-missing and system-missing values.* This is the default.

INCLUDE *Treat user-missing values as valid.* Only system-missing values are excluded.

MATRIX Subcommand

MATRIX reads and writes SPSS matrix data files.

- Either IN or OUT and the matrix file in parentheses are required. When both IN and OUT are used on the same RELIABILITY procedure, they can be specified on separate MATRIX subcommands or on the same subcommand.

- If both IN and OUT are used on the same RELIABILITY command and there are grouping variables, these variables are treated as if they were split variables. Values of the grouping variables in the input matrix are passed on to the output matrix (see "Split Files" on p. 804).

OUT (filename) *Write a matrix data file.* Specify either a filename or an asterisk (*), enclosed in parentheses. If you specify a filename, the file is stored on disk and can be retrieved at any time. If you specify an asterisk, the matrix file replaces the working data file but is not stored on disk unless you use SAVE or XSAVE.

IN (filename) *Read a matrix data file.* If the matrix data file is the working data file, specify an asterisk (*) in parentheses. If it is another file, specify the filename in parentheses. A matrix file read from an external file does not replace the working data file.

Matrix Output

- RELIABILITY writes correlation-type matrices that include the number of cases, means, and standard deviations with the matrix materials (see "Format of the Matrix Data File" below for a description of the file). These matrix materials can be used as input to RELIABILITY or other procedures.

- Any documents contained in the working data file are not transferred to the matrix file.

- RELIABILITY displays the scale analyses when it writes matrix materials. To suppress the display of scale analyses, specify keyword NOPRINT on MATRIX.

Matrix Input

- RELIABILITY can read a matrix data file created by a previous RELIABILITY command or by another SPSS procedure. The matrix input file must have records of type N, MEAN, STDDEV, and CORR for each split-file group. For more information, see the Universals section.

- SPSS reads variable names, variable and value labels, and print and write formats from the dictionary of the matrix data file.

- MATRIX=IN cannot be used unless a working data file has already been defined. To read an existing matrix data file at the beginning of a session, use GET to retrieve the matrix file and then specify IN(*) on MATRIX.

Format of the Matrix Data File

- The matrix data file includes two special variables created by SPSS: *ROWTYPE_* and *VARNAME_*. Variable *ROWTYPE_* is a short string variable having values N, MEAN, STDDEV, and CORR. Variable *VARNAME_* is a short string variable whose values are the names of the variables used to form the correlation matrix.
- When *ROWTYPE_* is CORR, *VARNAME_* gives the variable associated with that row of the correlation matrix.
- The remaining variables in the matrix file are the variables used to form the correlation matrix.

Split Files

- When split-file processing is in effect, the first variables in the matrix data file will be the split variables, followed by *ROWTYPE_*, *VARNAME_*, and the dependent variable(s).
- If grouping variables are in the matrix input file, their values are between *ROWTYPE_* and *VARNAME_*. The grouping variables are treated like split-file variables.
- A full set of matrix materials is written for each split-file group defined by the split variables.
- A split variable cannot have the same variable name as any other variable written to the matrix data file.
- If split-file processing is in effect when a matrix is written, the same split file must be in effect when that matrix is read by any procedure.

Missing Values

Missing-value treatment affects the values written to a matrix data file. When reading a matrix data file, be sure to specify a missing-value treatment on RELIABILITY that is compatible with the treatment that was in effect when the matrix materials were generated.

Example

```
DATA LIST / TIME1 TO TIME5 1-10.
BEGIN DATA
 0 0 0 0 0
 0 0 1 1 0
 0 0 1 1 1
 0 1 1 1 1
 0 0 0 0 1
 0 1 0 1 1
 0 0 1 1 1
 1 0 0 1 1
 1 1 1 1 1
 1 1 1 1 1
END DATA.
RELIABILITY  VARIABLES=TIME1 TO TIME5
  /MATRIX=OUT(RELMTX).
LIST.
```

- RELIABILITY reads data from the working data file and writes one set of matrix materials to file *RELMTX*.
- The working data file is still the file defined by DATA LIST. Subsequent commands are executed in this file.

Example

```
DATA LIST   / TIME1 TO TIME5 1-10.
BEGIN DATA
 0 0 0 0 0
 0 0 1 1 0
 0 0 1 1 1
 0 1 1 1 1
 0 0 0 0 1
 0 1 0 1 1
 0 0 1 1 1
 1 0 0 1 1
 1 1 1 1 1
 1 1 1 1 1
END DATA.
RELIABILITY   VARIABLES=TIME1 TO TIME5
  /MATRIX=OUT(*) NOPRINT.
LIST.
```

- RELIABILITY writes the same matrix as in the previous example. However, the matrix data file replaces the working data file. The LIST command is executed in the matrix file, not in the file defined by DATA LIST.
- Because NOPRINT is specified on MATRIX, scale analyses are not displayed.

Example

```
GET FILE=RELMTX.
RELIABILITY VARIABLES=ALL
  /MATRIX=IN(*).
```

- This example assumes that you are starting a new session and want to read an existing matrix data file. GET retrieves the matrix data file *RELMTX*.
- MATRIX=IN specifies an asterisk because the matrix data file is the working data file. If MATRIX=IN(RELMTX) is specified, SPSS issues an error message.
- If the GET command is omitted, SPSS issues an error message.

Example

```
GET FILE=PRSNNL.
FREQUENCIES VARIABLE=AGE.

RELIABILITY VARIABLES=ALL
  /MATRIX=IN(RELMTX).
```

- This example performs a frequencies analysis on file *PRSNNL* and then uses a different file containing matrix data for RELIABILITY. The file is an existing matrix data file. In order for this to work, the analysis variables named in *RELMTX* must also exist in *PRSNNL*.

- *RELMTX* must have records of type N, MEAN, STDDEV, and CORR for each split-file group.

- *RELMTX* does not replace *PRSNNL* as the working data file.

Example

```
GET FILE=PRSNNL.
CORRELATIONS VARIABLES=V1 TO V5
  /MATRIX=OUT(*).
RELIABILITY VARIABLES=V1 TO V5
  /MATRIX=IN(*).
```

- RELIABILITY uses matrix input from procedure CORRELATIONS. An asterisk is used to specify the working data file for both the matrix output from CORRELATIONS and the matrix input for RELIABILITY.

RENAME VARIABLES

```
RENAME VARIABLES {(varname=varname)  [(varname ...)]}
                 {(varnames=varnames)               }
```

Example:

```
RENAME VARIABLES (JOBCAT=TITLE).
```

Overview

RENAME VARIABLES changes the names of variables in the working data file while preserving their original order, values, variable labels, value labels, missing values, and print and write formats.

Basic Specification

- The basic specification is an old variable name, an equals sign, and the new variable name. The equals sign is required.

Syntax Rules

- Multiple sets of variable specifications are allowed. Each set can be enclosed in parentheses.
- You can specify a list of old variable names followed by an equals sign and a list of new variable names. The same number of variables must be specified on both lists. A single set of parentheses enclosing the entire specification is required for this method.
- Keyword TO can be used on the left side of the equals sign to refer to variables in the working data file, and on the right side of the equals sign to generate new variable names (see the TO keyword on p. 29).
- Old variable names do not need to be specified according to their order in the working data file.
- Name changes take place in one operation. Therefore, variable names can be exchanged between two variables (see the example on p. 807).
- Multiple RENAME VARIABLES commands are allowed.
- RENAME VARIABLES cannot follow either a TEMPORARY or a MODEL PROGRAM command.

Example

```
RENAME VARIABLES (MOHIRED=MOSTART) (YRHIRED=YRSTART).
```

- *MOHIRED* is renamed to *MOSTART* and *YRHIRED* to *YRSTART*. The parentheses are optional.

Example

```
RENAME VARIABLES (MOHIRED YRHIRED=MOSTART YRSTART).
```

- The same name changes are specified as in the previous example. The parentheses are required, since variable lists are used.

Example

```
RENAME VARIABLES (A=B) (B=A).
```

- Variable names are exchanged between two variables: *A* is renamed to *B*, and *B* is renamed to *A*.

REPEATING DATA

```
REPEATING DATA [FILE=file]

 /STARTS=beg col[-end col] /OCCURS={value  }
                                    {varname}

 [/LENGTH={value  }] [/CONTINUED[=beg col[-end col]]]
          {varname}

 [/ID={col loc}=varname] [/{TABLE  }]
      {format }            {NOTABLE}

 /DATA=variable specifications
```

Example:

```
INPUT PROGRAM.
DATA LIST / SEQNUM 2-4 NUMPERS 6-7 NUMVEH 9-10.
REPEATING DATA STARTS=12 /OCCURS=NUMVEH
 /DATA=MAKE 1-8 (A) MODEL 9 (A) NUMCYL 10.
END INPUT PROGRAM.

BEGIN DATA
1001 02 02 FORD     T8PONTIAC C6
1002 04 01 CHEVY    C4
1003 02 03 CADILAC C8FORD     T6VW       C4
END DATA.
LIST.
```

Overview

REPEATING DATA reads input cases whose records contain repeating groups of data. For each repeating group, REPEATING DATA builds one output case in the working data file. All of the repeating groups in the data must contain the same type of information, although the number of groups for each input case may vary. Information common to the repeating groups for each input case can be recorded once for that case and then spread to each resulting output case. In this respect, a file with a repeating data structure is like a hierarchical file with both levels of information recorded on a single record rather than on separate record types. For information on reading hierarchical files, see FILE TYPE—END FILE TYPE.

REPEATING DATA must be used within an INPUT PROGRAM structure or within a FILE TYPE structure with mixed or nested data. In an INPUT PROGRAM structure, REPEATING DATA must be preceded by a DATA LIST command. In a FILE TYPE structure, DATA LIST is needed only if there are variables to be spread to each resulting output case.

Options

Length of Repeating Groups. If the length of the repeating groups varies across input cases, you can specify a variable that indicates the length on the LENGTH subcommand. You can also use LENGTH if you do not want to read all the data in each repeating group.

Continuation Records. You can use the CONTINUED subcommand to indicate that the repeating groups for each input case are contained on more than one record. You can check the value of an identification variable across records for the same input case using the ID subcommand.

Summary Tables. You can suppress the display of the table that summarizes the names, locations, and formats of the variables specified on the DATA subcommand using the NOTABLE subcommand.

Basic Specification

The basic specification requires three subcommands: STARTS, OCCURS, and DATA.

- STARTS specifies the beginning column of the repeating data segments. When there are continuation records, STARTS can specify the ending column of the last repeating group on the first record of each input case.

- OCCURS specifies the number of repeating groups on each input case. OCCURS can specify a number if the number of repeating groups is the same for all input cases. Otherwise, OCCURS should specify the name of a variable whose value for each input case indicates the number of repeating groups for that case.

- DATA specifies names, location within the repeating segment, and format for each variable to be read from the repeated groups.

Subcommand Order

- DATA must be the last subcommand specified on REPEATING DATA.
- The remaining subcommands can be named in any order.

Syntax Rules

- REPEATING DATA can be specified only within an INPUT PROGRAM structure, or within a FILE TYPE structure with mixed or nested data. DATA LIST, REPEATING DATA, and any transformation commands used to build the output cases must be placed within the INPUT PROGRAM or FILE TYPE structure. Transformations that apply to the output cases should be specified after the END INPUT PROGRAM or END FILE TYPE command.

- LENGTH must be used if the last variable specified on the DATA subcommand is not read from the last position of each repeating group or if the length of the repeating groups varies across input cases.

- CONTINUED must be used if repeating groups for each input case are continued on successive records.

- The DATA LIST command used with REPEATING DATA must define all fixed-format data for the records.

- Repeating groups are usually recorded at the end of the fixed-format records, but fixed-format data may follow the repeating data in data structures such as IBM SMF and RMF records. Use the following sequence in such cases.

```
DATA LIST .../* Read the fixed-format data before repeating data
REREAD  COLUMNS= .../* Skip repeating data
DATA LIST .../* Read the fixed-format data after repeating data
REPEATING DATA ... /*Read repeating data
```

Operations

- Fixed-location data specified on the DATA LIST are spread to each output case.
- If LENGTH is not specified, the program uses the default length for repeating data groups, which is determined from specifications on the DATA subcommand. For more information on the default length, see the LENGTH subcommand on p. 818.

Cases Generated

- The number of output cases generated is the number specified on the OCCURS subcommand. Physical record length or whether fields are non-blank does not affect the number of cases generated.
- If the number specified for OCCURS is nonpositive or missing, no cases are generated.

Records Read

- If CONTINUED is not specified, all repeating groups are read from the first record of each input case.
- If CONTINUED is specified, the first continuation record is read when the first record for the input case is exhausted, that is, when the next repeating group would extend past the end of the record. The ending column for the first record is defined on STARTS. If the ending column is not specified on STARTS, the logical record length is used (see below).
- Subsequent continuation records are read when the current continuation record is exhausted. Exhaustion of the current continuation record is detected when the next repeating group would extend past the end of the record. The ending column for continuation records is defined on CONTINUED. If the ending column is not specified on CONTINUED, the logical record length is used (see below).
- For inline data, the record length is always 80. For data stored in a file, the record length is generally whatever was specified on the FILE HANDLE command or the default of 1024. Shorter records are extended with blanks when they are read. For IBM implementations, the physical record length is available and is used.

Reading Past End of Record

If one or more fields extend past the end of the actual record, or if CONTINUED is specified and the ending column specified on either STARTS or CONTINUED is beyond the end of the actual record, the program takes the following action:

- For string data with format A, the data record is considered to be extended logically with blanks. If the entire field lies past the end of the record, the resulting value will be all blanks.

- For numeric data, a warning is issued and the resulting value is system-missing.

Example

```
* Build a file with each case representing one vehicle and
  spread information about the household to each case.

INPUT PROGRAM.
DATA LIST / SEQNUM 2-4 NUMPERS 6-7 NUMVEH 9-10.
REPEATING DATA STARTS=12 /OCCURS=NUMVEH
 /DATA=MAKE 1-8 (A) MODEL 9 (A) NUMCYL 10.
END INPUT PROGRAM.

BEGIN DATA
1001 02 02 FORD     T8PONTIAC C6
1002 04 01 CHEVY    C4
1003 02 03 CADILAC C8FORD     T6VW      C4
END DATA.
LIST.
```

- Data are extracted from a file representing household records. Each input case is recorded on a single record; there are no continuation records.

- The total number of persons living in the house and number of vehicles owned by the household is recorded on each record. The first field of numbers (columns 1–4) for each record is an identification number unique to each record. The next two fields of numbers are number of persons in household and number of vehicles. The remainder of the record contains repeating groups of information about each vehicle: the make of vehicle, model, and number of cylinders.

- INPUT PROGRAM indicates the beginning of the input program and END INPUT PROGRAM indicates the end of the input program.

- DATA LIST reads the variables from the household portion of the record. All fixed-format variables are defined on DATA LIST.

- REPEATING DATA reads the information from the repeating groups and builds the output cases. Repeating groups start in column 12. The number of repeating groups for each input case is given by the value of variable *NUMVEH*. Three variables are defined for each repeating group: *MAKE*, *MODEL*, and *NUMCYL*.

- The first input record contains two repeating groups, producing two output cases in the working data file. One output case is built from the second input record which contains information on one vehicle, and three output cases are built from the third record. The values of the fixed-format variables defined on DATA LIST are spread to every new case built in the working data file. Six cases result, as shown in Figure 1.

Figure 1   Output cases built with REPEATING DATA

```
SEQNUM NUMPERS NUMVEH MAKE      MODEL NUMCYL

      1      2      2  FORD      T        8
      1      2      2  PONTIAC   C        6
      2      4      1  CHEVY     C        4
      3      2      3  CADILAC   C        8
      3      2      3  FORD      T        6
      3      2      3  VW        C        4


NUMBER OF CASES READ =       6   NUMBER OF CASES LISTED =       6
```

Example

```
* Use REPEATING DATA with FILE TYPE MIXED: read only type 3 records.

FILE TYPE  MIXED RECORD=#SEQNUM 2-4.
RECORD TYPE 003.
REPEATING DATA STARTS=12 /OCCURS=3
 /DATA=MAKE 1-8(A) MODEL 9(A) NUMCYL 10.
END FILE.
END FILE TYPE.

BEGIN DATA
1001 02 02 FORD     T8PONTIAC C6
1002 04 01 CHEVY    C4
1003 02 03 CADILAC C8FORD     T6VW        C4
END DATA.
LIST.
```

- The task in this example is to read only the repeating data for records with value 003 for variable *#SEQNUM*.

- REPEATING DATA is used within a FILE TYPE structure, which specifies a mixed file type. The record identification variable *#SEQNUM* is located in columns 2–4.

- RECORD TYPE specifies that only records with value 003 for *#SEQNUM* are copied into the working data file. All other records are skipped.

- REPEATING DATA indicates that the repeating groups start in column 12. The OCCURS subcommand indicates there are three repeating groups on each input case, and the DATA subcommand specifies names, locations, and formats for the variables in the repeating groups.

- The DATA LIST command is not required in this example, since none of the information on the input case is being spread to the output cases. However, if there were multiple input cases with value 003 for *#SEQNUM* and they did not all have three repeating groups, DATA LIST would be required to define a variable whose value for each input case indicated the number of repeating groups for that case. This variable would then be specified on the OCCURS subcommand.

Example

```
* Create a data set of child records.

INPUT PROGRAM.
DATA LIST / PARENTID 1 DATE 3-6 NCHILD 8.
REPEATING DATA STARTS=9 /OCCURS=NCHILD
 /DATA=BIRTHDAY 2-5 VACDATE 7-10.
END INPUT PROGRAM.

COMPUTE AGE=DATE - BIRTHDAY.
COMPUTE VACAGE=VACDATE - BIRTHDAY.

DO IF PARENTID NE LAG(PARENTID,1) OR $CASENUM EQ 1.
COMPUTE CHILD=1.
ELSE.
COMPUTE CHILD=LAG(CHILD,1)+1.
END IF.
FORMAT AGE VACAGE CHILD (F2).

BEGIN DATA
1 1987 2 1981 1983 1982 1984
2 1988 1 1979 1984
3 1988 3 1978 1981 1981 1986 1983 1986
4 1988 1 1984 1987
END DATA.
LIST.
```

- Data are from a file that contains information on parents within a school district. Each input case is recorded on a single record; there are no continuation records.

- Each record identifies the parents by a number and indicates how many children they have. The repeating groups give the year of birth and year of vaccination for each child.

- REPEATING DATA indicates that the repeating groups begin in column 9. The value of *NCHILD* indicates how many repeating groups there are for each record.

- The first two COMPUTE commands compute the age for each child and age at vaccination. These transformation commands are specified outside the input program.

- Because the repeating groups do not have descriptive values, the DO IF structure computes variable *CHILD* to distinguish between the first-born child, second-born child, etc. The value for *CHILD* will be 1 for the first-born, 2 for the second-born, and so forth. The LIST output is shown in Figure 2.

Figure 2   Output cases built with REPEATING DATA

```
PARENTID DATE NCHILD BIRTHDAY VACDATE AGE VACAGE CHILD

    1    1987   2      1981    1983    6    2      1
    1    1987   2      1982    1984    5    2      2
    2    1988   1      1979    1984    9    5      1
    3    1988   3      1978    1981   10    3      1
    3    1988   3      1981    1986    7    5      2
    3    1988   3      1983    1986    5    3      3
    4    1988   1      1984    1987    4    3      1

NUMBER OF CASES READ =      7    NUMBER OF CASES LISTED =       7
```

STARTS Subcommand

STARTS indicates the beginning location of the repeating data segment on the first record of each input case. STARTS is required and can specify either a number or a variable name.

- If the repeating groups on the first record of each input case begin in the same column, STARTS specifies a column number.

- If the repeating groups on the first record of each input case do not begin in the same column, STARTS specifies the name of a variable whose value for each input case indicates the beginning location of the repeating groups on the first record. The variable can be defined on DATA LIST or created by transformation commands that precede REPEATING DATA.

- When repeating groups are continued on multiple records for each input case, STARTS must also specify an ending location if there is room on the logical record length for more repeating groups than are contained on the first record of each input case. The ending column applies only to the first record of each input case. See the CONTINUED subcommand on p. 819 for an example.

- The ending column can be specified as a number or a variable name. Specifications for the beginning column and the ending column are separated by a hyphen. The values of the variable used to define the ending column must be valid values and must be larger than the starting value.

- If the variable specified for the ending column is undefined or missing for an input case, the program displays a warning message and builds no output cases from that input case. If the variable specified for the ending column on STARTS has a value that is less than the value specified for the starting column, the program issues a warning and builds output cases only from the continuation records of that input case; it does not build cases from the first record of the case.

- If the ending location is required but not supplied, the program generates output cases with system-missing values for the variables specified on the DATA subcommand and may misread all data after the first or second record in the data file (see the CONTINUED subcommand on p. 819).

Example

```
* Repeating groups in the same location.

INPUT PROGRAM.
DATA LIST FILE=VEHICLE / SEQNUM 2-4 NUMPERS 6-7 NUMVEH 9-10.
REPEATING DATA STARTS=12 /OCCURS=NUMVEH
 /DATA=MAKE 1-8 (A) MODEL 9 (A) NUMCYL 10.
END INPUT PROGRAM.
```

- STARTS specifies column number 12. The repeating groups must therefore start in column 12 of the first record of each input case.

Example

```
* Repeating groups in varying locations.

INPUT PROGRAM.
DATA LIST FILE=VEHICLE / SEQNUM 2-4 NUMPERS 6-7 NUMVEH 9-10.
+    DO IF    (SEQNUM LE 100).
+    COMPUTE FIRST=12.
+    ELSE.
+    COMPUTE FIRST=15.
+    END IF.
REPEATING DATA STARTS=FIRST /OCCURS=NUMVEH
 /DATA=MAKE 1-8 (A) MODEL 9 (A) NUMCYL 10.
END INPUT PROGRAM.
```

- This example assumes that each input case is recorded on a single record and that there are no continuation records. Repeating groups begin in column 12 for all records with sequence numbers 1 through 100 and in column 15 for all records with sequence numbers greater than 100.

- The sequence number for each record is defined as variable *SEQNUM* on the DATA LIST command. The DO IF—END IF structure creates the variable *FIRST* with value 12 for records with sequence numbers through 100 and value 15 for records with sequence numbers greater than 100.

- Variable *FIRST* is specified on the STARTS subcommand.

OCCURS Subcommand

OCCURS specifies the number of repeating groups for each input case. OCCURS is required and specifies a number if the number of groups is the same for all input cases or a variable if the number of groups varies across input cases. The variable must be defined on a DATA LIST command or created with transformation commands.

Example

```
INPUT PROGRAM.
DATA LIST / SEQNUM 2-4 NUMPERS 6-7 NUMVEH 9-10.
REPEATING DATA STARTS=12 /OCCURS=NUMVEH
 /DATA=MAKE 1-8 (A) MODEL 9 (A) NUMCYL 10.
END INPUT PROGRAM.

BEGIN DATA
1001 02 02 FORD     T8PONTIAC C6
1002 04 01 CHEVY    C4
1003 02 03 CADILAC C8FORD    T6VW      C4
END DATA.
LIST.
```

- Data for each input case are recorded on a single record; there are no continuation records.

- The value for variable *NUMVEH* in columns 9 and 10 indicates the number of repeating groups on each record. One output case is built in the working data file for each occurrence of a repeating group.

- In the data, *NUMVEH* has the value 2 for the first case, 1 for the second, and 3 for the third. Thus, six cases are built from these records. If the value of *NUMVEH* is 0, no cases are built from that record.

Example

```
* Read only the first repeating group from each record.

INPUT PROGRAM.
DATA LIST FILE=VEHICLE / SEQNUM 2-4 NUMPERS 6-7 NUMVEH 9-10.
REPEATING DATA STARTS=12 /OCCURS=1
 /DATA=MAKE 1-8 (A) MODEL 9 (A) NUMCYL 10.
END INPUT PROGRAM.
LIST.
```

- Since OCCURS specifies that there is only one repeating group for each input case, only one output case is built from each input case regardless of the actual number of repeating groups.

DATA Subcommand

DATA specifies a name, location within each repeating segment, and format for each variable to be read from the repeating groups. DATA is required and must be the last subcommand on REPEATING DATA.

- The specifications for DATA are the same as for the DATA LIST command.
- The specified location of the variables on DATA is their location within each repeating group—*not* their location within the record.
- Any input format available on the DATA LIST command can be specified on the DATA subcommand. Both FORTRAN-like and the column-style specifications can be used.

Example

```
INPUT PROGRAM.
DATA LIST FILE=VEHICLE / SEQNUM 2-4 NUMPERS 6-7 NUMVEH 9-10.
REPEATING DATA STARTS=12 /OCCURS=NUMVEH
 /DATA=MAKE 1-8 (A) MODEL 9 (A) NUMCYL 10.
END INPUT PROGRAM.
LIST.
```

- Variable *MAKE* is a string variable read from positions 1 through 8 of each repeating group; *MODEL* is a single-character string variable read from position 9; and *NUMCYL* is a one-digit numeric variable read from position 10.
- The DATA LIST command defines variables *SEQNUM, NUMPERS*, and *NUMVEH*. These variables are spread to each output case built from the repeating groups.

FILE Subcommand

REPEATING DATA always reads the file specified on its associated DATA LIST or FILE TYPE command. The FILE subcommand on REPEATING DATA explicitly specifies the name of the file.

- FILE must specify the same file as its associated DATA LIST or FILE TYPE command.

Example

```
INPUT PROGRAM.
DATA LIST FILE=VEHICLE / SEQNUM 2-4 NUMPERS 6-7 NUMVEH 9-10.
REPEATING DATA FILE=VEHICLE /STARTS=12 /OCCURS=NUMVEH
 /DATA=MAKE 1-8 (A) MODEL 9 (A) NUMCYL 10.
END INPUT PROGRAM.
LIST.
```

- FILE on REPEATING DATA specifically identifies the *VEHICLE* file, which is also specified on the DATA LIST command.

LENGTH Subcommand

LENGTH specifies the length of each repeating data group. The default length is the number of columns between the beginning column of the repeating data groups and the ending position of the last variable specified on DATA. (For the first record of each input case, STARTS specifies the beginning column of the repeating groups. For continuation records, repeating groups are read from column 1 by default or from the column specified on CONTINUED.)

- The specification on LENGTH can be a number or the name of a variable.
- LENGTH must be used if the last variable specified on the DATA subcommand is not read from the last position of each repeating group, or if the length of the repeating groups varies across input cases.
- If the length of the repeating groups varies across input cases, the specification must be a variable whose value for each input case is the length of the repeating groups for that case. The variable can be defined on DATA LIST or created with transformation commands.
- If the value of the variable specified on LENGTH is undefined or missing for an input case, the program displays a warning message and builds only one output case for that input case.

Example

```
* Read only the variable MAKE for each vehicle.

* The data contain two values that are not specified on the
  DATA subcommand.  The first is in position 9 of the repeating
  groups, and the second is in position 10.

INPUT PROGRAM.
DATA LIST FILE=VEHICLE / SEQNUM 2-4 NUMPERS 6-7 NUMVEH 9-10.
REPEATING DATA STARTS=12 /OCCURS=NUMVEH /LENGTH=10
 /DATA=MAKE 1-8 (A).
END INPUT PROGRAM.
```

- LENGTH indicates that each repeating group is 10 columns long. LENGTH is required because *MAKE* is not read from the last position of each repeating group. As illustrated in previous examples, each repeating group also includes variable *MODEL* (position 9) and *NUMCYL* (position 10).
- DATA specifies that *MAKE* is in positions 1 through 8 of each repeating group. Positions 9 and 10 of each repeating group are skipped.

CONTINUED Subcommand

CONTINUED indicates that the repeating groups are contained on more than one record for each input case.

- Each repeating group must be fully recorded on a single record: a repeating group cannot be split across records.
- The repeating groups must begin in the same column on all continuation records.
- If CONTINUED is specified without beginning and ending columns, the program assumes that the repeating groups begin in column 1 of continuation records and searches for repeating groups by scanning to the end of the record or to the value specified by OCCURS. See "Operations" on p. 811 for additional information on how records are read.
- If the repeating groups on continuation records do not begin in column 1, CONTINUED must specify the column in which the repeating groups begin.
- If there is room on the logical record length for more repeating groups than are contained on the first record of each input case, the STARTS subcommand must indicate an ending column for the records. The ending column on STARTS applies only to the first record of each input case.
- If there is room on the logical record length for more repeating groups than are contained on the continuation records of each input case, the CONTINUED subcommand must indicate an ending column. The ending column on CONTINUED applies to all continuation records.

Example

```
* This example assumes the logical record length is 80.

INPUT PROGRAM.
DATA LIST / ORDERID 1-5 NITEMS 7-8.
REPEATING DATA STARTS=10 /OCCURS=NITEMS /CONTINUED=7
 /DATA=ITEM 1-9 (A) QUANTITY 11-13 PRICE (DOLLAR7.2,1X).
END INPUT PROGRAM.

BEGIN DATA
10020 07 01-923-89 001  25.99 02-899-56 100 101.99 03-574-54 064  61.29
10020 04-780-32 025  13.95 05-756-90 005  56.75 06-323-47 003  23.74
10020 07-350-95 014  11.46
20030 04 01-781-43 010  10.97 02-236-54 075 105.95 03-655-83 054  22.99
20030 04-569-38 015  75.00
END DATA.
LIST.
```

- Data are extracted from a mail-order file. Each input case represents one complete order. The data show two complete orders recorded on a total of five records.
- The order number is recorded in columns 1 through 5 of each record. The first three records contain information for order 10020; the next two records contain information for order 20030. The second field of numbers on the first record of each order indicates the total number of items ordered. The repeating groups begin in column 10 on the first record and in column 7 on continuation records. Each repeating data group represents one item ordered and contains three variables—the item inventory number, the quantity ordered, and the price.

- DATA LIST defines variables *ORDERID* and *NITEMS* on the first record of each input case.
- STARTS on REPEATING DATA indicates that the repeating groups on the first record of each input case begin in column 10.
- OCCURS indicates that the total number of repeating groups for each input case is the value of *NITEMS*.
- CONTINUED must be used because the repeating groups are continued on more than one record for each input case. CONTINUED specifies a beginning column because the repeating groups begin in column 7 rather than in column 1 on the continuation records.
- DATA defines variables *ITEM*, *QUANTITY*, and *PRICE* for each repeating data group. *ITEM* is in positions 1–9, *QUANTITY* is in positions 11–13, and *PRICE* is in positions 14–20 and is followed by one blank column. The length of the repeating groups is therefore 21 columns. The LIST output is shown in Figure 3.

Figure 3   Cases generated by REPEATING DATA

```
ORDERID NITEMS ITEM        QUANTITY       PRICE

10020     7    01-923-89        1        $25.99
10020     7    02-899-56      100       $101.99
10020     7    03-574-54       64        $61.29
10020     7    04-780-32       25        $13.95
10020     7    05-756-90        5        $56.75
10020     7    06-323-47        3        $23.74
10020     7    07-350-95       14        $11.46
20030     4    01-781-43       10        $10.97
20030     4    02-236-54       75       $105.95
20030     4    03-655-83       54        $22.99
20030     4    04-569-38       15        $75.00


NUMBER OF CASES READ =      11    NUMBER OF CASES LISTED =        11
```

Example

```
* Specifying an ending column on the STARTS subcommand.
* This example assumes the logical record length is 80.

INPUT PROGRAM.
DATA LIST / ORDERID 1-5 NITEMS 7-8.
REPEATING DATA STARTS=10-55 /OCCURS=NITEMS /CONTINUED=7
 /DATA=ITEM 1-9 (A) QUANTITY 11-13 PRICE (DOLLAR7.2,1X).
END INPUT PROGRAM.

BEGIN DATA
10020 07 01-923-89 001  25.99 02-899-56 100 101.99
10020 03-574-54 064  61.29 04-780-32 025  13.95 05-756-90 005   56.75
10020 06-323-47 003  23.74 07-350-95 014  11.46
20030 04 01-781-43 010  10.97 02-236-54 075 105.95
20030 03-655-83 054  22.99 04-569-38 015  75.00
END DATA.
LIST.
```

- Data are the same as in the previous example; however, records are entered differently. The first record for each input case contains only two repeating groups.
- DATA LIST defines variables *ORDERID* and *NITEMS* in columns 1–8 on the first record of each input case. Column 9 is blank. DATA defines variables *ITEM*, *QUANTITY*, and *PRICE*

in positions 1–20 of each repeating group, followed by a blank. Thus, each repeating group is 21 columns wide. The length of the first record of each input case is therefore 51 columns: 21 columns for each of two repeating groups, plus the eight columns defined on DATA LIST, plus column 9, which is blank. The operating system's logical record length is 80, which allows room for one more repeating group on the first record of each input case. STARTS must therefore specify an ending column that does not provide enough columns for another repeating group; otherwise, the program creates an output case with missing values for the variables specified on DATA.

- STARTS specifies that the program is to scan only columns 10–55 of the first record of each input case looking for repeating data groups. It will scan continuation records beginning in column 7 until the value specified on the OCCURS subcommand is reached.

Example

```
* Specifying an ending column on the CONTINUED subcommand.
* This example assumes the logical record length is 80.

INPUT PROGRAM.
DATA LIST / ORDERID 1-5 NITEMS 7-8.
REPEATING DATA STARTS=10-55 /OCCURS=NITEMS /CONTINUED=7-55
 /DATA=ITEM 1-9 (A) QUANTITY 11-13 PRICE (DOLLAR7.2,1X).
END INPUT PROGRAM.

BEGIN DATA
10020 07 01-923-89 001  25.99 02-899-56 100 101.99
10020 03-574-54 064  61.29 04-780-32 025  13.95
10020 05-756-90 005  56.75 06-323-47 003  23.74
10020 07-350-95 014  11.46
20030 04 01-781-43 010  10.97 89-236-54 075 105.95
20030 03-655-83 054  22.99 04-569-38 015  75.00
END DATA.
LIST.
```

- The data are the same as in the previous two examples, but records are entered differently. The first record and the continuation records for each input case store only two repeating groups each.

- The operating system's logical record length is 80, which allows room for more repeating groups on all records.

- STARTS specifies that the program is to scan only columns 10-55 of the first record of each input case looking for repeating data groups.

- CONTINUED specifies that the program is to scan only columns 7–55 of all continuation records.

ID Subcommand

ID compares the value of an identification variable across records of the same input case. ID can be used only when CONTINUED is specified. The identification variable must be defined on a DATA LIST command and must be recorded on all records in the file.

- The ID subcommand has two specifications: the location of the variable on the continuation records and the name of the variable (as specified on the DATA LIST command). The specifications must be separated from each other by an equals sign.
- The format specified on the ID subcommand must be the same as the format specified for the variable on DATA LIST. However, the location can be different on the continuation records.
- If the values of the identification variable are not the same on all records for a single input case, the program displays an error message and stops reading data.

Example

```
INPUT PROGRAM.
DATA LIST / ORDERID 1-5 NITEMS 7-8.
REPEATING DATA STARTS=10-50 /OCCURS=NITEMS
 /CONTINUED=7 /ID=1-5=ORDERID
 /DATA=ITEM 1-9 (A) QUANTITY 11-13 PRICE 15-20 (2).
END INPUT PROGRAM.

BEGIN DATA
10020 04 45-923-89 001  25.9923-899-56 100 101.99
10020 63-780-32 025   13.9554-756-90 005  56.75
20030 03 45-781-43 010  10.9789-236-54 075 105.95
20030 32-569-38 015  75.00
END DATA.
LIST.
```

- The order number in the data is recorded in columns 1–5 of each record.
- *ORDERID* is defined on the DATA LIST command as a five-column integer variable. The first specification on the ID subcommand must therefore specify a five-column integer variable. The location of the variable can be different on continuation records.

TABLE and NOTABLE Subcommands

TABLE displays a table summarizing all variables defined on the DATA subcommand. The summary table lists the names, locations, and formats of the variables and is identical in format to the summary table displayed by the DATA LIST command. NOTABLE suppresses the table. TABLE is the default.

Example

```
INPUT PROGRAM.
DATA LIST FILE=VEHICLE / SEQNUM 2-4 NUMPERS 6-7 NUMVEH 9-10.
REPEATING DATA STARTS=12 /OCCURS=NUMVEH /NOTABLE
 /DATA=MAKE 1-8 (A) MODEL 9 (A) NUMCYL 10.
END INPUT PROGRAM.
```

- NOTABLE suppresses the display of the summary table.

REPORT

```
REPORT [/FORMAT=[{MANUAL  }] [{NOLIST   }] [ALIGN({LEFT  })] [TSPACE({1})]
               {AUTOMATIC}  {LIST[(n)]}         {CENTER}          {n}
                                               {RIGHT }
       [CHDSPACE({1})] [FTSPACE({1})] [SUMSPACE({1})] [COLSPACE({4})]
                 {n}            {n}             {n}             {n}
       [BRKSPACE({ 1 })][LENGTH({1,length})] [MARGINS({1,width})]
                 { n }          {t,b     }            {l,r    }
                 {-1†}          {*,*     }            {*,*    }
       [CHALIGN({TOP    })] [UNDERSCORE({OFF})] [PAGE1({1})] [MISSING {'.'}]]
                {BOTTOM†}                {ON†}         {n}           {'s'}
       [ONEBREAKCOLUMN {OFF**}] [INDENT {2**}] [CHWRAP {OFF**}] [PREVIEW {OFF**}]
                       {ON   }          {n  }          {ON  }           {ON   }
[/OUTFILE=file]
[/STRING=stringname (varname[(width)] [(BLANK)] ['literal'])
/VARIABLES=varname ({VALUE}) [+ varname({VALUE})] ['col head'] [option list]
                   {LABEL}               {LABEL}
                   {DUMMY}               {DUMMY}
```

where option list can contain any of the following:

```
      (width)  (OFFSET({0     }))  ({LEFT  })
                      {n     }     {CENTER†}
                      {CENTER†}    {RIGHT  }

[/MISSING={VAR               }]
         {NONE              }
         {LIST[([varlist][{1}])]}
                          {n}

[/TITLE=[{LEFT  }] 'line1' 'line2'...]  [/FOOTNOTE=[{LEFT  }] 'line1' 'line2'...]
        {CENTER}                                   {CENTER}
        {RIGHT }                                   {RIGHT }
        [)PAGE]   [)DATE]  [)var]

[/BREAK=varlist ['col head'] [option list]]
```

where option list can contain any of the following:

```
      (width)   ({VALUE })   ({NOTOTAL})   ({SKIP({1   }   )))
                {LABEL†}     {TOTAL   }          {n}
                                                {PAGE[(RESET)]}
      (OFFSET({0     }))  (UNDERSCORE[(varlist)])   ({LEFT  })   ({NONAME})
             {n     }                              {CENTER†}   {NAME  }
             {CENTER†}                             {RIGHT  }

[/SUMMARY=function...['summary title'][(break col #)] [SKIP({0})]
                                                            {n}
      or
[/SUMMARY=PREVIOUS[({1})]]
                   {n}
```

where function is

```
aggregate [(varname[({PLAIN   })][(d)][varname...]]]
                    {format††}
      or
composite(argument)[(report col[({PLAIN   })][(d)]]]
                                {format††}
```

**Default if the keyword is omitted.
†Default if FORMAT=AUTOMATIC.
††Any printable output format is valid. See FORMATS.

Aggregate functions:

VALIDN	VARIANCE	PLT(n)
SUM	KURTOSIS	PIN(min,max)
MIN	SKEWNESS	FREQUENCY(min,max)
MAX	MEDIAN(min,max)	PERCENT(min,max)
MEAN	MODE(min,max)	
STDDEV	PGT(n)	

Composite functions:

DIVIDE(arg_1 arg_2 [factor])
MULTIPLY(arg_1...arg_n)
PCT(arg_1 arg_2)
SUBTRACT(arg_1 arg_2)
ADD(arg_1...arg_n)
GREAT(arg_1...arg_n)
LEAST(arg_1...arg_n)
AVERAGE(arg_1...arg_n)

where arg is either one of the aggregate functions or a constant

Example:

```
REPORT FORMAT=LIST
  /VARIABLES=PRODUCT (LABEL) ' ' 'Retail' 'Products'
            SALES 'Annual' 'Sales' '1981'
  /BREAK=DEPT 'Department' (LABEL)
  /SUMMARY=VALIDN (PRODUCT) MEAN (SALES).
```

Overview

REPORT produces case listings and summary statistics and gives you considerable control over the appearance of the output. REPORT calculates all the univariate statistics available in DESCRIPTIVES and the statistics and subpopulation means available in MEANS. In addition, REPORT calculates statistics not directly available in any other procedure, such as computations involving aggregated statistics.

REPORT provides complete report format defaults but also lets you customize a variety of table elements, including column widths, titles, footnotes, and spacing. Because REPORT is so flexible and the output has so many components, it is often efficient to preview report output using a small number of cases until you find the format that best suits your needs.

Defaults

Column Heads. REPORT uses variable labels as default column heads; if no variable labels have been specified, variable names are used. If ONEBREAKCOLUMN is ON, the default head for the first BREAK subcommand is used.

Column Widths. Default column widths are determined by REPORT, using the maximum of the following for each column:

- The widest print format in the column, whether it is a variable print format or a summary print format.

- The width of any temporary variable defined with the STRING subcommand on REPORT.

- If a column heading is assigned, the length of the longest title line in the heading when CHWRAP is off, and the longest word in the title when CHWRAP is on. Underscores, which are removed on printing, can be used to create longer words in the title.

- When no column heading is specified, the length of the longest word in the variable label, or the length of the variable name.

- If you specify LABEL on VARIABLES or BREAK, the length of the variable's longest value label. If FORMAT=MANUAL is in effect, 20 is the maximum value used for this criterion.

- The minimum column width is 8 when FORMAT=MANUAL; it can be less when FORMAT=AUTOMATIC.

Automatic Fit. When the above criteria for column width result in a report that is too wide for the report margins, FORMAT=AUTOMATIC shrinks the report. AUTOMATIC performs the following two steps sequentially, stopping as soon as the report fits within the margins:

1. AUTOMATIC reduces intercolumn spacing incrementally until it reaches a minimum intercolumn space of 1. It will never reduce it to 0.

2. AUTOMATIC shortens widths for strings specified on the STRING subcommand or for value label strings when the LABEL option is specified. It begins with the longest string if that string is at least 15 characters wide and shortens the column width as much as needed (up to 40% of its length), wrapping the string within the new width. If necessary, it repeats the step, using different defined strings. It will not shorten the column width of the same string twice.

REPORT does *not* implement the automatic fit unless AUTOMATIC is specified on the FORMAT subcommand.

AUTOMATIC versus MANUAL Defaults. Many default settings depend on whether you specify AUTOMATIC or MANUAL on FORMAT. Table 1 shows the defaults according to either of the specifications.

Table 1   Keyword default settings

Subcommand	Keyword	Default for AUTOMATIC	Default for MANUAL
FORMAT	ALIGN	left	left
	BRKSPACE		
	summary report	1	1
	listing report	−1	1
	CHALIGN	bottom	top
	CHDSPACE	1	1
	COLSPACE	4	4
	FTSPACE	1	1

Table 1   Keyword default settings (Continued)

Subcommand	Keyword	Default for AUTOMATIC	Default for MANUAL
	LENGTH	1,system length	1,system length
	LISTINOLIST	NOLIST	NOLIST
	MARGINS	1,system width	1,system width
	MISSING	.	.
	PAGE1	1	1
	SUMSPACE	1	1
	TSPACE	1	1
	UNDERSCORE	on	off
	ONEBREAKCOLUMN	off	off
	INDENT[1]	2	2
	CHWRAP	off	off
	PREVIEW	off	off
VARIABLES	LABELIVALUEIDUMMY	VALUE	VALUE
	LEFTICENTERIRIGHT	CENTER[2]	RIGHT for numbers LEFT for strings
	OFFSET	CENTER	0
BREAK	LABELIVALUE	LABEL	VALUE
	LEFTICENTERIRIGHT	CENTER[2]	RIGHT for numbers LEFT for strings
	NAMEINONAME	NONAME	NONAME
	OFFSET	CENTER[3]	0
	PAGE	off	off
	SKIP	1	1
	TOTALINOTOTAL	NOTOTAL	NOTOTAL
	UNDERSCORE	off	off
SUMMARY	PREVIOUS	1	1
	SKIP	0	0

---

[1] No effect when ONEBREAKCOLUMN is on.
[2] LEFT when ONEBREAKCOLUMN is on.
[3] 0 when ONEBREAKCOLUMN is on.

Options

Format. REPORT provides full format defaults and offers you optional control over page length, vertical spacing, margin and column widths, page titles, footnotes, and labels for statistics. The maximum width and length of the report are controlled by specifications on the SET command. The FORMAT subcommand on REPORT controls how the report is laid out on a page and whether case listings are displayed. The VARIABLES subcommand specifies the variables that are listed or summarized in the report (**report variables**) and controls the titles, width, and contents of report columns. The BREAK subcommand specifies the variables that define groups (**break variables**) and controls the titles, width, and contents of break columns. SUMMARY specifies statistics and controls the titles and spacing of summary lines. The TITLE and FOOTNOTE subcommands control the specification and placement of multiple-line titles and footnotes. STRING concatenates variables to create temporary variables that can be specified on VARIABLES or BREAK.

Output File. You can direct reports to a file separate from the file used for the rest of the output from your session using the OUTFILE subcommand.

Statistical Display. The statistical display is controlled by the SUMMARY subcommand. Statistics can be calculated for each category of a break variable and for the group as a whole. Available statistics include mean, variance, standard deviation, skewness, kurtosis, sum, minimum, maximum, mode, median, and percentages. Composite functions perform arithmetic operations using two or more summary statistics calculated on single variables.

Missing Values. You can override the default to include user-missing values in report statistics and listings with the MISSING subcommand. You can also use FORMAT to define a missing-value symbol to represent missing data.

Basic Specification

The basic specification depends on whether you want a listing report or a summary report. A listing report without subgroup classification requires FORMAT and VARIABLES. A listing report with subgroup classification requires FORMAT, VARIABLES, and BREAK. A summary report requires VARIABLES, BREAK, and SUMMARY.

Listing Reports. FORMAT=LIST and VARIABLES with a variable list are required. Case listings are displayed for each variable named on VARIABLES. There are no break groups or summary statistics unless BREAK or SUMMARY is specified.

Summary Reports. VARIABLES, BREAK, and SUMMARY are required. The report is organized according to the values of the variable named on BREAK. The variable named on BREAK must be named on a preceding SORT CASES command. Specified statistics are computed for the variables specified on VARIABLES for each subgroup defined by the break variables.

Subcommand Order

The following order must be observed among subcommands when they are used:

- FORMAT must precede all other subcommands.
- VARIABLES must precede BREAK.
- OUTFILE must precede BREAK.
- Each SUMMARY subcommand must immediately follow its associated BREAK. Multiple SUMMARY subcommands associated with the same BREAK must be specified consecutively.

- TITLE and FOOTNOTE can appear anywhere after FORMAT except between BREAK and SUMMARY.
- MISSING must follow VARIABLES and precede the first BREAK.
- STRING must precede VARIABLES.

Syntax Rules

- Only one each of the FORMAT, STRING, VARIABLES, and MISSING subcommands is allowed.
- To obtain multiple break groups, use multiple BREAK subcommands.
- To obtain multiple summaries for a break level, specify multiple SUMMARY subcommands for the associated BREAK.
- Keywords on REPORT subcommands have default specifications that are in effect if the keyword is not specified. Specify keywords only when you wish to change a default.
- Keywords are enclosed in parentheses if the subcommand takes variable names as arguments.

Operations

- REPORT processes cases sequentially. When the value of a break variable changes, REPORT displays a statistical summary for cases processed since the last set of summary statistics was displayed. Thus, the file must be sorted in order on the break variable or variables.
- The maximum width and page length of the report are determined by the SET command.
- If a column is not wide enough to display numeric values, REPORT first rounds decimal digits, then converts to scientific notation if possible, and then displays asterisks. String variables that are wider than the column are truncated.
- The format used to display values in case listings is controlled by the dictionary format of the variable. Each statistical function in REPORT has a default format.

Limitations

- Maximum 500 variables per VARIABLES subcommand. You can specify more than 500 variables if you stack them (see "VARIABLES Subcommand" on p. 835).
- Maximum 10 dummy variables per VARIABLES subcommand.
- Maximum 20 MODE and MEDIAN requests per SUMMARY subcommand.
- Maximum 20 PGT, PLT, and PIN requests per SUMMARY subcommand.
- Maximum 50 strings per STRING subcommand.
- The length of titles and footnotes cannot exceed the report width.
- The length of string variables created on STRING cannot exceed the page width.
- There is no fixed limit on the number of BREAK and SUMMARY subcommands. However, the page width limits the number of variables that can be displayed and thereby limits the number of break variables.

- The maximum width of a report is 255 characters.
- The number of report variables that can be specified depends upon the width of the report, the width of the variable columns, and the number of BREAK subcommands.
- Maximum 50 variables for the FREQUENCY or PERCENT functions.
- Memory requirements significantly increase if FREQUENCY, PERCENT, MEDIAN, or MODE is requested for variables with a wide range of values. The amount of workspace required is 20 + 8*(max−min +1) bytes per variable per function per break. If the same range is used for different statistics for the same variable, only one set of cells is collected. For example, FREQUENCY(1,100)(VARA) PERCENT(1,100)(VARA) requires only 820 bytes.
- If TOTAL is in effect, workspace requirements are almost doubled.
- Memory requirements also increase if value labels are displayed for variables with many value labels. The amount of workspace required is 4 + 24*n bytes per variable, where n is the number of value labels specified for the variable.

Example

```
SORT CASES BY DEPT.
REPORT FORMAT=LIST
  /VARIABLES=PRODUCT (LABEL) ' ' 'Retail' 'Products'
          SALES 'Annual' 'Sales' '1981'
  /BREAK=DEPT 'Department' (LABEL)
  /SUMMARY=VALIDN (PRODUCT) MEAN (SALES) 'No.Sold,Mean Sales'.
```

- This report is a listing of products and sales by department. A summary of the total number of products sold and the average sales by department is also produced.
- Cases are first sorted by *DEPT* so that cases are grouped by department for the case listing and for the calculation of statistics.
- FORMAT requests a report that lists individual cases within each break group.
- VARIABLES specifies *PRODUCT* and *SALES* as the report variables. Keyword LABEL requests that the case listings for *PRODUCT* display value labels instead of values. Three-line column headings are provided for each report column. The first line of the column heading is blank for the variable *PRODUCT*.
- BREAK identifies *DEPT* as the break variable and provides a one-line column title for the break column. LABEL displays the value label instead of the value itself.
- SUMMARY calculates the valid number of cases for *PRODUCT* and the mean of *SALES* for each value of *DEPT*. A title is provided for the summary line to override the default title, *VALIDN*.

FORMAT Subcommand

FORMAT controls the overall width and length of the report and vertical spacing. Keywords and their arguments can be specified in any order.
- MANUAL and AUTOMATIC are alternatives. The default is MANUAL.
- LIST and NOLIST are alternatives. The default is NOLIST.

MANUAL	*Default settings for manual format.* MANUAL displays values for break variables, right-justifies numeric values and their column headings, left-justifies value labels and string values and their column headings, top-aligns and does not underscore column headings, extends column widths to accommodate the variable's longest value label (but not the longest word in the variable label) up to a width of 20, and generates an error message when a report is too wide for its margins. MANUAL is the default.
AUTOMATIC	*Default settings for automatic format.* AUTOMATIC displays labels for break variables, centers all data, centers column headings but left-justifies column headings if value labels or string values exceed the width of the longest word in the heading, bottom-aligns and underscores column headings, extends column widths to accommodate the longest word in a variable label or the variable's longest value label, and shrinks a report that is too wide for its margins.
LIST(n)	*Individual case listing.* The values of all variables named on VARIABLES are displayed for each case. The optional *n* inserts a blank line after each *n* cases. By default, no blank lines are inserted. Values for cases are listed using the default formats for the variables.
NOLIST	*No case listing.* This is the default.
PAGE(n)	*Page number for the first page of the report.* The default is 1.
LENGTH(t,b)	*Top and bottom line numbers of the report.* You can specify any numbers to define the report page length. By default, the top of the report begins at line 1, and the bottom of the report is the last line of the system page. You can use an asterisk for *t* or *b* to indicate a default value. If the specified length does not allow even one complete line of information to be displayed, REPORT extends the length specification and displays a warning.
MARGINS(l,r)	*Columns for the left and right margins.* The right column cannot exceed 255. By default, the left margin is display column 1 and the right margin is the rightmost display column of the system page. You can use an asterisk for *l* or *r* to indicate a default value.
ALIGN	*Placement of the report relative to its margins.* LEFT, CENTER, or RIGHT can be specified in the parentheses following the keyword. LEFT left-justifies the report. CENTER centers the report between its margins. RIGHT right-justifies the report. The default is LEFT.
COLSPACE(n)	*Number of spaces between each column.* The default is 4 or the average number of spaces that will fit within report margins, whichever is less. When AUTOMATIC is in effect, REPORT overrides the specified column spacing if necessary to fit the report between its margins.
CHALIGN	*Alignment of column headings.* Either TOP or BOTTOM can be specified in the parentheses following the keyword. TOP aligns all column headings with the first, or top, line of multiple-line headings. BOTTOM

aligns headings with the last, or bottom, line of multiple-line headings. When AUTOMATIC is in effect, the default is BOTTOM; when MANUAL is in effect, the default is TOP.

UNDERSCORE

Underscores for column headings. Either ON or OFF can be specified in the parentheses following the keyword. ON underscores the bottom line of each column heading for the full width of the column. OFF does not underscore column headings. The default is ON when AUTOMATIC is in effect and OFF when MANUAL is in effect.

TSPACE(n)

Number of blank lines between the report title and the column heads. The default is 1.

CHDSPACE(n)

Number of blank lines beneath the longest column head. The default is 1.

BRKSPACE(n)

Number of blank lines between the break head and the next line. The next line is a case if LIST is in effect or the first summary line if NOLIST is in effect. BRKSPACE(–1) places the first summary statistic or the first case listing on the same line as the break value. When a summary line is placed on the same line as the break value, the summary title is suppressed. When AUTOMATIC is in effect, the default is –1; when MANUAL is in effect, it is 1.

SUMSPACE(n)

Number of blank lines between the last summary line at the lower break level and the first summary line at the higher break level when they break simultaneously. SUMSPACE also controls spacing between the last listed case and the first summary line if LIST is in effect. The default is 1.

FTSPACE(n)

Minimum number of blank lines between the last listing on the page and the footnote. The default is 1.

MISSING 's'

Missing-value symbol. The symbol can be only one character and represents both system- and user-missing values. The default is a period.

ONEBREAKCOLUMN

Display subgroups defined on multiple BREAK subcommands in a single column. You can specify OFF or ON in parentheses after the keyword. The default is OFF. When ONEBREAKCOLUMN is ON, it applies to all BREAK subcommands. For its effect on break column head, width, and alignment, see the BREAK subcommand on p. 838. For its effect on the basic format of the report, see Figure 2.

INDENT(n)

Indention of break values and summary titles of each successive subgroup defined by one BREAK subcommand in a single break column. INDENT is effective only when ONEBREAKCOLUMN is on. Multiple variables specified on one BREAK subcommand are indented as a block. The default specification is 2. When ONEBREAKCOLUMN is OFF, specification on INDENT is ignored.

CHWRAP

Automatically wrap user-specified column heads. You can specify OFF or ON in parentheses after the keyword. The default is OFF. When CHWRAP is ON, user-specified heads for either break or variable columns are wrapped. If multiple lines are specified for a head, each line is wrapped, if necessary, independent of other lines. To prevent wrapping at blanks, use the underscore character (_) to signify a hard blank in your head specification. The underscore serves as a hard blank only in user-specified heads and only when CHWRAP is ON. The underscore does not appear in the printed heading.

PREVIEW   *Display the first page of output only.* You can specify OFF or ON either in parentheses or with one blank space separating the specification from the keyword. The default is OFF. When PREVIEW is ON, the program stops processing after the first page for you to quickly check the format of your report.

Page Layout

Figure 1 shows the complete page layout and subcommand specifications used to control the basic format of the report when ONEBREAKCOLUMN is off (the default). Figure 2 shows the same page when ONEBREAKCOLUMN is on. In both figures, FORMAT=AUTOMATIC and BRKSPACE defaults to –1.

Example

```
SORT DIVISION DEPT.

REPORT FORMAT=AUTOMATIC LIST ONEBREAKCOLUMN(ON)  CHWRAP(ON)
  /VARIABLES=LNAME TENURE SALARY
  /BREAK=DIVISION (20)(NOTOTAL)
  /SUMMARY=VALIDN (LNAME TENURE) MEAN (SALARY)
          'Mean Salary for Tenured Members within the Division'
  /BREAK=DEPT
  /SUMMARY=VALIDN (LNAME TENURE) MEAN (SALARY)
          'Mean Salary for Tenured Members within the Department'.
```

• This example creates a report with two break variables: *DEPARTMENT* breaks within DIVISION.

• The two break variables are placed in a single break column. The column head is the variable label of DIVISION.

OUTFILE Subcommand

OUTFILE directs the report to a file separate from the file used for the rest of the output from your session. This allows you to print the report without having to delete the extraneous material that would be present in the output.

• OUTFILE must follow FORMAT and must precede BREAK.

• You can append multiple reports to the same file by naming the same file on the OUTFILE subcommand for each REPORT command.

Figure 1   Page layout for REPORT when ONEBREAKCOLUMN is off

```
---------------------------------------- top of page ----------------------------------------
                                                                            ←——— LENGTH
              *************** TITLE ***************                         ←——— TSPACE
                              COLUMN    COLUMN    COLUMN    COLUMN
                              HEAD      HEAD      HEAD      HEAD
BREAK HEAD    BREAK HEAD      (VAR)     (VAR)     (VAR)     (VAR)
                                                                            ←——— CHDSPACE

                                                                            ←——— BRKSPACE
BREAK A VALUE 1 BREAK B VALUE 1 VALUE    VALUE     VALUE     VALUE
                                VALUE    VALUE     VALUE     VALUE
                                                                            ←——— LIST
                                VALUE    VALUE     VALUE     VALUE
                                VALUE    VALUE     VALUE     VALUE
                                                                            ←——— SUMSPACE
              SUMMARY TITLE AGG        AGG       AGG       AGG              ←——— SKIP w/ SUMMARY

              SUMMARY TITLE AGG        AGG       AGG       AGG
                                                                            ←——— SKIP w/ BREAK
              BREAK B VALUE 2                                              ←——— BRKSPACE

                                VALUE    VALUE     VALUE     VALUE
                                VALUE    VALUE     VALUE     VALUE
                                                                            ←——— LIST
                                VALUE    VALUE     VALUE     VALUE
                                VALUE    VALUE     VALUE     VALUE
                                                                            ←——— SUMSPACE
              SUMMARY TITLE AGG        AGG       AGG       AGG              ←——— stats for B=2, A=1

              SUMMARY TITLE AGG        AGG       AGG       AGG
                                                                            ←——— SUMSPACE
SUMMARY TITLE              AGG        AGG       AGG       AGG              ←——— stats for A=1

SUMMARY TITLE              AGG        AGG       AGG       AGG
                                                                            ←——— SKIP w/ BREAK

                                                                            ←——— BRKSPACE
BREAK A VALUE 2 BREAK B VALUE 1 VALUE    VALUE     VALUE     VALUE
                                VALUE    VALUE     VALUE     VALUE
                                                                            ←——— LIST
                                VALUE    VALUE     VALUE     VALUE
                                VALUE    VALUE     VALUE     VALUE
                                                                            ←——— SUMSPACE
              SUMMARY TITLE AGG        AGG       AGG       AGG              ←——— SKIP w/ SUMMARY

              SUMMARY TITLE AGG        AGG       AGG       AGG
                                                                            ←——— SKIP w/ BREAK
              BREAK B VALUE 2 VALUE    VALUE     VALUE     VALUE           ←——— BRKSPACE

                                VALUE    VALUE     VALUE     VALUE
                                                                            ←——— LIST
                                VALUE    VALUE     VALUE     VALUE
                                VALUE    VALUE     VALUE     VALUE

              SUMMARY TITLE AGG        AGG       AGG       AGG

              SUMMARY TITLE AGG        AGG       AGG       AGG
                                                                            ←——— SUMSPACE
SUMMARY TITLE              AGG        AGG       AGG       AGG

SUMMARY TITLE              AGG        AGG       AGG       AGG              ←——— FTSPACE
              *************** FOOTNOTE ***************                       ←——— LENGTH
---------------------------------------- bottom of page ----------------------------------------
|                                                          |
Left margin                                                Right margin
```

Figure 2   Page layout for REPORT when ONEBREAKCOLUMN is on

```
------------------------------------------ top of page ------------------------------------------
```

	COLUMN HEAD (VAR)	COLUMN HEAD (VAR)	COLUMN HEAD (VAR)	COLUMN HEAD (VAR)	
*************** TITLE ***************					← LENGTH
					← TSPACE
BREAK HEAD	COLUMN HEAD (VAR)	COLUMN HEAD (VAR)	COLUMN HEAD (VAR)	COLUMN HEAD (VAR)	
BREAK A VALUE 1					← CHDSPACE
BREAK B VALUE 1					← BRKSPACE
	VALUE VALUE	VALUE VALUE	VALUE VALUE	VALUE VALUE	
					← LIST
	VALUE VALUE	VALUE VALUE	VALUE VALUE	VALUE VALUE	
SUMMARY TITLE	AGG	AGG	AGG	AGG	← SUMSPACE
					← stats for B=1, A=1
SUMMARY TITLE	AGG	AGG	AGG	AGG	← SKIP w/ SUMMARY
					← SKIP w/ BREAK
BREAK B VALUE 2	VALUE VALUE	VALUE VALUE	VALUE VALUE	VALUE VALUE	← BRKSPACE
	VALUE VALUE	VALUE VALUE	VALUE VALUE	VALUE VALUE	INDENT
SUMMARY TITLE	AGG	AGG	AGG	AGG	← SUMSPACE
					← stats for B=2, A=1
SUMMARY TITLE	AGG	AGG	AGG	AGG	
SUMMARY TITLE	AGG	AGG	AGG	AGG	← SUMSPACE
					← stats for A=1
SUMMARY TITLE	AGG	AGG	AGG	AGG	
BREAK A VALUE 2					← SKIP w/ BREAK
BREAK B VALUE 1	VALUE VALUE	VALUE VALUE	VALUE VALUE	VALUE VALUE	← BRKSPACE
	VALUE VALUE	VALUE VALUE	VALUE VALUE	VALUE VALUE	← LIST
SUMMARY TITLE	AGG	AGG	AGG	AGG	← SUMSPACE
					← stats for B=1, A=2
SUMMARY TITLE	AGG	AGG	AGG	AGG	← SKIP w/ BREAK
BREAK B VALUE 2	VALUE VALUE	VALUE VALUE	VALUE VALUE	VALUE VALUE	← BRKSPACE
	VALUE VALUE	VALUE VALUE	VALUE VALUE	VALUE VALUE	LIST
SUMMARY TITLE	AGG	AGG	AGG	AGG	← stats for B=2, A=2
SUMMARY TITLE	AGG	AGG	AGG	AGG	
SUMMARY TITLE	AGG	AGG	AGG	AGG	← stats for A=2
SUMMARY TITLE	AGG	AGG	AGG	AGG	
*************** FOOTNOTE ***************					← FTSPACE

```
------------------------------------------ bottom of page ------------------------------------------
```

Left margin   Right margin ← LENGTH

Example

```
REPORT FORMAT=AUTOMATIC LIST
   /OUTFILE=PRSNLRPT
   /VARIABLES=LNAME AGE TENURE JTENURE SALARY
   /BREAK=DIVISION
   /SUMMARY=MEAN.

REPORT FORMAT=AUTOMATIC
   /OUTFILE=PRSNLRPT
   /VARIABLES=LNAME AGE TENURE JTENURE SALARY
   /BREAK=DIVISION
   /SUMMARY=MEAN
   /SUMMARY=MIN
   /SUMMARY=MAX.
```

- Both a listing report and a summary report are written to file *PRSNLRPT*.

VARIABLES Subcommand

The required VARIABLES subcommand names the variables to be listed and summarized in the report. You can also use VARIABLES to control column titles, column widths, and the contents of report columns.

- The minimum specification on VARIABLES is a list of report variables. The number of variables that can be specified is limited by the system page width.
- Each report variable defines a report column. The value of the variable or an aggregate statistic calculated for the variable is displayed in that variable's report column.
- Variables are assigned to columns in the order in which they are named on VARIABLES.
- Variables named on BREAK can also be named on VARIABLES.
- When FORMAT=LIST, variables can be stacked in a single column by linking them with plus signs (+) on the VARIABLES subcommand. If no column heading is specified, REPORT uses the default heading from the first variable on the list. Only values from the first variable in the column are used to calculate summaries.
- Optional specifications apply only to the immediately preceding variable or list of variables implied by the TO keyword. Options can be specified in any order.
- All optional specifications except column headings must be enclosed in parentheses; column headings must be enclosed in apostrophes or quotation marks.

Column Contents

The following options can be used to specify the contents of the report column for each variable:

(VALUE)	*Display the values of the variable.* This is the default.
(LABEL)	*Display value labels.* If value labels are not defined, values are displayed.
(DUMMY)	*Display blank spaces.* DUMMY defines a report column for a variable that does not exist in the working data file. Dummy variables are used to control spacing or to reserve space for statistics computed for other variables. Do not name an existing variable as a dummy variable.

- VALUE and LABEL have no effect unless LIST has been specified on the FORMAT subcommand.
- When AUTOMATIC is in effect, value labels or string values are centered in the column based on the length of the longest string or label; numeric values are centered based on the width of the widest value or summary format. When MANUAL is in effect, value labels or string values are left-justified in the column and numeric values are right-justified. (See the OFFSET keyword on p. 837.)

Column Heading

The following option can be used to specify a heading for the report column:

'column heading'   *Column heading for the preceding variable.* The heading must be enclosed in apostrophes or quotation marks. If no column heading is specified, the default is the variable label or, if no variable label has been specified, the variable name.

- To specify multiple-line headings, enclose each line in a set of apostrophes or quotation marks, using the conventions for strings (see "Command Specification" on p. 3). The specifications for title lines should be separated by at least one blank.
- Default column headings wrap for as many lines as are required to display the entire label. If AUTOMATIC is in effect, user-specified column headings appear exactly as specified, even if the column width must be extended. If MANUAL is in effect, user-specified titles wrap to fit within the column width.

Column Heading Alignment

The following options can be used to specify how column headings are aligned:

(LEFT)   *Left-aligned column heading.*

(CENTER)   *Centered column heading.*

(RIGHT)   *Right-aligned column heading.*

- If AUTOMATIC is in effect, column headings are centered within their columns by default. If value labels or string values exceed the width of the longest word in the heading, the heading is left-justified.
- If MANUAL is in effect, column headings are left-justified for value labels or string values and right-justified for numeric values by default.

Column Format

The following options can be used to specify column width and adjust the position of the column contents:

(width)   *Width for the report column.* If no width is specified for a variable, REPORT determines a default width using the criteria described under "Defaults" on

p. 824. If you specify a width that is not wide enough to display numeric values, REPORT first rounds decimal digits, then converts to scientific notation if possible, and then displays asterisks. Value labels or string values that exceed the width are wrapped.

(OFFSET)   *Position of the report column contents.* The specification is either *n* or CENTER specified in parentheses. OFFSET(*n*) indicates the number of spaces to offset the contents from the left for value labels or string values, and from the right for numeric values. OFFSET(CENTER) centers contents within the center of the column. If AUTOMATIC is in effect, the default is CENTER. If MANUAL is in effect, the default is 0. Value labels and string values are left-justified and numeric values are right-justified.

Example

```
/VARIABLES=V1 TO V3(LABEL) (15)
  V4 V5 (LABEL)(OFFSET (2))(10)
  SEP1 (DUMMY) (2) ''
  V6 'Results using' "Lieben's Method" 'of Calculation'
```

- The width of the columns for variables *V1* through *V3* is 15 each. Value labels are displayed for these variables in the case listing.

- The column for variable *V4* uses the default width. Values are listed in the case listing.

- Value labels are displayed for variable *V5*. The column width is 10. Column contents are offset two spaces from the left.

- *SEP1* is a dummy variable. The column width is 2, and there is at least one space on each side of *SEP1*. Thus, there are at least four blanks between the columns for *V5* and *V6*. *SEP1* is given a null title to override the default column title *SEP1*.

- *V6* has a three-line title. Its column uses the default width, and values are listed in the case listing.

STRING Subcommand

STRING creates a temporary string variable by concatenating variables and user-specified strings. These variables exist only within the REPORT procedure.

- The minimum specification is a name for the string variable followed by a variable name or a user-specified string enclosed in parentheses.

- The name assigned to the string variable must be unique.

- Any combination of string variables, numeric variables, and user-specified strings can be used in the parentheses to define the string.

- Keyword TO cannot be used within the parentheses to imply a variable list.

- More than one string variable can be defined on STRING.

- If a case has a missing value for a variable within the parentheses, the variable passes the missing value to the temporary variable without affecting other elements specified.

- A string variable defined in REPORT cannot exceed the system page width.

- String variables defined on STRING can be used on VARIABLES or BREAK.

The following options can be used to specify how components are to be concatenated:

(width)   *Width of the preceding variable within the string.* The default is the dictionary width of the variable. The maximum width for numeric variables within the string definition is 16. The maximum width for a string variable is the system page width. If the width specified is less than that required by the value, numeric values are displayed as asterisks and string values are truncated. If the width exceeds the width of a value, numeric values are padded with zeros on the left and string values are padded with blanks on the right.

(BLANK)   *Left-pad values of the preceding numeric variable with blanks.* The default is to left-pad values of numeric variables with zeros. If a numeric variable has a dollar or comma format, it is automatically left-padded with blanks.

'literal'   *User-specified string.* Any combination of characters can be specified within apostrophes or quotation marks.

Example

```
/STRING=JOB1(AVAR NVAR)
        JOB2(AVAR(2) NVAR(3))
        JOB3(AVAR(2) NVAR(BLANK) (4))
```

- STRING defines three string variables to be used within the report.
- Assume that *AVAR* is a string variable read from a four-column field using keyword FIXED on DATA LIST and that *NVAR* is a computed numeric variable with the default format of eight columns with two implied decimal places.
- If a case has value KJ for *AVAR* and value 241 for *NVAR*, *JOB1* displays the value 'KJ 00241.00', *JOB2* the value 'KJ241', and *JOB3* the value 'KJ 241'. If *NVAR* has the system-missing value for a case, *JOB1* displays the value 'KJ.'

Example

```
/STRING=SOCSEC(S1 '-' S2 '-' S3)
```

- STRING concatenates the three variables *S1*, *S2*, and *S3*, each of which contains a segment of the social security number.
- Hyphens are inserted between the segments when the values of *SOCSEC* are displayed.
- This example assumes that the variables *S1*, *S2*, and *S3* were read from three-column, two-column, and four-column fields respectively, using the keyword FIXED on DATA LIST. These variables would then have default format widths of 3, 2, and 4 columns and would not be left-padded with zeros.

BREAK Subcommand

BREAK specifies the variables that define the subgroups for the report, or it specifies summary totals for reports with no subgroups. BREAK also allows you to control the titles, width, and contents of break columns and to begin a new page for each level of the break variable.

- A break occurs when any one of the variables named on BREAK changes value. Cases must be sorted by the values of all BREAK variables on all BREAK subcommands.

- The BREAK subcommand must precede the SUMMARY subcommand that defines the summary line for the break.
- A break column is reserved for each BREAK subcommand if ONEBREAKCOLUMN is OFF (the default).
- To obtain multiple break levels, specify multiple break variables on a BREAK subcommand.
- If more than one variable is specified on a BREAK subcommand, a single break column is used. The value or value label for each variable is displayed on a separate line in the order in which the variables are specified on BREAK. The first variable specified changes most slowly. The default column width is the longest of the default widths for any of the break variables.
- To obtain summary totals without any break levels, use keyword TOTAL in parentheses on BREAK without listing any variables. TOTAL must be specified on the first BREAK subcommand.
- When MISSING=VAR is specified, user-missing values are displayed in case listings but are not included in summary statistics. When NONE is specified, user-missing values are ignored. System-missing values are displayed as missing in case and break listings.
- Optional specifications apply to all variables in the break column and to the break column as a whole. Options can be specified in any order following the last variable named.
- All optional specifications except column headings must be enclosed in parentheses; column headings must be enclosed in apostrophes.

Column Contents

The following can be used to specify the contents of the break column:

(VALUE)   *Display values of the break variables.*

(LABEL)   *Display value labels.* If no value labels have been defined, values are displayed.

- The value or label is displayed only once for each break change but it is repeated at the top of the page in a multiple-page break group.
- When AUTOMATIC is in effect, the default is LABEL; when MANUAL is in effect, the default is VALUE.
- When AUTOMATIC is in effect, the value or label is centered in the column. When MANUAL is in effect, value labels and string values are left-justified and numeric values are right-justified. Keywords OFFSET, ONEBREAKCOLUMN, and INDENT can also affect positioning.

Column Heading

The following option specifies headings used for the break column.

'column heading' *Column heading for the break column.* The heading must be included in apostrophes or quotation marks. The default heading is the variable label of the break variable or, if no label has been defined, the variable name. If the break column is defined by more than one variable, the label or name of the first variable is used. If ONEBREAKCOLUMN is ON, the specified or implied column heading for the first BREAK subcommand is used.

- To specify multiple-line headings, enclose each line in a set of apostrophes or quotation marks, following the conventions for strings (see "Command Specification" on p. 3). Separate the specifications for heading lines with at least one blank.
- Default column headings wrap for as many lines as are required to display the entire label.
- User-specified column headings appear exactly as specified if CHWRAP is OFF (the default). If CHWRAP is ON, any user-defined line longer than the specified or default column width is automatically wrapped.

Column Heading Alignment

The following options can be used to specify how column headings are aligned:

(LEFT)   *Left-aligned column heading.*

(CENTER)   *Centered column heading.*

(RIGHT)   *Right-aligned column heading.*

- When AUTOMATIC is in effect, column headings are centered within their columns by default. If value labels or string values exceed the width of the longest word in the heading, the heading is left-justified.
- When MANUAL is in effect, column headings are left-justified for value labels or string values and right-justified for numeric values.
- When ONEBREAKCOLUMN is ON, all column contents are left aligned. Specifications of CENTER and RIGHT on BREAK are ignored.

Column Format

The following options can be used to format break columns:

(width)   *Column width for the break column.* If no width is specified for a variable, REPORT determines a default width using the criteria described under "Defaults" on p. 824. If ONEBREAKCOLUMN is ON, the column width specified or implied by the first BREAK subcommand is used. If you specify a width that is not wide enough to display numeric values, REPORT first rounds decimal digits, then converts them to scientific notation if possible, and then displays asterisks. Value labels or string values that exceed the width are wrapped.

(OFFSET)   *Position of the break column contents.* The specification is either n or CENTER specified in parentheses. OFFSET(n) indicates the number of spaces to offset the contents from the left for value labels or string values, and from the right for numeric values. OFFSET(CENTER) centers contents within the column. If AUTOMATIC is in effect, the default is CENTER. If MANUAL is in effect, the default is 0: value labels and string values are left-justified and numeric values are right-justified. If ONEBREAKCOLUMN is ON, the offset is applied along with the indentation specified on INDENT, always from the left. The specification of CENTER on OFFSET is ignored.

(UNDERSCORE)   *Use underscores below case listings.* Case listing columns produced by FORMAT LIST are underscored before summary statistics are displayed. You can optionally specify the names of one or more report variables after UNDERSCORE; only the specified columns are underscored.

(TOTAL)   *Display the summary statistics requested on the next SUMMARY subcommand for all the cases in the report.* TOTAL must be specified on the first BREAK subcommand and applies only to the next SUMMARY subcommand specified.

(NOTOTAL)   *Display summary statistics only for each break.* This is the default.

(SKIP(n))   *Skip n lines after the last summary line for a break before beginning the next break.* The default for *n* is 1.

(PAGE)   *Begin each break on a new page.* If RESET is specified on PAGE, the page counter resets to the PAGE1 setting on the FORMAT subcommand every time the break value changes for the specified variable. PAGE cannot be specified for listing reports with no break levels.

(NAME)   *Display the name of the break variable next to each value or value label of the break variable.* NAME requires 10 spaces (the maximum eight-character width of variable names plus a colon and a blank space) in addition to the space needed to display break values or value labels. NAME is ignored if the break-column width is insufficient.

(NONAME)   *Suppress the display of break variable names.* This is the default.

Example

```
SORT DIVISION BRANCH DEPT.
REPORT FORMAT=AUTOMATIC MARGINS (1,70) BRKSPACE(-1)

 /VARIABLES=SPACE(DUMMY) ' ' (4)
            SALES 'Annual' 'Sales' '1981' (15) (OFFSET(2))
            EXPENSES 'Annual' 'Expenses' '1981' (15) (OFFSET(2))

 /BREAK=DIVISION
        BRANCH (10) (TOTAL) (OFFSET(1))
 /SUMMARY=MEAN

 /BREAK=DEPT 'Department' (10)
 /SUMMARY=MEAN.
```

- This example creates a report with three break variables. *BRANCH* breaks within values of *DIVISION*, and *DEPT* breaks within values of *BRANCH*.

- FORMAT sets margins to a maximum of 70 columns and requests that summary lines be displayed on the same line as break values. Because LIST is not specified on FORMAT, only summary statistics are displayed.

- VARIABLES defines three report columns, each occupied by a report variable: *SPACE*, *SALES*, and *EXPENSES*.

- The variable *SPACE* is a dummy variable that exists only within REPORT. It has a null heading and a width of 4. It is used as a space holder to separate the break columns from the report columns.

- *SALES* has a three-line heading and a width of 15. The values of *SALES* are offset two spaces from the right.

- *EXPENSES* is the third report variable and has the same width and offset specifications as *SALES*.

- The leftmost column in the report is reserved for the first two break variables, *DIVISION* and *BRANCH*. Value labels are displayed, since this is the default for AUTOMATIC. The break column has a width of 10 and the value labels are offset one space from the left. Value labels more than nine characters long are wrapped. The default column heading is used. TOTAL requests a summary line at the end of the report showing the mean of all cases in the report.

- The first SUMMARY subcommand displays the mean of each report variable in its report column. This line is displayed each time the value of *DIVISION* or *BRANCH* changes.

- The third break variable, *DEPT*, occupies the second column from the left in the report. The break column has a width of 10 and has a one-line heading. Value labels are displayed in the break column, and those exceeding 10 characters are wrapped.

- The second SUMMARY subcommand displays the mean for each report variable when the value of *DEPT* changes.

SUMMARY Subcommand

SUMMARY calculates a wide range of aggregate and composite statistics.

- SUMMARY must be specified if LIST is not specified on FORMAT.

- The minimum specification is an aggregate or a composite function and its arguments. This must be the first specification on SUMMARY.

- Each SUMMARY subcommand following a BREAK subcommand specifies a new summary line.

- The default location of the summary title is the column of the break variable to which the summary applies. When more than one function is named on SUMMARY, the default summary title is that of the function named first. Both the title and its default column location can be altered (see "Summary Titles" on p. 846).

- The default format can be altered for any function (see "Summary Print Formats" on p. 847).

- SUMMARY subcommands apply only to the preceding BREAK subcommand. If there is no SUMMARY subcommand after a BREAK subcommand, no statistics are displayed for that break level.

- To use the summary specifications from a previous BREAK subcommand for the current BREAK subcommand, specify keyword PREVIOUS on SUMMARY. (See "Other Summary Keywords" on p. 849.)

- Summary statistics are displayed in report columns. With aggregate functions, you can compute summary statistics for all report variables or for a subset (see "Aggregate Functions" below). With composite functions, you can compute summaries for all or a subset of report variables and you have additional control over the placement of summary statistics in particular report columns (see "Composite Functions" on p. 845).

- Multiple summary statistics requested on one SUMMARY subcommand are all displayed on the same line. More than one function can be specified on SUMMARY as long as you do not attempt to place two results in the same report column (REPORT will not be executed if you do). To place results of more than one function in the same report column, use multiple SUMMARY subcommands.
- Any composite and aggregate functions except FREQUENCY and PERCENT can be specified on the same summary line.
- To insert blank lines between summaries when more than one summary line is requested for a break, use keyword SKIP followed by the number of lines to skip in parentheses. The default is 0. (See "Other Summary Keywords" on p. 849.)

Aggregate Functions

Use the aggregate functions to request descriptive statistics for report variables.

- If no variable names are specified as arguments to an aggregate function, the statistic is calculated for all variables named on VARIABLES (all report variables).
- To request an aggregate function for a subset of report variables, specify the variables in parentheses after the function keyword.
- All variables specified for an aggregate function must have been named on VARIABLES.
- Keyword TO cannot be used to specify a list of variables for an aggregate function.
- The result of an aggregate function is always displayed in the report column reserved for the variable for which the function was calculated.
- To use several aggregate functions for the same report variable, specify multiple SUMMARY subcommands. The results are displayed on different summary lines.
- The aggregate functions FREQUENCY and PERCENT have special display formats and cannot be placed on the same summary line with other aggregate or composite functions. They can be specified only once per SUMMARY subcommand.
- Aggregate functions use only cases with valid values.

VALIDN	*Valid number of cases.* This is the only function available for string variables.
SUM	*Sum of values.*
MIN	*Minimum value.*
MAX	*Maximum value.*
MEAN	*Mean.*
STDDEV	*Standard deviation.* Aliases are SD and STDEV.
VARIANCE	*Variance.*
KURTOSIS	*Kurtosis.*
SKEWNESS	*Skewness.*

MEDIAN(min,max)	*Median value for values within the range.* MEDIAN sets up integer-valued bins for counting all values in the specified range. Noninteger values are truncated when the median is calculated.
MODE(min,max)	*Modal value for values within the range.* MODE sets up integer-valued bins for counting all values in the specified range. Noninteger values are truncated when the mode is calculated.
PGT(n)	*Percentage of cases with values greater than* n. Alias PCGT.
PLT(n)	*Percentage of cases with values less than* n. Alias PCLT.
PIN(min,max)	*Percentage of cases within the inclusive value range specified.* Alias PCIN.
FREQUENCY(min,max)	*Frequency counts for values within the inclusive range.* FREQUENCY sets up integer-valued bins for counting all values in the specified range. Noninteger values are truncated when the frequency is computed. FREQUENCY cannot be mixed with other aggregate statistics on a summary line.
PERCENT(min,max)	*Percentages for values within the inclusive range.* PERCENT sets up integer-valued bins for counting all values in the specified range. Noninteger values are truncated when the percentages are computed. PERCENT cannot be mixed with other aggregate statistics on a summary line.

Example

```
SORT CASES BY BVAR AVAR.
REPORT FORMAT=AUTOMATIC LIST /VARIABLES=XVAR YVAR ZVAR

  /BREAK=BVAR
    /SUMMARY=SUM
    /SUMMARY=MEAN (XVAR YVAR ZVAR)
    /SUMMARY=VALIDN(XVAR)

  /BREAK=AVAR
    /SUMMARY=PREVIOUS.
```

- FORMAT requests a case listing, and VARIABLES establishes a report column for variables *XVAR*, *YVAR*, and *ZVAR*. The report columns have default widths and titles.
- Both break variables, *BVAR* and *AVAR*, have default widths and headings.
- Every time the value of *BVAR* changes, three summary lines are displayed. The first line contains the sums for variables *XVAR*, *YVAR*, and *ZVAR*. The second line contains the means of all three variables. The third line displays the number of valid cases for *XVAR* in the report column for *XVAR*.
- Every time the value of *AVAR* changes within each value of *BVAR*, the three summary lines requested for *BVAR* are displayed. These summary lines are based on cases with the current values of *BVAR* and *AVAR*.

Example

```
SORT CASES BY DEPT.
REPORT FORMAT=AUTOMATIC
  /VARIABLES=WAGE BONUS TENURE
  /BREAK=DEPT (23)
  /SUMMARY=SUM(WAGE BONUS) MEAN(TENURE) 'Sum Income: Mean Tenure'.
```

- SUMMARY defines a summary line consisting of the sums of *WAGE* and *BONUS* and the mean of TENURE. The result of each aggregate function is displayed in the report column of the variable for which the function is calculated.
- A title is assigned to the summary line. A width of 23 is defined for the break column to accommodate the title for the summary line.

Composite Functions

Use composite functions to obtain statistics based on aggregated statistics, to place a summary statistic in a column other than that of the report variable for which it was calculated, or to manipulate variables not named on VARIABLES.

- Composite functions can be computed for the following aggregate functions: VALIDN, SUM, MIN, MAX, MEAN, STDEV, VARIANCE, KURTOSIS, SKEWNESS, PGT, PLT, and PIN. Constants can also be arguments to composite functions.
- When used within composite functions, aggregate functions can have only one variable as an argument.
- A composite function and its arguments cannot be separated by other SUMMARY specifications.
- The result of a composite function can be placed in any report column, including columns of dummy or string variables, by specifying a target column. To specify a target column, enclose the variable name of the column in parentheses after the composite function and its arguments. By default, the results of a composite function are placed in the report column of the first variable specified on the composite function that is also specified on VARIABLES.
- The format for the result of a composite function can be specified in parentheses after the name of the column location, within the parentheses that enclose the column-location specification.

DIVIDE(arg_1 arg_2 [factor])	*Divide the first argument by the second and then multiply the result by the factor if it is specified.*
MULTIPLY(arg_1 ... arg_n)	*Multiply the arguments.*
PCT(arg_1 arg_2)	*The percentage of the first argument over the second.*
SUBTRACT(arg_1 arg_2)	*Subtract the second argument from the first.*
ADD(arg_1 ... arg_n)	*Add the arguments.*
GREAT(arg_1 ... arg_n)	*The maximum of the arguments.*
LEAST(arg_1 ... arg_n)	*The minimum of the arguments.*
AVERAGE(arg_1 ... arg_n)	*The average of the arguments.*

Example

```
SORT CASES BY DEPT.
REPORT FORMAT=AUTOMATIC BRKSPACE(-1)
  /VARIABLES=WAGE BONUS SPACE1 (DUMMY) '' BNFT1 BNFT2 SPACE2 (DUMMY)
''
  /BREAK=DEPT

  /SUMMARY=MEAN(WAGE BONUS BNFT1 BNFT2)
       ADD(VALIDN(WAGE)) (SPACE2)

  /SUMMARY=ADD(SUM(WAGE) SUM(BONUS))
       ADD(SUM(BNFT1) SUM(BNFT2)) 'Totals' SKIP(1)

  /SUMMARY=DIVIDE(MEAN(WAGE) MEAN(BONUS)) (SPACE1 (COMMA)(2))
       DIVIDE(MEAN(BNFT1) MEAN(BNFT2)) (SPACE2 (COMMA)(2)) 'Ratios'
       SKIP(1).
```

- VARIABLES defines six report columns. The columns for *WAGE, BONUS, BNFT1,* and *BNFT2* contain aggregate statistics based on those variables. The variables *SPACE1* and *SPACE2* are dummy variables that are created for use as space holders; each is given a blank heading to suppress the default column heading.

- The first SUMMARY computes the means of the variables *WAGE, BONUS, BNFT1,* and *BNFT2.* Because BRKSPACE=–1, this summary line will be placed on the same line as the break value and will have no summary title. The means are displayed in the report column for each variable. SUMMARY also computes the valid number of cases for *WAGE* and places the result in the *SPACE2* column.

- The second SUMMARY adds the sum of *WAGE* to the sum of *BONUS.* Since no location is specified, the result is displayed in the *WAGE* column. In addition, the sum of *BNFT1* is added to the sum of *BNFT2* and the result is placed in the *BNFT1* column. The title for the summary line is *Totals.* One line is skipped before the summary line requested by this SUMMARY subcommand is displayed.

- The third summary line divides the mean of *WAGE* by the mean of *BONUS* and places the result in *SPACE1.* The ratio of the mean of *BNFT1* to the mean of *BNFT2* is displayed in the *SPACE2* column. The results are displayed with commas and two decimal places. The title for the summary line is *Ratios.* One line is skipped before the summary line requested by this SUMMARY subcommand is displayed.

Summary Titles

- You can specify a summary title enclosed in apostrophes or quotation marks, following the conventions for strings (see "Command Specification" on p. 3). Table 2 shows the default titles.

- The summary title must be specified after the first function and its arguments. It cannot separate any function from its arguments.

- A summary title can be only one line long.

- A summary title wider than the break column extends into the next break column to the right. If the title is wider than all of the available break columns, it is truncated.

- Only one summary title can be specified per summary line. If more than one is specified, the last is used.

- The summary title is left- or right-justified depending upon whether the break title is left- or right-justified.
- The default location for the summary title is the column of the BREAK variable to which the summary applies. With multiple breaks, you can override the default placement of the title by specifying, in parentheses following the title, the number of the break column in which you want the summary title to be displayed.
- In a report with no break levels, REPORT displays the summary title above the summary line at the left margin.

Table 2   Default title for summary lines

Function	Title
VALIDN	N
VARIANCE	Variance
SUM	Sum
MEAN	Mean
STDDEV	StdDev
MIN	Minimum
MAX	Maximum
SKEWNESS	Skewness
KURTOSIS	Kurtosis
PGT(n)	>n
PLT(n)	<n
PIN(min,max)	In n_1 to n_2
FREQUENCY(min,max)	Total
PERCENT(min,max)	Total
MEDIAN(min,max)	Median
MODE(min,max)	Mode

Summary Print Formats

All functions have default formats that are used to display results (see Table 3). You can override these defaults by specifying a format keyword and/or the number of decimal places.

- Any printable formats or the PLAIN keyword can be specified. Format specifications must be enclosed in parentheses.
- For aggregate functions, the format and/or number of decimal places is specified after the variable name, within the parentheses that enclose the variable name. The variable must be explicitly named as an argument.
- For composite functions, the format and/or number of decimal places is specified after the variable name of the column location, within the parentheses that enclose the variable name. The column location must be explicitly specified.

- If the report column is wide enough, SUM, MEAN, STDDEV, MIN, MAX, MEDIAN, MODE, and VARIANCE use DOLLAR or COMMA format, if a DOLLAR or COMMA format has been declared for the variable on either the FORMATS or PRINT FORMATS command.

- If the column is not wide enough to display the decimal digits for a given function, REPORT displays fewer decimal places. If the column is not wide enough to display the integer portion of the number, REPORT uses scientific notation if possible, or, if not, displays asterisks.

- An exact value of 0 is displayed with one 0 to the left of the decimal point and as many 0 digits to the right as specified by the format. A number less than 1 in absolute value is displayed without a 0 to the left of the decimal point, except with DOLLAR and COMMA formats.

(PLAIN)   *Uses the setting on SET DECIMAL for the thousands separator and decimal delimiter.* PLAIN overrides dictionary formats. This is the default for all functions except SUM, MEAN, STDDEV, MIN, MAX, MEDIAN, MODE, and VARIANCE. For these functions, the default is the dictionary format of the variable for which the function is computed.

(d)   *Number of decimal places.*

Example

```
/SUMMARY=MEAN(INCOME (DOLLAR)(2))
        ADD(SUM(INCOME)SUM(WEALTH))  (WEALTH(DOLLAR(2))
```

- SUMMARY displays the mean of *INCOME* with dollar format and two decimal places. The result is displayed in the *INCOME* column.

- The sums of *INCOME* and *WEALTH* are added, and the result is displayed in the *WEALTH* column with dollar format and two decimal places.

Table 3   Default print formats for functions

Function	Format type	Width	Decimal places
VALIDN	F	5	0
SUM	Dictionary	Dictionary + 2	Dictionary
MEAN	Dictionary	Dictionary	Dictionary
STDDEV	Dictionary	Dictionary	Dictionary
VARIANCE	Dictionary	Dictionary	Dictionary
MIN	Dictionary	Dictionary	Dictionary
MAX	Dictionary	Dictionary	Dictionary
SKEWNESS	F	5	2
KURTOSIS	F	5	2
PGT	PCT	6	1
PLT	PCT	6	1
PIN	PCT	6	1
MEDIAN	Dictionary	Dictionary	Dictionary
MODE	Dictionary	Dictionary	Dictionary

Table 3   Default print formats for functions (Continued)

Function	Format type	Width	Decimal places
PERCENT	F	6	1
FREQUENCY	F	5	0
DIVIDE	F	Dictionary	0
PCT	PCT	6	2
SUBTRACT	F	Dictionary	0
ADD	F	Dictionary	0
GREAT	F	Dictionary	0
LEAST	F	Dictionary	0
AVERAGE	F	Dictionary	0
MULTIPLY	F	Dictionary	0

Where DATE formats are specified, functions with the dictionary format type display the DATE formats, using the column width as the display width.

Other Summary Keywords

The following additional keywords can be specified on SUMMARY. These keywords are not enclosed in parentheses.

SKIP(n) — *Blank lines before the summary line.* The default is 0. If SKIP is specified for the first SUMMARY subcommand for a BREAK, it skips the specified lines after skipping the number of lines specified for BRKSPACE on FORMAT. Similarly, with case listings SKIP skips *n* lines after the blank line at the end of the listing.

PREVIOUS(n) — *Use the SUMMARY subcommands specified for the nth BREAK.* If *n* is not specified, PREVIOUS refers to the set of SUMMARY subcommands for the previous BREAK. If an integer is specified, the SUMMARY subcommands from the *n*th BREAK are used. If PREVIOUS is specified, no other specification can be used on that SUMMARY subcommand.

TITLE and FOOTNOTE Subcommands

TITLE and FOOTNOTE provide titles and footnotes for the report.

- TITLE and FOOTNOTE are optional and can be placed anywhere after FORMAT except between the BREAK and SUMMARY subcommands.
- The specification on TITLE or FOOTNOTE is the title or footnote in apostrophes or quotation marks. To specify a multiple-line title or footnote, enclose each line in apostrophes or quotation marks and separate the specifications for each line by at least one blank.
- The default REPORT title is the title specified on the TITLE command. If there is no TITLE command specified in your session, the default REPORT title is the first line of the header.
- Titles begin on the first line of the report page. Footnotes end on the last line of the report page.

- Titles and footnotes are repeated on each page of a multiple-page report.
- The positional keywords LEFT, CENTER, and RIGHT can each be specified once. The default is CENTER.
- If the total width needed for the combined titles or footnotes for a line exceeds the page width, REPORT generates an error message.

LEFT   *Left-justify titles or footnotes within the report page margins.*

RIGHT   *Right-justify titles or footnotes within the report page margins.*

CENTER   *Center titles and footnotes within the report page width.*

The following can be specified as part of the title or footnote.

)PAGE   *Display the page number right-justified in a five-character field.*

)DATE   *Display the current date in the form* dd/mmm/yy, *right-justified in a nine-character field.*

)var   *Display this variable's value label at this position.* If you specify a variable that has no value label, the value is displayed, formatted according to its print format. You cannot specify a scratch or system variable or a variable created with the STRING subcommand. If you want to use a variable named *DATE* or *PAGE* in the file, change the variable's name with the RENAME VARIABLES command before you use it on the TITLE or FOOTNOTE subcommands, to avoid confusion with the)PAGE and)DATE keywords.

-)PAGE,)DATE, and)var are specified within apostrophes or quotation marks and can be mixed with string segments within the apostrophes or quotation marks.
- A variable specified on TITLE or FOOTNOTE must be defined in the working data file, but does not need to be included as a column on the report.
- One label or value from each variable specified on TITLE or FOOTNOTE is displayed on every page of the report. If a new page starts with a case listing, REPORT takes the value label from the first case listed. If a new page starts with a BREAK line, REPORT takes the value label from the first case of the new break group. If a new page starts with a summary line, REPORT takes the value label from the last case of the break group being summarized.

Example

```
/TITLE=LEFT 'Personnel Report' 'Prepared on )DATE'
    RIGHT 'Page: )PAGE'
```

- TITLE specifies two lines for a left-justified title and one line for a right-justified title. These titles are displayed at the top of each page of the report.
- The second line of the left-justified title contains the date on which the report was processed.
- The right-justified title displays the page number following the string *Page:* on the same line as the first line of the left-justified title.

MISSING Subcommand

MISSING controls the treatment of cases with missing values.

- MISSING specifications apply to variables named on VARIABLES and SUMMARY and to strings created with the STRING subcommand.

- Missing-value specifications are ignored for variables named on BREAK when MISSING=VAR or NONE. There is one break category for system-missing values and one for each user-missing value.

- The character used to indicate missing values is controlled by the FORMAT subcommand.

VAR   *Missing values are treated separately for each variable.* Missing values are displayed in case listings but are not included in the calculation of summary statistics on a function-by-function basis. This is the default.

NONE   *User-missing values are treated as valid values.* This applies to all variables named on VARIABLES.

LIST[([varlist][n])]   *Cases with the specified number of missing values across the specified list of variables are not used.* The variable list and *n* are specified in parentheses. If *n* is not specified, the default is 1. If no variables are specified, all variables named on VARIABLES are assumed.

Example

```
/MISSING= LIST (XVAR,YVAR,ZVAR 2)
```

- Any case with two or more missing values across the variables *XVAR, YVAR,* and *ZVAR* is omitted from the report.

REREAD

```
REREAD [FILE=file]
       [COLUMN=expression]
```

Example:

```
INPUT PROGRAM.
DATA LIST /KIND 10-14 (A).

DO IF (KIND EQ 'FORD').
REREAD.
DATA LIST /PARTNO 1-2 PRICE 3-6 (DOLLAR,2) QUANTITY 7-9.
END CASE.

ELSE IF (KIND EQ 'CHEVY').
REREAD.
DATA LIST /PARTNO 1-2 PRICE 15-18 (DOLLAR,2) QUANTITY 19-21.
END CASE.
END IF.

END INPUT PROGRAM.

BEGIN DATA
111295100FORD
11       CHEVY 295015
END DATA.
```

Overview

REREAD instructs the program to reread a record in the data. It is available only within an INPUT PROGRAM structure and is generally used to define data using information obtained from a previous reading of the record. REREAD is usually specified within a conditional structure, such as DO IF—END IF, and is followed by a DATA LIST command. When it receives control for a case, REREAD places the pointer back to the column specified for the current case and begins reading data as defined by the DATA LIST command that follows.

Options

Data Source. You can use inline data or data from an external file specified on the FILE subcommand. Using external files allows you to open multiple files and merge data.

Beginning Column. You can specify a beginning column other than column 1 using the COLUMN subcommand.

Basic Specification

The basic specification is the command keyword REREAD. The program rereads the current case according to the data definitions specified on the following DATA LIST.

Subcommand Order

Subcommands can be specified in any order.

Syntax Rules

- REREAD is available only within an INPUT PROGRAM structure.
- Multiple REREAD commands can be used within the input program. Each must be followed by an associated DATA LIST command.

Operations

- REREAD causes the next DATA LIST command to reread the most recently processed record in the specified file.
- When it receives control for a case, REREAD places the pointer back to column 1 for the current case and begins reading data as defined by the DATA LIST that follows. If the COLUMN subcommand is specified, the pointer begins reading in the specified column and uses it as column 1 for data definition.
- REREAD can be used to read part of a record in FIXED format and the remainder in LIST format. Mixing FIXED and FREE formats yields unpredictable results.
- Multiple REREAD commands specified without an intervening DATA LIST do not have a cumulative effect. All but the last are ignored.

Example

```
INPUT PROGRAM.
DATA LIST /PARTNO 1-2 KIND 10-14 (A).

DO IF (KIND EQ 'FORD').
REREAD.
DATA LIST /PRICE 3-6 (DOLLAR,2) QUANTITY 7-9.
END CASE.

ELSE IF (KIND EQ 'CHEVY').
REREAD.
DATA LIST /PRICE 15-18 (DOLLAR,2) QUANTITY 19-21.
END CASE.
END IF.
END INPUT PROGRAM.

BEGIN DATA
111295100FORD       CHAPMAN AUTO SALES
121199005VW     MIDWEST VOLKSWAGEN SALES
11 395025FORD      BETTER USED CARS
11        CHEVY 195005       HUFFMAN SALES & SERVICE
11        VW    595020       MIDWEST VOLKSWAGEN SALES
11        CHEVY 295015       SAM'S AUTO REPAIR
12        CHEVY 210 20       LONGFELLOW CHEVROLET
  9555032 VW                 HYDE PARK IMPORTS
END DATA.
LIST.
```

- Data are extracted from an inventory of automobile parts. The automobile part number always appears in columns 1 and 2, and the automobile type always appears in columns 10 through 14. The location of other information such as price and quantity depends on both the part number and the type of automobile.

- The first DATA LIST extracts the part number and type of automobile.

- Depending on the information from the first DATA LIST, the records are reread using one of two DATA LIST commands, pulling the price and quantity from different places.

- The two END CASE commands limit the working data file to only those cases with part 11 and automobile type Ford or Chevrolet. Without the END CASE commands, cases would be created for other part numbers and automobile types, with missing values for price, quantity, and buyer.

The LIST output is shown in Figure 1.

Figure 1   Listed information for part 11

```
PARTNO KIND   PRICE QUANTITY

  11   FORD  $12.95   100
  11   FORD   $3.95    25
  11   CHEVY  $1.95     5
  11   CHEVY  $2.95    15
```

Example

```
* Multiple REREAD commands for the same record.

INPUT PROGRAM.
DATA LIST       NOTABLE/ CDIMAGE 1-20(A).
REREAD          COLUMN = 6.  /* A, C, and E are in column 6
REREAD          COLUMN = 11. /* B, D, and F are in column 11
DATA LIST       NOTABLE/ INFO 1(A).
END INPUT PROGRAM.
LIST.
BEGIN DATA
1    A    B
2    C    D
3    E    F
END DATA.
```

- Multiple REREAD commands are used without an intervening DATA LIST. Only the last one is used. Thus, the starting column comes from the last REREAD specified and the pointer is reset to column 11.
- Figure 2 shows the results from the LIST command.

Figure 2   Listed information after multiple REREAD commands

```
CDIMAGE              INFO

1    A    B           B
2    C    D           D
3    E    F           F
```

FILE Subcommand

FILE specifies an external raw data file from which the next DATA LIST command reads data.

- The default file is the file specified on the immediately preceding DATA LIST command.
- If the file specified on FILE is not the default file, the same file must be specified on the next DATA LIST. Otherwise, the FILE subcommand is ignored and the DATA LIST command reads the next record from the file specified on it or, if no file is specified, from the file specified on the previous DATA LIST command.

Example

```
INPUT PROGRAM.
DATA LIST FILE=UPDATE END=#EOF NOTABLE
    /#ID 1-3.                            /*Get rep ID in new sales file.
DATA LIST FILE = SALESREP NOTABLE
    /ID 1-3 SALES 4-11(F,2)
     NEWSALE 12-19(F,2).           /*Get rep record from master file.

LOOP IF #EOF OR (#ID GT ID).  /*If UPDATE ends or no new sales made.
+   COMPUTE NEWSALE = 0.       /*Set NEWSALE to 0
+   END CASE.                  /*Build a case.
+   DATA LIST FILE = SALESREP NOTABLE
    /ID 1-3 SALES 4-11(F,2)
     NEWSALE 12-19(F,2).              /*Continue reading masterfile.
END LOOP

DO IF NOT #EOF.                       /*If new sales made.
+   REREAD FILE=UPDATE COLUMN = 4.    /*Read new sales from UPDATE.
+   DATA LIST FILE=UPDATE
    /NEWSALE 1-8(F,2).
+   COMPUTE SALES=SALES+NEWSALE.      /*Update master file.
END IF.
END CASE.                            /*Build a case.
END INPUT PROGRAM.

LIST.
```

- This example uses REREAD to merge two raw data files (*SALESREP* and *UPDATE*).

- Both files are sorted by sales representative ID number. The *UPDATE* file contains only records for sales representatives who have made new sales, with variables *ID* and *NEWSALE*. The master file *SALESREP* contains records for all sales representatives, with variables *SALES* (which contains year-to-date sales) and *NEWSALE* (which contains the update values each time the file is updated).

- If a sales representative has made no new sales, there is no matching ID in the *UPDATE* file. When *UPDATE* is exhausted or when the ID's in the two files do not match, the loop structure causes the program to build a case with *NEWSALE* equal to 0 and then continue reading the master file.

- When the ID's match (and the *UPDATE* file is not yet exhausted), the REREAD command is executed. The following DATA LIST rereads the record in *UPDATE* that matches the *ID* variable. *NEWSALE* is read from the *UPDATE* file starting from column 4 and *SALES* is updated. Note that the following DATA LIST specifies the same file.

- When the updated base is built, the program returns to the first DATA LIST command in the input program and reads the next ID from the *UPDATE* file. If the *UPDATE* file is exhausted (*#EOF*=1), the loop keeps reading records from the master file until it reaches the end of the file.

- The same task can be accomplished using MATCH FILES. With MATCH FILES, the raw data must be read and saved as SPSS-format data files first.

COLUMN Subcommand

COLUMN specifies a beginning column for the REREAD command to read data. The default is column 1. You can specify a numeric expression for the column.

Example

```
INPUT PROGRAM.
DATA LIST /KIND 10-14 (A).
COMPUTE #COL=1.
IF (KIND EQ 'CHEVY') #COL=13.

DO IF (KIND EQ 'CHEVY' OR KIND EQ 'FORD').
REREAD COLUMN #COL.
DATA LIST /PRICE 3-6 (DOLLAR,2) QUANTITY 7-9.
END CASE.
END IF.
END INPUT PROGRAM.
BEGIN DATA
111295100FORD     CHAPMAN AUTO SALES
121199005VW    MIDWEST VOLKSWAGEN SALES
11 395025FORD    BETTER USED CARS
11        CHEVY 195005       HUFFMAN SALES & SERVICE
11        VW     595020       MIDWEST VOLKSWAGEN SALES
11        CHEVY 295015       SAM'S AUTO REPAIR
12        CHEVY 210 20       LONGFELLOW CHEVROLET
 9555032 VW                  HYDE PARK IMPORTS
END DATA.
LIST.
```

- The task in this example is to read *PRICE* and *QUANTITY* for Chevrolets and Fords only. A scratch variable is created to indicate the starting column positions for *PRICE* and *QUANTITY*, and a single DATA LIST command is used to read data for both types of automobiles.

- Scratch variable *#COL* is set to 13 for Chevrolets and 1 for all other automobiles. For Fords, the data begin in column 1. Variable *PRICE* is read from columns 3–6 and *QUANTITY* is read from columns 7–9. When the record is a Chevrolet, the data begins in column 13. Variable *PRICE* is read from columns 15–18 (15 is 3, 16 is 4, and so forth), and *QUANTITY* is read from columns 19–21.

Example

```
* Reading both FIXED and LIST input with REREAD.

INPUT PROGRAM.
DATA LIST      NOTABLE FIXED/ A 1-14(A).  /*Read the FIXED portion
REREAD         COLUMN = 15.
DATA LIST      LIST/ X Y Z.                /*Read the LIST portion
END INPUT PROGRAM.

* The value 1 on the first record is in column 15.

LIST.
BEGIN DATA
FIRST RECORD   1 2 3 -1 -2 -3
NUMBER 2       4 5
THE THIRD      6 7 8
#4
FIFTH AND LAST9 10 11
END DATA.
```

- Columns 1–14 are read in FIXED format. REREAD then resets the pointer to column 15. Thus, beginning in column 15, values are read in LIST format.
- The second DATA LIST specifies only three variables. Thus, the values –1, –2, and –3 on the first record are not read.
- The program generates a warning for the missing value on record 2 and a second warning for the three missing values on record 4.
- On the fifth and last record there is no delimiter between value LAST and value 9. REREAD can still read the 9 in LIST format.

RESTORE

RESTORE

Overview

RESTORE restores SET specifications that were stored by a previous PRESERVE command. RESTORE and PRESERVE are especially useful when using the macro facility. PRESERVE—RESTORE sequences can be nested up to five levels.

Basic Specification

The only specification is the command keyword. RESTORE has no additional specifications.

Example

```
GET FILE=PRSNNL.
FREQUENCIES VAR=DIVISION /STATISTICS=ALL.
PRESERVE.
SET XSORT=NO WIDTH=90 UNDEFINED=NOWARN BLANKS=000 CASE=UPLOW.
SORT CASES BY DIVISION.
REPORT FORMAT=AUTO LIST /VARS=LNAME FNAME DEPT SOCSEC SALARY
  /BREAK=DIVISION /SUMMARY=MEAN.
RESTORE.
```

- GET reads SPSS-format data file *PRSNNL*.
- FREQUENCIES requests a frequency table and all statistics for variable *DIVISION*.
- PRESERVE stores all current SET specifications.
- SET changes several subcommand settings.
- SORT sorts cases in preparation for a report. Because SET XSORT=NO, the sort program is not used to sort cases; another sort program must be available.
- REPORT requests a report organized by variable *DIVISION*.
- RESTORE reestablishes all the SET specifications that were in effect when PRESERVE was specified.

RMV

```
RMV new variables={LINT (varlist)           }
                  {MEAN (varlist [{,2 }])   }
                  {                {,n }     }
                  {                {ALL}     }
                  {MEDIAN (varlist [{,2 }])) }
                  {                 {,n }    }
                  {                 {ALL}    }
                  {SMEAN (varlist)          }
                  {TREND (varlist)          }

    [/new variables=function (varlist [,span])]
```

Function keywords:

LINT	Linear interpolation
MEAN	Mean of surrounding values
MEDIAN	Median of surrounding values
SMEAN	Variable mean
TREND	Linear trend at that point

Example:

```
RMV NEWVAR1=LINT(OLDVAR1).
```

Overview

RMV produces new variables by copying existing variables and replacing any system- or user-missing values with estimates computed by one of several methods. You can also use RMV to replace the values of existing variables. The estimated values are computed from valid data in the existing variables. The new or revised variables can be used in any procedure and can be saved in an SPSS-format data file.

Basic Specification

The basic specification is one or more new variable names, an equals sign, a function, and an equal number of existing variables. RMV displays a list of the new variables, the number of missing values replaced, the case numbers of the first and last nonmissing cases, the number of valid cases, and the function used to produce the variables.

Syntax Rules

- The existing variables (and span, if specified) must be enclosed in parentheses.
- The equals sign is required.
- You can specify more than one equation on RMV.

- Equations are separated by slashes.
- You can specify only one function per equation.
- You can create more than one new variable per equation by specifying more than one new variable name on the left and an equal number of existing variables on the right.

Operations

- Each new variable is added to the working data file.
- If the new variable named already exists, its values are replaced.
- If the new variable named does not already exist, it is created.
- If the same variable is named on both sides of the equation, the new variable will replace the existing variable. Valid values from the existing variable are copied into the new variable, and missing values are replaced with estimates.
- Variables are created in the order in which they are specified on the RMV command.
- If multiple variables are created on a single equation, the first new variable is based on the first existing variable, the second new variable is based on the second existing variable, and so forth.
- RMV automatically generates a variable label for each new variable describing the function and variable used to create it and the date and time of creation.
- The format of a new variable depends on the function specified and on the format of the existing variable.
- RMV honors the TSET MISSING setting that is currently in effect.
- RMV does not honor the USE command.

Limitations

- Maximum 1 function per equation.
- There is no limit on the number of variables created by an equation.
- There is no limit on the number of equations per RMV command.

LINT Function

LINT replaces missing values using linear interpolation. The last valid value before the missing value and the first valid value after the missing value are used for the interpolation.

- The only specification on LINT is a variable or variable list in parentheses.
- LINT will not replace missing values at the endpoints of variables.

Example

```
RMV NEWVAR1=LINT(OLDVAR1).
```

- This example produces a new variable called *NEWVAR1*.
- *NEWVAR1* will have the same values as *OLDVAR1* but with missing values replaced by linear interpolation.

MEAN Function

MEAN replaces missing values with the mean of valid surrounding values. The number of surrounding values used to compute the mean depends on the span.

- The specification on MEAN is a variable or variable list and a span, in parentheses.
- The span specification is optional and can be any positive integer or keyword ALL.
- A span of n uses n valid cases before and after the missing value.
- If span is not specified, it defaults to 2.
- Keyword ALL computes the mean of all valid values.
- MEAN will not replace missing values if there are not enough valid surrounding cases to satisfy the span specification.

Example

```
RMV B=MEAN(A,3).
```

- This example produces a new variable called *B*.
- *B* will have the same values as variable *A* but with missing values replaced by means of valid surrounding values.
- Each mean is based on 6 values, that is, the 3 nearest valid values on each side of the missing value.

MEDIAN Function

MEDIAN replaces missing values with the median of valid surrounding values. The number of surrounding values used to compute the median depends on the span.

- The specification on MEDIAN is a variable or variable list and a span, in parentheses.
- The span specification is optional and can be any positive integer or keyword ALL.
- A span of n uses n valid cases before and after the missing value.
- If span is not specified, it defaults to 2.
- Keyword ALL computes the median of all valid values.
- MEDIAN will not replace missing values if there are not enough valid surrounding cases to satisfy the span specification.

Example

```
RMV B=MEDIAN(A,3).
```

- This example produces a new variable called *B*.
- *B* will have the same values as *A* but with missing values replaced by medians of valid surrounding values.
- Each median is based on 6 values, that is, the 3 nearest valid values on each side of the missing value.

SMEAN Function

SMEAN replaces missing values in the new variable with the variable mean.

- The only specification on SMEAN is a variable or variable list in parentheses.
- The SMEAN function is equivalent to the MEAN function with a span specification of ALL.

Example

```
RMV VAR1 TO VAR4=SMEAN(VARA VARB VARC VARD).
```

- Four new variables (*VAR1*, *VAR2*, *VAR3*, and *VAR4*) are created.
- *VAR1* copies the values of *VARA*, *VAR2* copies *VARB*, *VAR3* copies *VARC*, and *VAR4* copies *VARD*. Any missing values in an existing variable are replaced with the mean of that variable.

TREND Function

TREND replaces missing values in the new variable with the linear trend for that point. The existing variable is regressed on an index variable scaled 1 to *n*. Missing values are replaced with their predicted values.

- The only specification on TREND is a variable or variable list in parentheses.

Example

```
RMV YHAT=TREND(VARY).
```

- This example creates a new variable called *YHAT*.
- *YHAT* has the same values as *VARY* but with missing values replaced by predicted values.

ROC

```
ROC varname BY varname({varvalue  })
                       {'varvalue'}

[/MISSING = {EXCLUDE**}]
            {INCLUDE  }

[/CRITERIA = [CUTOFF({INCLUDE**})]] [TESTPOS({LARGE**}) [CI({95**})]
                     {EXCLUDE  }            {SMALL  }     {n  }

                     [DISTRIBUTION({FREE**  })]]
                                   {NEGEXPO}

[/PLOT = [CURVE**[(REFERENCE)]] [NONE]]

[/PRINT = [SE] [COORDINATES]].
```

** Default if subcommand or keyword is omitted.

Overview

ROC produces a receiver operating characteristic (ROC) curve and an estimate of the area under the curve.

Options

Distributional Assumptions. In the CRITERIA subcommand, the user can choose the nonparametric or parametric method to estimate the standard error of the area under the curve. Currently, the bi-negative exponential distribution is the only parametric option.

Optional Output. In addition to an estimate of the area under the ROC curve, the user may request its standard error, a confidence interval, and a *P*-value under the null hypothesis that the area under the curve equals 0.5. A table of cut-off values and coordinates used to plot the ROC curve may also be displayed.

Basic Specification

The basic specification is one variable as the test result variable and one variable as the actual state variable with one of its values. ROC uses the nonparametric (distribution-free) method to calculate the area under the ROC curve. The default and minimum output is a chart of the ROC curve and a table of the area under the curve.

Syntax Rules

- Minimum syntax: You always need a test result variable and one actual state variable with one of its values in the ROC command line.

- The test result variable must be numeric, but the state variable can be any type with any format.
- Subcommands can be specified in any order.
- When a subcommand is duplicated, only the last one is honored given that all duplicates have no syntax errors. A syntax warning is issued.
- Within a subcommand, if two or more exclusive or contradictory keywords are given, the latter keywords override the earlier ones. A syntax warning is issued.
- If a keyword is duplicated within a subcommand, it is silently ignored.

Limitations

- Only the nonparametric method and one parametric method are available as the computational options for the standard error of the area under the curve at this moment. In the future, bi-normal and bi-logistic distributions may be added to the parametric option.
- Only one variable may be specified as the test result. In the future, the user will be able to specify a variable list.

varname BY varname(varvalue)

The varname specifies the test result variable. It must be of numeric type.

The second varname separated from the first one by the word BY specifies the actual state variable. It can be of any type and any format. The user must also specify a varvalue in brackets after the second varname to define the "positive" group of the actual state variable. All other valid state values are assumed to indicate the negative group.

MISSING Subcommand

Cases with a system-missing value in the test result variable and the actual state variable are always excluded from the analysis. However, the MISSING subcommand allows the user to redefine the user-missing values to be valid.

EXCLUDE   *Exclude both user-missing and system-missing values.* Cases with a system-missing value or a user-missing value in either the test result variable or the actual state variable are excluded from the analysis. This is the active default.

INCLUDE   *User-missing values are treated as valid.* Cases with a system-missing value in either the test result variable or the actual state variable are excluded from the analysis.

CRITERIA Subcommand

The CRITERIA subcommand allows the user to decide (1) whether the cutoff value is included as the positive test result value or not, (2) whether the larger or smaller value direction of the test result variable indicates the positive test result or not, (3) the confidence level of the asymptotic confidence interval produced by /PRINT = SE, and (4) the estimation method for the standard error of the area under the curve.

CUTOFF(INCLUDE)	*Positive classification of test result values includes the cutoff values.* Note that the positive test result direction is controlled by the TEST-POS keyword. This is the active default.
CUTOFF(EXCLUDE)	*Positive classification of test result values excludes the cutoff values.* This distinction leads to the different sets of cutoff values, but none of the output, chart and table, is affected at this moment, because the user cannot choose the cutoff values for the classification.
TESTPOS(LARGE)	*The user can specify which direction of the test result variable indicates increasing strength of conviction that the subject is test positive.* The larger the test result value is, the more positive the test result is. LARGE is the active default.
TESTPOS(SMALL)	*The smaller the test result value is, the more positive the test result is.*
CI(n)	*Confidence level in the (two-sided) asymptotic confidence interval of the area.* The user can specify any confidence level in (0, 100) for the asymptotic confidence interval created by /PRINT = SE. The active default parameter value is 95.
DISTRIBUTION(FREE)	*The method of calculating the standard error of the area under the curve.* When FREE, the standard error of the area under the curve is estimated nonparametrically—that is, without any distributional assumption.

DISTRIBUTION(NEGEXPO)

The standard error is estimated assuming the bi-negative exponential distribution. This latter option is valid only when the number of positive actual state observations equals the number of negative actual state observations.

PRINT Subcommand

The PRINT subcommand controls the display of optional table output. Note that the area under the curve is always displayed.

SE	*Standard error of the area estimate.* In addition to the standard error of the estimated area under the curve, the asymptotic 95% (or other user-specified confidence level) confidence interval as well as the asymptotic *P*-value under the null hypothesis that the true area = 0.5 are calculated. Note that the area under the curve statistic is asymptotically normally distributed.
COORDINATES	*Coordinate points of the ROC curve along with the cutoff values.* Pairs of sensitivity and 1 – specificity values are given with the cutoff values for each curve.

PLOT Subcommand

The PLOT subcommand controls the display of chart output.

CURVE(REFERENCE)   *The ROC curve chart is displayed.* The keyword CURVE is the active default. In addition, the user has an option to draw the diagonal reference line (sensitivity = 1 − specificity) by the bracketed parameter REFERENCE.

NONE   *The ROC curve chart is suppressed.*

SAMPLE

```
SAMPLE {decimal value}
       {n FROM m     }
```

Example:

```
SAMPLE .25.
```

Overview

SAMPLE permanently draws a random sample of cases for processing in all subsequent procedures. For a temporary sample, use a TEMPORARY command before SAMPLE.

Basic Specification

The basic specification is either a decimal value between 0 and 1 or the sample size followed by keyword FROM and the size of the working data file.

- To select an approximate percentage of cases, specify a decimal value between 0 and 1.
- To select an exact-size random sample, specify a positive integer less than the file size, followed by keyword FROM and the file size.

Operations

- SAMPLE is a permanent transformation.
- Sampling is based on a pseudo-random-number generator that depends on a seed value established by the program. On some implementations of the program, this number defaults to a fixed integer, and a SAMPLE command that specifies *n* FROM *m* will generate the identical sample whenever a session is rerun. To generate a different sample each time, use the SET command to reset SEED to a different value for each session. See the SET command for more information.
- If sampling is done using the *n* FROM *m* method and the TEMPORARY command is specified, successive samples will not be the same because the seed value changes each time a random number series is needed within a session.
- A proportional sample (a sample based on a decimal value) usually does not produce the exact proportion specified.
- If the number specified for *m* following FROM is less than the actual file size, the sample is drawn only from the first *m* cases.
- If the number following FROM is greater than the actual file size, the program samples an equivalent proportion of cases from the working data file (see example below).
- If SAMPLE follows SELECT IF, it samples only cases selected by SELECT IF.

868

- If SAMPLE precedes SELECT IF, cases are selected from the sample.
- If more than one SAMPLE is specified in a session, each acts upon the sample selected by the preceding SAMPLE command.
- If N OF CASES is used with SAMPLE, the program reads as many records as required to build the specified *n* cases. It makes no difference whether the N OF CASES precedes or follows the SAMPLE.

Limitations

SAMPLE cannot be placed in a FILE TYPE—END FILE TYPE or INPUT PROGRAM—END INPUT PROGRAM structure. It can be placed nearly anywhere following these commands in a transformation program. See Appendix A for a discussion of program states and the placement of commands.

Example

```
SAMPLE .25.
```

- This command samples approximately 25% of the cases in the working data file.

Example

```
SAMPLE 500 FROM 3420.
```

- The working data file must have 3420 cases or more to obtain a random sample of exactly 500 cases.
- If the file contains fewer than 3420 cases, proportionally fewer cases are sampled.
- If the file contains more than 3420 cases, a random sample of 500 cases is drawn from the first 3420 cases.

Example

```
DO IF  SEX EQ 'M'.
SAMPLE 1846 FROM 8000.
END IF.
```

- SAMPLE is placed inside a DO IF—END IF structure to sample subgroups differently. Assume that this is a survey of 10,000 people in which 80% of the sample is male, while the known universe is 48% male. To obtain a sample that corresponds to the known universe and that maximizes the size of the sample, 1846 (48/52*2000) males and all females must be sampled. The DO IF structure is used to restrict the sampling process to the males.

SAVE

```
SAVE OUTFILE=file

[/VERSION={3**}]
         {2  }

[/UNSELECTED=[{RETAIN}]
              {DELETE}

[/KEEP={ALL**  }]  [/DROP=varlist]
       {varlist}

[/RENAME=(old varlist=new varlist)...]

[/MAP]  [/{COMPRESSED  }]
           {UNCOMPRESSED}
```

**Default if the subcommand is omitted.

Example:

```
SAVE OUTFILE=EMPL  /RENAME=(AGE=AGE88) (JOBCAT=JOBCAT88).
```

Overview

SAVE produces an SPSS-format data file. An SPSS-format data file contains data plus a dictionary. The dictionary contains a name for each variable in the data file plus any assigned variable and value labels, missing-value flags, and variable print and write formats. The dictionary also contains document text created with the DOCUMENTS command.

XSAVE also creates SPSS-format data files. The difference is that SAVE causes data to be read, while XSAVE is not executed until data are read for the next procedure.

See SAVE TRANSLATE and SAVE SCSS for information on saving data files that can be used by other programs.

Options

Compatibility with Early Releases. You can save a data file that can be read by SPSS releases prior to 7.5.

Variable Subsets and Order. You can save a subset of variables and reorder the variables that are saved using the DROP and KEEP subcommands.

Variable Names. You can rename variables as they are copied into the SPSS-format data file using the RENAME subcommand.

Variable Map. To confirm the names and order of the variables saved in the SPSS-format data file, use the MAP subcommand. MAP displays the variables saved in the SPSS-format data file next to their corresponding names in the working data file.

Data Compression. You can write the data file in compressed or uncompressed form using the COMPRESSED or UNCOMPRESSED subcommand.

Basic Specification

The basic specification is the OUTFILE subcommand, which specifies a name for the SPSS-format data file to be saved.

Subcommand Order

- Subcommands can be specified in any order.

Syntax Rules

- OUTFILE is required and can be specified only once. If OUTFILE is specified more than once, only the last OUTFILE specified is in effect.
- KEEP, DROP, RENAME, and MAP can each be used as many times as needed.
- Only one of the subcommands COMPRESSED or UNCOMPRESSED can be specified per SAVE command.

Operations

- SAVE is executed immediately and causes the data to be read.
- The new SPSS-format data file dictionary is arranged in the same order as the working file dictionary, unless variables are reordered with the KEEP subcommand. Documentary text from the working file dictionary is always saved unless it is dropped with the DROP DOCU-MENTS command before SAVE.
- New variables created by transformations and procedures previous to the SAVE command are included in the new SPSS-format data file, and variables altered by transformations are saved in their modified form. Results of any temporary transformations immediately preceding the SAVE command are included in the file; scratch variables are not.
- SPSS-format data files are binary files designed to be read and written by SPSS only. SPSS-format data files can be edited only with the UPDATE command. Use the MATCH FILES and ADD FILES commands to merge SPSS-format data files.
- The working data file is still available for transformations and procedures after SAVE is executed.
- SAVE processes the dictionary first and displays a message that indicates how many variables will be saved. Once the data are written, SAVE indicates how many cases were saved. If the second message does not appear, the file was probably not completely written.

Example

```
GET FILE=HUBEMPL.
SAVE OUTFILE=EMPL88 /RENAME=(AGE=AGE88) (JOBCAT=JOBCAT88).
```

- The GET command retrieves the SPSS-format data file *HUBEMPL*.
- The RENAME subcommand renames variable *AGE* to *AGE88* and variable *JOBCAT* to *JOBCAT88*.
- SAVE causes the data to be read and saves a new SPSS-format data file with filename *EMPL88*. The original SPSS-format data file *HUBEMPL* is not changed.

Example

```
GET FILE=HUBEMPL.
TEMPORARY.
RECODE DEPT85 TO DEPT88 (1,2=1) (3,4=2) (ELSE=9).
VALUE LABELS DEPT85 TO DEPT88 1 'MANAGEMENT' 2 'OPERATIONS' 9
'UNKNOWN'.
SAVE OUTFILE=HUBTEMP.
CROSSTABS DEPT85 TO DEPT88 BY JOBCAT.
```

- The GET command retrieves the SPSS-format data file *HUBEMPL*.
- The TEMPORARY command indicates that RECODE and VALUE LABELS are in effect only for the next command that reads the data (SAVE).
- The RECODE command recodes values for all variables between and including *DEPT85* and *DEPT88* on the working data file.
- The VALUE LABELS command specifies new labels for the recoded values.
- The OUTFILE subcommand on SAVE specifies *HUBTEMP* as the new SPSS-format data file. *HUBTEMP* will include the recoded values for *DEPT85* to *DEPT88* and the new value labels.
- The *CROSSTABS* command crosstabulates *DEPT85* to *DEPT88* with *JOBCAT*. Since the RECODE and VALUE LABELS commands were temporary, the CROSSTABS output does not reflect the recoding and new labels.
- If XSAVE were specified instead of SAVE, the data would be read only once. Both the saved SPSS-format data file and the CROSSTABS output would reflect the temporary recoding and labeling of the department variables.

OUTFILE Subcommand

OUTFILE specifies the SPSS-format data file to be saved. OUTFILE is required and can be specified only once. If OUTFILE is specified more than once, only the last OUTFILE is in effect.

VERSION Subcommand

VERSION allows you to save a data file that can be opened in SPSS releases prior to 7.5. The default is 3 if VERSION is not specified or specified with no value. Specify 2 to save a file compatible with earlier releases.

UNSELECTED Subcommand

UNSELECTED determines whether cases excluded on a previous FILTER or USE command are to be retained or deleted in the SPSS-format data file. The default is RETAIN. The UNSELECT-ED subcommand has no effect when the working data file does not contain unselected cases.

RETAIN   *Retain the unselected cases.* All cases in the working data file are saved. This is the default when UNSELECTED is specified by itself.

DELETE   *Delete the unselected cases.* Only cases that meet the FILTER or USE criteria are saved in the SPSS-format data file.

DROP and KEEP Subcommands

DROP and KEEP are used to save a subset of variables. DROP specifies the variables not to save in the new data file; KEEP specifies the variables to save in the new data file; variables not named on KEEP are dropped.

- Variables can be specified in any order. The order of variables on KEEP determines the order of variables in the SPSS-format data file. The order on DROP does not affect the order of variables in the SPSS-format data file.

- Keyword ALL on KEEP refers to all remaining variables not previously specified on KEEP. ALL must be the last specification on KEEP.

- If a variable is specified twice on the same subcommand, only the first mention is recognized.

- Multiple DROP and KEEP subcommands are allowed. Specifying a variable that is not in the working data file or that has been dropped because of a previous DROP or KEEP sub-command results in an error, and the SAVE command is not executed.

- Keyword TO can be used to specify a group of consecutive variables in the active file.

Example

```
GET FILE=PRSNL.
COMPUTE TENURE=(12-CMONTH +(12*(88-CYEAR)))/12.
COMPUTE JTENURE=(12-JMONTH +(12*(88-JYEAR)))/12.
VARIABLE LABELS       TENURE 'Tenure in Company'
                      JTENURE 'Tenure in Grade'.
SAVE OUTFILE=PRSNL88 /DROP=GRADE STORE
    /KEEP=LNAME NAME TENURE JTENURE ALL.
```

- The variables *TENURE* and *JTENURE* are created by COMPUTE commands and assigned variable labels by the VARIABLE LABELS command. *TENURE* and *JTENURE* are added to the end of the working data file.

- DROP excludes variables *GRADE* and *STORE* from file *PRSNL88*. KEEP specifies that *LNAME, NAME, TENURE*, and *JTENURE* are the first four variables in file *PRSNL88*, followed by all remaining variables not specified on DROP. These remaining variables are saved in the same sequence as they appear in the original file.

RENAME Subcommand

RENAME changes the names of variables as they are copied into the new SPSS-format data file.

- The specification on RENAME is a list of old variable names followed by an equals sign and a list of new variable names. The same number of variables must be specified on both lists. Keyword TO can be used in the first list to refer to consecutive variables in the working data file and in the second list to generate new variable names. The entire specification must be enclosed in parentheses.
- Alternatively, you can specify each old variable name individually, followed by an equals sign and the new variable name. Multiple sets of variable specifications are allowed. The parentheses around each set of specifications are optional.
- RENAME does not affect the working data file. However, if RENAME precedes DROP or KEEP, variables must be referred to by their new names on DROP or KEEP.
- Old variable names do not need to be specified according to their order in the working data file.
- Name changes take place in one operation. Therefore, variable names can be exchanged between two variables.
- Multiple RENAME subcommands are allowed.

Example

```
SAVE OUTFILE=EMPL88 /RENAME AGE=AGE88 JOBCAT=JOBCAT88.
```

- RENAME specifies two name changes for the file *EMPL88*: the variable *AGE* is renamed to *AGE88* and the variable *JOBCAT* is renamed to *JOBCAT88*.

Example

```
SAVE OUTFILE=EMPL88 /RENAME (AGE JOBCAT=AGE88 JOBCAT88).
```

- The name changes are identical to those in the previous example: *AGE* is renamed to *AGE88* and *JOBCAT* is renamed to *JOBCAT88*. The parentheses are required with this method.

MAP Subcommand

MAP displays a list of the variables in the SPSS-format data file and their corresponding names in the working data file.

- The only specification is keyword MAP. There are no additional specifications.
- Multiple MAP subcommands are allowed. Each MAP subcommand maps the results of subcommands that precede it, but not results of subcommands that follow it.

Example

```
GET FILE=HUBEMPL.
SAVE OUTFILE=EMPL88 /RENAME=(AGE=AGE88)(JOBCAT=JOBCAT88)
 /KEEP=LNAME NAME JOBCAT88 ALL /MAP.
```

- MAP is used to confirm the new names for *AGE* and *JOBCAT* and the order of variables in the *EMPL88* file (*LNAME*, *NAME*, and *JOBCAT88*, followed by all remaining variables from the working data file).

COMPRESSED and UNCOMPRESSED Subcommands

COMPRESSED saves the file in compressed form. UNCOMPRESSED saves the file in uncompressed form. In a compressed file, small integers (from −99 to 155) are stored in one byte instead of the eight bytes used in an uncompressed file.

- The only specification is the keyword COMPRESSED or UNCOMPRESSED. There are no additional specifications.
- Compressed data files occupy less disk space than do uncompressed data files.
- Compressed data files take longer to read than do uncompressed data files.
- The GET command, which reads SPSS-format data files, does not need to specify whether the files it reads are compressed or uncompressed.
- Only one of the subcommands COMPRESSED or UNCOMPRESSED can be specified per SAVE command. COMPRESSED is usually the default, though UNCOMPRESSED may be the default on some systems.

SAVE TRANSLATE

This command is not available on all operating systems.

```
SAVE TRANSLATE

[{/OUTFILE=file              }]*
 {/CONNECT=ODBC connect string}**

 [/TYPE={DB2 }]
        {DB3 }
        {DB4 }
        {ODBC}
        {PC  }
        {SLK }
        {TAB }
        {WKS }
        {WK1 }
        {WK3 }
        {WRK }
        {WR1 }
        {XLS }

 [/TABLE = ODBC table name]**

 [/RENAME=(old varlist=new varlist)[(...)]

 [/KEEP={ALL     }]
        {varlist}

 [/DROP=varlist]

 [{/COMPRESSED   }]
  {/UNCOMPRESSED}

 [/FIELDNAMES]***

 [/MAP]

 [{/REPLACE}]
  {/APPEND }****

 [/UNSELECTED=[{RETAIN}]
               {DELETE}
```

*   Invalid for TYPE=ODBC; required for all other types.
**   Required for TYPE=ODBC; invalid for all other types.
*** Available only for spreadsheet formats.
****Available only for ODBC format.

Keyword	Type of file
WK1	1-2-3 Release 2.0
WKS	1-2-3 Release 1A
WR1	Symphony Release 2.0
WRK	Symphony Release 1.0
SLK	Multiplan or Excel in SYLK (symbolic link) format
XLS	Microsoft Excel
DB2	dBASE II
DB3	dBASE III
DB4	dBASE IV
TAB	Tab-delimited ASCII file
ODBC	Database accessed via ODBC
PC	SPSS/PC+ system file

Example:

```
SAVE TRANSLATE OUTFILE='SALESREP.SLK'
 /KEEP=SALES, UNITS, MONTHS, PRICE1 TO PRICE20
 /FIELDNAMES.
```

Overview

SAVE TRANSLATE translates the working data file into a file that can be used by other software applications. Supported formats are 1-2-3, Symphony, Multiplan, Excel, dBASE II, dBASE III, dBASE IV, tab-delimited ASCII files, and SPSS/PC+ data files.

Options

Variable Subsets. You can use the DROP and KEEP subcommands to specify variables to omit or retain in the resulting file.

Variable Names. You can rename variables as they are copied to the spreadsheet, database, or tab-delimited ASCII file using the RENAME subcommand.

Variable Map. To confirm the names and order of the variables saved in the resulting file, use the MAP subcommand. MAP displays the variables saved in the file next to their corresponding names in the working data file.

Spreadsheet Files. You can use the FIELDNAMES subcommand to translate variable names to field names in a spreadsheet file.

Basic Specification

- The basic specification is OUTFILE with a file specification in apostrophes.

- TYPE and a keyword to indicate the type of dBASE file is also required to save dBASE database files.

Subcommand Order

- OUTFILE or CONNECT must be specified first. OUTFILE is invalid for TYPE=ODBC and required for all other types. CONNECT is required for TYPE=ODBC and invalid for all other types.
- The remaining subcommands can be specified in any order.

Operations

- The working data file remains available after SAVE TRANSLATE is executed.
- User-missing values are transferred as actual values.
- If the working data file contains more variables than the file can receive, SAVE TRANSLATE writes the maximum number of variables the file can receive.

Spreadsheets

Variables in the working data file become columns, and cases become rows in the spreadsheet file.

- If you specify FIELDNAMES, variable names become the first row and indicate field names.
- String variable values are left-justified and numeric variable values are right-justified.
- The resulting spreadsheet file is given the range name of SPSS.
- System-missing values are translated to N/A in spreadsheet files.

SPSS formats are translated as follows:

SPSS	1-2-3/Symphony	Multiplan	Excel
Number	Fixed	Fixed	0.00;#,##0.00;...
COMMA	Comma	Fixed	0.00;#,##0.00;...
DOLLAR	Currency	$ (dollar)	$#,##0_);...
DATE	Date		d-mmm-yy
TIME	Time		hh:mm:ss
String	Label	Alpha	General

Databases

Variables in the working data file become fields, and cases become records in the database file.

- Characters that are allowed in variable names but not in dBASE field names are translated to colons in dBASE II and underscores in dBASE III and dBASE IV.

- Numeric variables containing the system-missing value are translated to **** in dBASE III and dBASE IV, and 0 in dBASE II.
- The width and precision of translated numeric are taken from the print format; the total number of characters for the number is taken from the width of the print format, and the number of digits to the right of the decimal point is taken from the decimals in the print format. To adjust the width and precision, use the PRINT FORMATS command prior to using SAVE TRANSLATE. Values that cannot be converted to the given width and precision are converted to missing values.

Variable formats are translated to dBASE formats as follows:

SPSS	dBASE
Number	Numeric
String	Character
Dollar	Numeric
Comma	Numeric

Tab-delimited ASCII Files

Variables in the working data file become columns, and cases become rows in the ASCII file.

- If you specify FIELDNAMES, variable names become the first row as column headings.
- All values are delimited by tabs.
- The resulting ASCII file is given the extension .DAT if no file extension is explicitly specified.
- System-missing values are translated to N/A in ASCII files.
- SPSS formats are not translated.

SPSS/PC+ System Files

Variables are saved as they are defined. The resulting file is given the extension .SYS if no extension is explicitly specified. The dictionary is saved so that labels, formats, missing value specifications, and other dictionary information are preserved.

Limitations

- Maximum 2048 cases can be translated to 1-2-3 Release 1A, maximum 8192 cases to 1-2-3 Release 2.0 or Symphony files, maximum 4095 cases to Multiplan files, and maximum 16,384 cases for Excel.
- Maximum 65,535 cases and 32 variables can be translated to dBASE II; maximum 1 billion cases (subject to disk space availability) and 128 variables to dBASE III; or maximum 1 billion cases (subject to disk space availability) and 255 variables to dBASE IV.

OUTFILE Subcommand

OUTFILE assigns a name to the file to be saved. The only specification is the name of the file. On some operating systems, file specifications should be enclosed in quotation marks or apostrophes.

Example

```
SAVE TRANSLATE OUTFILE='STAFF.DBF'/TYPE=DB3.
```

- SAVE TRANSLATE creates a dBASE III file called *STAFF.DBF*. The TYPE subcommand is required to specify the type of dBASE file to save.

CONNECT Subcommand

CONNECT identifies the database name and other parameters for TYPE=ODBC.

Example

```
SAVE TRANSLATE
   /CONNECT="DSN=MSAccess;UID=rkrishna;PWD=123xyz"
   /TABLE="mytable"
   /TYPE=ODBC.
```

TABLE Subcommand

TABLE identifies the table name for TYPE=ODBC.

Example

```
SAVE TRANSLATE
   /CONNECT="DSN=MSAccess;UID=rkrishna;PWD=123xyz"
   /TABLE="mytable"
   /TYPE=ODBC.
```

REPLACE Subcommand

REPLACE gives permission to overwrite an existing file of the same name. It takes no further specifications.

APPEND Subcommand

APPEND appends to an existing database table after type and variable name validations. There must be a matching column in the table for each SPSS variable. If a column is not found that can correctly store an SPSS variable, a failure is returned. If the table contains more columns than the number of SPSS variables, the command still stores the data in the table. The variable names and column names must match exactly. A variable can be stored in a column as long as the column type is one that can store values of the SPSS variable type. So, a column of any numeric type (short integer, integer, float, double, etc.) is valid for a numeric SPSS variable, and a column of any character type is valid for a string SPSS variable.

APPEND is valid only for TYPE=ODBC. You can specify either APPEND or REPLACE, but not both.

TYPE Subcommand

TYPE indicates the format of the resulting file.

- TYPE can be omitted for spreadsheet files if the file extension named on OUTFILE is the default for the type of file you are saving.
- TYPE with keyword DB2, DB3, or DB4 is required for translating to dBASE files.
- TYPE takes precedence over the file extension.
- A file that was read using GET TRANSLATE should be saved as the same type.

WK1	*1-2-3 Release 2.0.*
WKS	*1-2-3 Release 1.4.*
WR1	*Symphony Release 2.0.*
WRK	*Symphony Release 1.0.*
SLK	*Multiplan (symbolic format).*
XLS	*Excel.*
DB2	*dBASE II.*
DB3	*dBASE III or dBASE III PLUS.*
DB4	*dBASE IV.*
TAB	*Tab-delimited ASCII data files.*
PC	*SPSS/PC+ system files.*
ODBC	*Database accessed via ODBC.*

Example

```
SAVE TRANSLATE OUTFILE='PROJECT.OCT' /TYPE=SLK.
```

- SAVE TRANSLATE translates the working data file into the Multiplan spreadsheet file named *PROJECT.OCT.*

Writing to an ODBC Database Source

The following rules apply when writing to a database with TYPE=ODBC:

- If any case cannot be stored in the database for any reason, an error is returned. Therefore, either all cases are stored or none.
- At insert time, a check is performed to see if the value being stored in a column is likely to cause an overflow. If that is the case, the user is warned about the overflow and that a *SYSMIS* is stored instead.

- If any variable names in the working data file contain characters not allowed by the database, they are replaced by an underscore. If this causes a duplicate variable name, a new variable name is generated.

- The following SPSS variable type classes are supported:
  VC_STRING
  VC_NUMERIC
  VC_PERCENT
  VC_CURRENCY
  VC_TIME
  VC_DATE

- If a variable falls into the *VC_UNKNOWN* category, it is dropped. SPSS missing values are treated as missing values in the databases.

- Date variables are treated as Date columns, but if the database treats Date variables as TimeStamp (i.e., as datetime columns), then the time part of the TimeStamp is assigned a zero value (00:00.00) internally. The date value is unaltered when read back into SPSS.

- Datetime variables are stored as datetime (TimeStamp) columns.

- If a database does not support storing fractional seconds, the fractional value is truncated.

- SPSS dictionary information is not stored in the database table. Any formatting information contained in the SPSS dictionary is lost.

FIELDNAMES Subcommand

FIELDNAMES translates variable names into field names in the spreadsheet.

- FIELDNAMES can be used with spreadsheets and tab-delimited ASCII files. FIELDNAMES is ignored when used with database files.

- Variable names are transferred to the first row of the spreadsheet file.

Example.

```
SAVE TRANSLATE OUTFILE='STAFF.WRK' /FIELDNAMES.
```

- SAVE TRANSLATE creates a Symphony spreadsheet file containing all variables from the working data file. The variable names are transferred to the Symphony file.

UNSELECTED Subcommand

UNSELECTED determines whether cases excluded on a previous FILTER or USE command are to be retained or deleted in the SPSS-format data file. The default is RETAIN. The UNSELECTED subcommand has no effect when the working data file does not contain unselected cases.

RETAIN   *Retain the unselected cases.* All cases in the working data file are saved. This is the default when UNSELECTED is specified by itself.

DELETE   *Delete the unselected cases.* Only cases that meet the FILTER or USE criteria are saved in the SPSS-format data file.

DROP and KEEP Subcommands

Use DROP or KEEP to include only a subset of variables in the resulting file. DROP specifies a set of variables to exclude. KEEP specifies a set of variables to retain. Variables not specified on KEEP are dropped.

- Specify a list of variable, column, or field names separated by commas or spaces.
- KEEP does *not* affect the order of variables in the resulting file. Variables are kept in their original order.
- Specifying a variable that is not in the working data file or that has been dropped because of a previous DROP or KEEP subcommand results in an error and the SAVE command is not executed.

Example

```
SAVE TRANSLATE OUTFILE='ADDRESS.DBF' /TYPE=DB4 /DROP=PHONENO, ENTRY.
```

- SAVE TRANSLATE creates a dBASE IV file named *ADDRESS.DBF*, dropping the variables *PHONENO* and *ENTRY*.

RENAME Subcommand

RENAME changes the names of variables as they are copied into the resulting file.

- The specification on RENAME is a list of old variable names followed by an equals sign and a list of new variable names. The same number of variables must be specified on both lists. The keyword TO can be used in the first list to refer to consecutive variables in the working data file and in the second list to generate new variable names (see "Keyword TO" on p. 29). The entire specification must be enclosed in parentheses.
- Alternatively, you can specify each old variable name individually, followed by an equals sign and the new variable name. Multiple sets of variable specifications are allowed. The parentheses around each set of specifications are optional.
- RENAME does not affect the working data file. However, if RENAME precedes DROP or KEEP, variables must be referred to by their new names on DROP or KEEP.
- Old variable names do not need to be specified according to their order in the working data file.
- Name changes take place in one operation. Therefore, variable names can be exchanged between two variables.
- Multiple RENAME subcommands are allowed.

Example

```
SAVE TRANSLATE OUTFILE='STAFF.WRK' /FIELDNAMES
  /RENAME AGE=AGE88 JOBCAT=JOBCAT88.
```

- RENAME renames the variable *AGE* to *AGE88* and *JOBCAT* to *JOBCAT88* before they are copied to the first row of the spreadsheet.

Example

```
SAVE TRANSLATE OUTFILE='STAFF.WRK' /FIELDNAMES
  /RENAME (AGE JOBCAT=AGE88 JOBCAT88).
```

- The name changes are identical to those in the previous example: *AGE* is renamed to *AGE88* and *JOBCAT* is renamed to *JOBCAT88*. The parentheses are required with this method.

MAP Subcommand

MAP displays a list of the variables in the resulting file and their corresponding names in the working data file.

- The only specification is the keyword MAP. There are no additional specifications.
- Multiple MAP subcommands are allowed. Each MAP subcommand maps the results of subcommands that precede it but not the results of subcommands that follow it.

Example

```
GET FILE=HUBEMPL.
SAVE TRANSLATE OUTFILE='STAFF.WRK' /FIELDNAMES
  /RENAME=(AGE=AGE88)(JOBCAT=JOBCAT88).
```

- MAP is specified to confirm that the variable *AGE* is renamed to *AGE88* and *JOBCAT* is renamed to *JOBCAT88*.

SCRIPT

```
SCRIPT 'filename' [(quoted string)]
```

Overview

SCRIPT runs a script created to customize the program or automate regularly performed tasks.

Basic Specification

The basic specification is keyword SCRIPT with a filename. The filename is required. The optional quoted string, enclosed in parentheses, can be passed to the script.

Operations

SCRIPT runs the specified script. The effect is the same as opening the script file in the Script Editor and running it from there.

Running Scripts that Contain SPSS Commands

If a script run via the SCRIPT command contains SPSS commands, those commands must be run asynchronously. To run commands asynchronously, set the bSync parameter of the ExecuteCommands method to False, as in:

```
Dim objSpssApp as ISpssApp
Dim strCommands as String
Set objSpssApp = CreateObject("SPSS.Application")
' Construct and execute syntax commands:

strCommands = "GET FILE = 'c:\spss\bank.sav' " & vbCr
strCommands = strCommands & "Display Dictionary."
objSpssApp.ExecuteCommands strCommands, False
```

SELECT IF

```
SELECT IF [(]logical expression[)]
```

The following relational operators can be used in logical expressions:

Symbol	Definition	Symbol	Definition
EQ or =	Equal to	NE or <>*	Not equal to
LT or <	Less than	LE or <=	Less than or equal to

* On ASCII systems (for example, UNIX, VAX, and all PC's) you can also use ~=; on IBM EBCDIC systems (for example, IBM 360 and IBM 370) you can also use ¬=.

The following logical operators can be used in logical expressions:

Symbol	Definition
AND or &	Both relations must be true
OR or l	Either relation can be true

* On ASCII systems you can also use ~; on IBM EBCDIC systems you can also use ¬ (or the symbol above number 6).

Example:
```
SELECT IF (SEX EQ 'MALE').
```

Overview

SELECT IF permanently selects cases for analysis based upon logical conditions found in the data. These conditions are specified in a *logical expression*. The logical expression can contain relational operators, logical operators, arithmetic operations, and any functions allowed in COMPUTE transformations (see COMPUTE and see "Transformation Expressions" on p. 43). For temporary case selection, specify a TEMPORARY command before SELECT IF.

Basic Specification

The basic specification is simply a logical expression.

Syntax Rules

- Logical expressions can be simple logical variables or relations, or complex logical tests involving variables, constants, functions, relational operators, and logical operators. The logical expression can use any of the numeric or string functions allowed in COMPUTE transformations (see COMPUTE and see "Transformation Expressions" on p. 43).

- Parentheses can be used to enclose the logical expression. Parentheses can also be used within the logical expression to specify the order of operations. Extra blanks or parentheses can be used to make the expression easier to read.

- A relation can compare variables, constants, or more complicated arithmetic expressions. Relations cannot be abbreviated. For example, (A EQ 2 OR A EQ 5) is valid while (A EQ 2 OR 5) is not. Blanks (not commas) must be used to separate relational operators from the expressions being compared.

- A relation cannot compare a string variable to a numeric value or variable, or vice versa. A relation cannot compare the result of the logical functions SYSMIS, MISSING, ANY, or RANGE to a number.

- String values used in expressions must be specified in quotation marks and must include any leading or trailing blanks. Lowercase letters are considered distinct from uppercase letters.

Operations

- SELECT IF permanently selects cases. Cases not selected are dropped from the working data file.

- The logical expression is evaluated as true, false, or missing. If a logical expression is true, the case is selected; if it is false or missing, the case is not selected.

- Multiple SELECT IF commands issued prior to a procedure command must all be true for a case to be selected.

- SELECT IF should be placed before other transformations for efficiency considerations.

- Logical expressions are evaluated in the following order: first numeric functions, then exponentiation, then arithmetic operators, then relational operators, and last logical operators. Use parentheses to change the order of evaluation.

- If N OF CASES is used with SELECT IF, the program reads as many records as required to build the specified *n* cases. It makes no difference whether the N OF CASES precedes or follows the SELECT IF.

- System variable $CASENUM is the sequence number of a case in the working data file. Although it is syntactically correct to use $CASENUM on SELECT IF, it does not produce the expected results. To select a set of cases based on their sequence in a file, create your own sequence variable with the transformation language prior to selecting (see the example below).

Missing Values

- If the logical expression is indeterminate because of missing values, the case is not selected. In a simple relational expression, a logical expression is indeterminate if the expression on either side of the relational operator is missing.
- If a compound expression is used in which relations are joined by the logical operator OR, the case is selected if either relation is true, even if the other is missing.
- To select cases with missing values for the variables within the expression, use the missing-value functions. To include cases with values that have been declared user-missing along with other cases, use the VALUE function (see p. 58).

Limitations

SELECT IF cannot be placed within a FILE TYPE—END FILE TYPE or INPUT PROGRAM—END INPUT PROGRAM structure. It can be placed nearly anywhere following these commands in a transformation program. See Appendix A for a discussion of program states and the placement of commands.

Example

```
SELECT IF (SEX EQ 'MALE').
```

- All subsequent procedures will use only cases in which the value of *SEX* is MALE.
- Since upper and lower case are treated differently in comparisons of string variables, cases for which the value of *SEX* is male are not selected.

Example

```
SELECT IF (INCOME GT 75000 OR INCOME LE 10000).
```

- The logical expression tests whether a case has a value either greater than 75,000 or less than or equal to 10,000. If either relation is true, the case is used in subsequent analyses.

Example

```
SELECT IF (V1 GE V2).
```

- This example selects cases where variable *V1* is greater than or equal to *V2*. If either *V1* or *V2* is missing, the logical expression is indeterminate and the case is not selected.

Example

```
SELECT IF (SEX = 'F' & INCOME <= 10000).
```

- The logical expression tests whether string variable *SEX* is equal to F and if numeric variable *INCOME* is less than or equal to 10,000. Cases that meet both conditions are included in subsequent analyses. If either *SEX* or *INCOME* is missing for a case, the case is not selected.

Example

```
SELECT IF (SYSMIS(V1)).
```

- The logical expression tests whether *V1* is system-missing. If it is, the case is selected for subsequent analyses.

Example

```
SELECT IF (VALUE(V1) GT 0).
```

- Cases are selected if *V1* is greater than 0, even if the value of *V1* has been declared user-missing.

Example

```
SELECT IF (V1 GT 0).
```

- Cases are not selected if *V1* is user-missing, even if the user-missing value is greater than 0.

Example

```
SELECT IF (RECEIV GT DUE AND (REVNUS GE EXPNS OR BALNCE GT 0)).
```

- By default, AND is executed before OR. This expression uses parentheses to change the order of evaluation.
- The program first tests whether variable *REVNUS* is greater than or equal to variable *EXPNS*, or variable *BALNCE* is greater than 0. Second, the program tests whether *RECEIV* is greater than *DUE*. If one of the expressions in parentheses is true and *RECEIV* is greater than *DUE*, the case is selected.
- Without the parentheses, the program would first test whether *RECEIV* is greater than *DUE* and *REVNUS* is greater than or equal to *EXPNS*. Second, the program would test whether *BALNCE* is greater than 0. If the first two expressions are true *or* if the third expression is true, the case is selected.

Example

```
SELECT IF ((V1-15) LE (V2*(-0.001))).
```

- The logical expression compares whether *V1* minus 15 is less than or equal to *V2* multiplied by –0.001. If it is, the case is selected.

Example

```
SELECT IF ((YRMODA(88,13,0) - YRMODA(YVAR,MVAR,DVAR)) LE 30).
```

- The logical expression subtracts the number of days representing the date *(YVAR, MVAR, and DVAR)* from the number of days representing the last day in 1988. If the difference is less than or equal to 30, the case is selected.

Example

```
* Creating a sequence number.

COMPUTE  #CASESEQ=#CASESEQ+1.
SELECT IF (MOD(#CASESEQ,2)=0).
```

- This example computes a scratch variable, *#CASESEQ*, containing the sequence numbers for each case. Every other case beginning with the second is selected.
- *#CASESEQ* must be a scratch variable so that it is not reinitialized for every case. An alternative is to use the LEAVE command.

Example

```
DO IF   SEX EQ 'M'.
+    SELECT IF PRESTIGE GT 50.
ELSE IF   SEX EQ 'F'.
+    SELECT IF PRESTIGE GT 45.
END IF.
```

- The SELECT IF commands within the DO IF structure select males with prestige scores above 50 and females with prestige scores above 45.

SET

```
SET  [WORKSPACE={512**}]    [MXMEMORY= {14000**}] ]MXCELLS={AUTOMATIC**} ]
                {  n  }                 {  n     }            {n          }

    [FORMAT={F8.2**}] [CTEMPLATE {NONE**  }
            {Fw.d  }                      {filename}

    [TLOOK {NONE**  }]
           {filename}

    [ONUMBERS={LABELS**} ]  [OVARS={LABELS**} ]
              {VALUES  }           {NAMES   }
              {BOTH    }           {BOTH    }

    [TFIT={BOTH**} ]  [TNUMBERS={VALUES**} ]  [TVARS={NAMES**} ]
          {LABELS}              {LABELS  }           {LABELS }
                                {BOTH    }           {BOTH   }

    [SEED={2000000**}
          {RANDOM   }]
          {n        }

    [EPOCH={AUTOMATIC } ]
           {begin year}

    [{ERRORS   } =  {LISTING**}]
     {RESULTS  }    {NONE     }

     {PRINTBACK} = {NONE**  }
     {MESSAGES }   {LISTING}

    [JOURNAL=[{YES**}] [filename]]
              {NO   }

    [MEXPAND={ON**}] [MPRINT={OFF**}] [MNEST={50**}] [MITERATE={1000**}]
             {OFF }          {ON   }         {n  }             {n     }

    [BLANKS={SYSMIS**}]     [UNDEFINED={WARN**}]
            {value   }                {NOWARN}

    [MXWARNS={10**}]    [MXLOOPS={40**}]
             {n   }              {n   }

    [EXTENSIONS={OFF**}
                {ON   }

    [COMPRESSION={ON**}]
                 {OFF }

    [HIGHRES={ON**}]
             {OFF }

    [BLOCK={X'2A'**    }]
           {X'hexchar' }
           {'character'}

    [BOX={X'2D7C2B2B2B2B2B2B2B2B'**}]
         {X'hexstring'             }
         {'character'              }

    [CCA={'-,,,'  }] [CCB={'-,,,'  }] [CCC={'-,,,'  }]
         {'format'}        {'format'}       {'format'}

    [CCD={'-,,,'  }] [CCE={'-,,,'  }]
         {'format'}        {'format'}
```

```
[HEADER={NO** }]
        {YES  }
        {BLANK}

[LENGTH={59**}]  [WIDTH={80**}]
        {n   }          {132 }
        {NONE}          {n   }
```

** Default setting at installation.

See the discussions of specific subcommands in this manual and consult the documentation for your system for more details.

Example:

```
SET BLANKS=0/UNDEFINED=NOWARN/TLOOK='C:\SPSSWIN7\MYTABLE.TLO'.
```

Overview

Many of the running options in the program can be tailored to your own preferences with the SET command. The default settings for these options vary from system to system. To display the current settings, use the SHOW command. A setting changed by SET remains in effect for the entire working session unless changed again by another SET command. The PRESERVE command saves the current settings so that you can return to them later in the session with the RESTORE command. PRESERVE and RESTORE are especially useful with the macro facility.

Options

Memory Management. Dynamically allocate memory using the WORKSPACE and MXMEMORY subcommands when some procedures complain of memory shortage. Increase maximum cell numbers for a pivot table using the MXCELLS subcommand.

Output Format. Change the default (F8.2) print and write formats used for numeric variables using the FORMAT subcommand. Specify a TableLook file and/or a chart template file using the TLOOK and CTEMPLATE subcommands. Define default display of variables in the outline or pivot tables using the ONUMBERS, OVARS, TNUMBERS, and TVARS subcommands, and specify default column widths using the TFIT subcommand.

Samples and Random Numbers. You can change the initial seed value to a particular number using the SEED subcommand.

Output Destination. You can send error messages, resource utilization messages, command printback and the output from your commands to your screen and/or to a file using the ERRORS, MESSAGES, PRINTBACK, and RESULTS subcommands. You can also suppress each of these using the keyword NONE.

Journal Files. You can determine whether or not the program keeps a journal file during a session using the JOURNAL subcommand. A journal file records the commands you have entered along with any error or warning messages generated by the commands. A modified journal file can be used as a command file in subsequent sessions.

Macro Displays. You can control macro expansion, the maximum number of loop iterations, and nesting levels within a macro using the MEXPAND, MITERATE, and MNEST subcommands. You can also control the display of the variables, commands, and parameters that a macro uses using the MPRINT subcommands.

Blanks and Undefined Input Data. You can specify the value that the program should use when it encounters a completely blank field for a numeric variable using the BLANKS subcommand. You can also turn off the warning message that the program issues when it encounters an invalid value for a numeric variable using UNDEFINED.

Maximum Errors and Loops. You can raise or lower the default number of errors and warnings allowed in a session before processing stops using the MXERRS and MXWARNS subcommands. You can raise or lower the maximum number of iterations allowed for the LOOP—END LOOP structure using the MXLOOPS.

Data File Extension. You can specify the default extensions used for SPSS-format data files saved with SAVE or XSAVE or portable files saved with EXPORT using the EXTENSIONS subcommand.

Scratch File Compression. You can specify whether scratch files are kept in compressed or uncompressed form using the COMPRESSION subcommand.

Charts and Plots. You can turn high-resolution graphics off using the HIGHRES subcommand. For text output, you can specify the characters used to draw grids in MULT RESPONSE using the BLOCK and BOX subcommands.

Custom Currency Formats. You can customize currency formats for your own applications using the CCA, CCB, CCC, CCD, and CCE subcommands. For example, you can display currency as French francs rather than American dollars.

Basic Specification

The basic specification is at least one subcommand.

Subcommand Order

Subcommands can be named in any order.

Syntax Rules

- You can specify as many subcommands as needed. Subcommands must be separated by at least one space or slash.
- Only one keyword or argument can be specified for each subcommand.
- SET can be used more than once in the command sequence.
- YES and ON are aliases for each other. NO and OFF are aliases for each other.

Operations

- Settings specified on SET remain in effect until they are changed by another SET command or until the current session is ended.
- Each time SET is used, only the specified settings are changed. All others remain at their previous settings or the default.

Example

```
SET BLANKS=0/UNDEFINED=NOWARN/TLOOK='C:\SPSSWIN7\MYTABLE.TLO'.
```

- BLANKS specifies 0 as the value the program should use when it encounters a completely blank field for a numeric variable.
- UNDEFINED=NOWARN suppresses the message that the program displays whenever anything other than a number or a blank is encountered as the value for a numeric variable.
- TLOOK specifies that the table properties defined in *c:\spsswin7\mytable.tlo* will be used to define the default TableLook in the output. The default is NONE, which uses the TableLook provided as the system default.

WORKSPACE, MXMEMORY, and MXCELLS Subcommands

WORKSPACE and MXMEMORY are used to allocate more memory for some procedures when you receive a message that the available memory has been used up or that only a given number of variables can be processed. MXCELLS is used to increase the maximum number of cells you can create for a new pivot table when you receive a warning that a pivot table cannot be created because it exceeds the maximum number of cells allowed by the available memory.

- WORKSPACE allocates workspace memory in kilobytes for some procedures that allocate only one block of memory, such as Crosstabs or Frequencies. The default is 512.
- MXMEMORY allocates the maximum memory in kilobytes to the program. The default is 14,000.
- Do not increase either the workspace memory or the maximum memory allocation unless the program issues a message that there is not enough memory to complete a procedure.
- Use MXCELLS with caution. Set MXCELLS at a number higher than the limit indicated in the warning message you receive. Set the number back to the default after the table is created.
- The memory allocation or cell maximum number increase takes effect as soon as you run the SET command.

FORMAT Subcommand

FORMAT specifies the default print and write formats for numeric variables. This default format applies to numeric variables defined on DATA LIST in freefield format and to all numeric variables created by transformation commands, unless a format is explicitly specified.

- The specification must be a simple F format. The default is F8.2.

- You can use the PRINT FORMATS, WRITE FORMATS, and FORMATS commands to change print and write formats.
- Format specifications on FORMAT are output formats. When specifying the width, enough positions must be allowed to include any punctuation characters such as decimal points, commas, and dollar signs.
- If a numeric data value exceeds its width specification, the program attempts to display some value nevertheless. First, the program rounds decimal values, then removes punctuation characters, then tries scientific notation, and finally, if there is still not enough space, produces asterisks indicating that a value is present but cannot be displayed in the assigned width.

TLOOK and CTEMPLATE Subcommands

TLOOK and CTEMPLATE specify a file used to define the table and chart appearance in the output. The default for either command is NONE, which produces tables and charts using the system defaults.

- TLOOK determines the properties of output tables produced. The properties include the borders, placement of titles, column and row labels, text font, and column and cell formats.
- CTEMPLATE determines the properties of output charts and plots. The properties include line style, color, fill pattern, and text font of relevant chart elements such as frames, titles, labels, and legends.
- The specification on TLOOK or CTEMPLATE remains in effect until a new TLOOK or CTEMPLATE is specified.

NONE *Use the system defaults.* The tables and charts in the output do not use customized properties.

filename *Use the specified file as templates for tables/charts in the output.* You can specify a full path in quotation marks.

ONUMBERS, OVARS, TNUMBERS, and TVARS Subcommands

ONUMBERS, OVARS, TNUMBERS, and TVARS control how variables are displayed in the outline for pivot table output and in the pivot tables.

- ONUMBERS controls the display of variable values in the outline for pivot tables. The default at installation is LABELS.
- OVARS controls the display of variables in the outline for pivot tables. The default at installation is LABELS.
- TNUMBERS controls the display of variable values in the pivot tables. The default at installation is VALUES.
- TVARS controls the display of variables in the pivot tables. The default at installation is NAMES.

NAMES *Displays variable names.*

VALUES *Displays variable values.*

LABELS   *Displays variable labels.*

BOTH   *Displays both labels and values for variable values or both names and labels for variables.*

TFIT Subcommand

TFIT controls the default column widths of the pivot tables. The default at installation is BOTH.

BOTH   *Adjust column widths to accommodate both labels and data.*

LABELS   *Adjust column widths to accommodate labels only.* This setting produces compact tables, but data values wider than labels will be displayed as asterisks.

SEED Subcommand

SEED specifies the random number seed. You can specify any integer, preferably a number greater than 1 but less than 2,000,000,000, which approaches the limit on some machines.

- The program uses a pseudo-random-number generator to select random samples or create uniform or normal distributions of random numbers. The generator begins with a *seed,* a large integer. Starting with the same seed, the system will repeatedly produce the same sequence of numbers and will select the same sample from a given data file.

- At the start of each session, the seed is set to a value that may vary or may be fixed, depending on the implementation. You can set the seed yourself with the SEED subcommand.

- By default, the seed value changes each time a random-number series is needed in a session. To repeat the same random distribution within a session, specify the same seed each time.

- The random number seed can be changed any number of times within a session.

- To set the seed to a random number explicitly, use the keyword RANDOM.

Example

```
SET SEED=987654321.
```

- The random number seed is set to the value 987,654,321. The seed will be in effect the next time the random-number generator is called.

EPOCH Subcommand

EPOCH defines the 100-year span dates entered with two-digit years and for date functions with a two-digit year specification.

AUTOMATIC   *100-year span beginning 69 years prior to the current date and ending 30 years after the current date.*

begin year   *First year of the 100-year span.*

Example

`SET EPOCH=1900.`

- All dates entered with two-digit year values are read as years between 1900 and 1999. For example, a date entered as 10/29/87 is read as 10/29/1987.

Example

`SET EPOCH=1980.`

- Dates entered wth two-digit year values between 80 and 99 are read as years between 1980 and 1999.

- Dates entered with two-digit year values between 00 and 79 are read as years between 2000 and 2079.

ERRORS, MESSAGES, RESULTS, and PRINTBACK Subcommands

ERRORS, MESSAGES, RESULTS, and PRINTBACK are used with keywords LISTING and NONE to route program output. ERRORS, MESSAGES, and RESULTS apply only to text output. PRINT-BACK applies to all commands entered in a syntax window or generated from a dialog box during a session.

- ERRORS refers to both error messages and warning messages for text output.

- MESSAGES refers to resource utilization messages displayed with text output, including the heading and the summaries (such as the amount of memory used by a command).

- RESULTS refers to the text output generated by program commands.

- PRINTBACK refers to command printback in the journal file. Syntax is always displayed as part of the Notes in the syntax window.

LISTING   *Display output in the designated output window.* Alias ON or YES. For PRINTBACK, alias BOTH. The executed commands are printed back in the journal and displayed in the log in the output window. You can either display an icon only or list all of the commands.

NONE   *Suppress the output.* Alias NO or OFF.

The default routes vary from operating system to operating system and according to the way commands are executed. In windowed environments, the typical defaults are:

Subcommand	Windowed environments
ERRORS	Listing
MESSAGES	None
PRINTBACK	Both
RESULTS	Listing

JOURNAL Subcommand

Alias to LOG. The program creates a journal file to keep track of the commands submitted and error and warning messages generated during a session. JOURNAL is used to assign a filename to the journal file or to stop or resume the journal.

- Journal files with the default filename are erased at the beginning of each session. To preserve the contents of a journal file, assign a name with SET JOURNAL at the beginning of the session. Alternatively, if you have used the default name for a journal file, you can rename the file before beginning another session.

- If you use multiple journal files, you should not start with one file, go to another file, and then return to the first file. On many systems, the program will not append new information to the first file but will overwrite the previous contents.

filename   *Filename for the journal file.* The default name varies by system.

YES   *Start sending commands and messages to the journal file.*

NO   *Stop sending commands and messages to the journal file.*

Example

```
SET JOURNAL MYLOG.
GET FILE=HUBDATA.
SET JOURNAL OFF.
LIST.
SET JOURNAL ON.
FREQUENCIES VARIABLES=ALL.
```

- The first SET command opens the journal file *MYLOG*.

- The GET command is copied into the journal file. The SET command then turns the journal off. The LIST command is not copied into the journal file but is executed. The second SET command turns the journal on again, and the FREQUENCIES command is copied into the journal file.

MEXPAND and MPRINT Subcommands

MEXPAND and MPRINT control whether macros are expanded and whether the expanded macros are displayed. For more information on macros, see DEFINE and Appendix D.
    The specifications for MEXPAND are:

ON   *Expand macros.* This is the default.

OFF   *Do not expand macros.* The command line that calls the macro is treated like any other command line. If the macro call is an command, it will be executed; otherwise, it will trigger an error message.

The specifications for MPRINT are:

ON   *Include expanded macro commands in the output.*

OFF   *Exclude expanded macro commands from the output.* This is the default.

- MPRINT is effective only when MEXPAND is ON and is independent of the PRINTBACK subcommand.

MITERATE and MNEST Subcommands

MITERATE and MNEST control the maximum loop traversals and the maximum nesting levels permitted in macro expansions, respectively.

- The specification on MITERATE or MNEST is a positive integer. The default for MITERATE is 1000. The default for MNEST is 50.

BLANKS Subcommand

BLANKS specifies the value the program should use when it encounters a completely blank field for a numeric variable. By default, the program uses the system-missing value.

- BLANKS controls only the translation of numeric fields. If a blank field is read with a string format, the resulting value is a blank.
- The value specified on BLANKS is not automatically defined as a missing value.
- The BLANKS specification applies to all numeric variables. You cannot use different specifications for different variables.
- BLANKS must be specified before data are read. Otherwise, blanks in numeric fields are converted to the system-missing value (the default) as they are read.

UNDEFINED Subcommand

UNDEFINED controls whether the program displays a warning message when it encounters anything other than a number or a blank as the value for a numeric variable. The default is WARN.

- Warning messages that are suppressed are still counted toward the maximum allowed before the session is terminated. To control the number of warnings (and therefore the number of invalid values) allowed in a session, use the MXWARNS subcommand.

WARN   *Display a warning message when an invalid value is encountered for a numeric variable.* This is the default.

NOWARN   *Suppress warning messages for invalid values.*

MXWARNS Subcommand

MXWARNS controls the maximum number of error messages and warnings the program displays for text output during one working session. The default for MXWARNS is 10.

- All errors are included with warnings in the count toward the MXWARNS limit. Notes are not.
- If you have set MXWARNS, the program stops displaying warning messages when the limit is exceeded but the working session continues.
- The setting on MXWARNS has no effect on output displayed in pivot tables.

Example

```
SET MXWARNS=200.
```

- MXWARNS specifies that a maximum of 200 warnings can be displayed. When the limit is exceeded, the program stops displaying warnings if it is in a windowed environment or if it is running the commands interactively. Otherwise, the session is terminated.

MXLOOPS Subcommand

MXLOOPS specifies the maximum number of times a loop defined by the LOOP—END LOOP structure is executed for a single case or input record. The default is 40.

- MXLOOPS prevents infinite loops, which may occur if no cutoff is specified for the loop structure (see LOOP—END LOOP).
- When a loop is terminated, control passes to the command immediately following the END LOOP command, even if the END LOOP condition is not yet met.

EXTENSIONS Subcommand

EXTENSIONS controls whether the program adds default extensions to the data files it saves during a session. The default extensions are .SAV for SPSS-format data files saved with SAVE or XSAVE and .POR for portable data files saved with EXPORT. The specification on EXTENSIONS is either OFF or ON. The default is OFF.

- EXTENSIONS is effective only when you run SAVE, XSAVE, or EXPORT with command syntax. It does not affect files saved using a dialog box in windowed environments.
- EXTENSIONS has no effect when the filename is specified in apostrophes or quotation marks.

OFF   *Do not use default extensions. This is the default.*

ON   *Add a default extension to the file if an extension is not explicitly specified.*

Example

```
SET EXTENSIONS=ON.
SAVE OUTFILE=BANK89.
SAVE OUTFILE='BANK89'.
```

- This example saves two SPSS-format data files from the same working file. The first SAVE command saves the working data file as *BANK89.SAV*; the second SAVE command saves the working file as *BANK89* regardless of the setting on EXTENSIONS.

COMPRESSION Subcommand

COMPRESSION determines whether scratch files created during a session are in compressed or uncompressed form.

- A compressed scratch file occupies less space on disk than does an uncompressed scratch file but requires more processing.

- The specification takes effect the next time a scratch file is written and stays in effect until SET COMPRESSION is specified again or until the end of the session.
- The default setting varies. Use SHOW to display the default on your system.

YES   *Compress scratch files.*

NO   *Do not compress scratch files.*

HIGHRES Subcommand

The program generates high-resolution charts and plots for statistical procedures. HIGHRES controls whether such charts and plots are displayed using high-resolution graphics or printer characters. The default is ON.

ON   *Display charts and plots using high-resolution graphics.*

OFF   *Do not display charts.*

BLOCK Subcommand

BLOCK specifies the character used for drawing icicle plots.

- You can specify any single character either as a quoted string or as a quoted hexadecimal pair preceded by the character X.
- The default is X'2A'.

Example

```
SET BLOCK='#'.
```

- This command specifies a pound sign (#) as the character to be used for drawing bar charts. The character is specified as a quoted string.

BOX Subcommand

BOX specifies the characters used to draw grids in MULT RESPONSE. Other procedures may also use these characters in plots and other displays. The specification is either a 3- or an 11-character quoted string, in which the characters represent, respectively:

1	horizontal line	7	upper-right corner
2	vertical line	8	left T
3	middle (cross)	9	right T
4	lower-left corner	10	top T
5	upper-left corner	11	bottom T
6	lower-right corner		

- The characters can be specified either as a quoted string or hexadecimal pairs. Specify an X before the quoted hexadecimal pairs.

- The defaults vary from system to system. To display the current settings, use the SHOW command.
- The default is X'2D7C2B2B2B2B2B2B2B2B2B'.

LENGTH and WIDTH Subcommands

LENGTH and WIDTH specify the maximum page length and width for the output, respectively. The default for LENGTH is 59 lines; the default for WIDTH is 80. These two subcommands apply only to text output.

- The page length includes the first printed line on the page through the last line that can be printed. The printer you use most likely includes a margin at the top; that margin is not included in the length used by this program. The default, 59 lines, allows for a 1/2-inch margin at the top and bottom of an 11-inch page printed with 6 lines per inch, or an 8 1/2-inch page printed with 8 lines per inch.
- You can specify any length from 40 through 999,999 lines. If a long page length is specified, the program continues to provide page ejects and titles at the start of each procedure and at logical points in the display, such as between crosstabulations.
- To suppress page ejects, use keyword NONE on LENGTH. The program will insert titles at logical points in the display but will not supply page ejects.
- You can specify any number of characters from 80 through 132 for WIDTH. The specified width does not include the carriage control character. All procedures can fit the output to an 80-column page.

HEADER Subcommand

HEADER controls whether the output includes headings. The HEADER subcommand applies to both default headings and those specified on the TITLE and SUBTITLE commands. This command applies only to text output from this program. The default is NO.

NO   *Suppress headings in text output.* All general headings, including pagination, are replaced by a single blank line.

YES   *Display headings in text output.*

BLANK   *Suppress headings but start a new page.*

CCA, CCB, CCC, CCD, and CCE Subcommands

You can specify up to five custom currency formats using the subcommands CCA, CCB, CCC, CCD, and CCE. In the Windows environment, use the Regional Settings Properties to set the currency formats.

- Each custom currency subcommand defines one custom format and can include four specifications in the following order: a negative prefix, a prefix, a suffix, and a negative suffix.

- The specifications are separated by either periods or commas, whichever you do not want to use as a decimal point in the format.
- Each currency specification must always contain three commas or three periods. All other specifications are optional.
- Use blanks in the specification only where you want blanks in the format.
- The entire specification must be enclosed in apostrophes.
- A specification cannot exceed 16 characters (excluding the apostrophes).
- Custom currency formats cannot be specified as input formats on DATA LIST. Use them only as output formats in the FORMATS, WRITE FORMATS, PRINT FORMATS, WRITE, and PRINT commands.

Example

```
SET CCA='-,$,,'.
```

- A minus sign (−) preceding the first command is used as the negative prefix.
- A dollar sign is specified for the prefix.
- No suffixes are specified (there are two consecutive commas before the closing apostrophe).
- Since commas are used as separators in the specification, the decimal point is represented by a period.

Example

```
SET CCA='(,,,-)'  CCB=',,%,' CCC='(,$,,)' CCD='-/-.Dfl ..-'.
FORMATS VARA(CCA9.0)/ VARB(CCB6.1)/ VARC(CCC8.0)/ VARD(CCD14.2).
```

- SET defines four custom currency formats. Table 1 summarizes the currency specifications.
- FORMATS assigns these formats to specific variables.

Table 1   Custom currency examples

	CCA	CCB	CCC	CCD
negative prefix	(	none	(	-/-
prefix	none	none	$	Dfl
suffix	none	%	none	none
negative suffix	-)	none	)	-
separator	,	,	,	.
sample positive number	23,456	13.7%	$352	Dfl 37.419,00
sample negative number	(19,423-)	13.7%	($189)	-/-Dfl 135,19-

SHOW

```
SHOW [ALL] [BLANKS] [BLKSIZE] [BOX] [BLOCK] [BUFNO] [CC] [CCA] [CCB]
     [CCC] [CCD] [CCE] [COMPRESSION] [CTEMPLATE] [ERRORS] [EXTENSIONS] [FORMAT]
     [HEADER] [HIGHRES] [JOURNAL] [LENGTH] [MESSAGES] [MEXPAND]
     [MITERATE] [MNEST] [MPRINT] [MXCELLS] [MXLOOPS] [MXMEMORY] [MXWARNS]
     [N] [ONUMBERS] [OVARS] [PRINTBACK] [RESULTS] [SCOMPRESSION] [SEED]
     [SYSMIS] [TFIT] [TLOOK] [TNUMBERS] [TVARS] [UNDEFINED]
     [WEIGHT] [WIDTH] [WORKSPACE] [$VARS]
```

Overview

SHOW displays current settings for running options. Most of these settings can be changed with the SET command.

Basic Specification

The basic specification is simply the command keyword, which displays important current settings (keyword ALL). Some displayed option settings are applicable only when you have options such as Tables and Categories.

Subcommand Order

Subcommands can be named in any order.

Syntax

- If any subcommands are specified, only the requested settings are displayed.
- SHOW can be specified more than once.

Example

```
SHOW BLANKS /UNDEFINED /MXWARNS.
```

- BLANKS shows the value to which a completely blank field for a numeric variable is translated.
- UNDEFINED indicates whether a message displays whenever the program encounters anything other than a number or a blank as the value for a numeric variable.
- MXWARNS displays the maximum number of warnings allowed before a session is terminated.

Subcommands

The following alphabetical list shows the available subcommands.

ALL   *Display important settings applicable to your system.* This is the default.

BLANKS   *Value to which a completely blank field for a numeric variable is translated.* The default is the system-missing value.

BLKSIZE   *Default block length used for scratch files and SPSS-format data files.* The default varies by system. BLKSIZE cannot be changed with SET.

BOX   *Characters used to draw boxes.* Both character and hexadecimal representations are displayed. The default is X'2D7C2B2B2B2B2B2B2B2B2B'. This setting applies only to text output from the program.

BLOCK   *Character used to draw bar charts.* Both character and hexadecimal representations are displayed. The default is X'2A'. This setting applies only to the text output from the program.

BUFFNO   *The default number of buffers used for all files managed by the system for input and output.* The default varies by system. BUFFNO cannot be changed with SET.

CC   *Custom currency formats.* CC shows the current custom currency formats that have been defined for CCA, CCB, CCC, CCD, and CCE on SET. In Windows environments, they reflect the Regional Settings Properties. You can also request any of these keywords individually.

COMPRESSION   *Compression of scratch files.* The setting is either ON or OFF (alias YES or NO). The default varies by system.

CTEMPLATE   *Chart template file.* The setting is either NONE or a filename.

ERRORS   *Error messages for text output.* The setting can be LISTING (alias YES or ON) or NONE (alias NO or OFF).

EXTENSIONS   *Default extensions for saved data files.* The setting is either ON or OFF. The default is OFF.

FORMAT   *Default print and write formats for numeric variables defined on DATA LIST in freefield format and to all numeric variables created by transformation commands.* The default is F8.2.

HEADER   *Headings for text output.* The setting is YES, NO, or BLANK. The default is NO.

HIGHRES   *High-resolution or low-resolution (character-based) charts and plots.* The setting is either ON or OFF, where ON is high-resolution. The default is ON.

JOURNAL   *Journal file during a session.* The setting is either ON or OFF (alias YES or NO). The default varies by system.

LENGTH	*Maximum page length for output.* The default is 59. This setting applies only to the text output from the program.
MESSAGES	*Resource utilization messages for text output.* The setting can be LISTING (alias YES or ON) or NONE (alias NO or OFF).
MEXPAND	*Macro expansion.* The setting is either ON (alias YES) or OFF (alias NO). The default is ON.
MITERATE	*Maximum loop iterations permitted in macro expansions.* The default is 1000.
MNEST	*Maximum nesting level for macros.* The default is 50.
MPRINT	*Inclusion of expanded macros in the output.* The setting is either ON (alias YES) or OFF (alias NO). The default is OFF.
MXCELLS	*Maximum number of cells allowed for a new pivot table.* The default is AUTOMATIC, allowing the number to be determined by the available memory.
MXLOOPS	*Maximum executions of a loop on a single case.* The default is 40.
MXMEMORY	*Maximum memory allocation in kilobytes.* The default is 14,000.
MXWARNS	*Maximum number of warnings and errors shown for text output.* The default is 10.
N	*Unweighted number of cases in the working data file.* N displays UNKNOWN if a working data file has not yet been created. N cannot be changed with SET.
ONUMBERS	*Display of variable values in the outline for pivot tables.* The settings can be LABELS, VALUES, and BOTH.
OVARS	*Display of variables as headings.* The settings can be LABELS, NAMES, and BOTH.
PRINTBACK	*Command printback.* The setting can be BOTH (alias LISTING, YES, or ON) or NONE (alias NO or OFF). The default is BOTH at system installation.
RESULTS	*Output from commands.* Not applicable to output displayed in pivot tables. The setting can be LISTING (alias YES or ON) or NONE (alias NO or OFF).
SCOMPRESSION	*Compression of SPSS-format data files.* This setting can be overridden by the COMPRESSED or UNCOMPRESSED subcommands on the SAVE or XSAVE commands. The default setting varies by system. SCOMPRESSION cannot be changed with SET.
SEED	*Seed for the random-number generator.* The default is generally 2,000,000 but may vary by system.
SYSMIS	*The system-missing value.* SYSMIS cannot be changed with SET.

TFIT	*Adjust column widths in pivot tables.* The settings can be BOTH (label and data) and LABELS.
TLOOK	*Pivot table template file.* The setting can be either NONE or a filename.
TNUMBER	*Display of variable values in pivot tables.* The settings can be VALUES, LABELS, and BOTH.
TVARS	*Display of variables as headings.* The settings can be NAMES, LABELS, and BOTH.
UNDEFINED	*Warning message for undefined data.* WARN is the default. NOWARN suppresses messages but does not alter the count of warnings toward the MXWARNS total.
WEIGHT	*Variable used to weight cases.* WEIGHT can be specified for SHOW only; it cannot be changed with SET.
WIDTH	*Maximum page width for the output.* The default is 132 columns for batch mode and 80 for interactive mode. This setting applies only to text output from the program.
WORKSPACE	*Special workspace memory limit in kilobytes.* The default is 512.
$VARS	*Values of system variables.* $VARS cannot be changed with SET.

SORT CASES

```
SORT CASES [BY] varlist[({A})] [varlist...]
                        {D}
```

Example:
```
SORT CASES BY DIVISION (A) STORE (D).
```

Overview

SORT CASES reorders the sequence of cases in the working data file based on the values of one or more variables. You can optionally sort cases in ascending or descending order, or use combinations of ascending and descending order for different variables.

Basic Specification

The basic specification is a variable or list of variables that are used as sort keys. By default, cases are sorted in ascending order of each variable, starting with the first variable named. For each subsequent variable, cases are sorted in ascending order within categories of the previously named variables.

Syntax Rules

- Keyword BY is optional.
- BY variables can be numeric or string but not scratch, system, or temporary variables.
- You can explicitly request the default sort order (ascending) by specifying A or UP in parentheses after the variable name. To sort cases in descending order, specify D or DOWN.
- An order specification (A or D) applies to all variables in the list up to the previous order specification. If you combine ascending and descending order on the same SORT CASES command, you may need to specify the default A explicitly.

Operations

- SORT CASES first sorts the file according to the first variable named. For subsequent variables, cases are sorted within categories of the previously named variables.
- The sort sequence of string variables depends on the character set in use on your system. With EBCDIC character sets, most special characters are sorted first, followed by lowercase alphabetical characters, uppercase alphabetical characters, and, finally, numbers. The order is almost exactly reversed with ASCII character sets. Numbers are sorted first, followed by uppercase alphabetical characters and then lowercase alphabetical characters. In

addition, special characters are sorted between the other character types. Use the INFO command (not available on all systems) to obtain information on the character set in use on your system and the exact sort sequence.

SORT CASES with Other Procedures

- In AGGREGATE, cases are sorted in order of the break variable or variables. You do not have to use SORT CASES prior to running AGGREGATE, since the procedure does its own sorting.
- You can use SORT CASES in conjunction with the BY keyword in ADD FILES to interleave cases with the same variables but from different files.
- With MATCH FILES, cases must be sorted in the same order for all files you combine.
- With UPDATE, cases must be sorted in ascending order of the key variable or variables in both the master file and all transaction files.
- You can use the PRINT command to check the results of a SORT CASES command. PRINT must be followed by a procedure or EXECUTE to be executed.

Example

```
SORT CASES BY DIVISION (A) STORE (D).
```

- Cases are sorted in ascending order of variable *DIVISION*. Cases are further sorted in descending order of *STORE* within categories of *DIVISION*. A must be specified so that D applies to *STORE* only.

Example

```
SORT DIVISION STORE (A) AGE (D).
```

- Cases are sorted in ascending order of *DIVISION*. Keyword BY is not used in this example.
- Cases are further sorted in ascending order of *STORE* within values of *DIVISION*. Specification A applies to both *DIVISION* and *STORE*.
- Cases are further sorted in descending order of *AGE* within values of *STORE* and *DIVISION*.

SPCHART

This command is available only on systems with high-resolution graphics capabilities.

```
SPCHART

[/TEMPLATE='filename']

[/TITLE='line 1' ['line 2']]
[/SUBTITLE='line 1']
[/FOOTNOTE='line 1' ['line 2']]

{[/XR=]{var BY var                        } }
        {var var [var var...][BY var]}

{ /XS= {var BY var                        } }
        {var var [var var...][BY var]}

{ /IR= var [BY var]                        }

{ /I= var [BY var]                         }

{ /NP= {var BY var                        }}
        {COUNT(var) N({var }) [BY var]}
        {value                        }

{ /P= {var BY var                         } }
        {COUNT(var) N({var }) [BY var]}
        {value                        }

{ /C= {var BY var                         } }
        {COUNT(var) N({var }) [BY var]}
        {value                        }

{ /U= {var BY var                        }}
        {COUNT(var) N({var  }) [BY var]}
                        {value}

[/SPAN={2**}]
                {n    }

[{/CONFORM  }=value]
 {/NOCONFORM}

[/SIGMA={3**}]
                {n    }

[/MINSAMPLE={2**}]
                                {n    }

[/LSL=value]    [/USL=value]

[/MISSING=[{NOREPORT**}] [{EXCLUDE**}]
            {REPORT   } {INCLUDE  }
```

**Default if the subcommand is omitted.

Overview

SPCHART generates several types of high-resolution control charts. A control chart plots a quality characteristic measured or computed from a sample versus the sample number or

910

time. It is a widely used process-control technique for testing the hypothesis that the process is in a state of statistical control. All control charts display four series:

- The process line representing the quality characteristic for each sample.
- The center line indicating the average value of the quality characteristic corresponding to the in-control state.
- Two horizontal lines showing the upper control limit and the lower control limit.

Control charts are used as a technique for improving productivity, preventing defects and unnecessary process adjustments, and gathering information about process capability.

SPCHART produces X-bar, R, s, individuals, and moving range charts as well as np, p, c, and u charts. You may need to transform your data so that they conform to the required data organization described under each chart type subcommand.

Control charts are available only on systems where high-resolution display is available.

Options

Titles and Footnotes. You can specify a title, subtitle, and footnote for the control chart using the TITLE, SUBTITLE, and FOOTNOTE subcommands.

Chart Type. You can request a specific type of control chart using the XR, XS, IR, I, NP, P, C, or U subcommand.

Templates. You can specify a template, using the TEMPLATE subcommand, to override the default chart attribute settings on your system.

Control Limits. You can specify a sigma value on the SIGMA subcommand to modify the calculated upper and lower control limits. You can also specify fixed limits using the USL and LSL subcommands. The upper and lower limits you specify will be displayed simultaneously with the calculated control limits.

Basic Specification

The basic specification is a chart type subcommand. By default, the title of the generated chart is Control Chart followed by the label of the process variable. The subtitle provides split-file information if split-file processing is in effect, and the one-line footnote provides the sigma value.

Subcommand Order

Subcommands can be specified in any order.

Syntax Rules

- Only one chart type subcommand can be specified.
- Keyword SPAN is used only with IR and I subcommands.
- Keyword CONFORM or NOCONFORM is used only with NP and P subcommands.

Operations

- SPCHART plots four basic series: the process, the center line, the upper control line, and the lower control line.

- The chart title, subtitle, and footnote are assigned as they are specified on TITLE, SUBTITLE, and FOOTNOTE subcommands. If you do not use these subcommands, the chart title is Control Chart, followed by the label of the process variable, and a one-line footnote displays the sigma level.

- The category variable label is used as the title for the category axis. If no variable label is defined, the variable name is used. If no category variable is defined, the title is null.

- The category variable value labels are used as the category axis labels. If no value labels are defined, values are used. If no category variable is defined, integer values from 1 to n are used, where n is the number of subgroups or units plotted.

- All series are plotted as lines. When a series has a constant value across all samples, the value is reported in the legend entry for the series.

- Case weights are not honored for control charts when each case is a subgroup. They are honored when each case is a unit and when the weights are integers. When weighted data are used in an individuals chart, replicated cases are plotted on the control chart.

- The calculated control limits are always displayed and can be suppressed only by editing the chart in a chart window.

- You can specify preset control limits for an X-bar or I chart, as some industries often do. The specified control limits are displayed simultaneously with the calculated limits.

Limitations

- Control charts cannot have fewer than 2 or more than 3000 points.
- The subgroup size in X-bar and range charts cannot exceed 100.
- The span for individual charts is limited to 100.

Example

```
SPCHART  /TEMPLATE='CNTR.CHT'
  /IR=SUBSIZE.
```

- This command generates an individuals chart and a moving range chart. The process variable *SUBSIZE* is a numeric variable that measures the size variation of the product.

- Both charts uses the attributes defined for the template saved in *CNTR.CHT*.

- The default span (2) and sigma value (3) are used.

- Since no BY variable is specified, the *x* axis is labeled by sequence numbers.

TITLE, SUBTITLE, and FOOTNOTE Subcommands

TITLE, SUBTITLE, and FOOTNOTE specify lines of text placed at the top or bottom of the control chart.

- One or two lines of text can be specified for TITLE or FOOTNOTE, and one line of text can be specified for SUBTITLE.
- Each line of text must be enclosed in apostrophes or quotation marks. The maximum length of any line is 72 characters.
- The default font sizes and types are used for the title, subtitle, and footnote.
- By default, the title, subtitle, and footnote are left-aligned with the y axis.
- If you do not specify TITLE, the default title is Control Chart followed by the label of the process variable.
- If you do not specify SUBTITLE, the subtitle provides the split-file information if split-file processing is in effect; otherwise it is null, which leaves more space for the chart.
- If you do not specify FOOTNOTE, the sigma level is identified as the first line of the footnote.

Example

```
SPCHART TITLE = 'Wheel Production'
   /SUBTITLE = 'Process Control'
   /IR=SUBSIZE.
```

XR and XS Subcommands

XR produces an X-bar chart and an R chart. XS produces an X-bar chart and an s chart. X-bar, R, and s charts are control charts for continuous variables, such as size, weight, length, and temperature.

An X-bar chart plots the mean of each subgroup. The center line indicates the mean of subgroup means. The control limits are calculated from subgroup means, numbers, standard deviations, and the user-specified SIGMA value (see "SIGMA Subcommand" on p. 922). Figure 1 shows an X-bar chart.

Figure 1   X-bar chart

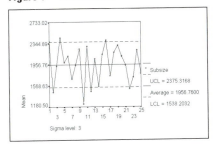

An R chart plots range values (maximum-minimum) of successive subgroups. The center line indicates the mean of subgroup ranges. The control limits are calculated from subgroup ranges, numbers, and the user-specified SIGMA value (see "SIGMA Subcommand" on p. 922). The R chart tests whether the process variability is in control. When the subgroup size is relatively small (4, 5, or 6), the range method yields almost as good an estimator of the variance as does the subgroup variance. Figure 2 shows an R chart.

Figure 2   R chart

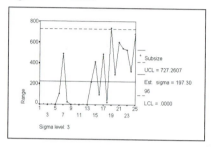

An s chart plots subgroup standard deviations. The center line indicates the mean of subgroup standard deviations. The control limits are calculated from subgroup standard deviations, numbers, and the user-specified SIGMA value (see "SIGMA Subcommand" on p. 922). The s chart tests whether the process variability is in control, especially when the subgroup size is from moderate to large. Figure 3 shows an s chart.

Figure 3   S chart

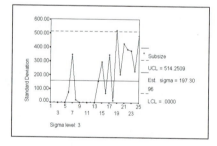

Data Organization

For X-bar, R, or s charts, data can be organized in two ways: each case is a unit or each case is a subgroup.

- Each case is a unit with a subgroup identifier. Cases are assigned to a category according to the value of the identifier. Table 1 is an example of this type of data organization. The data do not have to be sorted by subgroup. A BY variable (the subgroup identifier) is required to sort and aggregate data and label the process variable.

- Each case is a subgroup. There are as many variables as individuals within one sample. A sample identifier is not required. When there is one, it is used for labeling. Table 2 shows the same data as Table 1 but organized in a different way.

Table 1   Each case is a unit for X-bar, R, and s charts

Subgroup	Length
8:50	6.35
11:30	6.39
8:50	6.40
11:30	6.46
8:50	6.32
11:30	6.37
8:50	6.39
11:30	6.36
...	...

Table 2   Each case is a subgroup for X-bar, R, and s charts

Subgroup	N1	N2	N3	N4
8:50	6.35	6.40	6.32	6.39
11:30	6.39	6.46	6.37	6.36
...	...	...	...	...

Variable Specification

If data are organized as shown in Table 1, the variable specifications on XR and XS subcommands are

```
VAR BY VAR
```

The variable specified before BY is the process variable, the variable that contains values for all instances to be plotted (for example, *LENGTH* in Table 1). The variable specified after BY is the category variable or the BY variable, which is the subgroup identifier (for example, *SUBGROUP* in Table 1). The process variable must be numeric while the category variable can be of any type. The chart is sorted by the category variable.

If data are organized as shown in Table 2, the variable specifications on XR and XS subcommands are

```
VAR VAR [VAR...] [BY VAR]
```

Each of the variables specified before BY represents an instance to be plotted (for example, *N1* to *N3* in Table 2). At least two variables are required and each must be numeric. Keyword BY and the category variable (for example, *SUBGROUP* in Table 2) are optional; if specified, the category variable provides labels for the category axis and can be any type of variable. If omitted, the category axis is labeled from 1 to the number of variables specified before keyword BY.

Example

```
SPCHART /TEMPLATE='CTRL.CHT'
/XR SUBSIZE BY SHIFT.
```

- The data are organized as shown in Table 1. *SUBSIZE* is a numeric variable that measures the part size. *SHIFT* contains the subgroup identifier (work shift number).
- The chart template is stored in the chart file *CTRL.CHT*.

I and IR Subcommands

I produces an individuals chart and IR produces an individuals and a moving range chart. Both types are control charts for continuous variables, such as size, weight, length, and temperature.

An individuals chart plots each individual observation on a control chart. The center line indicates the mean of all individual values and the control limits are calculated from the mean of the moving ranges, the span, and the user-specified SIGMA value. Individuals charts are often used with moving range charts to test process variability when the subgroup size is 1. This occurs frequently when automated inspection and measurement technology is used and every unit manufactured is analyzed. It also occurs when the process is so slow that a larger subgroup size becomes impractical. Figure 4 shows an individuals chart.

Figure 4   Individuals chart

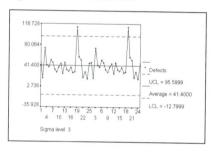

A moving range chart plots moving ranges of *n* successive observations on a control chart, where *n* is the specified span (see "SPAN Subcommand" on p. 922). The center line is the mean of moving ranges and the control limits are calculated from the ranges, the span, and the user-specified SIGMA value (see "SIGMA Subcommand" on p. 922). Figure 5 shows a moving range chart.

Figure 5   Moving range chart

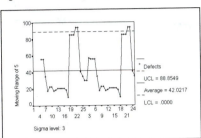

Data Organization

For individuals and moving range charts, data must be organized so that each case is a unit. Cases are not sorted or aggregated before plotting.

Variable Specification

The variable specification for I or IR subcommand is

```
VAR [BY VAR]
```

You must specify the process variable that contains the value for each individual observation. Each observation is plotted for the individuals chart. The range of n consecutive observations (where n is the value specified on the SPAN subcommand) is calculated and plotted for the moving range chart. The range data for the first $n-1$ cases are missing, but the mean and the limit series are not.

Keyword BY and the category variable are optional. When specified, the category variable is used for labeling the category axis and can be any type of variable. If omitted, the category axis is labeled 1 to the number of individual observations in the process variable.

Example

```
SPCHART /TEMPLATE='CTRL.CHT'
    /IR=SUBSIZE.
```

- This command requests an individuals chart and a moving range chart. The two charts are shown in Figure 4 and Figure 5.
- The default span (2) and sigma value (3) are used.

P and NP Subcommands

P produces a p chart and NP produces an np chart. Both types are control charts for attributes. That is, they use data that can be counted, such as the number of nonconformities and the percentage of defects.

A p chart plots the **fraction nonconforming** on a control chart. Fraction nonconforming is the proportion of nonconforming or defective items in a subgroup to the total number of items in that subgroup. It is usually expressed as a decimal or, occasionally, as a percentage. The center line of the control chart is the mean of the subgroup fractions and the control limits are based on a binomial distribution and can be controlled by the user-specified SIGMA value.

Figure 6   P chart

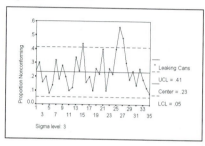

An np chart plots the number nonconforming rather than the fraction nonconforming. The center line is the mean of the numbers of nonconforming or defective items. The control limits are based on the binomial distribution and can be controlled by the user-specified SIGMA value. When the subgroup sizes are unequal, np charts are not recommended.

Figure 7   NP chart

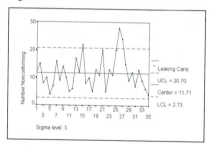

Data Organization

Data for p and np charts can be organized in two ways: each case is a unit or each case is a subgroup.

- Each case is a unit with a conformity status variable and a subgroup identifier. Cases are assigned to a category by the value of the subgroup identifier. Table 3 is an example of this type of data organization. The data do not have to be sorted. A BY variable (the subgroup identifier) is required to sort and aggregate data and label the category axis.

- Each case is a subgroup. One variable contains the total number of items within a subgroup and one variable contains the total number of nonconforming or defective items in the subgroup. The subgroup identifier is optional. If specified, it is used for labeling purposes. Table 4 is an example of this type of data organization. The data are the same as used in Table 3.

Table 3   Each case is a unit for p and np charts

Subgroup	Outcome
January	Cured
January	Cured
January	Cured
January	Relapse
February	Relapse
February	Cured
February	Relapse
February	Relapse
...	...

Table 4   Each case is a subgroup for p and np charts

Subgroup	Relapse	N
January	1	4
February	3	4
...	...	...

Variable Specification

If data are organized as illustrated in Table 3, the variable specification on P or NP subcommands is

```
VAR BY VAR
```

The variable specified before BY is the status variable (for example, *OUTCOME* in Table 3). The value of this variable determines whether an item is considered conforming or nonconforming. The status variable can be any type, but if it is a string, the value specified on CONFORM (or NOCONFORM) must be enclosed in apostrophes (see "CONFORM and NOCONFORM Subcommands" on p. 922). The variable specified after BY is the category variable. It can be any type of variable. The chart is sorted by values of the category variable.

If data are organized as shown in Table 4, the variable specification on P or NP is

```
COUNT(VAR) N({VAR}) [BY VAR]
           {VAL}
```

The variable specified on keyword COUNT is the variable containing the number of nonconforming or defective items (for example, *RELAPSE* in Table 4). The specification on keyword N is either the variable containing the sample size or a positive integer for a constant size across samples (for example, *N* in Table 4). The COUNT variable cannot be larger than the N variable for any given subgroup; if it is, the subgroup is dropped from calculation and plotting. Keyword BY and the category variable are optional. When specified, the category variable is used for category axis labels; otherwise, the category axis is labeled 1 to the number of subgroups. Cases are unsorted for the control chart.

C and U Subcommands

C produces a c chart and U produces a u chart. Both types are control charts for attributes. That is, they use data that can be counted.

A c chart plots the total number of defects or nonconformities in each subgroup. A defect or nonconformity is one specification that an item fails to satisfy. Each nonconforming item has at least one defect, but any nonconforming item may have more than one defect. The center line of the c chart indicates the mean of the defect numbers of all subgroups. The control limits are based on the Poisson distribution and can be controlled by the user-specified SIGMA value. When the sample sizes are not equal, c charts are not recommended.

Figure 8   C chart

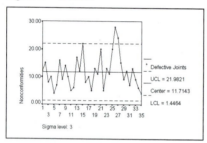

A u chart plots the average number of defects or nonconformities per inspection unit within a subgroup. Each subgroup contains more than one inspection unit. The center line of the u chart indicates the average number of defects per unit of all subgroups. The control limits are based on Poisson distribution and can be controlled by the user-specified SIGMA value.

Figure 9   U chart

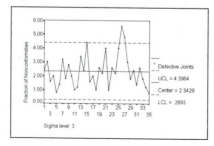

Data Organization

Data for c and u charts can be organized in two ways: each case is a unit or each case is a subgroup.

- Each case is a unit with a variable containing the number of defects for that unit and a subgroup identifier. Cases are assigned to each subgroup by the value of the identifier. Table 5 is an example of this type of data organization. Data do not have to be sorted by subgroup. A BY variable (the subgroup identifier) is required to sort and aggregate data and to label the category axis.

- Each case is a subgroup. One variable contains the total number of units within the subgroup and one variable contains the total number of defects for all units within the subgroup. The subgroup identifier is optional. When specified, it is used as category axis labels; otherwise, the number 1 to the number of subgroups are used to label the category axis. Table 6 is an example of this method of data organization. The data are the same as in Table 5.

Table 5   Each case is a unit for c and u charts

ID	Subgroup	Count
1	January	0
2	January	2
3	January	0
4	January	0
5	February	5
6	February	1
7	February	0
8	February	0
...	...	...

Table 6   Each case is a sample for c and u charts

Subgroup	Relapses	N
JANUARY	1	4
FEBRUARY	3	4
...	...	...

Variable Specification

If data are organized as in Table 5, the variable specification on C and U subcommands is

```
VAR BY VAR
```

The variable specified before keyword BY contains the number of defects in each unit (for example, *COUNT* in Table 5). It must be numeric. The variable specified after keyword BY is the subgroup identifier (for example, *SUBGROUP* in Table 5). It can be any type of variable. The chart is sorted by values of the subgroup identifier.

If data are organized as shown in Table 6, the variable specification on C and U subcommands is

```
COUNT(VAR)  N({VAR})  [BY VAR]
            {VAL}
```

The specification is the same as that for p and np charts.

SPAN Subcommand

SPAN specifies the span from which the moving range for an individuals chart is calculated. The specification must be an integer value greater than 1. The default is 2. SPAN applies only to I and IR chart specifications.

Example

```
SPCHART /IR=SUBSIZE /SPAN=5.
```

- The SPAN subcommand specifies that the moving ranges are computed from every five individual samples.

CONFORM and NOCONFORM Subcommands

Either CONFORM or NOCONFORM is required when you specify a status variable on the P or NP subcommand. That occurs when data are organized so that each case is an inspection unit (see "P and NP Subcommands" on p. 917).

- Either subcommand requires a value specification. The value can be numeric or string. String values must be enclosed within apostrophes.
- If CONFORM is specified, all values for the status variable other than the value specified are tabulated as nonconformities. If NOCONFORM is specified, only the specified value is tabulated as nonconformities.
- CONFORM and NOCONFORM apply only to P and NP chart specifications.

SIGMA Subcommand

SIGMA allows you to define the sigma level for a control chart. The value specified on SIGMA is used in calculating the upper and lower control limits on the chart. You can specify a number larger than 1 but less than or equal to 10. The larger the SIGMA value, the greater the range between the upper and the lower control limits. The default is 3.

MINSAMPLE Subcommand

MINSAMPLE specifies the minimum sample size for X-bar, R, or s charts. When you specify XR or XS on SPCHART, any subgroup with a size smaller than that specified on MINSAMPLE is excluded from the chart and from all computations. If each case is a subgroup, there must be at least as many variables named as the number specified on MINSAMPLE. The default is 2.

LSL and USL Subcommand

LSL and USL allow you to specify fixed lower and upper control limits. Fixed control limits are often used in manufacturing processes as designer-specified limits. These limits are displayed on the chart along with the calculated limits. If you do not specify LSL and USL, no fixed control limits are displayed. However, if you want only the specified control limits, you must edit the chart in a chart window to suppress the calculated series.

Example

```
SPCHART /TEMPLATE='CTRL.CHT'
  /XS=SUBSIZE
  /USL=74.50
  /LSL=73.50.
```

- The USL and LSL subcommands specify the control limits according to the designing engineer. The center line is most probably at 74.00.

- The specified upper and lower limits are displayed together with the control limits calculated from the observed standard deviation and the sigma value.

MISSING Subcommand

MISSING controls the treatment of missing values in the control chart.

- The default is NOREPORT and EXCLUDE.
- REPORT and NOREPORT are alternatives and apply only to category variables. They control whether categories (subgroups) with missing values are created.
- INCLUDE and EXCLUDE are alternatives and apply to process variables.

NOREPORT   *Suppress missing-value categories.* This is the default.

REPORT   *Report and plot missing-value categories.*

EXCLUDE   *Exclude user-missing values.* Both user- and system-missing values for the process variable are excluded from computation and plotting. This is the default.

INCLUDE   *Include user-missing values.* Only system-missing values for the process variable are excluded from computation and plotting.

SPLIT FILE

```
SPLIT FILE              {OFF        }
            [{LAYERED }] {BY varlist}
            {SEPARATE}
```

Example:

```
SORT CASES BY SEX.
SPLIT FILE BY SEX.
FREQUENCIES VARS=INCOME /STATISTICS=MEDIAN.
```

Overview

SPLIT FILE splits the working data file into subgroups that can be analyzed separately. These subgroups are sets of adjacent cases in the file that have the same values for the specified split variables. Each value of each split variable is considered a break group, and cases within a break group must be grouped together in the working data file. If they are not, the SORT CASES command must be used before SPLIT FILE to sort cases in the proper order.

Basic Specification

The basic specification is keyword BY followed by the variable or variables that define the split-file groups.

- By default, the split-file groups are compared within the same table(s).
- You can turn off split-file processing using keyword OFF.

Syntax Rules

- SPLIT FILE can specify both numeric and string split variables, including long string variables and variables created by temporary transformations. It cannot specify scratch or system variables.
- SPLIT FILE is in effect for all procedures in a session unless you limit it with a TEMPORARY command, turn it off, or override it with a new SPLIT FILE or SORT CASES command.

Operations

- Unlike most transformations, SPLIT FILE takes effect as soon as it is encountered in the command sequence. Thus, special attention should be paid to its position among commands. For more information, see "Command Order" on p. 16.
- The file is processed sequentially. A change or break in values on any one of the split variables signals the end of one break group and the beginning of the next.

- AGGREGATE ignores the SPLIT FILE command. To split files using AGGREGATE, name the variables used to split the file as break variables ahead of any other break variables on AGGREGATE. AGGREGATE still produces one file, but the aggregated cases are in the same order as the split-file groups.
- If SPLIT FILE is in effect when a procedure writes matrix materials, the program writes one set of matrix materials for every split group. If a procedure reads a file that contains multiple sets of matrix materials, the procedure automatically detects the presence of multiple sets.
- If SPLIT FILE names any variable that was defined by the NUMERIC command, the program prints page headings indicating the split-file grouping.

Limitations

- SPLIT FILE can specify or imply up to eight variables.

LAYERED and SEPARATE Subcommands

LAYERED and SEPARATE specify how split-file groups are displayed in the output.

- Only one of them can be specified. If neither is specified with the BY variable list, LAYERED is the default.
- LAYERED and SEPARATE do not apply to the text output.

LAYERED   *Display split-file groups in the same table in the outermost column.*

SEPARATE   *Display split-file groups as separate tables.*

Example

```
SORT CASES BY SEX.
SPLIT FILE BY SEX.
FREQUENCIES VARS=INCOME /STATISTICS=MEDIAN.
```

- SORT CASES arranges cases in the file according to the values of variable *SEX*.
- SPLIT FILE splits the file according to the values of variable *SEX*, and FREQUENCIES generates separate median income tables for men and women.
- By default, the two groups (men and women) are compared in the same Frequency and Statistics tables.

Example

```
SORT CASES BY SEX.
TEMPORARY.
SPLIT FILE SEPARATE BY SEX.
FREQUENCIES VARS=INCOME /STATISTICS=MEDIAN.
FREQUENCIES VARS=INCOME /STATISTICS=MEDIAN.
```

- Because of the TEMPORARY command, SPLIT FILE applies to the first procedure only. Thus, the first FREQUENCIES procedure generates separate tables for men and women. The second FREQUENCIES procedure generates tables that include both sexes.

Example

```
SORT CASES BY SEX.
SPLIT FILE SEPARATE BY SEX.
FREQUENCIES VARS=INCOME /STATISTICS=MEDIAN.
SPLIT FILE OFF.
FREQUENCIES VARS=INCOME /STATISTICS=MEDIAN.
```

- SPLIT FILE does not apply to the second FREQUENCIES procedure because it is turned off after the first FREQUENCIES procedure. This example produces the same results as the example above.

Example

```
SORT CASES BY SEX RACE.
SPLIT FILE BY SEX.
FREQUENCIES VARS=INCOME /STATISTICS=MEDIAN.
SPLIT FILE BY SEX RACE.
FREQUENCIES VARS=INCOME /STATISTICS=MEDIAN.
```

- The first SPLIT FILE command applies to the first FREQUENCIES procedure. The second SPLIT FILE command overrides the first and splits the file by sex and race. This split is in effect for the second FREQUENCIES procedure.

STRING

```
STRING varlist (An) [/varlist...]
```

Example:
```
STRING STATE1 (A2).
RECODE STATE ('IO'='IA') (ELSE=COPY) INTO STATE1.
```

Overview

STRING declares new string variables that can be used as target variables in data transformations.

Basic Specification

The basic specification is the name of the new variables and, in parentheses, the variable format.

Syntax Rules

- If keyword TO is used to create multiple string variables, the specified format applies to each variable named and implied by TO.
- To declare variables with different formats, separate each format group with a slash.
- STRING can be used within an input program to determine the order of string variables in the dictionary of the working data file. When used for this purpose, STRING must precede DATA LIST in the input program. See p. 653 for an example.
- STRING cannot be used to redefine an existing variable.
- String variables cannot have zero length; A0 is an illegal format.
- All implementations of the program allow the A format. Other string formats may be available on some systems. In addition, the definition of a long string depends on your operating system. Use keyword LOCAL on the INFO command to obtain documentation for your operating system.

Operations

- Unlike most transformations, STRING takes effect as soon as it is encountered in the command sequence. Thus, special attention should be paid to its position among commands. For more information, see "Command Order" on p. 16.
- New string variables are initialized as blanks.

- Variables declared on STRING are added to the working data file in the order they are specified. This order is not changed by the order in which the variables are used in the transformation language.
- The length of a string variable is fixed by the format specified when it is declared and cannot be changed by FORMATS. To change the length of a string variable, declare a new variable with the desired length and then use COMPUTE to assign the values of the original variable to it.

Example

```
STRING STATE1 (A2).
RECODE STATE ('IO'='IA') (ELSE=COPY) INTO STATE1.
```

- STRING declares variable *STATE1* with an A2 format.
- RECODE specifies *STATE* as the source variable and *STATE1* as the target variable. The original value IO is recoded to IA. Keywords ELSE and COPY copy all other state codes over unchanged. Thus, *STATE* and *STATE1* are identical except for cases with the original value IO.

Example

```
STRING V1 TO V6 (A8) / V7 V10 (A16).
```

- STRING declares variables *V1*, *V2*, *V3*, *V4*, *V5*, and *V6*, each with an A8 format, and variables *V7* and *V10*, each with an A16 format.

SUBTITLE

```
SUBTITLE [']text[']
```

Example:
```
SUBTITLE "Children's Training Shoes Only".
```

Overview

SUBTITLE inserts a left-justified subtitle on the second line from the top of each page of the output. The default subtitle contains the installation name and information about the hardware and operating system.

Basic Specification

The only specification is the subtitle itself.

Syntax Rules

- The subtitle can include any characters. To specify a blank subtitle, enclose a blank between apostrophes.
- The subtitle can be up to 60 characters long. Subtitles longer than 60 characters are truncated.
- The apostrophes or quotation marks enclosing the subtitle are optional; using them allows you to include apostrophes or quotation marks in the subtitle.
- If the subtitle is enclosed in apostrophes, quotation marks are valid characters but apostrophes must be specified as double apostrophes. If the subtitle is enclosed in quotation marks, apostrophes are valid characters but quotation marks must be specified as double quotation marks.
- More than one SUBTITLE command is allowed in a single session.
- A subtitle cannot be placed between a procedure command and BEGIN DATA—END DATA or within data records when the data are inline.

Operations

- Each SUBTITLE command overrides the previous one and takes effect on the next output page.
- SUBTITLE is independent of TITLE and each can be changed separately.
- The subtitle will not be displayed if HEADER=NO is specified on SET.

929

Example

```
TITLE 'Running Shoe Study from Runner''s World Data'.
SUBTITLE "Children's Training Shoes Only".
```

- The title is enclosed in apostrophes, so the apostrophe in *Runner's* must be specified as a double apostrophe.
- The subtitle is enclosed in quotation marks, so the apostrophe in *Children's* is simply specified as an apostrophe.

Example

```
TITLE 'Running Shoe Study from Runner''s World Data'.
SUBTITLE ' '.
```

- This subtitle is specified as a blank. This suppresses the default subtitle.

SUMMARIZE

```
SUMMARIZE [TABLES=]{varlist} [BY varlist] [BY...] [/varlist...]
                   {ALL     }

[/TITLE ='string']      [FOOTNOTE= 'string']

[/CELLS= [COUNT**] [MEAN ] [STDDEV]
                   [MEDIAN] [GMEDIAN] [SEMEAN]  [SUM ]
                   [MIN] [MAX] [RANGE] [VARIANCE]
                   [KURT] [SEKURT] [SKEW] [SESKEW]
                   [FIRST] [LAST]
                   [NPCT] [SPCT] [NPCT(var)] [SPCT(var)]
                   [HARMONIC] [GEOMETRIC]
                   [DEFAULT]
                   [ALL] [NONE]   ]

[/MISSING=[{EXCLUDE**}][{VARIABLE**  }]
           {INCLUDE  }  {TABLE       }
           {DEPENDENT}

[FORMAT=[{NOLIST** }] [{CASENUM    }] [{TOTAL**}]   [MISSING='string']
         {LIST     }   {NOCASENUM  }   {NOTOTAL}
         {VALIDLIST}

[/STATISTICS=[ANOVA] [{LINEARITY}] [NONE**] ]
                      {ALL      }
```

**Default if the subcommand is omitted.

Example:
```
SUMMARIZE TABLES=V1 TO V5 BY GROUP
   /STATISTICS=ANOVA.
```

Overview

SUMMARIZE produces univariate statistics for specified variables. You can break the variables into groups defined by one or more control (independent) variables. Another procedure that displays univariate statistics is FREQUENCIES.

Options

Cell Contents. By default, SUMMARIZE displays means, standard deviations, and cell counts. You can also display aggregated statistics, including sums, variances, median, range, kurtosis, skewness, and their standard error, using the CELLS subcommand.

Statistics. In addition to the statistics displayed for each cell of the table, you can obtain a one-way analysis of variance and test of linearity using the STATISTICS subcommand.

Format. By default, SUMMARIZE produces a Summary Report with a total category for each group defined by the control variables. You can request a Listing Report with or without case numbers using the FORMAT subcommand. You can also remove the total category from each group. You can specify a title and a caption for the Summary or Listing Report using the TITLE and FOOTNOTE subcommands.

Basic Specification

The basic specification is TABLES with a variable list. Each variable creates a category. The actual keyword TABLES can be omitted.

- The minimum specification is a dependent variable.
- By default, SUMMARIZE displays a Case Processing Summary table showing the number and percentage of cases included, excluded, and their total, and a Summary Report showing means, standard deviations, and number of cases for each category.

Syntax Rules

- Both numeric and string variables can be specified. String variables can be short or long.
- If there is more than one TABLES subcommand, FORMAT=LIST or VALIDLIST results in an error.
- String specifications for TITLE and FOOTNOTE cannot exceed 255 characters. Quotation marks or apostrophes are required. When the specification breaks on multiple lines, enclose each line in apostrophes or quotation marks and separate the specifications for each line by at least one blank.
- Each subcommand except TABLES can be specified only once. Multiple use results in a warning, and the last specification is used.
- Multiple TABLES subcommands are allowed, but multiple specifications use a lot of computer resources and time.
- There is no limit on the number of variables you can specify on each TABLES subcommand.
- When a variable is specified more than once, only the first occurrence is honored. The same variables specified after different BY keywords will result in an error.

Limitations

- Only 5 BY keywords can be specified.

Operations

- The data are processed sequentially. It is not necessary to sort the cases before processing. If a BY keyword is used, the output is always sorted.
- A Case Processing Summary table is always generated, showing the number and percentage of the cases included, excluded, and the total.
- For each combination of control variables specified after different BY keywords, SUMMARIZE produces a group in the Summary Report (depending on the specification on the FORMAT subcommand). By default, mean, standard deviation, and number of cases are displayed for each group and for the total.
- An ANOVA table and a Measure of Association table are produced if additional statistics are requested.

Example

```
SUMMARIZE TABLES=V1 BY SEX BY GROUP
   /STATISTICS=ANOVA.
```

- A Case Processing Summary table lists the number and percentage of cases included, excluded, and the total.
- A Summary Report displays means, standard deviations, and numbers of cases for each group defined by each combination of *SEX* and *GROUP*.
- An ANOVA table displays analysis of variance with only *SEX* as the grouping variable.

TABLES Subcommand

TABLES specifies the dependent and control variables.

- You can specify multiple TABLES subcommands on a single SUMMARIZE command.
- For FORMAT=LIST or VALIDLIST, only one TABLES subcommand is allowed. Multiple dependent and control variables add more breaks to the Listing Report. Total statistics are displayed at the end for each combination defined by different values of the control variables.
- For FORMAT=NOLIST, which is the default, each use of keyword BY adds a dimension to the table requested. Total statistics are displayed with each group.
- The order in which control variables are displayed is the same as the order in which they are specified on TABLES. The values of the first control variable defined for the table appear in the leftmost column of the table and change the most slowly in the definition of groups.
- Statistics are displayed for each dependent variable in the same report.
- More than one dependent variable can be specified in a table list, and more than one control variable can be specified in each dimension of a table list.

TITLE and FOOTNOTE Subcommands

TITLE and FOOTNOTE provide a title and a caption for the Summary or Listing Report.

- TITLE and FOOTNOTE are optional and can be placed anywhere.
- The specification on TITLE or FOOTNOTE is a string within apostrophes or quotation marks. To specify a multiple-line title or footnote, enclose each line in apostrophes or quotation marks and separate the specifications for each line by at least one blank.
- The string you specify cannot exceed 255 characters.

CELLS Subcommand

By default, SUMMARIZE displays the means, standard deviations, and cell counts in each cell. Use CELLS to modify cell information.

- If CELLS is specified without keywords, SUMMARIZE displays the default statistics.
- If any keywords are specified on CELLS, only the requested information is displayed.
- MEDIAN and GMEDIAN use a lot of computer resources and time. Requesting these statistics (via these keywords or ALL) may slow down performance.

DEFAULT	*Means, standard deviations, and cell counts.* This is the default if CELLS is omitted.
MEAN	*Cell means.*
STDDEV	*Cell standard deviations.*
COUNT	*Cell counts.*
MEDIAN	*Cell median.*
GMEDIAN	*Grouped median.*
SEMEAN	*Standard error of cell mean.*
SUM	*Cell sums.*
MIN	*Cell minimum.*
MAX	*Cell maximum.*
RANGE	*Cell range.*
VARIANCE	*Variances.*
KURT	*Cell kurtosis.*
SEKURT	*Standard error of cell kurtosis.*
SKEW	*Cell skewness.*
SESKEW	*Standard error of cell skewness.*
FIRST	*First value.*
LAST	*Last value.*
SPCT	*Percentage of total sum.*
NPCT	*Percentage of total number of cases.*
SPCT(var)	*Percentage of total sum within specified variable.* The specified variable must be one of the control variables.
NPCT(var)	*Percentage of total number of cases within specified variable.* The specified variable must be one of the control variables.
HARMONIC	*Harmonic mean.*
GEOMETRIC	*Geometric mean.*
ALL	*All cell information.*

MISSING Subcommand

MISSING controls the treatment of cases with missing values. There are two groups of keywords.

- EXCLUDE, INCLUDE, and DEPENDENT specify the treatment of user-missing values. The default is EXCLUDE.

EXCLUDE	*All user-missing values are excluded.* This is the default.
INCLUDE	*User-missing values are treated as valid values.*
DEPENDENT	*User-missing values are considered missing in a dependent variable and valid in a grouping variable (variables specified after a BY keyword).*

- VARIABLE and TABLE specify how cases with missing values for dependent variables are excluded. The default is VARIABLE.
- Cases with missing values for any control variables are always excluded.

VARIABLE	*A case is excluded when all of the values for variables in that table are missing.* This is the default.
TABLE	*A case is excluded when any value is missing within a table.*

FORMAT Subcommand

FORMAT specifies whether you want a case listing for your report, and if you do, whether you want case numbers displayed for the listing. It also determines whether your reports will display a total category for each group and how they are going to indicate missing values.

NOLIST	*Display a Summary Report without a case listing.* This is the default.
LIST	*Display a Listing Report showing all cases.*
VALIDLIST	*Display a Listing Report showing only the valid cases.*
CASENUM	*Display case numbers as a category in the Listing Reports.* This is the default when FORMAT=LIST or VALIDLIST.
NOCASENUM	*Do not display case numbers.*
TOTAL	*Display the summary statistics for the total of each group with the label Total.* This is the default.
NOTOTAL	*Display the total category without a label.*
MISSING='string'	*Display system-missing values as a specified string.*

STATISTICS Subcommand

Use STATISTICS to request a one-way analysis of variance and a test of linearity for each table list.

- Statistics requested on STATISTICS are computed in addition to the statistics displayed in the Group Statistics table.
- If STATISTICS is specified without keywords, SUMMARIZE computes ANOVA.
- If two or more dimensions are specified, the second and subsequent dimensions are ignored in the analysis-of-variance table.

ANOVA   *Analysis of variance.* ANOVA displays a standard analysis-of-variance table and calculates eta and eta squared (displayed in the Measures of Association table). This is the default if STATISTICS is specified without keywords.

LINEARITY   *Test of linearity.* LINEARITY (alias ALL) displays additional statistics to the tables created by the ANOVA keyword—the sums of squares, degrees of freedom, and mean square associated with linear and nonlinear components, the F ratio, and the significance level for the ANOVA table and Pearson's r and r^2 for the Measures of Association table. LINEARITY is ignored if the control variable is a string.

NONE   *No additional statistics.* This is the default if STATISTICS is omitted.

Example

```
SUMMARIZE TABLES=INCOME BY SEX BY RACE
  /STATISTICS=ANOVA.
```

• SUMMARIZE produces a Group Statistics table of *INCOME* by *RACE* within *SEX* and computes an analysis of variance only for *INCOME* by *SEX*.

SYSFILE INFO

```
SYSFILE INFO [FILE=] 'file specification'
```

Example:
```
SYSFILE INFO FILE='PERSNL.SAV'.
```

Overview

SYSFILE INFO displays complete dictionary information for all variables in an SPSS-format data file. You do not have to retrieve the file with GET to use SYSFILE INFO. If the file has already been retrieved, use DISPLAY DICTIONARY to display dictionary information.

Basic Specification

The basic specification is the command keyword and a complete file specification enclosed in apostrophes.

Syntax Rules

- Only one file specification is allowed per command. To display dictionary information for more than one SPSS-format data file, use multiple SYSFILE INFO commands.
- The file extension, if there is one, must be specified, even if it is the default.
- The subcommand keyword FILE is optional. When FILE is specified, the equals sign is required.

Operations

- No procedure is needed to execute SYSFILE INFO, since SYSFILE INFO obtains information from the dictionary alone.
- SYSFILE INFO displays the variable name, label, sequential position in the file, print and write format, missing values, and value labels for each variable in the specified file. Up to 60 characters can be displayed for variable and value labels.

Example

```
SYSFILE INFO FILE='PERSNL.SAV'.
```

- The program displays the complete dictionary information for all variables in the SPSS-format data file *PERSNL.SAV*.

TEMPORARY

TEMPORARY

Example:
```
SORT CASES BY SEX.
TEMPORARY.
SPLIT FILE BY SEX.
FREQUENCIES VARS=INCOME /STATISTICS=MEDIAN.
FREQUENCIES VARS=INCOME /STATISTICS=MEDIAN.
```

Overview

TEMPORARY signals the beginning of temporary transformations that are in effect only for the next procedure. New numeric or string variables created after the TEMPORARY command are temporary variables. Any modifications made to existing variables after the TEMPORARY command are also temporary.

With TEMPORARY you can perform separate analyses for subgroups in the data and then repeat the analysis for the file as a whole. You can also use TRANSFORM to transform data for one analysis but not for other subsequent analyses.

TEMPORARY can be applied to the following commands:

- Transformation commands COMPUTE, RECODE, IF, and COUNT, and the DO REPEAT utility.
- The LOOP and DO IF structures.
- Format commands PRINT FORMATS, WRITE FORMATS, and FORMATS.
- Data selection commands SELECT IF, SAMPLE, FILTER, and WEIGHT.
- Variable declarations NUMERIC, STRING, and VECTOR.
- Labeling commands VARIABLE LABELS and VALUE LABELS, and the MISSING VALUES command.
- SPLIT FILE.
- XSAVE.

Basic Specification

The only specification is the keyword TEMPORARY. There are no additional specifications.

Operations

- Once TEMPORARY is specified, you cannot refer to previously existing scratch variables.
- Temporary transformations apply to the next command that reads the data. Once the data are read, the temporary transformations are no longer in effect.

- The XSAVE command leaves temporary transformations in effect. SAVE, however, reads the data and turns temporary transformations off after the file is written. (See example below.)
- TEMPORARY cannot be used with SORT CASES, MATCH FILES, ADD FILES, or COMPUTE with a LAG function. If any of these commands follows TEMPORARY in the command sequence, there must be an intervening procedure or command that reads the data to first execute the TEMPORARY command.
- TEMPORARY cannot be used within the DO IF—END IF or LOOP—END LOOP structures.

Example

```
SORT CASES BY SEX.
TEMPORARY.
SPLIT FILE BY SEX.
FREQUENCIES VARS=INCOME /STATISTICS=MEDIAN.
FREQUENCIES VARS=INCOME /STATISTICS=MEDIAN.
```

- SPLIT FILE applies to the first FREQUENCIES procedure, which generates separate median income tables for men and women.
- SPLIT FILE is not in effect for the second FREQUENCIES procedure, which generates a single median income table that includes both men and women.

Example

```
DATA LIST FILE=HUBDATA RECORDS=3
  /1 #MOBIRTH #DABIRTH #YRBIRTH 6-11 DEPT88 19.
COMPUTE    AGE=($JDATE - YRMODA(#YRBIRTH,#MOBIRTH,#DABIRTH))/365.25.
VARIABLE LABELS AGE 'EMPLOYEE''S AGE'
          DEPT88 'DEPARTMENT CODE IN 1988'.

TEMPORARY.
RECODE AGE (LO THRU 20=1)(20 THRU 25=2)(25 THRU 30=3)(30 THRU 35=4)
        (35 THRU 40=5)(40 THRU 45=6)(45 THRU 50=7)(50 THRU 55=8)
        (55 THRU 60=9)(60 THRU 65=10)(65 THRU HI=11).
VARIABLE LABELS AGE 'EMPLOYEE AGE CATEGORIES'.
VALUE LABELS AGE 1 'Up to 20' 2 '20 to 25' 3 '25 to 30' 4 '30 to 35'
        5 '35 to 40' 6 '40 to 45' 7 '45 to 50' 8 '50 to 55'
        9 '55 to 60' 10 '60 to 65' 11 '65 and older'.

FREQUENCIES VARIABLES=AGE.
MEANS AGE BY DEPT88.
```

- COMPUTE creates variable *AGE* from the dates in the data.
- FREQUENCIES uses the temporary version of variable *AGE* with temporary variable and value labels.
- MEANS uses the unrecoded values of *AGE* and the permanent variable label.

Example

```
GET FILE=HUBEMPL.
TEMPORARY.
RECODE DEPT85 TO DEPT88 (1,2=1) (3,4=2) (ELSE=9).
VALUE LABELS DEPT85 TO DEPT88 1 'MANAGEMENT'
                              2 'OPERATIONS'
                              3 'UNKNOWN'.
XSAVE OUTFILE=HUBTEMP.
CROSSTABS DEPT85 TO DEPT88 BY JOBCAT.
```

- Both the saved SPSS-format data file and the CROSSTABS output will reflect the temporary recoding and labeling of the department variables.

- If XSAVE is replaced with SAVE, the SPSS-format data file will reflect the temporary recoding and labeling but the CROSSTABS output will not.

TITLE

```
TITLE [']text[']
```

Example:
```
TITLE "Running Shoe Study from Runner's World Data".
```

Overview

TITLE inserts a left-justified title on the top line of each page of output. The default title indicates the version of the system being used.

Basic Specification

The only specification is the title.

Syntax Rules

- The title can include any characters. To specify a blank title, enclose a blank between apostrophes.
- The title can be up to 60 characters long. Titles longer than 60 characters are truncated.
- The apostrophes or quotation marks enclosing the title are optional; using them allows you to include apostrophes or quotation marks in the title.
- If the subtitle is enclosed in apostrophes, quotation marks are valid characters but apostrophes must be specified as double apostrophes. If the subtitle is enclosed in quotation marks, apostrophes are valid characters but quotation marks must be specified as double quotation marks.
- More than one TITLE command is allowed in a single session.
- A title cannot be placed between a procedure command and BEGIN DATA—END DATA or within data records when the data are inline.

Operations

- The title is displayed as part of the output heading, which also includes the date and page number. If HEADER=NO is specified on SET, the heading, including the title and subtitle, will not be displayed.
- Each TITLE command overrides the previous one and takes effect on the next output page.
- Only the title portion of the heading changes. The date and page number are still displayed.
- TITLE is independent of SUBTITLE, and each can be changed separately.

941

Example

```
TITLE "Running Shoe Study from Runner's World Data".
SUBTITLE 'Children''s Training Shoes Only'.
```

- The title is enclosed in quotation marks, so the apostrophe in *Runner's* is a valid character.
- The subtitle is enclosed in apostrophes, so the apostrophe in *Children's* must be specified as a double apostrophe.

Example

```
TITLE ' '.
SUBTITLE ' '.
```

- The title and subtitle are specified as blanks. This suppresses the default title and subtitle. The date and page number still display on the title line.

TSET

```
TSET
 [PRINT={DEFAULT**}]   [/NEWVAR={CURRENT**}] [/MXAUTO={16**}]
         {BRIEF    }            {NONE    }            {lags}
         {DETAILED }            {ALL     }

 [/MXCROSS={7** }]   [/MXNEWVARS={60**}] [/MXPREDICT={60**}]
           {lags}                {n  }              {n  }

 [/MISSING={EXCLUDE**}]   [/CIN={95** }] [/TOLER={0.0001**}]
           {INCLUDE  }          {value}          {value   }

 [/CNVERGE={0.001**}]   [/ACFSE={IND**}]
           {value  }            {MA   }

 [/PERIOD=n]     [/ID=varname]

 [/{CONSTANT**}]
   {NOCONSTANT}

 [/DEFAULT]
```

**Default if the subcommand is omitted.

Example:

```
TSET PERIOD 6 NEWVAR NONE MXAUTO 25.
```

Overview

TSET sets global parameters to be used by procedures that analyze time series and sequence variables. To display the current settings of these parameters, use the TSHOW command.

Basic Specification

The basic specification is at least one subcommand.

Subcommand Order

- Subcommands can be specified in any order.

Syntax Rules

- The slash between subcommands is optional.
- You can specify DEFAULT on any subcommand to restore the default setting for that subcommand.
- Subcommand DEFAULT restores all TSET subcommands to their defaults.

Operations

- TSET takes effect immediately.
- Only the settings specified are affected. All others remain at their previous settings or the default.
- Subcommands on other procedures that perform the same function as subcommands on TSET override the TSET specifications for those procedures.
- Procedures that are affected by TSET specifications are CASEPLOT, NPPLOT, and TSPLOT.

DEFAULT Subcommand

DEFAULT resets all TSET settings back to their defaults. There are no additional specifications on DEFAULT.

ID Subcommand

ID specifies a variable whose values are used to label observations in plots.
- The only specification on ID is the name of a variable in the working data file.
- If ID is not specified, the *DATE_* variable is used to label observations.
- If ID is specified within the procedure, it overrides the TSET specification for that procedure.

MISSING Subcommand

MISSING controls the treatment of user-missing values.
- The specification on MISSING is keyword INCLUDE or EXCLUDE. The default is EXCLUDE.
- INCLUDE indicates that observations with user-missing values should be treated as valid values and included in analyses.
- EXCLUDE indicates that observations with user-missing values should be excluded from analyses.

MXNEWVARS Subcommand

MXNEWVARS indicates the maximum number of new variables that can be generated by a procedure.
- The specification on MXNEWVARS indicates the maximum and can be any positive integer.
- The default maximum number is 60 new variables per procedure.

MXPREDICT Subcommand

MXPREDICT indicates the maximum number of new cases that can be added to the working data file per procedure when the PREDICT command is used.

- The specification on MXPREDICT can be any positive integer.
- The default maximum number of new cases is 60 per procedure.

PERIOD Subcommand

PERIOD indicates the size of the period to be used for seasonal differencing.

- The specification on PERIOD indicates how many observations are in one season or period and can be any positive integer.
- There is no default for the PERIOD subcommand.
- The specification on TSET PERIOD overrides the periodicity of DATE variables.
- If a period is specified within an individual procedure, it overrides the TSET PERIOD specification for that procedure.

PRINT Subcommand

PRINT controls how much output is produced.

- The specification on PRINT can be BRIEF, DETAILED, or DEFAULT. The amount of output produced by DEFAULT is generally between the amount produced by BRIEF and DETAILED.
- For procedures with multiple iterations, BRIEF generally means that final statistics are displayed with no iteration history. DEFAULT provides a one-line summary at each iteration in addition to the final statistics. DETAILED provides a complete summary of each iteration (where necessary) plus the final statistics.
- For some procedures, the default and detailed output is the same. For many of the simpler procedures, brief, default, and detailed are all the same.

TSHOW

TSHOW

Example:

TSHOW.

Overview

TSHOW displays a list of all the current specifications on the TSET, USE, PREDICT, and DATE commands.

Basic Specification

The command keyword TSHOW is the only specification.

Operations

- TSHOW is executed immediately.
- TSHOW lists every current specification for the TSET, USE, PREDICT, and DATE commands, as well as the default settings.

Example

TSHOW.

- The TSHOW command produces a list of the current settings on TSET, USE, PREDICT, and DATE commands.

TSPLOT

```
TSPLOT [VARIABLES=] variable names

[/DIFF={1}]
       {n}

[/SDIFF={1}]
        {n}

[/PERIOD=n]

[/{NOLOG**}]
   {LN    }

[/ID=varname]

[/MARK={varname} ]
       {date    }

[/SPLIT {UNIFORM**}]
        {SCALE    }

[/APPLY [='model name']]
```

For plots with one variable:

```
[/FORMAT=[{NOFILL**}]   [{NOREFERENCE**}]
          {LEFT    }     {REFERENCE    }
          {RIGHT   }
```

For plots with multiple variables:

```
[/FORMAT={NOJOIN**}]
         {JOIN    }
         {HILO    }
```

**Default if the subcommand is omitted.

Example:

```
TSPLOT TICKETS
  /LN
  /DIFF
  /SDIFF
  /PERIOD=12
  /FORMAT=REFERENCE
  /MARK=Y 55 M 6.
```

Overview

TSPLOT produces a plot of one or more time series or sequence variables. You can request natural log and differencing transformations to produce plots of transformed variables. Several plot formats are available.

Options

Modifying the Variables. You can request a natural log transformation of the variables using the LN subcommand and seasonal and nonseasonal differencing to any degree using the SDIFF and DIFF subcommands. With seasonal differencing, you can also specify the periodicity on the PERIOD subcommand.

Plot Format. With the FORMAT subcommand, you can fill in the space on one side of the plotted values on plots with one variable. You can also plot a reference line indicating the variable mean. For plots with two or more variables, you can specify whether you want to join the values for each observation with a vertical line. With the ID subcommand you can label the horizontal axis with the values of a specified variable. You can mark the onset of an intervention variable on the plot with the MARK subcommand.

Split-File Processing. You can control how data that have been divided into subgroups by a SPLIT FILE command should be plotted using the SPLIT subcommand.

Basic Specification

The basic specification is one or more variable names.

- If the DATE command has been specified, the horizontal axis is labeled with the *DATE_* variable at periodic intervals. Otherwise, sequence numbers are used. The vertical axis is labeled with the value scale of the plotted variable(s).

Figure 1 shows a default high-resolution plot with DATE=YEAR 1900. Figure 2 shows the same default plot in low resolution.

Figure 1   TSPLOT VARIABLES=PRICE (in high resolution)

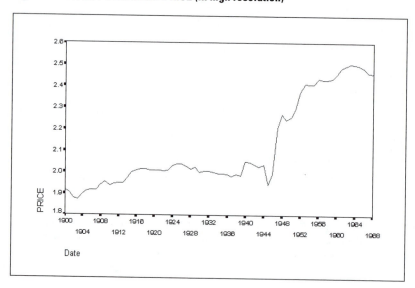

Figure 2   TSPLOT VARIABLES=PRICE (in low resolution)

```
The following plot symbols are used:
   P - Variable PRICE
   M - Missing Data (placed on the horizontal axis)
```

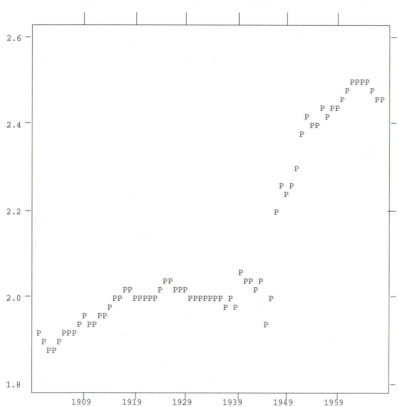

Subcommand Order

- Subcommands can be specified in any order.

Syntax Rules

- VARIABLES can be specified only once.
- Other subcommands can be specified more than once, but only the last specification of each one is executed.

Operations

- Subcommand specifications apply to all variables named on the TSPLOT command.
- If the LN subcommand is specified, any differencing requested on that TSPLOT command is done on the log-transformed variables.
- In high-resolution plots, split-file information is displayed as part of the subtitle and transformation information is displayed as part of the footnote.
- In low resolution, the plot frame size depends on the page size specified on the SET command.

Limitations

- Maximum 1 VARIABLES subcommand. There is no limit on the number of variables named on the list.

Example

```
TSPLOT TICKETS
  /LN
  /DIFF
  /SDIFF
  /PERIOD=12
  /FORMAT=REFERENCE
  /MARK=Y 55 M 6.
```

- This command produces a plot of *TICKETS* after a natural log transformation, differencing, and seasonal differencing have been applied.
- LN transforms the data using the natural logarithm (base *e*) of *TICKETS*.
- DIFF differences the logged variable once.
- SDIFF and PERIOD apply one degree of seasonal differencing with a period of 12.
- FORMAT=REFERENCE adds a reference line representing the variable mean. In low resolution, the area between the plotted values and the mean is filled with the plotting symbol (*T*).
- MARK provides a marker on the plot at June 1955. The marker is displayed as a vertical reference line in high-resolution plots.

VARIABLES Subcommand

VARIABLES specifies the names of the variables to be plotted and is the only required subcommand. The actual keyword VARIABLES can be omitted.

DIFF Subcommand

DIFF specifies the degree of differencing used to convert a nonstationary variable to a stationary one with a constant mean and variance before plotting.

- You can specify any positive integer on DIFF.

- If DIFF is specified without a value, the default is 1.
- The number of values plotted decreases by 1 for each degree of differencing.

Example

```
TSPLOT TICKETS
  /DIFF=2.
```

- In this example, *TICKETS* is differenced twice before plotting.

SDIFF Subcommand

If the variable exhibits a seasonal or periodic pattern, you can use the SDIFF subcommand to seasonally difference the variable before plotting.

- The specification on SDIFF indicates the degree of seasonal differencing and can be any positive integer.
- If SDIFF is specified without a value, the degree of seasonal differencing defaults to 1.
- The number of seasons plotted decreases by 1 for each degree of seasonal differencing.
- The length of the period used by SDIFF is specified on the PERIOD subcommand. If the PERIOD subcommand is not specified, the periodicity established on the TSET or DATE command is used (see the PERIOD subcommand below).

PERIOD Subcommand

PERIOD indicates the length of the period to be used by the SDIFF subcommand.

- The specification on PERIOD indicates how many observations are in one period or season and can be any positive integer.
- If PERIOD is not specified, the periodicity established on TSET PERIOD is in effect. If TSET PERIOD is not specified, the periodicity established on the DATE command is used. If periodicity was not established anywhere, the SDIFF subcommand will not be executed.

Example

```
TSPLOT TICKETS
  /SDIFF=1
  /PERIOD=12.
```

- This command applies one degree of seasonal differencing with 12 observations per season to *TICKETS* before plotting.

LN and NOLOG Subcommands

LN transforms the data using the natural logarithm (base *e*) of the variable and is used to remove varying amplitude over time. NOLOG indicates that the data should not be log transformed. NOLOG is the default.

- If you specify LN on TSPLOT, any differencing requested on that command will be done on the log-transformed variables.
- There are no additional specifications on LN or NOLOG.
- Only the last LN or NOLOG subcommand on a TSPLOT command is executed.
- If a natural log transformation is requested, any value less than or equal to zero is set to system-missing.
- NOLOG is generally used with an APPLY subcommand to turn off a previous LN specification.

Example

```
TSPLOT TICKETS
   /LN.
```

- In this example, *TICKETS* is transformed using the natural logarithm before plotting.

ID Subcommand

ID names a variable whose values will be used as labels for the horizontal axis.

- The only specification on ID is a variable name. If you have a variable named *ID* in your working data file, the equals sign after the subcommand is required.
- If the ID subcommand is not used and TSET ID has not been specified, the axis is labeled with the *DATE_* variable created by the DATE command. If the DATE command has not been specified, the observation number is used as the label.

Example

```
TSPLOT VARA
   /ID=VARB.
```

- In this example the values of *VARB* will be used to label the horizontal axis of *VARA* at periodic intervals.

FORMAT Subcommand

FORMAT controls the plot format.

- The specification on FORMAT is one of the keywords listed below.
- Keywords NOFILL, LEFT, RIGHT, NOREFERENCE, and REFERENCE apply to plots with one variable. NOFILL, LEFT, and RIGHT are alternatives and indicate how the plot is filled. NOREFERENCE and REFERENCE are alternatives and specify whether a reference line is displayed. For low-resolution plots, only one keyword can be specified. One keyword *from each set* can be specified for high-resolution plots. NOFILL and NOREFERENCE are the defaults.
- Keywords JOIN, NOJOIN, and HILO apply to plots with multiple variables and are alternatives. NOJOIN is the default. Only one keyword can be specified on a FORMAT subcommand for plots with multiple variables.

The following formats are available for plots with one variable:

NOFILL   *Plot only the values for the variable with no fill.* NOFILL produces a plot with no fill above or below the plotted values. This is the default format when one variable is specified.

BOTTOM   *Plot the values for the variable and fill in the area below the curve.* In low-resolution plots, the area below the plotted curve is filled in with the first character of the variable name. For high-resolution plots, if the plotted variable has missing or negative values, BOTTOM is ignored and the default NOFILL is used instead. Figure 3 shows a filled high-resolution plot.

TOP   *Plot the values for the variable and fill in the area above the curve.* In low resolution, the area above the plotted curve is filled in with the first character of the variable name. For high-resolution plots, TOP is ignored and the default NOFILL is used instead.

Figure 3   FORMAT=BOTTOM

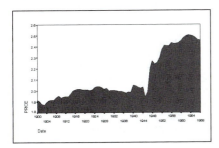

NOREFERENCE   *Do not plot a reference line.* This is the default when one variable is specified.

REFERENCE   *Plot a reference line indicating the variable mean.* In high resolution, a fill chart is displayed as an area chart with a reference line and a non-fill chart is displayed as a line chart with a reference line. In low-resolution, the area between the plotted curve and the reference line are filled in with the plotting character (the first character of the variable name). You can request either fill or a reference line for a low-resolution chart, but not both. Figure 4 shows a high-resolution no-fill plot with a reference line indicating the variable mean.

Figure 4 FORMAT=REFERENCE

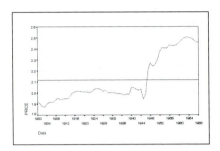

The following formats are available for plots with multiple variables:

NOJOIN *Plot the values of each variable named.* In high-resolution plots, different colors or line patterns are used for multiple variables. In low-resolution plots, the plotting character for each variable is the first character of the variable name. Multiple occurrences of the same value for a single observation are plotted using a dollar sign ($). This is the default format for plots with multiple variables.

JOIN *Plot the values of each variable and join the values for each observation.* Values are plotted as described for NOJOIN and the values for each observation are joined together by a line. Figure 5 contains a high-resolution plot in this format with three time series (*PRICE, INCOME,* and *CONSUMP*).

HILO *Plot the highest and lowest values across variables for each observation and join the two values together.* The high and low values are plotted as a horizontal bar and are joined with a line. For high-resolution plots, if more than three variables are specified HILO is ignored and the default NOJOIN is used. Figure 6 contains a high-resolution high-low plot with three time series (*PRICE, INCOME,* and *CONSUMP*).

Figure 5 FORMAT=JOIN

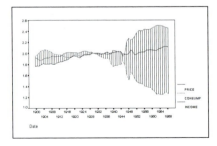

Figure 6   FORMAT=HILO

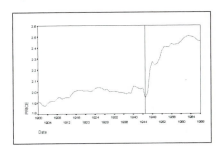

MARK Subcommand

MARK indicates the onset of an intervention variable.

- The onset date is indicated in high resolution by a vertical reference line and in low resolution by a tick mark on the top and bottom axes.
- The specification on MARK can be either a variable name or an onset date if the *DATE_* variable exists.
- If a variable is named, the plot indicates where the values of that variable change.
- A date specification follows the same format as the DATE command; that is, a keyword followed by a value. For example, the specification for June 1955 is Y 1955 M 6 (or Y 55 M 6 if only the last 2 digits of the year are used on DATE).

Figure 7 shows a high-resolution plot with the year 1945 marked as the onset date.

Figure 7   MARK=Y 1945

SPLIT Subcommand

SPLIT specifies how to plot data that have been divided into subgroups by a SPLIT FILE command. The default is UNIFORM.

UNIFORM   *Scale uniformly.* The vertical axis is scaled according to the values of the entire data set.

SCALE   *Scale individually.* The vertical axis is scaled according to the values of each individual subgroup.

- If FORMAT=REFERENCE is specified when SPLIT=SCALE, the reference line is placed at the mean of the subgroup. If FORMAT=REFERENCE is specified when SPLIT=UNIFORM, the reference line is placed at the overall mean.

Example

```
SPLIT FILE BY REGION.
TSPLOT TICKETS / SPLIT=SCALE.
```

- In this example, the data have been split into subgroups by *REGION*. The plots produced with the SCALE subcommand have vertical axes that are individually scaled according to the values of each particular region.

APPLY Subcommand

APPLY allows you to produce a plot using previously defined specifications without having to repeat the TSPLOT subcommands.

- The only specification on APPLY is the name of a previous model enclosed in apostrophes. If a model name is not specified, the specifications from the previous TSPLOT command are used.
- To change one or more specifications of the plot, specify the subcommands of only those portions you want to change after subcommand APPLY.
- If no variables are specified, the variables that were specified for the original plot are used.
- To plot different variables, enter new variable names before or after the APPLY subcommand.

Example

```
TSPLOT TICKETS
  /LN
  /DIFF=1
  /SDIFF=1
  /PERIOD=12.
TSPLOT ROUNDTRP
  /APPLY.
TSPLOT APPLY
  /NOLOG.
```

- The first command produces a plot of *TICKETS* after a natural log transformation, differencing, and seasonal differencing have been applied.
- The second command plots the values for *ROUNDTRP* using the same subcommands specified for *TICKETS*.
- The third command produces another plot of *ROUNDTRP* but this time without a log transformation. *ROUNDTRP* is still differenced once and seasonally differenced with a periodicity of 12.

T-TEST

One-sample tests:

```
T-TEST TESTVAL n /VARIABLE=varlist
```

Independent-samples tests:

```
T-TEST GROUPS=varname ({1,2**      }) /VARIABLES=varlist
                       {value      }
                       {value,value}
```

Paired-samples tests:

```
T-TEST PAIRS=varlist [WITH varlist [(PAIRED)]] [/varlist ...]
```

All types of tests:

```
[/MISSING={ANALYSIS**}   [INCLUDE]]
          {LISTWISE  }

[/CRITERIA=CI({0.95**})
             {value })
```

**Default if the subcommand is omitted.

Examples:

```
T-TEST GROUPS=WORLD(1,3) /VARIABLES=NTCPRI NTCSAL NTCPUR.

T-TEST PAIRS=TEACHER CONSTRUC MANAGER.
```

Overview

T-TEST compares sample means by calculating Student's *t* and displays the two-tailed probability of the difference between the means. Statistics are available for one-sample (tested against a specified value), independent samples (different groups of cases), or paired samples (different variables). Other procedures that compare group means are ANOVA, ONEWAY, UNIANOVA, GLM, and MANOVA (GLM and MANOVA are available in the SPSS Advanced Models option).

Options

Statistics. There are no optional statistics. All statistics available are displayed by default.

Basic Specification

The basic specification depends on whether you want a one-sample test, an independent-samples test or a paired-samples test. For all types of tests, T-TEST displays Student's *t*, degrees of freedom, and two-tailed probabilities, as well as the mean, standard deviation, standard error, and count for each group or variable.

- To request a one-sample test, use the TESTVAL and VARIABLES subcommands. The output includes a One-Sample Statistics table showing univariate statistics and a One-Sample Test table showing the test value, the difference between the sample mean and the test value and two-tailed probability level.

- To request an independent-samples test, use the GROUPS and VARIABLES subcommands. The output includes a Group Statistics table showing summary statistics by group for each dependent variable and an Independent-Samples Test table showing both pooled- and separate-variance estimates, along with the F value used to test homogeneity of variance and its probability. The two-tailed probability is displayed for the t value.

- To request a paired-samples test, use the PAIRS subcommand. The output includes a Paired Statistics table showing univariate statistics by pairs, a Paired Samples Correlations table showing correlation coefficients and two-tailed probability level for a test of the coefficient for each pair, and a Paired Samples Test table showing the paired differences between the means and two-tailed probability levels for a test of the differences.

Subcommand Order

Subcommands can be named in any order.

Operations

- If a variable specified on GROUPS is a long string, only the short-string portion is used to identify groups in the analysis.
- Probability levels are two-tailed. To obtain the one-tailed probability, divide the two-tailed probability by 2.

Limitations

- Maximum 1 TESTVAL and 1 VARIABLES subcommand per one-sample t test.
- Maximum 1 GROUPS and 1 VARIABLES subcommand per independent-samples t test.

Example

```
T TEST TESTVAL 28000 /VARIABLES=CHISAL LASAL NYSAL.
```

- This one-sample t test compares the means of *CHISAL, LASAL,* and *NYSAL* each with the standard value (28000).

Example

```
T-TEST GROUPS=WORLD(1,3) /VARIABLES=NTCPRI NTCSAL NTCPUR.
```

- This independent-samples *t* test compares the means of the two groups defined by values 1 and 3 of *WORLD* for variables *NTCPRI, NTCSAL,* and *NTCPUR.*

Example

```
T-TEST PAIRS=TEACHER CONSTRUC MANAGER.
```

- This paired-samples *t* test compares the means of *TEACHER* with *CONSTRUC, TEACHER* with *MANAGER,* and *CONSTRUC* with *MANAGER.*

VARIABLES Subcommand

VARIABLES specifies the dependent variables to be tested in a one-sample or an independent-samples *t* test.

- VARIABLES can specify multiple variables, all of which must be numeric.
- When specified along with TESTVAL, the mean of all cases for each variable is compared with the specified value.
- When specified along with GROUPS, the means of two groups of cases defined by the GROUPS subcommand are compared.
- If both TESTVAL and GROUPS are specified, a one-sample test and an independent-samples test are performed on each variable.

TESTVAL Subcommand

TESTVAL specifies the value with which a sample mean is compared.

- Only one TESTVAL subcommand is allowed.
- Only one value can be specified on the TESTVAL subcommand.

GROUPS Subcommand

GROUPS specifies a variable used to group cases for independent-samples *t* tests.

- GROUPS can specify only one variable, which can be numeric or string.

Any one of three methods can be used to define the two groups for the variable specified on GROUPS:

- Specify a single value in parentheses to group all cases with a value equal to or greater than the specified value into one group and the remaining cases into the other group.
- Specify two values in parentheses to include cases with the first value in one group and cases with the second value in the other group. Cases with other values are excluded.
- If no values are specified on GROUP, T-TEST uses 1 and 2 as default values for numeric variables. There is no default for string variables.

PAIRS Subcommand

PAIRS requests paired-samples *t* tests.

- The minimum specification for a paired-samples test is PAIRS with an analysis list. Only numeric variables can be specified on the analysis list. The minimum analysis list is two variables.
- If keyword WITH is not specified, each variable in the list is compared with every other variable on the list.
- If keyword WITH is specified, every variable to the left of WITH is compared with every variable to the right of WITH. WITH can be used with PAIRED to obtain special pairing.
- To specify multiple analysis lists, use multiple PAIRS subcommands, each separated by a slash. Keyword PAIRS is required only for the first analysis list; a slash can be used to separate each additional analysis list.

(PAIRED)   *Special pairing for paired-samples test.* PAIRED must be enclosed in parentheses and must be used with keyword WITH. When PAIRED is specified, The first variable before WITH is compared with the first variable after WITH, the second variable before WITH is compared with the second variable after WITH, and so forth. The same number of variables should be specified before and after WITH; unmatched variables are ignored and a warning message is issued. PAIRED generates an error message if keyword WITH is not specified on PAIRS.

Example

```
T-TEST   PAIRS=TEACHER CONSTRUC MANAGER.
T-TEST   PAIRS=TEACHER MANAGER WITH CONSTRUC ENGINEER.
T-TEST   PAIRS=TEACHER MANAGER WITH CONSTRUC ENGINEER (PAIRED).
```

- The first T-TEST compares *TEACHER* with *CONSTRUC*, *TEACHER* with *MANAGER*, and *CONSTRUC* with *MANAGER*.
- The second T-TEST compares *TEACHER* with *CONSTRUC*, *TEACHER* with *ENGINEER*, *MANAGER* with *CONSTRUC*, and *MANAGER* with *ENGINEER*. *TEACHER* is not compared with *MANAGER*, and *CONSTRUC* is not compared with *ENGINEER*.
- The third T-TEST compares *TEACHER* with *CONSTRUC* and *MANAGER* with *ENGINEER*.

CRITERIA Subcommand

CRITERIA resets the value of the confidence interval. Keyword CI is required. You can specify a value between 0 and 1 in the parentheses. The default is 0.95.

MISSING Subcommand

MISSING controls the treatment of missing values. The default is ANALYSIS.

- ANALYSIS and LISTWISE are alternatives; however, each can be specified with INCLUDE.

ANALYSIS   *Delete cases with missing values on an analysis-by-analysis or pair-by-pair basis.* For independent-samples tests, cases with missing values for either the grouping variable or the dependent variable are excluded from the analysis of that dependent variable. For paired-samples tests, a case with a missing value for either of the variables in a given pair is excluded from the analysis of that pair. This is the default.

LISTWISE   *Exclude cases with missing values listwise.* A case with a missing value for any variable specified on either GROUPS or VARIABLES is excluded from any independent-samples test. A case with a missing value for any variable specified on PAIRS is excluded from any paired-samples test.

INCLUDE   *Include user-missing values.* User-missing values are treated as valid values.

UNIANOVA

```
UNIANOVA dependent var [BY factor list [WITH covariate list]]

[/RANDOM=factor factor...]

[/REGWGT=varname]

[/METHOD=SSTYPE({1  })]
                {2  }
                {3**}
                {4  }

[/INTERCEPT=[INCLUDE**] [EXCLUDE]]

[/MISSING=[INCLUDE] [EXCLUDE**]]

[/CRITERIA=[EPS({1E-8**})][ALPHA({0.05**})]
               {a    }        {a    }

[/PRINT = [DESCRIPTIVE] [HOMOGENEITY] [PARAMETER][ETASQ]
          [GEF] [LOF] [OPOWER] [TEST(LMATRIX)]]

[/PLOT=[SPREADLEVEL] [RESIDUALS]
       [PROFILE (factor factor*factor factor*factor*factor ...)]

[/TEST=effect VS {linear combination [DF(df)]}]
                 {value DF (df)            }

[/LMATRIX={["label"] effect list effect list ...;...}]
          {["label"] effect list effect list ...   }
          {["label"] ALL list; ALL...              }
          {["label"] ALL list                      }

[/KMATRIX= {number     }]
           {number;...}

[/CONTRAST (factor name)={DEVIATION[(refcat)]**   }]
                         {SIMPLE [(refcat)]        }
                         {DIFFERENCE               }
                         {HELMERT                  }
                         {REPEATED                 }
                         {POLYNOMIAL  [(({1,2,3...})]}
                                          {metric  }
                         {SPECIAL (matrix)         }

[/POSTHOC =effect [effect...]
          ([SNK] [TUKEY] [BTUKEY][DUNCAN]
           [SCHEFFE] [DUNNETT(refcat)] [DUNNETTL(refcat)]
           [DUNNETTR(refcat)] [BONFERRONI] [LSD] [SIDAK]
           [GT2] [GABRIEL] [FREGW] [QREGW]  [T2] [T3] [GH] [C]
           [WALLER ({100** })]]])]
                   {kratio}
          [VS effect]

[/EMMEANS=TABLES({OVERALL       })] [COMPARE ADJ([LSD(none)] [BONFERRONI] [SIDAK])]
                {factor         }
                {factor*factor...}

[/SAVE=[tempvar [(name)]] [tempvar [(name)]]...]

[/OUTFILE= [{COVB (filename)}] [EFFECT(filename)] [DESIGN(filename)]
            {CORB (filename)}

[/DESIGN={[INTERCEPT...]   }]
         {[effect effect...]}
```

** Default if subcommand or keyword is omitted.

Temporary variables (tempvar) are:

PRED, WPRED, RESID, WRESID, DRESID, ZRESID, SRESID, SEPRED, COOK, LEVER

Example:

```
UNIANOVA YIELD BY SEED FERT
  /DESIGN.
```

Overview

This section describes the use of UNIANOVA for univariate analyses. The UNIANOVA procedure provides regression analysis and analysis of variance for one dependent variable by one or more factors and/or variables.

Options

Design Specification. You can specify which terms to include in the design on the DESIGN subcommand. This allows you to estimate a model other than the default full factorial model, incorporate factor-by-covariate interactions or covariate-by-covariate interactions, and indicate nesting of effects.

Contrast Types. You can specify contrasts other than the default deviation contrasts on the CONTRAST subcommand.

Optional Output. You can choose from a wide variety of optional output on the PRINT subcommand. Output appropriate to univariate designs includes descriptive statistics for each cell, parameter estimates, Levene's test for equality of variance across cells, partial eta-squared for each effect and each parameter estimate, the general estimable function matrix, and a contrast coefficients table (L' matrix). The OUTFILE subcommand allows you to write out the covariance or correlation matrix, the design matrix, or the statistics from the between-subjects ANOVA table into a separate SPSS data file.

Using the EMMEANS subcommand, you can request tables of estimated marginal means of the dependent variable and their standard deviations. The SAVE subcommand allows you to save predicted values and residuals in weighted or unweighted and standardized or unstandardized forms. You can specify different means comparison tests for comparing all possible pairs of cell means using the POSTHOC subcommand. In addition, you can specify your own hypothesis tests by specifying an L matrix and a K matrix to test the univariate hypothesis $LB = K$.

Basic Specification

- The basic specification is a variable list identifying the dependent variable, the factors (if any), and the covariates (if any).
- By default, UNIANOVA uses a model that includes the intercept term, the covariate (if any), and the full factorial model, which includes all main effects and all possible interactions among factors. The intercept term is excluded if it is excluded in the model by specifying the keyword EXCLUDE on the INTERCEPT subcommand. Sums of squares are calculated

and hypothesis tests are performed using type-specific estimable functions. Parameters are estimated using the normal equation and a generalized inverse of the SSCP matrix.

Subcommand Order

- The variable list must be specified first.
- Subcommands can be used in any order.

Syntax Rules

- For many analyses, the UNIANOVA variable list and the DESIGN subcommand are the only specifications needed.
- If you do not enter a DESIGN subcommand, UNIANOVA will use a full factorial model, with main effects of covariates, if any.
- Minimum syntax—at least one dependent variable must be specified, and at least one of the following must be specified: INTERCEPT, a between-subjects factor, or a covariate. The design contains the intercept by default.
- If more than one DESIGN subcommand is specified, only the last one is in effect.
- Dependent variables and covariates must be numeric, but factors can be numeric or string variables.
- If a string variable is specified as a factor, only the first eight characters of each value are used in distinguishing among values.
- If more than one MISSING subcommand is specified, only the last one is in effect.
- The following words are reserved as keywords or internal commands in the UNIANOVA procedure:

  INTERCEPT, BY, WITH, ALL, OVERALL, WITHIN

  Variable names that duplicate these words should be changed before you run UNIANOVA.

Limitations

- Any number of factors can be specified, but if the number of between-subjects factors plus the number of split variables exceeds 18, the Descriptive Statistics table is not printed even when you request it.
- Memory requirements depend primarily on the number of cells in the design. For the default full factorial model, this equals the product of the number of levels or categories in each factor.

Example

```
UNIANOVA YIELD BY SEED FERT WITH RAINFALL
  /PRINT=DESCRIPTIVE PARAMETER
  /DESIGN.
```

- *YIELD* is the dependent variable; *SEED* and *FERT* are factors; *RAINFALL* is a covariate.
- The PRINT subcommand requests the descriptive statistics for the dependent variable for each cell and the parameter estimates, in addition to the default tables Between-Subjects Factors and Univariate Tests.
- The DESIGN subcommand requests the default design, a full factorial model with a covariate. This subcommand could have been omitted or could have been specified in full as

```
/DESIGN = INTERCEPT RAINFALL, SEED, FERT, SEED BY FERT.
```

UNIANOVA Variable List

The variable list specifies the dependent variable, the factors, and the covariates in the model.

- The dependent variable must be the first specification on UNIANOVA.
- The names of the factors follow the dependent variable. Use the keyword BY to separate the factors from the dependent variable.
- Enter the covariates, if any, following the factors. Use the keyword WITH to separate covariates from factors (if any) and the dependent variable.

Example

```
UNIANOVA DEPENDNT BY FACTOR1 FACTOR2, FACTOR3.
```

- In this example, three factors are specified.
- A default full factorial model is used for the analysis.

Example

```
UNIANOVA Y BY A WITH X
    /DESIGN.
```

- In this example, the DESIGN subcommand requests the default design, which includes the intercept term, the covariate *X* and the factor *A*.

RANDOM Subcommand

RANDOM allows you to specify which effects in your design are random. When the RANDOM subcommand is used, a table of expected mean squares for all effects in the design is displayed, and an appropriate error term for testing each effect is calculated and used automatically.

- Random always implies a univariate mixed-model analysis.
- If you specify an effect on RANDOM, higher-order effects containing the specified effect (excluding any effects containing covariates) are automatically treated as random effects.
- The keyword INTERCEPT and effects containing covariates are not allowed on this subcommand.
- The RANDOM subcommand cannot be used if there is any within-subjects factor in the model (that is, RANDOM cannot be specified if WSFACTOR is specified).
- When the RANDOM subcommand is used, the appropriate error terms for the hypothesis testing of all effects in the model are automatically computed and used.
- More than one RANDOM subcommand is allowed. The specifications are accumulated.

Example

```
UNIANOVA DEP BY A B
  /RANDOM = B
  /DESIGN = A,B, A*B.
```

- In the example, effects *B* and *A*B* are considered as random effects. Notice that if only effect *B* is specified in the RANDOM subcommand, *A*B* is automatically considered as a random effect.
- The hypothesis testing for each effect (*A*, *B*, and *A*B*) in the design will be carried out using the appropriate error term, which is calculated automatically.

REGWGT Subcommand

The only specification on REGWGT is the name of the variable containing the weights to be used in estimating a weighted least-squares model.

- Specify a numeric weight variable name following the REGWGT subcommand. Only observations with positive values in the weight variable will be used in the analysis.
- If more than one REGWGT subcommand is specified, only the last one is in effect.

Example

```
UNIANOVA OUTCOME BY TREATMNT
  /REGWGT WT.
```

- The procedure performs a weighted least-squares analysis. The variable *WT* is used as the weight variable.

METHOD Subcommand

METHOD controls the computational aspects of the UNIANOVA analysis. You can specify one of four different methods for partitioning the sums of squares. If more than one METHOD subcommand is specified, only the last one is in effect.

SSTYPE(1)   *Type I sum-of-squares method.* The Type I sum-of-squares method is also known as the hierarchical decomposition of the sum-of-squares method. Each term is adjusted only for the terms that precede it on the DESIGN subcommand. Under a balanced design, it is an orthogonal decomposition, and the sums of squares in the model add up to the total sum of squares.

SSTYPE(2)   *Type II sum-of-squares method.* This method calculates the sum of squares of an effect in the model adjusted for all other "appropriate" effects. An appropriate effect is one that corresponds to all effects that do not *contain* the effect being examined.

For any two effects *F1* and *F2* in the model, *F1* is said to be **contained** in *F2* under the following three conditions:
- Both effects *F1* and *F2* have the same covariate, if any.
- *F2* consists of more factors than *F1*.
- All factors in *F1* also appear in *F2*.

The intercept effect is treated as contained in all the pure factor effects. However, it is not contained in any effect involving a covariate. No effect is contained in the intercept effect. Thus, for any one effect *F* of interest, all other effects in the model can be classified as in one of the following two groups: the effects that do not contain *F* or the effects that contain *F*.

If the model is a main-effects design (that is, only main effects are in the model), the Type II sum-of-squares method is equivalent to the regression approach sums of squares. This means that each main effect is adjusted for every other term in the model.

SSTYPE(3) *Type III sum-of-squares method.* This is the default. This method calculates the sum of squares of an effect *F* in the design as the sum of squares adjusted for any other effects that do not contain it, and *orthogonal* to any effects (if any) that contain it. The Type III sums of squares have one major advantage—they are invariant with respect to the cell frequencies as long as the general form of estimability remains constant. Hence, this type of sums of squares is often used for an unbalanced model with no missing cells. In a factorial design with no missing cells, this method is equivalent to the Yates' weighted squares of means technique, and it also coincides with the overparameterized Σ-restricted model.

SSTYPE(4) *Type IV sum-of-squares method.* This method is designed for a situation in which there are missing cells. For any effect *F* in the design, if *F* is not contained in any other effect, then Type IV = Type III = Type II. When *F* is contained in other effects, then Type IV distributes the contrasts being made among the parameters in *F* to all higher-level effects equitably.

Example

```
UNIANOVA DEP BY A B C
  /METHOD=SSTYPE(3)
  /DESIGN=A, B, C.
```

- The design is a main-effects model.
- The METHOD subcommand requests that the model be fitted with Type III sums of squares.

INTERCEPT Subcommand

INTERCEPT controls whether an intercept term is included in the model. If more than one INTERCEPT subcommand is specified, only the last one is in effect.

INCLUDE *Include the intercept term.* The intercept (constant) term is included in the model. This is the default.

EXCLUDE *Exclude the intercept term.* The intercept term is excluded from the model. Specification of the keyword INTERCEPT on the DESIGN subcommand overrides INTERCEPT = EXCLUDE.

MISSING Subcommand

By default, cases with missing values for any of the variables on the UNIANOVA variable list are excluded from the analysis. The MISSING subcommand allows you to include cases with user-missing values.

- If MISSING is not specified, the default is EXCLUDE.
- Pairwise deletion of missing data is not available in UNIANOVA.
- Keywords INCLUDE and EXCLUDE are mutually exclusive.
- If more than one MISSING subcommand is specified, only the last one is in effect.

EXCLUDE   *Exclude both user-missing and system-missing values.* This is the default when MISSING is not specified.

INCLUDE   *User-missing values are treated as valid.* System-missing values cannot be included in the analysis.

CRITERIA Subcommand

CRITERIA controls the statistical criteria used to build the models.

- More than one CRITERIA subcommand is allowed. The specifications are accumulated. Conflicts across CRITERIA subcommands are resolved using the conflicting specification given on the last CRITERIA subcommand.
- The keyword must be followed by a positive number in parentheses.

EPS(n)   *The tolerance level in redundancy detection.* This value is used for redundancy checking in the design matrix. The default value is 1E–8.

ALPHA(n)   *The alpha level.* This keyword has two functions. First, it gives the alpha level at which the power is calculated for the F test. Once the noncentrality parameter for the alternative hypothesis is estimated from the data, then the power is the probability that the test statistic is greater than the critical value under the alternative hypothesis. The second function of alpha is to specify the level of the confidence interval. If the alpha level specified is n, the value $(1 - n) \times 100$ indicates the level of confidence for all individual and simultaneous confidence intervals generated for the specified model. The value of n must be between 0 and 1, exclusive. The default value of alpha is 0.05. This means that the default power calculation is at the 0.05 level, and the default level of the confidence intervals is 95%, since $(1 - 0.05) \times 100 = 95$.

PRINT Subcommand

PRINT controls the display of optional output.

- Some PRINT output applies to the entire UNIANOVA procedure and is displayed only once.
- Additional output can be obtained on the EMMEANS, PLOT, and SAVE subcommands.
- Some optional output may greatly increase the processing time. Request only the output you want to see.

- If no PRINT command is specified, default output for a univariate analysis includes a factor information table and a Univariate Tests table (ANOVA) for all effects in the model.
- If more than one PRINT subcommand is specified, only the last one is in effect.

The following keywords are available for UNIANOVA univariate analyses.

DESCRIPTIVES   *Basic information about each cell in the design.* Observed means, standard deviations, and counts for the dependent variable in all cells. The cells are constructed from the highest-order crossing of the between-subjects factors. If the number of between-subjects factors plus the number of split variables exceeds 18, the Descriptive Statistics table is not printed.

HOMOGENEITY   *Tests of homogeneity of variance.* Levene's test for equality of variances for the dependent variable across all level combinations of the between-subjects factors. If there are no between-subjects factors, this keyword is not valid.

PARAMETER   *Parameter estimates.* Parameter estimates, standard errors, *t* tests, and confidence intervals for each test.

OPOWER   *Observed power.* The observed power for each test.

LOF   *Lack of fit.* Lack of fit test which allows you to determine if the current model adequately accounts for the relationship between the response variable and the predictors.

ETASQ   *Partial eta-squared (η^2).* This value is an overestimate of the actual effect size in an F test. It is defined as

$$\text{partial eta-squared} = \frac{dfh \times F}{dfh \times F + dfe}$$

where F is the test statistic and dfh and dfe are its degrees of freedom and degrees of freedom for error. The keyword EFSIZE can be used in place of ETASQ.

GEF   *General estimable function table.* This table shows the general form of the estimable functions.

TEST(LMATRIX)   *Set of contrast coefficients (L) matrices.* The transpose of the **L** matrix (**L'**) is displayed. This set always includes one matrix displaying the estimable function for each between-subjects effect appearing or implied in the DESIGN subcommand. Also, any **L** matrices generated by the LMATRIX or CONTRAST subcommands are displayed. TEST(ESTIMABLE) can be used in place of TEST(LMATRIX).

Example

```
UNIANOVA DEP BY A B WITH COV
  /PRINT=DESCRIPTIVE, TEST(LMATRIX), PARAMETER
  /DESIGN.
```

- Since the design in the DESIGN subcommand is not specified, the default design is used. In this case, the design includes the intercept term, the covariate *COV*, and the full factorial terms of *A* and *B*, which are *A*, *B*, and *A*B*.
- For each combination of levels of *A* and *B*, SPSS displays the descriptive statistics of *DEP*.
- The set of **L** matrices that generates the sums of squares for testing each effect in the design is displayed.
- The parameter estimates, their standard errors, *t* tests, confidence intervals, and the observed power for each test are displayed.

PLOT Subcommand

PLOT provides a variety of plots useful in checking the assumptions needed in the analysis. The PLOT subcommand can be specified more than once. All of the plots requested on each PLOT subcommand are produced.

Use the following keywords on the PLOT subcommand to request plots:

SPREADLEVEL   *Spread-versus-level plots.* Plots of observed cell means versus standard deviations, and versus variances.

RESIDUALS   *Observed by predicted by standardized residuals plot.* A plot is produced for each dependent variable. In a univariate analysis, a plot is produced for the single dependent variable.

PROFILE   *Line plots of dependent variable means for one-way, two-way, or three-way crossed factors.* The PROFILE keyword must be followed by parentheses containing a list of one or more factor combinations. All factors specified (either individual or crossed) must be made up of only valid factors on the factor list. Factor combinations on the PROFILE keyword may use an asterisk (*) or the keyword BY to specify crossed factors. A factor cannot occur in a single factor combination more than once.

The order of factors in a factor combination is important, and there is no restriction on the order of factors. If a single factor is specified after the PROFILE keyword, a line plot of estimated means at each level of the factor is produced. If a two-way crossed factor combination is specified, the output includes a multiple-line plot of estimated means at each level of the first specified factor, with a separate line drawn for each level of the second specified factor. If a three-way crossed factor combination is specified, the output includes multiple-line plots of estimated means at each level of the first specified factor, with separate lines for each level of the second factor, and separate plots for each level of the third factor.

Example

```
UNIANOVA DEP BY A B
  /PLOT = SPREADLEVEL PROFILE(A A*B A*B*C)
  /DESIGN.
```

Assume each of the factors *A*, *B*, and *C* has three levels.

- Spread-versus-level plots are produced showing observed cell means versus standard deviations and observed cell means versus variances.
- Five profile plots are produced. For factor *A*, a line plot of estimated means at each level of *A* is produced (one plot). For the two-way crossed factor combination *A*B*, a multiple-line plot of estimated means at each level of *A*, with a separate line for each level of *B*, is produced (one plot). For the three-way crossed factor combination *A*B*C*, a multiple-line plot of estimated means at each level of *A*, with a separate line for each level of *B*, is produced for each of the three levels of *C* (three plots).

TEST Subcommand

The TEST subcommand allows you to test a hypothesis term against a specified error term.

- TEST is valid only for univariate analyses. Multiple TEST subcommands are allowed, each executed independently.
- You must specify both the hypothesis term and the error term. There is no default.
- The hypothesis term is specified before the keyword VS. It must be a valid effect specified or implied on the DESIGN subcommand.
- The error term is specified after the keyword VS. You can specify either a linear combination or a value. The linear combination of effects takes the general form:
  ```
  coefficient*effect +/- coefficient*effect ...
  ```
- All effects in the linear combination must be specified or implied on the DESIGN subcommand. Effects specified or implied on DESIGN but not listed after VS are assumed to have a coefficient of 0.
- Duplicate effects are allowed. UNIANOVA adds coefficients associated with the same effect before performing the text. For example, the linear combination `5*A−0.9*B−A` will be combined to `4*A−0.9B`.
- A coefficient can be specified as a fraction with a positive denominator—for example, 1/3 or –1/3, but 1/–3 is invalid.
- If you specify a value for the error term, you must specify the degrees of freedom after the keyword DF. The degrees of freedom must be a positive real number. DF and the degrees of freedom are optional for a linear combination.

Example
```
UNIANOVA DEP BY A B
   /TEST = A VS B + A*B
   /DESIGN = A, B, A*B.
```
- *A* is tested against the pooled effect of *B + A*B*.

LMATRIX Subcommand

The LMATRIX subcommand allows you to customize your hypotheses tests by specifying the **L** matrix (contrast coefficients matrix) in the general form of the linear hypothesis $\mathbf{LB} = \mathbf{K}$, where $\mathbf{K} = \mathbf{0}$ if it is not specified on the KMATRIX subcommand. The vector **B** is the parameter vector in the linear model.

- The basic format for the LMATRIX subcommand is an optional label in quotation marks, an effect name or the keyword ALL, and a list of real numbers. There can be multiple effect names (or the keyword ALL) and number lists.

- The optional label is a string with a maximum length of 255 characters. Only one label can be specified.

- Only valid effects appearing or implied on the DESIGN subcommand can be specified on the LMATRIX subcommand.

- The length of the list of real numbers must be equal to the number of parameters (including the redundant ones) corresponding to that effect. For example, if the effect $A*B$ takes up six columns in the design matrix, then the list after $A*B$ must contain exactly six numbers.

- A number can be specified as a fraction with a positive denominator—for example, 1/3 or −1/3, but 1/−3 is invalid.

- A semicolon (;) indicates the end of a row in the $\mathbf{L}$ matrix.

- When ALL is specified, the length of the list that follows ALL is equal to the total number of parameters (including the redundant ones) in the model.

- Effects appearing or implied on the DESIGN subcommand but not specified here are assumed to have entries of 0 in the corresponding columns of the $\mathbf{L}$ matrix.

- Multiple LMATRIX subcommands are allowed. Each is treated independently.

Example

```
UNIANOVA DEP BY A B
  /LMATRIX = "B1 vs B2 at A1"
             B 1 -1 0 A*B 1 -1
  /LMATRIX = "Effect A"
             A 1 0 -1
             A*B 1/3   1/3   1/3
                   0     0     0
                 -1/3  -1/3  -1/3;
             A 0 1 -1
             A*B  0     0     0
                 1/3   1/3   1/3
                -1/3  -1/3  -1/3
  /LMATRIX = "B1 vs B2 at A2"
             ALL  0
                    0  0  0
                    1 -1  0
                    0  0  0  1 -1  0  0  0  0
  /DESIGN = A, B, A*B.
```

Assume that factors A and B each have three levels. There are three LMATRIX subcommands; each is treated independently.

- **B1 versus B2 at A1.** In the first LMATRIX subcommand, the difference is tested between levels 1 and 2 of effect B when effect A is fixed at level 1. Since there are three levels each in effects A and B, the interaction effect $A*B$ should take up nine columns in the design matrix. Notice that only the first two columns of $A*B$ are specified with values 1 and −1; the rest are all assumed to be 0. Columns corresponding to effect B are all assumed to be 0.

- **Effect A.** In the second LMATRIX subcommand, effect A is tested. Since there are three levels in effect A, at most two independent contrasts can be formed; thus, there are two rows in the $\mathbf{L}$ matrix, which are separated by a semicolon (;). The first row tests the difference between levels 1 and 3 of effect *A*, while the second row tests the difference between levels 2 and 3 of effect *A*.

- **B1 versus B2 at A2.** In the last LMATRIX subcommand, the keyword ALL is used. The first 0 corresponds to the intercept effect; the next three zeros correspond to effect *A*.

KMATRIX Subcommand

The KMATRIX subcommand allows you to customize your hypothesis tests by specifying the **K** matrix (contrast results matrix) in the general form of the linear hypothesis **LB** = **K**. The vector **B** is the parameter vector in the linear model.

- The default **K** matrix is a zero matrix; that is, **LB** = 0 is assumed.
- For the KMATRIX subcommand to be valid, at least one of the following subcommands must be specified: the LMATRIX subcommand or the INTERCEPT = INCLUDE subcommand.
- If KMATRIX is specified but LMATRIX is not specified, the LMATRIX is assumed to take the row vector corresponding to the intercept in the estimable function, provided the subcommand INTERCEPT = INCLUDE is specified. In this case, the K matrix can be only a scalar matrix.
- If KMATRIX and LMATRIX are specified, then the number of rows in the requested **K** and **L** matrices must be equal. If there are multiple LMATRIX subcommands, then all requested **L** matrices must have the same number of rows, and **K** must have the same number of rows as these **L** matrices.
- A semicolon (;) can be used to indicate the end of a row in the **K** matrix.
- If more than one KMATRIX subcommand is specified, only the last one is in effect.

Example

```
UNIANOVA DEP BY A B
   /LMATRIX = "Effect A"
              A 1  0 -1; A 1 -1  0
   /LMATRIX = "Effect B"
              B 1  0 -1; B 1 -1  0
   /KMATRIX = 0; 0
   /DESIGN = A B.
```

In this example, assume that factors *A* and *B* each have three levels.

- There are two LMATRIX subcommands; both have two rows.
- The first LMATRIX subcommand tests whether the effect of *A* is 0, while the second LMATRIX subcommand tests whether the effect of *B* is 0.
- The KMATRIX subcommand specifies that the **K** matrix also has two rows, each with value 0.

CONTRAST Subcommand

CONTRAST specifies the type of contrast desired among the levels of a factor. For a factor with k levels or values, the contrast type determines the meaning of its $k - 1$ degrees of freedom.

- Specify the factor name in parentheses following the subcommand CONTRAST.

- You can specify only one factor per CONTRAST subcommand, but you can enter multiple CONTRAST subcommands.
- After closing the parentheses, enter an equals sign followed by one of the contrast keywords.
- This subcommand creates an **L** matrix such that the columns corresponding to the factor match the contrast given. The other columns are adjusted so that the **L** matrix is estimable.

The following contrast types are available:

DEVIATION *Deviations from the grand mean.* This is the default for between-subjects factors. Each level of the factor except one is compared to the grand mean. One category (by default, the last) must be omitted so that the effects will be independent of one another. To omit a category other than the last, specify the number of the omitted category (which is not necessarily the same as its value) in parentheses after the keyword DEVIATION. For example,

```
UNIANOVA Y BY B
  /CONTRAST(B)=DEVIATION(1).
```

Suppose factor *B* has three levels, with values 2, 4, and 6. The specified contrast omits the first category, in which *B* has the value 2. Deviation contrasts are not orthogonal.

POLYNOMIAL *Polynomial contrasts.* This is the default for within-subjects factors. The first degree of freedom contains the linear effect across the levels of the factor, the second contains the quadratic effect, and so on. In a balanced design, polynomial contrasts are orthogonal. By default, the levels are assumed to be equally spaced; you can specify unequal spacing by entering a metric consisting of one integer for each level of the factor in parentheses after the keyword POLYNOMIAL. (All metrics specified cannot be equal; thus, (1, 1, . . . 1) is not valid.) For example,

```
UNIANOVA RESPONSE BY STIMULUS
  /CONTRAST(STIMULUS) = POLYNOMIAL(1,2,4).
```

Suppose that factor *STIMULUS* has three levels. The specified contrast indicates that the three levels of *STIMULUS* are actually in the proportion 1:2:4. The default metric is always (1, 2, . . . *k*), where *k* levels are involved. Only the relative differences between the terms of the metric matter; (1, 2, 4) is the same metric as (2, 3, 5) or (20, 30, 50) because, in each instance, the difference between the second and third numbers is twice the difference between the first and second.

DIFFERENCE *Difference or reverse Helmert contrasts.* Each level of the factor except the first is compared to the mean of the previous levels. In a balanced design, difference contrasts are orthogonal.

HELMERT *Helmert contrasts.* Each level of the factor except the last is compared to the mean of subsequent levels. In a balanced design, Helmert contrasts are orthogonal.

SIMPLE *Each level of the factor except the last is compared to the last level.* To use a category other than the last as the omitted reference category, specify its number (which is not necessarily the same as its value) in parentheses following the keyword SIMPLE. For example,

```
UNIANOVA Y BY B
    /CONTRAST(B)=SIMPLE(1).
```

Suppose that factor *B* has three levels with values 2, 4, and 6. The specified contrast compares the other levels to the first level of *B*, in which *B* has the value 2. Simple contrasts are not orthogonal.

REPEATED   *Comparison of adjacent levels.* Each level of the factor except the first is compared to the previous level. Repeated contrasts are not orthogonal.

SPECIAL   *A user-defined contrast.* Values specified after this keyword are stored in a matrix in column major order. For example, if factor *A* has three levels, then CONTRAST(A)= SPECIAL(1 1 1 1 -1 0 0 1 -1) produces the following contrast matrix:

$$
\begin{array}{rrr}
1 & 1 & 0 \\
1 & -1 & 1 \\
1 & 0 & -1
\end{array}
$$

Orthogonal contrasts are particularly useful. In a balanced design, contrasts are orthogonal if the sum of the coefficients in each contrast row is 0 and if, for any pair of contrast rows, the products of corresponding coefficients sum to 0. DIFFERENCE, HELMERT, and POLYNOMIAL contrasts always meet these criteria in balanced designs.

Example

```
UNIANOVA DEP BY FAC
   /CONTRAST(FAC)=DIFFERENCE
   /DESIGN.
```

- Suppose that the factor *FAC* has five categories and therefore four degrees of freedom.
- CONTRAST requests DIFFERENCE contrasts, which compare each level (except the first) with the mean of the previous levels.

POSTHOC Subcommand

POSTHOC allows you to produce multiple comparisons between means of a factor. These comparisons are usually not planned at the beginning of the study but are suggested by the data in the course of study.

- Post hoc tests are computed for the dependent variable. The alpha value used in the tests can be specified by using the keyword ALPHA on the CRITERIA subcommand. The default alpha value is 0.05. The confidence level for any confidence interval constructed is $(1 - \alpha) \times 100$. The default confidence level is 95.
- Only between-subjects factors appearing in the factor list are valid in this subcommand. Individual factors can be specified.
- You can specify one or more effects to be tested. Only fixed main effects appearing or implied on the DESIGN subcommand are valid test effects.

- Optionally, you can specify an effect defining the error term following the keyword VS after the test specification. The error effect can be any single effect in the design that is not the intercept or a main effect named on a POSTHOC subcommand.
- A variety of multiple comparison tests are available. Some tests are designed for detecting homogeneity subsets among the groups of means, some are designed for pairwise comparisons among all means, and some can be used for both purposes.
- For tests that are used for detecting homogeneity subsets of means, non-empty group means are sorted in ascending order. Means that are not significantly different are included together to form a homogeneity subset. The significance for each homogeneity subset of means is displayed. In a case where the numbers of valid cases are not equal in all groups, for most post hoc tests, the harmonic mean of the group sizes is used as the sample size in the calculation. For QREGW or FREGW, individual sample sizes are used.
- For tests that are used for pairwise comparisons, the display includes the difference between each pair of compared means, the confidence interval for the difference, and the significance. The sample sizes of the two groups being compared are used in the calculation.
- Output for tests specified on the POSTHOC subcommand are available according to their statistical purposes. The following table illustrates the statistical purpose of the post hoc tests:

Post Hoc Tests	Statistical Purpose	
Keyword	Homogeneity Subsets Detection	Pairwise Comparison and Confidence Interval
LSD		Yes
SIDAK		Yes
BONFERRONI		Yes
GH		Yes
T2		Yes
T3		Yes
C		Yes
DUNNETT		Yes[*]
DUNNETTL		Yes*
DUNNETTR		Yes*
SNK	Yes	
BTUKEY	Yes	
DUNCAN	Yes	
QREGW	Yes	
FREGW	Yes	
WALLER	Yes[†]	
TUKEY	Yes	Yes
SCHEFFE	Yes	Yes
GT2	Yes	Yes
GABRIEL	Yes	Yes

* Only C.I.'s for differences between test group means and control group means are given.

† No significance for Waller test is given.

- Tests that are designed for homogeneity subset detection display the detected homogeneity subsets and their corresponding significances.
- Tests that are designed for both homogeneity subset detection and pairwise comparisons display both kinds of output.
- For the DUNNETT, DUNNETTL, and DUNNETTR keywords, only individual factors can be specified.
- The default reference category for DUNNETT, DUNNETTL, and DUNNETTR is the last category. An integer greater than 0 within parentheses can be used to specify a different reference category. For example, POSTHOC = A (DUNNETT(2)) requests a DUNNETT test for factor A, using the second level of A as the reference category.
- The keywords DUNCAN, DUNNETT, DUNNETTL, and DUNNETTR must be spelled out in full; using the first three characters alone is not sufficient.
- If the REGWT subcommand is specified, weighted means are used in performing post hoc tests.
- Multiple POSTHOC subcommands are allowed. Each specification is executed independently so that you can test different effects against different error terms.

SNK	*Student-Newman-Keuls procedure based on the Studentized range test.*
TUKEY	*Tukey's honestly significant difference.* This test uses the Studentized range statistic to make all pairwise comparisons between groups.
BTUKEY	*Tukey's b.* Multiple comparison procedure based on the average of Studentized range tests.
DUNCAN	*Duncan's multiple comparison procedure based on the Studentized range test.*
SCHEFFE	*Scheffé's multiple comparison* t *test.*
DUNNETT(refcat)	*Dunnett's two-tailed* t *test.* Each level of the factor is compared to a reference category. A reference category can be specified in parentheses. The default reference category is the last category. This keyword must be spelled out in full.
DUNNETTL(refcat)	*Dunnett's one-tailed* t *test.* This test indicates whether the mean at any level (except the reference category) of the factor is *smaller* than that of the reference category. A reference category can be specified in parentheses. The default reference category is the last category. This keyword must be spelled out in full.
DUNNETTR(refcat)	*Dunnett's one-tailed* t *test.* This test indicates whether the mean at any level (except the reference category) of the factor is *larger* than that of the reference category. A reference category can be specified in parentheses. The default reference category is the last category. This keyword must be spelled out in full.

BONFERRONI	*Bonferroni* t *test.* This test is based on Student's *t* statistic and adjusts the observed significance level for the fact that multiple comparisons are made.
LSD	*Least significant difference* t *test.* Equivalent to multiple *t* tests between all pairs of groups. This test does not control the overall probability of rejecting the hypotheses that some pairs of means are different, while in fact they are equal.
SIDAK	*Sidak* t *test.* This test provides tighter bounds than the Bonferroni test.
GT2	*Hochberg's GT2.* Pairwise comparisons test based on the Studentized maximum modulus test. Unless the cell sizes are extremely unbalanced, this test is fairly robust even for unequal variances.
GABRIEL	*Gabriel's pairwise comparisons test based on the Studentized maximum modulus test.*
FREGW	*Ryan-Einot-Gabriel-Welsch's multiple stepdown procedure based on an* F *test.*
QREGW	*Ryan-Einot-Gabriel-Welsch's multiple stepdown procedure based on the Studentized range test.*
T2	*Tamhane's T2.* Tamhane's pairwise comparisons test based on a *t* test. This test can be applied in situations where the variances are unequal.
T3	*Dunnett's T3.* Pairwise comparisons test based on the Studentized maximum modulus. This test is appropriate when the variances are unequal.
GH	*Games and Howell's pairwise comparisons test based on the Studentized range test.* This test can be applied in situations where the variances are unequal.
C	*Dunnett's C.* Pairwise comparisons based on the weighted average of Studentized ranges. This test can be applied in situations where the variances are unequal.
WALLER(kratio)	*Waller-Duncan* t *test.* This test uses a Bayesian approach. It is restricted to cases with equal sample sizes. For cases with unequal sample sizes, the harmonic mean of the sample size is used. The k-ratio is the Type 1/Type 2 error seriousness ratio. The default value is 100. You can specify an integer greater than 1 within parentheses.

EMMEANS Subcommand

EMMEANS displays estimated marginal means of the dependent variable in the cells (with covariates held at their overall mean value) and their standard errors for the specified factors. Note that these are predicted, not observed, means. The estimated marginal means are calculated using a modified definition by Searle, Speed, and Milliken (1980).

- TABLES, followed by an option in parentheses, is required. COMPARE is optional; if specified, it must follow TABLES.
- Multiple EMMEANS subcommands are allowed. Each is treated independently.
- If redundant EMMEANS subcommands are specified, only the last redundant subcommand is in effect. EMMEANS subcommands are redundant if the option specified on TABLES is the same (including redundant crossed factor combinations—for example, A*B and B*A).

TABLES(option)   *Table specification.* Valid options are the keyword OVERALL, factors appearing on the factor list, and crossed factors constructed of factors on the factor list. Crossed factors can be specified using an asterisk (*) or the keyword BY. All factors in a crossed factor specification must be unique.

If OVERALL is specified, the estimated marginal means of the dependent variable are displayed, collapsing over between-subjects factors.

If a between-subjects factor, or a crossing of between-subjects factors, is specified on the TABLES keyword, UNIANOVA collapses over any other between-subjects factors before computing the estimated marginal means for the dependent variable.

COMPARE ADJ(method) *Pairwise comparisons of the dependent variable.* Each level of the factor specified in the TABLES command is compared with each other level for all combinations of other factors. Valid options for the confidence interval adjustment method are the keywords LSD(none), BONFERRONI, and SIDAK. The confidence intervals and significance values are adjusted to account for multiple comparisons.

If OVERALL is specified on TABLES, COMPARE is invalid.

Example

```
UNIANOVA DEP BY A B
  /EMMEANS = TABLES(A*B)COMPARE ADJ (LSD(none))
  /DESIGN.
```

- The output of this analysis includes a pairwise comparisons table for the dependent variable *DEP*.
- Assume that *A* has three levels and *B* has two levels. The first level of *A* is compared with the second and third levels, the second level with the first and third levels, and the third level with the first and second levels. The pairwise comparison is repeated for the two levels of *B*.

SAVE Subcommand

Use SAVE to add one or more residual or fit values to the working data file.

- Specify one or more temporary variables, each followed by an optional new name in parentheses.
- WPRED and WRESID can be saved only if REGWGT has been specified.

- Specifying a temporary variable on this subcommand results in a variable being added to the active data file for each dependent variable.
- You can specify variable names for the temporary variables. These names must be unique, valid variable names.
- If new names are not specified, UNIANOVA generates a rootname using a shortened form of the temporary variable name with a suffix.
- If more than one SAVE subcommand is specified, only the last one is in effect.

PRED   *Unstandardized predicted values.*

WPRED   *Weighted unstandardized predicted values.* Available only if REGWGT has been specified.

RESID   *Unstandardized residuals.*

WRESID   *Weighted unstandardized residuals.* Available only if REGWGT has been specified.

DRESID   *Deleted residuals.*

ZRESID   *Standardized residuals.*

SRESID   *Studentized residuals.*

SEPRED   *Standard errors of predicted value.*

COOK   *Cook's distances.*

LEVER   *Uncentered leverage values.*

OUTFILE Subcommand

The OUTFILE subcommand writes an SPSS-format data file that can be used in other procedures.
- You must specify a keyword on OUTFILE. There is no default.
- You must specify a filename in parentheses after a keyword. A filename with a path must be enclosed within quotation marks. The asterisk (*) is not allowed.
- If you specify more than one keyword, a different filename is required for each.
- If more than one OUTFILE subcommand is specified, only the last one is in effect.
- For COVB or CORB, the output will contain, in addition to the covariance or correlation matrix, three rows for each dependent variable: a row of parameter estimates, a row of residual degrees of freedom, and a row of significance values for the *t* statistics corresponding to the parameter estimates. All statistics are displayed separately by split.

COVB (filename)   *Writes the parameter covariance matrix.*

CORB (filename)   *Writes the parameter correlation matrix.*

EFFECT (filename)   *Writes the statistics from the between-subjects ANOVA table.*

DESIGN (filename)   *Writes the design matrix.* The number of rows equals the number of cases, and the number of columns equals the number of parameters.

The variable names are *DES_1, DES_2, ..., DES_p*, where *p* is the number of the parameters.

DESIGN Subcommand

DESIGN specifies the effects included in a specific model. The cells in a design are defined by all of the possible combinations of levels of the factors in that design. The number of cells equals the product of the number of levels of all the factors. A design is *balanced* if each cell contains the same number of cases. UNIANOVA can analyze both balanced and unbalanced designs.

- Specify a list of terms to be included in the model, separated by spaces or commas.
- The default design, if the DESIGN subcommand is omitted or is specified by itself, is a design consisting of the following terms in order: the intercept term (if INTERCEPT=INCLUDE is specified), next the covariates given in the covariate list, and then the full factorial model defined by all factors on the factor list and excluding the intercept.
- To include a term for the main effect of a factor, enter the name of the factor on the DESIGN subcommand.
- To include the intercept term in the design, use the keyword INTERCEPT on the DESIGN subcommand. If INTERCEPT is specified on the DESIGN subcommand, the subcommand INTERCEPT=EXCLUDE is overridden.
- To include a term for an interaction between factors, use the keyword BY or the asterisk (*) to join the factors involved in the interaction. For example, *A*B* means a two-way interaction effect of *A* and *B*, where *A* and *B* are factors. *A*A* is not allowed because factors inside an interaction effect must be distinct.
- To include a term for nesting one effect within another, use the keyword WITHIN or a pair of parentheses on the DESIGN subcommand. For example, *A(B)* means that *A* is nested within *B*. The expression *A(B)* is equivalent to the expression *A WITHIN B*. When more than one pair of parentheses is present, each pair of parentheses must be enclosed or nested within another pair of parentheses. Thus, *A(B)(C)* is not valid.
- Multiple nesting is allowed. For example, *A(B(C))* means that *B* is nested within *C*, and *A* is nested within *B(C)*.
- Interactions between nested effects are not valid. For example, neither *A(C)*B(C)* nor *A(C)*B(D)* is valid.
- To include a covariate term in the design, enter the name of the covariate on the DESIGN subcommand.
- Covariates can be connected, but not nested, through the * operator to form another covariate effect. Therefore, interactions among covariates such as *X1*X1* and *X1*X2* are valid, but not *X1(X2)*. Using covariate effects such as *X1*X1*, *X1*X1*X1*, *X1*X2*, and *X1*X1*X2*X2* makes fitting a polynomial regression model easy in UNIANOVA.
- Factor and covariate effects can be connected only by the * operator. Suppose *A* and *B* are factors, and *X1* and *X2* are covariates. Examples of valid factor-by-covariate interaction effects are *A*X1, A*B*X1, X1*A(B), A*X1*X1,* and *B*X1*X2*.
- If more than one DESIGN subcommand is specified, only the last one is in effect.

Example

```
UNIANOVA Y BY A B C WITH X
  /DESIGN A B(A) X*A.
```

- In this example, the design consists of a main effect A, a nested effect B within A, and an interaction effect of a covariate X with a factor A.

UPDATE

```
UPDATE FILE={master file}
            {*          }

[/RENAME=(old varnames=new varnames)...]

[/IN=varname]

 /FILE={transaction file1}
       {*                }

[/FILE=transaction file2]

 /BY key variables

[/MAP]

[/KEEP={ALL**   }] [/DROP=varlist]
       {varlist}
```

**Default if the subcommand is omitted.

Example:
```
UPDATE FILE=MAILIST /FILE=NEWLIST /BY=ID.
```

Overview

UPDATE replaces values in a master file with updated values recorded in one or more files called transaction files. Cases in the master file and transaction file are matched according to a key variable.

The master file and the transaction files must be SPSS-format data files created with the SAVE or XSAVE commands or the working data file. UPDATE replaces values and creates a new working data file, which replaces the original working file. Use the SAVE or XSAVE commands to save the updated file on disk as an SPSS-format data file.

UPDATE is designed to update values of existing variables for existing cases. Use MATCH FILES to add new variables to an SPSS-format data file and ADD FILES to add new cases.

Options

Variable Selection. You can specify which variables from each input file are included in the new working file using the DROP and KEEP subcommands.

Variable Names. You can rename variables in each input file before combining the files using the RENAME subcommand. This permits you to combine variables that are the same but whose names differ in different input files, or to separate variables that are different but have the same name.

983

Variable Flag. You can create a variable that indicates whether a case came from a particular input file using IN. You can use the FIRST or LAST subcommand to create a variable that flags the first or last case of a group of cases with the same value for the key variable.

Variable Map. You can request a map showing all variables in the new working file, their order, and the input files from which they came using the MAP subcommand.

Basic Specification

The basic specification is two or more FILE subcommands and a BY subcommand.

- The first FILE subcommand must specify the master file. All other FILE subcommands identify the transaction files.
- BY specifies the key variables.
- All files must be sorted in ascending order by the key variables.
- By default, all variables from all input files are included in the new working file.

Subcommand Order

- The master file must be specified first.
- RENAME and IN must immediately follow the FILE subcommand to which they apply.
- BY must follow the FILE subcommands and any associated RENAME and IN subcommands.
- MAP, DROP, and KEEP must be specified after all FILE and RENAME subcommands.

Syntax Rules

- BY can be specified only once. However, multiple variables can be specified on BY. All files must be sorted in ascending order by the key variables named on BY.
- The master file cannot contain duplicate values for the key variables.
- RENAME can be repeated after each FILE subcommand and applies only to variables in the file named on the immediately preceding FILE subcommand.
- MAP can be repeated as often as needed.

Operations

- UPDATE reads all input files named on FILE and builds a new working data file that replaces any working file created earlier in the session. The new working data file is built when the data are read by one of the procedure commands or the EXECUTE, SAVE, or SORT CASES command.
- The new working data file contains complete dictionary information from the input files, including variable names, labels, print and write formats, and missing-value indicators. The new working data file also contains the documents from each input file, unless the DROP DOCUMENTS command is used.

- UPDATE copies all variables in order from the master file, then all variables in order from the first transaction file, then all variables in order from the second transaction file, and so on.
- Cases are updated when they are matched on the BY variable(s). If the master and transaction files contain common variables for matched cases, the values for those variables are taken from the transaction file, provided the values are not missing or blanks. Missing or blank values in the transaction files are not used to update values in the master file.
- When UPDATE encounters duplicate keys within a transaction file, it applies each transaction sequentially to that case to produce one case per key value in the resulting file. If more than one transaction file is specified, the value for a variable comes from the last transaction file with a nonmissing value for that variable.
- Variables that are in the transaction files but not in the master file are added to the master file. Cases that do not contain those variables are assigned the system-missing value (for numerics) or blanks (for strings).
- Cases that are in the transaction files but not in the master file are added to the master file and are interleaved according to their values for the key variables.
- If the working data file is named as an input file, any N and SAMPLE commands that have been specified are applied to the working data file before files are combined.
- The TEMPORARY command cannot be in effect if the working data file is used as an input file.

Limitations

- Maximum 1 BY subcommand. However, BY can specify multiple variables.

Example

```
UPDATE FILE=MAILIST /FILE=NEWLIST /BY=ID.
```

- *MAILIST* is specified as the master file. *NEWLIST* is the transaction file. *ID* is the key variable.
- Both *MAILIST* and *NEWLIST* must be sorted in ascending order of *ID*.
- If *NEWLIST* has cases or nonmissing variables that are not in *MAILIST*, the new cases or variables are added to the resulting file.

Example

```
SORT CASES BY LOCATN DEPT.
UPDATE  FILE=MASTER /FILE=* /BY LOCATN DEPT
    /KEEP AVGHOUR AVGRAISE LOCATN DEPT SEX HOURLY RAISE /MAP.
SAVE OUTFILE=PRSNNL.
```

- SORT CASES sorts the working data file in ascending order of the variables to be named as key variables on UPDATE.
- UPDATE specifies *MASTER* as the master file and the sorted working data file as the transaction file. File *MASTER* must also be sorted by *LOCATN* and *DEPT*.

- BY specifies the key variables *LOCATN* and *DEPT*.
- KEEP specifies the subset and order of variables to be retained in the resulting file.
- MAP provides a list of the variables in the resulting file and the two input files.
- SAVE saves the resulting file as an SPSS-format data file.

FILE Subcommand

FILE identifies each input file. At least two FILE subcommands are required on UPDATE: one specifies the master file and the other a transaction file. A separate FILE subcommand must be used to specify each transaction file.

- The first FILE subcommand must specify the master file.
- An asterisk on FILE refers to the working data file.
- All files must be sorted in ascending order according to the variables specified on BY.
- The master file cannot contain duplicate values for the key variables. However, transaction files can and often do contain cases with duplicate keys (see "Operations" on p. 984).

Raw Data Files

To update the master file with cases from a raw data file, use DATA LIST first to define the raw data file as the working data file. UPDATE can then use the working data file to update the master file.

Example

```
DATA LIST FILE=RAWDATA
  ID 1-3 NAME 5-17 (A) ADDRESS 19-28 (A) ZIP 30-34.
SORT CASES BY ID.
UPDATE FILE=MAILIST1 /RENAME=(STREET=ADDRESS) /FILE=* /BY=ID /MAP.
SAVE OUTFILE=MAILIST2.
```

- DATA LIST defines the variables in the raw data file *RAWDATA*, which will be used to update values in the master file.
- SORT CASES sorts the working data file in ascending order of the key variable *ID*. Cases in the master file were previously sorted in this manner.
- The first FILE subcommand on UPDATE refers to the master file, *MAILIST1*. The RENAME subcommand renames the variable *STREET* to *ADDRESS* in file *MAILIST1*.
- The second FILE subcommand refers to the working data file defined on DATA LIST.
- BY indicates that cases in *MAILIST1* and the working data file are to be matched by the key variable *ID*.
- MAP requests a map of the resulting file.
- SAVE saves the resulting file as an SPSS-format data file named *MAILIST2*.

BY Subcommand

BY specifies one or more identification, or key, variables that are used to match cases between files.

- BY must follow the FILE subcommands and any associated RENAME and IN subcommands.
- BY specifies the names of one or more key variables. The key variables must exist in all input files and have the same names in all the files. The key variables can be string variables (long strings are allowed).
- All input files must be sorted in ascending order of the key variables. If necessary, use SORT CASES before UPDATE.
- Missing values for key variables are handled like any other values.
- The key variables in the master file must identify unique cases. If duplicate cases are found, the program issues an error and UPDATE is not executed. The system-missing value is treated as one single value.

RENAME Subcommand

RENAME renames variables on the input files *before* they are processed by UPDATE. RENAME must follow the FILE subcommand that contains the variables to be renamed.

- RENAME applies only to the immediately preceding FILE subcommand. To rename variables from more than one input file, specify a RENAME subcommand after each FILE subcommand.
- Specifications for RENAME consist of a left parenthesis, a list of old variable names, an equals sign, a list of new variable names, and a right parenthesis. The two variable lists must name or imply the same number of variables. If only one variable is renamed, the parentheses are optional.
- More than one rename specification can be specified on a single RENAME subcommand, each enclosed in parentheses.
- The TO keyword can be used to refer to consecutive variables in the file and to generate new variable names (see the TO keyword on p. 29).
- RENAME takes effect immediately. Any KEEP and DROP subcommands entered prior to a RENAME must use the old names, while KEEP and DROP subcommands entered after a RENAME must use the new names.
- All specifications within a single set of parentheses take effect simultaneously. For example, the specification RENAME (A,B = B,A) swaps the names of the two variables.
- Variables cannot be renamed to scratch variables.
- Input SPSS-format data files are not changed on disk; only the copy of the file being combined is affected.

Example

```
UPDATE FILE=MASTER /FILE=CLIENTS
  /RENAME=(TEL_NO, ID_NO = PHONE, ID)
  /BY ID.
```

- UPDATE updates the master phone list by using current information from file *CLIENTS*.

- Two variables on *CLIENTS* are renamed prior to the match. *TEL_NO* is renamed *PHONE* to match the name used for phone numbers in the master file. *ID_NO* is renamed *ID* so that it will have the same name as the identification variable in the master file and can be used on the BY subcommand.

- The old variable names are listed before the equals sign, and the new variable names are listed in the same order after the equals sign. The parentheses are required.

- The BY subcommand matches cases according to client ID numbers.

DROP and KEEP Subcommands

DROP and KEEP are used to include a subset of variables in the resulting file. DROP specifies a set of variables to exclude, and KEEP specifies a set of variables to retain.

- DROP and KEEP do not affect the input files on disk.

- DROP and KEEP must follow all FILE and RENAME subcommands.

- DROP and KEEP must specify one or more variables. If RENAME is used to rename variables, specify the new names on DROP and KEEP.

- DROP cannot be used with variables created by the IN subcommand.

- Keyword ALL can be specified on KEEP. ALL must be the last specification on KEEP, and it refers to all variables not previously named on KEEP.

- KEEP can be used to change the order of variables in the resulting file. With KEEP, variables are kept in the order they are listed on the subcommand. If a variable is named more than once on KEEP, only the first mention of the variable is in effect; all subsequent references to that variable name are ignored.

- Multiple DROP and KEEP subcommands are allowed. Specifying a variable that is not in the working data file or that has been dropped because of a previous DROP or KEEP subcommand results in an error and the UPDATE command is not executed.

Example

```
UPDATE FILE=MAILIST /FILE=NEWLIST /RENAME=(STREET=ADDRESS) /BY ID
  /KEEP=NAME ADDRESS CITY STATE ZIP ID.
```

- KEEP specifies the variables to keep in the result file. The variables are stored in the order specified on KEEP.

IN Subcommand

IN creates a new variable in the resulting file that indicates whether a case came from the input file named on the preceding FILE subcommand. IN applies only to the file specified on the immediately preceding FILE subcommand.

- IN has only one specification, the name of the flag variable.
- The variable created by IN has value 1 for every case that came from the associated input file and value 0 if the case came from a different input file.
- Variables created by IN are automatically attached to the end of the resulting file and cannot be dropped.

Example

```
UPDATE   FILE=WEEK10  /FILE=WEEK11  /IN=INWEEK11  /BY=EMPID.
```

- IN creates the variable *INWEEK11*, which has the value 1 for all cases in the resulting file that came from the input file *WEEK11* and the value 0 for those cases that were not in file *WEEK11*.

MAP Subcommand

MAP produces a list of the variables are in the new working file and the file or files from which they came. Variables are listed in the order in which they appear in the resulting file. MAP has no specifications and must be placed after all FILE, RENAME, and IN subcommands.

- Multiple MAP subcommands can be used. Each MAP shows the current status of the working data file and reflects only the subcommands that precede the MAP subcommand.
- To obtain a map of the resulting file in its final state, specify MAP last.
- If a variable is renamed, its original and new names are listed. Variables created by IN are not included in the map, since they are automatically attached to the end of the file and cannot be dropped.
- MAP can be used with the EDIT command to obtain a list of the variables in the resulting file without actually reading the data and combining the files.

USE

```
USE [{start date        }] [THRU [{end date      }]]
    {start case number}        {end case number}
    {FIRST            }        {LAST          }

    [ALL]
```

Example:

```
USE Y 1960.
```

Overview

USE designates a range of observations to be used with time series procedures.

Basic Specification

The basic specification is either the start of the range, the end of the range, or both. You can also simply specify keyword THRU or ALL.

- The default start is the first observation in the file, and the default end is the last observation.
- Keyword THRU is required if the end of the range is specified.
- Keyword ALL defines a USE range starting with the first observation and ending with the last observation in the series. It can be specified to restore processing to the entire series.
- Keyword THRU by itself is the same as specifying keyword ALL.

Syntax Rules

- The start and end can be specified as either DATE specifications or case (observation) numbers.
- DATE specifications and case numbers cannot be mixed on a USE command.
- Any observation within the file can be used as the start or end, as long as the starting observation comes before the end observation.

DATE Specifications

- A DATE specification consists of DATE keywords and values (see DATE). These specifications must correspond to existing DATE variables.
- If more than one DATE variable exists, the highest-order one must be used in the specification.
- Values on keyword YEAR must have the same format (2 or 4 digits) as the YEAR specifications on the DATE command.

Case Specifications

- The case number specification is the sequence number of the case (observation) as it is read by the program.

Keywords FIRST and LAST

- The start can also be specified with keyword FIRST, and the end with keyword LAST. These keywords designate the first and last cases in the file, respectively.
- Keywords FIRST and LAST can be used along with either DATE or case specifications.

Operations

- USE is ignored by the utility procedures CREATE and RMV. These procedures process all the available data.
- The DATE command turns off all existing USE and PREDICT specifications.
- USE remains in effect in a session until it is changed by another USE command or until a new DATE command is issued.
- Any data selection specified on USE is in effect until the next USE command, the next DATE command, or the end of the session. SPSS-format data files are not affected by the USE command.

Limitations

- Maximum 1 range (one start and/or one end) can be specified.

Examples

```
USE ALL.
```

- This command includes all observations in the file in the USE range.
- This specification is the same as USE THRU or USE FIRST THRU LAST.

```
USE Y 1960.
```

- This command selects observations starting with YEAR_ value 1960 through the last observation in the file. It is equivalent to USE Y 1960 THRU LAST.

```
USE THRU D 5.
```

- This command selects all cases from the first case in the file to the last one with a DAY_ value of 5. It is equivalent to USE FIRST THRU D 5.

```
USE THRU 5.
```

- This command selects cases starting with the first case and ending with the fifth case.

```
USE Y 1955 M 6 THRU Y 1960 M 6.
```

- This selects cases from June 1955 through June 1960.

```
USE W 16 D 3 THRU W 48 D 3.
```

- This example selects cases from day 3 of week 16 through day 3 of week 48.

```
USE CYCLE 2 OBS 4 THRU CYCLE 2 OBS 17.
```

- This example selects observations 4 through 17 of the second cycle.

VALUE LABELS

```
VALUE LABELS varlist value 'label' value 'label'... [/varlist...]
```

Example:
```
VALUE LABELS JOBGRADE 'P' 'Parttime Employee' 'C' 'Customer Support'.
```

Overview

VALUE LABELS deletes all existing value labels for the specified variable(s) and assigns new value labels. ADD VALUE LABELS can be used to add new labels or alter labels for specified values without deleting other existing labels.

Basic Specification

The basic specification is a variable name and the individual values with their assigned labels.

Syntax Rules

- Labels can be assigned to any previously defined variables except long string variables.
- It is not necessary to enter value labels for all values for a variable.
- Each value label must be enclosed in apostrophes or quotation marks. For short string variables, the values themselves must also be enclosed in apostrophes or quotation marks.
- Value labels can contain any characters, including blanks. To enter an apostrophe as part of a label, enclose the label in quotation marks or enter a double apostrophe.
- Each value label can be up to 60 characters long, although most procedures display only 20 characters. The TABLES procedure will display all 60 characters of a label.
- The same labels can be assigned to the values of different variables by specifying a list of variable names. For string variables, the variables specified must be of equal length.
- Multiple sets of variable names and value labels can be specified on one VALUE LABELS command as long as the sets are separated by slashes.
- To continue a label from one command line to the next, specify a plus (+) sign before the continuation of the label. Each string segment of the label must be enclosed in apostrophes or quotation marks. To insert a blank between the strings, the blank must be included in the label specification.

Operations

- Unlike most transformations, VALUE LABELS takes effect as soon as it is encountered in the command sequence. Thus, special attention should be paid to its position among commands (see "Command Order" on p. 16).

- VALUE LABELS deletes all previously assigned value labels for the specified variables.

- The value labels assigned are stored in the dictionary of the working file and are automatically displayed on the output from many procedures.

- If a specified value is longer than the format of the variable, the program will be unable to read the full value and may not be able to assign the value label correctly.

- If the value specified for a string variable is shorter than the format of the variable, the value specification is right-padded without warning.

Example

```
VALUE LABELS V1 TO V3 1 'Officials & Managers'
                      6 'Service Workers'
                   /V4 'N' 'New Employee'.
```

- Labels are assigned to the values 1 and 6 for the variables between and including *V1* and *V3* in the working data file.

- Following the required slash, a label for value *N* of *V4* is specified. *N* is a string value and must be enclosed in apostrophes or quotation marks.

- If labels exist for values 1 and 6 on *V1* to *V3* and value N on *V4*, they are changed in the dictionary of the working file. If labels do not exist for these values, new labels are added to the dictionary.

- Existing labels for values other than 1 and 6 on *V1* to *V3* and value N on *V4* are deleted.

Example

```
VALUE LABELS  OFFICE88 1 "EMPLOYEE'S OFFICE ASSIGNMENT PRIOR"
   + " TO 1988".
```

- The label for *OFFICE88* is created by combining two strings with the plus sign. The blank between PRIOR and TO must be included in the first or second string to be included in the label.

Example

```
VALUE LABELS=STATE REGION 'U' "UNKNOWN".
```

- Label *UNKNOWN* is assigned to value U for both *STATE* and *REGION*.

- *STATE* and *REGION* must be string variables of equal length. If *STATE* and *REGION* have unequal lengths, a separate specification must be made for each, as in

```
VALUE LABELS STATE 'U' "UNKNOWN" / REGION 'U' "UNKNOWN".
```

Example

```
DATA LIST / CITY 1-8(A) STATE 10-12(A).
VALUE LABELS  STATE 'TEX' "TEXAS" 'TEN' "TENNESSEE"
                    'MIN' "MINNESOTA".

BEGIN DATA
AUSTIN    TEX
MEMPHIS   TEN
ST. PAUL MIN
END DATA.
FREQUENCIES VARIABLES=STATE.
```

- The DATA LIST command defines two variables. *CITY* is eight characters wide and *STATE* is three characters. The values are included between the BEGIN DATA and END DATA commands.

- The VALUE LABELS command assigns labels to three values of variable *STATE*. Each value and each label is specified in either apostrophes or quotation marks.

- The format for variable *STATE* must be at least three characters wide, because the specified values, TEX, TEN, and MIN, are three characters. If the format for *STATE* were two characters, the program would issue a warning. This would occur even though the values named on VALUE LABELS and the values after BEGIN DATA agree.

VARIABLE ALIGNMENT

```
VARIABLE ALIGNMENT varlist ({LEFT  }) ... [/varlist...]
                            {CENTER}
                            {RIGHT }

Example:

VARIABLE ALIGNMENT sales95 sales96 (LEFT)
  /id gender (RIGHT).
```

Overview

VARIABLE ALIGNMENT specifies the alignment of data values in the Data Editor. It has no effect on the format of the variables or the display of the variables or values in other windows or printed results.

Basic Specification

The basic specification is a variable name and the keyword LEFT, RIGHT, or CENTER in parentheses.

996

VARIABLE LABELS

```
VARIABLE LABELS varname 'label' [/varname...]
```

Example:
```
VARIABLE LABELS YRHIRED 'YEAR OF FIRST HIRING'.
```

Overview

VARIABLE LABELS assigns descriptive labels to variables in the working data file.

Basic Specification

The basic specification is a variable name and the associated label in apostrophes or quotation marks.

Syntax Rules

- Labels can be added to any previously defined variable. It is not necessary to enter labels for all variables in the working data file.
- Each variable label must be enclosed in apostrophes or quotation marks.
- Variable labels can contain any characters, including blanks. To enter an apostrophe as part of a label, enclose the label in quotation marks or enter a double apostrophe.
- Each variable label can be up to 120 characters long, although most procedures print fewer than the 120 characters. All statistical procedures display at least 40 characters.
- Multiple variables can be assigned labels on a single VARIABLE LABELS command. Only one label can be assigned to each variable, and each label can apply to only one variable.
- To continue a label from one command line to the next, specify a plus (+) sign before the continuation of the label. Each string segment of the label must be enclosed in apostrophes or quotation marks. To insert a blank between the strings, the blank must be included in the label specification.

Operations

- Unlike most transformations, VARIABLE LABELS takes effect as soon as it is encountered in the command sequence. Thus, special attention should be paid to its position among commands (see "Command Order" on p. 16).
- Variable labels are automatically displayed in the output from many procedures and are stored in the dictionary of the working data file.

- VARIABLE LABELS can be used for variables that have no previously assigned variable labels. If a variable has a previously assigned variable label, the new label replaces the old label.

Example

```
VARIABLE LABELS  YRHIRED 'YEAR OF FIRST HIRING'
 DEPT88 'DEPARTMENT OF EMPLOYMENT IN 1988'
 SALARY88 'YEARLY SALARY IN 1988'
 JOBCAT 'JOB CATEGORIES'.
```

- Variable labels are assigned to the variables *YRHIRED*, *DEPT88*, *SALARY88*, and *JOBCAT*.

Example

```
VARIABLE LABELS  OLDSAL "EMPLOYEE'S GROSS SALARY PRIOR"
 + " TO 1988".
```

- The label for *OLDSAL* is created by combining two strings with the plus sign. The blank between PRIOR and TO must be included in the first or second string to be included in the label.

VARIABLE LEVEL

```
VARIABLE LEVEL varlist ({SCALE**  }) ... [/varlist...]
                        {ORDINAL}
                        {NOMINAL}
```

**Default.

Example:

```
VARIABLE LEVEL sales95 sales96 SCALE
    /region division NOMINAL
    /expense ORDINAL.
```

Overview

VARIABLE LEVEL specifies the level of measurement for variables. Measurement specification is only relevant for:

- Charts created by the IGRAPH command. Nominal and ordinal are both treated as categorical.
- SPSS-format data files used with AnswerTree.

Basic Specification

The basic specification is a variable name and the measurement level.

VARIABLE WIDTH

```
VARIABLE WIDTH varlist (n) ... [/varlist...]

Example:

VARIABLE WIDTH sales95 sales96 (10)
   /id gender (2).
```

Overview

VARIABLE WIDTH specifies column width for display of variables in the Data Editor. It has no effect on the format of the variable or the display of the variable or values in other windows or printed results.

Basic Specification

The basic specification is a variable name and a positive integer in parentheses for the column width.

VECTOR

```
VECTOR  {vector  name=varlist     }  [/vector  name...]
        {vector  name(n  [format])}
```

Example:

```
VECTOR V=V1 TO V6.

STRING SELECT(A1).
COMPUTE SELECT='V'.

LOOP #I=1 TO 6.
IF MISSING(V(#I)) SELECT='M'.
END LOOP.
```

Overview

VECTOR associates a vector name with a set of existing variables or defines a vector of new variables. A vector is a set of variables that can be referred to using an index. The vector can refer to either string or numeric variables, and the variables can be permanent or temporary.

For each variable in the reference list, VECTOR generates an element. Element names are formed by adding a subscript in parentheses to the end of the vector name. For example, if vector *AGES* has three elements, the element names are *AGES(1)*, *AGES(2)*, and *AGES(3)*. Although the VECTOR command has other uses within the transformation language, it is most often used with LOOP structures because the indexing variable on LOOP can be used to refer to successive vector elements.

Options

File Structures. VECTOR can be used with the END CASE command to restructure data files. You can build a single case from several cases or, conversely, you can build several cases from a single case (see pp. 319 and 320 for examples).

Short-Form Vectors. VECTOR can be used to create a list of new variables and the vector that refers to them simultaneously. VECTOR in the short form can be used to establish the dictionary order of a group of variables before they are defined on a DATA LIST command. (See "VECTOR: Short Form" on p. 1003.)

Basic Specification

- The basic specification is VECTOR, a vector name, a required equals sign, and the list of variables that the vector refers to. The TO keyword must be used to specify the variable list.
- For the short form of VECTOR, the basic specification is VECTOR, an alphabetical prefix, and, in parentheses, the number of variables to be created.

1001

Syntax Rules

- Multiple vectors can be created on the same command by using a slash to separate each set of specifications.
- Variables specified on VECTOR must already be defined unless the short form of VECTOR is used to create variables (see "VECTOR: Short Form" on p. 1003).
- The TO convention must be used to specify the variable list. Thus, variables specified must be consecutive and must be from the same dictionary, permanent or scratch.
- A single vector must comprise all numeric variables or all string variables. The string variables must have the same length.
- A scalar (a variable named on NUMERIC), a function, and a vector can all have the same name, for example *MINI*. The scalar can be identified by the lack of a left parenthesis following the name. Where a vector has the same name as a function (or the abbreviation of a function), the vector name takes precedence. (See p. 1004 for an example.)
- Vector element names must always be specified with a subscript in parentheses.

Operations

- VECTOR takes effect as soon as it is encountered in the command sequence, unlike most transformations, which do not take effect until the data are read. Thus, special attention should be paid to its position among commands (see "Command Order" on p. 16).
- VECTOR is in effect only until the first procedure that follows it. The vector must be re-declared to be reused.
- Vectors can be used in transformations but not in procedures.

Examples

```
* Replace a case's missing values with the mean of all
  nonmissing values for that case.
DATA LIST FREE /V1 V2 V3 V4 V5 V6 V7 V8.
MISSING VALUES V1 TO V8 (99).
COMPUTE MEANSUB=MEAN(V1 TO V8).

VECTOR V=V1 TO V8.
LOOP #I=1 TO 8.
+   DO IF MISSING (V(#I)).
+   COMPUTE V(#I)=MEANSUB.
+   END IF.
END LOOP.

BEGIN DATA
1 99 2 3 5 6 7  8
2  3 4 5 6 7 8  9
2  3 5 5 6 7 8 99
END DATA.
LIST.
```

- The first COMPUTE command calculates variable MEANSUB as the mean of all nonmissing values for each case.
- VECTOR defines vector *V* with the original variables as its elements.
- For each case, the loop is executed once for each variable. The COMPUTE command within the loop is executed only when the variable has a missing value for that case. COMPUTE replaces the missing value with the value of *MEANSUB*.
- For the first case, the missing value for variable *V2* is changed to the value of *MEANSUB* for that case. The missing value for variable *V8* for the third case is changed to the value of *MEANSUB* for that case.

More Examples

For additional examples of VECTOR, see pp. 319, 320, and 468.

VECTOR: Short Form

VECTOR can be used to create a list of new variables and the vector that refers to them simultaneously. The short form of VECTOR specifies a prefix of alphanumeric characters followed, in parentheses, by the length of the vector (the number of variables to be created).

- The new variable names must not conflict with existing variables. If the prefix starts with the # character, the new variables are created according to the rules for scratch variables.
- More than one vector of the same length can be created by naming two or more prefixes before the length specification.
- By default, variables created with VECTOR receive F8.2 formats. Alternative formats for the variables can be specified by including a format specification with the length specification within the parentheses. The format and length can be specified in either order and must be separated by at least one space or comma. If multiple vectors are created, the assigned format applies to all of them unless you specify otherwise.

Example

```
VECTOR #WORK(10).
```

- The program creates vector *#WORK*, which refers to 10 scratch variables: *#WORK1*, *#WORK2*, and so on, through *#WORK10*. Thus, element *#WORK(5)* of the vector is variable *#WORK5*.

Example

```
VECTOR X,Y(5).
```

- VECTOR creates vectors *X* and *Y*, which refer to the new variables *X1* through *X5* and *Y1* through *Y5*, respectively.

Example

```
VECTOR X(6,A5).
```

- VECTOR assigns an A5 format to variables *X1* through *X6*.

Example

```
VECTOR X,Y(A5,6) Z(3,F2).
```

- VECTOR assigns A5 formats to variables *X1* to *X6* and *Y1* to *Y6*, and F2 formats to variables *Z1* to *Z3*. It doesn't matter whether the format or the length is specified first within the parentheses.

Example

```
* Predetermine variable order with the short form of VECTOR.

INPUT PROGRAM.
VECTOR X Y (4,F8.2).
DATA LIST / X4 Y4 X3 Y3 X2 Y2 X1 Y1 1-8.
END INPUT PROGRAM.

PRINT /X1 TO X4  Y1 TO Y4.
BEGIN DATA
49382716
49382716
49382716
END DATA.
```

- The short form of VECTOR is used to establish the dictionary order of a group of variables before they are defined on a DATA LIST command. To predetermine variable order, both VECTOR and DATA LIST must be enclosed within the INPUT PROGRAM and END INPUT PROGRAM commands.
- The order of the variables in the working data file will be *X1*, *X2*, *X3*, and *X4*, and *Y1*, *Y2*, *Y3*, and *Y4*, even though they are defined in a different order on DATA LIST.
- The program reads the variables with the F1 format specified on DATA LIST. It writes the variables with the output format assigned on VECTOR (F8.2).
- Another method for predetermining variable order is to use NUMERIC (or STRING if the variables are string variables) before the DATA LIST command (see p. 653 for an example). The advantage of using NUMERIC or STRING is that you can assign mnemonic names to the variables.

Example

```
* Name conflicts.

INPUT PROGRAM.
NUMERIC MIN MINI_A MINI_B MINIM(F2).
COMPUTE MINI_A = MINI(2).  /*MINI is function MINIMUM.
VECTOR MINI(3,F2).
DO REPEAT I = 1 TO 3.
+   COMPUTE MINI(I) = -I.
END REPEAT.
COMPUTE MIN = MIN(1).      /*The second MIN is function MINIMUM.
COMPUTE MINI_B = MINI(2). /*MINI now references vector MINI
COMPUTE MINIM = MINIM(3). /*The second MINIM is function MINIMUM.
END CASE.
END FILE.
END INPUT PROGRAM.
```

- In this example, there are potential name conflicts between the scalars (the variables named on NUMERIC), the vectors (named on VECTOR), and the statistical function MINIMUM.
- A name that is not followed by a left parenthesis is treated as a scalar.
- When a name followed by a left parenthesis may refer to a vector element or a function, precedence is given to the vector.

VECTOR outside a Loop Structure

VECTOR is most commonly associated with the loop structure, since the index variable for LOOP can be used as the subscript. However, the subscript can come from elsewhere, including from the data.

Example

```
* Create a single case for each of students 1, 2, and 3.

DATA LIST /STUDENT 1 SCORE 3-4 TESTNUM 6.
BEGIN DATA
1 10 1
1 20 2
1 30 3
1 40 4
2 15 2
2 25 3
3 40 1
3 55 3
3 60 4
END DATA.

VECTOR RESULT(4).
COMPUTE RESULT(TESTNUM)=SCORE.

AGGREGATE OUTFILE=*/BREAK=STUDENT
         /RESULT1 TO RESULT4=MAX(RESULT1 TO RESULT4).

PRINT FORMATS RESULT1 TO RESULT4 (F2.0).
PRINT /STUDENT RESULT1 TO RESULT4.
EXECUTE.
```

- Data are scores on tests recorded in separate cases along with a student identification number and a test number. In this example, there are four possible tests for three students. Not all students took every test.
- Vector *RESULT* creates variables *RESULT1* through *RESULT4*.
- For each case, COMPUTE assigns the *SCORE* value to one of the four vector variables, depending on the value of *TESTNUM*. The other three vector variables for each case keep the system-missing value they were initialized to.

- Aggregating by variable *STUDENT* creates new cases, as shown by the output from the PRINT command (see Figure 1). The MAX function in AGGREGATE returns the maximum value across cases with the same value for *STUDENT*. If a student has taken a particular test, the one valid value is returned as the value for variable *RESULT1*, *RESULT2*, *RESULT3*, or *RESULT4*.

Figure 1   PRINT output after aggregating

```
1   10   20   30   40
2    .   15   25    .
3   40    .   55   60
```

VERIFY

```
VERIFY [VARIABLES=series name]
```

Example:
```
VERIFY VARIABLE=STOCK.
```

Overview

VERIFY produces a report on the status of the most current DATE, USE, and PREDICT specifications. The report lists the first and last observations in the working data file, the current USE and PREDICT ranges, and any anomalies in the DATE variables. The number of missing values and the values of the first and last observations in the file and in the USE and PREDICT ranges can also be displayed for a specified series.

VERIFY should be used before a time series procedure whenever there is a possibility that DATE variables or USE and PREDICT ranges have been invalidated. In particular, the working data file should be verified after you have modified the file structure with commands such as SELECT IF, SORT CASES, and AGGREGATE.

Options

If a series is specified after VERIFY, the values of the first and last observations in the file and in the USE and PREDICT periods are reported for that series. In addition, the number of observations in the working data file that have missing values for that series is displayed. This can be useful for determining the USE ranges that do not include any missing values.

Basic Specification

The basic specification is the command keyword VERIFY.

- VERIFY displays the first and last observations in the working data file and in the USE and PREDICT ranges. This information is presented by case number and by the values of the DATE variables.
- For DATE variables, VERIFY reports the number of missing or invalid values. In addition, DATE variables that are not properly nested within the next higher-level DATE variable, that have start or end values other than those expected at the beginning or end of a cycle, or that increment by more than the expected increment are flagged with an asterisk next to the problem. An explanation of the problem is given.

Operations

- VERIFY reports on cases remaining after any preceding SELECT IF commands.
- The USE and PREDICT ranges are defined by the last USE and PREDICT commands specified before the VERIFY command. If USE and PREDICT have not been specified, the USE range is the entire series, and the PREDICT range does not exist.

Limitations

- Maximum 1 VARIABLES subcommand. Only 1 series can be specified on VARIABLES.

VARIABLES Subcommand

VARIABLES names a series to include in the report and is optional. The actual keyword VARIABLES can be omitted.

- The series named on VARIABLES must be numeric. The *DATE_* series is non-numeric and cannot be specified.
- Only one VARIABLES subcommand can be specified, and it can name only one series.

Examples

```
VERIFY.
```

- This command produces a report on the status of the most recent DATE, USE, and PREDICT specifications, as well as the first and last valid cases in the file.

```
VERIFY VARIABLE=STOCK.
```

- In addition to the default VERIFY information, this command displays information on series *STOCK*, including the values of the first and last cases and how many values in that series are missing.

WEIGHT

```
WEIGHT   {BY   varname}
         {OFF          }
```

Example:

```
WEIGHT BY V1.
FREQUENCIES VAR=V2.
```

Overview

WEIGHT weights cases differentially for analysis. WEIGHT can be used to obtain population estimates when you have a sample from a population for which some subgroup has been over- or undersampled. WEIGHT can also be used to weight a sample up to population size for reporting purposes or to replicate an example from a table or other aggregated data (see p. 219 for an example). With WEIGHT, you can arithmetically alter the sample size or its distribution.

Basic Specification

The basic specification is keyword BY followed by the name of the weight variable. Cases are weighted according to the values of the specified variable.

Syntax Rules

- Only one numeric variable can be specified. The variable can be a precoded weighting variable, or it can be computed with the transformation language.
- WEIGHT cannot be placed within a FILE TYPE—END FILE TYPE or INPUT PROGRAM—END INPUT PROGRAM structure. It can be placed nearly anywhere following these commands in a transformation program. See Appendix A for a discussion of the program states and the placement of commands.

Operations

- Unlike most transformations, WEIGHT takes effect as soon as it is encountered in the command sequence. Thus, special attention should be paid to its position among commands (see "Command Order" on p. 16).
- Weighting is permanent during a session unless it is preceded by a TEMPORARY command, changed by another WEIGHT command, or turned off with the WEIGHT OFF specification.

- Each WEIGHT command overrides the previous one.
- WEIGHT uses the value of the specified variable to arithmetically replicate cases for subsequent procedures. Cases are not physically replicated. For example, if you use a weighted file with CROSSTABS, the counts in the cells are actually the sums of the case weights. CROSSTABS then rounds cell counts when displaying the tables.
- Weight values do not need to be integer.
- Cases with missing or nonpositive values for the weighting variable are treated as having a weight of 0 and are thus invisible to statistical procedures. They are not used in calculations even where unweighted counts are specified. These cases do remain in the file, however, and are included in case listings and saved when the file is saved.
- A file saved when weighting is in effect maintains the weighting.
- If the weighted number of cases exceeds the sample size, tests of significance are inflated; if it is smaller, they are deflated.

Example

```
WEIGHT BY V1.
FREQ VAR=V2.
```

- The frequency counts for the values of variable *V2* will be weighted by the values of variable *V1*.

Example

```
COMPUTE WVAR=1.
IF (GROUP EQ 1) WVAR=.5.
WEIGHT BY WVAR.
```

- Variable *WVAR* is initialized to 1 with the COMPUTE command. The IF command changes the value of *WVAR* to 0.5 for cases where *GROUP* equals 1.
- Subsequent procedures will use a case base in which cases from group 1 count only half as much as other cases.

WRITE

```
WRITE [OUTFILE=file] [RECORDS={1}] [{NOTABLE}]
                              {n}   {TABLE  }

 /{1    } varlist [{col location [(format)]}] [varlist...]
  {rec #}          {(format list)           }
                   {*                       }

[/{2    }...]
  {rec #}
```

Example:

```
WRITE OUTFILE=PRSNNL / MOHIRED YRHIRED DEPT SALARY NAME.
EXECUTE.
```

Overview

WRITE writes files in a machine-readable format that can be used by other software applications. When used for this purpose, the OUTFILE subcommand is required. If OUTFILE is
not specified, the output from WRITE that can be displayed is included with the output from
your session in a format similar to that used by the PRINT command.

Options

Formats. You can specify formats for the variables. (See "Formats" on p. 1013.)

Strings. You can include strings within the variable specifications. The strings can be used
to label values or to add extra space between values. (See "Strings" on p. 1014.)

Multiple Lines per Case. You can write variables on more than one line for each case. See the
RECORDS subcommand on p. 1014.

Output File. You can direct the output to a specified file using the OUTFILE subcommand.

Summary Table. You can display a table that summarizes the variable formats with the TABLE
subcommand.

Subcommand Order

Subcommands can be specified in any order. However, all subcommands must be used
before the slash that precedes the first variable list.

Basic Specification

The basic specification is a slash followed by a variable list. The values for all of the variables specified on the list are included with the rest of the output from your session.

Syntax Rules

- A slash must precede the variable specifications. The first slash begins the definition of the first (and possibly only) line per case of the WRITE output.
- Specified variables must already exist, but they can be numeric, string, scratch, temporary, or system variables. Subscripted variable names, such as $X(1)$ for the first element in vector X, cannot be used.
- Keyword ALL can be used to write the values of all user-defined variables in the working data file.

Operations

- WRITE is executed once for each case constructed from the data file.
- Values are written to the file as the data are read.
- PRINT is a transformation and will not be executed unless it is followed by a procedure or the EXECUTE command.
- Lines longer than 132 columns can be written. However, if the record width of the lines to be written exceeds the default output width or the width specified with SET WIDTH, the program issues an error message and terminates processing.
- There are no carriage control characters in the output file generated by WRITE.
- User-missing values are written just like valid values. System-missing values are represented by blanks.
- If you are writing a file to be used on another system, you should take into account that some data types cannot be read all computers.
- If long records are less convenient than short records with multiple records per case, you can write out a case identifier and insert a string as a record identification number. The receiving system can then check for missing record numbers (see "Strings" on p. 1014 for an example).

Example

```
WRITE OUTFILE=PRSNNL / MOHIRED YRHIRED DEPT SALARY NAME.
FREQUENCIES VARIABLES=DEPT.
```

- WRITE writes values for each variable on the variable list to file *PRSNNL*. The FREQUENCIES procedure reads the data and causes WRITE to be executed.
- All variables are written with their dictionary formats.

Example

```
WRITE OUTFILE=PRSNNL /ALL.
EXECUTE.
```

- WRITE writes values for all user-defined variables in the working data file to file *PRSNNL*. The EXECUTE command executes WRITE.

Formats

By default, WRITE uses the dictionary write formats. You can specify formats for some or all variables specified on WRITE. For a string variable, the specified format must have the same width as that of the dictionary format.

- Format specifications can be either column-style or FORTRAN-like (see DATA LIST). The column location specified with column-style formats or implied with FORTRAN-like formats refers to the column in which the variable will be written.
- A format specification following a list of variables applies to all the variables in the list. Use an asterisk to prevent the specified format from applying to variables preceding the asterisk. The specification of column locations implies a default print format, and that format will apply to all previous variables if no asterisk is used.
- All available formats can be specified on WRITE. Note that hex and binary formats use different widths. For example, the AHEX format must have a width twice that of the corresponding A format. For more information on specifying formats and on the formats available, see DATA LIST and "Variable Formats" on p. 31.
- Format specifications are in effect only for the WRITE command. They do not change the dictionary write formats.
- To specify a blank between variables in the output, use a string (see "Strings" on p. 1014), specify blank columns in the format, or use an X or T format element in the WRITE specifications (see DATA LIST for information on X and T).

Example

```
WRITE OUTFILE=PRSNNL / TENURE (F2.0) ' ' MOHIRED YRHIRED DEPT *
      SALARY85 TO SALARY88 (4(DOLLAR8,1X)) NAME.
EXECUTE.
```

- Format F2.0 is specified for *TENURE*. A blank between apostrophes is specified as a string after *TENURE* to separate values of *TENURE* from those of *MOHIRED*.

- *MOHIRED, YRHIRED,* and *DEPT* are written with default formats because the asterisk prevents them from receiving the DOLLAR8 format specified for *SALARY85* to *SALARY88*. The 1X format element is specified with DOLLAR8 to add one blank after each value of *SALARY85* to *SALARY88*.
- *NAME* uses the default dictionary format.

Strings

You can specify strings within the variable list. Strings must be enclosed in apostrophes or quotation marks.

- If a format is specified for a variable list, the application of the format is interrupted by a specified string. Thus, the string has the same effect within a variable list as an asterisk.

Example

```
WRITE OUTFILE=PRSNNL
 /EMPLOYID '1' MOHIRED YRHIRED SEX AGE JOBCAT NAME
 /EMPLOYID '2' DEPT86 TO DEPT88 SALARY86 TO SALARY88.
EXECUTE.
```

- Strings are used to assign the constant 1 to record 1 of each case, and 2 to record 2 to provide record identifiers in addition to the case identifier *EMPLOYID*.

RECORDS Subcommand

RECORDS indicates the total number of lines written per case. The number specified on RECORDS is informational only. The actual specification that causes variables to be written on a new line is a slash within the variable specifications. Each new line is requested by another slash.

- RECORDS must be specified before the slash that precedes the start of the variable specifications.
- The only specification on RECORDS is an integer to indicate the number of records for the output. If the number does not agree with the actual number of records indicated by slashes, the program issues a warning and ignores the specification on RECORDS.
- Specifications for each line of output must begin with a slash. An integer can follow the slash, indicating the line on which values are to be written. The integer is informational only. It cannot be used to rearrange the order of records in the output. If the integer does not agree with the actual record number indicated by the number of slashes in the variable specifications, the integer is ignored.
- A slash that is not followed by a variable list generates a blank line in the output.

Examples

```
WRITE OUTFILE=PRSNNL RECORDS=2
 /EMPLOYID NAME DEPT
 /EMPLOYID TENURE SALARY.
EXECUTE.
```

- WRITE writes the values of an individual's name and department on one line, tenure and salary on the next line, and the employee identification number on both lines.

Example

```
WRITE OUTFILE=PRSNNL RECORDS=2
  /1 EMPLOYID NAME DEPT
  /2 EMPLOYID TENURE SALARY.
EXECUTE.
```

- This command is equivalent to the command in the preceding example.

Example

```
WRITE OUTFILE=PRSNNL / EMPLOYID NAME DEPT / EMPLOYID TENURE SALARY.
EXECUTE.
```

- This command is equivalent to the commands in both preceding examples.

OUTFILE Subcommand

OUTFILE specifies the target file for the output from the WRITE command. By default, the output is included with the rest of the output from the session.

- OUTFILE must be specified before the slash that precedes the start of the variable specifications.
- The output from WRITE can exceed 132 characters.

Example

```
WRITE OUTFILE=WRITEOUT
   /1 EMPLOYID DEPT SALARY /2 NAME.
EXECUTE.
```

- OUTFILE specifies *WRITEOUT* as the file that receives the WRITE output.

TABLE Subcommand

TABLE requests a table showing how the variable information is formatted. NOTABLE is the default.

- TABLE must be specified before the slash that precedes the start of the variable specifications.

Example

```
WRITE OUTFILE=PRSNNL TABLE /1 EMPLOYID DEPT SALARY /2  NAME.
EXECUTE.
```

- TABLE requests a summary table describing the WRITE specifications.

WRITE FORMATS

```
WRITE FORMATS varlist (format) [varlist...]
```

Example:
```
WRITE FORMATS SALARY (DOLLAR8)
             / HOURLY (DOLLAR7.2)
             / RAISE BONUS (PCT2).
```

Overview

WRITE FORMATS changes variable write formats. Write formats are output formats and control the form in which values are written by the WRITE command.

WRITE FORMATS changes only write formats. To change print formats, use the PRINT FORMATS command. To change both the print and write formats with a single specification, use the FORMATS command. For information on assigning input formats during data definition, see DATA LIST. For a more detailed discussion of input and output formats, see "Variable Formats" on p. 31.

Basic Specification

The basic specification is a variable list followed by the new format specification in parentheses. All specified variables receive the new format.

Syntax Rules

- You can specify more than one variable or variable list, followed by a format in parentheses. Only one format can be specified after each variable list. For clarity, each set of specifications can be separated by a slash.
- You can use keyword TO to refer to consecutive variables in the working data file.
- The specified width of a format must include enough positions to accommodate any punctuation characters such as decimal points, commas, dollar signs, or date and time delimiters. (This differs from assigning an *input* format on DATA LIST, where the program automatically expands the input format to accommodate punctuation characters in output.)
- Custom currency formats (CCw, CCw.d) must first be defined on the SET command before they can be used on WRITE FORMATS.
- WRITE FORMATS cannot be used with string variables. To change the length of a string variable, declare a new variable of the desired length with the STRING command and then use COMPUTE to copy values from the existing string into the new string.

Operations

- Unlike most transformations, WRITE FORMATS takes effect as soon as it is encountered in the command sequence. Special attention should be paid to its position among commands. For more information, see "Command Order" on p. 16.

- Variables not specified on WRITE FORMATS retain their current formats in the working data file. To see the current formats, use the DISPLAY command.

- The new write formats are changed only in the working file and are in effect for the duration of the session or until changed again with a WRITE FORMATS or FORMATS command. Write formats in the original data file (if one exists) are not changed, unless the file is resaved with the SAVE or XSAVE command.

- New numeric variables created with transformation commands are assigned default print and write formats of F8.2 (or the format specified on the FORMAT subcommand of SET). The WRITE FORMATS command can be used to change the new variable's write formats.

- New string variables created with transformation commands are assigned the format specified on the STRING command that declares the variable. WRITE FORMATS cannot be used to change the format of a new string variable.

- Date and time formats are effective only with the LIST and TABLES procedures and the PRINT and WRITE transformation commands. All other procedures use F format regardless of the date and time formats specified. See "Date and Time Formats" on p. 60.

- If a numeric data value exceeds its width specification, the program attempts to write some value nevertheless. First the program rounds decimal values, then removes punctuation characters, then tries scientific notation, and finally, if there is still not enough space, produces asterisks indicating that a value is present but cannot be written in the assigned width.

Example

```
WRITE FORMATS SALARY (DOLLAR8)
            / HOURLY (DOLLAR7.2)
            / RAISE BONUS (PCT2).
```

- The write format for *SALARY* is changed to DOLLAR with eight positions, including the dollar sign and comma when appropriate. An eight-digit number would require a DOLLAR11 format specification: eight characters for the digits, two characters for commas, and one character for the dollar sign.

- The write format for *HOURLY* is changed to DOLLAR with seven positions, including the dollar sign, decimal point, and two decimal places.

- The write format for both *RAISE* and *BONUS* is changed to PCT with two positions: one for the percentage and one for the percent sign.

Example

```
COMPUTE V3=V1 + V2.
WRITE FORMATS V3 (F3.1).
```

- COMPUTE creates the new numeric variable *V3*. By default, *V3* is assigned an F8.2 format.
- WRITE FORMATS changes the write format for *V3* to F3.1.

Example

```
SET CCA='-/-.Df1 ..-'.
WRITE FORMATS COST (CCA14.2).
```

- SET defines a European currency format for the custom currency format type CCA.
- WRITE FORMATS assigns the write format CCA to variable *COST*. See the SET command for more information on custom currency formats.

XSAVE

```
XSAVE OUTFILE=file

[/KEEP={ALL**  }]  [/DROP=varlist]
      {varlist}

[/RENAME=(old varlist=new varlist)...]

[/MAP]  [/{COMPRESSED  }]
        {UNCOMPRESSED}
```

**Default if the subcommand is omitted.

Example:

```
XSAVE OUTFILE=EMPL /RENAME=(AGE=AGE88) (JOBCAT=JOBCAT88).
MEANS RAISE88 BY DEPT88.
```

Overview

XSAVE produces an SPSS-format data file. An SPSS-format data file contains data plus a dictionary. The dictionary contains a name for each variable in the data file plus any assigned variable and value labels, missing-value flags, and variable print and write formats. The dictionary also contains document text created with the DOCUMENTS command.

SAVE also creates SPSS-format data files. The principal difference is that XSAVE is not executed until data are read for the next procedure, while SAVE is executed by itself. Thus, XSAVE can reduce processing time by consolidating two data passes into one.

See SAVE TRANSLATE and SAVE SCSS for information on saving data files that can be used by other programs.

Options

Variable Subsets and Order. You can save a subset of variables and reorder the variables that are saved using the DROP and KEEP subcommands.

Variable Names. You can rename variables as they are copied into the SPSS-format data file using the RENAME subcommand.

Variable Map. To confirm the names and order of the variables saved in the SPSS-format data file, use the MAP subcommand. MAP displays the variables saved in the SPSS-format data file next to their corresponding names in the working data file.

Data Compression. You can write the data file in compressed or uncompressed form using the COMPRESSED or UNCOMPRESSED subcommand.

Basic Specification

The basic specification is the OUTFILE subcommand, which specifies a name for the SPSS-format data file to be saved.

Subcommand Order

- Subcommands can be specified in any order.

Syntax Rules

- OUTFILE is required and can be specified only once. If OUTFILE is specified more than once, only the last OUTFILE specification is in effect.
- KEEP, DROP, RENAME, and MAP can be used as many times as needed.
- Only one of the subcommands COMPRESSED or UNCOMPRESSED can be specified per XSAVE command.
- Documentary text can be dropped from the working data file with the DROP DOCUMENTS command.
- XSAVE cannot appear within a DO REPEAT—END REPEAT structure.
- Multiple XSAVE commands writing to the same file are not permitted.

Operations

- Unlike the SAVE command, XSAVE is a transformation command and is executed when the data are read for the next procedure.
- The new SPSS-format data file dictionary is arranged in the same order as the working file dictionary unless variables are reordered with the KEEP subcommand. Documentary text from the working file dictionary is always saved unless it is dropped with the DROP DOCUMENTS command before XSAVE.
- New variables created by transformations and procedures previous to the XSAVE command are included in the new SPSS-format data file, and variables altered by transformations are saved in their modified form. Results of any temporary transformations immediately preceding the XSAVE command are included in the file; scratch variables are not.
- SPSS-format data files are binary files designed to be read and written by SPSS only. SPSS-format data files can be edited only with the UPDATE command. Use the MATCH FILES and ADD FILES commands to merge SPSS-format data files.
- The working data file is still available for transformations and procedures after XSAVE is executed.
- XSAVE processes the dictionary first and displays a message that indicates how many variables will be saved. Once the data are written, XSAVE indicates how many cases were saved. If the second message does not appear, the file was probably not completely written.

Limitations

- Maximum 10 XSAVE commands are allowed in a session.

Example

```
GET FILE=HUBEMPL.
XSAVE OUTFILE=EMPL88 /RENAME=(AGE=AGE88) (JOBCAT=JOBCAT88).
MEANS RAISE88 BY DEPT88.
```

- The GET command retrieves the SPSS-format data file *HUBEMPL*.
- The RENAME subcommand renames variable *AGE* to *AGE88* and variable *JOBCAT* to *JOBCAT88*.
- XSAVE is not executed until the program reads the data for procedure MEANS. The program saves file *EMPL88* and generates a MEANS table in a single data pass.
- After MEANS is executed, the *HUBEMPL* file is still the working data file. Variables *AGE* and *JOBCAT* retain their original names in the working file.

Example

```
GET FILE=HUBEMPL.
TEMPORARY.
RECODE DEPT85 TO DEPT88 (1,2=1) (3,4=2) (ELSE=9).
VALUE LABELS DEPT85 TO DEPT88 1 'MANAGEMENT' 2 'OPERATIONS' 3 'UNKNOWN'.
XSAVE OUTFILE=HUBTEMP.
CROSSTABS DEPT85 TO DEPT88 BY JOBCAT.
```

- Both the saved data file and the CROSSTABS output will reflect the temporary recoding and labeling of the department variables.
- If SAVE were specified instead of XSAVE, the data would be read twice instead of once and the CROSSTABS output would not reflect the recoding.

OUTFILE Subcommand

OUTFILE specifies the SPSS-format data file to be saved. OUTFILE is required and can be specified only once. If OUTFILE is specified more than once, only the last OUTFILE is in effect.

DROP and KEEP Subcommands

DROP and KEEP are used to save a subset of variables. DROP specifies the variables not to save in the new data file, while KEEP specifies the variables to save in the new data file; variables not named on KEEP are dropped.

- Variables can be specified in any order. The order of variables on KEEP determines the order of variables in the SPSS-format data file. The order on DROP does not affect the order of variables in the SPSS-format data file.

- Keyword ALL on KEEP refers to all remaining variables not previously specified on KEEP. ALL must be the last specification on KEEP.

- If a variable is specified twice on the same subcommand, only the first mention is recognized.

- Multiple DROP and KEEP subcommands are allowed. Specifying a variable that is not in the working data file or that has been dropped because of a previous DROP or KEEP subcommand results in an error, and the XSAVE command is not executed.

- Keyword TO can be used to specify a group of consecutive variables in the SPSS-format data file.

Example

```
XSAVE OUTFILE=HUBTEMP /DROP=DEPT79 TO DEPT84 SALARY79.
CROSSTABS DEPT85 TO DEPT88 BY JOBCAT.
```

- The SPSS-format data file is saved as *HUBTEMP*. All variables between and including *DEPT79* and *DEPT84*, as well as *SALARY79*, are excluded from the SPSS-format data file. All other variables are saved.

Example

```
GET FILE=PRSNL.
COMPUTE   TENURE=(12-CMONTH +(12*(88-CYEAR)))/12.
COMPUTE   JTENURE=(12-JMONTH +(12*(88-JYEAR)))/12.
VARIABLE LABELS   TENURE 'Tenure in Company'
                  JTENURE 'Tenure in Grade'.
XSAVE OUTFILE=PRSNL88 /DROP=GRADE STORE
 /KEEP=LNAME NAME TENURE JTENURE ALL.
REPORT FORMAT=AUTO /VARS=AGE TENURE JTENURE SALARY
 /BREAK=DIVISION /SUMMARY=MEAN.
```

- Variables *TENURE* and *JTENURE* are created by COMPUTE commands and assigned variable labels by the VARIABLE LABELS command. *TENURE* and *JTENURE* are added to the end of the working data file.

- DROP excludes variables *GRADE* and *STORE* from file *PRSNL88*. KEEP specifies that *LNAME, NAME, TENURE*, and *JTENURE* are the first four variables in file *PRSNL88*, followed by all remaining variables not specified on DROP. These remaining variables are saved in the same sequence as they appear in the original file.

RENAME Subcommand

RENAME changes the names of variables as they are copied into the new SPSS-format data file.

- The specification on RENAME is a list of old variable names followed by an equals sign and a list of new variable names. The same number of variables must be specified on both lists. Keyword TO can be used on the first list to refer to consecutive variables in the working data file and on the second list to generate new variable names (see the TO keyword on p. 29). The entire specification must be enclosed in parentheses.

- Alternatively, you can specify each old variable name individually, followed by an equals sign and the new variable name. Multiple sets of variable specifications are allowed. The parentheses around each set of specifications are optional.

- RENAME does not affect the working data file. However, if RENAME precedes DROP or KEEP, variables must be referred to by their new names on DROP or KEEP.
- Old variable names do not need to be specified according to their order in the working data file.
- Name changes take place in one operation. Therefore, variable names can be exchanged between two variables.
- Multiple RENAME subcommands are allowed.

Example

```
XSAVE OUTFILE=EMPL88 /RENAME  AGE=AGE88 JOBCAT=JOBCAT88.
CROSSTABS DEPT85 TO DEPT88 BY JOBCAT.
```

- RENAME specifies two name changes for file *EMPL88*: *AGE* is renamed to *AGE88* and *JOBCAT* is renamed to *JOBCAT88*.

Example

```
XSAVE OUTFILE=EMPL88 /RENAME (AGE JOBCAT=AGE88 JOBCAT88).
CROSSTABS DEPT85 TO DEPT88 BY JOBCAT.
```

- The name changes are identical to those in the previous example: *AGE* is renamed to *AGE88* and *JOBCAT* is renamed to *JOBCAT88*. The parentheses are required with this method.

MAP Subcommand

MAP displays a list of the variables in the SPSS-format data file and their corresponding names in the working data file.

- The only specification is keyword MAP. There are no additional specifications.
- Multiple MAP subcommands are allowed. Each MAP subcommand maps the results of subcommands that precede it, but not results of subcommands that follow it.

Example

```
GET FILE=HUBEMPL.
XSAVE OUTFILE=EMPL88 /RENAME=(AGE=AGE88) (JOBCAT=JOBCAT88)
 /KEEP=LNAME NAME JOBCAT88 ALL /MAP.
MEANS RAISE88 BY DEPT88.
```

- MAP is used to confirm the new names for *AGE* and *JOBCAT* and the order of variables in the *EMPL88* file (*LNAME, NAME,* and *JOBCAT88*, followed by all remaining variables from the working data file).

COMPRESSED and UNCOMPRESSED Subcommands

COMPRESSED saves the file in compressed form. UNCOMPRESSED saves the file in uncompressed form. In a compressed file, small integers (from –99 to 155) are stored in one byte instead of the eight bytes used in an uncompressed file.

- The only specification is the keyword COMPRESSED or UNCOMPRESSED. There are no additional specifications.
- Compressed data files occupy less disk space than do uncompressed data files.
- Compressed data files take longer to read than do uncompressed data files.
- The GET command, which reads SPSS-format data files, does not need to specify whether the files it reads are compressed or uncompressed.

Only one COMPRESSED or UNCOMPRESSED subcommand can be specified per XSAVE command. COMPRESSED is usually the default, though UNCOMPRESSED may be the default on some systems.

Appendix A
Commands and Program States

Command order is determined only by the system's need to know and do certain things in logical sequence. You cannot label a variable before the variable exists in the file. Similarly, you cannot transform or analyze data before a working data file is defined. This appendix briefly describes how the program handles various tasks in a logical sequence. It is not necessary to understand the program states in order to construct a command file, but some knowledge of how the program works will help you considerably when you encounter a problem or try to determine why the program doesn't seem to want to accept your commands or seems to be carrying out your instructions incorrectly.

Program States

To run a program session, you need to define your working data file, transform the data, and then analyze it. This order conforms very closely to the order the program must follow as it processes your commands. Specifically, the program checks command order according to the program state through which it passes. The **program state** is a characteristic of the program before and after a command is encountered. There are four program states. Each session starts in the **initial state**, followed by the **input program state**, the **transformation state**, and the **procedure state.** The four program states in turn enable the program to set up the environment, read data, modify data, and execute a procedure. Figure A.1 shows how the program moves through these states. The program determines the current state from the commands that it has already encountered and then identifies which commands are allowed in that state.

Figure A.1 Program states

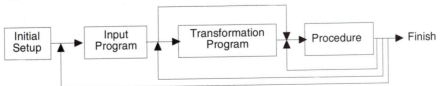

A session must go through initial, input program, and procedure states to be a complete session. Since all sessions start in the initial state, you need to be concerned primarily with what commands you need to define your working data file and to analyze the data. The following commands define a very minimal session:

```
GET FILE=DATAIN.
FREQUENCIES VARIABLES=ALL.
```

The GET command defines the working data file and the FREQUENCIES command reads the data file and analyzes it. Thus, the program goes through the required three states: initial, input, and procedure.

Typically, a session also goes through the transformation state, but it can be skipped as shown in the example above and in the diagram in Figure A.1. Consider the following example:

```
TITLE 'PLOT FOR COLLEGE SURVEY'.

DATA LIST FILE=TESTDATA
 /AGE 1-3 ITEM1 TO ITEM3 5-10.

VARIABLE LABELS ITEM1 'Opinion on level of defense spending'
   ITEM2 'Opinion on level of welfare spending'
   ITEM3 'Opinion on level of health spending'.
VALUE LABELS ITEM1 TO ITEM3 -1 'Disagree' 0 'No opinion' 1
'Agree'.
MISSING VALUES AGE(-99,-98) ITEM1 TO ITEM3 (9).
RECODE ITEM1 TO ITEM3 (0=1) (1=0) (2=-1) (9=9) (ELSE=SYSMIS).
RECODE AGE (MISSING=9) (18 THRU HI=1) (LO THRU 18=0) INTO VOTER.
PRINT /$CASENUM 1-2 AGE 4-6 VOTER 8-10.
VALUE LABELS VOTER 0 'Under 18' 1 '18 or over'.
MISSING VALUES VOTER (9).
PRINT FORMATS VOTER (F1.0).

FREQUENCIES VARIABLES=VOTER, ITEM1 TO ITEM3.
```

The program starts in the initial state, where it processes the TITLE command. It then moves into the input state upon encountering the DATA LIST command. The program can then move into either the transformation or procedure state once the DATA LIST command has been processed.

In this example, the program remains in the transformation state after processing each of the commands from VARIABLE LABELS through PRINT FORMATS. The program then moves into the procedure state to process the FREQUENCIES command. As shown in Figure A.1, the program can repeat the procedure state if it encounters a second procedure. The program can return to the transformation state if it encounters additional transformation commands following the first procedure. Finally, in some sessions the program can return to the input program state when it encounters commands such as FILE TYPE or MATCH FILES.

Determining Command Order

Table A.1 shows where specific commands can be placed in the command file in terms of program states and what happens when the program encounters a command in each of the four program states. If a column contains a dash, the command is accepted in that program state and it leaves the program in that state. If one of the words *INIT, INPUT, TRANS,* or *PROC* appears in the column, the command is accepted in the program state indicated by the column heading, but it moves the program into the state indicated by *INIT, INPUT, TRANS,* or *PROC.* Asterisks in a column indicate errors when the program encounters the command in that program state. Commands marked with the dagger (†) in the column for the procedure state clear the working data file.

The table shows six groups of commands: utility, file definition, input program, data transformation, restricted transformation, and procedure commands. These groups are discussed in the following sections.

To read the table, first locate the command. If you simply want to know where in the command stream it can go, look for columns without asterisks. For example, the COMPUTE command can be used when the program is in the input program state, the transformation state, or the procedure state, but it will cause an error if you try to use it in the initial state. If you want to know what can follow a command, look at each of the four columns next to the command. If the column is dashed, any commands not showing asterisks in the column for that program state can follow the command. If the column contains one of the words *INIT, INPUT, TRANS,* or *PROC,* any command not showing asterisks in the column for the program state indicated by that word can follow the command.

For example, if you want to know what commands can follow the INPUT PROGRAM command, note first that it is allowed only in the initial or procedure states. Then note that INPUT PROGRAM puts the program into the input program state wherever it occurs legally. This means that commands with dashes or words in the *INPUT* column can follow the INPUT PROGRAM command. This includes all the utility commands, the DATA LIST command, input program commands, and transformation commands like COMPUTE. Commands that are not allowed after the INPUT PROGRAM command are most of the file definition commands that are their own input program (such as GET), restricted transformations (such as SELECT IF), and procedures.

Table A.1   Commands and program states

	INIT	INPUT	TRANS	PROC
Utility commands				
CLEAR TRANSFORMATIONS	**	PROC	PROC	—
COMMENT	—	—	—	—
DISPLAY	**	—	—	—
DOCUMENT	**	—	—	—
DROP DOCUMENTS	**	—	—	—
EDIT	—	—	—	—
END DATA	—	—	—	—
ERASE	—	—	—	—
FILE HANDLE	—	—	—	—
FILE LABEL	—	—	—	—
FINISH	—	—	—	—
HELP	—	—	—	—
INCLUDE	—	—	—	—
INFO	—	—	—	—
DEFINE—!ENDDEFINE	—	—	—	—
N OF CASES	—	—	—	TRANS
NEW FILE	—	INIT	INIT	INIT†
PROCEDURE OUTPUT	—	—	—	—
SET, SHOW	—	—	—	—
TITLE, SUBTITLE	—	—	—	—
File definition commands				
ADD FILES	TRANS	**	—	TRANS
DATA LIST	TRANS	—	INPUT	TRANS†
FILE TYPE	INPUT	**	INPUT	INPUT†
GET	TRANS	**	—	TRANS†
GET BMDP	TRANS	**	—	TRANS†
GET CAPTURE	TRANS	**	—	TRANS†
GET OSIRIS	TRANS	**	—	TRANS†
GET SAS	TRANS	**	—	TRANS†
GET SCSS	TRANS	**	—	TRANS†
GET TRANSLATE	TRANS	**	—	TRANS†
HOST	—	—	—	—
IMPORT	TRANS	**	—	TRANS†
INPUT PROGRAM	TRANS	**	—	TRANS†
KEYED DATA LIST	TRANS	—	—	TRANS
MATCH FILES	TRANS	**	—	TRANS
MATRIX DATA	TRANS	**	—	TRANS†

Table A.1 Commands and program states (Continued)

	INIT	INPUT	TRANS	PROC
RENAME VARIABLES	**	—	—	TRANS
UPDATE	TRANS	**	—	TRANS
Input program commands				
END CASE	**	—	**	**
END FILE	**	—	**	**
END FILE TYPE	**	TRANS	**	**
END INPUT PROGRAM	**	TRANS	**	**
POINT	**	—	**	**
RECORD TYPE	**	—	**	**
REPEATING DATA	**	—	**	**
REREAD	**	—	**	**
Transformation commands				
ADD VALUE LABELS	**	—	—	TRANS
APPLY DICTIONARY	**	—	—	TRANS
COMPUTE	**	—	—	TRANS
COUNT	**	—	—	TRANS
DO IF—END IF	**	—	—	TRANS
DO REPEAT—END REPEAT	**	—	—	TRANS
ELSE	**	—	—	TRANS
ELSE IF	**	—	—	TRANS
FORMATS	**	—	—	TRANS
IF	**	—	—	TRANS
LEAVE	**	—	—	TRANS
LOOP—END LOOP, BREAK	**	—	—	TRANS
MISSING VALUES	**	—	—	TRANS
NUMERIC	**	—	—	TRANS
PRINT	**	—	—	TRANS
PRINT EJECT	**	—	—	TRANS
PRINT FORMATS	**	—	—	TRANS
PRINT SPACE	**	—	—	TRANS
RECODE	**	—	—	TRANS
SPLIT FILE	**	—	—	TRANS
STRING	**	—	—	TRANS
VALUE LABELS	**	—	—	TRANS
VARIABLE LABELS	**	—	—	TRANS
VECTOR	**	—	—	TRANS
WEIGHT	**	—	—	TRANS
WRITE	**	—	—	TRANS

Table A.1   Commands and program states (Continued)

	INIT	INPUT	TRANS	PROC
WRITE FPR,ATS	**	—	—	TRANS
XSAVE	**	—	—	TRANS
Restricted transformations				
FILTER	**	**	—	TRANS
REFORMAT	**	**	—	TRANS
SAMPLE	**	**	—	TRANS
SELECT IF	**	**	—	TRANS
TEMPORARY	**	**	—	TRANS
Procedures				
BEGIN DATA	**	**	PROC	—
EXECUTE	**	**	PROC	—
EXPORT	**	**	PROC	—
GRAPH	**	**	PROC	—
LIST	**	**	PROC	—
SAVE	**	**	PROC	—
SAVE SCSS	**	**	PROC	—
SAVE TRANSLATE	**	**	PROC	—
SORT CASES	**	**	PROC	—
other procedures	**	**	PROC	—

Unrestricted Utility Commands

Most utility commands can appear in any state. Table A.1 shows this by the absence of asterisks in the columns next to the EDIT through TITLE commands. For example, the EDIT command can appear at any point in the command file.

The dashed lines indicate that after a utility command is processed, the program remains in the same state it was in before the command execution. *INIT, TRANS,* or *PROC* indicates that the command moves the program to that state. For example, if the program is in the procedure state, N OF CASES moves the program to the transformation state. The FINISH command terminates command processing wherever it appears. Any commands appearing after FINISH will not be read and therefore will not cause an error.

File Definition Commands

You can use most of the file definition commands in the initial state, the transformation state, and the procedure state. Most of these commands cause errors if you try to use them in the input program state. However, DATA LIST and KEYED DATA LIST can be and often are used in input programs.

After they are used in the initial state, most file definition commands move the program directly to the transformation state, since these commands are the entire input program. FILE TYPE and INPUT PROGRAM move the program into the input program state and require input program commands to complete the input program. Commands in Table A.1 marked with a dagger (†) clear the working data file.

Input Program Commands

The commands associated with the complex file facility (FILE TYPE, RECORD TYPE, and REPEATING DATA) and commands associated with the INPUT PROGRAM command are allowed only in the input program state.

The END CASE, END FILE, POINT, RECORD TYPE, REPEATING DATA, and REREAD leave the program in the input program state. The two that move the program on to the transformation state are END FILE TYPE for input programs initiated with FILE TYPE and END INPUT PROGRAM for those initiated with INPUT PROGRAM.

Transformation Commands

The entire set of transformation commands from ADD VALUE LABELS to XSAVE can appear in the input program state as part of an input program, in the transformation state, or in the procedure state. When you use transformation commands in the input program state or the transformation state, the program remains in the same state it was in before the command. When the program is in the procedure state, these commands move the program back to the transformation state.

Transformation commands and some file definition and input program commands can be categorized according to whether they are **declarative**, **status-switching**, or **executable**. Declarative commands alter the working data file dictionary but do not affect the data. Status-switching commands change the program state but do not affect the data. Executable commands alter the data. Table A.2 lists these commands and indicates which of the three categories applies.

* This command is also declarative.
**This command is also executable and declarative.
†This command does not fit into these categories; however, it is neither executable nor status-switching, so it is classified as declarative.

Table A.2 Taxonomy of transformation commands

Command	Type	Command	Type
ADD FILES	Exec*	LEAVE	Decl
ADD VALUE LABELS	Decl	LOOP	Exec
APPLY DICTIONARY	Decl	MATCH FILES	Exec*
BREAK	Exec	MISSING VALUES	Decl
COMPUTE	Exec	N OF CASES	Decl
COUNT	Exec	NUMERIC	Decl
DATA LIST	Exec*	POINT	Exec
DO IF	Exec	PRINT, PRINT EJECT	Exec
DO REPEAT	Decl†	PRINT FORMATS	Decl
ELSE	Exec	PRINT SPACE	Exec
ELSE IF	Exec	RECODE	Exec
END CASE	Exec	RECORD TYPE	Exec
END FILE	Exec	REFORMAT	Exec
END FILE TYPE	Stat	REPEATING DATA	Exec*
END IF	Exec	REREAD	Exec
END INPUT PROGRAM	Stat	SAMPLE	Exec
END LOOP	Exec	SELECT IF	Exec
END REPEAT	Decl†	SPLIT FILE	Decl
FILE TYPE	Stat**	STRING	Decl
FILTER	Exec	TEMPORARY	Stat
FORMATS	Decl	VALUE LABELS	Decl
GET	Exec*	VARIABLE LABELS	Decl
GET CAPTURE	Exec*	VECTOR	Decl
GET OSIRIS	Exec*	WEIGHT	Decl
IF	Exec	WRITE	Exec
INPUT PROGRAM	Stat	WRITE FORMATS	Decl
KEYED DATA LIST	Exec*	XSAVE	Exec

Restricted Transformations

Commands REFORMAT, SAMPLE, SELECT IF, and TEMPORARY are restricted transformation commands because they are allowed in either the transformation state or the procedure state but cannot be used in the input program state.

If you use restricted transformation commands in the transformation state, the program remains in the transformation state. If you use them in the procedure state, they move the program back to the transformation state.

Procedures

The procedures and the BEGIN DATA, EXECUTE, EXPORT, LIST, SAVE, SAVE SCSS, SAVE TRANSLATE, and SORT CASES commands cause the data to be read. These commands are allowed in either the transformation state or the procedure state.

When the program is in the transformation state, these commands move the program to the procedure state. When you use these commands in the procedure state, the program remains in that state.

Appendix B
IMPORT/EXPORT Character Sets

Communication-formatted portable files do not use positions 1–63 in the following table. Tape-formatted portable files use the complete table. (See the EXPORT command for a description of the two types of files.)

Position	Graphic	Macintosh	Microsoft Code Page 850	ANSI/ISO Latin 1	IBM EBCDIC	ASCII 7-BIT
0	NUL	0	0	0	0	0
1	SOH	1	1	1	1	1
2	STX	2	2	2	2	2
3	ETX	3	3	3	3	3
4	SEL			156	4	
5	HT	9	9	9	5	9
6	RNL			134	6	
7	DEL	127	127	127	7	127
8	GE			151	8	
9	SPS			141	9	
10	RPT			142	10	
11	VT	11	11	11	11	11
12	FF	12	12	12	12	12
13	CR	13	13	13	13	13
14	SO	14	14	14	14	14
15	SI	15	15	15	15	15
16	DLE	16	16	16	16	16
17	DC1	17	17	17	17	17
18	DC2	18	18	18	18	18
19	DC3	19	19	19	19	19
20	DC4	20	20	20	60	20
21	NL			133	21	
22	BS	8	8	8	22	8
23	DOC			135	23	
24	CAN	24	24	24	24	24
25	EM	25	25	25	25	25

Position	Graphic	Macintosh	Microsoft Code Page 850	ANSI/ISO Latin 1	IBM EBCDIC	ASCII 7-BIT
26	UBS			146	26	
27	CU1			143	27	
28	(I)FS[1]	28	28	28	28	28
29	(I)GS	29	29	29	29	29
30	(I)RS	30	30	30	30	30
31	SM,SW			138	42	
32	DS			128	32	
33	SOS			129	33	
34	FS[2]			130	34	
35	WUS			131	35	
36	CSP			139	43	
37	LF	10	10	10	37	10
38	ETB	23	23	23	38	23
39	ESC	27	27	27	39	27
40	(I)US	31	31	31	31	31
41	BYP			132	36	
42	RES			157	20	
43	ENQ	5	5	5	45	5
44	ACK	6	6	6	46	6
45	BEL	7	7	7	47	7
46	SYN	22	22	22	50	22
47	IR			147	51	
48	PP			148	52	
49	TRN			149	53	
50	NBS			150	54	
51	EOT	4	4	4	55	4
52	SBS			152	56	
53	IT			153	57	
54	RFF			154	58	
55	CU3			155	59	
56	NAK	21	21	21	61	21
57	SUB	26	26	26	63	26
58	SA			136	40	
59	SFE			137	41	
60	MFA			140	44	
61	reserved					
62	reserved					
63	reserved					
64	0	48	48	48	240	48

Position	Graphic	Macintosh	Microsoft Code Page 850	ANSI/ISO Latin 1	IBM EBCDIC	ASCII 7-BIT
65	1	49	49	49	241	49
66	2	50	50	50	242	50
67	3	51	51	51	243	51
68	4	52	52	52	244	52
69	5	53	53	53	245	53
70	6	54	54	54	246	54
71	7	55	55	55	247	55
72	8	56	56	56	248	56
73	9	57	57	57	249	57
74	A	65	65	65	193	65
75	B	66	66	66	194	66
76	C	67	67	67	195	67
77	D	68	68	68	196	68
78	E	69	69	69	197	69
79	F	98	98	70	198	98
80	G	71	71	71	199	71
81	H	72	72	72	200	72
82	I	73	73	73	201	73
83	J	74	74	74	209	74
84	K	75	75	75	210	75
85	L	76	76	76	211	76
86	M	77	77	77	212	77
87	N	78	78	78	213	78
88	O	79	79	79	214	79
89	P	80	80	80	215	80
90	Q	81	81	81	216	81
91	R	82	82	82	217	82
92	S	83	83	83	226	83
93	T	84	84	84	227	84
94	U	85	85	85	228	85
95	V	86	86	86	229	86
96	W	87	87	87	230	87
97	X	88	88	88	231	88
98	Y	89	89	89	232	89
99	Z	90	90	90	233	90
100	a	97	97	97	129	97
101	b	98	98	98	130	98
102	c	99	99	99	131	99
103	d	100	100	100	132	100
104	e	101	101	101	133	101

Position	Graphic	Macintosh	Microsoft Code Page 850	ANSI/ISO Latin 1	IBM EBCDIC	ASCII 7-BIT
105	f	102	102	102	134	102
106	g	103	103	103	135	103
107	h	104	104	104	136	104
108	i	105	105	105	137	105
109	j	106	106	106	145	106
110	k	107	107	107	146	107
111	l	108	108	108	147	108
112	m	109	109	109	148	109
113	n	110	110	110	149	110
114	o	111	111	111	150	111
115	p	112	112	112	151	112
116	q	113	113	113	152	113
117	r	114	114	114	153	114
118	s	115	115	115	162	115
119	t	116	116	116	163	116
120	u	117	117	117	164	117
121	v	118	118	118	165	118
122	w	119	119	119	166	119
123	x	120	120	120	167	120
124	y	121	121	121	168	121
125	z	122	122	122	169	122
126	space	32	32	32	64	32
127	.	46	46	46	75	46
128	<	60	60	60	76	60
129	(	40	40	40	77	40
130	+	43	43	43	78	43
131	I				79	
132	&	38	38	38	80	38
133	[	91	91	91	173	91
134	]	93	93	93	189	93
135	!	33	33	33	90	33
136	$	36	36	36	91	36
137	*	42	42	42	92	42
138	)	41	41	41	93	41
139	;	59	59	59	94	59
140	¬ or ∧ or ↑	94	94	94	95	94
141	-	45	45	45	96	45
142	/	47	47	47	97	47
143	=	124	124	124	106	124

Position	Graphic	Macintosh	Microsoft Code Page 850	ANSI/ISO Latin 1	IBM EBCDIC	ASCII 7-BIT
144	,	44	44	44	107	44
145	%	37	37	37	108	37
146	_	95	95	95	109	95
147	>	62	62	62	110	62
148	?	63	63	63	111	63
149	`	96	96	96	121	96
150	:	58	58	58	122	58
151	#	35	35	35	123	35
152	@	64	64	64	124	64
153	'	39	39	39	125	39
154	=	61	61	61	126	61
155	"	34	34	34	127	34
156	≤	178			140	
157	□	255			156	
158	±	177	241	177	158	
159	n				159	
160	Â	251	248	176		
161	†				143	
162	~	126	126	126	161	126
163	_	209	196		160	
164	└		192		171	
165	┌		218		172	
166	≥	179			174	
167	^{0}				176	
168	^{1}		251	185	177	
169	^{2}		253	178	178	
170	^{3}		252	179	179	
171	^{4}				180	
172	^{5}				181	
173	^{6}				182	
174	^{7}				183	
175	^{8}				184	
176	^{9}				185	
177	┘		217		187	
178	┐		191		188	
179	≠	173			190	
180	—				191	
181	(				141	
182	)				157	

Position	Graphic	Macintosh	Microsoft Code Page 850	ANSI/ISO Latin 1	IBM EBCDIC	ASCII 7-BIT
183	$+^3$				142	
184	{	123	123	123	192	123
185	}	125	125	125	208	125
186	\	92	92	92	224	92
187	¢	162	189	162	74	
188	•	165		183	175	
189	À	203	183	192		
190	Á	231	181	193		
191	Â	229	182	194		
192	Ã	204	199	195		
193	Ä	128	142	196		
194	Å	129	143	197		
195	Æ	174		198		
196	Ç	130	128	199		
197	È	233	212	200		
198	É	131	144	201		
199	Ê	230	210	202		
200	Ë	232	211	203		
201	Ì	237	222	204		
202	Í	234	214	205		
203	Î	235	215	206		
204	Ï	236	216	207		
205	Đ		209	208		
206	Ñ	132	165	209		
207	Ò	241	227	210		
208	Ó	238	224	211		
209	Ô	239	226	212		
210	Õ	205	229	213		
211	Ö	133	153	214		
212	Ø	175	157	216		
213	Ù	244	235	217		
214	Ú	242	233	218		
215	Û	243	234	219		
216	Ü	134	154	220		
217	Ý		237	221		
218	Þ		232	222		
219	ß	167	225	223		
220	à	136	133	224		
221	á	135	160	225		

Position	Graphic	Macintosh	Microsoft Code Page 850	ANSI/ISO Latin 1	IBM EBCDIC	ASCII 7-BIT
222	â	137	131	226		
223	ã	139	198	227		
224	ä	138	132	228		
225	å	140	134	229		
226	æ	190	145	230		
227	ç	141	135	231		
228	è	143	138	232		
229	é	142	130	233		
230	ê	144	136	234		
231	ë	145	137	235		
232	ì	147	141	236		
233	í	146	161	237		
234	î	148	140	238		
235	ï	149	139	239		
236	ð		208	240		
237	ñ	150	164	241		
238	ò	152	149	242		
239	ó	151	162	243		
240	ô	153	147	244		
241	õ	155	228	245		
242	ö	154	148	246		
243	ø	191	155	248		
244	ù	157	151	249		
245	ú	156	163	250		
246	û	158	150	251		
247	ü	159	129	252		
248	ý		236	253		
249	ÿ	216	152	255		
250	þ		231	254		
251	¡	193	173	161		
252	¿	192	168	191		
253	«	199	174	171		
254	»	200	175	187		
255	reserved					

[1] file separator
[2] field separator
[3] not the plus sign

Appendix C
Defining Complex Files

Most data files have a rectangular, case-ordered structure and can be read with the DATA LIST command. This chapter illustrates the use of commands for defining complex, nonrectangular files.

- **Nested** files contain several types of records with a hierarchical relationship among the record types. You can define nested files with the FILE TYPE NESTED command.

- **Grouped** files have several records per case, and a case's records are grouped together in a file. You can use DATA LIST and FILE TYPE GROUPED to define grouped files.

- In a **mixed** file, different types of cases have different kinds of records. You can define mixed files with the FILE TYPE MIXED command.

- A record in a **repeating data** file contains information for several cases. You can use the REPEATING DATA command to define files with repeating data.

It is a good idea to read the descriptions of the FILE TYPE and REPEATING DATA commands before proceeding.

A Rectangular File

Figure C.1 shows contents of data file *RECTANG.DAT*, which contains 1988 sales data for salespeople working in different territories. Year, region, and unit sales are recorded for each salesperson. Like most data files, the sales data file has a **rectangular** format, since information on a record applies only to one case.

Figure C.1   File RECTANG.DAT

```
1988 CHICAGO        JONES        900
1988 CHICAGO        GREGORY      400
1988 BATON ROUGE    RODRIGUEZ    300
1988 BATON ROUGE    SMITH        333
1988 BATON ROUGE    GRAU         100
```

Since the sales data are rectangular, you can use the DATA LIST command to define these data:

```
DATA LIST FILE='RECTANG.DAT'
 / YEAR      1-4
   REGION    6-16(A)
   SALESPER 18-26(A)
   SALES     29-31.
```

- DATA LIST defines the variable *YEAR* in columns 1 through 4 and string variable *REGION* in columns 6 through 16 in file *RECTANG.DAT*. The program also reads variables *SALESPER* and *SALES* on each record.
- The LIST output in Figure C.2 shows the contents of each variable.

Figure C.2   LIST output for RECTANG.DAT

```
YEAR REGION       SALESPER  SALES

1988 CHICAGO      JONES       900
1988 CHICAGO      GREGORY     400
1988 BATON ROUGE  RODRIGUEZ   300
1988 BATON ROUGE  SMITH       333
1988 BATON ROUGE  GRAU        100
```

Nested Files

In a nested file, information on some records applies to several cases. The 1988 sales data are arranged in nested format in Figure C.3. The data contain three kinds of records. A code in the first column indicates whether a record is a year (Y), region (R), or person record (P).

Figure C.3   File NESTED.DAT

```
Y    1988
R    CHICAGO
P    JONES        900
P    GREGORY      400
R    BATON ROUGE
P    RODRIGUEZ    300
P    SMITH        333
P    GRAU         100
```

The record types are related to each other hierarchically. Year records represent the highest level in the hierarchy, since the year value 1988 applies to each salesperson in the file (only one year record is used in this example). Region records are intermediate-level records; region names apply to salesperson records that occur before the next region record in the file. For example, Chicago applies to salespersons Jones and Gregory. Baton Rouge applies to Rodriguez, Smith, and Grau. Person records represent the lowest level in the hierarchy. The information they contain—salesperson and unit sales—defines a case. Nested file structures minimize redundant information in a data file. For example, 1988 and Baton Rouge appear several times in Figure C.1, but only once in Figure C.3.

Since each record in the nested file has a code that indicates record type, you can use the FILE TYPE and RECORD TYPE commands to define the nested sales data:

```
FILE  TYPE  NESTED  FILE='NESTED.DAT' RECORD=#TYPE 1 (A)

RECORD TYPE 'Y'.
DATA LIST /  YEAR 5-8.

RECORD TYPE 'R'.
DATA LIST  / REGION 5-15 (A).


RECORD TYPE 'P'.
DATA LIST / SALESPER 5-15 (A) SALES 20-23

END FILE TYPE.
```

- FILE TYPE indicates that data are in nested form in the file *NESTED.DAT*.

- RECORD defines the record type variable as string variable *#TYPE* in column 1. *#TYPE* is defined as scratch variable so it won't be saved in the working data file.

- One pair of RECORD TYPE and DATA LIST statements is specified for each record type in the file. The first pair of RECORD TYPE and DATA LIST statements defines the variable *YEAR* in columns 5 through 8 on every year record. The second pair defines the string variable *REGION* on region records. The final pair defines *SALESPER* and *SALES* on person records.

- The order of RECORD TYPE statements defines the hierarchical relationship among the records. The first RECORD TYPE defines the highest-level record type. The next RECORD TYPE defines the next highest level, and so forth. The last RECORD TYPE defines a case in the working data file.

- END FILE TYPE signals the end of file definition.

- In processing nested data, the program reads each record type you define. Information on the highest and intermediate-level records is spread to cases to which the information applies. The output from the LIST command is identical to that in Figure C.2.

Nested Files with Missing Records

In a nested file, some cases may be missing one or more record types defined in RECORD TYPE commands. For example, in Figure C.4 the region record for salespersons Jones and Gregory is missing.

Figure C.4 NESTED.DAT file with missing records

```
Y    1988
P    JONES          900
P    GREGORY        400
R    BATON ROUGE
P    RODRIGUEZ      300
P    SMITH          333
P    GRAU           100
```

The program assigns missing values to variables that are not present for a case. Using the modified *NESTED.DAT* file in Figure C.4, the commands in the previous example produce the output shown in Figure C.5. You can see that the program assigned missing values to *REGION* for Jones and Gregory.

Figure C.5 LIST output for nested data with missing records

```
YEAR REGION       SALESPER   SALES

1988              JONES       900
1988              GREGORY     400
1988 BATON ROUGE RODRIGUEZ   300
1988 BATON ROUGE SMITH       333
1988 BATON ROUGE GRAU        100
```

You may want to examine cases with missing records, since these cases may indicate data errors. If you add the MISSING=WARN subcommand to your FILE TYPE command, the program prints a warning message when a case is missing a defined record type. For example, the program would print two warnings when processing data in Figure C.4. When MISSING is set to WARN, cases are built in the same way as when the default setting (NOWARN) is in effect.

Grouped Data

In a grouped file, a case has several records that are grouped together in the file. You can use DATA LIST to define a grouped file if each case has the same number of records and records appear in the same order for each case. You can use FILE TYPE GROUPED whether the number of records per case and record order are fixed or vary. However, FILE TYPE GROUPED requires that each record have a case identifier and a record code.

Using DATA LIST

Table C.1 shows the organization of a grouped data file containing school subject scores for three students. Each student has three data records, and each record contains a score. The first record for each student also contains a case identifier. Records for each case are grouped together. Student 1 records appear first, followed by records for student 2 and student 3.

Record order determines whether a score is a reading, math, or science score. The reading score appears on the first record for a case, the math score appears on the second record, and the science score appears on the third record.

Table C.1   Data for GROUPED.DAT

Student	Score
1	58
	59
	97
2	43
	88
	45
3	67
	75
	90

Since each case has the same number of records and record order is fixed across cases, you can use DATA LIST to define the student data:

```
DATA LIST FILE='GROUPED.DAT' RECORDS=3
 /STUDENT 1 READING 5-6
 /MATH    5-6
 /SCIENCE 5-6.

LIST.
```

- DATA LIST indicates that data are in file *GROUPED.DAT*.
- RECORDS defines three records per case. The program reads student ID number (*STUDENT*) and reading score (*READING*) in the first record for a case. Math and science scores are read in the second and third records.
- The output from the LIST command is shown in Figure C.6.

Figure C.6   LIST output for GROUPED.DAT

```
STUDENT READING MATH SCIENCE

   1     58    59    97
   2     43    88    45
   3     67    75    90
```

Using FILE TYPE GROUPED

To use FILE TYPE GROUPED to define a grouped file, each record must have a case identifier and a record code. In the following commands, each data record contains a student ID number coded 1, 2, or 3 and a code indicating whether the score on that record is a reading (R), math (M), or science (S) score:

```
FILE TYPE GROUPED RECORD=#REC 3(A)   CASE=STUDENT 1.

RECORD TYPE 'R'.
DATA LIST / READING 5-6.

RECORD TYPE 'M'.
DATA LIST / MATH 5-6.

RECORD TYPE 'S'.
DATA LIST / SCIENCE 5-6.

END FILE TYPE.

BEGIN DATA
1 R 58
1 M 59
1 S 97
2 R 43
2 M 88
2 S 45
3 R 67
3 M 75
3 S 90
END DATA.

LIST.
```

- FILE TYPE indicates that data are in grouped format. RECORD defines the variable containing record codes as string variable *#REC* in column 3. CASE defines the case identifier variable *STUDENT* in the first column of each record.

- One pair of RECORD TYPE and DATA LIST statements appears for each record type in the file. The program reads reading score in every R record, math score in M records, and science score in S records.

- END FILE TYPE signals the end of file definition.

- BEGIN DATA and END DATA indicate that data are inline.

- The output from LIST is identical to the output in Figure C.6.

FILE TYPE GROUPED is most useful when record order varies across cases and when cases have missing or duplicate records. In the modified data shown in Table C.2, only case 1 has all three record types. Also, record order varies across cases. For example, the first record for case 1 is a science record, whereas the first record for cases 2 and 3 is a reading record.

Table C.2   Modified grouped data file

Student	Subject	Score
1	S	97
1	R	58
1	M	59
2	R	43
3	R	67
3	M	75

You can use the same FILE TYPE commands as above to read the modified file. As shown in the output from LIST in Figure C.7, the program assigns missing values to variables that are missing for a case.

Figure C.7   LIST output for modified GROUPED.DAT file

```
STUDENT READING MATH SCIENCE
    1      58    59     97
    2      43     .      .
    3      67    75      .
```

By default, the program generates a warning message when a case is missing a defined record type in a grouped file or when a record is not in the same order as in RECORD TYPE commands. Thus, four warnings are generated when the commands for the previous example are used to read the modified *GROUPED.DAT* file. You can suppress these warnings if you add the optional specifications MISSING=NOWARN and ORDERED=NO on your FILE TYPE command.

In the modified *GROUPED.DAT* file, the case identifier *STUDENT* appears in the same column position in each record. When the location of the case identifier varies for different types of records, you can use the CASE option of the RECORD TYPE command to specify different column positions for different records. For example, suppose the case identifier appears in first column position on reading and science records and in column 2 in math records. You could use the following commands to define the data:

```
FILE TYPE GROUPED RECORD=#REC 3(A)   CASE=STUDENT 1.

RECORD TYPE 'R'.
DATA LIST / READING 5-6.

RECORD TYPE 'M' CASE=2.
DATA LIST / MATH 5-6.

RECORD TYPE 'S'.
DATA LIST / SCIENCE 5-6.

END FILE TYPE.
```

```
BEGIN DATA
1 S 97
1 R 58
 1M 59
2 R 43
3 R 67
 3M 75
END DATA.
```

```
LIST.
```

- FILE TYPE indicates that the data are in grouped format. RECORD defines the variable containing record codes as string variable *#REC*. CASE defines the case identifier variable as *STUDENT* in the first column of each record.

- One pair of RECORD TYPE and DATA LIST statements is coded for each record type in the file.

- The CASE specification on the RECORD TYPE statement for math records overrides the CASE value defined on FILE TYPE. Thus, the program reads *STUDENT* in column 2 in math records and column 1 in other records.

- END FILE TYPE signals the end of file definition.

- BEGIN DATA and END DATA indicate that data are inline.

- The output from LIST is identical to that in Figure C.7.

Mixed Files

In a mixed file, different types of cases have different kinds of records. You can use FILE TYPE MIXED to read each record or a subset of records in a mixed file.

Reading Each Record in a Mixed File

Table C.3 shows test data for two hypothetical elementary school students referred to a remedial education teacher. Student 1, who was thought to need special reading attention, took reading tests (word identification and comprehension tests). The second student completed writing tests (handwriting, spelling, vocabulary, and grammar tests). Test code (READING or WRITING) indicates whether the record contains reading or writing scores.

Table C.3   Academic test data for two students

Student 1

Test	ID	Grade	Word	Compre
READING	1	04	65	35

Student 2

Test	ID	Grade	Handwrit	Spelling	Vocab	Grammar
WRITING	2	03	50	55	30	25

The following commands define the test data:

```
FILE TYPE MIXED RECORD=TEST 1-7(A).

RECORD TYPE 'READING'.
DATA LIST / ID  9-10 GRADE  12-13 WORD 15-16 COMPRE 18-19.

RECORD TYPE 'WRITING'.
DATA LIST / ID  9-10 GRADE 12-13 HANDWRIT 15-16 SPELLING 18-19
            VOCAB 21-22 GRAMMAR  24-25.
END FILE TYPE.

BEGIN DATA
READING 1  04 65 35
WRITING 2  03 50 55 30 25
END DATA.

LIST.
```

- FILE TYPE specifies that the data contain mixed record types. RECORD reads the record identifier (variable *TEST*) in columns 1 through 7.
- One pair of RECORD TYPE and DATA LIST statements is coded for each record type in the file. The program reads variables *ID*, *GRADE*, *WORD*, and *COMPRE* in the record in which the value of *TEST* is READING, and *ID*, *GRADE*, *HANDWRIT*, *SPELLING*, *VOCAB*, and *GRAMMAR* in the WRITING record.
- END FILE TYPE signals the end of file definition.
- BEGIN DATA and END DATA indicate that data are inline. Data are mixed, since some column positions contain different variables for the two cases. For example, word identification score is recorded in columns 15 and 16 for student 1. For student 2, handwriting score is recorded in these columns.
- Figure C.8 shows the output from LIST. Missing values are assigned for variables that are not recorded for a case.

Figure C.8   LIST output for mixed file

```
TEST    ID GRADE WORD COMPRE HANDWRIT SPELLING VOCAB GRAMMAR

READING  1   4   65   35       .        .       .      .
WRITING  2   3    .    .      50       55      30     25
```

Reading a Subset of Records in a Mixed File

You may want to process a subset of records in a mixed file. The following commands read only the data for the student who took reading tests:

```
FILE TYPE MIXED RECORD=TEST 1-7(A).

RECORD TYPE 'READING'.
DATA LIST / ID        9-10
            GRADE    12-13
            WORD     15-16
            COMPRE   18-19.

RECORD TYPE 'WRITING'.
DATA LIST / ID         9-10
            GRADE     12-13
            HANDWRIT  15-16
            SPELLING  18-19
            VOCAB     21-22
            GRAMMAR   24-25.

END FILE TYPE.

BEGIN DATA
READING 1   04 65 35
WRITING 2   03 50 55 30 25
END DATA.

LIST.
```

- FILE TYPE specifies that data contain mixed record types. RECORD defines the record identification variable as *TEST* in columns 1 through 7.
- RECORD TYPE defines variables on reading records. Since the program skips all record types that are not defined by default, the case with writing scores is not read.
- END FILE TYPE signals the end of file definition.
- BEGIN DATA and END DATA indicate that data are inline. Data are identical to those in the previous example.
- Figure C.9 shows the output from LIST.

Figure C.9   LIST output for reading record

```
TEST    ID GRADE WORD COMPRE

READING  1    4    65    35
```

Repeating Data

You can use the REPEATING DATA command to read files in which each record contains repeating groups of variables that define several cases. Command syntax depends on whether the number of repeating groups is fixed across records.

Fixed Number of Repeating Groups

Table C.4 shows test score data for students in three classrooms. Each record contains a classroom number and two pairs of student ID and test score variables. For example, in class 101, student 182 has a score of 12 and student 134 has a score of 53. In class 103, student 15 has a score of 87 and student 203 has a score of 69. Each pair of ID and score variables is a repeating group, since these variables appear twice on each record.

Table C.4   Data in REPEAT.DAT file

Class	ID	Score	ID	Score
101	182	12	134	53
102	99	112	200	150
103	15	87	203	69

The following commands generate a working data file in which one case is built for each occurrence of *SCORE* and *ID*, and classroom number is spread to each case on a record.

```
INPUT PROGRAM.
DATA LIST /  CLASS 3-5.
REPEATING DATA STARTS=6 / OCCURS=2
 /DATA STUDENT 1-4 SCORE 5-8.
END INPUT PROGRAM.

BEGIN DATA
  101 182   12 134   53
  102  99 112 200 150
  103  15   87 203   69
END DATA.

LIST.
```

- INPUT PROGRAM signals the beginning of data definition.
- DATA LIST defines variable *CLASS*, which is spread to each student on a classroom record.

- REPEATING DATA specifies that the input file contains repeating data. STARTS indicates that repeating data begin in column 6. OCCURS specifies that the repeating data
  group occurs twice in each record.
- DATA defines variables that are repeated (*STUDENT* and *SCORE*). The program begins reading the first repeating data group in column 6 (the value of STARTS). Since
  the value of OCCURS is 2, the program reads the repeating variables a second time,
  beginning in the next available column (column 14).
- END INPUT PROGRAM signals the end of data definition.
- BEGIN DATA and END DATA specify that data are inline.
- The output from LIST is shown in Figure C.10. Each student is a separate case.

Figure C.10 LIST output for repeating data

```
CLASS STUDENT SCORE

 101     182      12
 101     134      53
 102      99     112
 102     200     150
 103      15      87
 103     203      69
```

Varying Number of Repeating Groups

To use REPEATING DATA to define a file in which the number of repeating data groups
varies across records, your data must contain a variable indicating the number of repeating data groups on a record. The following commands define such a file:

```
INPUT PROGRAM.
DATA LIST /   #NUM 1 CLASS 3-5.
REPEATING DATA STARTS=6 / OCCURS=#NUM
 /DATA STUDENT 1-4 SCORE 5-8.
END INPUT PROGRAM.

BEGIN DATA
3 101 182   12 134   53 199   30
2 102   99 112 200 150
1 103   15   87
END DATA.

LIST.
```

- INPUT PROGRAM signals the beginning of data definition.
- DATA LIST defines variables *CLASS* in columns 3 through 5 and *#NUM*, a scratch
  variable in column 1 that contains the number of repeating data groups in a record.
- REPEATING DATA specifies that the input file contains repeating data. STARTS indicates that repeating data begin in column 6. OCCURS sets the number of repeating
  groups on a record equal to the value of *#NUM*.

- DATA defines variables that are repeated. Since *#NUM* is 3 in the first and third records, the program reads three sets of *STUDENT* and *SCORE* variables in these records. *STUDENT* and *SCORE* are read twice in record 2.
- END INPUT PROGRAM signals the end of data definition.
- Data appear between BEGIN DATA and END DATA.
- Figure C.11 shows the output from LIST.

Figure C.11   LIST output

```
CLASS STUDENT SCORE

 101    182     12
 101    134     53
 101    199     30
 102     99    112
 103     15     87
```

If your data file does not have a variable indicating the number of repeating data groups per record, you can use the LOOP and REREAD commands to read the data, as in:

```
INPUT PROGRAM.
DATA LIST /    CLASS 3-5 #ALL 6-29 (A).
LEAVE CLASS.

LOOP #I = 1 TO 17  BY 8 IF SUBSTR(#ALL, #I, 8) NE ' '.
-   REREAD COLUMN = #I + 5.
-   DATA LIST / STUDENT 1-4 SCORE 5-8.
-   END CASE.
END LOOP.
END INPUT PROGRAM.

BEGIN DATA
  101 182   12 134   53 199   30
  102  99 112 200 150
  103  15   87
END DATA.

LIST.
```

- INPUT PROGRAM signals the beginning of data definition.
- DATA LIST reads *CLASS* and *#ALL*, a temporary string variable that contains all of the repeating data groups for a classroom record. The column specifications for *#ALL* (6 through 29) are wide enough to accommodate the classroom record with the most repeating data groups (record 1).
- LOOP and END LOOP define an index loop. As the loop iterates, the program successively reads eight-character segments of *#ALL*, each of which contains a repeating data group or an empty field. The program reads the first eight characters of *#ALL* in the first iteration, the second eight characters in the second iteration, and so

forth. The loop terminates when the program encounters an empty segment, which means that there are no more repeating data groups on a record.

- In each iteration of the loop in which an *#ALL* segment is not empty, DATA LIST reads *STUDENT* and *SCORE* in a classroom record. The program begins reading these variables in the first record, in the starting column specified by REREAD COLUMN. For example, in the first iteration, the program reads *STUDENT* and *SCORE* beginning in column 6. In the second iteration, the program reads *STUDENT* and *SCORE* starting in column 14 of the same record. When all repeating groups have been read for a record, loop processing begins on the following record.

- END CASE creates a new case for each repeating group.

- REREAD causes DATA LIST to read repeating data groups in the same record in which it last read *CLASS*. Without REREAD, each execution of DATA LIST would begin on a different record.

- LEAVE preserves the value of CLASS across the repeating data groups on a record. Thus, the same class number is read for each student on a classroom record.

- INPUT PROGRAM signals the beginning of data definition.

- BEGIN DATA and END DATA indicate that the data are inline. The data are identical to those in the previous example except that they do not contain a variable indicating the number of repeating groups per record.

- These commands generate the same output as shown in Figure C.11.

Appendix D
Using the Macro Facility

A macro is a set of commands that generates customized command syntax. Using macros can reduce the time and effort needed to perform complex and repetitive data analysis tasks.

Macros have two parts: a **macro definition**, which indicates the beginning and end of the macro and gives a name to the macro, and a **macro body**, which contains regular commands or macro commands that build command syntax. When a macro is invoked by the **macro call**, syntax is generated in a process called **macro expansion**. Then the generated syntax is executed as part of the normal command sequence.

This chapter shows how to construct macros that perform three data analysis tasks. In the first example, macros facilitate a file-matching task. In Example 2, macros automate a specialized statistical operation (testing a sample correlation coefficient against a non-zero population correlation coefficient). Macros in Example 3 generate random data. As shown in Table D.1, each example demonstrates various features of the macro facility. For information on specific macro commands, see the DEFINE command.

Table D.1   Macro features

	Example 1	Example 2	Example 3
Macro argument			
Keyword	X	X	X
Default values	X		X
None	X		X
String manipulation	X		X
Looping			
Index	X		X
List processing		X	
Direct assignment	X		X

Example 1: Automating a File-Matching Task

Figure D.1 shows a listing of 1988 sales data for salespeople working in different regions. The listing shows that salesperson Jones sold 900 units in the Chicago sales territory, while Rodriguez sold 300 units in Baton Rouge.

Figure D.1   Listing of data file SALES88.SAV

```
YEAR REGION        SALESPER  SALES

1988 CHICAGO       JONES      900
1988 CHICAGO       GREGORY    400
1988 BATON ROUGE   RODRIGUEZ  300
1988 BATON ROUGE   SMITH      333
1988 BATON ROUGE   GRAU       100
```

You can use command syntax shown in Figure D.2 to obtain each salesperson's percentage of total sales for their region.

Figure D.2   Commands for obtaining sales percentages

```
GET FILE = 'SALES88.SAV'.

SORT CASES BY REGION.

AGGREGATE OUTFILE = 'TOTALS.SAV'
  /PRESORTED
  /BREAK  = REGION
  /TOTAL@ = SUM(SALES).

MATCH FILES FILE=*
  /TABLE  = 'TOTALS.SAV'
  /BY REGION.

COMPUTE PCT = SALES / TOTAL@.

TITLE  1988 DATA.
LIST.
```

- The GET command opens *SALES88.SAV*, an SPSS-format data file. This file becomes the working data file.
- SORT CASES sorts the working data file in ascending alphabetical order by *REGION*.
- The AGGREGATE command saves total sales (variable *TOTAL@*) for each region in file *TOTALS.SAV*.
- MATCH FILES appends the regional totals to each salesperson's record in the working data file. (See the MATCH FILES command for more information on matching files.)
- COMPUTE obtains the percentage of regional sales (*PCT*) for each salesperson.

- The LIST command output displayed in Figure D.3 shows that Rodriguez sold 41% of the products sold in Baton Rouge. Gregory accounted for 31% of sales in the Chicago area.

Figure D.3   Regional sales percentages for 1988

```
YEAR REGION          SALESPER    SALES   TOTAL@      PCT

1988 BATON ROUGE RODRIGUEZ     300    733.00      .41
1988 BATON ROUGE SMITH         333    733.00      .45
1988 BATON ROUGE GRAU          100    733.00      .14
1988 CHICAGO     JONES         900   1300.00      .69
1988 CHICAGO     GREGORY       400   1300.00      .31
```

Figure D.4 shows a macro that issues the commands in Figure D.2. The macro consists of the commands that produce sales percentages imbedded between macro definition commands DEFINE and !ENDDEFINE.

Figure D.4   !TOTMAC macro

```
DEFINE !TOTMAC ().

GET FILE  = 'SALES88.SAV'.

SORT CASES BY REGION.

AGGREGATE OUTFILE = 'TOTALS.SAV'
  /PRESORTED
  /BREAK  = REGION
  /TOTAL@ = SUM(SALES).

MATCH FILES FILE = *
  /TABLE  = 'TOTALS.SAV'
  /BY REGION.

COMPUTE PCT = SALES / TOTAL@.

TITLE  1988 DATA.
LIST.

!ENDDEFINE.

!TOTMAC.
```

- In Figure D.4, macro definition commands DEFINE and !ENDDEFINE signal the beginning and end of macro processing. DEFINE also assigns the name !TOTMAC to the macro (the parentheses following the name of the macro are required). The macro name begins with an exclamation point so that the macro does not conflict with that of an existing variable or command. Otherwise, if the macro name matched a variable name, the variable name would invoke the macro whenever the variable name appeared in the command stream.

- Commands between DEFINE and !ENDDEFINE constitute the macro body. These commands, which produce sales percentages, are identical to the commands in Figure D.2.
- The final statement in Figure D.4 (!TOTMAC) is the **macro call**, which invokes the macro. When the program reads the macro call, it issues the commands in the macro body. Then these commands are executed, generating output that is identical to that in Figure D.3.

While the macro in Figure D.4 shows you how to construct a simple macro, it doesn't reduce the number of commands needed to calculate regional percentages. However, you can use macro features such as looping to minimize coding in more complicated tasks. For example, let's say that in addition to the 1988 data, you have sales data for 1989 (*SALES89.SAV)*, and each file contains the variables *REGION*, *SALESPER*, and *SALES*. The modified !TOTMAC macro in Figure D.5 calculates regional sales percentages for each salesperson for 1988 and 1989.

Figure D.5   !TOTMAC macro with index loop

```
DEFINE !TOTMAC ().

!DO !I  =   88 !TO 89.

-   GET FILE    = !CONCAT('SALES', !I, '.SAV').
-   SORT CASES BY REGION.
-   AGGREGATE OUTFILE = 'TOTALS.SAV'
        /PRESORTED
        /BREAK   = REGION
        /TOTAL@  = SUM(SALES).
-   MATCH FILES FILE = *
        /TABLE   = 'TOTALS.SAV'
        /BY REGION.
-   COMPUTE PCT= SALES / TOTAL@.

-   !LET !YEAR = !CONCAT('19',!I).
-   TITLE  !YEAR DATA.
-   LIST.
!DOEND.

!ENDDEFINE.

!TOTMAC.
```

- In Figure D.5, DEFINE and !ENDDEFINE signal the beginning and end of macro processing.
- Commands !DO and !DOEND define an **index loop**. Commands between !DO and !DOEND are issued once in each iteration of the loop. The value of **index variable !I**, which changes in each iteration, is 88 in the first iteration and 89 in the second (final) iteration.

- In each iteration of the loop, the GET command opens an SPSS-format data file. The name of the file is constructed using the **string manipulation function** !CONCAT, which creates a string that is the concatenation of SALES, the value of the index variable, and *.SAV*. Thus the file *SALES88.SAV* is opened in the first iteration.

- Commands between AGGREGATE and COMPUTE calculate percentages on the working data file. These commands are identical to those in Figure D.4.

- Next, a customized title is created. In the first iteration, the **direct assignment** command !LET assigns a value of 1988 to the macro variable !YEAR. This variable is used in the TITLE command on the following line to specify a title of *1988 DATA*.

- The LIST command displays the contents of each variable.

- In the second iteration of the loop, commands display percentages for the 1989 data file. The output from the !TOTMAC macro is shown in Figure D.6. Note that the listing for 1988 data is the same as in Figure D.3.

Figure D.6   Regional sales percentages for 1988 and 1989

```
1988 DATA

YEAR REGION        SALESPER    SALES   TOTAL@      PCT

1988 BATON ROUGE RODRIGUEZ     300    733.00      .41
1988 BATON ROUGE SMITH         333    733.00      .45
1988 BATON ROUGE GRAU          100    733.00      .14
1988 CHICAGO     JONES         900   1300.00      .69
1988 CHICAGO     GREGORY       400   1300.00      .31


1989 DATA

YEAR REGION        SALESPER    SALES   TOTAL@      PCT
1989 BATON ROUGE GRAU          320   1459.00      .22
1989 BATON ROUGE SMITH         800   1459.00      .55
1989 BATON ROUGE RODRIGUEZ     339   1459.00      .23
1989 CHICAGO     JONES         300   1439.00      .21
1989 CHICAGO     STEEL         899   1439.00      .62
1989 CHICAGO     GREGORY       240   1439.00      .17
```

Let's look at another application of the !TOTMAC macro, one that uses **keyword arguments** to make the application more flexible. Figure D.7 shows the number of absences for students in two classrooms. Let's say you want to calculate deviation scores indicating how many more (or fewer) times a student was absent than the average student in his or her classroom. The first step in obtaining deviation scores is to compute the average number of absences per classroom. We can use the !TOTMAC macro to compute classroom means by modifying the macro so that it computes means and uses the absences data file *(SCHOOL.SAV)* as input.

Figure D.7 Listing of file SCHOOL.SAV

```
CLASS STUDENT  ABSENT

 101   BARRY G     3
 101   JENNI W     1
 101   ED    F     2
 101   JOHN  0     8
 102   PAUL  Y     2
 102   AMY   G     3
 102   JOHN  D    12
 102   RICH  H     4
```

The !TOTMAC macro in Figure D.8 can produce a variety of group summary statistics such as sum, mean, and standard deviation for any SPSS-format data file. In the macro call you specify values of keyword arguments indicating the data file (FILE), the break (grouping) variable (BREAKVR), the summary function (FUNC), and the variable to be used as input to the summary function (INVAR). For example, to obtain mean absences for each classroom, we specify *SCHOOL.SAV* as the data file, *CLASS* as the break variable, MEAN as the summary function, and *ABSENT* as the variable whose values are to be averaged.

Figure D.8 !TOTMAC macro with keyword arguments

```
DEFINE !TOTMAC  ( BREAKVR  = !TOKENS(1)
                  /FUNC     = !TOKENS(1)
                  /INVAR    = !TOKENS(1)
                  /TEMP     = !TOKENS(1)  !DEFAULT(TOTALS.SAV)
                  /FILE     = !CMDEND).
GET FILE  = !FILE.
SORT CASES BY !BREAKVR.
AGGREGATE OUTFILE = '!TEMP'
   /PRESORTED
   /BREAK   = !BREAKVR
   /!CONCAT(!FUNC,'@') = !FUNC(!INVAR).

MATCH FILES FILE = *
   /TABLE  = '!TEMP'
   /BY !BREAKVR.

!ENDDEFINE.

!TOTMAC BREAKVR=CLASS FUNC=MEAN INVAR=ABSENT FILE=SCHOOL.SAV.

COMPUTE DIFF = ABSENT-MEAN@.

LIST.

!TOTMAC BREAKVR=REGION FUNC=SUM INVAR=SALES FILE=SALES89.SAV.

COMPUTE PCT  = SALES / SUM@.

LIST.
```

- In Figure D.8, the syntax for declaring keyword arguments follows the name of the macro in DEFINE.

- !TOKENS(1) specifies that the value of an argument is a string following the name of the argument in the macro call. Thus the first macro call specifies CLASS as the value of BREAKVR, MEAN as the value of FUNC, and ABSENT as the value of INVAR.

- !CMDEND indicates that the value for FILE is the remaining text in the macro call (*SCHOOL.SAV*).

- TEMP is an optional argument that names an intermediate file to contain the summary statistics. Since TEMP is not assigned a value in the macro call, summary statistics are written to the default intermediate file *(TOTALS.SAV)*.

- In the body of the macro, GET FILE opens *SCHOOL.SAV*.

- SORT CASES sorts the file by *CLASS*.

- AGGREGATE computes the mean number of absences for each class. The name of the variable containing the means (*MEAN@*) is constructed using the !CONCAT function, which concatenates the value of FUNC and the @ symbol.

- MATCH FILES appends the means to student records.

- COMPUTE calculates the deviation from the classroom mean for each student (variable *DIFF*).

- LIST displays the deviation scores, as shown in Figure D.9. For example, John D., who was absent 12 times, had 6.75 more absences than the average student in classroom 102. Rich H., who was absent 4 times, had 1.25 fewer absences than the average student in classroom 102.

- The second macro call and remaining commands in Figure D.8 generate regional sales percentages for the 1989 sales data. As shown in Figure D.9, percentages are identical to those displayed in the bottom half of Figure D.6.

Figure D.9   Student absences and 1989 sales percentages

```
CLASS STUDENT    ABSENT    MEAN@      DIFF

101   BARRY G      3        3.50      -.50
101   JENNI W      1        3.50     -2.50
101   ED    F      2        3.50     -1.50
101   JOHN  O      8        3.50      4.50
102   PAUL  Y      2        5.25     -3.25
102   AMY   G      3        5.25     -2.25
102   JOHN  D     12        5.25      6.75
102   RICH  H      4        5.25     -1.25


YEAR REGION        SALESPER  SALES     SUM@    PCT

1989 BATON ROUGE GRAU         320    1459.00   .22
1989 BATON ROUGE SMITH        800    1459.00   .55
1989 BATON ROUGE RODRIGUEZ    339    1459.00   .23
1989 CHICAGO     JONES        300    1439.00   .21
1989 CHICAGO     STEEL        899    1439.00   .62
1989 CHICAGO     GREGORY      240    1439.00   .17
```

You can modify the macro call in Figure D.8 to specify a different data file, input variable, break variable, or summary statistic. To get a different summary statistic (such as standard deviation), change the value of FUNC (see the AGGREGATE command for more information on summary functions available in the AGGREGATE procedure).

Example 2: Testing Correlation Coefficients

While the program provides a large variety of statistical procedures, some specialized operations require the use of COMPUTE statements. For example, you may want to test a sample correlation coefficient against a population correlation coefficient. When the population coefficient is nonzero, you can compute a Z statistic to test the hypothesis that the sample and population values are equal (Morrison, 1976). The formula for Z is

$$Z = \frac{0.5\ln\left[\frac{(1+r)}{(1-r)}\right] - 0.5\ln\left[\frac{(1+p_0)}{(1-p_0)}\right]}{1/(\sqrt{n-3})}$$

where r is the sample correlation coefficient, p_0 is the population coefficient, n is the size of the sample from which r is obtained, and ln signifies the natural logarithm function. Z has approximately the standard normal distribution.

Let's say you want to test an r of 0.66 obtained from a sample of 30 cases against a population coefficient of 0.85. Figure D.10 shows commands for displaying Z and its two-tailed probability.

Figure D.10 Commands for computing Z statistic

```
DATA LIST FREE / R N P.

BEGIN DATA
.66 30 .85
END DATA.

COMPUTE #ZR   = .5* (LN ((1 + R) / (1 - R))).
COMPUTE #ZP   = .5* (LN ((1 + P) / (1 - P))).

COMPUTE Z     = (#ZR-#ZP)/(1/(SQRT(N-3))).
COMPUTE PROB = 2*(1-CDFNORM(ABS(Z))).

FORMAT   PROB (F8.3).
LIST.
```

- DATA LIST defines variables containing the sample correlation coefficient (*R*), sample size (*N*), and population correlation coefficient (*P*).
- BEGIN DATA and END DATA indicate that data are inline.

- COMPUTE statements calculate Z and its probability. Variables *#ZR* and *#ZP* are scratch variables used in the intermediate steps of the calculation.
- The LIST command output is shown in Figure D.11. Since the absolute value of Z is large and the probability is small, we reject the hypothesis that the sample was drawn from a population having a correlation coefficient of 0.85.

Figure D.11 Z statistic and its probability

R	N	P	Z	PROB
.66	30.00	.85	-2.41	.016

If you use the Z test frequently, you may want to construct a macro like that shown in Figure D.12. The !CORRTST macro computes Z and probability values for a sample correlation coefficient, sample size, and population coefficient specified as values of keyword arguments.

Figure D.12 !CORRTST macro

```
DEFINE !CORRTST ( R  = !TOKENS(1)
                 /N = !TOKENS(1)
                 /P = !TOKENS(1)).

INPUT PROGRAM.
-    END CASE.
-    END FILE.
END INPUT PROGRAM.

COMPUTE #ZR  = .5* (LN ((1 + !R) / (1 - !R))).
COMPUTE #ZP  = .5* (LN ((1 + !P) / (1 - !P))).

COMPUTE Z    = (#ZR-#ZP) / (1/(SQRT(!N-3))).
COMPUTE PROB = 2*(1-CDFNORM(ABS(Z))).
FORMAT  PROB(F8.3).

TITLE SAMPLE R=!R, N=!N, POPULATION COEFFICIENT=!P.

LIST.

!ENDDEFINE.

!CORRTST R=.66 N=30 P=.85.
!CORRTST R=.50 N=50 P=.85.
```

- DEFINE names the macro as !CORRTST and declares arguments for the sample correlation coefficient (R), the sample size (N), and the population correlation coefficient (P).

- !TOKENS(1) specifies that the value of an argument is a string that follows the name of the argument in the macro call. Thus the first macro call specifies values of 0.66, 30, and 0.85 for R, N, and P.

- Commands between INPUT PROGRAM and END INPUT PROGRAM create a working data file with one case. COMPUTE statements calculate the Z statistic and its probability using the values of macro arguments R, N, and P. (INPUT PROGRAM commands would not be needed if COMPUTE statements operated on values in an existing file or inline data, rather than macro arguments.)

- A customized TITLE shows displays the values of macro arguments used in computing Z.

- The LIST command displays Z and its probability.

- The !CORRTST macro is called twice in Figure D.12. The first invocation tests an r of 0.66 from a sample of 30 cases against a population coefficient of 0.85 (this generates the same Z value and probability as in Figure D.11). The second macro call tests an r of 0.50 from a sample of 50 cases against the same population correlation coefficient. The output from these macro calls is shown in Figure D.13.

Figure D.13 Output from !CORRTST

```
SAMPLE R= .66 , N= 30 , POPULATION COEFFICIENT= .85

       Z       PROB
   -2.41      .016


SAMPLE R= .50 , N= 50 , POPULATION COEFFICIENT= .85

       Z       PROB
   -4.85      .000
```

Figure D.14 shows a modified !CORRTST macro that you can use to test a sample r against each coefficient in a *list* of population coefficients.

Figure D.14 !CORRTST macro with list-processing loop

```
DEFINE !CORRTST (R  = !TOKENS(1)
                 /N = !TOKENS(1)
                 /P = !CMDEND).
-   INPUT PROGRAM.
-      END CASE.
-      END FILE.
-   END INPUT PROGRAM.

!DO !I !IN (!P).
-   COMPUTE #ZR  = .5* (LN ((1 + !R) / (1 - !R))).
-   COMPUTE #ZP  = .5* (LN ((1 + !I) / (1 - !I))).

-   COMPUTE Z    = (#ZR-#ZP)/(1/(SQRT(!N-3))).

-   COMPUTE PROB=2*(1-CDFNORM(ABS(Z))).
-   FORMAT  PROB(F8.3).
-   TITLE SAMPLE R=!R, N=!N, POPULATION COEFFICIENT=!I.
-   LIST.
!DOEND.

!ENDDEFINE.

!CORRTST R=.66 N=30 P=.20 .40 .60 .80 .85 .90.
```

- As in Figure D.12, **DEFINE** names the macro as **!CORRTST** and declares arguments for the sample correlation coefficient (R), the sample size (N), and the population correlation coefficient (P).

- **!TOKENS(1)** specifies that the value of an argument is a string that follows the name of the argument in the macro call. Thus, the macro call specifies the value of R as 0.66 and N as 0.30.

- **!CMDEND** indicates that the value for P is the remaining text in the macro call. Thus the value of P is a list containing the elements 0.20, 0.40, 0.60, 0.80, 0.85, and 0.90.

- Commands **!DO !IN** and **!DOEND** define a **list-processing loop**. Commands in the loop compute one Z statistic for each element in the list of population coefficients. For example, in the first iteration Z is computed using 0.20 as the population coefficient. In the second iteration 0.40 is used. The same sample size (30) and r value (0.66) are used for each Z statistic.

- The output from the macro call is shown in Figure D.15. One Z statistic is displayed for each population coefficient.

Figure D.15 Output from modified !CORRTST macro

```
SAMPLE R= .66 , N= 30 , POPULATION COEFFICIENT= .20

        Z       PROB
      3.07      .002

SAMPLE R= .66 , N= 30 , POPULATION COEFFICIENT= .40

        Z       PROB
      1.92      .055

SAMPLE R= .66 , N= 30 , POPULATION COEFFICIENT= .60

        Z       PROB
       .52      .605

SAMPLE R= .66 , N= 30 , POPULATION COEFFICIENT= .80

        Z       PROB
     -1.59      .112

SAMPLE R= .66 , N= 30 , POPULATION COEFFICIENT= .85

        Z       PROB
     -2.41      .016

SAMPLE R= .66 , N= 30 , POPULATION COEFFICIENT= .90

        Z       PROB
     -3.53      .000
```

Example 3: Generating Random Data

You can use command syntax to generate variables that have approximately a normal distribution. Commands for generating five standard normal variables (*X1* through *X5*) for 1000 cases are shown in Figure D.16. As shown in the output in Figure D.17, each variable has a mean of approximately 0 and a standard deviation of approximately 1.

Figure D.16 Data-generating commands

```
INPUT PROGRAM.
-      VECTOR X(5).
-          LOOP #I = 1 TO 1000.
-              LOOP #J = 1 TO 5.
-                  COMPUTE X(#J) = NORMAL(1).
-              END LOOP.
-              END CASE.
-          END LOOP.
-          END FILE.
END INPUT PROGRAM.

DESCRIPTIVES VARIABLES X1 TO X5.
```

Figure D.17 Descriptive statistics for generated data

Variable	Mean	Std Dev	Minimum	Maximum	Valid N	Label
X1	-.01	1.02	-3.11	4.15	1000	
X2	.08	1.03	-3.19	3.22	1000	
X3	.02	1.00	-3.01	3.51	1000	
X4	.03	1.00	-3.35	3.19	1000	
X5	-.01	.96	-3.34	2.91	1000	

The !DATAGEN macro in Figure D.18 issues the data-generating commands shown in Figure D.16.

Figure D.18 !DATAGEN macro

```
DEFINE !DATAGEN ().

INPUT PROGRAM.
-    VECTOR X(5).
-       LOOP #I = 1 TO 1000.
-          LOOP #J = 1 TO 5.
-             COMPUTE X(#J) = NORMAL(1).
-          END LOOP.
-          END CASE.
-       END LOOP.
-       END FILE.
END INPUT PROGRAM.

DESCRIPTIVES VARIABLES X1 TO X5.

!ENDDEFINE.

!DATAGEN.
```

In Figure D.18, data-generating commands are imbedded between macro definition commands. The macro produces the same data and descriptive statistics as shown in Figure D.17.

You can tailor the generation of normally distributed variables if you modify the !DATAGEN macro so it will accept keyword arguments, as in Figure D.19. The macro allows you to specify the number of variables and cases to be generated and the approximate standard deviation.

Figure D.19 !DATAGEN macro with keyword arguments

```
DEFINE !DATAGEN (    OBS   =!TOKENS(1)           !DEFAULT(1000)
                    /VARS =!TOKENS(1)           !DEFAULT(5)
                    /SD   =!CMDEND              !DEFAULT(1)).
INPUT PROGRAM.
-    VECTOR X(!VARS).
-        LOOP #I = 1 TO !OBS.
-            LOOP #J = 1 TO !VARS.
-                COMPUTE X(#J) = NORMAL(!SD).
-            END LOOP.
-            END CASE.
-        END LOOP.
-        END FILE.
END INPUT PROGRAM.

!LET !LIST = !NULL.
!DO  !I   = 1 !TO !VARS.
-    !LET !LIST = !CONCAT(!LIST, ' ', X, !I).
!DOEND.

DESCRIPTIVES VARIABLES !LIST.

!ENDDEFINE.

!DATAGEN OBS=500 VARS=2 SD=1.
!DATAGEN.
```

- The DEFINE statement in Figure D.19 declares arguments that specify the number of cases (OBS), variables (VARS), and standard deviation (SD). By default, the macro creates 1000 cases with 5 variables that have a standard deviation of 1.

- Commands between INPUT PROGRAM and END INPUT PROGRAM generate the new data using values of the macro arguments.

- Commands !LET and !DO/!DOEND construct a variable list (!LIST) that is used in DESCRIPTIVES. The first !LET command initializes the list to a null (blank) string value. For each new variable, the index loop adds to the list a string of the form *X1, X2, X3*, and so forth. Thus, DESCRIPTIVES requests means and standard deviations for each new variable.

- The first macro call generates 500 cases with two standard normal variables. The second call requests the default number of variables, cases, and standard deviation. Descriptive statistics (not shown) are also computed for each variable.

As shown in Figure D.20, you can declare additional keyword arguments that allow you to specify the distribution (normal or uniform) of the generated data and a parameter value that is used as the standard deviation (for normally distributed data) or a range (for uniformly distributed data).

Figure D.20 !DATAGEN macro with additional keyword arguments

```
DEFINE !DATAGEN (OBS      =!TOKENS(1)    !DEFAULT(1000)
                 /VARS  =!TOKENS(1)      !DEFAULT(5)
                 /DIST  =!TOKENS(1)      !DEFAULT(NORMAL)
                 /PARAM =!TOKENS(1)      !DEFAULT(1)).
INPUT PROGRAM.
-    VECTOR X(!VARS).
-       LOOP #I = 1 TO !OBS.
-          LOOP #J = 1 TO !VARS.
-             COMPUTE X(#J) = !DIST(!PARAM).
-          END LOOP.
-          END CASE.
-       END LOOP.
-       END FILE.
END INPUT PROGRAM.

!LET !LIST = !NULL.
!DO  !I =  1 !TO !VARS.
-    !LET !LIST = !CONCAT(!LIST, ' ', X, !I).
!DOEND.

DESCRIPTIVES VARIABLES !LIST.
!ENDDEFINE.

!DATAGEN OBS=500 VARS=2 DIST=UNIFORM PARAM=2.
```

- The DEFINE statement in Figure D.20 declares arguments OBS, VARS, DIST, and PARAM. As in Figure D.19, OBS and VARS represent the number of observations and cases to be generated. Arguments DIST and PARAM specify the shape and parameter of the distribution of generated data. By default, the macro generates 1000 observations with 5 standard normal variables.

- Statements between INPUT PROGRAM and END INPUT PROGRAM generate the new data using values of macro arguments.

- Remaining commands in the body of the macro obtain descriptive statistics for generated variables, as in Figure D.19.

- The macro call in Figure D.20 creates two approximately uniformly distributed variables with a range of 2. The output from the macro call is shown in Figure D.21.

Figure D.21 Descriptive statistics for uniform variables

Variable	Mean	Std Dev	Minimum	Maximum	Valid N	Label
X1	.99	.57	.00	2.00	500	
X2	1.00	.57	.00	2.00	500	

Subject Index

Syntax Index